The Facts On File

DICTIONARY OF NONPROFIT ORGANIZATION MANAGEMENT

The Facts On File DICTIONARY OF NONPROFIT ORGANIZATION MANAGEMENT

J. STEVEN OTT
Applied Management Corporation
and
JAY M. SHAFRITZ
University of Colorado at Denver

Facts On File Publications
New York, New York • Oxford, England

The Facts On File Dictionary of Nonprofit
Organization Management

Library of Congress Cataloging-in-Publication Data

Ott, J. Steven.
The Facts on File dictionary of nonprofit organization management.

1. Corporations, Nonprofit—Management—Dictionaries.
I. Shafritz, Jay M. II. Facts on File, Inc.
III. Title. IV. Title: Dictionary of nonprofit organization management.

HD62.6.88 1986 658'.048'0321 85-25223
ISBN 0-8160-1282-2

Printed in the United States of America
10 9 8 7 6 5 4 3 2 1

FOREWORD

The nonprofit sector has finally arrived. Here is at last a dictionary devoted to terms that managers in this field need.

There are unique aspects of organizations in the nonprofit sector which require a vocabulary that is somewhat different from that found in government and profit making organizations. This dictionary represents the first attempt to reflect both the unique aspects of the sector and the aspects which are common to managers in all organizations.

Governance, funding, staffing and oversight are areas of the greatest difference. For example, nonprofits usually have boards of directors or trustees, who are responsible for the governance of organizations. Their role is more central and demanding than that of corporate directors, and they are generally unpaid volunteers who represent the community. The relationship of the board and staff is a complex one that requires skill, tact, and good judgment. Board members often are expected to contribute to the organization or, in the case of foundations, to approve final grant determinations.

"Nonprofit manager" used to be an oxymoron, like "jumbo shrimp." Service deliverers and volunteers ran the vast majority of nonprofit agencies. Managers were a luxury that few agencies wanted or could afford. Keeping expenses low and avoiding bureaucracy were of paramount concern. Times have changed. More nonprofits appreciate a skilled administrator who can help provide efficient and effective programs. The ongoing debate about whether and how to train managers, is becoming moot as more and more colleges, universities, and other organizations develop and offer a wide variety of courses for nonprofit management. Nonprofit organizations now hire persons with basic management skills and obtain training for their personnel.

Why the changes? Many factors have contributed. Services have expanded with the increase in population. They also expanded in response to government funding of basic human services in the postwar period. Governments contracted with nonprofits to provide services, increasing the scope, reach and revenues of many agencies. But government contracts also required accountability in the form of budgeting, accounting and reporting. Further, the sector is labor intensive; most of its costs involve staff, not equipment.

This period of expansion was followed by the difficult times of high inflation in the 1970's and federal government retrenchment in the 1980's. Both caused cutbacks and reduced revenues in many parts of the nonprofit sector. In the face of these hard times, nonprofit boards and private funders became increasingly concerned with building financial and administrative strength in nonprofit agencies.

Finally, there is a growing recognition of the vital role the nonprofit sector plays, and has historically played, in providing educational, health, cultural and social services in our country. Researchers have discovered the nonprofit sector and have begun to explore it. Recent work paints a picture of a vibrant collection of diverse entities that employ as many persons as the automobile industry, that deliver services to a wide spectrum of individuals across the country, and that are funded by fees, grants, contributions and contracts with government.

As the importance of the sector has become more evident, so has the realization that we lack adequate data, theory or understanding of nonprofit contributions to American life. Nor have we been sufficiently concerned about the efficiency and effectiveness of these organizations.

Why has the nonprofit sector been so neglected? Until recently, for example, the yearly compilation of figures published in *Giving USA* by the American Association of Fundraising Counsel, was virtually the only source of data on philanthropy. Many of these figures are rough estimates that are gradually becoming more sophisticated. Although there has long been a small group of dedicated scholars, such as Robert Bremner, research on philanthropy and nonprofit organizations has largely fallen through the cracks.

Research on the philanthropic sector was given impetus by the Filer Commission during the mid 1970's. Many of the studies sponsored by that Commission began the task of defining and measuring the sector. The banner was then taken up by the Program on Non-Profit Organizations (Ponpo) under the direction of John Simon at Yale. Ponpo became the only academic center of nonprofit research in the country. More recently, other organizations have begun to explore this field. Notably, Lester Salamon of the Urban Institute, who is conducting an indepth study of nonprofit organizations in 16 locations. The level of research activity is growing, but it is still very small compared with what needs to be done.

Even the government has neglected the nonprofit sector. The *Census of Services* presents basic data, but the Census Bureau has stopped publishing its compilation on nonprofits. The Internal Revenue Service does require information forms (Form 990) of all nonprofit organizations with revenues over $25,000. The IRS then makes computer tapes with certain limited data elements available for a fee. Unfortunately, the processing of these forms has been a low priority and, as a result, the data in recent years has been so inaccurate that—after a series of protests—the tape for 1983 has been withdrawn.

The dismal state of data about the nonprofit sector was a catalyst for the formation of the National Center for Charitable Statistics (NCCS). This organization, formed by a consortium of the Council on Foundations, Independent Sector, the National Charities Information Bureau, and United Way of America, is determined to improve the quality, quantity and accessibility of information on philanthropy.

NCCS compiled and published the discontinued Census data on the sector in a volume entitled, *Non-Profit Service Organizations: 1982*. In addition, INDEPENDENT SECTOR (a national membership organization of nonprofit organizations) has published a volume entitled, *Dimensions of the Independent Sector: A Statistical Profile*. This book combines existing data from all major sources to provide the first comprehensive view of what is known about American philanthropy.

Counting and defining the organizations that make up the nonprofit sector is a challenge in itself. *Dimensions* took on the task and estimated that there are probably several million organizations. These include religious organizations, private colleges and universities, foundations, hospitals, day care centers, youth agencies, advocacy organizations and many others that provide services. There is no good count of small churches or of nonprofits that fall under the floor of $5,000 in revenues.

In 1982 there were 1.18 million documented nonprofit organizations. From this, *Dimensions* concludes that there were 793,000 "independent sector" organizations in 1982. These include 323,000 organizations with 501 (c) (3) tax-exempt (charitable) status, 132,000 other tax-exempt organizations that serve primarily charitable purposes, and 339,000 churches. Nonprofit organizations not included in this definition are a diverse group of mutual insurance companies, credit unions, cemetery companies and others.

The "independent sector" organizations in 1980 accounted for $123 billion in national income, $71 billion in salaries, and an estimated $52 billion in volunteer time. Private contributions from individuals, bequests, foundations and corporations totaled $48.2 billion dollars in that year. Government provided $40.3 billion dollars.

Why the concern about the data on the nonprofit sector? First, the popular conception of the sector as independent from government and business masks the large and ongoing cooperative relationship that exists among the three sectors. Without accurate data, policy makers cannot appreciate the impact that various policies will have. Without accurate data, the capacity of the sector is a matter of guesswork, and the services provided and to whom are estimates. Lack of understanding of the relationship between government and nonprofits led to the phenomenon of government cutbacks to those very agencies that were being urged to take up the slack as the federal budget was trimmed. Exhortations to corporations and foundations to fill the gaps do not make sense when the size of their resources is compared with the needs. Together they provided about $7 billion to nonprofit organizations in 1982, not a major amount of revenue for the sector.

It is not widely recognized that nonprofit organizations are often the mechanism of choice for delivering government funded services. This relationship does not square neatly with the current image of the independence of the sector, on the one hand, or the dominance of government in welfare services on the other. Yet it does fit the historical American tradition of decentralized provision of public services.

There are, however, advantages and disadvantages of providing services in this way, aptly discussed by Lester Salamon in a recent paper entitled, "Partners in Public Service: Government and the Nonprofit Sector in Theory and Practice." Salamon's work suggests that nonprofit organizations do not generally serve the poorest people, but that government grants are often used to extend their reach to the poor. There is growing concern that as nonprofits adapt to current fiscal retrenchment by implementing revenue raising measures such as charging fees, fewer services will be accessible to the poor. Nonprofit agencies are challenged, as rarely before, to do more with less and to find creative ways to reach those who need their services most.

The nonprofit sector needs managers who appreciate their role within their communities and in the larger society. It also needs leaders who are aware of the larger picture, who realize how interdependent the sectors are, and who are able to effectively educate and advocate on their own behalf.

Funding of nonprofits is often precarious and usually a time-consuming preoccupation. Putting together a strategy that uses the best of available options to ensure the survival of the organization without detracting from the program, requires considerable skill and creativity. Options include grants, fees, contracts, appeals and endowment campaigns. The need to do this job well is leading to a growing cadre of "development" or fund-raising staff professionals. In addition, there are well-known private corporations that provide fund-raising services for a fee. But in most organizations the board and staff must raise the money themselves.

As the need for funds has intensified in recent years, so has the pressure to find additional sources of income. Many agencies are experimenting with unrelated activities to raise funds to support their programs. Universities and research institutions may sell computer time. Agencies may own a profit-making subsidiary such as a food franchise. Such activities are taxable above a certain limit, but more importantly, they are raising questions about unfair competition with small businesses.

Staffing in nonprofits is often a combination of paid and unpaid volunteer help. The voluntary aspect of the sector is one of its traditional hallmarks and one of its great strengths. Volunteers are on its boards in governance capacities and work with staff to provide services or administrative support. Managing volunteers is a delicate job. They must be motivated, used effectively and given a sense of satisfaction. This is not always an easy task, and professionals sometimes view volunteers as interlopers who take more time than they are worth. However the thousands of volunteer hours given to nonprofit organizations is staggering. They attest to the commitment of individuals to voluntary agencies and to the success of most agencies in attracting, training and keeping volunteers.

Managing paid staff in nonprofit agencies is somewhat different from the other sectors. Salaries are generally lower, benefits less generous and overwork routine. Dealing with staff burnout and turnover is common. Some observers feel that the nonprofit sector is the training ground for committed young persons, especially women, who then move on to jobs in government and profit-making corporations.

Oversight of the voluntary sector is somewhat different too. The Internal Revenue Service is the regulatory agency for most of the sector. Forms are filed with the IRS which attempts to monitor the activities of the sector based on these reports. As only private foundations are required to pay a tax on income (unless there is unrelated business income), the IRS has little motivation to be aggressive. The real federal impact comes in relation to activities that may threaten the tax-exempt status of agencies. If an organization loses its exempt status, donors cannot receive a tax deduction for gifts made to it.

The sections of the tax code defining nonprofit organizations are very complex, outdoing even the complexity and diversity of the organizations that make up the sector. Private foundations are the most highly regulated group of entities in the sector, and the rules governing them are particularly extensive. What is missing is a rational classification system that would make sense of the sector. The IRS uses an ad hoc list of types of organizations. Others use different terms. In response to this situation, the NCCS is supporting the development of a classification system by Russy Sumariwalla of United Way of America. If it becomes widely accepted, it will provide a logical and uniform method for categorizing the organizations in the sector.

State governments may also regulate nonprofit organizations. Some require registration and filing of an annual report (now a copy of the Federal 990, perhaps with additional schedules). Some have limitations on fund-raising costs and other requirements. The level of oversight varies considerably from state to state.

The complexity of the nonprofit sector and its regulations means that distilling its unique words is an effort that will be appreciated by many who work in this field and by those who are trying to learn about it. The management language from other sectors enhances communication, facilitates cooperation, and helps build job skills. All are worthy goals.

Elizabeth T. Boris, Ph. D.
Director of Research
Council on Foundations

AUTHORS' PREFACE

This dictionary is a tool and a reference source for all who wish to be knowledgeable about the theory, practices, terms, concepts, laws, codes, and institutions concerned with the management of nonprofit organizations. In short, it is a source of expertise for those who work with, or are concerned about, the operations of nonprofit organizations.

The first question the authors had to face in deciding to compile this dictionary was whether or not the nonprofit sector (or "third sector") has a sufficiently unique language to warrant a dictionary. Obviously, we decided affirmatively, but the answer is not that clear. Some aspects of nonprofit organizations are unique, while others overlap and coincide with private and public sector organization management.

In order to appreciate the scope of entries in this dictionary, it is necessary to consider the range of nonprofit organizations in the United States. Nonprofit organizations range from small, unincorporated, neighborhood, single purpose or goal associations to multistate hospital holding companies and international religious denominations. Many nonprofit organizations are similar to public sector organizations in that their primary purposes involve the advancement of the public good, public interests, or societal well-being rather than the private benefit of their owners or the financial advancement of their members. However, nonprofit organizations are more similar to private sector organizations in terms of their policy formation and decision processes: for example, nonprofit organizations usually make their own decisions about "what is the public good" and how to advance it. Also, most nonprofit organizations are directly accountable to their members through an elected board (of members) rather than to the general public or to publicly elected representatives. Furthermore, many nonprofit organizations compete in the general public, private sector, and public sector arenas for program and administrative funds and contributed effort as well as for markets (including clients or patrons) for their programs or services.

On the other hand, the nonprofit organization, while primarily accountable to its own board, usually, like the public sector organization, has multiple and often conflicting objectives. Frequently, the nonprofit organization may deliver services which originate from, for example, a legislative mandate. In these instances, the subcontracting relationship to public funders renders the nonprofit organization at least indirectly accountable to the general public. In many cases, nonprofit board decision making is quite similar to that of a public utility: the nonprofit board is free to make decisions within legislative paramaters. Where the nonprofit organization is not directly involved with a public funding agency, the argument for multiple and conflicting policy objectives still holds. The board's policy may seek to satisfice funders, client groups, collateral providers of service, and splinter advocacy groups within or without the organization. Thus, many would argue a similarity to the public sector or a unique stance for the nonprofit sector, rather than for a close resemblance to the private sector in policy formation and implementation.

To an outside observer, some nonprofit organizations are virtually indistinguishable from private for-profit enterprises in their inputs, structures, and functions; others are almost carbon copies of certain public sector organizations; still others have characteristics which make them separate and distinct from organizations in the other two sectors.

Many of the truly significant movements in our society originated through nonprofit organizations, including, for example, civil rights, care of—and creation of meaningful opportunities for—the physically and mentally disabled, and the abolition of slavery. Private foundations have a long and proud tradition of providing alternatives to government funding for creative projects and innovative ideas. This position or role of historical national leadership has at least partially resulted from the relative freedom from constraints on voluntary organizations relative to those that inhibit or bind public agencies and private enterprises. Nonprofit organizations provide opportunities for individuals to innovate, criticize, and reform—to direct their time, efforts and money to those societal needs, causes, and organizations they wish to support. Therefore, one can make a very convincing argument that nonprofit organizations in the United States are unique entities that reflect our basic values of individualism and freedom of choice.

One could also argue (but less convincingly) that nonprofit organizations are simply whatever private and public organizations are not, or that they are whatever the Congress, the courts, and the Internal Revenue Service have decided they are (or are not).

Nonprofit organizations are involved in an exhaustive array of activities—for example, the promotion and advancement of the arts, humanities, social services, religion, public welfare, education (elementary, secondary, higher, and continuing), research and development, health, political action, public policy analysis, the interests of employed people (such as labor organizations) and businesses with common interests (geographically, such as chambers of commerce, and by product lines, such as trade associations), and public safety. They engage in broadcasting, public information and education, programs, financing of other organizations' programs, and providing assistance, information, and support to public, nonprofit, and private organizations.

Just as nonprofit organizations vary in structure and culture according to their functions, they also vary by their primary sources of financial support. Some nonprofit organizations derive most of their financial support from private enterprises (for example, gifts from corporations, corporate foundation grants and contracts for services), others from the general public (for example, community fund-raising drives), others from members (for example, religious organizations), others from the public sector (for example, grants and contracts), and yet others from combinations of these sources. Therefore, a nonprofit organization that provides contract services to industry (for example, a sheltered workshop) will be more comfortable with the terminology of the private sector and may strive to be more "business-like." On the other hand, a nonprofit organization that receives most of its financial support from a state government to provide human services will tend to "look and feel" like a public human services agency. Yet, for example, a private foundation which receives most of its support from private corporations and supports primarily nonprofit organizations involved in the arts and preventive health may have its own unique personality that partially reflects the three worlds—but also the highly visible and tightly controlled (by the Internal Revenue Service) arena of private foundations.

Unless a subject is totally stagnant or reflects an expired technology, its language is constantly changing and evolving. This is certainly true of nonprofit organizations, and, in consequence, this dictionary is inherently a "work in progress." Every year, for example, new court decisions, rulings, and legislation change the terminology, the concepts, and the practice of nonprofit organizations. Even as this dictionary is being prepared, Congress, the administration, and interest groups are debating the merits of various "tax simplification" proposals—any of which could have significant implications for nonprofit, tax-exempt organizations. Therefore, although this dictionary seeks to capture and codify the language of nonprofit organizations, the authors are fully aware that even when it is finished it will be incomplete. The real world does not wait on a publisher's deadlines.

However inherently incomplete this dictionary may be, it is comprehensive by design. It contains all of the words, terms, phrases, processes, laws, and court cases with which people associated with nonprofit organizations should be familiar. The criteria for including and excluding definitions had to be rather loose because of the wide variation among nonprofit organizations and because the boundaries of nonprofit organizations overlap so many other fields. However loose the inclusion criteria may be, they are not arbitrary. For example:

- if a term is found in any of several score textbooks or handbooks on nonprofit organizations, it has been included;
- terms whose meanings in the context of nonprofit organizations do not differ from definitions found in any standard dictionary of the English language generally are not included;
- in general, terms which are central to the concerns of persons working in and with nonprofit organizations have received more thorough coverage than those that are more peripheral;
- terms which are specific to the private or public sector but which are encountered frequently by nonprofit organizations in their regular course of operations are included.

This last criterion required the authors to use considerable personal and professional discretion and judgment in determining how far to go into such related fields as business, law, accounting, public administration, economics, organization theory, and general management.

The rationale for some types of inclusions may not be self-evident and warrants a brief explanation:

- *Basic accounting and bookkeeping.* Some aspects of nonprofit accounting are unique (for example, restricted and unrestricted fund balances and distribution requirement formulas), but others are similar to those used in private enterprise (for example, billing, collections, journals, general ledger and subsidiary ledger accounts).
- *Basic business practices and law.* Many nonprofit organizations must function regularly in the worlds of mortgages, liens, bank accounts, civil suits, injunctions, embezzlement, etc.
- *Basic financial investments, securities, and insurance.* Many nonprofit organizations invest funds in a variety of securities and financial institutions. Further, it is common for nonprofit organizations to receive bequests of common stock, preferred convertible stock, properties with variable rate mortgates, etc. Most nonprofit organizations must deal with several types of insurance coverage.
- *Labor relations.* Although labor relations and unionism may appear remote to many nonprofit organizations, they are very real facts of life for others (for example, consider hospitals, educational institutions and social services agencies), and their penetration into white-collar and professional labor markets (particularly low-pay professional labor markets) cannot be ignored.
- *Management and organization theory.* Although aspects of nonprofit organization management differ from management in the private and public sectors, other aspects do not—or differ only to a minor degree. Certainly coordination of volunteers differs from management of employees, but the functions involved in supervision of faculty in a private nonprofit university are not that different from supervision of similar faculty in a state university. Nonprofit organizations are as susceptible to organizational entropy as private enterprises.
- *Personnel management.* In addition to general personnel management terms, this dictionary includes current definitions and important laws and court decisions related to sexual harassment, discrimination (age, sex, race, national origin, etc.), and affirmative action programs.

- *Program evaluation.* Foundations, boards of directors, and government agencies want to know what has been accomplished (and how efficiently) with their funds. Program evaluation designs, approaches, methods, and techniques form an area of vital knowledge for nonprofit organization managers—both granting and operating.
- *Project or program management.* Most charitable organizations plan, develop, and conduct programs which can benefit from project or program management techniques and tools (such as precedence diagrams, management by objectives, etc.)
- *Public administration.* The public administration terms and phrases have been limited to those which nonprofit organizations may encounter frequently in the course of normal operations. For example, *The Code of Federal Regulations* includes rules for organizations that contract with the federal government; the Federal Communications Commission administers the Federal Communications Act of 1934, which requires the electronic media to devote a portion of broadcast time to "the public interest"; and state and federal administrative practices acts define government agencies' obligations to solicit and receive public input prior to implementing rules and regulations.
- *Public relations.* This category of entries should require no explanation. Most nonprofit organizations of all types require public support at different times and in different forms.

The types of inclusions listed above are in addition to those one would expect to find in a dictionary of nonprofit organizations. Within the inherent limitations described previously, this dictionary presents a comprehensive set of definitions for terms and phrases related to the purposes, structures, functions, law, codes, ethics, and financing (especially fund-raising) of nonprofit organizations. It also focuses on the laws, practices, and tax implications of giving and bequesting. To the extent possible, the dictionary includes terms and phrases related to volunteerism, but frankly there are not many such words which differ in their nonprofit context from their general English language usage.

Inclusion-exclusion decisions were also required for court cases, laws, organizations, and publications. The same general rules described previously were used for court cases and laws: if they were mentioned with regularity in journals and textbooks, they have been included.

Nonprofit organizations have been listed only if they provide services or resources (such as information or technical assistance) to a variety of nonprofit organizations. Therefore, such umbrella organizations as the Council on Foundations, INDEPENDENT SECTOR, and the United Way are included, but specific foundations and operating charitable organizations are not, except occasionally in examples or in data tables. Once again, judgment was required with organizations such as area and regional associations of grantmakers. The inclusion criteria for newsletters and journals are even more subjective.

Authors and books have been cited only if a term or concept is generally credited or attributed to them. For example, one cannot discuss the "hierarchy of needs" without referencing Abraham Maslow, "segmentalism" without Rosabeth Moss Kanter, or "cognitive dissonance" without Leon Festinger.

Acknowledgments: No two people write a dictionary of nonprofit organization management by themselves—the field is too vast, complex, and changing. The authors owe so much to so many who contributed ideas, entries, insights, stimulation, challenges, and constructive criticism. Primary among those we wish to acknowledge are Elizabeth Boris of the Council on Foundations, Dave Gies and Robert Leduc with the Anschutz Family Foundation, Zadell Irene Loomis, CPA, of Stricklin, Loomis, Keena, P.C., Terry McAdam with the Hilton Foundation, Herb Paine with the United Way of California, and Jacke Wolf at the University of Manitoba—all of whom contributed insightful information and critiqued our drafts.

We express deep appreciation and admiration to the many current and past Applied Management Corporation people for their creative approaches to applying theory in a variety of organizations, many of which are included in this dictionary—particularly Charles A. Atler, CPA, Richard L. Subry, Patricia B. Trower, James W. Sawyer, and Richard E. Morrey.

Dean Marshall Kaplan and E. Sam Overman of the University of Colorado at Denver, Ronald S. Calinger with The Catholic University of America, Virginia A. Hodgkinson of INDEPENDENT SECTOR, and Albert C. Hyde at San Francisco State University provided encouragement and contributed invaluable information and materials. Special thanks to Daniel Oran for sharing his extensive knowledge on legal aspects of nonprofit organizations. We also appreciate his encouragement and critical suggestions.

Anna Lee Halsig, Delores Malloy, and Karen Rowe not only helped in preparing the manuscript but also were ingenious in deflecting distractions and tolerant of our periodically irrational behaviors and demands.

And thanks to Luise, Pat, Todd, Daren, Noah, and Terry, to whom we reintroduced ourselves periodically.

The Facts On File DICTIONARY OF NONPROFIT ORGANIZATION MANAGEMENT

A

AA: *see* AFFIRMATIVE ACTION.

AAA, American Accounting Association.
See also AMERICAN ARBITRATION ASSOCIATION.

AAAA, American Association of Advertising Agencies.

AACSB: *see* AMERICAN ASSEMBLY OF COLLEGIATE SCHOOLS OF BUSINESS.

AAFRC: *see* AMERICAN ASSOCIATION OF FUND-RAISING COUNSEL.

AAG: *see* AFFIRMATIVE ACTION GROUPS.

AAO: *see* AFFIRMATIVE ACTION OFFICER.

AAP: *see* AFFIRMATIVE ACTION PLAN or AFFIRMATIVE ACTION PROGRAM.

abandonment, elimination of a fixed asset from the financial records after its final retirement from service.

abandonment of position, quitting a job without formally resigning.

abate, to reduce, lessen, or diminish. For example, the IRS may abate a portion of an organization's tax liability.
See also ABATEMENT.

abatement, a reduction, decrease, alleviation, or mitigation. Also, an amount subtracted from a full tax. A reduction in a tax assessment.

ABC: *see* AUDIT BUREAU OF CIRCULATION.

abdication, giving up an office or responsibility by ceasing to perform its function rather than by formally resigning or relinquishing.

Abilene Paradox, a phenomenon of organizational behavior in which members assume that others favor an action or strategy, and no one questions or challenges it. Therefore, dysfunctional decisions are made and implemented. The Abilene Paradox is a form of "pluralistic ignorance." *See* Jerry B. Harvey, "The Abilene Paradox: The Management of Agreement," *Organizational Dynamics* (Summer, 1974).

ability, the present power to perform a physical or mental function.
See also APTITUDE.

ability test, performance test designed to reveal a measure of present ability (*e.g.*, a typing test).

ability to pay (labor relations), concept from collective bargaining referring to an employer's ability to tolerate the costs of requested wage and benefit increases. Factfinders and arbitrators frequently use the "ability to pay" concept in justifying their decisions.

ability to pay (taxation), the principle that the tax burden should be distributed according to a person's wealth. It is based on the assumption that as a person's income increases, the person can and should contribute a larger percentage of his/her income to support government activities. The progressive income tax is based on this principle.

abrogation of agreement, formal cancellation of an agreement or portion thereof.

abscond, to hide or sneak away to avoid arrest, a lawsuit, or creditors.
See also EMBEZZLEMENT.

absence, short-term unavailability for work, lasting at least one day or normal tour of duty. If an employee is absent from the job for a lesser period, it is usually considered a lateness.

absence rate, amount of absence, calculated by the U.S. Bureau of Labor Statistics using the following formula:
Absence rate =

$$\frac{\text{work days lost (per month)}}{\text{days worked plus days lost}} \times 100$$

absence without leave, absence without prior approval.

absentee, any employee not present for one or more scheduled days of work.

absenteeism, as defined by the U.S. Bureau of Labor Statistics:

> the failure of workers to appear on the job when they are scheduled to work. It is a broad term which is applied to time lost because sickness or accident prevents a worker from being on the job, as well as unauthorized time away from the job for other reasons. Workers who quit without notice are also counted as absentees until they are officially removed from the payroll.

Generally, absenteeism is associated with unnecessary, unexcused, or habitual absences from work.

absolution, freedom or release from an obligation or debt.

absorption accounting, an accounting system in which all costs (fixed or variable, direct or indirect) are "absorbed" by the goods or services produced within the accounting period.

abstract objective: *see* OBJECTIVE.

abuse, also FRAUD, furnishing excessive services to beneficiaries, violating regulations, or performing improper practices, none of which involves prosecutable fraud. *Fraud* is the obtaining of something of value by unlawful means through willful misrepresentation.

Academy of Management, nonprofit organization with primary objectives of advancing research, learning, teaching, and practice in the field of management and encouraging the extension and unification of knowledge pertaining to management. The Academy, most of whose members are college teachers, views itself as America's academic voice in U.S. management. The Academy of Management publishes the *Academy of Management Journal* and the *Academy of Management Review*.

acceleration clause, a section of a contract that makes an entire debt come immediately due because of a failure to pay on time or because of some other failure.

acceptance, agreeing to an offer and becoming bound to the terms of a contract.

acceptance theory of authority: *see* ZONE OF ACCEPTANCE.

accession, any addition to the work force of an organization.

accession rate, also called HIRING RATE, number of employees added to a payroll during a given time period, usually expressed as a percentage of total employment. The accession rate is a significant indicator of economic growth—an increase (decrease) tends to indicate economic recovery (recession). Statistics on the accession rates of major industries are gathered monthly by the Bureau of Labor Statistics of the U.S. Department of Labor. Accession rates can be computed using the following formula:
accession rate =

$$\frac{\text{total accessions} \times 100}{\text{total number of workers}}$$

access time, the time required for information to be inserted into or taken from computer storage.

accidental death benefit, feature found in some life insurance policies that provides for payment of additional amounts to the beneficiary if the insured party dies as a result of an accident. When such provisions allow for an accidental death benefit that is twice the normal value of the policy, they are known as "double-indemnity" provisions.

accident and sickness benefits, variety of regular payments made to employees who lose time from work due to off-the-job disabilities occasioned by accidents or sickness.

accident frequency rate, as computed by the Bureau of Labor Statistics, the total number of disabling injuries per million hours worked.

accident prevention, planned effort to eliminate the causes and severity of workplace injuries and accidents.

accident-proneness, concept that implies that certain kinds of personalities are more likely to have accidents than others. However, psychological research supports the assertion that accident-proneness is more related to situational factors than to personality factors.

accident severity rate, generally computed as the number of work days lost because of accidents per thousand hours worked.

account, a self-contained financial record keeping system for one particular subject or type of transaction.

accountability, extent to which one is responsible to higher authority—legal or organizational—for one's actions in society at large or within one's particular organizational position; also, in the nonprofit arena, an organizational value or concept which recognizes that in exchange for the public trust conferred upon nonprofit organizations, is the responsibility for full disclosure and review of program and financial performance and impact. Oftentimes, the concept is tied to that of stewardship.

See also STEWARDSHIP, CONCEPT OF.

accountant, a person who specializes in the accuracy of financial records.

See also BOOKKEEPING and CERTIFIED PUBLIC ACCOUNTANT.

accounting, also CASH ACCOUNTING and ACCRUAL ACCOUNTING, process of classifying, measuring, and interpreting financial transactions. *Cash accounting* is the recording of transactions at the time the payment is actually made or received. *Accrual Accounting* means that revenues are recorded when they are earned, and expenses are recorded as they are incurred.

accounting cycle, the repetitive processing of financial transactions during an accounting "cycle"—typically one month. The basic steps in the accounting cycle are: (1) enter transactions in a journal, (2) balance the journals and allocate costs, (3a) post information from the journals to the general ledger, (3b) post information from the journals to the subsidiary ledger accounts, (4) reconcile and balance the ledger accounts, (5) prepare financial statements, and (6) use the information to improve operations.

See also:
BALANCE SHEET
FINANCIAL STATEMENTS
GENERAL LEDGER
JOURNAL
JOURNALIZING
OPERATING STATEMENT
SUBSIDIARY LEDGER

accounting equation, a mathematical representation of the basic relationships between parts of a financial statement. For example, the accounting equation for the relationship among assets, liabilities, and fund balances (on a balance sheet) is:

A = L (+) FB
Assets = Liabilities (+) Fund Balances

accounting, noncyclic, an accounting approach in which books are not closed at the end of fiscal periods (for example, the end of a month or a year). Instead, information cycles through the accounting system continuously, and current financial reports are "pulled" at (and for) any point in time they are desired by management.

accounting principles: *see* GENERALLY ACCEPTED ACCOUNTING PRINCIPLES.

THE ACCOUNTING CYCLE

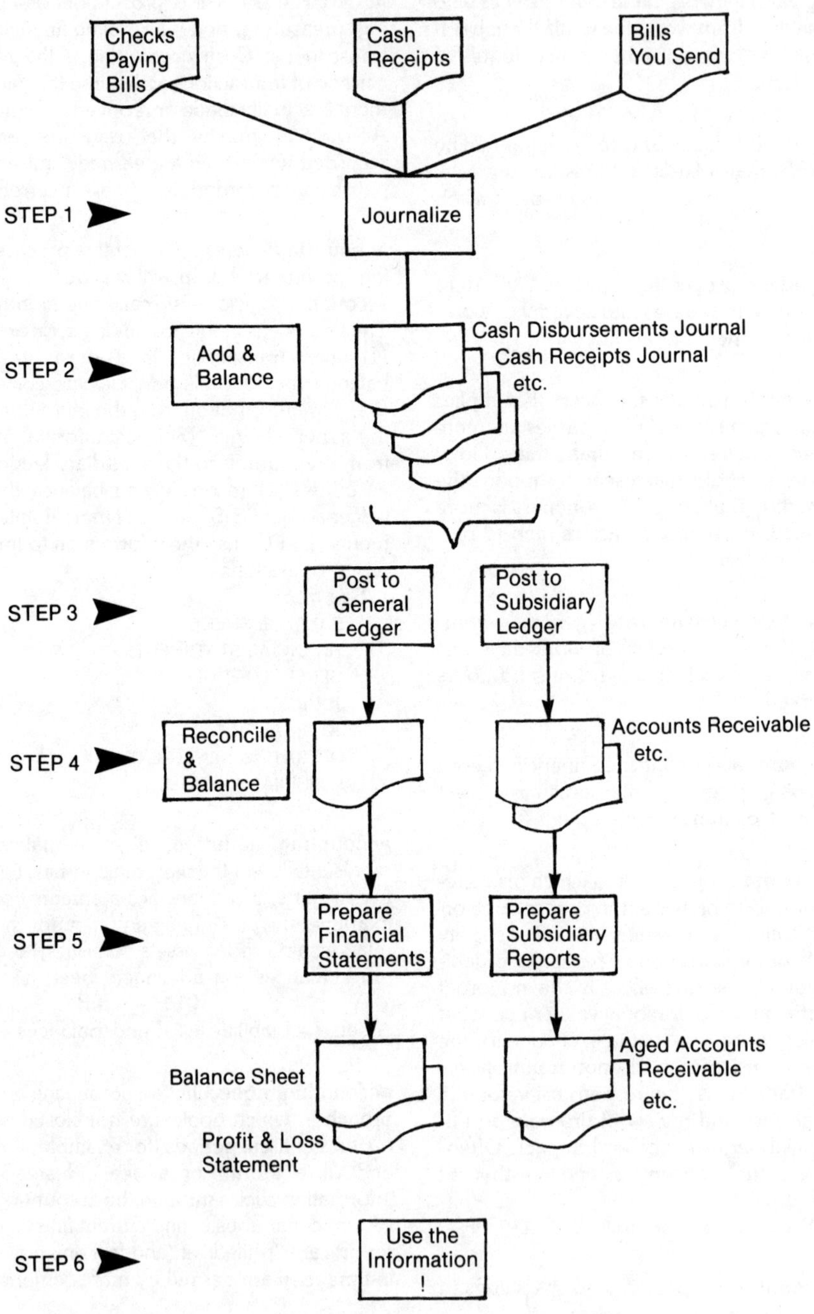

Accounting Principles Board, the body within the American Institute of Certified Public Accountants (AICPA) that establishes and revises generally accepted accounting principles.

See also FINANCIAL ACCOUNTING STANDARDS BOARD and GENERALLY ACCEPTED ACCOUNTING PRINCIPLES.

accounting ratio, any ratio used in analyzing an organization's financial condition. For example, a current ratio is the ratio of current assets to current liabilities.

See also RATIO and RATIO ACCOUNTING.

accounting system, a consistent way of organizing, recording, summarizing, and reporting financial transactions. The minimum requirements for an accounting system include the following:

1) It must provide financial information for management to make policy decisions, prepare budgets and grant proposals, and provide other useful financial reports.
2) Similar transactions must receive consistent accounting treatment.
3) It must be sufficiently flexible to handle hand- or machine-recorded accounting information without restricting the organization's accounting pattern.
4) It must be able to show whether or not the organization is in basic compliance with federal, state, and local laws, rules, and regulations, including tax laws and codes.
5) It must have a self-balancing group of accounts, a double entry system, and a general ledger and subsidiary ledgers.
6) It must match revenues and expenses for the same time periods—for example, a month or a year *(accrual accounting)*—or match cash received and expended for the same time periods *(cash accounting)*.

See also:

ACCOUNT
ACCOUNTING
ACCOUNTING CYCLE
DEBITS AND CREDITS
GENERAL LEDGER
SUBSIDIARY LEDGER

accounting system, double entry: *see* DEBITS AND CREDITS.

accounts payable, amounts owed to others for goods and services received and assets acquired.

accounts receivable, amounts due from others for goods furnished and services rendered, usually from customers or clients.

accreditation, the process by which an organization evaluates and recognizes a program of study or services or an institution as meeting certain predetermined standards. The recognition is called accreditation. Similar assessment of individuals is called *certification.*

accretion, a gradual accumulation; for example, the growth of a bank account due to continuing deposits and interest earned.

accrual accounting: *see* ACCOUNTING and ACCOUNTING SYSTEM.

accrued, due and payable but not yet paid.

accrued expenditures, charges during a given period that reflect liabilities incurred and the need to pay for services, goods, and other tangible property received, and amounts owed for which no current service or performance is required (such as annuities, insurance claims, other benefit payments, and some cash grants). Expenditures accrue regardless of when cash payments are made, whether invoices have been rendered, or, in some cases, whether goods or other tangible property have been physically delivered.

See also ACCOUNTING and LIABILITIES.

accumulated depreciation, the part of an asset's costs which have been depreciated (that is, for financial purposes, considered to have been consumed or used up).

See also DEPRECIATION.

achievement, accomplishment; past performance; what an individual or organization has accomplished in the past, in contrast with "ability," which refers to what an individual or organization can do now (in the present) or in the future.
See also ABILITY and APTITUDE.

achievement battery: *see* ACHIEVEMENT TEST.

achievement drive, also called ACHIEVEMENT NEED, motivation to strive for high standards of performance in a given area of endeavor.

achievement need: *see* ACHIEVEMENT DRIVE.

achievement test, test designed to measure an individual's level of proficiency in a specific subject or task. A collection of achievement tests designed to measure levels of skill or knowledge in a variety of areas is called an achievement battery.

acoustic coupler, a device that hooks a telephone handset into a computer to allow computer communication over telephone lines using a modem.
See also MODEM.

across-the-board increase, increase in wages, whether expressed in dollars or percentage of salary, given to an entire work force.

act, written bill formally passed by a legislature, such as the U.S. Congress. An act is a "bill" from its introduction until its passage by a house of a legislature. An act becomes law when it is signed by a chief executive, such as the U.S. President.

acting, holding a temporary position or rank; filling in temporarily for someone else.

Action, federal agency that provides centralized coordination and administration of domestic volunteer activities sponsored by the federal government. Action is the administrative home of Volunteers in Service to America (VISTA), the Foster Grandparent Program, the Retired Senior Volunteer Program (RSVP), and related programs.

actionable, an act or occurrence that provides adequate reason for a grievance or lawsuit.

action organization, an organization which devotes a substantial amount of effort seeking to influence legislation or participating in a political campaign to aid or oppose a candidate for public office. Action organizations do not meet the operational test for tax exemption for charitable organizations. An action organization is easier to define in theory than in practice, because it involves such difficult concepts as "substantially," "primarily," and "exclusively"—particularly related to legislative activities.
See also:
LEGISLATIVE ACTIVITIES
POLITICAL ACTION COMMITTEE
POLITICAL ACTIVITY
TAXABLE EXPENDITURE

action plan, a description of the specific steps and responsibilities involved in achieving a goal.

action research, in its broadest context, the application of the scientific method to practical problems. As the basic model underlying organization development, action research is the process of collecting data about an ongoing organizational system to feed it back into the system, then altering a variable within the organizational system in response to this data or to test a hypothesis and evaluate the results by collecting more data. The process is repeated as needed.
See also ORGANIZATION DEVELOPMENT.

action theory, a mode of analysis which seeks to unite theory and practice by taking the face-to-face encounter as the primary analytical unit.

active listening, counseling technique in which the counselor listens to both the facts and the feelings of the speaker. Such listening is called "active" because the counselor has the specific responsibilities of showing interest, of not passing judgment, and of helping the speaker to work out his problems.

The basic elements of active listening are:

1) Don't condone or condemn, agree or disagree.
2) Maintain a series of complementary transactions.
3) Use reflective phrases.
   - Paraphrase—sometimes overstate.
   - Some key phrases include:
     "Sounds like . . ."
     "I hear you saying . . ."
     "You feel like . . ."
     "In other words . . ."
4) Use reflective rather than accusative "you" messages.
5) Ask expansion-type questions.
6) Use reflective body language—for example, eye contact.
7) Be genuine and authentic.

When the other person gives positive or expanding responses, those are indicators of success in the active listening.

active trust, a trust for which the trustee must perform some services.

activity, a specific and distinguishable line of work performed by one or more individuals or organizational components for the purpose of discharging a function or subfunction for which the unit or individual is responsible. For example, food inspection is an activity performed in the discharge of the health function.

See also BUDGET ACTIVITY and FUNCTIONAL CLASSIFICATION.

activity (as in work plan), a detailed work step in a work plan; for example, for a project or a subtask. The most detailed and shortest duration statement of effort in a work plan.

activity charge, a checking account fee.

activity ratio, any measure of how well an organization manages its resources that uses ratios or rates.

See also RATIO and RATIO ACCOUNTING.

activity statement: *see* OPERATING STATEMENT.

actuarial projections, mathematical calculations involving the rate of mortality for a given group of people.

actuary, specialist in the mathematics of insurance.

adaptive-coping cycle, a seven-stage model which describes the processes used by organizations to adapt to change. According to J. A. Olmstead, H. E. Christensen, and L. L. Lackey's article, "Components of Organizational Competence: Test of a Conceptual Framework," RB 26-4 (Ft. Ord, Calif.: U.S. Army Organizational Effectiveness Training Center, Dec. 1977):

1) Sensing. The organization acquires and interprets data about its external and internal environments.
2) Communicating information. Transmitting interpreted data (information) to those parts of the organization which can act upon them.
3) Decision making. Using sensed information to make action decisions.
4) Communicating. Transmitting decisions, instructions, and directives to those parts of the organization that will implement them.
5) Stabilizing. Maintaining internal stability and integration in order to prevent disruption as the organization changes.
6) Coping actions. Implementing actions resulting from decisions.
7) Feedback. Assessing the results of actions by continuing to sense the environment. (Recycle to [1]).

addiction: *see* DRUG ADDICTION.

address (computers), the identifying name or symbol that locates the place where information is stored.

ad hoc, Latin word meaning for this special purpose or for this one time.

ad hoc arbitrator, arbitrator selected by the parties involved to serve on one case. Nothing prevents the arbitrator from being used again if both parties agree. *Ad hoc* or temporary, single-case arbitration is distinguished from "permanent" arbitration where arbitrators are named in an agreement to help resolve disputes about an agreement that may arise during the life of the agreement.

See also ARBITRATION.

ad hoc committee, committee created for a specific task or purpose whose existence ceases with the attainment of its goal.

ad-hocracy, Alvin Toffler's term, in *Future Shock* (NY: Random House, 1970), for "the fast-moving, information-rich, kinetic organization of the future, filled with transient cells and extremely mobile individuals." Ad-hocracy is obviously a contraction of ad hoc (Latin for "to this" or temporary) and bureaucracy.

See also FUTURE SHOCK.

adjournment, the putting off of business to another time or place; the decision to stop meeting.

adjudication, resolution of a dispute by means of judicial or quasijudicial proceedings.

adjunct account, an account that receives additions from another account (for example, interest).

adjustable rate mortgage, also FLEXIBLE RATE LOAN, a mortgage which can vary in any of its terms during its life, as agreed upon in the mortgage contract. Typically, the initial year(s) interest rate is lower than the rate offered on a standard fixed rate mortgage, and subsequent years' interest rates change with a contractually accepted index (for example, the U.S. Treasury bill rate).

See also MORTGAGE.

adjusted case, according to the National Labor Relations Board, cases in which an informal settlement agreement is executed and compliance with its terms is secured. A central element in an "adjusted" case is the agreement of the parties to settle differences without recourse to litigation.

adjusted gross income (AGI), federal income tax term referring, in general, to the money a person earns minus allowable deductions for certain travel, work, business, or moving expenses, etc. Deductions for contributions are limited to a percentage of AGI, thus, AGI frequently is called the "contribution base." In general the contribution deduction limit on gifts to most types of charitable organizations is fifty percent of AGI. The limits are tighter on gifts to private foundations.

adjusted net income (private foundation), gross income (with certain exclusions) less expenses incurred in the production of the income.

See also CHARITABLE ORGANIZATION.

adjusted trial balance, the trial balance taken immediately after adjusting entries have been posted.

See also ACCOUNTING CYCLE and TRIAL BALANCE.

adjustment assistance, financial and technical assistance to firms, workers, and communities to help them adjust to rising import competition. While the benefits of increased trade to the importing country generally exceed the costs of adjustments, the benefits are widely shared while the adjustment costs are sometimes narrowly concentrated on a few domestic producers and communities. Both import restraints and adjustment assistance are designed to reduce these hardships.

adjustment entries, also ADJUSTING JOURNAL ENTRIES, an accounting procedure used at the close of a fiscal period (for example, a month or a year) to record income and expenses in the proper period, to make the operating statement reflect the correct income, to adjust the balance sheet account balances to actual, and to correct errors.

See also:

ACCOUNTING CYCLE
DEPRECIATION
FINANCIAL STATEMENTS
FISCAL YEAR
OPERATING STATEMENTS

administration, management and direction of the affairs of institutions. Administration can also refer to administors collectively or to the execution of policy. For analyses of fifteen different meanings of the word, *see* A. Dunsire, *Administration: The Word and the Science* (New York: Halsted Press, John Wiley, 1973).

Administration & Society, quartery journal that seeks to further the understanding of public and human service organizations, their administrative processes, and their impacts upon the larger society.

administrative accountability, that aspect of administrative responsibility by which officials are held answerable for general notions of democracy and morality as well as for specific management responsibilities.

administrative advocacy, the recognition that administration is a highly political process involving severe differences of judgment in which the most feasible course of action is likely to emerge from the competition produced when each group pleads for the cause which it represents, whether that cause be more funds to carry out policies, the survival of a program, a particular piece of advice, or the desire for a more efficient system of administrative decision making.

administrative analysis, totality of the approaches and techniques that allow an organization to assess its present condition in order to make adjustments that further enhance the organization's ability to achieve its goals.

See also SYSTEMS ANALYSIS and STRATEGIC MANAGEMENT.

administrative behavior, human behavior in an organizational context. While administrative behavior tends to be used interchangeably with organizational behavior, the latter by implication restricts itself to work organizations while the former is rightly concerned with all of the organizations of society. The classic work on this subject is Herbert A. Simon, *Administrative Behavior: A Study of Decision-Making Processes in Administrative Organizations* (New York: Macmillan, 2nd ed., 1947, 1961).

administrative board, a governing body of a nonprofit organization which is mandated directly to govern the day-to-day administrative affairs, as well as policy, of the organization.

See also BOARD OF DIRECTORS GOVERNANCE.

administrative cost rate, the percent of total expenses budgeted, as in a grant, or expended for administrative costs.

administrative costs, also ADMINISTRATIVE EXPENSES, costs incurred to administer or manage an organization; costs which are not directly chargeable to a program. Often, a grantor will stipulate or negotiate maximum allowable administrative costs or an administrative cost rate.

See also ADMINISTRATIVE COST RATE and COST, INDIRECT.

administrative discretion, general principle of administration encompassing a number of points in administrative law; the requirement that the actions of any official be based upon a specific grant of authority which establishes strict limits on official action.

administrative due process, term encompassing a number of points in administrative law which require that the administrative procedures of government agencies and regulatory commissions, as they affect private parties, be based upon written guidelines that safeguard individual rights and protect against the arbitrary or inequitable exercise of bureaucratic power.

See also DUE PROCESS.

administrative law, the law concerning the powers and procedures of administrative agencies, particularly the law governing judicial review of administrative action; either the laws about the duties and proper conduct of an administrative agency that are handed to agencies by legislatures and courts or the rules and regulations set out by administrative agencies.

administrative law judge, also called HEARING EXAMINER and HEARING OFFICER, official who conducts hearings in the place of and in behalf of a more formal body.

administrative morality, use of religious, political, or social precepts to create standards by which the quality of administration may be judged; in the main, the standards of honesty, responsiveness, efficiency, effectiveness, competence, effect on individual rights, adherence to democratic procedures, and social equity.

administrative objective: *see* OBJECTIVE, ADMINISTRATIVE.

administrative order, a directive issued by an administrator or an administrative agency.

administrative planning, totality of deciding what an organization will do, who will do it, and how it will be done.

Administrative Procedure Act of 1946, basic law of how U.S. Government agencies must operate in order to provide adequate safeguards for agency clients and the general public.

administrative process, the planning, organizing, leading, and evaluating of others to achieve specific ends.

administrative remedy, a means of enforcing a right by going to an administrator or an administrative agency either for help or for a decision. Employees and clients often are required to "exhaust all administrative remedies" before taking their cases to court.

Administrative Science Quarterly, premier scholarly journal dedicated to advancing the understanding of administration through empirical investigation and theoretical analysis. Articles cover all phases of management, human relations, organizational behavior, and organizational communications.

administrative workweek, period of seven consecutive calendar days designated in advance. Usually an administrative workweek coincides with a calendar week.

administrator, any manager; the head of an organizational unit; or someone appointed by a court to handle a deceased person's estate.

See also MANAGEMENT and TRUSTEE.

admitted assets, assets of an insurance company that are recognized by a state regulatory or other examining body in determining the company's financial condition.

admonition, simple reproval of an employee by a supervisor.

See also REPRIMAND.

ADO: *see* ALLEGED DISCRIMINATORY OFFICIAL.

ADP, also **EDP,** automatic data processing or electronic data processing.

ad valorem tax: *see* TAX BASE.

advance appropriation, appropriation provided by the Congress for use in a fiscal year or more beyond the fiscal year for which the appropriation act is passed (*e.g.*, the 1976 appropriation for use in fiscal year 1976 for the Washington Metropolitan Area Transit Authority contained in the Department of Transportation and Related Agencies Appropriation Act, 1975, which was passed on August 28, 1974). Advance appropriations allow state and local governments, grantees, and contractors sufficient time to develop plans with assurance of future Federal funding.

See also ADVANCE FUNDING.

advance funding, authority to obligate and disburse funds during a fiscal year from a succeeding year's budget or appropriation. The funds so obligated increase the budget authority for the fiscal year in which obligated, and reduce the budget authority of the succeeding fiscal year.

advancement of religion, concept of, a broad, general term which has been viewed as a tax-exempt charitable purpose for many years. The concept includes the promotion of specific religions as well as religion in general. Permissible activities have included, for example, constructing a church building, paying staff salaries, supporting missions, etc.

advance on wages, wages/salaries drawn in advance of work performance or earned commissions. Also applies to payments in advance of the regular payday for sums already earned.

advances, amounts of money prepaid in contemplation of the later receipt of goods, services, or other assets. Advances are ordinarily made only to payees to whom an organization has an obligation, and not in excess of the amount of the obligation. A common example is travel advances, which are amounts made available to employees prior to the beginning of a trip for costs to be incurred.

adversary system, the system of law in the United States. The judge acts as the decision maker between opposing sides (for example, between two individuals, between a nonprofit organization and an individual, etc.) rather than acting as the person who also makes the state's case or independently seeks out evidence.

adverse action, personnel action considered unfavorable to an employee, such as discharge, suspension, demotion, etc.

See also DISCIPLINARY ACTION.

adverse effect, differential rate of selection (for hire, promotion, etc.) that works to the disadvantage of an applicant subgroup, particularly subgroups classified by race, sex, and other characteristics on the basis of which discrimination is prohibited by law.

adverse impact, term for a selection process for a particular job or group of jobs that results in the selection of members of any racial, ethnic, or sex group at a lower rate than members of other groups. Federal EEO enforcement agencies generally regard a selection rate for any group that is less than four fifths (4/5) or eighty percent of the rate for other groups as constituting evidence of adverse impact.

adverse-inference rule, an analytical tool used by the Equal Employment Opportunity Commission (EEOC) in its investigations. The EEOC holds that when relevant evidence is withheld by an organization and the EEOC feels that there is no valid reason for such a withholding, the EEOC may presume that the evidence in question is adverse to the organization being investigated. The EEOC Compliance Manual permits use of the adverse-inference rule only if "the requested evidence is relevant," the evidence was requested "with ample time to produce it and with notice that failure to produce it would result in an adverse inference," and the "respondent produced neither the evidence nor an acceptable explanation."

advertising, a marketing tool which has an identifiable sponsor who pays for a presentation of ideas, goods, or services to inform or persuade the public.

See also PUBLIC RELATIONS.

advertising agency, a company that creates and places advertising for clients. The agency generates its revenues by billing the client for creative or production services, and by commissions earned from publications and media in which it buys space on behalf of the client.

advertising campaign, a planned program using various media, conducted over a period of time, to sell ideas, goods, or services to the public.

Advertising Council, The, a nonprofit organization that produces public service advertising (for example, on behalf of nonprofit organizations).

See also:
INFORMATIONAL SPOT
MEDIA
PUBLIC RELATIONS

advertisement, display, an advertisement in a newspaper or magazine that uses graphics or pictures.

advertisement, institutional, an advertisement that is designed more to improve an organization's image than to sell its products or services.

See also PUBLIC RELATIONS.

advertorial, a paid editorial in which an organization presents its views on a social issue.

advised fund, a fund accounting arrangement for certain trusts under which, for example, the donor's authority relative to the distribution of trust funds is advisory only. Advised funds are but one of several types of funds which are commonly found in community foundations.

See also COMMUNITY FOUNDATION.

advisory arbitration, arbitration that recommends a solution of a dispute but is not binding upon either party.

advisory board, an elected or appointed body of a nonprofit organization which provides advice and expertise on administrative and/or program matters to the senior staff and/or the governing board of the organization.

advisory opinion, statement by a judge or regulatory agency about a question that has been informally submitted. The U.S. Supreme Court never issues advisory opinions.

advocacy, administrative: *see* ADMINISTRATIVE ADVOCACY.

advocacy case: *see* CASE ADVOCACY.

advocacy, class: *see* CLASS ADVOCACY.

advocacy organization, or ADVOCACY GROUP, a nonprofit organization that fills an important role as a social critic. The term includes cause- and issue-oriented organizations and groups including, for example, those involved in the environmental, consumer, civil rights, and women's movements, and those opposed to U.S. military involvement in different parts of the world.

See also CASE ADVOCACY and CLASS ADVOCACY.

AEI: *see* AMERICAN ENTERPRISE INSTITUTE FOR PUBLIC POLICY RESEARCH.

affected class, according to the U.S. Department of Labor's Office of Federal Court Compliance:

> persons who continue to suffer the present effects of past discrimination. An employee or group of employees may be members of an affected class when, because of discrimination based on race, religion, sex, or national origin, such employees, for example, were assigned initially to less desirable or lower paying jobs, were denied equal opportunity to advance to better paying or more desirable jobs, or were subject to layoff or displacement from their jobs.

affidavit, written statement made under oath before a person permitted by law to administer such an oath (*e.g.*, a notary public).

affiliated charities, two or more charities that are treated as one for certain purposes by the IRS, including, for example, for the expenditure tests.

See also AFFILIATED ORGANIZATIONS.

affiliated organizations, a general term meaning related organizations. For example, the IRS often views organizations as affiliated if they have interlocking directorates and if one (or more) of the organizations is committed to the actions of another by its governing instruments.

See also:
AFFILIATED CHARITIES
DIRECTORATES, INTERLOCKING
GOVERNING INSTRUMENT

affirmative action, term that first gained currency in the 1960s, meaning the removal of "artificial barriers" to the employment of women and minority group members. Toward the end of that decade, however, the term got lost in a fog of semantics and came out meaning the provision of compensatory opportunities for hitherto disadvantaged groups. In a formal, legal sense, affirmative action now refers to specific efforts to recruit, hire, and promote disadvantaged groups for the purpose of eliminating the present effects of past discrimination.

Affirmative Action Compliance Manual for Federal Contractors, publication of the Bureau of National Affairs, Inc., which includes a "News and Developments" report, plus the manual used by the Office of Federal Contract Compliance Programs (OFCCP), the OFCCP Construction Compliance Program Operations Manual, and material taken from the official compliance manuals used by the Department of Defense, the Department of the Treasury, the Department of Housing and Urban Development, and the Department of Health and Human Services—with appropriate excerpts from other official compliance manuals.

affirmative action groups, also called PROTECTED GROUPS, segments of the population that have been identified by federal, state, or local laws to be specifically protected from employment discrimination. Such groups include women, identified minorities, the elderly, and the handicapped.

affirmative action officer, individual with an organization who has the primary responsibility for the development, installation, and maintenance of the organization's affirmative action program.

affirmative action plan, an organization's written plan to remedy past discrimination against, or under utilization of, women and minorities. The plan itself usually consists of a statement of goals, timetables for achieving milestones, and specific program efforts.

affirmative action program, formal course of action undertaken by employers to hire and promote women and minorities in order to remedy past abuses or maintain present equity. The most basic tool of an affirmative action program is the affirmative action plan.

affirmative discrimination: *see* AFFIRMATIVE ACTION.

affirmative order, order issued by the National Labor Relations Board (NLRB) or similar state agency demanding that an employer or union take specific action to cease performing and/or undo the effects of an unfair labor practice. For example, the NLRB might issue an affirmative order to a company to "make whole" a wrongfully discharged employee by reinstating the employee with full back pay and reestablishing the employee's seniority and other rights.

affirmative recruitment, recruiting efforts undertaken to assure that adequate numbers of women and minorities are represented in applicant pools for positions in which they have been historically underutilized.

affirmative zoning, land use regulations which seek to require the construction of low income housing or other construction of use to the disadvantaged.

AFL-CIO: *see* AMERICAN FEDERATION OF LABOR-CONGRESS OF INDUSTRIAL ORGANIZATIONS.

agate line, a space measure used in newspaper, magazine, and journal advertising, one fourteenth of an inch high by the length of the printed line.

See also MILLINE RATE.

aged, home for the, under a 1972 IRS ruling, considered a charitable organization if it meets the residents' primary needs for housing, health care, and financial security.

age discrimination, disparate or unfavorable treatment of an individual in an employment situation because of age.

ageism, in the tradition of racism and sexism, discrimination against those who are considered old.

agency, any department, office, commission, authority, administration, board, government-owned corporation, or other independent establishment of any branch of government in the United States; also, commonly used when referring to local community-based organizations or service providers.

agency, employment: *see* EMPLOYMENT AGENCY.

agency and private trust transactions, receipt, holding, and disbursement of moneys by a government as agent or trustee for other governments or private persons, such as collection of local government taxes, collection of Federal income taxes and social security "taxes," receipt and return of guarantee deposits, and the like.

Agency for International Development (AID), unit of the U.S. International Development Cooperation Agency that carries out assistance programs designed to help the people of certain less developed countries develop their human and economic resources, increase productive capacities, and improve the quality of life. AID was a part of the U.S. Department of State until 1979.

agency shop, union security provision, found in some collective bargaining agreements, which requires that nonunion employees of the bargaining unit must pay the union a sum equal to union dues as a condition of continuing employment.

agenda, an order of business; a sequential listing of items to be addressed during a meeting. Preferably, a meeting's agenda should be prepared and distributed to directors or committee members several days in advance so that they may be prepared and better able to participate in deliberations and decisions. A typical agenda for a board of directors meeting and more formal committee meetings includes:

Call to order
Call and record attendance
Establish a quorum
Read and/or act to approve the (corrected) minutes of the previous meeting
Announcements
Additions or changes to the agenda
Reports (for example, staff, committees and/or officers)
Appointments (for example, to committees)
Old business (that is, business remaining from previous meeting[s])
New business
Announce or establish next meeting time and place
Adjournment

See also HIDDEN AGENDA.

agent, person who is formally designated to act on behalf of another person or organization.

aggregate cost method, also called AGGREGATE METHOD, projected funding technique that computes pension benefits and costs for an entire plan rather than for its individual participants.

aggregate liability, the total amount that an insurer will pay for liabilities assumed under a policy.

AGI: *see* ADJUSTED GROSS INCOME.

aging schedule, a report showing how long accounts receivable have been owed and which ones are overdue.

See also ACCOUNTS RECEIVABLE and COLLECTION RATE.

AGPA: *see* AMERICAN GROUP PSYCHOTHERAPY ASSOCIATION.

agreement, an intention of two or more parties to enter into a contract with one another, combined with an attempt to form a valid contract; also, a contract.

See also the following entries:

GENTLEMEN'S AGREEMENT
INDEX OF AGREEMENT
INDIVIDUAL AGREEMENT
MASTER AGREEMENT
MODEL AGREEMENT
OPEN-END AGREEMENT
SWEETHEART AGREEMENT

agricultural organization, a group organized and operated for agricultural purposes. For tax exemption purposes, agriculture is defined broadly. However, in order to qualify for tax-exempt status, organizations engaged in agricultural activities must also satisfy other criteria—including those relating to private inurement. Agricultural organizations may qualify for tax-exempt status under IRS Code 501(c)(5).

See also AGRICULTURE and PRIVATE INUREMENT.

agriculture, according to the Tax Reform Act of 1976, for federal tax purposes, agriculture includes, for example, "the act or science of cultivating land, harvesting crops or aquatic resources, or raising livestock." Because IRS Code 501(c)(5) authorizes tax exemptions for agricultural organizations, its definition is important.

AICPA: *see* AMERICAN INSTITUTE OF CERTIFIED PUBLIC ACCOUNTANTS.

AID: *see* AGENCY FOR INTERNATIONAL DEVELOPMENT.

AIM: *see* AMERICAN INSTITUTE OF MANAGEMENT.

air pollution, presence of contaminant substances or particulates in the atmosphere that do not disperse properly and that interfere with human, animal or plant life.

air quality control region, geographic area designated by a common air pollution situation.

air quality standards, levels measured by the amount of pollutants in the air prescribed by law or regulation that can not be exceeded in a defined area over a specific period of time. *Primary standards* are numerical levels of air pollution required to protect the public health. *Secondary standards* are numerical levels that would protect the public welfare and include effects on all geographic, social, and economic aspects.

air rights, the right to build above a piece of land or a structure (for example, a historic church).

Alabama Power Co.* v. *Davis, 431 U.S. 581 (1977), U.S. Supreme Court case which held that employers who rehire a returning veteran are required to credit the employee's military service toward the calculation of pension benefits. A unanimous court concluded that "pension payments are predominantly rewards for continuous employment with the same employer," rather than deferred compensation for services rendered. Thus, the purpose of Section 9 of the Selective Service Act, as explained by Justice Thurgood Marshall for the Court, is to protect veterans "from the loss of such rewards when the break in their employment resulted from their response to the country's military needs."

Albemarle Paper Co.* v. *Moody, 422 U.S. 405 (1975), U.S. Supreme Court case that established the principle that once discrimination has been proven in a Title VII (of the Civil Rights Act of 1964) case, the trial judge ordinarily does not have discretion to deny back pay.

alcoholism, detrimental dependency on alcoholic beverages. It was only in 1956 that the American Medical Association first recognized alcoholism as a disease. However, it is still not universally recognized as such. Almost all large organizations have some program to deal with alcoholic employees.

aleatory contract, a contract with effects and results that depend on an uncertain event; for example, insurance agreements are aleatory.

ALGOL, also ALGORITHMIC LANGUAGE, a computer language made up of both algebraic and English components.

algorithm, a repeatable, step-by-step procedure to solve a problem or to accomplish a task. Algorithms for computerized applications (and, in recent years, in general usage) make each step a yes-or-no decision with only two choices.

alienation, a concept originally from Marxism which held that industrial workers would experience feelings of disassociation because they lacked control of their work (and would thus be ripe for revolution). The word has lost its Marxist taint and now refers to feelings of estrangement from one's work, family, society, etc.

Alien Registration Act of 1940, also called the SMITH ACT, U.S. law that requires the annual registration of aliens. It also prohibits advocating the violent overthrow of the U.S. government.

alleged discriminatory official (ADO), individual charged in a formal equal employment opportunity complaint with having caused or tolerated discriminatory actions.

Alliance for Volunteerism, Inc., one of several recently formed national associations attempting to increase cooperation and collaboration among voluntary organizations.

See also NATIONAL CONGRESS ON VOLUNTEERISM AND CITIZENSHIP and VOLUNTEER.

allied health personnel, specially trained and licensed (when necessary) health workers other than physicians, dentists, podiatrists, and nurses. The term has no constant or agreed upon detailed meaning, sometimes being used synonymously with paramedical personnel, sometimes meaning all health workers who perform tasks which must otherwise be performed by a physician, and sometimes referring to health workers who do not usually engage in independent practice.

allocate, also REALLOCATE, to assign a position or class to a particular salary grade in the salary schedule based on an evaluation of its relative worth. To reallocate is to change the existing allocation of a position or class to a different salary grade in the schedule; also, a financial reporting term indicating the distribution of funds by a funding source to an agency.

allotment, an authorization to incur expenditures for a given amount of money for a specific purpose made on a monthly or quarterly basis.

allowable charge, generic term referring to the maximum fee that a third party will use in reimbursing a provider for a given service. An allowable charge may not be the same as either a reasonable, customary, or prevailing charge, as the terms are used under the Medicare program.

allowable costs: *see* COSTS, ALLOWABLE.

allowance, financial payment to compensate an employee for the extra expense of living at a hardship post, for special clothing such as uniforms, or for some other benefit that personnel policy allows.

allowances, amounts included in a budget request or projection to cover possible additional proposals, such as anticipated pay increases and contingencies for relatively uncontrollable programs and other requirements. Allowances remain undistributed until they occur or become firm, then they are distributed to the appropriate functional classification(s).

allowed time, also called NORMAL TIME, time given an employee to perform a task. Normally includes an allowance for fatigue and personal and/or unavoidable delays.

alphabetism, discrimination against those whose names begin with letters at the end of the alphabet.

alphanumeric, containing both letters and numbers.

alternate form, also called EQUIVALENT FORM or COMPARABLE FORM, any of two or more versions of a test that are the same with respect to the nature, number, and difficulty of the test items and that are designed to yield essentially the same scores and measures of variability for a given group.

alternate-form reliability, measure of the extent to which two parallel or equivalent forms of a test are consistent in measuring what they purport to measure.

alternation ranking, technique used in job evaluation and performance appraisal that ranks the highest and the lowest, then the next highest and the next lowest, etc., until all jobs have been ranked.

alternative cost: *see* OPPORTUNITY COST.

alternative technology: *see* APPROPRIATE TECHNOLOGY.

alumni association, an association of former students of an educational institution. Typically, alumni associations are involved in communications, student recruitment, member education, fund-raising, and social activities, usually through a network of "chapters." Alumni associations may qualify as educational organizations for federal tax purposes.

According to the *Associated Press Stylebook and Libel Manual* (Howard Angione, Editor), although "alumnae" and "alumni" are the plural forms of alumna (feminine) and alumnus (masculine), respectively, "Use *alumni* when referring to a group of men and women." However, "alumni/ae" is becoming the more commonly used term for organizations that include both alumni and alumnae.

AMA, American Marketing Association.

See also AMERICAN MANAGEMENT ASSOCIATION.

AMACOM: *see* AMERICAN MANAGEMENT ASSOCIATIONS.

amateur, a person or organization who participates in an activity for pleasure, generally without compensation or other financial benefit. Not to be confused with a volunteer or a paraprofessional.

amateur sports organization, a category of charitable organization established by the Tax Reform Act of 1976.

American Arbitration Association (AAA), formed in 1926, a public service, nonprofit organization dedicated to the resolution of disputes of all kinds through the use of arbitration, mediation, democratic election, and other voluntary methods. The AAA does not act as arbitrator. Its function is to submit to parties selected lists from which disputants may make their own choices and to provide impartial administration of arbitration.

The AAA is the most important single center of information, education, and research on arbitration.

The AAA's library serves other educational institutions as a clearinghouse of information and answers the research inquiries of AAA members and of students.

Although headquartered in New York, the AAA has regional offices throughout the United States.

American Assembly of Collegiate Schools of Business (AACSB), an organization of institutions devoted to higher education for business and administration, formally established in 1916. Its membership has grown to encompass not only educational institutions but business, government, and professional organizations as well, all seeking to improve and promote higher education for business and working to solve problems of mutual concern. Through its accrediting function, the AACSB provides guidelines to educational institutions in program, resource, and faculty planning. The Accreditation Council of AACSB is recognized by the Council on Postsecondary Accreditation and by the U.S. Department of Education as the sole accrediting agency for bachelor's and master's programs in business administration.

American Association for Counseling and Development, a professional association of 40,000 members, based in Alexandria, Va., concerned with personnel and guidance work at all educational levels from kindergarten through higher education, in community agencies, correction agencies, rehabilitation programs, government, business/industry, and research facilities. Formerly (until 1983) the American Personnel and Guidance Association.

American Association of Fund-Raising Counsel (AAFRC), the most widely known and probably the most prestigious association of fund-raising firms in the United States. In addition to other functions, AAFRC annually publishes *Giving USA*, a compilation of statistical information on numerous aspects of philanthropic activities.

American Association of Volunteer Service Coordinators, national association which provides educational and professional support to administrators of voluntary organizations.

American Enterprise Institute for Public Policy Research (AEI), independent, nonprofit, nonpartisan research and educational organization, based in Washington, D.C., whose basic purpose is to promote the competition of ideas. AEI, which tends to favor deregulation, decentralization, and a market economy, provided the Reagan administration with a fair share of both ideas and advisors. AEI frequently provides consultation and conducts research on public-private sector initiatives.

American Federation of Labor-Congress of Industrial Organizations (AFL-CIO), a voluntary federation of over one hundred national and international unions operating in the United States. The AFL-CIO is not itself a union; it does no bargaining. It is perhaps best thought of as a union of unions. The affiliated unions created the AFL-CIO to represent them in the creation and execution of broad national and international policies and in coordinating a wide range of joint activities.

Each member union of the AFL-CIO remains autonomous, conducting its own affairs in the manner determined by its own members. Each has its own headquarters, officers, and staff. Each decides its own economic policies, carries on its own contract negotiations, sets its own dues, and provides its own membership services. Each of the affiliated unions is free to withdraw at any time. But through its voluntary participation, it plays a role in establishing overall policies for the U.S. labor movement which in turn advances the interests of every union.

American Group Psychotherapy Association (AGPA), professional association organized in 1942 to provide a forum for the exchange of ideas among qualified professional persons interested in group psychotherapy; to publish and to make publications available on all subjects relating to group psychotherapy; to encourage the development of sound training programs in group psychotherapy for qualified mental health professionals; to establish and maintain high standards of ethical, professional group psychotherapy practice; and to encourage and promote research in group psychotherapy. It is headquartered in New York City.

American Institute of Certified Public Accountants (AICPA), the national standards setting and educational organization of the Certified Public Accounting (CPA) profession. The AICPA periodically issues accounting and audit guides for different types of organizations and industries, including nonprofit organizations.

American Institute of Management (AIM), group founded in 1948 to conduct studies in management research and to enhance the development of the managerial sciences as an educational discipline. AIM serves as a professional association for managers. Its purpose is to improve management thinking, practices, performances, and results through pertinent comments, studies, meetings, and publications that contribute to managerial knowledge, skill, and theory. AIM is located in Quincy, Mass.

American Journal of Public Health, official monthly journal of the American Public Health Association that is concerned with both health policy and administration.

American Management Associations (AMA), organization located in New York City. With over 85,000 members the AMA is by far the largest organization for professional managers. AMA programs operate principally through its divisions: Finance, General Management, Information Systems and Technology, Insurance and Employee Benefits, Manufacturing, Marketing, Management Systems, Research and Development, Human Resources, Packaging, International Management, Purchasing, Transportation and Physical Distribution, and General Administrative Services. AMACOM is its in-house publishing division.

American Municipal Association: *see* NATIONAL LEAGUE OF CITIES.

American Personnel and Guidance Association: *see* AMERICAN ASSOCIATION FOR COUNSELING AND DEVELOPMENT.

American Planning Association (APA), professional association of planning agency officials, professional planners, and planning educators. Formed in 1978 through a merger of the American Institute of Planners and the American Society of Planning Officials. APA's headquarters are in Chicago, Ill.

American Political Science Association (APSA), leading academic organization for American political scientists, located in Washington, D.C.

American Productivity Center, Inc., created in 1977, a privately funded, Houston based nonprofit organization dedicated to strengthening the free enterprise system by developing practical programs to improve productivity and the quality of working life in the United States.

American Psychological Association (APA), founded in 1892 and incorporated in 1925, the APA is the major psychological organization in the United States. With more than 58,000 members, it includes most of the qualified psychologists in the country.

The purpose of the APA is to advance psychology as a science and a profession and as a means of promoting human welfare by the encouragement of psychology in all its branches in the broadest and most liberal manner. It does so by the promotion of research in psychology and the improvement of research methods and conditions; by the continual improvement of the qualifications and competence of psychologists through high standards of ethical conduct, education, and achievement, and by the dissemination of psychological knowledge through meetings, psychological journals, and special reports. APA is located in Washington, D.C.

American Public Welfare Association (APWA), Washington, D.C. based professional association of welfare agencies and administrators.

American Public Works Association (APWA), professional association for city engineers and others involved in the construction, management, or maintenance of public works. Located in Chicago.

American Society for Personnel Administration (ASPA), a nonprofit professional association of personnel and industrial relations managers. Founded in 1948, ASPA today serves over 33,000 members with 380 chapters in the United States and thirty-seven other countries. It is the largest professional association devoted exclusively to human resource management.

ASPA's purpose is (1) to provide assistance for the professional development of members, (2) to provide international leadership in establishing and supporting standards of excellence in human resource management, (3) to provide the impetus for research to improve management techniques, (4) to serve as a focal point for the exchange of authoritative information, and (5) to publicize the human resource management field to create a better understanding of its functions and importance. ASPA is based in Alexandria, Va.

American Society for Public Administration (ASPA), a Washington, D.C. based, nationwide, nonprofit educational and professional organization dedicated to improved management in the public service through exchange, development, and dissemination of information about public administration. ASPA has over 18,000 members.

American Society for Training and Development (ASTD), national professional society of 22,000 members, based in Madison, Wisconsin, for persons with training and development responsibilities in business, industry, government, public service organizations, and educational institutions. Founded in 1944, ASTD is the only organization devoted exclusively to the comprehensive education, development, and expansion of the skills and standards of professionals in training and human resource development. Formerly (until 1964) the American Society of Training Directors.

American Society of Association Executives (ASAE), perhaps the best known and most prestigious of the organizations that provide educational programs, materials, and technical assistance for association executives. ASAE administers the Certified Association Executive (CAE) program—a certification program for association executives.

American Standard Code, a code for computer representation of letters, numbers, and typewriter symbols. A combination of eight computer bits can handle all 128 standard characters.

amicus curiae, literally, "friend of the court"; any person or organization allowed to participate in a lawsuit who would not otherwise have a right to do so. Participation is usually limited to filing a brief on behalf of one side or the other.

amortization, paying off a debt in regular and equal payments; breaking down the value and costs of an intangible asset (such as a copyright) year by year over the estimated useful life of the asset; any dividing up of benefits or costs by time periods, primarily for tax purposes. A gradual reduction of the principal of a loan, together with payment of interest, according to a known schedule of payments at regular intervals. By the end of the life of a loan, its principal balance will be fully paid off, in contrast to a loan involving a balloon payment.

analogies test, test that asks a series of questions such as: a foot is to a man as a paw is to what? The examinee is usually given four or five answers from which to choose.

analogue, individual's counterpart or opposite number in another organization.

analysis, backstep: *see* BACKSTEP ANALYSIS.

analysis, force field: *see* FORCE FIELD ANALYSIS.

analysis, incremental: *see* MARGINAL ANALYSIS.

analysis, marginal: *see* MARGINAL ANALYSIS.

analysis, sensitivity: *see* SENSITIVITY ANALYSIS.

analysis of variance, statistical procedure for determining whether the change noted in a variable that has been exposed to other variables exceeds what may be expected by chance.

analytical estimating, work measurement technique whereby the time required to perform a job is estimated on the basis of prior experience.

andragogy, an orientation to teaching adults which uses student-centered rather than instructor-centered learning experiences, problem solving-based rather than content-oriented curriculum, and an active rather than a passive learning environment. Andragogy is the opposite of pedagogy, and is becoming accepted as a more effective orientation for causing adults to learn.

A-95 review: *See* OFFICE OF MANAGEMENT AND BUDGET (OMB) CIRCULAR A-95.

Annals, The, bimonthly journal of the American Academy of Political and Social Science. Each issue focuses on a prominent social or political problem.

annual arrangements, tool to facilitate coordination among grant programs and to increase a city's capacity to set priorities. Involves negotiations between HUD field offices and cities aimed at packaging categorical programs into community development activities.

annual earnings, employee's total compensation during a calendar year—includes basic salary or wages, all overtime and premium pay, vacation pay, bonuses, etc.

annual exclusion or ANNUAL EXEMPTION (GIFT TAX): *see* GIFT EXEMPTION LIMIT and GIFT TAX.

annual giving, repeat contributions made by the same donor(s) to the same organization(s) each year.

annual giving program, a planned strategy conducted by a charitable organization to obtain repeat contributions from the same donors each year.

Annual Information Returns, the equivalent of income tax returns which tax-exempt organizations must file annually with the Internal Revenue Service and appropriate state agencies if their gross receipts normally are more than $25,000. Federal and state agencies usually mail Annual Information Return forms and instructions to tax-exempt organizations. The primary Annual Information Return forms are IRS Forms 990 (and Schedule A) and 990T.

annual interest rate, also ANNUAL PERCENTAGE RATE, the true cost of borrowing money, expressed in a standardized yearly way to make it easier to understand lending terms.

annualized cost, cost of something for a twelve-month period. Annualized costs may be figured on the calendar year, the fiscal year, the date a contract becomes effective, etc.

annual meeting, yearly meeting of the members or governing board of an organization. Annual meetings typically are specified in the articles of organization or by-laws.

annual report, a financial and programmatic report which summarizes the year's activities. Most incorporated organizations provide annual reports to their directors, members, and funding sources.

annuitant, one who is the recipient of annuity benefit payments.

See also REEMPLOYED ANNUITANT.

annuity, annual sum payable to a former employee who has retired; an agreement or contract by which a person purchases a claim to a future series of payments made at fixed intervals over a specified time period, often in the form of payments made by an insurance company during the remainder of a lifetime.

annuity trust: *see* CHARITABLE REMAINDER ANNUITY TRUST.

annulment, the act of making something void or eliminating it completely.

antecedent debt, a debt that is prior in time to another transaction.

antedate, to predate; to date a document earlier than the date it was actually signed. This is sometimes a crime.

anti-labor legislation, any law at any level of government that organized labor perceives to be to its disadvantage and to the disadvantage of prime union interests—better hours, wages, and working conditions. Leading examples would be "right-to-work" laws and "antistrike" laws.

antitrust laws, those federal and state statutes which limit the ability of businesses and unions to exercise monopoly control and cause restraint of trade.

A/P, accounts payable.

APA: *see* AMERICAN PLANNING ASSOCIATION and AMERICAN PSYCHOLOGICAL ASSOCIATION.

APB: *see* ACCOUNTING PRINCIPLES BOARD.

APGA: *see* AMERICAN PERSONNEL AND GUIDANCE ASSOCIATION.

apostolic groups, groups which have characteristics of the Biblical twelve apostles. Apostolic groups are subcategories of "church" and may qualify as tax-exempt religious organizations.

apparatchik, Russian word for a bureaucrat, now used colloquially to refer to any administrative functionary. The word as used in English seems to have no political connotations; it merely implies that the individual referred to mindlessly follows orders.

appeal, any proceeding or request to a higher authority that a lower authority's decision be reviewed.

appellant, one who appeals a case to a higher authority.

appellate jurisdiction, power of a tribunal to review cases that have previously been decided by a lower authority.

applicant, an individual seeking initial employment or an in-house promotional opportunity.

applicant pool, all those individuals who have applied for a particular job over a given period.

applicant population, the set of individuals within a geographical area, with identifiable characteristics or a mix of such characteristics, from which applicants for employment are obtained.

applicant tally, tally system by which the EEO status of applicants is recorded at the time of application or interview. By periodically comparing applicant tally rates with rates of appointment and/or rejection, the progress of affirmative action recruitment efforts can be measured.

application blank, frequently the first phase of the selection process. Properly completed, it can serve three purposes: (1) it is a formal request for employment; (2) it provides information that indicates the applicant's fitness for the position; and (3) it can become the basic personnel record for those applicants who are hired. Application blanks must conform to all EEOC guidelines; requested information must be a valid predictor of performance.

Application for Employer Identification Number: *see* EMPLOYER IDENTIFICATION NUMBER.

applied costs, the financial measure of resources consumed or applied within a given period of time to accomplish a specific purpose, such as performing a service, carrying out an activity, or completing a unit of work or a specific project, regardless of when ordered, received, or paid for.

applied psychology, generally, the practical use of the discoveries and principles of psychology.

appointing authority: *see* APPOINTING OFFICER.

appointing officer, also APPOINTING AUTHORITY, person having power to make appointments to positions in an organization.

apportionment (budgeting), executive budget function that takes place after passage of an appropriations bill when a jurisdiction's budget office creates a plan for expenditures to reconcile agency or department programs with available resources.

appraisal, also APPRAISEMENT, estimation by an impartial expert of the value of something; also, fixing the fair value of stock by a court when stockholders in a corporation quarrel and some must be bought out.

appraisal method of depreciation, method in which assets are valued by appraisals made at the beginning and end of each accounting period. Depreciation for the period, then, is the difference between the two appraised values.

appraiser, an impartial expert chosen to set a value on a piece of property.

appreciated property, items of property which have increased in value since their acquisition. Typical examples include art, stocks and bonds, and real estate. Historically, it has been more advantageous to donate stock or other property that has appreciated than to give cash, because the taxpayer obtains both a deduction for the full amount of the gift and also escapes the capital gains tax that would be incurred if the property was sold (except for gifts to private foundations). Therefore, it has been more advantageous to donate appreciated property than to sell it and to give the proceeds therefrom.

For years, many tax reformers have considered the right of donors to deduct the market value of a donated asset—without paying the capital gains tax—as a tax loophole. Several of the 1985 tax reform proposals, including the proposal presented by the U.S. Department of Treasury, contain provisions which reflect this point of view and would impose a (limited) capital gains tax on donated appreciated property.

See also BARGAIN SALE.

appreciation, the increase in the value of property since its acquisition (excluding value increases resulting from improvements).

approach-approach conflict, wanting two things at once, and the resulting indecision.

approach-avoidance conflict, wanting something which may cause pain or come at too high a cost, which causes indecision.

appropriate bargaining unit: *see* APPROPRIATE UNIT.

appropriate technology, also ALTERNATIVE TECHNOLOGY, concepts that involve the rejection of centralized control or direction for the use of technology, and the replacement of it with local determination of which technologies best fit the local environment.

appropriate unit, also known as BARGAINING UNIT and APPROPRIATE BARGAINING UNIT, group of employees that a labor organization seeks to represent for the purpose of negotiating agreements; an aggregation of employees that has a clear and identifiable community of interest and that promotes effective dealings and efficiency of operations. It may be established on a locational, craft, functional, or other basis.

appropriation, act of Congress that permits federal agencies to incur obligations and to make payments out of the Treasury for specified purposes. An appropriation usually follows enactment of authorizing legislation.

appropriation account, also called FUND ACCOUNT, a summary account for each appropriation and/or fund showing transactions to such accounts. Each such account provides the framework for establishing a set of balanced accounts on the books.

approval, a sale condition under which the buyer may return the goods if they are unsatisfactory, even if they are all the seller claims.

approval, membership: *see* MEMBERSHIP APPROVAL.

aptitude, capacity to acquire knowledge, skill, or ability with experience and/or a given amount of formal or informal education or training.

See also ABILITY and ACHIEVEMENT.

aptitude test, usually a battery of separate tests designed to measure an individual's overall ability to learn. A large variety of specialized aptitude tests have been developed to predict an applicant's performance on a particular job or course of study.

APWA: *see* AMERICAN PUBLIC WELFARE ASSOCIATION and AMERICAN PUBLIC WORKS ASSOCIATION.

A/R, accounts receivable.

arbiter, also ARBITRATOR, one chosen to decide a disagreement. In a formal sense an *arbiter* is one who has the power to decide while an *arbitrator* is one who is chosen to decide by the parties to the dispute, but the words tend to be used interchangeably.

arbitrary, said of an action decided by personal whim that was not guided by general principles or rules.

arbitration, means of settling a dispute by having an impartial third party (the arbitrator) hold a formal hearing and render a decision that may or may not be binding on both sides. The arbitrator may be a single individual or a board of three, five, or more. When boards are used, they may include, in addition to impartial members, representatives from both of the disputants.

arbitration acts, laws that help (and sometimes require) the submission of certain types of problems (often labor disputes) to an *arbitrator*.

arbitration clause, provision of a collective bargaining agreement stipulating that disputes arising during the life of the contract over its interpretation are subject to arbitration. The clause may be broad enough to include "any dispute" or restricted to specific concerns.

Arbitration Journal, quarterly journal of the American Arbitration Association, Inc. Includes articles written by practitioners and academics on all phases of arbitration and labor relations as well as reviews of related legal decisions.

arbitration standards, the four fundamental criteria that arbitrators must be concerned with in making their judgments: acceptability, equity, the public interest, and ability to pay. The mix of these factors that will be applied in any particular case of arbitration will depend upon the arbitrator's proclivities, the nature of the dispute, and, if it is in the public sector, the standards, if any, set forth in the pertinent legislation.

arbitration tribunal, panel created to decide a dispute that has been submitted to arbitration.

arbitrator, one who conducts an arbitration.

architectural barriers, physical aspects of a building that might hinder or prevent the employment of a physically handicapped person. The lack of a ramp, for example, may prevent a person in a wheelchair from entering a building having only stairways for access. The Architectural Barriers Act of 1968 (Public Law 90-480), as amended, requires that buildings constructed with federal funds be accessible to and usable by the physically handicapped.

Architectural Barriers Act of 1968: *see* ARCHITECTURAL BARRIERS.

archives, permanently available records created or received by an organization for its formal/official purposes.

area agreement, collective bargaining agreement that covers a variety of employers and their workers in a large geographical area.

area associations of grantmakers, groups of grantmaking organizations in geographical areas including private, public and corporate foundations and the United

Way, formed to increase their effectiveness by improving operations, sharing ideas, assessing needs, engaging in joint projects, etc. Currently, there are more than thirty such area associations, the majority of which are considered to be cooperating associations with the Council on Foundations. The area associations vary in size, geographic area of inclusion (such as a metropolitan area or a state), formality of organization, staffing (for example, some have no paid staff), and types of programming.

In 1980, the Council on Foundations identified

- two multi-state associations,
- seven state or multi-county associations,
- ten greater city associations, and
- six foundation luncheon groups.

See also REGIONAL ASSOCIATIONS OF GRANTMAKERS.

area labor-management committee, groups of local labor and business leaders who seek to solve problems affecting the economic well-being of an entire community, rather than just a particular work-site or industry.

area of consideration, geographic area within which all candidates who meet the basic requirements for promotion to a position are given the opportunity to be considered.

area sampling, a public surveying technique which involves marking off a geographical test area into blocks, choosing random sample blocks, and interviewing as many people as possible in those areas.

area standards picketing, picketing to demand that the primary employer pay "area standards" wages; that is, wages that are paid to union labor by other employers in the same geographic area.

area wage differences, differing pay rates for various occupations in differing geographic areas.

area wage survey: *see* WAGE SURVEY.

Argyris, Chris (1923-   ), one of the most influential advocates of the use of organization development (OD) techniques. His writings have provided the theoretical foundations for innumerable empirical research efforts dealing with the inherent conflict between the personality of a mature adult and the needs of modern organizations.

See also PSEUDO-EFFECTIVENESS.

arithmetic address, the place in a computer where computational results are stored.

arithmetic mean: *see* MEAN.

Arizona* v. *Norris, 77 L. Ed. 2d 1236 (1983), U.S. Supreme Court case which held that employers may not require female employees to make the same contributions to a pension plan as men while giving the males a larger benefit. The Court limited its ruling to plan contributions made after July 31, 1983, and did not specify how equalization of benefits must be achieved, which meant that it could be attained by raising women's benefits, lowering men's benefits, or a combination of the two approaches.

arm's-length, independently; as though not related.

arm's-length standards, IRS standards which defined self-dealing transactions with private foundations. The standards were deemed to be ineffective by Congress and were repealed by the Tax Reform Act of 1969. However, "self-dealing standards" remain in effect.

See also PRIVATE INUREMENT.

Army Alpha and Beta Tests, tests developed in 1917 by a special committee of the American Psychological Association to help the U.S. Army classify the abilities of its recruits. The committee developed the Army Alpha Intelligence Test (a verbal test for literate recruits) and the Army Beta Intelligence Test (a nonverbal test suited for illiterate and foreign-born recruits). After World War I, the tests were released for civilian use and became the progenitors of modern industrial and educational group intelligence/aptitude testing.

arrears, also ARREARAGES, money owed that is overdue and unpaid.

arrow network, a simplified variety of precedence diagram used to identify and display the chronological sequence of a project's activities and events.

See also:

CRITICAL PATH METHOD
PERT
PRECEDENCE DIAGRAM
PROJECT CONTROL CHART
PROJECT MANAGEMENT

articles, the separate parts of a document, book, set of rules, etc.

articles of association, also CHARTER, the articles of organization which are filed with the appropriate office of state government by some nonprofit associations. Articles of association serve the same purpose for a nonprofit organization as do articles of incorporation for a for-profit company.

See also:

ARTICLES OF INCORPORATION
ARTICLES OF ORGANIZATION
GOVERNING INSTRUMENT

articles of incorporation, the creating document for a corporation.

See also:

ARTICLES OF ASSOCIATION
ARTICLES OF ORGANIZATION
CREATING DOCUMENT
GOVERNING INSTRUMENT

articles of organization, the creating document for an organization. For example, articles of incorporation are the articles of organization for a corporation; for an unincorporated entity, the articles of organization may be, for example, a constitution or articles of association. Bylaws are not articles of organization.

See also:

ARTICLES OF ASSOCIATION
ARTICLES OF INCORPORATION
BYLAWS
CONSTITUTION
CREATING DOCUMENT
GOVERNING INSTRUMENT

Artificial barriers to employment, limitations (such as age, sex, race, national origin, parental status, credential requirements, criminal record, lack of child care, and absence of part-time or alternative working patterns/schedules) in hiring, firing, promotion, licensing, and conditions of employment which are not directly related to an individual's fitness or ability to perform the tasks required by the job.

artificial person, an entity to which the law gives some of the legal rights and duties of a person; for example, a corporation.

See also CORPORATION.

arts, the, the humanities.

ASAE: *see* AMERICAN SOCIETY OF ASSOCIATION EXECUTIVES.

ASCII: *see* AMERICAN STANDARD CODE.

as is, in its present condition. An *as is* sale is one in which the buyer agrees to accept the goods in the condition they are in at the time of purchase. No warranty applies to such a sale. The buyer bears all the risk as to the quality of the goods purchased, barring intentional fraud or misrepresentation by the seller.

ASPA: *see* AMERICAN SOCIETY FOR PERSONNEL ADMINISTRATION or AMERICAN SOCIETY FOR PUBLIC ADMINISTRATION.

ASQ: *see* ADMINISTRATIVE SCIENCE QUARTERLY.

assembly line, production method requiring workers to perform a repetitive task on a product as it moves along on a conveyor belt or tract.

assertiveness training, training program designed to help less assertive people communicate and express their ideas and feel-

BUILDING AN ARROW NETWORK

Each activity in a project or program is represented as an arrow with numbered circles (nodes) at its beginning and completion points.

Concurrent activities (activities that can be done simultaneously) are diagrammed as follows:

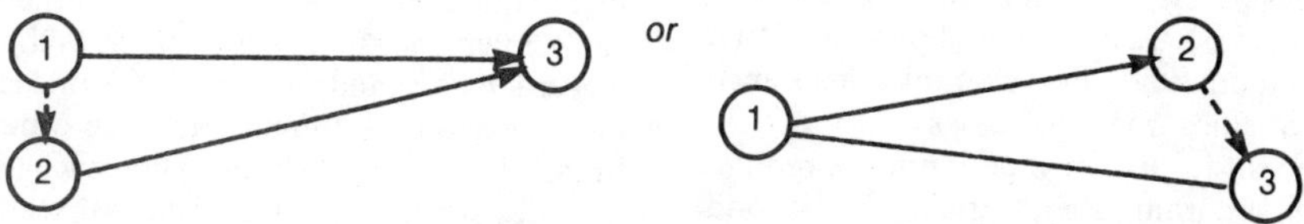

Sequential activities (activities that must follow each other in sequence) are diagrammed as:

A list is created of all activities needed to complete the project, then the sequence which is to be followed is noted. A partial list might be:

Activity	Must Follow
C	A & B
D	B

The example would be diagrammed as below:

The "dotted lines" are called "dummy activities" and serve two purposes. First, they provide unique identification for each activity; and, more important, they identify restraints (in other words, activities that restrain other activities). For example:

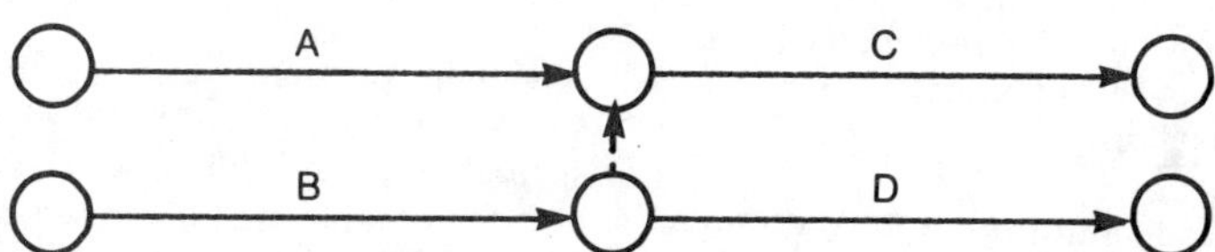

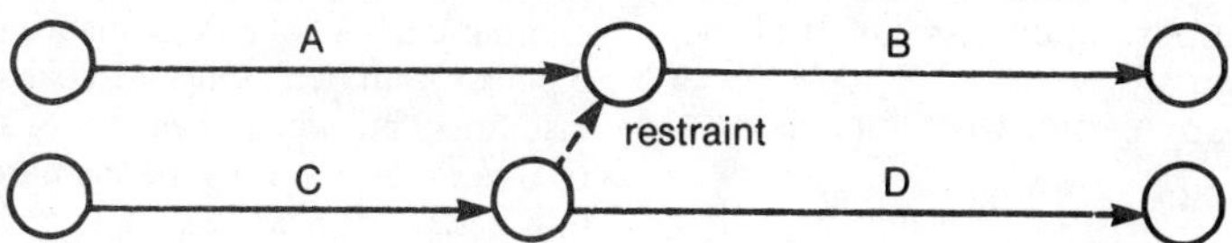

ings more effectively. The ideal level of assertiveness lies midway between passivity and aggressiveness.

assess, to set the value of something; to set the value of property for the purpose of taxing it; also, to charge part of the cost of a public improvement (such as a sidewalk) to each person or property directly benefiting from it.

assessed valuation, tax value assigned to property.

assessment, deciding on the amount to be paid by each of several persons into a common fund. For example, insurance companies may be assessed a certain amount to pay for a government regulatory program, also, a payment beyond what is normally required of members of a group; for example, a special assessment.

assessment center, a process consisting of the intense observation of a subject undergoing a variety of simulations and stress situations over a period of several days. Assessment centers have proven to be an increasingly popular way of identifying individuals with future executive potential so that they may be given the appropriate training and development assignments.

assessor, official of a jurisdiction who determines the value of property for the purpose of taxation.

asset-linked annuity: *see* VARIABLE ANNUITY.

asset, dedicated, assets of an organization whose articles of organization specify that the assets will be distributed for a specific exempt purpose upon dissolution of the organization.

See also DEDICATION OF ASSETS REQUIREMENT.

asset, unique: *see* UNIQUE ASSET.

asset depreciation range, the choice of "lifetimes" (or usable lives) the IRS permits when claiming depreciation on an asset.

See also DEPRECIATION.

assets, also CURRENT ASSETS and FIXED ASSETS, book value of items owned by an enterprise or jurisdiction as reflected on a balance sheet. Private foundations sometimes use market value rather than book value; also, all of the property of a person, association, corporation or estate which may be applied to or subject to paying his, her or its liabilities and other obligations. *Current assets* are cash or those highly liquid items which are convertible to a known amount of cash usually within a year (*i.e.*, accounts receivable, securities, inventory, and amounts due from other funds). *Fixed assets* are those items which normally are not convertible into cash within a year (*i.e.*, buildings, equipment, and machinery).

assets test, one of several tests or criteria used by the IRS to determine whether an organization qualifies as a private operating foundation. The test involves determining whether the organization's use of its assets is for the direct furtherance of its tax-exempt purposes. In essence, sixty-five percent or more of a private foundation's assets must be devoted directly to the carrying out of the foundation's exempt purpose.

assigned account, also PLEDGED ACCOUNTS RECEIVABLE, a debt owed to an organization (or individual) which it uses as security or a pledge for its own debt to a lender.

See also ACCOUNTS RECEIVABLE and PLEDGE.

assigned risk, a risk that an insurance company does not care to insure (such as a person with hypertension seeking health insurance) but which, because of state law or other reasons, must be insured. Insuring assigned risks usually is handled through a group of insurers (such as all companies licensed to issue health insurance in the state), and the individual assigned risks are assigned to the companies in turn or in proportion to their share of the total health insurance business in the state. Assignment of risk is quite common in casualty insurance and less common in health insurance.

assignment, the transfer of property, rights in property, or money to another person or organization.

assignment of income, an attempt to avoid income tax by having one's income diverted to someone else. The first person turns income or income-producing property over to the second person. Not to be confused with "assignment of wages."

See also ASSIGNMENT OF WAGES and TAX AVOIDANCE SCHEME.

assignment of wages, also called ATTACHMENT OF WAGES, procedure that has an employer, upon the authorization of the employee, automatically deduct a portion of the employee's wages and pay it to a third party, usually a creditor. When this is ordered by a court, the process is known as garnishment.

See also GARNISHMENT.

association, a general word meaning a group of people joined together for a particular purpose; also, a type of limited partnership, trust, or other financial entity that the IRS will tax as a corporation because it acts like a corporation.

association, unincorporated, a type of organization. Although it is a legal requirement, many smaller nonprofit organizations and associations do not bother incorporating—that is, filing articles of association or organization with the appropriate office of state government. These are referred to as unincorporated associations.

Association Management, the journal of the American Society of Association Executives (ASAE).

assumable mortgage, a mortgage that can be passed on to a new owner at the previous owner's rate of interest.

See also MORTGAGE.

assumption, also ASSUMPTION OF LIABILITY, acceptance of or incurring a debt. In most instances, nonprofit organizations are permitted to assume liabilities, for example, to purchase assets. However, there are limitations to the practice which have been established to prevent private inurement.

See also PRIVATE INUREMENT.

assumption fee, the cost charged for processing papers when a buyer assumes a loan from a seller (for example, assumes a mortgage).

See also ASSUMABLE MORTGAGE.

assumption-of-risk doctrine, common-law concept that an employer should not be held responsible for an accident to an employee if the employer can show that the injured employee had voluntarily accepted the hazards associated with a given job.

assurance: *see* PLEDGE.

ASTD: *see* AMERICAN SOCIETY FOR TRAINING AND DEVELOPMENT.

at risk, the special risk of injury or disease of certain groups, such as older women's risk of birth defects and coal miners' risk of black lung disease; also, the amount of money a person could lose if an investment goes bad, if an asset is not fully insured, if an obligation comes due, etc.

at-risk populations (discrimination), those identifiable groups that have been systematically denied on an economic, social, and political basis the opportunity and access to public and private goods and resources.

ATS: *see* AUTOMATIC TRANSFER SERVICE.

attachment of wages: *see* ASSIGNMENT OF WAGES.

attendance bonus, also called ATTENDANCE MONEY, payment to an employee that serves as inducement to regular attendance.

attest, to witness the signing of a document and to sign a document stating that the signing has been witnessed.

See also NOTARY PUBLIC.

attitude, learned predisposition to act in a consistent way toward particular persons, objects, or conditions.

attitude scale, any series of attitude indices that have given quantitative values relative to each other.

attitude survey, questionnaire, usually anonymous, that elicits the opinion of employees. Once completed they are summarized and analyzed to determine compliance with and attitudes towards current personnel management policies.

attribute, a non-quantitative characteristic; for example, a person's sex, rather than height.

attrition, reduction in the size of a work force through normal processes, such as voluntary resignations, retirements, discharges for cause, transfers, and deaths.

audio-visual media, those things that communicate information through human sight or sound sensors—films, slides, recordings, maps, etc.

audit, a review of the operations of an organization, especially its financial transactions, to determine whether it has spent moneys in accordance with the law, in the most efficient manner, and with desired results.

See also the following entries:

AUDIT PROGRAM
AUDIT STANDARDS
AUDIT TRAIL
COMPLIANCE
CONTRACT AUDIT
DESK AUDIT
FINANCIAL AUDIT
GENERALLY ACCEPTED ACCOUNTING PRINCIPLES
PROGRAM EVALUATION
PROGRAM RESULTS AUDITS
SOCIAL AUDIT

Audit Bureau of Circulation (ABC), an organization that verifies newspaper and magazine circulation claims.

Audit Guide, a publication of the American Institute of Certified Public Accountants which outlines the generally accepted accounting principles for nonprofit health and welfare voluntary organizations.

auditing, expanded scope of, function that, according to the Comptroller General of the United States, *Standards For Audit of Governmental Organizations, Programs, Activities, and Functions* (Washington, D.C.: U.S. General Accounting Office, 1981 Revision),

1. *Financial and compliance*—determines (a) whether the financial statements of an audited entity present fairly the financial position and the results of financial operations in accordance with generally accepted accounting principles and (b) whether the entity has complied with laws and regulations that may have a material effect upon the financial statements.
2. *Economy and efficiency*—determines (a) whether the entity is managing and utilizing its resources (such as personnel, property, space) economically and efficiently, (b) the causes of inefficiencies or uneconomical practices, and (c) whether the entity has complied with laws and regulations concerning matters of economy and efficiency.
3. *Program results*—determines (a) whether the desired results or benefits established by the legislature or other authorizing body are being achieved and (b) whether the agency has considered alternatives that might yield desired results at a lower cost.

auditor, person or organization conducting the audit.

auditor's opinion, an expression in an auditor's report as to whether the information in the financial statement is presented fairly in accordance with generally accepted accounting principles (or with other specified accounting principles applicable to the auditee) applied on a basis consistent with that of the preceding reporting period.

audit program, detailed steps and procedures to be followed in conducting the audit and preparing the report. A written audit program should be prepared for each audit and it should include such information as the purpose and scope, background information needed to understand the audit objectives and the entity's mission, definitions of unique terms, objectives, and reporting procedures.

audit standards, general measures of the quality and adequacy of the work performed. They also relate to the auditor's professional qualities.

audit trail, a systematic cross-referencing from an accounting record (a record of a transaction) to its source (for example, receipts) to properly explain it, document it, and/or check its accuracy—in other words, so that an auditor can "follow its trail."

authoritarian theory: *see* THEORY X AND THEORY Y.

authority, power inherent in a specific position or function that allows an incumbent to perform assigned duties and assume assigned responsibilities.

See also the following entries:
BUDGET AUTHORITY
POWER

authorization, also called AUTHORIZING LEGISLATION, basic substantive legislation enacted by Congress which sets up or continues the legal operation of a federal program or agency either indefinitely or for a specific period of time or sanctions a particular type of obligation or expenditure within a program.

authorization card, form signed by a worker to authorize a union to represent the worker for purposes of collective bargaining.

authorization election, or REPRESENTATION ELECTION, polls conducted by the National Labor Relations Board (or other administrative agency) to determine if a particular group of employees will be represented by a particular union or not.

authorizing committee, a standing committee of the House or Senate with legislative jurisdiction over the subject matter of those laws or parts of laws that set up or continue the legal operations of Federal programs or agencies. An authorizing committee also has jurisdiction in those instances where backdoor authority is provided in the substantive legislation.

See also SELECT COMMITTEE.

authorizing legislation: *see* AUTHORIZATION.

autocorrelation, the correlations among numbers ordered in a series.

See also CORRELATION.

automatic stabilizer, also called BUILT-IN STABILIZER, a mechanism having a countercyclical effect that automatically moderates changes in incomes and outputs in the economy without specific decisions to change government policy. Unemployment insurance and the income tax are among the most important of the automatic stabilizers in the United States.

See also COUNTERCYCLICAL.

Automatic Transfer Service (ATS), a service provided by the commercial banks through which they debit savings accounts to cover checks written against checking accounts. ATSs permit depositors to earn interest on the balances until they actually are spent.

See also DEBITS AND CREDITS.

automatic wage adjustment, raising or lowering of wage rates in direct response to previously determined factors such as an increase/decrease in the Consumer Price Index.

automatic wage progression, the increasing of wages premised on length of service.

automation, sometimes called MECHANIZATION, use of machines to do work that would otherwise have to be done by humans. As a word, automation has a considerable emotional charge since its manifestations have tended to create technological unemployment.

Automation tends to be popularly used interchangeably with mechanization—the use of machines. However, a production system is not truly automated unless the machinery is to some degree self-regulated—that is, capable of adjusting itself in response to feedback from its earlier outputs. This attribute lessens the need for human attendants.

automaton, person acting mechanically in a monotonous routine without the need to use any intellectual capacities.

autonomous work group, collection of individuals who have all the resources and abilities necessary to work independently.

auxiliary account, also ADJUNCT ACCOUNT and CONTRA ACCOUNT, an account that is closely related to another (major or principal) account.

auxiliary agency, also called HOUSEKEEPING AGENCY or OVERHEAD AGENCY, administrative unit whose prime responsibility is to serve other agencies of the greater organization. Personnel agencies are usually auxiliary, housekeeping, or overhead agencies.

auxiliary charitable organization, an organization which works in collaboration with a sponsoring organization to accomplish joint purposes. Nonprofit auxiliary organizations may be established, for example, by for-profit organizations to receive tax-exempt contributions; or tax-exempt organizations may establish separate auxiliary organizations to engage in activites which might jeopardize the sponsoring organization's tax-exempt status.

average deviation, also called MEAN DEVIATION, measure of dispersion that provides information on the extent of scatter, or the degree of clustering, in a set of data.

average earned rate, total earnings for a given time period divided by the number of hours worked during the period.

average hourly earnings, wages earned by an employee per hour of work during a specific time period. The average hourly earnings are computed by dividing total pay received by the total hours worked.

average incumbents, average work force strength figure found by adding the work force strengths at the beginning and end of a specified report period and dividing this sum by two. This type of computation is widely used in turnover analysis.

average straight-time hourly earnings, average wages earned per hour exclusive of premium payments.

avoidance-avoidance conflict, wanting to avoid two things when avoiding one may cause the other to happen—which causes indecision.

award, at the end of the arbitration process, the final decision of the arbitrator(s) when such arbitration is binding on both parties.

award fund, a type of fund used for making awards to recognize outstanding achievement or merit or contributions in public service. Award funds are frequently found in community foundations.

See also COMMUNITY FOUNDATION.

award incentive: *see* INCENTIVE AWARD.

B

Babbage, Charles (1792-1871), English mathematician and inventor. Best known as the father of the modern computer, he is also acclaimed for building upon the assembly line concepts of Adam Smith and anticipating the scientific management techniques of Frederick W. Taylor.

back, to endorse, sign, or assume financial responsibility for something; for example, to cosign a loan note.

backdoor authority, term generally used to denote legislation enacted outside the normal appropriation process that permits the obligation of funds. The most common forms of backdoor authority are *borrowing authority* (authority to spend debt receipts) and *contract authority*. Examples of accounts that have backdoor authority are the federal aid highways trust fund, the Environmental Protection Agency's construction grants, and the Social Security trust funds.

See also AUTHORIZATION.

backdoor spending, spending by a government unit that is not subject to legislative appropriation. For example, tax expenditures such as tax deductions and tax credits are often referred to as backdoor spending because taxpayers determine the extent (and the recipients) of the tax expenditures.

See also TAX CREDIT and TAX EXPENDITURES.

back loaded, a labor agreement providing for a greater wage increase in its later years; for example, a three-year contract that provides for a two percent increase in the first year and six percent in each of the remaining two years.

Also see FRONT LOADED.

back order, a request for an item for sale or inventory that is not available immediately.

back pay, delayed payment of wages for a particular time period.

backstep analysis, an analytical technique for diagraming a problem, its causes, and its consequences; used to help decide what a program can and should do to abate a problem, and to establish that a true problem is being attacked rather than its symptoms. Backstep analysis also serves as a guide for collecting information to validate a problem statement, causes, and consequences.

Backstep analysis assumes that there are cause-effect relationships (often very complex) between some underlying conditions, the problem of concern, and its consequences.

Following completion of a backstep analysis, the next logical program planning technique employed is "FAST" diagraming (Functional Analysis Systems Technique) to create an hierarchy of objectives.

See also FUNCTIONAL ANALYSIS SYSTEMS TECHNIQUE and HIERARCHY OF OBJECTIVES.

back-to-work movement, striking employees returning to their jobs before their union has formally ended the strike.

backward bending supply curve, the graphic depiction of the assumption that as wages increase, people will continue to offer to work only to a point; thereafter, the amount of offered work will decline as the demand for more leisure increases relative to the demand for more income.

bad debt, a debt that is completely uncollectable.

bad debt ratio, the ratio of bad debts to sales, typically for a year.

bad faith, dishonesty in dealing with another person or organization, whether or not actual fraud is involved.

EXAMPLE OF A BACKSTEP ANALYSIS FOR MUNICIPAL AIR POLLUTION

WHAT ARE THE CAUSES?

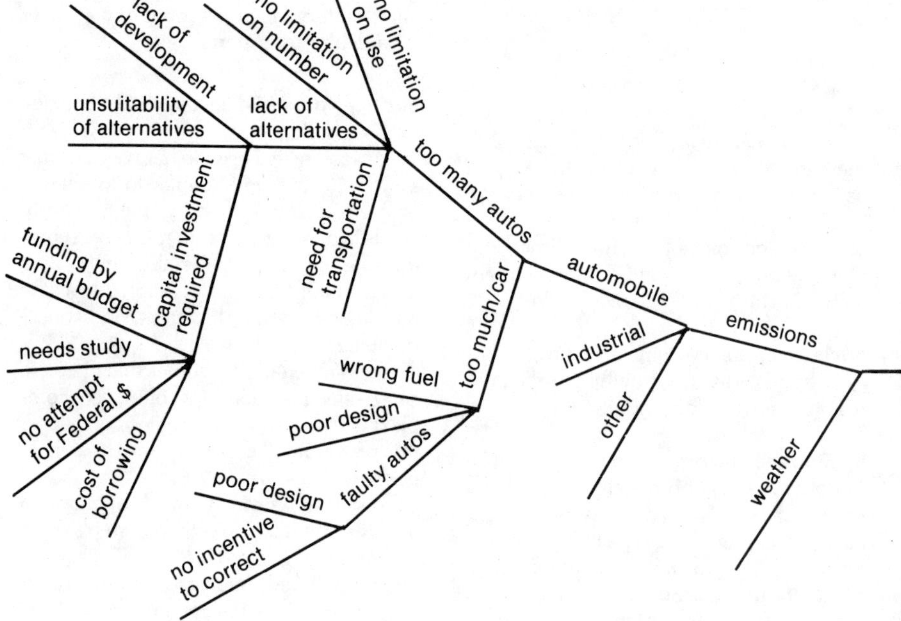

***Bakke* decision:** *see* REGENTS OF THE UNIVERSITY OF CALIFORNIA V. ALLAN BAKKE.

balanced budget, a budget in which receipts are equal to outlays.

balance of payments, tabulation of a nation's debt and credit transactions with foreign countries and international institutions.

balances, budget, the residual amounts remaining in budgeted accounts at the close of a fiscal period. An *obligated balance* is the amount of obligations incurred (formal commitments made) but for which payments have not been made. *Unobligated balance* is the portion of the budget which has not been obligated. *Unexpended balance* is the sum of the obligated and unobligated balances.

balance sheet, itemized accounting statement that reflects total assets, total liabilities, and residual balances as of a given date.

balloon payment, also BALLOON LOAN and BALLOON MORTGAGE, a loan or mortgage in which the last payment (or a limited number of intermediate payments) is much larger than any of the other regular payments.

band curve chart, or CUMULATIVE BAND CHART, chart on which the bands of a graph are plotted one above the other.

bank charge, a debit memorandum or notice of a charge made by a bank against an account.

bank credit, a written promise by a bank

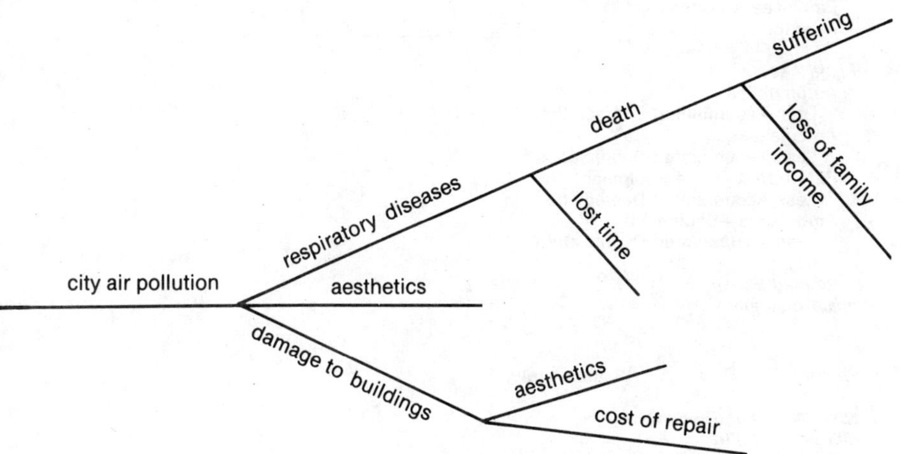

that an organization or person may borrow up to a specified amount.

banker's lien, a bank's right to take for its own the money or property left in its care by a customer if the customer owes an overdue debt to the bank and if the money, to the bank's knowledge, belongs to the customer.

bank holiday, any of the traditional legal holidays or other special occasions when banks as well as most, but not all, other organizations and businesses remain closed. The six essentially standard paid holidays are: Christmas Day, Thanksgiving Day, New Year's Day, Independence Day, Labor Day, and Memorial Day. Many organizations offer as many as twice this number of paid holidays for their employees, but the specific days vary with local customs.

BANs: *see* BOND ANTICIPATION NOTES.

bar chart: *see* HISTOGRAM and FREQUENCY DISTRIBUTION.

bar examination, written test that new lawyers must pass in order to practice law.

bargaining: *see* the following entries:
BLUE SKY BARGAINING
COALITION BARGAINING
COLLECTIVE BARGAINING
CRISIS BARGAINING
GOOD-FAITH BARGAINING
INDIVIDUAL BARGAINING

bargaining agent, the union organization (not an individual) that is the exclusive representative of all the workers, union as well as nonunion, in a bargaining unit.

bargaining agreement: *see* LABOR AGREEMENT.

EXAMPLE

ACE AMBULANCE SERVICE—BALANCE SHEET

Assets			
Current Assets			
Cash in Bank	$		
Petty Cash			
Accounts Receivable			
Less: Allowance for Bad Debts			
Employee Advances			
Inventory		$	
Fixed Assets			
Automobiles	$		
Less Accumulated Depreciation			
Ambulances			
Less Accumulated Depreciation			
Furniture & Office Equipment			
Less Accumulated Depreciation			
Ambulance—Equipment			
Less Accumulated Depreciation			
Prepaid Expenses	$		
Prepaid Insurance		$	
			$
Total Assets			
Liabilities + Fund Balances			
Current Liabilities			
Accounts Payable	$		
Notes Payable			
Accrued Taxes			
Withheld Taxes			
Accrued Payroll			$
Fund Balances			
A	$		
B			
C			
Total Liabilities + Fund Balances			$

bargaining chip, a phrase that came out of the Strategic Arms Limitations Talks of the 1970s meaning a military resource that one nation might discard or downgrade in return for a concession from a rival nation. But the term was so widely bandied about by the news media that it now refers to anything one might be willing to trade in a negotiation.

bargaining item, illegal: *see* ILLEGAL BARGAINING ITEMS.

bargaining rights, legal rights that all workers have to bargain collectively with their employers.

See also EXCLUSIVE BARGAINING RIGHTS.

bargaining strength, relative power that each of the parties holds during the negotiating process.

bargaining theory, the sum of several approaches to the study of how people negotiate and how to negotiate successfully. These approaches include mathematical modeling, game theory, various schools of psychology, and the study of bargaining in many different settings.

bargaining theory of wages, theory that wages are based on the supply and demand for labor, that wages can never be higher than a company's break-even point or lower than bare subsistence for the workers, and that the actual "price" of labor is determined by the relative strengths—the bargaining power—of employers and workers. While the bargaining theory does not explain wage determination over the long run, it is generally accepted as the most pragmatic explanation of short-run wage determination.

bargaining unit, or simply UNIT, group of employees, union members as well as others, that an employer has recognized and/or an administrative agency has certified as appropriate for representation by a union for purposes of collective bargaining. All of the employees in a bargaining unit are subsequently covered in the labor contract that the union negotiates on their behalf. Bargaining units may be as small as the handful of workers in a local shop or as large as the work force of an entire industry. The size of a bargaining unit is important in that it significantly affects the relative bargaining strength of both labor and management.

bargain sale, selling part and giving part of the same asset to a charitable organization. Under prior tax laws, bargain sales provided a way to sell appreciated property for an amount equal to its tax base, and then contribute the appreciated value to a charitable organization without generating taxable income. Current tax laws have restricted the appeal of bargain sales, but they still have limited applicability.
See also APPRECIATED PROPERTY.

Barnard, Chester I. (1886-1961), a Bell System executive closely associated with the Harvard Business School, best known for his sociological analyses of organizations that encouraged and foreshadowed the post World War II behavioral revolution, Barnard viewed organizations as cooperative systems where "the function of the executive" was to maintain the dynamic equilibrium between the needs of the organization and the needs of its employees. In order to do this, management had to be aware of the interdependent nature of the formal and informal organization. Barnard's analysis of the significance and role of informal organizations provided the theoretical foundations for a whole generation of empirical research.

BARS: *see* BEHAVIORALLY ANCHORED RATING SCALES.

base, point from which budgetary calculations usually begin, generally the level budgeted in the preceding fiscal year.
See also ZERO-BASE BUDGETING.

base period, time that an employee must work before becoming eligible for certain employment benefits.

base points, minimum point values given to the factors in a job evaluation system.

base rate: *see* BASE SALARY.

base salary, or BASE RATE, standard earnings before the addition of overtime or premium pay.

base time, time required for an employee to perform an operation while working normally with no allowance for personal/unavoidable delays or fatigue.

BASIC: *see* BEGINNERS' ALL-PURPOSE SYMBOLIC INSTRUCTION CODE.

basic workday, number of hours in a normal workday. Premium payments or compensatory time off may be made for time worked in excess of the basic workday. The eight-hour day is widely accepted as the standard basic workday.

basic workweek, number of hours in a normal workweek. Premium payments or compensatory time off must usually be made for time worked in excess of the basic workweek. The forty-hour week is widely accepted as the standard basic workweek.
See also FAIR LABOR STANDARDS ACT.

basis, the assumed cost of an item or property used in calculating gain or loss for tax purposes when property is donated, sold, or exchanged.

battery, or TEST BATTERY, two or more tests administered together and standardized on the same population so that the results on the various tests are comparable. The term battery is also used to refer to any tests administered as a group.

baud, signals sent and received per second; a measure of the flow speed of computer data over telecommunications lines, which is usually expressed in bits per second.

before and after study, an evaluation technique which measures a dependent variable before and after the application of, or a change in, a process. An example might be the installation of a new computerized system for generating follow-up letters to donors. The dependent variables measured might be the speed with which follow-up letters are mailed and the number of typographical errors. The variables would be measured before and after the installation. In order to reach a valid conclusion that the change was induced by the process, other variables either must be controlled or accounted for. One frequently used method for such control is through a control group.

See also CONTROL GROUP and EVALUATION TECHNIQUE.

beggar-thy-neighbor policy, a course of action through which a country tries to reduce unemployment and increase domestic output by raising tariffs and instituting nontariff measures that impede imports. Countries that pursued such policies in the early 1930s found that other countries retaliated by raising barriers against the first country's exports, which tended to worsen the economic difficulties that precipitated the initial protectionist action.

Beginners' All-Purpose Symbolic Instruction Code (BASIC), also EXTENDED BASIC, a widely used introductory computer language. *Extended BASIC* is more complex and more useful.

beginner's rate, or TRAINEE RATE, wage rate for an inexperienced employee. Once a previously established training period is completed, an employee is entitled to the regular rate of pay for the job.

behaviorally anchored rating scales (BARS), performance evaluation technique that is premised upon the scaling of critical incidents of work performance.

behavior modeling, training, usually for first or second line supervisors, that uses videotapes and/or role-playing sessions to give supervisors an opportunity to improve their supervisory abilities by imitating "models" who have already mastered such skills.

behavior models, diagrams used by social scientists to better explain their theories of human behavior. For examples, *see* JOHARI WINDOW and MANAGERIAL GRID.

behavior modification (BMod), use of positive or negative reinforcements to change the behavior of individuals or groups.

behavioral sciences, general term for all of the academic disciplines that study human and animal behavior by means of experimental research.

See also NATIONAL TRAINING LABORATORIES INSTITUTE FOR APPLIED BEHAVIORAL SCIENCE.

behavioral technology, emerging discipline that seeks to meld the technical and human aspects of the workplace. It places equal emphasis on social and technological sciences in order to foster the individual's fullest use as both a human and a technical resource.

behaviorism, school of psychology which holds that only overt behavior is the proper subject matter for the entire discipline. According to the foremost exponent of behaviorism, B. F. Skinner, in *About Behaviorism* (N.Y.: Alfred A. Knopf, 1974). "behaviorism is not the science of human behavior; it is the philosophy of that science."

EXAMPLE OF A BEHAVIORALLY ANCHORED NUMERICAL RATING SCALE

Rating	*Behavioral Anchor*
1	Knows rules of racquetball, can bounce ball and hit it with racquet
2	Hits forehand strokes with consistency, backhand is weak
3	Hits both forehand and backhand strokes with consistency
4	Can place ball accurately, including serves
5	All strokes are accurate, firm, and consistent; topspin and underspin strokes can be employed as required

bell curve: *see* NORMAL DISTRIBUTION.

Bell, Daniel (1919-), sociologist whose critiques of modern industrial societies have touched upon their politics and their management. Bell is considered to be both a major critic of the "machine civilization" of the scientific management era and a pioneer in social forecasting.

See also POST-INDUSTRIAL SOCIETY.

beltway bandits, term applied to consulting firms in the Washington, D.C., area because so many of them are located on the interstate beltway, Route 495, which surrounds the metro area.

benchmark, any standard that is identified with sufficient detail so that other similar classifications can be compared as being above, below, or comparable to the "benchmark" standard.

benchmark position, position used as a frame of reference in the evaluation of other positions.

beneficial interest, the right to receive a percentage of profit distributions from an organization (typically, an unincorporated organization) or a percentage of its assets following liquidation.

beneficial owner, the true owner of a security which may, for convenience, be recorded under the name of a nominee.

beneficiary, person, group, or organization to whom an insurance policy is payable.

benefit (insurance), a sum of money provided in an insurance policy payable for certain types of loss, or for covered services, under the terms of the policy. The benefits may be paid to the insured or on his behalf to others.

benefit (program), a measurable monetary return realized from a program or service rendered. Some programs operated by nonprofit organizations are not well suited to benefits analysis because some results cannot be adequately related to monetary value. For example, if each life saved is worth $ ________ (in, for exam-, ple lifetime earnings, nondependence on public assistance, etc.), then the estimated benefit achieved by a program to reduce vehicular fatalities is ________ lives saved (×) $ ________ per vehicular fatality.

benefit, death: *see* DEATH BENEFIT.

benefit, direct, also INDIRECT BENEFIT, a result attained which is related closely to a project or program in a cause and effect relationship; for example, an increase in literacy as a result of a reading program. An *indirect benefit* is a result which is achieved circuitously; for example, an increase in employment due to increased literacy arising from a reading program.

See also SPILLOVER EFFECT.

benefit, net: see NET BENEFIT.

benefit-cost analysis: *see* COST-BENEFIT ANALYSIS.

benefit district, method for financing construction of public works in which those who directly benefit are charged for the construction costs. For example, sidewalks are often financed through increases in property taxes of residents through whose property the sidewalk passes; that is, those owners are members of a sidewalk or benefit district that levies a tax and is dissolved when the construction costs have been recovered.

benefit of payor, a concept involved in the determination of related and unrelated business income. If a tax-exempt nonprofit organization performs useful services for and receives payment from an operating unit of government (an IRS Code 170 [c] [1] organization), and the services are compatible with the nonprofit organization's tax-exempt purposes, the money received from the government unit for the services is tax-exempt.

See also UNRELATED BUSINESS INCOME.

benefit period, the period of time for which payments for benefits covered by an insurance policy are available. The availability of certain benefits may be limited over a specified time period; for example, two well-baby visits during a one-year period. While the benefit period is usually defined by a set unit of time, such as a year, benefits may also be tied to a spell of illness.

benefit seniority, use of seniority in computing an employee's economic fringe benefits such as pensions, vacations, bonuses, etc.

benevolent organization, an organization such as a nonprofit organization that attempts to do good to, or for, others. The organization is for benefit rather than for profit. Also, a specific category of organizations which includes, for example, benevolent life insurance associations that may qualify for tax-exempt status under IRS Code 501 (c) (12).

See also:
CHARITABLE ORGANIZATION
ELEEMOSYNARY
PHILANTHROPIC

benign neglect: *see* MOYNIHAN, DANIEL PATRICK.

Bennis, Warren G. (1925-), a leading proponent of organization development, perhaps best known for his continuous sounding of the death knell of bureaucratic institutions. Bennis has indicted most present organizational formats as inadequate for a future that will demand rapid organizational and technological changes, participatory management, and the growth of a more professionalized work force. Organizations of the future, Bennis maintains, will be more responsive to these needs and, in consequence, decidedly less bureaucratic, less structured, and less rigid.

See also POSTBUREAUCRATIC ORGANIZATION.

Bentham, Jeremy (1748-1832), Utilitarian philosopher who held that self-interest was the prime motivator and that a government should strive to do the greatest good for the greatest numbers.

bequest, also LEGACY, instructions in a will to distribute personal property to an individual or organization.

bereavement leave: *see* FUNERAL LEAVE.

Berne, Eric (1910-1970), the psychoanalyst who founded the field of transactional analysis.

Bertalanffy, Ludwig von (1901-1972), Austrian-Canadian biologist considered to be the father of general systems theory.

Beth Israel Hospital* v. *National Labor Relations Board, 437 U.S. 483 (1978), U.S. Supreme Court case which upheld a National Labor Relations Board determination that employees seeking to organize a bargaining unit of hospital employees could not be prohibited from distributing leaflets in a hospital cafeteria patronized predominantly by hospital employees. To a limited extent, the court gave its approval to the NLRB's attempt to permit a substantial range for union communication to actual and potential members, provided such communication does not disrupt employer's business activities.

Better Business Bureau, a local business-supported organization that handles complaints about business practices, provides consumer information, and promotes ethical business dealings. National standards and support for the local bureaus are provided by the Council of Better Business Bureaus.

BFOQ: *see* BONA FIDE OCCUPATIONAL QUALIFICATION.

biannual, also SEMIANNUAL, twice a year.
See also BIENNIAL.

bias, tendency of a selection device to err in a particular direction.
See also CULTURAL BIAS.

biased sample, sample that does not truly represent the total population from which it was selected.

bidding, means by which an employee of an organization makes known his or her interest in a vacant position in that same organization.

bid shopping, disclosing low bids received for contract work in order to get lower bids from other vendors.

biennial, once every two years.
See also BIANNUAL.

Big Eight, slang term for the eight largest certified public accounting firms: Arthur Anderson and Co.; Coopers and Lybrand; Ernst and Ernst; Deloit, Haskins and Sells; Peat, Marwick, Mitchell and Company; Price Waterhouse and Company; Touche Ross and Company; and Arthur Young and Company.

***Big Mama Rag, Inc.* v. *United States*:** *see* FULL AND FAIR EXPOSITION REQUIREMENT.

bigotry: *see* DISCRIMINATION.

Big Seven: *see* PUBLIC INTEREST GROUP.

bill: *see* ACT.

billed revenue, also INVOICED REVENUE, the amount of earned revenue billed or invoiced to the recipient of services or a third-party payer. Many types of nonprofit organizations perform services-for-fees for individual clients or other organizations. Nonprofit ambulance services and sheltered workshops are typical examples.
See also:
BILLING
COLLECTED REVENUE
COLLECTION RATE
EARNED REVENUE
ESTIMATED INCOME
FEES-FOR-SERVICES
UNBILLED REVENUE
UNCOLLECTED REVENUE

billing, also INVOICING, the process of formally notifying recipients of services-for-fees or a third-party payer of the amount due. There are three general, elementary rules for billing recipients of services:
1) Bill promptly after providing services.
2) Send out bills that are accurate—without mistakes.
3) Bills should be complete and appear professional.

See the example of a Billing Accuracy Score Sheet, developed for rural volunteer ambulance services.
See also:
BILLED REVENUE
COLLECTED REVENUE
FEES-FOR-SERVICES
UNBILLED REVENUE
UNCOLLECTED REVENUE

billing cycle, the regular time interval (usually one month) between dates when bills are sent to customers or clients.

Billing Journal

Billing Accuracy Score Sheet

(1) Place an "X" on the line next to each statement that describes your billing procedures.

	Always	*Usually*	*Occasionally*	*Never*
Bills are checked by a second person before they are sent.	____	____	____	____
When an error is spotted on a bill, the bill is re-prepared rather than marked over or erased.	____	____	____	____
Our biller uses a calculator with paper tape.	____	____	____	____
Our charge sheet is posted prominently where bills are prepared.	____	____	____	____
When billing information is incomplete or illegible, we check with the people who made the run to make sure we have it right.	____	____	____	____
(2) Add the "X's" in each column	____	____	____	____
(3) Multiply the totals by	(X) 3	(X) 2	(X) 1	(X) 0
(4) Put the answers here; add them up.	____ (+)	____ (+)	____ (+)	____ = ☐

SCORING:

14–15	=	Excellent	(A+)
12–13	=	Very Good	(A)
10–11	=	Not bad, but	(B)
6– 9	=	You had better . . . . get to work	(C)
0– 5	=	You are in trouble	(D)

Source: Colorado Dept. of Health, Emergency Medical Services Division, Colorado Ambulance Service Management Handbook *(Denver, Colo.: 1984)*

billing journal, also SALES JOURNAL, an accounting journal used to record all billings (invoiced sales) for services provided to clients or other organizations. A billing journal should contain information on the date of each billing, the person or organization who was billed (for example, for a hospital or ambulance service, the patient, an insurance company, Medicaid, or Medicare), the amount due, when payment is due, and which subsidiary or general ledger accounts are affected (are debited or credited).

After the billing journal is totaled and balanced at the end of each fiscal period (for example, a month or a year), it is posted to the general ledger and to the accounts receivable subsidiary ledger.

See also:

ACCOUNTING CYCLE
DEBITS AND CREDITS
GENERAL LEDGER
JOURNAL
POSTING
SUBSIDIARY LEDGER
TRIAL BALANCE

billings, the amount that an advertising agency charges its clients for services.

See also BILLING.

EXAMPLE OF A BILLING JOURNAL

ACE AMBULANCE SERVICE—BILLING JOURNAL

		Invoice	CR	DR	Acct. Rec		
Date	Service Provided To	Number	Income	Desc. Acct. #	Amount	Gen'l. Descript'n	Amt.
8/22/83	Mrs. Jones	1234	$75.00	14-21	$75.00		
8/22/83	MRS. SMITH	1235	$125.00	16-27	$125.00		

Bill of Rights, first ten amendments to the U.S. Constitution.

Only a few individual rights were specified in the Constitution when it was ratified in 1788. Shortly after its adoption, however, ten amendments—called the Bill of Rights—were added to the Constitution to guarantee basic individual liberties. These liberties include freedom of speech, freedom of press, freedom of religion, and freedom to assemble and petition the government.

In 1868, the Fourteenth Amendment was added to the Constitution. In part, it provides that no state shall "deprive any person of life, liberty, or property without due process of law."

To place these rights in a broader perspective, one should realize that they make up only the core of what are considered to be our civil rights—those privileges and freedoms that are accorded all Americans by virtue of their citizenship. There are many other "civil" rights which are not specifically mentioned in the Constitution but which nonetheless have been recognized by the courts, guaranteed by statute, and now are embedded in our democratic traditions. The right to buy, sell, own, and bequeath property; the right to enter into contracts; the right to marry and have children; the right to live and work where one desires; and the right to participate in the political, social, and cultural processes of the society in which one lives are a few of those rights that are considered as fundamental to a democratic society as those specified by the Constitution.

bimodal distribution, frequency distribution in which there are two modes—two most frequently occurring scores. A graphic presentation would show two peaks.

binary number, a number using only the digits 0 and 1. The binary numbering system is used by computers because each logical or electronic choice can be made in yes-no or on-off form.

binder, a temporary, preliminary insurance contract.

binding arbitration, actually a redundancy! Arbitration, unless it is advisory, is by its nature binding upon the parties.

Binet, Alfred (1857-1911), French psychologist who originated the first modern intelligence test.

bingo game, a game of chance played simultaneously by many players for cash or noncash prizes. Some tax-exempt organizations use paid personnel to conduct regular bingo games as fund-raising events. However, for most tax-exempt organizations, the income therefrom is not defined as unrelated business income.

See also UNRELATED BUSINESS INCOME.

binomial variable, a variable that has only two attributes; for example, sex, where there is only male or female.

biofeedback, a new field; there is no single, widely accepted definition for the term. However, most authors use the term to mean a process for learning voluntary control over automatic body functions by "feeding back" physiological data to the person who creates it. Physiologic activities—often ones that are associated with stress, such as heart rate, blood pressure, muscle tension, etc.—are monitored with instruments and displayed (or signaled) to the person being monitored. If the biofeedback learning process is effective, the individual learns to recognize the physiologic activities without the use of monitoring equipment and, therefore, is able to voluntarily control them.
See also STRESS.

bi-partite board, labor-management committee established as part of a grievance process in order to resolve a dispute short of arbitration.

Birmingham Business College, Inc.* v. *Commissioner, a landmark 1960 decision by the U.S. Court of Appeals for the Fifth Circuit (276 F. 2d 476 [5th Cir. 1960]) in which the Birmingham Business College was denied tax-exempt status because some of its net earnings inured to the college's shareholders.
See also:
DISQUALIFIED PERSON
INSIDER
PRIVATE INUREMENT

birth leave, paid time off upon the birth of a child. This is generally available only to men. Women, should the occasion warrant, would necessarily take maternity leave.

biserial correlation, correlation between the score on a particular item and the total test score.

Bishop* v. *Wood, 426 U.S. 341 (1976), U.S. Supreme Court case which held that an employee's discharge did not deprive him of a property interest protected by the Due Process Clause of the U.S. Constitution's Fourteenth Amendment. The court further asserted that even assuming a false explanation for the employee's discharge, he was still not deprived of an interest in liberty protected by the clause if the reasons for his discharge were not made public.

bit, a single 0 or 1 character or symbol in the binary numbering system. This is the smallest unit of computer memory storage.
See also BYTE.

bit density, the number of bits stored in a given physical storage size; for example, bits per inch.

bit rate: *see* BAUD.

bivariate analysis, the analysis of two variables simultaneously in order to determine the relationship between them.

Bivens* v. *Six Unknown Named Federal Narcotics Agents, 403 U.S. 388 (1971), U.S. Supreme Court case establishing the principle that individuals could sue public officials for damages in connection with the violation of their constitutional rights under the Fourth Amendment. By implication, the same principle would apply to violations of other constitutional rights.

black lung benefits trust, a trust established by a coal mine operator to provide self-insurance protection against claims under various federal and state black lung benefits laws. Black lung benefits trusts may qualify for tax-exempt status under IRS Code 501 (c) (21).

black lung disease, scientific name PNEUMOCONIOSIS, chronic and disabling occupational disease (mostly of miners) resulting from the inhalation of dusts over a long period of time. Its popular name results from the tendency of the inhaled dusts to blacken lung tissue.

Blake, Robert R. (1918-) **and Jane S. Mouton** (1930-), industrial psychologists best known for their conceptualization of the "managerial grid"—a graphic description of the various managerial approaches. The grid itself represents leadership styles that reflect two prime dimensions, "concern for people" on the vertical axis and "concern for production" on the horizontal axis.

blank indorsement, signing a negotiable instrument—such as a check—without specifying to whom it is to be paid, and thus not limiting who can cash it.

bleeding shark, an employee in trouble at work who is attacked by others instead of helped.

blind trust, the placement of assets in a trust designed to prevent the owner from influencing or even knowing about its management. This is done when the owner wants to avoid the reality or perception of private inurement or conflict of interest or, for example, by a private foundation to avoid having a controlling interest in another organization.

See also:

PRIVATE FOUNDATION
PRIVATE INUREMENT

blockage discounting, the practice of discounting the fair market value of traded securities held by a private foundation in order to reduce the foundation's mandatory distribution amount. Because a private foundation's mandatory distribution amount is related to the value of its assets, discounting the fair market value of assets reduces the amount of money it would be required to distribute annually. The practice was restricted severely by provisions of the 1976 amendments to the Tax Reform Act.

See also MANDATORY DISTRIBUTION RULES.

block grant: *see* GRANT.

BLS: *see* BUREAU OF LABOR STATISTICS.

Blue Cross and Blue Shield, nonprofit group health insurance plans for, respectively, hospital and physician fees.

blue laws, state and local legislation banning commercial and related activities on particular days, usually Sunday.

Blue Shield: *see* BLUE CROSS AND BLUE SHIELD.

blue sky bargaining, unreasonable and unrealistic negotiating demands by either side, usually made at the beginning of the negotiating process.

BMod: *see* BEHAVIOR MODIFICATION.

BNA: *see* BUREAU OF NATIONAL AFFAIRS, INC.

BNA Pension Reporter, Bureau of National Affairs, Inc., information service that provides weekly notification of developments under the Employee Retirement Income Security Act of 1974, including enforcement actions, court decisions, labor and industry activities, and employee benefit trust fund regulation; activities of the Department of Labor, the Internal Revenue Service, the Pension Benefit Guaranty Corporation, and Congress; and state and local government actions.

BNA Policy and Practice Series, "common-sense" guide on the handling of employer-employee relations published by the Bureau of National Affairs, Inc. Covers personnel management, labor relations, fair employment practices, wages and hours, and compensation.

board basket, a file maintained by an organization's secretary with collected notes and materials to be used at the next meeting of the board of directors. The contents of the board basket are used to create the agenda.

See also AGENDA.

board of directors, the body of people which, under the authority of the organization's constitution and bylaws, controls and governs the affairs of the organization.

See also:

ADMINISTRATIVE BOARD
ADVISORY BOARD
CERTIFICATE OF INCORPORATION
DIRECTOR
GOVERNANCE.

board of trade, a type of association similar to but somewhat more narrow in purpose than a chamber of commerce. Boards of trade may qualify for tax exemption under IRS Code 501 (c) (6).

board of trustees, the equivalent of a board of directors for some charitable organizations.

A foundation may be a corporation or a trust, and the trustees of a trust foundation are designated legally by a foundation's trust instrument. For example, commercial banks are often trustees for community foundations.

Also, some nonprofit organizations, such as churches, have both a board of directors and a board of trustees. Under this arrangement, the board of directors is typically responsible for program and administrative policy, whereas the board of trustees is responsible for finances.

See also:
BOARD OF DIRECTORS
DIRECTOR
GOVERNANCE
TRUSTEE

board profile, an inventory of existing individual board (of directors) members' skills and experiences, areas of community contact and influence, important sociodemographic characteristics, and date of (board) term expiration. The profile is analyzed by, for example, a nominating committee to identify needed skills, contacts, and sociodemographic representation needs to be met by nominees. For example, the expiration of three board members' terms might deplete a board of all (1) skills and experience in public relations and strategic planning, (2) contacts with state legislative leaders and the print media, or (3) representation from the southwest part of the state and American Indians. The nominating committee thereby establishes its priorities in seeking candidates.

See also:
BOARD OF DIRECTORS
BOARD ROTATION
BOARD TERM
DIRECTOR
NOMINATING COMMITTEE

board rotation, also ROTATIONAL EXPIRATION OF TERM, a schedule for regular replacement of directors on a staggered basis (for example, one third of the members' terms expire every two years). Board rotation provides the organization with continuity of leadership and regular infusions of new ideas and talents. It provides directors with a finite board term and, therefore, a known period of obligation.

See also:
BOARD OF DIRECTORS
BOARD PROFILE
BOARD TERM
DIRECTOR

board term, the length of time for which

EXAMPLE OF A BOARD PROFILE

MEMBER	TERM EXPIRES	AREAS OF EXPERTISE	COMMUNITY CONNECTIONS	REPRESENTS

directors are elected. Typical board terms are three, five, and six years—or indefinite.

Bob Jones University* v. *Simon, (416 U.S. 725 [1974]), a landmark U.S. Supreme Court case which affirmed federal public policy against support for racial segregation (and, presumably, other forms of racial discrimination) in nonprofit educational institutions.

See also GREEN V. CONNALLY and WRIGHT V. REGAN.

bod biz, slang term for sensitivity training programs.

body chemistry, nebulous concept that refers to the fact that strangers, upon meeting, react to a variety of irrational and subliminal signals which, in turn, determine whether they like each other or not.

bogey, easily exceeded informal standard that employees may establish in order to restrict production.

bogus, false and intended to deceive. For example, a bogus check is a check written by a person who has no active account at the bank named on the check.

bona fide, (Latin) honest; in good faith; real.

bona fide member (charitable organization), a member of a charity or charitable organization who has more than a nominal connection with the organization. Also, to be considered a bona fide member, the individual should have taken some positive action toward the organization, such as paying dues or contributing. The concept is important in that, for example, a charitable organization is permitted to communicate with its bona fide members about legislative issues (with clear restrictions) without being deemed as participating in political activities.

bona fide occupational qualification (BFOQ or BOQ), a *necessary* occupational qualification. Title VII of the Civil Rights Act of 1964 allows employers to discriminate against applicants on the basis of religion, sex, or national origin when being considered for certain jobs if they lack a BFOQ. However, what constitutes a BFOQ has been interpreted very narrowly by the EEOC and the federal courts. Legitimate BFOQ's include female sex for a position as an actress or male sex for a sperm donor. There are no generally recognized BFOQ's with respect to race or color. Overall, a BFOQ is a job requirement that would be discriminatory and illegal were it not for its necessity for the performance of a particular job.

bona fide union, union that was freely chosen by employees and that is not unreasonably or illegally influenced by their employer.

bond, certificate of indebtedness issued by a borrower to a lender that constitutes a legal obligation to repay the principal of the loan plus accrued interest.

See also the following entries:

CALLABLE BONDS
MUNICIPAL BONDS
REVENUE BONDS
SERIAL BONDS

bond, fidelity: *see* FIDELITY BOND.

bond, industrial development, a bond put out by a local government unit to support building business facilities which then are leased to pay off the bond.

See also REVENUE BOND.

bond anticipation notes (BANs), form of short-term borrowing used to accelerate progress on approved capital projects. Once the revenues for a project have been realized from the sale of long-term bonds the BANs are repaid. BANs may also be used to allow a borrower to wait until the bond market becomes more favorable for the sale of long-term securities.

bond fund: *see* MUTUAL FUND.

bond funds, funds established to account for the proceeds of bond issues pending their disbursement.

bonding, a contract involving three parties: an insurance company, the beneficiary (who often pays the bond premium), and the principal (against whose acts the beneficiary is indemnified). The insurance company promises to pay the beneficiary for damages due to the failure of performance or dishonesty of the principal.

See also
BENEFICIARY
CORRUPTION
FIDELITY BOND

bond rating, the appraisal of the soundness and value assigned to a bond by one of several bond rating companies, such as Standard and Poor's or Moody. Rating systems differ, but the highest rating given usually is "AAA" and the lowest rating of an "investment quality bond" usually is "Baa."

bonus, also called SUPPLEMENTAL COMPENSATION, any compensation that is in addition to regular wages and salary. Because "bonus" has a mildly paternalistic connotation, it has been replaced in some organizations by "supplemental compensation."

See also the following entries:
NONPRODUCTION BONUS
STEP BONUS

bookkeeping, collecting, compiling, and retaining an organization's financial information in an organized fashion. Bookkeeping precedes the preparation of financial statements. A subset of accounting.

See also ACCOUNTANT and ACCOUNTING.

books of original entry, a journal in which transactions are recorded initially for subsequent posting in the organization's ledgers.

See also:
ACCOUNTING CYCLE
JOURNAL
LEDGER

book value, the worth of something as recorded on an organization's balance sheet, rather than its worth as established by the market; also, an organization's net worth, or its clearly proven assets minus its liabilities.

boondoggle, slang term for any wasteful and/or unproductive program.

boot, to enter a program into a computer.

bootleg wages, wages above union scale that an employer might pay in a tight labor market in order to retain and attract employees, as well as wages below union scale that an employee might accept in lieu of unemployment.

BOQ: *see* BONA FIDE OCCUPATIONAL QUALIFICATION.

borough, local government unit generally smaller than a city. New York City, for example, is divided into five boroughs: Manhattan, Brooklyn, Bronx, Queens, and Richmond.

See also TOWN.

borrowing authority, statutory authority (substantive or appropriation) that permits a public agency to incur obligations and to make payments for specified purposes out of borrowed moneys.

boss, slang term used by subordinates to refer to anyone from whom they are willing to take orders.

bossism, also POLITICAL MACHINE, informal system of local government in which political power is concentrated in the hands of a central figure, called a political boss, who may not have a formal government position. The power is concentrated through the use of a political machine, whereby a hierarchy is created and maintained by the use of patronage and government largesse to assure compliance with the wishes of the boss. It was a dominant system in American city government after the Civil War and was the main target of the American urban reform effort.

bottom line, the profit or loss from an activity; the final result of an activity, a final conclusion or responsibility.

bottom-line concept, in the context of equal employment opportunity, the suggestion that an employer whose total selection process has no adverse impact can be assured that EEO enforcement agencies will not examine the individual components of that process for evidence of adverse impact. However, not all EEO enforcement agencies subscribe to the concept.

bounded rationality: *see* SATISFICING.

bourgeois, in the context of Marxism, a member of the ruling class in capitalistic societies; one of the owners of the means of production. The plural is *bourgeoisie.* Marx distinguished between the *haute bourgeoisie,* the real leaders of industry, and the *petit bourgeoisie,* the small businessmen, whom he felt really belonged with the proletariat.

boycott, a refusal to deal with or buy the products of a business as a means of exerting pressure in a dispute. The U.S. Supreme Court has consistently held that boycotts are an illegal "restraint of trade" under the Sherman Antitrust Act of 1890.

See also SECONDARY BOYCOTT.

Boys Market* v. *Retail Clerks' Local 770, 398 U.S. 235 (1970), U.S. Supreme Court case which held that when a labor contract has a no-strike provision and provides an arbitration procedure, a federal court may, upon the request of an employer, issue an injunction to terminate a strike by employees covered by such a contract.

See also:
ARBITRATION
STRIKE

bracket: see TAX RATE.

Bradford, Leland P. (1905-   ), director of the National Training Laboratories from 1947 to 1967 who pioneered the development of "sensitivity training."

brain drain, pejorative term referring to the unfortunate flow of human capital—talent—from a country, an area, or an organization. While historically used to describe the exodus of doctors, scientists, and other professionals from a particular country, it is colloquially used to refer to the departure of any valued employee or group of employees.

brainstorming, term used to describe any group effort to generate ideas. It has a more formal definition—a creative conference for the sole purpose of producing suggestions or ideas that can serve as leads to problem solving.

branching: *see* DECISION TREE.

brass, slang term of military origin which now refers to the key executives in an organization.

breach, a failure or refusal to carry out the terms of an agreement or to do something that is required of one.

breach of contract, violation of an agreement by either party. If established dispute resolution machinery is not adequate, traditional lawsuits remain as a remedy.

breakdown: *see* NERVOUS BREAKDOWN.

break-even analysis, any of many methods for analyzing the relationships among costs (fixed, semifixed, and variable), volume of activity, and surplus or loss.

See also MARGINAL INCOME ANALYSIS.

break-even chart: *see* O'ROURKE'S BREAK-EVEN CHART.

break-even point, the sales volume at which income (or revenues) equals total costs; for example, the number of tickets which must be sold to a special event before a "profit" is realized.

break in service, the time between separation and reemployment that may cause a loss of rights or privileges.

bridge job, position specifically designed to facilitate the movement of individuals from one classification and/or job category to another classification and/or category. Such bridge jobs are an integral part of many career ladders and upward mobility programs.

bridge loan, temporary, short-term financing; for example, to build a new building before the old one is sold.

brief, a written statement prepared by each side in a formal lawsuit or hearing which summarizes the facts of the situation and makes arguments about how the law should be applied.

broken time, or SPLIT SHIFT, daily work schedule that is divided by a length of time considerably in excess of the time required for a normal meal break. For example, a school bus driver may work from 6 to 10 A.M. and then from 2 to 6 P.M.

Brookings Institution, nonprofit organization located in Washington, D.C., devoted to research, education, and publication in economics, government, foreign policy, and the social sciences generally.

brother-sister arrangement, a relationship between a sponsoring organization and an auxiliary charitable organization in which the two are operated as independent organizations rather than the latter being operated as a subsidiary of the former.

See also AUXILIARY CHARITABLE ORGANIZATION.

Brown* v. *Board of Education of Topeka, Kansas, 347 U.S. 483 (1954), landmark Supreme Court decision holding that the separation of children by race and according to law in public schools ". . . generates a feeling of inferiority as to their [the minority group's] status in the community that may affect their hearts and minds in a way unlikely ever to be undone." Consequently, it held that "separate educational facilities are inherently unequal" and therefore violate the equal protection clause of the Fourteenth Amendment.

B-school, slang for business school.

buddy system, on-the-job training technique that has a trainee assigned to work closely with an experienced worker until the trainee has gained enough experience to work alone.

budget, financial plan serving as a pattern for and control over future operations—hence, any estimate of future costs or any systematic plan for the utilization of the work force, material, or other resources, as well as the estimate of projected revenues.

Budget, Bureau of the, central budget agency of the United States from 1921 to 1970.

budget, current services, budget that projects estimated budget authority and outlays for the upcoming fiscal year at the same program level (and without policy changes) as the fiscal year in progress. Estimates take into account the budget impact of anticipated changes in economic conditions (such as unemployment or inflation), beneficiary levels, pay increases, and benefit changes.

budget, executive, process by which public agency requests for appropriations are prepared and submitted to a budget bureau under the chief executive for review, alteration, and consolidation into a single budget document that can be compared to expected revenues and executive priorities before submission to the legislature. Also refers to the methods for controlling departmental spending after the legal appropriations have been made.

budget, full-employment, estimated receipts, outlays, and surplus or deficit that would occur if the economy were continually operating at a rate defined as being at full capacity (traditionally defined as a certain percentage unemployment rate for the civilian labor force).

budget, line-item, classification of budgetary accounts according to narrow, detailed objects of expenditure (such as motor vehicles, clerical workers, or reams of paper), generally without reference to the ultimate purpose or objective served by the expenditure.

budget, operating, short-term plan for managing the resources necessary to carry out a program. "Short-term" can mean anything from a few weeks to a few years. Usually an operating budget is developed for each fiscal year with changes made as necessary.

budget, president's, budget for a particular fiscal year transmitted to the Congress by the president in accordance with the Budget and Accounting Act of 1921, as amended. Some elements of the budget, such as the estimates for the legislative branch and the judiciary, are required to be included without review by the Office of Management and Budget or approval by the president.

budget, tax-expenditures, enumeration of revenue losses resulting from tax expenditures under existing law for each fiscal year. Section 601 of the Congressional Budget and Impoundment Control Act of 1974 requires that estimated levels of tax expenditures be presented in the president's budget.

See also TAX EXPENDITURES.

budget activity, categories within most accounts that identify the purposes, projects, or types of activities financed.

Budget and Accounting Act of 1921, act that created the Bureau of the Budget (later OMB) and the General Accounting Office.

budget authority, authority to enter into obligations which generally result in immediate or future outlays of funds. Budget authority may be classified by the period of availability (one-year, multiple-year, no-year) or by the manner of determining the amount available (definite or indefinite).

1. Period of Availability. *One-year (annual) authority*—budget authority that is available for obligation only during a specified fiscal year and expires at the end of that time. *Multiple-year authority*—budget authority that is available for a specified period of time in excess of one fiscal year *No-year authority*—budget authority that remains available for obligation for an indefinite period of time, usually until the objectives have been obtained.
2. Determination of Amount. *Definite authority*—authority which is stated as a specifc sum at the time the authority is granted. This includes authority stated as "not to exceed" a specified amount. *Indefinite authority*—authority for which the amount is not stated, but is to be determined by subsequent circumstances such as an appropriation of all or part of the receipts from a certain source.

budget call: *see* BUDGET GUIDANCE.

budget committee: *see* FINANCE COMMITTEE.

budget cycle, timed steps of the budget process, including preparation, approval, execution, and audit.

budget deficit, amount by which budget outlays exceed budget receipts for any given period. Deficits are financed primarily by borrowing.

budget estimates, estimates of budget authority, outlays, receipts, or other budget measures that cover current and future years.

budget guidance, also BUDGET CALL, direction given by a board of directors at the time of the call for budget estimates for the forthcoming budget period. Guidance frequently includes specific instructions regarding the format and timing of the budget submissions as well as statements of executive policy concerning scope of requests and program emphasis for the coming year.

budgeting, no less than the single most important decision making process in U.S. nonprofit and public organizations today. The budget itself is also a most important reference document. In their increasingly voluminous formats, budgets simultaneously record policy decision outcomes, cite policy and program preferences (as well as program objectives), and delineate an organization's total program effort. At the national level—and, to a lesser extent, at the state and regional levels—government budgets are primary instruments for redistributing income, stimulating economic growth, promoting full employment, combating inflation, and maintaining economic stability. A budget is an accounting instrument that holds officials responsible for the expenditure of the funds with which they have been entrusted. Budgets also hold organizations accountable in the aggregate. The very concept of a budget implies that there is a ceiling or a spending limitation, which literally (but theoretically) requires organizations to live within their means.

See also the following entries:

APPROPRIATION
AUDIT
BACKDOOR AUTHORITY
BALANCED BUDGET
BUDGETING, PERFORMANCE
CROSSWALK
CURRENT SERVICES ESTIMATES
DEBT FINANCING
DISBURSEMENTS
FISCAL INTEGRITY
MISSION BUDGETING
PLANNING, PROGRAMMING, BUDGETING SYSTEMS
RECONCILIATION
UNCONTROLLABLE EXPENSES
ZERO-BASE BUDGETING

budgeting, capital, a budget process that deals with planning for large expenditures for capital items. Capital expenditures should be for long-term investments which yield returns for years after they are completed. Capital budgets typically cover five- to ten-year periods and are updated yearly. Items included in capital budgets may be financed through borrowing, capital funds drives, savings, grants, etc.

A capital budget provides for separating the financing of capital or investment expenditures from current or operating expenditures.

budgeting, continuous, an approach to financial management in which budgetary and financial decisions are made on an ad hoc rather than a long-range basis according to the current level of revenues and expenditures.

budgeting, cost-based, also OBLIGATION-BASED BUDGETING, budgeting in terms of costs to be incurred; that is, the resources to be consumed in carrying out a program, regardless of when the funds to acquire the resources were obligated or paid, and without regard to the source of funds. For example, inventory items become costs when they are withdrawn from inventory, and the cost of buildings is distributed over time, through periodic depreciation charges, rather than in a lump sum when the buildings are acquired.

budgeting, incremental, method of budget review focusing on the increments of increase or decrease in the budget of existing programs.

budgeting, performance, a type of budgeting that is concerned with performance work assessment and efficiency. Performance budgeting presents purposes and objectives for which funds are allocated, examines costs of programs and activities established to meet these objectives, and identifies and analyzes quantitative data measuring work performed and accomplishments.

Performance budgeting tends to be retrospective, focusing on previous performance and work accomplishment (for example, of a division or a program).

One problem of no small significance must be clarified. The terms *performance budgeting* and *program budgeting* tend to be used interchangeably, but they are not synonymous. In performance budgeting, programs are generally linked to the various higher levels of an organization and serve as labels that encompass and structure the subordinate performance units. These units—the central element of performance budgeting—are geared to an organization's operational levels, and information about them is concrete and meaningful to managers at all levels. Program budgeting, on the other hand might or might not incorporate performance measurement, yet still might be useful for delineating broad functional categories of expenditure for review at higher levels. Overall, performance budgeting tends to be retrospective—focusing on previous performance and work accomplishments—while program budgeting tends to be forward-looking—involving policy planning and forecasts.

budgeting, planning programming: *see* PLANNING, PROGRAMMING, BUDGETING SYSTEMS.

budgeting, program: *see* BUDGETING, PERFORMANCE.

budget period, the length of time for which a budget is effective. For nonprofit organizations, the budget period for most operating budgets is one year.

budget surplus, amount by which budget receipts exceed budget outlays for any given period.

budget update, statement summarizing amendments to or revisions in the budget requested, estimated outlays, and estimated receipts for a fiscal year that has not been completed.

budget year, fiscal year for which the budget is being considered.

buffer, organizational procedures or structures that absorb disruptive inputs and thus protect the continuity or equilibrium of some core group. For example, people in positions near the boundaries of organizations often absorb a wide variety of messages and demands. These inputs are filtered, processed, and passed to the technical core of the organization in a sequential and routine form. Because the inputs have been buffered, the central work processes are not disrupted.

bug, an error which occurs in a computer program.

built-in stabilizers, features of the economy (such as unemployment benefits, welfare payments, etc.) that automatically act to modify the severity of economic downturns.

See also AUTOMATIC STABILIZER and COUNTERCYCLICAL.

bump, or BUMPING, layoff procedure that gives an employee with greater seniority the right to displace or "bump" another employee. Sometimes bumping rights are restricted to one office or department. Because of bumping rights, the laying off of a single worker can lead to the sequential transfers of a dozen others.

burden of proof, requirement that a party to an issue show that the weight of evidence is on his or her side in order to have the issue decided in his or her favor.

***Burdine* v. *Texas Department of Community Affairs*,** 450 U.S. 248 (1980), U.S. Supreme Court case which held that employers charged with discrimination do not have to prove that a person hired or promoted was better qualified than the person passed over. Instead, the employer need only provide adequate evidence that race or sex was not a factor in the decision.

The unanimous opinion of the Supreme Court, written by Justice Lewis F. Powell Jr., said that although Federal law prohibits discrimination, it does not demand that an employer give preferential treatment to minorities or women; that an employer does not have to prove that its action is lawful, rather the employer need only produce evidence which would allow a judge to conclude that the decision had not been motivated by discriminatory animus.

bureau, government department, agency, or subdivision of same.

bureaucracy, a specific set of structural arrangements. The dominant structural definition of bureaucracy, indeed the point of departure for all further analyses on the subject, is that of the German sociologist, Max Weber. Weber's "ideal type" bureaucracy possesses the following characteristics:

1. The bureaucrats must be personally free and subject to authority only with respect to the impersonal duties of their offices.
2. They are arranged in a clearly defined hierarchy of offices.
3. The functions of each office are clearly specified.
4. Officials accept and maintain their appointments freely—without duress.
5. Appointments are made on the basis of technical qualifications which ideally are substantiated by examinations—administered by the appointing authority, a university, or both.
6. Officials should have a money salary as well as pension rights. Such salaries must reflect the varying levels of positions in the hierarchy. While officials are always free to leave the organization, they can be removed from their offices only under previously stated specific circumstances.
7. An incumbent's post must be his sole or at least his major occupation.
8. A career system is essential. While promotion may be the result of either seniority or merit, it must be premised on the judgment of hierarchical superiors.
9. The official may not have a property right to his position nor any personal claim to the resources which go with it.
10. An official's conduct must be subject to systematic control and strict discipline.

Definitions of bureaucracy apply equally to organizations in the public, nonprofit, and private sectors. However, public sector bureaucracies tend to operate in a somewhat different climate from those in the nonprofit private sectors. "Third sector"—not-for-profit organizations such as hospitals, universities, and foundations—are analytically classed with public organizations because of the lack of free-market forces upon them. In short, bureaucracy is best conceptualized as a specific form of organization, and public bureaucracy should be considered a special variant of bureaucratic organization. However, sometimes *bureaucracy* is used as a general invective to refer to any inefficient organization.

See also the following entries:

POSTBUREAUCRATIC ORGANIZATIONS
REALPOLITIK
RED TAPE
REPRESENTATIVE BUREAUCRACY
WEBER, MAX

bureaucrat, denizen of a bureaucracy.
See also APPARATCHIK.

Bureaucrat, The, quarterly journal of the National Area Chapter of the American Society for Public Administration and the Federal Executive Alumni Association.

bureaucratic impersonality, a feature of bureaucracy. Max Weber held that bureaucracy's "special virtue" was "dehumanization." Hardly anyone would argue that bureaucracy does not have dehumanizing consequences for its employees and, to a lesser extent, for its clients as well. By dehumanization, Weber meant eliminating "from official business love, hatred, and all purely personal, irrational, and emotional elements." In Weber's view, formalization, hierarchy, and the other central features of bureaucracy render the individual bureaucrat "only a single cog in an ever-moving mechanism which prescribes to him an essentially fixed route of march." Consequently, "the individual bureaucrat is forged to the community of all functionaries who are integrated into the mechanism." He cannot "squirm out of the apparatus in which he is harnessed." Today the term "impersonality" is generally used in referring to this aspect of bureaucratic behavior.

bureaucratic risk taking, extraordinary action, generally resisted by the persons in charge, taken by a bureaucrat who commits the organization to a profitable course of action, blocks the execution of an illegal or immoral order, or exposes corruption, deceit, or an unlawful act taking place within the bureaucracy.

Bureau of Labor Statistics (BLS), agency responsible for the economic and statistical research activities of the Department of Labor. The BLS is the government's principal fact-finding agency in the field of labor economics, particularly with respect to the collection and analysis of data on manpower and labor requirements, living conditions, labor-management relations, productivity and technological developments, occupational safety and health, structure and growth of the economy, urban conditions and related socioeconomic issues, and international aspects of certain of these subjects.

Bureau of National Affairs, Inc. (BNA), the largest private employer of information specialists in the nation's capital. Its function is to report, analyze, and explain the activities of the federal government and the courts to those persons who are directly affected—educators, attorneys, labor relations practitioners, business executives, accountants, union officials, personnel administrators, and scores of others. The BNA organization is universally recognized as a leading source of authoritative information services. Its information reports and services include:

Affirmative Action Compliance Manual for Federal Contractors
BNA Pension Reporter
BNA Policy and Practice Series
Collective Bargaining Negotiations & Contracts
Construction Labor Report
Daily Labor Report
EEOC Compliance Manual
Employment and Training Reporter
Fair Employment Practice Service
Government Employee Relations Report
Government Manager, The
Labor Arbitration Reports
Labor Relations Reporter
Retail/Services Labor Report
Union Labor Report
White Collar Report

BNA Communications, Inc. produces employee communication, motivational, and supervisory and sales training films, case studies for management development, and related instructional materials.

Bureau of the Census: *see* CENSUS, BUREAU OF THE.

bureaupathology, term used by Victor A. Thompson, in *Modern Organization* (N.Y.: Knopf, 1960), to describe the pathological or dysfunctional aspects of bureaucracy.

burnout, worker's feeling of mental and physical fatigue that causes indifference and emotional disengagement from his or her job.

business, a line of trade. Typically the line of trade with which an organization or individual is primarily concerned. For example, the purchase and sale of goods for the purpose of attempting to make a profit.
See also BUSINESS LEAGUE.

business agent, full-time officer of a local union, elected or appointed, who handles grievances, helps enforce agreements, and otherwise deals with the union's financial, administrative, or labor-management problems.

business cycles, the recurrent phases of expansion and contraction in overall business activity. Although no two business cycles are alike, they are all thought to follow a pattern of prosperity, recession (or depression), and recovery.

business games: *see* MANAGEMENT GAMES.

business holdings, excess: *see* EXCESS BUSINESS HOLDINGS.

business judgment rule, the principle of law which holds that if people running an organization make honest, careful decisions within their legal powers, no court will interfere with those decisions—even if the results of a decision are bad.

business league, an association formed to improve business conditions by people with a common business interest. Business leagues may qualify for tax exemption under IRS Code 501 (c) (6), but not if they are involved in a line of business which is typically conducted for profit.
See also BUSINESS.

business necessity, the major legal defense for using an employment practice that effectively excludes women and/or minorities. The leading court case, *Robinson* v. *Lorrilard Corp.* 444 F.2d 791 (4th Cir. 1971); *cert. denied,* 404 U.S. 1006 (1971), holds that the test of the business necessity defense "is whether there exists an overriding legitimate business purpose such that the practice is necessary to the safe and efficient operation of the business."

business unions, also called BREAD-AND-BUTTER UNIONS, the conservative U.S. trade unions. They have been called "bread-and-butter" or "business" unions because they have tended to concentrate on gaining better wages and working conditions for their members rather than devote significant efforts on political action, as many European unions have done.

Butz* v. *Economou, 438 U.S. 478 (1978), Supreme Court case that provided an immunity from suit for civil damages to federal administrative officials exercising adjudicatory functions.

buzz group, device that seeks to give all the individuals at a large meeting an equal opportunity to participate by breaking the larger meeting into small groups of from six to eight persons each. These "buzz groups" each designate one person to report on their consensus (and dissents, if any) when the total group reconvenes.

buzzwords, important-sounding words. Robert Kirk Mueller, in *Buzzwords: A Guide to the Language of Leaderships* (N.Y.: Van Nostrand Reinhold Co., 1974), credits the late Professor Ralph Hower of Harvard for first using "buzzwords" to mean "those phrases that have a pleasant buzzing sound in your ears while you roll them on your tongue and that may overwhelm you into believing you know what you're talking about when you don't." In spite of this "formal" definition, the technical vocabularies of any occupational specialty are often referred to as buzzwords.

bylaws, standing rules for the governance and regulation of an organization's affairs.
See also GOVERNING INSTRUMENT

byte, a combination of bits that forms a regular unit of usable computer data.
See also BIT.

C

cabinet, heads of the executive departments of an organization (*e.g.*, a college) who report to and advise its chief executive. For example, the president's cabinet, the mayor's cabinet, etc.

CAD, computer assisted design or computer assisted drafting.

cafeteria benefits plan, also called SMORGASBORD BENEFITS PLAN, any program that allows employees to choose their fringe benefits within the limits of the total benefit dollars for which they are eligible. This allows each employee to have, in effect, his own individualized benefit program. Because such programs cost more to administer, they tend to exist mainly as part of high-level managerial compensation packages. However, computer capabilities will make it increasingly likely that such plans will be more widely offered.

calendar, management: *see* MANAGEMENT CALENDAR.

***California Management Review* (CMR),** quarterly that seeks to serve as a bridge between creative thought about management and executive action. An authoritative source of information and ideas contributing to the advancement of management science, it is directed to active managers, scholars, teachers, and others concerned with management.

callable bonds, also NONCALLABLE BONDS, so designated because the issuer may repay part or all of the obligation prior to the maturity date. For this reason "callable" bonds ordinarily carry higher interest rates. *Noncallable bonds,* on the other hand, may not be repurchased until the date of maturation.

call-back pay, compensation, often at premium rates, paid to workers called back on the job after completing their normal shift.

called meeting, a special purpose meeting, as distinguished from a periodically scheduled regular meeting.

See also NOTICE OF MEETING.

Call memorandum, a memorandum requesting the submission of a document such as a program plan by a specified date.

CAM, computer assisted manufacturing.

campaign, political: *see* POLITICAL CAMPAIGN.

Canadian Centre for Philanthropy, an organization of Canadian foundations and nonprofit organizations begun in 1980 and headquartered in Toronto with a regional center in Winnipeg. The centre's mandate is to encourage philanthropy through lobbying, networking and management support activities. It maintains a computerized management information system and statistical service on philanthropic activity, encourages research, sponsors conferences and a certificate program in fundraising management. It publishes a journal abstracting service; a newsletter, the *Canadian Directory to Foundations and Granting Agencies;* and, with the Canadian Bar Association, *The Philanthropist,* a scholarly journal on nonprofit organization activities and issues.

candidate, applicant for a position.

candidate for public office, in the IRS's view, a contestant for an elective local, state, or national public office. An organization that engages in political activities on behalf of a candidate for public office is an "action organization."

See also ACTION ORGANIZATION and POLITICAL ACTIVITY.

candidate population, all of the individuals who apply for a particular position.

CAO: *see* CHIEF ADMINISTRATIVE OFFICER.

capability profile, a formal assessment of an organization's strengths and weaknesses in dealing with the opportunities and dangers presented by its external environment. A capability profile is usually prepared as part of a strategic planning process.

capacity building, term used to refer to any system, effort, or process—including a federal grant or contract and local management assistance or technical assistance program—which includes among its major objectives strengthening the capability of chief executive officers, chief administrative officers, and program managers to plan, implement, manage, or evaluate policies, strategies, or programs.

capital, the designation applied in economic theory to one of the three major factors of production, the others being land and labor. Capital can refer either to physical capital, such as plant and equipment, or to the financial resources required to purchase physical capital.

capital assets, almost all property owned by an individual or organization other than things held for sale.

capital budgeting: *see* BUDGETING, CAPITAL.

capital depreciation, the decline in value of *capital* assets (assets of a permanent or fixed nature, goods, and plant) over time with use. The rate and amount of depreciation is calculated by a variety of different methods (*e.g.*, straight line, sum of the digits, declining balance) which often give quite different results.

capital fund drive, also CAPITAL PROGRAM, a special fund-raising program to attract major gifts to improve the capital assets position of the organization; a drive for the purpose of capital improvements rather than for regular operating purposes. Typically, capital fund drives are conducted in addition to regular fund-raising activities and, ideally, should not diminish funds raised through the regular fund-raising program. Capital fund drives are often conducted over a period of one or more years; for example, a capital fund drive to build a new gymnasium or a new wing on a library building.

capital gain, the net income derived from the sale of a capital asset. Private foundations must pay a two percent excise tax on net investment income (unless they can satisfy certain payout requirements enabling them to reduce the tax rate to 1%) including short-term and long-term capital gains. Net short-term capital gains are also important to private foundations because they are included in adjusted net income and, therefore, in calculating the required income payout.

See also PAYOUT REQUIREMENT and TAX, EXCISE.

capital gains tax, tax on the income derived from the sale of a capital asset (for example, real estate, stocks, etc.)

capital giving, gifts that are given out of the donor's capital assets, usually over a period of years, rather than out of the donor's current income.

capital improvement, a modification, addition, restoration, or other improvement which increases the usefulness, productivity, or serviceable life of an existing building, structure, or major item of equipment, and the cost of which increases the recorded worth of the entity.

See also DEPRECIATION.

capital intensive, quality of any production process requiring a large proportion of capital relative to labor.

capitalism, private ownership of most means of production and trade combined with a generally unrestricted marketplace of goods and services.

capitalization of assets: *see* CAPITALIZE.

capitalize, to convert into capital; to compute the present value of a future stream of income to be realized from an asset.

capital outlay, direct expenditure for construction of buildings, roads, and other improvements, and for purchase of equipment, land, and existing structures. Includes amounts for additions, replacements, and major alterations to fixed works and structures.

capital program: *see* CAPITAL FUND DRIVE.

capitation, a method of payment for health services in which an individual or institutional provider is paid a fixed per capita amount for each person served without regard to the actual number or nature of services provided to each person.

capitation tax, a tax levied on a person at a fixed rate, regardless of income, assets, etc.; a head tax.

CAR: *see* CHAPTER ASSISTANCE REVIEW.

career, total work history of an individual.

career change, circumstance that occurs when individuals break with their present careers in order to enter other fields.

career counseling, guidance provided to employees in order to assist them in achieving occupational training, educational, and career goals. Services may include: (1) assessing skills, abilities, interests, and aptitudes; (2) determining qualifications required for different occupations and how the requirements relate to individual capabilities; (3) defining career goals and developing plans for reaching the goals; (4) identifying and assessing education and training opportunities and enrollment procedures; (5) identifying factors which may impair career development; and (6) learning about resources inside or outside the organization where additional help is available.

career curve: *see* MATURITY CURVE.

career development, systematic development designed to increase an employee's potential for advancement and career change. It may include classroom training, reading, work experience, etc.

career earnings formula, a formula which bases pension benefits on average earnings in all years of credited service.

career ladder, series of classifications in which an employee may advance through training and/or on-the-job experience into successively higher levels of responsibility and salary.

career lattice, a term that identifies horizontal and/or diagonal paths of occupational mobility leading from the entry level. Most often these paths link parallel paths of vertical or upward occupational mobility. A horizontal path of occupational mobility is often called a job transfer while a diagonal paths if often referred to as a transfer-promotional path. This lateral mobility usually occurs within an occupational field (*e.g.* engineering, accounting) but usually not the same specific occupational classification.

career management, aspect of personnel management that is concerned with the occupational growth of individuals within an organization.

career mobility, also called JOB MOBILITY, degree to which an individual is able to move or advance from one position to another.

career negotiation, that aspect of career planning that has both the individual employee and the organization, in the light of their respective interests and needs, develop (negotiate) a career plan that serves both parties.

career path, direction of an individual's career as indicated by career milestones. An employee following a career path may proceed up a single career ladder and then beyond it into a supervisory or executive position, or an employee may move from one career ladder to another.

career pattern, sequence of occupations of an individual or group of individuals. The study of career patterns has spawned the theory that an individual's work history is a good predictor of future vocational behavior.

career planning, the personal process of planning one's life work. Career planning usually involves assessing one's abilities and interests, weighing alternative career paths, establishing career objectives, and selecting practical implementation strategies.

career promotion, promotion made on the basis of merit, but without competition with other employees. An example is the promotion of an employee who, as he or she learns more about the job, can do more difficult kinds of work and assume greater responsibility, so that he or she is performing duties classified at a higher grade level.

career system, sequence of progressively more responsible positions in the same general occupation that an organization makes available to qualified individuals.

carrier, an insurance company; also, a person or organization that transports people or property.

carry back, also CARRY OVER, a tax rule that allows a person or organization to use losses to reduce taxes in the year prior to (or the years following) a loss; also, to carry forward to future years, a charitable contribution that exceeds the limits of the current year.

carrying charge, the cost of owning property, such as a land tax, mortgage payment, etc.; also, interest; also, a service charge to installment buyers to meet the extra expense of carrying the deferred account.

case, or CASE STATEMENT, as used in development and fund-raising programs, the written statement of activities that will be implemented to alleviate unmet education, public information, arts, humanities, social, etc. needs identified in the cause statement.

See also:
CAUSE
DEVELOPMENT
FUND-RAISING

CASE: *see* COUNCIL FOR ADVANCEMENT AND SUPPORT OF EDUCATION.

case advocacy, arguing on behalf of or attempting to find a solution to one person's—one case's—problems or service needs.

See also CLASS ADVOCACY.

casebook, collection of case studies on a given topic.

case law, all recorded judicial and administrative agency decisions.

case study, research design that focuses upon the in-depth analysis of a single subject. It is particularly useful when the researcher seeks an understanding of dynamic processes over time. A case study is usually more qualitative than quantitative in methodological approach and is more appropriate for generating hypotheses than for testing hypotheses. In a case study the researcher usually collects data through the review of records, interviews, questionnaires, and observations. It is particularly appropriate for generating insights in new areas of research.

cash, money plus all negotiable checks; money only.

cash accounting: *see* ACCOUNTING.

cash assistance, direct cash payments to beneficiaries of public welfare programs.

cash audit, an examination of cash transactions, the recording of cash receipts and disbursements, and cash in banks and on hand.

cash basis (accounting): *see* ACCOUNTING.

cash book, a journal in which cash receipts, disbursements, or both are recorded.

See also JOURNAL.

cash disbursements journal, also CHECK REGISTER, an accounting journal used to record payments made. It contains information about the date of each transaction (that is, when cash was paid or a check was written), to whom the payment was made, the check number, the purpose for the payment, the amount and which subsidiary and general ledger accounts are affected by the transaction (debited or credited).

In most cases, after the cash disbursements journal is totaled and balanced at the end of a fiscal period (a month or a year), it is posted to the general ledger and to the accounts payable subsidiary ledger.

EXAMPLE OF A CASH DISBURSEMENTS JOURNAL

ACE AMBULANCE SERVICE—CASH DISBURSEMENTS JOURNAL

		Check	CR	DR	Accts Pay	DR-General	Column
Date	Paid To	No.	Cash	A/P Acct #	Amount	Description	Amount
1-1	Acme Oil Co.	101	$175.00	#1616	$175.00		$
1-1	Ace Med. Supply	102	$500.00	# 120	$500.00		

See also:
ACCOUNTING CYCLE
DEBITS AND CREDITS
GENERAL LEDGER
JOURNAL
POSTING
SUBSIDIARY LEDGER
TRIAL BALANCE

cash flow: *see* CASH FLOW ANALYSIS.

cash flow analysis, an analysis of the timing of the movement of money in and out of an organization. In organizations that use a cash rather than an accrual method of accounting, a cash flow analysis is essentially equivalent to an operating statement.
See also OPERATING STATEMENT.

cashier's check, a certified check made out in a bank's own name and signed by a bank official.

cash management, the general strategy of managing the short-term timing of cash receipts, disbursements, and investments so as to maximize the use of the organization's liquid assets; particularly, maximizing returns on short-term investments and/or minimizing costs of short-term borrowing.

cash match, also HARD MATCH, the cash an organization will contribute to a project or program to match a grant received from a government agency or a foundation.
See also MATCHING SHARE.

cash projection worksheet: *see* CASH FLOW ANALYSIS.

cash receipts journal, an accounting journal used to record the receipt of cash. For each transaction, it should contain information about the date when cash was received, who paid the money, why the

EXAMPLE OF A CASH FLOW ANALYSIS

	Month 1		Month 2	
	Planned	Actual	Planned	Actual
Cash—Beginning Balance	$5,000	$5,000	$4,000	$3,000
Increase During Month	3,000	4,000	5,000	2,000
Cash Available During Month	8,000	9,000	9,000	5,000
Outflow During Month	4,000	6,000	7,000	7,000
Cash—Ending Balance	$4,000	$3,000	$2,000	$[2,000]*

* [ ] indicates a negative or minus cash balance.

EXAMPLE OF A CASH RECEIPTS JOURNAL

ACE AMBULANCE SERVICE—CASH RECEIPTS JOURNAL

		DR	CR	Acct. Rec.	CR—General Column	
Date	Received From	CASH	Acct. #	Amount	Description	Amount
1-1	John Doe	$100.00	# 210	$100.00		
1-5	Mary Smith	$75.00	# 650	$75.00		

money was paid and received, the amount of money received, and which subsidiary and general ledger accounts will be affected by the transaction.

See also:

ACCOUNTING CYCLE
GENERAL LEDGER
JOURNAL
SUBSIDIARY LEDGER

cash report, a regular report to an organization's officers showing the daily or weekly cash position.

casual labor, employees that are (1) essentially unskilled, (2) used only a few days at a time, or (3) needed seasonally.

casualty loss, a loss of property due to fire, storm, accident, or similar occurrence.

Catalog of Federal Domestic Assistance, a semiannual catalog published by the Office of Management and Budget which provides basic data on the federal government's domestic funding programs and agencies.

catalyst: *see* CHANGE AGENT.

catastrophic health insurance, health insurance which provides protection against the high cost of treating severe or lengthy illnesses or disabilities. Generally such policies cover all or a specified percentage of medical expenses above an amount that is the responsibility of the insured himself (or the responsibility of another insurance policy up to a maximum limit of liability).

catchmenting, designation of a geographic area whose residents will be provided specific government services.

Catch-22, an unreasonable combination of otherwise reasonable rules that prevents one from accomplishing something.

categorical grant: *see* GRANT.

Cato Institute, a conservatively-oriented public policy research organization based in Washington, D.C.

CATV, community antenna television system.

cause, short form of "just cause," reason given for removing someone from a job. The cause cited may or may not be the real reason for the removal.

cause, also CAUSE STATEMENT, as used in development and fund-raising, the written statement of currently unmet education, public information, arts, humanities, social, etc. needs which will be addressed with new funds.

See also:

CASE
DEVELOPMENT
FUND-RAISING

cause/effect evaluation, a type of evaluation that attempts to identify which process elements of a program affect the end results or outcomes, and to what extent. Cause/effect evaluation is a combination of performance and impact evaluation which usually requires complex, sophisticated, expensive, evaluation research procedures.

See also:
EVALUATION
OUTCOME
PROCESS EVALUATION
PROGRAM EVALUATION

cause-related marketing, a fundraising program in which a nonprofit organization links up with a corporation to promote a particular cause. For example, when the Jerry Lewis Telethon linked up with 7-Eleven stores (the Southland Corporation), both the corporation and the nonprofit organization benefited.

CBO: *see* CONGRESSIONAL BUDGET OFFICE.

CCH: *see* COMMERCE CLEARING HOUSE, INC.

CCL: *see* CHARITABLE CONTRIBUTIONS LAW and ECONOMIC RECOVERY TAX ACT.

cease-and-desist order, ruling which requires a charged party to stop conduct held to be illegal, and to take specific action to remedy the practice.

ceiling, upper limit of ability measured by a test. A test has a low ceiling for a given population if many examinees obtain perfect scores; it has a high ceiling if there are few or no perfect scores.

ceiling, job or **position:** *see* JOB CEILING.

cemetery company, a nonprofit membership-type company engaged in burials and cremations. Cemetery companies may qualify for tax-exempt status under IRS Code 501(c) (13).

census, a description of the characteristics of a population. A census differs from a survey in that all members of the population under consideration are included.

Census, Bureau of the, general purpose statistical agency of the U.S. federal government that collects, tabulates, and publishes a wide variety of statistical data about the people and the economy of the nation. These data are utilized by many organizations in the development and evaluation of economic and social programs.

centralization, also DECENTRALIZATION, any process by which the power and authority in an organization is concentrated. *Decentralization* is the reverse—power and authority are distributed more widely in an organization.

central processing unit (CPU), the part of a computer that contains facilities for control, memory, and calculations.

central tendency, series of statistical measures that provide a representative value for a distribution, or, more simply, refer to how scores tend to cluster in a distribution. The most common measures of central tendency are the mean, median, and mode.

CEO: *see* CHIEF EXECUTIVE OFFICER.

certificate, list of eligibles ranked according to regulations for appointment or promotion consideration. A more useful term is "candidate list."

certificate of incorporation, a document signed by the Secretary of State (or another appropriate state official) of the state in which an organization is incorporated, certifying as to its incorporation.

A certificate of incorporation should include:

a) a statement of charitable, educational, or similar purpose;
b) a statement that no part of the earnings shall inure to the benefit of its members, trustees, etc.;
c) a statement that the corporation's activities will not consist of substantial political or legislative activities;
d) a clause stating that upon dissolution, the organization's assets will be

disposed of for charitable purposes;
e) a statement that the organization will comply with the pertinent sections of the Internal Revenue Code.

certification (labor union), formal determination by the National Labor Relations Board or other administrative agency that a particular union is the majority choice, and thus the exclusive bargaining agent for a group of employees in a given bargaining unit. *Decertification* is the opposite process, where an administrative agency withdraws a union's official designation as the exclusive bargaining agent. In both cases, these actions are usually preceded by a formal polling of the union membership.

certification, selective, certifying only the names of eligibles who have special qualifications required to fill particular vacant positions.

certification of eligibles, procedure whereby those who have passed competitive employment examinations have their names ranked in order of score and placed on a list of those eligible for appointment.

certification proceeding, process by which the National Labor Relations Board discovers whether or not the employees of an organization want a particular union to represent them.

certified check, a check that a bank has marked as "guaranteed cashable" as to both signature and amount. In most situations, it is as good as cash.

certified financial statement, a financial statement which has been examined and reported upon with an opinion expressed by a certified public accountant (CPA).

certified funds, bank deposits held in suspension and awaiting claims by a certified check.

certified mail, mail that provides a receipt to the sender attesting to delivery.

certified public accountant (CPA), an accountant certified by a state government as having met specific education and experience requirements.
See also ACCOUNTING.

Certified Public Service Executive, a professional manager of a nonprofit public service organization who is a member of and is certified by the National Association of Public Service Organization Executives (NAPSOE).

certiorari, order or writ from a higher court demanding that a lower court send up the record of a case for review.

CETA: *see* COMPREHENSIVE EMPLOYMENT AND TRAINING ACT OF 1973.

CFR: *see* CODE OF FEDERAL REGULATIONS.

chain of command, a descriptive phrase for the authority systems and reporting relationships in an organization.

chain picketing, continuous, moving human chain sometimes formed by striking workers to prevent anyone from crossing their picket line.

chair, to function or preside as a chairperson, for example, over a meeting.

chairman: *see* CHAIR.

chairperson, the presiding officer of an organization, committee, task force, or meeting. "Chairperson" (or chair) has generally replaced "chairman."

chamber of commerce, a local association of businesses that promotes the area's trade.
See also BOARD OF TRADE.

chance score, score that has a significant probability of occurring on the basis of random selection of answers.

change agent, or CATALYST, descriptive way of referring to organization development consultants or facilitators.

change in duty station, personnel action that changes an employee from one geographical location to another in the same agency.

changes in financial position, statement of, a financial report which provides a summary of the resources available to an organization during the year and the uses made of those resources. A typical statement of changes in financial position is divided into three parts. The first part reports the excess of revenue and support over expenses both before and after capital additions. The second part shows the conversions of assets and liabilities. The final part displays the changes in working capital.

Channels: *see* NATIONAL COMMUNICATIONS COUNCIL FOR HUMAN SERVICES (NCCHS).

Chapter Assistance Review (CAR), a structured program used by a national (or international) nonprofit organization to review and assess the structure and operations of its subordinate affiliated organizations (for example, state chapters). Typically, a CAR results in a written report of the subordinate affiliated organization's strengths and weaknesses and recommendations for improvement. Many national nonprofit organizations use CAR teams comprised of national office personnel and staff and/or officers of other chapters (in other words, peers). When this design is employed, CARs also serve the purpose of peer education.

See also INTERNATIONAL NONPROFIT ORGANIZATION and SUBORDINATE AFFILIATED ORGANIZATION.

charge-off, also WRITE-OFF, lowering the worth of something in an organization's financial statements. For example, when a debt becomes uncollectable, it may be charged off.

See also FINANCIAL STATEMENT.

charging party, any individual who formally asserts that he or she is aggrieved because of an unlawful employment practice.

charismatic leadership, leadership that is based on the compelling personality of the leader rather than upon formal position.

charitable, a term with many definitions and uses, none of which are generally accepted or applicable to all situations. In its traditional use, charitable means for the relief of the poor. In this restricted context, charitable is a narrower term than philanthropy.

However, the meaning of "charitable" has been expanded through common usage and by Congress and the IRS to mean all those organizations whose primary purposes include charitable purposes—that is, the advancement of religion, education, science, etc. In this more general and more pragmatic context, charitable means simply "as defined in IRS Code 501(c) (3) and as upheld by the courts."

See also ELEEMOSYNARY and PHILANTHROPIC.

charitable contribution, a contribution to a charitable organization which is tax deductible.

charitable contributions credit: *see* TAX CREDIT.

Charitable Contributions Law (CCL), a term which encompasses those provisions of ERTA which established tax deductions through 1986 for charitable contributions by nonitemizing taxpayers, and also for myriad subsequent legislative efforts to make the deductions permanent.

See also ECONOMIC RECOVERY TAX ACT.

charitable deduction: *see* CHARITABLE CONTRIBUTION.

charitable donee, an organization which may receive tax-exempt contributions under IRS Code 501 (c) (3).

See also CHARITABLE ORGANIZATION.

charitable gift, a contribution to a charitable organization that is not subject to a gift or estate tax.

charitable grants economy, a concept of the third sector's role in the overall economy. It is used in comparison or conjunction with the public sector's coercive grants or tax economy and the private sector's market economy.

charitable lead trust, a trust that pays a guaranteed annuity or a unitrust interest to charitable beneficiary organizations for a specified period of time, but the balance of the trust eventually reverts to the beneficiaries of the trust creator (usually members of his or her family).

The creator of the trust is permitted to deduct the present value of the income interest payable to the charitable organization. Family members are permitted to be trustees.

When the trust is terminated, the family members (or other beneficiaries) receive the benefits of the unrealized appreciation in the trust assets and accumulated current income that exceeded the amount required to be paid to the charitable organizations. No further gift or estate tax is paid when the assets are distributed. (Not to be confused with a charitable remainder trust.)

See also:

ANNUITY
APPRECIATED PROPERTY
CHARITABLE REMAINDER TRUST
FAMILY MEMBER
PRESENT WORTH
TAX, ESTATE
TRUST
TRUSTEE
UNITRUST

charitable organization, a general term usually meaning any category of organization described in IRS Code 501(c) (3). When used in its broadest sense, there are two major categories of charitable organizations: public charities and private foundations. Public charities (which often are called charitable organizations, thereby creating confusion) include religious, scientific, educational and similar-purpose organizations. Private operating foundations are a subcategory of private foundations.

Precise operational definitions of "charitable organization" change with legislation, IRS regulations, and court rulings. Almost without exception, charitable organizations are eligible to receive tax-deductible charitable contributions. The theory behind tax exemption for charitable organizations is that in their absence, the government would need to provide the services with public funds.

See also ELEEMOSYNARY.

charitable remainder annuity trust, or ANNUITY TRUST, one of three types of charitable remainder trust under which the donor receives income in the form of an annuity that lasts either for the life of the beneficiary or for a defined period of time (not to exceed twenty years). The annuity payments may not be less than five percent of the initial fair market value of the trust assets. Subsequent contributions to the trust are not permitted. The other types of charitable remainder trusts are the pooled income fund and the unitrust (not to be confused with a charitable lead trust).

See also:

ANNUITY
ANNUITY TRUST
CHARITABLE LEAD TRUST
CHARITABLE REMAINDER TRUST
POOLED INCOME FUND
UNITRUST

charitable remainder trust, a trust which receives money or property for charitable purposes after others have had the use of the money. For example, a person establishes a charitable remainder trust, takes a tax deduction in the year of the trust's establishment, and receives income from the trust for the rest of his or her life. Then a designated foundation or other charitable organization receives the assets after the person's (donor's) death.

There are three types of charitable remainder trusts.

See:

CHARITABLE REMAINDER ANNUITY TRUST
POOLED INCOME FUND
UNITRUST

Charitable Solicitation Permit

No 801

Denver, Colo. March 27, 1985

By Authority of the Director of Excise & Licenses
Colorado Special Olympics, Inc.

Address 3615 So. Huron Sq. #101 Phone 762-1951

is hereby granted permission to solicit funds by registration fees for Cherry Creek Run

Expires July 1, 1985 Director of Excise & Licenses

Fee: $10.00

Retain this Permit for Inspection By Joyce Mulvany

ADMINISTRATIVE ASSISTANT

charitable solicitation permit, a document issued by a local unit of government permitting a charitable organization to solicit funds within its jurisdiction for a specified period of time.

See also:
DIRECT SOLICITATION
FUND-RAISING
SPECIAL EVENT

charitable trust, any trust established for a public service purpose, such as for a school, church, charity, etc.

charity: *see* CHARITABLE ORGANIZATION, and PHILANTHROPY.

charter: *see* ARTICLES OF ORGANIZATION.

charter, also CITY CHARTER and MODEL CHARTER, the articles of organization for a municipality. A city is legally a municipal corporation. In order to operate, a municipal corporation must have a charter, and like any other corporate charter the *city charter* spells out the purposes and powers of the corporation. The municipality can perform only those functions and exercise only those powers that are in the charter. If the particular state permits home rule, a city can develop and implement its own charter. Otherwise it is limited to statutory charters spelled out by the state legislature.

chart of accounts, a listing of the types of accounts used in an accounting system. A chart of accounts is organized so that similar accounts are grouped together (for example, current assets, travel, etc.). Each account in a chart of accounts should be given a number to simplify finding it. If the organization's accounting system is on a computer, a numerical coding system is mandatory. Each major account type is broken down until it provides the level of detail desired. For example, assets are usually broken down into current assets (like cash) and fixed assets (like equipment). Current assets and fixed assets may be further broken down. Similarly, income may be broken down into income from contributions, special events, grants, etc.

Establishing the chart of accounts is the first and most important step in starting an accounting system. The groupings of accounts must be created thoughtfully so that they support budgetary and management information needs.

check, a document by which an organization (or person) instructs its bank to pay a specified amount of money to another organization or person.

EXAMPLE
CHART OF ACCOUNTS FOR ACE AMBULANCE SERVICE

CLASSIFICATION	*ACCOUNT NUMBER*	*ACCOUNT TITLE*
Current Asset	101	Cash in Bank
	102	Petty Cash
	111	Accounts Receivable
	112	Allowance for Bad Debts
	120	Employee Advances
	130	Inventory
Fixed Assets	141	Automobiles
	142	Accumulated Depreciation
	143	Ambulances
	144	Accumulated Depreciation
	145	Furniture and Office Equipment
	146	Accumulated Depreciation
	147	Ambulance—Equipment
	148	Accumulated Depreciation
Prepaid Expenses	161	Prepaid Insurance
Current Liabilities	201	Accounts Payable
	211	Notes Payable
	230	Accrued Taxes
	240	Withheld Taxes
	250	Accrued Payroll
Fund Balances	290	Unrestricted
	292	Restricted—Program X
	293	Restricted—Program Y
Revenue	301	Income—Ambulance Service
	302	Income—Other Equipment Use
	303	Income—Supplies
	304	Income—Professional Services
	305	Income—Donations and Bequests
Expenses—Direct	401	Salaries—Ambulance Attendants
	402	Salaries—Other
	403	Supply Expense
	404	Oxygen Expense
	411	Ambulance Operating Expense—Gas and Oil
	412	Ambulance Operating Expense—Repairs
	413	Ambulance Operating Expense—Tires
	420	Depreciation Expense—Ambulance
	421	Depreciation Expense—Ambulance Equipment
	460	Communication Expenses
	461	Communication Equipment—Depreciation
	462	Communication Equipment—Repair and Maintenance
Expenses—General	601	Bad Debts
	610	Salaries—Administrative
	611	Depreciation—Office Equipment
	612	Administrative Travel
	613	Insurance
	614	Interest Expense
	615	Legal and Accounting Services
	617	Miscellaneous
	618	Repair and Maintenance—Office
	619	Rent—Office
	621	Stationery, Postage, and Office Supplies
	623	Telephone
	625	Training
	630	Employee Benefits

checklist, series of questions designed to take an inventory.

See also SPECIAL EVENTS ORGANIZING CHECKLIST.

checkoff, union security provision, commonly provided for in the collective bargaining agreement, that allows the employer to deduct union dues, assessments, and initiation fees from the pay of all union members. The deducted amounts are delivered to the union on a prearranged schedule. The Labor-Management Relations (Taft-Hartley) Act of 1947 requires that union members give written permission for these fees to be deducted.

check register: *see* CASH DISBURSEMENTS JOURNAL.

chief administrative officer (CAO), an alternative label for "chief executive officer" (CEO), usually attached to a nonprofit organization's executive director.

See also CHIEF EXECUTIVE OFFICER.

chief executive officer (CEO), individual who is personally accountable to the board of directors or the electorate for the activities of the organization or the jurisdiction.

chief steward, union representative who supervises the activities of a group of shop stewards.

childbirth: *see* PREGNANCY.

child care: *see* DAY CARE.

child labor, originally, employing children in a manner that was detrimental to their health and social development; but now that the law contains strong child labor prohibitions, the term refers to the employment of children below the legal age limit.

chilling effect, inhibiting atmosphere created by employment practices, government regulations, court decisions, or legislation (or the threat of these) that prevents the free exercise of individual employment rights. A chilling effect tends to keep minorities and women from seeking employment and advancement in an organization even in the absence of formal bars. Other chilling effects may be positive or negative, depending upon the "chillee's" perspective.

chi-square, statistical procedure that estimates whether the observed values in a distribution differ from the expected distribution and thus may be attributable to the operation of factors other than chance. Particular values of chi-square are usually identified by the symbol χ^2.

Christmas bonus: *see* NONPRODUCTION BONUS.

chronic unemployment, unemployment lasting longer than six months.

church, one form of religious organization. The IRS uses multiple criteria for testing whether an organization is a church for taxation purposes. Despite the existence of such criteria, both the IRS and the courts have been very reluctant to decide what is and is not a church (or a religious organization). For example, one 1980 U.S. Tax Court decision held that a church must have a religious-type function, hold regular meetings, have religious leaders, perform ceremonies and/or sacraments, have a place of worship, etc. Examples of subcategories of church include church-operated organizations, bible societies, conventions of churches, and associations of churches.

CIO: *see* AMERICAN FEDERATION OF LABOR-CONGRESS OF INDUSTRIAL ORGANIZATIONS

circuit court of appeals: *see* COURT OF APPEALS.

circuit rider, government official who travels from jurisdiction to jurisdiction providing any of a variety of technical services.

circular file, a wastebasket.

citation, a reference to a printed authority and where it is to be found; also, a notice of a violation of law.

citizen participation, means of empowering individuals/groups to represent their own interests and to plan and implement their own programs with a view towards social, economic, and political power and control.

city, also CENTRAL CITY and INDEPENDENT CITY, municipal corporation chartered by its state. A *central city* is the core of a metropolitan area, while an *independent city* is outside of or separate from a metropolitan area.

city charter: *see* CHARTER.

city manager, chief executive of the council/manager (originally commission/manager) system of local government. In contrast to other types of government, the city manager is an appointed chief executive serving at the pleasure of the council.

***City of Los Angeles, Department of Water & Power* v. *Manhart*,** 435 U.S. 703 (1978), U.S. Supreme Court case which held that a pension plan requiring female employees to contribute more from their wages to gain the same pension benefits as male employees was in violation of Title VII of the Civil Rights Act 1964. While the actual statistics were undisputed (women live longer than men), the court reasoned that Title VII prohibits treating individuals "as simply components of a racial, religious, sexual or national class."

city planner, also CITY PLANNING, administrative official charged with the development of blueprints for the planned growth of a political unit, such as a city.

civilian labor force: *see* LABOR FORCE.

civil rights, generally, the protections and privileges given to all citizens by the U.S. Constitution. However, "civil rights" frequently is used to refer to those positive acts of government that seek to make constitutional guarantees a reality for all citizens.

Civil Rights Act of 1964, designed to eliminate racial and sexual discrimination in most areas of U.S. life, the act affected employers of fifteen or more employees engaged in interstate commerce by providing for the withholding of federal funds from programs administered in a discriminatory manner and establishing a right to equal employment opportunity without regard to race, color, religion, sex, or national origin. It also created the Equal Employment Opportunity Commission (EEOC) to assist in implementing this right.
See also EQUAL EMPLOYMENT OPPORTUNITY COMMISSION and TITLE VII.

Civil Rights Acts of 1866, 1870, and 1971, laws that ensure equality before the law in a variety of functional areas (ability to enter into contracts, sue, give evidence, and secure equal protection of persons and property) and establish that individuals or governments denying any rights or privileges shall be liable for legal action. These acts are often used in conjunction with, but are not replaced by, the Civil Rights Act of 1964 as the basis for suits.

Civil Rights Acts of 1957 and 1960, civil rights laws. The Civil Rights Act of 1957 (Public Law 85-135) is generally considered to be the beginning of contemporary civil rights legislation. It established the U.S. Commission on Civil Rights and strengthened the judiciary's ability to protect civil rights. The Civil Rights Act of 1960 (Public Law 86-449) served mainly to plug legal loopholes in the 1957 law.

Civil Rights Commission: *see* COMMISSION ON CIVIL RIGHTS.

civil service, collective term for all of those employees of a government who are not members of the military services.

claim, a request to an insurer for payment of benefits under an insurance policy.

claim of right doctrine, a rule in tax law

that if a person receives money under a "claim of right" (that is, the assertion or honest impression that it belongs to or was owed to the person), he or she must pay tax on the money that year even if there is a good chance that the money must be returned later.

class, unique position or a group of positions sufficiently similar in respect to duties and responsibilities that the same title may be used to designate each position in the group, the same salary may be equitably applied, the same qualifications required, and the same examination used to select qualified employees.

See also the following entries:

SERIES OF CLASSES
SPECIFICATION
TITLE

class action, search for judicial remedy that one or more individuals may undertake on behalf of themselves and all others in similar situations. Rule 23(b) of the Federal Rules of Civil Procedure establishes the technical legal requirements for the definition of a class in federal court proceedings:

> One or more members of a class may sue or be sued as representative parties on behalf of all only if (1) the class is so numerous that joinder of all members is impractical, (2) there are questions of law or facts common to the class, (3) the claims or defenses of the representative parties are typical of the claims or defenses of the class, and (4) the representative parties will fairly and adequately protect the interests of the class.

class advocacy, arguing on behalf of or attempting to find solutions to problems or service needs for the whole population of people who are affected.

See also CASE ADVOCACY.

class directors, directors of an organization whose terms of office are staggered. This ensures continuity of leadership.

See also BOARD ROTATION and BOARD TERM.

classical organization theory: *see* ORGANIZATION THEORY.

classification: *see* POSITION CLASSIFICATION.

classification standards, descriptions of classes of positions that distinguish one class from another in a series. They are, in effect, the yardstick or benchmark against which positions are measured to determine the proper level within a series of titles to which a position should be assigned.

classified service, all those positions in a governmental jurisdiction that are included in a formal merit system. Excluded from the classified service are all exempt appointments. Classified service is a term that predates the concept of position classification and has no immediate bearing on position classification concepts or practices.

classify, to group positions according to their duties and responsibilities and assign a class title. To reclassify is to reassign a position to a different class based on a reexamination of the duties and responsibilities of the position.

See also the following entries:

DESK AUDIT
JOB ANALYSIS
POSITION CLASSIFICATION

clause, a single phrase, sentence, or paragraph in a document—often a legal document.

Clean Air Act, federal statute (passed in 1963 and amended in 1965, 1967, 1970, and 1977) intended to protect public health and welfare from the effects of air pollution. The act establishes national air quality standards and specific automobile emission standards to achieve these goals.

clear, free from doubt or restrictions; for example, clear title; also, free of taxes, liens, or other encumbrances,

clearinghouse, in the term's broad sense, a center or organization which collects, reviews, and disseminates information on topics of interest to certain people and/or organizations. Also, the term refers to the A-95 clearinghouse review process for area-wide coordination of federal grants. For this definition, *see* OFFICE OF MANAGEMENT AND BUDGET (OMB) CIRCULAR A-95.

***Cleveland Board of Education* v. *Lafleur*,** 414 U.S. 632 (1974), U.S. Supreme Court case which held that arbitrary mandatory maternity leaves were unconstitutional. The court held that requiring pregnant teachers to take unpaid maternity leave five months before expected childbirth was in violation of the due process clause of the Fourteenth Amendment.

clientele, also CONSUMERS, individuals or groups who benefit from the services provided by an organization.

clientele agency, loose term for government organizations whose prime mission is to promote, serve, or represent the interest of a particular group.

Clifford trust, a trust that is established to give the income to someone else, eventually return the principal (the original money put in) to the establisher, and provide tax benefits in the meantime. Money must be left in a Clifford trust for at least ten years and a day.

clipping service, a service usually provided by for-profit organizations which review selected newspapers and clip and forward articles about identified topics to the requesting organization. Typically, a clipping service charges the organization a flat monthly fee plus an amount for each article clipped. Clipping services can be very useful, for example, for nonprofit organizations that are involved in numerous activities in multiple communities or states (for example, a state Special Olympics chapter)—both for evaluating the effectiveness of their public information programs and for maintaining awareness of media exposure or responsiveness.

clique, informal organizational subgroup whose members prefer to associate with each other on the basis of common interests.

closed-end investment company: *see* MUTUAL FUND.

closed-end program, also OPEN-END PROGRAM (PUBLIC), program which has a limited legislative appropriation. A program for which Congress has established no limit on the amount of federal funds available for matching recipient expenditures is considered an *open-end program*. Examples are AFDC and Medicaid programs.

closeout procedures, grant: *see* GRANT CLOSEOUT PROCEDURES.

closing date, deadline. When a grant, pending contract or job opening is announced, submissions are accepted as long as the announcement is "open." The deadline for submitting is usually stated on the announcement.

closing entry, a final adjusting entry of an accounting cycle which results in net surplus and loss postings to equity accounts (in the financial statements).

See also:

ACCOUNTING CYCLE
ADJUSTMENT ENTRIES
FINANCIAL STATEMENTS

clothing allowance, funds provided by employers to employees so that they can buy special clothing, such as uniforms or safety garments.

clout, slang term for influence and/or power.

cluster laboratory, laboratory training experience for a group of people from the same organization. The group consists of several subgroups of individuals whose work in the larger organization is related.

cluster sampling (statistics), a sampling technique in which the population is first divided into groups or clusters based on geographic concentration or proximity. A sample is then taken from randomly selected clusters rather than from the entire population. The technique is used, for example, in public opinion polling.

coaching, also COACHING ANALYSIS, face-to-face discussions with a subordinate in order to effect a change in his or her behavior. *Coaching analysis* consists of analyzing the reasons why unsatisfactory performance is occurring. According to Ferdinand F. Fournies, in *Coaching for Improved Work Performance* (NY: Van Nostrand Reinhold, 1978), there are five steps in the coaching technique:

1. Getting the employee's agreement that a problem exists.
2. A mutual discussion of alternative solutions.
3. Mutual agreement on the action to be taken to solve the problem.
4. Measuring the results of subsequent performance.
5. Recognize achievement and improved performance when it occurs.

coalition bargaining, also COORDINATED BARGAINING, situation in which an employer negotiates with a group of unions whose goal is to gain one agreement covering all or identical agreements for each. *Coordinated bargaining* differs only in that bargaining sessions take place simultaneously at different locations.

Coalition of Concerned Charities, a coalition of eighty national charities with several million members, formed in 1973 to create a network of influential citizens to lobby for changes in the Tax Reform Act of 1969's restraints on lobbying by tax-exempt organizations. The Coalition was at least partially responsible for passage of 1976 legislation which authorized tax-exempt charities (except private foundations and religious groups) to spend a portion of their income on lobbying.

COB: *see* COORDINATION OF BENEFITS.

COBOL: *see* COMMON BUSINESS ORIENTED LANGUAGE.

code, a collection of laws, rules, or principles, especially a complete, interrelated, and exclusive set of laws.

code of ethics, statement of professional standards of conduct to which the practitioners of a profession say they subscribe.

The EMT
CODE OF ETHICS

Professional status as an Emergency Medical Technician and Emergency Medical Technician-Paramedic is maintained and enriched by the willingness of the individual practitioner to accept and fulfill obligations to society, other medical professionals, and the profession of Emergency Medical Technician. As an Emergency Medical Technician at the basic level or an Emergency Medical Technician-Paramedic, I solemnly pledge myself to the following code of professional ethics:

A fundamental responsibility of the Emergency Medical Technician is to conserve life, to alleviate suffering, to promote health, to do no harm, and to encourage the quality and equal availability of emergency medical care.

The Emergency Medical Technician provides services based on human need, with respect for human dignity, unrestricted by consideration of nationality, race, creed, color, or status.

The Emergency Medical Technician does not use professional knowledge and skills in any enterprise detrimental to the public well being.

The Emergency Medical Technician respects and holds in confidence all information of a confidential nature obtained in the course of professional work unless required by law to divulge such information.

The Emergency Medical Technician, as a citizen, understands and upholds the law and performs the duties of citizenship; as a professional, the Emergency Medical Technician has the never-ending responsibility to work with concerned citizens and other health care professionals in promoting a high standard of emergency medical care to all people.

The Emergency Medical Technician shall maintain professional competence and demonstrate concern for the competence of other members of the Emergency Medical services health care team.

An Emergency Medical Technician assumes responsibility in defining and upholding standards of professional practice and education.

The Emergency Medical Technician assumes responsibility for individual professional actions and judgement, both in dependent and independent emergency functions, and knows and upholds the laws which affect the practice of the Emergency Medical Technician.

An Emergency Medical Technician has the responsibility to be aware of and participate in, matters of legislation affecting the Emergency Medical Technician and the Emergency Medical services System.

The Emergency Medical Technician adheres to standards of personal ethics which reflect credit upon the profession.

Emergency Medical Technicians, or groups of Emergency Medical Technicians, who advertise professional services, do so in conformity with the dignity of the profession.

The Emergency Medical Technician has an obligation to protect the public by not delegating to a person, less qualified, any service which requires the professional competence of an Emergency Medical Technician.

The Emergency Medical Technician will work harmoniously with, and sustain confidence in Emergency Medical Technician associates, the nurse, the physician, and other members of the emergency medical services health care team.

The Emergency Medical Technician refuses to participate in unethical procedures, and assumes the responsibility to expose incompetence or unethical conduct of others to the appropriate authority in a proper and professional manner.

Code of Federal Regulations (CFR), annual cumulation of executive agency regulations published in the daily *Federal Register,* combined with regulations issued previously that are still in effect. Divided into fifty titles, each representing a broad subject area, individual volumes of the CFR are revised at least once each calendar year and issued on a staggered quarterly basis. An alphabetical listing by agency of subtitle and chapter assignments in the CFR is provided in the back of each volume under the heading "Finding Aids" and is accurate for the revision date of that volume.

codetermination, in German, MITBES-TIM-MUNGSRECHT, union participation in all aspects of management even to the extent of having union representatives share equal membership on an organization's board of directors.

codification, the process of collecting and arranging things into one complete system; for example, arranging laws, rules, policies and procedures, accounts, etc., by subject.

coding, changing raw data into a standardized form, usually numerical, for computer entry and analysis.

coefficient of correlation: *see* CORRELATION COEFFICIENT.

coefficient of determination, the proportion of the variation of one thing that is due to the variation of another thing.

coercive grants economy: *see* CHARITABLE GRANTS ECONOMY.

coffee break, also called TEA BREAK, popular term for any brief rest period.

COG: *see* COUNCIL OF GOVERNMENT.

cognition, the mental activities by which a person processes information. The basic mental processes of cognition are coding, structuring, and manipulating (or using) information (including thoughts).

cognitive dissonance, theory first postulated by Leon Festinger, in *A Theory of Cognitive Dissonance* (Evanston, Ill.: Row, Peterson Co., 1957), which holds that when an individual finds him or herself in a situation where s/he is expected to believe two mutually exclusive things, the subsequent tension and discomfort generates activity designed to reduce the dissonance or disharmony.

See also INEQUITY THEORY.

Cohan rule, the rule of tax law which states that while a taxpayer must keep adequate records of deductions, if a deduction is proven but the amount is uncertain, a reasonable amount should be allowed (often fifty percent of the amount claimed).

cohesiveness, commitment on the part of group members to group membership—a sense of belonging, of unity and collectivity.

cohort, also COHORT STUDY, an age group, such as from ten to fifteen; also, any group of similar people. A *cohort study* is one in which a specific group is studied over time.

coinsurance, a sharing of an insurance risk between an insurance company and the customer. For example, a health insurance policy may provide that the insurer will reimburse a specified percentage (usually eighty percent) of covered medical expenses in excess of a deductible amount.

COLA: *see* COST-OF-LIVING ADJUSTMENT.

cold-storage training, the preparation of employees for jobs in advance of the need for them in the particular jobs.

collateral, money or property put up as backing for a loan.

collected revenue, the amount of earned revenue which is billed (or invoiced) and received from the service recipient or a third party payer.

Many types of nonprofit organizations provide services-for-fees for individual clients or other organizations. Nonprofit ambulance services and sheltered workshops are typical examples.

See also:
BILLED REVENUE
COLLECTION RATE
EARNED REVENUE
ESTIMATED INCOME
FEES-FOR-SERVICES
UNBILLED REVENUE
UNCOLLECTED REVENUE

collection, a fund-raising method for obtaining small amounts of money from a large number of people; for example, placing collection cans in retail stores or "passing a collection plate" during a religious service.

collection agency, a company that specializes in collecting overdue accounts receivable.

collection rate, also COLLECTION RATIO, collected revenue divided by billed revenue (or invoiced revenue). The calculation for a collection rate, in formula format, is:

$__________

Collected
Revenue

(Divided by) = _____ (×) 100 = _____%

Billed Revenue   Collection Rate

$__________

See also:
BILLED REVENUE
COLLECTED REVENUE
EARNED REVENUE
ESTIMATED INCOME
UNBILLED REVENUE
UNCOLLECTED REVENUE

collections, the process of attempting to collect billed but unpaid monies due from recipient individuals or organizations for services performed. Common collections techniques include (a) reminder bills, (b) follow-up letters or telephone calls, (c) a series of follow-up letters (each more firm than the prior one), (d) threatening letters from an attorney, and (e) collection agencies.

collective bargaining, a comprehensive term that encompasses the negotiating process that leads to a contract between labor and management on wages, hours, and other conditions of employment as well as the subsequent administration and interpretation of the signed contract. Collective bargaining is, in effect, the continuous relationship that exists between union representatives and employers. The four basic stages of collective bargaining are (1) the establishment of organizations for bargaining, (2) the formulation of demands, (3) the negotiation of demands, and (4) the administration of the labor agreement.

EXAMPLE
FOLLOW-UP COLLECTION LETTER

TINCUP AMBULANCE SERVICE
1234 2nd Avenue
Tincup, Colorado 81234
(303) 333-1234

May 29, 1986

Mr. John Smith
425 Columbine Street
Denver, Colorado 80206

Dear Mr. Smith:

On March 10, you injured your right leg and hip in a skiing accident on Mt. Princeton. Your wife called us for help. We responded, stopped the bleeding, immobilized your leg, and carried you by ambulance to the Tincup Memorial Hospital.

We sent bills to you on March 25th and April 25th, but have not received payment. Copies of the bills are attached.

Please understand that the Tincup Ambulance Service is run by volunteers for the benefit of the residents of this community, travelers through it, and, people like yourself, who come to the mountains for pleasure. We have no income other than from bills for ambulance services we provide.

Please either send a check right away, or call me to explain why not. I work during the days, so please call after 5:00 P.M.

Sincerely,

William Jones
Secretary/Treasurer

enclosure

See also the following entries:

ABILITY TO PAY
PRODUCTIVITY BARGAINING
RETIREMENT AGE
REVERSE COLLECTIVE BARGAINING
SPLIT-THE-DIFFERENCE
UNFAIR LABOR PRACTICES (EMPLOYERS)
UNION SECURITY
WELFARE FUNDS
ZIPPER CLAUSE

Collective Bargaining Negotiations & Contracts, biweekly reference service published by the Bureau of National Affairs, Inc., which presents comprehensive coverage of wage rates and data and cost-of-living figures; bargaining issues, demands, counterproposals, and significant settlements; strategy, techniques, industry facts and figures, and equal employment opportunity activities as they affect collective bargaining.

College Placement Annual: *see* COLLEGE PLACEMENT COUNCIL, INC.

College Placement Council, Inc., nonprofit corporation that provides professional services to career planning and placement directors at four-year and two-year colleges and universities in the United States, as well as to employers who hire

EXAMPLE
THIRD IN A SERIES OF COLLECTION LETTERS

James R. Collecthard, Attorney-at-Law
101 15th St.
Tincup, Colorado 81234
(303) 333-4321

June 25, 1986

Mr. John Smith
425 Columbine Street
Denver, Colorado 80206

Dear Mr. Smith:

Your delinquent account with the Tincup Ambulance Service has been turned over to me for collection.

Unless I receive full payment from you within ten days, I will initiate legal action on behalf of my client.

I regret this action, but your lack of response to repeated notices leaves them and me with no other recourse.

James R. Collecthard

cc Mr. William Jones, Secretary/Treasurer
Tincup Ambulance Service
1234 2nd Avenue
Tincup, Colorado 81234

graduates of these institutions. Each year the Council publishes the *College Placement Annual,* which includes the occupational needs anticipated by approximately 1,300 corporate and governmental employers who normally recruit college graduates. The council is located in Bethlehem, Pa.

college relations, also UNIVERSITY RELATIONS, a more acceptable term for public relations in a college or university.

See also PUBLIC RELATIONS.

Collyer doctrine, the predisposition of the National Labor Relations Board to defer to arbitral awards in disputes involving unfair labor practices if certain conditions are met—one of them being that the arbitrator must have considered and resolved the statutory issues, if any, present in the case.

comaker, a second, third, or other party who signs a negotiable instrument (such as a check or a loan note) and by so doing promises to pay it in full.

combination, also PERMUTATION (STATISTICS), a group of things or symbols in which the order of arrangement is immaterial. A *permutation* is an arrangement reflecting a specific order or sequence.

combined voting power, the total voting power in an organization (*e.g.,* a company) directly controlled by one individual or organization. Combined voting power does not include votes acquired through stock held in trusteeship because the owner of the stock does not control the voting power of the shares. Combined voting power is an important concept related to private inurement.

See also PRIVATE INUREMENT and EXCESS BUSINESS HOLDINGS.

comer, slang term for younger managers who seem to have the potential to assume top management responsibilities.

comity, the constitutional provision that "the citizens of each state shall be entitled to all privileges and immunities of citizens in the several states."

Commerce Business Daily, a daily publication that identifies upcoming federal government contracts (requests for proposals) in excess of $25,000.

Commerce clause, the part of the U.S. Constitution that allows Congress to control trade with foreign countries and from state to state. This is called the *commerce power* (Article One, Section Eight of the Constitution). If anything "affects interstate commerce" (such as labor unions, product safety, etc.), it is fair game for the federal government to regulate what goes on or even to take over all regulation.

Commerce Clearing House, Inc. (CCH), publishers of a variety of looseleaf information services concerned with law, taxes, business, urban affairs, etc., located in Chicago, Illinois.

commercial market strategy, approach whereby government subsidizes the delivery of goods or services to a target group by serving as bill payer as clients seek designated benefits from existing market outlets. For example, in the case of Medicare, beneficiaries seek medical care from a broad range of physicians and hospitals and government pays a portion of their bills.

commingle, mix. Often used in the context of tax-exempt organizations' funds. Tax-exempt charitable organizations must keep their moneys separate from other organizations and must be financially self-supporting. For example, auxiliary charitable organizations must not commingle funds with their sponsoring organizations.

Commission on Civil Rights, also called CIVIL RIGHTS COMMISSION, body whose role is to encourage constructive steps toward equal opportunity for minority groups and women. The Commission investigates complaints, holds public hearings, and collects and studies information on denials of equal protection of the laws because of race, color, religion, sex, or national origin. Voting rights, administration of justice, and equality of opportunity in education, employment, and housing are among the many topics of specific Commission interest.

The Commission on Civil Rights, created by the Civil Rights Act of 1957, makes findings of fact but has no enforcement authority. Findings and recommendations are submitted to both the President and the Congress. Many of the Commission's recommendations have been enacted, either by statute, executive order, or regulation. The Commission evaluates federal laws and the effectiveness of government equal opportunity programs. It also serves as a national clearinghouse for civil rights information.

Commission on Private Philanthropy and Public Needs, or THE FILER COMMISSION, established in 1973, the commission studied the roles of philanthropic giving and of the voluntary sector in the United States. The Commission recommended ways in which the third sector and the practice of private giving should be strengthened and rendered more effective. The Commission argued that philanthropy plays a vital role, but the impacts of the Tax Reform Act of 1969 and other pressures on nonprofit organizations mean that the continued presence of an effective third sector can not be taken for granted.

The commission also sponsored ninety-one research studies which were published under the title *Research Papers* (1977). The studies established a base of information on giving trends, the relationship between public and private support for philanthropic activities, and the effects of the tax system on the ability of the third sector to meet public needs.

commitment, a psychological and sociological bond between people and organizations which results from the matching of personal needs with the organizational culture.

committee, also AD HOC COMMITTEE and STANDING COMMITTEE, a group of people designated to investigate, act on, or propose action in a defined area of responsibility. Committees typically do not have authority to bind the parent group (*e.g.*, the board of directors) to a course of action.

Standing committees are permanent committees—for example, an executive committee, finance committee, or personnel committee.

Ad hoc committees (or temporary committees or special committees) are formed to accomplish a time-limited task(s) and then disband—for example, a nominating committee or a committee to organize a single special event.

A typical nonprofit organization may have the following types of standing committees: budget, bylaws, executive, finance, fund-raising, government relations, membership, personnel (or staff-board relations), planning, policies and procedures, program, public information (or public relations), visitor hospitality, volunteer coordination. Temporary or ad hoc committees often include nominating, searching (for example, for a new executive director), and coordinating (for example, for specific special events or drives).

See also TASK FORCE.

Committee for Economic Development (CED), nonpartisan organization of business leaders and scholars who conduct research and formulate policy recommendations on economic and public policy issues.

Committee for Industrial Organization, committee established within the American Federation of Labor in 1935 that grew to be the Congress of Industrial Organizations in 1938. *See* AMERICAN FEDERATION OF LABOR-CONGRESS OF INDUSTRIAL ORGANIZATIONS.

committeeman, or COMMITTEEWOMAN, worker (usually) elected by coworkers to represent the union membership in the handling of grievances and the recruitment of new union members, among other duties.

Committee on Political Education (COPE), nonpartisan organization of the AFL-CIO made up of members of the AFL-CIO's Executive Council. COPE has the responsibility spelled out in the AFL-CIO Constitution of "encouraging workers to register and vote, to exercise their full rights and responsibilities of citizenship, and to perform their rightful part in the political life of the city, state and national communities."

Common Business Oriented Language (COBOL), a procedure-oriented computer language that resembles standard business English.

Common Cause, leading public interest lobby with headquarters in Washington, D.C.

Common Fund, The, a large cooperative educational service venture created in 1970 and operated by a number of institutions of higher education to invest their funds collectively.

common fund foundation, a variety of private foundation in which each contributor may decide each year on the tax-exempt recipient of his/her portion of the fund's distribution.

common law of the shop, or INDUSTRIAL RELATIONS COMMON LAW, the total body of law established by judicial precedent. The *common law of the shop* or *industrial relations common law* is that portion of the common law that applies to the workplace.

common situs picketing, picketing of an entire construction site by members of a single union to increase their strike's impact and to publicize a dispute with one or more contractors or subcontractors. In 1976, President Ford vetoed a bill that

Common-Size Balance Sheet

EXAMPLE OF A COMMON-SIZE BALANCE SHEET

BALANCE SHEET—AS OF JUNE 30, 1986

	$	%
ASSETS		
CURRENT ASSETS	$252,336.46	98.3%
Cash, Checking Account	437.32	.2
Cash, Savings Account	151,201.93	58.9
Petty Cash	300.00	.1
Savings	100,397.21	39.1
PROPERTY AND EQUIPMENT	4,321.58	1.7
Equipment	488.36	.2
Office Equipment	5,731.22	2.2
Accumulated Depreciation	[1,898.00]	[.7]
TOTAL ASSETS	$256,658.04	100.0%
LIABILITIES AND FUND BALANCE		
CURRENT LIABILITIES	$ 400.40	.2%
State Withholding	400.40	.2
LONG-TERM LIABILITIES	-0-	-0-
FUND BALANCE	256,257.64	99.8
TOTAL LIABILITIES AND FUND BALANCE	$256,658.04	100.0%

would have made common situs picketing legal.

common-size balance sheet, a financial reporting technique in which the ratios of each asset to total assets and the ratios of each liability to total liabilities and fund balance are shown. A statement of this type is known as a common-size statement because the totals of all accounts so constructed are equal to one hundred percent and, therefore, are of a common size (or comparable).

See also
ACCOUNTING RATIO
ASSET
BALANCE SHEET
LIABILITY

common-size operating statement: *see* COMMON-SIZE BALANCE SHEET and OPERATING STATEMENT.

common stock, shares in a for-profit corporation that depend for their worth on the value of the company.

See also SHAREHOLDER.

communication, process of exchanging information, ideas, and feelings between two or more individuals or groups. *Horizontal communication* refers to such an exchange among peers or people at the same organizational level. *Vertical communication* refers to such an exchange between individuals at differing levels of the organization.

See also GRAPEVINE and NONVERBAL COMMUNICATION.

Communications Act of 1934, the Act that created the Federal Communications Commission (FCC) and which contains significant electronic media-related provisions for nonprofit organizations. For example, Section 307 authorizes the FCC to issue licenses to radio and television stations ". . . if public convenience, interest, or necessity will be served (by the applying station). . ." Although the Act does not define "public convenience," the FCC considers the amount of noncommercial time—including public service time—allocated by stations when reviewing both new and renewal license applications.

communication theory, a body of knowledge and an area of exploration that seeks to explain how information (meaning all social interactions) is sent, received, stored, and used by an organization, a nation, etc.

community, a loose term generally used to mean a group of people who live in close proximity and who share a common cultural and/or historical heritage.

See also COMMUNITY FOUNDATION and COMMUNITY TRUST.

community chest, a fund for local social welfare or development purposes, typically supported by voluntary contributions.

community control, extreme form of citizen participation in which democratically selected representatives of a neighborhood-sized governmental jurisdiction are given administrative and financial control over local programs such as education, land use, and police protection.

community foundation, a public charity organized as a corporation or trust and operated to benefit charitable organizations in a particular community or area.

Community foundations are similar to other private foundations in purpose, but they have unique characteristics. For example, funds are secured from many donors rather than a single contributor. Second, investment portfolios are often managed by trustee banks. Third, grant programs almost always are directed to organizations in the immediate community or area. Fourth, the typical governing board is broadly representative of the community served.

In general, community foundations offer donors considerable freedom to designate areas of giving, central administration and continuity of leadership. Further, they encourage and manage funds which are held separately or as part of a general fund, and are maintained as permanent endowments for all purposes which are defined as charitable under the law.

A few of the types of funds which commonly are found in community foundations include

ADVISED FUND
AWARD FUND
DESIGNATED FUND
ENDOWMENT FUND
FIELD-OF-INTEREST FUND
SCHOLARSHIP FUND
UNRESTRICTED FUND

community health care, activities and programs intended to improve the healthfulness of, and general health status in, a specified community. The term is widely used with many different definitions, and thus must be used with caution. It is variously defined, as above, in a manner similar to public health, synonymously with environmental health, as all health services of any kind available to a given community, or even synonymously with a community's ambulatory care.

community health center, an ambulatory health care program usually serving a catchment area with scarce or nonexistent health services or a population with special health needs. Often known as neighborhood health centers.

community of interest (labor relations), criterion used to determine if a group of employees make up an appropriate bargaining unit.

community power, usually the study or description of the political order, both formal and informal, of a segment of U.S. local governance.

community relations: *see* PUBLIC RELATIONS.

Community Services Administration (CSA), federal agency whose overall purpose was to reduce poverty in the U.S. Agency guidelines fixed the incomes which qualified a family or person for participation in antipoverty programs. The Community Services Administration was created in 1974 as the successor to the Office of Economic Opportunity, the prime mover in the Johnson administration's "war on poverty." Abolished in 1981, its close-out functions were assigned to the Office of Community Services of the Department of Health and Human Services.

community trust, a trust which generally solicits funds from, is controlled by people from, and focuses its programmatic efforts on a particular community. Community trusts may qualify as publicly supported institutions.

See also COMMUNITY FOUNDATION and PUBLICLY SUPPORTED INSTITUTION.

community wage survey, any survey whose purpose is to ascertain the structure and level of wages among employers in a local area.

company foundation: *see* CORPORATE FOUNDATION.

company town, slang term for any community whose economy is dominated by one employer. True company towns, where the company literally owned all of the land, buildings, and stores, are practically nonexistent in the modern U.S.—with the possible exception of remote areas of Alaska.

comparable form test: *see* ALTERNATE FORM.

comparable worth, providing equitable compensation for performing work of a comparable value as determined by the relative worth of a given job to an organization. The basic issue of comparable worth is whether Title VII of the Civil Rights Act of 1964 makes it unlawful for an employer to pay one sex at a lesser rate than the other when job performance is of comparable worth or value. For example, should graduate nurses be paid less than gardeners, or should beginning librarians with a master's degree be paid less than beginning managers with a master's degree? Historically, nurses and librarians have been paid less than those in occupations of "comparable worth", because they were considered to be in "female" jobs. Comparable worth as a legal concept and as a social issue directly challenges traditional and market assumptions about the worth of a job.

See also EQUAL PAY FOR EQUAL WORK and COUNTY OF WASHINGTON V. GUNTHER.

comparative analysis (financial), the comparison of ratios from the financial statement of an organization with either the same organization's financial statement for a different time period or corresponding "standard" ratios of other, similar organizations. *See also* FINANCIAL STATEMENT and RATIO.

comparative financial statement: *see* FINANCIAL STATEMENT, COMPARATIVE.

comparative-norm principle, the notion that a particular organization's salary levels should neither fall substantially behind nor be greatly above those of other employer-employee relationships.

compassionate leave, any leave granted for urgent family reasons.

compensable factors, various elements of a job that, when put together, both define the job and determine its value to the organization.

compensable injury, work injury that qualifies an injured worker for workers' compensation benefits.

compensating balance, a minimum amount of money that an organization or person must keep in a no-interest checking account to compensate a bank for loans or other services; any required bank balance.

compensation, also PAY or REMUNERATION, generic terms that encompass all forms of organizational payments and rewards.

See also the following entries:

- BONUS
- DEFERRED COMPENSATION
- INDIRECT WAGES
- TOTAL COMPENSATION COMPARABILITY
- UNEMPLOYMENT BENEFITS

compensation (directors), payment of directors. The bylaws of most public charities prohibit compensation for directors, except reimbursement for reasonable expenses incurred directly on behalf of the organization. Conversely, many larger foundations do compensate their directors or trustees.

See also BYLAWS and CONTROLLING INSTRUMENTS.

compensation for services, reasonable, payments to employees and contractors. Although tax-exempt organizations are not allowed to allocate resources for the private benefit of insiders (such as a portion of its net earnings), the payment of "reasonable" compensation to, for example, its employees will not result in the organization being denied or losing tax-exempt status under ordinary circumstances. Unfortunately, the criteria for "reasonable" and "excessive" are not fixed.

compensation management, that facet of management concerned with the selection, development, and direction of the programs that implement an organization's financial reward system.

Compensation Review, quarterly journal covering all aspects of employee compensation. Also contains "condensations of noteworthy articles" from other business and professional publications that relate to compensation.

compensatory damages, payment for the actual loss suffered by a plaintiff, as opposed to punitive damages.

compensatory time, time off in lieu of overtime pay.

competence, ability to consistently perform a task or job to an acceptable standard.

See also INTERPERSONAL COMPETENCE.

competitive level, all positions of the same grade within a competitive area which are sufficiently alike in duties, responsibilities, pay systems, terms of appointment, requirements for experience, training, skills, and aptitudes that the incumbent of any of them could readily be shifted to any of the other positions without significant training or undue interruption to the work program.

competitive promotion, selection for promotion made from the employees rated *best* qualified in competition with others, all of whom have the *minimum* qualifications required for the position.

competitive seniority, use of seniority in determining an employee's right, relative to other employees, to job-related "rights" that cannot be supplied equally to any two employees.

competitive wages, rates of pay that an employer, in competition with other employers, must offer if he or she is to recruit and retain employees.

complaint examiner, official designated to conduct complaint hearings.

completion item, test question that calls for the examinee to complete or fill in the missing parts of a phrase, sentence, etc.

compliance, inducing individuals and/or organizations to act in accordance with prescribed rules or goals: a determination of whether there is compliance with laws and regulations.

compliance agency, generally, any government agency that administers laws and/or regulations.

complimentary interview, an interview designed to provide personnel with positive performance feedback, recognition, and praise. A complimentary interview focuses on an employee's potential.

composite score, score derived by combining scores obtained by an applicant on two or more tests or other measures.

compound interest, interest on interest. In other words, interest is paid on the principal (the loan or deposited amount) at regular intervals, and interest is computed on the interest on the last principal plus interest.

Comprehensive Employment and Training Act of 1973 (CETA), act that established a program of financial assistance to state and local governments to provide job training and employment opportunities for economically disadvantaged, unemployed, and underemployed persons. CETA provided funds for state and local jurisdictions to hire unemployed and underemployed persons in public service jobs. The CETA reauthorization legislation expired in September 1982. It was replaced by the Job Training Partnership Act of 1982, which was signed into law in October 1982. The legislation provides for job training programs which are planned and implemented under the joint control of local elected government officials and private industry councils in service delivery areas designated by the governor of each state. The new law took effect October 1, 1983, providing for a one-year transition period under the CETA system.

compressed time, the same number of hours worked in a week spread over fewer days than normal.

comp time: *see* COMPENSATORY TIME.

comptroller, *see* CONTROLLER.

compulsory arbitration, negotiating process whereby the parties are required by law to arbitrate their dispute.

compulsory retirement, automatic cessation of employment at a given age.

computer, an electronic device which follows programmed instructions (programs) for the performance of logical and arithmetical operations on data that is furnished to it directly or is stored in its memory. The basic sections of a computer include input devices (for example, a keyboard), memory (or storage), arithmetical and logical section (that is, the processor), output devices (for example, a printer or a television-like screen), and a control section (the computer's "traffic cop").

Computers are generally classified into three groupings, but the "borders" of the groupings are quite fuzzy: microcomputers, minicomputers and mainframe (or large) computers.

Microcomputer systems are small and deceptively simple. They consist of a television screen and a small, self-contained keyboard that looks like a typewriter. In 1986, a complete microcomputer system designed primarily for home use could be purchased for less than $500; one for use by a small nonprofit organization for as little as $1,000 to $2,000 (however, most organizations want more capability than $1,000 to $2,000 can purchase).

See also HARDWARE.

Comsearch Printouts, a computerized listing maintained by The Foundation Center which includes grants of $5,000 and larger made by reporting private foundations and community foundations in a year. The listing is by, for example, major types of grants, geographic location of recipients, etc.

See also FOUNDATION CENTER, THE.

conciliator, individual who is assigned or who assumes the responsibility for maintaining disputing parties until they reach a voluntary settlement. For example, the Federal Mediation and Conciliation Service (FMCS) has Commissioners of Conciliation located in its various regional offices available to assist parties in the settlement of labor-management disputes.

concrete objective: *see* OBJECTIVE.

concurrent power, a power held jointly by both federal and state governments. Taxation is a major example.

concurrent resolution on the budget, resolution passed by both houses of Congress, but not requiring the signature of the president, setting forth, reaffirming, or revising the Congressional Budget for the United States Government for a fiscal year.

concurrent validity, a quality of a test. To assess the concurrent validity of a prospective employment examination, it must be given to individuals already performing successfully on the job. Each incumbent must also be independently rated by supervisors on actual job performance. Then the test scores and the ratings are correlated. If the better workers also obtain the better test scores, then the examination can be said to have concurrent validity.

condition, a future uncertain event that creates or destroys rights and obligations. For example, a contract may contain a condition stating that if one person should die, the contract is terminated.

condominium, several organizations or individuals owning individual pieces of a building (for example, an apartment or office building) and managing it together.

conduit foundation, a foundation which distributes moneys equal to the total amount of contributions it receives during a year to other tax-exempt organizations.

Conference Board, Inc., The, independent, nonprofit business research organization located in New York City. Since 1916 it has continuously served as an institution for scientific research in the fields of business economics and business management. Its sole purpose is to promote prosperity and security by assisting in the effective operation and sound development of voluntary productive enterprise. It does continuing research in the fields of economic conditions, marketing, finance, personnel administration, international activities, public affairs, corporate contributions, antitrust, and various other related areas.

confidence level (statistics), a quantitative statement of the assurance or confidence used in estimating from a sample. A confidence level usually is expressed as a percentage.

confidence testing, testing approach that allows the subject to express his or her attraction to or confidence in possible answers in percentage terms.

confirmation, formal approval, especially formal written approval; a notice that something has been received, sent, ordered, etc.

conflict, situation in which individuals or collectivities adhere to and act upon incompatible values, perceptions, or feelings.

conflict of interest, any situation where a decision that may be made (or influenced) may (or may appear to) be to an individual's personal benefit.

See also:

ARM'S LENGTH
DISQUALIFIED PERSON
PRIVATE INUREMENT

conflict resolution, a conscious effort to keep conflicts constructive rather than to permit them to become destructive. The concept of conflict resolution views conflict as inevitable in organizations; the issue is to permit and control it for beneficial purposes.

conformity, expression or enactment of similar feelings or behaviors by the members of a collectivity.

confrontation, process in which opposing parties exchange information on points of difference in order to move towards compromise or resolution.

confrontation meeting, organization development technique that has an organizational group (usually the management corps) meet for a one-day effort to assay their organizational health.

Congressional Budget, budget as set forth by Congress in a concurrent resolution on the budget.

Congressional Budget and Impoundment Control Act of 1974, reform of the federal budget process. The significant features of the act include

(1) creation of two new budget committees: the House and Senate Budget Committees;
(2) creation of a Congressional Budget Office to support Congress just as the OMB serves the President;
(3) adoption of a new appropriations process for Congress;

(4) adoption of a new budget calendar for Congress;
(5) establishment of a new fiscal year (October 1 through September 30) to more rationally deal with the timing of budget cycles;
(6) creation of a Current Services Budget; and
(7) creation of two new forms of impoundments: recissions and deferrals, both of which must be submitted to the Congress.

From a nonprofit organization perspective, the Congressional Budget and Impoundment Control Act of 1974 was particularly important because it directed the Budget Committees of the House and Senate to focus attention on coordinating tax expenditures with the Congressional appropriations process. As one result of the Act, starting in 1976, the President's budget request has included an analysis of tax expenditures.

See also TAX EXPENDITURES.

Congressional Budget Office (CBO), support agency of the U.S. Congress created in 1974 by the Congressional Budget and Impoundment Act. It provides Congress with basic budget data and with analyses of alternative fiscal, budgetary, and programmatic policy issues.

Congressional Record, publication containing the proceedings of Congress. Issued daily when Congress is in session, publication of the *Record* began March 4, 1873. It was the first series officially reported, printed, and published directly by the federal government.

connect time, the time during which a remote computer terminal is in use on a time-sharing computer system.

consensual validation, procedure of using mutual agreement as the criterion for validity.

consent decree, approach to enforcing equal employment opportunity involving a negotiated settlement that allows an employer to not admit to any acts of discrimination yet agree to greater EEO efforts in the future. Consent decrees are usually negotiated with the Equal Employment Opportunity Commission or a federal court.

consent order, regulatory agency procedure to induce voluntary compliance with its policies. A consent order usually takes the form of a formal agreement whereby an organization agrees to stop a practice in exchange for the agency's cessation of legal action against it.

consignment, handing over things for sale, but retaining ownership. For example, a nonprofit organization might hold an art sale and obtain paintings (to sell) from artists on consignment. Those that are not sold are returned to the artists.

console, the user control portion of a computer.

consolidated decision packages, packages prepared at higher organizational and program levels that summarize and supplement information contained in decision packages received from subordinate units. Consolidated packages may reflect different priorities, including the addition of new programs or the abolition of existing ones.

See also DECISION PACKAGES and ZERO-BASE BUDGETING.

consolidated financial statement, a financial statement of legally separate organizations combined as though they were one organization.

See also FINANCIAL STATEMENTS.

consortium, a combination of people, groups, associations, or organizations. A consortium may be assembled, for example, to accomplish a single, short-term purpose, or as a semipermanent alliance to pursue multiple ends. Nonprofit organizations frequently utilize corsortia or cooperative ventures. Examples include higher education and hospital cooperative purchasing and laundry consortia.

The tax-exempt status of consortia has changed frequently through the years. In general, the IRS has been more supportive of tax exemptions for consortia (of tax-exempt organizations) than the courts and Congress.

constant dollar, a dollar value adjusted for changes in prices. Constant dollars are derived by dividing current dollar amounts by an appropriate price index, a process generally known as deflating. The result is a constant dollar series as it would presumably exist if prices and transactions were the same in all subsequent years as in the base year. Any changes in such a series would reflect only changes in the real volume of goods and services.

See also CURRENT DOLLAR.

constant payment mortgage, a mortgage in which equal monthly payments are made, with a portion of each payment going to principal (increasing) and a portion to interest (decreasing) until the mortgage is paid off.

constituency, individuals or groups having an interest in the activities of an organization.

constitution, one form which a nonprofit organization's articles of organization may take. Other forms include, for example, articles of association, articles of incorporation, and charter.

constitutional, consistent with and reflective of the Constitution.

constitutional law, that area of the law concerned with the interpretation and application of the nation's highest law—the Constitution.

constitutional right, prerogative guaranteed to the people by the Constitution.

construct, an idea or concept created or synthesized ("constructed") from available information and refined through scientific investigation. In psychological testing, a construct is usually dimensional, an attribute of people that varies in degree from one person to another. Tests are usually intended to be measures of intellectual, perceptual, psychomotor, or personality constructs (*e.g.*, a clerical test may measure the construct known as "perceptual speed and accuracy" or the performance of invoice clerks may be measured in terms of "ability to recognize errors").

constructive discharge theory, a legal theory. If an employer makes conditions of continued employment so intolerable that it results in a "constructive discharge" whereby the employee "voluntarily" leaves, the employer may still be subject to charges that the employer violated Title VII of the Civil Rights Act of 1964, which generally prohibits employers from discharging employees because of their race, color, sex, or national origin.

construct validity, measure of how adequate a test is for assessing the possession of particular psychological traits or qualities.

consultant, individual or organization temporarily employed by other individuals or organizations because of some presumed expertise. Consultants are typically used by nonprofit organizations, for example, to develop or improve financial management systems, management information systems, development or fund-raising programs, membership programs, staff compensation programs, public information or public relations programs, and for training staff, board members, committee members, and other volunteers. Consultants may also be useful for conducting evaluations of the organization or of selected programs.

consumer: *see* CLIENTELE.

Consumer Credit Protection Act of 1970, law that limits the amount of an employee's disposable income which may be garnisheed and protects employees from discharge because of one garnishment.

consumerism, a political movement which seeks to extend greater protections to consumers of goods and services through government regulation of the quality and safety of products.

Consumer Price Index (CPI), also called COST-OF-LIVING INDEX, monthly statistical measure of the average change in prices over time in a fixed market basket of goods and services.

The CPI is based on prices of food, clothing, shelter, fuels, transportation fares, charges for doctors' and dentists' services, drugs, and other goods and services that people buy for day-to-day living. Prices are collected in eighty-five urban areas across the country from over 18,000 tenants, 18,000 housing units for property taxes, and about 24,000 establishments—grocery and department stores, hospitals, filling stations, and other types of stores and service establishments.

In calculating the index, price changes for the various items in each location are averaged together with weights which represent their importance in the spending of the appropriate population group. Local data are then combined to obtain a U.S. city average. Separate indexes are also published for twenty-eight local areas. Area indexes do not measure differences in the level of prices among cities; they only measure the average change in prices for each area since the base period.

The index measures price changes from a designated reference date—1967—which equals 100.0. An increase of twenty-two percent, for example, is shown as 122.0. This change can also be expressed in dollars as follows: The prices of a base period "market basket" of goods and services in the CPI has risen from $10 in 1967 to $12.20.

Consumer Product Safety Commission (CPSC), federal commission created to protect the public against unreasonable risks of injury from consumer products; to assist consumers to evaluate comparative safety of consumer products; to develop uniform safety standards for consumer products and minimize conflicting state and local regulations; and to promote research and investigation into the causes and prevention of product-related deaths, illnesses, and injuries.

consumer taxes, taxes levied by all levels of government against the tax base of consumer spending. The two most prevalent types of consumer taxes are taxes on retail sales and taxes on selected commodities. These taxes have been found objectionable to many as they are regressive in nature, only moderately elastic, and have a more negative impact on the poor because they spend a larger portion of their income on taxed commodities. Examples of state and local consumer taxes include: retail sales taxes, liquor and tobacco taxes, utilities taxes, lodging taxes, entertainment and admissions taxes, automotive taxes including license and registration fees, etc. Federal consumer taxes include firearms taxes, transportation taxes, gambling taxes, narcotics taxes, and taxes on manufactured goods and imports.

See also TAXATION.

contempt, a willful disobeying of a judge's command or official court order.

content analysis, the process of systematically identifying and organizing written material (for example, from newspapers or from responses to open-ended questions on a public survey) in order to extract usable information.

content validity, a validity measure for tests. A selection device has content validity if it measures the specific abilities needed to perform the job.

contextual variable, a condition that may affect the validity of a test.

contingency management, also called SITUATIONAL MANAGEMENT, any management style that recognizes that the application of theory to practice must necessarily take into consideration, and be contingent upon, the given situation.

See also CONTINGENCY PLANNING.

contingency model of leadership effectiveness, Fred E. Fiedler's theory of leadership effectiveness. According to Fiedler, the appropriate leadership style is determined by three critical elements in the leader's situation: (1) the power position of the leader; (2) the task structure; (3) the leader-member personal relationships. The nature of these three factors determines the "favorableness" of the situation for the leader, which in turn requires a particular leadership style. Fiedler suggests that it may be to an organization's advantage to try to design jobs to fit leaders' styles rather than attempting to change leaders' behavior to fit the situation. For the original presentation, *see* Fred E. Fiedler, *A Theory of Leadership Effectiveness* (N.Y.: McGraw-Hill, 1967).

contingency planning, the process of developing a series of alternative plans for achieving an objective. Different alternatives are implemented depending upon future events, opportunities, or barriers.
See also CONTINGENCY MANAGEMENT.

contingency question, a survey or interview question that is asked of only some respondents. The decision is made whether to ask the question based on the response to another question(s).

contingency reserve, also CONTINGENCY FUND, a fund of money set aside (or budgeted) by an organization to cover possible unknown future expenses.

contingent liability, existing condition, situation, or set of circumstances involving uncertainty as to a possible loss that will ultimately be resolved when one or more future events occur or fail to occur. A contingent liability is a conditional commitment that may become an actual liability because of a future event.
See also LIABILITIES.

continuing education, general term that usually refers to graduate or undergraduate coursework undertaken on a part-time basis in order to keep up to date on new developments in one's occupational field, learn a new field, or contribute to one's general education.

continuing plans: *see* STANDING PLANS.

continuing resolution, legisation that provides budget authority for specific ongoing activities in cases where the regular fiscal year appropriation for such activities has not been enacted by the beginning of the fiscal year. The continuing resolution usually specifies a maximum rate at which the agency may incur obligations based on the rate of the prior year, the president's budget request, or an appropriation bill passed by either or both houses of the Congress.

continuous budgeting: *see* BUDGETING, CONTINUOUS.

continuous negotiating committee, labor-management committee established to review a collective bargaining agreement on a continuous basis.

contra (Latin), also CONTRA ACCOUNT AND CONTRA BALANCE, against. In accounting, *contra accounts* are established to show subtractions from other accounts, and *contra balances* are account balances that are the opposite (positive or negative) of what usually appears.

contraband, things that are illegal to import or export or that are illegal to possess.

contract: *see* the following entries:
- BREACH OF CONTRACT
- EMPLOYMENT CONTRACT
- INCENTIVE CONTRACT
- LABOR AGREEMENT
- MASTER AGREEMENT
- SWEETHEART CONTRACT
- TERMINATION CONTRACT

contract audit, an examination and evaluation of government contracts for goods and services with private as well as nonprofit organizations.

contract authority: *see* BACKDOOR AUTHORITY.

contract bar, an existing collective bargaining agreement that bars a representation election sought by a competing union.

contracting, legal process by which the government enters into relationships with firms in the nonprofit or private sector to administer programs or provide the government with goods or services. The contract may provide that the government reimburse the organization for the costs it incurs or that the government pay a fixed price for the product; both types of contracts may contain incentive provisions that reward the contractor for meeting deadlines and staying within cost estimates.

contracting-out, having work performed outside an organization's own work force.

contractor, an organization or person who takes on work but generally retains control over his or her own work. Usually, work must be performed to negotiated standards within a specific period of time. Other caveats regarding reporting or conditions of work performance frequently are stipulated.

See also CONSULTANT.

contributed services, also IN-KIND CONTRIBUTIONS, time and effort—often professional—donated to a nonprofit organization.

See also:
CONTRIBUTION
DONATED SERVICES

contribution, donation. From a nonprofit organization perspective, the most common use of the word contribution is "a gift"—most typically of money, but also of objects of value, time, effort, and skills.

According to the American Association of Fund-Raising Counsel, Inc., the approximate 1984 U.S. sources of charitable contributions were individuals ($62 billion), bequests ($5 billion), foundations ($4.5 billion), and corporations ($3.5 billion). In the same year, the primary recipients of charitable contributions were religion ($36 billion), health care ($10.5 billion), education ($10 billion), social services ($8 billion), arts and humanities ($4.5 billion), and civic causes ($2 billion).

contribution base, *see* ADJUSTED GROSS INCOME.

contribution, excess: *see* EXCESS CONTRIBUTIONS.

contribution margin, the excess of income (for example, from providing a service) over an organization's variable cost to produce the service, not including fixed costs (for example, space, supervision, etc.).

See also COST, VARIABLE.

contributory pension plan, any pension program that has employees contributing a portion of the cost.

control, that aspect of management concerned with the comparison of actual versus planned performance as well as the development and implementation of procedures to correct substandard performance. Control, which is inherent to all levels of management, is a feedback process which ideally should report only unexpected situations. This is the essence of management by exception. Some management control systems regularly report critical indicators of performance so that management will have advance notice of potential problems.

As the term is used in organization theory and behavior, control is an aspect of management in which it is assumed that cause-effect relationships are known and there is a high level of certainty. In *Management or Control? The Organizational Challenge* (Bloomington, Ind.: Indiana University Press, 1980) Russell Stout, Jr., asserts that there is a managerial tendency towards inappropriate use of control, particularly in public organizations. Preoccupation with accountability and avoidance of errors leads to increased controls and often "overcontrol," when a more experimental management orientation is needed.

control, statistical quality, *see* STATISTICAL QUALITY CONTROL.

control chart, a graphical display developed from sampled information which shows whether or not a process is under statistical control.

control group, in a research design, a group with characteristics similar to those of the experimental or subject group, which is not exposed to the experimental treatment and which is used for comparative purposes.

controlled circulation, the number of readers reached by a free publication with a selected readership which derives its income from advertising space sales.

controlled organization income, income received by an organization that is at least eighty percent controlled by a tax-exempt organization. Controlled organization income is used by the IRS in analyzing a tax-exempt organization's unrelated business income.
See also UNRELATED BUSINESS INCOME.

controller or COMPTROLLER, the financial officer of an organization.

controlling account, an account in a general ledger that shows in summary from what appears in detail in the corresponding subsidiary ledger. There is a separate controlling account for each subsidiary ledger.
See also:
ACCOUNTING CYCLE
FINANCIAL STATEMENTS
GENERAL LEDGER
SUBSIDIARY LEDGER ACCOUNT

controlling instruments, a general term for nonprofit organizations' articles of organization and bylaws.
See also:
ARTICLES OF ASSOCIATION
ARTICLES OF INCORPORATION
ARTICLES OF ORGANIZATION
BYLAWS

convergent validity, in testing, evidence that different measures of a construct will produce similar results.

converted score, general term referring to any of a variety of "transformed" scores, in terms of which raw scores on a test may be expressed for such reasons as facilitating interpretation and permitting comparison with scores on other test forms. For example, the raw scores obtained by candidates on the various College Board tests are converted to scores on a common scale that ranges from 200 to 800.

convertible bond, a bond which gives its holder the right to exchange or convert it into common stock (or, occasionally, some other form of security) under stipulated conditions and when the holder finds conversion to be advantageous.

convertible preferred stock, a class of stock in a company that gives its holder the privilege of converting the shares into some other form of security. Convertible preferred stock usually is convertible into a predetermined number of shares of common stock.

conveyance, a transfer of title.

cooling-off period, any legal provision that postpones a strike or lockout for a specific period of time in order to give the parties an additional opportunity to mediate their differences.

cooperative agreement, a form of assistance award from the federal government to a nonprofit organization, state or local government or other recipient to support and stimulate an activity or venture to accomplish a public purpose, and in which the federal government will be substantially involved during the performance of the contemplated activity.

cooperative education, an educational process wherein students alternate formal studies with actual work experiences. It is distinguished from other part-time employment in that successful completion of the off-campus experiences becomes a prerequisite for graduation.

cooperative educational service

organization, an organization which jointly invests funds of and for member educational organizations. Under IRS Code 501(f), cooperative educational service organizations may qualify as tax-exempt charitable organizations.

cooperative hospital service organization, an entity organized and operated cooperatively by and for at least two tax-exempt hospitals that provides allowable services to the member hospitals including, for example, food services, billing and collections, or purchasing and personnel functions. In general, cooperative hospital laundry services do not qualify. Under IRS Code 501(e), cooperative hospital service organizations are charitable organizations and, therefore, may qualify for tax-exempt status.

cooperative venture, a consortium of organizations established to advance the purposes of its member organizations. The tax-exempt status of cooperative ventures (whose members are themselves tax-exempt organizations) has changed frequently over the years and generally is not clear. Typical examples include cooperative purchasing ventures of hospitals and educational institutions.

See, for example, COOPERATIVE EDUCATIONAL SERVICE ORGANIZATION and COOPERATIVE HOSPITAL SERVICE ORGANIZATION.

cooptation, efforts of an organization to bring and subsume new elements into its policymaking process in order to prevent such elements from being a threat to the organization or its mission.

coordination of benefits (COB), provisions and procedures used by insurers to avoid duplicate payment for losses insured under more than one insurance policy.

copayment, a type of cost sharing whereby insured or covered persons pay a specified flat amount per unit of service or unit of time (*e.g.*, $2 per visit, $10 per inpatient hospital day), their insurer paying the rest of the cost. The copayment is incurred at the time the service is used. The amount paid does not vary with the cost of the service (unlike coinsurance, which is payment of some percentage of the cost).

COPE: *see* COMMITTEE ON POLITICAL EDUCATION.

coproduction, an emerging concept of public service delivery in which there is direct citizen collaboration in the design and delivery of municipal services.

copy, the written text of an advertisement, book, etc.; the spoken part of a public service announcement or an advertisement on radio or television.

copyright, the right of an author (or other originator) to control the copying and distributing of books, articles, movies, etc. This right is created, regulated, and limited by federal statute. The symbol for copyright is ©. The legal life of a copyright is the author's life plus fifty years, or a flat seventy-five years for one held by a company. Copyrights are registered in the Copyright Office of the Library of Congress.

copywriter, a person who writes copy for advertisements.

Cornelius* v. *NAACP-LDF, No. 84-312, (1985), U.S. Supreme Court case which held that the federal government may exclude legal defense funds from the annual charity drives conducted among federal workers as long as the government's goal is not to suppress a particular point of view.

Corning Glass Works* v. *Brennan, 417 U.S. 188 (1974), U.S. Supreme Court case which held that it was a violation of the Equal Pay Act of 1963 to continue to pay some men at a higher rate ("red circle") than women for the same work even though all new hires for these same positions would receive the same salary regardless of sex.

corporate, pertaining to or belonging to

a corporation. For example, corporate donor, corporate foundation, and corporate giving.

corporate contribution, a direct gift by a corporation—not through, for example, a corporate foundation.

corporate foundation or COMPANY FOUNDATION, a private foundation created by and—usually—financially supported by a single corporation. Corporate foundations frequently target their grant funds on programs with high public visibility and in geographical areas where the company operates or has subsidiaries. A corporate foundation usually functions as a conduit for its supporting company's philanthropic activities, although some have substantial endowments.

See also CONDUIT FOUNDATION.

Corporate Giving Profiles, a monthly newsletter-type report which presents in-depth profiles of selected corporations' giving practices. *Corporate Giving Profiles* reviews the corporations' grant types, how much they give, contact persons, their priorities and philosophies, and how to approach them.

corporate giving program, a private company's planned, scheduled program for philanthropic giving.

Corporate Giving Watch, a monthly newsletter-type report which contains news and ideas for nonprofit organizations seeking corporate funds.

corporate social responsibility (of foundation portfolio investment policies), ensuring that companies act in a socially responsible manner. In recent years, some foundations have been exercising responsibility related to the social responsibility of businesses in two ways: through grants to organizations that monitor corporate activities and as active stockholders.

corporation, an organization formed under state or federal law that exists, for legal purposes, as a separate being or an artificial person.

See also ARTIFICIAL PERSON.

corporation counsel, attorney for a corporation.

correctional institution, prisons, reformatories, houses of correction, and other institutions for the confinement and correction of convicted persons and juveniles.

correction for guessing, reduction in a test score for wrong answers—sometimes applied in scoring multiple-choice questions—that is intended to discourage guessing and to yield more accurate ranking of examinees in terms of their true knowledge.

corrections, generic term that includes all government agencies, facilities, programs, procedures, personnel, and techniques concerned with the investigation, intake, custody, confinement, supervision, or treatment of alleged or adjudicated adult offenders, delinquents, or status offenders.

correlation (statistics), the degree to which changes in one number vary with changes in another number. This association of changes may or may not be because one causes the other.

correlation, biserial: *see* BISERIAL CORRELATION.

correlation coefficient, a number which expresses the degree of correlation (closeness of association) between changes in two numbers. A correlation coefficient can range from -1.0 (a perfect negative correlation) to $+1.0$ (a perfect positive correlation). When there is no correlation between two measures, the coefficient is 0. The mathematical symbol for a correlation coefficient is r.

corruption, impairment of integrity, virtue, or moral responsibility. The most typical form of corruption encountered by nonprofit organizations is embezzlement.

See also EMBEZZLEMENT.

cosigner, a general term for a person who signs a document along with another person. Depending on the situation and the state, a cosigner may have primary responsibility or only a secondary responsibility (for example, to pay a debt).

cosmic search, in the context of equal employment opportunity, the endless search by an employer for an alternative selection procedure with less adverse impact.

cosmopolitan-local construct, two latent social roles that manifest themselves in organizational settings, according to Alvin W. Gouldner. The first role, *cosmopolitan,* tends to be adopted by true professionals. It assumes a small degree of loyalty to the employing organization, a high commitment to specialized skills, and an outer-reference group orientation. The second role, *local,* tends to be adopted by nonprofessionals. It assumes a high degree of loyalty to the employing organization, a low commitment to specialized skills, and an inner-reference group orientation. These role models are extremes and represent the two ends of a continuum. *See* Alvin W. Gouldner, "Cosmopolitans and Locals: Toward an Analysis of Latent Social Roles—I," *Administrative Science Quarterly* (December 1957).

cost, direct, a cost which is allocated for the direct operation or support of a program or project. The opposite of direct cost is indirect cost.

See also COST, INDIRECT.

cost, fixed, a cost which remains constant as the number of units of output changes.

See also COST, SEMI-FIXED and COST, VARIABLE.

cost, incremental: *see* COST, MARGINAL.

cost, indirect, a cost which is incurred, for example, by a grantee organization for nondirect support of a program or project. Typical indirect costs include payroll expenses for organizational supervision (payroll expenses), utilities and general legal expenses—services which are provided for the entire organization and which indirectly benefit the project. Indirect costs can not be directly attributed to a particular program but are indeed borne as part of the total operation.

Formulas for the distribution of indirect costs often are based on space or personnel allocations, and exist in order to achieve a more accurate reflection of true program costs.

Many government granting agencies stipulate or negotiate an indirect cost rate with larger grantee organizations such as colleges.

See also, COST, DIRECT.

cost, intangible, an undesirable, noncostable consequence of an action or a program.

cost, marginal, also INCREMENTAL COST, the dollar cost to produce one additional unit of output. *Incremental cost* is the dollar cost to produce two or more additional units of output.

In program planning, it is a common mistake to use average cost figures as the basis for making decisions about changing the level of output units. For example: A proposed decision to revise eligibility criteria for services provided by a mental health center would hypothetically result in twenty-five new clients. The center's total current cost of operations is $1,000,000, and 5,000 people are receiving services. Therefore, the current average cost per client is $200.

However, it is highly unlikely that that $200 will be the incremental cost for each new client, or that the total incremental costs will be $200 × 25 new clients ($5,000). The additional cost elements must be identified and calculated in order to determine the true incremental costs.

For example, to service the new clients, new records must be kept which will require one-half of a clerical person earning $10,000 per year ($5,000); one psychiatric social worker earning $15,000 per year ($15,000); three-fourths of a psychologist earning $24,000 per year ($18,000); and $2,000 in additional space and supplies

EXAMPLE OF SEMI-FIXED COSTS

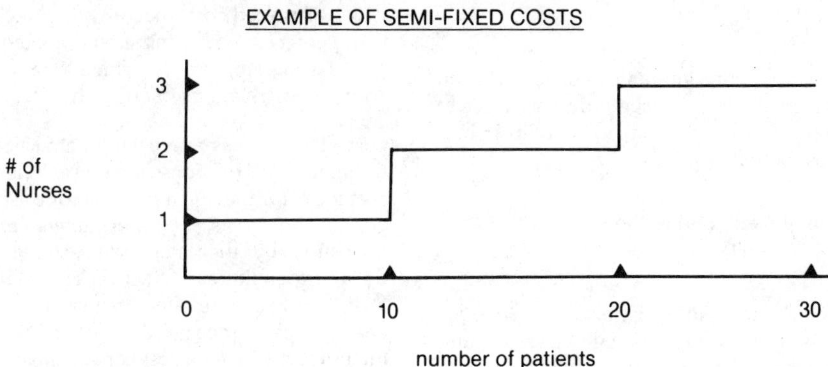

costs. These costs total $40,000—substantially different than the $50,000 arrived at by using average costs. The incremental cost per client is $1,600 rather than $2,000.

See also:
COST, FIXED
COST, SEMI-FIXED
COST, VARIABLE

cost, opportunity, the cost of pursuing one goal or implementing one program which consumes resources that are then no longer available for pursuing different goals or implementing other programs; the "cost" of opportunities lost.

cost, semi-fixed, a cost that remains constant over a limited range of output levels, but changes when the limits of that range are exceeded. For example, one nurse can provide care to ten patients, but another nurse must be added when the number of patients rises to between eleven and twenty, and still another nurse is needed to handle from twenty-one to thirty patients.

See also COST, FIXED and COST, VARIABLE.

cost, sunk, an irrevocable past cost. Because there is no decision which can change a sunk cost, it is irrelevant to current and future decisions.

cost, variable, a cost which changes with a change in the level of outputs. Each new output produced consumes more variable costs.

EXAMPLE OF VARIABLE COSTS

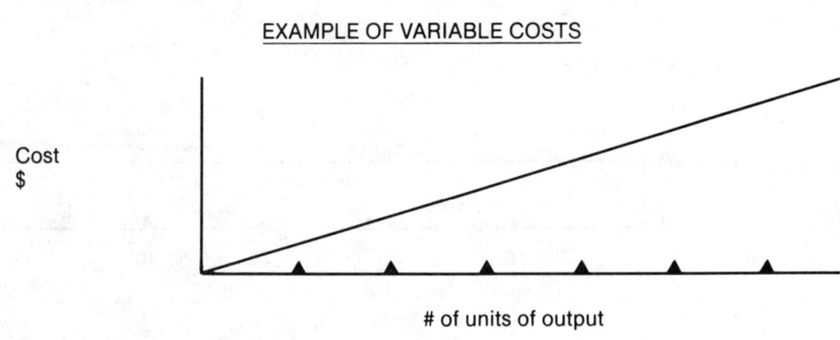

See also COST, FIXED and COST, SEMI-FIXED.

costable criterion, an evaluation criterion which allows definitive monetary costs to be derived and used, for example, in a cost-benefit analysis.

cost-based budgeting: *see* BUDGETING, COST-BASED.

cost-benefit analysis, also BENEFIT-COST ANALYSIS, a process by which organizations seek to determine the effectiveness of their spending, in relation to costs, in meeting outcome or impact objectives; a method of analysis that compares the dollar costs of resources used to achieve benefits when a monetary value can be assigned to the benefits achieved. The result of a cost-benefit analysis is a cost-benefit ratio. For example, if each life saved is worth $ ____ (in, for example, lifetime earnings, nondependence on public assistance, etc.), the estimated cost-benefit ratio for a program to reduce vehicular fatalities would be estimated by multiplying the number of lives saved by $ ____ and dividing the result by program costs.

See also COST-EFFECTIVENESS ANALYSIS.

cost-benefit ratio: *see* COST-BENEFIT ANALYSIS and COST-EFFECTIVENESS ANALYSIS

cost center, an accounting device by which all related costs that are attributable to a "center" in an organization (for example, a program) are segregated for accounting or reimbursement purposes.

cost-effectiveness analysis, an analytical technique used to choose the most efficient method for achieving a program or policy goal. The costs of alternatives are measured by their requisite estimated dollar expenditures. Effectiveness is defined by the degree of goal attainment. If effectiveness is measured in dollars, then the process is called a cost-benefit analysis.

Either the net effectiveness (effectiveness minus costs) or the cost-effectiveness ratios of alternatives are compared. The most cost-effective method chosen may involve one or more alternatives.

See also COST-BENEFIT ANALYSIS.

costing-out, determining the actual cost of a contract proposal (wages and fringe benefits).

cost of capital, what it costs an organization to pay for its financing; for example, a rate of interest or an opportunity cost.

cost of insurance, the amount which a policyholder pays to the insurer minus what he gets back from it. This should be distinguished from the rate for a given unit of insurance ($10 for a $1000 life insurance policy).

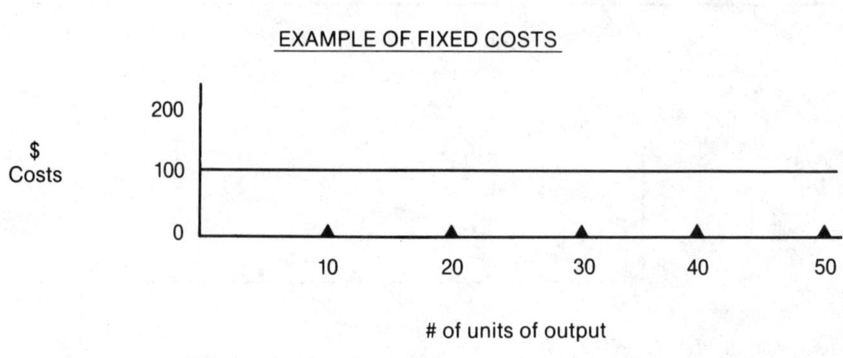

cost-of-living adjustment (COLA), also COST-OF-LIVING ALLOWANCE, an increase in compensation in response to increasing inflation. A *cost-of-living allowance* is additional compensation for accepting employment in high costs-of-living areas.

cost-of-living escalator: *see* ESCALATOR CLAUSE.

Cost-of-Living Index: *see* CONSUMER PRICE INDEX.

cost per unit, a cost accounting measure used in calculating the efficiency or effectiveness of a program. For example, cost per client served, cost per client placed, etc.

cost sharing: a provision of a health insurance policy which requires the insured to pay some portion of covered medical expenses.

See also MATCHING SHARE.

costs, allowable, expenses which are permitted under the conditions or stipulations of a grant. For example, FMC (Federal Management Circular) 74-4 includes the following allowable costs: accounting, advertising, advisory councils, bonding, compensation for personal services, legal expenses, materials and supplies, payroll preparation, printing and reproduction, transportation and travel, etc. FMC 74-4 also includes costs that are allowable with the approval of the granting agency.

See also COST, UNALLOWABLE.

costs, unallowable, expenses which are not permitted under the conditions or stipulations of a grant. For example, FMC (Federal Management Circular) 74-4 lists as unallowable costs bad debts, contingencies, contributions and donations, entertainment, interest and other financial costs, etc.

See also COSTS, ALLOWABLE.

Council for Advancement and Support of Education (CASE), an association of public relations officers in educational institutions. Approximately two thousand colleges, universities, two-year colleges, and independent schools belong to CASE. It was formed in 1974 through a merger of the American College Public Relations Association (ACPRA) and the American Alumni Council (AAC).

council of government (COG), multijurisdictional cooperative arrangements to permit a comprehensive approach to planning, development, transportation, environment, and similar problems that affect the region as a whole. They are comprised of designated policymaking representatives from each participating government within the region. COG's are substate regional planning agencies established by states and are responsible for areawide review of projects applying for Federal funds and for development of regional plans and other areawide special purpose arrangements.

Council of State Governments (CSG), joint agency of all state governments created, supported, and directed by them. Its purpose is to strengthen all branches of state government and preserve the state governmental role in the federal system through catalyzing the expression of states' views on major issues; conducting research on state programs and problems; assisting in federal-state liaison and state-regional-local cooperation; offering training, reference, and consultation services to state agencies, officials, and legislators; and serving as a broad instrument for bringing together all elements of state government. CSG is based in Lexington, KY.

Council on Environmental Quality federal agency that develops and recommends to the president national policies which further environmental quality, performs a continuing analysis of changes or trends in the national environment, administers the environmental impact statement process, provides an ongoing assessment of the nation's energy research and development from an environmental and conservation standpoint, and assists the president in the preparation of the annual environmental quality report to the Congress.

Council on Foundations, a Washington, D.C. based organization comprised of nearly 1,000 grantmakers, including community, operating, independent, and company-sponsored foundations; business firms with contributions programs; and other publicly supported organizations whose primary activity is grantmaking. Associations of grantmakers and several trust companies and banks are cooperating organizations of the Council.

The Council provides a variety of technical and advisory services for its members on matters including government legislation and regulation, improving administration, and identifying possible partners for joint funding. Programs and services include public policy analysis and development, education, information, and consultation.

counseling, crisis: *see* CRISIS INTERVENTION.

counseling, employee: *see* EMPLOYEE COUNSELING.

countercyclical, type of actions aimed at smoothing out swings in economic activity. Countercyclical actions may take the form of monetary and fiscal policy (such as countercyclical revenue sharing or jobs programs). Automatic (built-in) stabilizers have a countercyclical effect without necessitating changes in governmental policy.

See also AUTOMATIC STABILIZER.

counterpart requirement, requirement that the organization's purposes must be comparable to and not exceed those of a charitable, religious, educational, or similar tax-exempt organization. In order for a government instrumentality to qualify as a charitable organization for tax purposes, it must meet the counterpart requirement.

See GOVERNMENT INSTRUMENTALITY.

counterproposal, offer made by a party in response to an earlier offer made by another party.

County of Washington v. Gunther, 68 L. Ed. 2d 751 (1981), U.S. Supreme Court case which held that a claim of sex-based wage discrimination was not precluded by a failure to allege performance of work equal to that performed by male counterparts. This case involved female matrons of a county jail who performed substantially equal work to that performed by male guards, but were compensated less. Although they alleged in their complaint a violation of the equal pay standard of the Equal Pay Act as between themselves and the male guards, they did not allege that job performance was "substantially equal" as required under the Act. Suing under Title VII, the matrons' argument was that even if their job content was not substantially equal to that of the male guards, some of the difference in compensation paid to them was because of sex discrimination. While the Court agreed with the matrons, it dodged the issue of comparable worth. Justice Brennan in his majority opinion wrote that "respondent's claim is not based on the controversial concept of 'comparable worth'."

See also COMPARABLE WORTH.

court, agency of the judicial branch of government authorized or established by statute or constitution and consisting of one or more judicial officers which has the authority to decide upon controversies in law and disputed matters of fact brought before it.

court of appeals, also called FEDERAL COURT OF APPEALS and U.S. COURT OF APPEALS, appellate court below the U.S. Supreme Court which hears appeals from cases tried in federal district courts. In most cases, a decision by a court of appeals is final, since only a small fraction of their decisions are ever reviewed by the U.S. Supreme Court. Before 1948 the court of appeals was called the circuit court of appeals.

cousin laboratory, a laboratory training experience for people who have no direct working relationship with each other but come from the same organization.

covenant, a written promise, agreement, or restriction usually contained in a deed.

coverage, the guarantee against specific losses provided under the terms of an insurance policy, frequently used interchangeably with *benefits* or *protection*. The extent of the insurance afforded by a policy. Often used to mean insurance or an insurance contract.

covered jobs, all those positions that are affected and protected by specific labor legislation.

cover your ass (CYA), any bureaucratic technique that serves to hold the individual bureaucrat blameless for policies or actions with which he or she was once associated.

CPA: *see* CERTIFIED PUBLIC ACCOUNTANT.

CPI: *see* CONSUMER PRICE INDEX.

CPI Detailed Report, U.S. Bureau of Labor Statistics' monthly publication featuring detailed data and charts on the Consumer Price Index.

CPM: *see* CRITICAL PATH METHOD.

CP/M, a computer operating system for microcomputers, developed and marketed by Digital Research, Inc., which allows access to many standard computer programs.

CPSC: *see* CONSUMER PRODUCT SAFETY COMMISSION.

CPU: *see* CENTRAL PROCESSING UNIT.

cradle-to-the-grave, also called WOMB-TO-TOMB, slang phrases that refer to the total security offered citizens in the fully realized welfare state.

craft, any occupation requiring specific skills that must be acquired by training.

craft union, also called HORIZONTAL UNION and TRADE UNION, labor organization that restricts its membership to skilled craft workers (such as plumbers, carpenters, etc.), in contrast to an industrial union that seeks to recruit all workers in a particular industry.

craft unit, bargaining unit that consists of workers with the same specific skill (such as electricians, plumbers, or carpenters).

crash, an unplanned computer shutdown caused by a machine (hardware) malfunction or a bad program (software) instruction.

See also:

COMPUTER
HARDWARE

creating document, the legal document that creates an organization; for example, articles of organization, articles of incorporation, or a constitution. The IRS views the creating document as the only source document for satisfying the organizational test for tax exemption as a charitable organization—the bylaws will not suffice.

creative director, a person who is responsible for both advertising copy and pictures.

See also COPY.

creativity test, test that stresses divergent thinking or the ability to create new or original answers; considered useful for examining the culturally disadvantaged and certain ethnic groups whose command of English is not highly developed. Such tests utilize common and familiar objects in order to sample the testee's originality, flexibility, and fluency of thinking. Tasks include suggesting inprovements in familiar devices such as telephones or listing many possible uses for a broom handle. The tests are scored simply on the number of acceptable answers given by the subject.

credentialing, the process of recognizing professional or technical competence. The credentialing process may include registration, certification, licensure, professional association membership, or the award of a degree in the field.

credentialism, an emphasis on paper manifestations, such as college degrees, instead of actual ability to accomplish the tasks of a job.

credit, letter of, a formal document issued by a granting agency that authorizes a grantee to draw deposited grant funds from a selected commercial bank. The federal government tends to prefer distributing funds through letters of credit for larger grant awards when the grant is for at least one year and the grantee has demonstrated its financial management capabilities.

credit bureau, also CREDIT AGENCY, an organization that gathers and distributes information about the credit used by individuals and organizations and on their reported financial reliability. For example, Dun & Bradstreet, Inc. in the business world and retail credit bureaus in the consumer field.

credit check, reference check on a prospective employee's financial standing. Such checks are usually conducted only when financial status may bear upon the job, as with bank tellers, for example.

credit counseling, a formal effort to help overextended consumers manage their personal debts.

credited service, employment time that an employee has for benefit purposes.

creditor, a person to whom a debt is owed.

credit rating, the determination of an organization's creditworthiness. The ability of an organization to sell its bonds is often a function of the credit rating it enjoys. This credit rating translates into a rating for each issue which in turn determines the level of interest the jurisdiction must pay to entice buyers. The two major municipal bond rating services are Standard and Poor's Corporation and Moody's Investors Service.

credits (accounting): *see* DEBITS AND CREDITS.

credit union, according to a 1977 U.S. Court of Appeals decision, "a democratically controlled, cooperative, nonprofit society (which encourages) . . . thrift and self-reliance among its members, by creating a source of credit at a fair and reasonable rate of interest in order to improve the economic and social conditions of its members." Credit unions may qualify for tax-exempt status under IRS Code 501(c)(14).

crisis bargaining, collective bargaining negotiations conducted under the pressure of a severe deadline.

crisis intervention, a formal effort to help an individual experiencing a crisis to reestablish equilibrium. A crisis is a turning point in a person's life. It can be the death of a child, spouse, or parent. It can be a heart attack. It can be anything that tests the limits of an individual's ability to cope.

criterion, plural CRITERIA, measure of performance against which program or individual performance is compared.

criterion, qualifiable, an evaluation criterion or standard which is neither costed nor directly quantified, but which is described subjectively (*e.g.*, social and aesthetic values). Qualifiable criteria may be expressed in a structured form by the use of nonparametric statistics.

See:

CRITERION
CRITERION, QUANTIFIABLE
NONPARAMETRIC STATISTICS

criterion, quantifiable, an evaluation criterion or standard which is numerically measurable.

See also CRITERION, QUALIFIABLE and MEASURE, QUANTIFIED.

criterion contamination, influence on criterion measures of variables or factors not relevant to the work behavior being measured. If the criterion is, for example, a set of supervisory ratings of competence in job performance and if the ratings are correlated with the length of time the supervisor has known the individual people he/she rates, then the length of acquaintance is a contaminant of the criterion measure. Similarly, if the amount of production on a machine is counted as the criterion measure and if the amount of production depends in part on the age of the machine being used, then age of machinery is a contaminant of production counts.

criterion objective: *see* PERFORMANCE OBJECTIVE.

criterion-referenced test, test by which a candidate's performance is measured according to the degree a specified criterion has been met.

criterion related validation: *see* STATISTICAL VALIDATION.

criterion relevance, judgment of the degree to which a criterion measure reflects the important aspects of job performance. Such a judgment is based on an understanding of the measurement process itself, of the job and worker requirements as revealed through the needs of the organization.

critical-incident method, also called CRITICAL-INCIDENT TECHNIQUE, identifying, classifying, and recording significant examples—critical incidents—of an employee's behavior for purposes of performance evaluation. The theory behind the critical-incidents approach holds that there are certain key acts of behavior that make the difference between success and failure. After the incidents are collected they can be ranked in order of frequency and importance and assigned numerical weights. Once scored, they can be as useful for employee development and counseling as for formal appraisals.

Critical Path Method (CPM), a form of project management diagram (precedence diagram or flow chart) which identifies and displays a project's "critical path"—that is, the path of sequential activities which, if delayed, will delay completion of the total project.

See also PRECEDENCE DIAGRAM and PROJECT MANAGEMENT.

critical score: *see* CUTTING SCORE.

crop operations finance corporation, a membership corporation for financing member farmers' crop operations. In order to qualify for tax-exempt status under IRS Code 501(c)(16), a crop operations finance corporation must be organized and operated by a tax-exempt farmers' association or cooperative.

cross-check, procedure by which the National Labor Relations Board or an appropriate state agency compares union authorization cards to an employer's payroll to determine whether a majority of the employees wish union representation. With the employer's consent, such a cross-check can bring union recognition and certification without a formal hearing and election.

cross picketing, picketing by more than one union when each claims to represent the work force.

cross-sectional study, a study that is based on data collected at one point in time, in contrast with a longitudinal study in which data are collected over a period of time.

cross validation, process which seeks to apply the results of one validation study to another. As such, it is a check on the accuracy of the original validation study.

crosswalk, any procedure for expressing the relationship between budgetary data from one set of classifications to another.

crowding out, term that commonly refers to the displacement of private investment expenditures by increases in public expenditures financed by sales of government securities. The extent of the displacement depends on such factors as the responsive-

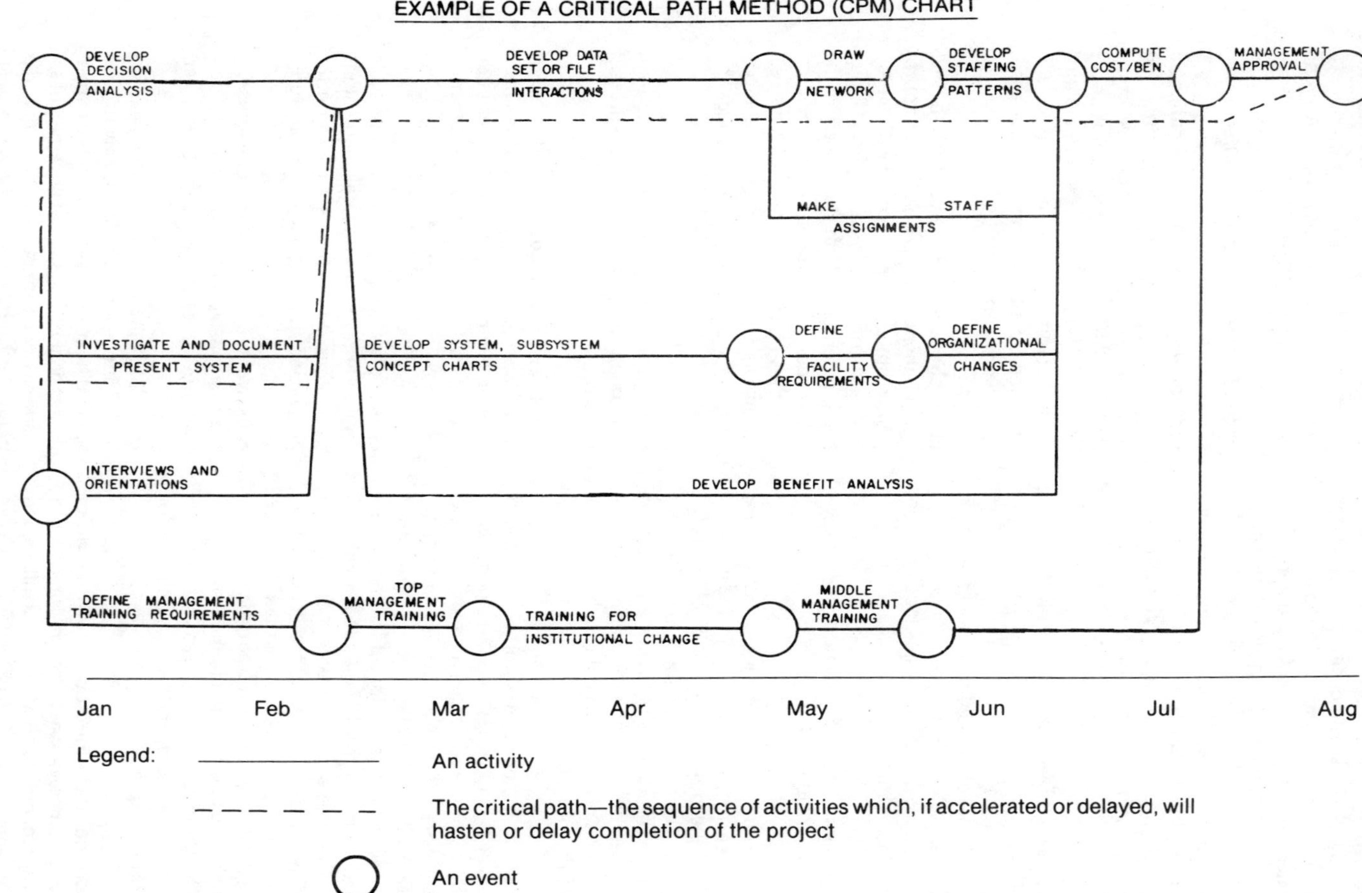
EXAMPLE OF A CRITICAL PATH METHOD (CPM) CHART
DEVELOP DECISION ANALYSIS
DEVELOP DATA SET OR FILE INTERACTIONS
DRAW NETWORK
DEVELOP STAFFING PATTERNS
COMPUTE COST/BEN.
MANAGEMENT APPROVAL
MAKE STAFF ASSIGNMENTS
INVESTIGATE AND DOCUMENT PRESENT SYSTEM
DEVELOP SYSTEM, SUBSYSTEM CONCEPT CHARTS
DEFINE FACILITY REQUIREMENTS
DEFINE ORGANIZATIONAL CHANGES
INTERVIEWS AND ORIENTATIONS
DEVELOP BENEFIT ANALYSIS
DEFINE MANAGEMENT TRAINING REQUIREMENTS
TOP MANAGEMENT TRAINING
TRAINING FOR INSTITUTIONAL CHANGE
MIDDLE MANAGEMENT TRAINING
Jan
Feb
Mar
Apr
May
Jun
Jul
Aug
Legend:
An activity
The critical path—the sequence of activities which, if accelerated or delayed, will hasten or delay completion of the project
An event

ness of private saving and investment to changes in interest rates and the degree to which the Federal Reserve monetizes the increase in public debt.

CRT, a cathode-ray tube; a television-like information display device often used with computers.

crude score: *see* RAW SCORE.

cruelty to animals, prevention, *see* ORGANIZATION, PREVENTION OF CRUELTY.

cruelty to children, prevention, *see* ORGANIZATION, PREVENTION OF CRUELTY.

CSA: *see* COMMUNITY SERVICES ADMINISTRATION.

CSG: *see* COUNCIL OF STATE GOVERNMENTS.

cult, a group bound together by devotion to the same thing, person, or ideal; an extravagant admiration for a principle or person. Typically, a religion and/or its followers which are perceived as invalid, unorthodox, and/or faddish.

cultural, a general term used to mean of, or pertaining to, the arts, humanities, etc.

cultural bias, in the context of employee selection, cultural bias refers to the indirect and incidental (as opposed to direct and deliberate) bias of individuals and instruments making selection decisions. Also, the propensity of a test to reflect favorable or unfavorable effects of certain types of cultural backgrounds.

cultural institution, an organization with primary purposes involving advancing the arts or humanities.

culturally disadvantaged, description of groups that do not have full participation in U.S. society because of low incomes, substandard housing, poor education, and other "atypical" environmental experiences.

culture, organizational: *see* ORGANIZATIONAL CULTURE.

culture-fair test, also called CULTURE-FREE TEST, a test yielding results that are not culturally biased.

cum rights, a stock in a company that comes with rights to buy other stock at a specified price.

cumulative band chart: *see* BAND CURVE CHART.

cumulative frequency, sum of successively added frequencies, usually of test scores.

cumulative frequency chart, graphic presentation of a cumulative frequency distribution which has the frequencies expressed in terms of the number of cases or as a percentage of all cases.

Cumulative List of Organizations (Publication 78), a listing of organizations which are defined as tax-exempt by the Internal Revenue Service. Each entry contains a code for organization type and limit on deductibility. Although this publication is not all-inclusive, it is the most comprehensive, readily available, list of tax-exempt organizations.

cumulative percentage, cumulative frequency expressed as a percentage.

cumulative preferred stock, a class of preferred stock which, if dividends are not paid in any given year or dividend period, entitles the owner to the arrearage in subsequent years.

See also ARREARS and PREFERRED STOCK.

current assets: *see* ASSETS.

current dollar, the dollar value of a good or service in terms of prices current at the time the good or service was sold. This is in contrast to the value of the good or service in constant dollars.

See also CONSTANT DOLLAR.

current fund: *see* GENERAL FUND.

current assets: *see* ASSETS.

current dollar, the dollar value of a good or service in terms of prices current at the time the good or service was sold. This is in contrast to the value of the good or service in constant dollars.
See also CONSTANT DOLLAR.

current fund: *see* GENERAL FUND.

current liabilities: *see* LIABILITIES.

current ratio, current assets (for example, cash and accounts receivable) divided by current liabilities (for example, accounts payable). The current ratio is a commonly used measure of an organization's liquidity.
See also LIQUIDITY.

current services budget: *see* BUDGET, CURRENT SERVICES.

current services estimates, estimated budget requirements for the ensuing fiscal year based on continuation of existing levels of programs or services. These estimates reflect the anticipated costs of continuing programs and activities at present spending levels without policy changes; that is, ignoring the budget impacts of new programs.

current value accounting, an accounting approach which reports assets at their present replacement cost rather than at their original purchase price.
See also ASSETS.

Current Wage Developments, U.S. Bureau of Labor Statistics's monthly report about collective bargaining settlements and unilateral management decisions about wages and benefits.

current year, the fiscal year in progress.

current yield, the annual rate of return from an investment calculated as a percent of the price actually paid for it.

curricular validity, degree to which an examination is representative of the body of knowledge for which it is testing.

curriculum vita: *see* RESUMÉ.

custodial funds, funds received for providing services for another organization (for example, custodial services) and over which the recipient organization has control.

cutback, work force reduction that results in layoffs.

cutback management: *see* MANAGEMENT, CUTBACK.

cutting score, also called CRITICAL SCORE, PASSING SCORE, or PASSING POINT, test score used as an employment requirement. Those at or above such a score are eligible for selection or promotion, whereas those below the score are not.

CYA: *see* COVER YOUR ASS.

cybernetics, the multidisciplinary study of the structures and functions of control and information processing systems in animals and machines. Developed by mathematician Norbert Weiner while working on antiaircraft systems during World War II, the basic concept behind cybernetics is self-regulation—creating a machine or system that can identify a problem, do something about it, and then receive feedback to adjust itself automatically and take further, more effective action.
See also FEEDBACK.

cycle, adaptive-coping: *see* ADAPTIVE-COPING CYCLE.

cyclical unemployment, unemployment caused by a downward trend in the business cycle.

D

Daily Labor Report, Bureau of National Affairs, Inc. report that gives Monday through Friday notification of all significant developments in the labor field. Covers congressional activities, court and NLRB decisions, arbitration, union developments, key contract negotiations, and settlements.

daily rate, basic pay earned by an employee for a standard work day.

daisy wheel, a circular typehead for a letter-quality printer.

data, the plural of datum. A *datum* is a single bit of information.

data bank, also called DATABASE, information stored in a computer system so that any particular item or set of items can be extracted or organized as needed. Data bank (or data base) is also used to refer to any data-storage system.

database management system, computer software that manages, updates, secures, and gains computer access to data banks (or databases). For example, DBase 2.

data bases (library), computer-accessible information files which usually contain bibliographic citations and abstracts that provide quick subject access to journal articles, conference papers, and other original sources. Most academic and some large public libraries provide access to data bases.

data processing, a broad term for manipulation of data—classifying, sorting, putting in, or taking out of a computer; preparing reports, calculating answers, etc.

date of issue, the day a document is formally put or takes effect. For example, the date of issue of an insurance policy is the first day the policy says it will take effect.

date of organization, the date on which an organization is legally organized. For example, a corporation is organized on the date on which its articles of incorporation are filed with the appropriate office of state government. The date of organization is important to nonprofit organizations because filing for tax exemption must be accomplished less than sixteen months after the end of the month in which the date of organization occurred.

datum: *see* DATA.

Davis-Bacon Act of 1931, also called PREVAILING WAGE LAW, federal law passed in 1931 which requires contractors on federal construction projects to pay the rates of pay and fringe benefits that prevail in their geographic areas. Prevailing rates are determined by the Secretary of Labor and must be paid on all federal contracts and subcontracts of $2,000 or more.

day book, also DAYTIMER, a book in which a person records each day's schedule, activities, etc.

day care, a newly emerging employee fringe benefit. More than half of all mothers with children under six are now in the labor force.

day wage, earnings for a set number of hours per day.

daywork, regular day shift that is paid on the basis of time rather than output.

day worker, casual, usually unskilled worker hired by the day.

DBA, doing business as; also Doctor of Business Administration.

dead time, time on the job lost by a worker through no fault of his or her own.

dead work, mining term that refers to required work (removing debris, rocks, etc.) that does not directly produce the material being mined.

***Dean* v. *Gadsden Times Publishing Corp.*,** 412 U.S. 543 (1973), Supreme Court case which upheld an Alabama law providing that an employee called to serve on a jury "shall be entitled to his usual compensation received from such employment less the fee or compensation he received for serving" as a juror.

death and gift taxes, taxes imposed on transfer of property at death, in contemplation of death, or as a gift.

death benefit, benefit provided under a pension plan that is paid to an employee's survivors or estate. Payments may be made in monthly installments or in a lump sum.

debenture, a corporation's obligation to pay money (usually in the form of a note or a bond) that is not secured (backed up) by any specific property. The common use of the word includes only long-term bonds.

See also BOND and LIABILITIES.

debits and credits, the basic entries in a double entry accounting system. Each transaction is entered in two places; each debit and its matching credit(s) should equal zero. If they do not, the accounting system is out of balance. A debit is usually abbreviated "DR" and a credit "CR."

All accounts are categorized as either assets, liabilities, fund balances, income, or expenses. Each category of accounts is defined as carrying a debit or a credit balance. Each accounting transaction changes an account balance according to a basic formula.

See also:

ACCOUNTING CYCLE
ACCOUNTING SYSTEM
ASSETS
BOOKKEEPING
LIABILITIES

debt, a sum of money owned.

debt, nonguaranteed, long-term debt payable solely from pledged specific sources—*e.g.*, from earnings of revenue-producing activities (university and college dormitories, toll highways and bridges, electric power projects, etc.). Includes only debt that does not constitute an obligation against any other resources if the pledged sources are insufficient.

debt-equity ratio, an accounting ratio obtained by dividing total debt by fund balances.

A CHART FOR UNDERSTANDING DEBITS AND CREDITS

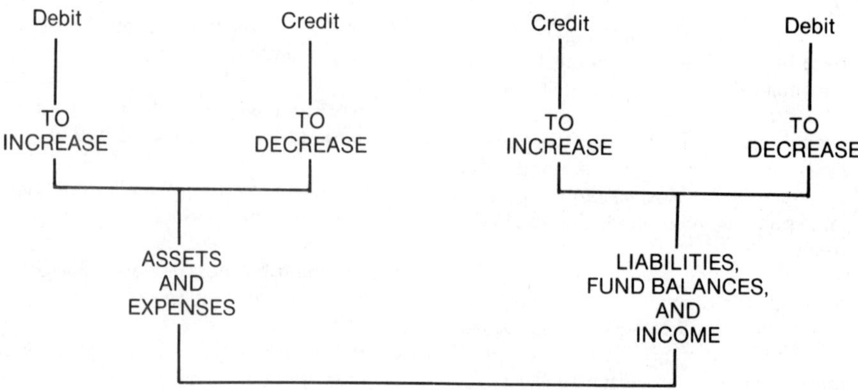

debt-financed income, income generated from debt-financed real or personal property that is owned for the purpose of generating income. The debt must have been incurred in order to acquire or improve the income-generating property, but does not need to have been incurred prior to acquiring or improving it. Debt-financed income is important in determining unrelated business income.

See also UNRELATED BUSINESS INCOME.

debt financing, paying for programs or capital improvements by borrowing.

debtor, a person or organization that owes money.

debt outstanding, all debt obligations remaining unpaid on the date specified.

debt service, regular payments of principal, interest, and other costs (such as insurance) made to pay off a financial obligation.

debugging, process of detecting, locating, and removing mistakes or imperfections from a computer program or any new system.

decentralization, *see* CENTRALIZATION.

decertification: *see* CERTIFICATION.

decile, division that contains one tenth of whatever is being divided.

decision analysis, the systematic analysis of alternative actions as the basis for making choices among them.

decision making, process of selecting the most desirable course of action from among alternatives. In a larger sense, decision making is the total process by which managers act to achieve organizational goals.

decision packages, mechanisms used in zero-base budgeting to look at the effects on programmatic resource requirements, products, and levels of performance of alternative levels of funding.

See also CONSOLIDATED DECISION PACKAGES and ZERO BASE BUDGETING.

Henry Kissinger on Decision Making

I have seen it happen more often than not that when one asks for choices one is always given three: two absurd ones and the preferred one. And the experienced bureaucrat, which I am slowly becoming, can usually tell the preferred one because it is almost always the one that is typed in the middle.

Source: The New York Times Magazine (October 28, 1973), p. 93.

decision rule, any directive established to make decisions in the face of uncertainty. For example, a payroll office might be given a decision rule to deduct one hour's pay from an employee's wages for each lateness that exceeds ten minutes but is less than one hour.

decision table, a tabular presentation of the various factors associated with, as well as the decision options for, a given problem.

decision theory, a body of knowledge concerned with the nature and processes of decision making. Decision theory abstracts given situations into a more structured problem which calls for the decision maker to deal with the situation by an objective judgment. Frequently dependent upon quantitative analysis, decision theory is also called *statistical decision theory* and *Bayesian decision theory*.

decision tree, graphic method of presenting various decisional alternatives so that the various risks, information needs, and courses of action are visually available to the decision maker. The various decisional alternatives are displayed in the form of a tree with nodes and branches. Each branch represents an alternative course of action or decision, which leads to a node, which represents an event. Thus, a decision tree shows both the different courses of action available as well as their possible outcomes. According to John F. Magee, in "Decision Trees for Decision Making," *Harvard Business Review* (July-August 1964), making a decision tree requires management to

1. identify the points of decision and alternatives available at each point;
2. identify the points of uncertainty and the type or range of alternative outcomes at each point;
3. estimate the values needed to make the analysis, especially the probabilities of different events or results of action and the costs and gains of various events and actions; and
4. analyze the alternative values to choose a course.

declaration, an announcement of a set-aside money. For example, a declaration of estimated tax is a statement and set-aside of money required by the IRS of persons who have income from which taxes have not been withheld, and a declaration of dividends is a corporation's setting aside part of its profits to pay stockholders.

declaration of trust, a trust agreement; articles of organization for a trust.

See also ARTICLES OF ORGANIZATION and CONTROLLING INSTRUMENTS.

declaratory judgment, a formal or express statement of opinion or judgment. For example, the Tax Reform Act of 1976 provides for declaratory judgments about an organization's tax-exempt status under certain circumstances.

declining balance, the decreasing amount owed on a debt as periodic payments are made.

declining-block pricing, the pricing of a service (*e.g.*, electricity) so that its unit price decreases as the consumption level increases.

deconstitutionalization, tendency of the U.S. Supreme Court to refuse to hear cases even though they may involve constitutional questions.

decruitment, slang term for the process of recycling older middle- and top-level managers into lower-level, lower-paying positions. The concept was pioneered in Denmark, where some employers freeze promotions for managers at age fifty and start decruiting them at age sixty.

dedicated asset: *see* ASSET, DEDICATED.

dedication of assets requirement, one element of the organizational test for tax exemption as a charitable organization. In the view of the IRS, if a charitable organization is dissolved, its assets should continue to be used for a charitable purpose.

See also ASSET, DEDICATED.

deductible, the amount of loss or expense that must be incurred by an insured or otherwise covered individual before an insurer will assume any liability for all or part of the remaining cost of covered services. Deductibles may be either fixed dollar amounts or the value of specified services (such as two days of hospital care or one physician visit); also, amounts that can be subtracted from income for calculating taxes owed.

deductible charitable contribution, a contribution or gift to a tax-exempt organization which, under tax laws and IRS rules, can be subtracted from income when calculating taxes owed. Under current law and rules, deductions for contributions are limited to a percentage of Adjusted Gross Income (AGI).

See also ADJUSTED GROSS INCOME.

deduction (workplace), any amount for any reason that is withheld from an employee's pay and credited toward a legitimate purpose such as taxes, insurance, United Way, etc.

deed, a document by which one person or organization transfers the legal ownership of land (and what is on it) to another person or organization.

deed of trust, a document that creates a trust; also, a document by which an organization or person transfers ownership of land to an independent trustee to be held until a debt on the land (a mortgage) is paid off.

defalcation, failure of a person to account for money trusted to his of her care. There is the assumption that the money was misused.

default, failure to pay legal debts.

defensive program evaluation: *see* PROGRAM EVALUATION.

deferred annuity, annuity that does not start until after a specified period or until the annuitant reaches a specified age.

deferred compensation, withholding of a portion of current earnings until a later time, usually retirement, when the receiver would likely be in a lower income tax bracket.

deferred full vesting, pension plan that provides that an employee retains rights to accrued benefits if he or she is terminated after a specified age and/or after he or she completes a specified period of service in the organization.

deferred giving, giving which occurs after the death of the donor. There are many forms and arrangements for deferred giving including gift annuities, pooled income funds, life estate contracts, short-term charitable trusts, revocable charitable trusts, charitable remainder annuity trusts, and charitable remainder unitrusts.

See also DEFERRED GIVING PROGRAM
LIFE INCOME GIFTS

deferred giving program, a planned development program for encouraging deferred giving, usually for the purpose of increasing an organization's endowment. Deferred giving programs range from relatively simple attempts to secure bequests to more polished and complex programs involving, for example, living trusts.

See also:
BEQUEST
ENDOWMENT
LIVING TRUST
TRUST

deferred graded vesting, pension plan that provides that an employee acquires a right to a specified percentage of accrued benefits if and when he or she meets the participation requirements stipulated by the plan.

deferred life annuity, annuity that becomes effective at a specified future date. If death occurs before the specified date, no benefits are paid. Once the annuity has started, it continues only for the life of the insured.

deferred stock, stock in a company on which no dividends are to be paid until after a certain other class of stock has received its dividends.

deferred wage increase, negotiated pay increase that does not become effective until a specified future date.

deficit, amount by which an organization's expenditures exceed its revenues.

defined benefit plan, a pension plan which includes a formula for calculating retirement benefits (such as a specified percent of earnings or flat dollar amount per year of service) and obligates the employer to provide the benefits so determined. Therefore, employer contributions are not fixed, but are whatever is needed, together with earnings of pension fund investments, to finance the required benefits.

defined contribution plan, a pension plan that obligates the employer to contribute money to a pension fund according to a formula (such as a specified percent of earnings). Benefits are not fixed, but depend on the amount of employer contributions and the earnings of pension fund investments.

deflation: see INFLATION.

DeFunis* v. *Odegaard, 416 U.S. 312 (1974), U.S. Supreme Court case concerning a white male who was denied admission to law school at the same time minority applicants with lesser academic credentials were accepted. DeFunis challenged the school's action on the grounds that it denied him equal protection of the laws in violation of the Fourteenth Amendment. He was successful in local court and was admitted. On appeal, the school won a reversal in the state supreme court. Nevertheless, DeFunis remained in law school pending further action by the U.S. Supreme Court. As the nation awaited a definitive resolution of the issue of reverse discrimination, the Supreme Court sought to avoid the problem. Since DeFunis had completed all but his last quarter of law school and was not in danger of being denied his diploma no matter what was decided, a majority of the justices seized upon this fact and declared that the case was consequently moot—that it was beyond the court's power to render decisions on hypothetical matters of only potential constitutional substance.

See also REGENTS OF THE UNIVERSITY OF CALIFORNIA V. ALLEN BAKKE and REVERSE DISCRIMINATION.

degree of freedom (statistics), the extent to which a statistic may vary, usually depending on the number of independent variables affecting it.

See also INDEPENDENT VARIABLE.

degrees, gradations used in the point-rating method of job evaluation to differentiate among job factors.

dehiring, generally, any means of encouraging a marginal or unsatisfactory employee to quit as an alternative to being fired. This face-saving technique allows an organization to (1) avoid the distasteful aftermath of firing an employee, (2) avoid the implication that someone made a mistake in hiring the employee, (3) avoid the adverse effect of the public thinking that the organization is not a secure place in which to be employed, and (4) protect the feelings of the employee involved.

deinstitutionalization, removal of individuals from institutional settings and returning them to community life.

delegate, a person who is chosen to represent another person, a group, or an organization; for example, a delegate to a national organization's annual convention.

delegation, designating or appointing of a person with the power to act as one's representative or agent in specified matters. A delegation of authority in an organizational sense may be implied in statements of responsibility for functional entities or group endeavors but can also be documented by other methods. Certain delegations that are granted to a single individual may be restricted as to any further redelegations (*e.g.*, it could restrict a senior clerk from delegating some disagreeable task that clerk was responsible for to a junior clerk). Delegation of authority begins at the executive level and filters down through an organization to workers themselves, who must have enough authority to make decisions called for in their daily tasks.

delinquency, failure, omission, or violation of duties; misconduct. For example, a debt that has fallen behind in payment is called a delinquency.

delinquent, overdue and unpaid; also, willfully and intentionally failing to carry out an obligation.

delphi method, a procedure for forecasting specific technological and social events. Experts are asked to give their best judgment as to the probability of a specific event occurring. The results are collated and then returned to the original experts for their perusal along with an opportunity to revise their own predictions. Revised estimates with supporting arguments are then recorded and recirculated again and again; in theory, the feedback always narrows the range of answers. In the end, a group prophecy will have been arrived at without the possibility of distortion from face-to-face contact, leadership influences, or the pressures of group dynamics.

EXAMPLE OF A SERIES OF DELPHI PROBES

DELPHI PROBE I

PLEASE PROVIDE ONE OR MORE RESPONSES TO THE FOLLOWING SENTENCE:

In the decade ahead, the (insert name of the organization) should concentrate its energies and resources on solving the problems of . . .

DELPHI PROBE II

In response to DELPHI probe #1, the following suggestions were received. In the space provided at the left of each problem (or goal) statement, code one of the following six values according to your qualitative judgment:

Value	
6	Strongly recommend concentration on solving
5	Recommend concentration on solving
4	Recommend concentration as secondary concern
3	No strong feelings either way / unsure
2	Do not recommend concentration on solving
1	Strongly against concentration on solving

Value	Problem (or Goal) Statement
______	1.
______	2.
______	3.
•	•
•	•
______	20.

DELPHI PROBE III

Shown below on the DELPHI tabulation form are the sums and ranks of each problem as determined on the previous probe. Fourteen problems have been classified as primary and secondary. In the space provided at the left of each problem statement, code one of the following six values according to your judgment. In the space provided at the right of each statement, indicate your reason, if you changed your response.

Value	
6	Strongly recommend concentration on solving
5	Recommend concentration on solving
4	Recommend concentration as secondary concern
3	No strong feelings either way / unsure
2	Do not recommend concentration on solving
1	Strongly against concentration on solving

Value	*Problem Statement*	*Reason for Change*
______	1.	______
______	2.	______
______	3.	______
______	4.	______

de minimus, short form of *de minimus non curat lex:* Latin for "the law does not bother with trifles."

de minimis rule, an exception to the excess business holdings limitation which permits a foundation to own two percent or less of a business enterprise.

demise, a lease; also, a transfer of property; also, death.

democratize, the concept of equalizing the tax benefits accruing to charitable donors who are in different tax brackets. Increased use of tax credits rather than charitable deductions is a frequently cited way to democratize the income tax system.

See also:
EQUITY (TAX)
TAX CREDIT
TAX EXPENDITURES

demographics, statistics showing an area's population characteristics such as age, income, education, etc.

Demonstration Cities and Metropolitan Development Act of 1966: *see* MODEL CITIES PROGRAM.

demotion, reassignment of an employee to a job of lower status, responsibility, and pay. There are three basic kinds of demotions; (1) *voluntary demotion,* usually the result of a reduction in force—the employee takes a job of lower status and pay rather than being laid off; (2) *involuntary demotion* results from a worker's inability to perform adequately on the job; (3) *disciplinary demotion* usually takes place after an employee has been repeatedly warned to stop some kind of misconduct or disruptive behavior.

dental plan, also called DENTAL INSURANCE, group insurance program, either contributory or noncontributory, that pays for some portion of dental services for an employee and his/her family.

See also SUPPLEMENTAL MEDICAL INSURANCE.

departmental seniority, also called UNIT SENIORITY, seniority based on years of service in a particular subsection of a larger organization as opposed to seniority based simply on total years of service to the larger organization.

dependent, an organization or person who relies on another for a significant portion of support; sometimes used to mean a dependent blood relative.

See also SUPPORT.

dependent variable, factor in an experimental relationship which has or shows variation that is hypothesized to be caused by an independent factor or variable.

depletion allowance, tax credit sometimes granted to owners of exhaustible natural resources.

deposit, (as a verb) to place money for safekeeping, for example, in a bank; also, a pledge, as in to *make a deposit* to hold a purchase; (as a noun) money placed for safekeeping or placed as a pledge.

deposit ceiling rate of interest, the maximum interest rate that can be paid on savings and time deposits at federally insured commercial banks, mutual savings banks, savings and loan associations, and credit unions. Deposit interest rate ceilings are being phased out under the oversight of the Depository Institutions Deregulation Committee.

deposition, the process of taking a witness's sworn testimony out of court; also, the written record of a witness's sworn testimony.

depreciation, also DEPRECIATION EXPENSE, STRAIGHT-LINE DEPRECIATION, and ACCELERATED DEPRECIATION, the cost of wear and tear on assets which are expected to last more than one year (fixed assets), such as buildings, vehicles, and equipment. Depreciation is not an out-of-pocket cost; rather, it is shown only in financial records. However, depreciation expenses are very important even to tax-exempt organizations, because they reflect the cost of services provided and, if there is a surplus, they provide the "source of funds" to replace worn out or obsolete fixed assets (in other words, non-spent moneys, because they are non-cash expenses). For accounting purposes, fixed assets should be depreciated even if the organization did not pay for them if they will need to be replaced in the future.

Straight line depreciation expense is computed by (a) subtracting the amount that may reasonably be expected to be realized from sale of the item at the end of its useful life (that is, its trade-in value, scrap value, or salvage value) from its purchase price, and (b) dividing the difference by the number of years or annual units (for example, miles driven) of its useful life.

Accelerated depreciation methods are used primarily by for-profit corporations for tax deduction/rapid capital accumulation purposes. Assets are depreciated more rapidly during the early years of their useful life and more slowly during their later years.

See also ACCUMULATED DEPRECIATION.

depth interview, a relatively unstructured research technique in which a person is encouraged to speak freely about his or her

EXAMPLE OF DEPRECIATION

A radio is purchased for $2,000. It should be usable for about five years, and we should be able to get $50 for it when we are done with it (scrap value).

1. Subtract the scrap value from the purchase price.	$2,000.00 (50.00)
	$ 1950.00
2. Divide $1,950.00 by 5 years	1,950.00 5
(EQUALS) Annual Depreciation Expense	$390.00

opinions of a product, a problem, a social issue, etc.

derived score, any test score that is obtained after some statistical treatment or manipulation of the raw score.

descriptive average, estimate of a mean based upon incomplete data.

descriptive statistics, statistics that describe the characteristics of a sample or the relationship among variables in a sample. Descriptive statistics do not attempt to move beyond the description of observations to make inferences about the population from which the sample was drawn.

See also INFERENTIAL STATISTICS.

designated fund, a type of fund used to continue support to designated charitable organizations after a person dies. Designated funds are often found in and managed by community foundations which send donations to the designated recipient charities. See also COMMUNITY FOUNDATION.

desk audit, also called JOB AUDIT, review of the duties and responsibilities of a position through an interview with the incumbent and/or the incumbent's supervisor made at the employee's desk or regular place of work.

See also POSITION CLASSIFICATION.

desk audit (IRS), the review of a federal tax return by an IRS employee who needs no additional information from the taxpaying individual.

destitute, completely poverty-stricken.

detail, temporary assignment of an employee to a different position for a specified period with the assumption that the employee will return to normal duties at the end of the detail.

determination letter, also RULING LETTER, a letter issued by the Internal Revenue Service defining an organization's tax-exempt status.

See also INTERNAL REVENUE SERVICE.

development, the planned promotion of understanding, participation, and support among potential donors. Usually *development* is used broadly and is considered to consist of three major, distinct groups of activities which need to be coordinated if development is to be effective: planning, public relations, and fund-raising.

development, moral: *see* MORAL DEVELOPMENT.

development director, a person who manages a development program. In larger nonprofit organizations, the development director position may be filled by a full-time person with a supporting staff; in smaller nonprofit organizations, the functions typically are performed on a part-time basis, for example, by the executive director.

deviation, amount by which a score differs from a reference value such as the mean or the norm.

dexterity test, also called PSYCHOMOTOR TEST, any testing device that seeks to determine the motor/mechanical skills of an individual.

DHHS: *see* HEALTH AND HUMAN SERVICES, DEPARTMENT OF.

diagnostic test, any testing device that is primarily designed to identify the nature and/or source of an individual's disabilities.

dialectical organization, postbureaucratic form of organization designed to be responsive to clientele needs; *dialectical* refers to the permanent state of tension between the tendency toward bureaucratization and the tendency toward responsiveness to clients, a tension the organization uses to continually renew itself.

dichotomy: *see* BINOMIAL VARIABLE.

dicta, in its most common usage, that portion of the opinion of a judge that is not the essence of the judge's decision. In the context of arbitration, dicta becomes any opinion or recommendation an arbitrator expresses in making an award that is not necessarily essential to the resolution of the dispute.

***Dictionary of Occupational Titles* (DOT),** a comprehensive body of standardized occupational information for purposes of job placement, employment counseling, and occupational career guidance. Now in its fourth edition, the DOT includes standardized and comprehensive descriptions of job duties and related information for 20,000 occupations; covers nearly all jobs in the U.S. economy; groups occupations into a systematic occupational classification structure based on interrelationships of job tasks and requirements; and is designed as a job placement tool to facilitate matching job requirements and worker skills. *See* Employment and Training Administration, U.S. Department of Labor, *Dictionary of Occupational Titles* (Washington, D.C.: Government Printing Office, 4th ed., 1977).

differential, displacement: *see* DISPLACEMENT DIFFERENTIAL.

differential piece work, also DIFFERENTIAL PIECE RATE, wage program in which the money rate per piece is determined by the total number of pieces produced over a time period—usually a day.

differentials, increases in wage rates because of shift work, or other conditions generally considered to be undesirable.
See also the following entries:
NIGHT PREMIUM
SKILL DIFFERENTIAL
WAGE DIFFERENTIALS

differential user charge, any user charge scaled to meet the requirements of different kinds of customers, levels of usage, time or season of use, etc.

differential validation, also called DIFFERENTIAL PREDICTION, assumption that different tests or test scores might predict differently for different groups. Some social groups, because of a variety of sociological factors, tend to score lower (higher) than other groups on the same test.

difficulty index, any of a variety of indexes used to indicate the difficulty of a test question. The percent of some specified group, such as students of a given age or grade, who answer an item correctly is an example of such an index.

diffusion index, a statistical measure of the overall behavior of a group of economic time series. It indicates the percentage of series expanding in the selected group. If one half of the series in the group are rising over a given time span, the diffusion index value equals 50. The limits of a diffusion index are 0 and 100. As an analytical measure, the diffusion index is helpful in indicating the spread of economic movements from one industry to another and from one economic process to another.

diffusion theory of taxation, theory that the real burden of an increase in taxes of any kind is eventually distributed throughout the population because of price changes.

digital, data represented by discrete individual numbers rather than as a continuous flow of information. The opposite of *analog*.

Dillon's Rule, criteria developed by state courts to determine the nature and extent of powers granted to municipal corporations. It is a very strict and limiting rule, stating that municipal corporations have only those powers (1) expressly granted in the charter; (2) necessarily or fairly implied by or incidental to the express powers; and (3) essential to the declared purposes of the corporation. "Any fair, reasonable, substantial doubt" about a power is to result in denying that power to the corporation. The rule was formulated by John F. Dillon in his *Commentaries on the Law of Municipal Corporations* (Boston: Little, Brown, 5th ed., 1911). In some states the rule has been relaxed, especially in dealing with home rule cities.

See also MUNICIPAL CORPORATION.

diminishing marginal utility of income, also ABILITY TO PAY PRINCIPLE OF TAXATION, the principle that suggests that the marginal value of an additional dollar of income to a rich person is less than to a poor person. This concept is a mainstay of progressive taxation because it suggests that graduated income taxes will have less of a negative effect on wealthier members of the community than on those with less wealth. Proportionally larger tax payments by those with higher incomes recognize the diminishing marginal utility of income.

direct comparison, a form of evaluation measure obtained by measuring results achieved against a predetermined standard or norm.

direct cost: *see* COST, DIRECT.

directed interview, also NONDIRECTIVE INTERVIEW, session where the interviewer is in full control of the interview content, typically soliciting answers to a variety of specific questions. In the *nondirective interview,* in contrast, it is more the responsibility of the interviewee to determine the subjects to be discussed.

directing federal funds, the concept that people in higher tax brackets, in effect, direct government funds to their own desired purposes because government "subsidizes" deductible charitable contributions.

See also:

EQUITY
TAX CREDIT
TAX EXPENDITURES

direct labor, also INDIRECT LABOR, work performed on a product that is a specific contribution to its completion. *Indirect labor* consists of all overhead and support activities that do not contribute directly to the completion of a product.

Direct Mail Advertising Association (DMAA), an association of organizations involved in advertising and fund-raising through direct mail. The Association publishes the *Direct Mail Manual* for member organizations.

direct mail campaign, a form of fund-raising which involves mailing large numbers of letters to potential donors asking for financial support. Most development officers contend that direct mail campaigns should be ongoing efforts rather than one-time appeals.

See also DEVELOPMENT and FUND-RAISING.

SUGGESTIONS FOR A DIRECT MAIL FUND-RAISING LETTER

A. The Letter
1. First two paragraphs are the most important.
2. Repeat request for money several times.
3. Make the letter as "person-to-person" as possible.
4. Do something in the letter to get their attention.
5. Have the "you's" in the letter outnumber the "we's."
6. Describe the work the money will accomplish.
7. Demonstrate the need for the money.
8. Touch their hearts.
9. Ask them to send a specific amount.
10. Remember to write from the donor's perspective.

11. Long, wordy letters for national appeals, shorter letters for local appeals.
12. Be up front on costs.
13. Introduce the reader to the rest of the package in the letter.
14. Draw their attention to the options for contributing.
15. Stress the importance of acting now.

B. The Paper
1. Soft color
2. Textured stock
3. Not expensive paper
4. Matte finish
5. 60 to 70 lb.

C. The Ink
1. High contrast with the paper
2. No more than two colors
3. The letter should look personally typed.
4. Use unjustified margins.

D. The Type
1. Large and easy to read
2. Use serif type
3. No more than 350 words per page

E. The Return Device
1. Easy to fill out
2. Self-addressed return envelope
3. Stamped—especially if it is a new mailing list

F. The Outside Envelope
1. Avoid junk mail look
2. Keep colors the same as the letter.
3. Use a stamp rather than a meter.
4. Keep the address as personal as possible.
5. Consider using a "teaser line" on the envelope.

director, one member of the board of directors, the body which—under an organization's constitution and bylaws—controls and governs the affairs of the organization. Many charitable organizations use *trustee* and *board of trustees* rather than director and board of directors. In this context, there is no meaningful difference between the two.

See also
BOARD OF DIRECTORS
BOARD OF TRUSTEES
TRUSTEE

directorates, interlocking, organizations with substantial overlapping membership on their boards of directors.

director of personnel: *see* PERSONNEL DIRECTOR.

directors, board of: *see* BOARD OF DIRECTORS.

direct placement, also PRIVATE PLACEMENT, when a company sells its stock or bonds directly to a buyer rather than to the public through underwriters.

direct relief: *see* RELIEF.

direct solicitation (of funds), a form of fund-raising which involves asking individuals, businesses, fraternal organizations, and other groups directly for contributions to support a nonprofit organization. In order for a direct solicitation to be effective, the solicitations should be made in person by well-prepared solicitors (that is, they know why the money is being solicited, know something about the person or organization being solicited, can answer basic questions about the soliciting organization, and have rehearsed both the presentation and answers to expected questions).

See also FUND-RAISING.

EFFECTIVENESS OF DIFFERENT APPROACHES TO DIRECT SOLICITATIONS OF FUNDS

Most Effective

- Personal solicitation by a team
- Personal solicitation by one person
- Personal letter with a telephone call
- Personal letter with no call
- Personal phone call with a follow-up letter
- Personal phone call without a follow-up letter
- Impersonal letter—mass-produced
- Impersonal phone call

Least Effective

direct tax, also INDIRECT TAX, tax paid to a government directly by a taxpayer. An *indirect tax (e.g.*, a sales tax) is paid to a third party who in turn pays it to a government.

direct writer, an insurance agent who generally deals with only one insurance company.

disability compensation, compensation made to disabled employees.

disability insurance, insurance designed to compensate individuals who lose wages because of illness or injuries.

disability retirement, retirement caused by a physical inability to perform on the job.

disabled veteran, veteran of the armed services who has a service-connected disability and is rated ten percent or more disabled by the Veterans Administration.
See also VETERANS PREFERENCE.

disadvantaged, culturally: *see* CULTURALLY DISADVANTAGED.

disadvantaged workers, workers who are usually unemployed or underemployed and either a member of a minority group, handicapped, or over forty-five years of age. They tend to have lower education rates and higher criminal arrest rates than the rest of the population.

disburse, to pay out money, for example, for expenses incurred.

disbursements, payments. Gross disbursements represent the amount of checks issued, cash, or other payments made, less refunds received. Net disbursements represent gross disbursements less income collected and credited to the appropriate account, such as amounts received for goods and services provided.

disc: *see* DISK.

discharge: *see* DISMISSAL.

discharge, discriminatory: *see* DISCRIMINATORY DISCHARGE.

discharge warning, formal notice to an employee that he or she will be discharged if unsatisfactory work behavior continues.

disciplinary action, any action short of dismissal taken by an employer against an employee for a violation of policy.

disciplinary demotion: *see* DEMOTION.

disciplinary fine, fine that a union or professional association may levy against a member for violating a provision of its bylaws.

disciplinary layoff, suspension of an employee as punishment for violating some rule or policy.

discipline: *see* the following entries:
ADMONITION
ADVERSE ACTION
DISCIPLINARY ACTION
PREVENTIVE DISCIPLINE
REPRIMAND
SLIDE-RULE DISCIPLINE

discipline clause, provision of a collective bargaining agreement that stipulates the means for disciplining workers who violate management or union rules.

discount, a deduction or lowering of an amount of money; for example, a lower price; also, paying interest in advance.

discount factor: see BLOCKAGE DISCOUNTING.

discounting, a decision analysis process which is used when alternative programs (or capital expenditures) have different costs and possibly dollar benefits in different years. Discounting brings dollar values (of costs and benefits) to a common point in time in order to allow direct comparison between or among the alternatives.

EXAMPLE OF DISCOUNTING

Yr.	Program A	Program B
0	$100,000	-0-
1	10,000	$25,000
2	10,000	25,000
3	10,000	25,000
4	10,000	25,000
5	60,000	60,000
6	15,000	20,000
7	15,000	20,000
8	15,000	20,000
9	15,000	20,000
10	15,000	20,000

Source: R. L. Subry, J. S. Ott, C. J. Peterson, and J. W. Sawyer, *Program Planning and Analysis* (Denver, Colo.: Applied Management Corporation, 1977, 1982).

In the example, it would be erroneous to simply add the costs for each alternative and compare the total costs. The $100,000 in total costs for years six through ten for alternative B do not have the same value as the $100,000 in initial costs for alternative A because they occur at different times.

See also PRESENT WORTH.

discount rate, the percentage of the face value of a commercial loan note, mortgage, etc. that is deducted from the payment by a buyer (such as a bank); also the interest rate that a commercial bank pays when it borrows from a Federal Reserve Bank. The discount rate is one of the tools of monetary policy used by the Federal Reserve System. The Federal Reserve customarily raises or lowers the discount rate to signal a shift toward restraining or easing its money and credit policy.

discouraged workers, also called HIDDEN UNEMPLOYED, persons who want to work but are not seeking employment because of a belief that such an effort would be fruitless.

discrete variable, a variable that can be expressed only as a whole number, such as the number of people in a family.

discretionary grant: *see* GRANT.

discriminant validity, evidence that a measure of a construct is indeed measuring that construct.

discrimination, in the context of employment, the failure to treat equals equally. Whether deliberate or unintentional, any action that has the effect of limiting employment and advancement opportunities because of an individual's sex, race, color, age, national origin, religion, physical handicap, or other irrelevant criteria is discrimination. Because of the EEO and civil rights legislation of recent years, individuals aggrieved by unlawful discrimination now have a variety of administrative and judicial remedies open to them. Employment discrimination has its origins in the less genteel concept of bigotry.

See also the following entries:

AGE DISCRIMINATION
CIVIL RIGHTS ACT OF 1964
EQUAL EMPLOYMENT OPPORTUNITY
IMPACT THEORY OF DISCRIMINATION
INSTITUTIONAL DISCRIMINATION
MCDONNELL DOUGLAS CORP. V. GREEN
NATIONAL ORIGIN DISCRIMINATION
RELIGIOUS DISCRIMINATION
REVERSE DISCRIMINATION
RIGHTFUL PLACE
SEX DISCRIMINATION
SYSTEMIC DISCRIMINATION
THIRD-PARTY ALLEGATIONS OF DISCRIMINATION
UNFAIR LABOR PRACTICES (EMPLOYERS)

discrimination index, any of a variety of indexes used to indicate the extent to which a test item differentiates among examinees with respect to some criterion (such as the test as a whole).

discriminatory discharge, dismissal of an employee for union activity. This is an unfair labor practice.

disinterested, impartial; not biased or prejudiced; not affected personally or financially by the outcome. (However, the word does not mean "uninterested" nor "lacking an opinion.")

disk, also DISKETTE, a rotating, circular, magnetic, random access storage device for computer data. A diskette is a soft plastic or "floppy" disk. In contrast with a disk, a computer tape is a storage device which is accessed serially (like a tape recorder).

disk drive, the part of a computer system that holds and "plays" disks much like a record player. A disk drive allows random access to information on a disk.

disk operating system (DOS), a set of programs stored on a disk that the computer reads in order to know how to run application programs (such as an accounts payable program, a mailing list, a spread sheet, etc.).

dismissal, also called DISCHARGE, management's removal of an employee from employment.

dismissal pay: *see* SEVERANCE PAY.

disparate effect, tendency of an employment screening device or criteria to limit the appointment opportunities of women and minorities at a greater rate than for nonminority males.

dispersion, the distribution of values around a central value such as a mean.

displaced homemaker, usually a woman who has been caring for a family and has lost her means of support through divorce, separation, death, or the disabling of a spouse and has only the briefest work experience outside the home.

displacement differential, compensation equal to the difference between an employee's regular pay and the rate of a temporary assignment caused by layoff or technological displacement. Such differentials are usually available only for a limited time.

disposable personal income, the net income available to persons for consumption, saving, or giving.

disqualified person, a person who is not permitted to conduct transactions with a tax-exempt organization in order to prevent self-dealing. Disqualified persons include insiders—for example, directors, trustees, members, officers, or shareholders of the organization—and substantial contributors. Prohibitions against transactions between disqualified persons and tax-exempt organizations are central to preventing private inurement.

See also:
PRIVATE INUREMENT
SELF-DEALING
TAX REFORM ACT OF 1969

distractors, also called FOILS, in multiple-choice examinations, the incorrect alternatives.

distributable amount, the amount a private foundation must distribute each year for charitable purposes. This amount is currently five percent of the foundation's assets.

See also:
PAYOUT
PRIVATE FOUNDATION
PUBLICLY SUPPORTED ORGANIZATION

distribution, bimodal: *see* BIMODAL DISTRIBUTION.

distribution, equity: *see* EQUITY DISTRIBUTION.

distribution, frequency: *see* FREQUENCY DISTRIBUTION.

distribution, qualifying: *see* QUALIFYING DISTRIBUTION.

distribution of income: *see* DISTRIBUTABLE AMOUNT.

district, subdivision of many different types of areas (such as national nonprofit organizations, states, or counties) for judicial, political, or administrative purposes. *Districting* is the process of drawing a district's boundary lines.

district council, a level of labor organization below the national union but above the locals. The district council is composed of local unions in a particular industry within a limited geographic area.

district court,- also called FEDERAL DISTRICT COURT and U.S. DISTRICT COURT, court of original jurisdiction for most federal cases. This is the only federal court that holds trials where juries and witnesses are used. Each state has at least one district court.

districting: *see* DISTRICT.

diversification, the process of spreading one's investments (for example, bank accounts, shares of stock, bonds, etc.), usually for the purpose of reducing the risk of one investment suddenly losing value; also, an organization expanding its scope of activities or going into new ventures.

dividend, a payment per share of a corporation's stock. There are many forms of dividends; for example, cumulative dividends, asset dividends, stock dividends, etc.

dividend reinvestment plan, a plan in which a corporation, at the request of a stockholder, automatically reinvests stock dividends in additional shares of the corporation's stock.

division of labor, also called FACTORY SYSTEM, production process that has individual workers specializing in the varying aspects of a larger task. The most famous and influential statement on the economic rationale of the factory system is found in Adam Smith's *The Wealth of Nations* (1776).

DMMA: *see* DIRECT MAIL ADVERTISING ASSOCIATION.

dock, deduct a part of an employee's wages as a penalty for tardiness, absenteeism, breakage, etc.

doctrine, legal principle or rule.

document and stock transfer taxes, taxes on the recording, registering, and transfer of documents such as mortgages, deeds, and securities.

See also TAXATION.

DOE: *see* EDUCATION, DEPARTMENT OF.

do-gooders, also GOO-GOOS, derisive terms for social and political reformers. Goo-Goos stood for good government.

DOI: *see* INTERIOR, DEPARTMENT OF THE.

DOL: *see* LABOR, DEPARTMENT OF.

domestic fraternal society, an association similar to a fraternal beneficiary society but which does not pay life, sickness, accident, or other insurance-type benefits to its members or their beneficiaries. Domestic fraternal societies may qualify for tax-exempt status under IRS Code 501 (c) (10).

domestic organization, an organization located and operating solely in the United States.

donated services, those contributed services which, if not contributed, would have to be paid for in order to operate a program. Thus, donated services are distinguished from other volunteered services such as service on boards of directors and committees. Donated services may be reflected as revenues and expenses on a nonprofit organization's operating statements, based on the fair market value of those services.

See also CONTRIBUTED SERVICES.

donative element test, a test or criterion used by the IRS to determine whether services are being donated (for example, by a cooperative venture to its members) or are, in fact, being charged as fees-for-services. In order to pass the donative elements test, services must be provided at a price significantly less than their actual costs. In other words, the organization must show a "donative intent."

donative intent: *see* DONATIVE ELEMENT TEST.

donee, the recipient of a gift or contribution.

donee, nominal, the recipient of a charitable contribution that is not the true user of the funds. For example, conduit organizations are nominal donees.

See also CONDUIT FOUNDATION.

donor, an individual or organization who donates or gives.

donors, potential, also POSSIBLE DONORS, the large pool of individuals, groups, associations, companies, foundations, and government agencies which might donate to a nonprofit organization if approached properly.

See DONORS, RECORDS OF POTENTIAL.

donors, records of potential, forms used to help plan, manage, and coordinate fund-raising activities with specific potential donors.

See also DONORS, POTENTIAL.

DOT: *see* DICTIONARY OF OCCUPATIONAL TITLES.

dot matrix, the use of combinations of dots to form, display, and print characters (such as letters and numbers). Dot matrix printers are frequently used with computers when letter-quality printing (printing that looks like a typewriter) is not required.

dotted-line responsibility, a customer's obligations after signing; also an obligation that organizational members have to consult with, but not report to, each other. This is reflective of the dotted-line connections that exist on organization charts.

double entry, method of bookkeeping that shows each transaction as both a debit and a credit by using both horizontal rows and vertical columns of numbers. The totals of the rows and columns should always be the same. This makes it easier to find out where mistakes are than if the records were kept with only one entry for each item.

See also DEBITS AND CREDITS.

Example of
RECORD OF POTENTIAL DONORS

C O N F I D E N T I A L

NAME OF INDIVIDUAL

Title, Position:

BUSINESS ADDRESS:	HOME ADDRESS:	*GIFT RECORD:* *Date* *Amount* *Purpose* __________ __________ __________ __________ __________
TELEPHONE:	TELEPHONE:	
KIND OF BUSINESS:	EDUCATION:	
MEMBER OF ORGANIZATIONS, CLUBS, COMMUNITY ACTIVITIES:	OUR CONTACTS:	
MARITAL STATUS:	INTERESTS:	
CHILDREN:	GIFT POTENTIAL RANGE: $ ________ to $ ________	

double indemnity: *see* ACCIDENTAL DEATH BENEFIT.

double taxation, either the illegal imposition of two taxes on the same property by the same government during the same time period for the same purpose, or any time the same money is taxed twice. A *legal* form of *double taxation* is taxing a corporation on its profits, then taxing its stockholders on their dividends from the corporation.

double time, penalty or premium rate of pay for overtime work, for holiday or Sunday work, etc., amounting to twice the employee's regular hourly wage.

downgrading, reassignment of an employee to a position having a lower rate of pay and/or lesser responsibilities.

down payment, the cash that must be paid at the time that something is bought by installments (on time).

Downs, Anthony (1930-), economist and policy analyst whose classic book on bureaucracy, *Inside Bureaucracy* (Boston: Little, Brown, 1967), sought to justify bureaucratic government on economic grounds and develop laws and propositions that would aid in predicting the behavior of bureaus and bureaucrats.

See also BUREAUCRACY and ISSUE ATTENTION CYCLE.

down time, periods of inactivity while waiting for the repair, setup, or adjustment of equipment.

down-time pay, payments for time spent idle because of equipment failures (or routine maintenance) that are clearly beyond the responsibility of the employee.

draft, a negotiable instrument for the payment of money drawn by one person on another: for example, an ordinary personal check is one type of a draft.

dramaturgy, manner in which an individual acts out or theatrically stages his or her organizational role. All organization members are involved in such impression management.

Drucker, Peter F. (1909-), the preeminent philosopher of management, the world's best-selling management author, and the man usually credited with having invented "management by objectives."

See also the following entries:
KNOWLEDGE WORKER
MANAGEMENT BY OBJECTIVES
PENSION FUND SOCIALISM

drug addiction, also DRUG ABUSE, any habitual use of a substance which leads to psychological and/or physiological dependence. *Drug abuse* consists of using drugs to one's physical, emotional, and/or social detriment without necessarily being addicted.

dual-career couple, a husband and wife pursuing professional careers that both feel are equally important. This has important implications for recruitment and transfer policies: for example, one spouse may be unwilling to accept a move unless an appropriate job is also found for the other.

dual ladder, also called PARALLEL LADDER, a variant of a career ladder that provides dual or parallel career hierarchies so that both professional and managerial employees will be afforded appropriate career advancement.

dual processor, a computer with two central processing units (CPUs), such as one to process eight-bit programs and another to handle sixteen-bit programs.

See also COMPUTER and HARDWARE.

dual unionism, situation where two rival unions claim the right to organize workers in a particular locality.

due process, the clause of the U.S. Constitution which requires that "no person shall be deprived of life, liberty, or property without due process of law." While the specific requirements of due process vary with new Supreme Court decisions, the essence of the idea is that individuals must be given adequate notice and a fair opportunity to present their side in a legal dispute and that no law or government procedure should be arbitrary or unfair.

dues, fees that must be periodically paid by association, club, and union members in order for them to remain in good standing. The dues are used to finance activities.

dues checkoff: *see* CHECKOFF.

dumb terminal, a typewriter, video display terminal, printer, etc., that can operate only when connected to a computer.

Dun & Bradstreet, Inc., a major supplier of business credit ratings. Also, through a subsidiary, developer and seller of sophisticated information for use in marketing and development programs (for example, highly targeted mailing lists).

See also MAILING LIST.

duplex, also FULL-DUPLEX, the simultaneous transmission of data in both directions, for example, over telephone wires. One-way transmission is called half-duplex.

duty of fair representation, obligation of a labor union to represent all of the members in a bargaining unit fairly and without discrimination.

duty to bargain, positive obligation under various state and federal laws that employers and employees bargain with each other in good faith. Section 8 (d) of the Labor-Management Relations (Taft-Hartley) Act of 1947 holds that the duty to bargain collectively

> is the performance of the mutual obligation of the employer and the representative of the employees to meet at reasonable times and confer in good faith with respect to wages, hours, and other terms and conditions of any employment, or the negotiation of an agreement, or any question arising thereunder, and the execution of a written contract incorporating any agreement reached if requested by either party, but such obligation does not compel either party to agree to a proposal or require the making of a concession.

dyad, interpersonal encounter or relationship between two people or two groups. Dyads are frequently artificially (as opposed to spontaneously) created for sensitivity training purposes.

dynamic psychology, school of psychology that is primarily concerned with motivation.

dynamic system, any system that has its parts interrelated in such a way that a change in one part necessarily affects other parts of the system. This is in contrast to a *static system,* whose parts can be affected independently of the rest of its system.

E

EAP: *see* EMPLOYEE ASSISTANCE PROGRAM.

earmark, also RED CIRCLE, terms used to designate a position for restudy when vacant to determine its proper classification before being refilled.

earned revenue, the total amount earned in a period (usually a month or a year) by providing services; for example, it is the amount an ambulance service would have billed if every run, every billable mile, every billable service provided, and every billable supply used had, in fact, been billed (or invoiced).

See also:

BILLED REVENUE
COLLECTED REVENUE
COLLECTION RATE
ESTIMATED INCOME
UNBILLED REVENUE
UNCOLLECTED REVENUE

earnings, remuneration of an employee or group of employees for work performed, including wages, bonuses, commissions, etc.

earnings, net: *see* NET EARNINGS.

earnings concept, one of several accounting perspectives for recognizing income in a nonprofit organization's operating statement. Under the earnings concept—in contrast with, for example, the stewardship concept—income is recognized in an operating statement only after the income has been earned. For example, restricted donations and endowment gifts are excluded from the operating statement until they are expended because they are restricted and, therefore, not available for general use. The earnings concept for recognizing income is analogous to the accounting practices used by private enterprises.

See also

OPERATING STATEMENT
STEWARDSHIP CONCEPT
INCOME, RECOGNITION OF

earnings multiple, the number by which an annual stock dividend is multiplied to equal the stock's selling price.

earnings per share, a company's profits available to pay dividends on its common stock, divided by the number of shares of stock owned by investors.

earthquake manager, one who shakes everything up.

easement: *see* RIGHT-OF-WAY.

Eastex, Inc.* v. *National Labor Relations Board, 437 U.S. 556 (1978), U.S. Supreme Court case which affirmed a National Labor Relations Board ruling that union members have the right to distribute, on their employers' property, leaflets, containing articles pertaining to political issues (such as right-to-work laws and minimum wages) as well as those directly connected to the union-employer relationship.

econometric model, a set of related equations used to analyze economic data through mathematical and statistical techniques. Such models are devised in order to depict the essential quantitative relationships that determine the behavior of output, income, employment, and prices. Econometric models are used for forecasting and estimating the likely quantitative impact of alternative assumptions, including various propositions about the way the economy works.

econometrics, a subdiscipline of economics which is known by its use of such mathematical techniques as regression analysis and modeling to test economic theories and forecast economic activity.

economic analysis, a systematic approach to the problem of choosing how to employ scarce resources and an investigation of the full implications of achieving a given objective in the most efficient and effective manner. The determination of efficiency and effectiveness is implicit in the assessment of the cost effectiveness of alternative approaches.

economic determinism, doctrine holding that economic concerns are the primary motivating factors of human behavior.

economic efficiency, the mix of alternative factors of production which results in maximum outputs, benefits, or utility for a given cost. Also, that mix of productive factors which represents the minimum cost at which a specified level of output can be obtained.

economic growth, an increase in a nation's productive capacity leading to an increase in the production of goods and services. Economic growth is usually measured by the annual rate of increase in real (constant dollars) gross national product.

economic indicators, measurements of various economic and business movements and activities in a community, such as employment, unemployment, hours worked, income, savings, volume of building permits, volume of sales, etc., whose fluctuations affect and may be used to determine overall economic trends. The economic time series can be segregated into leaders, laggers, and coinciders in relation to movements in aggregate economic activity.

economic loss, the aggregate adjusted dollar loss resulting from a social problem or need; for example, the economic loss from crime and the economic loss from people not being permitted to realize their full potential.

economic man, concept that finds humans motivated *solely* by economic factors—always seeking the greatest reward at the least possible cost. Any management philosophy assuming that workers are motivated by money and can be further motivated only by more money is premised on the "economic man" concept.

Economic Opportunity Act of 1964, the keystone of the Johnson Administration's "war on poverty." This act created the Jobs Corps and other work incentive programs.

economic policy, process by which a government manages its economy. Economic policy generally consists of three dimensions—fiscal policy, monetary policy, and any other facet of public policy that has economic implications (*e.g.*, energy policy, farm policy, labor union policy, etc.). The interaction of these dimensions of economic policy becomes crucial since none can operate in a vacuum.

Economic Recovery Tax Act (1981) (ERTA), also CHARITABLE CONTRIBUTIONS LAW (CCL), the law which culminated the Reagan administration's first major campaign to reduce the federal deficit and stimulate the economy by reducing federal income taxes. ERTA impacted nonprofit, tax-exempt organizations in several ways, including the following:

- It established the Charitable Contributions Law (CCL), under which nonitemizing taxpayers can deduct a percent of contributions to charity up to a maximum amount each year. The law increased the percentage each year—for example, from initially 25% of $25 to 25% of $300 in 1984, to 50% in 1985, and 100% in 1986. However, the law allowing these deductions is scheduled to expire on December 31, 1986.
- It relaxed the private foundation payout requirements from the greater of 5% of assets *or* all income, to 5% of assets.
- It further reduced private foundations' required payouts by changing the interest income calculation base from 12% to the prime rate.

See also:
DEDUCTION
PAYOUT REQUIREMENT

economic strike, strike that is undertaken for economic gain; that is, for better wages, hours, and working conditions.

economic time series, a set of quantitative data collected over regular time intervals (e.g., weekly, monthly, quarterly, annually) which measures some aspect of economic activity. The data may measure a broad aggregate such as the gross national product, or a narrow segment such as the sale of trucks or the price of labor.

economies of scale, cost savings resulting from aggregation of resources and/or mass production. In particular, it refers to decreases in average cost when all factors of production are expanded proportionately. For example, hospital costs for a unit of service are generally less in 300-bed than 30-bed hospitals.

economy and efficiency audits, audits that seek to determine (a) whether an organizational entity is managing and utilizing its resources (such as personnel, property, space) economically and efficiently, (b) the causes of inefficiencies or uneconomical practices, and (c) whether the entity has complied with laws and regulations concerning matters of economy and efficiency.

EDGAR: *See,* EDUCATION DEPARTMENT GENERAL ADMINISTRATIVE REGULATIONS.

EDP: *see* ELECTRONIC DATA PROCESSING.

education, cooperative: *see* COOPERATIVE EDUCATION.

Education, Department of (DOE), cabinet-level department that establishes policy for, administers, and coordinates most federal assistance to education. Created on October 17, 1979, when the Department of Health, Education and Welfare was divided in two.

educational expenses, employee expenses to gain skills for a current job or to meet an employer's educational requirements. They may be tax deductible, but expenses to gain skills for a new job or to meet minimum educational requirements are not deductible.

educational institution: *see* EDUCATIONAL ORGANIZATION.

educational leave: *see* LEAVE WITHOUT PAY.

educational organization, as defined by the Internal Revenue Service, an organization involved in "instruction or training of the individual for the purpose of improving or developing his capabilities" or the "instruction of the public on subjects useful to the individual and beneficial to the community." The definition is broad and extends beyond formal (or classroom) schooling. However, the government draws a tight line between educational and propaganda activities.

Education Department General Administrative Regulations (EDGAR), replaced the U.S. Department of Education's "Part 74, Administration of Federal Grants," in 1981, as the administrative guidelines for nonprofit organizations' expenditures of federal education funds.

EEOC: *see* EQUAL EMPLOYMENT OPPORTUNITY COMMISSION.

EEO Compliance Manual, publication of the Bureau of National Affairs, Inc., which provides a summary of the latest Equal Employment Opportunity Commission (EEOC) developments and the photographic text of the official operations manual that is followed by the staff of the EEOC.

EEO Counselor: *see* EQUAL EMPLOYMENT OPPORTUNITY COUNSELOR.

EEO Officer: *see* EQUAL EMPLOYMENT OPPORTUNITY OFFICER.

EEO-1, the annual report of the sex and minority status of various work force categories that is required of all employers with one hundred or more employees. The report must be filed with the Joint Reporting Committee of the Equal Employment Opportunity Commission and the Office of Federal Contract Compliance.

effective labor market, labor market from which an employer actually draws applicants, as distinct from the labor market from which an employer attempts to draw applicants.

effectiveness, *also* IMPACT and OUTCOME, traditionally, the extent to which an organization accomplishes some predetermined goal or objective; more recently, the overall performance of an organization from the viewpoint of some strategic constituency. Effectiveness is not synonymous with efficiency. Effectiveness is increased by strategies which employ resources to take advantage of changes in unmanageable factors in such a way that the greatest possible advancement of whatever one is seeking is achieved.

efficacy, commonly used synonym for effectiveness. *Efficacy* may usefully be distinguished from *effectiveness* by using *efficacy* for the results of actions undertaken under ideal circumstances and *effective-*

ness for their results under usual or normal circumstances. Actions can thus be efficacious and effective, or efficacious and ineffective, but not the reverse.

efficiency, also EFFICIENCY RATIO, measure generally determined by seeking the ratio of output to input, which is called the *efficiency ratio.*

$$\text{efficiency} = \frac{\text{output}}{\text{input}}$$

Generally speaking, efficiency refers to the promotion of administrative methods that will produce the largest store of results for a given objective at the least cost; the reduction of material and personnel costs while maximizing precision, speed, and simplicity in administration.

efficiency expert, mildly pejorative and decidedly dated term for a management or systems analyst.

efficiency rating, now-dated term for performance appraisal.

See also PERFORMANCE APPRAISAL.

efficiency ratio: *also* EFFICIENCY.

EFTS: *see* ELECTRONIC FUND TRANSFER SYSTEM.

egalitarianism: *see* EQUALITY.

eighty percent rule: *see* ADVERSE IMPACT.

elasticity of demand, measure of the sensitivity of demand for a product or service to changes in its price (price elasticity) or the income of the people demanding the product or service (income elasticity). Price elasticity is the ratio of the resulting percentage change in demand to a given percentage change in price.

electronic data processing (EDP), computer manipulation of data. The term is gradually being supplanted by "management information systems."

See also MANAGEMENT INFORMATION SYSTEM.

electronic fund transfer system (EFTS), a general term covering a variety of systems and technologies for transferring payments and credits electronically (for example, making payments without needing to write checks).

electronic mail, also ELECTRONIC MESSAGE SYSTEM, primarily the transmission of messages from computer to computer, but also telex, electronic funds transfer systems, computer conferencing, facsimile transmission, etc.

eleemosynary, related to charity or charitable donations; dependent on or supported by charity.

element, also called JOB ELEMENT, smallest unit into which a job can be divided without analyzing the physical and mental processes necessarily involved.

eligibility, criteria for determining which organizations—*e.g.,* Indian tribes, nonprofits, universities, individuals, etc.—are entitled to be recipients of federal assistance programs.

eligible, any applicant for a position or promotion who meets the minimum qualification requirements.

eligible list, also called ELIGIBLE ROSTER and ELIGIBLE REGISTER, list of qualified applicants in rank order.

See also REEMPLOYMENT LIST.

embezzlement, to fraudulently appropriate property that has been entrusted to one's care. An employee or volunteer might take money and cover it up by faking account books. Embezzlement is one of the most frequent forms of corruption encountered in nonprofit organizations.

See also CORRUPTION and FIDELITY BOND.

emergency management, public-private cooperative activities that are concerned with reducing the risk to life and property posed by natural and manmade hazardous events.

eminence grise, "gray eminence," the power behind the throne. Staff officers are sometimes accused of exercising such power.

eminent domain, a government's right to take private property for the public's use.

emolument, any monetary gain or other advantage achieved from employment; a more comprehensive term than wages and/or salaries.

empathy, projecting oneself mentally into the mind and feelings of another person; interpreting things from another person's viewpoint while holding one's own viewpoint in check. Not to be confused with *sympathy*.

empirical, description of findings or conclusions derived from direct and repeated observations of a phenomenon under study.

empirical validity, validity of a test according to how well the test actually measured what it was designed to measure. Most other kinds of validity are efforts to achieve empirical validity.

employ, hire the services of an individual and/or his or her equipment.

employee, general term for all those who let themselves for hire.
See also PROBATIONARY EMPLOYEE.

employee assistance program (EAP), formal program designed to assist employees with personal problems through both (1) internal counseling and aid and (2) a referral service to outside counseling resources. The thrust of such programs is to increase productivity by correcting distracting outside personal problems.

employee benefits: *see* FRINGE BENEFITS.

employee counseling, formal efforts on the part of an organization to help its members deal with their personal and professional problems and concerns so that they will be more effective in both their personal and organizational lives.
See also PRE-RETIREMENT COUNSELING.

employee development, term that may include career development and upward mobility. It may be oriented toward development for better performance on an employee's current job, for learning a new policy or procedure, or for enhancing an employee's potential for advancement.

employee relations, personnel function that centers upon the relationship between the supervisor and individual employees.

Employee Retirement Income Security Act of 1974 (ERISA), popularly known as PENSION REFORM ACT OF 1974, federal statute enacted to protect "the interest of participants in employee benefit plans and their beneficiaries . . . by establishing standards of conduct, responsibility and obligations for fiduciaries of employee benefit plans, and by providing for appropriate remedies, sanctions, and ready access to the Federal courts." The basic intent of ERISA is to insure that employees will eventually gain appropriate benefits from the pension plans in which they participate.

employee selection: *see* PERSONNEL SELECTION.

employees, exempt: *see* EXEMPT EMPLOYEES.

employer association, a voluntary organization of employers whose purpose is to deal with problems common to the industry, the area, etc.

Employer Identification Number, number issued by the IRS. Whether or not a tax-exempt organization has any employees, it must obtain an Employer Identification Number. Applications are filed with the IRS on Form SS-4.

employer paternalism: *see* PATERNALISM.

employer unit, any bargaining unit that holds all of the eligible employees of a single employer.

employment, occupational activity usually, but not necessarily, for pay. In economic statistics, employment refers to all persons who, during the week when the employment survey was taken, did any work for pay or profit, or who worked for fifteen hours or more without pay on a farm or in a business operated by a member of the person's family. Also included as employed are those who did not work or look for work but had a job or business from which they were temporarily absent during the week.

See also FULL EMPLOYMENT and SEASONAL EMPLOYMENT.

employment agency, private firm that provides brokerage services between employers and individuals seeking work. Fees or commissions are charged to the employer, the worker, or both.

Employment and Training Administration (ETA), agency of the Department of Labor that encompasses a group of offices and services. Major units include the U.S. Employment Service, the Office of Employment and Training, and the Bureau of Apprenticeship and Training.

Employment and Training Reporter, weekly notification and reference service published by the Bureau of National Affairs, Inc. Provides technical assistance on the effective utilization of the nation's human resources, including where and how to apply for employment and training funds and how to develop successful programs.

employment contract, generally, a promise or set of promises for which the law offers a remedy if the promise(s) is breached. An employment contract is the agreed-upon work (and other contributions) and total compensation (monetary and nonmonetary) commitments between an employer and an employee. Employment contracts are legally enforceable.

Employment Cost Index (ECI), measure of the rate of change in employee compensation which includes wages, salaries, and employers' cost for employee benefits. Several elements distinguish the ECI from other surveys of employee compensation. It is comprehensive in that it (1) includes costs incurred by employers for employee benefits in addition to wages and salaries; and (2) covers all establishments and occupations in both the private nonfarm and public sectors. It measures the change in a fixed set of labor costs so that it is not affected over time by changes in the composition of the labor force.

employment interview: *see* INTERVIEW.

employment manager, job title sometimes given to managers who function as personnel directors.

employment parity: *see* PARITY.

employment-population ratio (E-P ratio), also called EMPLOYMENT RATIO, ratio of employment to working-age population.

employment ratio: *see* EMPLOYMENT-POPULATION RATIO.

employment relations, general term for all relationships that occur in a worker-manager context. While used synonymously with labor relations and industrial relations, it is often applied in nonunion situations in order to emphasize "nonunion."

employment standard, a specific requirement for employment. An employment standard can be based on a wide variety of things. For example, if assessment is based on tests, the standard might be a specific cutting score. If education is assessed, the standard might be a specific class standing, or grades of B or better in certain courses of study.

Employment Standards Administration (ESA), agency of the Department of Labor that administers laws and regulations set-

Philanthropic employment as a percent of total private employment in service-producing activities[1], 1982
(Employment in thousands)

Service-producing activities	Total employment	Philanthropic employment	
		Number	As a percent of total
Total	49,886.0	6,523.1	13
Activities with a philanthropic component	8,974.6	6,523.1	73
Health services	4,411.8	3,052.5	69
Nursing and personal care	1,064.4	255.5	24
Hospitals	3,013.9	2,593.2	86
Other health services	333.5	203.6	61
Education and research	1,274.9	1,212.5	95
Elementary and secondary education	322.1	322.1	100
Colleges and universities	752.6	752.6	100
Libraries and information centers	12.4	12.4	100
Correspondence and vocational schools	50.7	13.0	26
Other educational, scientific, and research organizations	137.1	112.4	82
Social services	1,166.6	959.2	82
Individual and family services	230.4	220.7	96
Job training and related services	191.4	183.0	96
Child day care services	289.0	163.2	56
Residential care	237.1	181.6	77
Other social services	218.7	210.7	96
Culture, entertainment, recreation	338.1	79.7	24
Theater, orchestra, and other performing arts	86.0	22.4	26
Radio and television broadcasting	216.4	11.6	5
Visual arts (museums and botanical and zoological gardens)	35.7	35.7	100
Membership organizations	1,198.7	1,198.7	100
Civic, social, and fraternal associations	301.6	301.6	100
Religious organizations	897.1	897.1	100
Legal services	565.4	12.4	2
Educational, religious, and charitable trusts	18.3	18.3	100

[1]Includes full- and part-time employment.

Source: Gabriel Rudney and Murray Weitzman, "Trends in Employment and Earnings in the Philanthropic Sector," Monthly Labor Review *(September 1984).*

ting employment standards, providing workers' compensation to those injured on their jobs, and requiring federal contractors to provide equal employment opportunity. Its major divisions include the Wage and Hour Division, the Office of Federal Contract Compliance, and the Office of Workers' Compensation.

employment taxes, also called PAYROLL TAXES, any of a variety of taxes levied by governments on an employer's payroll. The most common employment tax is the employer's contribution to social security known as FICA taxes (after the Federal Insurance Contribution Act). There are also FUTA taxes (after the Federal Unemployment Tax Act) and sometimes other unemployment insurance contributions required by state law.

employment testing, any means of measuring the qualifications of applicants for employment in specific positions.

enabling instruments: *see* ARTICLES OF ORGANIZATION and BYLAWS.

encounter group, form of group psychotherapy in which body contact and/or emotional expression are the primary forms of interaction as opposed to traditional verbal interaction. Encounter groups seek to produce experiences which force individuals to examine themselves in new and different ways, aided by others. Part of the emphasis on body movement includes attention to nonverbal communications. An individual should learn to be more conscious of his/her own nonverbal communications, to read others' signs more adequately, and to practice being more adept in his/her body language.

encumbrance, a claim, charge, or liability on property, such as a lien or mortgage, that lowers the property's value.

Encyclopedia of Associations, a publication containing a comprehensive listing of associations and other nonprofit organizations. The *Encyclopedia* is published semiannually in Detroit, Michigan, by the Gale Research Company.

endowment (insurance), an insurance policy that pays a set amount at a set time or, if the person insured dies, pays the money to a beneficiary.

endowment fund, a restricted fund, the contents of which must be invested to generate income. Many foundations make grants only from their endowment income, but this is not necessarily true of smaller corporate foundations which often receive annual contributions from the corporation.

See also ENDOWMENT INCOME.

endowment income, income generated from the resources in a restricted endowment fund.

endowment test, one of several tests or criteria used by the IRS for determining whether an organization qualifies as a private operating foundation.

end-testing, examining individuals who have just completed a course of training on the subject in which they were trained in order to measure the individual's attainments and/or the effectiveness of the training.

enhancement, a term used to mean development or fundraising, particularly in colleges and universities.

See also DEVELOPMENT.

enjoin, require or command. A court's injunction directs (enjoins) a person or persons to do or not do certain acts.

enlistment (of volunteers), the process of securing volunteers to participate in an activity; for example, a fund-raising campaign.

enlistment of volunteers form, a form used to help manage the process of securing volunteers for an activity.

enterprise zone, also called URBAN ENTERPRISE ZONE, area of high unemployment and poverty which is granted business tax reductions by a state in order to lure industry and concomitant prosperity.

VOLUNTEER ENLISTMENT FORM

1984–1985 Tincup Volunteer Ambulance Service Fund-raising Committee

These people have agreed to work as ______________________________ on the Fund-raising Committee. They are willing to:

1. Attend meetings on ____________________
2. Enlist ____________________ committee people
3. Contact ____________________ about being contributors.

NAME	TITLE	COMPANY & ADDRESS	PHONE NUMBER

entitlement authority, legislation that requires the payment of benefits to any person or government meeting the requirements established by such law (*e.g.*, social security benefits and veterans' pensions). Section 401 of the Congressional Budget and Impoundment Control Act of 1974 places certain restrictions on the enactment of new entitlement authority.

See also BACKDOOR AUTHORITY.

entitlement program, any government program which pays benefits to individuals, organizations, or other governments who meet eligibility requirements set by law.

entrance level position, position in an occupation at the beginning level grade.

entrance rate, also called PROBATIONARY RATE and HIRING RATE, hourly rate of pay at which new employees are hired.

entropy, term from thermodynamics that is applicable to all physical systems and sometimes applied to social systems. It refers to the inherent tendency of all closed systems which do not interact with their environments to move toward a chaotic state in which there is no further potential for work.

See also ORGANIZATIONAL ENTROPY.

entry, the act of making or entering a formal record by writing it down; for example, to make an entry in an accounting journal.

entry level, the lowest position or performance level in a job promotional line.

environmental conservancy, efforts to preserve and protect the natural environment. Environmental conservancy is an example of a social welfare organizational purpose which may qualify an entity as a charitable organization for federal tax purposes.

environmental impact statement: *see* ENVIRONMENTAL POLICY.

environmental lobby, citizen groups that engage in information dissemination, public discussion, lobbying, litigation, and demonstrations on behalf of environmental protection. Generally consists of preservationists (who want to save the natural environment from man's use except for aesthetic and controlled recreational enjoyment) and utilitarians (who advocate the prudent use and renewal of environmental resources). In 1979, the combined membership of all environmental groups was estimated at eight million. The single largest group is the National Wildlife Federation; perhaps the best known is the Sierra Club.

environmental movement, a spontaneous grassroots mobilization of citizens that grew out of the earlier conservation movement, which is concerned with the quality of natural and human environment. The movement receives its organizational expression through the formation of interest groups that engage in lobbying, court litigation, and public information activities.

environmental policy, also NATIONAL ENVIRONMENTAL POLICY ACT OF 1969 and ENVIRONMENTAL IMPACT STATEMENT, a document which assesses the impact of a new program upon the environment. The National Environmental Policy Act of 1969 declared a federal responsibility for the protection of the environment. The act provides for the preparation of an *environmental impact statement* on all major federal actions significantly affecting the quality of the human environment.

Environmental Protection Agency (EPA), federal agency created to permit coordinated and effective governmental action on behalf of the environment. EPA endeavors to abate and control pollution systematically by proper integration of a variety of research, monitoring, standard setting, and enforcement activities. As a complement to its other activities, EPA coordinates and supports research and antipollution activities by state and local governments, private and public groups, individuals, and educational institutions.

EPA: *see* ENVIRONMENTAL PROTECTION AGENCY.

E-P ratio: *see* EMPLOYMENT-POPULATION RATIO.

equal employment opportunity (EEO), concept fraught with political, cultural, and emotional overtones. Generally, it applies to a set of employment procedures and practices that effectively prevent any individual from being adversely excluded from employment opportunities on the basis of race, color, sex, religion, age, national origin, or other factors that cannot lawfully be used in employment efforts. While the ideal of EEO is an employment system that is devoid of both intentional and unintentional discrimination, achieving this ideal may be a political impossibility because of the problem of definition. One man's equal opportunity may be seen by another as tainted with institutional racism or by a woman as institutional sexism. Because of this problem of definition, only the courts have been able to say if, when, and where EEO exists.

Environmental Impact Statement

As the story is told, Moses led the tribes of Israel from bondage in Egypt to the shores of the Red Sea. Looking behind him, he saw the rapidly approaching armies and chariots of the pharaoh and became alarmed. Looking then to the heavens, he called out for assistance. A voice from the heavens promptly answered: "Moses, be calm, for I have good news and bad news."

Moses replied, "Tell me quickly, for the armies grow nearer."

The voice answered: "The good news is that when you raise your staff to the sky, the Red Sea will open, creating a path for your people to cross over in safety. Then the walls of the sea shall come crashing down and destroy the armies."

Moses then queried, "That is marvelous, and the bad news?"

The voice replied, "The bad news is that you will first have to prepare an environmental impact statement."

See also the following entries:
ADVERSE EFFECT
ADVERSE IMPACT
ADVERSE-INFERENCE RULE
AFFECTED CLASS
AFFIRMATIVE ACTION
BONA FIDE OCCUPATIONAL QUALIFICATION
BOTTOM-LINE CONCEPT
BUSINESS NECESSITY
CHILLING EFFECT
CONSENT DECREE
DISCRIMINATION
DISPARATE EFFECT
FAIR EMPLOYMENT PRACTICE COMMISSION
MAKE WHOLE
READING ASSISTANT
REASONABLE ACCOMMODATION
RELIGIOUS DISCRIMINATION
REPRESENTATIVE BUREAUCRACY
REVERSE DISCRIMINATION
RIGHTFUL PLACE
SEX PLUS
THIRD PARTY ALLEGATIONS
TITLE VII
TOKENISM
UNDERUTILIZATION
UNFAIR LABOR PRACTICES (EMPLOYERS)
UPWARD MOBILITY PROGRAM

Equal Employment Opportunity Commission (EEOC), body created by Title VII of the Civil Rights Act of 1964. The EEOC is composed of five members (one designated chair) appointed for five-year terms by the president, subject to the advice and consent of the Senate. The EEOC's mission is to end discrimination based on race, color, religion, sex, or national origin in hiring, promotion, firing, wages, testing, training, apprenticeship, and all other conditions of employment and to promote voluntary action programs by employers, unions, and community organizations to make equal employment opportunity an actuality.

The EEOC's operations are decentralized to forty-eight field offices which receive written charges of discrimination against public and private employers, labor organizations, joint labor-management apprenticeship programs, and public and private employment agencies.

The EEOC encourages and assists in voluntary action by employers, unions, and employment agencies through affirmative action programs, providing the EEOC's services in identifying discriminatory systems and devising ways to change them. Such programs are designed to help organizations achieve EEO goals through nondiscriminatory recruiting, fair employee selection procedures, expanded training programs, and job upgrading.

equal employment opportunity counselor, specifically designated individual within an organization who provides an open and systematic channel through which employees may raise questions, discuss real and imagined grievances, and obtain information on their procedural rights. Counseling is the first stage in the discrimination complaint process. The counselor, through interviews and inquiries, attempts to informally resolve problems related to equal employment opportunity.

equal employment opportunity officer, official within an organization who is designated responsibility for monitoring EEO programs and assuring that both organizational and national EEO policies are being implemented.

equality, also EGALITARIANISM, philosophic disposition toward the greater political and social equality of the citizens within a state; this is, all citizens would have an equal claim on the political and economic rewards of the society.

Equal Pay Act of 1963, an amendment to the Fair Labor Standards Act of 1938. The Equal Pay Act of 1963 (Public Law 88-38) prohibits pay discrimination because of sex and provides that men and women working in the same establishment under similar conditions must receive the same pay if jobs require equal (similar) skill, effort, and responsibility.

See also COMPARABLE WORTH.

equal pay for equal work, principle that salary rates should not be dependent upon factors unrelated to the quantity or quality of work.
See also COMPARABLE WORTH.

equal protection clause: *see* BROWN V. BOARD OF EDUCATION OF TOPEKA, KANSAS.

equal protection of laws, constitutional requirement that the government will in no way fail to treat equals equally, set up illegal categories to justify treating persons unfairly, or give unfair or unequal treatment to a person based on that person's race, religion, etc.

Equal Rights Amendment (ERA), amendment passed by Congress in 1972 that never became law because not enough of the states ratified it. The proposed Twenty-seventh Amendment read: "Equality of rights under the law shall not be denied or abridged by the United States or any state on account of sex."

equated scores, scores from different tests of the same variable which are reduced by weighting in order to have a common basis for comparison.

equating, process of adjusting the raw statistics obtained from a particular sample to corresponding statistics obtained for a base group or reference population.

equilibrium, in balance; the stable condition of a management or organization which will continue until an important variable is altered.

equipercentile equating, process that treats as equivalent those raw scores that fall at the same percentile in different samples although the raw scores themselves may be different.

equity (corporate), a corporation's ownership value, including retained earnings. Charitable nonprofit organizations are not permitted to pay dividends (in other words, may not distribute the equivalent of equity) to "owners" as is done in for-profit organizations.

equity (tax), the conceptual basis for widespread criticism of charitable contribution deductions because the government, in effect, offsets contributions from people in higher tax brackets more than people in lower brackets.
See also:
DEMOCRATIZE
TAX EQUITY
TAX EXPENDITURES

equity, external/internal: *see* EXTERNAL EQUITY.

equity distribution, an allocation of an organization's equity (for example, retained earnings to shareholders). Tax-exempt charitable organizations are not permitted to distribute equity to owners.

equity theory: *see* INEQUITY THEORY.

equivalent form: *see* ALTERNATE FORM.

ergonomics: *see* HUMAN-FACTORS ENGINEERING.

ERISA: *see* EMPLOYEE RETIREMENT INCOME SECURITY ACT OF 1974.

ERTA: *see* ECONOMIC RECOVERY TAX ACT.

ESA: *see* EMPLOYMENT STANDARDS ADMINISTRATION.

escalator clause, also called COST-OF-LIVING ESCALATOR, provision of a wage agreement which allows for periodic adjustments in response to changes in the cost of living, usually as determined by the Consumer Price Index of the Bureau of Labor Statistics.

escape clause, a contract provision that allows a party to avoid doing something or to avoid liability if certain things happen. For example, in a maintenance-of-membership shop, a union contract may provide for a period of time during which union members may withdraw (escape) from the union without affecting their employment.

escrow, money, property, or documents that belong to organization A that are held by organization B until organization A takes care of an obligation to organization C. For example, a mortgage company may require a nonprofit organization with a mortgage on a building to make monthly payments into an escrow account to take care of a future balloon payment when it comes due.

See also MORTGAGE.

esprit de corps, strong feelings of unity and common purpose on the part of a group.

Establishment Clause (of the First Amendment to the U.S. Constitution), clause that prohibits the government from establishing or aiding a religion to its advantage over other religions. Court cases involving the Establishment Clause are typically concerned with governmental regulation or interference with religious organizations rather than an individual's religious expression.

See also FREE EXERCISE CLAUSE.

estate, property or possessions. From a nonprofit organization's perspective, estate is often used to mean the property of a deceased person.

estate planning, making plans for a person's property to be passed on at his or her death (for example, to a charitable organization) and gaining maximum legal benefit from that property by best using the laws of wills, trusts, insurance, property, and taxes.

estate tax, a tax on an estate; a federal or state tax paid on the property left by a dead person. This is in contrast to an inheritance tax, which is based on the money each individual (heir) receives and is paid by each heir separately.

FIGURE 1

PROJECTING ESTIMATES INTO THE FUTURE

FEE-FOR-SERVICES INCOME
NEXT YEAR'S PROJECTION

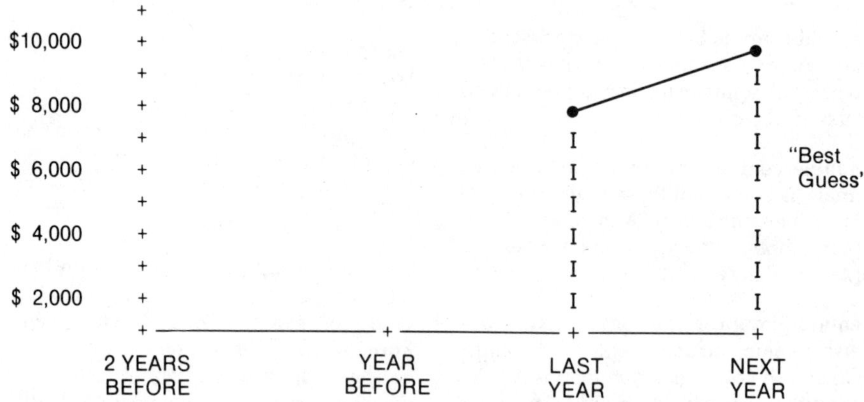

PROJECTED FEE-FOR-SERVICE INCOME FOR NEXT YEAR (BASED ON "BEST GUESS" FROM LAST YEAR ALONE) $10,000 (FROM ABOVE GRAPH)

estimated income, income predicted to be received in the future. Estimated income is important, for example, for formulating future budgets and deciding the need for fund-raising drives.

Income may be estimated in a variety of ways, ranging from simple guesses to the use of sophisticated statistical forecasting procedures. The most common method used by smaller nonprofit organizations involves projecting an educated guess from estimates or actual experience over the prior several years. Basically, projecting assumes that the next year is an imaginary target to be aimed at using the past years' information as "sights." Two or more years of historical information provide a fairly stable "sighting" into the future, whereas one year provides an unreliable "sighting."

If only one year of information is available to "aim" with, the projection accuracy depends exclusively on a best guess about the next year. Last year's level is plotted, next year's is guessed, and a connecting line is drawn between the two plotted points (Figure 1).

When more than one year of historical information is available, each prior year's level is plotted. The points are connected with a line, and the line is continued or extended out to the next year (or two) (Figure 2a).

In most cases, the prior year plottings will not lie on a straight line, and it is necessary to plot the connecting line "through the points" (Figure 2b).

The next year's projected income is read from the scale on the left side of the chart.

Sometimes, even with estimates from two or more years, the projected figure will not be reasonable. For example, a relatively new church has experienced a large in-

FIGURE 2a

PROJECTING ESTIMATES INTO THE FUTURE

DONATION INCOME
NEXT YEAR'S PROJECTION

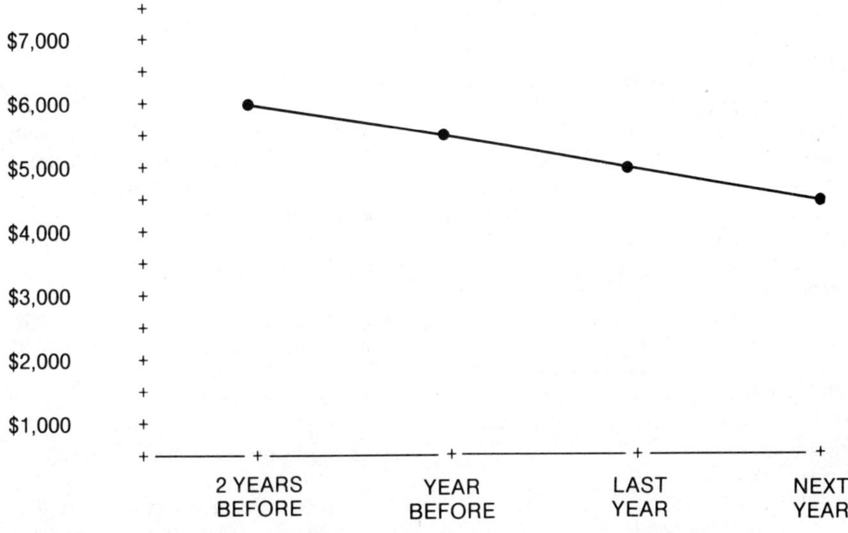

PROJECTED DONATION INCOME FOR NEXT YEAR [BASED ON THREE YEARS OF DATA ("SIGHTS")] $4,500 (FROM ABOVE GRAPH)

FIGURE 2b

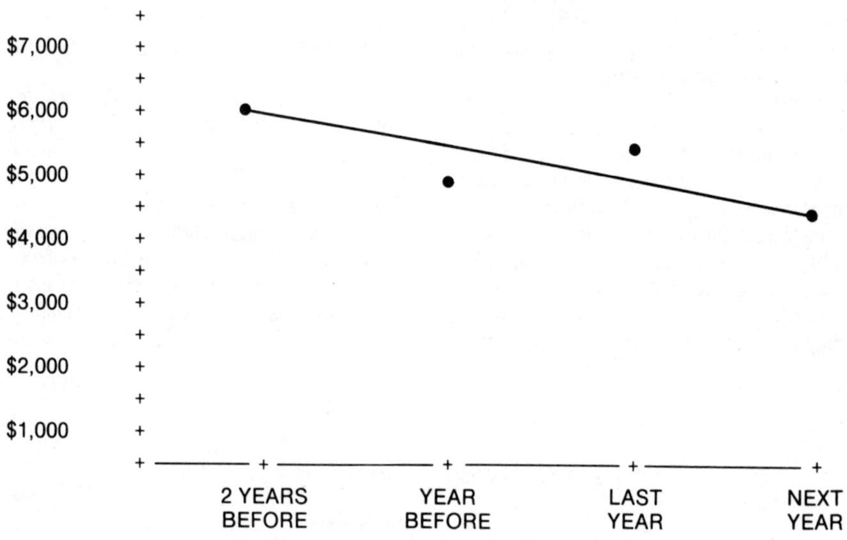

PROJECTED DONATION INCOME FOR NEXT YEAR [BASED ON THREE YEARS OF DATA ("SIGHTS")] $4,700 (FROM ABOVE GRAPH)

crease in pledges over the first two years of its existence. However, during the last few months of the second year, there are indications that new memberships are slowing. If the projection for the third year is made only on the basis of the prior two years, the estimate might be unreasonably optimistic (Figure 3).
By applying common sense judgment to the projection, it might be adjusted to a more conservative estimate (Figure 4).

Estimated changes in income resulting from changes in procedures can also be estimated. For example, increasing the collection rate will increase estimated income (Figure 5).

See also:

BILLED REVENUE
COLLECTED REVENUE
COLLECTION RATE
EARNED REVENUE
UNBILLED REVENUE
UNCOLLECTED REVENUE

estimated tax, tax which individuals with income other than salaries must "declare" and pay every three months.

See also TAXATION.

estimating: *see* ESTIMATED INCOME.

ethics, standards of fair and honest conduct; standards of conduct for a profession.

See also CODE OF ETHICS.

ethics, code of: *see* CODE OF ETHICS.

Ethics in Government Act of 1978, federal statute that seeks to deal with possible conflicts of interest by former federal executive branch employees by imposing

FIGURE 3

PROJECTION *BEFORE* ADJUSTMENT

NUMBER OF NEW MEMBERS—NEXT YEAR'S PROJECTION

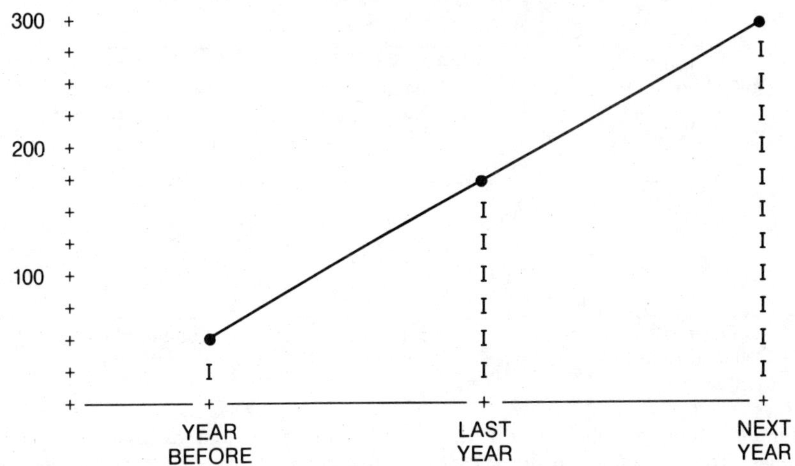

(Overestimation due to assumption that rapid growth rate will continue)

FIGURE 4

PROJECTION *AFTER* ADJUSTMENT

NUMBER OF NEW MEMBERS—NEXT YEAR'S PROJECTION

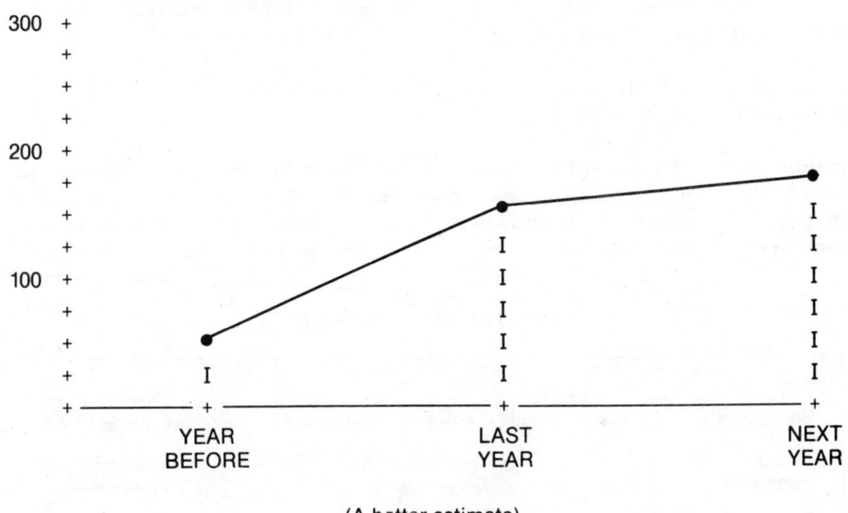

(A better estimate)

FIGURE 5

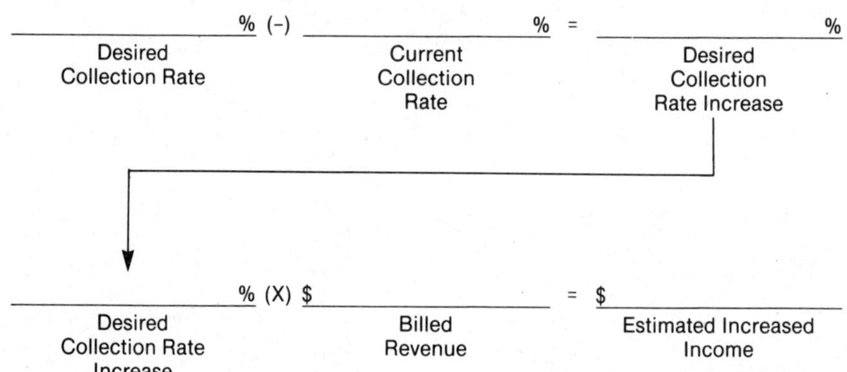

postemployment prohibitions on their activities. The restrictions in the law are concerned with former government employees' representations or attempts to influence federal agencies, not with their employment by others. What is prohibited depends on how involved a former employee was with a matter while with the government and whether he or she was one of a specified group of senior employees.

ethnic categories: *see* RACE CATEGORIES.

ethnic group, social, biological, or (sometimes) political division of humankind.

evaluation, use of research techniques to measure the past performance of a specific program—in particular, a program's use of its resources, its operations, and/or its impact on the conditions it seeks to ameliorate or modify. Evaluation is conducted for the purpose of changing the program to improve its effectiveness or efficiency in achieving its objectives. There are three major types of evaluation: outcome (or impact), process (or performance), and input (or administrative).

See also:

CAUSE-EFFECT EVALUATION
COST-BENEFIT ANALYSIS
COST-EFFECTIVENESS ANALYSIS
EVALUATION, ADMINISTRATIVE
PROCESS EVALUATION
PROGRAM EVALUATION

evaluation, administrative, also STRUCTURAL EVALUATION and INPUT EVALUATION, one form of evaluation which measures resources consumed; the

THREE TYPES OF EVALUATION

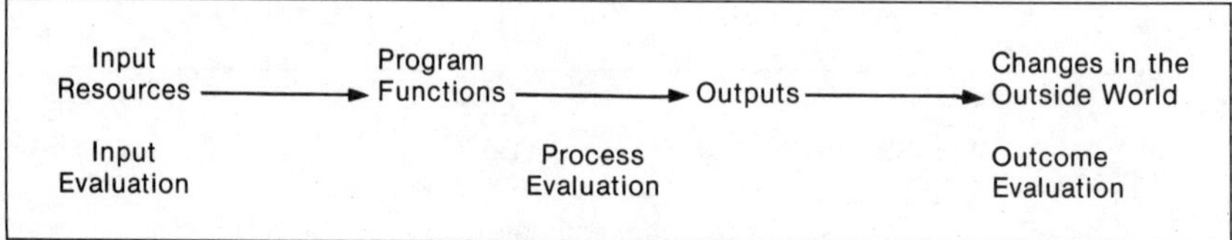

measurement of inputs to program processes. Of the three major types of evaluation (*i.e.*, program, process, and administrative), administrative evaluation is conceptually at the lowest level. For example, one focus of an administrative evaluation might be whether or not an organization successfully recruited and trained staff to conduct a new program in a reasonable period of time after receiving a grant.

See also EVALUATION and HIERARCHY OF OBJECTIVES.

evaluation, impact: *see* PROGRAM EVALUATION.

evaluation criterion, a standard for judging relative success or failure; a standard for measuring the degree of effectiveness or efficiency with which program or organizational objectives have been met. There are three major types of evaluation criteria: costable, quantifiable, and qualifiable.

See also

CRITERION, QUALIFIABLE
CRITERION, QUANTIFIABLE

evaluation design, a statement of an evaluation's (1) purposes, objectives, and probable limitations; (2) conceptual approach and evaluation technique; (3) data collection, analysis, and interpretative methods; (4) work plan, including tasks and activities to be accomplished, schedule, and milestones; (5) interim reports (written and oral) and final report. Sometimes anticipated costs also are included.

See also EVALUATION TECHNIQUE.

evaluation technique, one element in an evaluation design, usually used to mean the basic evaluation research approach which is to be used. For example, a two group before-and-after comparison, or a single group time series.

See also EVALUATION DESIGN.

event (work plan), a point in time on a work plan or project control chart (for example, a Critical Path Method or PERT chart); a starting or ending point of an activity. An event—in this limited sense—does not consume time or resources.

See also CRITICAL PATH METHOD and PERT.

FREQUENTLY USED EVALUATION TECHNIQUES AS DESCRIBED BY THEIR STANDARD NOTATIONS

NOTATION			
R—GROUP	R_1	R_N	Group #1 THROUGH GROUP #N
O—OBSERVATION	O_1	O_N	OBSERVATION #1 THROUGH OBSERVATION #N
X—TREATMENT	X_1	X_N	TREATMENT #1 THROUGH TREATMENT #N

Design Type		
Single Group		
Direct (one shot)	X O	
Before-After	O_1 X O_2	
Time Series	O_1 O_2 O_3 X O_4	
Multiple Group		
Direct	R_1 O_1 R_2 X O_2	
Before-After	R_1 O_1 O_2 R_2 O_3 X O_4	
Time Series	R_1 O_1 O_2 O_3 O_4 R_1 O_5 O_6 O_7 X O_8	Combination of 1, 2, 3, & 5
Four-Group Design	R_1 O_1 O_2 R_2 O_3 X O_4 R_3 O_5 R_4 X O_6	

evergreen contract, an agreement that automatically renews itself annually unless one side gives advance notice to the other side that it will end.

examination: *see* EMPLOYMENT TESTING.

examination, assembled, examination that includes as one of its parts a written or performance test for which applicants are required to assemble at appointed times and places.

examination, group oral: *see* GROUP ORAL INTERVIEW.

examination, unassembled, examination in which applicants are rated on their education, experience, and other qualifications as shown in the formal application and any supportive evidence that may be required, without assembling for a written or performance test.

excess business holdings, the limitation on the size of an investment that a private foundation may make in a business enterprise. In general, an excess business holding consists of combined ownership of more than twenty percent of the voting power in a business enterprise by a foundation and all disqualified persons.

In other words, while there are exceptions, excess business holdings consist of a private foundation's equity holdings in a private corporation which must be disposed of in order to avoid excise taxes and for the remainder of its holdings to be allowed by the IRS. One such exception is the *de minimis rule*, under which a foundation may own two percent or less of a business enterprise.

See also:

COMBINED VOTING POWER
DISQUALIFIED PERSON
EQUITY
PRIVATE FOUNDATION

excess contributions, contributions to tax-exempt organizations are limited to a percentage of Adjusted Gross Income (AGI) and, therefore, contributions in excess of that percentage may not be claimed as income tax deductions. Under current tax law and rules, excess contributions may be carried forward for use in future years.

See ADJUSTED GROSS INCOME.

excess policy, insurance that pays only for losses greater than those covered by another policy.

exchange theory, the concept that people in organizations are motivated by an expectation that favors will in some way, at some later time, be returned. The everyday expression "you owe me one!" is a succinct summary of the importance and pervasiveness of exchange theory.

See also ORGANIZATION THEORY.

excise tax: *see* TAX, EXCISE.

exclusion, not counting something. For example, a certain amount of money may be donated each year without paying a tax on the gift. This is called an exclusion.

See also:

DEDUCTION
EXEMPTION
TAX CREDIT

exclusion, lifetime: *see* LIFETIME EXCLUSION, GIFT TAX.

exclusionary clause, that part of a contract that tries to restrict the legal remedies available to one side if the contract is broken.

exclusively, as the term has been interpreted for tax-exemption purposes, it means primarily or substantially. Therefore, the language of IRS Code 501(c) (3), which requires organizations to be organized and operated exclusively for tax-exempt purposes, should be interpreted to mean "primarily or substantially for tax-exempt purposes."

See also ORGANIZED and OPERATED.

ex-con: *see* EX-OFFENDER.

execution, carrying out or completing; signing and finalizing a document, such as a contract.

executive, any of the highest managers in an organization.

See also GROUP EXECUTIVE and PLURAL EXECUTIVE.

executive committee, a standing committee of the board of directors, usually comprised of the board's elected officers plus a limited number of other board members. The functions and authority of executive committees varies widely among nonprofit organizations. Some executive committees function as the board of directors between board meetings; they have full authority to make binding decisions for the board on a broad range of issues. Some executive committees serve as the president's or executive director's "kitchen cabinet." Other executive committees are restricted to quasi-housekeeping functions like creating board meeting agendas and recommending committee appointments.

See also COMMITTEE and KITCHEN CABINET.

executive development: *see* MANAGEMENT DEVELOPMENT.

executive order, any rule cr regulation issued by a chief administrative authority.

Executive Order 10925, presidential executive order of March 6, 1961, which, for the first time, required that "affirmative action" be used to implement the policy of nondiscrimination in employment by the federal government and its contractors.

Executive Order 11141, presidential executive order of February 12, 1964, which prohibits employment discrimination because of age by federal government contractors.

Executive Order 11246, presidential executive order of September 24, 1965, which requires federal government contracts to contain provisions against employment discrimination because of race, color, religion, or national origin.

See also PHILADELPHIA PLAN.

Executive Order 11375, presidential executive order of October 17, 1967, which requires federal government contracts to contain provisions against employment discrimination because of sex.

executive oversight, total process by which an executive attempts to exercise control over his organization and hold individual managers responsible for the implementation of their programs.

executive session, any meeting of a board, commission, or legislative group or subgroup that is not open to the public.

executor, a person selected by a person making a will to administer the will and to distribute his or her estate (property) after the person making the will dies.

exempt, not included; not obligated to pay taxes on. For example, exempt income.

exempt activities, activities of a tax-exempt organization which will not jeopardize its tax-exempt status.

See also EXEMPT FUNCTION INCOME.

exempt employees, employees who, because of their administrative, professional, or executive status, are not covered by the overtime provisions of the Fair Labor Standards Act. In consequence, their employing organizations are not legally required to pay them for overtime work.

exempt from filing (for tax exemption), not required to file: churches, some church-related organizations, small private foundations, and a few other types of nonprofit organizations are not required to file for tax exemption; however, many do so of their own volition in order to have tangible evidence of their tax-exempt status.

exempt function income, income generated from the sale of services or goods produced through exempt activities.

See also EXEMPT ACTIVITIES and UNRELATED BUSINESS INCOME.

exemption, the state of being tax-exempt; also, a deduction from gross income for income tax purposes allowed for the support of one's self and dependents.

exempt organization, a general term for an organization that is not required to pay federal income tax. Typically, an organization that is exempt under federal law is also exempt under state and local laws.

Exempt Organizations Branch (of IRS) (EO), the office within the Internal Revenue Service which has responsibility for regulating tax-exempt organizations and enforcing the provisions of applicable federal tax laws.

exempt purposes, charitable, religious, scientific, and educational purposes. Within each of these broad categories there are numerous subcategories. For example, within charitable purposes, some of the subpurposes include promotion of social welfare and promotion of the arts.

exit interview, also called SEPARATION INTERVIEW, tool to monitor employee terminations that seeks information on why the employee is leaving and what he or she liked or disliked about his or her job, working conditions, company policy, etc. Exit interviews are usually, and most desirably, conducted by the personnel department and not by the supervisor of the exiting employee.

ex-offender, anyone who, having been convicted of a crime, served time in prison.

ex officio, Latin phrase ("by virtue of his office"). Many individuals hold positions on boards, commissions, councils, etc., because of an office that they temporarily occupy. For example, the mayor of a city may be an *ex officio* member of the board of trustees of a college in her city.

expectancy, probability of success on the job in terms of a specific criterion and associated with a known fact about an individual such as a test score, level of education, etc.

expectancy theory, also VALENCE, theory that individuals have cognitive "expectancies" regarding outcomes that are likely to occur as a result of what they do, and that individuals have preferences among these various outcomes. Consequently, motivation occurs on the basis of what the individual expects to occur as a result of what he chooses to do. An "expectancy" in this context refers to an employee's perceived probability that a given level of effort will result in a given outcome, such as a promotion or raise in salary.

expenditure, taxable: *see* TAXABLE EXPENDITURE.

expenditure responsibility, the responsibility of a private foundation for ensuring that the funds it grants to a 501(c) (3) organization, which—for any of several reasons—does not have public charity status, or to a non-501(c) (3) organization for a project which clearly is charitable in nature, are spent for the intended purposes and that accurate reportings of financial transactions are made to the Internal Revenue Service.

expenditures, term generally used interchangeably with *outlays*.

expense, the cost of resources (assets) used in operating an organization.

expense account, the advance or reimbursement of monies to an employee or a volunteer who incurs expenses in the ordinary course of the nonprofit organization's operations.

experience-based learning, *see* LABORATORY TRAINING.

experienced unemployed, term from the U.S. Bureau of the Census that refers to "unemployed persons who have worked at any time in the past."

experience rating, insurance term which refers to a review of a previous year's group claims experience in order to establish premium rates for the following year.

experimental group, a group in a research design that is exposed to the treatment or manipulation called for in that design.

experimenter effect, any distortion in an experiment's findings because of the behavior or attitudes of the experimenters.
See also HAWTHORNE EFFECT.

expert, efficiency: *see* EFFICIENCY EXPERT.

expiration date, time established by a collective bargaining agreement for the agreement to terminate.

expiration of term, rotational: *see* BOARD ROTATION.

expired account, an account in which authority to incur obligations has lapsed but from which outlays may be made to pay existing obligations and liabilities previously incurred, as well as valid adjustments thereto.

exploited exempt activity income, also ADVERTISING INCOME, income generated through business activities which typically are engaged in by for-profit business organizations. For example, the sale of advertising in a journal usually is considered exploited exempt activity (or advertising) income. Exploited exempt activity income is one consideration in determining unrelated business income.
See also UNRELATED BUSINESS INCOME.

external audit: *see* AUDIT.

external equity, also INTERNAL EQUITY, a measure of the justice of an employee's wages when the compensation for his/her position is compared to the labor market as a whole within a region, profession, or industry. *Internal equity* is a measure of the justice of an employee's wages when the compensation for his/her position is compared to similar positions within the same organization.

external house organ: *see* HOUSE ORGAN.

externalities: *see* SPILLOVER EFFECT.

external labor market, geographic region from which employers reasonably expect to recruit new workers.

extrapolation: *see* ESTIMATED INCOME.

extrinsic motivation, motivation not an inherent part of the work itself. When one works solely for the monetary rewards, one is extrinsically motivated.

F

face amount, in life insurance, this is the amount, stated on the front of the policy, that is payable upon the death of the insured. The actual amount payable to the beneficiary may differ according to the policy's specific provisions, such as double indemnity or subsequent riders.

face validity, also called FAITH VALIDITY, measure of the degree to which a test *appears* to be valid. While this is the most superficial kind of validity, it may contribute significantly to the legitimacy of the test in the eyes of the candidates (an important consideration in avoiding legal challenges).

facilitator, individual who serves as a catalyst, usually in a formal organization development effort, in order to improve the interactions and interpersonal relationships of a group.

facility, in general usage, something designed, built, installed, etc., to serve a specific function affording a convenience or service. However, in the world of third sector organizations, facility usually means working space in a building. A leased facility often is an allowable grant cost, and the effective lease costs of facilities are usually allowable for calculating in-kind match.

See also:
COSTS, ALLOWABLE
GRANT

facsimile, exact copy; for example, facsimile signatures are mechanically imprinted signatures on checks, stock certificates, and bonds. These signatures can be imprinted on checks with checkwriting machines.

factfinding, (labor relations), an impartial review of the issues in a dispute by a specially appointed third party, whether it be a single individual, panel, or board. The factfinder holds formal or informal hearings and submits a report to the parties involved. The factfinder's report, usually considered advisory, may contain specific recommendations.

factor analysis, any of several methods of analyzing the intercorrelations among test scores or other sets of variables.

factors: *see* JOB FACTORS.

facts and circumstances test, an IRS test to allow exceptions to its requirement that publicly supported institutions receive at least thirty-three percent of their support from public and governmental sources. In order to satisfy the facts and circumstances test, an organization must receive a percentage of its income from public support (but a smaller percentage than thirty-three percent); it must have a history of soliciting funds publicly; and it must demonstrate the public nature of its programs and organizational control.

Failure to satisfy the test may result in an organization being declared a private foundation or private operating foundation.

See also PRIVATE FOUNDATION and PRIVATE OPERATING FOUNDATION.

fact sheet, an informational piece used in media relations and development. A fact sheet provides a concise statement (not more than one typed page) about an organization or a project. For example, a nonprofit organization's fact sheet might include statements of its purpose, clientele served, its uniqueness, key staff members and board members, and contact person(s).

See also:
DEVELOPMENT
MEDIA RELATIONS
PUBLIC RELATIONS
PUBLIC RELATIONS KIT

Fair Credit Reporting Acts, federal and state laws regulating the organizations that investigate, store, and give out consumer credit and information, organizations that collect bills, etc. Consumers are given rights to know about investigations, see and dispute their files, etc.

fair day's work, generally, the amount of work produced in a work day by a qualified employee of average skill exerting average effort.

Fair Employment Practice Commission (FEPC), generic term for any state or local government agency responsible for administrating/enforcing laws prohibiting employment discrimination because of race, color, sex, religion, national origin, or other factors.

fair employment practice laws, all government requirements designed to prohibit discrimination in the various aspects of employment.

Fair Employment Practice Service, reference service published by the Bureau of National Affairs, Inc., which covers federal and state laws dealing with equal opportunity in employment. Full texts of federal and state FEP laws, orders, and regulations, as well as federal, state, and local court opinions, and decisions of the Equal Employment Opportunity Commission are included.

Fair Labor Standards Act (FLSA), also called WAGES AND HOURS ACT, federal statute of 1938 which, as amended, establishes minimum-wage, overtime-pay, equal-pay, recordkeeping, and child-labor standards affecting more than fifty million full-time and part-time workers.

See also, GARCIA V. SAN ANTONIO METROPOLITAN TRANSIT AUTHORITY.

fair market value, the price which an asset could command on the open market.

fair use, the limited use that may be made of something (for example, text in a book) without infringing the copyright.

faith validity: *see* FACE VALIDITY.

false negative, any incidence whereby an individual who is in fact qualified is excluded by a test or some other screening criteria.

false positive, any incidence whereby an individual who is in fact unqualified is selected because of a test or some other screening criteria.

family corporation, also FAMILY PARTNERSHIP, a corporation or partnership established to spread income among members of a family and thereby reduce the total tax obligation.

family-expense policy, health insurance policy that insures both the individual policyholder and his or her immediate dependents (usually spouse and children).

family foundation, a foundation established by, controlled by, and usually endowed or supported by one family. Most family foundations are small and target their funds on local charitable organizations which deal with favored causes.

See also FOUNDATION and PRIVATE FOUNDATION.

family members, a term defined in IRS Code 4946(d) as spouses, ancestors, children, grandchildren, great-grandchildren and their spouses. If an individual is a disqualified person (relative to dealing with a private foundation), the individual's family members are also disqualified.

See DISQUALIFIED PERSON and PRIVATE FOUNDATION.

family T-group, work team that undertakes a T-group effort as a unit.

See also T-GROUP.

Fannie Mae: *see* FEDERAL NATIONAL MORTGAGE ASSOCIATION.

Farm Credit Administration, an agency of the federal government that supervises the Farm Credit System of federal land banks and associated banks and cooperatives.

farmers' cooperative, an association of farmers, ranchers, or other agricultural producers that purchases and/or markets cooperatively. Farmers' cooperatives may qualify for tax-exempt status under IRS Code 521.

FASB: *see* FINANCIAL ACCOUNTING STANDARDS BOARD.

"FAST" diagram, a hierarchy of objectives created by using the Functional Analysis Systems Technique.

See also:

BACKSTEP ANALYSIS
FUNCTIONAL ANALYSIS SYSTEMS TECHNIQUE
HIERARCHY OF OBJECTIVES

"FAST" program planning: *see* FUNCTIONAL ANALYSIS SYSTEMS TECHNIQUE.

fatigue, weariness caused by physical or mental exertion that lessens the capacity to, and the will for, work.

fatigue curve, also MONOTONY CURVE, graphic representation of productivity increases and decreases influenced by fatigue. As workers "warm up" or practice their tasks, productivity increases; thereafter fatigue sets in and productivity decreases. After lunch or coffee breaks, productivity should rise again slightly, but thereafter continuously decline until the end of the day. This pattern varies with different kinds of work. Fatigue curve measurements are essential in establishing realistic work standards.

FUNCTION ANALYSIS SYSTEM TECHNIQUE DIAGRAM

(FAST DIAGRAM)

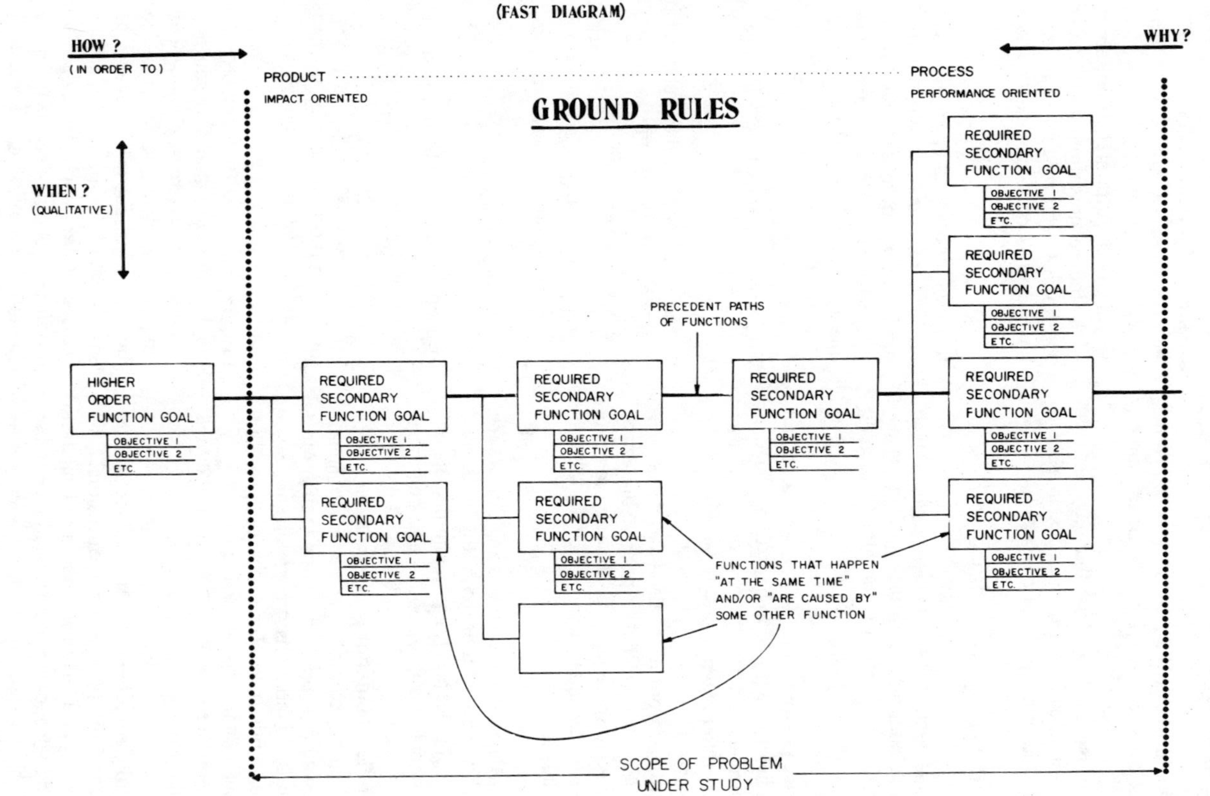

A *monotony curve* is characterized by a drop in productivity in the middle of the work period, great variability in the rate of productivity, and a tendency to "end spurt"—show an increase in productivity at the end of the work period due to a feeling of relief that the work period is almost over.

Fayol, Henri (1841-1925), French executive engineer who developed the first comprehensive theory of management. His *Administration Industrielle et Générale* (published in France in 1916) was almost ignored in the U.S. until Constance Storrs' English translation, *General and Industrial Management* (London: Pitman, 1949), appeared. Today his theoretical contributions are generally considered as significant as those of Frederick W. Taylor.

featherbedding, an easy or superfluous job; the term originated in the U.S. Army in the 1850s. Today featherbedding connotes any labor practice that requires an employer to pay for more workers than are truly needed for a job, or to pay for work that is not performed. Featherbedding provisions in labor contracts usually have their origin in work rules that were once efficient but have become obsolete due to newer technology. Union leaders often insist on maintaining the older practices in order to protect the jobs of those whose livelihoods are threatened by the new technology.

The Labor-Management Relations (Taft-Hartley) Act of 1947 makes it an unfair labor practice "to cause or attempt to cause an employer to pay or deliver or agree to pay or deliver any money or other thing of value in the nature of an exaction, for services which are not performed." This provision has not had much effect, however, because of the legal subtleties of defining featherbedding practices.

federal assistance programs, term used to refer to the variety of federal programs available to state and local governments including counties, cities, metropolitan, and regional governments; schools, colleges, and universities; health institutions; nonprofit and for-profit organizations; and individuals and families. Current federal assistance programs are listed in the annual *Catalogue of Federal Domestic Assistance*.

Federal Council on the Arts and Humanities: *see* NATIONAL FOUNDATION ON THE ARTS and THE HUMANITIES.

federal court of appeals: *see* COURT OF APPEALS.

federal courts, the integrated system of courts created by the U.S. Constitution and by Congress.

federal district court: *see* DISTRICT COURT.

Federal Emergency Management Agency (FEMA), the point of accountability for emergency preparedness and response by private, nonprofit, and public organizations and for all types of emergencies—natural, manmade, and nuclear.

Federal Home Loan Bank Board, also FEDERAL SAVINGS AND LOAN INSURANCE CORPORATION, body that supervises and regulates savings and loan associations, which specialize in lending out money on homes and are the country's major private source of funds to pay for building and buying homes. The Board operates the *Federal Savings and Loan Insurance Corporation*, which protects savings of the more than 75 million Americans with savings accounts in FSLIC-insured savings and loan associations. The Board also directs the *Federal Home Loan Bank System*, which, like the Federal Reserve System for banks, provides reserve credit and the assurance that member savings and loan associations will continue to be a source of financing for homes.

Federal Home Loan Mortgage Corporation, also FREDDIE MAC, corporation that, under the supervision of the Federal Home Loan Bank Board, maintains a secondary market principally for conventional mortgages (mortgages not guaranteed by the government). It purchases mortgages from primary lenders, including members of the Federal Home Loan Bank System and large mortgage bankers, for packaging into various sorts of securities. These securities are bought primarily by private investors such as pension funds, insurance companies, etc.

Federal Insurance Contributions Act, also the SOCIAL SECURITY ACT, act which states that personal services provided for an exempt organization may be exempted from the provisions of the Social Security Act.

federalism, creative, the Johnson Administration's term for its approach to intergovernmental relations, which was characterized by joint planning and decision making among all levels of government, nonprofit, and for-profit organizations.

federalism, horizontal, state-to-state interactions and relationships. Interstate relationships take many forms, including compacts and commissions which have been established for specific purposes: river basin management, transportation, extradition of criminals, conservation of forests and wildlife, and administration of parks and recreation.

Horizontal relationships between and among state and local governments also are numerous. Cities frequently contract for services from neighboring state and local governments. The Lakewood Plan, established in southern California in 1954, has been the most comprehensive example of interlocal contracting for services to date. Under this plan, the City of Lakewood contracted for a rather comprehensive package of services from Los Angeles County, where Lakewood is located.

federalism, new, term variously used, first as a reconceptualization of federalism as intergovernmental relations, thereafter referring to the actual relationships between the levels of government as they shared in the performance of expanding governmental functions in the early 1970s. New federalism, as developed by the Reagan administration, disregarded the Nixon approach of decentralized federal regional management entirely and turned to development of direct relationships of the federal government to state governments. The intent of new federalism under the Reagan administration has been to return power and responsibility to the state and to dramatically reduce the role of the federal government in domestic programs.

***Federal Management Circulars* (FMC)** and OFFICE OF MANAGEMENT AND BUDGET CIRCULARS (OMB), two extremely important series of management guidelines that define federal requirements for federal government grantees and contractors. FMC's are issued by the Office of Federal Management Policy and, obviously, the OMB circulars by the Office of Management and Budget. Each FMC and OMB circular addresses a specific topical area, for example, Cost Sharing of Federal Research or Coordinating Indirect Cost Rates; and Audit at Educational Institutions.

Federal Mediation and Conciliation Service (FMCS), body created by the Labor-Management Relations (Taft-Hartley) Act of 1947 as an independent agency of the federal government. FMCS helps prevent disruptions in the flow of interstate commerce caused by labor-management disputes by providing mediators to assist disputing parties in the resolution of their differences. FMCS can intervene on its own motion or by invitation of either side in a dispute. Mediators have no law enforcement authority and rely wholly on persuasive techniques. FMCS also helps provide qualified third-party neutrals as factfinders or arbitrators.

Federal National Mortgage Association, also FANNIE MAE and FNMA, a federally chartered but private, for-profit corporation owned by stockholders and regulated by the Department of Housing and Urban Development. Fannie Mae purchases government-guaranteed and other mortgages to add to its own portfolio and for limited resale. Fannie Mae issues its own securities, which are treated in financial markets as if they were those of a government agency rather than a private organization.

Federal Register, daily publication that is the medium for making available to the public federal agency regulations and other legal documents of the executive branch. These documents cover a wide range of government activities—environmental protection, consumer product safety, food and drug standards, occupational health and safety, and many more areas of concern to the public. Perhaps more important, the *Federal Register* includes *proposed* changes in regulated areas. Each proposed change published carries an invitation for any citizen or group to participate in the consideration of the proposed regulation through the submission of written data, views, or arguments, and sometimes by oral presentations.

Federal Register System, established in 1935 by the Federal Register Act; the means by which administrative rules and regulations issued by executive departments and agencies under authority of law are codified and made known to the public. It consists of the *Federal Register* published daily Tuesday through Saturday except for the day following a legal holiday; the *Code of Federal Regulations*, an annually issued multivolume cumulation of administrative regulations in force; and the annually published *United States Government Manual*. The System is administered by the National Archives and Records Service of the General Services Administration.

Federal Reserve System, colloquially known as the FED, central bank of the U.S., charged with administrating and making policy for the nation's credit and monetary affairs. Run by a seven member Board of Governors appointed by the president (who also appoints their chairman), the system includes twelve Federal Reserve Banks, twenty-four branches, all national banks, and many state banking institutions. Three major monetary tools are available to the Federal Reserve System to control the economy's supply of money and credit:

1. Open market operations which, through the purchase or sale of government bonds, increases or decreases the availability of dollars to member banks.
2. Discount rate adjustments which increase or decrease the interest rate charged to member banks for the money they borrow.
3. Reserve requirements which, through changes in levels of reserve, increase or decrease the number of dollars a bank may make available for loan.

Two less significant tools, moral suasion and selective controls over stock purchase margin requirements, are also used to help manage the economy.

Federal Savings and Loan Insurance Corporation: *see* FEDERAL HOME LOAN BANK BOARD.

Federal Supplemental Compensation, a program enacted in 1982 to provide benefits to individuals who exhaust all of their rights to benefits under the regular and extended unemployment insurance programs. In states where extended benefits are not in effect, exhaustees of regular unemployment insurance immediately become eligible for Federal Supplemental Compensation. In states on extended benefits, an individual must exhaust those benefits before collecting Federal Supplemental Compensation.

Federal Times, weekly newspaper that covers pending civil service legislation, compensation problems, corruption, labor/management concerns, and other issues of interest to federal government employees.

Federal Trade Commission (FTC), body whose objective is to prevent the free enterprise system from being stifled, substantially lessened or fettered by monopoly or restraints on trade, or corrupted by unfair or deceptive trade practices. As an administrative agency acting quasi-judicial-ly and quasi-legislatively, the Commission was established to deal with trade practices on a continuing and corrective basis. It has no authority to punish; its function is to "prevent," through cease-and-desist orders and other means, those practices condemned by the law of federal trade regulation; however, court ordered civil penalties up to $10,000 may be obtained for each violation of a commission order.

Federal Unemployment Tax Act, act which states that services provided for an exempt organization may be exempted from the provisions of the act.

feedback, information about the effect and/or results of the behavior of a person or system that is communicated back to that person or system so that human behavior or organization (mechanical) performance might be modified.

See also CYBERNETICS.

feeder account, those budgeted accounts whose resources are available only for transfer to other specified accounts.

fee-for-service plan (health care), a type of prepaid health care plan similar to a health care insurance plan. For example, Blue Cross and Blue Shield are fee-for-service health care plans.

fees-for-services, payments to an organization in return for services performed. A tax-exempt organization may charge fees for its services without necessarily jeopardizing its tax-exempt status. However, the concept has been controversial and difficult to define, and fees-for-service should be handled with caution. In general, the IRS has held that the general criteria are whether an organization is operated for a profit motive and/or for private interest.

fellow servant doctrine, common-law concept that an employer should not be held responsible for an accident to an employee if the accident resulted from the negligence of another employee.

FEMA, *see* FEDERAL EMERGENCY MANAGEMENT AGENCY.

FEPC: *see* FAIR EMPLOYMENT PRACTICE COMMISSION.

fictitious person: *see* ARTIFICIAL PERSON.

fidelity bond, insurance on a person against that person's dishonesty; a form of bonding, similar to insurance protection, against embezzlement. Fidelity bonding has two primary advantages: the organization is able to recover (up to) the amount of money embezzled; and fidelity bonding serves as a preventive measure against embezzlement by employees and volunteers.

field, a set of data-holding positions in computer storage that are treated as one unit of information.

See also:

BIT
BYTE
RECORD

field-of-interest fund, a type of fund which allows donors to direct contributions to a field (or area) of interest but not limit those donations to one or two specific charitable organizations. Field-of-interest funds are often found in and managed by community foundations. *See also* COMMUNITY FOUNDATION.

field survey, research method in which data are collected through interviews or questionnaries from a sample of people selected to represent some larger population. The selection process saves time and energy because it is not necessary to contact every member of the population. The method is most appropriate for gathering information about topics of which the respondents are consciously aware.

field theory, theory that holds that an individual's behavior at any given time is the result of his/her basic personality interacting with the psychological forces of the environment.

See also GROUP DYNAMICS and LEWIN, KURT.

file, circular: *see* CIRCULAR FILE.

Filer Commission: *see* COMMISSION ON PRIVATE PHILANTHROPY AND PUBLIC NEEDS.

final offer arbitration, also called LAST OFFER ARBITRATION, negotiating stratagem that has an arbitrator choose from among the disputing parties' final or last offers.

finance, the manipulation of money and credit; the fields of banking, taxes, insurance, and the money, foreign exchange, and investment markets. Finance directly involves other fields such as accounting, marketing, and production. It is an integral part of management in all three sectors of the economy.

As a broad managerial field, finance is the art or science of obtaining and managing funds.

finance charge, the interest or other payment made in addition to the price of goods or services, paid off in installments or "on time."

finance committee, a standing committee which is usually assigned responsibility for overseeing the organization's financial operations and status. The finance committee usually reviews financial statements with the staff prior to board of directors meetings; compares expenditures with budgets; questions certain expenditures and bookkeeping decisions; and advises the board to take (or not take) financially-related actions. Some finance committees are responsible for drafting and/or presenting budgets, whereas other nonprofit organizations have separate budget committees.

See also COMMITTEE.

finance company, a corporation that lends money to businesses and their customers in a wide variety of ways, involving such things as secured and unsecured loans, purchase of accounts receivable, etc.

financial accounting: *see* ACCOUNTING.

Financial Accounting Standards Board (FASB), a private organization that sets standards for financial accounting and reporting and promulgates generally accepted accounting principles. Its pronouncements are officially recognized as authoritative by the American Institute of Certified Public Accountants and the Securities and Exchange Commission.

financial administration, activities involving the management of finances. Includes accounting, auditing, and budgeting; the supervision of finances; collection, custody, and disbursement of funds; administration of employee retirement systems; debt and investment administration; and the like.

financial analysis, a general term referring to the process of extracting and studying information in financial statements for use in management decision making. For example, financial analysis typically involves the use of ratios, comparisons with prior periods and with the budget, etc.

financial audit, determination of (1) whether financial operations are properly conducted, (2) whether the financial reports of an audited entity are presented fairly, and (3) whether the entity has complied with applicable laws and regulations.

financial claim: *see* CLAIM.

financial institution, a broad term that includes banks, trust companies, credit unions, savings and loan associations, and similar organizations licensed by a state or the U.S. government to do financial business.

financially assisted programs, any activities, services, projects, or processes of any agencies, commissions, councils, administrations, government-owned corporations, or instrumentalities of any governments.

financial ratio: *see* RATIO and RATIO, ACCOUNTING.

financial service, a company that provides investment advice, often through subscription newsletters and other publications.

EXAMPLE OF A COMPARATIVE OPERATING STATEMENT FOR INCOME

INCOME	1985 Actual	1985 Budget	1984 Actual
Fund-raising			
Special Events	$ 98,073	$ 80,000	$ 53,123
Corporate Events	119,960	105,000	108,478
Sales	5,868	5,000	4,532
Memberships	19,821	10,000	9,741
Interest	17,469	15,000	14,398
Donations	4,721	5,000	5,256
Total Income	$365,209	$335,000	$280,882

Source: Colorado Department of Health, Emergency Medical Services Division, Colorado Ambulance Service Management Handbook *(Denver, Colorado, July 1984.)*

financial statement, comparative, a financial statement which presents comparable information for more than one time period, to allow comparisons; for example, this year and last year, or this month and last month.

financial statements, also FINANCIAL REPORTS, for nonprofit organizations, the balance sheet and the operating statement or activity statement. The operating statement is equivalent to a for-profit corporation's profit-and-loss statement.

See also BALANCE SHEET and OPERATING STATEMENT.

financing, the process of providing an organization with the money it needs to operate; also, obtaining something on credit.

fire, discharge from employment. The word has such a rude connotation that it is hardly ever used for formal purposes. It seems so much more genteel and antiseptic to terminate, discharge, dismiss, sever, or lay off an employee.

***Fire Fighters Local Union No. 1784* v. *Stotts*,** 81 L Ed 483 (1984), U.S. Supreme Court case which held that courts may not interfere with seniority systems to protect newly hired black employees from layoff.

first-dollar coverage, coverage under an insurance policy which begins with the first dollar of expense incurred by the insured for the covered benefits.

first-line management, level of management that is just above the workers (for example, a foreman).

first mortgage, also LIEN, the mortgage (or lien) that has the right to be paid off before all others.

See also LIEN and MORTGAGE.

first option: *see* RIGHT OF FIRST REFUSAL.

fiscal, having to do with taxation, public revenues, or public debt.

fiscal impact analysis, a projection of the public cost and revenues associated with residential or nonresidential growth in a given jurisdiction.

fiscal integrity, also FISCAL RESPONSIBILITY, reliability in fiscal matters.

fiscal responsibility: *see* FISCAL INTEGRITY.

fiscal stress: *see* MANAGEMENT, CUTBACK.

fiscal year, a financial year. A fiscal year consists of twelve consecutive months, which may start and end anytime during the calendar year. Some organizations select fiscal years to coincide with their program years and others with when officers take office. Many others use the calendar year as their fiscal year. The fiscal year should be established and formally incorporated in the organization's bylaws. The fiscal year is designated by the calendar year in which it ends (*e.g.*, fiscal year 1986 is the fiscal year ending, for example, September 30, 1986).

fixed annuity, annuity that provides constant, periodic dollar payments for its entire length.

fixed assets: *see* ASSETS.

fixed-benefit retirement plan, retirement plan whose benefits consist of a fixed amount or fixed percentage.

fixed costs: *see* COSTS, FIXED.

fixed price contract, technically, a contract in which an exact price is specified for goods or services.

fixed rate mortgage, a loan secured by property, whose interest rate is fixed for its life. Fixed rate mortgages are not as readily available as in the past. Because the market is highly changeable, some lenders are reluctant to lock themselves into rates that cannot adapt to changing conditions. Fixed rate mortgages are beginning to be replaced by adjustable, renegotiable, and variable rate mortgages.

See also MORTGAGE.

fixed shift, work shift to which an employee is assigned indefinitely.

fixture, anything attached to a building or to land. Attached things—once they are attached—may not be removed by a tenant. Conversely (and confusingly), the term is also used to mean those things which are attached and may be removed.

flagged rate, also called OVERRATE, compensation rates paid to employees whose positions warrant lower rates.

***Flast* v. *Cohen*,** 392 U.S. 83 (1968), Supreme Court case concerning the expenditure of federal funds for instructional purposes in religious schools under the Elementary and Secondary Education Act of 1965. The court found that parties had standing to challenge these expenditures if they could show that (1) they were taxpayers, and (2) the challenged enactment exceeded specific constitutional limitations imposed on the exercise of the congressional power to tax and spend.

flat-benefit plan, pension plan whose benefits are unrelated to earnings. Such a plan might provide a stipulated amount per month per year of service.

flat organization, one whose structure has comparatively few levels. In contrast, a *tall organization* is one whose structure has many levels.

See also TALL ORGANIZATION.

flat rate, also called STANDARD RATE and SINGLE RATE, pay structure offering only one rate of pay for each pay level.

flexible passing score: *see* CUTTING SCORE.

flexible rate mortgage: *see* ADJUSTABLE RATE MORTGAGE.

flexible working hours: *see* FLEXI-TIME.

flexi-time, flexible work schedule in which workers can, within a prescribed band of time in the morning and again in the afternoon, start and finish work at their discretion as long as they complete the total number of hours required for a given period, usually a month. That is, the workday can vary from day to day in its length as well as in the time that it begins and ends. The morning and evening bands of time are often designated as "quiet time." Telephone calls and staff meetings are confined to "core time," which generally runs from midmorning to midafternoon. Time clocks or other mechanical controls for keeping track of the hours worked are usually a part of flexi-time systems.

floating policy, also FLOATER POLICY, a supplemental insurance policy which covers items that frequently move (change location) or vary in quantity.

floppy, also FLOPPY DISK, a small, inexpensive plastic disk for random storage of

and access to computer data.
See also DISK.

flowchart, graphic representation of an analysis of, or solution to, a problem that uses symbols to indicate various operations, equipment, and data flow.
See also PRECEDENCE CHART and PROJECT CONTROL CHART.

FLSA: *see* FAIR LABOR STANDARDS ACT.

FMCS: *see* FEDERAL MEDIATION AND CONCILIATION SERVICE.

FNMA: *see* FEDERAL NATIONAL MORTGAGE ASSOCIATION.

focus job area, a unit of an establishment's work force (such as a seniority unit, job title, etc.) in which minorities or women are concentrated or underrepresented relative either to their overall representation in the relevant work force sector or to their availability for the jobs in question. This concept is more related to determining the existence of discrimination rather than to finding underutilization for the purpose of setting goals as part of an affirmative action program.

foils: *see* DISTRACTORS.

Follett, Mary Parker (1868-1933), early social psychologist who anticipated in the 1920s many of the conclusions of the Hawthorne experiments of the 1930s and the post-World War II behavioral movement. In calling for "power with," as opposed to "power over," she anticipated the movement toward more participatory management. Her "law of the situation" is contingency management in its humble origins.

follow-up letter (for contributions), a letter which should be sent to donors shortly after receiving a contribution.

forced choice, testing technique that requires the subject to choose from among a given set of alternatives.

TINCUP AMBULANCE SERVICE
1234 2nd Avenue
Tincup, Colorado 81234

December 1, 1985

Mr. Jonathon Doe
245 Columbine Street
Antero Junction, Colorado 84321

Dear Jonathon:

In December 1985, you gave $300 to the Tincup Ambulance Service. We greatly appreciate your generosity and were delighted to count you as one of our Sustaining Friends last year.

As we near the end of 1986, the Trustees of the Tincup Volunteer Ambulance Service are committed to having a balanced budget for the third consecutive year. As of today, we are $2,000 short of our "Sustaining Friends Contributions" goal, which must be reached in order for us to be in the black again.

Your support is needed. As you know, we cannot expect any financial help from the town, state, or federal government. We are entirely on our own. We only need enough contributions to cover the costs which are not raised through fees.

Please renew your gift so we can continue providing volunteer ambulance services for Tincup's residents and visitors. An addressed envelope is enclosed.

Sincerely,

Patricia B. Trower
President

forced-distribution method, performance appraisal technique that predetermines the percentage of ratees to be placed in the various performance categories.

forced sale, a sale made to pay off a court's judgment, ordered by that court, and done according to rules set by the court; a judicial sale.

force field analysis, a procedure for determining what factors or forces are contributing to a problem. Force field analysis can be used in a variety of situations occuring in program planning and analysis. Its greatest uses may be in (1) solving prob-

EXAMPLE OF A FORCED CHOICE INSTRUMENT

DIRECTIONS:

You will be given the start of a self-descriptive statement followed by four alternative endings. You are to indicate the order in which you feel each ending applies to you. In the parentheses to the right of each ending, fill in the number 4, 3, 2, or 1 according to which alternative is *most like you* (4) on to which alternative is *least like you* (1)

PLEASE FILL IN THIS EXAMPLE:

MOST OF THE TIME I AM: RANK 4, 3, 2, 1

good-natured and jolly .... ( )
hard-working and full of plans .... ( )
economical and thoughtful .... ( )
charming and popular .... ( )

Check the example above to see if each alternative ending is ranked with a different number and that you did not use 4, 3, 2, or 1 more than once.

If the statements that follow in this questionnaire have two or more alternative endings that seem equally like you, or if some are not like you at all, please rank them even though it may be difficult. All alternative endings must be ranked with 4, 3, 2, or 1; most like you (4), least like you (1).

I FEEL MOST PLEASED WITH MYSELF WHEN I:

1. act idealistically and with optimism .... ( )
2. see an opportunity for leadership and go right after it .... ( )
3. look after my own interests and let others look after theirs .... ( )
4. adjust myself to fit in with the group in which I find myself .... ( )

lems during the planning process and in the substantive areas of the program being analyzed, and (2) overcoming constraints that are impeding a program from being planned, implemented, or operated.

In the substantive program area, force field analysis might be used, for example, during the problem formulation phase to identify forces that are pushing to solve an identified problem and what forces are preventing the problem from being solved.

The basic steps involved in a force field analysis are:

1. Write a specific problem statement.
2. Write the desired goal or end result.
3. List the forces pushing toward achievement of the goal.
4. List the forces pushing against achievement of the goal.
5. Rank each force in order of importance.
6. Decide which forces can be changed to move toward the goal.
7. Decide upon a plan of action.

formal organization: *see* INFORMAL ORGANIZATION.

Form 990 (IRS) [Return of Organization Exempt from Income Tax], also FORM 990-SCHEDULE A [ORGANIZATION EXEMPT UNDER 501(c)(3)], forms which are charitable nonprofit organizations' equivalents of federal income tax returns.

See also ANNUAL INFORMATION RETURNS.

Form 990-PF (IRS), the IRS form on which private foundations submit their annual reports and their annual returns detailing finances, grants, and tax liabilities. Copies of Form 990-PF's are available for public review, for example, by grant-seekers, at major Foundation Center locations.

See also FOUNDATION CENTER, THE.

forms control, a set of procedures or a program for improving the use, work flow, storage, and disposition of forms.

Form 1023 (IRS), the IRS form which must be filed by an organization with the Internal Revenue Service in order to receive tax-exempt designation.

formula-based categorical grant: *see* GRANT.

formula-project categorical grant: *see* GRANT.

formula score, raw score on a multiple-choice test after a correction for guessing has been applied. With five-choice items, for example, the formula score is the number of correct answers minus one fourth the number of wrong answers. This makes zero the score that would most likely be obtained by random guessing.

Form W-2, also called W-2 FORM and WAGE AND TAX STATEMENT, statement which must be provided to employees by their employers by the end of January of each year. Form W-2 shows earnings for the preceding year and various deductions. Employees must file one copy of their Form W-2 with their federal income tax return.

FORTRAN, an acronym for Formula Translating System, a computer language closely resembling algebraic notation.

Fortune 500, a directory of the five hundred largest U.S. corporations published annually by *Fortune* magazine. The companies listed are called the "Fortune 500 companies."

forward funding, practice of obligating funds in one fiscal year for programs that are to operate in a subsequent year.

foundation, a general term that includes private foundations and other organizations, typically public charities, which have been established for charitable purposes. Foundations serve as important channels through which profits earned by corporations and individuals are distributed for the public benefit. Foundations also serve as informational clearinghouses about sources, needs, and new approaches to problems. The two major classifications of foundations are private and private operating. The most important forms of foundations include independent foundations, corporate foundations, and community foundations.

F. Emerson Andrews, in his pioneering work, *Philanthropic Foundations* (1956), defined a foundation as "a nonprofit organization, with funds (usually from a single source, either an individual, a family, or a corporation) and program managed by its own trustees or directors, established to maintain or aid social, educational, charitable, religious, or other activities serving the common welfare, primarily through the making of grants."

The Tax Reform Act of 1969 (as amended) defines private foundations by exclusion—in other words, as all organizations described by Section 501(c) (3) except

1. organizations described in section 170(b) (1) (A) (i) through (vi)—churches, schools, hospitals, some organizations affiliated with churches, schools, and hospitals, publicly supported organizations, and governmental units;
2. organizations which meet two support tests: (a) in general, they may not receive more than 33⅓% of their financial support from investment income and (b) in general, they must receive more than 33⅓% of their support from "public" sources; and
3. organizations involved in public safety testing.

According to *Foundations Today,* 1982, pg. 7, the five largest foundations of each major type, ranked by their 1980 assets, were:

Independent Foundations
- Ford Foundation
- Robert Wood Johnson Foundation
- Andrew W. Mellon Foundation
- John D. and Catherine T. MacArthur Foundation
- Pew Memorial Trust

Operating Foundations
- Norton Simon Foundation
- Robert A. Welch Foundation
- Norton Simon, Inc. Museum of Art
- Amherst H. Wilder Foundation(*)
- Charles F. Kettering Foundation

Company-sponsored Foundations
Alcoa Foundation
General Motors Foundation
Ford Motor Company Fund
Prudential Foundation
Amoco Foundation, Inc.
Community Foundations
San Francisco Foundation
New York Community Trust
Cleveland Foundation
Chicago Community Trust
Permanent Charity Fund of Boston(**)
(*) No longer is an operating foundtion.
(**) Since has been renamed the Boston Foundation.

See also:
COMMUNITY FOUNDATION
CORPORATE (OR COMPANY) FOUNDATION
FAMILY FOUNDATION
PRIVATE FOUNDATION
PRIVATE OPERATING FOUNDATION

foundation, community: *see* COMMUNITY FOUNDATION.

foundation, private: *see* PRIVATE FOUNDATION.

Foundation Center, The, probably the most highly respected organization in the United States which collects, interprets, and reports data and information about foundations. The Foundation Center is not affiliated with any other organization (including foundations), and its information is considered to be highly trustworthy. A few of its publications include *Foundation Grants Index Annual, The Foundation Center National Data Book, The Foundation Center Source Book Profiles,* and *The Foundation Directory.*

The Foundation Center has four major library centers (in Cleveland, New York, San Francisco, and Washington, D.C.) and has cooperating collections in more than 130 locations. The Center provides reference services.

See also:
COMSEARCH PRINTOUTS
FOUNDATION CENTER NATIONAL DATA BOOK
FOUNDATION CENTER SOURCE BOOK PROFILES,
FOUNDATION DIRECTORY
FOUNDATION GRANTS INDEX ANNUAL

Foundation Center National Data Book, a publication of The Foundation Center which provides information (names, addresses, and finances) on all private foundations which are known to be active—large and small.

Foundation Center Source Book Profiles, a reference document published by The Foundation Center which provides in-depth information about large foundations, their program preferences, previous grants awarded, and statistical profiles of recent granting histories.

See also FOUNDATION CENTER, THE.

Foundation Directory, The, the basic reference on foundations, published by The Foundation Center. It contains information about foundations with more than one million dollars in assets or which make more than $100,000 in annual grants.

Foundation Giving Watch, a monthly report in newsletter format. It is directed at nonprofit organizations that are seeking foundation support.

Foundation Grants Index Annual, a source of current information about recent grants made by (participating) larger foundations, including the grants' sizes, purposes, and recipients. *The Foundations Grants Index* is published in an annual, a bimonthly journal, and is available through *Comsearch Printouts.* The *Foundation Index* has several versions covering different time periods, ranging from the most recent months (inserted in the bimonthly *Foundation News*) to the prior six years.

See also FOUNDATION CENTER, THE and FOUNDATION NEWS.

foundation manager, a manager, director, or other significant official of a private foundation. According to IRS Code

4946(a) (1), foundation managers are disqualified persons.
See DISQUALIFIED PERSON.

Foundation News, a bimonthly publication of the Council on Foundations dedicated to philanthropy. *Foundation News* carries information of importance to third sector organizations such as recent issues and events, research findings, legislative and regulatory developments, innovative projects, etc.

Foundation Updates, a semimonthly newsletter-type report which provides in-depth profiles and analyses of private foundations and their activities. *Foundation Updates* profiles selected foundations in each issue including, for example, the types of grants they make, the geographical area they serve, contact persons, fiscal information, general descriptions, areas of interest, and examples of recent grants.

founders, those who established or initiated something; for example, the founders of a church.

Founding Church of Scientology v. United States, (412 F. 2d 1197 [Ct. Cl. 1969], cert. den. 397 U.S. 1009 [1970]), a landmark 1969 Court of Claims decision in which the Founding Church of Scientology was found not eligible for tax exemption because private inurements were being provided to the Church's founder and his family.
See also:
DISQUALIFIED PERSON
INSIDER
PRIVATE INUREMENT

four-day workweek, reallocation of the standard forty-hour workweek over four days instead of five. By lengthening the workday, employees get a three-day weekend every week with no loss of pay.
See also FLEXI-TIME.

four-fifths rule: *see* ADVERSE IMPACT.

franchise, a business arrangement in which a person buys the right to sell, rent, etc. the products or services of a company and use the company's name to do business.

fraternal beneficiary society, according to a U.S. Court of Appeals in the 1896 case of *National Union v. Marlow,* a society "whose members have adopted the same, or a very similar, calling, avocation, or profession, or who are working in unison to accomplish some worthy object, and who for that reason have banded themselves together as an association or society to aid and assist one another, and to promote the common cause." Fraternal beneficiary societies may qualify for tax-exempt status under IRS Code 501(c) (8).
See also DOMESTIC FRATERNAL SOCIETY.

fraternal society, domestic: *see* DOMESTIC FRATERNAL SOCIETY.

fraud, any kind of trickery used by one person to cheat another.
See also CORRUPTION.

Freddie Mac: *see* FEDERAL HOME LOAN MORTGAGE CORPORATION.

freedom of choice, the freedom of individuals to select and to financially support causes and organizations engaged in pursuing those causes; a basic philosophical underpinning of tax exemption as established in the U.S. tax codes.

Freedom of Information Act of 1966, the law which provides for making information held by federal agencies available to the public unless it comes within one of the specific categories of matters exempt from public disclosure. The legislative history of the act (particularly the recent amendments) makes it clear that the primary purpose was to make information maintained by the executive branch of the federal government more available to the public. At the same time, the act recognized that records that cannot be disclosed without impairing rights of privacy or important government operations must be protected from disclosure.

Virtually all agencies of the executive branch of the federal government have issued regulations to implement the Freedom of Information Act. These regulations inform the public where certain types of information may be readily obtained, how other information may be obtained on request, and what internal agency appeals are available if a member of the public is refused requested information. To locate specific agency regulations pertaining to freedom of information, consult the *Code of Federal Regulations* index under "Information Availability."

free enterprise, a political and economic system in which most of the society's goods and services are provided by the private sector.

Free Exercise Clause (of the First Amendment to the U.S. Constitution), one of the Constitutional protections against government interference with religion and religious activities. In the case of *Sherbert v. Verner* (374 U.S. 398 [1963]), the U.S. Supreme Court held: "Government may neither compel affirmation of a repugnant belief nor penalize or discriminate against individuals or groups because they hold religious views abhorrent to the authorities." Court cases which turn on the free exercise clause usually involve alleged government intrusion into individuals' religious beliefs rather than government interference with the operations of a religious organization.

See also ESTABLISHMENT CLAUSE and SHERBERT V. VERNER.

freelancer, an independent worker, usually a professional, who takes assignments from various organizations under contract.

See also CONSULTANT and CONTRACTOR.

free-response test, technique used in psychological testing that places no restriction on the kind of response an individual is to make, so long as it relates to the situation presented.

free rider, derogatory term for a person working in a bargaining unit and receiving substantially all of the benefits of union representation without belonging to the union.

frequency distribution, tabulation of scores (or other data) from high to low, or low to high, showing the number of units that fall in each score interval.

frequency polygon, a graphical way to present data that displays the relationship between two (or more) variables. A frequency polygon uses a vertical (Y) axis and a horizontal (X) axis to represent the variables. Data are plotted and connected by lines.

See also FREQUENCY DISTRIBUTION.

Friedman, Milton (1912-), Nobel Prize-winning conservative economist generally considered the leading proponent of a return to laissez-faire economics. As a leading advocate of positive economics, he has been a major influence on thinking about monetary policy, consumption, and government regulation.

friend of the court: *see* AMICUS CURIAE.

friends organization, an entity established to receive contributed funds in this country and expend them in another country either to further its own charitable purposes or on behalf of another charitable entity.

frontage assessment, a tax to pay for improvements (such as sidewalks or sewer lines) that is charged in proportion to the frontage (number of feet bordering the road) of each property.

front end, a terminal used to load data into a computer; a small computer hooked into a larger one to load data and handle specialized tasks.

front loaded, a labor agreement providing for a greater wage increase in its early period; for example, a three-year contract that provides for a ten percent increase in the first year and four percent in each of the remaining two years.

See also BACK LOADED.

front money, the initial capital needed to get a venture (such as a special event) started.

frozen account, an account (usually a bank account) from which no money may be removed until a court order is lifted.

FTC: *see* FEDERAL TRADE COMMISSION.

FUBAR, slang term meaning "fouled up beyond all recognition."

full and fair exposition requirement, also FULL AND FAIR EXPOSITION STANDARD, a standard that had been used by the IRS to distinguish between educational and propaganda activities. The standard required an organization to be willing to disseminate information on both sides of questions, not simply information to support one's own cause. The full and fair exposition requirement was declared unconstitutional in 1980 by the U.S. Court of Appeals for the District of Columbia in *Big Mama Rag, Inc. v. United States* (631 F. 2d 1030 [D.C. Cir. 1980]).

full coverage, insurance that pays for every dollar of a loss with no maximum and no deductible amount.

full employment, economic situation where all those who want to work are able to. In recent years, economists have been telling the public that "full" employment really means from three to six percent unemployment.

full field investigation, personal investigation of an applicant's background to determine whether he/she meets fitness standards for a critical or sensitive position.

full funding, providing budgetary resources to cover the total cost of a program or project at the time it is undertaken. Full funding differs from incremental funding, where a budget is established or provided for only a portion of total estimated obligations expected to be incurred during a single fiscal year. Full funding is generally discussed in terms of multi-year programs, whether or not obligations for the entire program are made in the first year.

Fullileve v. Klutznick, 448 U.S. 448 (1980), U.S. Supreme Court case which held that Congress has the authority to use quotas to remedy past discrimination, reasoning that the Fourteenth Amendment's requirement of equal protection means that groups historically denied this right may be given special treatment.

full responsibility, the complete burden. Nowhere is primitive ritual or Machiavellian feigning more apparent than in the periodic assumption of full responsibility by an organization's chief executive. Although one of the advantages of delegating a problem is the ease with which the cunning manager can shift the blame for the situation if it sours, modern executives are seldom so crude as to lay blame. The appropriate tactic would be to assume "full" responsibility for the situation. Paradoxically, in "assuming" full responsibility, the manager is seemingly relieved of it. It is expected that the top management of any organizational unit will occasionally declare its willingness, indeed eagerness, to take personal responsibility for the actions and especially the mistakes of subordinates.

full-time-worker rate, wage rate of regular full-time employees, as distinguished from the wage rate of temporary or part-time employees performing the same job.

full-time workers, also PART-TIME WORKERS, according to the Bureau of Labor Statistics, those employed at least thirty-five hours a week. *Part-time workers* are those who work fewer hours.

fully funded pension plan, pension plan whose assets are adequate to meet its obligations into the foreseeable future.

function, all, or a clearly identifiable segment, of an individual's or organization's mission, including all the parts of that mission (*e.g.*, procurement), regardless of how performed.

functional analysis, a research perspective in which the analyst attempts to discover those antecedent structures and processes that tend to cause, bring about, or reinforce a given pattern of behavior.

Functional Analysis Systems Technique ("FAST"), an analytical technique for determining and displaying the logical relationships between a program's inputs, processes, and outcomes, used in program planning, management, and evaluation; a structured procedure for creating a hierarchy of objectives. "FAST" is very useful in designing and developing new programs, preparing grant applications, communicating the essence of a complex program to a noninformed audience, and developing an evaluation design.

See also:

BACKSTEP ANALYSIS
"FAST" (EXAMPLE)
HIERARCHY OF OBJECTIVES

functional classification, a means of presenting budgeted income and expenditure data in terms of the principal purposes which programs are intended to serve. Each account is generally placed in the single function that best represents its major purpose, regardless of who administers the program. Functions are generally subdivided into narrower categories called *subfunctions*.

functional expense reporting: *see* BUDGETING, PERFORMANCE.

functional expenses, statement of, a financial report which shows the allocation of line-item expenses to each of an organization's functions or programs.

functional illiterate, individual whose reading and writing skills are so poor that he/she is incapable of functioning effectively in the most basic business, office, or factory situations. Because many functional illiterates are high school graduates, the value of such diplomas is increasingly being discounted by personnel offices.

functional job analysis, technology of work analysis that measures and describes a position's specific requirements. Functional job analysis can discard traditional-

EXAMPLE OF A STATEMENT OF FUNCTIONAL EXPENSES

LINCOLN COMMUNITY DEVELOPMENT ASSOCIATION
Statement of Functional Expenses
For the Year Ended June 30, 198X

		Programs			
Item	*Total All Expenses*	*"Industry for Lincoln"*	*Lake Jefferson Project*	*Total Program*	*Total Support*
Salaries	$	$	$	$	$
Payroll Taxes					
Employee Benefits					
Rent					
Telephone					
Depreciation					
Legal					
Accounting					
Supplies					
Misc.					
TOTAL	$	$	$	$	$

ly restrictive labels for positions. In their place, a variety of component descriptions are used to more accurately illustrate the specific and varied duties actually performed by an incumbent. Functional job analysis data readily lend themselves to computerized personnel management information systems.

functional leadership, concept holding that leadership emerges from the dynamics associated with the particular circumstances under which groups integrate and organize their activities, rather than from the personal characteristics or behavior of an individual.

functus officio, Latin term that can be applied to an official who has fulfilled the duties of an office that has expired and who, in consequence, has no further formal authority. Arbitrators are said to be *functus officio* concerning a particular case after they have declared their awards on it.

fund, accounting device established to control receipt and disbursement of income from sources set aside to support specific activities or attain certain objectives; a sum of money set aside for a particular purpose.
See also FUNDS.

fund, general: *see* GENERAL FUND.

fund, separate, a distinct fund. Tax-exempt organizations (except charitable organizations established under IRS Code 501(c) (3)) may create a separate fund solely for a tax-exempt purpose, and this "separate fund" may receive tax-exempt designation (and, therefore, tax-exempt donations) under Code 501(c) (3). As is usually the case with general statements about tax exemption, there are exceptions and restrictions.
See also CHARITABLE ORGANIZATION.

fund, unrestricted: see GENERAL FUND.

fund accounting, the traditional accounting approach used by nonprofit organizations. In essence, separate financial records are maintained on restricted funds or groups of restricted funds. The organization's financial statements include mini financial statements for each. Fund accounting helps to ensure that restricted funds are used for their intended purposes, grant and other donor restrictions are complied with, etc. Fund accounting is equally prevalent in the public sector.
See also ACCOUNTING CYCLE and FINANCIAL STATEMENTS.

funded pension plan, pension plan that provides for the periodic accumulation of money to meet the pension plan's obligations in future years.

funding method, any of the procedures by which money is accumulated to pay for pensions under a pension plan.

fund-raising, all activities that help create support for a nonprofit organization in the form of gifts, grants, contributions, and services. In addition to funds and services from individuals, corporations, groups, fraternal organizations, associations, foundations and governments, fund-raising also includes seeking intangible gifts that inspire confidence and enthusiasm and generate support for the nonprofit organization. Fund-raising is the "action" part of development.
See also:
DEVELOPMENT
DIRECT MAIL CAMPAIGN
DIRECT SOLICITATION
ENHANCEMENT
GRANT
SPECIAL EVENT

fund-raising committee, the standing committee responsible for coordinating and controlling an organization's fund-raising program, including its direct solicitations, special events, human resources, fund-raising calendar, etc.
See also COMMITTEE.

fund-raising event: *see* SPECIAL EVENT.

fund-raising firm, a company, typically for profit, which performs contractual fund-raising services for nonprofit organizations.

Examples of services include planning and organizing fund-raising campaigns, developing promotional literature, training volunteers, and soliciting contributions.

fund-raising goal, the target amount to be raised through a fund-raising campaign; an important element of a fund-raising plan.

Fund Raising Management, a monthly publication that carries articles on the how-to's of fund-raising campaigns.

fund-raising plan, the document for coordinating a fund-raising campaign or series of campaigns. A fund-raising plan should consist of (1) the overall fund-raising goal, (2) possible sources (that is, potential targeted donors), (3) previous year's actual fund-raising experience with the different possible sources, (4) this year's goal for each possible source, (4) the person responsible for each major activity and/or possible source, (5) the specific plan of action, and (6) a specific timetable. A well conceived fund-raising plan can be updated relatively easily for use in subsequent years.

funds, money and all other assets on hand (like stocks and bonds).

See also FUND.

FUND-RAISING PLANNING AND CONTROL CHART

Fund-raising Committee Chairperson ______________ This year's $ fund-raising goal ______________

SOURCE OF FUNDS	LAST YEAR'S ACTUAL	THIS YEAR'S GOAL	RECEIVED TO DATE:	PERSON RESPONSIBLE	PLAN OF ACTION & COMPLETION DATE
Board	$	$	$		
Industry Contracts	$	$	$		
Major Donors ($100 +)	$ This column is	$ The . Committee (& Board)	$ This column changes	Put NAMES in this column.	The Committee with each person
Contributors (under $100)	$ filled in from last	$ sets these goals.	$ every month.	This is probably the	responsible decides what plan of action
Subscriptions	$ year's records.	$ This column	$ At a	single most important part!	will achieve the goal, and the
Foundations	$	$ has to	$ glance		completion
Business	$	$ add up	$ everyone		date.
Benefits or Events	$	$ to the fund-raising needs.	$ can see what needs		Then it's
United Way, etc.	$	$	$ to be done and		easy to see if it's getting done.
Clubs/ Associations/ Churches	$	$	$ who's not doing the the job!		
Fees Collected					
TOTALS	$	$	$	______ Includes unpaid subscriptions of $ ______	

Source: Colorado Department of Health, Emergency Medical Services Division, Colorado Ambulance Service Management Handbook *(Denver, Colo.: 1984).*

funds, current: *see* GENERAL FUND.

funds, custodial: *see* CUSTODIAL FUNDS.

funds, mutual: *see* MUTUAL FUNDS.

funeral leave, also called BEREAVEMENT LEAVE, paid time off for an employee at the time of a death in his/her immediate family. The majority of all employers offer such time off, usually three or four days. The biggest problem with administering such a benefit is defining just what constitutes a member of the "immediate" family.

fungible, a description for things that are easily substituted for one another. For example, a grant is "fungible" when the recipient is able to use the grant moneys for purposes other than those specified in the grant authorization.

furlough, period of absence from work, initiated either by the employer as a layoff or the employee as a leave of absence.

future funding, the source(s) and method(s) by which a program will be funded after the termination of a supporting grant.

future shock, as defined in the leading work on future shock, Alvin Toffler's *Future Shock* (New York: Random House, 1970), "the distress, both physical and psychological, that arises from an overload of the human organism's physical adaptive systems and its decision making processes. Put more simply, future shock is the human response to over-stimulation."

futuristics, fledgling discipline that seeks to anticipate future societal developments and present alternative courses of action for society's consideration.

G

GAAP, *see* GENERALLY ACCEPTED ACCOUNTING PRINCIPLES.

GAAS, generally accepted auditing standards, as established by the American Institute of Certified Public Accountants.

gag rules, or GAG ORDERS, colloquial terms for any formal instructions from a competent authority, usually a judge, to refrain from discussing and/or advocating something.

gain sharing, any of a variety of wage payment methods in which the worker receives additional earnings due to increases in productivity.

See also:

INDUSTRIAL DEMOCRACY
WORKERS' COUNCILS

games: *see* MANAGEMENT GAMES.

game theory, a mathematical approach to decision making in situations involving two or more players with presumably conflicting interests. Because the theory of games assumes rationality on the part of the players, the strategies and decisions of one player are heavily dependent upon the anticipated behavior of the opposition. The possible outcomes of a two person game are frequently presented in a *payoff matrix* consisting of numbers arranged in rows and columns with the degrees of preference that each player assigns to each outcome. Of course, a player's overall strategy is a *game plan*.

gaming simulation, a model of reality with dynamic parts that can be manipulated to teach the manipulator(s) how to better cope with the represented processes in real life.

Gantt, Henry Lawrence (1861-1919), contemporary and protege of Frederick W. Taylor; a pioneer in the scientific management movement and inventor of the "Gantt Chart."

GAO: *see* GENERAL ACCOUNTING OFFICE.

Garcia* v. *San Antonio Metropolitan Transit Authority, No. 82-1913 (1985), case in which the U.S. Supreme Court held that the Federal Fair Labor Standards Act could be constitutionally applied to a municipally owned mass transit system. The Court overruled its decision in *National League of Cities v. Usery* (1976), which held that the Tenth Amendment prohibited the federal government from establishing wages and hours for state employees.

The full implications of the Garcia decision are not yet known, but it may have substantial impact on scheduling and pay practices in hospitals, volunteer fire departments, and ambulance services. If, as appears to be the case, the decision applies to these types of organizations, many commonly used personnel scheduling systems (for example, twenty-four hours on, twenty-four hours on call, and twenty-four hours off) will require overtime pay, and many "volunteers" will be redefined as "employees" who will be subject to the wages and hours provisions of the Fair Labor Standards Act.

See also FAIR LABOR STANDARDS ACT.

garnishment, any legal or equitable procedure through which earnings of any individual are required to be withheld for the payment of any debt. Most garnishments are made by court order.

The Federal Wage Garnishment Act limits the amount of an employee's disposable earnings subject to garnishment in any one week and protects the employee from discharge because of garnishment for any one indebtedness. It does not change other matters related to garnishment, such as the right of a creditor to collect the full amount owed, and most garnishment procedures established by state laws or rules. The largest amount of total disposable earnings subject to garnishment in any workweek may not exceed the lesser of: (1) twenty-five percent of the disposable earnings for that week or (2) the amount by which disposable earnings for that week exceeds thirty times the federal minimum hourly wage.

No court of the United States, or any state, may make, execute, or enforce any order or process in violation of these restrictions.

The restrictions on the amount that may be garnisheed in a week do not apply to: (1) court orders for the support of any person, such as child support and alimony; (2) bankruptcy court orders under Chapter XIII of the Bankruptcy Act; and (3) debts due for state or federal taxes. A levy against wages for a federal tax debt by the Internal Revenue Service is not restricted by this law.

The Federal Wage Garnishment Act is enforced by the Secretary of Labor, acting through the Wage and Hour Division, U.S. Department of Labor.

General Accounting Office (GAO), independent agency created by the Budget and Accounting Act of 1921 to audit federal government expenditures, including contract and grant expenditures, and to assist Congress with its legislative oversight responsibilities. The GAO also conducts program audits of grants and contracts.

General Electric Co.* v. *Gilbert, 429 U.S. 125 (1976), U.S. Supreme Court case which held that excluding pregnancies from sick leave and disability benefit programs is not "discrimination based on sex" and so is not a violation of Title VII of the Civil Rights Act of 1964. This decision led to a Title VII amendment (the Pregnancy Discrimination Act of 1978) that reversed the court's decision.

See also PREGNANCY.

general fund, also CURRENT FUND, unrestricted moneys and other liquid assets which are available for an organization's general use; a fund consisting of all receipts not earmarked for a specific purpose and from general borrowing. It is used for the general operations of an organization.

general increase, any upward salary adjustment governing the pay of most employees.

general ledger, the master accounting sheets which should exist for each account in an organization's chart of accounts. Postings are made to the general ledger from the journals. Information posted should include the transaction date, which journal the transaction was in, the dollar amount, and whether each transaction was a debit or a credit. After posting all journals to the general ledger for the cycle (usually one month), each general ledger account is totaled and the information is "tested" in a trial balance. Information from the general ledger is used to prepare the organization's financial statements.

See also

ACCOUNTING CYCLE
CHART OF ACCOUNTS
JOURNAL
POSTING
TRIAL BALANCE

generally accepted accounting principles (GAAP), the totality of the conventions, rules, standards, and procedures which collectively define the responsible practice of accounting. Since the 1930's, the Securities and Exchange Commission has had the authority to establish accounting standards, but has never done so. Instead, it has allowed the accounting profession to establish its own guidelines, first through the Committee on Accounting Principles (from 1939 to 1959), and later through the Accounting Principles Board (from 1959 to 1973), both of the American Institute of Certified Public Accountants (AICPA). In 1973 the Accounting Principles Board was superseded by the Financial Accounting Standards Board (FASB).

general manager, a person authorized to manage and control the day-to-day operations of an organization (or a subsidiary unit of an organization).

general revenue sharing: *see* GRANT.

General Services Administration (GSA), federal agency that establishes policy and provides for the management of the federal government's property and records, including construction and operation of buildings, procurement and distribution of supplies, utilization and disposal of property, transportation, traffic, and communications management, stockpiling of strategic materials, and the management of a government-wide automatic data processing resources program.

generic management, those areas and concerns of management that are of common concern to the nonprofit, public, and private sectors.

gentlemen's agreement, also INFORMAL AGREEMENT, a dated phrase for a transaction that is not enforceable and depends solely on the good faith of the people making it. *Informal agreement* is the preferred term.

EXAMPLE OF GENERAL LEDGER
ACE AMBULANCE SERVICE

Account # ____________ Account Title ____________

Date	Reference	DR	CR	Balance
1-31	Cash Receipts Summary	$5,175.00		
1-31	Cash Disbursements Journal		$3,500.00	
1-31	Payroll Register		$1,500.00	DR $175.00

gentrification, the gradual replacement of the poor by people with middle- and upper-class incomes in a given neighborhood.

geriatrics, also GERONTOLOGY and INDUSTRIAL GERONTOLOGY, that branch of medicine concerned with the special medical problems of older people. *Gerontology* is that branch of biology which is concerned with the nature of the aging process. *Industrial gerontology* is a far more comprehensive term that summarizes all of those areas of study concerned with the employment and retirement problems of workers who are middle-aged and beyond.

gerontology: *see* GERIATRICS.

Gestalt therapy, psychotherapy technique pioneered by Frederic S. Perls which emphasizes the treatment of a person as a biological and perceptual whole. "Gestalt" is a German word for a configuration, pattern, or otherwise organized whole whose parts have different qualities than the whole.

get the sack, be fired. At the dawn of the industrial revolution, factory workers had to use their own tools. When a worker was fired, he was given a sack in which to gather up his tools.

ghetto, area of a city inhabited exclusively by members of an ethnic, racial, religious, or social group. It often carries connotations of low income.

gift, something given voluntarily and without charge. From a nonprofit organization perspective, a gift is typically money or objects of value given for charitable or eleemosynary purposes. However, under current court interpretation, the definition is broader. For example, an interest-free loan made among family members is also a gift.

gift annuity agreement, an arrangement under which a person makes a gift to a charitable institution and receives annual payments for life. The donor is allowed a tax deduction for a portion of the gift amount, and only part of the payments must be reported as income for tax purposes. If appreciated stocks are given, the realized capital gains can be reported over the donor's life expectancy.

gift exemption limit, the maximum amount of gifts a person is permitted to make to, for example, a child in a year or a lifetime without being subject to federal gift taxes.

gift-leaseback, an arrangement in which a person transfers a building or equipment used in his or her business to a Clifford Trust established for someone else, typically his or her child, and then rents it back at a fair market rate. An amount equal to the trust's net rental income is shifted from the first person to the second person, usually so it can be taxed at lower rates.

See also LEASE-BACK.

gift of cash, cash gifts without restrictions or terms of trust. For federal income tax purposes, gifts of cash generally are deductible up to a percent of adjusted gross income, with a five year carry forward of excess contributions.

See also,
- ADJUSTED GROSS INCOME
- CARRY FORWARD
- EXCESS CONTRIBUTIONS

gift revenues, a nonprofit organization's total revenues or income from contributions, donations, and/or gifts.

gift tax, a tax on the transfer of a gift. As has been interpreted recently by the courts, the federal gift tax was intended to apply to all transfers of property and property rights that have significant value. For example, interest-free loans made among family members are gifts. In most cases, gift taxes are paid by the donor.

GIGO, an acronym used in the world of computers and data processing which means "garbage in, garbage out."

***Gilbert* case:** *see* GENERAL ELECTRIC CO. V. GILBERT.

Gilbreth, Frank Bunker (1868-1924) **and Lillian Moller** (1878-1972), husband and wife team who were the pioneers of time-and-motion study. Their influence on the scientific management movement was rivaled only by that of Frederick W. Taylor.

Ginnie Mae: *see* GOVERNMENT NATIONAL MORTGAGE ASSOCIATION.

girl Friday: *see* MAN FRIDAY.

giveback, any demand by management that a union accept a reduction in its present terms of employment.

Give But Give Wisely, a quarterly publication of the Philanthropic Advisory Services (PAS), Council of Better Business Bureaus, which rates the most active nonprofit organizations that do and do not meet PAS's charitable standards.

giving, annual, *see* ANNUAL GIVING.

giving, annual program, *see* ANNUAL GIVING PROGRAM.

giving principles, principles helpful in designing and developing a fund-raising program. Examples are (1) people give to people, not to impersonal organizations; (2) people give only what they have (that is, discretionary income); and (3) people give only when they are interested and feel involved.

Giving in America, the 1974 report of the President's Commission on Private Philanthropy and Public Needs.

See also COMMISSION ON PRIVATE PHILANTHROPY AND PUBLIC NEEDS

Giving USA, a report published annually by the American Association of Fund Raising Counsel (AAFRC) which documents the sources, types of recipients, and uses (for example, by purpose) of philanthropy in the United States.

See also AMERICAN ASSOCIATION OF FUND-RAISING COUNSEL.

GMAT, the Graduate Management Admission Test, administered by the Educational Testing Service, Princeton, NJ. GMAT is required for admission to most graduate schools of business and management.

GNMA: *see* GOVERNMENT NATIONAL MORTGAGE ASSOCIATION.

gnomes of Zurich, the secretive Swiss financial and banking institutions.

goal (organizational or program), a nonquantified, long range, visionary statement of intent. In contrast, an objective is a measurable statement of commitment to attempt to achieve a specific result.

See also OBJECTIVE.

goals, also QUOTAS and TIMETABLES (affirmative action), realistic objectives which an organization endeavors to achieve through affirmative action. A *quota,* in contrast, restricts employment or development opportunities to members of particular groups by establishing a required number or proportionate representation which managers are obligated to attain without regard to "equal" employment opportunity. To be meaningful, any program of goals or quotas must be associated with a specific *timetable*—a schedule of when the goals or quotas are to be achieved.

gobbledygook, also OFFICIALESE, and BAFFLEGAB, slang terms for the obtuse language so frequently used by bureaucrats.

going rate, wage rate most commonly paid to workers in a given occupation.

goldbricking, originally a slang term for something that had only a surface appearance of value well before it was adopted by the military to mean shirking or giving the appearance of working. The word has now come to imply work slowdowns, whether they be individual initiatives (or the lack of individual initiative) or group efforts (organized or otherwise).

Example of Gobbledygook

We respectfully petition, request, and entreat that due and adequate provision be made, this day and the date hereinafter subscribed, for the satisfying of these petitioners' nutritional requirements and for the organizing of such methods of allocation and distribution as may be deemed necessary and proper to assure the reception by and for said petitioners of such quantities of baked cereal products as shall, in the judgment of the aforesaid petitioners, constitute a sufficient supply thereof.

Translation: "Give us this day our daily bread."

golden handcuffs, the feeling of being bound to remain in a job because financial benefits would be forfeited upon resignation.

golden handshake, dismissing an employee while at the same time providing him/her with a large cash bonus.

good faith, in the context of equal employment opportunity, the absence of discriminating intent. The "good faith" of an employer is usually considered by the courts in fashioning an appropriate remedy to correct the wrongs of "unintentional" discrimination.

good-faith bargaining, honest negotiation. Section 8(a) (5) of the National Labor Relations Act makes it illegal for an employer to refuse to bargain in good faith about wages, hours, and other conditions of employment with the representative selected by a majority of the employees in a unit appropriate for collective bargaining. A bargaining representative seeking to enforce its right concerning an employer under this section must show that it has been designated by a majority of the employees, that the unit is appropriate, and that there has been both a demand that the employer bargain and a refusal by the employer to do so.

The duty to bargain covers all matters concerning rates of pay, wages, hours of employment, or other conditions of employment. These are called "mandatory" subjects of bargaining about which the employer, as well as the employees' representative, must bargain in good faith, although the law does not require "either party to agree to a proposal or require the making of a concession." These mandatory subjects of bargaining include, but are not limited to, such matters as pensions for present and retired employees, bonuses, group insurance, grievance procedure, safety practices, seniority, procedures for discharge, layoff, recall, or discipline, and the union shop.

An employer who is required to bargain under this section must, as stated in Section 8(d), "meet at reasonable times and confer in good faith with respect to wages, hours, and other terms and conditions of employment, or the negotiation of an agreement, or any question arising thereunder, and the execution of a written contract incorporating any agreement reached if requested by either party."

An employer, therefore, will be found to have violated Section 8 (a) (5) if its conduct in bargaining, viewed in its entirety, indicates that the employer did not negotiate with a good-faith intention to reach agreement. However, the employer's good faith is not at issue where its conduct constitutes an out-and-out refusal to bargain on a mandatory subject. For example, it is a violation for an employer, regardless of good faith, to refuse to bargain about a subject it believes is not a mandatory subject of bargaining, when in fact it is.

See also

UNFAIR LABOR PRACTICES (EMPLOYERS)

goodness of fit, how well a curve on a chart minimizes the error, which usually is defined as the difference between observed and predicted values at various points.

goodwill, the reputation and built-up support for an organization.

goo-goos: *see* DO GOODERS.

gopher, a menial. While this is not formally listed as a job title on anybody's resumé, many a successful manager will admit to having worked his way up from gopher—go for coffee, go for this, go for that, etc.

governance, a general term referring to the collective actions of a board of directors or board of trustees in its governing of a tax-exempt organization.

governing instrument, document that governs an organization's actions. IRS regulations identify two types of governing instruments: Creating documents (for example, articles of organization) and operating documents (for example, bylaws).

See also:

ARTICLES OF INCORPORATION
ARTICLES OF ORGANIZATION
BYLAWS
DECLARATION OF TRUST

government corporation, government-owned corporation or an agency of government that administers a self-supporting enterprise. Such a structure is used (1) when an agency's business is essentially commercial, (2) when an agency can generate its own revenue, and (3) when the agency's mission requires greater flexibility than government agencies normally have. Examples of federal government corporations include the Saint Lawrence Seaway Development Corporation, the Federal Deposit Insurance Corporation, the National Railroad Passenger Corporation (AMTRAK), and the Tennessee Valley Authority. At the state and municipal levels, corporations, often bearing different names, such as "authorities," operate enterprises such as turnpikes, airports, and harbors (such as the Port of New York Authority).

government instrumentality, an organization owned by but separate from a municipality or a state. A government instrumentality may qualify as a charitable organization for tax purposes if it is a clear counterpart of a charitable, religious, educational, or similar organization.

See COUNTERPART REQUIREMENT and UNITED STATES INSTRUMENTALITIES.

Government National Mortgage Association, also GINNIE MAE (GNMA), a federal corporation that assists the financing of federally-guaranteed mortgages. GNMA also purchases mortgages at above-market prices (low interest rates) from their originators, for sale to the Federal National Mortgage Association (Fannie Mae) and other investors.

government relations committee, a standing committee which is frequently found in nonprofit organizations. Typically, government relations committees collect, analyze, and maintain current information about proposed legislation that may impact on the organization or its program, recommend legislative policy positions, educate volunteers about legislative issues, train volunteers in legislative strategies, and advise the organization about political activities which might jeopardize the organization's tax-exempt status.

See also COMMITTEE.

government-sponsored enterprises, federal budget term for enterprises with completely private ownership established and chartered by the federal government to perform specialized credit functions. Examples include the Federal National Mortgage Association, institutions in the Farm Credit System, Federal Home Loan Banks, and the Federal Home Loan Mortgage Corporation.

grace, a holding off on demanding payment of a debt or enforcing some other right; for example, a "grace period."

Grace Commission, formally the President's Private Sector Survey on Cost Control. Chaired by J. Peter Grace, it was created in 1982 to examine the federal government's operations and policies from a business perspective. Its final report, prepared by over 1,500 volunteer private-sector executives, contained over two thousand recommendations for improving the efficiency of the federal government.

grade, established level or zone of difficulty. Positions of the same difficulty and responsibility tend to be placed in the same grade even though the content of the work differs greatly.

grade creep, also called GRADE ESCALATION, long-term tendency for positions to be reallocated upward.

gradual pressure strike, concerted effort by employees to influence management by gradually reducing production until their objectives are met.

graduated lease, a commercial lease with payments that vary according to the money made by the renter or by some other standard (for example, the number of people who enter the store).

See also LEASE.

graduated payment mortgage, a mortgage in which payments go up by a set formula over the years.

See also MORTGAGE and VARIABLE RATE MORTGAGE.

graduated tax: *see* TAX RATE.

graduated wages, wages adjusted on the basis of length of service and performance.

grandfather clause, a colloquial expression for any provision or policy that exempts a category of individuals from meeting new standards. For example, if a hospital were to establish a policy that all nursing supervisors had to have a master's degree as of a certain date, it would probably exempt nurses without such degrees who were in supervisory positions prior to that date. This statement of exemption would be a grandfather clause.

grant, a financial award made to support a project, program, individual, or organization in general. A grant differs from a contract in that specific goods or services are not purchased; rather, programs are supported. Many federal agencies and private foundations will make grants only to nonprofit, tax-exempt organizations.

The Advisory Commission on Intergovernmental Relations has identified the following types of grants, some of which are applicable to both nonprofit and public organizations. Others are applicable to public agencies only.

1. *Block Grant.* A grant that is distributed in accordance with a statutory formula for use in a variety of activities within a broad functional area largely at the recipient's discretion.
2. *Categorical Grant.* A grant that can be used only for specific, narrowly defined activities. Usually legislation details the parameters of the program and specifies the types of eligible activities, but sometimes these may be determined by administrators.
3. *Conditional Grant.* A grant that is awarded with limitations (conditions) attached to use of the funds. Both categorical and block grants are conditional, although the categorical grant generally has a greater number and severity of conditions.
4. *Formula-Based Categorical Grant.* A categorical grant under which funds are allocated among recipients according to factors specified in legislation or in administrative regulations.
5. *Project Categorical Grant.* Nonformula categorical grants awarded on a competitive basis to recipients who submit specific, individual applications in the form and at the times indicated by the grantor.
6. *Formula-Project Categorical Grant.* A project grant for which a formula specified in statutes or regulations is used to determine the amount available for a state area, and then funds are distributed at the discretion of the administrator in response to project applications submitted by substate entities.
7. *Open-end Reimbursement Grant.* Often regarded as a formula grant, but characterized by an arrangement wherein the federal govern-

ment commits itself to reimbursing a specified portion of state-local program expenditures with no limit on the amount of such expenditures.

8. *Discretionary Grant.* A grant awarded at the discretion of a federal administrator subject to conditions specified by legislation. Generally used interchangeably with project grant.
9. *General Revenue Sharing.* A financial assistance program for states and their general purpose political subdivision under which funds are distributed by formula with few or no limits on the purposes for which they may be spent and few restrictions on the procedures by which they are spent.
10. *Special Revenue Sharing.* Usually used interchangeably with the term block grant. The term was employed by the Nixon administration in connection with its grant consolidation proposals. Those who consider special revenue sharing a separate form usually differentiate it from the block grant by its lack of a matching requirement and imposition of fewer conditions on recipient performance.
11. *Target Grant.* A grant which packages and coordinates funds for wide-ranging public services directed at a specific clientele group or geographic area. Major examples include the Appalachian Regional Development Program, the Community Action Program, and the discontinued Model Cities Program.

Foundation grants also can be grouped into categories, such as endowment grants, capital support grants, matching grants, general support grants and project grants.

See also the following entries:

ANNUAL ARRANGEMENTS
FUNGIBLE
STIMULATIVE
TARGETED

grant, general support, a grant made to an operating charitable organization in a particular area of concern to the grantmaking organization (for example, the performing arts or early child development) for its general support, rather than to support a specific project. The logic for general support grants is that the agencies supported are better able to establish program priorities than the grantmaking organization.

grant, project, a grant which directs funding to a specific project, in contrast to a general support grant.

grant closeout procedures, the procedures specified by granting public agencies which define financial, reporting, and asset retention or protection steps which must be taken at the termination of a grant.

grantee, a recipient of grant funds.

grant-in-aid, federal transfers of payments to states or federal or state transfers to local governments for specified purposes, usually subject to a measure of supervision and review by the granting government agency in accordance with prescribed standards and requirements.

grantmaking organization, a general term which refers to any foundation, corporation, or government agency that regularly makes grants to operating charitable organizations, individuals, etc.

grant proposal, also GRANT REQUEST, a document written and submitted to a foundation or government agency requesting grant funds, usually for specific uses. Many foundations and agencies require specific grant proposal inclusions and formats, but most request: (1) title of the project and the submitting organization, (2) a proposal abstract or very short summary, (3) an introduction to the submitting organization (a little about its history, anything unique about it, some of its major accomplishments, its major long-term goals and support received from other sources), (4) a problem statement (that is, what needs or problems the grant will be used to address), (5) specific project objectives, (6) the project's methods or strategy, (7) an evaluation strategy, (8) a project budget, and (9) appendices containing, for example, documents, resumés, maps, and other information helpful to the proposal reviewers but which would detract from the flow of the proposal's narrative.

See also:

GRANT
GRANT PROPOSAL ABSTRACT
GRANT PROPOSAL BUDGET
OBJECTIVE
PROJECT CONTROL CHART

grant proposal abstract, a very brief summary of a grant proposal's purpose, needs to be addressed, description of the project's approach, and the total amount of grant funds required or requested.

grant proposal budget, the proposed project budget included in a grant proposal submitted to a foundation or government agency. Many granting organizations require grant proposal budgets to be submitted in a specific format, but most include: (1) the total project budget (by line item), (2) the amount requested from the granting organization, and (3) the amount to be contributed from other sources.

grant request: *see* GRANT PROPOSAL.

grants-in-kind, donations of surplus property or commodities.

Examples of Grant Proposal Abstracts

A NOT-SO-GOOD EXAMPLE:

Summary:

The long-range goal of this proposed program is to help students develop into adults who think creatively and independently, learn by observation, work together in inquiring teams, develop judgment and decision making abilities, and, most importantly, adults who can conceive of more satisfactory alternatives to social problems than passive acceptance or militant violence. In short, this program's aim is to help students to grow into adults who actively practice and participate in democratic citizenship.

Not only does this summary leave out just about all the basic information, but it's impossible to figure out what they're trying to say.

A GOOD EXAMPLE:

Summary:

Brown Memorial Hospital, located in the barrio section of Maybell, Colorado, has planned a community health education and screening program to be brought directly to residents of the area as a means of reducing the rate of communicable and chronic diseases. Programs will be conducted at local parish halls, schools, Head Start Centers, and other community facilities, in close cooperation with more than twenty-five local community organizations.

Two bilingual outreach workers with community involvement experience will work with individuals and organizations to promote participation by the Spanish-speaking residents of the area. These community-based workers will also resolve obstacles to attendance, such as the need for child care. They will conduct follow-ups by contacting participants to determine whether the information gained through the program is being applied to their daily lives.

The program is budgeted at $14,435 for a six-month period. Of this total, $7,000 is requested and the rest is being donated by the medical society.

EXAMPLE OF A GRANT PROPOSAL BUDGET

BUDGET SUMMARY

Total This Grant	Total $10,067.12	Total Requested $7,836.62	Total Pledged By Other Sources $2,230.50
1. Personnel	$ 7,776.62	$5,847.12	$1,928.50
A. Salaries & Wages	4,995.00	4,320.00	675.00
B. Fringe Benefits	1,214.62	1,047.12	166.50
C. Contract Services	1,566.00	480.00	1,086.00
2. Non-Personnel			
A. Space Costs	1,230.00	990.00	240.00
B. Equipment Rental, Lease, or Purchase	271.00	208.00	63.00
C. Supplies	128.50	128.50	-0-
D. Travel	176.00	176.00	-0-
E. Telephone	350.00	350.00	-0-
F. Other Costs	135.00	135.00	-0-

Grants Magazine, a quarterly journal of sponsored research and related programs. *Grants Magazine* provides a forum for discussion of issues that affect public and private philanthropy. Articles tend to address government, foundation, and corporate grants, including information on current programs and trends and the technical aspects of researching sources of funds.

grantsmanship, the art (or science, depending on one's viewpoint) of writing successful grant proposals.

See also GRANT PROPOSAL.

Grantsmanship Center News, a bimonthly publication of the Grantsmanship Center which provides substantive information and helpful suggestions about public and private grants and how to get them.

grants receivable, an asset account in a nonprofit organization's chart of accounts and balance sheet. Grants receivable are posted when formal notification of a grant award has been received.

See also:
BALANCE SHEET
CHART OF ACCOUNTS
FINANCIAL STATEMENTS

grants to individuals, grants made to individuals rather than to organizations; for example, for educational and charitable purposes. Grants to individuals may not be deducted by taxpayers, but deductions may be made by private foundations, with restrictions.

grapevine, informal means by which organizational members give or receive information.

graphic rating scale, performance appraisal chart that lists traits (such as promptness, knowledge, helpfulness, etc.) with a range of performance to be indicated with each (unsatisfactory, satisfactory, etc.).

Grassroots Fundraising Journal, a semimonthly "how-to" journal. Typical articles cover how to seek pledges through the mail, conduct poltical action appeals, produce brochures, and attract new members.

graveyard shift, also called LOBSTER SHIFT, slang terms for the tour of duty of employers who work from 11 P.M. or midnight until dawn.

Great Society, label for the 1960s domestic policies of the Johnson administration that were premised on the belief that social and/or economic problems could be solved by new federal programs.

green card, a small document which identifies an alien as a permanent resident of the U.S. The "green card" was originally green, but now is white and salmon.

green-circle rate, also called BLUE-CIRCLE RATE, pay rate that is below the minimum rate of an employee's evaluated pay level.

green hands, slang term for inexperienced workers.

Green River Ordinance, legal provision allowing local government to control soliciting. Named for the Wyoming city in which it was initiated.

Green v. Connally, (330 F. Supp. 1150 [D.D.C. 1971], aff'd sub nom. *Coit v. Green,* 404 U.S. 997 [1971]), a 1971 federal court decision which held that the IRS Code "does not contemplate the granting of special Federal tax benefits to trusts or organizations'... whose organization or operation contravene Federal public policy."

See also BOB JONES UNIVERSITY V. SIMON and WRIGHT V. REGAN

grey market, organizational transactions that are legal but hardly ethical.

grievance, any dissatisfaction felt by an employee in connection with his/her employment. The word generally refers to a formal complaint initiated by an employee, by a union, or by management concerning the interpretation or application of a collective bargaining agreement or established employment practice.

grievance arbitration, also called RIGHTS ARBITRATION, arbitration concerned with disputes that arise over the interpretation/application of an existing agreement. The grievance arbitrator interprets the contract for the parties.

grievance committee (labor), those employee, union, and/or management representatives who are formally designated to review grievances left unresolved by lower elements of the grievance machinery.

grievance machinery, totality of the methods, usually enumerated in an agreement, used to resolve the problems of interpretation arising during the life of an agreement. Grievance machinery is usually designed so that those closest to the dispute have the first opportunity to reach a settlement.

grievance procedure, specific means by which grievances are channeled for their adjustment through progressively higher levels of authority in an organization. Grievance procedures, while long considered the "heart" of a labor contract, are increasingly found in nonunionized organizations as managers realize the need for a process to appeal the decisions of supervisors that employees consider unjust.

grievant, one who files a formal grievance; one who grieves. This person is not in a state of mourning, but one of complaining.

Griggs, et al.* v. *Duke Power Company, 401 U.S. 424 (1971), the most significant single Supreme Court decision concerning the validity of employment examinations. The court unanimously ruled that Title VII of the Civil Rights Act of 1964 "proscribes not only overt discrimination but also practices that are discriminatory in operation." Thus, if employment practices operating to exclude minorities "cannot be shown to be related to job performance, the practice is prohibited." The ruling dealt a blow to restrictive credentialism, stating that, while diplomas and tests are useful, the "Congress had mandated the commonsense proposition that they are not to become masters of reality." In essence, the court held that the law requires that tests used for employment purposes "must measure the person for the job and not the person in the abstract."

The *Griggs* decision applied only to the private sector until the Equal Employment Opportunity Act of 1972 extended the provisions of Title VII of the Civil Rights Act of 1964 to cover public as well as private employees.

gross domestic product, the value of the total output of final goods and services produced in a country in a specific period, usually a year. It differs from Gross National Product in that GDP excludes (and GNP includes) the value of net income accruing to factors of production from abroad.

gross lease, a lease in which the landlord pays all ownership and maintenance costs and the tenant pays rent.

See also NET LEASE.

gross national product (GNP), monetary value of all of the goods and services produced in a nation in a given year.

gross national product gap, the difference between the economy's output of goods and services and its potential output at full employment—that is, the difference between actual GNP (gross national product) and potential GNP.

ground rent, rent paid for land when the tenant has constructed the building.

group: *see:*

GROUP, PRIMARY
GROUP DYNAMICS
SMALL-GROUP RESEARCH

group, primary, also SECONDARY GROUP, group that consists of people who communicate often over a period of time and who are few enough in number that each can communicate with all the others face-to-face. A *secondary group* is a group which does not satisfy the criteria for a primary group; a group which is too large to permit face-to-face communication over time among its members.

See also GROUP DYNAMICS and SMALL GROUP RESEARCH.

group annuity, any of a variety of pension plans designed by insurance companies for a group of persons to cover all of those qualified under one contract.

group cohesiveness, measure of the degree of unity and solidarity that a group possesses.

group development, loose term concerned with the various processes and circumstances that occur when individuals organize themselves into goal-oriented groups.

group dynamics, the study of the nature of groups, how they develop, and their relationships to individuals, other groups, and larger institutions. It is generally accepted that Kurt Lewin invented the field of group dynamics (that is, he was responsible, either directly or indirectly, for most of the pioneering research on group dynamics).

See also the following entries:

ALBILENE PARADOX
FIELD THEORY
GROUPTHINK
ORGANIZATION DEVELOPMENT

group executive, manager responsible for the work of two or more organizational divisions.

group exemption letter, an IRS letter granting tax exemption to a central nonprofit organization and subordinate organizations under its direct control. Group exemption letters must be applied for—they are not granted automatically.

group incentive plan: *see* INCENTIVE-WAGE PLAN.

group insurance, also GROUP HEALTH INSURANCE and GROUP LIFE INSURANCE, any insurance plan that covers individuals (and usually their dependents) by means of a single policy issued to the employer or association with which the insured individuals are affiliated. The cost of group insurance is usually significantly lower than the costs for equivalent individual policies. Group insurance policies are written in the name of the employer so that individual employees are covered only as long as they remain with the insuring employer. Sometimes group insurance policies provide that an employee can continue his/her coverage upon resignation by buying an individual policy. The most common kinds of group insurance are *group health insurance, group life insurance,* and *group disability insurance.* Many employers pay a substantial portion or all of the cost of group insurance.

group of classes, two or more closely related job classes having a common basis of duties, responsibilities, and qualification requirements but differing in some particular (such as the nature of specialization) that is essential from the standpoint of recruitment and selection and requires that each class in the group be treated individually. Such classes have the same basic title but may be distinguished by a parenthetic. For example: Engineer (Chemical), Engineer (Electrical), etc.

group oral interview, also called GROUP ORAL EXAMINATION, measurement tool that involves a group of candidates (ideally 5-7) discussing a job-related problem. The evaluators do not actively participate in the group discussion; their role is to observe and evaluate the behavior of the participants. The value of this technique is heavily dependent on the ability of the evaluators.

group psychotherapy, any form of psychological treatment involving more than one subject. Organization development efforts can be considered a form of group psychotherapy.

groupthink, psychological drive for consensus at any cost which tends to suppress both dissent and the appraisal of alternatives in small decision making groups. Groupthink, because it refers to a deterioration of mental efficiency and moral judgment due to in-group pressures, has an invidious connotation.

See also ALBILENE PARADOX and GROUP DYNAMICS.

GSA: *see* GENERAL SERVICES ADMINISTRATION.

guaranteed base rate: *see* GUARANTEED RATE.

guaranteed mortgage, a mortgage made by a mortgage company that then sells the mortgage to an investor, guarantees payments to the investor, and manages the mortgage for a fee.

guaranteed rate, also called GUARANTEED BASE RATE, minimum wage guaranteed to an employee working under an incentive pay program.

guaranteed workweek, provision in some union contracts that an employee will be paid a full week's wages even when there is not enough actual work available to otherwise warrant a full week's pay.

guaranty, a promise to fulfill an obligation (or pay a debt) for another person or organization if that person or organization fails to fulfill it.

guideline method, job evaluation technique that determines the value of a position in an organization not by an analysis of the position's content, but by what the labor market says it is worth.

H

halo effect, bias in ratings arising from the tendency of a rater to be influenced in his/her rating of specific traits by a general impression of the person being rated.

handicapped individual, also QUALIFIED HANDICAPPED INDIVIDUAL, is any person who (1) has a physical or mental impairment which substantially limits one or more of such person's major life activities, (2) has a record of such an impairment, or (3) is regarded as having such an impairment. A *qualified handicapped individual,* with respect to employment, is one who with reasonable accommodation can perform the essential functions of a job in question. According to the Vocational Rehabilitation Act of 1973 (as amended), federal contractors and subcontractors are required to take affirmative action to seek out qualified handicapped individuals for employment.

hands-off policy, the unstated reluctance of the courts to attempt to define the term "religious" or to determine that particular organizations are not organized or operated for religious purposes. This reluctance has been called the hands-off policy.

See also RELIGIOUS and RELIGIOUS ORGANIZATION.

hands-on test, performance test that uses the actual tools of the job.

harassment, words and/or actions that unlawfully annoy or alarm another. Harassment may include anonymous, repeated, offensively coarse or late-night phone calls; insulting, taunting, or physically challenging approaches; etc.

See also SEXUAL HARASSMENT.

hard cases, cases where fairness may require judges to be loose with legal principles; that's why "hard cases make bad law."

hard copy, typed or printed information, as opposed to information stored in computer memory, tape, or disk.

hard-core unemployed, those individuals who, because of racial discrimination, an impoverished background, or the lack of appropriate education, have never been able to hold a job for a substantial length of time.

hard funding, also SOFT FUNDING, money obtained from an organization's regular sources of operating funds that is budgeted for activities. In contrast, *soft funding* implies that the money comes from a grant or other source that will not continue indefinitely.

hardware, formally, the mechanical, magnetic, electrical, and electronic devices or components of a computer. Informally, any piece of computer or automatic data processing equipment.

See also COMPUTER.

***Harvard Business Review* (HBR),** journal for professional managers, published bimonthly by the faculty of the Harvard University Graduate School of Business Administration. The editors modestly state that, in selecting articles for publication, they "try to pick those that are timeless rather than just timely." The *Harvard Business Review* is almost universally considered the foremost business journal in the United States.

Harvard Business School (HBS), the most prestigious of the prestigious "B" schools. Robert Townsend, in *Up the Organization* (N.Y.: Knopf, 1970), suggests that you "don't hire Harvard Business School graduates. This worthy enterprise confesses that it trains its students for only three posts—executive vice-president, president, and board chairman. The faculty does not blush when HBS is called the West Point of capitalism." HBS also conducts a variety of continuing education programs, including some for managers of nonprofit and public organizations.

hatchet man, a subordinate who does "dirty work" for a higher administrator, such as firing long-term employees. Occasionally, a board of directors deliberately selects a new executive director as a hatchet man to "clean house" of "deadwood." After the blood has been let by the hatchet man, the board replaces him or her with someone who can start as a "nice guy" with a "clean slate."

Hawthorne Effect, any production increase due to known presence of benign observers. Elton Mayo and his associates, while conducting their now famous Hawthorne Studies, discovered that the researchers' concern for and attention to the workers led to increases in production.

Work group behavior, output restriction, supervisory training, personnel research, interviewing methodology, employee counseling, socio-technical systems theory, small group incentive plans, and organizational theory became prime concerns of management, because, in one way or another, they were brought to the fore or elucidated by the Hawthorne Studies.

Hay System, job evaluation method developed by Edward N. Hay. Essentially a modification of the factor-comparison technique, Hay's Guide Chart-Profile Method is based on three factors: know-how, problem solving, and accountability. Many organizations have adopted variations of the Hay System.

See also POINT SYSTEM.

hazard pay, compensation paid to an employee above regular wages for work that is potentially dangerous to his/her health.

HBR: *see* HARVARD BUSINESS REVIEW.

HBS: *see* HARVARD BUSINESS SCHOOL.

headhunter, a slang term for an executive recruiter.

Health and Human Services, Department of (DHHS), cabinet-level department of the federal government most concerned with health, welfare, and income security plans, policies, and programs. It was created on October 17, 1979, when the Department of Health, Education and Welfare was divided in two.

health benefits, total health service and health insurance programs that an organization provides for its employees.

health care plan, prepaid, a general category of organizations that typically have been able to qualify for tax exemption as social welfare organizations. Common types of prepaid health care plans include fees-for-services health care plans and health maintenance organizations (HMOs).

See also:

FEE-FOR-SERVICES PLAN
HEALTH MAINTENANCE ORGANIZATION
SOCIAL WELFARE ORGANIZATION

Health, Education and Welfare, Department of (HEW), former cabinet-level department of the federal government. Created in 1953, HEW was reorganized into the Department of Education and the Department of Health and Human Services in 1979.

See also EDUCATION, DEPARTMENT OF and HEALTH AND HUMAN SERVICES, DEPARTMENT OF.

health facilities, collectively, all buildings and facilities used in the provision of health services. Usually limited to facilities which were built for the purpose of providing health care, such as hospitals and nursing homes; does not include an office building which includes a physician's office.

health insurance, group: *see* GROUP INSURANCE.

health maintenance organization (HMO), an organized system for prepaid health care in a geographic area which delivers an agreed-upon set of basic and supplemental health maintenance and treatment services to a voluntarily enrolled group of people. The HMO is reimbursed for these services through a predetermined, fixed, periodic prepayment made by or on behalf of each person or family unit enrolled in the HMO, without regard to the amounts of services provided or received. The HMO then hires or contracts with health care providers. A federal law requires that employers of twenty-five or more who currently offer a medical benefit plan also offer the option of joining a qualified HMO, if one exists in the area.

Participating health care providers are paid a fixed fee for their services. HMO's may qualify for tax exemption as either social welfare or charitable organizations.

Health Maintenance Organization Act of 1973, federal statue that sets standards of qualifications for an HMO and mandates that employers of twenty-five or more who currently offer a medical benefit plan offer the additional option of joining a qualified HMO, if one exists in the area.

Health Systems Agencies (HSAs), organizations established by the National Health Planning and Resources Development Act of 1974 to conduct health systems planning and resources development activities in state or substate geographical areas.

hearing, legal or quasi-legal proceeding in which arguments, witnesses, or evidence are heard by a judicial officer, administrative body, or legislative committee.

hearing examiner/officer: *see* ADMINISTRATIVE LAW JUDGE.

hedge fund, a mutual fund that seeks capital gains as a hedge against inflation.
See also MUTUAL FUND.

helping interview, interview that consists of a genuine dialogue between the interviewer and the interviewee; the interviewer is an empathic listener rather than a mere technician recording information.

Herzberg, Frederick (1923-   ), a major influence on the conceptualization of job design, especially job enrichment. His motivation-hygiene or two-factor theory of motivation is the point of departure and a common reference point for analyses of the subject.
See also JOB ENRICHMENT and MOTIVATION-HYGIENE THEORY.

heuristic, shortcut process of reasoning that searches for a satisfactory, rather than an optimal, solution to a very large, complex, and/or poorly defined problem.

hidden agenda, unannounced or unconscious goals, personal needs, expectations, and strategies that each individual brings with his/her participation in a group. Parallel to the group's open agenda are the private or hidden agendas of each of its members.

hidden unemployed: *see* DISCOURAGED WORKERS.

hierarchy, any ordering of persons, things, or ideas by rank or level.

hierarchy of objectives, also HIERARCHY OF GOALS, a graphic display of the assumed linkages between a program's inputs, processes, and outcomes. The hierarchies also are useful for designing an evaluation process. According to Edward A. Suchman in *Evaluative Research: Principles and Practice in Public Service and Social Action Programs* (New York: Russell Sage Foundation, 1967):

> A distinction is often made between "objectives," "activities," and "steps" arranged in a descending order, with each of the latter terms used to denote action taken to implement a former one. In this sense, the objectives make up an ordered series, each of which is dependent for its existence upon an objective at the next higher level, while each is, in turn, implemented by means of lower-level objectives. In this framework there is a descending order of objectives, beginning with the idealized objective and ending, at the lowest level, with a subdivision of administrative tasks.

The Functional Analysis System Technique ("FAST" program planning) can be used to create hierarchies of objectives for complex programs—including programs that involve several organizations—relatively quickly.
See also FUNCTIONAL ANALYSIS SYSTEMS TECHNIQUE.

high match: *see* MATCHING SHARE.

hire: *see* EMPLOY.

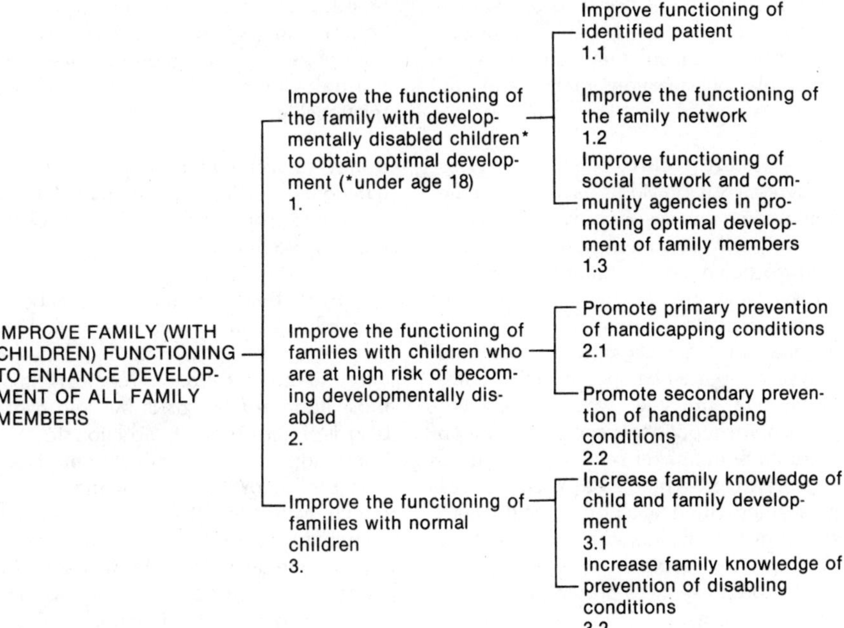
EXAMPLE OF A GOALS HIERARCHY
FOR A DEVELOPMENT CENTER
IMPROVE FAMILY (WITH CHILDREN) FUNCTIONING TO ENHANCE DEVELOPMENT OF ALL FAMILY MEMBERS
Improve the functioning of the family with developmentally disabled children* to obtain optimal development (*under age 18) 1.
Improve functioning of identified patient 1.1
Improve the functioning of the family network 1.2
Improve functioning of social network and community agencies in promoting optimal development of family members 1.3
Improve the functioning of families with children who are at high risk of becoming developmentally disabled 2.
Promote primary prevention of handicapping conditions 2.1
Promote secondary prevention of handicapping conditions 2.2
Improve the functioning of families with normal children 3.
Increase family knowledge of child and family development 3.1
Increase family knowledge of prevention of disabling conditions 3.2

hiring rate: *see* ACCESSION RATE and ENTRANCE RATE.

histogram, a bar chart used to display frequency distributions.

See also FREQUENCY DISTRIBUTION.

historical society, a nonprofit organization dedicated to restoring, preserving, maintaining, and disseminating or displaying an area's history.

HMO: *see* HEALTH MAINTENANCE ORGANIZATION.

holdback, amount of money withheld from periodic payments to contractors to assure compliance with contract terms. Usually the amount to be withheld is expressed as a percentage in the contract provisions. The amounts withheld are paid to the contractor after a designated official certifies that the contractor has completed work pursuant to the contract terms.

holding gain, also HOLDING LOSS, the difference in the worth of an asset from the time it was bought to another subsequent time (usually when it is sold, donated, or otherwise disposed of).

See also CAPITAL GAINS TAX.

holding period, the length of time a capital asset must be owned to make the federal taxation more favorable as a capital gain.

holiday pay, premium rate paid for work performed on holidays.

Hollerith cards, punched cards used by computers which were first developed by Herman Hollerith of the U.S. Bureau of the Census in 1889.

home health agency, an agency which provides home health care. To be certified under Medicare an agency must provide skilled nursing services and at least one additional therapeutic service (physical, speech or occupational therapy, medical social services, or home health aide services) in the home. A home health agency is an example of a health provider organization which may qualify as a charitable organization for federal tax purposes.

home health care, health services rendered to an individual as needed in the home. Such services are provided to aged, disabled, sick, or convalescent individuals who do not need institutional care. The services may be provided by a visiting nurse association, home health agency, hospital, or other organized community group. They may be specialized or comprehensive (nursing services, speech, physical, occupational, and rehabilitation therapy, homemaker services, and social services). Under Medicare, such services must be provided by a home health agency. Under Medicaid, states may, but do not have to, restrict coverage of home health care to services provided by home health agencies.

homemaker services, nonmedical support services (*e.g.*, food preparation, bathing) given a homebound individual who is unable to perform these tasks himself. Such services have not been covered under the Medicare and Medicaid programs or most other health insurance programs, but may be included in the social service programs developed by the States under Title XX of the Social Security Act. Homemaker services are intended to preserve independent living and normal family life for the aged, disabled, sick, or convalescent.

homogeneity principle, principle of administration that advises the executive to group the major functions of an organization according to their purpose, the process used, the persons served, or the places where it takes place, with each constituted as a single unit under the direction of a single administrator guided by a single plan of action.

honeymoon period, that period of time immediately following, for example, the appointment of a new executive by a board of directors or a major agreement between management and labor when both sides may seek to de-emphasize the normal difficulties inherent in their relationship.

honor, to accept (in other words, to pay) a negotiable instrument, such as a check, when it is properly presented for acceptance (or payment).

honorary board of directors, a board established to honor individuals who have contributed substantially (funds or time and effort) to the organization. Membership on most honorary boards is by vote of the board of directors. In addition to their honoring function, honorary boards are also useful for (a) maintaining a community-wide network of people who have contributed in the past and who can be called upon again, and (b) increasing the organization's credibility through association with community influentials. For example, many organizations print the names of honorary board members on their letterhead, or on letterhead used in fund-raising.

horizontal communication: *see* COMMUNICATION.

horizontal conflict, bureaucratic conflict between units of an agency that are located at similar hierarchical levels.

horizontal equity: *see* TAX EQUITY.

horizontal loading: *see* JOB LOADING.

horizontal occupational mobility: *see* OCCUPATIONAL MOBILITY.

horizontal promotion, advancement for an employee within his/her basic job category. For example, a promotion from Window Washer I to Window Washer II or from Junior Accountant to Intermediate Accountant.

horizontal union: *see* CRAFT UNION.

horizontal work group, work group that contains individuals whose positions are essentially the same in terms of rank, prestige, and level of skill.

horticultural organization, an organization which has as its primary purpose the study or the actual cultivation of flowers, fruits, vegetables, and/or plants. Horticultural organizations may qualify for tax exemption under IRS Code 501 (c) (5).

hospital, charitable, hospital which has been declared tax-exempt and which can receive tax-exempt contributions. A hospital is an institution for providing sick and injured persons with medical, surgical, and/or therapeutic treatment. In common usage, *charitable hospital* often means one which provides substantial amounts of care to the poor and destitute who cannot afford the costs of hospitalization. In recent years, the courts have been more liberal in their interpretation of *charitable* relative to hospitals.

See also COOPERATIVE HOSPITAL SERVICE ORGANIZATION.

hospitalization, group insurance program that pays employees for all or part of their hospital, nursing, surgical, and other related medical expenses due to injury or illness to them or their dependents.

hot stove discipline, disciplinary practices that are immediate, painful, and impersonal.

hourly-rate workers, employees whose weekly pay is determined soley by the actual number of hours worked during a week.

housekeeping agency: *see* AUXILIARY AGENCY.

house organ, also INTERNAL HOUSE ORGAN and EXTERNAL HOUSE ORGAN, any publication—magazine, newspaper, newsletter, etc.—produced by an organization to keep its volunteers, clients, donors, and employees informed about the activities of the organization. *Internal house organs* are directed primarily to an organization's volunteers and employees; *external house organs* find a wider distribution as part of the organization's public relations program.

See also INTERNAL PUBLIC RELATIONS and PUBLIC RELATIONS.

housing allowance, special compensation consisting of a flat rate or a salary percentage for the purpose of subsidizing the living expenses of an employee. For example, a church may pay a housing allowance to its minister in lieu of providing housing (such as a parsonage).

Housing and Urban Development, Department of (HUD), principal federal agency responsible for programs concerned with housing needs and improving and developing the nation's communities.

H.R. 10 Plan: *see* KEOGH PLAN.

HSA, Health Systems Agency, Health Systems Authority, or Health Systems Area.

See HEALTH SYSTEMS AGENCIES.

HUD: *see* HOUSING AND URBAN DEVELOPMENT, DEPARTMENT OF.

HUD "701", Section 701 of the Housing Act of 1954 (and subsequent amendments), which provides for grants to strengthen the "planning and decision making capabilities of the chief executives of state, area-wide, and local agencies to promote more effective use of the nation's physical, economic, and human resources."

human capital, a concept that views employees as assets in the same sense as financial capital. It presupposes that an investment in human potential will yield significant returns for the organization.

human-factors engineering, also called ERGONOMICS, design for human use. The objective of human factors engineering, usually called ergonomics in Europe, is to increase the effective use of physical objects and facilities by people at work, while at the same time attending to concerns such as health, safety, job satisfaction, etc. These objectives are sought by the systematic application of relevant information about human behavior to the design of the things (usually machines) that people use and to the environments in which they work.

humanist, an individual with an intense concern for human dignity and well-being; a person who is involved and concerned with the humanities.

See also HUMANITIES.

humanitarian, concerned with improving the health, welfare, and happiness of humankind; a person engaged in activities to improve the health, welfare, and happiness of humankind; a true philanthropist.

humanities, art, philosophy, and literature, in contrast with the sciences; the study of classical literature and languages.

human relations, discipline concerned with the application of the behavioral sciences to the analysis and understanding of human behavior in organizations.

Personnel operations still tend to live in the shadow of the old-style human-relations approach to management that emphasized sympathetic attitudes on the part of managers. Its critics contended that the human-relations approach (most popular during the late 1940s and 1950s) was little more than a gimmick—that there was sincere interest in the workers only to the extent that they could be manipulated for management's ends. The goal was to adjust the worker—the same old interchangeable part of the scientific management movement—so that he or she would be content in the industrial situation, not to change the situation so that the worker would find more contentment in his or her work.

Today, human relations is in a more mature period. Like the caterpillar that turned into the butterfly, it simply evolved into something much more desirable. By expropriating advances in the behavioral sciences as its own, it grew into its current definition.

human resource accounting, concept that views the employees of an organization as capital assets similar to plant and equipment. While the concept is intuitively attractive, calculating the value, replacement cost, and depreciation of human assets poses significant problems. Consequently, it is viewed with considerable skepticism by managers and accountants.

human resources, also called MANPOWER, general term for all of the employees in an organization or the workers in a society. It is gradually replacing the more sexist "manpower."

human resources administration, increasingly popular euphemism for the management of social welfare programs. Many jurisdictions that had Departments of Welfare have replaced them with Departments of Human Resources.

human resources development, a more impressive-sounding phrase for the training and development function of personnel management.

human resources management (HRM), the administration of human resources. Although often used synonymously with personnel management, HRM transcends traditional personnel concerns, taking the most expansive view of the personnel department's mandate. Instead of viewing the personnel function as simply that collection of disparate duties necessary to recruit, pay, and discharge employees, a HRM approach assumes that personnel's appropriate mission is the maximum utilization of its organization's human resources.

human resources planning, also called MANPOWER PLANNING, planning for personnel allocation and training. There is no universally accepted definition of what human resources planning (or its more sexist equivalent, "manpower planning") is or consensus on what activities should be associated with it. Organizations claiming that they do such planning appear to use a wide variety of methods to approach their own unique problems.

Historically, manpower planning was most associated with the Johnson Administration's Great Society Programs of the 1960s. It was and remains an integral part of numerous government programs whose objective is to affect the labor market in order to improve the employment status and welfare of individuals. All such programs have a macro focus—they deal with the aggregate labor force of the country (all employed and unemployed individuals). At roughly the same time as the new manpower initiatives of the Johnson Administration, parallel thinking on human resources planning began to emerge at the firm and organizational level. Both situations involve projecting and managing the supply and demand of human resources, only at different levels. Both are concerned with future demand aspects; that is, what will be the requirements for the future work force. At the macro level, this means projecting what skills will be in demand to service the economy. At the micro level, this entails projecting specific requirements for the work force of the organization, or what quantities and qualities of personnel will be needed to carry out organizational objectives. Both levels are concerned with future supply aspects. At the macro level this means that projections must be made on what the national work force will consist of in terms of future skills, both surpluses and deficits. For the micro level, the organization must forecast what its future work force will consist of as well as evaluate its competitive position in order to decide what quantities and qualities of personnel it can encourage to enter the organization as replacements.

human resources planning models, also called MANPOWER PLANNING MODELS, models which use systems analysis techniques to forecast future human resources requirements, analyze the impact of proposed changes in human resources policy, test the rationale of historical human resources policies, explore possible policy changes, assess the relative organizational/human resources operational problems, design systems that balance human resources and requirements, and structure the human resources information system for policy analysis and planning.

human resources requirements analysis, also called MANPOWER REQUIREMENTS ANALYSIS, analysis and projection of (a) the personnel movements and (b) the numbers and kinds of vacancies to be expected during each stage of management's work force plan. According to the federal Office of Personnel Management, the essential steps in manpower requirements analysis are:

- *First*, to estimate what portion of the work force present at the start of the planning period, or hired during the period, will leave their positions during the period.
- *Second*, to estimate how many of these position leavers will move to other positions in the work force during the period and how many will leave the service entirely.
- *Third*, to estimate the positions to be occupied by in-service movers to the end of the planning period.
- *Fourth*, by comparison of this retained work force with the work force specified in management's work force plan, to identify the numbers and kinds of positions to be filled during the planning period.

human resources utilization, also called MANPOWER UTILIZATION, general terms for the selection, development, and placement of human resources within an economic or organizational system in order to use these resources in the most efficient manner.

human services, general term for organizations that seek to improve the quality of their client's lives by providing counseling, rehabilitative, nutritional, informational, and related services.

hype, extreme advertising and public relations promotion of an event.

hypothesis, testable assertion, statement, or proposition about the relationship between two variables that are in some way related to each other. For example, a personnel manager might hypothesize that a specific kind of job performance can be predicted from a particular kind of knowledge about an applicant (such as scores on tests or grades in school). Hypotheses of this kind are proven—one way or another—by validation studies.

hypothesis testing, the process of formally assessing whether the expectations presented in a hypothesis exist (or hold true) in the real world.

I

ICMA: *see* INTERNATIONAL CITY MANAGEMENT ASSOCATION.

ICMA Retirement Corporation, nonprofit, tax-exempt organization providing a deferred compensation retirement plan for the mobile employees of state and local government.

The plan was developed by the International City Management Association, which underwrote the Retirement Corporation. In recognition of the plan's importance, most of the major public interest and professional associations related to state and local government have become sponsors of the plan.

idle time, time for which employees are paid but not able to work because of factors not within their control.

IDP: *see* INDIVIDUAL DEVELOPMENT PLAN.

illegal aliens, also called UNDOCUMENTED WORKERS, individuals from other countries who are living/working in the United States unlawfully. The U.S. Department of Labor prefers to refer to these individuals as "undocumented workers."

illegal bargaining items, any proposal made during the collective bargaining process that is expressly forbidden by law; for example, a union shop in a "right-to-work" state.

illegal strike, strike that violates existing law. While most public sector strikes are illegal, so are strikes that violate a contract, that are not properly authorized by the union membership, and that violate a court injunction.

illusion: *see* PERCEPTION.

image consultant, a public relations practitioner who specializes in teaching executives how to project a more impressive image (both inside and outside of the organization) by dressing, speaking, socializing, etc. in a more "executive-like" manner.

immediate full vesting, pension plan that entitles an employee to all of the retirement income—both his/her contributions as well as those of his/her employer—accrued during his/her time of participation in the plan.

immigrant association, an association of people who immigrated from another country that provides members with mutual support, social integration assistance, fellowship, and—intentionally or unintentionally—helps to maintain aspects of the group's cultural heritage.

Immigration and Naturalization Service (INS), federal agency responsible for administering the immigration and naturalization laws relating to the admission, exclusion, deportation, and naturalization of aliens. Specifically, the INS inspects aliens to determine their admissibility into the U.S.; adjudicates requests of aliens for benefits under the law; guards against illegal entry into the United States; investigates, apprehends, and removes aliens in this country who are in violation of the law; and examines alien applicants wishing to become citizens.

immunity, an exemption from ordinary legal culpability while holding office. For example, directors of organizations generally need some protections against lawsuits, whether frivolous or not, which might be brought against them by individuals who are dissatisfied with their actions or adversely affected by them.

impact: *see* OUTCOME.

impact evaluation: *see* PROGRAM EVALUATION.

impact-incidence matrix, an analytical decision making tool which attempts to ensure that noncostable impacts are considered. The matrix lays out all identifiable, important impacts of a proposed program or project on different sectors of society (such as human, biological, physical, etc.).

The use of impact-incidence matrices is increasing, primarily as an alternative to cost/benefit analysis, cost/effectiveness analysis, and single social cost indices. The latter three techniques are not particularly well suited for decision analyses involving multiple noncostable potential impacts.

See also COST/BENEFIT ANALYSIS and COST/EFFECTIVENESS ANALYSIS.

impact ratio, for employment decisions that offer people employment opportunities (such as hiring, training, promotion, etc.), the selection rate for that group divided by the selection rate for the group with the highest selection rate. For any adverse employment decision (such as disciplinary action, layoff, termination, etc.), the impact ratio is the rate for the group in question. Impact ratios are compared to the eighty percent rule of thumb to determine adverse impact.

impact theory of discrimination, concept that asserts it is the consequences of employment practices that are relevant, not their intent. Even though an intent is

EXAMPLE OF AN IMPACT-INCIDENCE MATRIX FOR A NEW DOWNTOWN PERFORMING ARTS CENTER

	Patrons							
	In Town	Out of Town	Performers	Producers	Vendors	Local Bsns	Tourists	Public Trsnpt.
Dollar Impacts								
Construction $				X	X			
Access time & $	X	X	X		X			X
Center finac'l feasibility	X	X		X	X	X		
Community econ. benefits					X	X		X
Quantitative Impacts								
Location re patrons	X	X	X	X	X	X		X
Increased traffic congest'n	X	X	X	X	X	X	X	X
Increased volume to downtown businesses						X		
Qualitative Impacts								
Air Pollution	X	X	X	X	X	X	X	X
Displacement of businesses	X					X	X	X

benign, its consequences could foster systemic discrimination.

impasse, a condition that exists during negotiations when either party feels that no further progress can be made toward reaching a settlement.

impeachment, a quasi-judicial process for removing public officials from office.

implementation, those activities involved in putting policies and goals into action; an interactive process among policies or goals and action, in which policies provide direction for action and, in turn, the experience (or learning) gained through acting causes modifications to policies and goals.

Implementation is a complex political process. Like board members, administrators and those with whom they interact during the implementation process (for example, clients, volunteers, and community organizations) exert power over program objectives and influence program outputs and outcomes. Further, implementation involves administrators, volunteers, clients, and other actors with diverse values, mobilizing power resources, forming coalitions, consciously plotting strategies, and generally engaging in strategic behavior designed to assure that their point of view prevails.

implicit price deflator, a price index for the gross national product (GNP); the ratio of GNP in current prices to GNP in constant prices.

implied, known indirectly; known by analyzing surrounding circumstances or the actions of the persons involved; the opposite of *express*.

TYPES OF IMPASSE RESOLUTION

	Mediation	*Fact-Finding*	*Arbitration*
Process	Intervention by Federal Mediation and Conciliation Service or other appropriate third party at request of negotiating parties or on own proffering of services.	A procedure for compelling settlement, frequently a final alternative to arbritration	A terminal procedure alternative to or following fact-finding
Subject Matter	Terms of new agreement being negotiated	Terms of agreement being negotiated	Terms of agreement being negotiated (also final step in grievance procedure)
Setting	*Mediator* tries to determine basis for agreement and persuade parties to reach agreement	*Parties* try to persuade fact-finder by arguments	*Parties* try to persuade arbitrator by arguments (same as fact-finding)
Third Party	*Mediator*—a Federal Commissioner of Mediation and Conciliation or other third party	*Fact-finder*—a public employee or a private citizen selected by parties or by an administrative agency	*Arbitrator*—a public employee or a private citizen selected by parties or by an administrative agency
Power Factor	*Mediator* limited to persuasion and ability to find compromise	*Fact-finder* may make recommendations for impasse resolution	*Arbitrator* makes binding decision
Publicity	Confidential process —no public record kept	Quasi-public process with recommendations recorded and reported	Quasi-public process with decisions recorded and reported

implied authority, the authority one person "grants" to another to accomplish a job, even if the authority is not given directly.

implied terms, parts of a contract that do not exist on paper, but are part of the contract nonetheless (because the law requires them, because usual contracts in that business have them, etc.).

implied warranty, the legal conclusion that a merchant promises that what is sold is fit for normal use or, if the merchant knows what the buyer wants the thing for, that it is fit for that particular purpose. Unless these implied warranties are expressly excluded (for example, by clearly labeling an item "as is"), a merchant will be held to them.

See also AS IS.

impoundment, tactic available to fiscal strategists—the withholding by executives of funds budgeted or appropriated. There are several types of impoundment decisions. One is to confiscate funds when the program objective has been accomplished. Presidents Eisenhower and Truman both made use of impoundment to take back "extra" funds from programs whose objectives had been met or were clearly not in need of funds. Another mode of impoundment is for legal compliance. President Lyndon Johnson impounded and threatened to impound funds for local governments and school districts who were in violation of the Civil Rights Act or federal court orders.

imprest, also IMPREST FUND, a loan or advance. An *imprest fund* is a petty cash fund.

improvement, an addition or change to land or buildings that increases their worth; more than a repair or replacement.

improvement curve: *see* LEARNING CURVE.

imputed, also IMPUTED COST, a cost not recognized as an actual cost by an accountant. Imputed costs do not result in transfers of cash, but they may still affect management decisions; for example, the cost of donated services.

in-basket exercise, training technique and type of test frequently used in management assessment centers to simulate managerial problems by presenting the subject with an array of written materials (the kinds of items that might accumulate in an "in-basket") so that responses to the various items and problems can be evaluated.

See also ASSESSMENT CENTER.

incentive, reward, whether monetary or psychic, that motivates and/or compensates an employee for performance above standard.

incentive awards, also called INCENTIVE SCHEME, formal plan or program designed to motivate individual or group efforts to improve the economy and efficiency of organizational operations. There are essentially two kinds of awards—monetary and honorary.

incentive contract, that portion or clause of a collective bargaining agreement that establishes the terms and conditions of an incentive-wage system.

incentive pay, wage system that rewards a worker for productivity above an established standard.

incentive plan, individual/group: *see* INCENTIVE-WAGE PLAN.

incentive rate, special wage rate for production above a previously fixed standard of performance.

incentive scheme: *see* INCENTIVE AWARD.

incentive-wage plan, also GROUP INCENTIVE PLAN, wage program that has wages rise with increases in productivity. Individual incentive plans are based on the performance of the individual employee, while *group incentive plans* are based on the performance of the total work group.

incidental learning, also called LATENT LEARNING, learning that takes place without formal instruction, intent to learn, or ascertainable motive. The information obtained tends to lie dormant until an occasion for its use arises.

incidental private inurement, private inurement that is incidential (small and tangential) to the entity's public benefit purposes. It will not automatically disqualify a nonprofit organization from tax-exempt status. However, as a general rule, private inurement—incidental or not—should be avoided to prevent jeopardizing tax exemption.
See also PRIVATE INUREMENT.

income, estimated: *see* ESTIMATED INCOME.

income, indirect: *see* INDIRECT WAGES.

income, recognition of (accounting), the point in time at which income is recognized for accounting purposes. There are different conceptual approaches to recognizing income in nonprofit organizations.
See, for example, EARNINGS CONCEPT and STEWARDSHIP CONCEPT.

income averaging, reducing a tax liability by showing that income in prior years was far lower than the current year, and by paying tax on the basis of the average income for several years.

income bond, also ADJUSTMENT BOND, a bond on which interest is paid only when the issuing company has earnings sufficient to pay it.

income fund, a mutual fund whose prime objective is to maximize current income (not, for example, to maximize future growth).
See also MUTUAL FUND.

income in-kind, the receipt of goods or services as payment for something.

income property, property which is purchased more for current income generation than for capital appreciation.
See also APPRECIATION.

income return, either the annual gain from an investment or the percentage figure found by dividing the annual gain by the initial price.

income splitting, reducing a family's total tax liability by giving income-producing property to a family member who pays taxes at a lower rate (or selling it to a family member and extending the buyer a no-interest loan).
See also GIFT.

income statement: *see* OPERATING STATEMENT.

income tax, from a business perspective, a tax on profits from business or work, but not on the growth in value of investments or property. For an individual, an income tax is a tax on personal income from work, less allowable deductions, credits, etc.

income test, one of several tests or criteria used by the IRS to determine whether an organization qualifies as a private operating foundation. The test involves the relationship between income and the amount of funds distributed directly for the advancement of the organization's purposes.
See PRIVATE OPERATING FOUNDATION.

incompetence, demonstrated failure of an employee to meet minimum standards of job performance.

incorporated, also UNINCORPORATED, legally organized under the laws of a state.

incorporators, the people who organize an organization and file its initial articles of organization with a state.

increment, also called STEP INCREASE, established salary increase between steps of a given salary grade, marking a steady progression from the minimum of the grade to the maximum.

incremental analysis: *see* MARGINAL ANALYSIS.

incremental budgeting: *see* BUDGETING, INCREMENTAL.

incremental cost: *see* COST, MARGINAL.

incremental funding, the provision (or recording) of budgetary resources for a program or project based on obligations estimated to be incurred within a fiscal year when such budgetary resources will cover only a portion of the obligations to be incurred in completing the program or project as programmed. This differs from full funding, where budgetary resources are provided or recorded for the total estimated obligations for a program or project in the initial year of funding.
See also FULL FUNDING.

incrementalism, an approach to decision making in which executives begin with the current situation, consider a limited number of changes in that situation based upon a restricted range of alternatives, and test those changes by instituting them one at a time; a normative theory of organizations that views policy making as a process of bargaining and competition involving the participation of different persons with conflicting points of view.

incumbent, person presently serving in a position.

indemnify, act of compensating insured individuals for their losses.

indemnity, insurance contract to reimburse an individual or organization for possible losses of a particular type.

independent contractor, a person or organization who contracts with another organization to do a particular piece of work by his or her own methods and under his or her own control. An independent contractor is neither an agent nor an employee.
See also CONSULTANT and CONTRACTOR.

independent foundation, a private foundation established and funded by an individual or a family. The term was coined by the Council on Foundations to differentiate such foundations from private foundations which are funded by corporations. The term appears to be gaining general acceptance.
See also:
COMMUNITY FOUNDATION
CORPORATE FOUNDATION
FOUNDATION
PRIVATE FOUNDATION

independent sector: *see* THIRD SECTOR.

INDEPENDENT SECTOR, a national coalition of 580 voluntary organizations, foundations, and corporations which seeks to preserve and enhance the American traditions of giving, volunteering, and not-for-profit initiative. Formed in 1980 through the merger of the National Council on Philanthropy and the Coalition of National Voluntary Organizations, INDEPENDENT SECTOR is located in Washington, D.C.

independent union, a union that is not affiliated with the AFL-CIO.

independent variable, a factor in a hypothesized relationship that is thought to cause or bring about variation in the performance of the dependent factor.

index, a bibliographic resource; for example, *Human Resources Abstracts, Index to Legal Periodicals,* and *Business Periodicals Index.*

indexing, system by which salaries, pensions, welfare payments, and other kinds of income are automatically adjusted to account for inflation.

index number, measure of relative value compared with a base figure for the same series. In a time series in index form, the base period usually is set equal to 100, and data for other periods are expressed as percentages of the value in the base period.

Index numbers possess advantages over the raw data from which they are derived. First, they facilitate analysis by their simplicity. Second, they are a more useful basis for comparison of changes in data originally expressed in dissimilar units. Third, they permit comparisons over time with some common starting point—the index base period.

See also TIME SERIES ANALYSIS.

index of agreement, index, usually expressed as a percentage, showing the extent to which examiners agree on a candidate's scores.

Indian tribe, an aggregation of American Indians united by ties of descent from common ancestors and by a community of values, beliefs, customs, rituals, and traditions. Also, sometimes used to refer to the elected governing structure of an Indian tribe (for example, a tribal council).

indirect costs: *see* COSTS, INDIRECT.

indirect labor: *see* DIRECT LABOR.

indirect labor costs, loose term for the wages of nonproduction employees.

indirect self-dealing, an attempt by a disqualified person to circumvent laws and regulations against self-dealing with private foundations, typically attempted by transacting through an intermediate entity controlled by a foundation.

See SELF-DEALING and TAX-AVOIDANCE SCHEME.

indirect tax: *see* DIRECT TAX.

indirect validity: *see* SYNTHETIC VALIDITY.

indirect wages, also called INDIRECT INCOME and INDIRECT COMPENSATION, nonfinancial benefits employees receive from their work situations—favorable organizational environment, nontaxable benefits, perquisites, and the authority, power, and/or status that may come with their jobs.

individual agreement, also called INDIVIDUAL CONTRACT, formal agreement between a single employee and his/her employer that determines the employee's conditions and terms of employment.

individual-contract pension trust, pension plan that creates a trust to buy and hold title to employees' individual insurance and/or annuity contracts. The employer makes payments to the trust, which then pays the insurance premiums on its various contracts.

individual development plan (IDP), periodically prepared schedule of developmental experiences, including both work assignments and formal training, designed to meet particular developmental objectives needed to improve current performance and/or to prepare the individual for positions of greater responsibility.

Individual Retirement Account (IRA), an individual pension that the Pension Reform Act of 1974, as amended, allows each person to create in order to put aside money that builds up tax-free until retirement. Funds can be invested in savings accounts, mutual funds, annuities, government bonds, etc. Individuals *may* start withdrawing funds at age 59½ and *must* begin withdrawals by age 70½. Funds are taxed in the year they are withdrawn.

individual test, testing device designed to be administered (usually by a specially trained person) to only one subject at a time.

indorsement, signing a negotiable instrument, such as a check, so that the piece of paper and the rights it stands for transfer to another person.

industrial accident insurance: *see* WORKMEN'S COMPENSATION.

industrial and organizational psychology: *see* INDUSTRIAL PSYCHOLOGY.

industrial democracy, also PARTICIPATIVE MANAGEMENT, any of a variety of efforts designed to encourage employees to participate in an organization's decision making processes by identifying problems and suggesting solutions to them in a formal manner. While the terms "industrial democracy" and "participative management" tend to be used almost interchangeably, there is a distinction. The modern usage of *industrial democracy* to cover innumerable types of joint or cooperative management programs dates from World War I. Then it connoted a scheme to avoid labor-management disputes which might adversely affect war production. Today *industrial democracy* connotes joint action by management and employees. *Participative management,* in contrast, connotes cooperative programs that are unilaterally implemented from on high. Nevertheless, both terms seem to be rapidly losing their distinctive connotations.

industrial engineering, term defined by the American Institute of Industrial Engineers as being

> concerned with the design, improvement, and installation of integrated systems of men, materials, and equipment; drawing upon specialized knowledge and skill in the mathematical, physical, and social sciences together with the principles and methods of engineering analysis and design, to specify, predict, and evaluate the results to be obtained from such systems.

industrial gerontology: *see* GERIATRICS.

industrial health services, or OCCUPATIONAL HEALTH SERVICES, health services provided by physicians, dentists, nurses, or other health personnel in a work setting for the appraisal, protection, and promotion of the health of employees while on the job. *Occupational health services* is now the preferred term.

industrial medicine, that branch of medicine that is concerned with protecting workers from hazards in the workplace and with dealing with health problems/emergencies that may occur during working hours.

industrial psychology, also called OCCUPATIONAL PSYCHOLOGY, INDUSTRIAL AND ORGANIZATIONAL PSYCHOLOGY, and I/O PSYCHOLOGY, psychology traditionally concerned with those aspects of human behavior related to work organizations. Its focus has been on the basic relations in organizations between (1) employees and their coworkers, (2) employees and machines, and (3) employees and the organization. Because the term *industrial psychology* holds a restrictive connotation, the field is increasingly referred to as *industrial and organizational psychology* or *I/O psychology*.

industrial relations, term generally used to refer to all matters of mutual concern to employers and employees and their representatives. In a more technical sense, its use should be limited to labor-management relationships.

industrial revenue bond, a tax-exempt local government-issued bond, used to pay for a plant formally owned by the government unit but leased to a firm(s) on a long-term basis. A locality uses these bonds to help attract new industry and, thereby, strengthen the local economy.

See also REVENUE BONDS.

inequity theory, also EQUITY THEORY, theory most fully developed by J. Stacy Adams (he premised his work upon Leon Festinger's theory of cognitive dissonance), who holds that inequity exists for Worker A whenever his/her perceived job inputs and outcomes are inconsistent with Worker B's job inputs and outcomes. Inequity would exist if a person perceived that he/she was working much harder than another person who received the same pay. Adams suggests that the presence of inequity creates tension within Person A to reduce the inequity by, for example, increasing (or decreasing) one's efforts if it is perceived to be low (or high) relative to others' work effort.

See also COGNITIVE DISSONANCE.

inferential statistics, that portion of the field of statistics concerned with making in-

ferences to a larger population from findings obtained through the use of sampling.
See also DESCRIPTIVE STATISTICS.

inflation, also DEFLATION, is a rise in the costs of goods and services which is equated to a fall in the value of a nation's currency. *Deflation* is the reverse, a fall in costs and a rise in the value of money. Cost-push inflation is inflation caused by increases in the costs of production which are independent of the state of demand. Demand-pull inflation is inflation caused by increased demand rather than by increases in the cost of production. Hidden inflation is a price increase achieved by selling smaller quanties (or a poorer quality) of a product for the same price as before. Hyperinflation is inflation so extreme that it practically destroys the value of paper money.

influencing legislation, attempting to persuade legislators to initiate, support, reject, or otherwise oppose proposed legislation. If a substantial portion of a nonprofit organization's activities involve attempting to influence legislation, it is known as an "action organization." Action organizations are not charitable organizations.
See also:
ACTION ORGANIZATION
LEGISLATION
LEGISLATIVE ACTIVITIES

informal organization, spontaneously developed relationships and patterns of interaction among employees.

informational spot (electronic media), a short, attention-catching, support-generating public service announcement on a radio or television station. An informational spot is differentiated from a sales spot by its lack of an appeal for a specific act (such as a contribution). Informational spots are used for general development rather than for specific fund-raising purposes. They are used by stations to help meet the public interest time requirement specified in their FCC license applications.
See also:
COMMUNICATIONS ACT OF 1934
PUBLIC INTEREST
SALES SPOT

information management: *see* RECORDS MANAGEMENT.

infrastructure, the core of an organization's effectiveness—whether expressed as volunteers, staff, endowments, public support, etc.—which is essential for the organization's continuing successful operations; also, physical assets of a nation that relate to its industrial productivity, such as roads, dams, bridges, etc.

infringement, a breach or violation of a right; also, the unauthorized making, using, selling, or distributing of something protected by a patent, copyright, or trademark.

initiation fees, payments required by clubs, associations, and unions of all new members and/or of employees who, having once disassociated, wish to return. Initiation fees serve several purposes: (1) they are a source of revenue, (2) they force the new member to pay for the advantages secured by those who built the organization, and (3) they (when the fees are high enough) can be used as a device to restrict membership.

initiative, procedure that allows citizens, as opposed to legislators, to propose the enactment of laws; or a very high-level organizational goal (for example, a rural health initiative, an Indian health initiative, or a community economic development initiative).

injury, work related, for compensation under the Federal Employees' Compensation Act, a personal injury sustained while in the performance of duty. The term "injury" includes diseases proximately caused by the employment.

ink-blot test: *see* RORSCHACH TEST.

in-kind grant: *see* GRANTS-IN-KIND.

in-kind match, also called SOFT MATCH,

grant recipient's fulfilling of its cost-sharing obligation by a contribution other than cash, such as the rental of space or equipment or staff services.

***Inland Steel Co.* v. *National Labor Relations Board*,** decision by the U.S. Court of Appeals, 7th Circuit (1948), which held that a company was required to bargain with its union over retirement and pension matters. The decision was indirectly upheld by the U.S. Supreme Court when it denied certiorari in the case, 336 U.S. 960 (1949).

inner-directed, David Riesman's description of people with strong personal value systems as opposed to those who are other-directed (who more easily accept the values of their peers). *See* his *The Lonely Crowd* (1950).

See also REFERENCE GROUP.

INS: *see* IMMIGRATION AND NATURALIZATION SERVICE.

insecurity clause, a section of a contract that allows a creditor to make an entire debt come due if there is a good reason to believe that the debtor cannot or will not pay.

in-service training, term used mainly to refer to job-related instruction and educational experiences made available to employees. In-service training programs are usually offered during normal working hours. However, some programs, especially those offering college credit, are available to the employee only on his/her own time.

insider (corporate), a person who has business knowledge not available to the general public.

insider (tax-exempt organization), a person with a substantial relationship to a tax-exempt organization, typically as a director, trustee, member, contributor, or stockholder, and who is prohibited from conducting many types of transactions with it (particularly financial transactions which might result in private inurement). Insiders are disqualified persons.

See DISQUALIFIED PERSON and PRIVATE INUREMENT.

insolvent, the condition of a person or organization who either cannot pay debts as they come due or whose assets are less than liabilities.

See also ASSETS and LIABILITIES.

installment credit, an arrangement in which a buyer pays the purchase price (plus, usually, interest and other finance charges) in regular (usually monthly) payments.

institutional advertising: *see* ADVERTISEMENT, INSTITUTIONAL.

institutional discrimination, practices contrary to EEO policies that occur even though there was no intent to discriminate. Institutional discrimination exists whenever a practice or procedure has the effect of treating one group of employees differently from another.

instrument, a written document; a formal or legal document such as a contract or a will. Also, a negotiable instrument (such as a check).

instrument, controlling: *see* CONTROLLING INSTRUMENTS.

instrument, governing: *see* GOVERNING INSTRUMENT.

instrumentality, government: *see* GOVERNMENT INSTRUMENTALITY.

instrumentality, United States: *see* UNITED STATES INSTRUMENTALITY.

instrumentality rule, the legal rule that a subsidiary organization must be an independent entity and not a mere instrument or tool of its parent organization if the separate legal entity of the subsidiary is to be recognized. If the subsidiary is not an independent entity, the parent organization may be liable for its debts.

See also SUBORDINATE AFFILIATED ORGANIZATION.

instrumented laboratory, laboratory training experience that uses feedback from measurements taken during laboratory sessions of the behavior and feelings of the group and/or its component individuals.

insubordination, disobedience to higher authorities in an organization; refusing to take orders from those who are properly designated to give them.

insubstantial: *see:*
EXCLUSIVELY

insurable risk, a risk which has the following attributes: it is one of a large homogeneous group of similar risks; the loss produced by the risk is definable and quantifiable; the occurrence of loss in individual cases is accidental or fortuitous; the potential loss is large enough to cause hardship; the cost of insuring is economically feasible; the chance of loss is calculable; and it is sufficiently unlikely that loss will occur in many individual cases at the same time.

insurance, also INSURANCE PREMIUM, contractual arrangement that has a customer pay a specified sum, the *insurance premium,* in return for which the insurer will pay compensation if specific events occur (*e.g.*, death for life insurance, fire for fire insurance, hospitalization for health insurance, etc.). The insurance premiums are calculated so that their total return to the insurance company is sufficient to cover all policyholder claims plus administrative costs and profit.

See also the following entries:
DENTAL PLAN
DISABILITY INSURANCE
GROUP INSURANCE
LIFE INSURANCE
PLAN TERMINATION INSURANCE

insurance commissioner, the state official charged with the enforcement of laws pertaining to insurance in the respective states. The commissioner's title, status in government, and responsibilities differ somewhat from state to state, but all states have an official having such responsibilities regardless of his or her title. Sometimes called superintendent or director.

insurance pool, an organization of insurers or reinsurers through which particular types of risks are shared or pooled. The risk of high loss by any particular insurance company is transferred to the group as a whole (the insurance pool) with premiums, losses, and expenses shared in agreed amounts. The advantage of a pool is that the size of expected losses can be predicted for the pool with much more certainty than for any individual party to it. Pooling arrangements are often used for catastrophic coverage or for certain high risk populations like the disabled. Pooling may also be done within a single company by pooling the risks insured under various different policies so that high losses incurred by one policy are shared with others.

insurance premium: *see* INSURANCE.

insurance trust contributions, amounts derived from contributions, assessments, premiums, "taxes," etc.

insured, person who buys insurance on property, or the person whose life or health is insured.

insured loan, in the context of federal credit programs, a loan in which a private lender is assured of repayment by the federal government on part or all of the principal or interest due; for example, a guaranteed student loan.

insurer, person, company, or governmental agency that provides insurance.

intangible cost: *see* COST, INTANGIBLE.

intangible objective: *see* OBJECTIVE.

intangible rewards, satisfactions of no monetary value that an individual gains from a job.

intangibles, those benefits and costs which cannot be converted into dollar values.

integrated auxiliary (of a religious organization), an organization affiliated with or controlled by a church which engages solely in religious activities. Integrated auxiliaries may qualify as tax-exempt organizations. Examples include missionary societies, theological seminaries, and religious fellowship associations.

See also CHURCH and RELIGIOUS ORGANIZATION.

integrative bargaining: *see* PRODUCTIVITY BARGAINING.

intelligence, a hypothetical construct. Generally, it refers to an individual's ability to cope with his/her environment and deal with mental abstractions. The military, as well as some other organizations, use the word "intelligence" in its original Latin sense—as information.

intelligence function, use of techniques that encourage organizational advocacy and competitiveness in the gathering, interpreting, and communicating of information in order to give executives accurate and up-to-date information for use in decision making and administration.

intelligence quotient (IQ), measure of an individual's general intellectual capability. IQ tests have come under severe criticism because of their declining relevancy as a measurement tool for individuals past the age of adolescence and because of their inherent cultural bias, which has tended to discriminate against minorities.

intelligence test, any of a variety of standardized tests that seek to measure a range of mental abilities and social skills.

intelligent terminal, a typewriter, monitor, etc., containing a computer for stand-alone computational operations. The opposite of "dumb terminal."

intent, letter of: *see* LETTER OF INTENT.

IQ Classifications

The following table illustrates a partial classification of IQ's and indicates the percentage of persons in a normal population who would fall into each classification.

Classification	IQ	Percentage of Population
Gifted	140 and above	1
Very Superior	130–139	2.5
Superior	120–129	8
Above Average	110–119	16
Average	90–109	45
Below Average	80–89	16
Borderline	70–79	8

Interagency Committee on Handicapped Employees: *see* VOCATIONAL REHABILITATION ACT OF 1973.

interdisciplinary team: *see* TASK GROUP.

interest, the price received for loaning money; money paid for the use of money; also, a broad term for any right in property. For example, both an owner who mortgages land and the person who lends the owner money on the mortgage have an interest in the land.

interest, community of: *see* COMMUNITY OF INTEREST.

interest arbitration, arbitration of a dispute arising during the course of contract negotiations where the arbitrator must decide what will or will not be contained in the agreement.

interest-free loan (gift tax exemption): *see* GIFT and GIFT TAX.

interest group: *see* PUBLIC INTEREST GROUP.

interest group liberalism, a theory of policy making maintaining that public authority is parceled out to private interest groups, resulting in weak, decentralized government incapable of long-range planing. Powerful interest groups operate to promote private goals, but do not compete to promote the public interest. Government becomes not an institution that makes hard choices among conflicting values, but a holding company for interests. *See also* PLURALISM.

interest inventory, questionnaire designed to measure the intensity of interest that an individual has in various objects and activities. Interest inventories are widely used in vocational guidance.

interest test, battery of questions designed to determine the interest patterns of an individual, particularly with regard to vocational choice.

interexaminer reliability: *see* INTERRATER RELIABILITY.

interface, point of contact, or the boundary between organizations, people, jobs, and/or systems; the way that parts of a computer system link together, the way systems link together, or the way the operator links into the system. This includes computer hardware and software.

See also:

PARALLEL INTERFACE
PORT
SERIAL INTERFACE

Interfaith Center on Corporate Responsibility, a nonprofit organization that analyzes and informs foundations (and others) about specific corporations' lines of business, products, and issues to be raised at stockholders' meetings. By so doing, the Center attempts to equip foundations and others so that they can argue for socially responsible corporate actions.

interference, an unfair labor practice. Section 8 (a) (1) of the Labor-Management Relations (Taft-Hartley) Act of 1947 makes it unlawful for an employer "to interfere with, restrain, or coerce employees" who are exercising their right to organize and bargain collectively.

Intergovernmental Personnel Act of 1970 (IPA), federal statute (Public Law 91-648), designed to strengthen the personnel resources of state and local governments by making available to them a wide range of assistance. Among its provisions, the Act provides for the temporary assignment of personnel between federal agencies and state and local governments or institutions of higher education.

intergovernmental relations, fiscal and administrative processes by which higher units of government share revenues and other resources with lower units of government, generally accompanied by special conditions that the lower units must satisfy as prerequisites to receiving the assistance.

interim financing, a short-term construction loan with final financing provided later by a mortgage; any form of bridge financing. For nonprofit organizations particularly, the situation in which one funding source provides interim or bridge financing for an agency until it receives funds from another source (private or public).

interim report, a report issued before a project or a reporting period (for example, a fiscal year) has been completed; a progress report.

See also REPORT.

Interior, Department of the (DOI), cabinet-level federal department. As the nation's principal conservation agency, the DOI has responsibility for most of our nationally owned public lands and natural resources; also has a major responsibility for American Indian reservation communities and for people who live in island territories under U.S. administration.

interlocking directorate: *see* DIRECTORATE, INTERLOCKING.

intermittent, less than full-time employment requiring irregular work hours that cannot be prescheduled.

intern: *see* INTERNSHIP.

internal alignment, relationship among positions in an organization in terms of rank and pay. In theory, the most desirable internal alignment calls for similar treatment of like positions, with the differences in treatment in direct proportion to differences in the difficulty, responsibilities, and qualifications needed for a position.

internal audit: *see* AUDIT.

internal consistency reliability, measure of the reliability of a test based on the extent to which items in the test measure the same traits.

internal controls, a system of accounting procedures for protecting a nonprofit organization's assets and ensuring the accuracy and validity of financial reports; the plan of organization and all of the coordinate methods and measures adopted within an organization to safeguard its assets, check the accuracy and reliability of its accounting data, promote operational efficiency, and encourage adherence to prescribed managerial policies.

internal equity: *see* EXTERNAL EQUITY.

internal house organ: *see* HOUSE ORGAN.

internal public relations, a program of communications with an organization's staff and members, typically utilizing newsletters and bulletins. Internal public relations programs are intended to create and maintain morale, enthusiasm, etc.

See also PUBLIC RELATIONS.

Internal Revenue Bulletin, a weekly bulletin published by the Internal Revenue Service which announces official rulings, Executive Orders, court decisions, and other developments related to federal tax issues.

Internal Revenue Code of 1954, the code which included IRS Code 501 (c) (3)—the keystone of modern tax exemption regulations and practices. The Act also added several new categories of organizations eligible for tax exemption, including those involved in testing products for safe use by the general public. It prohibited tax-exempt organizations from participating or intervening in political campaigns on behalf of candidates for public office. The 1954 Code used the "popular and ordinary" definition of the concept *charitable*.

See also

CHARITABLE
POPULAR AND ORDINARY
INTERNAL REVENUE SERVICE CODES.

Internal Revenue Service (IRS), federal agency within the Treasury Department. The IRS is responsible for administering and enforcing the internal revenue laws, except those relating to alcohol, tobacco, firearms, and explosives (which is the responsibility of the Bureau of Alcohol, Tobacco and Firearms). The IRS mission is to encourage and achieve the highest possible degree of voluntary compliance with the tax laws and regulations. Basic IRS activities include providing taxpayer service and education; determination, assessment, and collection of internal revenue taxes; determination of pension plan qualifications and exempt organization status; and preparation and issuance of rulings and regulations to supplement the provisions of the Internal Revenue Code.

Internal Revenue Service Codes, also IRS CODES, the IRS's system of published rules and regulations. Different sections of the Codes govern all aspects of, for example, types of tax-exempt organizations, criteria or tests for determining tax-exempt status, permitted activities, etc. Sections of the Code which are pertinent to nonprofit organizations fall into two general classifications: Definitional Code Sections, which have three-digit primary code numbers (for example, what is a religious organization?), and Operational Code Sections, which have either three- or four-digit primary code numbers (for example, how does one terminate a private foundation? or, what are the excise tax implications of self-dealing?). In this *Dictionary*, the various Sections of the IRS Codes are noted as in the following examples: Definitional Code Section—IRS Code 501 (c) (3); Operational Code Sections—IRS Code 507 (b) (1) (A) and IRS Code 4947.

IRS Code Sections

Following is a partial, summarized listing of important IRS Code Sections.

Definitional Code Sections

401 (a)	Qualified Pension and Profit-Sharing Trusts
408 (e)	Individual Retirement Accounts (IRAs)
501 (c) (1)	U.S. Instrumentalities
(c) (2)	Title Holding Companies of Tax-Exempt Organizations
(c) (3)	Publicly Supported Charitable Organizations
(c) (4)	Civic Leagues and Social Welfare Organizations
(c) (5)	Labor, Agricultural, and Horticultural Organizations
(c) (6)	Business Leagues, Chambers of Commerce, and Boards of Trade
(c) (7)	Social Clubs
(c) (8)	Fraternal Beneficiary Societies
(c) (9)	Voluntary Employees' Beneficiary Associations
(c) (10)	Domestic Fraternal Societies
(c) (11)	Teachers' Retirement Fund Associations
(c) (12)	Benevolent Life Insurance Associations
(c) (13)	Cemetery Companies
(c) (14)	State Chartered Credit Unions and Mutual Reserve Funds
(c) (15)	Mutual Insurance Companies
(c) (16)	Cooperative Crop Financing Organizations
(c) (17)	Supplemental Unemployment Benefit Trusts
(c) (18)	Employee-funded Pension Trusts
(c) (19)	Veterans' Organizations
(c) (21)	Black Lung Benefit Trusts
501 (d)	Religious Organizations
501 (e)	Cooperative Hospital Services Organizations
501 (f)	Cooperative Operating Educational Services Organizations
521 (b) (1)	Farmers' Cooperatives
527 (e)	Political Organizations
(g)	Newsletter Funds
528 (c)	Homeowners' Associations
664	Charitable Remainder Trusts

Operational Code Sections

41	Contributions to Political Organizations
170, 2055 & 2522	Contributions to Charitable Organizations
192	Black Lung Benefit Trust Contributions
218	Contributions to Political Organizations
501 (h)	Restrictions on Charitable Organization Expenditures to Influence Legislation
507	Termination of Private Foundations
511 to 515	Taxes on Certain Types of Unrelated Business Income
527 (f)	Taxes on Charitable Organizations' Investment Income Used for Political Activities Expenditures
4940	Excise Tax on Private Foundations' Investment Income
4941	Excise Tax on Private Foundations' Self-Dealing
4943	Excise Tax on Private Foundations' Excess Business Holdings

Internal Revenue Service (IRS) Sections: *See* INTERNAL REVENUE SERVICE CODES.

International Association of Volunteer Education (IAVE), an organization dedicated to the education of volunteers and of people in volunteerism. IAVE sponsors conferences, exchanges, and visitations in many parts of the world.

International City Management Association (ICMA), professional organization for appointed chief executives in cities, counties, towns, and other local governments. Its primary goals include strengthening the quality of urban government through professional management and developing and disseminating new concepts and approaches to management through a wide range of information services, training programs, and publications. It is based in Washington, D.C.

international nonprofit organization, a nonprofit organization which is involved in charitable activities that affect people and organizations in other nations, and/or relationships between other nations and the United States.

See also TRANSNATIONAL NONPROFIT ORGANIZATION.

international union, also called NATIONAL

UNION, parent union composed of affiliated unions known as "locals." Many international unions in the United States are "international" solely because of their affiliates in Canada. The international or national union is supported by a per capita tax on each of its locals' members.

internship, any of a variety of formal training programs for new employees or students that allows them to learn on the job by working closely with professionals in their field. Almost all professional educational programs at universities require or allow their students to undertake internships of one kind or another.

interpersonal competence, measure of an individual's ability to work well with people in a variety of situations. To have interpersonal competence while occupying any given position, one would have to be proficient in meeting all of a position's role demands.

interpersonal perceptual cycle: *see* PERCEPTUAL CYCLE, INTERPERSONAL.

interpolation, process of estimating intermediate values between two known values.

interrater reliability, also called INTEREXAMINER RELIABILITY, extent to which examiners give the same score to like-performing candidates.

interval estimate, an estimate which states that, subject to a given confidence level, the characteristic of interest has a value that is located within a range (or interval) of values.

interval scale, ranking data in order, with the size difference between each two pieces of data being equal and fixed.

intervention, one of the most basic techniques of organization development. According to Chris Argyris, *Intervention Theory and Method: A Behavioral Science View* (Reading, Mass.: Addison-Wesley, 1970),

to intervene is to enter into an ongoing system of relationship, to come between or among persons, groups, or objects for the purpose of helping them. There is an important implicit assumption in the definition that should be made explicit: the system exists independently of the intervenor. There are many reasons one might wish to intervene. These reasons may range from helping the clients make their own decisions about the kind of help they need to coercing the clients to do what the intervenor wishes them to do. Examples of the latter are . . . executives who invite interventionists into their system to manipulate subordinates for them; trade union leaders who for years have resisted systematic research in their own bureaucratic functioning at the highest levels because they fear that valid information might lead to entrenched interests—especially at the top—being unfrozen.

interview, also EMPLOYMENT INTERVIEW and SELECTION INTERVIEW, a data collection conversation between two or more persons in which one person (an interviewer) asks questions of another(s) (a respondent[s]). The purpose of an *employment interview* or *selection interview* is evaluation, and it is designed to accomplish three basic purposes: (1) to assess the relevance of an applicant's experience and training, (2) to appraise his or her personality, motivation, and presence, and (3) to evaluate his or her intellectual functioning.

See also:

COMPLIMENTARY INTERVIEW
DIRECTED INTERVIEW
EXIT INTERVIEW
HELPING INTERVIEW
PATTERNED INTERVIEW
SCREENING INTERVIEW
STRESS INTERVIEW

interview guide, an instrument containing preselected questions which are to be asked in an interview. Interview guides may be very detailed or may simply identify major topics to be addressed.

Interview Schedule

Example of an Interview Guide

	Attachment
Program Name ______________________	
Program Affiliation (Sponsorship) ______________________	
______________________	
Address ______________________	
______________________	
Phone number ______________________	
Contact Person(s) ______________________	
1. What are the program's goals and objectives?	
2. How did the program develop? (How was the program initiated?) (What are the historical and theoretical foundations?)	
3. What are the instructional approaches? lecture case study small group exercises audio/visual materials other	

interview schedule, formal list of questions that an interviewer puts to an interviewee.

inter vivos gift, a gift made during the lifetime of the donor and donee.

inter vivos trust, a trust established during the lifetime of the parties involved.

intestate, dying without making a will; dying without making a valid will; also, a person who dies without making a valid will.

intrinsic reward, also called PSYCHIC INCOME, reward contained in the job itself, such as personal satisfaction, a sense of achievement, and the prestige of office.

inurement, something that accrues to the benefit or for the advantage of someone.

inurement, private, *see* PRIVATE INUREMENT.

inventory, the total items in a group of material (for example, office supplies, brochures, souvenirs for sale, etc.) or their value, usually based on cost; also, the process of counting, listing, and pricing such items; also, a questionnaire designed to obtain nonintellectual information about a subject. Inventories are often used to gain information on an individual's personality traits, interests, attitude, etc.

inventory, interest: *see* INTEREST INVENTORY.

inventory control, maintaining supplies of inventory at appropriate levels to meet needs.

inverse seniority, concept that allows workers with the greatest seniority to elect temporary layoff so the most recently hired (who would normally be subject to layoff) can continue working. The key to making the concept practical is the provision that senior workers who are laid off receive supplementary compensation in excess of state unemployment compensation and have the right to return to their previous jobs.

investing institutions, institutions that invest other people's money. These include banks, trust companies, investment companies, etc.

investment, using money to make money by, for example, lending it for interest, buying property for gain in value, leasing property, etc.

investment club, a formal or informal group of people who meet to learn more about investing, pool their money to invest, or both.

investment company, a financial institution that invests the funds of a large number of individuals and organizations in different types of securities and other forms of investments (such as, for example, real estate).

investment credit, also INVESTMENT TAX CREDIT, either a credit given to a business for the purchase of fixed assets or a tax break on fixed assets bought for business purposes. A tax credit is more than a deduction. It is a direct subtraction from income of a percentage of the purchase price of major equipment, buildings, etc.

Prior to 1985, investment credits sometimes made sale-leaseback arrangements attractive for nonprofit organizations and private individuals or organizations. However, the Tax Equity and Fiscal Responsibility Act (TEFRA) now disallows the investment credit for property leased to or otherwise used by a tax-exempt organization.

See also:
EQUITY, TAX
LEASEBACK
TAX CREDIT
TAX EQUITY AND FISCAL RESPONSIBILITY ACT

investment grade, a rating (or grade) given to securities based on their predicted safety and return on investment; for example Standard & Poor's and Moody's ratings of AAA to BBB and Aaa and Baa respectively.

investment income test, one of several tests or criteria for determining whether a nonprofit organization may qualify as a publicly supported institution rather than as a private foundation. In order to satisfy the test for tax exemption, an organization may not receive more than one third of its income from investments and unrelated business income.

Investor Responsibility Research Center, a nonprofit organization that analyzes and informs foundations (and others) about specific corporations' lines of business, products, and issues to be raised at stockholders' meetings. By so doing, the Center attempts to equip foundations and others so that they can argue for socially responsible corporate actions.

invoice, *see* BILLING.

involuntary demotion: *see* DEMOTION.

Involvement Corps, The, a national association whose goal is to increase cooperation and coordination between charitable organizations and the private sector.

I/O (computers), input/output.

I/O (psychology), *see* INDUSTRIAL PSYCHOLOGY.

iron law of oligarchy, according to the French sociologist Robert Michels, in *Political Parties* (1915), the fact that organizations are by their nature oligarchic because majorities within an organization are not capable of ruling themselves and, "as a result of organization, every party or professional union becomes divided into a minority of directors and a majority of the directed."

iron law of wages, also called SUBSISTENCE THEORY OF WAGES, concept, variously stated as a law or theory, which holds that in the long run workers will be paid merely the wages that they require for bare survival. It is premised upon the notion that as wages rise, workers have larger families. This increases the labor force and, in turn, drives down wages. The ensuing poverty causes family sizes to decline and, in turn, drives wages higher.

irrevocable, incapable of being stopped, called back, revoked, or changed.

IRS: *see* INTERNAL REVENUE SERVICE.

IRS Publication 557, the IRS document which specifies how an organization applies for tax-exempt status. No organization should attempt to apply without first consulting it.

issue, a group of stocks or bonds that are offered or sold at the same time.

issue attention cycle, a model developed by Anthony Downs that attempts to explain how many policy problems evolve on the political agenda. The cycle is premised on the proposition that the public's attention rarely remains focused on any one issue for a very long period of time, regardless of the objective nature of the problem.

The cycle consists of five steps: the preproblem stage (an undesirable social condition exists, but has not captured public attention); alarmed discovery and euphoric enthusiasm (a dramatic event catalyzes the public attention, accompanied by an enthusiasm to solve the problem); recognition of the cost of change (gradual realization of the difficulty of implementing meaningful change); decline of public interest (people become discouraged or bored and/or new issue claims attention); and the post-problem stage (although the issue has a higher level of attention than in stage one, it has been displaced, but not solved, on the nation's agenda).

item, a test question.

See also RECALL ITEM and RECOGNITION ITEM.

item analysis, statistical description of how a particular question functioned when used in a particular test. An item analysis provides information about the difficulty of the question for the sample on which it is based, the relative attractiveness of the options, and how well the question discriminated among the examinees with respect to a chosen criterion. The criterion most frequently used is the total score on the test of which the item is a part. However, the criterion may be the score on a subtest, on some other test, or, in general, on any appropriate measure that ranks the examinee from high to low.

itemize, to list by separate articles or items; also, to list and claim each deductible contribution and expense for income tax purposes; to not claim a standard deduction.

itemized deduction: *see* ITEMIZE and ITEMIZER.

itemizer, one who lists and claims deductions rather than using the standard deduction in calculating income tax owed.

item validity, extent to which a test item measures what it is supposed to measure.

iteration, repetition of a computer instruction or series of instructions (a program) until a specific task is completed.

itinerant worker, employee who finds work by traveling from one employer or community to another.

J

jargon: *see* BUZZWORDS.

jargonaphasia, physiological disorder manifested by the intermingling of correct words with unintelligible speech. Many writers of organization memoranda and government regulations seem to suffer from this ailment.

Jarvis-Gann Amendment: *see* PROPOSITION 13.

jeopardizing investments rules, rules prohibiting private foundations from making investments which may endanger the foundation's financial security. For example, trading in commodities is generally subject to close scrutiny. The jeopardizing investments rules were initiated by the Tax Reform Act of 1969. The general test for a jeopardy investment is whether a foundation manager used ordinary business care and prudence when making an investment.

See also PRUDENT RULE.

jeopardy investment: *see* JEOPARDIZING INVESTMENTS RULES.

JIC files, files containing information and documents "just in case" they are needed; files containing defensive or protective information.

Jim Crow, a name given to any law requiring the segregation of the races. All such statutes are now unconstitutional.

job, one of three common usages: (1) colloquial term for one's position or occupation, (2) group of positions that are identical with respect to their major duties and responsibilities, (3) discrete unit of work within an occupational specialty. Historically, jobs were restricted to manual labor. Samuel Johnson's *English Dictionary* (1755) defines a job as "petty, piddling work; a piece of chance work." Anyone not dwelling in the lowest strata of employment had a position, a profession, a calling, or (at the very least) an occupation. However, our language strives ever toward egalitarianism and now even an executive at the highest level would quite properly refer to his position as a job.

job, bridge: *see* BRIDGE JOB.

job, covered: *see* COVERED JOBS.

job analysis, determination of a position's specific tasks and of the knowledges, skills, and abilities that an incumbent should possess. This information can then be used in making recruitment and selection decisions, creating selection devices, developing compensation systems, approving training needs, etc.

job analysis, functional: *see* FUNCTIONAL JOB ANALYSIS.

job area acceptance range, a sliding scale of minority or female representation in job areas based on their percentages in the work force; a mathematical formula used to identify possible affected classes and the concentration and underrepresentation of minorities and women.

job audit: *see* DESK AUDIT.

job bank, tool first developed in the late 1960s by the U.S. Employment Service so that its local offices could provide applicants with greater access to job openings and employers with a greater choice of workers from which to choose. The job bank itself is a computer. Each day the computer is fed information on new job openings and on jobs just filled. Its daily printout provides up-to-the-minute information for all job seekers, greater exposure of employers' needs, and a faster referral of job applicants.

job ceiling, maximum number of employees authorized at a given time.

job classification evaluation method, method by which jobs are grouped into classes based on the job's level of difficulty.
See also POSITION CLASSIFICATION.

job coding, numbering system used to categorize jobs according to their job families or other areas of similarity. For example, all positions in a clerical series might be given numbers from 200 to 299, or all management positions might be numbered from 500 to 599. Higher numbers usually indicate higher skill levels within a series.

job content, duties and responsibilities of a specific position.

Job Corps, federal program for the administration of a nationwide training program offering comprehensive development for disadvantaged youth through centers with the unique feature of residential facilities for all or most enrollees. Its purpose is to prepare these youth for the responsibilities of citizenship and to increase their employability by providing them with education, vocational training, and useful work experience in rural, urban, or innercity centers.

Job Corps recruiting is accomplished primarily through state employment services. In certain areas, private organizations are the principal source of referrals. State employment services and private, nonprofit organizations provide assistance to enrollees in locating jobs after completion of training.

job definition, formal statement of the task requirements of a job. The term is frequently used interchangeably with job description.

job depth, measure of the relative freedom that the incumbent of a position has in the performance of assigned duties.

job description, also called POSITION GUIDE, summary of the duties and responsibilities of a job. According to Robert Townsend, in *Up the Organization*, (N.Y.: Knopf, 1970), at best, a job description freezes the job as the writer understood it at a particular instant in the past. At worst, they're prepared by personnel people who can't write and don't understand the jobs.
See also SPECIFICATION.

job design, also called JOB REDESIGN, one of the central concerns of industrial society. In addition to providing all of our goods and services, work provides our social identities and is the single most significant determinant of our physical and emotional health. Organizing work in a manner consistent with societal goals has been the basic task of management since prehistory. This task is made more difficult today by the ever-increasing educational levels and expectations of employees. During the first phase of industrialization, workers were content to be interchangeable human parts of machines (it was more desirable than the alternative of subsistence agriculture). But the modern day archetypical organizational citizens are highly educated individuals who exhibit little resemblance to their illiterate forebearers. The scientific management movement, which grew up as an adjunct of industrial engineering, concerned itself solely with the physical considerations of work; it was human engineering. The research findings of medicine and the behavioral sciences of the last half century have thoroughly demonstrated that the social and psychological basis of work is as significant to long-term productivity and efficiency as are the traditional physiological factors. A modern job design purview seeks to address the totality of these concerns.

job diagnostic survey, research instrument developed by Hackman and Oldham to measure job characteristics and outcomes that might result from job redesign. The Hackman and Oldham approach is particularly concerned with the level of skill variety, task identity, task significance, autonomy, and feedback that characterize a job. *See* J. R. Hackman and G. R. Oldham, "Development of the Job Diagnostic Survey," *Journal of Applied Psychology* (April 1975).

	GIVEN A SIMPLE, ROUTINE JOB	GIVEN AN "ENRICHED" JOB
HIGH-GROWTH NEED INDIVIDUALS	INDIVIDUAL FEELS UNDERUTILIZED AND BORED. HIGH FRUSTRATION, DISSATISFACTION, AND TURNOVER.	VERY HIGH QUALITY PERFORMANCE. HIGH SATISFACTION, LOW ABSENTEEISM AND LOW TURNOVER.
LOW-GROWTH NEED INDIVIDUALS	EFFECTIVE PERFORMANCE, ADEQUATE LEVELS OF SATISFACTION, LOW ABSENTEEISM	INDIVIDUAL OVERWHELMED BY JOB DEMANDS. PSYCHOLOGICAL WITHDRAWAL FROM JOB OR OVERT HOSTILITY AND INADEQUATE JOB PERFORMANCE.

Relationship Between Job Design Effort and Individual Growth Need Level

Source: Leadership in Organizations, *The Department of Behavioral Sciences and Leadership, United States Military Academy, West Point, N.Y., 1981.*

job dilution, dividing a relatively sophisticated job into parts that can be performed by less skilled labor.

job element: *see* ELEMENT.

job enlargement: *see* JOB ENRICHMENT.

job enrichment, also JOB ENLARGEMENT, term often confused or used interchangeably with *job enlargement*. Enlarging a job—adding additional but similar duties—does not substantively change and by no means enriches it. For example, a maintenance person performing menial tasks is not going to have his/her attitudes affected in any significant way if he /she is allowed to perform additional menial tasks. Job enrichment can only occur when motivational factors are designed into the work. Job enlargement is nothing more than horizontal loading—similar tasks laid alongside one another. But job enrichment comes only with vertical loading—building into lower level jobs the very factors that make work at the higher levels of the organization more satisfying, more responsible, even more fun. Two such factors would be personal responsibility for discrete units of work and the ability to set one's own pace within an overall schedule.

job evaluation, process that seeks to determine the relative worth of a position. It implies a formal comparison of the duties and responsibilities of various positions in order to ascertain the worth, rank, or classification of one position relative to all others in an organization. While job content is obviously the primary factor in evaluation, market conditions must also be considered.

See also WHOLE-JOB RANKING.

job factors, also called FACTORS, factors that pertain to different jobs. The factors themselves can usually be categorized within the following groupings:

I. *Job Requirements*—the knowledges, skills, and abilities needed to perform the duties of a specific job.
II. *Difficulty of Work*—the complexity or intricacy of the work and the associated mental demands of the job.
III. *Responsibility*—the freedom of action required by a job and the impact of the work performed upon the organizational mission.

IV. *Personal Relationships*—the importance of interpersonal relationships to the success of mission accomplishment.
V. *Other Factors*—specific job-oriented elements which should be considered in the evaluation process; for example, physical demands, working conditions, accountability, number of workers directed.

job family, group or series of jobs in the same general occupational area, such as accounting.

job freeze, formal halt to an organization's discretionary hiring and promoting. Such an action is inherently temporary.

job grading: *see* POSITION RANKING.

job hopper, person who frequently changes jobs.

job loading, also HORIZONTAL LOADING and VERTICAL LOADING, assigning a greater variety of duties and responsibilities to a job. It is *horizontal loading* when the newly assigned tasks are at the same level of interest and responsibility as the job's original tasks. It is *vertical loading* when the newly assigned tasks allow for increased responsibility, recognition, and personal achievement.
See also JOB ENRICHMENT.

job mobility, a measure of the degree to which an individual can move from job to job within one organization; or the degree to which an individual can market his or her skills to another organization.

job placement, assigning an individual to a job.

job posting, system that allows and encourages employees to apply for other jobs in their organization.

job preview: *see* WORK PREVIEW.

job pricing, determining the dollar value of a particular job.

job range, a measure of the number of different tasks that a job has.

job ranking, also called RANKING, most rudimentary method of job evaluation, which simply ranks jobs in order of their importance to an organization.

job redesign: *see* JOB DESIGN.

job-relatedness, degree to which an applicant appraisal procedure's knowledges, skills, abilities, and other qualification requirements have been determined to be necessary for successful job performance through a careful job analysis.

job restructuring, also called WORK RESTRUCTURING, element of job analysis that involves the identification of jobs within the context of the system of which they are a part and the analysis and rearrangement of their tasks to achieve a desired purpose. Although the term is relatively new, the concept is familiar. Employers frequently find it necessary to rearrange or adjust the contents (tasks performed) of jobs within a system because of economic conditions, technological changes, and the inability to fill vacant positions, among other reasons. Because the interdependencies and relationships among jobs in a system cannot be ignored, job restructuring should be thought of not as changing one job but, rather, as rearranging the contents of jobs within a system.

job rotation, transferring a worker from one assignment to another in order to minimize boredom and/or enhance skills.

job sample: *see* WORK SAMPLING.

job sampling: *see* WORK SAMPLING.

job satisfaction, the totality of an employee's feelings about the various aspects of his or her work; an emotional appraisal of whether one's job lives up to one's values.

job security, presence of safeguards that protect an employee from capricious assignments, demotion, or discharge.

job-sharing, concept that has two persons—each working part-time—sharing the same job.

See also WORK SHARING.

job specification: *see* SPECIFICATION.

Job Training Partnership Act of 1983, *see* COMPREHENSIVE EMPLOYMENT AND TRAINING ACT OF 1973.

job upgrading, reclassifying a position from a lower to a higher classification.

job vacancy, also called JOB VACANCY RATE, an available job for which an organization is actively seeking to recruit a worker. The *job vacancy rate* is the ratio of the number of job vacancies to the sum of actual employment plus job vacancies.

Johari Window, model, frequently used in laboratory training, for examining the mirror image of oneself. The window, developed by Joseph Luft and Harry Ingham (Joe + Harry = Johari), consists of the following four quadrants:

1. The first quadrant, the *public self*, contains knowledge that is known to both the subject and others.
2. The second quadrant, the *blind self*, contains knowledge that is known to others and unknown to the subject.
3. The third quadrant, the *private self*, contains all of those things that a subject keeps secret.
4. The fourth quadrant, the *unknown area*, contains information that neither the subject nor others know.

The Johari Window model is usually used as a visual aid for explaining the concepts of interpersonal feedback and disclosure.

joint and several, both together and individually. For example, a debt is joint and several if the creditor may sue the debtors either as a group (with the result that the debtors would have to split the loss) or individually (with the result that one debtor might have to pay the whole thing).

joint bank account, a bank account held in the names of two or more people, each of whom has full authority to put money in or take it out, and all of whom share equally in the money.

joint correlation (statistics), two variables that are dependent upon a third variable.

joint council, labor-management committee established to resolve disputes arising during the life of a contract.

joint purchasing agreement, a formal agreement among two or more organizations to purchase professional services, equipment, supplies, etc. The agreements simplify purchasing and result in economies of scale, which lower costs.

See also COOPERATIVE VENTURE.

joint return, a single income tax report filed by both husband and wife.

See also TAX RETURN.

joint tenant: *see* TENANT.

journal, a chronological recording of accounting transactions. After the journals are balanced at the end of an accounting cycle (usually a month), they are posted to the general ledger and to the subsidiary ledger accounts.

For example, a purchases journal is used to keep track of items ordered and purchased. It contains information on the date of the purchases or placing orders, from whom the purchase was made, what was purchased, the purchase order number, the amount, and which subsidiary and general ledger accounts will be affected by the purchase (debited or credited).

See also:

ACCOUNTING CYCLE

ACE AMBULANCE SERVICE—PURCHASES JOURNAL

		Purchase	CR		DR—General Col.	
Date	Purchase From	Order Number	Acct. #	Accts. Pay	Description	Amount
1-1	Acme Oil Co.	2001	1616	$175.00	Gas & Oil	$175.00

GENERAL LEDGER
JOURNALIZING
SUBSIDIARY LEDGER

journalizing, the initial recording of an accounting transaction in a journal.

See also ACCOUNTING CYCLE and JOURNAL.

Journal of Counseling and Development, monthly journal of the American Association for Counseling and Development which publishes articles of common interest to counselors and personnel workers in schools, colleges, community agencies, and government.

Journal of Human Resources, quarterly that provides a forum for analysis of the role of education and training in enhancing production skills, employment opportunities, and income, as well as of manpower, health, and welfare policies as they relate to the labor market and to economic and social development.

judgmental sample or PURPOSIVE SAMPLE, a type of nonprobability sample in which one selects the units to be observed based on judgment about which will be the most useful or representative.

judicial review, any court's power to review legislative acts or lower court (or quasi-judicial entities, such as arbitration panels) decisions in order to either confirm or overturn them.

junior, an interest or a right that is subordinate to another interest or right.

jurisdiction, either (1) a union's exclusive right to represent particular workers within specified industrial, occupational, or geographical boundaries, or (2) a territory, subject matter, or person over which lawful authority may be exercised.

jurisdictional dispute, disagreement between two unions over which should control a particular job or activity.

jury-duty pay, the practice of giving employees leave with pay if they are called to jury duty. Many organizations reduce such pay by the amount the employee is paid by the court for his jury service.

K

K, one thousand; in "computerese," either 1,000 or 1,024.

Kafkaesque, bureaucratic to a ridiculous extreme. Franz Kafka's (1883-1924) novels and short stories often dealt with the theme of bureaucratic frustration.

***Kaiser Aluminum & Chemical Corp.* v. *Weber, et. al.*:** *see* UNITED STEELWORKERS OF AMERICA V. WEBER, ET. AL.

Kentucky rule, the principle that all dividends (except for some stock dividends) are income to a trust, not an addition to principal.

See also:
DIVIDEND
TRUST

Keogh Plan, also called H.R. 10 PLAN, a type of pension plan. The Self-Employed Individuals Tax Retirement Act of 1962 encourages the establishment of voluntary pension plans by self-employed individuals. The act allows individuals to have tax advantages similar to those allowed for corporate pension plans. Congressman Eugene J. Keogh was the prime sponsor of the act. H.R. 10 was the number assigned to the bill prior to its passage.

Kerr-Mills, popular name for the Social Security Amendment of 1960 which expanded and modified the federal government's existing responsibility for assisting the states in paying for medical care for the aged poor.

Kepner-Tregoe Model, a model for organizational decision making that includes four major components: (1) situational appraisal, (2) problem analysis, (3) decision analysis, and (4) potential problem analysis. *See* C. H. Kepner and B. B. Tregoe, *The New Rational Manager* (Princeton, N.J.: Kepner-Tregoe, Inc., 1981).

key class, occupations or positions for which data are gathered from other employers (via a salary survey) in order to serve as a basis for establishing wage rates.

keying, measuring the effectiveness of an advertising or public relations medium by having people respond to different box or department numbers. For example, the same request for volunteers in each of several newspapers might have responses sent to different post office boxes, or calls to different phone numbers.

Keynes, John Maynard (1883-1946), English economist who wrote the most influential book on economics of this century, *The General Theory of Employment, Interest and Money* (London: Macmillan, 1936), founded a school of thought known as *Keynesian economics,* which called for using a government's fiscal and monetary policies to positively influence a capitalistic economy, and developed the framework of modern macroeconomic theory. Keynes observed that "practical men, who believe themselves to be quite exempt from any intellectual influences, are usually the slaves of some defunct economist" and provided the definitive economic forecast when he asserted that "in the long run we are all dead."

key result area, a major area or grouping of activities and their results which are "key" to the organization's continuing survival and success. Key results areas are integral to organizational planning, management, and evaluation and are absolutely essential for managing by objectives. Key result areas vary among nonprofit organizations; there is no standardization. In general, however, most nonprofit organizations tend to define key result areas which involve program (such as services to clients), community (such as public support in terms of fund-raising and volunteer recruitment; public recognition and credibility; and legislative action), and internal organization management (such as staff performance, volunteer performance, and financial management and control).
See also MANAGEMENT BY OBJECTIVES.

keywords, words in a document's title that can be used to find types of documents in a computerized information (reference) system.
See also INDEX.

kickback, money extorted from employees or contractors by employers or third parties who threaten to sever or have severed a relationship. Most kickbacks are obviously unethical, if not illegal. The Anti-Kickback Act of 1934 (or the Copeland Act, as amended) prohibits kickbacks by federal contractors and subcontractors.

kicked upstairs, slang term for the removal of an individual from a position where his or her performance is not thought satisfactory by promoting him or her to a higher position in the organization.

kicker, loan charges in addition to the interest; any extra charge or penalty.

kick-in-the-ass motivation: *see* KITA.

Kirkland v. New York State Department of Correctional Services, federal court of appeals case, 520 F. 2d 420 (2d Cir. 1975), cert. denied, 429 U.S. 974 (1976), that dealt with the permissible range of remedies for illegal employment discrimination. While approving portions of a lower court ruling ordering New York State to develop an unbiased, job-related test for hiring correctional officials and instituting temporary hiring and promotion quotas until such a test could be developed, the appeals court overturned the portion of the order requiring a "permanent" quota to be followed until members of minority groups reached a specified proportion of correctional sergeants.

KISS principle, Keep it Simple, Stupid.

kit, public relations: *see* PUBLIC RELATIONS KIT.

KITA, mnemonic device used by Frederick Herzberg to refer to "kick-in-the-ass" attempts at worker motivation. Variants of KITA include "negative physical KITA" (literally using physical force); "negative psychological KITA" (hurting someone with a psychic blow); and "positive KITA" (offering rewards for performance). Herzberg states that KITA cannot create motivation; its only ability is to create movement.

kitchen cabinet, informal advisors of a chief executive, first used as derisive term for some of President Andrew Jackson's advisors. The word "kitchen" originally implied that such advisors were not respectable enough to visit in the more formal rooms of the White House. Over the years the term has lost its derisive quality.

kiting, writing checks on an account before money is deposited to cover them.

knock off work, stop work. It is thought that the phrase "knocking off" has its origins in the slave galleys of old. So that the oarsmen would row with the proper timing, an overseer would beat rhythmically on a block or drum. When it was time to stop, a special knock would indicate that the oarsmen could knock off or stop their work.

knowledge, understanding of facts or principles relating to a particular subject or subject area.

knowledge worker, Peter F. Drucker's term, in *The New Society: The Anatomy of Industrial Order* (1949), for the largest and most rapidly growing group in the working population of the developed countries: "It is a group of 'workers' though it will never identify itself with the 'proletariat,' and will always consider itself 'middle-class' if not 'part of management.' And it is an independent group because it owns the one essential resource of production—knowledge. It is this group whose emergence makes ours a 'new' society."

L

labor, collective term for an organization's work force exclusive of management.

See also the following entries:

CASUAL LABOR
CHILD LABOR
DIRECT LABOR
DIVISION OF LABOR
SKILLED LABOR

Labor, Department of (DOL), U.S. federal agency whose purpose is to foster, promote, and develop the welfare of the wage earners of the United States, to improve their working conditions, and to advance their opportunities for profitable employment. In carrying out this mission, DOL administers more than 130 federal labor laws guaranteeing workers' rights to safe and healthful working conditions; a minimum hourly wage and overtime pay; freedom from employment discrimination; unemployment insurance; and workers' compensation. DOL also protects workers' pension rights; sponsors job training programs; helps workers find jobs; works to strengthen free collective bargaining; and keeps track of changes in employment, prices, and other national economic measurements.

labor agreement, formal results achieved by collective bargaining.

Labor Arbitration Reports, weekly published by the Bureau of National Affairs, Inc. This is the standard authority on awards and recommended settlements by arbitrators, emergency boards, fact-finding bodies, permanent referees, and umpires.

laboratory education, also called LABORATORY METHOD, terms which are used interchangeably for all of the formal means of learning about human behavior through experiencing group activities that have been specially created for such a purpose.
See also LABORATORY TRAINING.

laboratory experiment, research method in which a researcher consciously manipulates an independent variable in order to observe the effects of the manipulation on a dependent variable. While a laboratory experiment maximizes control over the research process, it is often questioned in terms of generalizability to normal conditions in the real world.

laboratory training, also SENSITIVITY TRAINING and T-GROUP, generic term for those educational/training experiences that are designed (1) to increase an individual's sensitivity to his/her own motives and behavior, (2) to increase sensitivity to the behavior of others, and (3) to ascertain those elements of interpersonal interactions that either facilitate or impede a group's effectiveness. While laboratory training and *sensitivity training* tend to be used interchangeably, sensitivity training is the subordinate term (being the most common method of laboratory training) and the popular name given to almost all experience-based learning exercises. The basic vehicle for the sensitivity training experience is the *T-Group* (T for Training). According to Chris Argyris, in "T-Groups for Organizational Effectiveness," *Harvard Business Review* (March-April 1964), the T-Group experience is designed to provide maximum possible opportunity for the individuals to expose their behavior, give and receive feedbacks, experiment with new behavior, and develop everlasting awareness and acceptance of self and others. The T-group, when effective, also provides individuals with the opportunity to learn the nature of effective group functioning. They are able to learn how to develop a group that achieves specific goals with minimum possible human cost.
See also:
INSTRUMENTED LABORATORY
NATIONAL TRAINING LABORATORIES
INSTITUTE FOR APPLIED BEHAVIORAL SCIENCE
ROLE
TRAINERLESS LABORATORY

labor certification, certification by the U.S. Department of Labor which certain aliens (such as foreign medical graduates) seeking to immigrate to the United States in order to work must obtain before they may obtain a visa. People in occupations which the Department of Labor feels are in short supply throughout the country (such as physicians and nurses but not dentists) are given such certification after review of the applicant's qualifications.

labor cost, that part of the cost of a product or service that is attributable to wages.

labor costs, also UNIT LABOR COST, total expenses an employer must meet in order to retain the services of employees. The *unit labor cost* is the expense for labor divided by the number of units of output produced.

labor costs, indirect: *see* INDIRECT LABOR COSTS.

labor dispute, according to Section 2(9) of the National Labor Relations Act, as amended, term that includes

> any controversy concerning terms, tenure or conditions of employment, or concerning the association or representation of persons in negotiating, fixing, maintaining, changing, or seeking to arrange terms or conditions of employment.

labor economics, the subfield of economics concerned with wages and the supply/allocation of manpower.

labor force, also CIVILIAN LABOR FORCE and TOTAL LABOR FORCE, according to the Bureau of Labor Statistics, all employed or unemployed persons in the civilian non-institutional population; the *total labor force* includes military personnel. Persons not in the labor force are those not classified as employed or unemployed; this group includes persons retired, those engaged in their own housework, those not working while attending school, those unable to work because of long-term illness, those discouraged from seeking work because of personal or job market factors, and those who are voluntarily idle. The non-institutional population comprises all persons sixteen years and older who are not inmates of penal or mental institutions, sanitariums, or homes for the aged, infirm, or needy.

labor force participation, rate at which a given group (women, blacks, handicapped, etc.) is represented (either nationally, regionally, or locally) in the labor force.

labor grade, one of a series of steps in a wage-rate structure established by a process of job evaluation or collective bargaining.

labor intensive, any production process requiring a large proportion of human effort relative to capital investment.

labor law, body of law applied to concerns of employment, wages, conditions of work, unions, labor-management relations, etc.

labor lobby, those elements of organized labor that seek to influence legislation affecting labor's interests.

labor-management relations, general term referring to the formal and informal dealings and agreements between employees or employee organizations and managers.

Labor-Management Relations Act of 1947 (LMRA), also called TAFT-HARTLEY ACT, federal statute that modified what the Congress thought was pro-union bias of the National Labor Relations (Wagner) Act of 1935. Essentially a series of amendments to the National Labor Relations Act, Taft-Hartley provided

1. that "National Emergency Strikes" could be put off for an eighty-day cooling-off period during which the president might make recommendations to Congress for legislation that might cope with the dispute;
2. a list of unfair labor practices by unions, which balanced the list of unfair labor practices by employers delineated in the Wagner Act;
3. that the "closed shop" was illegal (this provision allowed states to pass "right-to-work" laws);
4. that supervisory employees be excluded from coverage under the act;
5. that suits against unions for contract violations were allowable (judgments enforceable only against union assets);

6. that a party seeking to cancel an existing collective bargaining agreement is required to give sixty days' notice;
7. that employers have the right to seek a representation election if a union claimed recognition as a bargaining agent;
8. that the National Labor Relations Board was reorganized and enlarged from three to five members; and
9. that the Federal Mediation and Conciliation Service be created to mediate labor disputes.

The Taft-Hartley Act was passed over the veto of President Truman.

Labor-Management Reporting and Disclosure Act of 1959, also called LANDRUM-GRIFFIN ACT, federal statute enacted in response to findings of corruption in the management of some unions. The purpose of the act is to provide for the reporting and disclosure of certain financial transactions and administrative practices of labor organizations and employers, to prevent abuses in the administration of trusteeships by labor organizations, to provide standards with respect to the election of officers of labor organizations and for other purposes.

labor mobility, degree of ease with which workers can change jobs and occupations.

labor monopoly, dominance over the supply of labor by a union or group of unions.

labor movement, inclusive term for the progressive history of U.S. unionism. Sometimes it is used in a broader sense to encompass the fate of the "workers."

labor organization, as defined by Section 2(5) of the National Labor Relations act (as amended),

> any organization of any kind, or any agency or employee representation committee or plan, in which employees participate and which exists for the purpose, in whole or part, of dealing with employers concerning grievances, labor disputes, wages, rates of pay, hours of employment, or conditions of work.

An association of workers formed to advance or maintain the interests of its members, the labor union is the most typical form of labor organization—as defined in IRS Code 501(c) (5)—but other types of labor associations may also qualify for tax exemption.

labor organizer: *see* ORGANIZER.

labor piracy, attracting employees away from one organization and into another by offering better wages and benefits.

labor pool, set of trained workers from which prospective employees are recruited.

labor relations, totality of the interactions between an organization's management and organized labor.

labor reserve, general term that refers to potential members of the work force. Historically, the concept has been applied to the least skilled and the least able.

labor-saving equipment, any device that reduces an organization's need for human labor.

labor slowdown: *see* SLOWDOWN.

Labor Statistics, Bureau of: *see* BUREAU OF LABOR STATISTICS.

labor surplus area, an area of high unemployment for which the federal government sets aside procurement contracts for competition among firms that agree to perform a substantial portion of the production of the contract in the labor surplus area.

labor theory of value, notion that the value of a product is dependent on or determined by the amount (or value) of the labor needed to produce it. Karl Marx used this concept (developed earlier by Adam Smith and David Ricardo) to denounce capitalists who exploited the working class by selling products at higher prices than the cost of the labor that went into them.

Laffer curve, purported relationship between tax rates and government revenues "discovered" by economist Arthur B. Laffer. According to Laffer, higher taxes reduce government revenues because high tax rates discourage taxable activity. Following this logic, a government can raise its total revenues by cutting taxes. This should stimulate new taxable activity, and the revenue from this should more than offset the loss from lower tax rates.

laissez-faire, "hands off" style of leadership that emphasizes loose supervision.

lame duck, any officeholder who is serving out the remainder of a fixed term after declining to run, or being defeated, for reelection. since he/she will soon be leaving, his/her authority is considered impaired or "lame." The term is used in an organizational sense to refer to anyone whose leaving has been announced, whether for retirement, promotion, transfer, etc.

land bank, also SOIL BANK, a federal program in which land is taken out of agricultural production and used for conservation or trees (also known as a *soil bank*); also, a federally created bank that makes low-interest farm loans.

Landrum-Griffin Act: *See* LABOR-MANAGEMENT REPORTING AND DISCLOSURE ACT OF 1959.

land sales contract, also CONTRACT FOR DEED and INSTALLMENT CONTRACT, a contract for the sale of real estate (including buildings—not just land) which is not recorded in the land records. The seller retains title (or puts it into escrow) until an agreed future time (for example, when the mortgage has been paid off). This practice is used to keep a low interest rate on an existing mortgage.

language, a set of symbols for communication and rules for their use. Languages for instructing a computer and transferring data in and out include, for example, Algol, Basic, Cobol, Fortran, Lisp, and Pascal.

last dollar coverage, insurance coverage without upper limits or maximums no matter how great the benefits payable.

last offer arbitration: *see* FINAL OFFER ARBITRATION.

latent learning: *see* INCIDENTAL LEARNING.

lateral entry, appointment of an individual from outside of the organization to a position above the bottom level of a generally recognized career ladder.

lateral transfer: *see* TRANSFER.

law firm, public interest: *see* PUBLIC INTEREST LAW FIRM.

law of the situation, Mary Parker Follett's idea that one person should not give orders to another person, but both should agree to take their orders from the situation. If orders are simply part of the situation, the question of someone giving and someone receiving does not come up.

law of triviality, C. Northcote Parkinson's discovery that "the time spent on any item of the agenda will be in inverse proportion to the sum involved." For more, *see* C. Northcote Parkinson, *Parkinson's Law and other Studies in Administration* (Boston: Houghton Mifflin Co., 1957).

See also PARKINSON'S LAW.

layoff, temporary or indefinite separation from employment, without prejudice or loss of seniority, resulting from factors over which the worker has no control. The Bureau of Labor Statistics compiles monthly layoff rates by industry.

The "last hired-first fired" policy of layoffs has come under increasing criticism because of the disparate impact that it has had upon minorities.

See also the following entries:

DISCIPLINARY LAYOFF
RECALL
RE-EMPLOYMENT LIST
RETENTION STANDING

leadership, exercise of authority, whether formal or informal, in directing and coordinating the work of others.

See also the following entries:

CHARISMATIC LEADERSHIP
CONTINGENCY MODEL OF LEADERSHIP EFFECTIVENESS
FULL RESPONSIBILITY
FUNCTIONAL LEADERSHIP
PATH-GOAL THEORY OF LEADERSHIP

leadership, transformational, leadership that strives to change organizational culture and directions, rather than continuing to move along historical paths. It reflects the ability of a leader to develop a values-based vision for the organization, convert the vision into reality, and maintain it over time. Transformational leadership is a 1980's concept, closely identified with the concepts of symbolic management and organizational culture.

leadership effectiveness, contingency model of: *see* CONTINGENCY MODEL OF LEADERSHIP EFFECTIVENESS.

leadership style, an imprecise term which refers to the blending of a person's knowledge of leadership theory and skills with his or her own personality and values under different organizational circumstances to yield a "style" of leadership behavior. Some people are relatively rigid and can use only one or two styles; others are more flexible and may have many style options available to them. Many authors have proposed typologies, continuums, and matrices of leadership styles, but none has met with general acceptance.

lead time, the time expected between the completion of planning and the start of a venture; for example, between planning a fund-raising concert and "pulling it off."

learning, generally, any behavior change occurring because of interaction with the environment.

learning curve, the concept that holds that when people repeatedly perform a task, the amount of effort and time required per unit of output decreases according to a constant pattern.

The learning curve as a concept in training describes a learning process in which increases of performance are large at the beginning but become smaller with continued practice. Learning of any new thing eventually levels off as mastery is attained, at which point the curve becomes horizontal.

learning plateau, that flat part of a learning curve that indicates there has been little or no additional learning.

lease, a contract renting land, a building, space in a building, or equipment, typically for at least one year but often longer. Under a lease, title (or ownership) does not change. Leasing is an alternative to purchasing capital items (that is, an alternative to incurring capital costs). Under some circumstances, private enterprises lease rather than purchase because tax considerations make it less expensive. Obviously, tax-exempt organizations need a different justification.

See also LEASEBACK and LEASE-PURCHASE.

leaseback, also SALE AND LEASEBACK, an arrangement by which a nonprofit organization sells a capital asset (such as a building or piece of equipment) to another organization, and the asset is leased back immediately to the nonprofit organization for its use. Some lease-back arrangements can be extremely complex and sophisticated as the parties attempt to maximize their respective benefits through the transaction. For example, leasebacks can allow

a nonprofit organization to protect its capital assets and a commercial enterprise or individual to gain certain tax advantages. The IRS tends to review leaseback arrangements involving nonprofit organizations rather carefully in order to ensure that self-dealing or other forms of private inurement are not occurring.
See also:
CAPITAL ASSETS
GIFT-LEASEBACK
LEASE
PRIVATE INUREMENT
SELF-DEALING
TAX-AVOIDANCE SCHEME

leaseholder, a tenant under a lease.
See also LEASE.

lease-purchase, a lease which includes a provision whereby the leaseholder may purchase the leased asset during the term of the lease—usually at a favorable price—or a portion of the lease payments that have been made up to the time of purchase may be applied against the purchase price.
See also:
CAPITAL ASSETS
LEASE
LEASEBACK

leave, birth: *see* BIRTH LEAVE.

leave of absence: *see* FURLOUGH and LEAVE WITHOUT PAY.

leave without pay, a temporary nonpay status and short-term absence from duty granted upon the employee's request. The permissive nature of leave without pay distinguishes it from absence without leave. A *leave of absence* is the same as leave without pay except for duration. A leave of absence implies a more substantial amount of time away from one's position.

LEDC: *see* LOCAL ECONOMIC DEVELOPMENT CORPORATION.

ledger, a business account book used to record day-to-day transactions, usually showing debits and credits separately.
See also:
ACCOUNTING CYCLE
DEBITS AND CREDITS
GENERAL LEDGER
SUBSIDIARY LEDGER

ledger card, a card which holds one subsidiary ledger account, typically on 5″ × 8″ heavy stock paper.
See also SUBSIDIARY LEDGER.

legacy: *see* BEQUEST.

legal aid program, a program that provides legal representation to persons or organizations which cannot afford to pay. Legal aid programs may be supported by public, private, and/or third sector organizations.

legal reserves, the percentage of total funds that an insurance company or a bank must set aside to meet possible claims.

legal services trust, prepaid, a trust which may qualify for tax exemption under IRS Code 501 (c) (20) and which may receive funds from employees and their employer to support prepaid legal services. A prepaid legal services trust must be established in conjunction with a qualified group legal services plan.

legatee, a person who inherits something in a will.

legislation, under IRS regulations, actions by the United States Congress, state legislatures, city or town councils, boards of county commissioners, and public referendums, initiatives, recalls, and constitutional amendments. Typically included are acts, bills, laws, and resolutions.
See also:
ACTION ORGANIZATION
LEGISLATIVE ACTIVITIES
TAXABLE EXPENDITURE

legislative activities, activities undertaken by a nonprofit organization to influence the actions of a local, state, or national legislative body or a public referendum. Legislative activities are generally taxable expenditures.

See also:
- ACTION ORGANIZATION
- INFLUENCING LEGISLATION
- LEGISLATION
- TAXABLE EXPENDITURE

legislative intent, supposed real meaning of a statute as it can be interpreted from the legislative history.

legislative oversight, total means by which a legislature monitors the activities of agencies in order to see that laws are faithfully executed.

legitimacy, characteristic of a social institution whereby it has both a legal and a perceived right to make binding decisions for its members. Legitimacy is granted to an institution by its public.

leptokurtic, frequency distribution or curve that is more peaked, as opposed to flat-topped, than a normal curve.

lese majesty, in French LESE MAJESTE, literally *injured majesty;* originally an offense against one's sovereign or ruler. Now it quite properly refers to an insolent or slighting behavior towards one's organizational superiors.

lessee, a person who leases or rents something from someone; a tenant.

See also LEASE.

lessening the burdens of government, concept of, one of the fundamental theoretical bases for having tax exemptions for organizations which advance public interests. The concept is that tax-exempt organizations perform public services which, in their absence, the government would have to do or pay to accomplish.

lessor, a person who leases or rents something to someone; a landlord.

See also LEASE.

let, to award a contract to one of several bidders; also, to lease.

letter, group exemption: *see* GROUP EXEMPTION LETTER.

letter of credit: *see* CREDIT, LETTER OF.

letter of intent, a preliminary understanding that forms the basis of an intended contract; for example, a letter from a foundation or a granting agency stating that a contract or grant will be made.

letter-writing campaign, a campaign to influence action or policies (for example, by a legislature, by a government agency, or by a private individual or organization). At its lowest level, a nonprofit organization may provide background information on an issue or policy to its members, volunteers, and friends and encourage or request them to write letters to the appropriate parties. At higher levels, an organization may provide sample letters, or even letters which are ready to be signed and mailed in (provided) addressed, stamped envelopes.

level annual premium funding method, pension contributions or premiums that are paid into a fund (or to an insurance company) in equal installments during the employee's remaining working life so that upon retirement the pension benefit is fully funded.

level of difficulty, classification term used to indicate the relative ranking of duties and responsibilities.

leverage, borrowing, especially for investment purposes.

leveraged lease, an arrangement in which leased items are financed by a third party. This is often done to shift tax benefits from users of the property to the owners, who gain more.

See also PRIVATE INUREMENT.

leverage ratio, also DEBT RATIO, an organization's total debt divided by its total assets; one of many accounting ratios used for assessing an organization's financial health.

See also RATIO and RATIO, ACCOUNTING.

Lewin, Kurt (1890-1947), the most influential experimental psychologist of the twentieth century, popularly noted for his assertion that "there is nothing so practical as a good theory." His research originated the modern concepts of group dynamics, action research, field theory, and sensitivity training.

liabilities, also CURRENT LIABILITIES and LONG-TERM LIABILITIES, the current and long-term debts owed by a jurisdiction or enterprise. *Current liabilities* are due and payable within a year and include such items as accounts payable, wages, and short-term debt. *Long-term liabilities* are payable more than a year hence and include items such as bonds.

See also CONTINGENT LIABILITY.

liberality of construction, doctrine of, a common judicial stance relative to charitable exemptions which holds that ambiguities relative to organizational purpose should be resolved in favor of the taxpayer rather than the government.

license, a permission granted to an individual or organization by competent authority, usually public, to engage in a practice, occupation, or activity otherwise unlawful. Licensure is the process by which the license is granted. Since a license is needed to begin lawful practice, it is usually granted on the basis of examination and/or proof of education rather than measures of performance. License when given is usually permanent but may be conditioned on annual payment of a fee, proof of continuing education, or proof of competence. Common grounds for revocation of a license include incompetence, commission of a crime (whether or not related to the licensed practice), or moral turpitude.

See also OCCUPATIONAL LICENSING.

lie detector, also called POLYGRAPH; also VOICE STRESS ANALYZER and PSYCHOLOGICAL STRESS ANALYZER, an instrument for recording physiological phenomena such as blood pressure, pulse rate, and respiration rate of individuals as they answer questions put to them by an operator. The technique is based on the assumption that when an individual experiences apprehension, fear, or emotional excitement, his/her respiration rate, blood pressure, etc. will increase sharply.

Many state and local legislative actions have placed legal limitations on employers' use of lie detectors. Thirteen states prohibit the use of polygraphs as a condition of employment or continued employment. In addition, labor arbitrators often refuse to admit test results as evidence of "just cause" for discharge and have upheld a worker's right to refuse to take such a test.

The *voice stress analyzer* or *psychological stress analyzer* is a lie detector that can be used without the subject knowing that he/she is being tested. By simply analyzing the stress in the subject's voice it purports to tell whether or not the truth is being told. As such devices have only been available since the mid-1970s, their use should still be considered experimental.

lien, a claim, charge, or liability against property that is allowed by law, rather than one that is part of a contract or agreement. For example, a tax lien is the government's placing of a financial obligation on a piece of property that must be paid because taxes are delinquent.

life estate contract, an arrangement under which a person transfers title to his or her home or farm to a charitable organization, and continues to use the real estate for life. The donor is entitled to any income the real estate produces and is responsible for its upkeep. An income tax deduction is available in the year of the gift.

life income gift, a form of deferred giving. An irrevocable gift of cash, securities or real estate to an exempt organization, with the donor reserving income from the donated assets for himself or herself or other beneficiaries. Common forms of life income gifts include unitrusts, annuity trusts, pooled income funds, gift annuities, deferred payment gift annuities, and charitable lead trusts.

life insurance, insurance that provides for the payment of a specific amount to a designated beneficiary in the event of the death of the insured.

See also the following entries:

ACCIDENTAL DEATH BENEFIT
GROUP INSURANCE
INSURANCE
SPLIT-DOLLAR LIFE INSURANCE
TERM LIFE INSURANCE
VARIABLE LIFE INSURANCE

life position, a transactional analysis concept of one's basic "position" that establishes or predetermines the pattern of a person's relations with others. The four life positions are:

I'm OK—You're OK
I'm OK—You're Not OK
I'm Not OK—You're OK
I'm Not OK—You're Not OK

See also SCRIPT and TRANSACTIONAL ANALYSIS.

life script: *see* SCRIPT.

lifetime exclusion, gift tax, the maximum amount of gifts an individual may make to, for example, a child without being subject to a gift tax. For federal gift tax purposes, there are two primary types of exclusions: annual and lifetime.

See also GIFT EXEMPTION LIMIT.

Likert, Rensis (1903-1981), one of the pioneers of organizational survey research and director of the Institute of Social Research at the University of Michigan from 1948 to 1970. He is perhaps best known for his linking-pin theory and his concepts of Systems 1, 2, 3, and 4.

Likert Scale, also called LIKERT-TYPE SCALE, one of the most widely used scales in social research. Named after Rensis Likert, who first presented it in "A Technique for the Measurement of Attitudes, *Archives of Psychology* (No. 140, 1932), the scale presents a subject with a statement to which the subject expresses his/her reaction or opinion by selecting one of five (or more) possible responses arranged at equidistant intervals.

Questions Using a Likert Scale

1. The sick-leave policies of this organization are not liberal enough.
   (a) strongly agree
   (b) agree
   (c) no opinion
   (d) disagree
   (e) strongly disagree
2. My supervisor is a good leader.
   (a) strongly agree
   (b) agree
   (c) uncertain
   (d) disagree
   (e) strongly disagree

limited partnership: *see* PARTNERSHIP.

Lindblom, Charles E. (1917-   ), the leading proponent of the incremental approach to policy/decision making. In his most famous work, "The Science of Muddling Through," *Public Administration Review* (Spring 1959), Lindblom took a hard look at the rational models of decisional processes. He rejected the notion that most decisions are made by rational—total information—processes. Instead he saw such decisions—indeed, the whole policy making process—as dependent upon small incremental decisions that tended to be made in response to short-term political conditions. Lindblom's thesis essentially held that decision making was controlled infinitely more by events and circumstances than by the will of those in policy making positions.

linear programming, a mathematical technique for analyzing a problem.

linear responsibility chart: *see* ORGANIZATION CHART.

line-item budget: *see* BUDGET, LINE-ITEM.

line of authority: *see* SCALAR CHAIN.

line of business requirement, a principle enunciated by the U.S. Supreme Court requiring business leagues to represent an entire industry rather than a particular segment of it in order to qualify for tax exemption under IRS Code 501 (c) (6). The landmark Supreme Court Case was *National Muffler Dealers Association, Inc. v. United States* (440 U.S. 472 [1979], aff'g 565 F. 2d 845 [2nd Cir. 1977]).

line organization, those segments of a larger organization that perform the major functions of the organization and have the most direct responsibilities for achieving organizational goals.

line printer, a high-speed computer printer that prints a line at a time rather than a character at a time.

linkage, strategy relating two or more issues in negotiations and then using them as tradeoffs or pressure points, much as in a "carrot and stick" technique.

linking pin, concept developed by Rensis Likert in his *New Patterns of Management* (New York: McGraw-Hill, 1961). A "linking pin" is anyone who belongs to two groups within the same organization, usually as a superior in one and as a subordinate in the other.

See also LIKERT, RENSIS.

liquid, having enough money to carry on normal operations; also, easily converted into cash.

liquid assets, cash and other current assets which can be converted rapidly to cash.

See also ASSETS.

liquidate, to settle or pay a debt; to abolish or do away with; for example, to liquidate a company.

liquidity, the rapidity and facility with which assets can be converted to cash.

See also ASSETS and LIQUID.

liquidity ratio: *see:*

CURRENT RATIO
RATIO, ACCOUNTING

list, mailing: *see* MAILING LIST.

list, membership: *see* MEMBERSHIP LIST.

listening, one of the oldest and most useful management techniques. According to John A. Wilson, in *The Culture of Ancient Egypt* (1951), the ancient Egyptians advised their leaders to "be calm as thou listenest to what the petitioner has to say. Do not rebuff him before he has swept out his body or before he has said that for which he came. . . . It is not [necessary] that everything about which he has petitioned should come to pass, [for] a good hearing is soothing to the heart."

list of eligibles: *see* ELIGIBLE LIST.

living trust, also INTER VIVOS TRUST, a trust that will take effect while the person setting it up is still alive, as opposed to one set up under a will.

See also DEFERRED GIVING PROGRAM and DEVELOPMENT.

LMRA: *see* LABOR-MANAGEMENT RELATIONS ACT OF 1947.

load, that part of insurance, mutual fund, or other business charges that represents sales commissions; also, to put data or instructions into a computer—in particular, to transfer data from external storage (such as a disk) to internal computer storage.

loading, in insurance, the amount added to the actuarial value of the coverage (expected or average amounts) payable to the insured to cover the expense to the insurer of securing and maintaining the business; *i.e.*, the amount added to the pure premium needed to meet anticipated liabilities for expenses, contingencies, profits, or special situations.

loading, job/horizontal/vertical: *see* JOB LOADING.

loan, to lend or advance money or other property or persons for temporary use; borrowed money. For accounting purposes, a loan is an account receivable to the lender and an account payable to the recipient.

loan guarantee, an agreement by which the government pledges to pay part or all of the loan principal and interest to a lender or holder of a security in the event of default by a third party borrower; for example, guaranteed student loans. The purpose of a guaranteed loan is to reduce the risk borne by a private lender by shifting all or part of the risk to the federal government. If it becomes necessary for the government to pay part or all of the loan principal or interest, the payment is a direct outlay. Otherwise, the guarantee does not directly affect federal budget outlays.

loan insurance, a type of loan guarantee whereby a government agency operates a program of pooled risks, pledging the use of accumulated insurance premiums to secure a lender against default on the part of the borrower.

loan value, the maximum amount that can be borrowed against the cash value of a life insurance policy.

lobby, also FEDERAL REGULATION OF LOBBYING ACT OF 1946, any individual, group, or organization that seeks to influence legislation or administrative action. The term arose from the use of lobbies, or corridors, in legislative halls as places to meet with and persuade legislators to vote a certain way. Lobbying in general is not an evil; many lobbies provide legislatures with reliable firsthand information of considerable value. However, some lobbies have given the practice an undesirable connotation.

The Federal Regulation of Lobbying Act of 1946 requires that persons who solicit or accept contributions for lobbying purposes keep accounts, present receipts and statements to the clerk of the House, and register with the clerk of the House and the secretary of the Senate. The information received is published quarterly in the *Congressional Record.* The purpose of this registration is to disclose the sponsorship and source of funds of lobbyists, but not to curtail the right of persons to act as lobbyists.

Lobbying activities by charitable organizations are restricted, and if a nonprofit organization is not careful, such activities can jeopardize its tax-exempt status; for example, if its lobbying efforts are not directly in its own behalf.

lobster shift: *see* GRAVEYARD SHIFT.

local: *see* COSMOPOLITAN-LOCAL CONSTRUCT.

local affairs, department of, generic name of a state agency with oversight responsibilities for local government. Sometimes local governments are required to submit audit and budget reports to such an agency, with the exact requirements varying from state to state.

local economic development corporation (LEDC), an organization formed to help improve the economy in a depressed area. Although LEDC's have "alleviation of poverty" as a primary purpose (clearly a charitable purpose), they typically accomplish their mission by aiding local businesses and attempting to attract new businesses to the area. Therefore, the tax-exempt status of LEDC's has been controversial.

local employees' associations, according to IRS code 501 (c) (4), "local associations of employees, the membership of which is limited to . . . person or persons in a particular municipality, and the net earnings of which are devoted exclusively to charitable, educational or recreational purposes." Local employees' associations may qualify for tax-exempt status under IRS Code 501 (c) (4).

Local Government Funding Report, a publication of Government Information Services which provides extensive information on local government program funding trends and developments.

local independent union, local union not affiliated with a national or international union.

local union, regional organization of union members who are part of a national or international union. A local union is chartered by the national or international union with which it is affiliated.

lockout, employer's version of a strike—the closing of a business in order to pressure the employees and/or the union to accept the employer's offered terms of employment. This early weapon against the union movement lost much of its effect when locked-out employees became eligible for unemployment compensation. Almost all union contracts with a no-strike clause contain a similar ban against lockouts.

lodge, the meeting place of a chapter of a society or association—often a secret society; the membership of a chapter.

lodge (labor union), organizational unit of some labor unions, equivalent to a local union.

logic, the principles behind the interconnection of circuits in a computer.

logo, a symbol used by an organization as its identifying emblem.

longevity pay, also called LONGEVITY RATE, salary additions based on length of service. Pay plans frequently state specific time periods to qualify for such upward wage adjustments.

longitudinal survey, study of a group of subjects that follows them through time.

long-range planning, consideration in the present time period (today) of what capability must be provided in the future to meet the anticipated objectives that are inherent in a predicted situation, condition, or event and the courses of action that might be involved.

See also STRATEGIC PLANNING.

long-term debt, debt payable more than one year after date of issue.

long-term debt offsets, cash and investment assets of sinking funds and other reserve funds, however designated, which are specifically held for redemption of long-term debt.

long-term debt retired, par value of long-term debt obligations liquidated by repayment or exchange, including debt retired by refunding operations.

long-term liabilities: *see* LIABILITIES.

long-term original issues, all long-term debt issued other than that issued to refund existing long-term debt. Includes long-term debt issued for funding of existing short-term obligations.

loophole, someone else's way of legally avoiding taxes. For your way, *see:*

DEDUCTION
EXCLUSION
TAX CREDIT

loser: *see* WINNERS AND LOSERS.

low match: *see* MATCHING SHARE.

loyalty, also LOYALTY OATH, allegiance. A *loyalty oath* is an affirmation of allegiance.

M

machine language, a set of instructions which can be directly understood and obeyed by a computer. Machine language programs are very flexible but have the disadvantages of being difficult and time-consuming to write and highly susceptible to errors.

macro, large-scale.

macroeconomics, study of the relationships among broad economic aggregates such as national income, consumer savings and expenditures, capital investment, employment, money supply, prices, and balance of payments. Macroeconomics is especially concerned with government's role in affecting these aggregates.

mag card, a magnetized card for data storage, usually used with a memory typewriter.

Magnuson-Moss Act, a federal law that set standards for warranties on consumer products. The act requires clear, simple, written warranties, defines what "full warranty" and "limited warranty" mean, etc.
See also CONSUMERISM.

mail, direct campaign: *see* DIRECT MAIL CAMPAIGN.

mailing list, a list containing the names and mailing addresses of people and/or organizations who are to be contacted regularly by mail. Most mailing lists used by all except the smallest nonprofit organizations are stored on computers for ease of maintenance, updating, sorting (by purpose), and retrieval.
A list of active members and a list of people who have contributed to the organization in recent years are examples of mailing lists. However, for major direct mail campaigns, mailing lists are usually purchased from other organizations or associations of organizations, or from companies that specialize in compiling lists for different purposes. Mailing lists may be very general (such as everyone in a geographical area) or very targeted (such as the presidents of all manufacturing companies in a specified area with sales in excess of a certain amount).

Maimonides, a twelfth century Jewish scholar who defined eight ascending levels of charity. At the lowest level is charity given grudgingly, where donor and recipient know each other. The levels ascend according to willingness to give and anonymity. At the highest level, a donor gladly helps a stranger until he can break free of the need for assistance.

mainframe, the hardware of a large computer.
See also COMPUTER and HARDWARE.

maintenance, preventive, periodic inspection and correction of harmful conditions in machinery and equipment, before they occur or while they are still minor; the analysis of equipment and facilities in order to minimize required maintenance.

maintenance of effort, a requirement that grant recipients maintain the level of program expenditures financed from their own resources prior to receipt of a grant and use the grant funds to supplement expenditures for the aided activities.

maintenance review, formal periodic review (usually annual) of all positions in an organization, or portion of an organization, to insure that classifications are correct and position descriptions are current.

major duty, any duty or responsibility or group of closely related tasks of a position that (1) determines qualification requirements for the position, (2) occupies a significant amount of the employee's time, and (3) is a regular or recurring duty.

major medical insurance, insurance designed to offset the heavy medical expenses resulting from catastrophic or prolonged illness or injuries. Generally, such policies do not provide first dollar coverage, but do provide benefit payments of seventy-five to eighty percent of all types of medical expenses above a certain base amount paid by the insured. Most major medical policies sold as private insurance contain maximums on the total amount that will be paid (such as $50,000); thus, they do not provide last dollar coverage or complete protection against catastrophic costs. However, there is a trend toward $250,000 limits or even unlimited plans. In addition, benefit payments are often one hundred percent of expenses after the individidual has incurred some large amount ($500 to $2,000) of out-of-pocket expenses.

maker, a person who signs a negotiable instrument (such as a loan note) and by so doing promises to pay on it.

make-up pay, allowances paid to piece workers to make up the difference between actual piecework earnings and guaranteed rates (or statutory minimum wages).

make whole, legal remedy that provides for an injured party to be placed, as near as may be possible, in the situation he or she would have occupied if the wrong had not been committed.

make-work, any effort to reduce or limit labor output so that more labor must be employed.

malpractice, professional misconduct or lack of ordinary skill in the performance of a professional act. A practitioner is liable for damages or injuries caused by malpractice. Such liability for some professions, like medicine, can be covered by malpractice insurance against the costs of defending suits instituted against the professional and/or any damages assessed by the court, usually up to a maximum limit.

malpractice insurance, insurance against the risk of suffering financial damage because of malpractice.

management, (1) the people responsible for running an organization and (2) the running process itself—the utilizing of numerous resources to accomplish organizational goals.

See also the following entries:

CAREER MANAGEMENT
CONTINGENCY MANAGEMENT
FIRST-LINE MANAGEMENT
INDUSTRIAL DEMOCRACY
MANAGEMENT PRINCIPLES
MUSHROOM MANAGEMENT
PRINCIPLES OF MANAGEMENT
PROJECT MANAGEMENT
REACTIVE MANAGEMENT
SCIENTIFIC MANAGEMENT
STRATEGIC MANAGEMENT
SYSTEMS MANAGEMENT

management, cutback, phrase that describes the management of organizations in times of fiscal stress.

management, personnel: *see* PERSONNEL MANAGEMENT.

management, project, also PROGRAM MANAGEMENT: *see* PROJECT MANAGEMENT.

management, program: *see* PROJECT MANAGEMENT.

management, public: *see* PUBLIC MANAGEMENT.

managment, symbolic: *see* SYMBOLIC MANAGEMENT.

management audit, any comprehensive examination of the administrative operations and organizational arrangements which uses generally accepted standards of practice for the purpose of evaluation.

management by exception, management control process that has a subordinate report to an organizational superior only for exceptional or unusual events that might call for decision making on the part of the superior. In this way, a manager may avoid unnecessary detail that only confirms that all is going according to plan.

management by objectives (MBO), an approach to managing which controls by outputs and/or results rather than by inputs. The approach's hallmark is a mutual—by both organizational subordinate and superior—setting of measurable, time-limited goals to be accomplished by an individual or team over a period of time. According to George S. Odiorne, in *Management by Objectives* (New York: Pitman Publishing Company, 1965), "The superior and subordinate managers of an organization jointly define its common goals, define each individual's major areas of responsibility in terms of the results expected of him, and use these measures as guides for operating the unit and assessing the contribution of each of the members." One of the major uses—and misuses—of MBO is for formal performance appraisals.

management by objectives form, a record used to document, monitor, and evaluate results (individual, project, or organizational) in an organization or program that uses a management by objectives process.

See also MANAGEMENT BY OBJECTIVES.

management calendar, a working calendar which displays significant events, periods of heavy work load, etc., used for planning by staff, committee members, and directors.

Management Center, The, a nonprofit, tax-exempt San Francisco area organization whose purpose is to help executive directors and boards of directors of nonprofit organizations become more informed, responsible, and effective managers of their organizations.

management clause: *see* MANAGEMENT RIGHTS CLAUSE.

management control: *see* CONTROL.

management cycle, also MANAGEMENT WHEEL, a conception of the program management processes or functions in which the "center thrusts of power" are innovation/motivation and staff development.

management development, also called EXECUTIVE DEVELOPMENT, any conscious effort on the part of an organization to provide a manager with skills that he or she might need for future duties, such as rotational assignments or formal educational experience. The semantic difference between training workers and developing managers is significant. A manager is trained so that he or she can be of greater organizational value not only in present but in future assignments. In such a context the development investment made by the organization in a junior manager may only pay off when and if that individual grows into a bureau or division chief.

management games, also called BUSINESS GAMES, any of a variety of simulation exercises used in management development and education.

management information system (MIS), any formal process in an organization that provides managers with facts that they need for decision making. Modern management information systems are almost invariably dependent upon computers.

management letter: *see* AUDITOR'S OPINION.

management of committees, the process of ensuring that committees are formed, function, and are disbanded efficiently and effectively.

management official, an individual whose duties and responsibilities require or authorize the individual to formulate, determine, or influence policies.

EXAMPLE OF A MANAGEMENT CALENDAR

MONTH	JAN	FEB	MAR	APR	MAY	JUN	JUL	AUG	SEP	OCT	NOV	DEC
Board Mtgs & Agenda Items												
Executive Committee												
Finance Committee												
Fund-raising Committee												
Personnel Committee												
Policy & Planning Committee												
Public Relations Committee												
Temporary Committees												
Executive Director												
Division Heads												

management prerogatives: *see* MANAGEMENT RIGHTS.

management principles, the outdated view that there are "basic principles" which underlie the successful practice of management in organizations. Over the years, many authors, managers, and consultants have sought such simplistic and universal rules or principles of management unsuccessfully.

See also POSDCORB.

management rights, also called MANAGEMENT PREROGATIVES and RESERVED RIGHTS, those rights reserved to management that management feels are intrinsic to its ability to manage and, consequently, not subject to collective bargaining.

management rights clause, also called MANAGEMENT CLAUSE, that portion of a

MANAGEMENT CYCLE

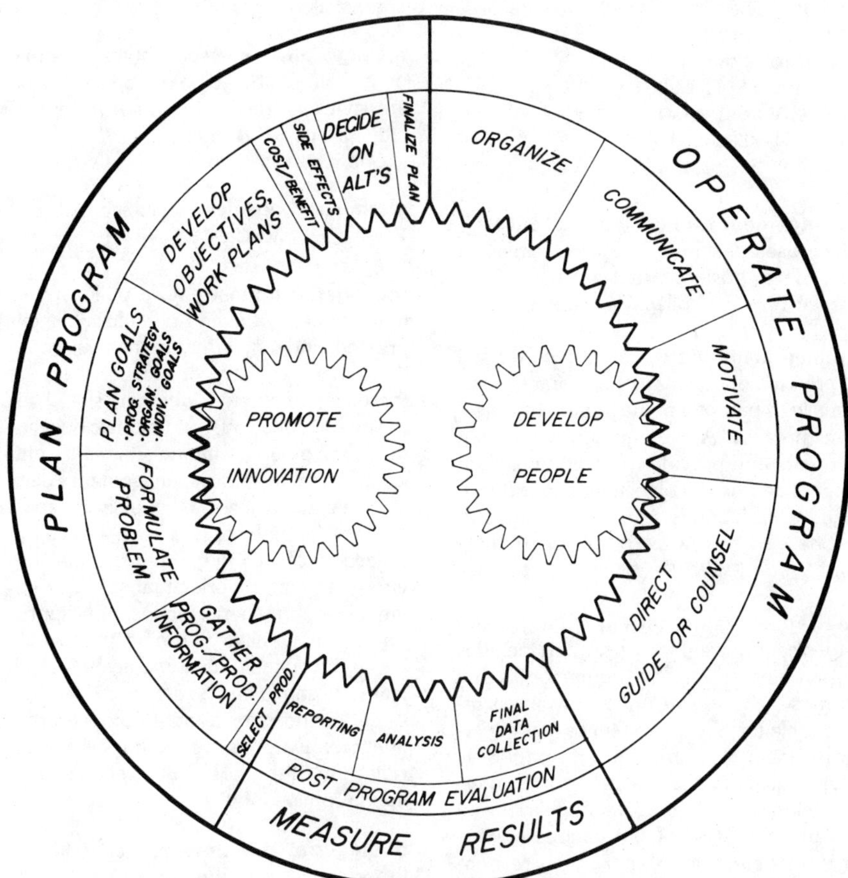

Source: R. L. Subry, J. S. Ott, C. J. Peterson, and J. W. Sawyer, Program Planning and Analysis *(Denver, Colo.: Applied Management Corporation, 1977, 1982.)*

collective bargaining agreement that defines the scope of management rights, functions, and responsibilities—essentially all those activities which management can undertake without the consent of the union. A typical management rights clause might read: "It is the intention hereof that all of the rights, powers, prerogatives, authorities that the company had prior to the signing of this agreement are retained by the company except those, and only to the extent that they are specifically abridged, delegated, granted, or modified by the agreement."

management science, also called OPERATIONS RESEARCH, approach to management dating from World War II that seeks to apply the scientific method to managerial problems. Because of its emphasis on mathematical techniques, *management science* as a term is frequently used interchangeably with *operations research.* Management science should not be confused with Frederick W. Taylor's Scientific Management Movement.

management support organization, general term used to refer to nonprofit organizations that provide an array of training, technical assistance, and support to nonprofit organizations in the general area of management.

See for example:

INDEPENDENT SECTOR, THE
REGIONAL ASSOCIATIONS OF GRANTMAKERS
SUPPORT CENTER, THE

management trainee, administrative job title loosely assigned to a wide variety of entry-level positions that are usually reserved for new college graduates.

management work plan, a record used in program or organizational management, usually as part of a management by objectives process. A management work plan supports and provides greater detail than a management by objectives form. It emphasizes task and resources management.

See also MANAGEMENT BY OBJECTIVES and MANAGEMENT BY OBJECTIVES FORM.

manager, generally speaking, any organization member whose job includes supervising others. A *top manager* is one of those who makes policy for, and is responsible for, the overall success of the organization. A *middle manager* is responsible for the execution and interpretation of top management policies and for the operation of the various departments. A *supervisory manager* is responsible for the final implementation of policies by rank and file employees.

manager, project: *see* PROJECT MANAGER.

managerial grid, the basis of Robert R. Blake and Jane S. Mouton's widely implemented organization development program. By using a graphic gridiron format, which has an X axis locating various degrees of orientation toward production and a Y axis locating various degrees of orientation toward people, individuals scoring this "managerial grid" can place themselves at one of eighty-one available positions that register their relative orientations toward people or production. Grid scores can then be used as the point of departure for a discussion of individual and organizational growth needs.

managerialist, a person who believes that organizations should be run by those who are specially trained to do so; for example, MBAs, MPAs, etc.

See also MBA and MPA.

managerial obsolescence: *see* OCCUPATIONAL OBSOLESCENCE.

managerial philosophy, a philosopy of management. It need not be formally expressed; indeed, many managers would deny that they have one. But it's always there, somewhere—whether stated or unstated, conscious or unconscious, intentional or unintentional. It is this philosophy that facilitates management's decision making process. Of course, different managerial philosophies have evolved in reflection of differing organizational environments and work situations. For example, a managerial philosophy appropriate for a military combat unit would hardly be suitable for a medical research team seeking to find a cure for cancer. The sincerity and rigor of an employee's motivation toward his or her duties is a direct reflection of the host organization's managerial philosophy.

managerial psychology, generally, all those concepts of human behavior in organizations that are relevant to managerial problems.

mandamus, also call WRIT OF MANDAMUS, court order that compels the performance of an act.

mandatory bargaining items, those collective bargaining items that each party must bargain over if introduced by the other party.

mandatory distribution rules, IRS rules requiring private foundations to distribute a minimum amount to charitable purposes each year. The amount is called the "distributable amount" and is equal to five percent of the foundation's assets.

man-day, amount of work that can be accomplished in a single normal day of work.

man Friday or GIRL FRIDAY, a general and cheerful helper. In Daniel Defoe's 1719 novel, *Robinson Crusoe,* the hero, a castaway on a desolate island, was fortunate to find a black man who developed into a hardworking helper. He was named Friday because that was the day of the week when Crusoe rescued him from acquaintances who thought he was good enough to eat.

manning table, also called PERSONNEL INVENTORY, listing of all of the employees in an organization by job and personal characteristics which serves as a basic reference for planning and other purposes.

manpower: *see* HUMAN RESOURCES.

Manpower Development and Training Act of 1962 (MDTA), federal statute that authorized the U.S. Department of Labor to identify the skills and capability needs of the economy and to initiate and find appropriate training programs. It was superseded by the Comprehensive Employment and Training Act of 1973.

manpower planning: *see* HUMAN RESOURCES PLANNING.

manpower planning models: *see* HUMAN RESOURCES PLANNING MODELS.

manpower requirements analysis: *see* HUMAN RESOURCES REQUIREMENTS ANALYSIS.

manpower utilization: *see* HUMAN RESOURCES UTILIZATION.

manual, a handbook of instructions. Manuals are published and sold on all varieties of topics related to nonprofit organizations, including, for example, how to raise funds, how to recruit and train volunteers, how to set up an accounting system, etc. Many nonprofit organizations develop their own manuals, such as a *Policy and Procedures Manual,* a *Volunteers Manual,* and a *Program Manual.*

See also POLICIES AND PROCEDURES MANUAL.

marginal analysis, also INCREMENTAL ANALYSIS, a decision analysis procedure which compares marginal costs and marginal benefits of alternative programs (for example, alternative ways to accomplish an objective or solve a problem); also, any technique that seeks to determine the point at which the cost of something (for example, an additional employee or machine) will be worthwhile or pay for itself.

marginal cost: *see* COST, MARGINAL.

marginal cost pricing, pricing equal to the marginal (additional) costs of the last unit of a good or service produced.

marginal employees, those members of an organization who contribute least to the organization's mission because of their personal sloth or the inherent nature of their duties.

marginal income analysis, an approach to financial planning which seeks to break down costs according to how they behave in order to quickly determine break-even points, gain a measure of a product's or service's profitability or loss level, and obtain a basis for sound pricing.

See also BREAK-EVEN ANALYSIS.

marginal productivity theory of wages, theory holding that the wages of workers will be determined by the value of the productivity of the marginal worker; additional workers will not be hired if the value of the added production is less than the wages that must be paid them. Consequently, wages will tend to equal the value of the product contributed by the last (the marginal) worker hired.

marginal tax rate, the tax rate, or percentage, which is applied on the last increment of income for purposes of computing federal or other income taxes.

EXAMPLE OF A MARGINAL ANALYSIS

ALTERNATIVE PROGRAMS	COST	BENEFIT
A	$300	$400
B	400	515
C	800	850
D	600	750

Calculate the marginal costs and benefits associated with each alternative, starting with the lowest cost program and proceeding to the highest cost program.

ALTERNATIVE PROGRAMS	COST	MARGINAL COST	BENEFIT	MARGINAL BENEFIT
A	$300		$400	
		$100		$115
B	400		515	
		200		235
C	800		850	
		200		100
D	600		750	

The analysis is continued until the marginal benefit is less than the marginal cost. In the example, marginal benefits exceed marginal costs until the analyst moves from program alternative C to D. There, the marginal cost of $200 exceeds the marginal benefit of $100. For this analysis, program alternative C is the preferred decision.

market, the geographical area in which an organization, product, or service can be (or is being) sold; the economic and social characteristics of potential donors (or service buyers), etc.

marketable, easily sold; for example, a marketable fund-raising idea, a marketable security.

market analysis, the process of systematically determining the characteristics of the market and the measurement of its capacity to contribute or buy.

See also MARKET RESEARCH.

marketing, demonstrating how it is in potential donors' best interests to contribute to a nonprofit organization. Marketing is a broader term than fund-raising and includes public relations-type activities; similar to development.

See also DEVELOPMENT and FUND-RAISING.

market penetration: *see* PENETRATION.

market price, fair: *see* FAIR MARKET VALUE.

market research, also MARKETING RESEARCH, the systematic gathering and analyzing of information about who is likely to give or buy what, in order to help development and marketing people make better decisions about public relations and advertising programs, follow-up methods, etc.

See also MARKET ANALYSIS.

market segmentation, the identification of subsets of a nonprofit organization's market, followed by the development of an effective marketing program (or development program) for the different subsets. For example, *see* MAILING LIST and MARKET RESEARCH.

Markoff chain or MARKOV CHAIN, a series (or "chain") of probabilities in which the events, numbers, times, or choices involved are discontinuous. For an example of a Markoff chain, *see* DECISION TREE.

martinet, strict disciplinarian.

Maslow, Abraham, H. (1908-1970), psychologist best known for his theory of human motivation, which was premised upon a "needs hierarchy" within which an individual moved up or down as the needs of each level were satisfied or threatened.

mass picketing, technique used when a union wants to indicate broad support for a strike. A "mass" of strikers is assembled to picket a place of business in order to discourage nonstrikers from entering the premises.

mass transit, the public provision of transportation in an urban area, typically governed by a special district. It is financially aided by the national government and usually susidized by state or local governments.

master, special, a person appointed by a court to carry out the court's orders in certain types of lawsuits or following certain court decisions.

master agreement, also called MASTER CONTRACT, collective bargaining contract that serves as a model for an entire industry or segment of that industry. While the master agreement serves to standardize the economic benefits of all of the employees covered by it, it is often supplemented by a local contract which deals with the varying circumstances of the various local unions.

matching, an accounting concept which holds that expenses should be recognized in the same accounting period that is used to recognize the income they produced.
See also RECOGNITION OF INCOME.

matching funds: *see:*
CASH MATCH
IN-KIND MATCH
MATCHING SHARE

matching grant, a grant made under the condition that additional funds are raised from other sources. For example, a foundation might make a matching grant to a college up to an amount (for example, $10,000) if the remainder of the needed funds for a project (for example, $20,000) is raised from alumni, corporations, and other foundations. Matching grants provide the potential recipient with demonstrable evidence of a foundation's willingness to participate, which is useful in raising funds from other sources.

matching grant approach (to taxation), an alternative to charitable deductions and tax credits for increasing tax equity. Under a matching grant approach the government would, in effect, "match" gifts to tax-exempt organizations.
See also DEMOCRATIZE and EQUITY.

matching item, test item that asks which one of a group of words, pictures, etc. matches up with those of another group.

matching share, also HIGH MATCH and LOW MATCH, the contribution that grant recipients are required to make to supplement the grantor's grant moneys. *A high match* is a recipient's contribution that is fifty percent or greater. A *low match* is a recipient's contribution that is less than fifty percent of the total cost.
See also CASH MATCH and IN-KIND MATCH.

maternity benefits, insurance coverage for the costs of pregnancy and delivery and, in some cases, family planning, postpartum care, and complications of pregnancy.

maternity leave, formally approved temporary absence from work for childbirth and its aftermath.
See also BIRTH LEAVE.

matrix diamond, basic structural form of matrix organizations; this is in contrast to the pyramid—the basic structural form of traditional organizations.

matrix manager, any manager who shares former authority over a subordinate with another manager.

matrix organization, any organization using a multiple command system whereby an employee might be accountable to one superior for overall performance as well as to one or more leaders of particular projects. "Matrix" is a generic term that is used to refer to various organizational structures.

See also PROJECT MANAGEMENT and TASK FORCE.

matrix printer: *see* DOT MATRIX.

maturity, the time when a debt or other obligation becomes due or a right becomes enforceable. It is usually the date when the borrower on a loan, note, or bond must pay the full amount of the debt.

maturity curve, also called CAREER CURVE and SALARY CURVE, technique for determining the salaries of professional and technical employees that relates the employee's education and experience to on-the-job performance. For example, after it is determined what the average compensation for a professional employee is for each of various categories of experience, the individual employee is assigned a salary based upon whether he or she is considered average, below average, or above average in performance.

Mayo, Elton (1880-1949), principal organizer and researcher of the famous Hawthorne experiments and considered the founder of the human relations approach in industry.

mayor-council system, also STRONG MAYOR and WEAK MAYOR, system of urban government with a separately elected executive, the mayor, and an urban legislature, or council, usually elected in partisan ward elections. It is called a *strong mayor* system if the office of mayor is filled by separate citywide elections and has powers such as veto, appointment and removal, etc. In contrast, where the office of mayor lacks such powers it is called a *weak mayor* system. This designation does not take into account any informal powers possessed by the incumbent mayor, only the formal powers of the office.

MBA, Master of Business Administration degree.

See also MPA.

MBO: *see* MANAGEMENT BY OBJECTIVES.

***McDonnell Douglas Corporation* v. *Green*,** 411 U.S. 792 (1973), U.S. Supreme Court case which held that an employee could establish a prima facie case of discrimination by initially showing (1) that he or she was a member of a racial minority; (2) that he or she applied and was qualified in an opening for which the employer sought applicants; (3) that despite qualifications he or she was rejected; (4) that after rejection the position remained open and the employer continued to seek applicants.

McGregor, Douglas M. (1906-1964), organizational humanist and managerial philosopher who is best known for his conceptualization of Theory X and Theory Y.

MDTA: *see* MANPOWER DEVELOPMENT AND TRAINING ACT OF 1962.

mean, simple average of a set of measurements obtained by summing the measurements and dividing by the number of them.

mean deviation: *see* AVERAGE DEVIATION.

measure, direct, an evaluation variable which is measured directly—not through an intervening variable or indicator. For example, as vehicle miles driven increases, the accident rate will probably change. The change—increase or decrease—is a direct measure of the relationship between accident rate and vehicle miles driven.

See also:

MEASURE, INDIRECT
MEASURE, PROXY

measure, indirect, tangential measurement. When a chain of relationships exists among evaluation variables, where variable C depends on variable B which depends on variable A, then a change in dependent variable C is an indirect measure of the relationship between dependent variable B and independent variable A. For example, if a nonprofit organization initiates a major community anti-drinking and driving campaign (independent variable A), it should have a direct effect on the number of drinking drivers on the roads (dependent variable B). An indirect measure would be the number of convictions or citations issued for drinking driving (dependent variable C).

measure, proxy, intermediate measurement. When a chain of relationships exists among evaluation variables where variable C depends on variable B which depends on variable A, a change in variable A causes a change in variable C. When this change in variable C cannot be measured directly, it may be inferred by measuring the change in the proxy (or intermediate) variable B. For example, implementation of a new ambulance dispatch communications system (independent variable A) should reduce response time (proxy or indirect variable B) which, in turn, should reduce mortality and morbidity resulting from certain types of injuries and illnesses (dependent variable C). The response time is an easily obtained proxy measure of the changes in mortality and morbidity, which are very difficult and expensive to measure directly.

See also MEASURE, DIRECT and MEASURE, INDIRECT.

measure, quantified, an evaluation or research variable, indicator, or measure which is expressed in numerical terms.

See also:
BEFORE-AND-AFTER STUDY
EVALUATION
EVALUATION DESIGN
EVALUATION TECHNIQUE
TIME SERIES ANALYSIS

EXAMPLES OF QUANTIFIED MEASURES FOR USE IN AN EVALUATION STUDY
volume amounts
units of production
time units
frequency rates
ratios
index numbers
percentages
proportions
averages
number of aggregates
degrees
phases or stages
percentiles
quartiles
deciles
mean deviations
ranges
correlations

measure of dispersion, also called MEASURE OF VARIABILITY, any statistical measure showing the extent to which individual test scores are concentrated about or spread out from a measure of central tendency.

mechanical aptitude tests, tests designed to measure how well an individual can learn to perform tasks that involve the understanding and manipulation of mechanical devices. Classified into two subgroups—mechanical reasoning and spatial relations.

mechanic's lien, a worker's legal claim to hold property (for example, a repaired car) until repair charges are paid or to file formal papers securing a right to property (such as a car or an office building) until charges for work done are paid.

mechanistic system, organization form, proven to be most appropriate under stable conditions, which is characterized by: (1) a high degree of task differentiation and specialization with a precise delineation of rights and responsibilities; (2) a high degree of reliance on the traditional hierarchical structure; (3) a tendency for the top of the hierarchy to control all incoming and outgoing communications; (4) an emphasis on vertical interactions between superiors and subordinates; (5) a demand for loyalty to the organization and to superiors; and (6) a greater importance placed on internal (local) knowledge, skill, and experience, in contrast to more general (cosmopolitan) knowledge, experience, and skill.

See also ORGANIC SYSTEM.

mechanization: *see* AUTOMATION.

med-arb, a combination of mediation and arbitration which engages a third party neutral in both mediation and arbitration. The main idea is to mediate in an effort to resolve the impasse or at least reduce the number of issues going to arbitration. Then, where mediation is unsuccessful, some form of binding arbitration is used.

media, a general term for the mass communication industry, including newspapers, radio, and television.

media, electronic, a general term for radio and television.

media, print, also PRINTED MEDIA, a general term for daily and weekly newspapers and, in some instances, periodicals.

median, middle score in a distribution; the fiftieth percentile; the point that divides the group into two equal parts. Half of a group of scores fall below the median and half above it.

media relations, a broad, continuing, carefully developed relationship with the media which is necessary for obtaining responsive, accurate, and—sometimes—friendly media coverage of organization programs, drives, and other activities; a subfunction of public information or public relations.

See also MEDIA and PUBLIC RELATIONS.

mediation, also CONCILIATION, any attempt by an impartial third party to help settle disputes. A mediator has no power but that of persuasion. The mediator's suggestions are advisory in nature and may be rejected by both parties. Mediation and conciliation tend to be used interchangeably to denote the entrance of an impartial third party into a dispute. However, there is a distinction. *Conciliation* is the less active term. It technically refers simply to efforts to bring the parties together so that they may resolve their problems themselves. *Mediation,* in contrast, is a more active term. It implies that an active effort will be made to help the parties reach agreement by clarifying issues, asking questions, and making specific proposals. However, the usage of the two terms has been so blurred that the only place where it is absolutely necessary to distinguish between them is in a dictionary.

See also PREVENTIVE MEDIATION.

Mediation Service, abbreviated way of referring to the Federal Mediation and Conciliation Service or state agencies performing a similar function.

mediator, individual who acts as an impartial third party in order to help resolve disputes. The mediator's role is to help the parties reach an agreement.

Medicaid, a federally aided, state operated and administered program which provides medical benefits for certain low-income people in need of health and medical care.

medical insurance, supplemental: *see* SUPPLEMENTAL MEDICAL INSURANCE.

Medicare, the National Health Insurance Program for the elderly and the disabled. The two parts of Medicare—hospital insurance and medical insurance—help protect people sixty-five and over from the high costs of health care. Also eligible for Medicare are disabled people under sixty-five who have been entitled to social security disability benefits for twenty-four or more consecutive months (including adults who are receiving benefits because they have been disabled since childhood). Insured workers and their dependents who need dialysis treatment or a kidney transplant because of permanent kidney failure also have Medicare protection.

megatrends, term popularized by John Naisbitt in his 1982 book bearing the same title. Megatrends are basic socio/economic/technological trends that influence basic public, nonprofit, and for-profit organization strategies.

melioration, improvements, rather than repairs, to property.

See also IMPROVEMENT.

member, bona fide (charitable organization): *see* BONA FIDE MEMBER.

membership approval, agreement of the full membership. The articles and bylaws of many nonprofit organizations require the board of directors to submit certain important decisions to the membership for approval. Although the decisions vary among organizations, typical ones include amending the bylaws, adopting the annual budget, dissolving the organization, approving the annual financial reports, incurring a substantial debt (for example, to acquire a building), etc.

membership corporation, a nonprofit, non-stock company created for social, political, charitable, or other public benefit purposes. In most membership corporations, the primary function of the members is to elect directors or trustees.

memory, the area in a computer where programs (instructions) and data are stored.

See also:
COMPUTER
RANDOM ACCESS
ROM

menu, a list of computer programs, operations, options, instructions, files, questions, etc. displayed on a computer monitor to assist an operator.

merger, the union of two or more things, including organizations. Sometimes (but not always) the smaller or less important thing ceases to exist once it is a part of the other; for example, the merger of the Unitarian and Universalist denominations into the Unitarian-Universalist denomination.

merit increase, raise in pay based upon a favorable review of an employee's performance. This is the way most organizations seek to relate quality of performance to financial rewards.

merit pay system, also called MERIT PAY PROGRAM, set of procedures designed to reward employees with salary increases reflective of their on-the-job performance.

merit principle, the concept that members of an organization are selected and promoted based on achievements measured in a standard way through open competition.

merit promotion, selection to a higher position made solely on the basis of job-related qualifications without regard to factors such as race, color, religion, national origin, sex, age, political belief, marital status, or physical handicap.

merit raise: *see* MERIT INCREASE.

M-Form Society, normative concept of U.S. society popularized by William Ouchi in *The M-Form Society: How American Teamwork Can Recapture the Competitive Edge* (Reading, Mass.: Addison-Wesley Publishing Company, 1984). The M-Form Society conceptually parallels a multidivisional corporation in structure and method of functioning. According to Ouchi, business and trade associations must be the essential elements for revitalizing the nation's economic strength.

MGD data: *see* MINORITY GROUPS DESIGNATOR DATA.

Mickey Mouse, pejorative term for many aspects of administration. When Walt Disney's famous mouse made it big in the 1930s, he appeared in a variety of cartoon shorts that had him building something that would later fall apart (such as a house or boat) or generally going to a great deal of trouble for little result. So Mickey Mouse gradually gave his name to anything requiring considerable effort for slight result. The term is also applied to policies or regulations felt to be needless, silly, or mildly offensive.

microeconomics, the study of how small economic units (*e.g.*, the consumer, the household, etc.) interrelate with the market in determining the relative price of goods and the factors of production.

microfiche, a 4″ by 6″ film with 270 pages of print readable when it is put on a fiche reader. Microfiche is used to store large quantities of printed materials; for example, archives, journals, newspapers, etc.

microprocessor, a computer chip that acts as a full computer; the core of a microcomputer.

See also COMPUTER and HARDWARE.

mid-career change: *see* CAREER CHANGE.

mid-career crisis, also MID-LIFE CRISIS, terms used to refer to a period in a person's life, usually during his/her thirties, which is marked by feelings of personal frustration and professional failure. Such feelings may or may not have a basis in fact.

See also STRESS.

middle management, vague delineation of organizational authority and leadership that lies below top management and above first-level supervisors.

mid-level managers: *see* MIDDLE MANAGEMENT.

mid-life crisis: *see* MID-CAREER CRISIS.

midnight shift, tour of duty that usually runs from midnight to 8 A.M.

migratory worker, individual whose principal income is earned from temporary employment (typically in agriculture) and who, in order to find work, moves several times a year through as many states.

mileage allowance, specific amount an employee is reimbursed for each mile that his/her personal automobile is used on company business.

milestone, a signficant event in a work plan or a project control chart. Milestones are used to predict whether or not program or organizational objectives will be accomplished. There are two major types of milestones: *Percent complete milestones* and *significant event milestones. Percent complete milestones* are used with quantifiable objectives, such as dollars to be raised through pledges, number of visitors to a zoo, and number of column inches of an organization's print media coverage. *Percent complete milestones* might be, for example, respectively, the dollar amount raised through the first three months of a year, the number of visitors through the first six months, and the number of column inches through the first nine months. *Significant event milestones* are major subaccomplishments which if not achieved probably predict that the objectives will not be accomplished. For example, if an objective is to attract a number of new members or volunteers, a significant event milestone might be the successful launching of a membership or volunteer recruitment drive.

See also OBJECTIVE and PROJECT CONTROL CHART.

military leave, lengthy leave of absence for service in the armed forces of the United States, or a short-term leave of absence for service in the military reserves.

mill, also MILL RATE and MILL LEVY, one tenth of one cent. Many local property taxes (*mill levies*) are expressed in mills or *mill rates*.

milline rate, the cost of reaching one million readers with one agate line of advertising.

See also AGATE LINE.

minimax, an approach to decision making from game theory which calls for choosing the alternative that minimizes the chances of the maximum loss (the worst case). It is a relatively conservative decision approach.

See also GAME THEORY.

minimum wage, smallest hourly rate that may be paid to a worker. The minimum wage usually refers to the federal minimum wage law—the Fair Labor Standards Act (FLSA). The minimum wage at any given time is established by Congress via FLSA amendments. The Secretary of Labor regulates some exceptions to the minimum wage. Persons with impaired earning or production capacity because of age, physical or mental deficiences, or injury may be paid as low as fifty percent of the wage paid to a nonhandicapped worker for the same type, quality, and quantity of work.

Forty-one states, the District of Columbia, and Puerto Rico have minimum wage laws for adults with minimum rates currently in effect. State minimum wage laws are of two basic types: those that contain a minimum in the law itself (a statutory rate) and those that authorize an administrator or wage board to set minimum rates by occupation or industry. Several states combine the two types and have both a statutory minimum for most employment and provisions for wage orders to establish rates and/or working conditions for certain occupations or industries. Only the legislature can change statutory rates, but wage orders can be modified by the administrator or wage board. Under both types of minimum wage law, lower rates are generally payable to learners and apprentices, handicapped persons, and minors.

Statutory state minimum wage rates for experienced adults varied widely in mid-1982, from a low of $1.25 an hour in Georgia to a high of $3.85 in Alaska. Some states provide for automatic upward adjustment if the federal minimum wage rate is increased. When workers are covered by both the federal minimum wage law and a state law, they are entitled to the higher rate.

Full-time students may be employed at eighty-five percent of the minimum wage under certain conditions.

FLSA Minimum Wage Standards

Legislation	Hourly Rate	Effective Date
Act of 1938	$ .25	Oct. 24, 1938
	.30	Oct. 24, 1939
	.40	Oct. 24, 1945
Amendments of:		
1949	.75	Jan. 25, 1950
1955	1.00	Mar. 1, 1956
1961	1.15	Sept. 3, 1961
	1.25	Sept. 3, 1963
1966	1.40	Feb. 1, 1967
	1.60	Feb. 1, 1968
1974	2.00	May 1, 1974
	2.10	Jan. 1, 1975
	2.30	Jan. 1, 1976
1977	2.65	Jan. 1, 1978
	2.90	Jan. 1, 1979
	3.10	Jan. 1, 1980
	3.35	Jan. 1, 1981

minority groups designator data, also called MGD DATA, data base or system which provides statistical employment information by race or national origin. In theory, such data should only be used in studies and analyses that evaluate an organization's equal employment opportunity programs.

minutes, the official written record of a meeting.

MIS: *see* MANAGEMENT INFORMATION SYSTEM.

misery index, the sum of the rates of inflation and unemployment.

misrepresentation, a false or misleading statement.

mission (organizational), a statement of an organization's macro-level purposes and philosophy.

See also INITIATIVE.

mission agency, any government department or agency whose legislation gives it responsibility for promotion of some cause or operation of some system as its primary reason for existence (mission) and which is appropriated funds for the conduct of this mission.

missionary organization, a category of religious organization which carries on religious work, typically evangelization or proselytizing, in conjunction with operating schools or hospitals in underdeveloped foreign countries or in economically depressed areas of this country.

See also RELIGIOUS ORGANIZATION.

mission budgeting, an end-purpose approach to budgeting. The basic idea is that a mission budget would categorize programs and activities by end-purposes.

mixed-scanning, decision making model that uses both incrementalism and the rational-comprehensive approach to seek best short-term solutions.

mobility: *see* OCCUPATIONAL MOBILITY.

mode, score or value that occurs most frequently in a distribution.

model, a simplification of reality; a reduction in time and space that allows for a better understanding of reality. The representation may be expressed in words, numbers, or diagrams. For example, a textbook may have several paragraphs describing a model of leadership. In the next chapter it may have several diagrams representing a model of motivation. These are both simplified representations of more complex phenomena and are intended to facilitate understanding.

model agreement, collective bargaining agreement developed by a national or international union to serve as a standard for its locals.

Model Cities Program, also DEMONSTRATION CITIES AND METROPOLITAN DEVELOPMENT ACT OF 1966, national government program creating demonstration cities which would designate particular areas for intensive use of coordinated federal programs. Though originally programmed for only a dozen or so cities as part of Lyndon Johnson's Great Society, it quickly grew to include more than 150 cities. It was dismantled under Richard Nixon and replaced by revenue sharing.

modeling, identifying the fixed and variable components in a system, assigning them numerical or economic values, and relating them to each other in a logical fashion so that one can derive optimal solutions to operational problems by manipulating the components of the model.

modem, modulator/demodulator; a device that converts a computer's digital signals to analog signals (and back) for transmission between computer systems, frequently over telephone lines.
See also ACOUSTIC COUPLER.

mom and pop operation, an organization so small that its work force consists primarily of immediate family members. For example, many nonprofit day programs for people with developmental disabilities were mom and pop operations up through the 1960s.

money broker, a firm or individual who helps find people to lend large quantities of money to those who need it.

money market certificate, a savings certificate sold by banks and other savings institutions that is usually held for at least six months. The interest rate is usually based on the current U.S. Treasury bill rate.

money market fund, a mutual fund that invests in short-term securities such as Treasury bills.
See also MUTUAL FUND.

money order, a type of draft (or guaranteed check) sold by banks, post offices, and other companies who want to make payments in check form, but who do not use their own checks.

money purchase benefit, pension that is entirely dependent on contributions made to an individual's account.

money purchase plan, a pension plan in which an employer contributes a fixed amount each year. The ultimate worth of the benefits paid will vary depending on how much the invested sums earn.

monitoring, any process for reviewing and assessing programs and activities.

monotony curve: *see* FATIGUE CURVE.

moonlighting, slang term for holding a

second job. Employee moonlighting may impede primary job productivity and otherwise cause problems when there are questions about sick leave claims, absenteeism, tardiness, overtime scheduling, and potential conflicts of interest. Many employers formally restrict moonlighting by their employees. Typically, such restrictions require advance approval and stipulate that moonlighting be done outside of regularly scheduled work periods.

moral development, the stages through which a person passes in developing a personal ethical system. The three major theories that attempt to describe moral development are psychoanalytic, cognitive-developmental, and social learning.

morale, collective attitude of the work force toward their work environment; a crude measure of the organizational climate. Peter F. Drucker insists that the only true test of morale is performance. As such, morale is one of the most significant indicators of organizational health.

morality, administrative: *see* ADMINISTRATIVE MORALITY.

moratorium, an enforced delay; a deliberate delay.

morphological analysis, any technique which seeks to systematically find all of the possible means for achieving a goal.

mortgage, a loan arrangement under which the borrower conveys title to a capital asset to the lender as security for the loan.

mortgage company, a company that makes mortgage loans, then sells them to others.

mortgagee, a lender who takes a mortgage.

mortgagor, a person or organization that borrows on a mortgage.

motion study, the study of the body motions used to perform an operation for the purpose of improving the operation by removing unnecessary motions and simplifying necessary motions.

motivation, also WORK MOTIVATION, an emotional stimulus that causes a person to act. *Work motivation* is an amalgam of all of the factors in one's working environment that foster (positively or negatively) productive efforts.

See also the following entries:

EXTRINSIC MOTIVATION
REINFORCEMENT
SELF-ACTUALIZATION
STROKING

Motivation-Hygiene Theory, also called TWO-FACTOR THEORY, theory put forth in a landmark study by Frederick Herzberg, Bernard Mausner, and Barbara Snyderman, in *The Motivation to Work* (N.Y.: John Wiley & Sons, 1959). It was one of the first extensive empirical demonstrations of the primacy of internal worker motivation. Five factors were isolated as determiners of job satisfaction: achievement, recognition, work itself, responsibility, and advancement. Similarly, the factors associated with job dissatisfaction were realized: company policy and administration, supervision, salary, interpersonal relations, and working conditions. The satisfying factors were all related to job content, the dissatisfying factors to the environmental context of the job. The factors that were associated with job satisfaction were quite separate from those factors associated with job dissatisfaction. According to Herzberg, in "The Motivation-Hygiene Concept and the Problems of Manpower," *Personnel Administration* (January-February 1964):

> Since separate factors needed to be considered depending on whether job satisfaction or job dissatisfaction was involved, it followed that these two feelings were not the obverse of each other. The opposite of job satisfaction would not be job dissatisfaction but rather NO job satisfaction; and similarly the opposite of job dissatisfaction is NO job dissatisfaction—not job satisfaction.

Because the environmental context of jobs, such as working conditions, interpersonal relations, and salary, served primarily as preventatives, they were termed hygiene factors, as an analogy to the medical use of hygiene, meaning preventative and environmental. The job-content factors such as achievement, advancement, and responsibility were termed motivators because these are the things that motivate people to superior performance. Again according to Herzberg, in *Work and the Nature of Man* (Cleveland: World Publishers, 1966):

> The principal result of the analysis of this data was to suggest that the hygiene or maintenance events led to job dissatisfaction because of a need to avoid unpleasantness; the motivator events led to job satisfaction because of a need for growth or self-actualization. At the psychological level, the two dimensions of job attitudes reflected a two-dimensional need structure: one need system for the avoidance of unpleasantness and a parallel need system for personal growth.

Since its original presentation, a considerable number of empirical investigations by a wide variety of researchers has tended to confirm the Motivation-Hygiene Theory. Its chief fault seems to be its rejection of the view that pay is a unique incentive capable in different circumstances of being a hygiene as well as a motivator factor. But the theory's main holding—that worker motivation is essentially internal—remains largely unchallenged.

See also HERZBERG, FREDERICK.

Mt. Healthy Board of Education* v. *Doyle, 429 U.S. 274 (1977), U.S. Supreme Court case which held that the first amendment does not demand that a discharged employee be placed "in a better position as a result of the exercise of constitutionally protected activity than he would have occupied had he done nothing." An employer should not be inhibited from evaluating an employee's performance and "reaching a decision not to rehire on the basis of that record, simply because the protected conduct makes the employer more certain of the correctness of its decision."

Mouton, Jane S: *see* BLAKE, ROBERT R. AND JANE S. MOUTON.

Moynihan, Daniel Patrick (1927-   ), U.S. Senator from New York elected in 1976; former Ambassador to the United Nations (1975-76); former Ambassador to India (1973-75); former urban affairs advisor to President Nixon (1969-73). Moynihan first came to national attention in 1965 when as an Assistant Secretary of Labor he wrote a report suggesting instability in black families—"The Negro Family: The Case for National Action." Moynihan once again ran afoul of black leaders when in 1970 he wrote in a memorandum to President Nixon that "The time may have come when the issue of race could benefit from a period of 'benign neglect'." When the memorandum was leaked to the press, its misinterpretation once again angered the black community.

MPA or **MBA,** Master of Public Administration and Master of Business Administration, respectively. These are the leading managerial degrees for organizational practitioners.

Ms. tile of courtesy for a woman which is used without regard to her marital status.

muddling through: *see* INCREMENTALISM and LINDBLOM, CHARLES E.

multiemployer pension plan trust, a trust formed to provide funds for multiemployer pension funds. Multiemployer pension plan trusts may qualify for tax-exempt status under IRS Code 501 (c) (22) since passage of the Multiemployer Pension Plan Amendments Act of 1980.

multiple-choice test, test consisting entirely of multiple-choice items, which require the examinee to choose the best or correct answer from several that are given as options.

multiple management, a loose term used to describe programs in which workers participate in the development and implementation of policy and programs.

multiple regression analysis: *see* REGRESSION ANALYSIS.

municipal bonds, also TAX-EXEMPT MUNICIPAL BONDS, terms used interchangeably with public borrowing and debt financing. This causes some confusion because they appear to refer only to bonds issued by local government. Yet bonds issued by states, territories, or possessions of the United States or by any municipality, political subdivision (including cities, counties, school districts, and special districts for fire prevention, water sewer, irrigation, and other purposes) or public agency or instrumentality (such as an authority or commission) are subsumed under the rubric "municipal bonds." While the interest on municipal bonds is exempt from federal taxes, state and local exemptions may vary.

municipal corporation, city corporation. Cities are legally corporations, bound by their charter and any relevant state and federal legislation. As a charter, even if developed and implemented through a home rule process, it is a document bestowed by the state. Cities are not legally comparable to state governments, which have the ability to obtain powers from the people.

See also DILLON'S RULE.

municipal revenue bonds, state and local government debt securities whose interest and principal are paid from the revenues of rents, tolls, or other user charges flowing from specific projects financed by the bonds.

Munsterberg, Hugo (1863-1916), German psychologist who spent his later years at Harvard and earned the title of "father" of industrial or applied psychology by proposing the use of psychology for practical purposes.

Murphy's Law, any of the rules published in *Public Administration Review* (July 1976):

1. Anything that can go wrong will go wrong.
2. Anything that can go wrong will—at the worst possible time.
3. Nothing is as easy as it seems.
4. If there is a possibility of several things going wrong, the one that will go wrong is the one that will do the most damage.
5. Everything takes longer than it should.
6. Left to themselves, things will go from bad to worse.
7. Nature always sides with the hidden flaw.
8. If everything seems to be going well, you have obviously overlooked something.

Murphy seems related to that famous literary wit, Anonymous. Only one thing seems certain—Murphy's laws were not written by Murphy, but by another person with the same name.

mushroom management, a poor management style. All that mushrooms need in order to grow is to be left undisturbed in the dark and fed fertilizer frequently. Mushroom managers keep subordinates in the dark and feed them lots of manure.

mutual benefit association, a social organization or corporation for the relief of its members from specified problems or costs (such as the costs of illness or injury). Mutual benefit associations pay losses with assessments on their members for specific losses rather than by fixed premiums payable in advance.

mutual company, a company in which the customers are the owners and receive the profits.

mutual fund, also OPEN-END INVESTMENT COMPANY, CLOSED-END INVESTMENT COMPANY, organization that issues and sells shares continuously and without limits (hence "open-end") and is required to repurchase them from shareholders on demand or request. The best known mutual funds trade in stock market equities, bonds, or cash instruments, so there are varieties of stock mutual funds, bond mutual funds, etc.

In contrast to an open-end investment company, a *closed-end investment company* issues and sells its shares infrequently, usually in large amounts or blocks, and is not required to repurchase them on demand or request.

A *no-load mutual fund* does not charge brokerage fees or sales commissions.

mutual insurance company, a member-controlled, nonprofit insurance company with no stock which provides insurance to its members essentially at cost. Mutual insurance companies may qualify for tax-exempt status under IRS Code 501 (c) (15).

mutual organization: *see* BENEVOLENT ORGANIZATION.

mutual will, a will in which a husband and wife leave all assets to each other.

N

N, mathematical symbol commonly used to represent the number of cases in a distribution, study, etc. The symbol of the number of cases in a subgroup of *N* is *n*.

NAACP: *see* NATIONAL ASSOCIATION FOR THE ADVANCEMENT OF COLORED PEOPLE.

NAB: *see* NATIONAL ALLIANCE OF BUSINESS.

NAB: *see* NATIONAL ASSOCIATION OF BROADCASTERS.

NAPSOE: *see* NATIONAL ASSOCIATION OF PUBLIC SERVICE ORGANIZATION EXECUTIVES.

Nashville Gas Co.* v. *Satty, 434 U.S. 136 (1977), U.S. Supreme Court case which held that pregnant women forced to take maternity leave cannot be denied their previously accumulated seniority rights when they return to work.

See also PREGNANCY.

NASPAA: *see* NATIONAL ASSOCIATION OF SCHOOLS OF PUBLIC AFFAIRS AND ADMINISTRATION.

NASS: *see* NATIONAL ASSOCIATION OF SUGGESTION SYSTEMS.

National Alliance of Business (NAB), business group formed in 1968 to work in partnership with the federal government in order to find permanent jobs for the hard core unemployed. It is located in Washington, D.C.

national association, also NATIONAL ORGANIZATION and INTERNATIONAL ASSOCIATION, organization that attempts to address issues and solve problems which affect the entire nation, usually through a network of regional, state, and substate chapters or affiliates (subordinate organizations). National associations and organizations vary structurally from loose confederations of separately incorporated affiliates to highly centralized organizations which exercise strong control over subordinate chapters.

International associations are similar to national associations in purpose, structure, and functions, but have chapters or affiliates in other countries.

National Association for the Advancement of Colored People (NAACP), founded in 1909, the largest and historically most influential of the black interest groups.

National Association of Broadcasters (NAB), body whose Radio and Television Codes are general advisory standards of decency, decorum, etc. for voluntary use by radio and television stations. Although the Codes are not binding, most stations attempt to abide by them.

National Association of Manufacturers (NAM), the largest non-trade employer's association in the United States.

National Association of Public Service Organization Executives (NAPSOE), a leading nonprofit association of professional managers of nonprofit public service organizations. In addition to its other educational and professional advancement functions, NAPSOE administers a certification program leading to designation as a Certified Public Service Executive (CPSE).

See also CERTIFIED PUBLIC SERVICE EXECUTIVE.

National Association of Schools of Public Affairs and Administration (NASPAA), organization of academic programs in public administration and public affairs with a stated objective of advancing education and training in public affairs and public administration. NASPAA serves as a national center for information on programs and developments in this field and represents the concerns and interests of member institutions in the formulation and support of national policies for education in public affairs and public administration. NASPAA is in Washington, D.C.

National Association of Securities Dealers (NASD), an association of dealers in securities.

National Association of Suggestion Systems (NASS), Chicago based nonprofit organization founded in 1942 to promote and develop suggestion systems. NASS seeks to develop new technology and disseminate information about suggestion systems to its more than 800 members and to all others interested in suggestion systems.

National Center for Charitable Statistics (NCCS), the first continuing effort to track the scope of the charitable sector in the United States. It began as an independent, nonprofit organization sponsored by a consortium of the Council on Foundations, INDEPENDENT SECTOR, National Information Bureau, and United Way of America. In-kind contributions from these four consortium members provide support for the core administration and services of the Center, which is now a program of the INDEPENDENT SECTOR.

NCCS facilitated the development and national acceptance in 1981 of a revised Internal Revenue Service (IRS) Form 990 as a substitute for varying reporting requirements among the states and the IRS.

The Center is developing a comprehensive national data base on charitable statistics.

See also INDEPENDENT SECTOR.

National Center for Community Action (NCCA), a national clearinghouse concerned with community action and community development issues and trends.

National Center for Voluntary Action (NCVA), a national clearinghouse on volunteerism.

National Charities Information Bureau, a New York City based organization which provides comparable data and information about tax-exempt organizational giving practices, costs, etc.

National Communications Council for Human Services (NCCHS), an association that provides public relations literature and services to member nonprofit organizations. Its periodical, *Channels,* carries new information for public relations people in nonprofit organizations. NCCHS is associated with the Public Relations Society of America.

National Conference of State Legislatures (NCSL), body founded in 1975 to replace three previously-existing organizations (National Legislative Conference, National Conference of State Legislative Leaders, National Society of State Legislators). The NCSL is the only nationwide organization representing all state legislators (7,600) and their staffs (approximately 10,000); it seeks to advance the effectiveness, independence and integrity of the state legislature as an equal coordinate branch of government. It also fosters interstate cooperation and represents states and their legislatures with Congress and federal agencies. NCSL is headquartered in Denver, Colo.

National Congress on Volunteerism and Citizenship (NCVC), one of many newer national organizations established to attempt to increase cooperation and collaboration among nonprofit organizations involved in public service activities.

National Consumer Cooperative Bank, bank that provides loans and technical assistance with special emphasis on providers of health care, housing, and consumer goods.

National Credit Union Administration, body that charters, supervises, and provides deposit insurance for credit unions.
See also CREDIT UNION.

National Employ the Handicapped Week, also called NETH WEEK, the first full week in October, which has been set aside by the U.S. Congress to emphasize the employment of the handicapped.

National Endowment for the Arts/Humanities: *see* NATIONAL FOUNDATION ON THE ARTS AND THE HUMANITIES.

National Foundation on the Arts and the Humanities, an independent federal agency created in 1965. The foundation consists of national endowments for the arts and humanities as well as a *Federal Council on the Arts and Humanities*.

The activities of the *National Endowment for the Arts* are designed to foster the growth and development of the arts in the U.S. The endowment awards grants to individuals, state and regional arts agencies, and nonprofit organizations representing the highest quality in the fields of architecture and environmental arts, crafts, dance, education, expansion arts, folk arts, literature, museums, music, media arts (film, radio, and television), theatre, and the visual arts.

The activities of the *National Endowment for the Humanities* are designed to promote and support the production and dissemination of knowledge in the humanities, especially as it relates to the serious study and discussion of contemporary values and public issues. The endowment makes grants to individuals, groups or institutions—schools, colleges, universities, museums, public television stations, libraries, public agencies, and private nonprofit groups—to increase understanding and appreciation of the humanities. It makes grants in support of research productive of humanistic knowledge of value to the scholarly and general public.

National Health Planning and Resources Development Act of 1974, the federal law that established Health Systems Agencies (HSAs) to conduct health system planning and resource development activities in state or substate geographic areas.

National Institute for Occupational Safety and Health (NIOSH), body established under the provisions of the Occupational Safety and Health Act of 1970. NIOSH is the federal agency responsible for formulating new or improved occupational safety and health standards. It is located in Atlanta.

Under the Occupational Safety and Health Act, NIOSH has the responsibility for conducting research designed to produce recommendations for new occupational safety and health standards. These recommendations are transmitted to the Department of Labor, which has the responsibility for the final setting, promulgation, and enforcement of the standards.

National Labor Relations Act of 1935 (NLRA), also called WAGNER-CONNERY ACT and WAGNER ACT, the nation's principal labor relations law applying to all interstate commerce except railroad and airline operations. The NLRA seeks to protect the rights of employees and employers, to encourage collective bargaining, and to eliminate certain practices on the part of labor and management that are harmful to the general welfare. It states and defines the rights of employees to organize and to bargain collectively with their employers through representatives of their own choosing. To ensure that employees can freely choose their own representatives for the purpose of collective bargaining, the act establishes a procedure by which they can exercise their choice at a secret ballot election conducted by the National Labor Relations Board. Further, to protect the rights of employees and employers and to prevent labor disputes that would adversely affect the rights of the public, Congress has defined certain practices of employers and unions as unfair labor practices. The NLRA is administered and enforced principally by the National Labor Relations Board, which was created by the act.

In common usage, the National Labor Relations Act refers not to the act of 1935, but to the act as amended by the Labor-Management Relations (Taft-Hartley) Act of 1947 and the Labor-Management Reporting and Disclosure (Landrum-Griffin) Act of 1959.

National Labor Relations Board (NLRB), federal agency that administers the nation's laws relating to labor relations in the private and nonprofit sectors. (There are some public sector organizations also under its jurisdiction, most notably the U.S. Postal Service.) The NLRB is vested with the power to safeguard employees' rights to organize, to determine through elections whether workers want unions as their bargaining representatives, and to prevent and remedy unfair labor practices.

The NLRB has two principal functions—preventing and remedying unfair labor practices by employers and labor organizations or their agents, and conducting secret ballot elections among employees in appropriate collective bargaining units to determine whether or not they desire to be represented by a labor organization. The NLRB also conducts secret ballot elections among employees who have been covered by a union shop agreement to determine whether or not they wish to revoke their union's authority to make such agreements; in jurisdictional disputes, the NLRB decides and determines which competing group of workers is entitled to perform the work involved; and it conducts secret ballot elections among employees concerning employers' final settlement offers in national emergency labor disputes.

***National Labor Relations Board* v. *Yeshiva University*,** 444 U.S. 672 (1980), U.S. Supreme Court case which held that university faculty members who are involved in the governance (management) of their institutions are excluded from the protections and rights offered nonmanagerial employees by the National Labor Relations Act.

National League of Cities (NLC), formerly AMERICAN MUNICIPAL ASSOCIATION, known until 1964 as the American Municipal Association, group founded in 1924 by and for reform-minded state municipal leagues. Membership in NLC was opened to individual cities in 1947, and NLC now has more than 1,100 direct member cities. The twenty-seven U.S. cities with populations greater than 500,000 are all NLC direct members, as are eighty-seven percent of all cities with more than 100,000 residents. NLC is an advocate for municipal interests before Congress, the executive branch, and the federal agencies and in state capitals across the nation where matters of importance to cities are decided. NLC is based in Washington, D.C.

National Municipal League, New York based membership organization that serves as a clearinghouse and lobby for urban concerns.

national origin discrimination, discrimination based on a person's place of birth. Title VII of the Civil Rights Act of 1964 prohibits disparate treatment, whether overt or covert, of any individual or group of individuals because of their national origin except when such treatment is necessary because of a bona fide occupational qualification; for example, it might be lawful to require native fluency in Spanish for a position as a translator. The Equal Employment Opportunity Commission (EEOC) gives as examples of national origin discrimination

> the use of tests in the English language where the individual tested came from circumstances where English was not that person's first language or mother tongue, and where English language skill is not a requirement of the work to be performed; denial of equal opportunity to persons married to or associated with persons of a specific national origin; denial of equal opportunity because of membership in lawful organizations identified with or seeking to promote the interests of national groups; denial of equal opportunity because of attendance at schools or churches commonly utilized by persons of a given national origin; denial of equal opportunity because their name or that of their spouse reflects a certain national origin, and denial of equal opportunity to persons who as a class of persons tend to fall outside national norms for height and weight where such height and weight specifications are not necessary for the performance of the work involved.

Some states have laws prohibiting the employment of noncitizens in varying circumstances. According to the EEOC, "where such laws have the purpose or effect of discriminating on the basis of national origin, they are in direct conflict with and are, therefore, superseded by Title VII of the Civil Rights Act of 1964, as amended."

national planning, the concept of centralized, government conducted or coordinated economic planning and development. The concept has been highly controversial because of its identification with socialistic and communistic approaches to government management of national economies. National planning was advocated by Frederick Winslow Taylor in the 1920s, but he was unsuccessful in gaining acceptance for it in the United States. In the 1980s, various forms, approaches, and government and industry roles in national planning have been suggested for revitalizing the U.S. industrial economy.

See also PLANNED ECONOMY.

National Planning Association (NPA), nonpartisan, nonprofit Washington, D.C., based organization whose goal is to encourage joint economic planning and cooperation by leaders from business, labor, agriculture, and the professions.

National Public Radio (NPR), the national network of public radio stations. NPR was incorporated in 1970 and started providing network programming to local stations in 1971. NPR accepts underwriting from foundations and companies.

National Rehabilitation Association (NRA), founded in 1925, a private, nonprofit organization of 18,000 people whose purpose is to advance the rehabilitation of all handicapped persons. It is based in Washington, D.C.

National Right to Work Committee, also NATIONAL RIGHT TO WORK LEGAL DEFENSE FOUNDATION, INC., the *National Right to Work Committee,* located in Springfield, Virginia, advocates legislation to prohibit all forms of forced union membership. The *National Right to Work Legal Defense Foundation, Inc.* seeks to establish legal precedents protecting workers against compulsory unionism.

National Safety Council, Chicago based nonprofit public service organization dedicated to reducing the number and severity of all kinds of accidents by gathering and distributing information about the causes of accidents and ways to prevent them.

National Technical Information Service (NTIS), body established in 1970 to simplify and improve public access to Department of Commerce publications and to data files and scientific and technical reports sponsored by federal agencies. It is the central point in the United States for the public sale of government-funded research and development reports and other analyses prepared by federal agencies, their contractors, or grantees.

National Training Laboratories Institute for Applied Behavioral Science (NTL), also called NTL INSTITUTE, organization founded as the National Training Laboratories in 1947 in Bethel, Maine, now located in Arlington, Va. The early years at Bethel were devoted to the development of human relations laboratories. It was during this period that NTL proved the effectiveness of the new concept of the T Group ("T" for training). NTL's concept of the T Group—in which individuals working in small groups develop new insights into self and others—is still an important element in NTL programs and has been widely imitated. During the 1950s and 1960s, major areas for experimentation and development were expanded to include group dynamics, organization development and community development. During the 1960s and early 1970s the development of individual potential in personal growth programs became an added thrust, as did innovation in working with large systems. In the late 1970s, NTL helped men and women recognize and develop their potential in response to the array of alternatives in lifestyles, careers, and patterns of interaction available to them. It works toward keeping change from becoming chaos by promoting flexibility and innovation and by providing help in planning for individuals, organizations, and large systems.

Today, NTL Institute is internationally recognized as a focal agency for experience-based learning programs. It is also known as the institution which has had most to do with developing the new profession of laboratory education, with exploring new means of relating, with new approaches to social change, and with new methods of managing organizations. Interest in laboratory education has grown rapidly, and NTL defines as one of its roles helping to maintain professional standards in a field now popularized and often misunderstood.

National Transportation Safety Board (NTSB), group that seeks to assure that all types of transportation in the United States are conducted safely. The board investigates accidents and makes recommendations to government agencies, the transportation industry, and others on safety measures and practices. The board also regulates the procedures for reporting accidents and promotes the safe transport of hazardous materials by government and private industry.

national union, union composed of a variety of widely dispersed affiliated local unions. The Bureau of Labor Statistics defines a national union as one with agreements with different employers in more than one state.

See also INTERNATIONAL UNION.

National Urban League, also called the URBAN LEAGUE, nonpartisan community service agency (115 local units) devoted to the economic and social concerns of blacks. The league is based in New York City.

National Voluntary Organizations Coalition NVO, in the U.S. formerly an organization which was a founding member of The Independent Sector; in Canada, an umbrella organization which encompasses a majority of the country's 50,000 registered charities, founded in 1974 and headquartered in Ottawa. Canada's NVO works to identify and build on the common interests of the Canadian voluntary sector and to promote consistent and supportive government policies for the sector.

native ability, actual ability. A test score is usually interpreted to mean that an individual's native ability lies somewhere in a range (plus or minus fifty points, for example) surrounding the score.

natural business year, a fiscal or program year that ends with the close of the month in which the organization's activities are at or near their lowest point.

NCCA: *see* NATIONAL CENTER FOR COMMUNITY ACTION.

NCCHS: *see* NATIONAL COMMUNICATIONS COUNCIL FOR HUMAN SERVICES.

NCVA: *see* NATIONAL CENTER FOR VOLUNTARY ACTION.

NCVC: *see* NATIONAL CONGRESS ON VOLUNTEERISM AND CITIZENSHIP.

need, the gap between an existing status and a desired status. When developing a program or writing a grant, the first step should be to define the need.
See also NEEDS ASSESSMENT.

needs assessment or NEEDS ANALYSIS, any of a variety of approaches that seek to establish the requirements of a particular situation in order to determine what, if any, program activity should be initiated; the first step in formulating the purposes for a new program or program activities. A needs assessment should be conducted prior to establishing program goals or objectives.
See also NEED.

needs hierarchy, a theoretical construct. In the July 1943 issue of *Psychological Review,* Abraham H. Maslow published his now classic, "A Theory of Human Motivation," in which he put forth his hierarchical conception of human needs. Maslow asserted that humans had five sets of goals or basic needs arranged in a hierarchy of prepotency: physiological needs, safety needs, love or affiliation needs, esteem needs, and the need for self-actualization—the desire "to become everything that one is capable of becoming." Once lower needs are satisfied, they cease to be motivators of behavior. Conversely, higher needs cannot motivate until lower needs are satisfied. It is commonly recognized that there are some inescapable incongruities in Maslow's needs hierarchy. Some lower needs in some people, such as security, love, and status, never seem to be satiated. However, this does not take away from the importance of the desire for higher level needs as a motivational force in others.

negative income tax, a proposed (but not yet implemented) welfare alternative which would use the federal income tax structure. Citizens with incomes below a specified level would receive cash payments (or pay negative income tax).

negatively skewed: *see* SKEWNESS.

negative pledge clause, a restriction (usually in a bond issue) that prohibits the issuing company from allowing any subsequent debt to take priority over the restricted debt.

negative reinforcement: *see* REINFORCEMENT.

negative strike: *see* POSITIVE STRIKE.

negative stroking: *see* STROKING.

negative transfer: *see* TRANSFER OF TRAINING.

negotiable instrument, a signed document that contains a promise to pay an exact sum of money; for example, a check.

Negotiable Order of Withdrawal (NOW) Account, an interest-earning, check-like bank account on which people can write orders of withdrawal that are treated as if they were checks. Technically they are not checking accounts, however, because the offering institution (for example, a bank) can impose a hold before honoring the orders.

negotiating committee, continuous: *see* CONTINUOUS NEGOTIATING COMMITTEE.

negotiation, process by which people and organizations bargain.

negotiation, career: *see* CAREER NEGOTIATION.

negotiations, collective: *see* COLLECTIVE BARGAINING.

neighborhood association, also NEIGHBORHOOD MOVEMENT, an organization of residents of an area. In many American cities, neighbors in a particular area have formally organized into associations. These associations often play important political roles, lobbying local government and protecting neighborhood interests at all levels of government. They often reflect a movement calling for a decentralization of local government. At the extreme are advocates for neighborhood self-sufficiency, seeing both economic and political power only possible for poorer neighborhoods to the extent they can become independent of the dominant urban government.

neighborhood community association, an association for improving business conditions in a general community. Neighborhood community associations are examples of associations which may qualify for tax-exempt status as chambers of commerce or boards of trade [under IRS Code 501 (c) (6)].

neighborhood reinvestment corporation, a public corporation that promotes reinvestment in older neighborhoods by local financial institutions working cooperatively with community people and local governments, largely relying on local initiative for specific program designs.

neoclassical organization theory: *see* ORGANIZATION THEORY.

nepotism, any practice by which officeholders award positions to members of their immediate family. It is derived from the Latin *nepós*, meaning nephew or grandson. The rulers of the medieval church were often thought to give special preference to their nephews in distributing churchly offices. At that time, "nephew" became a euphemism for their illegitimate sons.

nervous breakdown, catch-all expression for mental illness that does not refer to any particular disorder. Individuals in high pressure jobs who can no longer cope with the associated mental strains are frequently said to have had nervous breakdowns, but the actual clinical reason for their incapacity could be any of a large variety of mental and/or physical maladies.

See also STRESS.

net benefit, also NET BENEFIT ANALYSIS, a decision criterion which uses the same information and is used for the same basic purposes as a cost/benefit analysis. A net benefit is calculated by subtracting costs from benefits &a cost benefit analysis divides benefits by costs). If the result of the subtraction is positive, the program is considered to be economically beneficial.

See also COST/BENEFIT ANALYSIS.

net earnings, gross earnings less expenses. However, the courts have construed net earnings more restrictively relative to nonprofit organizations in order to prevent private inurement.

See also PRIVATE INUREMENT.

NETH Week: *see* NATIONAL EMPLOY THE HANDICAPPED WEEK.

net income, revenue and gains minus expenses and losses.

net lease, also NET NET LEASE, a lease in which the tenant pays rent plus all costs of ownership, such as taxes and maintenance. Sometimes a distinction is made between a *net lease* (rent plus some costs, such as heat) and a *net net lease* (rent plus all expenses, such as taxes).

See also GROSS LEASE.

net pay, take-home pay.

net realizable value, the net cash or equivalent that can be expected from the sale of an asset.

See also ASSETS.

net social benefit, the social benefits minus the social costs of a proposed program or project.

network, pattern of interrelated and interconnected individuals, groups, and/or organizations that form a system of communication. At present more is known about the structure of networks than is known about the dynamics of network interaction. Large networks are known to show great complexity and structural variation, with actors performing specialized functions as gatekeepers or linking pins.

neutral, any third party who is actively engaged in negotiations in order to facilitate an agreement.

neutral competence, concept that envisions a continuous, politically uncommitted cadre of bureaucrats at the disposal of elected or appointed executives.

new girls' network: *see* OLD BOYS' NETWORK.

new hire, individual who has just joined an organization as an employee.
See also PROBATIONARY EMPLOYEE.

new industrial state, John Kenneth Galbraith's concept (from his 1967 book of the same name) which holds that modern organizations have become so complex that traditional leaders are no longer able to "make" major decisions; they can only ratify the decisions made for them by a technostructure of specialists who may be more interested in maintaining themselves than generating profits.

newsletter: *see* HOUSE ORGAN.

news media: *see* MEDIA.

news release: *see* PRESS RELEASE.

NGT: *see* NOMINAL GROUP TECHNIQUE.

night premium, also called NIGHT DIFFERENTIAL, addition to regular wage rates that is paid to employees who work on shifts other than the regular day shift.

ninety day letter, a notice from the IRS claiming that taxes are owed. During the ninety days after receiving the notice, a person or organization must either pay the taxes (and claim a refund) or challenge the IRS's decision in a tax court.

NIOSH: *see* NATIONAL INSTITUTE FOR OCCUPATIONAL SAFETY AND HEALTH.

NLRA: *see* NATIONAL LABOR RELATIONS ACT OF 1935.

NLRB: *see* NATIONAL LABOR RELATIONS BOARD.

NOI: *see* NOTIFICATION OF INTENT.

no-load fund: *see* MUTUAL FUND.

nominal, in name only; not real or substantial.

Nominal Group Technique (NGT), also NOMINAL GROUP, a group process or technique for generating ideas and achieving group consensus. NGT attempts to maximize creativity of the participants and to balance participation by group members (minimize the chances that a group will be dominated by a few people). NGT is often used in the needs assessment and problem formulation stages of a project to identify problems and assess the causes and consequences of problems. NGT also is useful for establishing goals and prioritizing needs, goals, and programs.

The basic steps involved in the Nominal Group Technique are:

1. silent listing of ideas on paper;
2. round-robin listing of ideas in a group;
3. group discussion of ideas; and
4. silent voting or prioritizing.

See also:
BACKSTEP ANALYSIS
GOAL
NEED
NEEDS ASSESSMENT
PRIORITIZING

nominating committee, a standing committee which prepares an annual slate of candidates for a nonprofit organization's elected positions. Most nominating committees are responsible for identifying candidates, screening, obtaining assurances of willingness from potential nominees, and formally nominating officers for the board of directors, new members for the board of directors, chairpersons for selected committees, and, in many organizations, successor members of the nominating committee.

See also COMMITTEE.

nominee trust, an arrangement in which one person agrees to hold land, stock, etc. for the benefit of another undisclosed person.

noncallable bonds: *see* CALLABLE BONDS.

noncontributory pension plan, pension program that has the employer paying the entire cost.

noncumulative preferred stock: *see* CUMULATIVE PREFERRED STOCK.

non-cyclic accounting: *see* ACCOUNTING, NON-CYCLIC.

nondirective interview: *see* DIRECTED INTERVIEW.

nondistribution constraint: *see* PRIVATE INUREMENT.

nonguaranteed debt: *see* DEBT, NON-GUARANTEED.

nonparametric statistics, statistics for variables that do not have a normal (or other known, regular) distribution.

nonproduction bonus, also called CHRISTMAS BONUS and YEAR-END BONUS, payments to workers that are, in effect, gratuities upon which employees cannot regularly depend.

Nonprofit Executive, The, a monthly publication of the Taft Corporation designed to bring timely and useful information to high-level management and fund-raising personnel working within all areas of nonprofit enterprise.

nonprofit organization, also NONPROFIT ASSOCIATION and NONPROFIT CORPORATION, a broad term—in many respects a concept rather than a specific entity—which can be defined in many different ways. The primary essence of a nonprofit organization, however, is that it is organized and operated for public or societal purposes (such as alleviation of poverty) rather than private benefit purposes (such as return on shareholders' investments). A second essential element of a nonprofit organization is its reliance on voluntary action for most of its financial and human resources. From a relatively narrow, legalistic point of view, one could argue that a nonprofit organization is, in effect, an organization prescribed by the laws, rules, and codes of tax exemption.

Despite common misconceptions to the contrary—and within well-defined limitations—nonprofit organizations can realize profits from their activities and programs, and they can engage in commercial-type enterprises. However, such profits must be returned to the operations of the agency.

From a tax exemption viewpoint, there are two basic types of nonprofit organizations: (1) publicly supported charitable organizations which engage directly in religious, educational, social welfare, etc. programs and activities; and (2) private foundations, which tend to support other tax-exempt organizations' programs.

Nonprofit organizations range in size and structure from large international religious denominations and seminational hospital chains to small, local, nonincorporated associations of people with common interests, goals, or concerns.

See also:

ARTICLES OF ASSOCIATION
ARTICLES OF ORGANIZATION
ASSOCIATION
CHARITABLE GRANTS ECONOMY CONCEPT
CHARITABLE ORGANIZATION
CORPORATION
FREEDOM OF CHOICE
INTERNAL REVENUE SERVICE CODES
OPERATED
ORGANIZED
PRIVATE FOUNDATION
PRIVATE INUREMENT

PRIVATE OPERATING FOUNDATION
PUBLIC BENEFIT
PUBLICLY SUPPORTED ORGANIZATION
THIRD SECTOR

**Private Not-For-Profit Organizations:
Estimates of Current Operating Expenditures 1960-1982**

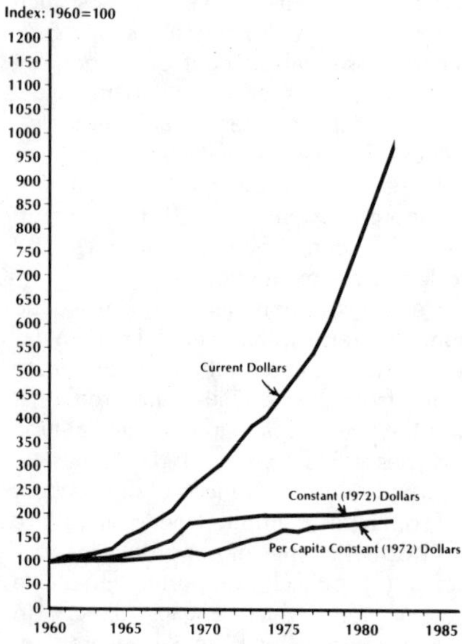

Source: Hodgkinson, V. A. and M. S. Weitzman, Dimensions of the Independent Sector: A Statistical Profile *(Washington, D.C.: INDEPENDENT SECTOR, 1984), p. 15.*

nonprofit sector: *see* THIRD SECTOR and INDEPENDENT SECTOR.

Nonprofit World Report, a bimonthly journal published by the Society for Nonprofit Organizations. The journal typically carries articles on general aspects of nonprofit organization management, project management, applied technology, and marketing research.

nonrecourse loan, a loan in which the lender cannot take more than the property borrowed on as repayment for the loan. Occasionally mortgages are nonrecourse, but not normally.

nonsupplant provision, provision in grant agreements that does not clearly specify an actual level of spending to be maintained (as in a maintenance of effort provision) but merely stipulates that recipients shall maintain spending from their own resources at the level that would have existed in the absence of aid.

nonverbal communication, any means of projecting opinion, attitudes, and desires through the use of body postures, movements, expressions, gestures, eye contact, use of space and time, or other means of expressing such ideas short of written and/or verbal communications.

norm, standard or criteria against which an individual's test score or performance can be compared and evaluated.
See also NORMS.

normal distribution, frequency distribution that follows the pattern of the normal "bell shaped" curve, characterized by symmetry about the mean and a standard relationship between width and height of the curve.

normally, concept of, tax concept. An organization may continue to qualify as a tax-exempt, publicly supported organization even if it fails to satisfy all applicable IRS criteria in a given year if it can demonstrate that "normally" in the past it has done so.

normative, description of judgments, findings, opinions, and conclusions that are based upon morally established norms of right and wrong.

normative standard, standard of performance obtained by examining the relative performance of a group or sample of candidates.

norm-referenced test, any test that describes a candidate's performance in terms of its relation to the performance of other candidates.

norms, also PIVOTAL NORMS and

PERIPHERAL NORMS, socially enforced requirements and expectations about basic responsibilities, behavior, and thought patterns of members in their organizational roles. Edgar H. Schein distinguishes between two types of organizational norms based on their centrality to the organization's values: *a pivotal norm* is one to which adherence is a requirement of continued membership in an organization. *A peripheral norm* is one which is considered desirable, but adherence to it is not essential for continued membership. *See* Schein's "Organizational Socialization and the Profession of Management," *Sloan Management Review,* Vol. 9, No. 2., Winter 1968.

See also ROLE and VALUE.

norms (psychological testing), tables of scores from a large number of people who have taken a particular test.

no ruling letter, a letter from the Internal Revenue Service informing an organization which applied for tax-exempt status that its application was incomplete, needs to be revised, and, therefore, that the IRS has not issued a determination ruling.

no-solicitation rule, employer's rule that prohibits solicitation of employees for any purpose during working hours.

notary public, semipublic official who can administer oaths, certify the validity of documents, and perform a variety of formal witnessing duties.

See also ATTEST.

note, a written promise to pay a certain sum of money.

not-for-profit organization, a tax-exempt nonprofit organization. Although some states' tax laws use the "not-for-profit" terminology, in common usage it tends to be used interchangeably with "nonprofit organization."

See also NONPROFIT ORGANIZATION.

nothing job, a job that offers nothing (no satisfaction, prestige, etc.) to an employee except wages; or an easy task that can be quickly done.

notice of meeting, a written notification stating the date, time, location, and purpose of a forthcoming meeting. Most nonprofit organizations' bylaws specify the required lead time and contents for notices of different kinds of meetings (membership meetings, board of directors meetings, etc.).

See also BYLAWS.

notification of intent (NOI), usually, a written notification to a granting agency or an area clearinghouse of an organization's intention to submit a grant. NOIs typically include a brief statement of the proposed project's purpose, rationale, approach, and approximate budget.

See also:

CLEARINGHOUSE
GRANT
GRANT PROPOSAL

NOW Account: *see* NEGOTIABLE ORDER OF WITHDRAWAL (NOW) ACCOUNT.

NPA: *see* NATIONAL PLANNING ASSOCIATION.

NPO: *see* NONPROFIT ORGANIZATION.

NPR: *see* NATIONAL PUBLIC RADIO.

NTIS: *see* NATIONAL TECHNICAL INFORMATION SERVICE.

NTL: *see* NATIONAL TRAINING LABORATORIES INSTITUTE FOR APPLIED BEHAVIORAL SCIENCE.

NTSB: *see* NATIONAL TRANSPORTATION SAFETY BOARD.

null hypothesis, hypothesis used in statistics that asserts there is no difference between two populations that cannot be explained by chance.

NVO: *see* NATIONAL VOLUNTARY ORGANIZATIONS.

O

OASDI: *see* OLD AGE, SURVIVORS, AND DISABILITY INSURANCE.

objective, a statement of a specific intended accomplishment or result; a commitment to attempt to achieve. There are three types of objectives: administrative, process, and outcome.

An objective should specify three things: the desired performance or behavior, the criteria or standards of quality and/or quantity, and the conditions under which successful performance will be demonstrated. Objectives should be attainable within a specified time frame and measurable or observable.

Abstract or *intangible objectives* are the qualities one seeks to attain in people and the environment that examplify the application of the highest management principles. They are the broad, general goals cited by management as theoretical considerations, ideals, or qualities to be attained. These abstractions or ideals are found in such objectives as: improve employee morale, increase individual employee productivity, be cost-conscious, provide better on-the-job training, etc.

Concrete or *tangible objectives* are the translation of broad, strategic goals into the specific, realistic goals containing identifiable and/or measurable performance from the application of resources.

See also:

EVALUATION
FUNCTIONAL ANALYSIS SYSTEM TECHNIQUE
MANAGEMENT BY OBJECTIVES
MEASURE
OBJECTIVE, ADMINISTRATIVE
OBJECTIVE, OUTCOME
OBJECTIVE, PROCESS

objective, administrative, also INPUT OBJECTIVE and STRUCTURAL OBJECTIVE, a type of objective which is concerned with inputs of resources. For example:

> To hire three social workers for X program by July 1.

The example objective does not state what the social workers will accomplish; therefore, it is a statement of resource gathering (and, therefore, future resource consumption) rather than a statement of outputs or outcomes.

Administrative objectives are useful during the early start-up months of a project or organization, while things are "getting organized." However, once a project or organization is moving, the accomplishment of administrative objectives leaves one with the feeling of "so what?"

See also:

EVALUATION
FUNCTIONAL ANALYSIS SYSTEM TECHNIQUE
HIERARCHY OF OBJECTIVES
MANAGEMENT BY OBJECTIVES
MEASURE
OBJECTIVE, OUTCOME
OBJECTIVE, PROCESS

objective, outcome, also PRODUCT OBJECTIVE and IMPACT OBJECTIVE, a type of objective which is concerned with desired changes in the status of a program or an organization's clientele after the program or organization has delivered its services. For example:

> At least sixty percent of the sheltered workshop employees who move to regular industry worksites during 1986 will retain employment with their employer for at least two years.

> All students who complete the CPR (cardiopulmonary resuscitation) segment of the Emergency Medical Technician course will demonstrate correct procedures on a recording Resci-Annie.

Note that the service-providing organization does not have control over the accomplishment of the objective. The organization does—and should—influence accomplishment through its service delivery, but success is dependent upon subsequent behaviors of people who have been served.

See also:
EVALUATION
FUNCTIONAL ANALYSIS SYSTEM TECHNIQUE
HIERARCHY OF OBJECTIVES
MANAGEMENT BY OBJECTIVES
MEASURE
OBJECTIVE
OBJECTIVE, ADMINISTRATIVE
OBJECTIVE, PROCESS
OUTCOME

objective, process, also PERFORMANCE OBJECTIVE, a type of objective which is concerned with the results of work processes. For example,

To contract with private businesses for at least thirty supported worksites for our sheltered workshop employees during 1986.

Process objectives are commonly written erroneously as task statements instead of as result statements. For example,

To talk with at least fifty private businesses about contracting worksites for our sheltered workshop employees.

This is a task statement rather than a process objective, because there is no result—just activity.

See also:
EVALUATION
FUNCTIONAL ANALYSIS SYSTEM TECHNIQUE
HIERARCHY OF OBJECTIVES
MEASURE
OBJECTIVE
OBJECTIVE, ADMINISTRATIVE
OBJECTIVE, OUTCOME

objective test, any examining device whose scoring is not dependent upon the discretion of the examiners.

objectivity, quality that seeks to remove personal opinion by reducing the impact of individual judgment; the opposite of subjectivity.

obligations, orders placed, contracts awarded, services rendered, or other commitments made during a given period which will require outlay during the same or some future period.

obligatory arbitration, arbitration requested by one party in a situation where the other party is obligated (for example, by a contract provision) to accept it.

obsolescence, the loss in value of an asset due to new inventions, changes in styles, and other causes, not including the wear and tear of ordinary usage.

See also OCCUPATIONAL OBSOLESCENCE.

occupation, relatively continuous pattern of activity that (1) provides a livelihood for an individual and (2) serves to define an individual's general social status.

occupational certification, also called CERTIFICATION, practice that permits practitioners in a particular occupation to claim minimum levels of competence. While certification enables some practitioners to claim a competency which others cannot, this type of regulation does not prevent uncertified people from supplying the same services as certified people.

See also OCCUPATIONAL LICENSING.

occupational disease: *see* OCCUPATIONAL ILLNESS.

occupational grouping, grouping of classes within the same broad occupational category, such as nursing, accounting, etc.

occupational hazard, any danger directly associated with one's work.

occupational health, all the activities related to protecting and maintaining the health and safety of employees.

occupational illness, also called OCCUPATIONAL DISEASE, any abnormal condition or disorder, other than one resulting from an occupational injury, caused by exposure to environmental factors associated with employment. It includes acute and chronic illnesses or diseases which may be caused by inhalation, absorption, ingestion, or direct contact.

occupational injury, any injury (such as a cut, fracture, sprain, amputation, etc.) that results from a work accident or from exposure involving a single incident in the work environment.

occupational licensing, also called LICENSING, the requirement that all nonlicensed persons be excluded from practicing a particular licensed profession.
See also CERTIFICATION.

occupational mobility, also HORIZONTAL and VERTICAL OCCUPATIONAL MOBILITY, the movement of individuals from one occupation to another. A change from one occupation to another of similar occupational status is an example of *horizontal occupational mobility*. A change of occupational status levels within the same occupation is an example of *vertical occupational mobility*.

occupational obsolescence, concept usually associated with professional employees who lack currency with their discipline. For example, an engineer who has served as an administrator for a significant number of years may, in consequence, be unable to function in his/her engineering specialty because the "state of the art" has moved too far.

Occupational Outlook Handbook, the Bureau of Labor Statistics' biennial survey of employment trends that contains descriptive information and employment prospects for hundreds of occupational categories.

Occupational Outlook Quarterly, the U.S. Bureau of Labor Statistics's magazine designed to help high school students and guidance counselors assess career opportunities.

occupational parity: *see* PARITY.

occupational prestige, also called OCCUPATIONAL STATUS, ascribed status associated with an individual's employment. Opinion surveys typically find physicians, college professors, psychologists, bankers, and architects at the top of a hierarchy of occupational prestige, while unskilled farm workers and garbage collectors compete for the lowest rankings.

occupational psychiatry, also called INDUSTRIAL PSYCHIATRY, any of the professional activities of psychiatry conducted at the workplace of the clients.

occupational psychology: *see* INDUSTRIAL PSYCHOLOGY.

Occupational Safety and Health Act of 1970, also called WILLIAMS-STEIGER ACT, federal government's basic legislation for providing for the health and safety of employees on the job. The act created the Occupational Safety and Health Review Commission, the Occupational and Health Administration, and the National Institute for Occupational Safety and Health.
See also WORKMEN'S COMPENSATION.

Occupational Safety and Health Administration (OSHA), body established by the Occupational Safety and Health Act of 1970. OSHA develops and promulgates occupational safety and health standards, develops and issues regulations, conducts investigations and inspections to determine the status of compliance with safety and health standards and regulations, and issues citations and proposes penalties for noncompliance with safety and health standards and regulations.

Occupational Safety & Health Reporter, weekly notification and reference service published by the Bureau of National Affairs, Inc. that covers significant legislative, administrative, judicial, and industrial developments under the Occupational Safety and Health Act. Includes information on standards, legislation, regulations, enforcement, research, advisory committee recommendations, union activities, and state programs.
See also BUREAU OF NATIONAL AFFAIRS, INC.

Occupational Safety and Health Review Commission (OSHRC), independent adjudicatory agency established by the Occupational Safety and Health Act of 1970 to adjudicate enforcement actions initiated under the act when they are contested by employers, employees, or representatives of employees.

The Occupational Safety and Health Act covers virtually every employer in the country. It requires employers to furnish their employees with employment and a place of employment free from recognized hazards that are causing or are likely to cause death or serious physical harm to employees and to comply with occupational safety and health standards promulgated under the act.

The Secretary of Labor has promulgated a substantial number of occupational safety and health standards which, pursuant to the act, have the force and effect of law. He has also initiated a regular program of inspections in order to check on compliance. A case for adjudication by OSHRC arises when a citation is issued against an employer as the result of such an inspection and it is contested within fifteen working days thereafter.

occupational socialization, process by which an individual absorbs and adopts the values, norms, and behavior of the occupational role models with whom he/she interacts. Occupational socialization is complete when an individual internalizes the values and norms of the occupational group.

occupational sociology, also called INDUSTRIAL SOCIOLOGY and SOCIOLOGY OF WORK, subspecialty of sociology concerned with examining the social structures and institutions which a society develops to facilitate its work.

occupational status: *see* OCCUPATIONAL PRESTIGE.

occupational survey, an organization's study of all positions in a given class, series of classes, or occupational group in whatever departments or divisions they may be located.

occupational therapy, health profession providing services to people whose lives have been disrupted by physical injury or illness, developmental problems, the aging process, and social or psychological difficulties.

occupation-related nonprofit organization, a nonprofit organization organized and operated to promote the well-being of people engaged in a particular occupation or trade; for example, nonprofit organizations of paramedics, government employees, college professors, nurses, retail merchants, etc.

OD: *see* ORGANIZATION DEVELOPMENT.

OFCCP: *see* OFFICE OF FEDERAL CONTRACT COMPLIANCE PROGRAMS.

offer, a proposal to make a transaction.

office: *see* OPEN OFFICE

office audit: *see* AUDIT.

office automation, a loose term for any significant use of machines in offices. In the 1960s it referred to any use of computers to process paperwork. Today it refers to word processing and other information retrieval equipment, but it has also taken on a larger connotation—the "office of the future," in which electronic office devices are linked by telecommunications to other offices throughout an organization, a region, or the world.

Office of Federal Contract Compliance Programs (OFCCP), agency within the Department of Labor delegated the responsibility for ensuring that there is no employment discrimination by government contractors because of race, religion, color, sex, or national origin, and to ensure affirmative action efforts in employing Vietnam Era veterans and handicapped workers.

Office of Federal Management Policy (OFMP), the office of the federal government which issues Federal Management Circulars (FMC's).

See also FEDERAL MANAGEMENT CIRCULARS.

Office of Management and Budget (OMB) Circular A-95, a regulation designed to promote maximum coordination of federal programs and projects with state, areawide, and local plans and programs by providing an opportunity to governors, mayors, county elected officials, and other state and local officials, through clearinghouses, to influence federal decisions on proposed projects that may affect their own plans and programs.

The circular sets forth procedures under which applicants for federal grants and other forms of assistance must give state and local governments, through state and areawide clearinghouses, an opportunity to assess the relationship of their proposals to state, areawide, and local plans and programs for the development of their area. Federal agencies are required to consider these assessments in deciding whether or not to proceed with a proposed project. However, clearinghouse recommendations on federal or federally assisted development proposals are advisory only.

Office of Management and Budget Circulars (OMB Circulars), a series of regulations issued by the Office of Management and Budget covering a wide range of requirements, procedures, etc., including requirements for recipients of federal grants and contracts.

See also FEDERAL MANAGEMENT CIRCULARS and OFFICE OF MANAGEMENT AND BUDGET (OMB) CIRCULAR A-95.

Office of Technology Assessment (OTA), also TECHNOLOGY ASSESSMENT ACT OF 1972, office created by the Technology Assessment Act of 1972 to help the Congress anticipate and plan for the consequences of uses of technology. The OTA provides an independent and objective source of information about the impacts, both beneficial and adverse, of technological applications and identifies policy alternatives for technology-related issues.

officer, a person elected (or, in some circumstances, appointed) to a position of responsibility and authority in an organization. Typical officers in a nonprofit organization include a president, one or more vice-presidents, a secretary, and a treasurer (or a single secretary/treasurer). Many organizations have other officers, including, for example, a past-president, a president-elect, a parliamentarian, etc. An organization's articles of organization specify its officers, method of selection, and term of office. An organization's bylaws provide more explicit information about the officers' responsibilities, authorities, duties, etc.

See also ARTICLES OF ORGANIZATION and BYLAWS.

office title, job title that differs from the classified title assigned to a job and is used to describe a particular position for other than payroll, budget, or official purposes. For example, a Head Clerk position might have an "office" title of Office Supervisor.

off-line, computer system whose operations are not under the control of a central processing unit, or a computer system that does not process information as it is received, but stores and processes it at a later time.

offset account, an accounting procedure used to balance one set of figures against another to make the books come out even.

offshore fund, a mutual fund outside of the United States; an investment made outside of the United States to avoid taxes, SEC regulations, etc.

See also MUTUAL FUND.

off-the-books, description of wages or other payments for which no records are kept.

Old Age, Survivors, and Disability Insurance (OASDI), federal program created by the Social Security Act which taxes both workers and employers to pay benefits to retired and disabled people, their dependents, widows, widowers, and children of deceased workers.

See also SOCIAL SECURITY.

old boys' network, also NEW GIRLS' NETWORK, colloquial way of referring to the fact that men who went to school together or belong to the same clubs tend to help each other as the occasion arises. Many a career was advanced because a college roommate was in a critical position twenty years later. In an effort to develop similar ties for similar advantages, some women have been purposely trying to create a "new girls' network" by sponsoring appropriate social events. As Sarah Weddington, President Carter's "women's advisor," told one such group, "where you are tomorrow may well depend upon whom you meet tonight."

Older Americans Act of 1965, federal statute that as amended attempts to provide a national policy for assisting older Americans in securing equal opportunity and an enhanced quality of life. The act provides assistance to states for new and improved programs, planning, training, and research.

old money, substantial wealth that was accumulated by earlier generations.

oligarchy: *see* IRON LAW OF OLIGARCHY.

OMB Circular A-95: *see* OFFICE OF MANAGEMENT AND BUDGET CIRCULAR A-95.

ombudsman, also ORGANIZATION OMBUDSMAN, official whose job is to investigate the complaints of an organization's clients and staff.

An *organization ombudsman* is a high-level staff officer who receives complaints and grievances about his organization directly from the employees. Such an officer mainly serves as an open channel of communication between employees and top management.

on-line, computer system whose operations are under the control of a central processing unit or a computer system in which information is processed as received.

See also OFF-LINE.

on-the-job training, any training that takes place during regular working hours and for which normal wages are paid.

open account, a charge account in which purchases and loans can be made without going through separate credit arrangements each time. This is often done on credit cards and with revolving charges, where a person pays a part of the amount owed on several different purchases each month.

See also OPEN-END MORTGAGE.

open-book test, test that allows candidates to consult textbooks or other relevant material while the examination is in progress.

open-end agreement, bargaining agreement providing for a contract that will remain in effect until one of the parties wants to reopen negotiations.

open-end company, a mutual fund.

See also MUTUAL FUND.

open-end lease, a lease that may involve a balloon payment based upon the value of the item leased when it is returned to the lessor.

See also:

BALLOON LOAN
LEASE
LESSOR

open-end mortgage, a mortgage agreement in which amounts of money may be borrowed from time to time on the same agreement.

open-end program, entitlement program for which eligibility requirements are determined by law (*e.g.*, Medicaid). Actual obligations and resultant outlays are limited only by the number of eligible persons who apply for benefits and the actual benefits received.

See also CLOSED-END PROGRAM.

open-end reimbursement grant: *see* GRANT.

open enrollment, a period when new subscribers may elect to enroll in a health insurance plan or prepaid group practice. Open enrollment periods may be used in the sale of either group or individual insurance and be the only period of a year when insurance is available.

open mortgage, a mortgage that can be paid off without a penalty at any time before maturity (the time it ends).

See also CLOSED-END MORTGAGE and OPEN-END MORTGAGE.

open office, completely open room without walls, doors, or dividers; room with partitions and potted plants where walls once were; room with partitioned cubicles that curve and connect; and/or an office laid out according to how information flows from one person to the next.

open shop, any work organization that is not unionized. The term also applies to organizations that have unions but do not have union membership as a condition of employment. Historically, an "open shop" was one that tended to discriminate against unions.

open system, any organism or organization that interacts with its environment.

operated, as used most frequently relative to nonprofit organizations, "functioning for the purpose(s) of," in contrast with "organized" or "established for the purpose(s) of."

See also OPERATIONAL TEST and ORGANIZATIONAL TEST.

operating budget: *see* BUDGET, OPERATING.

operating expense, also OPERATING COST, an expense (or cost) incurred in conducting the ordinary activities of an organization, including running its programs, raising funds, and administering the organization.

operating foundation: *see* PRIVATE OPERATING FOUNDATION.

operating profit, a profit realized from the ongoing operations of an organization.

See also PROFIT.

operating ratio, operating expenses divided by income from operations.

operating report: *see* OPERATING STATEMENT.

operating statement, also ACTIVITY STATEMENT, a financial statement showing a nonprofit organization's revenues and expenses and—preferably for each—budgeted and actual figures and the discrepancy or variance between them in dollars and/or percentages.

See also FINANCIAL STATEMENTS.

operating system, a computer's internal programs that allow it to respond to the user's commands and to run "application programs."

operational data, a form of secondary evaluation data which are collected and maintained by an organization as an integral part of its ongoing need for information (such as hospital patient records). Because operational data are used by an organization for operational purposes, they tend to be more reliable and valid than nonoperational data. Unfortunately, however, operational date are often maintained in a form that does not lend itself to evaluation. Also, they tend to be voluminous.

See also:

PRIMARY DATA
SECONDARY DATA
SOURCES OF DATA

operational planning, decision making that implements the larger goals and strategies of an organization.

See also PLANNING and STRATEGIC PLANNING.

operational test (for exemption as a charitable organization), test that as-

EXAMPLE OF AN OPERATING STATEMENT

ACE AMBULANCE SERVICE—OPERATING STATEMENT

Revenue	
Income—Ambulance Services	$
Income—Other Equipment Use	
Income—Supplies	
Income—Professional Services	
Total	$
Direct Expenses	
Salaries—Ambulance Attendants	$
Salaries—Other	
Supply Expense	
Oxygen Expense	
Ambulance Operating Expenses—Gas & Oil	
Ambulance Operating Expenses—Repairs	
Ambulance Operating Expenses—Tires	
Depreciation Expense—Ambulance	
Depreciation Expense—Ambulance Equipment	
Communication Expenses	
Communication Equipment—Depreciation	
Communication Equipment—Repair & Maintenance	
General Expenses	
Salaries—Administrative	$
Bad Debts	
Depreciation—Office Equipment	
Administrative Travel	
Interest Expense	
Insurance	
Legal and Accounting Services	
Miscellaneous	
Repair and Maintenance—Office	
Rent—Office	
Stationery, Postage, and Office Supplies	
Telephone	
Employee Benefits	
Total Expenses	$
Excess (deficit) of Revenues Less Expenses	$

sesses whether an organization is operated "primarily" for exempt purposes. In order for an organization to be tax-exempt as a charitable organization, it must meet both an organizational and an operational test. If more than an insubstantial portion of its activities do not advance an exempt purpose, the organization will not pass the operational test. In general, for an organization to satisfy the operational test, it must be engaged in activities which advance public purposes.

See also:

EXCLUSIVELY

ORGANIZATIONAL TEST

operational validity, procedures used to assure maximum prediction within the limits of a test. The three basic elements in operational validity are test administration, interpretation, and application.

operations research, a group of mathematical methods for the efficient allocation of scarce resources such as capital, labor, and materials.

See also MANAGEMENT SCIENCE.

opinion poll: *see* PUBLIC OPINION POLL.

opportunity cost, also called ALTERNA-

TIVE COST, true cost of choosing one alternative rather than another; represents the implicit cost of the highest forgone alternative.

optimization, any attempt to maximize or minimize a specific quantity, usually called an "objective." Also, a determination of the best mix of inputs to achieve an objective.

option, a contract in which one person pays money for the right to buy something from, or sell something to, another person at a certain price and within a certain time period.

optional bond: *see* CALLABLE BOND.

optional dividend, a dividend payable in either cash or stock, as the stockholder prefers. The stockholder is usually given a certain number of days to choose.

oral board, committee formed for the purpose of interviewing candidates for employment, promotion, or evaluation.

oral contract, also ORAL AGREEMENT, an agreement or contract that is not written.

oral test, any test that has an examiner ask a set of oral questions, as opposed to a paper-and-pencil test.

order, a directive.

ordinance, a local (for example; city or county) law, rule, or regulation.

ordinary income, income from business profits, wages, interest, dividends, etc., as opposed to income from capital gains.

organic system, that organization form that has proved to be most appropriate under changing conditions. It is characterized by: (1) constant reassessment of tasks, assignments, and the use of organizational expertise; (2) authority, control, and communication that are frequently *ad hoc* depending upon specific commitments and tasks; (3) communications and interactions among members that are both very open and extensive; (4) leadership stressing consultation and group decisional processes; and (5) greater commitment to the organization's tasks and goals than to traditional hierarchical loyalty.

See also MECHANISTIC SYSTEM.

organization, any structure and process of allocating jobs so that common objectives may be achieved.

organization, action: *see* ACTION ORGANIZATION.

organization, agricultural: *see* AGRICULTURAL ORGANIZATION.

organization, benevolent or mutual: *see* BENEVOLENT ORGANIZATION.

organization, charitable: *see* CHARITABLE ORGANIZATION.

organization, cooperative educational service: *see* COOPERATIVE EDUCATIONAL SERVICE ORGANIZATION.

organization, cooperative hospital service: *see* COOPERATIVE HOSPITAL SERVICE ORGANIZATION.

organization, date of: *see* DATE OF ORGANIZATION.

organization, flat/tall: *see* FLAT ORGANIZATION.

organization, formal/informal: *see* INFORMAL ORGANIZATION.

organization, horticultural: *see* HORTICULTURAL ORGANIZATION.

organization, labor: *see* LABOR ORGANIZATION.

organization, prevention of cruelty, a category of organization which may qualify for tax exemption under IRS code 501(c)(3). Prevention of cruelty organizations are usually concerned with protecting animals and children.

organization, professional: *see* PROFESSIONAL ORGANIZATION.

organization, publicly supported: *see* PUBLICLY SUPPORTED ORGANIZATION.

organization, public safety, also PUBLIC SAFETY TESTING: *see* PUBLIC SAFETY TESTING ORGANIZATION.

organization, religious: *see* RELIGIOUS ORGANIZATION.

organization, scientific: *see* SCIENTIFIC ORGANIZATION.

organization, social welfare: *see* SOCIAL WELFARE ORGANIZATION.

organizational behavior, academic discipline consisting of those aspects of the behavioral sciences that focus on the understanding of human behavior in organizations.

organizational climate: *see* ORGANIZATIONAL CULTURE.

organizational conflict: *see* CONFLICT RESOLUTION.

organizational culture, the pattern of fundamental beliefs and attitudes which powerfully affects members' behaviors in and around the organization, persists over extended periods of time, and pervades the organization (to different extents and with varying intensity). The organizational culture is transmitted to new members through socialization (or enculturation) processes; is maintained and transmitted through a network of rituals, rites, myths, communication, and interaction patterns; is enforced and reinforced by group norms and the organization's system of rewards and controls. Organizational cultures vary in intensity, contents, and compatibility with the primary pattern of attitudes.

Sources of organizational culture include the attitudes and behaviors of dominant, early organization "shapers" and "heroes"; the organization's nature of work (or business), including its functions and interactions with the external environment; attitudes, values, and willingness to act of new members. The organizational culture serves useful purposes, including, for example: (1) providing a framework for shared understanding of events, (2) defining behavioral expectations, (3) providing a source of and focus for members' commitment, and (4) functioning as an organizational control system (*i.e.*, through group norms). According to Stanley M. Davis, in *Managing Corporate Culture* (Cambridge, Mass.: Ballinger, 1984), "The culture of an organization is the point of contact at which philosophy comes to bear on the problems of organizations. . . .the culture is the meeting place of ethics with organization."

Although the concept of organizational culture has similarities to that of organizational climate, the latter typically is limited in use to the "feeling tone" or the "psychological climate." In contrast, organizational culture is typically used more as it is in the traditional anthropological sense.

organizational entropy, a basic tendency for organizations to disintegrate slowly which is in accord with the second law of thermodynamics. The term's origin is generally credited to organization theorist Chris Argyris.

organizational humanism, movement to create more humane work environments.

organizational iceberg, concept that the formal or overt aspects of an organization are just the proverbial tip of the iceberg. The greater part of the organization—the feelings, attitudes, and values of its members, for example—remain covert or hidden from obvious view. In short, the formal organization is visible, while the informal is hidden and waiting to sink any ship that ignores it.

organizational identification, the process through which the goals of the individual and the organization become congruent.

organizational mirror, a term coined by

Jack K. Fordyce and Raymond Weil, in *Managing with People* (1971), for a type of meeting used to collect feedback about an organizational unit from the key organizations to which it relates.

organizational picketing, picketing an employer in order to encourage union membership. The Landrum-Griffin Act severely limited such picketing.

organizational politics, the use of influence and power to affect the allocation of organization resources, typically through the informal organization. B.T. Mayes and R.W. Allen limit the definition to those actions in which the desired ends may not be sanctioned by the organization or, if the ends are sanctioned, the influence means may not be sanctioned. See their "Toward a Definition of Organizational Politics," *The Academy of Management Review* (October 1977).

Also see REALPOLITIK.

organizational pyramids: *see* PYRAMIDS.

organizational socialization, the implicit and/or explicit processes used by organizations to prepare or shape members to conform (preferably voluntarily) to the organization or suborganization's values and desired patterns of behavior.

organizational test, test of whether an organization's creating document (such as its articles of organization) limits its purpose(s) to exempt purposes and does not expressly authorize it to participate in non-exempt activities to any substantial extent. An organization must satisfy both an organizational and an operational test in order to qualify as a tax-exempt charitable organization.

See also:

OPERATED
OPERATIONAL TEST
ORGANIZED

organization chart, a graphic or pictorial representation of an organization's formal structure (who formally reports to whom). Organization charts seldom depict the informal organization (who actually works with and for whom).

See also INFORMAL ORGANIZATION.

organization design, formal structure of the organization. Organization design is a relatively new term that implies that the structure is a consciously manipulatable variable. The term emerges from a resurgence of concern about the question, "what is the most appropriate structure in a given situation?"

organization development (OD), set of activities premised upon the notion that any organization wishing to survive must periodically divest itself of those parts or characteristics that contribute to its malaise. OD is a process for increasing an organization's effectiveness. As a process it has no value bias, yet it is usually associated with the idea that maximum effectiveness is to be found by integrating an individual's desire for personal growth with organizational goals. Wendell L. French and Cecil H. Bell, Jr., in *Organization Development: Behavioral Science Interventions for Organization Improvement* (Englewood Cliffs, N.J.: Prentice-Hall, 1973), provide a formal definition:

> Organization development is a long-range effort to improve an organization's problem-solving and renewal processes, particularly through a more effective and collaborative management of organization culture—with special emphasis on the culture of formal work teams—with the assistance of a change agent, or catalyst, and the use of the theory and technology of applied behavioral science, including action research.

See also the following entries:

ARGYRIS, CHRIS
BENNIS, WARREN
BLAKE, ROBERT R. AND JANE S. MOUTON
CONFRONTATION MEETING
NATIONAL TRAINING LABORATORIES INSTITUTE FOR APPLIED BEHAVIORAL SCIENCE
PROCESS CONSULTATION
SMALL-GROUP RESEARCH
TEAM BUILDING

organization man, also ORGANIZATION WOMAN, now-generic term to describe any individual within an organization who accepts the values of the organization and finds harmony in conforming to its policies. The term was popularized by William H. Whyte, Jr., in his best selling book, *The Organization Man* (New York: Simon & Schuster, 1956). Whyte wrote that these individuals were "the ones of our middle class who have left home, spiritually as well as physically, to take the vows of organization life, and it is they who are the mind and soul of our great self-perpetuating institutions."

organization ombudsman: *see* OMBUDSMAN.

organization, script: *see* SCRIPT.

organization theory, also CLASSICAL ORGANIZATION THEORY and NEOCLASSICAL ORGANIZATION THEORY, theory that seeks to explain how groups and individuals behave in varying organizational structures and circumstances.

Classical organization theory, as its name implies, was the first theory of its kind, is considered traditional, and will continue to be the base upon which subsequent theories are built. The development of any theory must be viewed in the context of its time. The beliefs of early management theorists about how organizations worked or should work was a direct reflection of the social values of their times. And the times were harsh. Individual workers were not viewed as individuals, but as the interchangeable parts in an industrial machine whose parts were made of flesh when it was impractical to make them of steel. Consequently, the first theories of organizations were concerned with the anatomy, with the structure, of formal organizations. This is the hallmark of classical organization theory—a concern for organizational structure that is premised upon the assumed rational behavior of its human parts.

There is no firm definition as to just what "neoclassical" means in *neoclassical organization theory*, but the general connotation is that of a theoretical perspective that revises and/or is critical of traditional (classical) organization theory because it does not pay enough attention to the needs and interactions of organizational members. The watershed between classical and neoclassical organization theory is World War II. The major writers of the classical school (Taylor, Fayol, Weber, Gulick, etc.) did their most significant work before World War II. The major neoclassical writers (Simon, March, Selznick, Parsons, etc.) gained their reputations as organization theorists by attacking the classical writers after the war.

organized, in the sense in which the term is used most frequently in relation to nonprofit organizations, incorporated under the laws of a state and established for the purpose(s) of or created to perform charitable purposes—in contrast with being operated for the purpose(s) of.

See also:

OPERATED
OPERATIONAL TEST
ORGANIZATIONAL TEST

organized, date: *see* DATE OF ORGANIZATION.

Organized Crime Control Act, a United States law that prohibits illegal gambling. The law exempts games of chance conducted by organizations which are tax-exempt under IRS Code 501(c)(3).

organized labor, collective term for members of labor unions.

organizer, also called LABOR ORGANIZER and UNION ORGANIZER, individual employed by a union who acts to encourage employees of a particular organization to join the union that the organizer represents.

orientation, formal introduction and guided adjustment of new employees to their new jobs, new coworkers, and new working environment.

orientation checklist, a listing in an orderly and logical sequence of all the items about which a new employee should be informed or must do as part of the orientation process.

O'Rourke's Breakeven Chart, a chart developed by John O'Rourke for use by large membership-type nonprofit organizations in balancing the costs and revenues associated with new member drives and dues. *See* John O'Rourke, "Planning Association Membership Drives," *Association Management* (November 1969).

OSHA: *see* OCCUPATIONAL SAFETY AND HEALTH ADMINISTRATION.

OSHRC: *see* OCCUPATIONAL SAFETY AND HEALTH REVIEW COMMISSION.

ostensible, apparent; visible. For example, ostensible authority is the power a person appears to have (especially the power someone else attributes to the person).

other directed: *see* INNER DIRECTED.

outage, unaccounted-for money.

outcome, also IMPACT and PRODUCT, the desired result of an organization's or program's processes. A change in, for example, the status or well-being of the clientele, the community, or the environment; for example, counseling (the process) to reduce clients' antisocial behavior (the outcome); distributing literature (the process) to reduce the incidence of alcohol-related accidents (the outcome).

See also:

EVALUATION
OBJECTIVE, OUTCOME
PROGRAM EVALUATION

outcome evaluation: *see* PROGRAM EVALUATION.

outcome objective: *see* OBJECTIVE, OUTCOME.

outlays, checks issued, interest accrued, or other payments, net of refunds and reimbursements. Total budget outlays consist of the sum of the outlays less offsetting receipts.

out-of-pocket, a small cash payment; also, a loss measured by the difference between the price paid for an item and the (true, lower) value of that item.

out-of-title work, also called OUT-OF-CLASS EXPERIENCE, duties performed by an incumbent of a position that are not appropriate to the class to which the position has been assigned.

outplacement, counseling and career planning services offered to terminated employees to reduce the impact of being fired, improve job search skills, and ultimately place the displaced person in a new job in another organization.

See also DEHIRING.

output, end result of any process; in a project management or project control sense, the results of an organization's or program's final process over which it has control, and which contributes directly to a desired outcome or impact—for example, pamplets distributed (output), pamphlets are read (outcome); clients counseled (output), client behavior changes (outcome).

See also:

HIERARCHY OF OBJECTIVES
OBJECTIVE, PROCESS
OUTCOME
PROCESS

output curve: *see* WORK CURVE.

outreach, process of systematically extending resources and activities to identified populations at risk for the purpose of enhancing their level and quality of participation and their utilization of specified services.

outstanding, unpaid; not collected (for example, an outstanding account receivable); also, remaining in existence.

outstationing, placement of direct service personnel of one organization into another organization's physical facility. However, the service personnel remain accountable to and are paid by their own organization.

overachievement, also UNDERACHIEVEMENT, psychological concepts that describe a discrepancy between predicted and actual achievement/performance. Individuals whose performance exceeds or goes below expectations are described as overachievers or underachievers, respectively.

overdraft, also OVERDRAW, taking more money from a bank account by check than one has in the account.

overdraft checking account, a line of credit that allows an organization or person to write checks for more than the actual balance in the account, with a finance charge on the overdraft.

overhead, the general and administrative expenses of an organization that cannot be allocated directly to a particular product or service produced. Overhead typically includes, for example, power, water, heat, supervision, facilities maintenance, rent, etc.

See also ADMINISTRATIVE COSTS and COST, INDIRECT.

overhead agency: *see* AUXILIARY AGENCY.

overrate: *see* FLAGGED RATE.

overtime, work performed in excess of the basic workday/workweek.

overtime computations, for employees covered by the Fair Labor Standards Act, payments at a rate of at least 1½ times the employee's regular pay rate for each hour worked in a workweek in excess of the maximum allowable in a given type of employment. Generally, the regular rate includes all payments made by the employer to or on behalf of the employee (excluding certain statutory exceptions). The following examples are based on a maximum forty-hour workweek:

1. **Hourly rate** (regular pay rate for an employee paid by the hour). If more than forty hours are worked, at least 1½ times the regular rate for each hour over forty is due. *Example:* An employee paid $3.80 an hour works forty-four hours in a workweek. The employee is entitled to at least 1½ times $3.80, or $5.70, for each hour over forty. Pay for the week would be $152 for the first forty hours, plus $22.80 for the four hours of overtime—a total of $174.80.
2. **Piece rate.** The regular rate of pay for an employee paid on a piecework basis is obtained by dividing the total weekly earnings by the total number of hours worked in the same week. The employee is entitled to an additional ½ of this regular rate for each hour over forty, besides the full piecework earnings. *Example:* An employee paid on a piecework basis works forty-five hours in a week and earns $162. The regular pay rate for that week is $162 divided by forty-five, or $3.60 an hour. In addition to the straight time pay, the employee is entitled to $1.80 (half the regular rate) for each hour over forty. Another way to compensate pieceworkers for overtime, if agreed to before the work is performed, is to pay 1½ times the piece rate for each piece produced during overtime hours. The piece rate must be the one actually paid during non-overtime hours and must be enough to yield at least the minimum wage per hour.
3. **Salaries.** The regular rate for an employee paid a salary for a regular or specified number of hours a week is obtained by dividing the salary by the number of hours. If, under the employment agreement, a salary sufficient to meet the minimum wage requirement in every workweek is paid as straight time for whatever number of hours are worked in a workweek, the regular

rate is obtained by dividing the salary by the number of hours worked each week. To illustrate, suppose an employee's hours of work vary each week and the agreement with the employer is that the employee will be paid $200 a week for whatever number of hours of work are required. Under this pay agreement, the regular rate will vary in overtime weeks. If the employee works fifty hours, the regular rate is $4 ($200 divided by 50 hours). In addition to the salary, ½ the regular rate, or $2, is due for each of the ten overtime hours, for a total of $220 for the week. If the employee works fifty-four hours, the regular rate will be $3.70 ($200 divided by fifty-four). In that case, an additional $1.85 is due for each of the fourteen overtime hours, for a total of $225.90 for the week.

In no case may the regular rate be less than the minimum wage required by the act. If a salary is paid on other than a weekly basis, the weekly pay must be determined in order to compute the regular rate and overtime. If the salary is for a half month, it must be multiplied by twenty-four and the product divided by fifty-two weeks to get the weekly equivalent. A monthly salary should be multiplied by twelve and the product divided by fifty-two.

P

PAC: *see* POLITICAL ACTION COMMITTEE.

package settlement, term that describes the total money value (usually quoted as cents per hour) of an increase in wages and benefits achieved through collective bargaining. For example, a new contract might give employees an increase of 50¢ an hour. However, when the value of increased medical and pension benefits are included, the "package settlement" might come to 74¢ an hour.

pact, an agreement.

PAIR, acronym for "personnel and industrial relations;" or for "personnel administration/industrial relations."

paper, short for commercial paper or for a negotiable instrument.

See also NEGOTIABLE INSTRUMENT.

PAQ: *see* POSITION ANALYSIS QUESTIONNAIRE.

par, the face value of a stock or bond. For example, if a one hundred-dollar bond sells in the bond market for one hundred dollars, it is selling "at par."

paradigm, a macro model that refers to a conception of a situation or condition; a "macro theory."

paradox of value, the fact that so many of the absolute necessities of life (such as water) are cheap or relatively inexpensive compared to the price of luxury items (such as diamonds); in effect, great utility does not necessarily yield economic value and economic value does not mean that an item is useful.

parallel forms, two or more forms of a test that are assembled as closely as possible to the same statistical and content specifications so that they will provide the same kind of measurement at different administrations.

parallel interface (or port), a printer or other computer peripheral device connected to a computer in such a way that all the bits of a byte of information are transmitted simultaneously.

See also INTERFACE and SERIAL INTERFACE.

parallel ladder: *see* DUAL LADDER.

paramedic, a person who is certified by a state agency (usually a state health department) to perform advance life support (ALS) procedures under the direction of a medical doctor (for example, administer drugs, perform defibrillation, start IVs, etc.). A paramedic functions (usually with an ambulance service) under a medical-legal extension of a specific physician's license to practice medicine. In contrast, an Emergency Medical Technician (EMT) is only allowed to perform basic life support procedures. (BLS).

parameter, the known limits within which an unknown quantity may vary; also, a numerical characteristic limiting, related to, or describing a population that can be estimated by sampling. It differs from a statistic, which is derived from a sample.

paraprofessional, any individual with less than standard professional credentials who assists a fully credentialed professional with the more routine aspects of his/her professional work. For example, paralegals assist lawyers and physician assistants assist medical doctors.

parity, also EMPLOYMENT PARITY, OCCUPATIONAL PARITY, and WAGE PARITY, long-term goal of all affirmative action efforts which will exist after all categories of an organization's employees are proportionately representative of the population in the organization's geographic region. *Employment parity* exists when the proportion of protected groups in the external labor market is equivalent to their proportion in an organization's total work force without regard to job classifications. *Occupational parity* exists when the proportion of an organization's protected group employees in all job classifications is equivalent to their respective availability in the external labor market.

Wage parity requires that the salary level of one occupational classification be the same as for another. The most common example of wage parity is the linkage between the salaries of police and firefighters.

Parkinson's Law, C. Northcote Parkinson's famous law that "work expands so as to fill the time available for its completion," which first appeared in his *Parkinson's Law and Other Studies in Administration* (Boston: Houghton Mifflin Co., 1957). With mathematical precision, he "discovered" that any public administrative department will invariably increase its staff an average of 5.75 percent per year. In anticipation of suggestions that he advise what might be done about this problem, he asserted that "it is not the business of the botanist to eradicate the weeds. Enough for him if he can tell us just how fast they grow."

See also LAW OF TRIVIALITY.

parliamentarian, a person, often elected, who rules on issues of parliamentary procedure during formal meetings.

See also OFFICER.

parliamentary procedure, the rules governing the methods of procedure, discussion, and debate during a formal meeting. An organization's bylaws should stipulate the parliamentary procedures to be followed; for example, "The latest edition of *Robert's Rules of Order* shall be in effect . . ."

See also ROBERT'S RULES OF ORDER.

participation, an insurance policy provision in which the insured person pays a certain percentage of any loss; also, a mortgage agreement in which the lender receives a share of the profits of the venture in addition to interest on the loan.

participative management: *see* INDUSTRIAL DEMOCRACY.

particular lien, a right to hold specific property because of a claim against that property; for example, a garage's right to hold a car until the repair bill is paid.

partner, also LIMITED PARTNER, one who is associated with another (or others) in an activity or endeavor. A *limited partner* is a partner with no (or limited) authority or responsibility for participating in operating decisions or to commit the partnership's resources.

partnership, also LIMITED PARTNERSHIP, an association of individuals to engage in activities or to accomplish a purpose; an unincorporated business organization consisting of two or more partners. A *limited partnership* is one in which a general partner has responsibility and authority to make operating decisions and binding commitments of the partnership's resources on behalf of the partnership, whereas the limited partner(s) has no (or limited) responsibility for operating decisions and actions.

part-time workers: *see* FULL-TIME WORKERS.

PAS: *see* PHILANTHROPIC ADVISORY SERVICE.

passbook account, an account at a commercial bank, a savings and loan institution, or other thrift institution whose ownership is evidenced by entries in a nonnegotiable book that must be presented with each deposit or withdrawal.

passing a dividend, omitting the declaration of a regular or expected dividend.

passing point: *see* CUTTING SCORE.

passing score: *see* CUTTING SCORE.

passionate leave: *see* COMPASSIONATE LEAVE.

pass rate, proportion of candidates who pass an examination.

pass-through, process by which a state government receives federal grants and passes the money through to substate grantees. Such action may be mandated by the grant statute or result from a state decision.

past practice, manner in which a similar issue was resolved before the occasion of a present grievance.

past year, fiscal year immediately preceeding the current year; the last completed fiscal year.

paternalism, also called INDUSTRIAL PATERNALISM and EMPLOYER PATERNALISM, in the United States, a derogatory reference to an organization's "fatherly" efforts to better the lot of its employees. In other societies where there are well-established paternalistic traditions, the derogatory connotations of the word may be absent. Japan is undoubtedly the most paternalistic of all the major industrial societies.

paternity leave, *see* BIRTH LEAVE.

path-goal theory of leadership, a leadership style that has the leader indicate to his or her followers the path by which to accomplish their individual and organizational goals, then help to make that path as easy to follow as possible.

patterned interview, also UNPATTERNED INTERVIEW, interview that seeks to ask the same questions of all applicants. An *unpatterned interview* does not seek such uniformity.

pay: *see* the following entries:
- BACK PAY
- CALL-BACK PAY
- COMPARABLE WORTH
- COMPENSATION
- DOWN-TIME PAY
- EQUAL PAY FOR EQUAL WORK
- HAZARD PAY
- HOLIDAY PAY
- INCENTIVE PAY
- JURY-DUTY PAY
- LONGEVITY PAY
- MAKE-UP PAY
- RETROACTIVE PAY
- SEVERANCE PAY
- STRIKE PAY
- TAKE-HOME PAY
- VACATION PAY
- WAGES
- WELL PAY
- WORK PREMIUM

payable: *see* ACCOUNTS PAYABLE.

pay-as-you-go plan, pension plan that has employers paying pension benefits to retired employees out of current income.

payback, also PAYBACK PERIOD or CASH RECOVERY PERIOD, the length of time it will take an investment to return what was put in.

pay compression, a situation where the salaries of all employees are forced so close together that there cease to be meaningful differences in the various pay rates.

pay criteria: *see* WAGE CRITERIA.

payee, the person to whom a negotiable instrument (such as a check) is made out. For example, "pay to the order of John Smith."

pay for performance, concept of paying an employee on the basis of job performance—all bonuses, raises, promotions, etc. would be directly related to the measurable results of the employee's efforts.

pay grade, also called PAY LEVEL, an increment that makes up a pay structure. Each represents a range of pay or a standard rate of pay for a specific class of jobs.

pay increase, any permanent raise in an employee's basic salary or wage level.

paying your dues, the experiences that one must have before being ready for advancement. In effect, "you have to pay your dues" before you can be perceived as a legitimate occupant of a higher position.

pay level: *see* PAY GRADE.

payment cap, a ceiling on the amount by which monthly adjustable rate mortgage payments (interest and principal) are allowed to rise in any one period of time.

See ADJUSTABLE RATE MORTGAGE.

payments in kind, noncash payments for services rendered.

payout, the amounts granted and expended by a foundation for charitable purposes during a twelve month period.

See also PAYOUT REQUIREMENT.

payout ratio, the dividend a company pays on each share of common stock divided by its earnings per share.

payout requirement, the requirement that foundations must pay out in grants and/or other qualifying distributions, five percent of the market value of their year's investment assets. Payouts must be made within twelve months following the end of a foundation's tax year.

See also DISTRIBUTABLE AMOUNT and QUALIFYING DISTRIBUTION.

pay plan, a listing of rates of pay for each job category in an organization. A *pay range,* also known as *salary* or *wage range,* indicates the minimum through maximum rates of pay for a job. The various increments that makes up the pay range are known as the *pay steps*. The *pay grade* or *pay level* is the range of pay or a standard rate of pay for a specific job. The totality of the pay grades makes up the *pay structure*.

While a position classification plan essentially arranges positions in classes on the basis of their similarities, a pay plan establishes rates of pay for each class of positions. Consequently, if a position is improperly classified, the corresponding salary cannot be in accord with the principle of "equal pay for equal work."

payroll, listing of all the wages and/or salaries earned by employees within an organization for a specific time period (usually weekly, bimonthly, or monthly).

payroll register, a separate, special form of the cash disbursements journal (or check register) used to record wages and salaries paid, payroll withholding taxes, and other payroll deductions.

The payroll register should contain the date of each payroll check, the name of each person paid (employee or paid volunteer), check number, net amount of the check after withholding taxes and other deductions, details for payroll withholding taxes (for example, Social Security Taxes; federal [FWT] and state [SWT] withholding taxes), details for other withholdings

ACE AMBULANCE SERVICE—PAYROLL REGISTER

Date	Employee	Check No.	CR Amount	CR FICA	CR FWT	CR SWT	CR Health Ins.	DR Wages
1-15	Henry Abbott	3002	$ 126.60	$ 13.40	$ 50.00	$ 10.00	$	$ 200.00
1-15	Richard Avery	3003	$ 119.95	$ 10.05	$ 20.00			$ 150.00

(for example, employee contributions to medical insurance), gross pay (before withholding), and which subsidiary and/or general ledger accounts are affected by each transaction.

At the end of each accounting period (for example, each month), all columns in the payroll register are totaled, balanced, and posted to the general ledger.

See also:
- CASH DISBURSEMENTS JOURNAL
- GENERAL LEDGER
- JOURNAL
- SUBSIDIARY LEDGER
- TRIAL BALANCE

payroll taxes: *see* EMPLOYMENT TAXES.

pay satisfaction, the difference between a person's level of pay and his or her belief about what the level of pay should be. If employees find themselves assuming substantially similar duties and responsibilities as coworkers who, because of seniority or education, receive higher pay, they are going to be dissatisfied. It is very difficult to convince employees that their pay is determined fairly if they have before them on a daily basis other more highly paid employees who serve not as role models that one should strive to emulate, but rather as glaring examples of the inequities of the pay program.

pay step, each of the various increments that make up a pay range.

pay survey: *see* WAGE SURVEY.

PBGC: *see* PENSION BENEFIT GUARANTY CORPORATION.

P-C: *see* PROCESS CONSULTATION.

Peace Corps, body established by the Peace Corps Act of 1961 and made an independent agency by title VI of the International Security and Development Cooperation Act of 1981. The Peace Corps consists of a Washington, D.C., headquarters; three recruitment service centers, supporting fifteen area offices; and overseas operations in more than sixty-two countries.

The Peace Corps' purpose is to promote world peace and friendship and to help the peoples of other countries in meeting their needs for trained manpower.

To fulfill the Peace Corps' mandate, men and women of all ages and walks of life are trained for a nine- to fourteen-week period in the appropriate local language, the technical skills necessary for their particular job, and the cross-cultural skills needed to adjust to a society with traditions and attitudes different from their own. Volunteers serve for a period of two years, living among the people with whom they work.

peaked out, negative way of referring to an employee who has reached the maximum step in his salary range or has already made his or her maximum contributions to the organization.

pecking order, hierarchy. Ever since social psychologists discovered that chickens have a pecking order—the strongest or most aggressive fowl get to eat, or to peck, first—the term has been used to describe the comparative ranks that humans hold in their social organizations. No aspect of our society is immune from the pecking order's fowl antics. According to Lyndon Johnson's former press secretary, George E. Reedy, in *The Twilight of the Presidency* (Cleveland: World Publishing, 1970),

> the inner life of the White House is essentially the life of the barnyard, as set forth so graphically in the study of the pecking order among chickens which every freshman sociology student must read. It is a question of who has the right to peck whom and who must submit to being pecked. There are only two important differences. The first is that the pecking order is determined by the individual strength and forcefulness of each chicken, whereas in the White House it depends upon the relationship to the barnyard keeper. The second is that no one outside the barnyard glorifies the chickens and expects them to order the affairs of mankind. They are destined for the frying pan and that is that.

peer rating, also called MUTUAL RATING, performance evaluation technique that calls for each employee to evaluate other employees in his/her work unit.

penalty, a requirement to pay. IRS penalties assessed against nonprofit organizations are usually imposed taxes.

penalty clause, a contract provision that requires payment of an exact sum of money if something is done to vary the contract's requirements; for example, paying off a mortgage before it is due to avoid further interest payments.

penetration rate, a nonprofit organization's sucess rate in raising funds in a community or area (either number of donors or amount of money received) relative to the estimated amount that could be raised; also, its number of clients served relative to the estimated number who are eligible to receive services.

penetration rate, also PENETRATION RATIO (EQUAL EMPLOYMENT OPPORTUNITY), the proportion of a work force belonging to a particular minority group. The *penetration ratio* is the ratio of an organization's penetration rate to the penetration rate for its geographic region (usually the standard metropolitan statistical area or SMSA). The rate and ratio are derived as follows:

$$\text{Penetration Rate} = \frac{\text{Total Minority Employment}}{\text{Total Employment}}$$

$$\text{Penetration Ratio} = \frac{\text{Penetration Rate for an Organization}}{\text{Penetration Rate for the SMSA}}$$

See also REPRESENTATIVE BUREAUCRACY.

penny stock, a speculative stock selling at less than a dollar a share.

pension, periodic payments to an individual who retires from employment (or simply from a particular organization) because of age, disability, or the completion of a specific period of service. Such payments usually continue for the rest of the recipient's life and sometimes extend to legal survivors.

Pension plans generally have either defined benefits or defined contributions. In *defined benefit plans* the amount of the benefit is fixed, but not the amount of contribution. These plans usually gear benefits to years of service and earnings or a stated dollar amount. About sixty percent of all pension plan participants are covered by defined benefit plans. In *defined contribution plans,* the amount of contributions is fixed, but the amount of benefit is not. These plans usually involve profit sharing, stock bonus, or money purchase arrangements where the employer contributes an agreed percentage of profits or wages to the worker's individual account. The eventual benefit is determined by the amount of total contributions and investment earnings in the years during which the employee is covered.

Pension Benefit Guaranty Corporation (PBGC), federal agency that guarantees basic pension benefits in covered private plans if they terminate with insufficient assets. Title IV of the Employee Retirement Income Security Act of 1974 (ERISA) established the corporation to guarantee payment of insured benefits if covered plans terminate without sufficient assets to pay such benefits. The PBGC, a self-financing, wholly-owned government corporation, is governed by a Board of Directors consisting of the secretaries of Labor, Commerce, and the Treasury. The Secretary of Labor is chairman of the board and is responsible for administering the PBGC in accordance with policies established by the board. A seven-member Advisory Committee, composed of two labor, two business, and three public members, appointed by the President, advises the PBGC on various matters.

Title IV of ERISA provides for mandatory coverage of most private defined benefit plans. These are those plans that provide a benefit the amount of which can be determined from a formula in the plan; for example, based on factors such as age, years of service, average or highest salary, etc.

pension fund socialism, Peter F. Drucker's term for the phenomenon that is turning traditional thinking about the "inherent" and historical separation of capital and labor upside down—namely, that the "workers" of the United States are rapidly and literally becoming the owners of the nation's industry through their pension fund investments in diverse common stocks. According to Drucker, by 1985 pension funds "will own at least fifty—if not sixty—percent of equity capital."

pension plan, contributory: *see* CONTRIBUTORY PENSION PLAN.

pension plan, fully funded: *see* FULLY FUNDED PENSION PLAN.

pension plan, funded: *see* FUNDED PENSION PLAN.

Pension Reform Act of 1974: *see* EMPLOYEES RETIREMENT INCOME SECURITY ACT OF 1974.

Pension Reporter: *see* BNA PENSION REPORTER.

pension trust, individual-contract: *see* INDIVIDUAL-CONTRACT PENSION TRUST.

per capita, Latin meaning "by heads." In a per capita election, each member would have one vote.

per capita income, the mean income computed for every man, woman, and child in a particular group. It is derived by dividing the total income of a particular group by the total population (including patients or inmates in institutional quarters) in that group.

per capita tax, tax on each head or person.

percentage of completion method, an accounting process used when a period of activity (for example, a concert series) goes beyond an accounting period. The revenues and expenses are recorded proportionately to the costs incurred in relation to the total expected costs of the activity.

percentile, that point or score in a distribution below which falls the percent of cases indicated by the given percentile. Thus the fifteenth percentile denotes the score or point below which fifteen percent of the scores fall.

percentile band, interval between percentiles corresponding to score limits one standard error of measurement above and below an obtained score. The chances are approximately two out of three that the true score of an examinee with a particular obtained score is within these score limits.

percentile rank, percent of scores in a distribution equal to or lower than a particular obtained score.

perception, also PERCEPTUAL ILLUSION, a mental image; a person's consciousness of the things that exist or are taking place; an interpretation of something observed (for example, an event) or encountered (for example, a conversation) in light of one's

Naval Education and Training Program Development Center, Human Behavior *(Washington, D.C.: United States Government Printing Office, 1984), page 3-1.*

experiences and feelings; a concept used to explain why people sometimes see and interpret the same things differently.

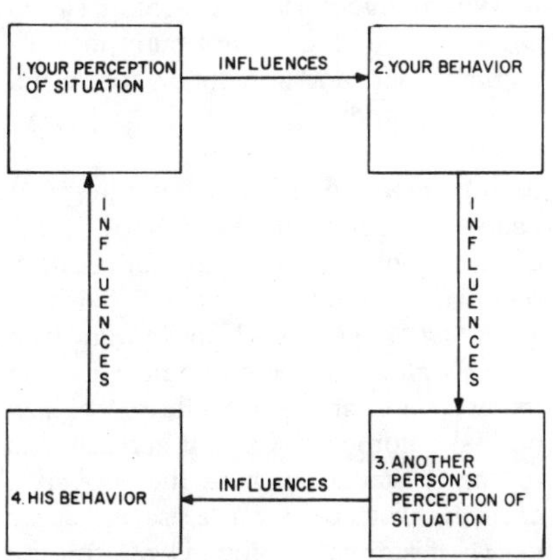

Naval Education and Training Program Development Center, Human Behavior *(Washington, D.C.: United States Government Printing Office, 1984), page 3-6.*

Perceptions play a major role in determining people's behaviors, because they often restructure "reality" to suit their motives, desires, beliefs, and attitudes (often without knowingly doing so).

See also PERCEPTUAL CYCLE, INTERPERSONAL and PHENOMENOLOGY.

perceptual cycle, interpersonal, a destructive cycle that develops between people who have different perceptions.

See also PERCEPTION and PHENOMENOLOGY.

per diem, Latin for "by the day." Temporary employees may be paid a "per-diem" rate or a travel expense program may reimburse employees using a flat "per-diem" amount.

performance appraisal, also called PERFORMANCE EVALUATION and PERFORMANCE REPORTING, title usually given to the formal method by which an organization documents the work performance of its employees. Performance appraisals are designed to serve a variety of functions, such as:

1. changing or modifying dysfunctional work behavior;
2. communicating to employees managerial perceptions of the quality and quantity of their work;
3. assessing future potential of an employee in order to recommend appropriate training or developmental assignments;
4. assessing whether the present duties of an employee's position have an appropriate compensation level; and
5. providing a documented record for disciplinary and separation actions.

See also the following entries:

BEHAVIORALLY ANCHORED RATING SCALES
EFFICIENCY RATING
SELF-APPRAISAL

performance bond, a bond which guarantees that a contractor will complete a job correctly and on time.

performance budgeting: *see* BUDGETING, PERFORMANCE.

performance evaluation: *see* PERFORMANCE APPRAISAL.

performance incentive: *see* INCENTIVE.

performance measure, a measurable indicator of performance by an individual, a project or an organization. Performance measures usually are derived from objectives or from generally accepted standards (such as those developed by a national organization.) Performance measures may be expressed as absolute numbers, percentages and ratios. For example: number of new members recruited, average response time following receipt of a call for assistance, percent of eligible clients served, and number of columnar inches of favorable print media coverage per dollar of budgeted public relations monies spent, etc.

See also,

ACCOUNTABILITY
FUND-RAISING
KEY RESULTS AREA
MANAGEMENT BY OBJECTIVES
OBJECTIVE
PERFORMANCE APPRAISAL

performance objective, also called CRITERION OBJECTIVE, statement specifying exactly what behavior is to be exhibited, the conditions under which behavior will be accomplished, and the minimum standard of acceptable performance.

performance reporting: *see* PERFORMANCE APPRAISAL.

performance standards: *see* STANDARDS OF PERFORMANCE.

performance test, examination that has candidates perform a sample of the actual work that would be found on the job.

peril, a risk or accident insured against in an insurance policy.

periodic cost: *see* COST, FIXED.

periodic increase: *see* WITHIN-GRADE INCREASE.

periodic tenancy, a lease that continues from month to month or year to year unless ended by the landlord or the tenant giving notice that it will be ended.

peripheral, computer input, output, or auxiliary equipment, such as a printer, a monitor, etc.

perks: *see* PERQUISITES.

permanent arbitrator, arbitrator who hears all disputes during the life of a contract or other stipulated term.

permanent injunction: *see* INJUNCTION.

permit, charitable solicitation: *see* CHARITABLE SOLICITATION PERMIT.

permutation: *see* COMBINATION.

perpetual care trust fund, a trust fund established to provide for the perpetual care of, for example, a gravesite.

perpetual inventory, an inventory system whose accounting is kept current by recording each addition to or subtraction from it immediately.

perquisites, also called PERKS, the special benefits, frequently tax-exempt, made available only to the top executives of an organization. There are two basic kinds of executive perquisites: (1) those with "take-home" value (such as company cars, club memberships, etc.) and (2) those that have no "take-home" value, but serve mainly to confer status (such as the proverbial executive washroom, office size and decor, etc.). Historically, the U.S. Internal Revenue Service has striven to restrict the tax-exempt status of executives perquisites.

See also TOTAL COMPENSATION COMPARABILITY.

persona, term developed by Carl Jung that refers to the personality or facade that each individual shows to the world. The persona is distinguished from our inner being because it is adopted and put on like a mask to meet the demands of social life. *Persona* is the word for the masks that actors wore in ancient Greece.

personal, having to do with a human being's thoughts, possessions, feelings, and things.

personal contact, probably the single most effective method for securing new members, volunteers, and contributions.
See also DIRECT SOLICITATION.

personal income, disposable, the income remaining to individuals or households after tax and nontax payments that is available for discretionary spending, savings, and donations.

personality inventory, also called SELF-REPORT INVENTORY, questionnaire concerned with personal characteristics and behavior that an individual answers about himself/herself. Then, the individual's self report is compared to norms based upon the responses given to the same questionnaire by a large representative group.

personality test, also PERSONALITY INVENTORY, test designed to measure any of the nonintellectual aspects of an individual's psychological disposition. It seeks information on a person's motivations and attitudes as opposed to his or her abilities.

personal property tax: *see* TAX, PERSONAL PROPERTY.

personal-rank system: *see* RANK-IN-MAN SYSTEM.

personal space, the area that individuals actively maintain around themselves into which others cannot intrude without arousing discomfort.

personal time, that time an employee uses to tend to personal needs. This time is usually separate from lunch and rest breaks.

personnel, collective term for all of the employees of an organization. The word is of military origin—the two basic components of a traditional army being materiel and personnel. Personnel is also commonly used to refer to the personnel management function or the organizational unit responsible for administering personnel programs.

personnel action, process necessary to hire, separate, reinstate, or make other changes affecting an employee (*e.g.*, change in position assignment, tenure, etc.).

personnel administration, also PERSONNEL MANAGEMENT, that aspect of management concerned with the recruitment, selection, development, utilization, and compensation of the members of an organization. While the terms *personnel administration* and *personnel management* tend to be used interchangeably, there is a distinction. The former is mainly concerned with the technical aspects of maintaining a full complement of employees within an organization, while the latter concerns itself as well with the larger problems of the viability of an organization's human resources.

Personnel Administrator of Massachusetts v. Feeney, 442 U.S. 256 (1979), U.S. Supreme Court case which held that a state law operating to the advantage of males by giving veterans lifetime preference for state employment was not in violation of the equal protection clause of the fourteenth Amendment. The court found that a veterans preference law's disproportionate impact on women did not prove intentional bias.
See also VETERANS PREFERENCE.

Personnel and Guidance Journal, The, *see Journal of Counseling and Development* (its new name).

personnel audit, evaluation of one or more aspects of the personnel function.

personnel committee, usually a standing committee of the board of directors charged with responsibility for developing and maintaining an organization's personnel policies and procedures; assisting staff in the development of annual performance targets (often through a management-by-objectives process, reviewing or monitoring staff performance, and conducting staff performance appraisals); analyzing and recommending changes in staff salaries, the compensation plan, staffing levels, and staff position responsibilities. In some organizations, the personnel committee also is responsible for analyzing and initiating action relative to volunteer resources and needs.

See also:
COMMITTEE
COMPENSATION
MANAGEMENT BY OBJECTIVES
PERFORMANCE APPRAISAL

personnel costs, the total cost to the organization of employees' salaries, fringe benefits, and all other direct and indirect components of the total compensation package.

See also COMPENSATION MANAGEMENT.

personnel director, manager responsible for all of an organization's personnel programs.

personnel examiner, job title for an individual who is a professional staff member of that unit of a personnel department which is concerned with selection.

personnel function, a service to line management that typically includes assistance in staffing needs planning, recruiting, selection, training, evaluation, compensation, discipline, and termination. The personnel function also usually includes assistance to management in such areas as labor (or union) relations, affirmative action programs, prevention of sexual, racial, age, etc. discrimination, etc.

The issue of how the overall personnel function should be organized in nonprofit and public organizations has been plagued by the attempt to realize several values at once. Foremost among these values have been those of "merit" or neutral competence, executive leadership, managerial flexibility, and representativeness. The main problem of the structure and policy thrusts of personnel units has been that maximizing some of these values requires arrangements ill-suited for the achievement of others. Thus, achieving neutral competence requires the creation of a relatively independent personnel unit to help insulate employees from the whims and demands of executives and directors. Yet the same structural arrangement will tend to frustrate the ability of executives to manage their agencies.

personnel game, the way some personnel directors, personnel officers, and personnel technicians refer to their occupation.

personnel generalist, personnelist who, instead of concentrating in one subspeciality, is minimally competent in a variety of personnel management subspecialities.

personnel inventory, a listing of all employees in an organization by job and personal characteristics which serves as a basic reference for planning and other purposes.

personnelist, also called PERSONNEL MANAGER, one who is professionally engaged in the practice of personnel management.

personnel jacket, file folder containing all personnel data on, and personnel actions pertaining to, an employee.

personnel management evaluation, formal effort to determine the effectiveness of any or all of an organization's personnel management program.

personnel manager: *see* PERSONNELIST.

personnel manual, written record of an organization's personnel policies and procedures.

personnel officer, common job title for the individual responsible for administering the personnel program of an organizational unit.

personnel planning, process that (1) forecasts future supply and demand for various categories of personnel, (2) determines net shortages or excesses, and (3) develops plans for remedying or balancing these forecasted situations.

See also HUMAN RESOURCES PLANNING.

personnel ratio, number of full-time employees of a personnel department (usually exclusive of clerical support) per hundred employees of the total organization.

personnel records, also called PERSONNEL FILES, all recorded information about employees kept by an employer, usually in the form of, and under the name, "personnel files."

personnel research, also called INDUSTRIAL RELATIONS RESEARCH, systematic inquiry into any or all of those problems, policies, programs, and procedures growing out of the employee-employer relationship.

personnel runaround, what happens to job applicants who apply for positions for which individuals have been preselected.

See also REALPOLITIK.

personnel selection, also called SELECTION and EMPLOYEE SELECTION, program the object of which is to choose for employment those applicants who best meet an organization's needs in particular jobs.

personnel technician, job title for an individual who is a professional staff member of a specialized unit (recruitment, classification and pay, examinations, etc.) of a personnel department.

PERT, acronym for "program evaluation and review technique," a planning and control process that requires identifying the accomplishments of programs and the time and resources needed to go from one accomplishment to the next. A PERT diagram shows the sequence and interrelationships of activities from the beginning of a project to the end and uses probabilities for activity start and completion dates.

See also CRITICAL PATH METHOD and PRECEDENCE DIAGRAM.

Peter Principle, principle promulgated by Laurence J. Peter, in his worldwide best-seller, *The Peter Principle: Why Things Always Go Wrong,* with Raymond Hull (N.Y.: William Morrow, 1969). The "principle" held that "in a hierarchy every employee tends to rise to his level of incompetence." Corollaries of the Peter Principle hold that "in time, every post tends to be occupied by an employee who is incompetent to carry out its duties." In answer to the logical question of who then does the work that has to be done, Peter asserts that "work is accomplished by those employees who have not yet reached their level of incompetence."

See also REALPOLITIK.

petty cash, also PETTY CASH FUND, a small revolving cash fund (usually twenty to fifty dollars) usually kept in a cash box and maintained by one staff person. The petty cash fund is used to pay for small, unexpected, incidental items as the need arises, without prior authorization and without the necessity for writing a check; for example, to purchase donuts for an early morning executive committee meeting or to pay for a C.O.D. package. When cash is withdrawn from the petty cash fund, a voucher or note is made and signed. It is called a "revolving fund" because each time the fund is drawn down to a predetermined minimum level, the vouchers or notes are reconciled with the remaining cash and the fund is replenished.

phantom unemployment, jobless citizens who, for a variety of reasons, fall between the statistical cracks and are never officially counted among the unemployed. They have the double misfortune of being both unemployed and "invisible."

phased testing, also called PROGRESS TESTING, testing of those in a training program after specific phases of the program.

phenomenology, frame of reference with which to view organizational phenomena. To a phenomenologist, an organization exists on two planes—in reality and in the mind of the person perceiving its actions. Phenomenology is the integrated study of reality as well as its perceptions.

Philadelphia Plan, equal opportunity compliance program that requires bidders on all federal and federally-assisted construction projects exceeding $500,000 to submit affirmative action plans setting specific goals for the utilization of minority employees. The plan went into effect on July 18, 1969 in the Philadelphia area and affected six of the higher-paying trades in construction—iron work, plumbing and pipefitting, steamfitting, sheetmetal work, electrical work, and elevator construction work.

The plan was issued under Executive Order 11246 of 1965, which charges the Secretary of Labor with responsibility for administering the government's policy requiring equal employment opportunity in federal contracts and federally-assisted construction work.

philanthropic, benevolent; for example, a philanthropic organization. Philanthropic is a broader concept than charitable.

See also:

BENEVOLENT
CHARITABLE
ELEEMOSYNARY
PHILANTHROPY

Philanthropic Advisory Service (PAS), a program of the Council of the Better Business Bureaus which analyzes and reports on the financial and program operations of operating charities that receive business client support.

Philanthropic Digest, a published listing of grants, bequests, gifts, and corporate gifts in the arts, education, health, etc.

philanthropy, donations and gifts of money, property, and time or effort to needy and/or socially desirable purposes. Philanthropy is a broader term than charity in that a return is expected from the donation in terms of some form of improvement in the public's welfare or general benefit. Whereas *chairty* traditionally has been used to mean the alleviation of individual cases of physical illness, poverty, etc., *philanthropy* has referred to efforts to eliminate the causes of those problems which charity seeks to alleviate.

See also:

BENEVOLENT
CHARITABLE GRANTS ECONOMY CONCEPT
CHARITABLE ORGANIZATION
DONOR
ELEEMOSYNARY
FREEDOM OF CHOICE
PUBLIC BENEFIT
THIRD SECTOR
VOLUNTEERISM

Philanthropy Monthly, a monthly magazine that contains articles and editorials on topics of current interest to foundations and other nonprofit organizations.

Phillips Curve, graphic presentation of the theory, put forth in 1958 by the British economist A. W. Phillips, holding that there is a measurable, direct relationship between unemployment and inflation. In short, as unemployment declines, wages and prices can be expected to rise.

philosophy: *see* MANAGERIAL PHILOSOPHY.

physical examination, medical review to determine if an applicant is able to perform the duties of a position.

picketing, activity that occurs when one or more persons are present at an employer's business in order (1) to publicize a labor dispute, (2) to influence others (both employees and customers) to withhold their services or business, and/or (3) to demonstrate a union's desire to represent the employees of the business being picketed.

The U.S. Supreme Court held, in the case of *Thornhill* v. *Alabama,* 310 U.S. 88 (1940), that the dissemination of information concerning the facts of a labor dispute was within the rights guaranteed by the First Amendment. However, picketing may be lawfully enjoined if it is for an unlawful purpose, not peaceful, or in violation of some specific state or federal law.

PIGs: *see* PUBLIC INTEREST GROUP.

pilot study, method of testing and validating a survey research instrument by administering it to a small sample of the subject population.

pilot testing, experimental testing of a newly devised program, system, or test in order to discover any problems before it is put into operational use.

pink-collar jobs, those jobs in which women form the bulk of the labor force, in which the pay is usually low in comparison to men of the same or lower educational levels, and where "equal-pay-for-equal work" provisions are of little effect because women tend to compete only with other women. *Pink-collar workers* include nurses, elementary school teachers, typists, telephone operators, secretaries, hairdressers, waitresses, private household workers, etc.

placement, acceptance by an employer of a candidate for a position as a direct result of the efforts of an employment agency, screening committee or personnel office.

planned economy, an economic system under which the major decisions as to the use of resources are made and controlled by government.

See also NATIONAL PLANNING.

planning, the formal process of making decisions for the future of individuals and organizations. There are two basic kinds of planning: *strategic* and *operational. Strategic planning,* also known as long-range, comprehensive, corporate, integrated, overall, and managerial planning, has three dimensions: the identification and examination of future opportunities, threats, and consequences; the process of analyzing an organization's environment and developing compatible objectives along with the appropriate strategies and policies capable of achieving those objectives; and the integration of the various elements of planning into an overall structure of plans so that each unit of the organization knows in advance what must be done, when, and by whom. *Operational planning* is concerned with the implementation of the larger goals and strategies that have been determined by strategic planning; improving current operations; and the allocation of resources through the operating budget.

See also the following entries:

ADMINISTRATIVE PLANNING
AMERICAN PLANNING ASSOCIATION
LONG-RANGE PLANNING
NATIONAL PLANNING ASSOCIATION
OPERATIONAL PLANNING
STRATEGIC PLANNING

planning, career: *see* CAREER PLANNING.

planning, tax: *see* TAX PLANNING.

planning horizon, the time limit of organizational planning beyond which the future is considered too uncertain or unimportant to waste time on.

planning model: *see:*

ESTIMATED INCOME
MODEL
PLANNING
TIME SERIES ANALYSIS

Planning Programming Budgeting Systems (PPBS), an elaborate version of program budgeting which requires agency directors to identify program objectives, develop methods of measuring program output, calculate total program costs over the long run, prepare detailed multiyear

program and financial plans, and analyze the costs and benefits of alternative program designs.
See also BUDGETING.

plan termination insurance, pension insurance available through the Pension Benefit Guarantee Corporation which provides that, in the event of the financial collapse of a private pension fund wherein the pension fund assets are not sufficient to meet its obligations, the interests of vested employees will be protected.

plat, also PLOT, a map showing how a piece of land will be subdivided (divided up) and built upon.

platykurtic, frequency distribution or curve that is more flat-topped, as opposed to peaked, than a normal curve.

pledge, a promise. As the word is used most frequently in relation to nonprofit organizations, a commitment to give an amount of money or services over a period of time (such as one year). Usually a portion of the pledge is due in regular installments, for example, monthly or quarterly.
See also ASSIGNED ACCOUNT.

plural executive, concept that has a committee assuming the normal responsibilities of an executive.

pluralism, in the U.S. context, a theory of government that attempts to reaffirm the democratic character of society by asserting that open, multiple, competing, and responsive groups preserve traditional democratic values in a mass industrial state. Thus, traditional democratic theory, with its emphasis on individual responsibility and development, is transformed into a model that emphasizes the role of the group in society.

However, power-elite theory argues that if democracy is defined as popular participation in public affairs, then pluralist theory is inadequate as an explanation of modern U.S. government. Pluralism, according to this view, offers little direct participation, since the elite structure is closed, pyramidal, consensual, and unresponsive. Society is divided into two classes: the few who govern and the many who are governed. That is, pluralism is covert elitism, instead of a practical solution to preserve democracy in a mass society.

PMO, a profit-making organization.

PNRS: *see* PROJECT NOTIFICATION AND REVIEW SYSTEM.

point, one percent; a term used by mortgage companies to describe an initial, one-time charge made for lending money.

point system, also called POINT METHOD, most widely used method of job evaluation, in which the relative worth of the jobs being evaluated is determined by totaling the number of points assigned to the various factors applicable to each of the jobs.
See also BEDAUX POINT SYSTEM and HAY SYSTEM.

policies: *see* POLICY.

policies and procedures manual, a manual which is a compendium of an organization's currently operable, formally adopted policies and the supporting methodological procedures. Most policies and procedures manuals are codified.
See also:
MANUAL
POLICY
PROCEDURE

policy, statement of goals that can be translated into a plan or program by specifying the objectives to be obtained. Goals are a far more general statement of aims than are objectives. Goal/objective ambiguity may exist for a variety of reasons. The original sponsors of the policy or program may not have had a precise idea of the end results desired. Formal statements of objectives may be intentionally ambiguous if it is easier to obtain a consensus on action. Value judgments underlying the objectives may not be shared by important

PARTIAL TABLE OF CONTENTS FROM A POLICIES AND PROCEDURES MANUAL

Table of Contents

1.6	DRESS CODE AND APPEARANCE		
	.1	Uniforms and Insignia	
		.1	Drivers and Attendants
		.2	Others
	.2	Off-duty Wearing of Uniform	
	.3	Personal Cleanliness and Hygiene	
1.7	COMMUNITY SERVICE/SPECIAL EVENTS		
1.8	INCIDENTS AND DISCIPLINE		
	.1	Reporting Incidents and Concerns	
	.2	Grounds for Discipline	
	.3	Disciplinary Steps/Appeals Process	

groups. Consequently, the end results intended may be perceived by some as implying ill effects for them; explicit statements of objectives tend to imply a specific assignment of priorities and commitment of resources.

policy analysis, set of techniques that seek to answer the question of what the probable effects of a policy will be before they actually occur. Policy analysis involves the application of systematic research techniques, drawn largely from the social sciences and based on measurements of program effectiveness, quality, cost, and impact on the formulation, execution, and evaluation of policy in order to create a more rational or optimal administration.

policy analyst, individual employed to study the effects of a proposed or actual policy.

Policy and Practice Series: *see* BNA POLICY AND PRACTICE SERIES.

policy committee, a standing committee of a board of directors, usually charged with responsibility for ensuring that the organization is focusing on appropriate needs and clientele and that its allocation of programs and resources is maximally supportive of its missions and public benefit purposes. The policy committee recommends desirable changes to the board of directors for action.

See also COMMITTEE and POLICY.

policy making, the totality of the decisional processes by which an organization decides to act or deliberately not act to deal with a particular problem, concern, or opportunity.

In seeking an explanation for the mechanisms that produce policy decisions or nondecisions, one is immediately confronted with two early, distinct, and opposite theories. What might be called the rational decision-making approach has generally been attributed to Harold Lasswell's *The Future of Political Science* (New York: Atherton, 1963), which posited seven significant phases for every decision:

1. the intelligence phase, involving an influx of information,
2. the promoting or recommending phase, involving activities designed to influence the outcome,
3. the prescribing phase, involving the articulation of norms,
4. the invoking phase, involving establishing correspondence between prescriptions and concrete circumstances,
5. the application phase, in which the prescription is executed,
6. the appraisal phase, assessing intent in relation to effect, and
7. the terminating phase, treating expectations (rights) established while the prescription was in force.

The rejection of this approach was urged by Charles E. Lindblom, who proposed the incremental decision-making theory popularly known as the "science of muddling through." Lindblom sees a rational model as unrealistic. The policy-making process was above all, he asserted, complex and disorderly. Disjointed incrementalism as a policy course was in reality the only truly feasible route, since incrementalism "concentrated the policymaker's analysis on familiar, better-known experiences, sharply reduced the number of different alternative policies to be explored, and sharply reduced the number and complexity of factors to be analyzed."

A question then remains—how can one accept the incremental model as a reality but use the rational model as a conceptual framework for policy analysis? There is no ready answer to such a question other than the utility of the rational model in producing change, or more information-oriented policy action. Scholars will use the rational model because it affords a dissective capability that can be used to focus on policy specifics and stages, regardless of how well constructed or formulated any given decisions may be.

It seems fair to conclude that there is no single policy-making process that produces all policies. Rather, there are numerous policy processes, each capable of producing different policy contents and applicable only in a particular environment.

policy management, term used to refer to the capacity of elected officials or board members to perform on an integrated, cross-cutting basis the needs assessment, goal setting, and evaluation functions of management; to mobilize and allocate resources; and to initiate and guide the planning, development, and implementation of policies, strategies, and programs.

policy management assistance, term used to refer to any system, effort, or process which has among its major objectives strengthening the capability of elected board members or officials to exercise the strategic needs assessment, goal-setting, and evaluation functions of management.

policy studies, imprecise term for interdisciplinary academic programs which focus on any or all aspects of policy.

policy termination, cessation of a policy or program.

political action committee (PAC), a nonprofit organization which raises and distributes funds to candidates for political office in the hope that supported candidates will act favorably on legislative or policy issues. PACs are separate and distinct from any political candidate's election or reelection committee. Most PAC's are established and supported by an organization or association of, for example, businesses, labor unions, or other interest groups.

See also:

ACTION ORGANIZATION
POLITICAL ACTIVITY
POLITICAL ORGANIZATION

political activity, a type of activity prohibited for tax-exempt organizations. Under the Internal Revenue Code of 1954, tax-exempt charitable organizations may not "participate in, or intervene in . . . any political campaign on behalf of any candidate for public office." Noninvolvement in political activities is one of four basic criteria for determining tax-exempt status under IRS Code 501 (c) (3).

political campaign, an organized effort to secure the election of a candidate for public office.

political campaign activity: *see* POLITICAL ACTIVITY.

political culture, a community's attitudes towards the quality and vigor of its nonprofit and governmental operations is determined largely by its political culture. Indeed, the only way to explain the extreme variations found in organizations and bureaucracies is to examine the cultural context of the community. The quality of organizational operations varies for a variety of reasons, not the last of which is the substantial disagreement as to just what constitutes a quality operation. But the quality or style of operations is determined only in the lesser part by well-meaning critics or even by administrators themselves; the crucial determinant is the will of the community as expressed by its political culture and shown by the administrative style of its organizations and programs.

political economy, the conjunction of economics and political science. It could be said that the major problem with an economy is that there is only one to be had and a great many individuals that would like to have it. Political economy is of concern to many nonprofit and most public organizations because of the primacy of economic prosperity. Maintaining economic prosperity remains a primary, though unspoken, objective in the United States.

political organization, an organization or association which accepts contributions and spends funds for political activities. Political organizations may qualify for tax-exempt status under IRS Code 527, but they remain subject to other restrictions.

political process, efforts of individuals and groups to gain and use power to achieve their goals.
See also POWER.

politics/administration dichotomy, the belief, growing out of the early administrative reform movement and its reaction against the spoils system which held that political interference in administration would erode the opportunity for administrative efficiency, that policy-making activities ought to be wholly separated from administrative functions, and that administrators had to have an explicit assignment of objectives before they could begin to develop an efficient administrative system. The dichotomy is still alive among those who contend that nonprofit boards should set policies and staff should implement such policies.

polygon, frequency: *see* FREQUENCY POLYGON.

polygraph: *see* LIE DETECTOR.

Ponpo: *see* PROGRAM ON NON-PROFIT ORGANIZATIONS.

pool, a joining together of resources (by individuals or organizations) in a common venture.

pooled income fund, one of three types of charitable remainder trusts in which a person makes a gift to a trust maintained by a charitable organization. The trust contains contributions made by many donors which are commingled to reduce risks and to benefit from professional management and planning. The annual distribution to the donor is the donor's pro rata share of the trust fund's earnings for the year. As is true of all charitable remainder trusts, the trust lasts for the life of the beneficiary and, upon his or her death, the trust assets are distributed to a qualified charity. The other types of charitable remainder trust are the charitable remainder annuity trust and the unitrust.
See also:
CHARITABLE REMAINDER ANNUITY TRUST
CHARITABLE REMAINDER TRUST
TRUST
UNITRUST

poor, having little or no money, goods, or means of support; dependent upon charity or public support; in poverty or destitute.

popular and ordinary, a narrow connotation of the term *charitable,* limiting its meaning to "for the relief of the poor."

population, also called SET and UNIVERSE, all of the cases in a class of things under statistical examination.

populism, recurring political theme in the U.S. that stresses the role of government in defending small voices against the powerful and wealthy.

port, a plug that connects parts of a computer system; a type of computer system interface.
See also INTERFACE.

portability, characteristic of a pension plan that allows participating employees to have the monetary value of accrued pension benefits transferred to a succeeding pension plan should they leave their present organization.

portfolio, all of the investments (usually stocks, bonds, etc.) held by one person or organization.

POSDCORB, mnemonic device invented by Luther Gulick in 1937 to call attention to the various functional elements of the work of a chief executive. POSDCORB stands for the following activities:

Planning; that is, working out in broad outline the things that need to be done and the methods for doing them to accomplish the purpose set for the enterprise;

Organizing; that is, the establishment of the formal structure of authority through which work subdivisions are arranged, defined, and coordinated for the defined objective;

Staffing; that is, the whole personnel function of bringing in and training the staff and maintaining favorable conditions of work;

Directing; that is, the continuous task of making decisions and embodying them in specific and general orders and instructions and serving as the leader of the enterprise;

Coordinating; that is, the all-important duty of interrelating the various parts of the work;

Reporting; that is, keeping those to whom the executive is responsible informed as to what is going on, which thus includes keeping himself and his subordinates informed through records, research and inspection;

Budgeting, with all that goes with budgeting in the form of fiscal planning, accounting, and control.

Source: Luther Gulick, "Notes on the Theory of Organization," in Luther Gulick and L. Urwick (eds.), *Papers on the Science of Administration* (N.Y.: Institute of Public Administration, 1937).

position, group of duties and responsibilities requiring the full- or part-time employment of one individual. A position may, at any given time, be occupied or vacant.

position, benchmark: *see* BENCHMARK POSITION.

position analysis, a systematic method of identifying, summarizing, and documenting the most important elements of an individual position, including (1) the results expected from the incumbent's work activity, (2) a summary of that work activity in terms of the tasks performed, and (3) a description of the qualifications needed to perform the necessary tasks. Position analysis is distinguished from job analysis in that the latter focuses on an analysis of a representative sample of positions included in a job classification.

Position Analysis Questionnaire (PAQ), job analysis questionnaire that is a tool for quantitatively describing the various aspects of a job. It was developed and copyrighted by the Purdue University Research Foundation.

position ceiling: *see* JOB CEILING.

position change, promotion, demotion, or reassignment.

position classification, process of using formal job descriptions to organize all jobs in a given organization into classes on the basis of duties and responsibilities for the purpose of delineating authority, establishing chains of command, and providing equitable salary scales.

To a program manager, budget maker or board member, positions are neat packages that represent specific salaries. Ultimately, the management of positions is a budgetary process. If position classification is thought of as essentially an accounting procedure, the whole system becomes more rational.

The principles and practices of position classification that are generally used are throwbacks to the heyday of the scientific management movement. They were conceived at a point in time—the second two decades of this century—when this school of management thought held sway, and they have never really been adapted to modern currents of management thought. After all, a classification plan is essentially a time-and-motion study for an organizational function. The duties of the larger organization are divided into positions in order to prevent duplication and enhance efficiency. A position is not a person but a set of duties and responsibilities fully equivalent to an interchangeable machine part because that is exactly what it represents—a human interchangeable part.

Current position classification practices are best thought of as being of mixed parentage, being derived more or less equally from two contemporary early twentieth century movements—scientific management and civil service reform.

As control devices, position classifications are doubly unsuccessful. First, they prevent program managers from having the discretion essential for the optimum success of their mission. Second, they generate an astounding amount of dysfunctional activity whose sole purpose is to get around the control devices. Although the controls are frequently and successfully cirumvented, the costs of such activity take away resources from the organization's prime goals.

See also the following entries:
CLASSIFICATION STANDARDS
SERIES OF CLASSES
SPECIFICATION

position classifier, a specialist in job analysis who determines the titles, occupational groups, series, and grades of positions.

position description, formal statement of the duties and responsibilities assigned to a position.

position guide: *see* JOB DESCRIPTION.

position management, term used to describe the key management actions involved in the process of organizing work to accomplish missions. It involves, essentially, the determination of the needs for positions, the determination of required skills and knowledges, and the organization, grouping, and assignment of duties and responsibilities among positions. There are no absolute rules for managers to follow in the complex and evolving art of position management; however, there are basic *system* requirements for position management which are designed to assure that work structures and organizational designs are systematically being assessed for improvement, that positions are correctly classified, and that the allocation of positions and deployment of people reflect the best that is known about managing human resources.

position paper, a formal statement of opinion on, for example, an organizational, social, or public issue.

position ranking, also called JOB GRADING, method of comparing jobs on a "whole job" basis in order to rank such jobs in a hierarchy from highest to lowest.

position survey, organizational review of positions to determine whether the positions are still needed and, if so, whether the classification and position description are correct.

positive law, a law that has been passed by a legislature.

positively skewed: *see* SKEWNESS.

positive recruitment, aggressive action designed to encourage qualified individuals to apply for positions, as opposed to just waiting for the right person to "knock on the door."

positive reinforcement: *see* REINFORCEMENT.

positive strike, also NEGATIVE STRIKE, a strike whose purpose is to gain new benefits. A *negative strike* is one whose purpose is to prevent the loss of present benefits.

positive stroking: *see* STROKING.

positive transfer: *see* TRANSFER OF TRAINING.

postbureaucratic organization, imagined organizations of the future. In 1952, Dwight Waldo, in the *American Political Science Review*, prophesied a future society in which "bureaucracy in the Weberian sense would have been replaced by more democratic, more flexible, though more complex, forms of large-scale organization." Waldo called such a society "post-bureaucratic." However, it remained for Warren G. Bennis, in the 1960s, to make the term particularly his own with a series of articles and books predicting the "end of bureaucracy." In its place, "there will be adaptive, rapidly changing *temporary systems*. These will be task forces composed of groups of relative strangers with diverse professional backgrounds and skills organized around problems to be solved. The groups will be arranged in an organic, rather than mechanical, model, meaning that they will evolve in response to a problem rather than to preset, programmed expectations. People will be evaluated not vertically according to rank and status, but flexibly according to competence. Organizational charts will consist of project groups rather than stratified functional groups." *See* Warren G. Bennis and Philip E. Slater, *The Temporary Society* (N.Y.: Harper & Row, 1968).

See also BENNIS, WARREN G.

postdate, to put a date on a document that is later than the date the document is signed; for example, to postdate a check.

post-entry training and CONTINUING EDUCATION, activities designed to upgrade the capabilities of an employee once he or she has joined an organization. Everything from executive development seminars constructed to improve the decision-making skills of top management to an orientation program which has as its objective acquainting new employees with the purposes and structure of the organization may be identified as post-entry training.

post-industrial society, term coined by Daniel Bell to describe the new social structures evolving in modern societies in the second half of the twentieth century. Bell holds that the "axial principle" of post-industrial society is the centrality of theoretical knowledge as the source of innovation and policy formation for the society. Hallmarks of post-industrial society include a change from a goods-producing to a service economy, the preeminence of a professional and technical class, and the creation of a new "intellectual" technology.

posting, writing down an entry (such as an expense) in an accounting journal; also, transferring the information from a journal into a ledger account.

See also:

ACCOUNTING CYCLE
JOURNAL
LEDGER

post-test, test given at the end of a training program or evaluation period to determine if the objectives have been met.

potential donors: *see* DONORS, POTENTIAL.

potential donors, records of: *see* DONORS, RECORD OF POTENTIAL.

poverty, the condition of having an inadequate supply of money, resources, goods, or means of subsistence. A difficult concept to define in practice, there is no single definition of poverty.

poverty area, an urban or rural geographic area with a high proportion of low income families. Normally, average income is used to define a poverty area, but other indicators, such as housing conditions, illegitimate birth rates, and incidence of juvenile delinquency are sometimes added to define geographic areas with poverty conditions.

power, the ability or the right (or both) to do something; the latent ability to influence others. Power enables leaders to exercise influence over other people. John R. P. French and Bertram Raven, in "The Bases of Social Power," suggest that there are five major bases of power: (1) *expert power,* which is based on the perception that the leader possesses some special knowledge or expertise; (2) *referent power,* which is based on the follower's liking, admiring, or identifying with the leader; (3) *reward power,* which is based on the leader's ability to mediate rewards for the follower; (4) *legitimate power,* which is based on the follower's perception that the leader has the legitimate right or authority to exercise influence over him or her; and (5) *coercive power,* which is based on the follower's fear that non-compliance with the leader's wishes will lead to punishment. Subsequent research on these power bases has indicated that emphasis on expert and referent power are more positively related to subordinate performance and satisfaction than utilization of reward, legitimate, or coercive power. For the French and Raven study, *see* Dorwin Cartwright (ed.), *Studies in Social Power* (Ann Arbor, Michigan: Institute for Social Research, University of Michigan 1959).

power base, the organizational or interpersonal support one has to advance one's self, policies, or programs.

power broker, a trader in influence.

power-elite theory: *see* PLURALISM.

power of attorney, document authorizing one person to act as attorney for, or in the place of, the person signing the document.

power structure, the people who make basic decisions for an organization or a community.

power test, test intended to measure level of performance unaffected by speed of response—there is either no time limit or a very generous one.

PPBS: *see* PLANNING PROGRAMING BUDGETING SYSTEMS.

practice, the use of one's knowledge in a particular profession. The practice of medicine is the exercise of one's knowledge in the promotion of health and treatment of disease.

practice effect, the influence of previous experience with a test on a later administration of the same test or a similar test—usually an increase in score on the second testing that can be attributed to increased familiarity with the directions, kinds of questions, or content of particular questions. Practice effect is greatest when the interval between testings is small, when the materials in the two tests are very similar, and when the initial test taking represents a relatively novel experience for the subjects.

precedence diagram, a diagrammatic representation of chronologically sequential activities or steps in a project or to accomplish an objective; a simplified version of a Critical Path Method diagram.

See also:

ARROW NETWORK
CRITICAL PATH METHOD
PERT

precedent, a legal decision on a question of law that gives authority and direction on how similar cases should be decided in the future.

prediction, differential: *see* DIFFERENTIAL VALIDATION.

predictive efficiency, measure of accuracy of a test or other predictive device in terms of the proportion of its predictions that have been shown to be correct.

predictive validity, measure obtained by giving a test to a group of subjects and then comparing the test results with the job performance of those tested.

predictor, any test or other procedure from which predictions of future performance or events may be made.

preference, a creditor's right to be paid before other creditors.

See also PRIORITY and VALUE.

preferred creditor: *see* PREFERENCE.

preferred stock, a category of stock that

is entitled to a fixed rate of income that is paid before dividends are paid on the company's common stock. Preferred stock makes for a more conservative investment than common stock, but less conservative than bonds.

See also CUMULATIVE PREFERRED STOCK.

pregnancy, the condition of expecting a child. According to Equal Employment Opportunity Commission guidelines,

> a written or unwritten employment policy or practice which excludes from employment applicants or employees because of pregnancy is in prima facie violation of Title VII (of the Civil Rights Act of 1964).
>
> Disabilities caused or contributed to by pregnancy, miscarriage, abortion, childbirth, and recovery therefrom are, for all job-related purposes, temporary disabilities and should be treated as such under any health or temporary disability insurance or sick leave plan available in connection with employment. Written and unwritten employment policies and practices involving matters such as the commencement and duration of leave, the availability of extensions, and the accrual of seniority and other benefits and privileges, reinstatement and payment under any health or temporary disability insurance or sick leave plan, formal or informal, shall be applied to disability due to pregnancy or childbirth on the same terms and conditions as they are applied to other temporary disabilities. Where the termination of an employee who is temporarily disabled is caused by an employment policy under which insufficient or no leave is available, such a termination violates the Act if it has a disparate impact on employees of one sex and is not justified by business necessity.

See also the following entries:

GENERAL ELECTRIC CO. V. GILBERT
MATERNITY LEAVE
NASHVILLE GAS CO. V. SATTY
SEX DISCRIMINATION
TITLE VII

Pregnancy Discrimination Act of 1978, an amendment to Title VII of the Civil Rights Act of 1964, which holds that discrimination on the basis of pregnancy, childbirth, or related medical conditions constitutes unlawful sex discrimination. The amendment was enacted in response to the Supreme Court's ruling in *General Electric Co.* v. *Gilbert,* 429 U.S. 125 (1976) that an employer's exclusion of pregnancy-related disabilities from its comprehensive disability plan did not violate Title VII. The amendment asserts that:

1. A written or unwritten employment policy or practice which excludes from employment opportunities applicants or employees because of pregnancy, childbirth or related medical conditions is in prime facie violation of Title VII.
2. Disabilities caused or contributed to by pregnancy, childbirth, or related medical conditions, for all job-related purposes, shall be treated the same as disabilities caused or contributed to by other medical conditions, under any health or disability insurance or sick leave plan available in connection with employment. Written or unwritten employment policies and practices involving matters such as the commencement and duration of leave, the availability of extensions, the accrual of seniority and other benefits and privileges, reinstatement, and payment under any health or disability insurance or sick leave plan, formal or informal, shall be applied to disability due to pregnancy, childbirth, or related medical conditions on the same terms and conditions as they are applied to other disabilities. Health insurance benefits for abortion, except where the life of the mother would be endangered if the fetus were carried to term or where medical complications have arisen from an abortion, are not required to be paid by an employer; nothing herein, however, precludes an employer from providing abortion benefits or otherwise affects bar-

gaining agreements in regard to abortion.

3. Where the termination of an employee who is temporarily disabled is caused by an employment policy under which insufficient or no leave is available, such a termination violates the Act if it has a disparate impact on employees of one sex and is not justified by business necessity.

premium, the money paid for insurance coverage, usually annually; also, the amount by which a stock, bond, or other security sells above its par value (face value).
See also PAR.

premium pay: *see* WORK PREMIUM.

prepaid expense, any expense or debt paid before it is due; for example, a travel advance to an employee.

prepaid health care plan: *see* HEALTH CARE PLAN, PREPAID.

prepaid legal services, employee benefit that has the employee and/or employer contribute to a fund that pays for legal services in the same way medical insurance pays for hospitalization.

prepaid legal services trust: *see* LEGAL SERVICES TRUST, PREPAID.

prepayment penalty, an extra charge that must be paid if a loan is paid off early.

pre-retirement counseling, efforts on the part of an organization to give to those of its employees who will be eligible to retire information about all of the options that retirement entails.
See also RETIREMENT COUNSELING.

preselection, process by which a person is informally selected for a position prior to the normal selection procedures. The ensuing selection process is necessarily a sham.

presentment, request for payment on a negotiable instrument, such as a check.

present worth, also PRESENT VALUE, future payments, earnings, or debts discounted to their value today (as if a sum of money was invested today to make future payments).
See also DISCOUNTING.

pre-service training, training provided to staff or volunteers before they start to work.
See also:
CONTINUING EDUCATION
ORIENTATION
TRAINING

president, chief elected or appointed officer of an organization. In public charitable organizations, the president is usually the chief elected officer of the board of directors—not the chief executive officer. However, the president of a foundation may be the chief executive officer.
See also CHIEF EXECUTIVE OFFICER and OFFICER.

President's Commission on Executive Interchange, federal government program, established in 1969 by Executive Order 11451, which arranges for managers from the public, nonprofit, and private sectors to work in a different sector for a year or more.

President's Commission on Private Philanthropy and Public Needs: *see* COMMISSION ON PRIVATE PHILANTHROPY AND PUBLIC NEEDS.

presort, to arrange mail in zip code order in order to take advantage of lower postage rates.

press kit: *see* PUBLIC RELATIONS KIT.

press release, a formal statement made by an organization to representatives of the media in hopes that it will be publicly disseminated (published or broadcast). Press releases are written descriptions of past or upcoming events or activities of significance or statements about the organization's position on, for example, a controversial public policy. The process of having press releases published or broadcast accurately and timely is a difficult one and requires considerable planning and development of media relations.

See also:

MEDIA
MEDIA, ELECTRONIC
MEDIA, PRINT
MEDIA RELATIONS
PUBLIC RELATIONS

pressure group, also called INTEREST GROUP, less kind ways of referring to legitimate lobbying organizations.

pre-tax income, also NET PROFIT BEFORE TAXES, a for-profit corporation's net profit exlusive of income tax due or paid.

pre-test, a test given, for example, before initiating a training program or implementing an evaluation in order to measure existing levels of proficiency or performance. Such levels should later be compared to end-test scores in order to evaluate the quality of the program or the attainments of the participants.

Also, a test designed for the purpose of validating new items and obtaining statistics for them before they are used in a final form.

See also BEFORE AND AFTER STUDY.

prevention of cruelty organization: *see* ORGANIZATION, PREVENTION OF CRUELTY.

preventive discipline, activity premised on the notion that knowledge of disciplinary policies tends to inhibit infractions. Preventive discipline seeks to heighten employees' awareness of organizational rules and policies.

preventive mediation, action used in order to avoid last-minute crisis bargaining. Negotiating parties sometimes seek preventive mediation—the use of a mediator before an impasse has been reached.

previously taxed income, earnings that have been taxed but not yet distributed. This usually happens when a Subchapter S corporation holds onto its earnings. This income will not be taxed a second time when distributed to the company's owners.

See also SUBCHAPTER S CORPORATION.

price/earnings ratio, the cost of a share of stock divided by the yearly dividend paid on that stock. For example, a $20 stock that pays a $2 dividend has a ten to one ratio. The price/earnings ratio is a standard measure used in comparing stocks for investment.

prima facie (Latin), at first sight; on the face of it; presumably.

primarily: *see* EXCLUSIVELY.

primary data, evaluation data which do not exist prior to initiating an evaluation study. The creation and collection of primary data is accomplished by the evaluator; for example, responses to a questionnaire or public survey.

See also:

OPERATIONAL DATA
SECONDARY DATA
SOURCES OF DATA

primary group: *see* GROUP, PRIMARY.

primary purpose rule, a general principle for determining tax exemption established by the U.S. Supreme Court in the 1945 case of *Better Business Bureau of Washington, D.C.* v. *United States* (326 U.S. 279, 283 [1945]). The court stated: "[The] presence of a single . . . [non-exempt] purpose, if substantial in nature, will destroy the exemption [of the organization in question] regardless of the number or importance of [its other] truly . . . [exempt] purposes."

prime rate, the rate of interest charged by commercial banks for short-term loans to their most creditworthy customers.

principal, chief, primary, or most important; also, a sum of money (for example, loaned or borrowed), rather than the profits (for example, interest) made on that money.

principles of management, fundamental truths or working hyptheses that serve as guidelines to management thinking and action.

See also the following entries:
MANAGEMENT PRINCIPLES
POSDCORB
PROVERBS OF ADMINISTRATION
SPAN OF CONTROL

printers ink statute, a state law that makes it illegal to advertise anything that is false or deceptive.

prioritize, the process of ranking alternative competing uses of scarce resources.

priority, precedence in importance; the right to take precedence over alternative uses of scarce resources. A priority may be, for example, a need, a program, public credibility, a staff position, a piece of equipment, etc.

Prisoner Rehabilitation Act of 1965, federal statute that permits selected federal prisoners to work in the community while still having an inmate status.

Privacy Act of 1974, (Public Law 93-579), federal statute that reasserts the fundamental right to privacy as derived from the Constitution of the United States and provides a series of basic safeguards for the individual to prevent the misuse of personal information by the federal government.

The act provides for making known to the public the existence and characteristics of all personal information systems kept by every federal agency. It permits an individual to have access to records containing personal information on that individual and allows the individual to control the transfer of that information to other federal agencies for nonroutine uses. The act also requires all federal agencies to keep accurate accountings of transfers of personal records to other agencies and outsiders and to make the accountings available to the individual. It further provides for civil remedies for the individual whose records are kept or used in contravention of the requirements of the act.

private, concerning individuals, not the general public and not the government.

private benefit: *see* PRIVATE INUREMENT.

private benefit test: *see* PRIVATE INUREMENT.

private foundation, a corporation or trust the endowments of which are dedicated to philanthropy and the proceeds of which are directed to the public good. Private foundations are controlled by and usually financially supported by a single source, such as an individual, a family, or a corporation. Private foundations were defined statutorily in the Tax Reform Act of 1969. Tax deductions for contributions to private foundations are more restricted than are contributions to other types of tax-exempt organizations.

See also:
CHARITABLE ORGANIZATION
EQUITY
FOUNDATION
PHILANTHROPY
PRIVATE OPERATING FOUNDATION
PUBLICLY SUPPORTED ORGANIZATION

private inurement, an important concept of tax-exemption meaning for the benefit of private individuals, typically organization members or shareholders. According to IRS Code 501(c) (3), no part of a tax-exempt organization's net earnings may inure to the benefit of any private shareholder or individual. The private inurement concept is to ensure that tax-exempt organizations serve public rather than private interests. Private inurement is similar in concept to self-dealing and is one of the most important concepts for distinguishing between for-profit and nonprofit organizations and activities.

See also:
ARM'S-LENGTH
NONPROFIT ORGANIZATION
PUBLIC BENEFIT
SELF-DEALING

private inurement, incidental: *see* INCIDENTAL PRIVATE INUREMENT.

private inurement doctrine: *see* PRIVATE INUREMENT .

private law, statute passed to affect only one person or group, in contrast to a public law.

private operating foundation, a type of private foundation which primarily operates programs directly rather than making grants to other entities. However, some private operating foundations also make a small number of grants.

See also PRIVATE FOUNDATION and PUBLICLY SUPPORTED ORGANIZATION.

private sector organization, all of those industries or activities considered to be within the domain of free enterprise.

privatization, the process of returning to the private sector property (such as public lands) or functions owned or performed by government.

privilege, an advantage or a right to preferential treatment; also, an exemption from a duty that others must perform; also, a basic right, for example, as guaranteed to all by Article Four and the Fourteenth Amendment of the U.S. Constitution.

privity, private or inside knowledge. Privity may determine, for example, who may be sued in certain circumstances.

proactive, an administrative or organizational style which encourages taking risks on behalf of one's clients or one's moral values; the opposite of reactive.

probability, chance of an occurrence—the likelihood that an event will occur, expressed as a number from 0 to 1.

probate, the process of proving that a will is genuine and distributing the property of an estate as provided in a will; also, in some states, the name for a court that handles the distribution of decedents' estates (dead persons' property) and other matters.

probationary employee, also PROBATIONARY PERIOD, period of time during which new employees are considered probationary. During this time they have no seniority rights and may be discharged without cause, so long as such a discharge does not violate laws concerning union membership and equal employment opportunity.

probationary rate: *see* ENTRANCE RATE.

pro bono publico, Latin phrase meaning "for the public good." When abbreviated to *pro bono*, it usually stands for work done by lawyers without pay for some charitable or public purpose; the representation of low-income people by law firms in voluntary legal aid efforts or projects.

See also PUBLIC INTEREST LAW FIRM.

procedural rights, various protections that all citizens have against arbitrary actions by public officials.

procedure, the method by which activities are to be performed; a particular direction or method of action. Procedures are more detailed and methodological than policies but are supposed to be derived from policies. Most nonprofit organizations merge policies and procedures into a single manual.

See also POLICIES AND PROCEDURES MANUAL and POLICY.

procedures manual: *see* POLICIES AND PROCEDURES MANUAL.

proceeds, money or property gained through sales or fund-raising activities.

process, the procedure used to yield program or organizational outcomes or impacts. For example, counseling (a process) to change clients' behaviors (an outcome); distributing literature (a process) to reduce the incidence of alcohol-related accidents (an outcome).

See also OUTCOME.

process consultation (P-C), according to the standard work on process consultation, Edgar H. Schein's *Process Consultation: Its Role in Organization Development* (Reading, Mass.: Addison-Wesley Publishing Co., 1969), "a set of activities on the part of the consultant which help the client to perceive, understand, and act upon process events which occur in the client's environment."

According to Schein, P-C makes the following seven assumptions:

1. Managers often do not know what is wrong and need special help in diagnosing what their problems actually are.
2. Managers often do not know what kinds of help consultants can give to them; they need to be helped to know what kind of help to seek.
3. Most managers have a constructive intent to improve things but need help in identifying what to improve and how to improve it.
4. Most organizations can be more effective if they learn to diagnose their own strengths and weaknesses. No organizational form is perfect; hence every form of organization will have some weaknesses for which compensatory mechanisms need to be found.
5. A consultant could probably not, without exhaustive and time-consuming study, learn enough about the culture of the organization to suggest reliable new courses of action. Therefore, he must work jointly with members of the organization who do know the culture intimately from having lived within it.
6. The client must learn to see the problem for himself, to share in the diagnosis, and to be actively involved in generating a remedy. One of the process consultant's roles is to provide new and challenging alternatives for the client to consider. Decision making about these alternatives must, however, remain in the hands of the client.
7. It is of prime importance that the process consultant be expert in how to diagnose and how to establish effective helping relationships with clients. Effective P-C involves the passing on of both these skills.

process objective: *see* PERFORMANCE OBJECTIVE.

process quality control: *see* STATISTICAL QUALITY CONTROL.

procurement standards, rules governing purchasing practices and procedures.

product: *see* IMPACT and OUTCOME.

productivity, measured relationship between the quantity (and quality) of results produced and the quantity of resources required for production. Productivity is, in essence, a measure of the work efficiency of an individual, a work unit, or a whole organization.

Productivity can be measured in two ways. One way relates the output of an enterprise, industry, or economic sector to a single input such as labor or capital. The other relates output to a composite of inputs, combined so as to account for their relative importance. The choice of a particular productivity measure depends on the purpose for which it is to be used.

The most generally useful measure of productivity relates output to the input of labor time—output per hour, or its reciprocal, unit labor requirements. This kind of measure is used widely because labor productivity is relevant to most economic analyses, and because labor is the most easily measured input. Relating output to labor input provides a tool not only for analyzing productivity, but also for examining labor costs, real income, and employment trends.

Labor productivity can be measured readily at several levels of aggregation: The business economy, its component sectors, industries, or plants. Depending on the components of the measure used and the context, labor productivity will be called output per hour of all persons engaged in the productive process, output per employee hour, or just output per hour.

The use of labor productivity indexes does not imply that labor is solely or primarily responsible for productivity growth. In a technologically advanced society, labor effort is only one of many sources of productivity improvement. Trends in output per hour also reflect technological innovation, changes in capital stock and capacity utilization, scale of production, materials flow, management skills, and other factors whose contribution often cannot be measured.

The output side of the output per hour ratio refers to the finished product or the amount of real value added in various enterprises, industries, sectors, or the economy as a whole. Few plants or industries produce a single homogeneous commodity that can be measured by simply counting the number of units produced. Consequently, for the purpose of measurement, the various units of a plant's or an industry's output are combined on some common basis—either their unit labor requirements in a base period or their dollar value. When information on the number of units produced is not available, as is often the case, output must be expressed in terms of the dollar value of production, adjusted for price changes.

See also the following entries:
NATIONAL ASSOCIATION OF SUGGESTION SYSTEM(S)
SUGGESTION SYSTEM

productivity bargaining, collective bargaining that seeks increases in productivity in exchange for increases in wages and benefits. There are two basic approaches to productivity bargaining—integrative bargaining and pressure bargaining. The latter is the stuff of confrontation and is best illustrated by the adversary model of labor relations—the most commonly adopted model in the United States. Its dysfunctional consequences—strikes and hostility—are well known. The other approach—integrative bargaining—is, in essence, participative management. It is premised upon the notions that a decrease in hostility is mutually advantageous and that management does not have a natural monopoly on brains. The crucial aspect of

**THE LITTLE RED HEN:
A PRODUCTIVITY FABLE**

Once upon a time there was a little red hen who scratched about the barnyard until she uncovered some grains of wheat. She turned to other workers on the farm and said: "If we plant this wheat, we'll have bread to eat. Who will help me plant it?"

"We never did that before," said the horse, who was the supervisor.

"I'm too busy," said the duck.

"I'd need complete training," said the pig.

"It's not in my job description," said the goose.

"Well, I'll do it myself," said the little red hen. And she did. The wheat grew tall and ripened into grain. "Who will help me reap the wheat?" asked the little red hen.

"Let's check the regulations first," said the horse.

"I'd lose my seniority," said the duck.

"I'm on my lunch break," said the goose.

"Out of my classification," said the pig.

"Then I will," said the little red hen, and she did.

At last it came time to bake the bread.

"Who will help me bake the bread?" asked the little red hen.

"That would be overtime for me," said the horse.

"I've got to run some errands," said the duck.

"I've never learned how," said the pig.

"If I'm to be the only helper, that's unfair," said the goose.

"Then I will," said the little red hen.

She baked five loaves and was ready to turn them in to the farmer when the other workers stepped up. They wanted to be sure the farmer knew it was a group project.

"It needs to be cleared by someone else," said the horse.

"I'm calling the shop steward," said the duck.

"I demand equal rights," said the goose.

"We'd better file a copy," said the pig.

But the little red hen turned in the loaves by herself. When it came time for the farmer to reward the effort, he gave one loaf to each worker.

"But I earned all the bread myself!" said the little red hen.

"I know," said the farmer, "but it takes too much paperwork to justify giving you all the bread. It's much easier to distribute it equally, and that way the others won't complain."

So the little red hen shared the bread, but her co-workers and the farmer wondered why she never baked any more.

SOURCE: *Federal News Clip Sheet* (June 1979)

integrative bargaining is its joint procedures in defining problems, searching for alternatives, and selecting solutions.

productivity measurement, measuring the productivity of any organization, program, or individual. This is particularly problematic in the nonprofit and public sectors because of the problem of defining outputs and of quantifying measures of efficiency, effectiveness, and impact.

Nonprofit and public organizations often have multiple and sometimes intangible outputs. In evaluating efficiency, selecting from among the many possible input/output ratios is troublesome. A considerable danger exists in selecting only certain input and output variables because a single efficiency measure may be, in truth, a meaningless or oversimplified measure of performance.

The productivity measurement issue is further complicated by the fact that different efficiency and effectiveness measures must be selected depending upon certain organizational variables: highly routine work vs. nonroutine work; high or low degrees of employee discretion; outputs that are standard or novel; or a work process which is simple vs. complex. Another way of stating this problem is that from the variety of available productivity measures, those selected must differentiate between intermediate outputs (outputs used by other members of the organization) and final outputs (those absorbed by the outside environment) and between staff and line functions (some individuals/units perform support functions whose impact can be assessed only in terms of increased performance of line departments). The question remains: how can these varied contributions be isolated and measured? Productivity measurement is beset by many obstacles, not the least of which is the insecurity felt by managers attempting to undertake productivity assessments.

profession, occupation requiring specialized knowledge that can only be gained via intensive preparation. Professional occupations tend to possess three features: (1) a body of erudite knowledge which is applied to the service of society; (2) a standard of success measured by accomplishments in serving the needs of society rather than purely serving personal gain; and (3) a system of control over the professional practice which regulates the education of its new members and maintains both a code of ethics and appropriate sanctions. The primary characteristic that differentiates it from a vocation is its theoretical commitment to rendering a public service.

professionalism, conducting oneself in a manner that characterizes a particular occupation. For example, a professional fireman is a full-time fireman who is thoroughly skilled in the trade. Nevertheless, a fireman is not a "professional" in the traditional sense.

professionalization, process by which occupations acquire professional status. For example, U.S. police departments are becoming more professional as increasing numbers of their members gain advanced degrees and take their ethical responsibilities more seriously. This process of professionalization will be complete only when the overwhelming majority of police officers meet the high standards of the present minority.

professional organization, also PROFESSIONAL ASSOCIATION, an organization that promotes a particular profession, for example, a medical society. Professional organizations may qualify for tax-exempt status as business leagues under IRS Code 501(c)(6).

Professional Standards Review Organizations (PSROs), a type of organization established by the Social Security Amendments of 1972 to control costs, quality, and unnecessary medical treatment provided in hospitals under Medicare and Medicaid financing. PSROs are required to be nonprofit organizations, and their members must be licensed physicians.

proficiency test, device to measure the skill or knowledge that a person has acquired in an occupation.

profile, board: *see* BOARD PROFILE.

profit, all gains, including both money and increases in the value of property; also, the return on invested capital; also, income minus expenses; a monetary surplus left to the owners of an organization after all expenses have been paid or accounted for. Profits of a for-profit company, for example, may be distributed to the owners, shared voluntarily with employees, or retained to finance future corporate growth or cash needs.

profit and loss statement, the operating statement used by for-profit companies. The equivalent of a profit and loss statement for nonprofit organizations is called simply an operating statement or a statement of activity.

See also FINANCIAL STATEMENTS and OPERATING STATEMENT.

profit motive, the concept that the desire for private inurement or personal benefit is the moving force for creativity and productivity in the private sector. The profit motive is often cited as the underlying reason why private sector organizations are supposedly inherently more efficient and effective than public sector organizations.

profit sharing, a plan set up by a private employer to distribute part of the firm's profits to some or all of its employees based on the profitability of the business. A *qualified profit sharing plan* (one that meets IRS requirements for tax benefits) must provide specific criteria and formulas for who gets what, how, and when.

pro forma, Latin phrase meaning "as a matter of form" or "a mere formality."

program, major organizational endeavor, mission oriented, that is defined in terms of the principal actions required to achieve a significant objective. A program is an organized set of activities designed to produce a particular result or set of results that will have a certain impact upon a problem.

program, also PROGRAMMER and PROGRAMMING, in computer terminology, a set of instructions telling the computer what to do. A *programmer* is a person who writes a computer program. As the programmer does his or her job, he or she can be said to be *programming* the computer.

program budgeting: *see* BUDGETING, PERFORMANCE.

program evaluation, also IMPACT EVALUATION and OUTCOME EVALUATION, systematic evaluation of any activity or group of activities undertaken to make a determination about their impacts or effects, both short- and long-range. A program evaluation should be distinguished from a performance or administrative evaluation because these are limited to concentrating on a program's internal administrative procedures. While program evaluations will use information such as workload measures, staffing levels, or operational procedural data, the main thrust is necessarily on overall program objectives and impact.

The concept of efficiency and effectiveness are the standard criteria against which programs are pitted by evaluation. In addition these concepts helped to forge a workable distinction between audits and evaluations. Audits, primarily financial accounting audits, are geared to control—to insure that funds are accounted for and that every regulation is complied with. This law enforcement type of management style is being increasingly displaced by program evaluation—a far more comprehensive management tool. We still expect programs to be administered efficiently, just as we expect fiscal accountability for funds and receipts. But efficiency isn't enough. A work unit could be terribly efficient while working toward the wrong goals. Because of this, evaluations, if they are themselves to be effective, must also deal with the questions of effectiveness and relevance. It is not unreasonable to demand that pro-

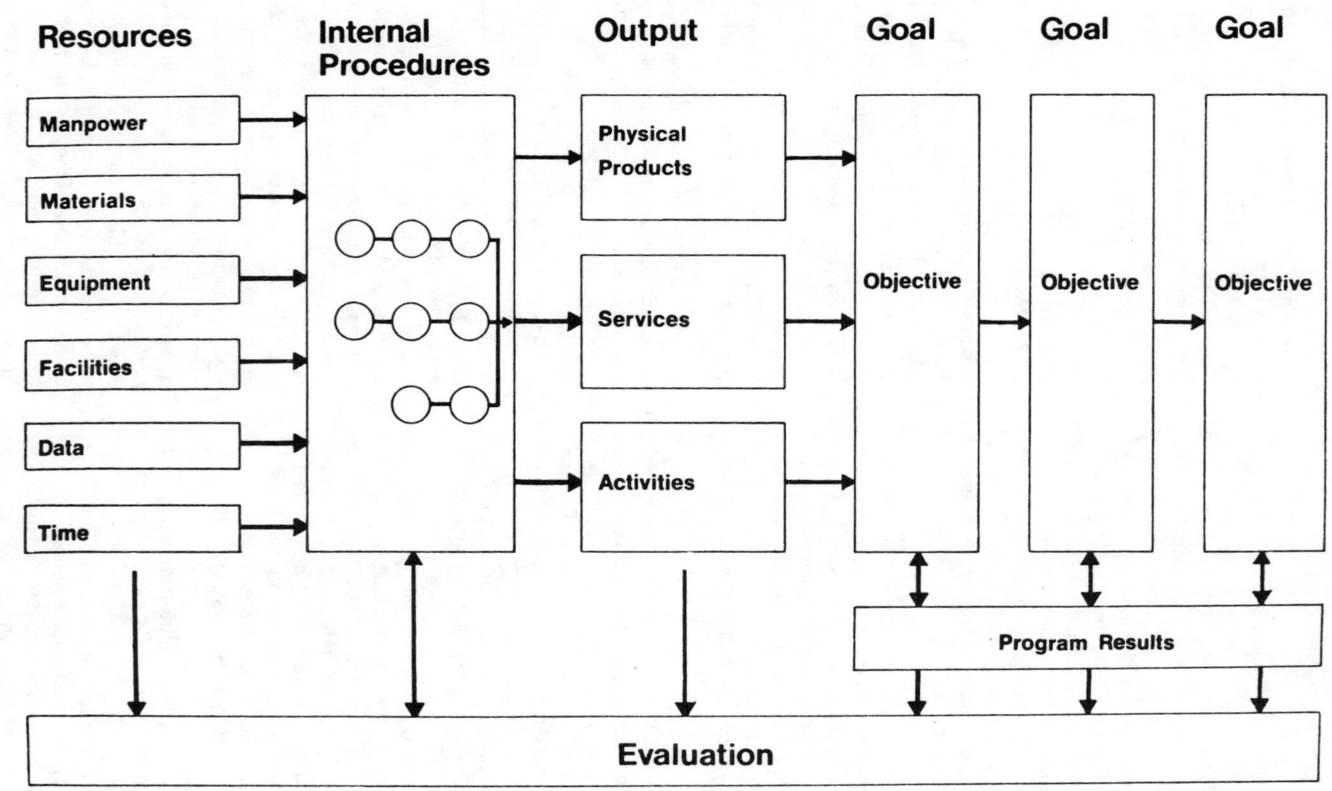

Source: R. L. Subry, J. S. Ott, C. J. Peterson, and J. W. Sawyer, Program Planning and Analysis *(Denver, Colo.: Applied Management Corporation, 1977, 1982.)*

grams have an effect on problems, and the right problems, at that. Simply put, the most basic objective of a program evaluation is to assay the impact of a program on its target problems or needs.

Program evaluation is not the sole province of any sector or organization. Evaluations are even being done by the courts in response to petitions by client groups. Of course, the press conducts evaluations with every exposé of a mismanaged organization. However, accurate or not, journalistic evaluations often tend to be too superficial to serve as instruments of reform, although they do serve to provide impetus for full-scale evaluation efforts by objective outsiders.

Program Evaluation and Review Technique: *see* PERT.

program management: *see* PROJECT MANAGEMENT.

programmed instruction: *see* PROGRAMMED LEARNING.

programmed learning, also called PROGRAMMED INSTRUCTION, technique that has learning materials presented in a predetermined order with provisions that permit the learner to proceed at his/her own pace and gain immediate feedback on his/her answers. Programmed learning usually requires the use of a teaching machine (computer) or programmed text. The rationale for and methodology of programmed learning is generally credited to B. F. Skinner. *See* J. G. Holland and B. F. Skinner, *The Analysis of Behavior: A Program for Self-Instruction* (N.Y.: McGraw-Hill 1961).

programmer: *see* PROGRAM.

programming: *see* PROGRAM.

Program on Non-profit Organizations (Ponpo), the only university-based research center on the nonprofit sector, located at Yale University in New Haven, Conn.

program-related investment, financial investments made by tax-exempt organizations for charitable purposes, which are made to nonprofit or nonexempt for-profit organizations. For example, an LEDC may invest in a local business in an economically depressed area to help save it from going out of business and, therefore, to help alleviate poverty in the area. The LEDC will not lose its tax-exempt status automatically. Foundations were first permitted to make program-related investments by the Tax Reform Act of 1969.

program results audits, audits which determine (a) whether the desired results or benefits are being achieved and (b) whether the organization has considered alternatives that might yield desired results at a lower cost.

program structure: *see* HIERARCHY OF OBJECTIVES.

program structure chart, a diagrammatic presentation of a hierarchy of objectives.

See also FAST and HIERARCHY OF OBJECTIVES.

progression line charts, lists of job titles in a broad job family, generally starting with the less difficult, lower paying jobs and progressing to the more difficult, higher paying jobs.

progression sequences, a hierarchy of job titles through which an employee may progress in following a career path or ladder. Such sequences generally begin with lower paying job titles and ascend through intermediate job titles to higher paying job titles.

progressive rate structure (income tax), system in which individuals and organizations with larger incomes are generally in higher tax brackets and, therefore, pay a larger percent of their taxable income in taxes than people and organizations in lower tax brackets.

progressive tax: *see* TAX EQUITY.

progress payments, periodic payments made as work on a contract progresses.

Program Evaluation Flow Chart

Planning for the Evaluation

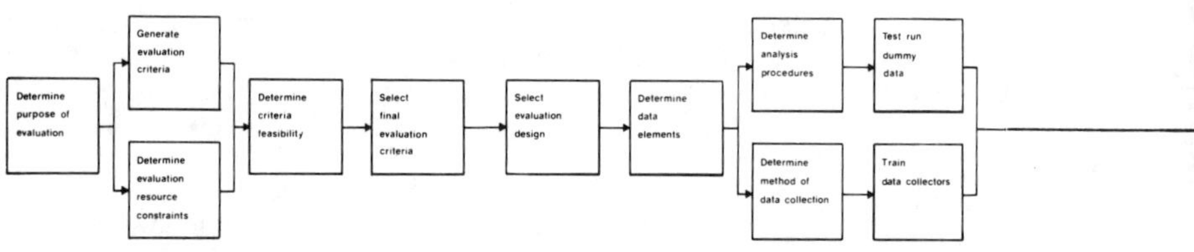

Used with permission of Applied Management Corporation.

progress testing: *see* PHASED TESTING.

project categorical grant: *see* GRANT.

project control chart, also FLOW CHART and WORK PLAN CHART, any one of several alternative diagrammatic approaches for displaying the chronological relationships among a project's or program's tasks, activities, and events.

See also:

CRITICAL PATH METHOD
GANTT CHART
PERT
PRECEDENCE DIAGRAM
PROJECT MANAGEMENT

projective test, also called PROJECTIVE TECHNIQUE, any method which seeks to discover an individual's attitudes, motivations, and characteristic traits through responses to unstructured stimuli such as ambiguous pictures or inkblots.

project management, also called PROGRAM MANAGEMENT, management of an organizational unit created to achieve a specific goal. While a project may last from a few months to a few years, it has no further future. Indeed, a primary measure of its success is its dissolution. The project staff necessarily consists of a mix of skills from the larger organization. The success of project management is most dependent upon the unambiguous nature of the project's goal and the larger organization's willingness to delegate sufficient authority and resources to the project manager. Project or program management is an integral part of matrix organizations.

project manager, manager whose task is to achieve a temporary organizational goal using as his/her primary tool the talents of diverse specialists from the larger organization. The authority and responsibility of a project manager vary enormously with differing projects and organizations.

Project Notification and Review System (PNRS), the procedure by which an organization notifies an A-95 clearinghouse of its intent (NOI) to submit a grant proposal in advance of submittal. PNRS provides the clearinghouse with advance notice of pending grant applications so it can prepare to review and circulate the grant proposals for review and comment.

See also:

GRANT PROPOSAL
NOTIFICATION OF INTENT
OFFICE OF MANAGEMENT AND BUDGET CIRCULAR A-95

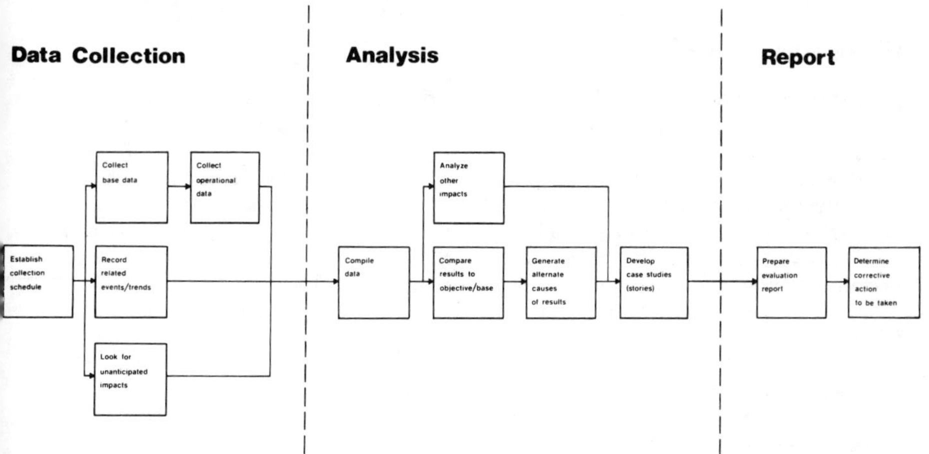

promissory note, a written promise, with no strings attached, to pay a certain sum of money by a certain time.

promotion (external relations), a very broad term meaning the presentation of a product (in the broadest sense of the word "product") for consumer or public acceptance through a program of direct contact methods (such as direct mail) and/or a media relations program. The term has both positive and negative uses, for example: *positive*—to promote the cause of world peace; *negative*—to promote by cunning or trickery, or the shady activities of a "promoter."

promotion (personnel management), process of advancing employees to positions that usually carry more responsibilities and greater salaries.

See also the following entries:
CAREER PROMOTION
COMPETITIVE PROMOTION
HORIZONTAL PROMOTION
MERIT PROMOTION

promotion certificate, list of best qualified candidates to be considered to fill a position under competitive promotion procedures.

promotion plan, the methods to be followed in locating, evaluating, and selecting employees for promotion. It also explains what records will be kept, how information will be given to employees about the promotion program, etc.

promulgate, to publish; to announce officially; to put out formally.

proof of claim, a sworn statement in a bankruptcy or probate proceeding of how much a creditor is owed.

proof of loss, a sworn statement made to an insurance company of a loss suffered under an insurance policy.

propaganda, the doctrines, beliefs, or principles propagated or advanced by an organization or movement and its members. Propaganda connotes spreading one-sided information to advance the purposes of the organization or movement. Other terms typically associated with propaganda include "selfish purpose," "ulterior purpose," and "colored facts."

property management, performing all of a landlord's functions, such as upkeep, rent collection, finding tenants, etc., for another person's building, for a fee.

property tax: *see* TAX, REAL PROPERTY and TAXATION.

proportional tax: *see* TAX EQUITY.

proposal: *see* GRANT PROPOSAL.

Proposition 13, also called the JARVIS-GANN INITIATIVE, state constitutional ammendment approved by California voters in 1978 that rolled back and set ceilings on property taxes. Proposition 13 is an important landmark in a national tax-relief movement and has significant implications for nonprofit organizations.

Proposition 2½, a 1980 tax limitation measure approved by the voters of Massachusetts which requires local governments to lower property taxes by fifteen percent a year until they reach 2½ percent of fair market value.

prorate, to divide or share proportionately or by shares.

prosecutor, attorney employed by a government agency or subunit whose official duty is to initiate and maintain criminal proceedings on behalf of the government against persons accused of committing criminal offenses.

prosecutorial agency, a federal, state, or local criminal justice agency of which the principal function is the prosecution of alleged offenders.

prospectus, a short document which "advertises" a forthcoming grant proposal; a preview of a grant proposal submitted to a potential grantor to test its potential willingness to consider funding a project—before the submitting organization fully develops or submits a complete grant proposal.

See also GRANT ABSTRACT and GRANT PROPOSAL.

protected classes/groups: *see* AFFIRMATIVE ACTION GROUPS.

protest, a written statement that a person or organization does not agree to the legality, justice, or correctness of a payment, but that it will pay while reserving the right to get the payment back later.

Protestant ethic, also called WORK ETHIC, Max Weber's term from his 1904-05 book, *The Protestant Ethic and the Spirit of Capitalism*, which refers to his theory that modern capitalism has its origins in the Calvinistic concern for moral obligation and economic success. While some dispute Weber's historical analysis, any society whose members have a strong drive for work and the accumulation of wealth is colloquially said to have a "Protestant" or work ethic.

protocol, the conventions about computer software, content, format, speed, etc. that allow different parts of a computer system and different computer systems to communicate.

See also COMPUTER.

proverbs of administration, contradictory adages. A significant landmark in the history of administrative theory was Herbert A. Simon's refutation of the principles approach that dominated administrative thinking until after World War II. Simon asserted, in "The Proverbs of Administration," *Public Administration Review* (Winter 1946), that the principles of administration, like proverbs, almost always occur in mutually contradictory pairs:

> Most of the propositions that make up the body of administrative theory today share, unfortunately, this defect of proverbs. For almost every principle one can find an equally plausible and acceptable contradictory principle. Although the two principles of the pair will lead to exactly opposite organizational recommendations, there is nothing in the theory to indicate which is the proper one to apply.

proxy, also PROXY STATEMENT, a person who acts for another person; a written authorization permitting another person to vote or to act for the signer of the authorizing document.

proxy measure: *see* MEASURE, PROXY.

prudent person rule, rule that a trustee may invest trust funds only in traditionally safe investments or risk being personally responsible for losses.

pseudo-effectiveness, according to Chris Argyris, in *Integrating the Individual and the Organization* (N.Y.: John Wiley & Sons, 1964), "a state in which no discomfort is reported but in which, upon diagnosis, ineffectiveness is found." Since the underlying ineffectiveness is not evident, the true costs of continuing in such a state remain hidden by compensatory mechanisms. Eventually, such compensatory mechanisms will require so much energy that they will influence the organization negatively and call attention to the underlying problem.

See also ARGYRIS, CHRIS.

PSO: *see* PUBLIC SERVICE ORGANIZATION.

PSRO: *see* PROFESSIONAL STANDARDS REVIEW ORGANIZATION. *Note*: In a few states PSRO's are called "Peer Standards Review Organizations."

psychobabble, indiscriminate use of psychological concepts and terms as an affected style of speech.

psychological contract, a concept proposed by Edgar H. Schein, in *Organizational Psychology* (Englewood Cliffs, N.J., 3rd ed., 1980), that involves the individual's and organization's expectations about the whole "pattern of rights, privileges, and obligations between worker and organization." Such expectations are not documented in formal agreements, but they function as powerful determinants of behavior.

psychological stress analyzer: *see* LIE DETECTOR.

psychological test, a general term for any effort (usually a standardized test) that is designed to measure the abilities or personality traits of individuals or groups.

psychology, generally, the scientific study of human and animal behavior, cognitions, and affects.

See also the following entries:

DYNAMIC PSYCHOLOGY
INDUSTRIAL PSYCHOLOGY

psychometrician, psychologist who deals with mental tests and their associated statistical procedures.

psychometrics, that branch of psychology that deals with mental tests and their associated statistical procedures.

psychometry, mental measurements and/or testing.

psychomotor test: *see* DEXTERITY TEST.

public, having to do with a state, nation, or the community as a whole. For example, a tax or a government function that will benefit the community as a whole rather than individual members has a public purpose.

public administration, the study of or the practice of organizing and managing people and other resources to achieve the goals of government; also, the art and science of management applied to the public sector.

Public administration is a broader term than "public management" because it also incorporates the political, social, cultural, etc. environments and influences which affect the management of public institutions.

See also PUBLIC MANAGEMENT.

public affairs, that aspect of public relations which deals with political and social issues and, most importantly, relations with governments; also, a more genteel-sounding name for public relations; also, an expansive view of the academic field of public administration. Accordingly, a Graduate School of Public Affairs might include, in addition to public administration, programs in nonprofit organization management, police administration, urban studies, etc.

public agency, any federal, state, or local government organization, or branch thereof. Not to be confused with a public institution or publicly supported institution.
See also PUBLIC INSTITUTION.

public charge, a person who is supported at public expense.

public charity, an organization which is tax-exempt under the provisions of the Tax Reform Act, Section 509(a)(1), 509(a)(2) or 509(a)(3). Public charities are not subject to the restrictions of the Act's sections which apply to private foundations. Further, they are eligible for fifty percent of adjusted gross income contribution deductions; grants to them need not be disbursed in the following year; etc.
See also:
CHARITABLE ORGANIZATION
PUBLIC INSTITUTION
TAX REFORM ACT OF 1969

public-choice economics, an approach to public administration based on microeconomic theory which views the citizen as a consumer of government goods and services and would attempt to maximize administrative responsiveness to citizen demand by creating a market system for governmental activities in which public agencies would compete to provide citizens with goods and services. This would replace the current system under which administrative agencies in effect act as monopolies under the influence of organized pressure groups which, the public-choice economists argue, are institutionally incapable of representing the demands of individual citizens.

public defender, attorney employed by a government agency or subdivision whose official duty is to represent defendants unable to hire private counsel.

public domain, land owned by the government or any property right that is held in common by all citizens; for example, the content of U.S. government publications, expired copyrights, or expired patents.

public enterprise (revolving) funds, federally owned funds that are credited with receipts, primarily from the public, generated by and earmarked to finance a continuing cycle of business-type operations (*e.g.*, the Federal Deposit Insurance Corporation).

public finance, imprecise term that refers to the totality (1) of the gaining and spending of funds by governments and (2) of the management of government debt.

public goods, commodities typically provided by government that cannot, or would not, be separately parceled out to individuals since no one can be excluded from their benefits. Public goods such as national defense, clean air, or public safety are neither divisible nor exclusive.

public health, the science dealing with the protection and improvement of community health by organized community effort. Public health activities are generally those which are less amenable to being undertaken or less effective when undertaken on an individual basis, and do not typically include direct personal health services. Immunizations, sanitation, preventive medicine, quarantine, and other disease control activities, occupational health and safety programs, assurance of the healthfulness of air, water and food, health education, and epidemiology are recognized public health activities.

public health administration, that area of public administration generally concerned with preventing disease, prolonging life, and promoting health by means of organized community efforts.

public hearing, a meeting to receive public input—both informational and opinion—on a designated need, issue, problem, or a pending policy or program. Public hearings are held by local, state, and national elected bodies (such as a Senate subcommittee or a board of county commissioners) and public agencies (for example, the Environmental Protection Agency or a state highway department).

public institution, also PUBLICLY SUPPORTED INSTITUTION, a general category of tax-exempt organization that receives financial support from multiple public and/or government sources. Public institutions were essentially created by the Tax Reform Act of 1969 and replaced what had been known as "thirty percent organizations." Public institutions are defined in IRS Code 170(b)(1)(A)(i) through (v). Not to be confused with a public agency.

See also:

PRIVATE FOUNDATION
PUBLIC AGENCY
PUBLICLY SUPPORTED ORGANIZATION
TAX REFORM ACT OF 1969
THIRTY PERCENT ORGANIZATION

public interest, an extremely general and vague phrase meaning for the betterment of the general public's or society's well-being; a universal label in which people and organizations wrap the policies and programs that they advocate. Would any board member, manager, or legislator ever propose a program that was not "in the public interest?" Because "the public interest" is generally taken to mean a commonly accepted good, the phrase is used both to further policies that are indeed for the common good as well as to obscure policies that may not be so commonly accepted as good. A considerable body of literature has developed about this phrase because it represents an important philosophic point that, if found, could provide considerable guidance for nonprofit and public administrators.

public interest group, an organized pressure group seeking to develop positions and support causes relating to a broader definition of the public good as opposed to any specific social or economic interest. Such groups are often characterized by efforts to obtain a national membership with a high level of participation by members and dissemination of information and authority. Examples of public interest groups are Common Cause, the Nader organizations, the League of Women Voters, the Sierra Club, and Consumer's Union.

See also INTEREST GROUP.

public-interest law, that portion of legal practice devoted to broad societal interests rather than the problems of individual clients.

public interest law firm, a law firm that provides services to advance or protect important public interests in cases which are not economically feasible or desirable for private law firms. Examples of public interests which have been represented by public interest law firms include environmental policy and freedom of information issues.

See also PRO BONO PUBLICO.

public interest requirement: *see* REQUIREMENT, PUBLIC INTEREST.

publicly supported organization, a category of tax-exempt public institution which receives at least thirty-three percent of its financial support from public and governmental sources and, in general, not more than two percent of its income from any single contributor. Typical examples of publicly supported organizations include arts and humanities organizations and the American Red Cross. An organization must meet several "tests" to qualify as a publicly supported organization.

For examples, *see*:

INVESTMENT INCOME TEST
PRIVATE FOUNDATION
SUPPORT
SUPPORT FRACTION
SUPPORT TEST

public management, a general term referring to a major segment of public administration. Typically, the phrase "public management" is used to identify those functions of public and nonprofit organizations which are more internally than externally oriented; for example, personnel management, procedures management, and organizational control functions. Whereas "policy management" typically focuses on policy formation and the selection of basic strategies, "public management" focuses on the organizational "machinery" for achieving policy goals.

Planning, organizing, and controlling are

the major means or functions by which the public manager shapes services (see POSDCORB). These functions constitute the primary knowledges and skills of public management and are applied in the form of budgets, performance appraisals, management information systems, program evaluations, organizational charts, cost/benefit analyses, and similar management tools. Public management also requires behavioral skills. Communications, negotiation, motivation, leadership, and interpersonal skills are equally important aspects of the job.

Public Management Institute, a San Francisco-based firm that publishes a wide array of "how to" handbooks for nonprofit organizations, for example, *How to Get Corporate Grants, How to Build a Big Endowment,* and *Computers for Nonprofits*.

public opinion, the collective opinion of a population on a need, issue, problem, policy, etc.

public opinion poll, a scientifically designed process to measure public opinion using a statistically sampled cross-section of the population in question. Public opinion polls are used descriptively—for example, to describe public attitudes about crime in America—and predictively—for example, to project voting patterns in a forthcoming election, or to gauge public support for a pending bond issue.

public radio: *see* NATIONAL PUBLIC RADIO.

public relations, a broad, continuing program to promote a reservoir of community good will for an organization and/or its programs which will benefit specific future development campaigns for funding, services, etc. Public relations encompasses, for example, public information and education, media relations, etc.

public relations, internal: *see* INTERNAL PUBLIC RELATIONS.

public relations committee, a standing committee charged with responsibility for developing, coordinating, and sustaining an organization's public relations program.
See also PUBLIC RELATIONS PROGRAM.

public relations consultant, also PUBLIC RELATIONS FIRM, a for-profit individual or organization that provides contracted technical assistance in developing, implementing, and evaluating a public relations program. A public relations firm may or not be associated with an advertising agency.

public relations kit, a package of public relations and public service advertising literature. The kits often are prepared by national (and international) and state nonprofit organizations and distributed to their subordinate affiliates (for example, chapters) for use with, for example, local media and speakers bureaus, and to help in assembling background information for grant proposals.
See also:
GRANT PROPOSAL
MEDIA
SUBORDINATE AFFILIATED ORGANIZATION

public relations program, a continuing program of information and communication with an organization's external publics. Public relations programs should be planned carefully to achieve specific long-term objectives involving public support. All communications within the public relations program should be compatible with the overall program objectives. Each communication should focus its message to evoke desired actions or sentiments from targeted segments of the public.
See also INTERNAL PUBLIC RELATIONS and PUBLIC RELATIONS.

public safety testing organization, a category of tax-exempt organization under IRS Code 501(c)(3). Organizations may be exempt if, for example, they test consumer products for safety in use.

public sector organization, any agency or institution funded, directly or indirectly, by public taxation.

See also PRIVATE SECTOR ORGANIZATION and THIRD SECTOR.

public service announcement: *see:*
COMMUNICATIONS ACT OF 1934
INFORMATIONAL SPOT
SPOT ANNOUNCEMENT

public service corporation, a private, regulated corporation which provides an essential service or commodity to the public, such as an electric or gas utility company; not to be confused with a public service organization or a publicly supported organization.
See also PUBLICLY SUPPORTED ORGANIZATION.

public service organization (nonprofit): *see* PUBLIC INSTITUTION and PUBLICLY SUPPORTED ORGANIZATION.

public support, general term meaning the willingness and potential willingness of people to provide moral, financial, and/or human support to an organization and its programs.

public support, revenue, expense and change in fund balances statement, an operating statement (or income and expense statement) often used by nonprofit organizations.
See also OPERATING STATEMENT.

public support (tax exemption): *see* PUBLIC INSTITUTION.

public support test: *see* SUPPORT TEST.

public utilities, legal designation encompassing those organizations producing essential services, usually in a monopolistic fashion. The designation requires these organizations to be highly regulated by government. Examples are electricity, natural gas, etc.

public utilities commission (PUC), state agency that regulates power companies, railroads, etc.

public welfare, support of and assistance to needy persons contingent upon their need.
See also RELIEF and WELFARE.

Public Welfare, quarterly journal of the American Public Welfare Association.

public works, generic term for government-sponsored construction and some types of maintenance and sanitation functions.

PUC: *see* PUBLIC UTILITIES COMMISSIONS.

punitive damages, also EXEMPLARY DAMAGES money awarded by a court to an organization or person who has been harmed in a particularly malicious or willful way by another person or organization. This money is not necessarily related to the actual cost of the injury or harm suffered. Its purpose is to prevent that sort of act from happening again by serving as a warning.

purchase order, a document that authorizes a person or organization to deliver goods or perform services for the issuing organization. It promises to pay for them.

purchases journal, the journal used to record items ordered and purchased. It contains information about the date of each item ordered and purchased, what the item is, the purchase order number, the dollar amount of the purchase, and which subsidiary or general ledger accounts are affected by the purchase (debited or credited).

At the end of each accounting period (usually monthly), all purchases are totaled by account, balanced, and posted to the accounts payable subsidiary ledger and to the general ledger.
See also:
DEBITS AND CREDITS
GENERAL LEDGER
JOURNAL
SUBSIDIARY LEDGER
TRIAL BALANCE

purposive sample: *see* JUDGMENTAL SAMPLE.

ACE AMBULANCE SERVICE—PURCHASES JOURNAL

		Purchase CR			DR—General Col.	
Date	Purchase From	Order Number	Acct. #	Accts. Pay	Description	Amount
1-1	Acme Oil Co	2001	1616	$175.00	GAS & OIL	$175.00

pyramid, also called ORGANIZATIONAL PYRAMID, colloquial term for an organization's hierarchy. According to Vance Packard, *The Pyramid Climbers* (N.Y.: McGraw-Hill, 1962),

> The number of ledges—or steps—in a company's hierarchy varies of course with the company's size and philosophy of organization. Some like tall, slender pyramids, with only a few people under each leader; others prefer short, squat pyramids. Occasionally, one literally sees these modern pyramids in brick and mortar, where the home office occupies a skyscraper with the suites of the highest officers at the pinnacle.

See also FLAT ORGANIZATION.

Q

qualification, also QUALIFYING A PROSPECT, making certain that a person or organization is a genuine prospect (target) for a fund-raising program.

qualification requirements, education, experience, and other prerequisites to employment or placement in a position.

qualified circulation: *see* CONTROLLED CIRCULATION.

qualified report, an opinion of an auditor which cannot be given full credence because the auditor was unable to examine, or has some doubts about, some relevant financial matters.

qualified research: *see* RESEARCH, QUALIFIED.

qualifying distribution, a financial outlay by a private foundation that satisfies the requirements of the mandatory distribution rules. Qualifying distributions include appropriate administrative and related expenses as well as contributions to tax-exempt organizations.

See also

ADJUSTED NET INCOME
DISTRIBUTABLE AMOUNT
FAIR MARKET VALUE
MANDATORY DISTRIBUTION RULES
PAYOUT REQUIREMENTS

qualifying test, examination used to simply qualify or disqualify individuals for employment or promotion, in contrast to tests that rank order individuals in terms of their scores.

qualitative research methods, a general term that incorporates a wide array of research methodologies which do not use quantitative data or analytical procedures. As applied to the study of organizations, qualitative research has been rooted in the tradition of cultural anthropology's "ethnographic paradigms" (*see* P.R. Sanday, "The Ethnographic Paradigms," in John VanMannen (ed.), *Qualitative Methodology* (Beverly Hills, Ca.: Sage Publications, 1979). During the late 1970s and 1980s, qualitative research methods have been experiencing a rebirth of interest and attention for studying organizations, largely because of dissatisfaction with the lack of useful knowledge produced during the last two decades through quantitative research methods, such as experimental and quasi-experimental designs.

quality circles, small groups of employees working in the same organizational unit who, with the approval of management, voluntarily meet on a regular basis to identify and solve problems that directly affect their work.

quality control, the totality of concern for, including the inspection of, the goods and services that are produced by an organization. See also STATISTICAL QUALITY CONTROL.

quality of working life, area of concern that addresses the problem of creating more humane working environments.

quantified measure: *see* MEASURE, QUANTIFIED.

quartile, one of three points that divide the test scores in a distribution into four equal groups.

quasi-experimental design, use of experimental methods and modes of analysis in situations lacking the full requirements of experimental control. The methodology for research and evaluation in many social organizations and programs is necessarily quasi-experimental.

See also QUALITATIVE RESEARCH METHODS.

quasi-judicial agency, agency such as a regulatory commission that may perform many courtlike functions in the course of enforcing its rules. For example, it may bring charges, hold hearings, and render judgments.

quasi-legislative, description of the rule-making functions of administrative agencies.

questionnaire, an instrument containing a set of questions to be answered by a subject.

questionnaire, exit: *see* EXIT INTERVIEW.

queuing theory, mathematical technique used in simulation and operations research that allows an analyst to identify the optimal use of agency personnel and equipment in situations that have the characteristics of a waiting line.

quick assets: *see* ASSETS.

quickie strike, spontaneous or unannounced strike of short duration.

quid pro quo, Latin meaning "something for something"; the giving of one valuable thing for another.

quit, normally, a volunteered resignation, but it can be considered a dismissal for the purposes of arbitral review if evidence suggests that there was not free intent.

quorum, the number of members of an elected body (*e.g.*, a board of directors) or eligible-to-vote members of an organization (*e.g.*, members of a religious congregation who pledged during the prior twelve months) who must be present at a meeting in order to transact business. If a quorum is not present at a meeting, business cannot be transacted legally.

The number or percent of voting members that comprises a quorum is specified in the organization's bylaws, and the number may differ for different types of transactions. For example, in nonprofit organizations, the quorum required for a vote on the acquisition or sale of capital assets is often larger than that required for conducting other types of business.

The most typical quorum for a board of directors is one person more than fifty percent of either the authorized or actual number of directors. So long as there is a quorum present, a simple majority of those voting determines the outcome of an issue (or a different majority if the bylaws so specify, such as a two-thirds majority.) When a quorum is defined as an absolute number or as a percentage of the authorized number of directors, vacancies on the board can create problems in gathering a quorum—particularly during summer months and holiday seasons.

quota: *see* GOAL.

R

®, registered, as in registered trademark.

r: *see* CORRELATION COEFFICIENT.

race, according to a United Nations publication, *Race and Science* (N.Y.: UNESCO, 1961),

> designates a group or population characterized by some concentrations, relative as to frequency and distribution, of hereditary particles (genes) or physical characters, which appear, fluctuate, and often disappear in the course of time by reason of geographic and/or cultural isolation. The varying manifestations of these traits in different populations are perceived in different ways by each group. What is perceived is largely preconceived, so that each group arbitrarily tends to misinterpret the variability which occurs as a fundamental difference which separates that group from all others.

race categories, also ETHNIC CATEGORIES, the race/ethnic categories that the Equal Employment Opportunity Commission insists be used for EEO reporting purposes.

White, not of Hispanic Origin. Persons having origins in any of the original peoples of Europe, North Africa, or the Middle East.

Black, not of Hispanic Origin. Persons having origins in any of the black racial groups of Africa.

Hispanic. Persons of Mexican, Puerto Rican, Cuban, Central or South American or other Spanish culture or origin, regardless of race.

American Indian or Alaskan Native. Persons having origins in any of the original peoples of North America and who maintain cultural identification through tribal affiliation or community recognition.

Asian or Pacific Islander. Persons having origins in any of the original peoples of the Far East, Southeast Asia, the Indian subcontinent, or the Pacific Islands. This area includes, for example, China, Japan, Korea, the Philippine Islands and Samoa.

race differential: *see* SEX DIFFERENTIAL.

racist, any person or organization that consciously or unconsciously practices racial discrimination.

raiding, generally, efforts by one organization to gain members of a competing organization for their own.

RAM, random access memory. Computer storage that can give (write) or take (read) information quickly because it need not be transferred in any set order.

See also ROM.

RAM: *see* REVERSE ANNUITY MORTGAGE.

RAMPS, Resource Allocation and Multi-Project Planning; a technique for planning large, multiple projects simultaneously, and especially for resolving conflicts among competing priorities.

RAND Corporation, Santa Monica, Calif. based "think tank" that periodically issues analyses of public policies and problems.

R & D: *see* RESEARCH AND DEVELOPMENT.

random access, a way to get data into and out of a computer that does not depend on the order in which it is stored. Random access is much faster than data storage and retrieval in only a set order (for example, serially).

See also RAM.

random sample, sample of members of

a population drawn in such a way that every member of the population has an equal chance of being included in the sample.

random selection, research procedure in which every potential subject has an equal chance to be included in the research sample. Random selection is a process that allows the scientist to collect information from a sample of subjects who represent the total population and then to generalize the findings to the entire population. By employing the techniques of random selection, the scientist saves time, energy, and money.

range, difference between the lowest and highest scores obtained on a test by some group.

rank, place in a hierarchical ordering of positions.

rank and file, colloquial expression referring to the masses. When used in an organizational context, it refers to those members of the organization who are not part of management. Rank and file was originally a military term referring to the enlisted men who had to line up in ranks, side by side, and files, one behind the other. Officers, being gentlemen, were spared such indignities.

ranking: *see* JOB RANKING.

ranking test, examination used to rank individuals according to their scores so that those with the higher scores have an advantage in gaining employment or promotion.

rank-in-man system, also called PERSONAL-RANK SYSTEM, method of establishing pay primarily on the basis of an employee's qualifications without consideration given to the specific duties and responsibilities that would be performed by the employee. Such personal rank systems tend to be restricted to the military, the U.S. Foreign Service, and other similar officer corps systems.

rank performance rating, method of performance appraisal that requires superiors to rank order employees according to their merit.

rapport, generally, a spirit of harmony, accord, and mutual confidence between individuals.

rate, beginner's: *see* BEGINNER'S RATE.

rate, incentive: *see* INCENTIVE RATE.

rate, trainee: *see* BEGINNER'S RATE.

ratebuster, also called JOB SPOILER, general term for any employee whose production level far exceeds the norms established by the majority of the employees. Ratebusters usually face considerable peer pressure to conform to average production levels, and sometimes this pressure can be physical. A *job spoiler* is a British ratebuster.

rate fixing, the power to set the prices an organization may charge for its services. This differs from price fixing, which may be illegal.

rate of return, a profit or yield as a percentage of the money and/or property invested. See also YIELD.

ratification, formal confirmation by the union membership of a contract that has been signed on their behalf by union representatives.

rating, efficiency: *see* EFFICIENCY RATING.

rating, rank performance: *see* RANK-PERFORMANCE RATING.

rating chart, graphic: *see* GRAPHIC RATING CHART.

ratio, a proportional relationship or rate, similar to a percentage; for example, the ratio of minorities to nonminorities served by a program, the ratio of administrative costs to program costs, and the ratio of funds raised to the cost of raising funds.
See also RATIO, ACCOUNTING.

ratio, accounting, any ratio used in financial analysis; an account or group of accounts divided by another. Accounting ratios are used as indicators of organizational performance and financial strength. They provide a common denominator for comparing the operations of one organization (or one chapter) with those of another. For example, *see:*

COLLECTION RATE
LIQUIDITY
RATIO

ratio, efficiency: *see* EFFICIENCY.

ratio analysis: *see* RATIO, ACCOUNTING.

ratio delay, work sampling technique that uses a large number of observations taken at random intervals in order to determine the parts of the workday (expressed in minutes or hours) during which an employee is working productively or is engaged in activities other than productive work.

rational-comprehensive approach, decision-making model requiring a complete assessment of all factors (costs, benefits, alternatives, etc.) in order to discover the best possible decision.

rational validity, measure that involves the use of a detailed job analysis to determine the knowledges, skills, and abilities that are necessary for effective performance in a particular job. Measurement instruments are then designed to measure such factors. For example, if a job requirement is the ability to type errorless copy at fifty words a minute, a test can be designed to measure that ability.

raw score, also called CRUDE SCORE, number of items correct, when there is no correction for guessing, or the formula score, when a correction for guessing has been applied.

reactive management, also REACTION MANAGEMENT, a management style that is limited to responding to immediate problems and pressures.

See also PROACTIVE.

reading assistant, reader for a blind employee. Public Law 87-614 of 1962 authorizes the employment of readers for blind federal employees. These reading assistants serve without compensation from the government, but they can be paid by the blind employees, nonprofit organizations, or state offices of vocational rehabilitation. They may also serve on a volunteer basis.

read only memory: *see* ROM.

reaffirmation, agreement to pay a prior, possibly uncollectable debt. Under bankruptcy and contract law, if a person or organization reaffirms a debt (with court approval in the case of bankruptcy), he or she is again liable for it.

Reaganomics: *see* SUPPLY-SIDE ECONOMICS.

real estate, land, buildings, and things permanently attached to land and buildings.

real estate investment trust (REIT), an arrangement in which investors buy shares in a trust that invests in real estate. In order to qualify for special income tax benefits, a REIT must meet certain requirements, such as being unincorporated, having fewer than a specified number of investors, and gaining most of its income from real estate and related financial ventures.

real estate tax: *see* TAX, REAL PROPERTY.

realized, also RECOGNIZED, actual; cashed in. For example, a realized investment is one made, not merely planned; a realized profit is a cash-in-hand gain as opposed to a paper profit.

From a tax point of view, *realization* means "now is the time to see whether income or loss will have tax consequences." Income and losses are realized when a "taxable event" takes place, such as the sale of a security or a building.

Recognized means "the income or loss has tax consequences." In general, realization and recognition are used to mean the same thing.

See also RECOGNITION.

reallocate: *see* ALLOCATE.

reallocation, also called RECLASSIFICATION, change in the position classification of an existing position resulting from significant changes in assigned duties and responsibilities.

Realpolitik, originally a German word meaning "realist politics"; applied to politics—whether of the organizational or societal variety—that are premised upon material or practical factors rather than theoretical or ethical considerations.

real property tax: *see* TAX, REAL-PROPERTY.

real rate of interest, the nominal rate of interest corrected for inflation. For example, if inflation is five percent and the nominal rate of interest is twelve percent, then the real rate of interest is seven percent.

real time, computer term that describes an information processing speed sufficient to control an ongoing process.

real time processing, immediate computations or changes made when information is put into a computer—the information or changes are not held for later processing.

realty, real estate.

real wages, wages after they have been adjusted for changes in the level of prices. The buying power of wages, the "real" wage, is computed by dividing the dollar amount by an index measuring changes in prices (such as the Consumer Price Index).

reasonable accommodation, requirement that employers provide a certain level of assistance to handicapped employees. Once a handicapped employee is hired, an employer is required to take reasonable steps to accommodate the individual's disability unless such steps would cause the employer undue hardship. Examples of "reasonable accommodations" include providing a reader for a blind employee, an interpreter for a deaf person requiring telephone contacts, or adequate work space for an employee confined to a wheelchair.

reassessment, a government's re-estimating of the value of property and changing the official value it gives to that property for tax purposes.

reassignment, transfer of an employee from one position to another without promotion or demotion.

rebate, a discount, deduction, or refund.

recall, (1) procedure that allows citizens to vote officeholders out of office between regularly scheduled elections, or (2) the rehiring of employees from a layoff.

recall item, test question that requires the examinee to supply the correct answer from memory, in contrast to a recognition item, where the examinee need only identify the correct answer.

recapture, the IRS requirement that a company or person pay taxes on profits created by a prior deduction or credit, such as the investment tax credit. For example, when accelerated depreciation is taken on property that is later sold at no loss, the IRS recaptures this depreciation by treating it as taxable income.

Also, a recapture is a lease provision giving a landlord a percentage of profits and allowing the landlord to end the lease if profits are not high enough.

See:

DEPRECIATION
TAXABLE INCOME
TAX CREDIT

receipt, a written acknowledgment and record of having received money, property, etc. Organizations use receipts both for financial control purposes and to provide payors and donors with a record to support deductions and expenses for income tax purposes.

See also:

ITEMIZE

ITEMIZER

receipts: *see* INCOME RECOGNITION OF.

receivables: *see* ACCOUNTS RECEIVABLE.

receiver, person appointed by a court to manage the affairs of an organization facing litigation and/or reorganization.

receivership, also RECEIVER, a court placement of money or property into the management of a *receiver* (a court-appointed, independent manager) to preserve it for the people who are ultimately entitled to it. This is done when the creditors of a business suspect fraud or gross mismanagement and ask the court to step in and watch over the business to protect them.

recession, a decline in overall business activity that is pervasive, substantial, and of at least several months duration. Historically, a decline in real gross national product for at least two consecutive quarters has been considered a recession.

reciprocity, the giving of privileges to the citizens of one jurisdiction by the government of another and vice versa.

reclassification: *see* REALLOCATION.

reclassify: *see* CLASSIFY.

recognition, acknowledgment. In most cases, when a taxpayer has received a financial gain, it is "recognized." This means that it must be reported on tax forms, and tax must be paid on it.

See also REALIZED.

Also, acknowledgment that something done by another person or organization was authorized by you; for example, selling magazine subscriptions in the name of a nonprofit organization.

For the psychological meaning of recognition, *see* STROKING.

Also, employer's acceptance of a union as the bargaining agent for all of the employees in a particular bargaining unit.

recognition item, test question that calls for the examinee to recognize or select the correct answer from among two or more alternatives.

reconciliation, bringing two accounts into agreement; for example, adjusting the balance in a checking account to agree with the bank's monthly statement.

record, a set of related information or facts. For example, an organization's records include its articles of organization, bylaws, and minutes of meetings (typically board of directors and membership meetings.)

In the computer sense of the word, a *record* is a set of related data fields treated as a single unit (for example, a donor's contribution history).

record, for the, a statement intended for public dissemination.

record, off the, a statement not intended for public dissemination; confidential.

record, on, a public statement of an individual's or organization's stand or position on an issue.

record, public, document filed with, or put out by, a government agency and open for public preview.

record copy, copy of a document that is regarded by an organization as the most important or the key official copy.

record cycle, the period of time during which a record is created, used, stored for easy retrieval, transferred to inactive status, and destroyed.

See also RECORDS MANAGEMENT.

record date, the date on which members of an organization (or stockholders) must be registered as members (or record owners of a company) on the organization's books in order to vote (or receive dividends). A nonprofit organization should define the record date in its bylaws; for example, "the record date shall be sixty days prior to the annual membership meeting."

recorder of deeds, official who is responsible for properly filing public land records.

records management, also INFORMATION MANAGEMENT, the total process of creating, maintaining, storing, and disposing of an organization's records.

recourse, the right of a person or organization who holds a negotiable instrument to receive payment on it from *anyone who has endorsed (signed) it* when the person who originally signed it fails to pay up.

red circle (position classification): *see* EARMARK.

red-circle rate, also called RINGED RATE, rate of pay that is higher than the established rate for a particular job.

redeem, buy back; gather up and pay off; reclaim from mortgage or pledge; turn in for cash.

redeemable bond, a callable bond; also a bond that has a maturity date.

See also CALLABLE BONDS.

redemption period, the time during which a mortgage or other debt that has gone into default can be paid off without losing the property. Some states have mandatory redemption periods for home mortgages.

redlining, practice alleged to be followed by urban financial institutions in which they refuse loans for home mortgages and home improvements to areas thought to be poor risks. Consequently, people living or wishing to live in these designated areas are denied such loans regardless of their particular financial situation. The name *redlining* derives from the drawing of red lines around such areas on a map.

red tape, the despised symbol of excessive formality and attention to routine that has its origins in the red ribbon with which clerks bound up official documents in the last century. The ribbon has disappeared, but the practices it represents linger on.

Herbert Kaufman's *Red Tape: Its Origins, Uses, and Abuses* (Washington, D.C.: The Brookings Institution, 1977) finds that the term "is applied to a bewildering variety of organizational practices and features." After all, "one person's 'red tape' may be another's treasured procedural safeguard." Kaufman concludes that "red tape turns out to be at the core of our institutions rather than an excrescence on them."

reduction in force: *see* RIF.

redundant, duplicative; repetitive; no longer needed.

reemployed annuitant, employee who, having retired with a pension from an organization, is again employed by that same organization.

reemployment list, also called REEMPLOYMENT ELIGIBILITY LIST, list on which employees will be ranked in the event of lay-offs, usually in order of their seniority. Usually, reemployment lists must be exhausted before new hires can be considered.

See also the following entries:

ELIGIBLE LIST
LAYOFF
RECALL
RIF

referee in bankruptcy, a federal judge who conducts bankruptcy hearings.

reference checking, verifying information provided by a job or loan applicant.

reference group, also called SOCIAL REFERENCE GROUP, social group with which an individual identifies to the extent that his/her personal values are derived from the group's norms and attitudes.

referendum, procedure for submitting proposed laws to the voters for ratification.

refinance, also REFUNDING, to pay off a debt with money from a new loan; for example, to refinance a home with a new long-term mortgage.

refunding, issuance of long-term debt in exchange for, or to provide funds for, the retirement of long-term debt already outstanding.

***Regents of the University of California* v. *Allan Bakke*,** 438 U.S. 265 (1978), U.S. Supreme Court case which upheld a white applicant's claim of reverse discrimination because he was denied admission to the University of California Medical School at Davis when sixteen out of the school's one-hundred class spaces were set aside for minority applicants. The court ruled that Bakke must be admitted to the Davis Medical School as soon as possible, but that the university had the right to take race into account in its admissions criteria. The imprecise nature of taking race into account as one factor among many has created considerable speculation about the potential impact this case may have on voluntary affirmative action programs concerning employment.

Regional Associations of Grantmakers, associations that support grantmaking organizations in carrying out their charitable endeavors more effectively. Seventeen Regional Associations of Grantmakers form a national network throughout the country, serving thirty states and representing approximately 1500 members. Private, community, and corporate foundations, corporations with giving programs, charitable trusts, and banks serving foundations are the typical members of Regional Associations.

Regional Associations offer a variety of programs and services which reflect the interests and needs of their memberships. Some of the activities conducted by Regional Associations include sponsoring seminars and workshops; publishing newsletters, annual reports, and directories of grantmaking organizations; researching data on grantmaking; monitoring legislative activity; and communicating to the general public about the philanthropic world.

In addition to organized Associations, there are also many informal foundation and corporate luncheon groups. These groups, located throughout the country, include individuals from foundations and corporations interested in sharing information and discussing issues related to philanthropy.

Regional Associations frequently cooperate with each other and with the Council on Foundations, a national membership organization headquartered in Washington, D.C. These organizations work to encourage private giving to serve the public good and to promote broader public understanding of the role of philanthropy in American life.

See also COUNCIL ON FOUNDATIONS.

register, to formally enroll as a student, a participant in an event or program, etc.; also any book of public facts such as births, deaths, and marriages. Other examples of public record books are the register of patents, the register of ships, the register of deeds, and the register of wills.

See also REGISTRY.

registered, listed in an official record.

registered bonds, bonds that require registration of the owner with the organization issuing the bond.

registered check, a check sold by a bank but not certified.

register of eligibles: *see* ELIGIBLE LIST.

registration, the act of registering.

See also OCCUPATIONAL REGISTRATION and REGISTER.

registry, also REGISTER, a roster of registered persons.

regression analysis, also MULTIPLE REGRESSION ANALYSIS, method for describing the nature of the relationship between two variables so that the value of one can be predicted if the value of the other is known. *Multiple regression analysis* involves more than two variables.

regression line, a graph of the mathematical relationship between two variables showing correlations and trends.

See also TIME SERIES ANALYSIS.

regressive tax: *see* TAX EQUITY.

regulation, the rulemaking process of those administrative agencies charged with the official interpretation of a statute. These agencies, most typically independent regulatory commissions, in addition to issuing rules, also tend to administer their implementation and adjudicate interpretive disputes.

regulatory tax: *see* TAX, REGULATORY.

rehabilitation: *see* VOCATIONAL REHABILITATION ACT.

reimbursement, repayment for expenses incurred; for example, reimbursement for travel expenses.

reinforcement, also POSITIVE REINFORCEMENT and NEGATIVE REINFORCEMENT, inducement to perform in a particular manner. *Positive reinforcement* occurs when an individual receives a desired reward that is contingent upon some prescribed behavior. *Negative reinforcement* occurs when an individual works to avoid an undesirable reward.

reinstatement, restoration of an employee to his/her previous position without any loss of seniority or other benefits. Also, the reinstatement of organization members who have been suspended, for example, for non-payment of dues. Terms and conditions for reinstating members should be specified in the bylaws.

reinvest, to use dividends, interest, or proceeds from the sale of securities to buy more securities. Arrangements are often made to automatically reinvest dividends in additional shares of common stock or shares of a mutual fund.

REIT: *see* REAL ESTATE INVESTMENT TRUST.

release, the giving up or relinquishing of a claim or a right by the person who has it to the person against whom it might have been enforced. For example, most people demand a written release in exchange for paying money to settle an accident claim.

relevance: *see* CRITERION RELEVANCE.

relevant market, the geographical area in which a nonprofit organization solicits funds or members, and/or in which it provides services to clientele.

reliability, dependability of a measuring device, as reflected in the consistency of its scores when repeated measurements are made of the same group. When a test is said to have a high degree of reliability, it means that an individual tested today and tested again at a later time with the same test and under the same conditions will get approximately the same score. In short, a measure is reliable if it gives a dependable measure of whatever it seeks to measure.

See also INTERNAL CONSISTENCY RELIABILITY and INTERRATER RELIABILITY.

reliability coefficient, numerical index of reliability that is obtained by correlating scores on two forms of a test, from statistical data on individual test items, or by correlating scores on different administrations of the same test. A reliability coefficient can be a perfect 1.00 or a perfectly unreliable—1.00. A reliability of .90 or greater is generally considered adequate for a test used as a personnel selection device.

relief, also WORK RELIEF, terms that usually refer to the public assistance program available during the depression of the 1930s. *Relief* or *direct relief* referred to straight welfare payments. *Work relief* referred to any of the numerous public works projects initiated specifically to provide jobs for the unemployed.

religious, a term that has been defined very broadly by the courts and the IRS for tax exemption purposes. The courts have been extremely reluctant to limit the term for fear of infringing on First Amendment guarantees and protections.

See also CHURCH and HANDS-OFF POLICY.

religious discrimination, any act that manifests unfavorable or inequitable treatment toward employees or prospective employees because of their religious convictions. Because of section 703(a) (1) of the Civil Rights Act of 1964, an individual's religious beliefs or practices cannot be given any consideration in making employment decisions. The argument that a religious practice may place an undue hardship upon an employer—for example, where such practices require special religious holidays and hence absence from work—has been upheld by the courts. However, because of the sensitive nature of discharging or refusing to hire an individual on religious grounds, the burden of proof to show that such a hardship exists is placed upon the employer.

religious institution: *see* RELIGIOUS ORGANIZATION.

religious order: *see* RELIGIOUS ORGANIZATION.

religious organization, organization formed for religious purposes. Under IRS Code 501(c) (3), an organization may be tax-exempt if it is organized and operated solely for religious purposes. The courts and the IRS have defined *religious* very broadly. Examples of types of organizations that have been accepted as religious for tax exemption purposes include churches, religious orders, and apostolic organizations.

Despite the courts' general reluctance to limit the definition of religious organizations, there have been notable exceptions. For example, in *United States* v. *Kuch* (288 F. Supp 439 [D.D.C. 1968]), the Neo-American Church was declared not a religious organization. According to the court, the Neo-American Church declared that it was the "religious duty of all members to partake of the sacraments on regular occasions." (The sacraments were psychedelic substances.) The church's symbol was a three-eyed toad; one of its hymns was "Puff the Magic Dragon."

See also HANDS-OFF POLICY and RELIGIOUS.

relocation allowance, payment by an employer of all or part of the cost of moving oneself and one's household to a distant place of employment.

remainder, any interest or estate in land or trust property that takes effect only when another interest in the land or trust property ends.

See also REVERSIONARY INTEREST.

remittance, money (or a check, etc.) sent by one person to another, usually as payment for a debt owed.

removal, separation of an employee for cause or because of continual unacceptable performance.

removal from office: *see* IMPEACHMENT.

remuneration: *see* COMPENSATION.

renegotiable rate mortgage (RRM), a fully amortized long-term mortgage whose interest rates and monthly payments are renegotiated (or "rolled over") once every three to five years. Within each of these intervals, the monthly payments stay level. Under 1980 regulations, federal savings and loan associations' changes in RRM rates are limited to .5 percentage point per year and up to five percentage points in all (either up or down).

rental, a lease or to lease. Sometimes used to mean a shorter term arrangement than

a lease; for example, a rental car rather than a leased car.
See also LEASE.

rental income, income derived from the rental of an asset.
See also:
LEASE
RENTAL

reorganization, changes in administrative structure or formal procedures, traditionally in the areas of departmental consolidation or functional realignment, generally for the purpose of promoting bureaucratic responsiveness and, secondarily, to simplify or professionalize administrative affairs.

report, a detailed statement describing an event, occurrence, or incident (such as a speech, debate, or meeting); the written result of a study or investigation; an announcement; to give a formal accounting (for example, to report a budget surplus); to notify, for example, organizational superiors of one's whereabouts.

reporting pay: *see* CALL-IN PAY.

repossession, also REPO, taking back something that has been sold because payments have not been made.

representation election: *see* AUTHORIZATION ELECTION.

representative action, a class action; also, a lawsuit brought by one stockholder in a corporation to claim rights or to fix wrongs done to many or all stockholders in the company.

representative bureaucracy, concept originated by J. Donald Kingsley, in *Representative Bureaucracy* (Yellow Springs, Ohio: Antioch Press, 1944), which asserts that all social groups have a right to participation in their governing institutions. In recent years, the concept has developed a normative overlay—that all social groups should occupy bureaucratic positions in direct proportion to their numbers in the general population.

representative sample, sample that corresponds to or matches the population of which it is a sample with respect to characteristics important for the purposes under investigation. For example, a representative national sample of secondary school students should probably contain students from each state, from large and small schools, and from public and independent schools in approximately the same proportions as these exist in the nation as a whole.

reprimand, formal censure for some job-related behavior. A reprimand is less severe than an adverse action, more forceful than an admonition.

reprivatization, assignment of functions to the private and nonprofit sectors that were previously performed by government (e.g., trash collection, fire protection, etc.).

repudiate, to reject or refuse.

repurchase agreement, an agreement by a seller to repurchase something sold to a buyer for a specific price, under certain circumstances or conditions, and usually on a specified date.

requirement, public interest, the fact that, in most instances, organizations must be organized and operated for the benefit of the public interest in order to qualify for tax-exempt status. For example, in order for a nonprofit organization engaged in scientific research to be tax-exempt, the organization must demonstrate that the results of its research are generally available to the public (in other words, they do not benefit only the researching organization or its owners).

requisite skills, those skills that make a person eligible for consideration for employment in a particular job.

requisition, a routine written request for supplies or services, usually made from one person or department in an organization to another.

rescind, to take back; unmake; annul. For example, a board may rescind a previous action.

research, a process of scientific inquiry.
See also EVALUATION and NEEDS ASSESSMENT.

research, qualified, research conducted for a purpose that qualifies for tax exemption.

research, scientific, an organizational purpose which may qualify a scientific organization for tax exemption. Basically, the criterion is whether the results of the scientific research benefit public rather than private interests.
See also REQUIREMENT, PUBLIC INTEREST.

research and development, the systematic and intensive study of a subject in order to direct that knowledge toward the production of new materials, systems, methods, or processes. Corporate research uncovers facts and principles in order to benefit development. *Pure* or *basic* research attempts to uncover new scientific knowledge and understanding with little regard to when, or specifically how, the new facts will be used: and *applied* research is conducted with a special purpose in mind. It is usually directed toward a specific problem, or toward a series of problems that stand in the way of progress in a particular area.

research center, also RESEARCH INSTITUTE, an organization which conducts research as its primary mission. Research centers may be independent or affiliated with other organizations such as colleges, universities, and hospitals. Funding for research centers may be from combinations of contracts, grants, and public appropriations. Staff members of university-affiliated research centers often carry faculty appointments, and costs are borne in part by the educational institution.

research design, plan of investigation developed by a scientist to provide an answer to a research question. It is important that the plan meet the basic requirements of the scientific approach and that the selected procedures for gathering information are appropriate to the purposes of the research effort.

reserved rights: *see* MANAGEMENT RIGHTS.

residual unemployment, no matter how many jobs are available, there will always be some people out of work because of illness, indolence, movement from one job or community to another, etc. The total number of these individuals is a measure of residual unemployment.

residual value, the difference between the original worth of an asset (for example, the purchase price or fair market value of a donated automobile) and that portion of it that has been amortized or written off (as a depreciation expense or loss).
See also:
AMORTIZATION
DEPRECIATION
FAIR MARKET VALUE

resignation, employee's formal notice that his or her relationship with the employing organization is being terminated.

resignation, volunteered: *see* QUIT.

resolution, a formal statement of an organization's position, stand, or opinion, usually as voted by the board of directors or the membership.

resource allocation: *see* BUDGET.

resources, a broad term meaning the inputs to an organization or program which permit its processes to be performed. Some examples of resources include money, people, a well-developed information network, and a current mailing list of potential donors.

response rate, in survey research, the

percentage of those given questionnaires who complete and return them. In fund-raising, the percentage of those to whom an appeal was made, who responded (or responded affirmatively).

responsibility, full: *see* FULL RESPONSIBILITY.

restitution, giving something back; making good on something.

restraining order, temporary: *see* INJUNCTION.

restricted security, a stock or bond that is issued in a private sale or other transaction not registered with the Securities and Exchange Commission.

restriction of output, reduced productivity on the part of a worker or work force because of informal group norms, personal grievances, or sloth.

restrictive covenant, a clause in a group of deeds (for example, in a housing subdivision) that forbids all of the current and future owners from doing certain things. Restrictive covenants have been serious impediments, for example, to establishing group homes and halfway houses by social services organizations.

restrictive credentialism, general term for any selection policy adversely affecting disadvantaged groups because they lack the formal qualifications for positions that, in the opinion of those adversely affected, do not truly need such formal qualifications.

restrictive indorsement, signing a negotiable instrument (such as a check) in a way that limits its negotiability; for example, to endorse a check, "Pay to Jim Smith only."

resumé, also CURRICULUM VITA, brief account of education and experience that job applicants typically prepare for prospective employers to review. In the academic world, a resumé is more pompously called a *curriculum vita.*

retail credit: *see* CONSUMER CREDIT.

retained earnings, a for-profit company's net profit minus the dividends it pays to shareholders during a year.

retention, keeping or retaining; for example, volunteer retention, staff retention, and retention of assets. Retention is often expressed as a rate or ratio.

retention period, stated period of time during which records are to be retained.

retention preference, relative standing of employees competing in a reduction-in-force. Their standing is determined by veterans preference, tenure group, length of service, performance appraisal, and critical skills.

retention schedule, a timetable showing how long an organization's records are to be kept. The period of retention for each record is affected by the organization's need for the information (for example, some records may be retained indefinitely for historical purposes), legal requirements, etc.

See also RECORDS MANAGEMENT.

retention standing, precise rank among employees competing for a position in the event of a reduction-in-force or layoff. It is determined by tenure groups and subgroups and by length of creditable service.

retirement, voluntary or involuntary termination of employment or voluntary service because of age, disability, illness, or personal choice. Also, making the final payment owed on a bond or a loan note, and thereby ending its existence and all obligations under it.

Also, the removal of fixed assets from service accompanied by adjustments of the accounts containing their costs and accumulated depreciation. It is immaterial whether the retired asset is sold for use, for junk, or just abandoned.

See also DEPRECIATION.

retirement age, age at which employees cease working. A 1978 amendment to the Age Discrimination in Employment Act raised the minimum mandatory retirement age to seventy years.

retirement counseling, systematic efforts by an organization to help its employees who are retiring to adjust to their new situation.

Retirement Equity Act of 1984, law that broadens the conditions under which spouses receive retirement benefits. Under the act, spouses of employees who die after attaining eligibility for pensions are guaranteed a benefit beginning at age fifty-five. Also, the act requires employers to count all service from age eighteen in calculating when an employee becomes vested (legally entitled to a pension), permits pension plan members to leave the work force for up to five consecutive years without losing pension credits, and allows plan members to take maternity or paternity leave without loss of service credit.

retirement fund, a fund established and maintained to pay employees following their retirement, under terms specified in the organization's retirement plan. Retirement funds, established in conformance with qualified retirement plans, may be tax-exempt or tax-deferred.

retirement plan, fixed-benefit: *see* FIXED-BENEFIT RETIREMENT PLAN.

retreating, assigning an employee to a position from or through which the employee was promoted when the position is occupied by someone with lower retention standing.

retroactive, effective as of a previous date; for example, a retroactive pay increase.

retroactive pay, wages for work performed during an earlier time at a lower rate. Retroactive pay would make up the difference between the new and old rates of pay.

retroactive seniority, seniority status that is retroactively awarded back to the date that a woman or minority group member was proven to have been discriminatorily refused employment. The U.S. Supreme Court has interpreted the "make whole" provision of Title VII of the Civil Rights Act of 1964 to include the award of retroactive seniority to proven discriminatees; however, retroactive seniority cannot be awarded further back than 1964—the date of the act.

retrospective study, an inquiry planned to observe events that have already occurred (a case-control study is usually retrospective); compare with a *prospective study,* which is planned to observe events that have not yet occurred.

return, yield or profit; for example, the return on a public relations campaign.

return, tax: *see* TAX RETURN.

return on investment, the profit an investor makes on shares of stock or other investments, such as rental office space.

revenue, also GROSS RECEIPTS, receipts from all sources. Unless otherwise stated, gross receipts represent receipts prior to the deduction of expenses.

Revenue Act of 1918, act that expanded the then existing list of tax-exempt organizations by adding those organized and operated for the purpose of preventing cruelty to children and animals.

Revenue Act of 1921, act that established community chests, funds, foundations, and literary groups as categories of tax-exempt organizations.

Revenue Act of 1934, act that prohibited tax-exempt organizations from attempting to influence legislation and from engaging in propaganda activities.

Revenue Act of 1978, act that tightened the rules for deducting appreciation on capital gain donations to private foundations and reduced the excise tax on private foundations' net investment income to two percent.

Revenue and Expenditure Control Act of 1968, act that established requirements for cooperative hospital and educational service organizations.

revenue anticipation notes, forms of short-term borrowing used to resolve a cash flow problem occasioned by a shortage of necessary revenues to cover planned or unplanned expenditures.

revenue bonds, municipal bonds whose repayment and dividends are guaranteed by revenues derived from the facility constructed from the proceeds of the sale of the bonds (*e.g.*, stadium bonds, toll road bonds, etc.). As revenue bonds are not pledged against the tax base of the issuing jurisdiction, they are usually not regulated by the same debt limitations imposed by most states on the sale of general obligation bonds. Additionally, revenue bond questions do not have to be submitted to the voters for approval as they do not commit the full faith and credit of the jurisdiction.

revenue gainers, also REVENUE ENHANCEMENT, euphemisms for tax increases.

revenue systems: *see* TAXATION.

reverse annuity mortgage (RAM), a mortgage that allows elderly homeowners to recover the equity in their residence without forcing them to sell the property; RAM combines a mortgage and an annuity.

See also:

ANNUITY
EQUITY
MORTGAGE

reverse art auction, a popular new fund-raising special event in which people sell the worst art they can find.

reverse collective bargaining, activity that occurs when economic conditions force collective bargaining agreements to be renegotiated so that employees end up with a less favorable wage package.

reverse discrimination, practice that, although generally understood to mean preferential treatment for women and minorities as opposed to white males, has no legal standing. Indeed, Section 703 (j) of Title VII of the Civil Rights Act of 1964 holds that nothing in the title shall be interpreted to require any employer to "grant preferential treatment to any individual or group on the basis of race, color, religion, sex or national origin." Yet affirmative action programs necessarily put some otherwise innocent white males at a disadvantage that they would not have otherwise had. The whole matter may have been summed up by George Orwell in his 1945 novella, *Animal Farm*, when he observed that "All animals are equal, but some animals are more equal than others."

reverse stock split, the act of a company calling in its shares of stock, reissuing a smaller number of shares of new stock (for example, issuing one share of new stock for each two shares of old stock), and thereby increasing the value of each share outstanding without changing the total value of all of the stock.

reversion, any future interest kept by a person who transfers away property.

See also REMAINDER.

reversionary interest, an arrangement under which the assets of a nonprofit organization revert to a private individual(s) or private organization upon its dissolution (in other words, private inurement after the nonprofit organization's demise). Tax-exempt organizations may not be organized so that interests are reversionary. Rather, they must be organized so that their assets flow to charitable and/or public purposes upon dissolution.

See also PRIVATE INUREMENT and REMAINDER.

Review, A-95: *see* OFFICE OF MANAGEMENT AND BUDGET (OMB) CIRCULAR A-95.

revocation, also REVOCABLE, the taking back of power or authority; also, wiping out or rescinding.

revolving charge, credit, often provided through credit cards or department stores, by which purchases may be charged and partially paid off month by month.

revolving fund, fund established to finance a cycle of operations through amounts received by the fund.

RIF, acronym for "reduction in force"—the elimination of specific job categories in organizations. While an employee who has been "riffed" has not been fired, he or she is nevertheless without a job. This acronym has become so common that it is often used as a verb.

right, the legally ability of a person or organization to control certain actions of another person.

rightful place, judicial doctrine that an individual who has been discriminated against should be restored to the job—to his or her "rightful place"—as if there had been no discrimination and given appropriate seniority, merit increases, and promotions.

right of first refusal, the right to have the first opportunity to buy property when it goes on sale; also, the right to meet any other offer.

right-of-way, also EASEMENT and SCENIC EASEMENT, legal right to use the land of another, typically for right of passage of a person or vehicle. In the case of *scenic easement,* it is the right to a view and therefore controls the land over which easement is held.

rights arbitration: *see* GRIEVANCE ARBITRATION.

right-to-work laws, state laws that make it illegal for collective bargaining agreements to contain maintenance of membership, preferential hiring, union shop, or any other clauses calling for compulsory union membership. A typical "right-to-work" law might read: "No person may be denied employment and employers may not be denied the right to employ any person because of that person's membership or nonmembership in any labor organization."

It was the Labor-Management Relations (Taft-Hartley) Act of 1947 that authorized right-to-work laws when it provided in section 14(b) that "nothing in this Act shall be construed as authorizing the execution or application of agreements requiring membership in a labor organization as a condition of employment in any State or Territory in which such execution or application is prohibited by State or Territorial law."

The law does not prohibit the union or closed shop; it simply gives each state the option of doing so. Twenty states have done so: Alabama, Arizona, Arkansas, Florida, Georgia, Iowa, Kansas, Louisiana, Mississippi, Nebraska, Nevada, North Carolina, North Dakota, South Carolina, South Dakota, Tennessee, Texas, Utah, Virginia, and Wyoming.

ringed rate: *see* RED-CIRCLE RATE.

ring theory of urban development, theory depicting growth of urban areas in concentric rings, much like ripples in a pond.

risk, the specific possible hazard or loss mentioned in an insurance policy; also, predictable or measurable uncertainty, as in decision theory. In decision theory, risk is defined as a predictable (for example, a statistical probability) chance (or unknown), whereas uncertainty is an unpredictable or unmeasurable chance or unknown.

See also AT RISK.

risk management, all of an organization's efforts to protect its assets, reputation, and human resources against loss.

Robert's Rules of Order, the standard reference on issues of parliamentary procedure. Consult Sarah Corbin Robert, *Robert's Rules of Order Newly Revised* (Palo Alto, Calif.: Scott, Foresman and Company, 1981).

See also PARLIAMENTARY PROCEDURE.

robot, general term for any machine that does the work that a person would otherwise have to do. The word comes from *robotnik,* the Czech word for slave.

robotics, the use of robots.

ROI: *see* RETURN ON INVESTMENT.

role, also ROLE PLAYING, in social psychology, the behavior expected of an individual occupying a particular position. Just as an actor acts out his role on the stage, a manager, for example, performs. Acting out a role will enable an individual to gain insights concerning the behavior of others that cannot be realized by reading a book or listening to a lecture.

role conception: *see* ROLE PERCEPTION.

role conflict, condition that occurs when an individual is called upon to perform mutually exclusive acts by parties having legitimate "holds" on him/her. For example, a rising young manager may not make it to the big meeting if he must at that moment rush his child to the hospital for an emergency appendectomy. When such conflicts arise, most individuals invoke a hierarchy of role obligations that gives some roles precedence over others. To most fathers, their child's life would be more important than a business meeting, no matter how big. Real life is not always so unambiguous, however, and role conflict is a common dilemma in the world of work.

role expectations, the behavioral expectations placed on a person by others around him or her that result from or are consequences of the person's roles or positions in life—in and out of an organization. To a considerable extent, role expectations are determined by the broader organizational context, including the organizational structure, functional specialization, culture, division of labor, and the formal reward system.

See also ROLE and ROLE CONFLICT.

role negotiation, an organization development (OD) technique which involves changing the role an individual or group performs in an organization. In contrast with many other OD intervention techniques, role negotiation goes beyond exposing and understanding issues (such as conflict) and attempts to achieve commitments to changed ways of working through mutually negotiated agreements.

The process openly acknowledges and works with competition, conflict, and struggles for power and influence in organizations. Role negotiation focuses on working relationships and expectations and avoids probing into feelings.

role perception, also called ROLE CONCEPTION, perception that delineates the position that the individual occupies in his/her organization and establishes for the individual the minimum and maximum ranges of permissible behavior in acting out his/her organizational role.

role playing: *see* ROLE and STRUCTURED ROLE PLAYING.

roll, a record of official proceedings; also, a list of members or taxable persons or property; for example, to call the roll.

roll over, to extend a short-term loan or membership for another short period. For example, to roll over the existing officers for one additional month beyond the expiration of their terms.

ROM, read-only memory. A computer memory and storage term.

See also RANDOM ACCESS.

Rorschach test, also called INK-BLOT TEST, projective test in which the responses to standard ink blots are interpreted to gain clues to the subject's personality. Developed by the Swiss psychiatrist Hermann Rorschach (1884-1922), the Rorschach test is no longer considered to be a valid tool for predicting vocational success.

See also PROJECTIVE TEST and THEMATIC APPERCEPTION TEST.

roster of eligibles: *see* ELIGIBLE LIST.

rotating shift, work schedule designed to give employees an equal share of day and night work.

rotation, board: *see* BOARD ROTATION.

rotational expiration of term: *see* BOARD ROTATION.

round lot, a normal unit of trading in stocks or bonds. Fewer shares are an odd lot.

routine, a set of instructions for a computer to perform certain tasks; one part of a computer program.

See also COMPUTER.

royalty, a payment made to an author, an inventor, an owner of oil or other mineral lands, etc. for the use of the property.

RRM: *see* RENEGOTIABLE RATE MORTGAGE.

rule, a regulation.

rule-making authority, powers exercised by administrative agencies that have the force of law.

rule of three, also RULE OF ONE and RULE OF THE LIST, practice of certifying the top three candidates for a position on an eligible list. The rule of three is intended to give the appointing official an opportunity to weigh intangible factors, such as personality, before making a decision. The *rule of one* has only the single highest ranking person on the eligible list certified. The *rule of the list* gives the appointing authority the opportunity to choose from the entire list of eligibles.

See also APPOINTMENT CLAUSE.

run, one complete cycle of a task, such as a computer completing a program.

running account, an open and as yet unpaid account; a charge account.

run-off election, election held when no one person (or union) receives a majority in an election. In the run-off election, participants choose between the two candidates that received the most votes in the first election.

S

sabbatical, lengthy paid leave for professional, intellectual, or emotional refurbishment. It was an ancient Hebrew tradition to allow fields to lie fallow every seventh year. The words sabbath and sabbatical both come from the Hebrew word *shabath,* meaning to rest. In modern times, a sabbatical has been a period of paid leave and rejuvenation for teachers at colleges and universities, but it has recently gained a broader meaning.

sabotage, deliberate destruction of property or the slowing down of work in order to damage a business. During a 1910 railway strike in France, strikers destroyed some of the wooden shoes or *sabots* that held the rails in place. Sabotage soon came into English, but it wasn't until World War II that the word gained widespread popularity as a description of the efforts of secret agents to hinder an enemy's industrial/military capabilities.

There is also the story of the French wool finishers who, in the 1820's, rioted to protest the use of machinery that might supplant them. They were said to have used their wooden shoes or *sabots* to kick the machines to pieces. While this may have been the first instance of sabotage, the use of the word in English dates from the 1910 railway strike.

safe harbor guidelines, rules established by the Tax Reform Act of 1976 defining permissible legislative activities by tax-exempt organizations.

safe haven criteria, criteria for determining unusual grants (that is, grants which satisfy the "unusual grant rule").
See also UNUSUAL GRANT RULE.

safe investment rule: *see* PRUDENT PERSON RULE.

safety, also SAFETY DEPARTMENT, an organization's total effort to prevent and eliminate the causes of accidents. Some organizations have a safety department responsible for administering the various aspects of the safety program.

safety net, President Ronald Reagan's term for the totality of social welfare programs which, in his opinion, assure at least a subsistence standard of living for all Americans.

salary: *see* WAGES.

salary compression, also WAGE COMPRESSION, the shrinking difference between pay to newcomers and the amount paid to experienced employees.

salary curve: *see* MATURITY CURVE.

salary review, formal examination of an employee's rate of pay in terms of his or her recent performance, changes in the cost of living, and other factors.

salary survey: *see* WAGE SURVEY.

salary survey, community: *see* COMMUNITY WAGE SURVEY.

sale, an exchange of property or services for money; a contract in which property or services are exchanged for money.

sale and leaseback: *see* LEASEBACK.

sales budget: *see* BUDGET.

sales journal: *see* BILLING JOURNAL.

sales tax, a tax on goods and services sold. Sales taxes are major sources of revenue for municipal and state governments. Organizations which are exempt for federal income tax purposes usually may also apply for and be exempted from state and local sales taxes.

sale value, the price an asset will bring if sold, less any selling costs.

salvage, to save; for example, to salvage a life.

salvage value, the worth (or predicted worth) of an asset that is disposed of because it has been replaced or is of no further use.
See also DEPRECIATION.

SAM: *see* SOCIETY FOR THE ADVANCEMENT OF MANAGEMENT.

SAM Advanced Management Journal, quarterly offering articles on all phases of management and career development.

sample, any deliberately chosen portion of a larger population that is representative of that population as a whole.

sample size, the number of people or items selected from a population to be studied.

sampling error, error caused by generalizing the behavior of a population from a sample of that population that is not representative of the population as a whole.

Sampling

The devastating effect of biased sampling is illustrated by an incident which attracted national attention a third of a century ago. The summer before the 1936 Presidential election, the *Literary Digest* undertook an extensive poll of the U.S. population to determine who the next President would be. The *Digest* did things in a big way. More than 10 million double postcards were mailed to persons living in every county in the United States. The list was made up of names taken from every telephone book in the United States, from the rosters of clubs and associations, from state directories, lists of registered voters, mail order lists, etc. The recipients were asked to indicate whether they intended to vote for Franklin D. Roosevelt or Alfred M. Landon for President. A sampling of 10 million people established an all-time record. The response was disappointing: Only 2 million cards were returned. Tabulating the returned cards, the *Digest* predicted the election of Landon by a substantial majority. When the votes were counted, Governor Landon carried only two states. The debacle was fatal to the *Digest*. It went out of business shortly thereafter.

This gargantuan poll suffered from two fatal deficiencies. In the first place, the list was made up predominantly of persons who had telephones or who belonged to clubs and associations. Millions of other citizens who did not enjoy the blessings of either a telephone or a membership were underrepresented in the sample. Those who did not get cards comprised a very different "statistical universe" from those who did. In the second place, the one-fifth of those polled who did respond doubtless also represented a different "universe" from the four-fifths who did not bother to answer, thus contributing a further—and unmeasurable—source of error.

The *Digest* discovered the hard way that mere size of a sample carries no guarantee of producing a representative response. Only if care is taken to assure that the sample drawn constitutes a true cross section of the entire population can it be relied on to produce usefully accurate information.

Source: Charles P. Kaplan and Thomas L. Van Valey, *Census '80: Continuing the Factfinder Tradition* (Washington, D.C.: U.S. Department of Commerce, Bureau of the Census, 1980), p. 27.

sampling population, entire set or universe from which a sample is drawn.

sanction: *see* PENALTY.

sandwich lease, a lease in which the person or organization leases property, then sublets it for more money; for example, leasing an office building and renting out space in it to others.

satisfactory-performance increase, annual incremental salary step increase awarded for satisfactory performance within a single salary grade.

satisficing, also called BOUNDED RATIONALITY, term coined by Herbert A. Simon, in *Administrative Behavior* (N.Y.: Macmillan 1947), while explaining his concept of *bounded rationality*. Simon asserts that it is impossible to ever know all of the facts that bear upon any given decision. Because truly rational research on any problem can never be completed, humans put bounds on their rationality and make decisions, not on the basis of optimal information, but on the basis of satisfactory information. Humans tend to make their decisions by satisficing—choosing a course of action that meets one's minimum standards for satisfaction.

saturation, the point at which further penetration of a market is improbable or excessively costly.

See also MARKET and PENETRATION RATE.

savings account, an interest-bearing account (usually at a bank, credit union, or savings and loan association) on which advance notice of intent to withdraw funds may be required.

savings account loan, a loan that is secured by funds on deposit in the financial institution.

savings and loan association (S&L), a financial institution that primarily makes loans to home buyers. Some S&L's are cooperatives; some banks; some state chartered; some federally chartered under the Federal Home Loan Bank Board.

savings bank, any bank that accepts savings accounts, other than a "full service" commercial bank.

savings bank trust: *see* TOTTEN TRUST.

SBA: *see* SMALL BUSINESS ADMINISTRATION.

SBIC: *see* SMALL BUSINESS INVESTMENT COMPANY.

scab, also called BLACKLEG, generally, an employee who continues to work for an organization while it is being struck by coworkers.

scalar chain, also LINE OF AUTHORITY, according to Henri Fayol, *General and Industrial Management*, trans. by Constance Storrs (London: Pitman Publishing, Ltd., 1949),

> the scalar chain is the chain of superiors ranging from the ultimate authority to the lowest ranks. The *line of authority* is the route followed—via every link in the chain—by all communications which start from or go to the ultimate authority. This path is dictated both by the need for some transmission and by the principle of unity of command, but it is not always the swiftest. It is even at times disastrously lengthy in large concerns, notably in governmental ones.

scaled score, score on a test when the raw score obtained has been converted to a number or position on a standard reference scale. Test scores reported to examinees and users of tests are usually scaled scores. The purpose of converting scores to a scale is to make reported scores as independent as possible of the particular form of a test an examinee has taken and of the composition of the candidate group at a particular administration. For example, the College Board Achievement tests are all reported on a scale of 200 to 800. A score of 600 on a College Board Achievement test is intended to indicate the same level of ability from year to year.

scapegoating, shifting the blame for a problem or failure to another person, group or organization—a common bureaucratic and political tactic.

scatter diagram, display of the relationship between variables using dots on a graph.

scenario, a narrative description of a problem or operation under analysis including the sequence of events, environment, purpose, and timing of actions.

scenic easement: *see* RIGHT-OF-WAY.

schedule, a series of items to be handled or of events to occur at or during a particular period of time; a timetable.

Also, any list; a list attached to a document that explains in detail things mentioned generally in the document. For example, the supporting pages of calculations attached to an IRS tax form are called schedules.

scheduled payment, a payment due at a specified time, such as installment payments in a credit agreement.

Schein, Edgar H. (1928-), psychologist who has written some of the most influential work on organizational psychology, organization development, organizational culture and career management.

schemes, tax avoidance: *see* TAX AVOIDANCE SCHEME.

scholarship fund, a type of fund used to establish scholarships in the name of donors. Scholarship funds are often found in and managed by community foundations.

See also, COMMUNITY FOUNDATION.

science policy, generic term referring to government decision making, usually at a national level, which relates to the furtherance, uses, and implications of science and scientific research. The beginnings of modern science policy making are traditionally dated at the beginning of World War II, with the establishment of the Office of Scientific Research and Development, which was responsible for, among other things, the development of the atomic bomb. The establishment of the National Science Foundation in 1951 institutionalized federal concerns for the control and direction of scientific research, and led to the development of a huge and growing number of agencies in the federal bureaucracy concerned with science and technology issues.

See also TECHNOLOGY ASSESSMENT.

scientific approach, procedure for collecting and analyzing data in a systematic and unbiased manner. The three major steps in the scientific approach are observation, measurement, and prediction.

scientific management, systematic approach to managing that seeks the "one best way" of accomplishing any given task by discovering the fastest, most efficient, and least fatiguing production methods. The job of the scientific manager, once the "one best way" was found, was to impose this procedure upon the work force. Frederick W. Taylor is considered to be the "father" of scientific management. *See* his *Principles of Scientific Management* (N.Y.: Harper & Bros., 1911).

See also the following entries:

GILBRETH, FRANK BUNKER AND LILLIAN MOLLER
MOTION STUDY
TAYLOR, FREDERICK W.
TIME STUDY

scientific method, an approach to research which starts with the observation of a phenomenon, then develops an hypothesis about it, and finally tests the hypothesis through experimentation. Then the process or cycle of observation-hypothesis-experimentation begins all over again.

See also RESEARCH, SCIENTIFIC.

scientific organization, a category of tax-exempt organizations which serve a public purpose by undertaking scientific research and disseminating scientific information.

See also PUBLIC INTEREST and RESEARCH, SCIENTIFIC.

scope of bargaining, the issues over which management and labor negotiate during the collective bargaining process.

score, crude/raw: *see* RAW SCORE.

score, formula: *see* FORMULA SCORE.

score, scaled: *see* SCALED SCORE.

score, standard: *see* STANDARD SCORE.

screening interview, initial interview for a job that serves to determine which applicants are to be given further consideration.

scrip, a piece of paper that is a temporary indication of a right to something valuable. Scrip includes paper money issued for temporary use, partial shares of stock after a stock split, etc.

script, also LIFE SCRIPT, according to transactional analysis theory, a set of messages received from parents and other authority figures which predetermines a person's learned, rehearsed, and acted-out roles in his or her dramatic life events (usually, scripts are triggered at times of stress). Once the roles are established, the individual selects and manipulates other people to join his or her cast of characters.

Most organizations also have and live scripts, which they receive from their founders and dominant early leaders.

See also LIFE POSITION and TRANSACTIONAL ANALYSIS.

scroll, to move text up or down a computer screen to read earlier or later text.

SCSA: *see* STANDARD CONSOLIDATED STATISTICAL AREA.

seal, corporate, a circular, embossed symbol used to indicate the authenticity of an organization's formal documents (including legal documents). In most organizations, the corporate seal is maintained and used by the secretary of the organization.

sealed bid, a potential contractor's offer (bid) to perform work which is submitted in a closed (sealed) envelope. All sealed bids are opened at the same time, and the "best" bid is selected.

seasonal adjustments, statistical modifications made to compensate for fluctuations in a time series which recur more or less regularly each year. The cause of these movements may be climatic (farm income, for example, is highest in the fall) or institutional (retail sales reach a peak just before Christmas). These seasonal movements are often so strong that they distort the underlying changes in economic data and tend to obscure trends that might be developing.

seasonal employment, also SEASONAL UNEMPLOYMENT, work that is available only during certain times of the year, such as jobs picking or canning fruit in the fall, jobs playing Santa Claus in a shopping mall, and jobs as lifeguards at summer resorts. *Seasonal unemployment* is unemployment occasioned by the seasonal variations of particular industries. Jobs affected by the weather such as those in construction and agriculture are particularly susceptible to seasonal unemployment.

SEC: *see* SECURITIES AND EXCHANGE COMMISSION.

secondary boycott, concerted effort by a union engaged in a dispute with an employer to seek another union to boycott a fourth party (usually their employers) who, in response to such pressure, might put like pressure on the original offending employer. Secondary boycotts are forbidden by the Labor-Management Relations (Taft-Hartley) Act of 1947.

secondary data, evaluation data which already exist prior to initiating an evaluation study; for example, health department statistics on births and deaths by county.

See also:

OPERATIONAL DATA
PRIMARY DATA
SOURCES OF DATA

secondary group: *see* GROUP, PRIMARY.

secondary strike, strike against an employer because it is doing business with another employer whose workers are on strike.

second career: *see* CAREER CHANGE.

second mortgage, also SECOND TRUST, a mortgage that is subordinate to another (or first) mortgage on a property, and that usually bears a higher rate of interest.

second-order effects, also called SECOND-ORDER CONSEQUENCES, side effects from a program or project.

secrete, to hide something, especially to keep it from creditors by putting title in someone else's name.

secured loan, a debt that is protected by a mortgage, lien, pledge, etc.

Securities and Exchange Commission (SEC), federal commission that seeks the fullest possible disclosure to the investing public and seeks to protect the interests of the public and investors against malpractices in the securities and financial markets.

securities rating: *see* BOND RATING and STANDARD & POOR'S CORP.

security, property that has been pledged or mortgaged as financial backing for a loan or other obligation; also, a share of stock, a bond, a note, or other forms of documents showing a share of ownership in a company or a debt owed.

security deposit, money put up in advance by a tenant to pay for possible damage to property or for leaving before the end of a lease.

seed money, initial financing to start a project which is to be supplemented with larger, more permanent funding at a later date.

select committee, committee established for a limited period and generally for a strictly temporary purpose. When that function has been carried out the select committee automatically expires. A *standing committee*, on the other hand, is a regular, permanent unit.

selection: *see* PERSONNEL SELECTION.

Selection Guidelines: *see* UNIFORM GUIDELINES ON EMPLOYEE SELECTION.

selection interview: *see* INTERVIEW.

selection out, euphemism for terminating an employee from a training program or employment.

selection procedure, according to the "Uniform Guidelines on Employee Selection,"

> any measure, combination of measures, or procedures used as a basis for any employment decision. Selection procedures include the full range of assessment techniques from traditional paper and pencil tests, performance tests, training programs, or probationary periods and physical, educational, and work experience requirements through informal or casual interviews and unscored application forms.

See also UNIFORM GUIDELINES ON EMPLOYEE SELECTION.

selection ratio, number of job applicants selected compared to the number of job applicants who were available.

selectman, member of some local legislatures or town councils.

self-actualization, apex of Abraham Maslow's needs hierarchy, where an individual theoretically reaches self-fulfillment and becomes all that he or she is capable of becoming. The importance of the concept of self-actualization was established long before Maslow gave it voice. The nineteenth century poet, Robert Browning, described its essence when he said, "a man's reach should exceed his grasp, or what's a heaven for?" Maslow's needs hierarchy was originally presented in "A Theory of Human Motivation," *Psychological Review* (July 1943).

self-appraisal, performance evaluation technique in which the employee takes the initiative in appraising his/her own performance.

self-dealing, conducting financial transactions with a tax-exempt organization (particularly a foundation) for one's own benefit. Self-dealing is similar to private inurement. Self-dealing includes virtually all financial transactions between "disqualified persons" and a private foundation.

See also DISQUALIFIED PERSON and PRIVATE INUREMENT.

self-dealing, indirect: *see* INDIRECT SELF-DEALING.

self-dealing transaction, a financial transaction between a disqualified person(s) and a private foundation for the purpose of self-inurement.

See PRIVATE INUREMENT and SELF DEALING.

self-employed, members of the work force who work for themselves—in their own trade or business—as opposed to wage earners who are in the employ of others.

Self-Employed Individuals Tax Retirement Act of 1962: *see* KEOGH PLAN.

self-employment tax, means by which persons who work for themselves are provided social security coverage. Each self-employed person must pay self-employment tax on part or all of his or her income to help finance social security benefits, which are payable to self-employed persons as well as wage earners.

See also TAXATION.

self-fulfilling prophecy, causing something to happen by believing it will. If a manager or teacher believes that his or her employees or students are not capable, they will eventually live up or down to the manager's or teacher's expectations.

self-insurance, setting aside a fund of money to pay for possible future losses rather than purchasing an insurance policy.

self-liquidating loan, a loan to buy or produce things (for example, a sheltered workshop to buy production equipment) which will be sold to obtain cash with which to repay the loan.

semi-fixed cost: *see* COST, SEMI-FIXED.

semiskilled workers, employees whose jobs are confined to well-established work routines, usually requiring a considerable degree of manipulative ability and a limited exercise of independent judgment.

semi-variable cost: *see* COST, SEMI-FIXED.

seniority, social mechanism that gives priority to the individuals who are the most senior—have the longest service—in an organization. Seniority is often used to determine which employees will be promoted, subjected to layoff, or given/denied other employment advantages.

See also the following entries:

BENEFIT SENIORITY
COMPETITIVE SENIORITY
DEPARTMENTAL SENIORITY
INVERSE SENIORITY
RETROACTIVE SENIORITY
SUPERSENIORITY

sensitivity analysis, a complex analytical procedure for assessing the costs, benefits, outputs, effectiveness, and other desirable and undesirable impacts of alternative decisions resulting from changes in the underlying assumptions. The steps leading to and in a sensitivity analysis include:

1. Construct cost-benefit and/or cost-effectiveness models.
2. Identify the important factors in the models. (There is an almost infinite variety of things which can affect the results of a proposed alternative, but there are only a few which should have a significant effect on the result.)
3. Determine the range of quantitative values or possible states which could occur. (For the important factors, determine the range which could reasonably be expected to occur. For example, the cost of a piece of equipment could range between $150 and $200. The chances of the cost being outside of the range are low.)
4. Select quantitative and qualitative values or states to use in the sensitivity analysis. (In the above example, you might select $150, $175, and $200 for inclusion in the sensitivity analysis. Assess the states of nature, social, psychological, and/or political aspects which might affect the results of the alternatives.)
5. Conduct the sensitivity analysis. [Run the three (or however many) quantitative values through the original cost-benefit or cost-effectiveness model. Make subjective estimates of the intangible factors which might occur (that is, how might they affect the decision we are facing?).]
6. Arrange the results in a useful format for decision maker(s). (Only a limited range of alternatives that should bear on the decision should be presented to decision makers. Assumptions should be stated explicitly.)

sensitivity training: *see* LABORATORY TRAINING and BRADFORD, LELAND P.

separate fund: *see* FUND, SEPARATE.

separation, termination of an individual's employment for whatever reason.

separation interview: *see* EXIT INTERVIEW.

separation pay: *see* SEVERANCE PAY.

separation rate, ratio of the number of separations per hundred employees over a specified time span.

serial bonds, bonds of the same issue, put out at the same time, that have varying dates of maturity so that the entire debt does not fall due at once. Usually, the group of bonds carrying the longest term (in years) pays a higher rate of interest than those with shorter terms. Serial bonds should not be confused with series bonds.

See also SERIES BONDS.

serial interface, a printer or other peripheral device connected to a computer that transmits the bits of a byte of information sequentially, or one after another.
For contrast, *see* PARALLEL INTERFACE.

series bonds, groups of bonds put out at different times with different cash-in dates, but all part of the same deal; often, a complex mortgage. Not to be confused with serial bonds.

series of classes, all classes of positions involving the same kind of work, but which may vary as to the level of difficulty and responsibility and have differing grade and salary ranges. The classes in a series either have differing titles (*e.g.*, assistant accountant, associate accountant, senior accountant) or numerical designations (*e.g.* Accountant I, Accountant II, Accountant III). Be wary of numerical designations, however. There is no uniformity in their use; an Accountant I could be either the most junior or most senior level.
See also POSITION CLASSIFICATION.

service, useful work; also, regular payments on a debt.

service delivery system, deliberately established set of social, economic, political, and/or cultural arrangements designed to provide a designated set of goods and/or services to consumers who are adjudged to have particular needs.

services, contracted, services provided for an organization by other than its own employees under a contractual arrangement. Typical types of services which are contracted by nonprofit organizations include design of a fund-raising campaign, implementation of a direct mail campaign, program development, legal services, accounting services, program evaluation, etc.
See also CONSULTANT and CONTRACTOR.

services, contributed: *see* CONTRIBUTED SERVICES.

set: *see* POPULATION.

set-aside, funds which a private foundation is permitted to earmark for a specific project which will not be initiated until a future year. The set-aside may be included as a part of the mandatory distribution requirement for the current year.
See also MANDATORY DISTRIBUTION REQUIREMENT.

set-aside rules, congressionally established rules governing the use of set-asides by private foundations.
See also SET-ASIDE.

settlement, also SETTLEMENT SHEET, a meeting in which the ownership of property (for example, a building) transfers from seller to buyer. All payments and debts are adjusted and taken care of at this time. These financial matters are written on a *settlement sheet*, which is also known as a closing statement.

seventy-percent syndrome: *see* CUTTING SCORE.

706 agency, state and local fair employment practices agency named for Section 706(c) of Title VII of the Civil Rights Act of 1964, which requires aggrieved individuals to submit claims to state or local fair employment practices agencies before they are eligible to present their cases to the federal government's Equal Employment Opportunity Commission. State and local agencies that have the ability to provide the same protections provided by Title VII as would the EEOC are termed 706 agencies. The EEOC maintains a list of the 706 agencies that it formally recognizes.

sever: *see* FIRE.

severance pay, also called DISMISSAL PAY, SEPARATION PAY, and TERMINATION PAY, lump-sum payment by an employer to an employee who has been permanently separated from the organization because of a work force reduction, the introduction of labor-saving machinery, or for any reason other than "cause." The amount of a severance payment is usually determined by a schedule based on years of service and earnings. About forty percent of all union contracts contain provisions for severance pay.

sex differential, also RACE DIFFERENTIAL, lower than "regular" wage rate paid by an employer to female and/or black employees. Such differentials were paid before the advent of current equal employment opportunity laws and are now illegal.

sex discrimination, any disparate or unfavorable treatment of an individual in an employment situation because of his or her sex. The Civil Rights Act of 1964 makes sex discrimination illegal except where a bona fide occupational qualification is involved.

sexist, person or organization that consciously or unconsciously practices sex discrimination.

sex plus, situation where an employer does not discriminate against all males or all females, but discriminates against a subset of either sex. *Phillips* v. *Martin Marietta*, 400 U.S. 542 (1971), is the U.S. Supreme Court case that dealt with the "sex plus" criterion for evaluating applicants for employment. Martin Marietta had a policy of hiring both sexes for a particular job but refused to hire any women with preschoolaged children. The court found this "sex plus" policy to be in violation of Title VII of the Civil Rights Act of 1964.

sexual harassment, activity that exists whenever an individual in a position to control or influence another's job, career, or grade uses such power to gain sexual favors or punish the refusal of such favors. Sexual harassment on the job varies from inappropriate sexual innuendo to coerced sexual relations.

share, one piece of stock in a for-profit corporation.

See also SHAREHOLDER.

share account, a type of account offered by a credit union which is similar to the time and savings accounts offered by commercial banks and thrift institutions.

share draft, a type of account offered by credit unions that is similar to a NOW account.

See NEGOTIABLE ORDER OF WITHDRAWAL.

shareholder, an owner of a corporation. Typically, owners are issued shares of stock. Most states do not permit nonprofit corporations to be organized as stock corporations.

shell corporation: *see* TAX AVOIDANCE SCHEME.

shelter, a way of investing money to minimize tax liabilities.

See also LOOPHOLE, TAX and TAX AVOIDANCE SCHEME.

sheltered workshop, place of employment that offers a controlled, noncompetitive environment for persons unable or not ready to compete in the regular world of work because of physical or mental disability.

***Sherbert* v. *Verner*,** 374 U.S. 398 (1963), U.S. Supreme Court case which held it was unconstitutional to disqualify a person for unemployment compensation benefits solely because that person refused to accept employment that would require working on Saturday contrary to his or her religious belief.

See also FREE EXERCISE CLAUSE.

shift, fixed: *see* FIXED SHIFT.

shift, split: *see* BROKEN TIME.

shift premium, also called SHIFT DIFFERENTIAL, extra compensation paid as an inducement to accept shift work.

shift work, formal tour of duty that is mostly outside of normal daytime business hours.

shop steward: *see* STEWARD.

short-term debt, interest-bearing debt due within one year from date of issue, such as bond anticipation notes and bank loans.

showing of interest, evidence of membership—the requirement that a union must show that it has adequate support from employees in a proposed bargaining unit before a representation election can be held. A "showing of interest" is usually demonstrated by signed authorization cards.

sick leave, leave of absence, usually with pay, granted to employees who cannot attend work because of illness.

sick-leave bank, arrangement that allows employees to pool some of their paid sick-leave days in a common fund so that they may draw upon that fund if extensive illness uses up their remaining paid time off. Sick-leave banks have tended to discourage absenteeism, because with everyone jointly owning days in the bank, there is some psychological pressure on workers not to use their sick leave unless they are really sick.

sight, payable when shown and requested; for example, a sight draft.

significance, also called STATISTICAL SIGNIFICANCE, degree to which one can be confident in the reliability of a statistical measure. For example, a confidence level of .05 means that the statistical finding would occur by chance in only one sample out of every twenty.

silver-circle rate, higher than standard pay rate based upon length of service.

Simon, Herbert A. (1916-), scholar awarded the Nobel Prize for Economics in 1978 for his pioneering work in management decision making. Simon is best known to the administrative world for his impressive contributions to our understanding of organizational behavior.

See also PROVERBS OF ADMINISTRATION and SATISFICING.

simple interest, interest on the original principal (invested money) only.

For comparison, *see* COMPOUND INTEREST.

simulation: *see* GAMING SIMULATION.

sinecure, any position for which a salary is extracted but little or no work is expected. This was originally an ecclesiastical term which meant a church office that did not require the care of souls. *Sinecure* is Latin for "without care."

single rate: *see* FLAT RATE.

single-use plans, plans used up or defunct when the goals are accomplished for which that plan was designed (*e.g.*, construction projects, research and development projects, fabrication of equipment or structures, etc.).

sinking fund, money or other assets put aside for a special purpose, such as to pay off bonds as they come due or to replace worn-out or outdated machinery or buildings.

sit-down strike, also STAY-IN STRIKE, any work stoppage during which the strikers remain at their work stations and refuse to leave the employer's premises in order to forestall the employment of strikebreakers. This kind of strike gained widespread publicity in the 1930s as a tactic of the unions in the rubber and automobile industries. A sit-down strike that lasts for a substantial period of time is then called a *stay-in strike*. Sit-down strikes now are illegal.

situational leadership: *see* CONTINGENCY MODEL OF LEADERSHIP EFFECTIVENESS.

situational management: *see* CONTINGENCY MANAGEMENT.

situation audit, a strategic planning technique for assessing an organization's performance. Major aspects of a situation audit include a capability profile and a WOTS-UP analysis.

See also:
CAPABILITY PROFILE
PLANNING
STRATEGIC PLANNING
WOTS-UP ANALYSIS

skewness, tendency of a distribution to depart from symmetry or balance around the mean. If the scores tend to cluster at the lower end of the distribution, the distribution is said to be positively skewed; if they tend to cluster at the upper end of the distribution, the distribution is said to be negatively skewed.

skill differential, differences in wage rates paid to workers employed in occupational categories requiring varying levels of skill.

skilled labor, workers who, having trained for a relatively long time, have mastered jobs of considerable skill requiring the exercise of substantial independent judgment.

skills, physical or manipulative activities requiring knowledge for their execution.

skills survey, also called SKILLS AUDIT and SKILLS INVENTORY, comprehensive collection and examination of data on the work force to determine the composition and level of employees' skills, knowledges, and abilities so that they can be more fully utilized and/or developed to fill the staffing needs of an organization. A skills survey or inventory may at times be the process of collecting data and at other times the product as represented by a collection of data in a variety of forms. To be effective, skills data must also be arranged in such a manner that the information gathered can be readily accessible for management use.

skimming, a slang term for illegally concealing business income from partners or tax authorities.

Skinner, B. F. (1904-), one of the most influential of behavioral psychologists, inventor of the teaching machine, and generally considered to be the "father" of programmed instruction.

slide-rule discipline, approach to discipline that eliminates supervisory discretion and sets very specific quantitative standards for the consequences of specific violations. For example, a discipline policy based on this concept might hold that any employee who is late for work more than four times in a thirty-day period would be automatically suspended for three days.

Sloan Management Review, professional management journal of the Alfred P. Sloan School of Management at the Massachusetts Institute of Technology. It is published three times each academic year (fall, winter, and spring) and has as its principal goal the exchange of information between academic and business communities.

slot, position in an organization.

slowdown, deliberate reduction of output by employees. Such efforts are usually designed to bring economic pressure upon an employer without incurring the costs of a strike.

Small Business Administration (SBA), federal agency whose purposes are to aid, counsel, assist, and protect the interests of small business; ensure that small business concerns receive a fair proportion of government purchases, contracts, and subcontracts, as well as of the sales of government property; make loans to small business concerns, state and local development companies, and the victims of floods or other catastrophes, or of certain types of economic injury; license, regulate, and make loans to small business investment companies; improve the management skills of small business owners, potential owners, and managers; conduct studies of the economic environment; and guarantee surety bonds for small contractors.

small business investment company (SBIC), a nonprofit corporation established under the provisions of the Small Business Investment Act which is subject to SBA regulation. SBICs loan money to small businesses that cannot secure financing through conventional commercial sources in order to accomplish charitable purposes (such as the alleviation of poverty). SBICs may be tax-exempt, but their tax status generally is neither clear nor certain.

small group: *see* GROUP, PRIMARY.

small-group research, also GROUP, study of small groups. A *group* consists of a number of individuals who interact with each other in a particular social setting. Generally, groups are classified as "small" when each member can at least take personal cognizance of all other members. This distinguishes small groups from social units that are so large that it is impossible for each member to be aware of all others.

See also:

GROUP, PRIMARY
GROUP DYNAMICS
ORGANIZATION DEVELOPMENT

Smithsonian Institution, an independent trust establishment that performs fundamental research; publishes the results of studies, explorations, and investigations; preserves for study and reference over seventy million items of scientific, cultural, and historical interest; maintains exhibits representative of the arts, U.S. history, technology, aeronautics and space explorations, and natural history; participates in the international exchange of learned publications; and engages in programs of education and national and international cooperation research and training, supported by its trust endowments and gifts, grants, and contracts, and funds appropriated to it by Congress.

smorgasbord benefits plan: *see* CAFETERIA BENEFITS PLAN.

SMSA: *see* STANDARD METROPOLITAN STATISTICAL AREA.

social audit, a corporate commitment to systematic assessments of and reporting on activities that have social impacts.

social benefits, public gains, both quantifiable and nonquantifiable, which result from a specific program or project.

social darwinism, Charles Darwin's concept of the "survival of the fittest" applied to human society.

social equity, normative standard holding that equity, rather than efficiency, is the major criterion for evaluating the desirability of a policy or program.

social indicators, statistical measures that aid in the description of conditions in the social environment (*e.g.*, measures of income distribution, poverty, health, physical environment).

social insurance, any benefit program that a state makes available to the members of its society in time of need and as a matter of right.

socialism, a system of government in which many of the means of production and trade are owned or run by the government and in which many human welfare needs are provided directly by the government. *Socialism* may or may not be democratic.

socialization, organizational: *see* ORGANIZATIONAL SOCIALIZATION.

socialized medicine, a medical care system where the organization and provision of medical care services are under direct government control, and providers are employed by or contract for the provision of services directly with the government; also, a term used more generally, without recognized or constant definition, referring to any existing or proposed medical care system believed to be subject to excessive governmental control.

Social Readjustment Rating Scale (SRRS), a widely used instrument for measuring the impact of life changes and events on people. The SRRS is used to assess a person's susceptibility to stress and, therefore, to predict physical and emotional problems. The SRRS is scaled in Life Change Units (LCUs) from 0 to 100. *See* Holmes, T. H. and R. H. Rahe, "The Social Readjustment Rating Scale," *Journal of Psychometric Research,* Vol. 11, 1967.

See also STRESS.

social reference group: *see* REFERENCE GROUP.

social security, term once defined by Britain's Lord Beveridge as "a job when you can work and an income when you can't." In the United States, social security is the popular name for the Old Age, Survivors, and Disability Insurance (OASDI) system established by the Social Security Act of 1935. At first, social security only covered private sector employees upon retirement. In 1939, the law was changed to pay survivors when the worker died, as well as certain dependents, when the worker retired. In the 1950s, coverage was extended to include most self-employed persons, most state and local employees, household and farm employees, members of the armed forces, and members of the clergy. Today, almost all U.S. jobs are covered by social security.

Disability insurance was added in 1954 to give workers protection against loss of earnings due to total disability. The social security program was expanded again in 1965 with the enactment of Medicare, which assured hospital and medical insurance protection to people sixty-five and over. Since 1973, Medicare coverage has been available to people under sixty-five who have been entitled to disability checks for two or more consecutive years and to people with permanent kidney failure who need dialysis or kidney transplants. Amendments enacted in 1972 provide that social security benefits will increase automatically with the cost of living.

See also the following entries:

MEDICARE
OLD AGE, SURVIVORS, AND DISABILITY INSURANCE
SOCIAL SECURITY ADMINISTRATION

Social Security Administration (SSA), U.S. government agency, part of the Department of Health and Human Services, that administers the national program of contributory social insurance whereby employees, employers, and the self-employed pay contributions that are pooled in special trust funds.

social service organization, a general label for nonprofit organizations which work to preserve and improve nonmembers' physical and/or mental health; for example, accident prevention, treatment of illness, and provision of rehabilitation services.

See also SOCIAL WELFARE ORGANIZATION.

social welfare, promotion of, the least well defined of the tax-exempt charitable purposes. In general, the test of whether an activity is for the promotion of the social welfare turns on whether the specific purpose reasonably appears to be in the community's social interest. IRS regulations have defined general types of promotion of social welfare efforts, including lessening neighborhood tensions, eliminating prejudice and discrimination, defending human and civil rights, and fighting community deterioration and juvenile delinquency.

See also SOCIAL WELFARE ORGANIZATION.

social welfare organization, a category of tax-exempt organizations that are organized and operated to promote the social welfare of specific groupings of people; for example, providing for the general welfare of a specific grouping of nonmembers who face social problems because of their social situation. Social welfare organizations focus on particular groups of people who have special needs, problems, or requirements. Social welfare organizations may qualify for tax-exempt status under IRS Code 501(c) (4).

Social welfare organizations may engage in activist-type activities that are not permissible for charitable organizations; however, they remain subject to most other prohibitions that apply to other categories of charitable organizations, such as those prohibiting participation in political campaign activities and private inurement transactions.

See also:

CHARITABLE ORGANIZATION
OPERATED
ORGANIZED
POLITICAL ACTIVITIES
PRIVATE INUREMENT
SOCIAL SERVICE ORGANIZATION
SOCIAL WELFARE, PROMOTION OF

social work, nonprofit and governmental administration of services for the old or for those who are socially handicapped.

social worker, a professionally trained person who provides social services to enable clients, patients, family members, or others to deal with problems of social functioning that affect (or are affected by) the status or well-being of the patient or client.

Society for Nonprofit Organizations, an association dedicated to bringing together those who work within and those who serve the nonprofit world in order to build a strong network of professionals throughout the United States.

Society for the Advancement of Management (SAM), professional society formed in 1912 by colleagues of Frederick W. Taylor, dedicated to the discussion and promotion of scientific management. SAM is now a peer training organization "devoted to helping managers develop professionally through communication and interaction with other managers." It is based in New York City.

sociogram, diagram showing the interactions between members of a group. Typically, it has circles representing people and arrows extending from those circles pointing out the other people (circles) that are liked, disliked, etc.

sociology, occupational: *see* OCCUPATIONAL SOCIOLOGY.

sociology of work: *see* OCCUPATIONAL SOCIOLOGY.

sociometry, technique for discovering the patterns of interpersonal relationships that exist within a group. A sociometric analysis typically has each member of the group express his or her choices for or against other members of the group. A common question on such surveys is, "Who should be the leader of the group?" The ensuing preference and rejection patterns can be used to construct sociograms or social maps.

socio-technical systems, concept that a work group is neither a technical nor a social system, but an interdependent socio-technical system. Research on this concept was pioneered in the early 1950s by the Tavistock Institute of Human Relations in London.

soft match: *see* IN-KIND MATCH.

soldier, in the industrial world, to malinger, to shirk one's duty, to feign illness, or to make a pretense of working. The usage comes from naval history. In earlier centuries, soldiers aboard ship did not have duties as arduous as those of the regular ship's company, so the sailors made soldiering synonymous with loafing and other nonproductive activities.

sole proprietorship, a business owned by one person. For contrast, *see* CORPORATION and PARTNERSHIP.

solid waste management, methods used to deal with the residential and commercial solid byproducts of consumption and production. Management techniques include solid waste reduction (*e.g.*, returnable beverage bottles), recycling (*e.g.*, the remanufacture of a new product from an old one such as paper), burning (*e.g.*, waste heat from incinerators to heat buildings) and burial (*e.g.*, landfills).

solvent, having the ability to pay debts as they come due; also, having more assets than liabilities.

sources of data (evaluation or research), the three most basic types of sources of data for use in evaluation research are primary data, secondary data, and operational data. Operational data are one form of secondary data but are sufficiently important to warrant separate consideration.

See also:

EVALUATION DESIGN
OPERATIONAL DATA
PRIMARY DATA
SECONDARY DATA

sovereignty, the quality of being supreme in power, rank, or authority.

space costs: *see* FACILITIES and COST, INDIRECT.

Spanish Speaking Program, also HISPANIC EMPLOYMENT PROGRAM, federal government program established on November 5, 1970 to call attention to the needs of the Spanish-speaking in federal employment. It is an integral part of the government's total EEO effort and is designed to assure equal employment opportunity for the Spanish-speaking in all aspects of federal employment. In March 1978, the name of the Spanish Speaking Program was changed to the Hispanic Employment Program.

span of control, extent of a manager's responsibility. The span of control has usually been expressed as the number of subordinates that a manager should supervise. Sir Ian Hamilton, *The Soul and Body of an Army* (London: Edward Arnold & Co., 1921), is generally credited with having first asserted that the "average human brain finds its effective scope in handling from three to six other brains." A. V. Graicunas took a mathematical approach to the concept and demonstrated, in "Relationship in Organization," Luther Gulick and Lyndall Urwick (eds.), *Papers on the Science of Administration* (N.Y.: Institute of Public Administration, 1937), that as the number of subordinates reporting to a manager increases arithmetically, the number of possible interpersonal interactions increases geometrically. Building upon Graicunas' work, Lyndall F. Urwick boldly asserts, in "The Manager's Span of Control," *Harvard Business Review* (May-June 1956), that "no superior can supervise directly the work of more than five or, at the most, six subordinates whose work interlocks." Studies on the concept of span of control abound, but there is no consensus on an ideal span.

spatial relations, measure of an individual's ability for rapid and dexterous manipulation of pieces and parts relative to one another (*i.e.*, perceiving geometric relationships).

Spearman-Brown Formula, formula for determining the relationship between the reliability of a test and its length.

special assessment, a real estate tax on certain landowners to pay for improvements that will, at least in theory, benefit them all; for example, a paved street.

See also BENEFIT DISTRICT.

special event, a fund-raising event usually involving entertainment or recreational activities, with a purchased ticket or a fixed donation required to attend. Food, beverages, and/or souvenirs (*e.g.*, T-shirts, pins, bumper stickers) and chances (such as lottery tickets) may be sold at the event to increase income. Types of special events are as varied as the sponsoring organization's members' imaginations. Some examples of special events include community carnivals, donkey basketball games, races/marathons, garage sales, swap meets, auctions, barbecues/steak fries, dances, raffles, bake sales, house parties, progressive dinners, fashion shows, wine tasting parties, baseball or football games, rodeos, dances (*e.g.*, formal or square), concerts, Christmas decorating festivals, walk-a-thons, chain parties, flea markets, and Trivial Pursuit parties.

Advantages of special events include: increases in the organization's visibility in a community, stimulation of interest of volunteers, and involvement of volunteers who do not like to solicit contributions directly.

On the negative side, special events tend to produce smaller than expected profits, consume considerable amounts of volunteer and staff time and energy, and often distract the nonprofit organization and potential donors from other, more fruitful fund-raising efforts. Like any other complex fund-raising activity, special events need to be planned carefully.

See FUND-RAISING and SPECIAL EVENTS ORGANIZING CHECKLIST.

special events organizing checklist, a checklist of things to be done and considered when planning, organizing, and conducting a special event.

See also CHECKLIST.

special funds, federal funds credited with receipts that are earmarked for a specific purpose.

special interest group, a group that has common interests, such as consumers, parents of people with developmental disabilities, people concerned about environmental conservancy, etc. Special interest groups attempt to influence legislators to pass laws and government administrators to interpret and administer laws.

See also:

ACTION ORGANIZATION
LEGISLATIVE ACTIVITIES
POLITICAL ACTION COMMITTEE
POLITICAL ACTIVITY

specification, also called JOB SPECIFICATION and CLASS SPECIFICATION, written description of the duties and responsibilities of a class of positions. Specifications usually include: the title of the position; a general statement of the nature of the work; examples of typical tasks; the minimum requirements and qualifications for the position; the knowledges, skills, and abilities essential for satisfactory performance; and the assigned salary range.

Specifications are designed to highlight those aspects of a position that are significant for classification purposes. They are descriptive, not restrictive. They are not expected to include all of the possible duties that might make up an individual position.

See also POSITION CLASSIFICATION.

SPECIAL EVENTS ORGANIZING CHECKLIST

The key to a successful event is organization, and one good way to become organized is to develop and follow checklists. These are basic checklists that apply to any type of fund-raising special event.

CHECKLIST FOR ASSETS

What do we already have in the organization to make this fund-raising project a success? What factors should we consider in choosing a special event?

People	Money	Time
___ Leaders, their time and talents	___ Seed money available for the event—from treasury, loan, advance sales	___ How much time do we want to spend fund-raising? Is there a way to shorten it?
___ Members with experience with this kind of event	___ When will we have to spend the money? (When will it come in?) What is our break-even point?	___ Are there any major conflicts with the service's calendar? The community calendar?
___ Total number of members who will work	___ Who will handle the money coming in? Who will control money going out?	___ How much staff time do we want to allocate to this?
___ Total number of members who will attend and contribute	___ Bank—will we need a separate account? Do we need any special arrangements to handle lots of cash?	___ If the event is to be repeated annually, is this the best time of year?
___ Possible allies and new members who will get involved		___ What consideration should we make for bad weather? (*e.g.*, an alternate rain/snow date, inside location, insurance)
___ Staff		

CHECKLIST FOR GOALS

What do we want to realize from this special event?

___ Amount of money. Net profit. Percent of annual budget
___ Number of new volunteers brought in
___ How will it challenge the leadership?
___ Can it be repeated? What is the probable increase next time?
___ Advantages to the service—morale, new people, new area, new style event

___ Number of people involved. Where and how
___ Experience. What new skills will we learn? What do we want to know for the next event and for this event next year?

What new sources of income will we reach?
___ New members
___ Non-member individuals
___ Institutions—businesses, clubs, churches
___ Foundations

___ Number of leadership roles possible
___ Who will take the leadership positions?

What will be the psychological effects of the event?
___ In the service
___ With people we hope will join?
___ To the staff
___ Fun

BASICS FOR ALL EVENTS

___ Notify police
___ Cash boxes
___ Receipts
___ Sign-up list (can be accomplished with a door prize)
___ Emergency numbers for police and fire
___ Pens
___ Errand runner for emergencies and forgotten things
___ Sense of humor, tact, patience, and imagination

___ Proper insurance
___ Cash in proper denominations for each cash box
___ Name tags for committee, all service members, or everyone
___ Cash for emergencies; coins for pay phone
___ Tape
___ Comfortable shoes
___ All necessary phone numbers—band, host, speakers, ice, etc.
___ Fire extinguisher

Literature about the service
___ Current newsletter or fact sheet
___ Notice of next meeting or event
___ How to join
___ Sale merchandise—buttons, T-shirts, etc.
___ First aid kit
___ Poster board and black markers
___ Aspirin
___ Name of doctor or nurse who will be present
___ Sound system

The last thing to do is to mentally walk through the event as though you were the customer.

What would make you more comfortable, especially if you were new? There are several things you can do to make newcomers feel welcome.

Use name tags to help everyone learn names.

Have several outgoing people serve as hosts and hostesses to make sure each new member is introduced to a veteran member.

Put up a display of photographs or recent clippings to serve as a conversation starter.

Station a few pleasant young people to help the oldsters with stairs and coats.

Recruit an enthusiastic master of ceremonies to make frequent announcements and introductions.

Print a simple program so everyone knows what will happen and when.

Mark an area for lost and found.

If you are selling anything, be sure you have enough bags.

Double-check to make sure the washrooms are well-stocked and clean.

Anything you can do to make people feel wanted will make everyone have a better time and spend more money, and will guarantee they will return next time.

Source: Colorado Department of Health, Emergency Medical Services Division, Colorado Ambulance Management Handbook *(Denver, Colo., July 1984). Adapted from Joan Flanagan,* The Grass Roots Fundraising Book *(Chicago: The Swallow Press, Inc., 1977).*

specific tax: *see* TAX BASE.

speededness, appropriateness of a test in terms of the length of time allotted. For most purposes, a good test will make full use of the examination period but not be so speeded that an examinee's rate of work will have an undue influence on the score received.

speed rating, performance rating that compares the speed with which an employee performs specific tasks against an observer's standard or norm.

speed test, term loosely applied to any test that few can complete within the allotted time or, more technically, a test consisting of a large number of relatively easy items so that a high score depends on how fast an examinee can work within a time limit.

speed-up, also STRETCH-OUT, terms referring to any effort by employers to obtain an increase in productivity without a corresponding increase in wages.

spillover effect, also EXTERNALITIES, benefits or costs that accrue to parties other than the buyer of a good or service. For the most part, the benefits of private goods and services enure to the exclusive benefit of the buyer (*e.g.*, new clothes, a television set, etc.). In the case of public goods, however, the benefit or cost usually spills over onto third parties. A new airport, for example, not only benefits its users but spills over onto the population at large in both positive and negative ways. Benefits might include improved air service for a community, increased tourism, and attraction of new businesses, while costs might include noise pollution and traffic congestion.

spiral-omnibus test, test in which the various kinds of tasks are distributed throughout the test (instead of being grouped together) and are in cycles of increasing difficulty. There is only one timing and one score for such a test.

split, stock, the division of a for-profit company's outstanding shares of stock into a larger or smaller (negative stock split) number of shares. Although each shareholder receives a different number of shares, overall equity remains the same.

split-dollar life insurance, also called SUPPLEMENTAL LIFE INSURANCE, life insurance for employees paid for by an employer. In the event of the covered employee's death, the employer totally recovers the paid premiums from the benefit sum with the remainder distributed to the employee's beneficiaries.

split-half reliability, measure of the reliability of a test obtained by correlating scores on one half of a test with scores on the other half and correcting for the reduced size.

split interest rules: *see* TAX REFORM ACT OF 1984.

split interest trust, a trust which itself is not tax-exempt, but some of whose funds—but only a portion of them—are tax-exempt.

split shift: *see* BROKEN TIME.

split-the-difference, bargaining tactic in which both sides agree to a settlement halfway between their bargaining positions.

spot announcement, a short, attention-grabbing public service announcement broadcast on radio or television. Spot announcements are designed to stimulate a specific action, such as a donation, a call to volunteer assistance, etc.

See also:

COMMUNICATIONS ACT OF 1934
INFORMATIONAL SPOT

spot zoning, changing the zoning of a parcel of land, without regard for the zoning plan of the entire area.

spousal remainder trust, a trust that is funded by a parent, a child receives the income from it for its term, and the princi-

pal passes to the founder's spouse at the end of its term. Spousal remainder trusts are advantageous because the change in ownership nullifies the ten-year minimum trust period mandated for Clifford Trusts.
See also CLIFFORD TRUST and CHARITABLE REMAINDER TRUST.

SRRS: *see* SOCIAL READJUSTMENT RATING SCALE.

SSA: *see* SOCIAL SECURITY ADMINISTRATION.

SSI: *see* SUPPLEMENTAL SECURITY INCOME.

stabilized bond, a bond that has its principal or interest adjusted to reflect changes in inflation or deflation as indicated by an index.

staff, specialists who assist line managers in carrying out their duties. Generally, staff units do not have the power of decision, command, or control of operations. Rather, they make recommendations (which may or may not be adopted) to the line personnel.

staff committee: *see* PERSONNEL COMMITTEE.

staffing, one of the most basic functions of management and usually considered synonymous with employment—that is, the process of hiring people to perform work for the organization. Staffing defines the organization by translating its objectives and goals into a specific work plan. It structures the responsibilities of the organization's human resources into a work system by establishing who will perform what function and have what authority. Staffing must also make the employment, advancement, and compensation processes satisfy the criteria of equity and due process while at the same time relating their processes to the overall organizational structure in order to ensure their relevance. Staffing is the essence of the personnel management process.

staffing dynamics, phrase used by those who are not content with calling turnover turnover.

staffing plan, planning document that minimally (1) lists an organization's projected personnel needs by occupation and grade level and (2) identifies how these needs will be met.

staffing program planning, determination by organization personnel management of the numbers and kinds of personnel management actions necessary during each stage of the planning period to staff the work force required in management's program plan.

staff organization, those segments of a larger organization that provide support services and have no direct responsibilities for line operations or production. For example, personnel administration has traditionally been a staff function.

staff out, process that involves soliciting a variety of views or recommendations on an issue so that a decision maker will be aware of all reasonable options.

staff principle, the principle of administration which states that the executive should be assisted by officers who are not in the line of operations but are essentially extensions of the personality of the executive and whose duties consist primarily of assisting the executive in controlling and coordinating the organization and, secondly, of offering advice.

staff responsibilities chart (Management by Objectives), a form for identifying and displaying responsibilities for coordinating a management by objectives process in an ongoing program.
See also MANAGEMENT BY OBJECTIVES.

stagflation, high levels of unemployment and inflation at the same time.
See also PHILLIPS CURVE.

stale check, a check that has been made uncashable because it has been held too long. This time period is usually established by state law.

standard, a model, example, or measurement unit established by authority, custom, or general consent.

standard, employment: *see* EMPLOYMENT STANDARD.

standard allowance, established amount of time by which the normal time for employees to complete their tasks is increased in order to compensate for the expected amount of personal and/or unavoidable delays.

Standard & Poor's Corp., a major publisher of financial information that is best known for its ratings of bonds and other securities.
See also SECURITY.

Standard Consolidated Statistical Area (SCSA), creation of the U.S. Census Bureau combining contiguous standard metropolitan statistical areas in order to more accurately portray urban population patterns.

standard deduction, a term that is no longer used that meant a fixed amount of money subtracted from taxable income by people who did not want to itemize (list) all their individual deductions on their income tax returns. This has been replaced by the zero bracket amount.
See also:
ITEMIZE
ZERO BRACKET AMOUNT

standard deviation, measure of the variability of a distribution about its mean or average. In distributions of test scores, for example, a low standard deviation would indicate a tendency of scores to cluster about the mean; a high standard deviation would indicate a wide variation in scores. In a normal distribution, approximately sixty-eight percent of the cases lie between +1 S.D. and −1 S.D. from the mean and approximately ninety-six percent of the cases between +2 S.D. and −2 S.D. from the mean.

standard error of measurement, number expresed in score units that serves as another index of test reliability. It can be interpreted as indicating the probability that if an error of measurement of a test is twenty points, there are approximately two chances out of three that an individual's "true score" will be within ± 20 points of his/her "obtained score" on the test. Similarly, the chances are approximately ninety-six out of one hundred that his/her "true score" will be within ± 40 points of his/her "obtained score."

standard federal regions, geographic subdivisions of the U.S. established to achieve more uniformity in the location and geographic jurisdiction of federal field offices as a basis for promoting more systematic coordination among agencies and among federal-state-local governments and for securing management improvements and economies through greater interagency and intergovernmental cooperation. Boundaries were drawn and regional office locations designed for ten regions, and agencies are required to adopt the uniform system when changes are made or new offices established.

standard hour, the normally expected amount of work to be done in an hour.

standard-hour plan, incentive plan that rewards an employee by a percent premium that equals the percent by which performance beats the standard.

standardization, specification of consistent procedures to be followed in administering, scoring, and interpreting tests.

standardized test, any objective test given under constant conditions and/or any test for which a set of norms is available.

Standard Metropolitan Statistical Area (SMSA), creation of the U.S. Census Bureau so as to more accurately portray urban population. It includes the population in all counties contiguous to an urban county (that is, one with a city over 50,000, in a common total) if the population of those counties is involved in the urban county work force. Being designated a SMSA is important to cities and counties because only SMSAs are eligible for certain federal government grants.

standard mileage rate, the amount the IRS allows taxpayers to deduct for charitable and business use of their personal vehicles.

standard of living, measure of the material affluence enjoyed by a nation or by an individual.

standard rate: *see* FLAT RATE.

Standard Rate and Data Service (SRDS), a widely accepted source of authoritative data on radio and television station markets, advertising rates, etc.
See also MEDIA, ELECTRONIC.

standards: *see* CLASSIFICATION STANDARDS.

standard score, any transformed test score in terms of which raw scores are expressed for convenience and ease of interpretation.

Standards of Accounting and Financial Reporting for Voluntary Health and Welfare Organizations, an authoritative, widely accepted set of accounting standards sponsored by the National Health Council and the National Social Welfare Assembly.

standards of conduct, an organization's formal guidelines for ethical behavior.
See also ETHICS and CODE OF ETHICS.

standards of performance, statements that tell an employee how well he or she must perform a task to be considered a satisfactory employee. Standards cover how much, how accurately, in what time period, or in what manner the various job tasks are to be performed. The performance standards, whether written or unwritten, will specify the minimum level of performance at which an employee must work in order to attain a satisfactory performance rating. Written performance standards are usually required only when an employee is warned that he or she may receive an unsatisfactory rating.

standby letter of credit: *see* CREDIT, LETTER OF.

standing, a person's right to initiate legal action because he or she is directly affected by the issues raised.

standing committee: *see* COMMITTEE.

standing plans, also called CONTINUING PLANS, plans designed to guide organizations in policies, standard methods, or procedures when dealing with objectives or problems of a recurring nature.

state bank, a commercial bank chartered by a state and subject to regulation by the state, and also (in many instances) by the federal financial regulatory agencies.

statement of activity: *see* OPERATING STATEMENT.

statement of financial position: *see* BALANCE SHEET and FINANCIAL STATEMENTS.

statements, financial: *see* FINANCIAL STATEMENTS.

state of the art, level of development in a given scientific or technological field at a given time, usually the present.

static system: *see* DYNAMIC SYSTEM.

statistical inference, use of information observed in a sample to make predictions about a larger population.

statistical quality control, also PROCESS QUALITY CONTROL, the use of statistical and other mathematical problem solving techniques to maintain the quality of an operation (for example, a production process, screening applications for services, ensuring that clients are receiving services, etc.).

Statistical quality control uses acceptance sampling to determine whether a batch of finished products (for example, invoices, claims, etc.) meets preestablished quality levels. Using statistical techniques, a random sample is taken from the batch, and the sample is inspected. From this analysis, an inference is made about the quality of the entire batch. *See* Ellis R. Ott, *Process Quality Control* (New York: McGraw-Hill, 1975).

statistical significance: *see* SIGNIFICANCE.

statistical validation, also called CRITERION RELATED VALIDATION, validation that involves definition of what is to be measured (*i.e.*, criterion) by some systematic method based upon observations of the job behavior of individuals. Possible measures of the knowledges, skills, abilities, and other employee characteristics are then obtained for individuals. Through statistical means, the strength of the relationship between the criterion and the measures is evaluated (validity).

If the criterion has been defined rationally through a careful empirical analysis of job duties, job-relatedness of the appraisal procedure is considered to be present. If the criterion has not been defined in this way, job-relatedness is inferred but not assured.

See also VALIDATION and VALIDITY.

statistics, any gathered numerical data and any of the processes of analyzing and of making inferences from the data. While there are innumerable works on the collection and interpretation of statistics, the classic work on statistical presentation is Darrell Huff's *How to Lie with Statistics* (N.Y.: W. W. Norton & Co., 1954). This work is valuable for those who would lie, those who would not, and those who would like not to be lied to.

statistics, nonparametric, *see* NONPARAMETRIC STATISTICS.

status, abstraction of one's relative position or ranking within an organization or society.

status symbols, visible signs of an individual's social status or importance in an organization. Status symbols are a significant element of the psychic compensation of every job. Under varying circumstances almost anything can be a status symbol—a private secretary, a key to the executive washroom, an assigned parking space, wood as opposed to metal office furniture, etc. For an account of the relentless search for greater status, *see* Vance Packard, *The Status Seekers* (N.Y.: David McKay Co., 1959).

Statute of Charitable Uses of 1601, historic British statute that lists such charitable purposes as: ". . . for relief of aged, impotent and poor people, . . . maintenance of sick and maimed soldiers and mariners, schools of learning, free schools, and scholars in universities, . . . preferment of orphans, some for or towards relief, stock or maintenance for houses of correction, some for marriages of poor maids . . ." The act serves to demonstrate the minimal material change that has occurred in the basic concept of charity during the last 280 years.

stay-in strike: *see* SIT-DOWN STRIKE.

step bonus, feature of wage incentive plans that call for a substantial increase in incentive payments when the quantity and/or quality of output reaches a specified level.

step increases: *see* INCREMENT and WITHIN-GRADE INCREASE.

step up basis, also STEP DOWN BASIS, an increase (or reduction) in the basis of a property for income tax purposes. This usually occurs when heirs take a dead person's property and their basis becomes market value.

steward, also called SHOP STEWARD and UNION STEWARD, local union's most immediate representative in a plant or department. Usually elected by fellow employees (but sometimes appointed by the union leadership), the shop steward handles grievances, collects dues, solicits new members, etc. A shop steward usually continues to work at his or her regular job and handles union matters on a part-time basis, frequently on the employer's time.

stewardship, concept of (income recognition), an accounting approach which recognizes a nonprofit organization's income (in its financial records) when it is received, whether or not it is restricted. This accounting approach reflects the organization's "stewardship responsibility" for funds.

See also EARNINGS CONCEPT and INCOME, RECOGNITION OF.

stimulative, description of a grant that increases the expenditures of the grantee for the specified activities over and above what they would have been in the absence of the grant.

stint-plan wage system, system that assigns a definite output as an employee's day's work; and, if the work is completed in less than normal time, the employee is credited with a full day's work and allowed to go home.

stochastic (statistics), random, but subject to probability analysis.

stock, a share of ownership in a for-profit company.

stock dividend: *see* DIVIDEND.

stockholder: *see* SHAREHOLDER.

stockholder's equity: *see* EQUITY.

stock power, a power of attorney which allows someone other than the shareholder to legally transfer ownership of the stock.

See also POWER OF ATTORNEY.

stop order, a customer's notice to his or her bank instructing it to refuse payment on a check the customer has written to another person or organization.

straight-line depreciation: *see* DEPRECIATION.

stranger laboratory, laboratory experience for individuals from differing organizations.

See also LABORATORY TRAINING.

stranger pickets, workers who picket an employee who has never employed them.

strategic-contingency model of power, a model of organizational behavior which holds that the use of noninstitutionalized power is necessary for aligning organizations with their realities. When power becomes institutionalized, the organization becomes buffered from its realities and cannot respond appropriately to its contexts. Internal power should shift with context changes, but institutionalized power allows the organization to resist needed changes.

See also POWER.

strategic management, a decisional process that combines an organization's capabilities with the opportunities and threats found in both the internal and external organizational environment.

strategic planning, long-range, comprehensive, integrated, overall organizational planning that has three dimensions: the identification and examination of future opportunities, threats, and consequences; the process of analyzing an organization's environment (including the internal and external environments) and developing compatible objectives along with strategies and policies capable of achieving those objectives; the integration of the various elements of organizational planning into an overall structure of plans so that each unit of the organization knows in advance what must be done, when, and by whom.

See also PLANNING.

stratified sample, a sampling procedure that "forces" inclusion of data from each important grouping of elements in the population. For example, an evaluation research study might use stratified sampling to ensure inclusion of minorities, disabled people, households in rural counties, etc. Then random samples are drawn from each of the stratified groupings. Stratified sampling is also used frequently in designing public opinion polls, marketing research studies, etc.

See also:
EVALUATION
MARKET RESEARCH
PUBLIC OPINION POLL
SAMPLING

straw boss, colloquial term for a supervisor who has no real authority, power, or status with which to back up his orders.

stress, engineering term applied to humans in reference to any condition or situation that forces the body to respond to it. Prolonged stress can overtax an individual's emotional and/or physical ability to cope with it. The pioneering work on "stress on the whole person" was done by Hans Seyle, *The Stress of Life* (N.Y.: McGraw-Hill, rev. ed., 1976).

See also the following entries:
BIOFEEDBACK
MID-CAREER CRISIS
NERVOUS BREAKDOWN

stress carriers, fellow workers who are crisis oriented and tend to induce stress in others in addition to suffering from it themselves.

stress interview, interview in which the interviewer deliberately creates a stressful situation for the interviewee in order to see how the interviewee might behave under such pressure. Common tactics used to induce stress include critically questioning the opinions of the interviewee, frequent interruptions of interviewee's answers to possibly hostile questions, silence on the part of the interviewer for an extended period, etc.

stretch-out: *see* SPEED-UP.

strike, also called WALKOUT, mutual agreement among workers (whether members of a union or not) to a temporary work stoppage in order to obtain or resist a change in their working conditions.

strike authorization, also called STRIKE VOTE, formal vote by union members that (if passed) invests the union leadership with the right to call a strike without additional consultation with the union membership.

strike benefits, payments by a union to its striking members or to nonmembers who are out on strike in support of the union.

strike-bound, any organization that is being struck by its employees and/or attempting to function in spite of the strike.

strikebreaker, person who accepts a position vacated by a worker on strike or a worker who continues to work while others are on strike.

strike counselors: *see* UNION COUNSELORS.

strike duty, tasks assigned to union members by the union leadership during the course of a strike (for example, picketing, distributing food, preventing violence, creating violence, etc.).

strike fund, moneys reserved by a union to be used during a strike to cover costs such as strike benefits or legal fees. Strike funds are not necessarily separate from a union's general fund. The amount of strike funds available may mean the success or failure of a strike.

strike pay, union payments to union members as partial compensation for income loss during a strike.

strike vote: *see* STRIKE AUTHORIZATION.

stroking, attention, also POSITIVE-STROKING and NEGATIVE STROKING. Eric Berne, in *Games People Play: The Psychology of Human Relationships* (N.Y.: Grove Press, 1964), took the intimate physical act of stroking and developed its psychological analogy in conversation. All of human intercourse can be viewed from the narrow perspective of the giving and receiving of physical and psychological strokes. In an organizational context, *positive stroking* consists of the laying of kind words on employees. *Negative stroking* involves using less than kind words—being critical.

structural change, alterations in the relative significance of the productive components of a national or international economy that take place over time. Expansion in the economy as a whole or temporary shifts in the relationship of its components as a result of cyclical developments would *not* be considered structural changes. Since the industrial revolution, structural change in most countries has resulted principally from changes in comparative advantage associated with technological advance, but also to a lesser degree from changes in consumer preference. It has involved shifts from subsistence agriculture to commercial agriculture, an increase in the relative significance of manufacturing and, at a later stage, a further shift toward service industries. Other major structural changes involve shifts in economic importance between various industries, shifts between regions of large national economies, and changes in the composition of exports and imports.

structural-functional theory, also called STRUCTURAL-FUNCTIONALISM, an approach in sociology in which societies, communities, or organizations are viewed as systems; then their particular features are explained in terms of their contributions—their functions—in maintaining the system.

structural unemployment, unemployment resulting from changes in technology, consumption patterns, or government policies—a mismatch between available labor and demand for skills. Structural unemployment can be said to be an inherent part of a dynamic economic system. The "cure" for structural unemployment is worker retraining.

structure, formal arrangement of positions, authority relations, and information flows in an organization.

structured role playing, role-play exercise or simulation in which the players receive oral or written instruction giving them cues as to their roles.

study committee, usually, a temporary committee assembled and charged to gather information on a single issue.

See also COMMITTEE.

SUB: *see* SUPPLEMENTAL UNEMPLOYMENT BENEFIT.

subchapter S corporation, a corporate form used by for-profit companies that allows them to be taxed as though they were partnerships.

subcommittee, a committee which is formed by, generally comprised of members of, and reports to another (regular) committee. Subcommittees usually focus on a portion of the responsibilities assigned to the regular committee, for example, the salary subcommittee of the personnel committee.

See also COMMITTEE.

subcontractor, an organization or person who contracts to do a part of a job for another person or organization (the prime contractor), who has a contract with a third person or organization to perform work.

See also CONSULTANT and CONTRACTOR.

subdivision, land divided into many lots by a developer and sold to different persons under a common plan.

See also RESTRICTIVE COVENANT.

subemployment, concept that tries to capture two major dimensions of labor market functioning that produce and reproduce poverty—the lack of opportunity for work and substandard wage employment.

subfunction: *see* FUNCTION.

subgovernment, unofficial body. Because chief executives cannot provide bureaucrats with all of the political support that they need through the official hierarchy, bureaucrats join, or create, subgovernments or partnerships with independent groups and agencies who share a common interest in a specialized policy.

subletting, a tenant renting property (or part of it) to another person.

suboptimization, accepting a decision that is less than ideal, but that accommodates the conflicting objectives of the various organizational interests.
See SIMON, HERBERT A.

subordinate affiliated organization, an organization which is associated with and is at least somewhat controlled by another organization; for example, the Missouri Affiliate of the American Heart Association.
See also GROUP EXEMPTION LETTER.

subordinate rating, the evaluation of one member of an organization by someone lower in the organization.

subordination, a ranking of rights; for example, signing a document that admits that one's claim or interest (for example, in a lien) is weaker than another person's.

subpoena, written order issued by a judicial officer requiring a specified person to appear in a designated court at a specified time in order to serve as a witness in a case under the jurisdiction of that court, or to bring material to that court.

subscription drive (publications), a form of fund-raising in which an organization's staff and/or volunteers sell subscriptions to periodicals directly, or the organization allows a for-profit company to use the organization's name to help sell subscriptions and, in exchange, receives a portion of the proceeds.
See also DIRECT SOLICITATION and FUND-RAISING.

subscription drive (subscription service), a form of fund-raising in which a nonprofit organization "sells subscriptions" to services it provides: for example, nonprofit, volunteer ambulance services. Most subscription drives are conducted annually, using either in-person or direct mail solicitations, often kicked off with a special event. Some nonprofit organizations have been able to persuade municipalities and public utilities to insert flyers describing subscription drives in water, trash, and/or electric bills.
See also:
DIRECT MAIL CAMPAIGN
DIRECT SOLICITATION
FUND-RAISING
SPECIAL EVENT
SUBSCRIPTION SERVICE

subscription service, a nonprofit service-providing organization which sells prepaid services. Subscription services are not uncommon, for example, among nonprofit ambulance services. The use of subscriptions as a fund-raising technique tends to increase a nonprofit organization's short-term financial/budgetary stability and predictability *(i.e.,* within the fiscal year), and the subscription records can be used as a mailing list for other purposes.

Households and businesses that subscribe to a subscription service receive free service, usually for a year, whereas nonsubscribers must pay. For example, a subscription ambulance service typically sells subscriptions to households for $50 to $250 per year. Then the ambulance service will transport anyone in the household (including visitors) to a hospital. Under the subscription agreement, the household may use the service as many times as needed during the year, unless it is determined that there has been abuse of the use privilege. Long-distance transfers are usually billed at a reduced rate or are not included in the subscription agreement. Businesses, including motels and hotels, pay a higher rate to cover on-site employees and customers. Nonsubscribers pay standard rates for service.
See also FUND-RAISING.

EXAMPLE OF A SUBSIDIARY LEDGER

ACE AMBULANCE SERVICE—ACCOUNTS PAYABLE SUBSIDIARY LEDGER

Name ______________________
Address ______________________
____
Telephone ______________________

Date	Reference	DR	CR	Balance
1-1	P.O. # 2001		175.00	
1-1	CK. # 101	175.00		Ø
	etc			

subsidiary ledger, ledger used when more detail is needed on accounts than can be given in a general ledger. For example, the accounts receivable subsidiary ledger would show each individual who owes money to the organization. In contrast, the general ledger accounts receivable total would include only the total of the accounts receivable subsidiary accounts, or the total amount owed by all individuals.

See also ACCOUNTING CYCLE and GENERAL LEDGER.

subsistence allowance, also PER DIEM ALLOWANCE, payment for an employee's or volunteer's reasonable expenses (for example, meals and lodging) while traveling on behalf of the organization.

substandard rate, wage rate below established occupational, prevailing, or legal levels.

substantial contributor, a person who donates more than $5,000 to a tax-exempt organization, when the contribution amounts to more than two percent of the organization's income during the year. A substantial contributor is a disqualified person (1) and is not permitted to transact business with that private foundation, and (2) and is disqualified for the purpose of determining whether an organization is publicly supported.

See also PUBLICLY SUPPORTED ORGANIZATION.

substantially: *see* EXCLUSIVELY.

substantial threat, jeopardy. In order for the courts to condone government intervention or regulation of a religious institution, there must be a "substantial threat to public safety, place or order."

substantive law, the basic law of rights and duties (contract law, criminal law, accident law, law of wills, etc.) as opposed to procedural law (law of pleading, law of evidence, law of jurisdiction, etc.).

substitutive, grant used by the recipient to reduce spending from the recipient's own sources for the aided activity, freeing these own-source funds for other programs.

subsystem, one of the various parts of a larger system.

succession, intestate, the transfer of property by law to heirs if the deceased person does not leave a will.

Sugarman* v. *Dougall, 413 U.S. 634 (1973), U.S. Supreme Court case which held that a ban on the employment of resident aliens by a state was unconstitutional because it encompassed positions that had little, if any, relation to a legitimate state interest in treating aliens differently from citizens. However, the court also stated that alienage might reasonably be taken into account with regard to specific positions.

suggestion system, formal effort to encourage employees to make recommendations that would improve the operations of their organizations.

summons, written order issued by a judicial officer requiring a person accused of a criminal offense to appear in a designated court at a specified time to answer charge(s).

sumptuary laws, laws which attempt to control the sale or use of socially undesirable, wasteful, or harmful products.

sunk costs, resources committed to the achievement of an organizational objective that cannot be regained if the objective is abandoned.

sunset laws, laws pioneered by Colorado and encouraged by a major lobbying effort by Common Cause. Many jurisdictions are enacting "sunset laws," which fix termination dates on programs or agencies. Formal evaluations and subsequent affirmative legislation are required if the agency or program is to continue. Although the purpose of a finite life span of, say, five years is meant to force evaluation and toughen legislative oversight, the effect is to subject programs to automatic termination unless the "clock" is reset.

superannuation, a pension.

supernumerary, someone who is extra and is not needed immediately.

supernumerary income, that portion of a worker's income which is not needed for the essentials of everyday life and consequently is available for luxuries and other optional spending.

superseniority, also called SYNTHETIC SENIORITY, seniority that supersedes ordinary seniority, which is dependent on an individual's length of service. Because a union may be detrimentally affected if its key officials are subject to layoffs, union contracts often grant them superseniority. This synthetic seniority is designed to ensure continued representation for workers remaining following a reduction in force. Superseniority also provides an advantage to management since established lines of communication with the union and its members continues without interruption. Sometimes union contracts provide for superseniority for special categories of employees (such as the aged or physically handicapped and key personnel essential if production is to be maintained).

supervision, directing the performance of one or more workers towards the accomplishment of organizational goals.

supervisor, according to Section 2(11) of the National Labor Relations Act, as amended,

> any individual having authority, in the interest of the employer, to hire, transfer, suspend, lay off, recall, promote, discharge, assign, reward, or discipline other employees, or responsibly to direct them, or to adjust their grievances, or effectively to recommend such action, if in connection with the foregoing the exercise of such authority is not of a merely routine or clerical nature, but requires the use of independent judgment.

supervisors, board of, governing body for a county unit of government in which membership on the board is determined by election or appointment to a particular office. For example, in some counties the board includes officials such as county judges.

supplemental compensation: *see* BONUS and FEDERAL SUPPLEMENTAL COMPENSATION.

supplemental compensation, executive: *see* EXECUTIVE SUPPLEMENTAL COMPENSATION.

supplemental dental insurance: *see* SUPPLEMENTAL MEDICAL INSURANCE.

supplemental life insurance: *see* SPLIT-DOLLAR LIFE INSURANCE.

supplemental medical insurance, also SUPPLEMENTAL DENTAL INSURANCE, fringe benefit usually offered only to top management whereby all expenses from medical and/or dental care not covered by the general medical/dental policy offered by the company are reimbursable.

Supplemental Security Income (SSI), federal program that assures a minimum monthly income to needy people with limited income and resources who are sixty-five or older, blind, or disabled. Eligibility is based on income and assets. Although the program is administered by the Social Security Administration, it is financed from general revenues, not from social security contributions.

supplemental unemployment benefit (SUB), payments to laid-off workers from private unemployment insurance plans that are supplements to state unemployment insurance compensation. The first SUB plan was negotiated by the Ford Motor Company and the United Auto Workers in 1955. By 1973, about twenty-nine percent of the members of major unions worked under contracts containing SUB plans. There are two basic SUB plans—the individual account and the pooled fund. With the former, contributions are credited to each employee's account and a terminated employee may take his benefits with him. With the latter, benefits are paid from a common fund and individual employees have no vested rights should they leave the company.

supplemental unemployment benefit trust, a trust that pays supplemental unemployment compensation benefits to laid-off employees. Supplemental unemployment benefit trusts may qualify for tax-exempt status under IRS Code 501(c)(17).

supply, in economics, the quantity of goods and services available for purchase if income and other factors are held constant. Increases in price either induce increases in supply or serve to ration the supply.

supply-side economics, also called Reaganomics, a belief that lower tax rates, especially on marginal income, will encourage fresh capital to flow into the economy, which will, in turn, generate jobs and growth and new tax revenue. Because this concept was widely adopted by President Reagan and his advisors, it has been popularly called "Reaganomics." Economist Arthur Laffer is generally credited with having "discovered" supply-side economics.

support, a general term which usually means income contributed to a tax-exempt organization.

Support Center, The, a national network of centers providing information and assistance to nonprofit organizations in such areas as planning, financial management, organizational design and staffing, organizational process, legal and tax compliance, and resource development. The Support Center also claims to be the largest trainer of nonprofit managers and board members in America. Centers are located in California, Illinois, New Jersey, Oklahoma, Rhode Island, Texas, and Washington, D.C.

support fraction, also SUPPORT RATIO, the dollar amount of a nonprofit organization's public support divided by its total support; one of the support tests used to distinguish between a private foundation and a publicly supported organization.

See also:
- PRIVATE FOUNDATION
- PUBLICLY SUPPORTED ORGANIZATION
- SUPPORT
- SUPPORT TESTS

supporting organization, an organization created to fund the activities of one or more existing public charities with which there is a close relationship. Supporting organizations are defined in Section 509(a)(3) of the Tax Reform Act of 1969.

supportive, a grant whose reduction or withdrawal is unlikely to weaken support for the aided activity from the recipient's own resources.

support tests, criteria used by the IRS for determining whether an organization qualifies, for example, as a publicly supported institution rather than as a private foundation. The essence of the support tests for publicly supported institutions is whether an organization receives more or less than thirty-three percent of its total support from permitted general public sources including, for example, donations, grants, and fees for performing tax-exempt services; or if it fulfills the facts and circumstances test.

See also:
PRIVATE FOUNDATION
PUBLICLY SUPPORTED ORGANIZATION
SUPPORT
SUPPORT FRACTION

Supreme Court, United States, the highest United States court.

surcharge, an extra charge on something already charged; a special payment; an overcharge.

surety, a company or person that insures or guarantees that another person's debt will be paid by accepting liability (responsibility) for the debt when it is made.

See also GUARANTY.

surplus, money left over; for example, a budget surplus.

surtax, an additional tax on what has already been taxed; that is, a tax on a tax. For example, if you must pay a $1,000 tax on a $10,000 income (ten percent), a ten percent surtax would be an additional $100.

survey: *see* PUBLIC OPINION POLL.

survivors benefits, totality of the benefits that are paid upon the death of an employee to his/her legal survivors. Employees are frequently required to make a decision at the time of retirement whether or not to take a reduced pension that allows for survivors benefits.

survivorship, the right to property that is held by more than one person, when one of those people dies.

suspension, removing an individual from employment for a specified period. Suspensions, by their nature temporary, are disciplinary acts—more severe than a reprimand yet less severe than a discharge.

sweat shop, work site where employees worked long hours for low wages, usually under unsanitary conditions. While sweat shop conditions have been mostly eliminated in the United States because of the union movement and labor legislation, the term is still used informally to refer to various working conditions that employees might find distasteful.

sweetheart agreement, also called SWEETHEART CONTRACT, expressions for any agreement between an employer and a union or union official that benefits them but not the workers. Incidences of employer bribes to labor officials in order to gain their agreement to substandard or "sweetheart" contracts are well known in American labor history.

swing shift, extra shift of workers in an organization operating on a continuous or seven-day basis. The swing crew rotates among the various shifts to compensate for those employees who are absent, sick, on vacation, etc.

symbols and SYMBOLIC MANAGEMENT, signs. Since prehistory people have been effectively controlled by their leaders by means of announced taboos and mandated rituals. The associated symbolism portends either terror or hope. Political leaders in the United States have evoked terror with dire predictions about the "international communist conspiracy" and hope with a call to arms to fight the "war on poverty." Similarly, U.S. business leaders evoke terror by reminding us of the perils of bad breath, dull teeth, and unsprayed bodily areas. These fears fade when the various sprays, creams, gels, and pastes are purchased and used. The public is assured that they too can be "beautiful people" if they take the right vitamin supplements, drive the appropriate car, and drink the correct diet cola. We are all subliminally, if not consciously, aware of symbolism utilized in political rhetoric and business advertising. However, the vital role that symbolism plays in policy making and managerial control in organizational and political situations is frequently unnoticed.

Symbolic management is the management of an organization through the development and transmittal of shared organizational beliefs and guiding values rather than through, for example, the coordination of tasks or manipulation of resources. For example, an executive wishing to impose a sanction upon a committee of the board that is holding up funding of a program might suggest that the committee is not acting in "the clients' interests." The notion of "the clients' interests," while vague, is a powerful symbol because it represents a commonly accepted good. Because it is so widely revered, it has great legitimacy. By wrapping the program in a symbol of hefty weight and using that symbol punitively against those in opposition to her program, an executive may succeed. The success or failure of such a calculated gambit depends upon a large variety of factors. How susceptible to this particular symbol were the committee members that she was trying to influence? Was the symbol of appropriate weight in comparison to the symbols of the opposition (for example, "fiscal responsibility")? While the executive might have wished to use a heavier symbol, such a tactic might also backfire. For example, one does not fight the opposition's symbol of "economy and efficiency" by calling them "bigots."

Conversely, symbols can be used to reward favorable action. After the executive gets her desired funding, she might applaud the committee members involved by publicly stating that they have shown "fiscal and moral responsibility."

synagogue: *see* RELIGIOUS ORGANIZATION.

syndication, in real estate, a limited partnership.

synectics, originally a Greek word meaning the joining together of different and apparently irrelevant elements. It is now used to describe an experimental process of observing and recording the unrestrained exchange of ideas among a group in order to methodically develop new ideas, solve problems, and/or make discoveries. As an effort to induce creativity, it is akin to brainstorming.

synergy, the dynamics that cause the whole (for example, organization) to be greater (in capability) than the sum of its individual parts (for example, its people).

synthetic basic-motion times, time standards for fundamental motions and groups of motions.

synthetic seniority: *see* SUPERSENIORITY.

synthetic time study, time study not dependent upon direct observation in which time elements are obtained from other sources of time data.

synthetic validity, also called INDIRECT VALIDITY, inferring validity by means of a systematic analysis of a job and its elements, obtaining test validity for the various elements, then combining the elemental validities into a whole synthetic validity.

system, any organized collection of parts that is united by prescribed interactions and designed for the accomplishment of a specific goal or general purpose.

See also OPEN SYSTEM.

system, career: *see* CAREER SYSTEM.

System 4, Rensis Likert's term for a participative-democratic managerial style.

systemic discrimination, use of employment practices (recruiting methods, selection tests, promotion policies, etc.) that have the unintended effect of excluding or limiting the employment prospects of women and minorities. Because of court interpretations of Title VII of the Civil Rights Act of 1964, all such systemic discrimination, despite its "innocence," must be eliminated where it cannot be shown that such action would place an unreasonable burden on the employer or that such practices cannot be replaced by other practices which would not have such an adverse effect.

systemism, belief that systems can actually be designed and managed to achieve their expressed goals.

systems analysis, methodologically rigorous collection, manipulation, and evaluation of organizational data in order to determine the best way to improve the functioning of the organization (the system) and to aid a decision maker in selecting a preferred choice among alternatives.

systems analyst, specialist in systems analysis.

systems approach, also called SYSTEMS PERSPECTIVE, philosophy that can help a manager cope with complex situations by providing an analytical framework which conceives of an enterprise as a set of objects with a given set of relationships and attributes all connected to each other and to their environment in such a way as to form an entirety. Because organizations (as well as the whole world) are constantly changing, approaches to dealing with such systems must have a corresponding evolution.

systems management, the application of systems theory to managing organizational systems. Systems management involves the recognition of a general model of input-throughputs-outputs-outcomes and also the interrelationships among subsystems and the suprasystem to which an organization belongs.

systems philosophy: *see* SYSTEMS APPROACH.

T

TA: *see* TRANSACTIONAL ANALYSIS and TECHNICAL ASSISTANCE.

Taft-Hartley Act: *see* LABOR-MANAGEMENT RELATIONS ACT OF 1947.

take-home pay, also called NET PAY, employee's wages minus deductions that are either required (such as taxes) or requested (such as savings bonds).

tall organization: *see* FLAT ORGANIZATION.

tandem, organizations operating in, organizations which are not operating independently or in an arm's-length fashion.

tangible objective: *see* OBJECTIVE.

tardiness, reporting to work later than the scheduled time.

target, expected earnings under a piece-rate wage system. The earnings target is usually fixed at ten to fifteen percent above the base rate.

targeted (grant), a grant whose eligibility and allocation provisions are drawn tightly so that only the most needy cases are assisted and the amounts of aid are directly proportional to program needs.
See also GRANT.

targeted job credit, a tax credit for employing a member of a target group (usually a group of disadvantaged workers) who have been so designated by an appropriate state employment agency.

Tariff Act of 1894, act that specified that

". . . nothing herein contained shall apply to . . . corporations, companies, or associations organized and conducted solely for charitable, religious, or educational purposes." Many aspects of tax exemption currently found in IRS Code 501(c)(3) can be traced directly to this act.

Tariff Act of 1913, act that exempted corporations and associations from the federal income tax if they were organized and operated solely for religious, charitable, scientific, or educational purposes, and if no part of the net income benefited any private shareholder or individual.

task, a unit of work.
See also ACTIVITY.

task, also FUNCTION (WORK PLAN OR PROJECT CONTROL CHART), a combination of activities. A series of tasks comprises a work plan.
See also ACTIVITY.

task analysis, identifying the various elements essential to the accomplishment of a task.

task-and-bonus plan, wage incentive plan paying a specific percent of the base wage rate (in addition to the base wage rate) when a specified level of production is maintained or exceeded for a specified period of time.

task force, temporary organizational unit charged with accomplishing a specific mission. Committees tend to be chiefly concerned with the assessment of information in order to reach a conclusion. In contrast, a task group, task force, or interdisciplinary team is aggressively oriented.
See also COMMITTEE.

task group: *see* WORK GROUP.

TAT: *see* THEMATIC APPERCEPTION TEST.

tax, compulsory contribution exacted by a government for public purposes, except employee and employer assessments for retirement and social insurance purposes, which are classified as insurance trust revenue. All tax revenue is classified as general revenue and comprises amounts received (including interest and penalties but excluding protested amounts and refunds) from all taxes imposed by a government.

tax, earmarked, tax whose revenues must, by law, be spent for specific purposes.

tax, employment/payroll: *see* EMPLOYMENT TAXES.

tax, estate, tax on a deceased person's estate made prior to the estate's distribution.

tax, excise, tax on the manufacture, sale, or consumption of a product. The Revenue Act of 1978 instituted a two percent excise tax on private foundations' net investment income. The 1984 Act reduced the excise tax to one percent when certain criteria are met.

tax, flat, a tax that charges the same rate to each taxpayer. This term is also used to refer to any of a wide variety of proposals for reform of the federal income tax.

tax, income, a tax on the income, earnings, and/or profits (for example, capital gains) of individuals and corporations. The income tax is the federal government's primary source of revenues.

tax, inheritance, tax, usually progressive, on an individual's share of a deceased person's estate.

tax, license, tax exacted (either for revenue raising or for regulation) as a condition to the exercise of a business or nonbusiness privilege, at a flat rate or measured by such bases as capital stock, capital surplus, number of business units, or capacity. Excludes taxes measured directly by transactions, gross or net income, or value of property except those to which only nominal rates apply. "Licenses" based on these latter measures, other than those at nominal rates, are classified according to the measure concerned. Includes "fees" related to licensing activities, automobile inspection, gasoline and oil inspection, professional examinations and licenses, etc., as well as license taxes producing substantial revenues.

tax, negative income, welfare program in which citizens with incomes below a specified level would receive cash payments.

tax, personal property, tax on the assessed value (1) of tangible property such as furniture, animals, or jewelry, or (2) of intangible property such as stocks and bonds.

tax, real-property, any tax on land and its improvements; usually referred to as simply "property tax."

tax, regulatory, tax levied for a purpose other than that of raising revenue.

tax, sales: *see* SALES TAX.

tax, stamp, a tax on certain legal documents, such as deeds, when it is required that revenue stamps be bought and put on the documents in order to make them valid.

tax, transfer, a tax on large transfers of property or money which are made without something of value given in return.
See also GIFT TAX.

tax, withholding, sums of money that an employer takes out of an employee's pay and turns over to a government as prepayment of the employee's income tax obligation.

taxable estate, *also* TAXABLE GIFT, the property of a deceased person (or a gift) that will be taxed after subtracting allowable expenses.

taxable expenditure, an expenditure by a tax-exempt organization which is in violation of federal tax code rules. For example, charitable organizations are not permitted to expend funds to attempt to influence legislation, intervene in political campaigns, make grants to nonexempt organizations, etc. Not to be confused with "tax expenditures."
See also TAX EXPENDITURES.

taxable income, under federal tax law, either the "gross income" of businesses or the "adjusted gross income" of individuals minus deductions and exemptions. It is the income against which tax rates are applied in order to compute one's tax obligation.

tax anticipation notes: see REVENUE ANTICIPATION NOTES.

taxation, also REVENUE SYSTEMS, means for raising government funds. There are major differences between the federal and state/local revenue systems. The federal system has experienced a trend towards less diversity. Over two thirds of its general revenues are provided by the federal income tax and the several insurance trust funds (*e.g.*, social security). State and local revenue systems, in contrast, depend on a greater variety of revenue sources, for example, property taxes, income taxes, sales taxes, user charges, lotteries, and federal grants. While local governments still rely primarily on the property tax, states—with a few exceptions—rely largely on the state personal income tax. In addition, state sales and business taxes provide a significant source of income. This melange of taxing authorities creates great disparities for the taxpayer. There is significant variance in the state-local tax burden. A resident of New York may pay hundreds of thousands of dollars in state income taxes while a resident of Texas—which has no state income tax—will pay none. Virginians have to pay more than double the sales taxes paid by Vermonters. There are even greater variations with property taxes. The identical house assessed X dollars in one jurisdiction may be taxed three times that amount in another.

These are the major methods of taxation:

1. *Personal Income Tax.* Based on ability to pay in that the tax rate is

applied against income. But income is more than just money; it is any asset that increases one's net worth. But income taxes are not necessarily a straight tax on all of one's income in a given year. Remember all of those millionaires that the press annually discovers who do not pay any tax on their income? They are able to do this because it is not their large incomes that are subject to taxation, but their adjusted gross incomes. All taxpayers have the right to exclude certain kinds of incomes from their gross incomes for tax purposes. For example, interest from state and local bonds is exempt from federal taxation. Thus, a millionaire whose sole income came from investments in such bonds would pay no federal income tax. Once adjusted gross income is realized, the taxpayer may subtract deductions and exemptions from his taxable income. Exemptions of so many dollars each are counted for the individual taxpayer(s) and his (their) exemptions. Then the taxpayer can deduct a host of expenses as long as they are allowed by the tax laws. Common deductions are those for medical care, state and local taxes (if a federal return), home mortgage interest, child care, and charitable contributions. Progressive tax rates are then applied to the taxable income to determine how much tax is due.

2. *Corporation Income Tax.* A tax on the privilege of operating a business. Various deductions can be made for depreciation, capital gains, research and development costs, etc., to finally determine taxable income.
3. *Capital Gains Tax.* The profits from investments (*i.e.*, capital gains) held more than a year are taxed at a fifty percent rate by the federal government. Capital gains achieved in less than a year are taxed as ordinary income.
4. *Sales Tax.* A favorite of many state and local governments, this is a tax on consumption, rather than income. Some fixed tax rate ranging from two to nine percent is charged on most purchases. A variety of items tend to be excluded from sales taxation—medicine, clothing, foods. The major difficulty with the sales tax is its equity. Sales taxes tend towards regressivity since higher income groups pay a lesser percentage of their income in tax than do lower income groups. For example, a family of four with an income of $8,000 would spend half of that in direct consumption and might pay a five percent sales tax of $200, or 2.5 percent of their income. But another family of four with an $80,000 income will have a much lower percentage of direct consumption (say twenty-five percent), and although they pay five percent on $20,000 (or $1,000), the proportion of their income taken by the sale tax is 1.2 percent, or half that of the lower income family.
5. *Property Tax.* The mainstay of most local governments; provides nearly half of the revenues that local governments get from their own sources. To administer a property tax, the tax base must first be defined—*i.e.*, housing and land, automobiles, other assets, whatever. Then an evaluation of the worth of the tax base must be made—this is the assessment. Finally, a tax rate, usually an amount to be paid per $100 value of the tax base, is levied. Since the value of the tax base will appreciate or depreciate substantially over time, continuing assessments must be made.

Arguments for the property tax resemble a good news/bad news joke. The good news is that the property tax provides a stable revenue source and has a good track record as a strong revenue raiser. The bad news is that its stability can also be considered inflexibility, as it does not keep pace with income growth. The good news is that since property is generally unmovable, it is hard to miss and therefore provides a good, visible tax base for relatively unskilled local tax offices to administer. The bad news is that the administration and assessment of property tax is at best erratic and at worst a horrendous mess. The result is that the property tax base tends to erode over time, that most errors are made in undervaluing the property of the wealthy or the politically influential, that there is a strong incidence effect on new people, and that old people are being increasingly pressed to meet property tax burdens.

See related entries under REVENUE, TAX, and the following entries:

ABILITY TO PAY
CONSUMER TAXES
DIRECT TAX
DOCUMENT AND STOCK TRANSFER TAXES
SELF-EMPLOYMENT TAX

tax avoidance, planning one's personal finances carefully so as to take advantage of all legal tax breaks, such as deductions and exemptions.

tax avoidance scheme, an attempt by a private individual(s) or organization(s) to circumvent or reduce a tax liability. Tax avoidance schemes often involve transactions between disqualified persons and tax-exempt organizations.

See also DISQUALIFIED PERSON and TAX EVASION.

tax base, also AD VALOREM TAX, the thing or value on which taxes are levied. Some of the more common tax bases include: individual income, corporate income, real property, wealth, motor vehicles, sales of commodities and services, utilities, events, imports, estates, gifts, etc. The rate of a tax to be imposed against a given tax base may be either specific or *ad valorem*. Specific taxes, for example, raise a specific, nonvariable, amount of revenue from each unit (*e.g.*, ten cents per gallon of gasoline). *Ad valorem* taxes, on the other hand, are expressed as a percentage, and the revenue yield varies according to the value of the tax base (*i.e.*, mill levy against real property).

tax bracket, the percentage of taxable income which must be paid in taxes. Tax brackets are progressive in that they increase with the level of taxable income (up to a specified maximum percentage).

See also:

EQUITY TAX
PROGRESSIVE TAX

tax collections: *see* TAX YIELD.

tax credit, an amount subtracted directly from the amount of taxes owed. In contrast, a tax deduction is subtracted from taxable income, and it varies in its impact depending upon the person's or organization's tax bracket. Tax credits are generally considered to be more equitable than tax deductions. As a side note, people in higher tax brackets tend to contribute proportionately more to education, the arts, and cultural organizations than do people in lower tax brackets, so any moves to replace tax deductions with tax credits would favor religious groups and social services-type organizations to the detriment of educational, arts, and cultural organizations.

See also:

DEMOCRATIZE
EXCLUSION
EXEMPTION
PROGRESSIVE RATE STRUCTURE
TAX BRACKET
TAX EQUITY

tax deduction: *see* DEDUCTION.

tax deferred annuity, an annuity with employee contributions not subject to taxes at the time that the contributions are made. Contributions are taxed later as they are paid out after retirement, when the annuitant presumably is in a lower tax bracket. 403(b) annuities are specifically geared to nonprofit organizations.

See also ANNUITY and TAX BRACKET.

tax efficiency, a basic productivity measurement; specifically, how much does it cost to collect the tax, what is its political practicality, what is its long-range and its short-range ability to raise revenue?

tax equity, also HORIZONTAL EQUITY and VERTICAL EQUITY, insuring that taxes treat equals as equals, and that unequals are treated unequally or comparably. These treatments are generally referred to, respectively, as horizontal equity and vertical equity. An equitable tax system would be one that requires all taxpayers with equal incomes to pay the same amount of taxes—this is horizontal equity. But since not all citizens have the same income, vertical equity is applied—as personal income gets higher, so does the percentage of taxes. The degree or percentage of tax increase compared to the increase in the tax base yields another criterion with which to judge the equity of fiscal institutions: their use of progressive, proportional, and regressive taxes. All three criteria can satisfy vertical equity in a very simple sense, if the only requirement is higher taxes for higher incomes. But it is the comparison of the increase in tax rate against the increase in the tax base that establishes progressive taxation as the only true vertical equity criterion. The federal graduated personal income tax is the best example of progressive taxation. Each successive higher income bracket pays a progressively higher tax rate. Proportional taxes are those that require an identical percentage increase in tax rates. Regressive taxes are those where the tax rate falls as the tax base increases. Some taxes that are actually proportional in structure, such as sales taxes or property taxes, function as regressive taxes when the tax paid is compared against income; the point is that individuals in a low income bracket will pay a higher percentage of their income for sales tax than will individuals with higher incomes.

Equity is premised on two classical economic concepts by which taxation is justified. The first concept is benefit—those who benefit from a public service should pay for it. A common example is the earmarking of gasoline taxes to finance highway construction and maintenance costs. The benefit concept is much more difficult to apply to national defense, clean air, prisons, and other public services where there is no direct link from usage to revenue source. The second concept is ability to pay—that the amount of tax should consider income, wealth, or other factors that determine how much an individual can afford. This is the essence of progressive taxation; higher incomes are taxed more, proportionately, than lower incomes. Here it is assumed that even the burden of paying fifty to seventy percent on taxable incomes over $200,000 will not deprive any individuals of the basic necessities of life.

Tax Equity and Fiscal Responsibility Act (1982) (TEFRA), law signed as P.L. 97-248 by President R. Reagan on September 3, 1982. TEFRA contained several provisions which were important to tax-exempt, nonprofit organizations:

- Withholding on dividend and interest income was established at a rate of ten percent.
- Nonprofit organizations' income was exempted from withholding.
- The use of the medical expense and casualty loss deductions was restricted, thereby increasing the number of nonitemizing taxpayers with tax incentives to make charitable contributions over the "floors" established by the Economic Recovery Tax Act (ERTA) of 1981.

See also ECONOMIC RECOVERY TAX ACT.

tax evasion, illegally paying less in taxes than the law allows; committing fraud in filing or paying taxes.

See also TAX AVOIDANCE SCHEME.

tax-exempt: *see* TAX-EXEMPT STATUS.

tax-exempt municipal bonds: *see* MUNICIPAL BONDS.

Tax Exempt News, monthly publication of Capital Publications, Inc., which presents and analyzes current congressional, I.R.S., judicial, foundation, etc. activities, events, and trends which are of interest to third sector organizations.

tax-exempt status, a determination or ruling granted to an organization which frees it from obligation(s) to pay taxes and also permits donors to deduct contributions made to it. Usually, tax-exempt status refers to a determination by the federal Internal Revenue Service, but the term also is applicable to tax-exempt status as determined by state and local government units (although they usually follow the IRS's lead).

See also CONTRIBUTION and DEDUCTION.

tax expenditures, government revenue losses resulting from tax deductions, tax exemptions, etc. Deductions and exemptions represent negative income or "opportunity costs" to the taxing government unit. Tax expenditures have been receiving substantial attention in Congress during the last decade as methods have been sought to find additional sources of tax income and to increase Congressional control over budgets and priorities. Not to be confused with "taxable expenditure."

See also:

BACKDOOR SPENDING
DEDUCTION
EQUITY, TAX
EXEMPTION
TAXABLE EXPENDITURE
TAX-EXEMPT STATUS

Tax Foundation, Washington, D.C.-based organization devoted to nonpartisan research and public education on the fiscal aspects of government.

tax fraud: *see* TAX AVOIDANCE SCHEME and TAX EVASION.

tax incidence, the effects of a particular tax burden on various socioeconomic levels.

tax-increment financing, the ability of local government to finance large-scale development through the expected rise in the property tax to be collected after the development is completed. This permits the issuance of bonds based on the expected tax increase.

tax loophole, an inconsistency in the tax laws, whether intentional or unintentional, that allows the avoidance of some taxes.

tax planning, arranging one's finances and investments so as to minimize tax liabilities.

tax rate, also TAX BRACKET, the percentage of taxable income (or of inherited money, things purchased subject to sales tax, etc.) paid in taxes. The federal income tax has a graduated tax rate. This means that the first ten thousand dollars of a person's taxable income might be taxed at a twenty percent rate, or two thousand dollars, and the next one thousand to two thousand dollars at a twenty-five percent rate. This percentage rate is what most people think of as their "tax bracket."

tax reform, the recurrent effort to produce a more equitable or efficient tax system.

Tax Reform Act of 1969, an important piece of legislation for nonprofit organizations. The act separated nonprofit organizations into two primary categories: publicly supported organizations and private foundations (and the subcategory of private foundations, private operating foundations). The act focused on private foundations in general and placed numerous restrictions and requirements on them.

See also:

EXCESS BUSINESS HOLDINGS
PRIVATE OPERATING FOUNDATION
PUBLIC CHARITY
PUBLICLY SUPPORTED ORGANIZATION
SELF DEALING
TAX, EXCISE
TAX REFORM ACT OF 1976

Tax Reform Act of 1976, act with provisions (a) establishing tax-exempt status for organizations that foster or promote national or international sports competition and for group legal service plan organizations, (b) permitting certain public charities to engage in restricted legislative activities (the act defined safe harbor guidelines), (c) tying mandatory distribution requirements to private foundation assets, and (d) allowing special employee annuity contributions to be made to closed-end mutual funds.

See also:

LEGAL SERVICES TRUST, PREPAID

LEGISLATIVE ACTIVITIES
MANDATORY DISTRIBUTION REQUIREMENT
MUTUAL FUND
PUBLICLY SUPPORTED ORGANIZATION
SAFE HARBOR GUIDELINES
TAX REFORM ACT OF 1969

Tax Reform Act of 1984, act which affects nonprofit, tax-exempt organizations in the following ways:

- a trust having both charitable and noncharitable beneficiaries (split interest trust) does not qualify for a charitable deduction unless it is structured as a charitable remainder annuity trust, unitrust, or pooled income fund; and
- redefined inclusion and exclusion from taxation of certain fringe benefits and established withholding for nonexcluded fringe benefits.

The act also contained provisions affecting private foundations. For example, the limit on gifts of cash was raised from twenty percent of AGI to thirty percent, a five year carryover provision was instituted, and private foundations were permitted to reduce their excise tax from two percent to one percent if they can meet a maintenance of effort test.

See also:

CHARITABLE REMAINDER ANNUITY TRUST
POOLED INCOME FUND
SPLIT INTEREST TRUST
UNITRUST

tax return, a form used to report income, deductions, etc. and to accompany tax payments and requests for tax refunds from the IRS.

tax shelter, investment in which any profits are fully or partially tax free; or an investment which creates deductions and credits that reduce one's overall taxes.

tax sheltered annuity: *see* TAX DEFERRED ANNUITY.

tax subsidy, tax advantage designed to encourage specific behavior that furthers public policy; for example, mortgage interest deductions to encourage citizens to buy houses, investment tax credits to encourage businesses to expand and create new jobs, etc.

tax yield, also TAX COLLECTIONS, the amount of tax which could potentially be collected. *Tax collections* are the portion of the tax yield that is actually collected.

Taylor, Frederick W. (1856-1915), originally an engineer, now considered the "father of scientific management." He did pioneering work on time-and-motion studies and led the search for the "one best way" of accomplishing any given task. *See Shop Management* (N.Y.: Harper & Bros., 1903); *The Principles of Scientific Management* (N.Y.: Harper & Bros., 1911).

See also SCIENTIFIC MANAGEMENT.

Taylorism, term used to describe the "scientific management" advocated by Frederick W. Taylor; it is also used as a general description for the mechanistic and authoritarian style of management common in American industry.

Teachers Insurance and Annuity Association (TIAA), organization that manages portable pension plans for professional employees of colleges and universities.

teachers' retirement fund association: *see* TEACHERS INSURANCE AND ANNUITY ASSOCIATION (TIAA).

team building, any planned and managed change involving a group of people in order to improve communications and working relationships. Team building is most effective when used as a part of a long-range strategy for organizational and personal development.

technical assistance (TA), term used to refer to the programs, activities, and services provided by a public interest group, a unit of government, or another third party to strengthen the capacity of recipients to improve their performance with respect to an inherent or assigned function.

technocrat, a term of disparagement. A technocrat is an individual in a decision making position of a technoscience organization whose background includes specialized technical training in a substantive field of science and/or technology.
See also TECHNOSCIENCE AGENCIES.

technological unemployment, unemployment that results from the displacement of workers by machinery or by the introduction of more efficient methods of production.

technology assessment, planning and evaluation device with which to judge the impact of technology in society. It is a tool that can be used to empirically evaluate the performance and the physical, ecological, political, and economic effects of any particular technology either presently in use or contemplated in the future.

Technology Assessment Act of 1972: *see* OFFICE OF TECHNOLOGY ASSESSMENT.

technology forecasting, use of techniques, such as surveys of experts or the assessment of a future demand, to anticipate technological developments.

technology transfer, application of technologies developed in one area of research or endeavor to another, frequently involving a concomitant shift in institutional setting (*e.g.*, from a federal agency to the private or third sector). Examples include the application of space technology developed under the auspices of NASA to the problems of transportation or weather prediction. Claims regarding the future possibilities for transfer are frequently factors in decisions concerning continuing financial support for technology development.

technoscience agencies, federal government agencies involved with science and technology policy making. These agencies generate ideas for scientific research and technological development, sponsor research in universities, corporations, and federal laboratories, and direct deployment projects. Examples include: National Science Foundation, National Aeronautics and Space Administration, Office of Science and Technology, Department of Defense, and Department of Energy (DOE).

technostructure, term that implies a growing influence of technical specialists in policy decisions. Technostructure is increasingly used as a technical term in the study of science and technology policy making to refer to the decision making structure in organizations.

TEFRA: *see* TAX EQUITY AND FISCAL RESPONSIBILITY ACT.

teleconferencing, connecting several people for a meeting by computer and telephone lines.

television: *see:*
COMMUNICATIONS ACT OF 1934
INFORMATIONAL SPOT
MEDIA, ELECTRONIC
PUBLIC INTEREST
SPOT ANNOUNCEMENT

temporary appointment: *see* APPOINTMENT.

temporary committee: *see* COMMITTEE.

temporary restraining order: *see* INJUNCTION.

tenant, a person who rents land, a building, or space in a building.

tenants' association, an association of renters, typically formed to advance the tenants' rights vis-à-vis the property owner(s).

tenure, period of time that one occupies a position. In the academic world, to have tenure means that an individual may continue in his or her position until retirement, subject, of course, to adequate behavior and the continued viability of the organization.

term, board: *see* BOARD TERM.

term, lease, the length of a lease.

term, rotational expiration of: *see* BOARD ROTATION.

term bonds: *see* SERIAL BONDS.

terminal, a device for computerized information exchange. It may include a typewriter keyboard, printer, keyboard plus monitor, etc.

See also DUMB TERMINAL and INTELLIGENT TERMINAL.

terminal arbitration, arbitration that is called for as the final step in a grievance procedure.

terminal earnings formula, a formula that bases pension benefits on average earnings in the final years of credited service—often the last three or five years.

termination, dismissal from employment. There is no general law which prohibits nonprofit or private employers from discharging employees without good cause. Employers have historically had the right to fire employees at will unless there was a written contract which protected against it. This broad right to discharge employees at will has been limited by a number of federal laws which prohibit discrimination based on sex, race, color, religion, national origin, age, physical or mental handicap, union or other protected concerted activities, wage garnishment, and filing complaints or assisting in procedures related to enforcing these laws.

In addition, some states and municipalities have passed laws which prohibit discharge for serving on jury duty, filing workers' compensation claims, refusing to take lie detector tests, or for discrimination based on marital status or sexual orientation. Collective bargaining agreements between employers and unions, and employee complaint procedures, also impose limitations on the absolute right of an employer to fire workers.

termination contract, agreement between an employer and a new employee that provides for salary continuation for the employee in the event of termination. The length of time that compensation continues to be paid typically varies from six months to two years.

termination pay: *see* SEVERANCE PAY.

termination requirements, requirements for terminating a private foundation which were established by the Tax Reform Act of 1969 and enunciated in IRS Code 507. The Code includes requirements for both voluntary and involuntary terminations.

See also PRIVATE FOUNDATION.

term life insurance, temporary insurance that offers protection for a limited number of years and has no cash value.

term loan, a bank loan for more than one year.

terms and conditions of employment, the entirety of the environment in which an employee works; all aspects of an employee's relationship with his or her employer and fellow employees, including compensation, fringe benefits, physical environment, work-related rules, work assignments, training and education, and opportunities to serve on committees and decision-making bodies.

test: *see* TESTS and TESTING.

testament, a will.

testamentary, contained in a will; given, bequeathed, done, or appointed through a will.

testamentary trust, a trust established through a will.

test anxiety, nervousness that an examinee experiences before and during the administration of a test.

testator, a person who has made a will; a person who died leaving a valid will.

test fidelity, extent to which a test represents the actual duties of a job.

test-retest reliability, measure of the reliability obtained by giving individuals the same test for a second time after an interval and correlating the sets of scores.

tests and testing: *see* the following entries:

CONFIDENCE TESTING
CREATIVITY TEST
CRITERION-REFERENCED TEST
CULTURE-FAIR TEST
DEXTERITY TEST
DIAGNOSTIC TEST
EMPLOYMENT TESTING
HANDS-ON TEST
INDIVIDUAL TEST
INTELLIGENCE TEST
INTEREST TEST
MULTIPLE-CHOICE TEST
NORM-REFERENCED TEST
PERFORMANCE TEST
PERSONALITY TEST
POST-TEST
POWER TEST
PRE-TEST
PROFICIENCY TEST
PSYCHOLOGICAL TEST
QUALIFYING TEST
RANKING TEST
RORSCHACH TEST
SPEED TEST
SPIRAL-OMNIBUS TEST
STANDARDIZED TEST
TEST ANXIETY
TEST FIDELITY
TEST-RETEST RELIABILITY

Texas Trade School* v. *Commissioner 30 T.C. 642 [1958], aff'd 272 F. 2d 168 [5th Cir. 1959], a landmark 1958 decision by the United States Tax Court in which the Texas Trade School was denied tax-exempt status because officers and past officers of the school were involved in real estate leasing and construction transactions (or schemes) with it. The court ruled the transactions were for the private inurement of insiders.

See also:

DISQUALIFIED PERSON
INSIDER
LEASE
PRIVATE INUREMENT
TAX AVOIDANCE SCHEME

T-Group: *see* LABORATORY TRAINING.

T-Group, family: *see* FAMILY T-GROUP.

Thematic Apperception Test (TAT), projective test that uses a standard set of pictures and calls for the subject to reveal his or her personality by making up stories about them. Variations of the TAT have been successfully used for vocational counseling and executive selection, as well as for determining attitudes toward labor problems, minority groups, and authority.

Theory X and Theory Y, contrasting sets of assumptions made by managers about human behavior that Douglas McGregor distilled and labeled in *The Human Side of Enterprise* (N.Y.: McGraw-Hill, 1960).

Theory X holds that:

1. The average human being has an inherent dislike of work and will avoid it if possible.
2. Because of this human characteristic of dislike of work, most people must be coerced, controlled, directed, or threatened with punishment to get them to put forth adequate effort toward the achievement of organizational objectives.
3. The average human being prefers to be directed, wishes to avoid responsibility, has relatively little ambition, wants security above all.

Theory X assumptions are essentially a restatement of the premises of the scientific management movement, not a flattering picture of the average citizen of modern industrial society. While McGregor's portrait can be criticized for implying greater pessimism concerning the nature of man on the part of managers than is perhaps warranted, Theory X is all the more valuable as a memorable theoretical construct because it serves as such a polar opposite of Theory Y. (McGregor would later deny that the theories were polar opposites and assert that they were "simply different cosmologies.")

Theory Y holds that:

1. The expenditure of physical and mental effort in work is as natural as play or rest. The average human

being does not inherently dislike work. Depending upon controllable conditions, work may be a source of satisfaction (and will be voluntarily performed) or a source of punishment (and will be avoided if possible).
2. External control and the threat of punishment are not the only means for bringing about effort toward organizational objectives. Men and women will exercise self-direction and self-control in the service of objectives to which they are committed.
3. Commitment to objectives is a function of the rewards associated with their achievement. The most significant of such rewards (*e.g.*, the satisfaction of ego and self-actualization needs) can be direct products of effort directed toward organizational objectives.
4. The average human being learns, under proper conditions, not only to accept but to seek responsibility. Avoidance of responsibility, lack of ambition, and emphasis on security are generally consequences of experience, not inherent human characteristics.
5. The capacity to exercise a relatively high degree of imagination, ingenuity, and creativity in the solution of organizational problems is widely, not narrowly, distributed in the population.
6. Under the conditions of modern industrial life, the intellectual potentialities of the average human being are only partially utilized.

While McGregor admitted that the assumptions of Theory Y were not finally validated, he found them "far more consistent with the existing knowledge in the social sciences than are the assumptions of Theory X." A central motif in both Theory X and Theory Y is control. With Theory X, control comes down from management via strict supervision. Theory Y, on the contrary, assumes that employees will be internally rather than externally controlled. Such internal control presumably comes from an inward motivation to perform effectively.

Theory Z, an approach to management generally associated with the Japanese that emphasizes participative management from employees who are committed to their work through cultural tradition, shared socioeconomic values, and communal forms of decision making. Theory Z personnel policies are characterized by high levels of trust, lifetime or long-term job security, and holistic career planning.

therblig, basic element of work motions first classified by the "inventor" of motion study, Frank G. Gilbreth. Therbligs (Gilbreth spelled backward) came in seventeen varieties and remain the foundation of the science of motion study. The basic therbligs, as modified by the Society for the Advancement of Management, are: search, select, grasp, reach, move, hold, release, position, pre-position, inspect, assemble, disassemble, use, unavoidable delay, avoidable delay, plan, and rest to overcome fatigue.

think tank, colloquial term that refers to an organization or organizational segment whose sole function is research. Some of the better known "think tanks" include The RAND Corporation, The Hudson Institute, and The Stanford Research Institute.

third-party allegations of discrimination, allegations of discrimination in employment brought by third parties—that is, groups or individuals not alleging discrimination against themselves and not seeking relief on their own behalf. The purpose of third-party procedures is to permit organizations with an interest in furthering equal opportunity to call attention to equal employment opportunity problems that appear to require correction or remedial action and that are unrelated to individual complaints of discrimination.

third party payment, a payment by a health insurance company or the government for health services (provided by, for example, a doctor, an ambulance company, etc.) for a patient.

third sector, all those organizations that fit neither in the public sector (government) nor the private sector (business); a generic phrase for the collectivity of nonprofit organizations, or organizations that institutionalize activism to deal with issues and problems that are being ignored by the public and private sectors.

See also NONPROFIT ORGANIZATION.

thirty day letter, an IRS letter to a taxpayer stating a tax deficiency (or refusing a refund request) and explaining appeal rights. The taxpayer has thirty days in which to respond.

thirty percent organization, former category of nonprofit organization. During the five years prior to passage of the Tax Reform Act of 1969, donors were permitted to contribute up to thirty percent of their adjusted gross income to certain types of religious, charitable, and other public organizations. These organizations came to be known as "thirty percent organizations." In contrast, donors could contribute only up to twenty percent to private foundations.

The applicable IRS Code was changed by the Tax Reform Act of 1969. The old thirty percent organizations are now generally known as public institutions (or fifty percent organizations) and are addressed by IRS Code 170(b)(1)(A)(i) through (v).

See also PUBLIC INSTITUTION.

Thomas* v. *Review Board of the Indiana Employment Security Division, 67 L.Ed. 2d 624 (1981), U.S. Supreme Court case which held the denial of unemployment compensation to a member of Jehovah's Witnesses who voluntarily quit his job because of his religious beliefs was violative of free exercise clause of the First Amendment.

See also FREE EXERCISE CLAUSE.

threshold effect, total impression a job applicant or a client makes by his or her bearing, dress, manners, etc. as he or she comes through the door.

throughput, middle step in data processing or a system's operation; it comes after input and before output.

Thurstone Scale, attitude scale created by Louis L. Thurstone that has judges rate the favorability of statements, then has subjects select those statements with which they agree.

TIAA: *see* TEACHERS INSURANCE AND ANNUITY ASSOCIATION.

tickler, a file in which documents are arranged by the dates when the next follow-up actions are required.

tiger team, a task force or work group assigned to solve a specific problem or generate new ideas.

time, broken: *see* BROKEN TIME.

time card, most basic payroll form on which is recorded, either manually or by means of a mechanical time clock, the hours that an employee has worked during a particular pay period.

time deposit, an account at a bank or other depository institution on which limitations on withdrawal are imposed. The depositor contracts to leave the funds on deposit for a specified period of time in return for receiving a certain rate of interest. Time deposits include, for example, certificates of deposit and savings accounts.

time horizon, that distance into the future to which a planner looks when seeking to evaluate the consequences of a proposed action.

time series analysis, a useful technique for forecasting and for program evaluations. When used for program evaluation purposes, historical trend data are plotted and projected into the future. The projected data points are subsequently compared with actual data, and the distance between them is used as a measure of program impact. For example, an American Heart Association chapter might create a time series showing the historical and projected trend in the number of people who survive certain types of heart attacks in a city (for example, ventricular fibrillation). Then, a massive citizen education program is conducted in CPR (cardio-pulmonary resuscitation). Six months later, the actual number of survivors is compared with the projected number. The difference between the two numbers is the measure of the program's success or lack of success.

See also:
EVALUATION
EVALUATION DESIGN
EVALUATION TECHNIQUE

time-sharing, simultaneous use of a central computer by two or more remote users, each of whom has direct and individual use of the central computer through the use of a terminal. The first commercial computer time-sharing services began in 1965.

time study, the technique of establishing an allowed time standard to perform a work task.

timetable: *see* GOAL.

time wage rate, any pay structure providing for wage payments in terms of an hourly, weekly, or monthly time interval. This is in contrast to a piece-rate structure where an employee is paid only for the amount that he or she produces.

titles, formal job descriptions, and useful management tools (and cheap, too). The appropriate title can provide incalculable psychic income and a decided advantage when dealing with the outside world. A fund-raiser may be more effective as an associate executive director. A secretary may be more effective as an administrative assistant. Some housewives are even slightly more content to be known as domestic engineers. Shakespeare's Juliet was wrong. A rose by any other name would not necessarily smell as sweet; sometimes it smells better!

Title VII, in the context of equal employment opportunity, Title VII of the Civil Rights Act of 1964 (as amended)—the backbone of the nation's EEO effort. It prohibits employment discrimination because of race, color, religion, sex, or national origin and created the Equal Employment Opportunity Commission as its enforcement vehicle. The federal courts have relied heavily upon Title VII in mandating remedial action on the part of employers.

See also the following entries:
CITY OF LOS ANGELES, DEPARTMENT OF WATER & POWER V. MANHART
CONSTRUCTIVE DISCHARGE THEORY
DISCRIMINATION
MAKE WHOLE
NATIONAL ORIGIN DISCRIMINATION
PREGNANCY DISCRIMINATION ACT OF 1978
RELIGIOUS DISCRIMINATION
RETROACTIVE SENIORITY
706 AGENCY
SEX PLUS
SEXUAL HARASSMENT
SYSTEMIC DISCRIMINATION
TOWER AMENDMENT

title-structure change, elimination of a title by substitution of a more appropriate title without any change in duties or responsibilities of the position involved.

tokenism, in the context of Equal Employment Opportunity, an insincere EEO effort by which a few minority group members are hired in order to satisfy government affirmative action mandates or the demands of pressure groups.

total compensation comparability, major means of incorporating fringe benefits into overall pay policy. The comparability principle, which holds that public and nonprofit employees should be paid wages comparable to those of similar workers in the private sector, has not kept pace with changing conditions. Consequently, in some cases, while actual wages and salaries may be comparable to or lower than those of private sector counterparts, the total package of pay plus fringe benefits plus time off often gives the public sector (and, in some cases, the third sector) employee a greater total return than that gained by a private sector counterpart.

In response to this situation, boards of directors and public jurisdictions are increasingly calling for total compensation comparability.

total labor force: *see* LABOR FORCE.

totem-pole ranking, rank ordering of employees, usually for purposes of evaluation, where each is placed above or below another with no more than one individual per rank.

Totten Trust, a trust arrangement in which a person puts money into a bank account in his or her name as trustee for a second person (or, typically, a nonprofit organization). The first person can take the money out at any time, but if he or she does not do so before dying, the money becomes the property of the second person or organization.

tour of duty, hours that an employee is scheduled to work.

Tower Amendment, portion of Title VII of the Civil Rights Act of 1964 that was introduced by Senator John Tower of Texas during Senate debate on the act. The Tower Amendment, Section 703(h), had the effect of establishing, in legal terms, the right of an employer to give "professionally developed ability tests" as long as they were not intentionally discriminatory.

town, also BOROUGH and VILLAGE, urban entities with powers less than those possessed by cities. These are strictly controlled by state statutes.

town meeting, a method of self-government, now suitable for only the smallest jurisdictions, where the entire citizenry meets to decide local issues of public policy.

township, a division of state land having six miles on each side and varying in importance as a unit of government from state to state.

track record, athletic metaphor for an individual's history of performance in any given field or endeavor.

trade association, an organization of people or organizations engaged in the same line of business that attempts to promote or strengthen that business. Trade associations may qualify for tax-exempt status as business leagues under IRS Code 501(c)(6).

See also BUSINESS and BUSINESS LEAGUE.

trade-off, the selection of one of several alternatives; also, a concession made to induce or in response to the other side's concession (for example, in negotiating).

trade union: *see* CRAFT UNION.

Tragedy of the Commons, a story illustrative of the principle that the maximization of private gain will not result in the maximization of social benefit. When herdsmen sought to maximize individual gain by adding more and more cattle to a common pasture, this overgrazed the common. The resulting tragedy was that no one was able to effectively use the common for grazing. The concepts involved with the tragedy of the commons apply to societal problems such as pollution, overpopulation, etc.

trainee rate: *see* BEGINNER'S RATE.

trainerless laboratory, laboratory training experience conducted by the participants themselves.

training, organized effort to increase the capabilities of individuals and modify their behavior in order to achieve previously determined objectives.

See also the following entries:

AMERICAN SOCIETY FOR TRAINING AND DEVELOPMENT
ASSERTIVENESS TRAINING
COLD-STORAGE TRAINING
COMPREHENSIVE EMPLOYMENT AND TRAINING ACT OF 1973
IN-SERVICE TRAINING

LABORATORY TRAINING
NATIONAL TRAINING LABORATORIES INSTITUTE FOR APPLIED BEHAVIORAL SCIENCE
POST-ENTRY TRAINING
PRE-SERVICE TRAINING
ROLE
TRANSFER OF TRAINING
VERTICAL TRAINING
VESTIBULE TRAINING
VOCATIONAL TRAINING

Training and Development Journal, monthly journal of the American Society for Training and Development, Inc. Articles written both by practitioners and academics emphasize all phases of training and organization development. Selections tend to be more practical than theoretical.

training by objectives, method that allows employees to establish their own developmental goals (compatible with organizational goals) and direct their activities toward these goals, much as a management by objectives system establishes objectives and breaks down all subordinate activity into subdivisions that contribute to the overall objectives.

training demand, also TRAINING NEED, expressed preferences for training programs by individuals. *Training need* reflects some form of skill deficit that is directly related to job performance. If an organization's sole criterion for initiating a training program is demand, the danger will persist that what is demanded is not necessarily what is needed.

training evaluation, also TRAINING MEASUREMENT, determination of the extent to which a training program is justified by its results. *Training measurement* must precede training evaluation, because it reveals the changes that may have occurred as a result of training. The essential question is whether or not a training effort has met its objective. Annual reports frequently boast of the number of employees trained during the preceding year, but such "facts" should be looked upon with great suspicion. It is a common mistake to assume that the number of people who have been subjected to training is equal to the number who have been trained. No statement of training accomplishment can confidently be made unless it is supported by sophisticated measures of evaluation.

training measurement: *see* TRAINING EVALUATION.

training need: *see* TRAINING DEMAND and NEED.

Training: The Magazine of Human Resources Development, monthly trade magazine dealing with all aspects of training and human resource development. Articles tend to be written by practitioners in order to help managers of training development functions use the behavioral sciences to solve human performance problems.

trait theory, an approach to the study of leaders and leadership based on the concept that more effective leaders have certain characteristics that differ from less effective leaders; for example, height, intelligence, appearance, etc.

transactional analysis (TA), approach to psychotherapy first developed by Eric Berne. Transactional analysis defines the basic unit of social intercourse as a "transaction." There are three "ego states" from which transactions emanate—that of a "parent," an "adult," or a "child." The transactions between individuals can be classified as complementary, crossed, simple, or ulterior, based upon the response that an individual receives to a "transactional stimulus"—any action that consciously or unconsciously acknowledges the presence of other individuals. The transactional analysis framework has become a popular means of helping managers to assess the nature and effectiveness of their interpersonal behavior. By striving for more adult-to-adult transactions, managers may eliminate many of the "games people play."

See also LIFE POSITION and SCRIPT.

transcendental meditation, technique utilizing biofeedback which seeks to expand an individual's intellectual growth and consciousness.

transfer, also called LATERAL TRANSFER, job reassignment in which the employee retains approximately the same pay, status, and responsibility as in his or her previous assignment.

transfer of training, theory that knowledge or abilities acquired in one area aid the acquisition of knowledge or abilities in other areas. When prior learning is helpful, it is called *positive transfer*.

transfer payments, payments by government to individuals who provide no goods or services in return.

transfer tax, the name for such different types of taxes as estate tax, gift tax, tax on the sale of stock, etc.

transformational leadership, *see* LEADERSHIP, TRANSFORMATIONAL.

transnational nonprofit organization, a nonprofit organization which focuses its activities on people in a single other nation and/or on the relationship between this country and one other nation; for example, Ethiopia, Afghanistan, South Africa, or Northern Ireland.

See also INTERNATIONAL NONPROFIT ORGANIZATION.

Trans World Airlines* v. *Hardison, 432 U.S. 63 (1977), U.S. Supreme Court case which ruled

> that an employer is not required to arrange Saturdays off for an employee so that he may observe his Sabbath, if in doing so the employer would incur more than minimal costs—such as overtime pay for a replacement. The Court also ruled that, if employees' work schedules are determined on the basis of seniority, an employer is not required to violate the seniority privileges of others so that an employee can observe a Saturday Sabbath.

travel expenses: *see* REIMBURSEMENT.

treasurer, the elected officer of a nonprofit organization who is responsible for the organization's finances and funds.

See also OFFICER.

treasury bills, the shortest term federal security. Treasury bills have maturity dates normally varying from three to twelve months and are sold at a discount from face value rather than carrying an explicit rate of interest.

trend projections, the examination and study of the behavioral patterns of both past and present statistical data, and also the projecting or predicting of the possible range of that data over a future period of time. Predicting trends consists of using usually quantitative methods for plotting data as a function of time to see what happened to it in the past and determine if the trend or character of the (plotted) data will continue unchanged for some future period. The three major types of predictions used are:

1. *Cyclic predictions,* which may be based on the principle that history repeats itself. Such data when displayed may show periodic fluctuations such as temperature changes throughout the year or the use of electricity in the same period. This can be used only when you are sure how the periodicity comes about and why.
2. *Trajectory predictions,* which are based on changes that occur in data that remain stable in character (*e.g.*, population growths, gross national product, etc.).
3. *Associative predictions,* which are data from one event that are used to predict a second event. Cause and effect relationships must exist to predict these situations (*e.g.*, unemployment vs. increase in the welfare rolls).

See also TIME SERIES ANALYSIS.

trial balance, an interim financial report used for checking the accuracy of bookkeeping system entries before preparing financial statements. A trial balance is created by totalling all credit entries and debit entries, and comparing them for equality.

trickle-down economics, description for government policies that seek to benefit the wealthy in hopes that prosperity will in turn "trickle down" to the middle and lower economic classes. The term was first coined by humorist Will Rogers (1879-1935) when he analyzed some of the depression remedies of the Hoover administration and noted that "the money was all appropriated for the top in the hopes it would trickle down to the needy."
See also SUPPLY-SIDE ECONOMICS.

trickle-down housing theory, belief that housing will be upgraded for all groups as they progress through housing left vacant by other groups as *they* progress up the economic ladder.

true-false item, test question that calls for the examinee to indicate whether a given statement is true or false.

true score, score entirely free of measurement errors. True scores are hypothetical values never obtained in actual testing, which always involves some measurement error. A true score is sometimes defined as the average score that would result from an infinite series of measurements with the same or exactly equivalent tests, assuming no practice or change in the examinee during the testings.

trust, a legal fiduciary relationship in which one organization or person (the trustee) holds the title and accepts responsibility for managing property (such as a trust estate) for the benefit of another or others (the beneficiary[s]).
See also:
BENEFICIARY
TRUSTEE

trust, community: *see* COMMUNITY TRUST.

trust account, an account with a trust company established by a depositor or trustee. The depositor or trustee controls the trust account during his/her lifetime. After the donor's death, the balance of the trust account is payable to the beneficiary(ies).

trust agreement: *see* DECLARATION OF TRUST.

trust certificate, a document showing that property is held in trust as security for a debt based on money used to buy the property.

trust company, a corporation established and operated to perform the functions of a trustee. Most trust companies also engage in other banking and/or financial business.
See also TRUST and TRUSTEE.

trustee, a person or organization (such as a trust company) that administers the affairs of a trust, an individual, or an organization; for example, the trustee of an estate; a trustee of an organization (for example, a church). Trustees of a trust may be held to a higher standard of fiduciary responsibility than directors of nonprofit corporations.
See also:
BOARD OF DIRECTORS
DIRECTOR
TRUST

trusteeship, the position or functions of a trustee.

trust fund, money or property set aside in a trust or set aside for a special purpose.
See also TRUST.

trust funds (government), funds collected and used by the federal government for carrying out specific purposes and programs according to terms of a trust agreement or statute, such as the social security and unemployment trust funds. Trust funds are administered by the government in a fiduciary capacity and are not available for the general purposes of the government. Trust fund receipts that are not anticipated to be used in the immediate future are generally invested in interest-bearing government securities and earn interest for the trust fund. A special category of trust funds called *trust revolving funds* is used to carry out a cycle of business-type operations (*e.g.*,Federal Deposit Insurance Corporation).

trust indenture, the creating document for a trust. A trust indenture is to a trust as articles of incorporation are to a corporation.

tuition aid, also TUITION REFUND, training program that partially or fully reimburses employees for the expenses of taking job-related part-time courses at local colleges or universities.

turnover, movement of individuals into, through, and out of an organization. Turnover can be statistically defined as the total number (or percentage) of separations that occurs over a given time period. The turnover rate is an important indicator of the morale and health of an organization.

two-career couple, *see* DUAL-CAREER COUPLE.

Two-Factor Theory: *see* MOTIVATION-HYGIENE THEORY.

two percent limitation: *see* PUBLICLY SUPPORTED ORGANIZATION.

Type I error, rejection of a statistical test or assumption that should be accepted in this case.

Type II error, acceptance of a statistical test or assumption that should be rejected in this case.

Type I publicly supported organization: *see* PUBLICLY SUPPORTED ORGANIZATION.

Type II publicly supported organization: *see* PUBLICLY SUPPORTED ORGANIZATION.

U

UBI: *see* UNRELATED BUSINESS INCOME.

ultrafiche: *see* MICROFICHE.

unaffiliated union, union not affiliated with the AFL-CIO.

unassembled examination, examination in which applicants are rated solely on their education, experience, and other requisite qualifications as shown in the formal application and on any supporting evidence that may be required.

unauthorized strike: *see* WILDCAT STRIKE.

unbilled revenue or NON-INVOICED REVENUE, the amount earned by providing services, but not billed (or invoiced). The calculation for unbilled revenue, in a formula format, is:

$______	(−)	$______	=	$______
Earned Revenue		Billed Revenue		Unbilled Revenue

Many types of nonprofit organizations perform services-for-fees for individual clients or other organizations. Nonprofit ambulance services, hospitals, and sheltered workshops are typical examples.

See also:

BILLED REVENUE
COLLECTED REVENUE
COLLECTION RATE
EARNED REVENUE
ESTIMATED INCOME
UNCOLLECTED REVENUE

uncollected revenue, the amount billed for services but not collected. The calculation for uncollected revenue, in formula format, is:

$______	(−)	$______	=	$______
Billed Revenue		Collected Revenue		Uncollected Revenue

See also:
BILLED REVENUE
COLLECTED REVENUE
COLLECTION RATE
EARNED REVENUE
ESTIMATED INCOME
UNBILLED REVENUE

uncontrollable expenses, also UNCONTROLLABLE SPENDING, generally, obligations where an organization has granted long-term contracts and is therefore unable to control the associated expenses.

underachievement: *see* OVERACHIEVEMENT.

underemployment, those workers who are involuntarily working less than a normal workweek and those who are situated in jobs that do not make efficient use of their skills and educational backgrounds. Examples of the latter would include a Ph.D. driving a taxi or an engineer working as a file clerk.

underground economy, the totality of economic activity undertaken in order to evade tax obligations.

understudy, individual who is engaged in on-the-job training under the direction of an experienced employee; also, an individual who is specifically hired to replace someone planning to resign or retire.

underutilization, in the context of equal employment opportunity, state that occurs when there are fewer minorities or women in a particular job classification than would be reasonably expected by their general availability.

underwrite, to insure; to guarantee to purchase any stock or bonds that remain unsold after a public sale.

undistributed income, income not distributed by a private foundation.

undistributed profits tax, a tax on a for-profit company's profit that is retained rather than paid to shareholders—in excess of reasonable needs.

undivided interest, or UNDIVIDED PORTION OF AN INTEREST (IN PROPERTY), a percentage of all interests and rights owned in a property. In general, a taxpayer cannot claim a deduction for donating a partial interest in property unless the donation is made to a charitable remainder trust. However, a deduction is permitted for an *undivided portion of the total interest* in a specific property.

The undivided portion of the interest must extend over the complete term of the taxpayer's interest in the property and in other property to which it may be converted. Further, the charitable organization that receives it must have the right to possession and control of the property for a portion of each year appropriate to its interest in the property.

undocumented workers: *see* ILLEGAL ALIENS.

unearned income, money that has been received but not earned.

See also EARNED REVENUE and INCOME, RECOGNITION OF.

unemployed, experienced: *see* EXPERIENCED UNEMPLOYED.

unemployed, hard-core: *see* HARD-CORE UNEMPLOYED.

unemployed, hidden: *see* DISCOURAGED WORKERS.

unemployment, the state of persons able and willing to work who are actively (but unsuccessfully) seeking to work at the prevailing wage rate. The unemployment rate is probably the most significant indicator of the health of the economy. U.S. economists tend to consider an unemployment rate of about four percent of the total labor force as "full employment." Unemployment statistics are compiled monthly by the Bureau of Labor Statistics. These figures are obtained by surveys of a sample of all U.S. households. The Bureau of the Census, which actually conducts the surveys, defines an unemployed person as a civilian over sixteen years old who, during a given week, was available for work but had none, and (1) had been actively seeking employment during the past month, or (2) was waiting to be recalled from a layoff, or (3) was waiting to report to a new job within thirty days.

See also the following entries:

FRICTIONAL UNEMPLOYMENT
PHANTOM UNEMPLOYMENT
PHILLIPS CURVE
RESIDUAL UNEMPLOYMENT
SEASONAL EMPLOYMENT
STRUCTURAL UNEMPLOYMENT
TECHNOLOGICAL UNEMPLOYMENT

unemployment benefits, also called UNEMPLOYMENT COMPENSATION, specific payments available to workers from the various state unemployment insurance programs. Unemployment benefits are available as a matter of right (without a means test) to unemployed workers who have demonstrated their attachment to the labor force by a specified amount of recent work and/or earnings in covered employment. To be eligible for benefits, the worker must be ready, able, and willing to work and must be registered for work at a public employment office. A worker who meets these eligibility conditions may still be denied benefits if he or she is disqualified for an act that would indicate the worker is responsible for his or her own unemployment.

A worker's monetary benefit rights are determined on the basis of employment in covered work over a prior reference period (called the "base period"). Under all state laws, the weekly benefit amount—that is, the amount payable for a week of total unemployment—varies with the worker's past wages within certain minimum and maximum limits. In most of the states, the formula is designed to compensate for a fraction of the usual weekly wage (normally about fifty percent), subject to specified dollar maximums.

unemployment compensation: *see* UNEMPLOYMENT BENEFITS.

unemployment insurance, programs designed to provide cash benefits to regularly employed members of the labor force who become involuntarily unemployed and who are able and willing to accept suitable jobs.

unfair labor practices (employers), actions prohibited by the National Labor Relations (Wagner) Act of 1935. These prohibitions, which serve to protect the right of employees to organize themselves in labor unions, are: interference with, restraint, or coercion of employees in the exercise of their guaranteed rights under the law; domination of, interference with the organization and administration of, or financial support of any labor organization; discrimination in hiring or firing of employees or in the conditions of employment aimed at the encouragement or discouragement of membership in a labor organization; discrimination against an employee who files charges or gives testimony under the Wagner Act; refusal to submit to collective bargaining.

unified transfer credit, a credit against the unified transfer tax which replaced the lifetime gift and estate tax exemptions.

unified transfer tax, a federal tax on transfers by gift or death. It has replaced the separate federal gift and estate taxes.

Uniform Guidelines on Employee Selection, guidelines adopted in 1978 by the four federal agencies most concerned with employee selection processes: the Equal Employment Opportunity Commission, the Civil Service Commission, the Department of Justice, and the Department of Labor. The guidelines are designed to assist employers, labor organizations, employment agencies, and licensing and certification boards to comply with requirements of federal law prohibiting employment practices that discriminate on grounds of race, color, religion, sex, or national origin.

uniform user charge, any user charge that makes no pricing distinctions among different kinds of customers, their levels of service, etc.

unincorporated, not a corporation; articles of organization have not been filed with the appropriate state office.

unincorporated area, an urban area that has not become a city and therefore has no local governmental structure of its own other than its county.

union: *see* list under LABOR ORGANIZATION. *See also* the following entries:

BONA FIDE UNION
BUSINESS UNIONS
CRAFT UNION
INDEPENDENT UNION
INTERNATIONAL UNION
LABOR ORGANIZATION
LOCAL INDEPENDENT UNION
LOCAL UNION
NATIONAL UNION
UNAFFILIATED UNION
WHITE-COLLAR UNION

union counselors, also called STRIKE COUNSELORS, under ordinary circumstances, a union member who has volunteered to take a training course on the work of his or her community's social agencies. Training completed, the counselor serves as a referral agent in the local union, supplying information about the location, specific services, eligibility requirements, and application procedures to fellow union members who seek help in resolving some personal or family problem. In the event of a strike, the counselor advises strikers how they may best avail themselves of their community's social welfare programs.

union label, any imprint attached to an item that indicates that it was made by union labor. Unions naturally encourage their members and the public to buy only those products bearing a union label.

union organizer: *see* ORGANIZER.

union security, generally, any agreement between an employer and a union that requires every employee in the bargaining unit, as a condition of employment, to be a member of the union or to pay a specified sum to the union for its bargaining services.

union steward: *see* STEWARD.

union trusteeship: *see* TRUSTEESHIP.

unique asset, an asset held by a private foundation for which there is no readily determinable fair market value or for which sale thereof would negatively influence its market (such as a very large block of shares of stock in a corporation).

unit: *see* BARGAINING UNIT.

unit, employer: *see* EMPLOYER UNIT.

United Airlines* v. *Evans, 431 U.S. 553 (1977), U.S. Supreme Court case that limited an employer's liability for prior violations under Title VII. The court ruled that an employee who was illegally discriminated against after Title VII took effect could lose her right to retroactive seniority if she fails to file charges within the specified period (now 180 days) after the violation occurred.

***United States Code* (U.S.C.),** official lawbooks that contain all federal laws.

United States Court of Appeals: *see* COURT OF APPEALS.

United States District Court: *see* DISTRICT COURT.

United States Employment Services (USES), federal agency within the U.S. Department of Labor which provides assistance to states and territories in establishing and maintaining a system of over 2,500 local public employment offices. Established by the Wagner-Peyser Act of 1933, the USES is responsible for providing job placement and other employment services to unemployed individuals and other job seekers, providing employers and workers with job development, placement, recruitment, and similar assistance, including employment, counseling, and special services to youth, women, older workers, and handicapped persons, and related supportive services. The USES is also responsible for the development of state and local information on employment and unemployment and on occupational demand and supply necessary for the planning and operation of job training and vocational education programs throughout the country.

The USES develops policies and procedures to provide a complete placement service to workers and employers in rural areas. Migrant and seasonal farm workers receive assistance to help them maintain year-round employment through the federal-state employment services interstate clearance system. The USES is responsible for insuring that, in the interstate recruitment of farm and woods workers, applicable standards and regulations relating to housing, transportation, wages, and other conditions are met.

United States Government Manual, annual publication of the federal government that provides detailed information on all agencies of the executive, legislative, and judicial branches of government. The *Manual* includes the names of major federal office holders.

United States instrumentalities, according to IRS Code 501(c) (1), corporations

> organized under Act of Congress, if such corporations are instrumentalities of the United States and if, under such Act . . . such corporations are exempt from Federal income taxes.

Examples of United States instrumentalities include the Federal National Mortgage Association, the Federal Reserve Banks, and the Federal Deposit Insurance Corporation.

See also GOVERNMENT INSTRUMENTALITY.

United States Reports, official record of cases decided by the U.S. Supreme Court. When cases are cited, *United States Reports* is abbreviated to "U.S." For example, the legal citation for the case of *Pickering* v. *Board of Education* is 391 U.S. 563 (1968). This means that the case will be found on page 563 of volume 391 of the *United States Reports* and that it was decided in 1968.

United States Statutes at Large, bound volumes, issued annually, containing all public and private laws and concurrent resolutions enacted during a session of Congress, reorganization plans, proposed and ratified amendments to the Constitution, and presidential proclamations.

United States* v. *Students Challenging Regulatory Agency Procedures (SCRAP), 412 U.S. 669 (1973), Supreme Court case granting standing to five law school students challenging an Interstate Commerce Commission-sanctioned increase in freight rates on the grounds that the increase might reduce the recycling of cans and so forth, which in turn might pollute the national parks in the Washington, D.C. area and consequently injure the students who use these parks. The case suggests that under present standards one who is injured by governmental activity will have standing to challenge it in court.

United Steelworkers of America* v. *Weber, et al., 443 U.S. 193 (1979), decided together with KAISER ALUMINUM & CHEMICAL CORP. V. WEBER, ET AL., U.S. Supreme Court decison that upheld an affirmative action program giving blacks preference in selection of employees for a training program.

See also the following entries:

AFFIRMATIVE ACTION
CIVIL RIGHTS ACT OF 1964
REGENTS OF THE UNIVERSITY OF CALIFORNIA V. ALLAN BAKKE
REVERSE DISCRIMINATION
TITLE VII

United Way, also UNITED WAY OF AMERICA, a network of approximately 2,300 autonomous United Way organizations, each with its own approaches to improving the quality of life in the communities it serves. Local United Way organizations are dues-paying affiliates, each retaining its own autonomy. Most United Way organizations raise funds for participating charitable organizations, conduct community needs assessments, develop plans for meeting human care needs, engage in community problem solving, assist in recruiting and placing volunteers, and provide information and referral services to connect people in need with serving agencies. Many services are available to human care organizations that do not receive funding through the United Way.

Most local United Way organizations receive approximately thirty percent of their funds from corporate contributions and about seventy percent from employee workplace contributions.

United Way of America is an umbrella association for the United Way organizations located in Alexandria, Virginia. United Way of America coordinates and staffs national lobbying efforts, provides legislative information, conducts national media campaigns (for example, with the National Football League), and provides materials and technical assistance to local United Way organizations.

United Way of America Service Identification System, Second Edition (UWASIS II), an organized taxonomy of human service programs which classifies and defines programs in a hierarchical structure, descending from goals to service systems, to services, to programs.

unit labor cost: *see* LABOR COSTS.

unitrust, or unit trust, also UNIT INVESTMENT TRUST, one of three types of charitable remainder trusts. It is similar to a charitable remainder annuity trust, except a unitrust can receive additional contributions and the payments to the beneficiary are not fixed. The two other types of charitable remainder trusts are *charitable remainder annuity trusts* and *pooled income funds*.

unit seniority: *see* DEPARTMENTAL SENIORITY.

unity of command, concept that each individual in an organization should be accountable to only a single superior.

unity of direction, concept that there should be only one head and one plan for each organizational segment.

universe: *see* POPULATION.

university relations, a more acceptable term for public relations in a university.
See also PUBLIC RELATIONS.

unobtrusive measures, measures taken without the subject being aware that he or she is being observed.

unpatterned interview: *see* PATTERNED INTERVIEW.

unrelated business income (UBI), net income (that is, gross income less normal expenses required to carry on a business) derived from a nonprofit organization's regular (ongoing) business activities which are not related substantially and directly to the organization's tax-exempt purpose or function. Whether or not the unrelated business income is subsequently used to advance the organization's tax-exempt purpose is irrelevant. Almost all tax-exempt organizations must pay taxes on unrelated business income.

unrelated trade, also UNRELATED BUSINESS, business activities conducted by an organization that are not related to its primary, tax-exempt purposes. Conduct of business for a profit may jeopardize an organization's tax-exempt status and may result in unrelated trade or business tax consequences under the operational test for tax exemption as a charitable organization.

unrestricted funds: *see* GENERAL FUND.

unsecured note, also UNSECURED LOAN, a loan granted on the basis of a borrower's creditworthiness and signature; not secured by collateral.

unskilled workers, employees whose jobs are confined to manual operations limited to the performance of relatively simple duties requiring only the slightest exercise of independent judgment.

unstructured role playing, role-play exercise or simulation in which the players are not given specific information on the character of their roles.

unusual grant rule, a rule which establishes an exception to the IRS criteria for determining whether a tax-exempt organization is a publicly supported organization or a private foundation. The rule permits the receipt of an "unusual" or unexpected large grant or contribution which otherwise would cause the organization to fail to satisfy the support tests. The IRS rules for unusual grants are called the "safe haven criteria."

See also:
CONTRIBUTION
GRANT
PRIVATE FOUNDATION
PUBLICLY SUPPORTED INSTITUTION
SAFE HAVEN CRITERIA
SUPPORT FRACTION
SUPPORT TESTS

upward mobility program, systematic management effort that focuses on the development and implementation of specific career opportunities for lower-level employees who are in positions or occupational series which do not enable them to realize their full work potential. An upward mobility program is usually just one aspect of an organization's overall EEO effort.

urban development: *see* RING THEORY OF URBAN DEVELOPMENT.

urban enterprise zone: *see* ENTERPRISE ZONE.

urban homesteading, program that gives a family a substandard home in a distressed urban area on condition that it be renovated and lived in by that family. Sometimes these programs provide for low-interest home improvement loans and/or sell the home for token amounts.

Urban Institute, Washington, D.C.-based research organization founded in 1968 to provide independent studies of and solutions to urban problems.

Urban League: *see* NATIONAL URBAN LEAGUE.

urban planning, formal process of guiding the physical and social development of cities and their regions.

urban renewal, also called URBAN REDEVELOPMENT, national program started in 1949 to rejuvenate urban areas through large-scale physical projects. Originally a loan program primarily for housing, it was quickly transformed by political pressures into a grant program for redoing large sections of the central business district or other commercial areas. It has been severely criticized for its uprooting of communities, especially black ones, and replacing them with commercial developments.

U.S.: *see* UNITED STATES REPORTS.

U.S.C.: *see* UNITED STATES CODE.

useful life, the normal expected operating life of a fixed asset for a particular organization. For example, the useful life of an automobile may differ between two organizations. Determination of an asset's useful life is necessary for determining the depreciation expense.

See also:
ASSETS
DEPRECIATION
SALVAGE

user-friendly, description of a computer system (hardware and/or software) that is easy to learn and to use.

***Usery* v. *Turner Elkhorn Mining Co.*,** 428 U.S. 1 (1976), U.S. Supreme Court case which upheld that portion of the Federal Coal Mine Health and Safety Act of 1969 making coal mine operators liable for benefits to former miners (and their dependents) who have suffered from black-lung disease (pneumoconiosis).

USES: *see* UNITED STATES EMPLOYMENT SERVICE.

UWASIS II: *see* UNITED WAY OF AMERICA

SERVICE IDENTIFICATION SYSTEM, SECOND EDITION.

V

VA: *see* VETERANS ADMINISTRATION.

VAC: *see* VOLUNTARY ACTION CENTERS.

vacancy, available position for which an organization is actively seeking to recruit an employee.

vacate, to set aside; to move out.

vacating an award, court's setting aside of an arbitration award.

vacation pay, pay for specified periods of time off work. The vacation or leave time that an employee earns frequently varies with length of service.

valence, in Victor H. Vroom's "Expectancy Theory of Motivation," the value an employee places on an incentive or reward. For a full account of Vroom's theory, *see* his *Work and Motivation* (N.Y.: John Wiley & Sons, 1964).

See also EXPECTANCY THEORY.

validation, process of investigation by which the validity of a particular type of test use is estimated. What is important here is to identify an ambiguity in the term "to validate," which is responsible for much confusion in the area of employment testing. To validate in ordinary language may mean to mark with an indication of official approval. In this sense, it is also possible to "invalidate" or to indicate official disapproval. In the technical vocabulary of employment testing, to validate is to investigate, to conduct research. Thus, in validating a test (more properly, in validating a use of a test), one is conducting an inquiry. In this context, the term "invalidating" has no meaning at all.

See also the following entries:

CONSENSUAL VALIDATION
CROSS VALIDATION
DIFFERENTIAL VALIDATION
GRIGGS V. DUKE POWER CO.
STATISTICAL VALIDATION
VALIDITY

validity, extent to which a test measures what it is supposed to measure or the accuracy of inferences drawn from test scores.

See also the following entries:

CONCURRENT VALIDITY
CONSTRUCT VALIDITY
CONTENT VALIDITY
CONVERGENT VALIDITY
CURRICULAR VALIDITY
DISCRIMINANT VALIDITY
EMPIRICAL VALIDITY
FACE VALIDITY
ITEM VALIDITY
OPERATIONAL VALIDITY
PREDICTIVE VALIDITY
RATIONAL VALIDITY
SYNTHETIC VALIDITY
VALIDATION

validity coefficient, correlation coefficient that estimates the relationship between scores on a test (or test battery) and the criterion.

valuation, the process of reducing measurements that are made on different scales to a common base (for example, dollars). It involves establishing and making trade-offs between multiple objectives. The valuation of benefits should not be confused with the quantitative estimates of benefits. For example, it is one thing to estimate the number of lives saved by a program, but it is another matter to place a dollar value on lives saved and then make a funding value judgment between several programs, all of which save lives.

valuation rules: *see:*

BLOCKAGE DISCOUNTING
DISTRIBUTION REQUIREMENT
PAYOUT

value, to cherish; a preference; a component of an attitude; also, of worth, as in *valuable*.

See also ATTITUDE and BELIEF.

values, a system of preferences.

value survey, an instrument used to help people identify and clarify the priorities in their own value system. A typical value survey lists values and asks the survey taker to rank-order the values based on their importance to him or her.

EXAMPLES OF ITEMS IN A VALUE SURVEY

_________ An exciting, stimulating, active life
_________ Inner harmony or freedom from inner conflict
_________ A sense of accomplishment
_________ Self-respect or self esteem
_________ Wisdom
_________ True friendship
_________ Mature love
_________ Pleasure (an enjoyable life)

variable, any factor or condition subject to measurement, alteration, and/or control.

variable, contextual: *see* CONTEXTUAL VARIABLE.

variable annuity, also called ASSET-LINKED ANNUITY, annuity that varies with the value of assets. In an effort to protect the purchasing power of a pensioner, some pension plans link benefit accruals to the value of an associated asset portfolio. Upon retirement, the pensioner may have the option of continuing to receive asset-linked benefits or to convert total benefits to a conventional fixed-income annuity.

variable cost: *see* COST, VARIABLE.

variable life insurance, form of life insurance whose death benefit is dependent upon the performance of investments in a common portfolio.

variable rate mortgage (VRM), a mortgage whose interest rate varies in accordance with a predetermined index (for example, the prime rate). Since the interest rate fluctuates, the amount of the monthly payments on the mortgage increases and decreases over the life of the VRM.

variance, difference between an expected or standard value and an actual one; also, official permission to use land or buildings in a way that would otherwise violate the zoning regulations for a neighborhood.

variance analysis: *see* ANALYSIS OF VARIANCE.

velvet ghetto, organizational unit (such as a public relations department) that is overloaded with women in response to an affirmative action program and in compensation for their scarcity in other professional or management categories.

venture capital, money to be used for starting new organizations or programs, or for expanding old ones.

vertical communication: *see* COMMUNICATION.

vertical conflict, bureaucratic conflict between differing hierarchical levels of an agency.

vertical equity: *see* TAX EQUITY.

vertical loading: *see* JOB LOADING.

vertical occupational mobility: *see* OCCUPATIONAL MOBILITY.

vertical training, simultaneous training of people who work together, irrespective of their status in the organization.

vertical work group, work group containing individuals whose positions differ in rank, prestige, and level of skill.

vested benefit: *see* VESTING.

vestibule training, training that prepares

a new employee for an occupation after acceptance for employment but before the assumption of the new job's duties.

vesting, granting an employee the right to a pension at normal retirement age even if the employee leaves the organization before the age of normal retirement. A vested benefit is usually based on accrued pension credit, as opposed to the pension for which the employee would have been eligible had he/she remained in the organization until retirement.

See also DEFERRED FULL VESTING, DEFERRED GRADED VESTING, and IMMEDIATE FULL VESTING.

veteran, disabled: *see* DISABLED VETERAN.

Veterans Administration (VA), federal agency that administers benefits for veterans and their dependents. These benefits include compensation payments for disabilities or death related to military service; pensions based on financial need for totally disabled veterans or certain survivors for disabilities or death not related to military service; education and rehabilitation; home loan guaranty; burial, including cemeteries, markers, flags, etc.; and a comprehensive medical program involving a widespread system of nursing homes, clinics, and more than 170 medical centers.

veterans organization, an association of prior and current members of the armed forces which may qualify for tax-exempt status under IRS code 501(c) (19).

veterans preference, concept that dates from 1865, when Congress, toward the end of the Civil War, affirmed that "persons honorably discharged from the military or naval service by reason of disability resulting from wounds or sickness incurred in the line of duty, shall be preferred for appointments to civil offices, provided they are found to possess the business capacity necessary for the proper discharge of the duties of such offices." The 1865 law was superseded in 1919, when preference was extended to all "honorably discharged" veterans, their widows, and to wives of disabled veterans. The Veterans Preference Act of 1944 expanded the scope of veterans preference by providing a five-point bonus on federal examination scores for all honorably separated veterans (except for those with a service-connected disability, who are entitled to a ten-point bonus). Veterans also received other advantages in federal employment (such as protections against arbitrary dismissal and preference in the event of a reduction-in-force).

All states and many other jurisdictions have veterans preference laws of varying intensity. New Jersey, for an extreme example, offers veterans absolute preference: if a veteran passes an entrance examination, he/she must be hired no matter what his/her score before nonveterans can be hired. Veterans competing with each other are rank ordered, and all disabled veterans receive preference over other veterans. Veterans preference laws have been criticized because they have allegedly made it difficult for government agencies to hire and promote more women and minorities. Although the original version of the Civil Service Reform Act of 1978 sought to limit veterans preference in the federal service, the final version contained a variety of new provisions *strengthening* veterans preference.

See also PERSONNEL ADMINISTRATOR OF MASSACHUSETTS V. FEENEY.

Veterans Readjustment Assistance Act of 1974, federal statute that required contractors with federal contracts of $10,000 or more to establish programs to take "affirmative action" to employ and advance in employment all disabled veterans (with thirty percent or more disability) and other veterans for the first forty-eight months after discharge.

veterans reemployment rights, reemployment rights program, under provisions of Chapter 43 of Title 38, U.S. Code, for men and women who leave their jobs to perform training or service in the armed forces. The Office of Veterans Reemployment Rights of the Labor-Management Services Administration of the U.S. Department of Labor has responsibility for the program. In general terms, to be entitled to reemployment rights a veteran must leave a position (other than a temporary position) for the purpose of entering the armed forces, voluntarily or involuntarily. The employer is generally obligated to reemploy the veteran within a reasonable time after he/she makes application for the position he/she would have occupied if he/she had remained on the job instead of entering military service.

vice-president, a term that can mean anything from "second in command" to "one of innumerable second-level officers."

Vietnam Era Veterans Readjustment Act of 1974: *see* VETERANS READJUSTMENT ASSISTANCE ACT OF 1974.

VISTA: *see* ACTION.

vocational behavior, total realm of human actions and interactions related to the work environment, including preparatin for work, participation in the work force, and retirement.

vocational counseling, any professional assistance given to an individual preparing to enter the work force concerning the choice of occupation.

Vocational Education Act of 1963, federal statute that authorized federal grants to states to assist them to maintain, extend, and improve existing programs of vocational education; to develop new programs of vocational education; and to provide part-time employment for youths who need the earnings from such employment to continue their vocational training on a full-time basis.

vocational habilitation, the development of people with handicaps to the fullest physical, mental, social, vocational, and economic usefulness of which they are capable. *See also* VOCATIONAL REHABILITATION.

vocational maturity, term premised upon the belief that vocational behavior is a developmental process which implies a comparison of an individual's chronological and vocational ages.

vocational maturity quotient, ratio of vocational maturity to chronological age.

vocational psychology, scientific study of vocational behavior and development that grew out of the practice of vocational guidance.

vocational rehabilitation, restoration of the handicapped to the fullest physical, mental, social, vocational, and economic usefulness of which they are capable. *See also* VOCATIONAL HABILITATION.

Vocational Rehabilitation Act of 1973, federal statute that requires federal contactors with contracts in excess of $2,500 to "take affirmative action to employ and advance in employment qualified handicapped individuals." The act also established within the federal government an Interagency Committee on Handicapped Employees whose purpose is "(1) to provide a focus for Federal and other employment of handicapped individuals, and to review, on a periodic basis, in cooperation with the Civil Service Commission [now Office of Personnel Management], the adequacy of hiring, placement, and advancement practices with respect to handicapped individuals, by each department, agency, and instrumentality in the executive branch of Government, and to insure that the special needs of such individuals are being met; and (2) to consult with the Civil Service Commission to assist the Commission to carry out its responsibilities" in implementing affirmative action programs for the handicapped.

vocational training, formal preparation for a particular business or trade.

voice stress analyzer: *see* LIE DETECTOR.

void, without legal effect; of no binding force; wiped out.

voluntarism, also VOLUNTARYISM, the principle of supporting socially desirable ends and organizations independent of the public sector, through voluntary contributions and efforts.

voluntary (action), done without compulsion or requirement and generally without compensation.
See also VOLUNTEER.

Voluntary Action Centers (VAC), organizations in local communities which promote voluntarism primarily through training and referral programs.

voluntary (organization), an organization that depends on voluntary actions and contributions to support its operations.

voluntary arbitration, arbitration agreed to by two parties in the absence of any legal or contractual requirement.

voluntary association, a nonincorporated organization formed to pursue an objective or to advance an interest.

voluntary bargaining items, those items over which collective bargaining is neither mandatory nor illegal.

voluntary demotion: *see* DEMOTION.

voluntary employees' beneficiary association, a voluntary association of employees which pays life, sickness, accident, or other benefits to its members or their beneficiaries, Voluntary employees' beneficiary associations may qualify for tax-exempt status under IRS Code 501(c) (9).

voluntary sector, the "third sector." (The public and private sectors are the first two.) The voluntary sector is generally considered to consist of nonprofit organizations which pursue social welfare goals.
See also THIRD SECTOR.

voluntary termination (foundation): *see* TERMINATION REQUIREMENTS.

volunteer, a person who provides a service without compulsion or requirement and typically without compensation. However, with the growth of the voluntary sector, the definition of a volunteer appears to be changing. For example, many volunteer ambulance services and fire departments now pay volunteers for their standby time and/or for making runs. These paid persons are still called volunteers or paid volunteers so long as their work with the ambulance service is not their primary source of income.

VOLUNTEER, a national organization of local voluntary action centers (VAC's).

Volunteers in Service to America, also VISTA, "the domestic Peace Corps"; a federal program administered by ACTION which deploys volunteers into low-income areas to teach self-improvement and self-help skills. Originally, VISTA was in the federal Office of Economic Opportunity, a cornerstone agency in the Johnson administration's "war on poverty."

voucher, a document that authorizes the giving out of something (usually cash).
See also PETTY CASH FUND.

voucher, in staffing terms, a formal inquiry to employers, references, professors, and others who presumably know a job applicant well enough to describe job qualifications and personal character.

VRM: *see* VARIABLE RATE MORTGAGE.

vulnerability assessment, an evaluation of the susceptibility of organization functions, programs, or projects in question to future loss of revenues.

W

wage and hour laws, the federal and state laws which set minimum wages and maxi-

mum hours for workers.
See FAIR LABOR STANDARDS ACT.

wage and salary administration, planning, organizing, and conducting those functions that relate to the direct and indirect compensation of employees for work they perform or services they provide.

wage and salary survey: *see* WAGE SURVEY.

Wage and Tax Statement: *see* FORM W-2.

wage arbitration, referral of a wage dispute to an arbitrator.

wage area, national and/or regional area selected on the basis of population size, employment, location, or other criteria for wage surveys.

wage assignment, voluntary transfer of earned wages to a third party to pay debts, buy savings bonds, pay union dues, etc.

wage compression: *see* SALARY COMPRESSION.

wage criteria, those external and internal standards or factors that determine the internal pay structure of an organization.

wage differentials, differences in wages paid for identical or similar work that are justified because of differences in work schedules, hazards, cost of living, or other factors.

wage drift, concept that explains the gap between basic wage rates and actual earnings, which tend to be higher because of overtime, bonuses, and other monetary incentives.

wage floor, minimum wage established by contract or law.

wage garnishment: *see* GARNISHMENT.

wage increase, deferred: *see* DEFERRED WAGE INCREASE.

wage inequity: *see* COGNITIVE DISSONANCE.

wage parity: *see* PARITY.

wage progression, progressively higher wage rates that can be earned in the same job. Progression takes place on the basis of length of service, merit, or other criteria.

wages, also SALARY, the pay received by an employee or group of employees for work performed or services provided for a specific period of time—typically an hour, day, week, month, or year. The term *wages* sometimes is restricted to pay to those who are compensated on an hourly basis and who are eligible for overtime pay, whereas *salary* sometimes connotes compensation to those who are not eligible for overtime pay.
See also the following entries:
BARGAINING THEORY OF WAGES
BOOTLEG WAGES
COMPETITIVE WAGES
GRADUATED WAGES
INDIRECT WAGES
IRON LAW OF WAGES
PAY
REAL WAGES
SALARY

Wages and Hours Act: *see* FAIR LABOR STANDARDS ACT.

wage survey, also called WAGE AND SALARY SURVEY and AREA WAGE SURVEY, formal effort to gather data on compensation rates and/or ranges for comparable jobs within an area, industry, or occupation. Wage surveys on both a national and regional basis are available from such organizations as the American Management Association, the International Personnel Management Association, and the International City Management Association.

wage tax, any tax on wages and salaries levied by a government. Many cities have wage taxes that force suburban commuters to help pay for the services provided to the region by the central city.

Wagner Act: *see* NATIONAL LABOR RELATIONS ACT OF 1935.

Wagner-O'Day Act, federal statute which provides that sheltered workshops serving blind and severely handicapped persons shall receive special preference in bidding on federal government contracts for products and services.

waive, to give up, renounce, or disclaim a privilege, right, or benefit with full knowledge of the consequences; to surrender a right.

walkout: *see* STRIKE.

Walsh-Healey Public Contracts Act of 1936, federal statute establishing basic labor standards for work done on U.S. government contracts exceeding $10,000 in value.

warm-up effect, adjustment process that takes place at the start of work. The warm-up period is over when the work curve reaches its first peak.

War on Poverty: *see* ECONOMIC OPPORTUNITY ACT OF 1964.

warrant, a short-term obligation issued in anticipation of revenue. The instrument or draft, when presented to a disbursing officer, such as a bank, is payable only upon acceptance by the issuer. Warrants may be made payable on demand or at some time in the future. Local governments, in particular, have used delayed payment of warrants as a way to protect cash flow.

Also, to promise, especially in a deed; also, an option to buy stock that is initially sold along with the sale of other securities.

warranty, also CONSUMER WARRANTY and LIMITED WARRANTY, a promise that certain facts are true and, with *consumer warranties,* that goods sold as fit for a particular purpose are, in fact, fit for that purpose. A warranty may be explicit and in writing or "presumed" (an implied warranty). Under recent federal law, if a written consumer warranty is not a "full warranty," it must be labeled *limited warranty* in the sales contract.

Washington Foundation Journal, The, a monthly publication that presents brief notes on legislative and federal administrative developments that may affect foundations. The *Journal* also notes meetings, reviews current books, etc.

Weber, Max (1864-1920), German sociologist who produced an analysis of bureaucracy that is still the most influential statement—the point of departure for all further analyses—on the subject.

weighted application blank, system in which weights or numeric values are placed on the varying responses to application blank items. After a job analysis determines the knowledges, skills, and abilities necessary to perform the duties of a position, corresponding personal characteristics can be elicited. Applicants who scored highest on the weighted application blank would be given first consideration.

welfare, public financial assistance to certain categories of poor persons.

welfare funds, employer contributions, agreed to during collective bargaining, to a common fund to provide welfare benefits to the employees of all of the contributing employers.

welfare state, a governing system where it is public policy that government will strive for the maximum economic and social benefits for each of its citizens short of changing the operating premises of the society. The line between an extreme welfare state and socialism is so thin that its existence is debatable.

See also PUBLIC WELFARE.

wellness program, a formal effort on the part of an employer to maintain the mental and physical health of its work force.

well pay, also called SWEEP PAY, incentive payments to workers who are neither sick nor late over a specified time period. In some organizations, well pay is called "sweep pay" for "Stay at Work, Earn Extra Pay."

whipsawing: *see* WHIPSAW STRIKE.

whipsaw strike, strike stratagem that uses one struck employer as an example to others in order to encourage them to accede to union demands without the necessity of additional strikes.

whistle blower, individual who believes the public interest overrides the interests of his or her organization and publicly "blows the whistle" if the organization is involved in corrupt, illegal, fraudulent, or harmful activity.

white-collar crime, "office crime," like embezzlement and fraud.
See also EMBEZZLEMENT and FRAUD.

white-collar union, general term for a union whose members are more likely to wear street clothes and sit at a desk than wear work clothes and stand at a lathe.

white-collar worker, employee whose job requires slight physical effort and allows him/her to wear ordinary clothes.

white paper, any formal statement of an official organizational policy or position with its associated background documentation.

whole-job ranking, job evaluation method that simply ranks jobs as a whole. For example, a small organization might rank one person president, another as bookkeeper, two others as stock clerks, etc.

whole life insurance, also STRAIGHT LIFE INSURANCE and ORDINARY LIFE INSURANCE, an insurance policy that provides protection for the insured person's entire life, usually for a flat yearly premium. While the face value of a whole life policy will be paid only at death, a "cash surrender value" builds up, against which the insured person may borrow at very favorable rates.

whole-person concept, philosophic attitude that management should be concerned with an employee's physical and mental health both on and off the job.

Wiener, Norbert: *see* CYBERNETICS.

wildcat strike, also called UNAUTHORIZED STRIKE and OUTLAW STRIKE, work stoppage not sanctioned by union leadership and usually contrary to an existing labor contract. Unless it can be shown that unfair employer practices were the direct cause of the wildcat strike, the union could be liable for damages in a breach of contract suit by management.

winners and losers, according to transactional analysis a *winner* is a person who responds authentically by being credible, trustworthy, responsive, and genuine both as an individual and as a member of society. Obviously, a *loser* is the opposite. Whether one is a winner or a loser reflects his or her success in coping with life scripts and his or her "life position." A *winner* occupies an "I'm OK—You're OK" life position; a loser, any of the other three life positions.
According to Eric Berne, in *Games People Play,* "We are all born princes and princesses, but our parents turn us into frogs."
See also:
LIFE POSITION
SCRIPT
TRANSACTIONAL ANALYSIS

wire transfer, an electronic communications network used for transferring funds and messages. Examples include the Federal Reserve wire network and Bank Wire, a communications network owned by commercial banks.
See also ELECTRONIC FUND TRANSFER SYSTEM.

withdrawal, removal of money from a bank.

withholding tax, federal, state, or local tax withheld by employers from the paychecks of their employees and paid directly to the taxing jurisdiction.

within-grade increase, also known as PERIODIC INCREASE and STEP INCREASE, a salary increase provided in certain pay plans based upon time-in-grade and acceptable or satisfactory work performance.

womb to tomb: *see* CRADLE TO THE GRAVE.

Women's Bureau, agency of the U.S. Department of Labor that is responsible for formulating standards and policies to promote the welfare of wage-earning women, improve their working conditions, increase their efficiency, advance their opportunities for professional employment, and investigate and report on all matters pertinent to the welfare of women in industry. The Women's Bureau has regional offices established in ten areas throughout the United States.

word processing, computerized text creation, editing, and printing.

work, according to Mark Twain, in *The Adventures of Tom Sawyer,* "Work consists of whatever a body is obliged to do, and play consists of whatever a body is not obliged to do."

See also the following entries:

DEAD WORK
OUT-OF-TITLE WORK

work-activities centers, centers planned and designed exclusively to provide therapeutic activities for handicapped clients whose physical or mental impairment is so severe as to make their productive capacity inconsequential. The Secretary of Labor is authorized by the Fair Labor Standards Act to allow the employment of handicapped persons in work activities centers at less than the minimum wage.

workaholic, word first used by Wayne Oates, in his *Confessions of a Workaholic: The Facts About Work Addiction* (N.Y.: World Publishing, 1971), to describe the addiction, the compulsion, or the uncontrollable need to work incessantly. A workaholic is a person whose involvement in his/her work is so excessive that his/her health, personal happiness, interpersonal relations, and social functioning are adversely affected.

work curve, also called OUTPUT CURVE, graphic presentation of an organization's or individual's productivity over a specified period of time.

work design: *see* JOB DESIGN.

work disability: *see* DISABILITY.

workers, *see* EMPLOYEE. *See also* the following entries:

DISADVANTAGED WORKERS
DISCOURAGED WORKERS
EXEMPT EMPLOYEE
FULL-TIME WORKERS
HOURLY-RATE WORKERS
ILLEGAL ALIENS
ITINERANT WORKER
PINK-COLLAR JOBS
SEMISKILLED WORKERS
UNSKILLED WORKERS
WHITE-COLLAR WORKERS

workers' compensation, also called WORKMEN'S COMPENSATION and INDUSTRIAL ACCIDENT INSURANCE, plan designed to provide cash benefits and medical care when a worker is injured in connection with his/her job and monetary payments to his/her survivors if he/she is killed on the job. It was the first form of social insurance to develop widely in the United States. There are now fifty-four different workers' compensation programs in operation. Each of the fifty states and Puerto Rico has its own workmen's compensation program. In addition, there are three federal workers' compensation programs covering federal government and private employees in the District of Columbia and longshoremen and harbor workers throughout the country.

Before the passage of worker's compensation laws, an injured employee ordinarily had to file suit against his/her employer and prove that the injury was due to the employer's negligence in order to recover damages. The enactment of workmen's compensation laws introduced the principle that a worker incurring an occupational injury would be compensated regardless of fault or blame in the accident and with a minimum of delay and legal formality. In turn, the employer's liability was limited, because workmen's compensation benefits became the exclusive remedy for work-related injuries.

The usual condition for entitlement to benefits is that the injury or death "arises out of and in the course of employment." Most programs exclude injuries due to the employee's intoxication, willful misconduct, or gross negligence. Although virtually limited to injuries or diseases traceable to industrial "accidents" initially, the scope of the laws has broadened over the years to cover occupational diseases as well.

In most states, worker's compensation is paid for entirely by employers who either purchase insurance coverage or self-insure—that is, assume total financial liability for the work accidents of their employees.

The Occupational Health and Safety Act of 1970 created the National Commission on State Workmen's Compensation Laws to evaluate the various state worker's compensation programs. The commission reported that "the evidence compels us to conclude that state workmen's compensation laws are in general neither adequate nor equitable." (*Report of the National Commission on State Workmen's Compensation Laws* [Washington, D. C.: U.S. Government Printing Office, 1972])

workers' councils, also called WORKS COUNCILS, any of a variety of joint labor-management bodies serving as vehicles for the resolution of problems of mutual interest. Workers' councils are usually associated with concepts of industrial democracy and are found mostly in Europe.

work ethic: *see* PROTESTANT ETHIC.

workfare, any public welfare program that requires welfare payment recipients to work (work + welfare = workfare) or enroll in a formal job-training program.

work force planning, determination by organization management of the numbers, kinds, and costs of workers needed to carry out each stage of the organization's program plan.

See also HUMAN RESOURCES PLANNING.

work group, also called WORKING GROUP and TASK GROUP, task unit within a larger organizational social system charged with the responsibility for making a specific contribution to the goals of the larger organization.

See also GROUP DYNAMICS

work group, autonomous: *see* AUTONOMOUS WORK GROUP.

work group, horizontal: *see* HORIZONTAL WORK GROUP.

work-in, form of protest demonstration in which a group of employees report to work as usual but refuse to follow their normal routines.

Work in America Institute, a clearinghouse for information on quality of working life and productivity, located in Scarsdale, N.Y.

working capital, money available to meet regular short-term operating expenses.

See also:

ASSETS
CASH MANAGEMENT
LIQUIDITY

working conditions, those factors, both physical and psychological, which comprise an employee's work environment. Included are such things as arrangement of office and factory equipment, salary or wages, fringe benefits, supervision, work routine, fair employment practices, health and safety precautions, length of work day, and relationship with coworkers.

working group: *see* WORK GROUP.

working hours, flexible: *see* FLEXI-TIME.

working papers, also called WORKING

CERTIFICATE and WORK PERMIT, federal certificate of age showing that a minor is above the oppressive child-labor age applicable to the occupation in which he/she would be employed. Such proof of age is required under the provisions of the Fair Labor Standards Act and the Walsh-Healey Public Contracts Act. Working papers are issued by a designee of the administrator of the Wage and Hour Division of the U.S. Department of Labor.

working permit: *see* WORKING PAPERS.

workload, the result expected from an expenditure of any employee's time and energy performing tasks or functions which can be evaluated in terms of either units produced, yardsticks of progress, or through judging the application and utilization of his or her effort.

work measurement, any method used to establish an equitable relationship between the volume of work performed and the human resources devoted to its accomplishment. Concerned with both volume and time, a work measurement program is basically a means of setting standards to determine just what constitutes a fair day's work.

See also MOTION STUDY and TIME STUDY.

work measurement standard, a numerical value applied to the units of work an employee or group can be expected to produce in a given period of time.

work motivation: *see* MOTIVATION.

work plan chart: *see* PROJECT CONTROL CHART.

work premium, also called PREMIUM PAY, extra compensation for work that is considered unpleasant, hazardous, or inconvenient. Overtime is the most obvious example of a work premium.

work preview, also called JOB SAMPLE and JOB PREVIEW, management technique for presenting prospective employees with realistic information about the particular job that they are considering.

work-ready, term used to describe a handicapped person who, if given employment, would be able to perform adequately on the job without being a burden to others.

work relief: *see* RELIEF.

work restructuring: *see* JOB RESTRUCTURING.

work rules, formal regulations prescribing both on-the-job behavior and working conditions. Work rules are usually incorporated into a collective bargaining agreement at the insistence of the union in order to restrict management's ability to unilaterally set production standards and/or reassign employees. The union's goal is to maximize and protect the jobs available to its members, protect their health and safety, and maintain stable work assignments for union members.

work sampling, also called JOB SAMPLING, technique used to discover the proportions of total time devoted to the various components of a job. Data obtained from work sampling can be used to establish allowances applicable to a job, to determine machine utilization, and to provide the criteria for production standards. While this same information can be obtained by time-study procedures, work sampling—dependent as it is upon the laws of probability—will usually provide the information faster and at less cost.

works councils: *see* WORKERS' COUNCILS.

worksharing, procedure for dividing the available work (or hours of work) among all eligible employees as an alternative to layoffs during slow periods. Three types of worksharing procedures may be identified—reduction in hours (by far the most common), division of work, and rotation of employment. *Reduction in hours,* as its name implies, requires that weekly hours of work be reduced below normal (non-overtime) schedules, usually within stated limits, to spread the work. The second procedure—*division of work*—is normally found in agreements covering employees on piecework or incentive systems, and emphasizes earnings rather than hours of work (although reduced hours may also occur). All available work is divided equally among eligible employees; under some conditions, faster workers may work somewhat fewer hours than slower ones for the same pay. The last procedure—*rotation of employment* (or layoff)—provides that short, specific periods of layoff be rotated equally among all employees, in contrast to the more common practice of laying off junior employees for longer or indefinite periods.

work simplification, the industrial engineering function which seeks to find the one best way to do each job based upon economy of time, material, effort, etc.

work station, specific location and immediate surrounding area in which a job is performed.

work stoppage, according to the U.S. Departments of Commerce and Labor, a work stoppage is a concerted and complete withholding of services by employees that lasts for at least one workday or one work shift.

work to rule, work slowdown in which all of the formal work rules are so scrupulously obeyed that productivity suffers considerably. Those working to rule seek to place pressure on management without losing pay by going on strike. Work-to-rule protests are particularly popular in the public sector, where most formal strikes are illegal.

work values, importance that employees place on the various aspects of work, such as pay, prestige, security, responsibility, etc.

workweek, expected or actual period of employment for a normal week, usually expressed in number of hours. According to the Fair Labor Standards Act, a workweek is a period of 168 hours during seven consecutive twenty-four-hour periods. It may begin on any day of the week and any hour of the day established by the employer. For purposes of minimum wage and overtime payment, each workweek stands alone, and there can be no averaging of two or more workweeks (except for hospital or nursing home employees on an "eight-and-eighty" schedule or seamen on U.S. vessels). Employee coverage, compliance with wage payment requirements, and the application of most exemptions are determined on a workweek basis.

See also the following entries:

FOUR-DAY WORKWEEK
GUARANTEED WORKWEEK

WOTS-UP analysis, an acronym for weakness, opportunities, threats, and strengths analysis; an analysis which seeks to determine how an organization should best cope with its environment. A WOTS-UP analysis is usually prepared as part of a strategic plan.

See also PLANNING and STRATEGIC PLANNING.

wrap-up clause: *see* ZIPPER CLAUSE.

Wright* v. *Regan, [49 A.F.T.R. 2d 82-757 (D.C. Cir. 1982)], a landmark 1982 decision by the U.S. Circuit Court of Appeals in Washington, D.C. which prohibited the United States government from granting tax-exempt status to any private schools which practice racial discrimination. The case involved Bob Jones University and the Goldsboro Christian School. The case was appealed to and upheld by the U.S. Supreme Court.

See also BOB JONES UNIVERSITY V. SIMON and GREEN V. CONNALLY.

writeoff, an uncollectable debt; also, a loss that can be claimed as a tax loss by a for-profit organization.

writ of certiorari: *see* CERTIORARI.

writ of mandamus: *see* MANDAMUS.

W-2 Form: *see* FORM W-2.

Y

year, fiscal: *see* FISCAL YEAR.

yield, profit, as expressed as a percentage of money invested. For example, a twenty dollar profit on a one hundred dollar investment is a twenty percent yield. See also RATE OF RETURN.

Z

ZBB: *see* ZERO-BASE BUDGETING.

ZD: *see* ZERO DEFECTS PROGRAM.

zero-base budgeting (ZBB), a budgeting process that is first and foremost a rejection of the incremental decision making model of budgeting. It demands a re-justification of the entire budget submission (from ground zero), whereas incremental budgeting essentially respects the outcomes of previous budgetary decisions (collectively referred to as the budget base) and focuses examination on the margin of change from year to year.

See also the following entries:

BASE
BUDGETING
DECISION PACKAGES

zero bracket amount, a flat deduction from income on personal income taxes. It is built into tax tables and tax schedules, so some taxpayers must subtract it from their itemized deductions. It has replaced the standard deduction.

zero-defects program (ZD), formal effort at quality assuredness aimed at eliminating human errors during production.

zero growth, also ZERO POPULATION GROWTH, a conscious policy on the part of a community to maintain a present population and life-style and not grow appreciably larger; a socioeconomic policy that discourages growth to conserve natural resources and a life-style.

zero rate mortgage, a mortgage in which a large down payment is made and the rest of the purchase price is paid off in equal installments with no interest. Often, the sales price is increased to offset the loan costs.

zipper clause, also called WRAP-UP CLAUSE, portion of a collective bargaining contract that specifically states that the written agreement is complete and anything not contained in it is not agreed to. A typical zipper clause might read: "This contract is complete in itself and sets forth all the terms and conditions of the agreement between the parties hereto." The main purpose of the zipper or wrap-up clause is to prevent either party from demanding a renewal of negotiations during the life of the contract. It also serves to limit the freedom of a grievance arbitrator because his rulings must be based solely on the written agreement's contents.

zone of acceptance, also called ACCEPTANCE THEORY OF AUTHORITY, concept that authority stems from the bottom up, based on the extent to which individuals are willing to hold in abeyance their own critical faculties and accept the directives of their organizational superiors. The "zone of acceptance" itself is a theoretical range of tolerance within which organizational members will accept orders without question.

zone of employment, the physical area (usually the place of employment and surrounding areas controlled by the employer) within which an employee is eligible for workers' compensation benefits when injured, whether or not on the job at the time.

zone of indifference, concept that comes from Chester I. Barnard's *The Functions of the Executive* (Cambridge, Mass.: Harvard University Press, 1938). According to Barnard:

> If all the orders for actions reasonably practicable be arranged in the order of their acceptability to the person affected, it may be conceived that there are a number which are clearly unacceptable, that is, which certainly will not be obeyed; there is another group somewhat more or less on the neutral line, that is, either barely acceptable or barely unacceptable; and a third group unquestionably acceptable. This last group lies within the "zone of indifference." The person affected will accept orders lying within this zone and is relatively indifferent as to what the order is so far as the question of authority is concerned.

zone of uncertainty, range or zone of test scores within which it cannot truly be said that differing scores actually represent differing levels of attainment.

zoning, the process by which local government can designate the types of structures and activities that can be built and performed in a particular area. It started in the 1920s and involves a highly complex legal process which is often impacted by local politics.

zoning, inclusionary, zoning practice that requires builders to provide (at reduced rates) a portion of new housing units for moderate and low income families.

Z score, another way of referring to a standard score.

BIBLIOGRAPHY

Alcoholics Anonymous World Services. *Alcoholics Anonymous. The Story of How Many Thousands of Men and Women Have Recovered From Alcoholism* (3rd edition). New York: Alcoholics Anonymous World Services, 1976.

Alderson, George and Sentman, Everett. *How You Can Influence Congress: The Complete Handbook for the Citizen Lobbyist.* New York: E.P. Dutton, 1979.

Alinsky, Saul D. *Rules for Radicals.* New York: Vintage Paperbacks, 1971.

Allen, Herb (Editor). *The Bread Game.* San Francisco: Glide Publications, 1974.

Allen, Kerry Ken, et al. *Volunteers From the Workplace.* Washington, D.C.: National Center for Voluntary Action, 1979.

American Association of Fund-Raising Counsel, Inc. *Giving USA: A Compilation of Facts and Trends on American Philanthropy.* Annual Report.

American Institute of Certified Public Accountants. *Statement of Position 78-10: Accounting Principles and Reporting Practices for Certain Nonprofit Organizations.* New York: AICPA, 1979.

American Psychological Association. *Publication Manual* (3rd edition). Washington, D.C.: American Psychological Association, 1983.

Andrews, F. Emerson. *Philanthropic Foundations.* New York: Russell Sage Foundation, 1956.

Anthony, Robert N. and Herzlinger, Regina E. *Management Control in Nonprofit Organizations* (revised edition). Homewood, IL: Richard Irwin, 1980.

Arthur Andersen & Co. *Tax Economics of Charitable Giving.* Chicago: Arthur Andersen & Co., 1979.

Bakal, Carl. *Charity USA* (2nd edition). New York: Times Books, 1980.

Becker, Sarah and Glenn, Donna. *Off Your Duffs and Up the Assets: Common Sense for Nonprofit Managers.* Rockville Center, NY: Farnsworth, 1985.

Broce, Thomas E. *Fund Raising: The Guide to Raising Money from Private Sources.* Norman, OK: The University of Oklahoma Press, 1979.

Callaghan, Christopher and Connors, Tracy. *Financial Management for Nonprofit Organizations.* New York: American Management Association, 1982.

Colorado Department of Health. *Colorado Ambulance Service Management Handbook.* Denver, CO: Colorado Department of Health, 1984.

Commission on Private Philanthropy and Public Needs (The Filer Commission). *Giving in America.* Washington, D.C.: Department of the Treasury, 1975.

Bibliography

Commission on Private Philanthropy and Public Needs (the Filer Commission). *Research Papers*. Washington, D.C.: Department of the Treasury, 1977.

Commission on Foundations and Private Philanthropy (the Peterson Commission). *Foundations, Private Giving and Public Policy*. Chicago: University of Chicago Press, 1970.

Connors, Tracy D. (Editor in Chief). *The Nonprofit Organization Handbook*. New York: McGraw-Hill Book Company, 1980.

Conrad, William and Glenn, William. *The Effective Voluntary Board of Directors: What It Is and How It Works* (3rd edition). Chicago: The Swallow Press, 1980.

The Co-op Handbook Collective. *The Food Co-op Handbook: How to Bypass Supermarkets to Control the Quality and Price of the Food You Eat*. Boston: Houghton Mifflin, 1975.

Crimmins, James C. and Keil, Mary. *Enterprise in the Nonprofit Sector*. New York: Partners for Livable Places and the Rockefeller Brothers Fund, 1983.

Cuninggim, Merrimon. *Private Money and Public Service: The Role of Foundations in American Society*. New York: McGraw-Hill, 1972.

Curtis, Joan C. *I Love My Child But I Need Help. . ., How To Develop a Crisis Nursery*. Washington, D.C.: National Center on Child Abuse and Neglect, Children's Bureau, 1977.

Fisher, John. *How to Manage a Nonprofit Organization*. Toronto: Management and Fund Raising Centre, 1978.

Flanagan, Joan. *The Grass Roots Fundraising Book: How to Raise Money in a Community*. Chicago: The Swallow Press, 1977.

Flanagan, Joan. *The Successful Volunteer Organization: Getting Started and Getting Results in Nonprofit, Charitable, Grass Roots, and Community Groups*. Chicago: Contemporary Books, 1981.

Freeman, David F. *The Handbook on Private Foundations*. Washington, D.C.: Council on Foundations, 1981.

Gaby, Patricia V. and Gaby, Daniel M. *Nonprofit Organization Handbook: A Guide to Fundraising, Grants, Lobbying, Membership Building, Publicity and Public Relations*. Englewood Cliffs, NJ: Prentice-Hall, Inc., 1979.

Gross, Malvern J., Jr. and Warshauer, William, Jr. *Financial and Accounting Guide for Nonprofit Organizations* (3rd edition). New York: Ronald Press, 1979.

Hardy, James M. *Corporate Planning for Nonprofit Organizations*. New York: Association Press, 1972.

Heimann, Fritz F. (Editor). *The Future of Foundations*. Englewood Cliffs, NJ: Prentice-Hall, for the American Assembly, 1973.

Hopkins, Bruce R. *The Law of Tax Exempt Organizations* (4th edition). New York: John Wiley & Sons, Inc., 1980.

Horowitz, Laura, et al. *Community Action Tool Catalog: Techniques and Strategies for Successful Action Programs* (2nd edition). Washington, D.C.: American Association of University Women, 1978.

Horwitz, Tem. *Arts Administration: How to Set Up and Run a Successful Nonprofit Arts Organization*. Chicago: Chicago Review Press, 1978.

Internal Revenue Service, Department of the Treasury. "Tax Information for Private Foundations and Foundation Managers" Publication 578. Washington, D.C.: Government Printing Office, November 1978.

Internal Revenue Service, Department of the Treasury. "Application for Recognition of Exemption" (Federal Package 1023). Washington, D.C.: Government Printing Office, March 1979.

Internal Revenue Service, Department of the Treasury. "How to Apply for and Retain Exempt Status for Your Organization" (Publication 557). Washington, D.C.: Government Printing Office, February 1980.

Institute for Voluntary Organizations. *Designs for Creative Management* (revised edition). Chicago: Institute for Voluntary Organization, 1983.

Kahn, Si. *How People Get Power: Organizing Oppressed Communities for Action.* New York: McGraw-Hill Paperbacks, 1970.

Kiritz, Norton J. *Program Planning and Proposal Writing* (expanded version). Los Angeles: The Grantsmanship Center, 1980.

Koch, Frank. *The New Corporate Philanthropy: How Society and Business Can Profit.* New York: Plenum Press, 1979.

Kotler, Philip. *Marketing for Nonprofit Organizations* (2nd edition). Englewood Cliffs, NJ: Prentice-Hall, 1975.

Kurzig, Carol M. *Foundation Fundamentals: A Guide for Grantseekers.* New York: The Foundation Center, 1980.

Lesly, Philip (Editor). *Lesly's Public Relations Handbook* (2nd edition). Englewood Cliffs, NJ: Prentice-Hall, 1978.

Levin, Nora Jean and Steiger, Janet Dempsey. *To Light One Candle: A Manual for Organizing, Funding and Maintaining Public Service Projects.* Chicago: American Bar Association, 1978.

Levy, Howard and Ross-Molloy, Lynn. *Beginning a Community Museum.* New York: The Publishing Center for Cultural Resources, 1975.

Lindberg, Roy A. and Cohn, Theodore. *Survival and Growth: Management Strategies for the Small Firm.* New York: American Management Association, 1978.

Lohmann, Robert A. *Breaking Even: Financial Management in Human Service Organizations.* Philadelphia, PA: Temple University Press, 1980.

Mason, Diane, Jensen, Gayle and Ryzewocz, Carolyn. *How to Grow a Parents' Group.* Western Springs, IL: CDG Enterprises, 1979.

McConkey, Dale D. *MBO for Nonprofit Organizations.* New York: American Management Association, 1975.

Montana, Patrick J. *Marketing in Nonprofit Organizations.* New York: AMACOM, 1978.

Montana, Patrick J. and Borst, Diane (Editors). *Managing Nonprofit Organizations.* New York: American Management Association, 1977.

Nason, John W. *Trustees and the Future of Foundations.* New York: Council on Foundations, Inc., 1977.

Nelson, Charles A. and Turk, Frederick J. *Financial Management for the Arts—A Guidebook for Arts Organizations.* New York: Associated Councils of the Arts, 1975.

Newman, Danny. *Subscribe Now! Building Arts Audiences Through Dynamic Subscription Promotion.* New York: Publishing Center for Cultural Resources, 1977.

Nicholas, Ted. *Nonprofit Tax Exempt Corporations: The Alternative Tax Shelter.* Wilmington, DE: Enterprise Publishing, 1980, 1982.

Nielsen, Waldemar A. *The Endangered Sector.* New York: Columbia University Press, 1980.

O'Connell, Brian. *Effective Leadership in Voluntary Organizations.* Chicago: Follet Publishing, 1976.

O'Connell, Brian (Editor). *America's Voluntary Spirit.* New York: The Foundation Center, 1983.

Oleck, Howard L. *Non-Profit Corporations, Organizations, and Associations* (3rd edition). Englewood Cliffs, NJ: Prentice-Hall, Inc., 1980.

Oran, Daniel and Shafritz, Jay M. *The MBA's Dictionary.* Reston, VA: Reston Publishing Company, 1983.

Orlans, Harold (Editor). *Nonprofit Organizations: A Government Management Tool.* New York: Praeger Publishers, 1980.

Price, A. Rae (Editor). *Increasing the Impact: 1980s.* Battle Creek, MI: The W. K. Kellogg Foundation, August 1985.

Ramanthan, Kavasseri V. *Management Control in Nonprofit Organizations.* New York: John Wiley and Sons, 1982.

Ramanthan, Kavasseri V., and Hegstad, Larry P. (Editors). *Readings in Management Control of Nonprofit Organizations.* New York: John Wiley and Sons, 1982.

Robert, Gen. Henry M. *Robert's Rules of Order, Revised.* New York: Morrow Quill Paperbacks, 1971.

Robert, Sarah Corbin. *Robert's Rules of Order Newly Revised.* Palo Alto, CA: Scott, Foresman & Co., 1981.

Russell, John M. *Giving and Taking: Across the Foundation Desk.* New York: Teachers College Press, 1977.

Schindler-Rainman, Eva and Lippit, Ronald. *The Volunteer Community: Creative Use of Human Resource* (2nd edition). La Jolla, CA: University Associates, 1975.

Seymour, Harold J. *Designs for Fund-Raising: Principles, Patterns, Techniques.* New York: McGraw-Hill Book Co., 1966.

Shafritz, Jay M. *The Facts on File Dictionary of Public Administration.* New York: Facts on File, 1985.

Shellow, Jill R. *The Grantseekers Guide: A Directory for Social and Economic Justice Projects.* Chicago: National Network of Grantmakers, 1981.

Shields, Laurie. *Displaced Homemakers: Organizing for a New Life.* New York: McGraw-Hill Paperbacks, 1981.

Simon, John G., Powers, Charles W. and Gunnemann, Jon P. *The Ethical Investor.* New Haven, CT: Yale University Press, 1972.

Struckhoff, Eugene C. *The Handbook for Community Foundations: Their Formation, Development and Operation* (2 volumes). New York: Council on Foundations, Inc., 1977.

Strunk, William, Jr. and White, E.F. *The Elements of Style* (3rd edition). New York: Macmillan Paperbacks, 1979.

Subry, Richard L., et al. *Program Planning and Analysis.* Denver, CO: Applied Management Corporation, 1977.

Subry, Richard L., et al. *Results Management.* Denver, CO: Applied Management Corporation, 1977.

Thomas, Patricia. *Why Establish a Private Foundation?* Atlanta, GA: Southeastern Council of Foundations, 1980.

Traub, Jack. *Accounting and Reporting Practices of Private Foundations: A Critical Evaluation.* New York: Praeger Publications, 1977.

Treusch, Paul E. and Sugarman, Norman A. *Tax-Exempt Charitable Organizations.* Philadelphia, PA: The American Law Institute, 1979.

Vanguard Public Foundation. *Robin Hood was Right: A Guide to Giving Your Money for Social Change.* San Francisco: Vanguard Public Foundation, 1977.

Weaver, Warren. *U.S. Philanthropic Foundations: Their History, Structure, Management and Record.* New York: Harper and Row, 1967.

Weber, Joseph. *Managing the Board of Directors.* New York: Greater New York Fund, 1975.

Weiss, Carol. *Evaluation Research: Methods of Assessing Program Effectiveness.* Englewood Cliffs, NJ: Prentice-Hall, Inc., 1972.

Wholey, Joseph S., Abramson, Mark A., & Bellavita, Christopher. Performance and Credibility. Lexington, MA: Lexington Books, 1985.

Whitaker, Ben. *The Philanthropoids: Foundations and Society.* New York: William Morrow and Company, Inc., 1974.

Wholey, Joseph S., Abramson, Mark A., & Bellavita, Christopher. Performance and Credibility. Lexington, MA: Lexington Books, 1985.

Wilson, Marlene. *The Effective Management of Volunteer Programs.* Boulder, CO: Volunteer Management Associates, 1976.

Wolf, Thomas. *The Nonprofit Organization: An Operating Manual.* Englewood Cliffs, NJ: Prentice-Hall, Inc., 1984.

"Fergus is gifted in his ability to portray the perceptions and emotions of women. He writes with tremendous insight and sensitivity about the individual community and the political and religious issues of the time, many of which are still relevant today. This book is artistically rendered with meticulous attention to small details that bring to life the daily concerns of a group of hardy souls at a pivotal time in U.S. history." —*Booklist*

"[May] and the other brides rise from the underbelly of society, becoming the most noble characters in this imaginative tale of the American West reeling under the decline of one culture and the forcible ascent of another." —*Publishers Weekly*

"In a word, *One Thousand White Women* is terrific! What Jim Fergus has done within these pages is give life and voice to an aspect of the American West and its native peoples that has been, if not covered up, too long overlooked. It is a tremendous achievement by a remarkable writer." —David Seybold, editor of *Boats* and *Fathers and Sons*

"*One Thousand White Women* is definitely a fresh twist on the traditional Western. Fergus has started his career as a novelist with a book rich in the results of personal fervor and study, and one that reflects a sensitive imagination. Fans of Western fiction and students of American frontier history can confidently add this novel to their summer reading list." —*San Antonio Express News*

"Jim Fergus's powerful first novel is a surefire winner. I read it nonstop and would now like to propose a hundred-year moratorium on all books about white women in the Old West, since it will take the rest of us at least that long to amass the research—not to mention the compassion—needed to equal this fine work. A masterful job!" —Robert F. Jones, author of *Tie My Bones to Her Back*

"This is a rich, beautifully conceived, rollicking novel, literally bursting with original characters and with the profound joy and heartbreak of the real history of the American West. May Dodd may be the most compellingly alive fictional character of that history since Little Big Man." —Charles Gaines, author of *A Family Place, Stay Hungry, Pumping Iron,* and *Survival Games*

ONE THOUSAND WHITE WOMEN

The Journals of May Dodd

Jim Fergus

ST. MARTIN'S PRESS
NEW YORK

Bird drawings by Loren G. Smith

Design by Nancy Resnick

Library of Congress Cataloging-in-Publication Data

Fergus, Jim.
One thousand white women : the journals of May Dodd / Jim Fergus.—1st ed.
p. cm.
ISBN 0-312-18008-X
1. Cheyenne Indians—Fiction. I. Title.
PS3556.E66054 1998
813'.54—dc21 97-37118
CIP

10 9 8 7 6 5 4

To Dillon

→ ACKNOWLEDGMENTS ←

Writing careers in general, and the writing of novels in particular, can be accurately, if somewhat unromantically, likened to rolling large boulders uphill. Sometimes the writer needs a little help, and if we're very lucky, people come along at opportune moments and not only offer a word of encouragement, but actually put their shoulder to the boulder and help us to move it forward. I have been that lucky, and owe thanks to many people — friends, family, and colleagues — for the existence of this book. So special and grateful thanks to all of the following:

To Barney Donnelley, without whose faith and generosity I couldn't have been a writer. To my agent Al Zuckerman, the quintessential pro, whose unfailing instincts culled this story out of the rockpile. To my editor, Jennifer Enderlin, for her constant enthusiasm for this project, her hard work, good cheer, and impeccable editorial judgment. To Laton McCartney, for years of wise council and boundless optimism. To Jon Williams, whose early turn at this particular boulder encouraged me to continue pushing. To Bob Wallace, who gave me my first magazine assignment almost twenty years ago, and, remarkably, stepped back into my professional life once again as editor in chief just in time to oversee this much-belated "first" novel. To Bonny Hawley and Douglas Tate, for invaluable insights and information on British place, name, and character. To Laurie Morrow, for her precise woman's perspective on the subject of romantic attraction. To Rev. Rolland W. Hoverstock, for critical information about the Episcopal church and ceremonies circa 1875. To Sister Thérèse de la Valdène, for providing always cherished retreats at Dogwood Farms, and to Guy de la Valdène, for wonderful dinners and a large vote of confidence when it was most needed. Finally, thanks to Dillon for cheerfully occupying over the past fifteen years the nearly always thankless role of writer's spouse.

While the author acknowledges the help and support of all of the above people in the creation of this novel, he accepts full responsibilities for any of its shortcomings.

Five percent of the author's royalties earned on the sale of *One Thousand White Women* will be donated to the St. Labre Indian School, Ashland, Montana 59004.

Women will love her, that she is a woman
More worth than any man; men that she is
The rarest of all women.

—William Shakespeare,
The Winter's Tale V, 1

→ AUTHOR'S NOTE ←

In spite of efforts to convince the reader to the contrary, this book is entirely a work of fiction. However, the seed that grew into a novel was sown in the author's imagination by an actual historical event: in 1854 at a peace conference at Fort Laramie, a prominent Northern Cheyenne chief requested of the U.S. Army authorities the gift of one thousand white women as brides for his young warriors. Because theirs is a matrilineal society in which all children born belong to their mother's tribe, this seemed to the Cheyennes to be the perfect means of assimilation into the white man's world—a terrifying new world that even as early as 1854, the Native Americans clearly recognized held no place for them. Needless to say, the Cheyennes' request was not well received by the white authorities—the peace conference collapsed, the Cheyennes went home, and, of course, the white women did not come. In this novel they do.

Certain other historical events are here rendered, but in an entirely fictitious manner. At the same time, the real names of certain actual historical figures are used in this novel, but the characters themselves are fictional creations. In all other respects this book is a work of fiction. Names, characters, places, dates, geographical descriptions are all either the product of the author's imagination or are used fictitiously. Any resemblance to actual persons, living or dead, or to actual events or locales is entirely coincidental.

Finally, while a genuine attempt was made to render the Cheyenne language as accurately as possible, certain misspellings and misuses inevitably occur in this book. For these errors, the author offers sincere apologies to the Cheyenne people.

INTRODUCTION

by J. Will Dodd

As a child growing up in Chicago, I used to scare my kid brother, Jimmy, silly at night telling him stories about our mad ancestor, May Dodd, who lived in an insane asylum and ran off to live with Indians—at least that was the fertile, if somewhat vague, raw material of secret family legend.

We lived on Lake Shore Drive and our family was still quite wealthy in those days, descendants of "old" money—a fortune and a dynasty begun by our great-great-grandfather, J. Hamilton Dodd, who as a young man in the mid–nineteenth century began plowing up the vast Midwestern prairies around Chicago in order to cultivate grain in what was some of the most fertile farmland in the world. "Papa," as he is still known by his descendants, was one of the original founders of the Chicago Board of Trade; he was friend, crony, business partner, and competitor, as the case might be, of all the most prominent entrepreneurs in that booming Midwestern metropolis—among them Cyrus McCormick, inventor of the reaper, Philip Armour and Gustavus Swift, the famous pork and beef packers, and the brothers Charles and Nathan Mears, lumbermen who bought up and single-handedly destroyed the great old-growth white pine forests of Michigan.

No one in our family spoke much about my great-grandmother May Dodd. Among the wealthy, ancestral insanity has always been a source of deep-rooted embarrassment. Even these many generations later, when the razor-sharp robber-baron genes have been largely blunted by line-breeding and soft country-club living, by boarding school and Ivy League educations, even now no one in our social milieu likes to admit to being directly descended from a crazy woman. In the heavily edited official family history, May Dodd remains little more than a footnote: *"Born March 23, 1850... second daughter of J. Hamilton and Hortense Dodd. Hospitalized at age 23 for a nervous disorder. Died in hospital, February 17, 1876."* That's it.

But even old-money taciturnity—for which there is no competition on earth—and the equally unparalleled ability of the rich to keep dark secrets, could not completely obscure the whispered rumors that trickled down through the generations that May Dodd had actually died under somewhat mysterious circumstances—not in the hospital as officially stated, but somewhere out West. This was the story that fueled my and my brother Jimmy's imaginations.

By the time I was a junior in college, our father had squandered most of the family fortune, which had by then already been vastly diluted by a couple of generations of unproductive heirs—what people used to call "wastrels." Pop finished it off with a series of bad investments in Chicago commercial real estate just when that market was collapsing, and then he managed to break a trust and drink away the last bit of money that was to pay for his sons' higher education. Partly as a result of this Jimmy got drafted—which was almost unheard of in our circles—and sent to Vietnam, where he was killed when he stepped on a land mine in a rice paddy in the Mekong Delta. Less than six months later, Pop drank himself to death.

I was luckier than my brother and managed to stay in college, drew a high lottery number, and graduated with a degree in journalism, armed with which I eventually became the editor in chief of the city magazine *Chitown*.

It was while researching a piece for the magazine about the old scions of Chicago that I happened to come again across May Dodd's name. I remembered the tales that I used to tell Jimmy, and I wondered where I had first heard the rumor that she had gone "out West to live with Indians"—which in our family had become a kind of euphemism for insanity.

I started poking around in the family archives, casually at first, then with greater and greater interest—some might even say obsession. One letter, reportedly written by May Dodd from inside the asylum to her children, Hortense and William, who were just infants at the time of her incarceration, had survived. Source of both the old family rumor, as well as proof positive of how crazy May really was, this letter was for me the beginning of a long, strange journey.

I took a leave of absence from my job at the magazine in order to devote myself full-time to following the convoluted trail of May Dodd's life. My research led me eventually to the Tongue River Indian reservation in southeastern Montana. It was here, armed with my family letter as proof of my ancestry, that I was finally granted access to the following journals, which have remained among the Cheyennes—a sacred tribal treasure for well over a hundred years. I need hardly add that the tale they tell of U.S. government intrigue *cum* social experiment has also remained one of the best-kept secrets in Western American history.

The following prologue to the journals briefly describes the historical events that led to May Dodd's story, and is based on several sources, including newspaper accounts of the time, the *Congressional Record,* the *Annual Report to the Commissioner of Indian Affairs,* correspondence from the files of the Adjutant General's Office in the National Archives in Washington, D.C., as well as various materials available in Chicago's Newberry Library. The Indian point of view pertaining to Little Wolf's visit to Washington in 1874, and the subsequent chain of events is based on Northern Cheyenne oral history recounted to me by Harold Wild Plums in Lame Elk, Montana, in October 1996.

PROLOGUE

⇢⇠

In September of 1874, the great Cheyenne "Sweet Medicine Chief" Little Wolf made the long overland journey to Washington, D.C., with a delegation of his tribesmen for the express purpose of making a lasting peace with the whites. Having spent the weeks prior to his trip smoking and softly discussing various peace initiatives with his tribal council of forty-four chiefs, Little Wolf came to the nation's capital with a somewhat novel, though from the Cheyenne worldview, perfectly rational plan that would ensure a safe and prosperous future for his greatly beseiged people.

The Indian leader was received in Washington with all the pomp and circumstance accorded to the visiting head of state of a foreign land. At a formal ceremony in the Capitol building with President Ulysses S. Grant, and members of a specially appointed congressional commission, Little Wolf was presented with the Presidential Peace Medal—a large ornate silver medallion—that the Chief, with no intentional irony, a thing unknown to the Cheyennes, would later wear in battle against the U.S. Army in the Cheyennes' final desperate days as a free people. Grant's profile appeared on one side of the medal, ringed by the words: LET US HAVE PEACE LIBERTY JUSTICE AND EQUALITY; on the other side an open Bible lay atop a rake, a plow, an ax, a shovel, and sundry other farming implements with the words: ON EARTH PEACE GOOD WILL TOWARD MEN 1874.

Also in attendance on this historic occasion were the President's wife, Julia, who had begged her husband to be allowed to attend so that she might see the Indians in all their savage regalia, and a few favored members of the Washington press corps. The date was September 18, 1874.

Old daguerreotype photographs of the assembly show the Cheyennes dressed in their finest ceremonial attire—ornately beaded moccasins; hide leggings from the fringe of which dangled chattering elk teeth; deerskin war shirts, trimmed at the seams with the scalps of enemies and elaborately ornamented with beads and dyed porcupine quills. They wore hammered silver coins in their hair, and brass-wire and otter-fur bands in their braids. Washingtonians had never seen anything quite like it.

Although over fifty years old by this time, Little Wolf looked at least a decade younger than his age. He was lean and sinewy, with aquiline nose and flared nostrils, high, ruddy cheekbones, and burnished bronze skin that bore the deep pockmarks of a smallpox epidemic that had ravaged the Cheyenne tribe in 1865. The Chief was not a large man, but he carried himself with great bearing—head held high, an expression of innate fierceness and defiance on his face. His demeanor would later be characterized by newspaper accounts as "haughty" and "insolent."

Expressing himself through an interpreter by the name of Amos Chapman from Fort Supply, Kansas, Little Wolf came directly to the point. "It is the Cheyenne way that all children who enter this world belong to their mother's tribe," he began, addressing the President of the United States, though he did not look directly in Grant's eyes as this was considered bad manners among his people. "My father was Arapaho and my mother Cheyenne. Thus I was raised by my mother's people, and I am Cheyenne. But I have always been free to come and go among the Arapaho, and in this way I learned also their way of life. This, we believe, is a good thing." At this point in his address, Little Wolf would ordinarily have puffed on his pipe, giving all those present a chance to consider what he had thus far said. However, with usual white man bad manners, the Great White Father had neglected to provide a pipe at this important gathering.

The Chief continued: "The People [The Cheyennes referred to themselves simply as *Tsitsistas*—the People] are a small tribe, smaller than either the Sioux or the Arapaho; we have never been numerous because we understand that the earth can only carry a certain number of the People, just as it can only carry a certain number of the bears, the wolves, the elks, the pronghorns, and all the rest of the animals. For if there are too many of any animal, this animal starves until there is the right number again. We would rather be few in number and have enough for everyone to eat, than be too many and all starve. Because of the sickness you have brought us (here Little Wolf touched his pockmarked cheek), and the war you have waged upon us (here he touched his breast; he had been wounded numerous times in battle), we are now even fewer. Soon the People will disappear altogether, as the buffalo in our country disappear. I am the Sweet Medicine Chief. My duty is to see that my People survive. To do this we must enter the white man's world—our children must become members of your tribe. Therefore we ask the Great Father for the gift of one thousand white women as wives, to teach us and our children the new life that must be lived when the buffalo are gone."

Now a collective gasp rose from the room, peppered with scattered exclamations of astonishment. To interrupt a man while he was speaking, except to utter soft murmurs of approbation, was an act of gross impoliteness to the Cheyennes, and this outburst angered Little Wolf. But the Chief knew that white people did not know how to behave, and he was not surprised. Still, he paused for a moment to let the crowd settle and to allow his chiefly displeasure to be registered by all present.

"In this way," Little Wolf continued, "our warriors will plant the Cheyenne seed into the bellies of your white women. Our seed will sprout and grow inside their wombs, and the next generation of Cheyenne children will be born into your tribe, with the full privileges attendant to that position."

At exactly this point in Little Wolf's address, President Grant's wife, Julia, fainted dead away on the floor, swooned right from her chair with a long, gurgling sigh like the death rattle of a lung-shot buffalo cow. (It was unseasonably hot in the room that day, and in her memoirs, Julia Dent Grant would maintain that the heat, not moral squeamishness at the idea of the savages breeding with white girls, had caused her to faint.)

As aides rushed to the First Lady's side, the President, reddening in the face, began to rise unsteadily to his feet. Little Wolf recognized that Grant was drunk and, considering the solemnity of the occasion, the Chief felt that this constituted a fairly serious breach of etiquette.

"For your gift of one thousand white women," Little Wolf continued in a stern, louder voice over the rising clamor (although at this point interpreter Chapman was practically whispering), "we will give you one thousand horses. Five hundred wild horses and five hundred horses already broke."

Now Little Wolf raised his hand as if in papal benediction, concluding his speech with immense dignity and bearing. "From this day forward the blood of our people shall be forever joined."

But by then all hell had broken loose in the room and hardly anyone heard the great leader's final remarks. Senators blustered and pounded the table. "Arrest the heathens!" someone called out, and the row of soldiers flanking the hall fell into formation, bayonets at the ready position. In response, the Cheyenne chiefs all stood up in unison, instinctively drawing knives and forming a circle, shoulders touching, in the way that a bevy of quail beds down at night to protect itself from predators.

President Grant had also gained his feet, swaying slightly, his face scarlet, pointing his finger at Little Wolf, and thundering, *"Outrageous! Outrageous!"* Little Wolf had heard that the President was a great warrior and a man much respected by his enemies. Still, the Sweet Medicine Chief did not care to be pointed at in this impertinent manner, and if he'd had his quirt with him, he'd have knocked the Great Father, drunk or not, to his knees for this behavior. Little Wolf was infamous among his people for his temper—slow to be aroused but grizzlylike in ferocity.

Order was finally restored. The Cheyennes put their knives up, and the guards quickly ushered the Indian delegation out of the hall without further incident, the great chief striding proudly at their head.

That night doors were locked all over Washington, shades pulled, wives and daughters forbidden to go outside as word of the Cheyennes' blasphemous proposal swept the capital. The next day's newspaper headlines further fanned the flames of racist fears and civic hysteria: **"Savages Demand White Women Love Slaves!," "White Brides for the Red Devils!," "Grant to Swap Injuns: White Girls for Wild Horses!"** In what must surely have been every nineteenth-century American man's worst nightmare, those few citizens who did venture out with women on their arms over the next few days cast furtive glances over their shoulders, keeping an anxious watch out for the hordes of mounted redskins they secretly feared might swoop down upon them, wailing like banshees as they lifted scalps with a single slash of glinting knife blade, to carry off their shrieking womenfolk and populate the earth with half-breeds.

Official response to Little Wolf's unusual treaty offer was swift; a tone of high moral outrage dominated the proclamations of the Congress, while the administration itself moved quickly to assure a nervous citizenry that *no*, white women would certainly not be traded to the heathens and, *yes*, immediate steps were being taken by the U.S. military to ensure that the virtue of American womanhood would be well protected.

Two days later Little Wolf and his entourage were packed inside a cattle car and escorted by armed guard out of the nation's capital. Word of the Indians' peace initiative had leaked out over the telegraph wires, and angry citizens wielding denunciatory placards turned out in lynch mob–like crowds along the way to taunt the Cheyennes as they passed, pelting their train car with rotten fruit and racist epithets.

At the same time that the Northern Cheyennes were being booed from train platforms across the Midwest, another parallel, and far more interesting national phenomenon was gaining momentum. Women from all over the country were responding to the Cheyennes' marriage proposal—telegraphing and writing letters to the White House, volunteering their services as brides. Not all of these women were crackpots, and they seemed to cut a wide socioeconomic and racial swath: everything from single working girls in the cities looking to spice up their drab lives with some adventure; to recently emancipated former slaves hoping to escape the sheer drudgery of post-slavery life in the cotton mills, sweat shops, and factories of newly industrialized America; to young women widowed in the War

Between the States. We know now that the Grant administration did not turn a deaf ear to their inquiries.

In private and after the initial uproar had abated, the President and his advisors had to admit that Little Wolf's unprecedented plan for assimilation of the Cheyennes made a certain practical sense. Having already implemented his Indian Peace Policy, which gave over management of the Indian reservations to the American Church, Grant was willing to consider any peaceful solutions to the still explosive situation on the Great Plains—a situation that impeded economic progress and promised yet more bloodshed for frontier settlers.

Thus was born the "Brides for Indians" (or "BFI" program, as its secret acronym became known in the President's inner circle). Besides placating the savages with this generous gift of brides, the administration believed that the "Noble American Woman," working in concert with the church, might also exert a positive influence upon the Cheyennes—to educate and elevate them from barbarism to civilized life.

Other members of the President's cabinet continued to champion the original plan for resolution of the "Indian problem," and it was understood by all concerned that any recaltrant tribes would still be subject to the "final solution" of military annihilation.

Yet while the genocide of an entire race of native people was considered by many to be morally palatable and politically expedient, even the more progressive members of the Grant cabinet were aware that the notion of white women interbreeding with the savages would never wash with the American public. Thus, in a series of highly secretive, top-level meetings on the subject, the administration decided, in age-old fashion, to take matters into its own hands—to launch its own covert matrimonial operation.

Grant's people assuaged their political conscience with the proviso that all of the women involved in this audacious experiment be volunteers—really little different than mail-order brides—with the added moral legitimacy of being under the wing of the church. Official rationale had it that if these socially conscientious and adventuresome women chose to go West and live with the Indians of their own volition, and if in the process, the Cheyennes were distracted from their warlike ways, then everyone benefited; a perfect Jeffersonian example of government greasing the wheels of social altruism and individual initiative.

If the "Brides for Indians" program had an Achilles' heel, the administration knew that it lay in its plan to supplement an anticipated shortage of volunteers by recruiting women out of jails, penitentiaries, debtors' prisons, and mental institutions—offering full pardons or unconditional release, as the case might be, to those who agreed to sign on for the program. One fact that the government had finally learned in its dealings with the natives, was that these were a literal people who expected treaties to be fulfilled to the letter. When the Cheyennes negotiated for one thousand brides, they meant exactly that number—and in return would deliver exactly one thousand horses to fulfill their end of the bargain. Any discrepancy in these figures would be sufficient cause to send the Indians back on the warpath. The administration intended to ensure that this did not occur—even if it meant early release of a few low-level felons or minor mental defectives.

The first trainload of white women bound for the northern Great Plains and their new lives as brides of the Cheyenne nation left Washington under a veil of total secrecy late one night the following spring, early March 1875—just over six months after Chief Little Wolf made his startling public request of President Grant. Over the next several weeks trains departed stations in New York, Boston, Philadelphia, and Chicago.

On March 23, 1875, a young woman by the name of May Dodd, age twenty-five years to the day, formerly a patient in the Lake Forest Lunatic Asylum, a private facility thirty miles north of Chicago, boarded the Union Pacific train at Union Station, with forty-seven other volunteers and recruits from the Chicago region—their destination Camp Robinson, Nebraska Territory.

[NOTE: The following journals are largely unedited, and, except for very minor corrections in spelling and punctuation have been here transcribed exactly as written by their author, May Dodd. Contained within May Dodd's journals, are several letters addressed to family members and friends. There is no indication that any of these letters were ever mailed, and they appear to have served the author primarily as a way for her to "speak" to individuals in her notebooks. It is also probable that May left this correspondence, as she says of the journals themselves, to be read later by her family in the event that she not survive her adventure. These letters, too, are presented in the order and form in which they appear in the original notebooks.]

THE JOURNALS OF MAY DODD

NOTEBOOK I

A Train Bound for Glory

"Frankly, from the way I have been treated by the so-called 'civilized' people in my life, I rather look forward to residency among the savages."

(from the journals of May Dodd)

→←

[NOTE: The following entry, undated, appears on the first page of the first notebook of May Dodd's journal.]

I leave this record for my dear children, Hortense and William, in the event that they never see their loving mother again and so that they might one day know the truth of my unjust incarceration, my escape from Hell, and into whatever is to come in these pages . . .

23 March 1875

Today is my birthday, and I have received the greatest gift of all—freedom! I make these first poor scribblings aboard the westbound Union Pacific train which departed Union Station Chicago at 6:35 a.m. this morning, bound for Nebraska Territory. We are told that it will be a fourteen-day trip with many stops along the way, and with a change of trains in Omaha. Although our final destination was intended to have been concealed from us, I have ascertained from overhearing conversations among our military escort (they underestimate a woman's auditory powers) that we are being taken first to Fort Sidney aboard the train—from there transported by wagon train to Fort Laramie, Wyoming Territory, and then on to Camp Robinson, Nebraska Territory.

How strange is life. To think that I would find myself on this train, embarking upon this long journey, watching the city retreating behind me. I sit facing backwards on the train in order to have a last glimpse of Chicago, the layer of dense black coal smoke that daily creeps out over the beach of Lake Michigan like a giant parasol, the muddy, bustling city passing by me for the last time. How I have missed this loud, raucous city since my dark and silent incarceration. And now I feel like a character in a theater play, torn from the real world, acting out some terrible and as yet unwritten role. How I envy these people I watch from the train window, hurrying off to the safety of their daily travails while we are borne off, captives of fate into the great unknown void.

Now we pass the new shanties that ring the city, that have sprung up everywhere since the great fire of '71. Little more than cobbled-together scraps of lumber they teeter in the wind like houses of cards, to form a kind of rickety fence around the perimeters of Chicago—as if somehow trying to contain the sprawling metropolis. Filthy half-dressed children play in muddy yards and stare blankly at us as we pass, as if we, or perhaps they, are creatures from some other world. How I long for my own dear children! What I would give to see them one last time, to hold them . . . now I press my hand against the train window to wave to one tiny child who reminds me somehow of my own sweet son William, but this poor child's hair is fair and greasy, hanging in dirty ringlets around his mud-streaked face. His eyes are intensely blue and he raises his tiny hand tentatively as we pass to return my greeting . . . I should say my farewell . . . I watch him growing smaller and smaller and then we leave these last poor outposts behind as the eastern sun illuminates the retreating city—the stage fades smaller and smaller into the distance. I watch as long as I can and only then do I finally gain the courage to change seats, to give up my dark and troubled past and turn around to face an uncertain and terrifying future. And when I do so the breath catches in my throat at the immensity of earth that lies before us, the prairie unspeakable in its vast, lonely reaches. Dizzy and faint at the sight of it, I feel as if the air has been sucked from my lungs, as if I have fallen off the edge of the world, and am hurtling headlong through empty space. And perhaps I have . . . perhaps I am . . .

But dear God, forgive me, I shall never again utter a complaint, I shall always remind myself how wonderful it is to be free, how I prayed for this moment every day of my life, and my prayers are answered! The terror in my heart of what lies ahead seems of little consequence compared with the prospect of spending my lifetime as an "inmate" in that loathsome "prison"—for it was a prison far more than a hospital, we were prisoners rather than patients. Our "medical treatment" consisted of being held captive behind iron bars, like animals in the zoo, ignored by indifferent doctors, tortured, taunted, and assaulted by sadistic attendants.

My definition of LUNATIC ASYLUM: A place where lunatics are created.

"Why am I here?" I asked Dr. Kaiser, when he first came to see me, fully a fortnight after my "admittance."

"Why, due to your promiscuous behavior," he answered as if genuinely surprised that I dare to even pose such a query.

"But I am in love!" I protested, and then I told him about Harry Ames. "My family placed me here because I left home to live out of wedlock with a man whom they considered to be beneath my station. For no better reason than that. When they could not convince me to leave him, they tore me from him, and from my babies. Can you not see, Doctor, that I'm no more insane than you?"

Then the doctor raised his eyebrows and scribbled on his notepad, nodding with an infuriating air of sanctimony. "Ah," he said, "I see—you believe that you were sent here as part of a conspiracy among your family." And he rose and left me and I did not see him again for nearly six months.

During this initial period I was subject to excruciating "treatments" prescribed by the good doctor to cure me of my "illness." These consisted of daily injections of scalding water into my vagina—evidently intended to calm my deranged sexual desires. At the same time, I was confined to my bed for weeks on end—forbidden from fraternizing with the other patients, not allowed to read, write letters, or pursue any other diversion. The nurses and attendants did not speak to me, as if I did not exist. I endured the further humiliation of being forced to use a bedpan, although there was nothing whatsoever physically wrong with me. Were I to protest or if I was found by a nurse out of my bed, I would be strapped into it for the remainder of the day and night.

It was during this period of confinement that I truly lost my mind. If the daily torture weren't enough, the complete isolation and inactivity were in themselves insupportable. I longed for fresh air and exercise, to promenade along Lake Michigan as I once had . . . At great risk I would steal from my bed before dawn and stand on a chair in my room, straining to see out through the iron bars that covered the tiny shaded window—just to catch one glimpse of daylight, one patch of green grass on the lawn outside. I wept bitterly at my fate, but I struggled against the tears, willed them away. For I had also learned that I must not allow anyone on staff to see me weep, lest it be said in addition to the doctor's absurd diagnosis of promiscuity, that I was also victim of Hysteria or Melancholia . . . which would only be cause for further tortures.

Let me here set down, once and for ever, the true circumstances of my incarceration.

Four years ago I fell in love with a man named Harry Ames. Harry was several years my senior and foreman of Father's grain-elevator operations. We met at my parents' home, where Harry came regularly to consult with Father on business matters. Harry is a very attractive man, if somewhat rough around the edges, with strong masculine arms and a certain workingman's self-confidence. He was nothing like the insipid, privileged boys with whom girls of my station are reduced to socializing at tea and cotillion. Indeed, I was quite swept away by Harry's charms . . . one thing led to another . . . yes well, surely by the standards of some I might be called promiscuous.

I am not ashamed to admit that I have always been a woman of passionate emotions and powerful physical desires. I do not deny them. I came to full flower at an early age, and had always quite intimidated the awkward young men of my family's narrow social circle.

Harry was different. He was a man; I was drawn to him like a moth to flame. We began to see each other secretly. Both of us knew that Father would never condone our relationship and Harry was as anxious about being found out as I—for he knew that it would cost him his job. But we could not resist one another—we could not stay apart.

The very first time I lay with Harry I became with child—my daughter Hortense. Truly, I felt her burst into being in my womb in the consummation of our love. I must say, Harry behaved like a gentleman, and assumed full responsibility. He offered to marry me, which I flatly refused, for although I loved him, and still do, I am an independent, some might say, an unconventional woman. I was not prepared to marry. I would not, however, give up my child, and so without explanation I moved out of my parents' home and took up residence with my beloved in a shabby little house on the banks of the Chicago River, where we lived very simply and happily for a time.

Naturally, it was not long before Father learned about his foreman's deception, and promptly dismissed him. But Harry soon found work with one of Father's competitors and I, too, found employment. I went to work in a factory that processed prairie chickens for the Chicago market. It was filthy, exhausting work, for which my privileged upbringing had in no way prepared me. At the same time, and perhaps for the same reason, it was oddly liberating to be out in the real world, and making my own way there.

I gave birth to Hortense and almost immediately became pregnant again with my son William . . . sweet Willie. I tried to maintain contact with my parents—I wished them to know their grandchildren, and not to judge me too harshly for having chosen a different path for myself. But Mother was largely hysterical whenever I arranged to visit her—indeed, it is she, perhaps, who should have been institutionalized, not I—and Father was inflexible and refused to even see me when I came to the house. I finally stopped going there altogether, and kept up only a tenuous contact with the family through my older married sister, also named Hortense.

By the time I gave birth to Willie, Harry and I had begun to have some difficulties. I wonder now if Father's agents were already working on him, even then, for he seemed to change almost overnight, to become distant and remote. He began to drink and to stay out all night, and when he came home I could smell the other women on him. It broke my heart, for I still loved him. Still, I was more than ever glad that I had not married him.

It was on one such night when Harry was away that Father's blackguards came. They burst through the door of our house in the middle of the night accompanied by a nurse, who snatched up my babies and spirited them away as the men restrained me. I fought them for all I was worth—screaming, kicking, biting, and scratching, but, of course, to no avail. I have not seen my children since that dark night.

I was taken directly to the lunatic asylum, where I was consigned to lie in bed in my darkened room, day after day, week after week, month after month, with nothing to occupy my time but my daily torture and constant thoughts of my babies—I had no doubt they were living with Father and Mother. I did not know what had become of Harry and was haunted by thoughts of him . . . (Harry, my Harry, love of my life, father of my children, did Father reward you with pieces of gold to give me up to his ruffians in the middle of the night? Did you sell your own babies to him? Or did he simply have you murdered? Perhaps I shall never know the truth . . .)

All of my misery for the crime of falling in love with a common man. All of my heartbreak, torture, and punishment because I chose to bring you, my dearest children, into the world. All of my black and hopeless despair because I chose an unconventional life . . .

Ah, but surely nothing that has come before can be considered unconventional in light of where I am now going! Let me record the exact events that led me to be on this train: Two weeks ago, a man and a woman came into the ladies dayroom at the asylum. Owing to the nature of my "affliction"—my "moral perversion," as it was described in my commitment papers (a sham and a travesty—how many other women I wonder have been locked away like this for no just cause!), I was among those patients strictly segregated by gender, prohibited even from fraternizing with members of the opposite sex—presumably for fear that I might try to copulate with them. Good God! On the other hand, my diagnosis seemed to be considered an open invitation to certain male members of the asylum staff to visit my room in the middle of the night. How many times did I wake up, as if suffocating, with the weight of one particularly loathsome attendant named Franz pressed upon me, a fat stinking German, corpulent and sweating . . . God help me, I prayed to kill him.

The man and woman looked us over appraisingly as if we were cattle at auction, and then they chose six or seven among us to come with them to a private staff room. Conspicuously absent from this group were any of the older women or any of the hopelessly, irredeemably insane—those who sit rocking and moaning for hours on end, or who weep incessantly or hold querulous conversations with their demons. No, these poor afflicted were passed over and the more "presentable" of us lunatics chosen for an audience with our visitors.

After we had retired to the private staff room, the gentleman, a Mr. Benton, explained that he was interviewing potential recruits for a government program that involved the Indians of the Western plains. The woman, who he introduced as Nurse Crowley, would, with our consent, perform a physical examination upon us. Should we be judged, based on the interview and examination, to be suitable candidates for the program, we might be eligible for immediate release from this hospital. Yes! Naturally, I was intrigued by the proposal. Yet there was a further condition of family consent, which I had scant hope of ever obtaining.

Still I volunteered my full cooperation. Truly, even an interview and a physical examination seemed preferable to the endless hours of agonizing monotony spent sitting or lying in bed, with nothing to pass the time besides foreboding thoughts about the injustice of my sentence and the devastating loss of my babies—the utter hopelessness of my situation and the awful anticipation of my next "treatment."

"Did I have any reason to believe that I was not fruitful?"—this was the first question posed to me by Nurse Crowley at the beginning of her examination. I must say I was taken aback—but I answered promptly, already having set my mind to passing this test, whatever its purpose. *"Au contraire!"* I said, and I told the nurse of the two precious children I had already borne out of wedlock, the son and daughter, who were so cruelly torn from their mother's bosom.

"Indeed," I said, "so fruitful am I that if my beloved Harry Ames, Esq., simply gazed upon me with a certain romantic longing in his eyes, babes sprang from my loins like seed spilling from a grain sack!"

(I must mention the unmentionable: the sole reason I did not become with child by the repulsive attendant Franz, the monster who visited me by night, is that the pathetic cretin sprayed his revolting discharge on my bedcovers, humping and moaning and weeping bitterly in his premature agonies.)

I feared that I may have gone too far in my enthusiasm to impress Nurse Crowley with my fertility, for she looked at me with that tedious and by now all too familiar expression of guardedness with which people regard the insane—and the alleged insane alike—as if our maladies might be contagious.

But apparently I passed my initial examination, for next I was interviewed by Mr. Benton himself, who also asked me a series of distinctly queer questions: Did I know how to cook over a campfire? Did I enjoy spending time outdoors? Did I enjoy sleeping out overnight? What was my personal estimation of the western savage?

"The western savage?" I interrupted. "Having never met any western savages, Sir, it would be difficult for me to have formed any estimation of them one way or another."

Finally Mr. Benton got down to the business at hand: "Would you be willing to make a great personal sacrifice in the service of your government?" he asked.

"But of course," I answered without hesitation.

"Would you consider an arranged marriage to a western savage for the express purpose of bearing a child with him?"

"Hah!" I barked a laugh of utter astonishment. "But why on earth?" I asked, more curious than offended. "For what purpose?"

"To ensure a lasting peace on the Great Plains," Mr. Benton answered. "To provide safe passage to our courageous settlers from the constant depredations of the bloodthirsty barbarians."

"I see," I said, but of course, I did not altogether.

"As part of our agreement," added Mr. Benton, "your President will demonstrate his eternal gratitude to you by arranging for your immediate release from this institution."

"Truly? I would be released from this place?" I asked, trying to conceal the trembling in my voice.

"That is absolutely guaranteed," he said, "assuming that your legal guardian, if such exists, is willing to sign the necessary consent forms."

Already I was formulating my plan for this last major hurdle to my freedom, and again I answered without a moment's hesitation. I stood and curtsied deeply, weak in the knees, both from my months of idle confinement and pure excitement at the prospect of freedom: "I should be deeply honored, Sir, to perform this noble duty for my country," I said, "to offer my humble services to the President of the United States." The truth is that I would have gladly signed on for a trip to Hell to escape the lunatic asylum . . . and, yet, perhaps that is exactly what I have done . . .

As to the critical matter of obtaining my parents' consent, let me say in preface, that although I may have been accused of insanity and promiscuity, no one has ever taken me for an idiot.

It was the responsibility of the hospital's chief physician, my own preposterous diagnostician, Dr. Sidney Kaiser, to notify the families of those patients under consideration for the BFI program (these initials stand for "Brides for Indians" as Mr. Benton explained to us) and invite them to the hospital to be informed of the program and to obtain their signatures on the necessary release papers—at which time the patients would be free to participate in the program if they so chose. In the year and a half that I had been incarcerated there against my will, I had, as I may have mentioned, been visited only twice by the good doctor. However, through my repeated but futile efforts to obtain an audience with him, I had become acquainted with his assistant, Martha Atwood, a fine woman who took pity on me, who befriended me. Indeed, Martha became my sole friend and confidante in that wretched place. Without her sympathy and visits, and the many small kindnesses she bestowed upon me, I do not know how I could have survived.

As we came to know one another, Martha was more than ever convinced that I did not belong in the asylum, that I was no more insane than she, and that, like other women there, I had been committed unjustly by my family. When this opportunity presented itself for me to "escape," she agreed to help me in my desperate plan. First she "borrowed" correspondence from Father out of my file in Dr. Kaiser's office, and she had made a duplicate of his personal letterhead. Together we forged a letter in Father's hand, written to Dr. Kaiser, in which Father explained that he was traveling on business and would be unable to attend the proposed meeting at the institution. Dr. Kaiser would have no reason to question this; he was aware of Father's position as president of the Chicago and Northwestern Railroad, for which Father had designed and built the entire grain-elevator system—the largest and most advanced such warehouse in the city, as he is forever reminding us. Father's job involved nearly constant travel, and as a child I rarely saw him. In our forged letter to Dr. Kaiser, Martha and I, or I should say "Father," wrote that the family had recently been contacted directly by the government regarding my participation in the BFI program and that Agent Benton had personally guaranteed him my safety for the duration of my stay in Indian territory. Because Martha had been privy to the entire interview process, I knew that I had passed all the necessary requirements and had been judged to be a prime candidate for the program (not that this represents any great accomplishment on my part considering that the main criterion for acceptance was that one be of childbearing age and condition, and not so insane as to be incapacitated. It is, I believe, safe to say that the government was less interested in the success of these matrimonial unions than they were in meeting their quota—

something that Father, ever the businessman and pragmatist could appreciate).

Thus in our letter, Father gave his full blessing for me to participate in, as I believe we wrote "this exciting and high-minded plan to assimilate the heathens." I know that Father has always viewed the western savages primarily as an impediment to the growth of American agriculture—he detests the notion of all that fertile plain going to waste when it could be put to good Biblical use filling his grain elevators. The truth is, Father harbors a deep-seated hatred of the Red Man simply for being a poor businessman—a shortcoming which Father believes to be the most serious character flaw of all. At his and Mother's endless dinner parties he is fond of giving credit to his and his wealthy guests' great good fortunes by toasting the Sac Chief Black Hawk, who once said that "land cannot be sold. Nothing can be sold but for those things that can be carried away"—a notion that Father found enormously quaint and amusing.

Too—and I must acknowledge this fact—I believe that secretly Father might actually have appreciated this opportunity to be rid of me, of the shame that my behavior, my "condition" has brought on our family. For if the truth be known, Father is a terrible snob. In his circle of friends and business cronies the stigma of having a lunatic—or, even worse, a sexually promiscuous daughter—must have been nearly unbearable for him.

So he went on in his letter, in his typically overblown but distracted manner—in the same tone he might employ if he were giving permission for me to be sent off to finishing school for young ladies (perhaps it is simply due to the fact that the same blood flows through our veins, but it was almost diabolically simple for me to imitate Father's writing style)—to state his conviction that the "bracing Western air, the hearty native life in the glorious out-of-doors, and the fascinating cultural exchange might be just what my poor wayward daughter requires to set her addled mind right again." It is an astonishing thing, is it not, the notion of a father being asked (and giving!) permission for his daughter to copulate with savages?

Enclosed with Father's letter were the signed hospital release papers, all of which Martha had delivered by private messenger to Dr. Kaiser's office—a tidy and ultimately perfectly convincing little package.

Of course, when her part in the deception was discovered, as it surely would be, Martha knew that she faced immediate dismissal—possibly even criminal prosecution. And thus it is, that my true, intrepid friend—childless and loveless (and if the truth be told rather plain to look upon), facing in all probability a life of spinsterhood and loneliness—enlisted in the BFI program herself. She rides beside me on this very train . . . and so at least I do not embark alone on this greatest adventure of my life.

24 March 1875

It would be disingenuous of me to say that I have no trepidations about the new life that awaits us. Mr. Benton assured us that we are contractually obligated to bear but one child with our Indian husbands, after which time we are free to go, or stay, as we choose. Should we fail to become with child, we are required to remain with our husbands for two full years, after which time we are free to do as we wish . . . or, at least, so say the authorities. It has not failed to occur to me that perhaps our new husbands might have different thoughts about this arrangement. Still, it seems to me a rather small price to pay to escape that living Hell of an asylum to which I would quite likely have been committed for the rest of my life. But now that we have actually embarked upon this journey, our future so uncertain, and so unknown, it is impossible not to have misgivings. How ironic that in order to escape the lunatic asylum I have had to embark upon the most insane undertaking of my life.

But honestly, I believe that poor naive Martha is eager for the experience; excited about her matrimonial prospects, she seems to be fairly blooming in anticipation! Why just a few moments ago she asked me, in rather a breathless voice, if I might give her some advice about carnal matters! (It appears that, due to the reason given for my incarceration, everyone connected with the institution—even my one true friend—seems to consider me somewhat of an authority in such matters.)

"What sort of advice, dear friend?" I asked.

Now Martha became terribly shy, lowered her voice even further, leaned forward, and whispered. "Well . . . advice about . . . about how best to make a man happy . . . I mean to say, about how to satisfy the cravings of a man's flesh."

I laughed at her charming innocence. Martha hopes to carnally satisfy her savage! "Let us assume, first of all," I answered, "that the aboriginals are similar in their physical needs to men of our own noble race. And we have no reason to believe otherwise, do we? If indeed all men are similarly disposed in matters of the heart and of the flesh, it is my limited experience that the best way to make them happy—if that is your true goal—is to wait on them hand and foot, cook for them, have sexual congress whenever and wherever they desire—but never initiate the act yourself and do not demonstrate any forwardness or longings of your own; this appears to frighten men—most of whom are merely little boys pretending to be men.

And, perhaps most importantly, just as most men fear women who express their physical longings, so they dislike women who express opinions—of any sort and on any subject. All these things I learned from Mr. Harry Ames. Thus I would recommend that you agree unequivocably with everything your new husband says . . . oh, yes, one final thing—let him believe that he is extremely well endowed, even if, especially if, he is not."

"But how will I know whether or not he is well endowed?" asked my poor innocent Martha.

"My dear," I answered. "You do know the difference between, let us say a breakfast sausage and a bratwurst? A *cornichon* and a cucumber? A pencil and a pine tree?"

Martha blushed a deep shade of crimson, covered her mouth, and began to giggle uncontrollably. And I, too, laughed with her. It occurs to me how long it has been since I really laughed . . . it does feel wonderful to laugh again.

27 March 1875

My Dearest Sister Hortense,

You have by this time perhaps heard news of my sudden departure from Chicago. My sole regret is that I was unable to be present when the family was notified of the circumstances of my "escape" from the "prison" from which you had all conspired to commit me. I would especially have enjoyed seeing Father's reaction when he learned that I am soon to become a bride—yes, that's right, I am to wed, and perforce, couple with a genuine Savage of the Cheyenne Nation!—Hah! Speaking of moral perversion. I can just hear Father blustering: "My God, she really is insane!" What I would give to see his face!

Now, truly, haven't you always known that your poor wayward little sister would one day embark on such an adventure, perform such a momentous deed? Imagine me, if you are able, riding this rumbling train west into the great unknown void of the frontier. Can you picture two more different lives than ours? You within the snug (though how dreary it must be!) confines of the Chicago bourgeoisie, married to your pale banker Walter Woods, with your brood of pale offspring—how many are there now, I lose track, four, five, six of the little monsters?—each as colorless and shapeless as unkneaded bread dough.

But forgive me, my sister, if I appear to be attacking you. It is only that I may now, at last—freely and without censor or fear of recriminations—

anger to those among my own family who so ill-treated me; I can y mind without the constant worry of further confirming my insanity, without the ever-present danger that my children will be torn from me forever—for all this has come to pass, and I have nothing left to lose. At last I am free—in body, mind, and spirit . . . or as free as one can be who has purchased her freedom with her womb . . .

But enough of that . . . now I must tell you something of my adventure, of our long journey, of the extraordinary country I am seeing. I must tell you of all that is fascinating and lonely and desolate . . . you who have barely set foot outside Chicago, can simply not imagine it all. The city is bursting at its very seams, abustle with rebuilding out of the ashes of the devastating great fire, expanding like a living organism out into the prairie (well, is it any wonder then that the savages rebel as they are pushed ever further west?). You cannot imagine the crowds, the human congress, the sheer activity on what used to be wild prairie when we were children. Our train passed through the new stockyard district—very near the neighborhood where Harry and I lived. (You never did come to visit us, did you, Hortense? . . . Why does that not surprise me?) There the smokestacks spew clouds of all colors of the rainbow—blue and orange and red—which when they enter the air seem to intermingle like oil paints mixed on a palette. It is quite beautiful in a grotesque sort of way, like the paintings of a mad god. Past the slaughterhouses, where the terrified cries of dumb beasts can be heard even over the steady din of the train, their sickening stench filling the car like rancid syrup. Finally the train burst from the shroud of smoke that blankets the city, as though it had come out of a dense fog into the clear-plowed farm country, the freshly turned soil black and rich, Father's beloved grain crops just beginning to break ground.

I must tell you that in spite of Father's insistence to the contrary, the true beauty of the prairie lies not in the perfect symmetry of farmlands, but where the farmlands end and the real prairie begins—a sea of natural grass like a living, breathing thing undulating all the way to the horizon. Today I saw prairie chickens, flocks of what must have been hundreds, thousands, flushing away in clouds from the tracks as we passed. I could only imagine the sound of their wings over the roar of the train. How extraordinary to see them on the wing like this after the year I spent laboring in that wretched factory where we processed the birds and where I thought I could never bear to look at another chicken as long as I lived. I know that you and the rest of the family could not understand my decision to take such menial work or to live out of wedlock with a man so far beneath my station in life, and that this has always been spoken of among you as the first outward manifestation of my insanity. But, don't you see,

Hortense, it was precisely our cloistered upbringing under Mother and Father's roof that spurred me to seek contact with a larger world. I'd have suffocated, died of sheer boredom, if I stayed any longer in that dark and dreary house, and although the work I took in the factory was indeed loathsome, I will never regret having done it. I learned so much from the men and women with whom I toiled; I learned how the rest of the world—families less fortunate than ours, which, of course constitutes the vast majority of people—lives. This is something you can never know, dear sister, and which you will always be poorer in soul for having missed.

Not that I recommend to you a job in the chicken factory! Good God, I shall never get over the stink of it, my hands even now when I hold them up to my face seem to reek of chicken blood, feathers, and innards . . . I think that I shall never eat poultry again as long as I live! But I must say my interest in the birds is somewhat renewed in seeing the wild creatures flying up before the train like sparks from the wheels. They are so beautiful, fanning off against the setting sun, their tangents helping to break the long straight tedium of this journey. I have tried to interest my friend Martha, who sits beside me, in this spectacle of wings, but she is very soundly asleep, her head jostling gently against the train window.

But here has occurred an amusing encounter: As I was watching the birds flush from the tracks, a tall, angular, very pale woman with short-cropped sandy hair under an English tweed cap came hurrying down the aisle of our car, stooping to look out each window at the birds and then moving on to the next seat. She wears a man's knickerbocker suit of Irish thornproof, in which, with her short hair and cap it might be easy to mistake her for a member of the opposite sex. Her mannish outfit includes a waistcoat, stockings, and heavy walking brogues, and she carries an artist's sketch pad.

"Excuse me, please, won't you?" the woman asked of each occupant of each seat in front of which she leaned in order to improve her view out the window. She spoke with a distinct British accent. "Do please excuse me. Oh, my goodness!" she exclaimed, her eyebrows raised in an expression of delighted surprise. "Extraordinary! Magnificent! Glorious!"

By the time the Englishwoman reached the unoccupied seat beside me the prairie chickens had set their wings and sailed off over the horizon and she flopped down in the seat all gangly arms and legs. "Greater prairie chicken," she said. "That is to say, *Tympanuchus cupido*, actually a member of the grouse family, commonly referred to as the prairie chicken. The first I've ever seen in the wilds, although, of course, I've seen specimens. And of course I have studied extensively the species' eastern cousin, the heath hen, during my travels about New England. Named after the Greek *tym-*

pananon, 'kettledrum,' and *'echein,'* to have a drum, aluding both to the enlarged esophagus on the sides of the throat, which in the male becomes inflated during courtship, as well as to the booming sound which the males utter in their aroused state. And further named after the 'blind bow boy,' son of Venus—not, however with any illusion to erotic concerns, I should hasten to add, but because the long, erectile, stiff feathers are raised like small rounded wings over the head of the male in his courtship display, and have therefore been likened to Cupid's wings."

Now the woman suddenly turned as if noticing me for the first time, and with the same look of perpetual surprise still etched in her milk-pale English countenance—eyebrows raised and a delighted smile at her lips as if the world itself were not only wonderful, but absolutely startling. I liked her immediately. "Do please excuse me for prattling on, won't you? Helen Elizabeth Flight, here," she said, thrusting her hand forward with manly forthrightness. "Perhaps you're familiar with my work? My book *Birds of Britain* is currently in its third printing—letterpress provided by my dear companion and collaborator, Mrs. Ann Hall of Sunderland. Unfortunately, Mrs. Hall was too ill to accompany me when I embarked on my tour of America to gather specimens and make sketches for our next opus, *Birds of America*—not to be confused, of course, with Monsieur Audubon's series of the same name. An interesting artist, Mr. Audubon, if rather too fanciful for my tastes. I've always found his birds to be rendered with such . . . caprice! Clearly he threw biological accuracy to the wind. Wouldn't you agree?"

I could see that this question was intended to be somewhat more than rhetorical, but just as I was attempting to form an answer, Miss Flight asked: "And you are?" still looking at me with her eyebrows raised in astonished anticipation, as if my identity were not only a matter of the utmost urgency but also promised a great surprise.

"May Dodd," I answered.

"Ah, May Dodd! Quite," she said. "And a smart little picture of a girl you are, too. I suspected from your fair complexion that you might be of English descent."

"Scottish actually," I said, "but I'm thoroughly American, myself. I was born and raised in Chicago," I added somewhat wistfully.

"And don't tell me that a lovely creature like you has signed up to live with the savages?" asked Miss Flight.

"Why yes I have," I said. "And you?"

"I'm afraid that I've run a trifle short of research funds," explained Miss Flight with a small grimace of distaste for the subject. "My patrons were unwilling to advance me any more money for my American sojourn, and this seemed like quite the perfect opportunity for me to study the birdlife of the western prairies at no additional expense. A frightfully exciting adventure, don't you agree?"

"Yes," I said, with a laugh, "frightfully!"

"Although I must tell you a little secret," she said, looking around us to see that we were not overheard. "I am unable to have children myself. I'm quite sterile! The result of a childhood infection." Her eyebrows shot up with delight. "I lied to the examiner in order to be accepted into the program!

"Now you will excuse me, Miss Dodd, won't you?" said Miss Flight, suddenly all business again. "That is to say, I must quickly make some sketches and record my impressions of the magnificent greater prairie chicken while the experience is still fresh in mind. I hope, when the train next stops, to be able to descend and shoot a few as specimens. I've brought with me my scattergun, especially manufactured for this journey by Featherstone, Elder & Story of Newcastle upon Tyne. Perhaps you are interested in firearms? If so, I'd love to show it to you. My patrons, before they ran into financial difficulties and left me stranded on this vast continent, had the gun especially built for me, specifically for my travels in America. I'm rather proud of it. But do excuse me, won't you? I'm so terribly pleased to have met you. Wonderful that you're along! We must speak at greater length. I have a feeling that you and I are going to be spiffing good friends. You have the most extraordinarily blue eyes, you know, the color of an Eastern bluebird. I shall use them as a model to mix my palette when I paint that species if you don't terribly mind. And I'm fascinated to learn more of your opinion on Monsieur Audubon's work." And with that the daffy Englishwoman took her leave!

While we are on the subject, and since Martha is proving at present to be exceedingly dull company, let me describe to you, dear sister, some of my other fellow travelers, who provide the only other diversion on this long, straight, monotonous iron road through country that while beautiful in its vast and empty reaches, can hardly be described as scenic. I've barely had time yet to acquaint myself with all of the women, but our common purpose and destination seems to have fostered a certain easy familiarity among us—personal histories and intimacies are exchanged without the usual period of tedious social posturing or shyness. These women—hardly more than girls really—are all either from the Chicago area or other parts of the Middle West, and come from all circumstances. Some appear to be escaping poverty or failed romances, or, as in my case, unpleasant "living arrangements." Hah! While there is only one other girl from my asylum, there are several in our group from other such public facilities around the city. Some are considerably more eccentric even than I. But then it was my observation in the asylum that nearly every resident there took solace in the fact that they could point to someone else who was madder than they. One, named Ada Ware, dresses only in black, wears a widow's veil, and has perpetual dark circles of grief beneath her eyes. I have yet to see her smile or make any expression whatsoever. "Black Ada" the others call her.

You will, perhaps, remember Martha, whom you met on the sole occasion when you visited me in the asylum. She is a sweet thing, barely two years younger than I, though she seems younger, and homely as a stick. I am forever indebted to her, for it was Martha who was so invaluable in helping me to obtain my liberty.

As mentioned, one other girl from my own institution survived the selection process—while a number of others declined to accept Mr. Benton's offer. It seemed remarkable to me at the time that they would give up the opportunity for freedom from that ghastly place, simply because they were squeamish about conjugal relations with savages. Perhaps I will live to regret saying this, but how could it be any worse than incarceration in that dank hellhole for the rest of one's life?

This young girl's name is Sara Johnstone. She's a pretty, timid little creature, barely beyond the age of puberty. The poor thing evidently lacks the power of speech—by this I do not mean that she is simply the quiet sort—I mean that she seems unable, or at least unwilling, to utter a word. She and I had, perforce, very little contact at the hospital, and therefore hardly any opportunity to get to know one another. I have a suspicion that this will all change now, for she seems to have attached herself to me and Martha. She sits facing us on the train, and frequently leans forward with tears in her eyes to grasp my hand and squeeze it fiercely. I know nothing of her past or the reason why she was originally confined in the institution. She has no family and according to Martha had evidently been there long before I arrived—ever since she was a young child. Nor do I know who supported her there—as we both know that wretched place was not for charity cases. Martha has intimated that Dr. Kaiser himself, the director of the hospital, volunteered the poor girl for the program as a way of being rid of her—what Father might recognize as a cost-cutting measure—for according to Martha, the girl was treated very much like a "poor relation" in the hospital. Furthermore, though we are hardly free to discuss the matter with the poor thing sitting directly in front of us, Martha has suggested that the child may, in fact, have had some familial connection with the Good Doctor—possibly, we have speculated, she is the product of his own romantic liaison with a former patient? Although one must wonder what kind of man would send his own daughter away to live among savages . . . Whatever the child's situation, I find it troubling that she was accepted into this program. She is such a frail little thing, terrified of the world, and so obviously ill prepared for what must certainly prove to be an arduous duty. Indeed, how could she be prepared for any experience in the real world, having grown up behind brick walls and iron-barred windows? I am certain that, like Martha, the girl is without experience in carnal matters, unless the repulsive night monster Franz visited her, too, in the dark . . . which I pray for her sake that he did not. In any case, I intend to watch over the child, to protect her from harm if it is within my power to do so. Oddly, her very youth and fearfulness seem to give me strength and courage.

Ah, and here come the Kelly sisters of Chicago's Irish town, Margaret and Susan, swaggering down the aisle—redheaded, freckle-faced identical twin lassies, thick as thieves, which in their case is somewhat more than an idle expression. They take everything in these two; their shrewd pale green eyes miss nothing; I clutch my purse to breast for safekeeping.

One of them, I cannot yet tell them apart, slips into the seat beside me. " *'Ave* ya got some tobacco on ye, May?" she asks in a conspiratorial tone, as if we are the very best of friends though I hardly know the girl. "I'd be *loookin'* to roll me a smoke."

"I'm afraid I don't smoke," I answer.

"*Aye,* 'twas easier to get a smoke in prison, than it is on this damn train," she says. "Isn't that so, Meggie?"

"It's *sartain,* Susie," Meggie answers.

"Do you mind my asking why you girls were in prison?" I ask. I tilt my notebook toward them. "I'm writing a letter to my sister."

"Why, we don't mind *at-tall,* dear," says Meggie, who leans on the seat in front of me. "Prostitution and Grand Theft—ten-year sentences in the Illinois State Penitentiary." She says this with real bravado in her voice as if it is a thing of which to be very proud, and as I write she leans down closer to make sure that I record the details correctly. "*Aye,* don't forget the Grand Theft," she repeats, pointing her finger at my notebook.

"Right, Meggie," adds Susan, nodding her head with satisfaction. "And we'd not have been apprehended, either, if it weren't for the fact that the gentleman we turned over in Lincoln Park *'appened* to be a municipal *jeewdge. Aye,* the old reprobate tried to solicit us for sexual favors. 'Twins!' he said. 'Two halves of a bun around my sausage' he desired to make of us. Ah ya beggar!—we gave him two halves of a brick on either side of his damn head, we did! In two shakes of a lamb's tail we had his pocket watch and his wallet in our possession—thinking in our ignorance what great good fortune that he was carrying *sech* a large *soom* of cash. No doubt His *Jeewdgeship's* weekly bribe revenue."

"It's *sartain,* Susie, and that would've been the end of it," chimes in Margaret, "if it weren't for that damn cash. The *jeewdge* went directly to his great good pal the Commissioner of Police and a *manhoont* the likes of which Chicago has never before seen was launched to bring the infamous Kelly twins to *juicetice!"*

" *'Tis* the God's own truth, Meggie," says Susan, shaking her head. "You probably read about us in the newspaper, Missy," she says to me. "We were quite famous for a time, me and Meggie. After a short trial, which the public advocate charged with our defense spent nappin'—the old bugger—we were sentenced to ten years in the penitentiary. *Aye,* ten years just for defendin' our honor against a lecherous old *jeewdge,* with a pocket full of bribe money, if you can believe that, Missy."

"And your parents?" I ask. "Where are they?"

"Oh, we *'ave* no idea, darlin'," says Margaret. "We were foundlings, you see. Wee babies left on the steps of the church. Isn't that so, Susie? Grew up in the city's Irish orphanage, but we didn't really care for the place. *Aye,* we been living by our wits ever since we *roon* away from there when we were just ten years old."

Now Margaret stands straight again and scans the other passengers with a certain predatory interest. Her gaze comes to rest on the woman sitting across the aisle from us—a woman named Daisy Lovelace; I have only spoken to her briefly, but I know that she is a Southerner and has the distinct look of ruined gentry about her. She holds an ancient dirty white French poodle on her lap. The dog's hair is stained red around its butt and muzzle, and around its rheumy, leaking eyes.

"Wouldn't *'appen* to *'ave* a bit of tobacco, on ye, Missy, would *ya* now?" Margaret asks her.

"Ah'm afraid *naught,"* says the woman in a slow drawl, and in not a particularly friendly tone.

"Loovely little dog, you've got there," says Margaret, sliding into the seat beside the Southerner. "What's its name, if you don't mind *me* askin'?" The twin's insinuating manner is transparent; it is clear that she is not interested in the woman's dog.

Ignoring her, the Lovelace woman sets her dog down on the floor between their feet. "You go on now an' make *teetee, Feeern Loueeese,"* she coos to it in an accent as thick as cane molasses, *"Go wan* now sweet*haart*. You make *teetee* for Momma." And the wretched little creature totters stiffly up the aisle sniffling and snorting, finally squatting to pee by a vacant seat.

"Fern Louise, is it then?" says Meggie. "Isn't that a grand name, Susie?"

"*Loovely,* Meggie," Susan says. "A *loovely* little dog."

Still ignoring them, the Southern woman pulls a small silver flask from her purse and takes a quick sip, which act is of great interest to the twins.

"Is that whiskey you've got there, Missy?" Margaret asks.

"No, it is *naught* whiskey," says the woman coolly. "It is *mah nuurve* medicine, doctor's order, and *no,* you may not have a taste of it."

The twins have met their match with this one I can see!

Now here comes my friend, Gretchen Fathauer, bulling her way down the aisle of the train, swinging her arms and singing some Swiss folksong in a robust voice. Gretchen never fails to cheer us all up. She is a big-hearted, enthusiastic soul—a large, boisterous, buxom rosy-cheeked lass who looks like she might be able to spawn single-handedly all the babes that the Cheyenne nation might require.

By now we all know Gretchen's history almost as well as our own: Her family were immigrants from Switzerland, who settled on the upland prairie west of Chicago to farm wheat when Gretchen was a girl. But the family farm failed after a series of bad harvests caused by harsh winters, blight, and insect attack, and Gretchen was forced to leave home as a young woman and seek employment in the city. She found work as a domestic with the McCormick family—yes, the very same—Father's dear friend Cyrus McCormick, who invented the reaper . . . isn't it odd, Hortense, to think that we probably visited the McCormicks in our youth at the same time that Gretchen was employed there—but of course we would never have paid any attention to the bovine Swiss chambermaid.

Gretchen longed to have a family of her own and one day she answered an advertisement in the *Tribune* seeking "mail-order" brides for western settlers. She posted her application and several months later was notified that she had been paired with a homesteader from Oklahoma territory. Her intended was to meet her at the train station in St. Louis on an appointed day, and convey her to her new home. Gretchen gave notice to the McCormicks and two weeks later boarded the train to St. Louis. But alas, although she has a heart of gold, Gretchen is terribly plain . . . indeed, I must confess that she is rather more than plain, to the extent that one of the less kind members of our expedition has referred to the poor dear as "Miss Potato Face" . . . and even those more charitable among us must admit that her countenance does have a certain unfortunate tuberous quality.

Well, Gretchen's intended had only to take one look at her, with which he excused himself under pretense of fetching his baggage, and Gretchen never laid eyes on the miserable cur again. She tells the story now with great good humor, but she was clearly devastated. She had given up everything—and was now abandoned at the train station in a strange city, with only her suitcase, a few personal effects, and the meager savings from her former employment. She could not bear the humiliation of going back to Chicago and asking the McCormicks for her old job. Nor was the possibility of returning to her family, shamed thusly by matrimonial rejection, any more appealing to her. No, Gretchen was determined to have a husband and children one way or another. She sat on the bench at the train station and wept openly at her plight. It was at that very moment that a gentleman approached her. He handed her a small paper flyer on which was printed the following:

> *If you are a healthy young woman of childbearing age, who seeks matrimony, exotic travel, and adventure, please present yourself to the following address promptly at 9:00 a.m., Thursday morning on the twelfth day of February, the year of our Lord, 1875.*

Gretchen laughs when she tells the story—a great hearty bellow—and says in her heavy accent, "*Vell*, you know, I *tought* this young fellow must be a messenger from God, I truly do. And *ven* I go to to *dis* place, and *dey* ask me if I like to marry a Cheyenne Indian fellow and have his babies, I say: '*Vell*, I *tink de* savages not be so *chooosy*, as *dat* farmer *yah*? Sure, *vy* not? I make *beeg*, strong babies for my new *hustband*. *Yah*, I feed *da* whole damn nursery, *yah*?' " And Gretchen pounds her massive breast and laughs and laughs.

Which causes all the rest of us to laugh with her.

Unable to break the Southern woman's steely indifference to them, the Kelly sisters have moved on to try their luck in the next car. They remind me of a pair of red foxes prowling a meadow for whatever they might turn up.

Just now as I was writing, my new friend, Phemie, came to sit beside me. Euphemia Washington is her full name—a statuesque colored girl who came to Chicago via Canada. She is about my same age, and quite striking, I should say nearly fierce, in appearance, being over six feet in height, with beautiful skin, the color of burnished mahogany—a finely formed nose with fiercely flared nostrils, and full Negro lips. I'm sure, dear sister, that you and the family will find it perfectly scandalous to learn that I am now fraternizing with Negroes. But on this train all are equal, at least such is the case in my egalitarian mind.

"I am writing a letter to my sister at home," I said to her, "describing the circumstances of some of the girls on the train. Tell me how you came to be here, Phemie, so that I may make a full report to her."

At this she chuckled, a rich warm laugh that seemed to issue from deep in her chest. "You are the first person who has asked me that, May," she said. "And why would your sister be interested in the nigger girl? Some of the others seem quite distressed that I am along." Phemie is very well spoken, with the most lovely, melodic voice that I've ever heard—deep and resonant, her speech like a poem, a song.

It occurred to me that, truth be told, you, dear sister, probably would not be interested in hearing about the nigger girl. Of course, this I did not say to Phemie.

"How did you happen to go to Canada, Phemie?" I asked.

She chuckled again. "You don't think that I look like a native Canadian, May?"

"You look like an African, Phemie," I said bluntly. "An African princess!"

"Yes, my mother came from a tribe called the Ashanti," Phemie said. "The greatest warriors in all of Africa," she added. "One day when she was a young girl she was gathering firewood with her mother and the other women. She fell behind, and sat down to rest. She was not worried, for she knew that her mother would return for her. As she sat, leaning against a tree, she fell asleep. And when she woke up, men from another tribe, who spoke a tongue she did not understand, stood round her. She was only a child, and she was very frightened.

"They took her away to a strange place, and kept her there in chains. Finally she was put in the hold of a ship with hundreds of others. She was many weeks at sea. She did not know what was happening to her, and she still believed that her mother would come back for her. She never stopped believing that. It kept her alive.

"The ship finally reached a city the likes of which my mother had never before seen or imagined. Many had died on route but she had lived. In the city she was sold at auction to a white man, a cotton shipper, who owned a fleet of sailing vessels in the port city of Apalachicola, Florida.

"My mother's first master was very good to her," Phemie continued. "He took her into his home where she did domestic duties and even received a bit of education. She learned to read and write, a thing unheard of among the other slaves. And when she became a young woman, her master took her into his bed.

"I was the child born of this union," Phemie said. "I, too, grew up in that house, where I was given lessons in the kitchen by the tutor of Master's 'real' children—his white family. Eventually the mistress discovered the truth of my parentage—perhaps she finally saw some resemblance between the kitchen nigger's child and her own children. And one night when I was not yet seven years old, two men, slave merchants, came and took me away—just as my mother had been taken from her family. She wept and pleaded and fought the men, but they struck her and knocked her to the ground. That was the last time I ever saw my mother, lying unconscious with her face battered and bleeding . . ." Phemie paused here and looked out the train window, tears glistening in the corners of her eyes.

"I was sold to the owner of a plantation outside Savannah, Georgia," she continued. "He was a bad man, an evil man. He drank and treated his slaves with terrible cruelty. The first day that I arrived there he had me branded on the back with his own initials . . . Yes, he burned his initials into the flesh of all his slaves so that they would be easily identified if ever they ran away. I was still just a child, eight years old, but after the first week that I was there, the man began to have me sent to his private quarters at night. I do not need to tell you what happened there . . . I was badly hurt . . .

"Several years passed this way," she went on in a softer voice. "Then one day a Canadian natural scientist came to visit the plantation. He came under the guise of studying the flora and fauna there—but he was an abolitionist and his true purpose was to spread the word to the slaves about the underground railroad. He carried excellent letters of introduction and was unwittingly welcomed at all the plantations. Because I had a little education, and because I had always been fascinated with wild things of all kinds, my master charged me with accompanying the naturalist on his daily excursions to collect specimens. Over the several days of his visit, the man spoke to me often of Canada, told me that every man, woman, and child lived free and equal there—that none was owned by another. The scientist liked me and took pity on me. He told me that I was too young to attempt to escape alone but that I should encourage some of the older slaves to take me with them. He showed me maps of the best routes north and gave me the names of people along the way who would help us.

"I spoke to some of the others, but all were too terrified of the Master to attempt such an escape. They had seen what Master did to runaway slaves who were returned to him.

"One night a week or so after the man left, after I had returned weeping and in great pain to the slaves quarters from Master's bedroom, I made a bundle of a few clothes and what little food I could gather and I left alone. I did not care if I died trying to escape. Death seemed welcome compared to my life.

"I was young and strong," Phemie said, "and over the next several nights

I ran through the forest and swamps and canebrakes. I never stopped running. Sometimes I could hear the hounds baying behind me, but the naturalist had instructed me to wade up streambeds and across ponds, which would cause the dogs to lose the scent. I ran and I ran.

For weeks I traveled north, moving by night, hiding in the undergrowth during the day. I ate what I could scavenge in the forest and fields, wild roots and greens, sometimes a bit of fruit or vegetables stolen from farms or gardens. I was hungry and often I did not know where I was, but I kept the North Star always before me and I looked for landmarks which the scientist had described to me. Often I longed to go into the towns I passed to beg a little food, but I dared not. Upon my back I still wore Master's brand, and if captured I would surely be returned to him and terribly punished.

"In those weeks alone in the wilderness, I began to remember the stories my mother had told me of her own people, of the men hunting and the women gathering from the earth. I would never have survived my journey to the land of freedom were it not for what my mother had taught me about the wilds. My grandmother's knowledge, passed down through my mother, saved my life. It was as if, all these years later, my mother's mother came back for me just as she had always believed she would come for her . . .

"It was several months before I finally crossed into Canada," Phemie continued. "There I called on people whose names the naturalist had given me and eventually I was placed in the home of a doctor's family. I was well treated there and was able to continue my education. I lived with the doctor and his family for almost ten years—I worked for them and was paid an honest wage for my labors.

"One day I happened to see a small notice in the newspaper requesting young single women of any race, creed, or color to participate in an important volunteer program on the American frontier. I answered the advertisement . . . and, here we are . . . you and I."

"But if you were happy with the doctor's family in Canada," I asked Phemie, "why did you wish to leave there, to come on this mad adventure?"

"They were fine people," Phemie said. "I loved them and will be forever grateful to them. But you see, May, I was still a servant. I was paid for my work, that is true, but I was still a servant to white folks. I dreamed of more for myself, I dreamed to be a free woman, truly free, on my own and beholden to no others. I owed that to my mother, and to my people. I know that as a white woman, it must be difficult for you to understand this."

I patted Phemie on the back of her hand. "You'd be surprised, Phemie," I said, "at how well I understand the longing for freedom."

* * *

But now an ugly thing has occurred, spoiling the moment. As Phemie and I were sitting together, the Southern woman Daisy Lovelace, seated across the aisle, set her ancient miserable little poodle down on the seat beside her and said in a voice so loud that we couldn't help but turn to look. *"Feeern Loueeese,"* she said, "would you rather be a *niggah*, or would you rather be *daid*?" upon which cue the little dog teetered stiffly and then rolled over on its back with its little bowed legs sticking straight in the air. Miss Lovelace shrieked with mean-spirited laughter.

"Wretched woman!" I muttered. "Pay no attention to her, Phemie."

"Of course I don't," Phemie said, unconcerned. "The poor soul is drunk, May, and believe me, I've heard far worse than that. I'm sure that such a parlor trick was a source of great amusement to her plantation friends. And now she finds herself among our motley group, where she must at least assert her superiority over the nigger girl. I think we should not judge her just yet."

I have dozed off, with my head on Phemie's shoulder, only to be rudely awakened by the shrill voice of a dreadful woman named Narcissa White, an evangelical Episcopalian who is enrolled in the program under the auspices of the American Church Missionary Society. Now Miss White comes bustling down the aisle of the train passing out religious pamphlets. " 'Ye who enter the wilderness without faith shall perish' said the Lord Jesus Christ," she preaches, and other such nonsense, which only serves to further agitate the others—some of whom already seem as skittish as cattle going to the slaughterhouse.

I'm afraid that Miss White and I have taken an instant dislike to one another, and I fear that we are destined to become bitter enemies. She is enormously tiresome and bores us all witless with her sanctimonious attitudes and evangelical rantings. As you well know, Hortense, I have never had much interest in the church. Perhaps the hypocrisy inherent in Father's position as a church elder, while remaining one of the least Christ-like men I've ever known, has something to do with my general cynicism toward organized religion of all kinds.

The White woman has already stated that she has no intention of bearing a child with her Cheyenne husband, nor indeed of having conjugal relations with him, and she assures us that she signed up for this mission strictly as a means of giving herself to the Lord Jesus—to save the soul of her heathen intended by teaching him "the ways of Christ and the true path to salvation," as she puts it in her most pious manner. Evidently she intends to distribute her pamphlets among the savages, and seemed not in the least deterred when I pointed out to her that very likely they won't be able to read them. It may be blasphemous for me to say so, but personally, I believe that our Christian God as He is represented by the likes of Miss White may be of somewhat limited use to the savages . . .

I will write to you again soon, my dearest sister . . .

31 March 1875

We crossed the Missouri River three days ago, spending one night in a boardinghouse in Omaha. Our military escort, or "guard" as I prefer to call them, treat us more as prisoners than as volunteers in the service of our government—they are contemptuous and snide, and have a gratingly familiar air that suggests some knowledge of the Faustian bargain we have struck with our government. None of us was permitted to go abroad in Omaha, nor even allowed to leave the boardinghouse—perhaps they fear that we might have a change of heart and seek to escape.

The next morning we boarded another train, which for the past two days has followed along a bluff overlooking the Platte River—not much of a river really—wide, slow-moving, and turgid.

We passed through the little settlement of Grand Island, where we took on supplies but were not permitted to disembark, westward through the muddy village of North Platte, where we were once again forbidden to so much as stretch our legs at the station. We did witness a remarkable spectacle yesterday morning at dawn—thousands, no I would more accurately guess, millions of cranes on the river. As if by some signal, perhaps simply frightened by the passing of our train, they all suddenly took flight, rising off the water as one being, like an enormous sheet lifted by the wind. Our British ornithologist, Miss Flight, was absolutely beside herself, rendered all but speechless by the spectacle. "Glorious!" she said, patting her flat chest. "Absolutely glorious!" Truly I thought the woman's eyebrows were going to shoot right off the top of her head. "A masterpiece," she marveled. "God's masterpiece!" I found this at first to be an odd remark, but soon realized how accurate a description it really was. The birds made a noise we could hear even over the roar of our locomotive. A million wings—imagine it!—like the sound of rumbling thunder or a waterfall, punctuated by the strange, otherworldly cries of the cranes, their wingbeats at once ponderous and elegant, their bodies so large that flight seemed improbable, legs dangling awkwardly beneath them like the rag tails of a child's kite. God's masterpiece . . . and perhaps after my long, spartan confinement behind four walls and a locked door such a spectacle of freedom and fecundity seems even more wonderful. Ah, but on this morning the earth seems like an especially fine place to be alive and free! I think that I shall not mind living in the wilderness . . .

I have no true sense of this strange new country yet. Compared to Illinois, the vast prairies hereabouts seem more arid, less productive, and the few farms that we pass down in the river floodplain appear poor—boggy and undeveloped. The people working in the fields look gaunt-eyed and discouraged as if they have given up already any dreams of success or prosperity. We passed one poor fellow trying futilely to plow a flooded field with a team of oxen; it was clearly a hopeless endeavor, for his oxen were mired up to their chests in the mud, and the man finally sat down himself and put his head dejectedly in his arms, looking as though he was going to weep.

I suspect that the uplands are better suited to the cattle business than are these marshy lowlands to agriculture. Indeed, the further west we move the more bovines we encounter—a variety of cattle that is quite different from anything I have ever seen back in Illinois, longer-legged, rangier, and wilder, with long, gracefully arced horns. Yesterday we saw a colorful sight—a herd of what must have been several thousand cows being driven across the river by "cowboys." The engineer had to stop the train for fear of a collision with the beasts, thus giving us a wonderful opportunity to observe the scene. Of course, I have read about the cowboys in periodicals and I have seen artists' renderings of them and now I find that they are every bit as colorful and festive in the flesh. Martha blushed quite crimson at the sight of them—a charming habit she has when excited—and an exciting scene it was, too. The cowboys make a thrilling little yipping noise as they drive their charges, waving their hats in the air cheerfully. It all seems rather wild and romantic, with the herd splashing across the river, urged along by these gay cowboys. We are told by one of the soldiers that these men are on the way from Texas to Montana Territory, where a prosperous new ranching industry is springing up. Who knows, perhaps we "Indian brides" will also visit that country in time—we have been forewarned that the savages are a nomadic people, and that we are to be prepared for frequent and sudden moves.

3 April 1875

Today our train has been stopped for several hours while a number of the men aboard indulge in a bit of "sport"—the shooting of dozens of buffalo from the train windows. I fail to see myself where exactly the sport in this slaughter lies as the buffalo seem to be as stupid and trusting as dairy cows. The poor dumb beasts simply mill about as they are knocked down one by one like targets at a carnival shooting gallery, while the men aboard, including members of our military escort, behave like crazed children—whooping and hollering and congratulating themselves on their prowess with the long gun. The women for the most part are silent, holding handkerchiefs to their noses while the train car fills with acrid smoke from the guns. It is a grotesque spectacle and seems terribly wasteful to me—the animals are left where they fall, many of those that aren't killed outright, mortally wounded and bellowing pitifully. Some of the cows have newborn spring calves with them and these, too, are cheerfully dispatched by the shooters. I have noticed during the past day that the country we are passing through is littered with bones and carcasses in various stages of decay and that a noticeable stench of rotting flesh often pervades the air. Such an ugly, unnatural thing can come to no good in God's eyes or anyone else's for that matter. I can't help but think once again what a foolish, loutish creature is man. Is there another on earth that kills for the pure joy of it?

Now we are finally under way again, the bloodlust of the men evidently sated . . .

8 April 1875—Fort Sidney, Nebraska Territory

We have reached our first destination, and are being lodged in officers' homes while we await transportation on the next leg of our journey. Martha and I have been separated, and I am staying with the family of an officer named Lieutenant James. His wife Abigail is tight-lipped and cool and seems to have adopted the superior attitude with which those of us enrolled in this program have been treated by virtually everyone with whom we have come in contact since the beginning of our journey. Although "officially" we are going among the heathens as missionaries, everyone seems to know the real truth of our mission, and everyone seems to despise us for it. Perhaps I am naive to expect otherwise—that we might be accorded some measure of respect as volunteers in an important social and political experiment but of course small-minded souls like the Lieutenant's wife must have someone to look down upon, and so they have cast us in the role of whores.

Shortly after our arrival, my hostess knocked on the door to my room, and when I answered, refused to enter but demanded in a haughty tone that I not speak of our mission in front of her children at the dining table.

"As our mission is a secret one," I answered, "I had no intention of discussing it. May I ask why you make such a request, madam?"

"The children have been exposed to the drunken, degenerate savages who frequent the fort," the woman replied. "They are a filthy people whom I would not invite into my home, let alone allow to sit at my dinner table. Nor will I permit my children to fraternize with the savage urchins. We have been ordered by the fort commander to house you women and to feed you, but it is not by our choice, nor does it reflect our own moral judgment against you. I shall not have my children corrupted by any discussion of the shameful matter. Do I make myself clear?"

"Perfectly," I answered. "And may I add that I would rather starve to death than to sit at your dining table."

Thus I spent my short time at Mrs. James's home in my room. I did not eat. Early one morning I went out to walk on the fort grounds, but even then I was leered at by a group of soldiers and by some very rough-looking brigands in buckskin clothes who frequent the fort. Their lewd remarks caused me, however reluctantly, to give up even the small diversion of walking. Our mission appears to be the worst-kept secret on the frontier, and seems to threaten and terrify all who know of it. Ah, well, this is of scant consequence to me; I am rather accustomed to doing the unconventional, the unpopular . . . clearly to a fault . . . Frankly, from the way I have been treated by the so-called "civilized" people in my life, I rather look forward to residency among the savages. I should hope that at the very least they might appreciate us.

11 April 1875

We are under way again, on a military train to Fort Laramie. We have lost several more of our number at Sidney. They must have had a change of heart with our destination now so close, or perhaps the army families with whom they were lodged convinced them to abandon this "immoral" program.

Or perhaps—and most likely of all—they took to heart the pathetic sight of the poor savages who inhabit the environs of the fort. I must admit that these are as scurvy a lot of beggars and drunkards as ever I've witnessed. Filthy and dressed in rags, they fall down in the dirt and sleep in their own filth. My God, if I were told that one of these poor unfortunates was to be my new husband, I, too, would reconsider. How they must stink!

While at Fort Sidney, my friend Phemie was put up by the Negro blacksmith and his wife. Many of our women have refused to be housed with Phemie during our journey because she is a Negro. As we are all of us off to live and procreate with heathens of a different race and a darker color, such fine distinctions strike me as especially pointless—and I wager that they will become less and less pronounced once we are among the savages themselves. Indeed, I suspect that Phemie will come to seem more and more like one of us . . . like a white person.

The blacksmith and his wife were very kind to Phemie and gave her extra clothing for her journey. They told her that the "free" Indians with whom we will be living are not at all like these "fort sitters," and that the Cheyennes are regarded as among the most handsome and cleanly of the various plains tribes, and their women considered to be the very most virtuous. We were all greatly relieved by this news.

The new train is a considerably more spartan affair, the seats mere benches of rough wood; it is as if we are being slowly stripped of the luxuries of civilization. Martha seems increasingly anxious; the poor mute child Sara practically hysterical with anxiety—she has chewed her finger nearly raw . . . even the usually boisterous and cheerful Gretchen has fallen oddly silent and apprehensive. And all the others are in various states of distress. The Lovelace woman drinks her "medicine" furtively and silently from her flask, clutching her old white poodle to her bosom. Miss Flight still wears her perpetual expression of surprise, but it is now tinged with a certain anxiety. Our woman in black, Ada Ware, who rarely speaks, looks more than ever like an angel of death. The Kelly sisters, too, seem to have lost a good measure of their street-urchin cheekiness in the face of these endless, desolate prairies. The twins have stopped prowling the train and sit across from each other like mirror images, quietly staring out the window. Of great relief to all, the evangelist, Narcissa White, who is usually preaching loudly enough for everyone to hear, is now lost in fervent, silent prayer.

Only Phemie, God bless her, remains, as always, calm, unperturbed, her head held high, a slight smile at her lips. I think the trials and tribulations of her life have given her a nearly unshakable strength; she is a force to behold.

And just now she has done a very fine thing. Just as we have all sunk to our lowest ebb, exhausted from the long journey, discouraged and frightened of what lies ahead; riding silently, and staring out the window of the train, and seeing nothing but the most dreadfully barren landscape—dry, rocky, treeless—truly country with nothing to recommend it, country that increases our anxieties and seems to presage this terrible new world to which we are being born away. Just then Phemie began to sing, in her low melodic voice, a Negro slave song about the underground railroad:

This train is bound for glory, this train.
This train is bound for glory, this train.
This train is bound for glory,
Get on board and tell your story
This train is bound for glory, this train.

And now all eyes were watching Phemie, and some of our women smiled timidly, listening spellbound while she sang:

This train don't pull no extras, this train,
This train don't pull no extras, this train,
This train don't pull no extras,
Don't pull nothing but the midnight special,
This train don't pull no extras, this train . . .

The proud brave sorrow in Phemie's lovely voice gave us courage, and when she took up the first verse again: *"This train is bound for glory, this train"* . . . I, too, began to sing with her . . . *"This train is bound for glory, this train. . . ."* And a few others joined in, *"This train is bound for glory, Get on board and tell your story"* . . . and soon, nearly all the women—even I noticed "Black Ada"—were singing a rousing and joyous chorus, *"This train is bound for glory, this train . . ."* Ah, yes, glory . . . isn't it fine to think so . . .

➛ NOTEBOOK II ➛

Passage to the Wilderness

"A peace is of the nature of a conquest;
For then both parties nobly are subdu'd,
And neither party loser."

(William Shakespeare,
Henry VI, Part Two, Act IV, Scene 2,
from the journals of May Dodd)

⊹

13 April 1875

Well, here we are at last, Fort Laramie, a dusty godforsaken place if ever there was one. It seems a hundred years ago that we left the comparative lushness of the Chicago prairie to arrive in this veritable desert of rock and dust. Good God!

We are housed here together in barracks, sleeping on rough wooden cots—all very primitive and uncomfortable . . . and yet I should not speak those words just yet. How much more uncomfortable will our lives become in the ensuing weeks? A week's rest here, we are told, at which time we are to be escorted north by a U.S. Army detachment to Camp Robinson, where we are finally to meet our new Indian husbands. Sometimes I am convinced that I really must be insane—that we all are. Would not one have to be insane to come to a place like this of one's own free will? To agree to live with savages? To marry a heathen? My God, Harry, why did you let them take me away . . .

13 April 1875

My Dear Harry,

You have perhaps by now heard the news of my departure from the Chicago area. Of my relocation to the West. Or perhaps this news has not yet reached you? Perhaps you are dead, done in by Father's hooligans . . . Oh Harry, I have tried not to think of you, tried not to think of our sweet babies. Did you give us all up, Harry, for a handful of coins? I loved you so, and it tortures me not to know the answer to these questions. Were you with another woman on the night of our abduction from your life, drinking and unaware of our plight? I prefer to believe so, Harry, than to believe that you were in league with Father. Was I not your faithful lover, the mother of your children? Were we not happy for a time, you and I?

Did we not love our dear babies? How much money did he give you, Harry? How much was your family worth to you?

I'm sorry . . . surely I have unjustly accused you . . . perhaps I shall never know the truth . . . Oh, Harry, my sweet, my love, they have taken our babies . . . God, I miss them so, I ache for them at night, when I awaken with a start, their dear sweet faces in my dreams. I lie awake wondering how they are getting on, wondering if they have any memory of their poor mother who loves them so. If only I could have some news of them. Have you seen them? No, surely not. Father would never allow it, nor even allow the fact that such a lowborn man such as yourself could be the father of his grandchildren. They will grow up spoiled and privileged as I did, insufferable little monsters who will look down on the likes of you, Harry. Strange, isn't it? That our lives could be torn from us so suddenly, our children swept away in the middle of the night, their mother incarcerated in an insane asylum, their father . . . God only knows what has become of you, Harry. Did they kill you or did they pay you? Did you die or did you sell us to the highest bidder? Should I hate you or should I mourn you? I can hardly bear to think of you, Harry, without knowing . . . now I can only dream of someday returning to Chicago, after my mission here is fulfilled, of coming home to be again with my children, of finding you and seeking the truth in your eyes.

As it is, Harry, how fortunate that you and I were never officially married, for I am presently betrothed to another. Yes, that's right, I know it seems sudden. But my general objections to the institution of marriage notwithstanding, I have struck a strange bargain to purchase my freedom. And although I do not as yet know the lucky gentleman's name, I do know that he is an Indian of the Cheyenne tribe. Yes, well, I can only make this admission in a letter which even if I knew how to reach you, I would be forbidden to mail. This is all supposed to be very secret, though of course it is not . . . And while it may sound insane to say so, I felt that I had a duty to write to you, to tell you this news . . . even if I cannot post this letter. Having discharged my obligation, I remain, if nothing else . . .

The loving mother of your children,
May

17 April 1875

After a week here at Fort Laramie, I shall be happy to be under way at last. The boredom has been unrelieved. We are kept under virtual lock and key, prisoners in these barracks, allowed only an hour to walk around the grounds in the afternoons, escorted always by soldiers. Perhaps they fear that we will fraternize with the agency Indians and all of us have a change of heart. I must say these are every bit as abject as those at Sidney—a sorrier more disgraceful group of wretches could not exist on earth. Primarily Sioux, Arapaho, and Crows we are told. The men do nothing but drink, gamble, beg, and try to barter their poor ragged wives and daughters to the soldiers for a drink of whiskey, or to the half-breeds and other criminal white men who congregate around the fort. It is all unsavory and pathetic—many of the women are themselves too drunk to protest and, in any case, have very little say in these vile transactions.

Yet we must keep heart that these fort Indians are in no way representative of the people to whom we are being taken. At least so I continue to maintain for the sake of the child Sara and my friend Martha. As I pointed out to Martha, even in the unlikely event that her husband were to trade her to a soldier for a bottle of whiskey, it would only mean that she would be free, relieved of her duty, back among her own people. Ah, but then I had forgotten that dear Martha's heart is now firmly set on finding true love among the savages, and thus my attempt to comfort her with the possible failure of her union had quite the opposite effect.

The only other diversion in our otherwise tedious stay at Fort Laramie comes during the communal meals held in the officers' dining hall. We have been, presumably for reasons of security, isolated from the general civilian population at the fort, but some of the officers and their wives are allowed to take their meals with us. Once again the "official" version of our visit here is that we are off to do "missionary" work among the savages.

Today I had occasion to be seated at the table of one Captain John G. Bourke, to whose care our group has been assigned for the remainder of this journey. The Captain is aide-de-camp to General George Crook himself, the famous Indian fighter who recently subdued the savage Apache tribe in Arizona Territory. Some of our ladies had read about the General's exploits in the Chicago newspapers. Of course, I did not have access to such luxuries as newspapers in the asylum . . .

I am very favorably impressed with Captain Bourke. He is a true gentleman and treats us, finally, with proper courtesy and respect. The Captain is unmarried, but rumored to be engaged to the post commander's daughter, a pretty if somewhat uninteresting young lady named Lydia Bradley, who sat on his right at table, and tried to monopolize the Captain's attention by making the most vapid conversation imaginable. Although he was most solicitous of her, she clearly bores him witless.

Captain Bourke was far more interested in our group, and asked many penetrating, if delicately phrased, questions of us. He is clearly privy to the true nature of our mission—which is not to say that he approves of it. Having spent a good deal of time among the aboriginals during his former posting in Arizona Territory, the Captain prides himself on being something of an amateur ethnographer and seems quite knowledgeable about the savage way of life.

Apropos of nothing, I shall, by way of personal aside, mention my observation that the Captain appears to have rather an eye for the ladies. I confess that he is a most handsome fellow, with fine military bearing and a manly build. He is dark of hair that falls just over his collar, wears a moustache, and has deep-set, soulful, hazel eyes, with a fine mischievous glint to them as if he were perpetually amused about something. Indeed his eyes seem less those of a soldier than they do those of a poet—and are shadowed, somewhat romantically, by a slightly heavy brow. He is a man of obvious intelligence and sensitivity.

It amused me and pleased my vanity to notice further that Captain Bourke directed more of his conversation to me than to any of the other women at the table. This fact was not lost on his fiancée and only served to make the poor thing prattle on ever more inanely.

"John, dear," she interrupted him at one point just as he was making an interesting observation about the religious ceremonies of the Arizona savages. "I'm sure that the ladies would prefer conversation about more civilized topics at the dining table. For instance, you have very cavalierly neglected to compliment me on my new hat, which just arrived from St. Louis and is the very latest fashion in New York."

The Captain looked at her with a distracted and mildly amused air. "Your hat, Lydia?" he asked. "And what does your hat have to do with the Chiricahuas' medicine dance?"

Her efforts to turn the conversation to the topic of her hat thus rebuffed, the poor girl flushed with embarrassment. "Why, of course, nothing whatsoever, dear," she said. "I thought only that the ladies might be more interested in New York fashion as a topic of dinner conversation than in the frankly tedious subject of savage superstitions. Is that not so, Miss Dodd?" she asked.

I could not help uttering an astonished laugh. "Why yes, Miss Bradley, your hat is perfectly lovely," I said. "Tell me, Captain, do you think that we women might be able to impart to our savage hosts a finer appreciation of New York fashion?"

The Captain smiled at me and nodded gallantly. "How very deftly, madam, you have married the two topics of ladies headwear and savage customs," he said, his eyes sparkling with good humor. "Would that your upcoming missionary work among them be accomplished as smoothly."

"Do I detect a tone of skepticism in your voice, Captain?" I asked. "You do not believe that we might teach the savages the benefits of our culture and civilization?"

The Captain adopted a more serious tone. "It has been my experience, madam," he said, "that the American Indian is unable, by his very nature, to understand our culture—just as our race is unable fully to comprehend their ways."

"Which is precisely the intended purpose of our mission," I said, treading rather closely to the subject of our "secret." "To foster harmony and understanding among the races—the melding of future generations into one people."

"Ah, a noble notion, madam," said the Captain, nodding in full acknowledgment of my meaning, "but—and I hope you will forgive me for speaking bluntly—pure poppycock. What we risk creating when we tamper with God's natural separation of the races will not be one harmonious people, but a people dispossessed, adrift, a generation without identity or purpose, neither fish nor fowl, Indian nor Caucasian."

"A sobering thought, Captain," I said, "to a prospective mother of that generation. And you do not believe that we might exert any beneficent influence whatsoever over these unfortunate people?"

The Captain reddened in embarrassment at the boldness of my admission, and Miss Bradley looked confused by the turn in the conversation.

"It has been my unfortunate experience, Miss Dodd," he said, "that in spite of three hundred years of contact with civilization, the American Indian has never learned anything from us but our vices."

"By which you mean," I said, "that in your professional opinion our mission among them is hopeless."

The Captain looked at me with his intelligent soulful eyes, the furrow between his eyebrows deepening. I thought I detected in his gaze, not only concern, but something more. He spoke in a low voice and his words chilled me to the bone. "It would be treasonous for an officer to speak against the orders of his Commander in Chief, Miss Dodd."

A hush fell over the table, from which all parties were grateful to be rescued finally by Helen Flight. "I say, Miss Bradley," she said, "were you aware that the feathers on your hat are the breeding plumes of the snowy egret?"

"Why, no, I wasn't," answered Miss Bradley, who seemed relieved and somehow vindicated by the fact that the conversation had come back, after all, to the subject of her hat. "Isn't that fascinating!"

"Quite," Helen said. "Rather a nasty business, actually, which I had occasion to witness last spring while I was in the Florida swamps studying the wading birds of the Everglades for my *Birds of America* portfolio. As you correctly stated, the feather-festooned hat such as the one you wear is very much the vogue in New York fashion these days. The hatmakers there have commissioned the Seminole Indians who inhabit the Everglades to supply them with feathers for the trade. Unfortunately the adult birds grow the handsome plumage that adorns your chapeau only during the nesting season. The Indians have devised an ingenious method of netting the birds while they are on their nests—which the birds are reluctant to leave due to their instinct to protect their young. Of course, the Indians must kill the adult birds in order to pluck the few 'aigrettes' or nuptial plumes as they are more commonly known. Entire rookeries are thus destroyed, the young orphaned birds left to starve in the nest." Miss Flight gave a small shudder. "Pity . . . a terribly disagreeable sound that of a rookery full of nestlings crying for their parents," she said. "You can hear it across the swamp for miles . . ."

Poor Miss Bradley went quite ashen at this explanation and now touched her new hat with trembling fingers. I feared that the poor thing was going to burst into tears. "John," she said faintly, "would you please escort me back to my quarters. I'm feeling a bit unwell."

"Oh, dear, did I say something wrong?" asked Helen, her eyebrows raised expectantly. "That is to say, I'm frightfully sorry if I upset you, Miss Bradley."

I was anxious to speak to Captain Bourke at greater length, and in private, about his obvious objections to our mission among the savages, and after dinner I spied him sitting alone in a chair on the veranda of the dining room, smoking a cigar. The bald truth is, I am undeniably drawn to the Captain, which attraction perforce can come to naught . . . but what harm can there be in an innocent flirtation?

I must have startled the Captain, for he fairly leapt from his seat at my approach.

"Miss Dodd," he said, bowing politely.

"Good evening, Captain," I answered. "I trust that Miss Bradley is not too ill? I'm afraid Helen's remarks upset her."

The Captain waved his hand, dismissively. "I'm afraid that Miss Bradley finds many things upsetting about life on the frontier," he said with an amused glimmer in his eye. "She was sent here last year from New York, where she has lived most of her life with her mother. She is discovering that army forts are hardly suited to young ladies of refined sensibilities."

"Better suited, perhaps," I said jokingly, "to we rough-and-ready girls from the Middle West."

"Not well suited, I should say," answered the Captain, his brow knitted thoughtfully, "to womankind in general."

"Tell me, Captain," I asked, "if life at the fort is difficult for women, how much harder will our life be among the savages?"

"As you may have guessed, Miss Dodd, I have been fully briefed by my superiors about your mission," he said. "As I suggested in our dinner conversation on the subject, I would prefer not to express my opinion."

"But you already have, Captain," I answered. "And in any case, I do not ask your opinion. I merely ask you, as an expert on the subject of the savage culture, to describe something of what we might expect in our new lives."

"Am I to understand," said the Captain, his voice tightening in anger, "that our government did not provide you ladies with any such information when you were recruited for this mission?"

"They suggested that we should be prepared to do some camping," I said—not without a trace irony in my tone.

"Camping . . ." the Captain murmured. ". . . madness, the entire project is utter madness."

"Would this be a personal or a professional opinion, Captain?" I asked with an attempt at a laugh. "President Ulysses S. Grant himself has dispatched us on this noble undertaking, and you call it madness. Perhaps this is the treason to which you referred."

The Captain turned away from me, his hands crossed behind his back, the fingers of one still holding the smoldering cigar. His strong profile with long straight nose was outlined against the horizon; his nearly black hair fell in curls over his collar. Although this was hardly the time for such observation on my part, I confess that I could not help but notice again what a fine figure of a man the Captain is—broad of back, narrow of hip, straight of carriage . . . the breeches of the soldier's uniform displayed the Captain's physique in a most favorable light . . . watching him now, I felt a stab of something very like . . . desire—a sensation which I further attribute to the fact that I have been, for over a year, confined to an institution without benefit of masculine company, other than that of my loathsome tormentors.

Now Captain Bourke turned around to face me, looked down upon me with a penetrating gaze that quite literally brought the blood to my cheeks. "Yes," he said, nodding, "the President's men in Washington sent you women here, consigned you to marriage with barbarians as some sort of preposterous political experiment. Camping? The very least of your worries, Miss Dodd, I assure you. Of course, the Washingtonians have no idea what sort of hardships await you—and probably don't care. As usual, they have not bothered themselves to consult those of us who do know. Our orders are simply to see that you are delivered safely to your new husbands—offered up, as it were, as trade goods. To be traded for horses! Shame!" said the Captain, whose anger had come up now like a fast-moving squall. "Shame on them! It is an abomination in the eyes of God."

"Horses?" I replied in a small voice.

"Perhaps they neglected to mention that the savages offered horses for their white brides," the Captain said.

I recovered my composure quickly. "Perhaps we should be flattered," I said. "I understand that the savages hold their horses in the very highest esteem. Furthermore, you must remember, my dear Captain, that no one forced us to participate in this program. We are volunteers. If there is shame in our mission, then some of it must rest with those of us who signed up of our own free will."

The Captain looked at me searchingly, as if trying to ferret out some possible motive that might make such a thing comprehensible to him. His broad brow cast a shadow like a cloud over his eyes. "I watched you at table tonight, Miss Dodd," he said in a low voice.

"Your regard did not escape my attention, Captain," I said, the blood rising again in my cheeks . . . a certain tingling sensation.

"I was trying to understand what had possessed a lovely young woman like yourself to join such an unlikely enterprise with such a motley assortment of cohorts," he continued. "Some of the others . . . well, quite frankly it is easier to speculate why some of the others had signed up. Your British friend, Miss Flight, for instance, clearly has a pressing professional need to visit the prairies. And the Irish sisters, the Kelly twins, why they have the look of rogues about them if ever I've seen it—I'll wager that they were in trouble with the police back in Chicago. And the big German girl—well, surely her matrimonial prospects among men of her own race are somewhat limited . . ."

"That is most unkind, Captain," I snapped. "You disappoint me. I took you for too much of a gentleman to make such a remark. The fact is that we are none of us any better than the next. We all entered into this for our own personal reasons, none of which is superior to that of the others. Or necessarily any of your concern."

The Captain straightened his back and clicked his heels together with smart military precision. He inclined his head in a slight bow. "You're quite right, madam," he said. "Please accept my apology. My intention was not to insult your companions. I only meant that a pretty, intelligent, witty, and obviously well-brought-up young lady such as yourself hardly fits the description of the felons, lonely hearts, and mentally deranged women that we had been notified by the government to expect as volunteers in this bizarre experiment."

"I see," I said, and I laughed. "So this is how our little troupe was billed; no wonder that we have been treated with such disdain by all we encounter. Would it salve your conscience, Captain, to know that you were handing over only such misfits and riffraff to the savages?"

"Not in the least," said the Captain. "That isn't at all what I meant." And then Captain Bourke did a peculiar thing. He took me by the elbow, grasped my arm lightly but firmly in his hand. The gesture was at once oddly proprietary and intimate, like the touch of a lover, and I felt again the pulse of my own desire. He stepped closer to me, still holding my arm, close enough that I could smell the aura of cigar smoke about him, could smell his own rich manly odor. "It would still be possible for you to refuse, madam," he said.

I looked into his eyes, and stupidly, as if in a kind of trance, as if paralyzed by his touch, I took his words to mean that it would still be possible for me to refuse his amorous advances.

"And why would I do that, Captain?" I asked in a whisper. "How could I refuse you?"

And then it was the Captain's turn to laugh, releasing my arm suddenly and pulling away, clearly embarrassed by this misunderstanding . . . or was it? "Forgive me, Miss Dodd," he said. "I meant . . . I only meant that it would still be possible for you to refuse to participate in the Brides for Indians program."

I must have turned very red in the face. I excused myself then and returned forthwith to my quarters.

18 April 1875

Captain Bourke was noticeably absent at the dining table yesterday, as was his fiancée Miss Bradley . . . I suspect that they must have dined privately, perhaps in the Captain's own quarters . . . Hah! It suddenly occurs to me that my journal entries—like my entirely inappropriate romantic longings of the past twenty-four hours—begin to sound like those of a lovesick schoolgirl. I seem quite unable to get the good Captain out of my mind. I must be insane! . . . betrothed to a man whom I have not met, infatuated with a man whom I cannot have. Good God! Perhaps my family was correct in committing me to the asylum for promiscuity . . .

19 April 1875

Dear Hortense,

It is very late at night, and I write to you by the dim light of a single candle in our spartan Army barracks at Fort Laramie. I am unable to sleep. A very strange thing has happened tonight of which I can not breathe a word to any of my fellow brides. Yet I am bursting to confide in someone, and so I must write you, my sister . . . yes, it reminds me of when we were little girls and still close, you and I, and I would come into your room late at night and crawl into your bed and we would giggle and tell each other our deepest secrets . . . how I miss you, dear Hortense . . . miss the way we once were . . . do you remember?

Let me tell you my secret. At dinner this evening I was seated once again, and I think not by accident, at the table of one Captain John G. Bourke, who has been chosen to escort us to Indian territory. Indeed, we are scheduled to depart tomorrow for Camp Robinson, Nebraska Territory, where we are to meet our new Indian husbands.

Although he is only twenty-seven years of age, Captain Bourke is a very important officer, already a war hero, having won the Medal of Honor at the bloody battle of Stones River, Tennessee. He comes from a good middle-class family in Philadelphia, is well-educated and a complete gentleman. He is at once extremely witty, with a mischievous sense of humor, and truly one of the handsomest men I've ever set eyes on—dark with intelligent, piercing hazel eyes that seem able to gaze directly into my heart. It is most disconcerting.

Under the circumstances you might think that there is little opportunity for gaiety or flirtation among our group of lambs off to slaughter, but this is not so. Dinnertime especially offers us some diversion from the boredom and inactivity of fort life, and in the manner natural to any group of unmarried women, all have been vying for the Captain's attentions. And all are green with envy that he only has eyes for me.

Our mutual, and perforce, perfectly innocent attraction and good-natured banter has not been lost on Miss Lydia Bradley, the post commander's pretty, if vapid, daughter, to whom Captain Bourke is engaged to be married this summer. She watches her fiancé like a hawk—as I would if he were mine—and misses no opportunity to divert him from his attentions toward me.

As a painfully obvious tactic toward this end, Miss Bradley goes to great lengths to cast me in an unfavorable light in the Captain's eyes. Unfortunately she's not a terribly clever girl, and her efforts so far have been distinctly unsuccessful. Tonight at table, for instance, she said: "Tell me, Miss Dodd, as a member of the church missionary society, I am curious to know with which denomination you are affiliated?" Ah, so her first gambit would be to expose me as a Protestant in front of the Captain who, is himself, as he had just informed us, Catholic, having been educated as a boy by the Jesuits.

"Actually, Miss Bradley, I am neither a member of the missionary society," I said, "nor affiliated with any particular denomination. Truth be told, I'm a bit of an agnostic when it comes to organized religion." I have found that the best, and certainly simplest defense of one's faith, or lack thereof, is the truth. And while I hoped that this information did not prejudice the good Captain against me, it has also been my experience that the Roman Catholics often prefer those of no faith to those of the wrong faith.

"Oh?" said the girl, feigning confusion. "I would have thought that to go among the heathens as a missionary, membership in the church would be the very first requisite."

It was again obvious where Miss Bradley was trying so clumsily to lead me. I'm certain that the Captain's sense of duty and discretion would have prevented him from discussing professional matters with his fiancée, but clearly she had by now deduced the true nature of our enterprise.

"That would depend," I answered lightly, "on what sort of mission one was fulfilling, Miss Bradley. Of course, I am not at liberty to discuss the details of our upcoming work among the savages, but suffice it to say that we are . . . shall we say . . . ambassadors of peace."

"I see," said the girl, visibly disappointed that she had elicited from me no hint of embarrassment for being a wanton woman off to couple with heathens. Having spent over a year in a lunatic asylum for roughly this same "sin," I am scarcely intimidated by the transparent interrogations of a twit such as Miss Bradley. "Ambassadors of peace . . ." she added, trying for a trace of sarcasm in her voice.

"That's right," I said, and I quoted:

> "*'A peace is of the nature of a conquest;*
> *For then both parties nobly are subdu'd,*
> *And neither party loser.'*

So saith the great Shakespeare."

"*Henry VI,* Part Two, Act IV, Scene 2!" boomed the Captain, with a broad smile. And then he quoted himself:

> "*'You did know*
> *How much you were my conqueror, and that*
> *My sword, made weak by my affection, would*
> *Obey it on all cause.'* "

"*Antony and Cleopatra,* Act III, Scene 11," I said, with equal pleasure.

"Wonderful!" the Captain said. "You're a student of the Bard, Miss Dodd!"

I laughed heartily. "And you, too, sir!" And poor Miss Bradley, having inadvertently led us, like horses to water, toward yet another common interest, fell silent and brooding, as we embarked upon a lively discussion of the great Shakespeare, joined enthusiastically by Miss Flight. The Captain is bright and extremely well read—altogether a perfectly charming dinner companion, and the evening was very gay, without further mention of our rapidly approaching fate . . .

Yes, yes, I know, Hortense. I can hear your objections already. I am fully aware that this is hardly the time to be embarking upon romantic liaisons—especially as both Captain Bourke and I are, shall we say, "bespoke." On the other hand, perhaps there is no better time for just such innocent flirtation—which is certainly all that it can be. After my ghastly ordeal in the asylum, where I fully expected to die lying in a dark, sunless room, you cannot imagine how wonderful it is to be in the company of a dashing Army officer who finds me . . . desirable. You would have no way of knowing this dear, but often forbidden love is the sweetest of all . . . ah yes, I can just hear you saying, "Good Lord, now she speaks of love!"

After dinner, poor Miss Bradley was "unwell"—the second time she has fallen ill since she's dined with our group. The Captain maintains that she is simply too delicate for frontier life, but as we women well know, feigning illness is the last refuge of one who lacks imagination.

I was already on the porch waiting for him when, after escorting Miss Bradley home, Captain Bourke returned to smoke his evening cigar. It was a lovely spring evening, warm and mild. The days are lengthening and dusk was just beginning to settle over the land, so that the bare rocky buttes of this godforsaken country were softened in gentle outline against the horizon. There was still a bit of color in the sky where the sun had set over the western hills. I stood facing the day's last fading light when the Captain approached.

"Would you care to take a stroll around the fort grounds, Miss Dodd?" he asked, stepping beside me so that his arm brushed lightly against mine. His touch was like that of flesh on flesh. It made my knees weak.

"I'd be delighted, Captain," I said, but I did not move away from his touch . . . indeed, could not. "Are you certain that your fiancée would approve," I added only half-jokingly, "of your keeping company with another woman?"

"Unquestionably she would not," the Captain said. "I'm sure you must find her to be a silly thing, Miss Dodd."

"No, not silly," I said. "Quite charming actually. Perhaps only rather young for her years . . . a bit callow."

"And yet she is not, I suspect, very much younger than you, madam," he said.

"Ah, tread cautiously, Captain!" I said "—a delicate subject, a woman's age. In any case, I am old for my years. As you are for yours."

"In what way old, Miss Dodd?" he asked.

"In the way of experience, Captain Bourke," I said. "Perhaps you and I can more fully appreciate the great Shakespeare because we have both lived enough of life to understand the truth and wisdom of his words."

"In my case war was a stern teacher of truth, if not wisdom," said the Captain. "But how is it that a young woman of your obvious breeding knows so much of life, madam?"

"Captain, it is quite likely that you and I will not know each other long enough for my personal history to matter," I said.

"It matters to me already, Miss Dodd," he said. "Surely, you are aware of that."

I still stared at the horizon, but I could feel the Captain's dark eyes on my face, the heat of his arm against mine. My breath came in shallow draughts as if I could not take sufficient air into my lungs. "It is late, Captain," I managed to say. "Perhaps we should take our stroll another time." Where our arms had touched and now parted it was like tearing my own flesh from the bone.

My candle burns down, dear Hortense, I must rest my pen . . .

I am,

Your loving sister, May

20 April 1875

Under way at last, we ride in mule-drawn wagons, escorted by a very snappy company of cavalry, at the head of which Captain John G. Bourke, with perfect military carriage, rides a smart-stepping white mare. That the army has entrusted us to the care of such an illustrious Indian fighter as the Captain is testament, I believe, to the fact that our safety is of the utmost concern to the authorities.

A number of the fort residents have gathered to watch our procession out the gates, including the Captain's pretty young fiancée, Lydia Bradley, who is dressed in a lovely pale pink spring dress and a matching bonnet (noticeably unadorned by feathers) and who smiles and waves a white handerchief at her Captain as he passes. He tips his hat to her gallantly. How I envy them, the life they will lead together. How drab she makes me feel . . .

Then we are through the gates, and beyond the fort and into the great prairie itself. Here the road rapidly deteriorates until it is little more than two ruts and then seems to disappear altogether. The ride is rough, the wagon itself exceedingly uncomfortable, with only the most unforgiving benches on which to sit. We are constantly jostled, often so violently that it seems to shake our teeth loose in our heads. Dust seeps up through the floorboards so that a perpetual cloud roils inside. Poor Martha has been sneezing since we got under way. With fully a fortnight yet to go I fear that it will be a long, desperately unhappy journey for her.

21 April 1875

Spring is in full bloom today, which offers a bit of cheer to this otherwise difficult passage. Much to the shock of some of the other ladies, I have decided to ride up on the buckboard alongside our teamster, a rough-spoken young man named Jimmy. I prefer the open air to choking on dust inside the wagon, and I am able to see something of the countryside as we pass, to enjoy a bit of the springtime.

Beyond the vastly improved view, another advantage to riding up top with Jimmy is that he can educate me about this new country of ours. While he is a rough lad, he seems quite knowledgeable on the subject, and I think that secretly he rather enjoys the feminine company.

Whereas the country on our first day of travel was flat, tedious, and largely without vegetation of interest, we seem today to be gaining a more varied topography of gently rolling hills intersected by rivers and creeks.

It has been a damp spring and the grass is as green as mother always described Scotland to be when she was a girl—the prairie wildflowers are just now coming into bloom, the birds everywhere in full song, the meadowlarks trilling joyously as if announcing our passage. There are ducks and geese by the thousands in every pothole of water and upon every flooded plain. Helen Flight is terribly pleased with the fecundity of bird life, and periodically begs the Captain to halt our procession so that she may descend with her shotgun to shoot one of the poor things—which she first sketches and then expertly skins to keep as a specimen for her work.

The Captain, a sportsman himself, so enjoys watching Miss Flight's prowess with the shotgun that he hardly objects to the delays caused by our frequent stops. Jimmy, my new muleskinner friend, is equally admiring of our accomplished gunner, and takes every opportunity to halt the wagon when birds are in range so that Miss Flight can display her considerable skills.

Thus she swings to the ground with masculine authority, all business, standing with her legs firmly planted, slightly apart, toes pointing out, to charge her muzzle loader. Even though the weather is warming daily, Miss Flight still wears her knickerbocker suit and particularly from the rear looks far more like a man than a woman. From a flask she carries in her jacket, she pours gunpowder into the barrel; this she rams home using wadded cotton from discarded petticoats. This is followed by a measure of very fine shot and then another wad made of card, which prevents the shot from rolling out the gun barrel. To her credit Miss Flight will only shoot the birds on the wing—believing it "unsporting" to do otherwise.

Not only does she collect her specimens in this manner, but she is filling our larder with all manner of game birds and waterfowl, which we surprise out of the plum thickets or spring potholes along the route. These include ducks, geese, grouse, snipe, and plover—which fare will undoubtedly provide a much welcome addition to our Army rations.

In only the first two days out from Fort Laramie, we have also seen deer, elk, antelope, and a small herd of bison grazing, and while the Captain will not permit the soldiers to hunt at too great a distance from the wagon train owing to the threat of Indians, we should have no want of fresh game en route.

Because of the spring floodwaters, we try to keep to the higher ground, though sometimes we are forced to drop down into the bottoms to ford the rivers and streams. It is hard going for the mules, who do not like to walk in thick mud, or even to get their feet wet. "There ain't nothin' an old mule hates worse," Jimmy instructs me, "than to put their *goddamn* feet down in water. They ain't like a horse that way. They's just *goddamn* prissy about water is all. But in every other way, you can give me an old mule over a horse any day. *Any day.*" A strange, rough boy, Jimmy, but he seems to have a good heart.

Traversing these drainages is a wet, muddy experience for us all. Several times already today we have had to descend to lighten the mules' load, hike our dresses up, and make our own way across the streams on foot, soaking our feet through to the bone.

And yet the river bottoms strike me as the loveliest country, for everything lives here, or passes by here or comes to water here from the long empty reaches of desert plains between.

At night we make camp as near to the water as possible while still being on dry ground. The mules are hobbled or picketed in the grass meadow, which is already lush with tender green shoots. It is very pretty. I think that one day I should like to live in such a place . . . perhaps one day I shall return home to reclaim my dear babies and we shall all come here together . . . to live in a little house on the banks of a creek, on the edge of a meadow, surrounded by a grove of cottonwood trees . . . ah, sweet dreams keep me alive . . .

Yes, indeed, and instead I shall soon be living in a tent! Think of it! Camped out like a nomad, a gypsy! What an astonishing adventure we have embarked upon!

To my great disappointment, Captain Bourke has hardly met my eye and barely spoken to me since we departed Fort Laramie. I sense that he is intentionally avoiding me. Perhaps because he is officially "on duty" now, his strict, military deportment appears to have completely supplanted his charming social demeanor. I confess to preferring the latter.

Tonight at dinner in the "mess" tent as the Army insists upon calling it, the conversation turned as it does with ever greater frequency to the subject of our Cheyennes. The Captain admitted, if rather grudgingly, that the tribe is a superior race as the American Indians go—a handsome, proud, and independent people, who have kept to themselves as much as they have been able in these times, avoiding the missionaries, the agencies, and general commerce with the whites more than any of the other tribes. This, the Captain stated, has allowed them to remain less "spoiled" than the others.

"I find that to be an unfortunate choice of words, Captain," objected our official church representative Narcissa White, "for it implies that contact with Christian civilization is the root cause of the spoilation of heathens, rather than the ladder by which they might climb from the muck of paganism."

"I consider myself to be a devout man, Miss White," answered the Captain. "But I am also a military man. It is the lesson of history that in order for Christian civilization to extend her noble boundaries, barbarians must first be roundly defeated on the battlefield. By spoiled I mean only that in giving the Red Man gifts—rations and charity that are not earned by the sweat of his own brow—our government has never accomplished anything other than to encourage him, like a dog fed scraps at table, to beg more gifts, rations, and charity."

"And brides," I interjected good-naturedly. "Give the damn heathens one thousand white women, and soon they'll want a thousand more!"

"Although I think you mock me, Miss Dodd," said the Captain with an amused glint in his eye, "that is exactly correct. Such well-intentioned gifts will only make them bolder in their demands. The savages will never be convinced of the benefits of civilization until they are first subdued by superior force."

"Yes, and isn't that why the government is sending us among them?" I said, with a bit of false bravado.

"*Yah*, May, I *tink* so," Gretchen Fathauer said. "I *tink dey* not seen superior force until *dey* seen us!" And we all laughed. For what else is there to do?

22 April 1875

This evening after dinner our muleskinner Jimmy called at the tent in which I share extremely close quarters with Phemie, Martha, Gretchen, and the girl Sara. Jimmy asked me to step outside for a word, and then proceeded to inform me that Captain Bourke should like to see me in his own quarters. There is little opportunity for privacy in our camps at the end of the day's travels, and I must say his request startled me, especially given the Captain's recent coolness toward me. The lad led me there. He is such a strange boy . . . I cannot put a finger on it . . .

The Captain greeted me at the entrance to his tent, and seemed genuinely pleased that I had come. "I hope you will not consider my invitation to be too forward, Miss Dodd," he said, "but evening bivouacs in the field can be exceptionally dull, particularly to an old Army man such as myself who has endured so many of them. I always carry with me in the field my cherished volume of Shakespeare, which I amuse myself by reading at night. I thought this evening you might be willing to join me—far more interesting to read aloud with a fellow enthusiast."

"Why thank you, Captain, I'd love to," I answered. "And shall I invite Helen Flight to join us, to play yet a third part?"

I had set this small trap for the Captain, just to gauge his reaction. And I was not displeased to see that he was unable to mask the flicker of disappointment that crossed his brow. But he recovered quickly and was, as usual, the perfect gentleman. "Yes . . . yes, by all means, Miss Dodd, a fine idea, do please ask Miss Flight to please join us. Shall I send Jimmy to fetch her?"

And then our eyes met and we stared for some time at one another, and the charade melted away in the heat of our gaze like parchment paper held over a candle flame. "Or possibly, John," I said in a low voice, "may I call you John?—possibly, John, it might, after all, be more amusing if it were just the two of us reading tonight."

"Yes, May," he whispered, "I was thinking so myself. Though I fear to expose you in any way to the appearance of impropriety."

"Ah, yes, the appearance of impropriety," I said. "Certainly that dreadfully sanctimonious woman Narcissa White will have her spies abroad. She misses nothing, and no opportunity to meddle in the affairs of others. But truthfully, Captain, at this point the appearance of impropriety is quite low on my list of immediate concerns."

And so I entered John Bourke's tent, an event which caused, as we had both suspected, no small scandal among our traveling party—although the evening was passed in perfect . . . I should say near perfect . . . innocence, for both of us are well aware of the other's feelings and to spend such time alone in company is only to fan the embers of that which cannot be. But this night we read Shakespeare together—nothing more. Nothing less. The fact is that nothing else has transpired between us besides a mutual but unspoken longing. It hangs between us, as palpable as a spider's web connecting our fates. Possibly it is simply due to the bizarre circumstances, or the fact that we must be denied one another, but I have never in my life known such a powerful stirring of feelings . . .

When I returned several hours later to my tent, Martha lay awake in her cot beside mine. "May, dear God, are you quite mad?" she whispered, as I slipped beneath my blanket.

I smiled and moved my head close to hers, and quoted, also in a whisper, " 'Love is merely a madness, and, I tell you, deserves as well a dark house and a whip as madmen do.' *As You Like It,* Act III, Scene 2. Perhaps this is why each time I have fallen in love, I am accused of madness, Martha."

"Love? Good God, May," Martha said, "it's impossible! The man is engaged. You are engaged. It can never be."

"I know, Martha," I answered. "Of course it can't. I only play. 'We that are true lovers run into strange capers.' As you may have guessed we amused ourselves by reading from *As You Like It* tonight."

"You're not going to quit us, May?" Martha asked with a tremor in her voice. "You're not going to abandon me to the savages while you run off with the Captain, are you?"

"Of course not, dear," I said. "All for one and one for all. Isn't that the vow we made?"

"Because I never would have come, May, if it weren't for you," said poor timid Martha, and I could tell that she was near to tears. "Please don't leave me. I've been worried sick about it, ever since I noticed how you and the Captain look at each other. Everyone has noticed. All have spoken of it."

I reached out and took Martha's hand in mine. "All for one and one for all," I repeated. "I'll never leave you, Martha. I swear. Never."

23 April 1875

As I had suspected, the White woman has already been spreading lies about my so-called "tryst" with the Captain. She is abetted in these efforts by the Southerner, Daisy Lovelace, with whom Miss White seems to have struck up an unlikely friendship—possibly because they are both generally disliked by the others. But what possible difference can their opinion of me make? The scurrilous gossip they spread is fueled by dull envy, and I shall not let it concern me.

Everyone has also noticed that both Miss White and Miss Lovelace try at every opportunity to curry favor with the Captain—unaware apparently that he, being a strict Catholic, dislikes Protestants on general principle—

and, by reason of his wartime experience in the Union Army, is equally prejudiced against Southerners.

It is a pathetic thing, indeed, to listen to the poor Lovelace woman trying to impress the Captain at the dining table with stories about her "Daddy" and the plantation they once owned with the two hundred "*niggahs*." Such information serves no other purpose than to offend the Captain further. One night at dinner, he asked her politely what had become of her father's plantation.

"Why Daddy lost everythin' during the *wah, suh*," she said. "Damn Yankees burned the house to the ground and set the *niggahs* free. Daddy never did recover from the shock; he took to drink and died a broken and penniless man."

"I'm very sorry to hear that, madam," the Captain said with a polite incline of his head, but not without the usual spark of amusement in his eyes. "And did your father fight in the great war?" he asked.

"No *suh*, he did not," said the dreadful woman, who clutched her old decrepit poodle, Fern Louise, to her breast. She allows the wretched little creature to sit on her lap at meals, fussing over it like a baby and feeding it morsels of food from her plate. "*Mah* daddy felt that his *fust duty* was to stay home and protect his family and his property from the vicious rape and pillage for which the Yankee army was so infamous. And so Daddy sent two of his best buck *niggahs* to fight in his stead. Course, straightaway they run off to join the Union, like all *niggahs*'ll do given the very *fust* opportunity." An unseen glance passed between the Captain and me; already we have a way of communicating wordlessly and we were both thinking at that moment that the Bard himself could scarcely have penned a more deserved end for this woman's dear departed daddy.

24 April 1875

We have now entered Indian country, and are forbidden to venture away from the wagons unescorted by soldiers. We have just been informed that last month Lt. Levi Robinson, after whom the new camp to which we are being conducted was named, was ambushed and murdered by hostile Sioux Indians from the nearby Red Cloud Agency while accompanying a wood train from Fort Laramie on this very same route. Evidently this news has been kept from us until now, for fear of causing panic among our women, and, of course, further explains our large military escort and the fact that Captain Bourke is in command of it.

The proximity of danger has imparted a new sense of immediacy to our mission, almost as if until this very moment, we had been but half-aware of the true nature of our destination—or perhaps only half-willing to think about it. I suspect that this may also be the cause of the increasing gravity I have noticed in John Bourke's countenance since we departed Fort Laramie. Onward we go, closer and closer to our appointed fate . . .

25 April 1875

I have made an extraordinary discovery. This afternoon I went into the willows to do my business and there I surprised our teamster "Jimmy" in the same act. By obvious means I now know that "he" is a "she"—yes, not a young man at all, but a woman! I knew something was peculiar about him . . . her . . . from the beginning. Her real name, she has confessed to me, is Gertie, and she is known on the frontier as "Dirty Gertie." We have heard stories of this woman's escapades at the forts and trading posts all along the way. A saloon girl, turned gambler, turned gunslinger, turned muleskinner, she's as rough and eccentric a woman as ever I've encountered, but not at all a bad sort, I believe, only a bit rough around the edges. She has begged me not to tell her secret as the other muleskinners are entirely ignorant of her true identity, and she would surely lose her position if they knew of the deception.

"I'm just tryin' to make my way in the world, honey," she explained. "Ain't a mule outfit in the country that'll hire on a gal skinner—especially one named Dirty Gertie. And I *learnt* some time ago that if I go around as a boy, it keeps most a them fellas from tryin' to crawl into my bedroll all night long—and those that does is roughly served by their compadres. Now a gal can holler all she wants and *probly* the *only* thing'll happen is the others'll line up behind the first. But if they think you're a boy and one 'em tries to get in your britches, why the others enjoy to inflict hurt on that kind of pervert. Men are strange creatures, honey, that's all I know for sure."

Although I had some difficulty imagining the men beating a path to Dirty Gertie's bedroll, I do enjoy riding up on the buckboard with "Jimmy" all the more for knowing "his" secret. I have not told another soul. Not even the Captain—although I have a suspicion he already knows.

5 May 1875

Camp Robinson is just as it sounds—a camp, a tent camp. We are housed in large communal tents where we sleep upon wooden and canvas cots with the same coarse woolen Army blankets to which we have grown accustomed on the trail. Great security measures are being taken here as well, with guards posted everywhere at all hours—to the extent that we have less privacy than ever.

By all accounts there has been much unrest among the Indians at the agency throughout the spring. On the same day in February that poor Lieutenant Robinson was killed, the agent here, a man named Appleton, was murdered at Red Cloud and fourteen mules stolen from the government supplier's string. Our own Cheyennes have been implicated in these depradations, along with the Sioux. We seem to have arrived at a volatile, if perhaps timely moment, and Captain Bourke is all the more concerned for our welfare. Soon we shall have full opportunity to put to the test the notion that we women may exert some civilizing influence over the wayward savages.

After regular defections en route our little group now numbers well under forty women. We have been informed that we are the first installment of "payment" to the savages—thus we are truly pioneers in this strange experiment. Reportedly, more will immediately follow, as other groups have currently embarked to various forts across the region. As the first, we are to be "traded" to a very prominent band of the Cheyenne tribe—that of the great Chief Little Wolf. Vis-à-vis the Captain's ethnographic expertise, we are told that the Cheyennes live in small communal bands that come together at certain times of year, somewhat like the great flocks of migratory geese. This makes the logistics of such an exchange rather complex, for these nomadic people follow the buffalo herds hither and yon during the spring, summer, and fall months and then maintain more or less permanent winter villages along some of the major river courses. We will be going first to one of these winter encampments, the exact location of which is unknown, but the Captain warns that we must be prepared to be on the move almost constantly. This sounds ever more foreign and terrifying to those of us who have been accustomed to a generally sedentary existence. Indeed, I wonder if there could have been any preparation made to ready us for our coming ordeal. Perhaps the Captain is right and this is all madness. Thank God we have Phemie and Helen Flight along. And Gretchen, too. Their close familiarity with the wilds of Nature should be invaluable to us all on this adventure, for many of our women are strictly "city girls" with little knowledge of the out-of-doors. I begin to understand why the recruiter Mr. Benton asked if we enjoyed camping out overnight . . . the least of our worries as the Captain pointed out . . .

6 May 1875

Good God, we saw them today! Our adoptive people. A contingent of them rode in to inspect us as though we were trade goods . . . which, indeed, is precisely what we are. They quite succeeded in taking my breath away. I counted fifty-three in the party—although it was somewhat like trying to count grains of sand on the wind—all men, mounted, they rode as if they were extensions of the horses themselves, rode in together like a dust devil, like one being, whirling and wheeling their horses. Our guards, alarmed, stood at the arms-ready position, surrounding our tent quarters, but it was soon clear to all that the Indians had only come to inspect the trade goods.

They are, I am relieved to report, nothing at all like those pitiable wretches around the forts. They are a lean and healthy race of men, dark of face, brown as chestnuts, small-boned and with sinewy, ropy muscles. They have a true animal litheness about them, and a certain true nobility of countenance. My first impression is that they are somehow closer to the animal kingdom than are we Caucasians. I mean this not in any disparaging sense; I mean only to say that they seem more "natural" than we—completely at one with the elements. Somehow I had imagined them to be physically larger, hulking creatures—as the artists render them in the periodicals—not these slender, nearly elfin beings.

Which is not to suggest that the savages are unimposing. Many of our visitors had their faces painted in bizarre designs, and were resplendently attired in leggings and shirts made of hide, with all manner of fantastic adornment. Others were bare-chested and bare-legged, their torsos, too, painted fantastically. Some wore feathers and full headdresses and carried brilliantly decorated lances that flashed in the sunlight. They wore beads and hammered silver coins in their braided hair, necklaces of bones and animal teeth, brass buttons, and silver bells so that their grand entrance was accompanied by a kind of low musical chattering and tinkling that contributed to a general effect of otherworldliness.

They are magnificent horsemen and handled their small, quick-stepping ponies with perfect precision, the horses themselves spectacularly painted with designs, their manes and tails decorated with feathers and beads, pieces of animal fur, brass and copper wire, buttons and coins.

Some of the savages wore little more than loincloths in the way of clothing—these are immodest garments that leave little to the imagination and caused some of our young ladies to turn their heads away out of a sense of modesty. Not so I, having never been of a particularly modest disposition. Indeed, among the many other contradictory emotions that I experienced upon first laying eyes upon these whirling creatures—man and horse—I admit to having felt an eerie, terrifying sense of exhilaration.

The apparent leader of this contingent of Cheyennes, a proud and handsome man, conferred in rapid sign language with the sergeant in charge of our guard troops. We have been advised that we must all learn the sign language as soon as possible, and pamphlets prepared by Lt. W. P. Clarke describing some of the most common gestures have been distributed among us. Captain Bourke, who is well-versed himself in this skill, has been teaching us a few of the rudimentary gestures. In jest, the Captain and I have even attempted to act out a passage from *Romeo and Juliet* in sign talk—and not without some success, I might add—and a great deal of merry laughter—which activity seems ever more precious as our fate approaches!

Having heard the speech of some of the hangs-around-the-fort Indians and that of the Army's own native scouts, I do not very well see how we shall ever be able to learn the spoken language of these people. It sounds so primitive to the ear—grunting and guttural—obviously a tongue without familiar Latin roots . . . we may as well try to learn the speech of coyotes or cranes for all it has in common with ours.

Now some of our women could only bring themselves to peek timidly from behind the tent flaps as the Indians milled about making these dreadful sounds. Those more bold among us came out to stand in the yard in front of the tents for a better look at our new gentlemen friends. It was a peculiar moment, I can assure you: the women gathered together in small clusters facing these savage mounted men, both parties inspecting the other like packs of dogs sniffing the wind.

Poor Martha blushed crimson and was rendered completely speechless by the sight of the Indians.

Our Englishwoman, Helen Flight, her eyebrows raised as always in pure astonishment, was, as usual, at a less total loss for words. "Oh . . . my goodness! Colorful lot, aren't they? That is to say, the Indians of the Florida swamps with whom I had brief acquaintance were usually covered with a terribly unattractive brown mud against the ubiquitous mosquitos. But these chaps are an artist's dream!"

"Or a *guurl's wuuust naaghtmare,*" said Daisy Lovelace, who I'm certain had been drinking, and clutched her old tiny French poodle to her breast, her hooded eyes narrowed to slits. "Why they are as *daahk* as *niggahs, Feeern Loueeese.* Wouldn't Daddy *jest* die if he knew his little girl was going to marry a damn *niggah* Injun boy?"

The cheeky Kelly twins were also completely uncowed by the spectacle of savages, and pushed directly to the front of our group to face the Indians boldly. For their part the Cheyennes seemed fascinated by the sight of the twin redheads; the men grunted and sneaked furtive looks at them. The savages have the oddest way of looking at you, while not appearing to look at you. It is difficult to describe but the men did not stare directly at us in the same way that white men might, but rather seemed to study us in their peripheral vision. "Look, Meggie," said Susan. "See how charmed that one is with me! That handsome laddy there on the spotted white pony. *Aye,* I believe he *loykes* me!" And with this, the brazen girl hiked her dress up to reveal her bare leg to the young man. " *'Ave* a peek at that then, darlin'," she said with a raw laugh. "How'd ya like to rest your lance in that sweet *cooontry?*" Her bold gesture seemed to cause the poor fellow great distress, and he wheeled his horse in a tight circle.

"Ah, but you're a naughty girl, Susie, ye are!" said sister Margaret. "*Aye, lookit* how you've got the poor lad *roonnin'* in circles already! It's *sartain,* though, that he's got eyes for you."

Gretchen Fathauer stood, solid as a house, her hands on her broad hips, eyes squinted against the sun. Finally she raised her fist in the air, and shook it as if to get their attention, and cried out. "*Yah!* All you fellas there! I am a *goot* woman! I make someone of you a *goot* wife." And she pounded her breast. "I *yam* not a pretty girl but I make *bick,* strong babies!" And she laughed, bellowing like a cow.

Phemie, as always perfectly serene, only chuckled in her deep good-natured way and shook her head, seemingly quite pleased at the spectacle. Her dark Negro skin seemed to cause a bit of commotion among the savages, as well, for several milled around her, making sounds like conversation and touching their own faces as if discussing her skin color. Then someone called out to the crowd and a moment later a large Negro Indian rode to the front and presented himself to Phemie. I mean to say that he was dressed exactly like the savages but he was very clearly a black man, and a large black man at that, who, seated on his little Indian horse, made the thing look like a child's pony. "Well, I'll be," Phemie said, chuckling, "I thought I'd seen everything, but just look at you. What you doin' dressed up like an Indian, nigger?" But the black man did not appear to speak English any more than the other savages, and he only grunted something incomprehensible to her in their language.

There then ensued a spirited discussion among the heathens. Some began to shout out to one another; it reminded me a bit of the atmosphere of a cattle auction at the Chicago stockyards; I believe that the men were actually staking their claims to us! They never pointed their fingers, but studied us intently and called out. We could only imagine their discussion: *"I'll take that one with the yellow hair! I'll take the redhead. I'll take the big one! I'll take the black-skinned woman. I choose the one in the blue dress! I'll take the one with the white dog!* Had it not all been so perfectly dreamlike, perhaps we might have taken offense at their presumption. But it has been clear from the beginning, and never more so than at this moment, that we are in the process of entering a new world, that the civilization which we have inhabited all our lives is crumbling away beneath us like an enormous sinkhole opening under our feet.

I looked about trying to ascertain who, if anyone, had claimed me, when my eyes met the averted glance of the one who had ridden in at the head of this contingent, and now sat on his horse, perfectly motionless and silent. He held a lance and an elaborately decorated shield, and wore a magnificent headdress of eagle feathers that spilled down his back and across his horse's rump. White zigzag lightning bolts ran down the legs of his black horse, but he wore no paint on his own face. He looked somewhat older than most of the others, or perhaps more accurately only seemed older, for he owned a certain stillness and confidence that suggested maturity. He had dark skin and very fine features with a fierce set to his jaw. Nor did he call out as the others had, but sat his mount like a statue. Now he raised his lance, and made with it a single short shake toward me, an imperious, kinglike gesture of taking, a kind of feudal ownership by right, and I knew beyond a shadow of a doubt that this one, the headman, had chosen me to be his bride. I nodded . . . less to my future husband personally, than in simple resignation, a kind of final acceptance of this terrible bargain we have struck, and I confess that I thought to myself with pure womanly calculation and my bedrock sense of practicality: *I could do worse than this one.*

At that precise moment I looked across the yard at the company of mounted soldiers who watched over these strange proceedings in nervous formation. They were trying to control their nervous horses, who snorted and whinnied, pranced and pawed—the air pungent and dangerous with the foreign scents and sights of their wild counterparts. And there at the head of his battalion, standing straight in his stirrups as his own white mount slipped sideways, Captain John Bourke stared at me with a look of unbearable sadness in his eyes.

As suddenly as they had ridden in and as if by some unknown signal, the savages wheeled all as one in perfect synchronization, like a covey of blackbirds rising from the ground, and galloped off as they had come . . .

7 May 1875

This morning, Colonel Bradley, the post commander, came to see us, accompanied by Captain Bourke—the purpose of their visit, to explain to us the procedures of our impending "transfer." How little romance there is in that word! This is to be effected in the morning. The Cheyennes will come for us just past daybreak; we are advised to travel with as little luggage as possible—trunks are not a thing understood by the savages, and they have no practical means of transporting them. They have not yet, as the Captain points out wryly, invented the wheel.

More in our group have had eleventh-hour changes of heart—I'm certain from having viewed the aboriginals yesterday. Indeed, one poor girl, who like me was recruited from an institution in Chicago—to which she had been committed for "Nervousness"—seems to have had a complete mental breakdown, sobbing and uttering gibberish. She has been taken to the camp hospital tent. I suppose this behavior may be expected of one who did, after all, come from an asylum. Truly this is no place for the Nervous. Several others deserted in the middle of the night, but soldiers returned them to us this morning. The women had been found by the Indian scouts wandering in the hills, dazed and half-dead from exposure—for it is still quite cool at night. I do not know what is to become of them now. As far as I'm concerned, we have struck our bargain and now must live with it. God knows we've all had second thoughts . . .

Yes, tomorrow they come for us . . . Good God . . . what have we done?

A postscript to this day's entry: Late this evening "Jimmy" came again to our quarters and called me outside.

"Capn' needs to see you at his tent, honey," Gertie said to me. "I better warn you, he's in a terrible state."

I had noticed earlier at our briefing with Colonel Smith that the Captain seemed silent and preoccupied, but I had never seen him so agitated as when I arrived at his tent. He was seated in a chair with a glass and a bottle of whiskey before him, and when I arrived he stood and began to pace the floor like an angry caged lion.

"Do you know why I have sent for you?" he asked, without any of his usual civility.

"Presumably not to read Shakespeare," I answered.

"You may mock me all you like, May," he snapped angrily, "for you are a proud and foolish girl. But this is not a game. You are no longer an actor in a farce."

"I resent your words, John," I said. "No one knows that better than I. Let me restate my answer to your question: I suspect that you have asked me here in order to entreat me not to participate in tomorrow's transfer."

He stopped pacing and turned to face me. "To entreat?" he bellowed. "To entreat? No, madam, not to entreat—to forbid! You must not go through with this insanity! I will not permit it."

I confess that I did laugh then at the Captain's distress . . . but mine was purely the false bravado of a desperate woman. For if the truth be told, I, too, was beginning to lose heart for this venture, was nearly paralyzed with fear and apprehension for myself and my fellow travelers. Ever since we have seen the savages in the flesh, our morale has been shaken to its core. But I could not let the others, or the Captain, see my loss of faith, my failure of courage.

"My dear Captain," I answered. "May I remind you that I am not one of your soldiers, that it is hardly your position to forbid me to do anything. In any case, our orders come from a higher authority."

The Captain shook his head in something like disbelief, but his anger seemed to drain away. "How can you still laugh, May?" he asked in a soft voice of wonder.

"Do you honestly believe, John, that my laughter is lighthearted?" I said, "That I mock you? That I consider this to be a game, or myself a player on a stage? Don't you know that I laugh because it is my last defense against tears?" I quoted: " 'I will instruct my sorrows to be proud—' "

" 'For grief is proud and makes his owner stoop,' " John Bourke finished for me. And then he knelt beside me. "Listen to me, May," he said, taking my hands and pressing them hard in his. "You cannot imagine the hardship that will be yours. You will not survive the life these people live—cannot survive—any more than you could survive life with a pack of wolves or in a den of bears. This is how different they are from us. You must believe me when I tell you this. The savages are not just a race separate from ours; they are a species distinct."

"Are they not human beings, John?" I asked. "May we not at least hope to find some common ground as fellow men and women?"

"They are Stone Age people, May," said the Captain, "pagans who have never evolved beyond their original place in the animal kingdom, have never been uplifted by the beauty and nobility of civilization. They have no religion beyond superstition, no art beyond stick figures scratched on rock, no music besides that made by beating a drum. They do not read or write. I ask you this: Where is the savages' Shakespeare? Their Mozart? Their Plato? They are a wild, indolent race of men. Their history is written in blood, centuries of unrelieved savagery, thievery, and butchery, murder and degeneracy. Listen to me, May: they do not think as we do. They do not live as we do . . ." He hesitated, and seemed to struggle for the words . . . "They do not . . . love as we do."

The breath caught in my throat in terror and apprehension at the starkness of the Captain's words. "Love?" I asked, nearer than ever to breaking down completely. "Tell me, John, in what way do the savages not love as we do?"

Now he could only shake his head and avert his eyes from mine. "Like animals . . ." he finally murmured. "They make love like animals."

"Good God, John . . ." I said softly, with a sense of despair as complete as any I have ever known . . . or so I allowed myself to think for a brief moment. But then I remembered again the despair that I had escaped—and this brought me back from the abyss of my own cowardice.

"You wondered once why I had agreed to participate in this program," I said, "and now I must tell you, Captain. Perhaps it will help to put your mind to rest. I was recruited by our government from a lunatic asylum—given the choice between the very real possibility of spending the rest of my life locked up in that place, or going to live among the savages. Which would you have done, John, given such a choice?"

"Why you're no more insane than I, May," the Captain protested. "What was the nature of your illness if I may be so forward as to ask?"

"Love," I answered. "I was in love with a man whom my family found unsuitable. I bore his children out of wedlock."

I did not miss the flicker of disappointment that crossed John Bourke's face at this moment—his good Catholic rectitude clearly offended by news of my "sin." He looked away from me in some confusion. "People are not committed to lunatic asylums for making such mistakes," he said at last.

"Mistakes, John?" I said, "Love is no mistake. My dearest children, with whom I pray nightly to be reunited after this present adventure is over, were not mistakes."

"And what official diagnosis of your illness did the doctors give in order to have you committed?" he asked.

"Moral perversion," I answered directly. "Promiscuity, my family called it."

Now the Captain released my hand and stood from his kneeling position. He turned away from me again, a look of even greater distress on his face. I knew what he must be thinking.

"John," I said, "I feel no need to defend myself again against such lies, or to justify my behavior, past or present. You and I are friends, are we not? We have become, I think, in a short time, dear friends. Unless my feelings deceive me, had the circumstances of our meeting been different, we might have been much more than that. I may be a woman of strong passions, but I am not promiscuous. I have been with only one man in my life. He is the father of my children, Harry Ames."

"I could intervene with the authorities on your behalf, May," the Captain interrupted, turning back to me. "Perhaps I could arrange that you be excused from the program."

"Even if you could do so," I said, "you could not prevent my family from putting me back in that ghastly place. Just as you tell me that I cannot imagine life among the savages, so you cannot imagine the life that was mine there. Where every day was exactly like the last—an endless string of sunless, hopeless days, one after another after another. Whatever is to come in this strange new world we enter, cannot be worse than the tedium and monotony of existence in the asylum. I will never go back, John. I will die first."

Now I stood and went to him. I put my arms around his waist and my head on his chest. I held him, felt his beating heart. "Perhaps you hate me now, John," I said, "now that you have learned the truth. Perhaps you think that I deserve to be sent off to live with savages."

The Captain closed his arms around me, and for that moment and for the first time in longer than I could remember I felt completely safe, as if I had found there against his chest sanctuary at last from the tumult and heartbreak of my life. I smelled his strong man's scent like a forest in the fall and felt the muscles of his back and arms like the sturdy walls of a well-made house. The rhythmic beat of his heart against my own breast was like the pulse of the earth itself. Would that I could rest there forever, I thought, in the safe haven of this good man's arms.

"You must know that I am in love with you, May," he said, "that I could never hate you, or judge you. If I were able to stop this madness, I would. I would do anything to save you."

"You are engaged to marry another, John," I said. "As I am. Even if I required saving, it is too late."

But now I believe that perhaps it was John Bourke, after all, who required saving from me, from my own terrible need, my desire to disappear within him, and him within me, as one being together, inseparable. Who falls swifter or harder from grace and with such splendid soul-rending agony than an Irish Catholic boy raised by Jesuits? An honorable soldier engaged to another? What sweeter love is there than that which cannot be?

When John Bourke kissed me, I tasted the faint sweetness of whiskey on his lips, and felt his deep moral reluctance giving itself up to my more powerful need for him. I felt us both being swept away together, and I held tight, held on for dear life, as if only the contact of our bodies could fix me in this time and place, as if only when his flesh and mine became seamless, seared together as one, would I be truly anchored to this world, the only world I know. "Will you show me now, John," I whispered into his mouth, "dear John, will you show me now," I implored, "how a civilized man makes love?"

8 May 1875

My Dear Harry,

I must try to write you the breeziest, the chattiest letter possible this evening, for if ever I am to go completely mad it will be on this strange night, our first in Indian country. And if I write to you and imagine that you will actually read this letter, perhaps I can pretend for this one moment longer that all is well, that I am simply having a dream from which I will awaken in your arms, in our apartment, our babies sleeping beside us . . . and all will be well . . . yes . . . all will be well . . .

I am to be a Chief's wife. That's right, the head savage has chosen me to be his bride. His rank being the savage equivalent of royalty, this will make me something like a Queen, I should think . . . Hah! And what would you think of that, Harry, if you could only know where our actions have led me? A Chieftain's wife, Queen of the Cheyennes, future mother of the royal savage children. . . .

The man's name is Little Wolf—he is much celebrated among the Plains Indians and has had a personal audience in Washington, D.C., with President Ulysses S. Grant himself. Even my Captain admits that the Chief is by reputation a fearless warrior and a great leader of his people. And I must say, as savages go he is not altogether unpleasant to look upon. It is impossible to guess how old he is. Not a young man, certainly, and quite a bit older than I, but not old either . . . perhaps near forty years of age. But very fit and healthy-looking, with dark, almost black eyes, and strong features set in a kind of wolflike demeanor. Yet he strikes me as a gentle man with a soft pleasant manner of speaking that makes even the hideous Indian language seem less ugly.

They came early this morning, Harry, driving a herd of horses ahead of them with unimaginable fanfare, making strange yipping, animal-like sounds—exactly the noises one might expect savages to make. The horses were herded into the camp corral, where they were counted by the camp comptroller.

Yes, well, naturally, I have mixed feelings about being traded for a horse . . . although I suppose I should take some consolation from the fact that the mount Little Wolf presented to the post commander for my hand was, by all accounts, one of the finest in the string . . . not that I, personally, am any great judge of horseflesh, but so said my new muleskinner friend "Jimmy."

So perhaps I can take some solace in knowing that I have been traded for a particularly excellent specimen of equine flesh . . . does that sound better?

My true friend, Martha, is to marry a fearsome-looking fellow, aptly named Tangle Hair, whose wildly unkempt hair causes him to look quite like one of the maddest of the mad inmates from the asylum. But he, too, is by all accounts a distinguished warrior.

In one of the oddest circumstances of this bizarre situation our brave Negress Phemie has been chosen by a black man among the savages. Indeed, that is his name—Black Man. It was explained to us by the camp interpreter, a half-breed Frenchman-Sioux named Bruyere, that Phemie's prospective husband was captured from a wagon train of escaped Negro slaves when he was only a child. Brought up among the Cheyennes, he is considered to be as much one of them as if he were natural born to the tribe. He speaks no English and is treated in all ways as an equal. Perhaps in this regard the savages are more civilized than we. He is a handsome fellow, quite a bit taller than most of the others, well over six feet I should guess, and I must say he seems to be a fine match for our Phemie . . . forgive me if I appear to ramble on Harry . . . exhaustion and terror will do that to a girl . . . I try only to give some order and definition to this desperate affair . . .

Helen Elizabeth Flight, our artiste in residence, has been chosen by a famous Cheyenne warrior named Hog. "Yes, well I expect I'll keep my professional name," she says with great good humor. "That is to say, Helen Hog has rather a disagreeable ring to it, don't you agree?" However unattractive his name, Mr. Hog is a fine-looking fellow, taller and broader of shoulder than most of the others.

Sweet little Sara is to wed a slender young man named Yellow Wolf, a youth who appears to have barely reached adolescence. But again I must say that the Cheyennes seem to have chosen wisely, for the boy is extremely shy of countenance and altogether smitten with the girl—can hardly take his eyes off her. Perhaps he will succeed where we have failed in bringing Sara out of her silent, fearful world.

Captain Bourke tells us that among the savages madness is considered a gift from the gods, and as such the insane are accorded great respect, even reverence in their society. Thus some of our group should be held in very high esteem by our hosts, possibly even regarded as idols! Indeed, there was spirited competition among several of the savage men over which of them gets poor Ada Ware as his wife. A former asylum inmate herself, suffering from Melancholia, Ada would hardly be considered a "catch" by men in our own society. But according to the interpreter, Bruyere, the savages believe that she is some kind of holy woman because of her black attire. They have had just enough exposure to our sundry religions to have things all in a muddle.

Our valises were objects of great mirth to the Indians. Those less dignified among them, grasped them by the handles and made quite an exaggerated show of carrying them around for the amusement of their foolish compatriots, and then all fell down laughing and rolling on the ground. Truly these people are like unruly children! I was pleased to see that my own intended did not participate in this nonsense, but merely watched sternly.

Poor Daisy Lovelace was involved in a terrible scene with the fellow who chose her to be his bride. As the man was collecting her belongings, he tried to take from her her beloved pet poodle, Fern Louise. Daisy, who I suspect had been taking her "medicine," clutched the little dog to her breast, and said, "No you don't, *suh*, you do not so much as touch my *Feeern Louuuise. Evah*. You *heah* me? *Nevah, evah* do you lay a finger on my *darlin' dawg.*"

But the fellow reached out again, quick as a cat, and snatched the little thing from Daisy's arms, then held it up by the scruff of its neck and made quite a show of displaying it to the others, who gathered laughing to watch as the poor thing flailed the air helplessly. I confess that I do not much care for Miss Lovelace, and care even less for her wretched little poodle, but I hate to see any animal mistreated, and when Daisy tried to take back her pet, I went to her aid. "Give her back that dog!" I demanded of the savage. The fellow seemed to understand what I was after and only shrugged and dropped the poor old thing in the dirt as casually as one discards a piece of trash. The little dog sprawled to the ground but quickly regained its feet and began to run round and round in circles, which only made the savages laugh harder. But as if by centrifugal force, Fern Louise suddenly shot out of her circle in a straight line toward the savage who had so rudely abused her, latched on to the man's foot, snarling viciously and shaking her head like a tiny demon from Hell. Now the savage began hopping about comically and hollering in pain, trying without success to shake the tenacious little poodle loose, which scene caused the others ever greater mirth.

"Hang on, Feeern Louueeesse!" Daisy Lovelace called out triumphantly, "That's right, *honey, hang on to the niggah*! You teach the damn *heathen* not to fool with you *darlin'*." Finally exhausted from its efforts, the little dog released its hold on the savage, and trotted, panting and slavering pink bloody foam, back to her mistress. Meanwhile, the savage had fallen to the ground, clutching his wounded foot and making piteous howling noises—which elicted no sympathy whatsoever from his compatriots, who found his distress hilarious beyond compare. Indeed, the episode provided much needed comic relief for all of us, and the poodle Fern Louise has gained immeasurably in our esteem.

Because the horse trade was merely a formality to the authorities, the Army has supplied each of us with a good American horse to ride into Indian country, and with proper Army saddles to which we strapped our bags and the few small luxuries which we were permitted to carry with us. Anticipating the difficulty that we would encounter riding any great distance astride such saddles wearing dresses, the soldiers have also thoughtfully outfitted those of us who accepted them with specially, if hastily, tailored cavalrymans' breeches. Suffice it to say that in matters of fit some of us were more fortunate than others. In any case, those among our women who refused these came to regret their vanity almost immediately once we were under way. For their part, the savage men were as agitated by our breeches as they were amused by our valises and made much disproving grunting on the subject. As they don't wear trousers themselves, one can only assume that they've never before seen women so attired.

I have my precious notebooks and a good supply of sturdy lead pencils that Captain Bourke presented to me—for he wisely felt that ink would be a difficult commodity to obtain where we are bound. The Captain has also lent me his cherished copy of Shakespeare to carry with me into the wilderness. Knowing what it means to him, I could hardly accept it, but the Captain insisted. Together we wept, Harry, wept and held each other in the sorrow of our parting, a luxury you and I were never allowed.

Yes, this I offer as a final confession to you Harry—my first love, father of my children, wherever you are, whatever has became of you . . . you to whom, until last night, I have remained faithful . . . Yes, the Captain and I were quite swept away by passion, our emotions raw . . . we could not help ourselves, nor did I wish to . . . what strange propensity is it of mine, Harry, to involve myself with unsuitable men—a factory foreman, an engaged Catholic Army Captain, and now a savage chieftain. Good God, perhaps I really am mad . . .

As a desperate eleventh-hour attempt to forestall the inevitable, a hastily formed committee of our women called upon Colonel Bradley to see if we might be permitted to spend one last night at the camp. Emotions were running high, and I feared a mass defection. The Colonel in turn passed along our request to Chief Little Wolf, and he and several of the other head Indians conferred over the matter. Finally the great Chief returned and announced their decision: the horses had been delivered as agreed upon and now we must accompany them. There was still plenty of daylight left in which to reach their camp, and apparently the Indians saw no reason to delay our departure for another day. Colonel Bradley explained that if he did not release us to them as agreed upon his actions might be construed by the Cheyennes as an attempt to renege on the bargain we have struck. In which case, there would almost certainly be trouble. As the entire purpose of this bold venture is to try to avoid further trouble with the savages, the Colonel regretfully denied our request for one final night in the bosom of civilization. Well, this is what we signed on for, isn't it?

We have been joined at the last minute by one Reverend Hare, a corpulent Episcopal missionary who arrived here only yesterday from Fort Fetterman, and who is to accompany us into the wilderness. He is a most unusual-looking fellow who must weigh at least 350 pounds, and bald as a billiard ball. In his white clerical gowns, the Reverend looks like nothing so much as an enormous swaddled infant. He rode in on a huge white mule that fairly groaned under the missionary's weight.

Captain Bourke could only shake his head at the Episcopalian's arrival and mutter something under his breath about the "well-fed Protestants." The Captain is evidently familiar with the Reverend's evangelical activities among the savages, and has complained privately that the President's Indian Peace Plan has all the various denominations squabbling over the souls of the savages like dogs over a steak bone. Accordingly, the Reverend, a "White Robe," as the Indians refer to the Episcopalians, has been dispatched by his church to bring the Cheyennes into the fold, thus preventing their souls from being captured by the "Black Robes" as the Romanists are known. One of the first pronouncements that the enormous Reverend made was to voice his opinion in front of Colonel Bradley and Captain Bourke that it would be preferable in the eyes of his church for the savages to remain heathens than to be converted by the Catholics, a remark that, believe me, did not sit well with my Captain.

Still, we have been informed that Reverend Hare has worked among the

Indians for a number of years and is something of a linguist, speaking several of the native tongues fluently, including Cheyenne. His function then will be to serve as both translator and spiritual advisor to our strange assembly of lambs going off to slaughter.

And it was in just such a spirit that we rode out from Camp Robinson with our prospective husbands. Some of our women were wailing as though this were a funeral procession rather than a wedding march. For my part, I tried to maintain my composure—in spite of Captain Bourke's disapproval I have vowed to keep a positive face on this adventure, to keep foremost in my mind the thought that this is a temporary posting; we are soldiers off to do duty for our country and can at least look forward to the day when we might return home. Closest of all to my heart, Harry, I keep the memory of our precious children, the dream I shall harbor forever in my breast of one day returning to them; this dream will keep me alive and strong. I have tried from the start to hearten the others with the same comforting thought: that one day we shall return again to the bosom of civilization—free women at last.

So I rode at the head of our procession, proudly alongside my intended, nodding slightly to Captain Bourke, whose own consternation with the occasion was written clearly in his countenance. I started to lift my hand to him in a farewell wave but I saw that he had cast his dark eyes to the ground and did not look at me. Did I detect shame in his averted gaze? Catholic self-flagellation? That in our one moment of passion he had betrayed his God, his fiancée, his military duty? Did I detect, perhaps, even a glimmer of relief that the wanton instrument of his temptation, the Devil's own temptress, was being taken away to live with savages—the fitting punishment of a vengeful God for our sweet sins of the night. Yes, all that I witnessed in John Bourke's downcast eyes. This is a woman's lot on earth, Harry, that man's atonement can only be purchased by our banishment.

But I did not bow my head. I intend at all costs to maintain my dignity in this strange new life, and if I am to be the wife of a Chief, I shall fulfill that role with the utmost decorum. Thus before our departure I instructed my friend Martha and those of the others who seemed most fearful—instructed them with the advice given me by my muleskinner friend, Jimmy, aka Dirty Gertie, who herself has experience among the heathens: "Keep your head high, honey, and never let them see you cry," but, of course, this advice was more difficult for some to implement than others. I, personally, have resolved never to display weakness, to be always strong and firm and forthright, to show neither fear nor uncertainty—no matter how fearful and uncertain I may be inside; I see no other way to survive this ordeal.

Within a short time most of our women seemed to resign themselves to our fate. Their wailings subsided to an occasional choked whimper and there was very little conversation among us; we were like children, speechless and awestruck, being led passively, meekly into the wilderness.

What a strange procession we must have made, riding in a long lazy line—nearly one hundred strong, counting Indians and brides—our passage winding and undisciplined compared to our recent military processions. To God, if he should be watching over us, we must have resembled a trail of ants as we rode across the hills. Up into the pine timber on the slopes and down again through densely overgrown river bottoms, where our horses forded streams swollen with spring runoff, the muddy rushing water tapping our stirrups. My horse, a stout bay whom I have named Soldier after my Captain, is calm and surefooted, and picked deliberately through the deadfall and then broke into a gentle trot up the rocky slopes to gain the ridges above, where the going was easier.

It was a lovely spring afternoon, and we were all somewhat consoled by that, by the notion that no matter how foreign and uncertain our future we still lived under the same sky, the same sun still shone down upon us, our own God, if such we believed in, still watched over us . . .

The faint sweet acrid scent of woodsmoke on the air announced the Indian encampment long before we reached it. Soon we could see a light haze from its fires in the sky above, marking the camp. A group of small boys greeted us on the trail, chattering and making weird cooing noises of amazement. Some of the smallest of the children rode enormous leggy dogs the likes of which I have never before seen—shaggy wolfish beasts that more closely resembled Shetland ponies than they did canines. The dogs were decorated with feathers and beads, bells and trinkets, and painted to mimic the men's war ponies. Now I felt more than ever that we were entering some other world, one possessing its own race of men, its own creatures . . . and so we were . . . a fairy-tale world existing in the shadows of our own, or perhaps it is our world living in the shadow of this one . . . who can say? A few of the bolder boys ran up to furtively touch our feet, and then scampered off chattering like chipmunks.

The pack of urchins ran ahead to announce our arrival to the camp, and then we could hear a great commotion of rising voices and barking dogs—a cacophony of village sounds, all of it foreign to us, and, I confess, all of it terrifying.

Throngs of curious women, children, and old people gathered as we entered the camp. The tents—tipis, they are called—appear to be set in roughly circular formations, groups of four or five of them forming half circles which in turn form a larger circle. It was a colorful, noisy place—

a feast for the eyes—but so strange that we were unable to take it all in and were further distracted by the hordes of people who approached us babbling in their strange tongue and all trying to touch us gently about the legs and feet. Thus we rode the whole length of the camp, as if on parade for the residents, then turned at the end and rode back again. There rose such shouting and chattering among the heathens, such noise and chaos that my head began to whirl, I hardly knew what was happening to me. Soon we were separated from one another and I heard some of our women calling out in confused desperation. I attempted to call back to them, but my words were lost in the din. I even lost sight of poor Martha as the families of the savages claimed us, absorbed us, one by one, into their being. My head spun, all was a blur of unfamiliar motion, color, and sound . . . I seemed to lose myself.

Now I write to you, my Harry, no longer from the safety of an Army tent, but by the last fading light of day and by the faintest glow from the dying embers of a tipi fire in the center of a Cheyenne warrior's lodge. Yes, I have entered this strange dream life, a life that cannot be real, cannot be taking place in our world, a dream that perhaps only the insane might truly understand . . .

I sit now in this primitive tent, by the failing fire, surrounded by sullen squatting savages, and the reality of our situation becomes finally quite inescapable. Riding out of Camp Robinson this afternoon, it occurred to me for the first time that I may very well die out here in the vast emptiness of this prairie, surrounded by this strange, godforsaken people . . . a people truly like trolls out of a fairy tale, not human beings as I know them, but creatures from a different earth, an older one. John Bourke was right. As I look around the circle of this tipi, even the chokingly close walls of my old room at the asylum suddenly seem in memory to be somehow comforting, familiar . . . a square, solid room with four walls . . . but, no, these thoughts I banish. I live in a new world, on a new earth, among new people. Courage!

Good-bye, Harry, wherever you may be . . . never has it been more clear to me that the part of my life which you occupied is over forever . . . I could not be further away from you if I were on the moon . . . how odd to think of one's life not as chapters in a book but as complete volumes, separate and distinct. In this spirit, tomorrow I shall begin a new notebook. This next volume to be entitled: *My Life as an Indian Squaw*. I will not write to you again, Harry . . . for you are dead to me now, and I to you. But I did love you once . . .

NOTEBOOK III

My Life as an Indian Squaw

"I fell then into a deep slumber and I had the strangest dream . . . at least it happened like a dream . . . It must have been a dream, for my husband was now in the tent with me, he was still dancing softly, noiselessly, his moccasined feet rising and falling gracefully, soundlessly, he spun softly around the fire, danced like a spirit being around me where I lay sleeping. I began to become aroused, felt a tingling in my stomach, an erotic tickle between my legs, the immutable pull of desire as he displayed to me."

(from the journals of May Dodd)

→←

12 May 1875

Good Lord! Four days here, no time to make journal entries, exhausted, nearly insane from strangeness, sleeplessness, lack of privacy. I fear the Captain was right, this entire experiment is insane, a terrible mistake. Like moving into a den with a pack of wild dogs.

First of all, how utterly perverse is the notion of sharing a tent with one's future husband, his two other wives, an old crone, a young girl, a young boy, and an infant! Yes, that is how many live in our quarters. How, one might fairly inquire, are conjugal relations to be managed? Privacy, such as it is, is maintained by the simple fact that no one ever looks at the other, much less speaks. It is the most peculiar feeling, like being invisible. And I can hardly describe the odor of all these bodies living in such proximity.

I am being attended to by the Chief's "second" wife—a pretty girl not much older than myself whose name, according to Reverend Hare, is Feather on Head. As mentioned Little Wolf appears to have two other wives, but the older one serves largely the function of domestic help—she cooks and cleans and has yet to so much as acknowledge my presence in the lodge. This one's name is Quiet One, for she almost never speaks. Although she goes about her business as if I don't exist, my woman's instinct senses her hatred of me as keenly as if she were holding a knife blade to my throat. Indeed, I have had the same nightmare every night since we arrived. In my dream I awaken and the woman is crouched over me, squatting like a gargoyle, holding a knife to my throat. I try to scream, but I cannot, because to move is to cut my throat on the blade. I always wake from this dream unable to breathe, gasping for air, choking. I must watch out for this one . . .

Our women have been immediately pressed into action doing the most demeaning women's work around the camp—we are like children taught by our Indian mothers, little more than slaves if the truth be told. It was our understanding that we were to be instructing them in the ways of the civilized world, not being made beasts of burden, but, as Helen Flight has pointed out, of what use are table manners to those without tables. Indeed, the savage women seem to be taking full advantage of our situation as newcomers by making us do all the hardest labor. We haul water at dawn from the creek, gather firewood for the morning meal, and spend our afternoons digging roots in the fields. God, what drudgery! Only Phemie seems to have escaped the daily chores—I do not as yet know how she has managed this, for I have barely seen her. The camp is large and spread out, and we are all working so hard that it is all we can do to eat a morsel or two of revolting boiled meat from the pot and collapse on our sleeping places at the end of the day. For my part, I will cooperate with our hosts for a time, but I have no intention of being made a slave, or a servant, and several of us have already voiced our complaints to Reverend Hare about this treatment.

For their part, the savage men appear to spend an inordinate amount of time lounging around their lodges, smoking and gossiping among themselves . . . so that it occurs to me that perhaps our cultures are not so different after all: the women do all the real work while the men do all the talking.

14 May 1875

We are told that the savages are plotting some sort of group wedding ceremony which involves little more than an elaborate feast and a dance, but these plans have been complicated by the presence of Reverend Hare, who feels obligated to conduct a Christian ceremony. Speaking of whom, while it would be very useful, indeed, if the Reverend made himself available to translate and help us adapt to our strange new life, he is truly one of the most indolent individuals I've ever encountered and has spent most of our first few days here lounging like a minidiety on his buffalo robes in the tent he shares with one of the Cheyenne holy men—a fellow named Dog Woman . . . which peculiarity of name I shall attempt to explain in a later entry. Truly so much has happened, our senses have been so constantly assaulted by one bizarre occurrence and sight after another, and I am usually so exhausted, that I don't see how I shall ever be able properly to record this experience . . .

In any case, the Reverend has got things in an even greater turmoil; under the agreed upon arrangement we have the option of "divorcing" our Indian "husbands" after two years. But evidently certain of the denominations who are participating in this scheme under the auspices of the Church Missionary Society do not permit divorce—which presents a bit of a problem if we are to be married in a Christian ceremony. Such nonsense! It would seem to me better for all concerned if we merely entered into the heathen union—after all, "when in Rome . . ."—under which there would be no future legal or religious obligation. In any case, until all of this is sorted out no marital relationships are to be consummated—although I for one say, let's get down to the business at hand.

I have, I should here mention, quite put John Bourke out of my mind and am prepared to be a dutiful wife to my Chief. This is easier said than done, but it is clear to me that if I am to keep any hold at all on my sanity, I must not dwell on what might have been . . . to do so would be to go truly mad. It is the one lesson I learned well at the asylum—to live each day as it comes, day by day, and to dwell neither on regrets of the past nor worries about the future—both of which are beyond my power to influence. This lesson should be well applicable to life among the barbarians, for in a genuine sense I feel as though I have simply entered another kind of asylum—and this one the maddest of them all.

A few more words about our daily routine: in the morning the men gather at the creek to take a swim together. The women do not seem to observe this daily ritual, but occasionally go down to the creek in the afternoon to take a kind of cloth bath—which is hardly sufficient after a day of the filthiest labor imaginable. Personally, I enjoy a daily bath, something I missed more than anything at the asylum and during our long journey. And so on our third morning here I followed the Chief from the lodge. He has so far paid me little attention—has hardly spoken to me or even looked at me—let alone made any amorous advances toward me.

I have brought with me among my few meager possessions my old bathing costume that I once wore another lifetime ago at Sunday outings with Harry to the beach on Lake Michigan. It was in a trunk among my effects at the institution and it was partly as a sentimental gesture that I packed it with me here. However, I also had in the back of my mind just precisely this matter of bathing in the wilds. I had no idea what provisions the savages made for personal hygiene, but I assumed that we would be reduced to something as basic as a dip in the creek, and I certainly had no intention of appearing before everyone in a natural state. When I saw that the men made this swim every morning while the women hauled water and firewood, stoked the fires, and prepared the morning meal, I determined my own clear preference to join the men at the creek. Indeed, as a young girl I was rather an accomplished swimmer—a recreation that I deeply missed after my incarceration.

Thus I awoke early this morning and, beneath my buffalo robes, dressed in my bathing costume. (I must say, lack of privacy notwithstanding, the bed of pine boughs, buffalo robes, and trade blankets is not altogether uncomfortable.) When the Chief slipped from our tent for his morning dip I followed him to the creek. There the other men had gathered at a pool formed by a beaver dam, chattering away like schoolboys and taking deep preparatory breaths prior to plunging into the frigid (as I quickly discovered!) water. When I first joined them they issued a kind of collective murmur of disapproval, more of a grunting actually. Then one of them made some sort of a remark—I'm certain now that he was making reference to my bathing costume, and they all began to laugh, a horribly unattractive guffawing which soon had them clutching their sides and rolling on the ground like morons. Only Little Wolf maintained his chiefly composure.

The men's rudeness angered me and, I confess, wounded my vanity. I have always believed that my bathing costume shows my figure to its best advantage. Nor am I accustomed to being made an object of ridicule. I'm certain I blushed deeply, and I had to fight back tears of shame and rage. But I refused to be defeated by their idiocy. Instead, I gathered myself and walked out to the end of a log over the beaver pond, and executed the most graceful dive I could muster into the icy depths—praying all the while that it wasn't too shallow! Truly, I thought my heart would stop from the shock when I hit the water! I swam deeply and when I broke the surface the men were no longer laughing but standing all together watching me with expressions of some admiration.

Now this afternoon I learn, via Reverend Hare, that the Indian name given to me is *Mesoke* which means "Swallow," rather a charming name I think, and one for which I feel very fortunate. For instance, the Reverend tells me that our large, gregarious friend, Gretchen, has been named something unpronounceable that he translates as Speaks with Big Voice—which, I suppose, is a variation of our own more vulgar "loudmouth." My, but these are a literal-minded people . . .

After my dip, which once I had adapted to the frigidity of the water was magnificently invigorating, the men suddenly seemed too shy to enter the pool themselves . . . perhaps they objected to swimming with a woman. One by one, they drifted away to another section of the creek until only Little Wolf was left watching me. I suspect that I had violated some ridiculous code of heathen behavior by trying to swim with the men. How preposterous! It rather reminds me of the stuffy men's club in Chicago to which Father belongs . . . Yes . . . well, with that thought in mind I believe I'll call this The Savage Men's Bathing Club!

Little Wolf finally slipped into the water himself. He wore only a breechclout—an immodest article of clothing if such it can be called, little more than a flap of leather hanging from a string tied loosely about the waist. It barely conceals his . . .

Let me describe the Chief. He is a slender man, rather fine-boned and small-muscled, dark-eyed and dark-complected. His skin is extraordinarily smooth and unlined, the color of deeply burnished copper. He has very high cheekbones, that seem nearly Asian, perhaps Mongolian, and his hair is perfectly black, glossy as a raven's feathers. He is actually quite handsome in a "foreign" sort of way, and he appears to be a man of the utmost dignity and bearing. I have yet to see him behave in anything other than the most chiefly fashion. I do find him to be a bit stern of countenance. In fact, as he waded into the water I thought to myself, "I would like just once to see my intended smile." And, lo and behold, at precisely that moment, as if somehow he had read my mind, I thought that I saw the flicker of a smile cross the Chief's face, though certainly, I suppose it may just as easily have been an involuntary grimace in reaction to the icy waters.

Mr. Little Wolf plunged underwater, sleek and graceful as a river otter, came to the surface, shaking himself lightly like a dog, and exited the pool without another glance in my direction. Frankly, I was a bit disappointed as this seemed the perfect opportunity to become acquainted away from the others with whom we are in such constant proximity. Not that I expected, or indeed encouraged, romantic advances in the frigid waters of the swimming hole, but it would be lovely if the Chief at least spoke to me.

15 May 1875

We have determined to hold daily meetings in small groups, scattered about the camp. These are in order to share our experiences and, we hope, aid one another in the transition to savage life. The meetings are supposed to be organized by Reverend Hare, but, as I mentioned, His Corpulence seems to have permanently esconced himself in the lodge he is sharing with the Cheyenne holy man Dog Woman. Let me explain . . . Not only does this Dog Woman reputedly have the ability to turn himself into a canine, but he is also what the Cheyennes call a *he'emnane'e*—half-man/half-woman. I do not know if the holy man is one who simply dresses like a woman or is actually hermaphroditic and has the organs of both sexes, but a stranger creature I have never before encountered; in her/his buckskin dress, brightly colored shawl, and leggings he/she makes a very convincing, if not particularly attractive, woman. This is all terribly confusing and only reinforces the sense we are experiencing of having entered another world peopled by a different species of human beings. Again I cannot forget John Bourke's words to this effect.

This Dog Woman creature seems to be much respected by the Cheyennes and has been chosen to provide quarters to Reverend Hare. The two holy men, one savage and one civilized, one hugely fat and one got up like a woman, make an odd couple, indeed! They, too, have a cronish old woman—Sleeps with Dog Woman, is the manner in which Reverend Hare translates her name, which only confuses the issue further—who lives in their tipi and takes care of them, a kind of live-in servant, I suppose.

The Reverend has sufficient experience living among the Indian tribes of the Middle West that he hardly seems inconvenienced by the lack of amenities and appears to have already made himself quite comfortable here. While one might expect the big man to soon shed some of his excess poundage, the Reverend manages to have some culinary delicacy or other constantly at hand, having arranged for food to be carried to him by the Indian women of the camp. They arrive at his tent in a steady procession all day long bearing various dishes which they present to him as solemnly as if making offerings to an idol. I can't help but feel that the Reverend is taking some advantage of his position as a holy man.

Well, at least he speaks a bit of the Indian tongue, for which we are all grateful. The language barrier is proving to be a real hindrance to our settlement here; I am working diligently to learn the sign language of which I now know several useful gestures.

Our best intentions to meet daily notwithstanding, the constraints and pressures of our new lives here are already beginning to make themselves felt. After only a few days I sense our community ties loosening. As I mentioned, we are often simply too exhausted after the day's labors to assemble, and the camp being quite spread out makes it difficult for us to keep track of one another or to get news to and from each other. It is all I can do to steal a few minutes alone with those among my closest friends. The Indians have a camp crier, an old man who makes the rounds of the camp each morning calling out the day's "news" and "activities," and I have suggested that we do likewise for our women.

I confess that I was both shocked and thrilled when I finally saw Euphemia at our meeting yesterday. As I may have mentioned I have not seen her with the other women during the chores. Now she strode in like a princess, having already given up her civilized attire in favor of Indian garb—a deerhide dress stitched with sinew thread, moccasins, and leggings. I must say, the costume quite becomes her; she is completely striking.

Several of the women gathered about her to admire her costume. I went immediately to her and grasped her by the hands. "I have been so concerned about you, Phemie," I said. "I thought you might be ill. Why have I not seen you working with the others?"

Phemie laughed her deep rich laugh. "Oh May," she said, "I did not come here to be made a slave again. I already escaped once from that life, and when I did so I made the promise to myself that I would never toil for another. I'm a free woman. From now on I choose my work."

"And how were you able to manage that?" I asked. "While the rest of us do women's chores?"

"A simple act of refusal, an assertion of my freedom of choice," Phemie said. "I've decided that I should like to be a hunter, not a digger of roots, and so I explained to my husband that my efforts shall be devoted to that end. What can they do to me—put me in chains? Whip me? Let them try. I will always carry scars on my back from the whip and a brand as a reminder of a slave's life among tyrants, and I will not allow this to be repeated."

"Good for you, Phemie!" I said, "We must use your example in our meeting today."

"Let me show you something else, May," Phemie said, pulling her rawhide dress up to her waist to reveal that she was wearing a Cheyenne chastity string. We had each been presented with one of these ungodly devices by our women tentmates on the first day of our arrival. Apparently all the young Cheyenne girls wear them. It is a small rope which passes around the waist, is knotted in front, two ends passing down between the thighs, each branch wound around the thigh down nearly to the knees. Now several of the more prudish women present (I swear some are so prissy, that I cannot understand whatever possessed them to sign up for this program!) gasped in offended modesty. But Phemie paid them no mind. "No one visits here without a key," she said in her melodic voice, and she laughed. "I wish that I had had such a contraption when I was in bondage. Many nights at the whim of my master there was no sleep at all for this nigger girl. But now I'm in charge of this part of my life, as well."

"God Phemie," I said, "you're actually wearing the ghastly thing! The old crone who lives in our tent tried to get me to don mine, but I refused. It looks terribly uncomfortable."

"And she didn't force you, did she?" Phemie pointed out. "You see, May, these are a democratic people, after all. As to the subject of comfort, it is certainly no less comfortable than the corsets into which many of you strap yourselves daily."

"But we are here to procreate, Phemie," I said, "not to protect our chastity."

"Yes, but that moment, too, I shall decide for myself," Phemie said.

I must say, contrary to the popular reports in the newspapers and periodicals of the immoral, lurid, and rapacious savage, this hardly seems to be a carnally oriented society. By all accounts at our daily meeting, none of the other women have yet even been approached by their prospective husbands. Under the circumstances a chastity string seems quite superfluous . . .

"*Right ya* are, May," said cheeky Meggie Kelly on the subject. "I been trying to get me laddy's weapon charged since we got here, but he'll have *noone* of it. Shy as a bunny he is." In a kind of uncannily perfect symmetry, the twins have themselves been paired for matrimony with twin savage men. The four of them together look like some kind of strange mirror image. Twins are considered by the savages to bring good luck to the people, and as a result seem to have a certain special status. Naturally the Kelly girls have been in no hurry to disabuse our hosts of this superstition, as their major responsibility seems to be to saunter around camp with their twin fiancés, letting all the others admire them.

At Meggie's remarks several of us laughed, but the Reverend hushed us sternly. "I will remind you ladies that you are not yet married in the eyes of our Lord," he said. "And that fornication is forbidden until the marriage union is thus sanctified."

"*Aye*, in the eyes of your Lord perhaps, Reverend," said Susie Kelly, "but you're a damn Protestant! Doesn't mean a thing to us unless a holy Roman priest conducts the ceremony. And then me and Meggie'd be stuck here in the wilderness married for the rest of our life raising a brood of heathens. Two years is the bargain we *stroock*. And then Meggie and me has got important business back in Chicago. Right Meggie?"

"Right as rain, Susie," said Meggie, "but let the fat old heretic marry us in his devil's church. Like *ya* say, wouldn't be binding to a *coople* of good Catholic girls *loyke* us."

Now the Reverend turned very red in the face and began to stammer. "I will not be spoken to in that manner, young lady. I demand respect. It is the Episcopal Church, the only true faith, the true house of the Lord, that has been charged by our government with the task of saving the souls of the heathens!"

"That's a damn shame, it 'tis, Father, for the souls of the heathens, then," said Meggie, uncowed by the Reverend's wrath, "because everyone knows that Protestants go to Hell!"

"Blasphemer!" shouted the red-faced Reverend, pointing at the redheads as one. "Blasphemer! Satan's spawn!"

It occurred to me that the job of making Christians of the savages will certainly be complicated by the fact that we can't even agree on a common God among ourselves.

"I for one agree with Susan and Margaret," I spoke up. "The wedding ceremony is a mere formality and should not be binding to any of us. The fact is that we have been sent here to bear children by the savages, and the sooner we have fulfilled our part in this bargain, the sooner we will be free to go home if we so choose. I say, let's get on with it."

"And under whose authority, Miss Dodd, have you assumed the moral leadership of our contingent?" asked Narcissa White, who rarely misses an opportunity to undermine my efforts at maintaining unity among our women. I'm certain that her jealously of me is further fueled by the fact that Chief Little Wolf chose me to be his bride, while Miss White was herself taken by a man named Turkey Legs—a gangly, aptly named young fellow without any real stature in the tribe.

"Why, under no one's authority at all," I replied, surprised at the charge. "I try only to do my part to expedite our mission here."

"Your part, my dear," she said in her most santimonious way, "does not include advising the rest of us on matters of moral conduct or the sanctity of the marriage union. It is my responsibility as official representative of the American Church Missionary Society, and that of Reverend Hare as spiritual agent of the Episcopal Indian Commission, to render decisions on all such spiritual questions. Although it is doubtless true," she added in her insufferably insinuating tone, "that you have more practical experience in carnal matters."

At this last, a general tittering ran among the others. All know by now the reason for my incarceration in the asylum—the accusation of promiscuity alone sufficiently damning to ruin a woman's reputation, especially among other women. Too, it is possible that Captain Bourke and I were spied upon in our moment of passion . . .

"As the mother of two children," I answered, "I should certainly hope to be more knowledgable on that particular subject than a fat priest and a zealous spinster," I answered, "which hardly makes me an expert."

To which rejoinder, my own supporters laughed heartily.

"I think that some of us had not understood," I continued, "that our mission here was to be directed by the church. We were under the impression that our first authority was the United States government which hired us to bear children by the savages."

"Partly true," said Miss White. "But the government has in turn given over responsibility for the Indians to the care of the church and the Missionary Society. We are the ultimate authority here."

"Ah, go *wan ya* beggar," said Susie. "There isn't any authority out here."

I looked at the Reverend, who had returned to his bowl of food, his denominational outrage evidently slackened by the morsels of meat that he placed in his mouth with his fingers, like some kind of wilderness emperor.

Now he wiped his greasy mouth with the back of his hand, and smiled, the picture of fatherly benevolence. "My dear madams," he said, calmly, "the Episcopal Church has been charged with ministering to the souls of heathens—as well as to seeing that they are eventually settled under God's protective wing on the reservation."

"But the Cheyennes do not have a reservation," I said.

"They will have one soon enough," he said. "We are even now working toward that end. Then our real work begins."

"We were all told that our purpose here was to give birth to Cheyenne babies as a means of assimilating the savages," I said.

"Yes, that, too," admitted the Reverend, with a shrug. "Washington's idea. After which the Cheyenne children, yours included, will, at the earliest possible age, be sent to church-affiliated boarding schools which we are presently in the process of establishing across the region. This is all a part of the President's Indian Peace Plan. In this manner, the children's first influence at an impressionable age will be civilized white people and good Christians—*Protestants*, I might add. The hope of the church and the State is that being half-Caucasian by blood, your children will have a distinct spiritual and intellectual advantage over the purebred heathens, and that the savages will in turn peacefully follow this superior new generation into the bosom of civilization, and down the true path of Christian salvation. I am merely here to provide you with spiritual guidance." At this, the enormous Reverend again made a slight emperor-like incline of his head, which caught the morning light and glistened like a glazed ham.

"And the Kellys and I are only suggesting that we get down to the business at hand," I repeated.

"As Christians," said Narcissa White, "some of us may choose for ourselves a higher path upon which to elevate the savages from their lowly lot."

"Your prospective husband gave a horse for you, just like all the rest," I pointed out.

"I certainly have no intention of compromising my chastity with a heathen for a horse," she answered. "I intend to teach my husband that the true path to Christian salvation lies on a higher plane."

"Ah *yooor* a grand lady, aren't ya, Narcissa," said Meggie Kelly, "and won't *pooor* Mr. Turkey Legs be in for a rude surprise on his wedding night when he tries to digs his spurs into that stony *coontry*!"

"And what about you, Phemie?" I asked.

Phemie chuckled again. Truly I envy her calm. Nothing seems to bother her. "When I'm ready, May," she said. "And if I like my new husband and believe that he will make a good father to my children, then yes, I'll remove my chastity string. However, as he is both a heathen and a nigger, under the circumstances it will be difficult for me to give birth to the superior half-Caucasian child of which the Reverend refers to as the church and government's ideal."

"Aye, Phemie, and we won't be *'avin'* no Protestant babies, neither," said Susie Kelly. "Of that ya can be damn *shoore*. Right, Meggie?"

18 May 1875

Phemie was correct in saying that the savages are a democratic people, and using her example I have begun to make tiny inroads in liberating myself from the drudgery of women's chores. It seems useful if one displays some other talent, even if it is only perceived as such by the savages. Like those scamps, the Kelly girls, who are largely excused from manual labor for no better reason than that they are twins! In this same way the savages are fascinated with my notebook and may even be ascribing some supernatural quality to my writing in it—which may yet prove useful to me. Yet I will not be a shirker, for it would be unfair to the others and to my fellow tentmates if I did not do my fair share.

I have this also to say on behalf of the savages: they are a tremendously tolerant people, and though some of our ways and customs appear to amuse them to no end, they have yet to be condemnatory or censorious. Thus far they seem to be merely curious, but always respectful. The children are particularly fascinated with our presence and stop whatever they are doing to stare at us when we pass with round disbelieving eyes as if we are enormously odd creatures to them—and, indeed, I suppose we are! Sometimes they come forward shyly and touch our dresses, only to run away giggling. Often they follow us about at a slight distance, like a pack of hungry dogs. I brought with me a little hard candy from the supply store at Fort Laramie and often I carry a few pieces in my pockets to give to the children. They are precious little things, brown and full of healthful vigor. They seem for their age more mature, healthier, and better behaved than Caucasian children of comparable years. They are too shy to speak to us, and take my offerings of candy with great solemnity and then run off again posthaste chattering like magpies. I feel that the children may prove to be our bridge to the savage way of life and theirs to ours, for all children are good, are they not? All children are children finally—it hardly matters to which race or culture they belong—they belong first to the race and culture of children. I so look forward to learning this difficult language that I may speak to these tiny savage elves. How I love the sight of them! What joy, mixed with sorrow, they bring to my heart when I watch them playing their games about the camp. For I cannot help but think of my own dear babies . . . How I long to hold them in my arms . . . and how I find myself beginning to look forward to bearing one of these little heathens myself!

Speaking of children, I have tried as well as I can to keep watch over little Sara. A most extraordinary thing has occurred. We have heard the child speak, just a few words, and not in English, but in the Indian tongue—it is either that or pure gibberish, for neither Martha nor I was able to make any sense of it. Her young fiancé, Yellow Wolf, seems to understand her perfectly, and so I can only assume that he is teaching her his language—though I still cannot make her to utter one single word of ours. Isn't it strange? And wonderful . . . Perhaps romance is blooming here among the savages after all.

For her part Martha seems to be having some problems adjusting to the savage life and inevitably her own high expectations of romance with her fierce, unkempt warrior Mr. Tangle Hair, have been somewhat disappointed. "He seems to be a kind fellow, May," she said to me while we were digging roots with the other women yesterday morning. "But I do so wish he would groom himself." Then she paused in her work. "Something I've been wondering—after our marriage am I to be known as Mrs. Tangle Hair? Because you do know what the savages call me now, don't you? Reverend Hare has just translated it for me. They call me Falls Down Woman. It is because I'm so clumsy."

The savages do seem to seize upon some obvious physical characteristics in their choice of names, and, in fact, poor Martha is a bit clumsy—constantly stumbling and falling.

"It's only because you insist on wearing your high buttonshoes with the tall heels, Martha," I said. "These were fine on the boardwalks of Chicago but are entirely inappropriate for walking on the uneven ground of Nature. And they are certainly not intended for laboring in the root fields. Why just look at them!"

"I know, of course you're right, May," Martha said, "I've practically ruined them . . . but . . . but" and I could tell the poor thing was about to break down . . . "they remind me of home." And then she began to weep, terrible shuddering sobs. "I'm sorry, May," she blubbered, "I'm just tired . . . I'm homesick. I don't wish to be known as Falls Down Woman, or as Mrs. Tangle Hair. I want to go home."

"Well, dear," I said, trying to console her, "that you can't do right now. But you could teach your future husband to comb his hair. And if you're unhappy with your own new Indian name, we'll just see that it's changed."

"And how shall we do that?" asked Martha, wiping her nose with a handkerchief, her sobs subsiding.

"It seems to me that the Indians are forever changing names on the least whim or fancy," I said. "Perhaps if you perform some deed or other, or adopt some new habit, or even simply don some article of clothing—wear one of your scarves over your head, for instance. Then, no doubt they will begin to call you Woman who Wears Scarf on Head—"

"Why on earth would I wish to be named that?" Martha asked, rather petulantly. I'm afraid that the general strangeness and the homesickness we are all feeling, coupled with the exhaustion of our labors and the frequently sleepless nights, have caused all of our moods to be a bit erratic.

"I only use that as an example, Martha," I said. "Tell me, what would you like to be called?"

"Something more romantic—your name, for instance, Swallow—*Mesoke*—it's quite lovely in either language. Or the one they call Woman Who Moves Against the Wind. How much more charming that is than Falls Down Woman."

"Well then, we must think of a name that pleases you and that somehow suits you . . . God this is filthy work, is it not?" I said, pausing, and throwing down the crude little spadelike implement that the savages fashion out of wood and stone for this chore. "It's ruining my fingernails—look how cracked and dirt-encrusted they are. Had I known we were to be doing work as fieldhands I'd have brought with me a proper pair of gloves and a spade. Soon they'll be calling me Needs Manicure Woman."

"But who gives out these names?" asked Martha, unamused by my attempt at humor—and to my way of thinking somewhat preoccupied with the matter. "How is it that they come into general usage?"

"As I make it out, they just occur," I answered, "for the most banal reasons. Someone sees you stumble and fall down, for instance, in the high-buttoned shoes that you insist on wearing, and the next time your name comes up in general conversation, they say, 'Oh, you know the one I mean—the woman who falls down.' "

"Why can't they simply call me by my Christian name—Martha?"

"In case you haven't noticed, my friend," I said, "we are not presently among Christians. Now, let's put our heads together and think of a suitable name for you, and then we shall launch a campaign to bring it into general usage."

"But we are unable even to speak the language," Martha said. "It's hopeless." And I feared that she was going to start crying again.

"No matter," I said. "We're learning the sign language, and we can always enlist the assistance of Reverend Hare—assuming, that is, that we can get his enormous Episcopalian backside off the buffalo robes. In any case, as I have said, these names seem to come about more as a result of actions or physical characteristics."

We considered the matter for a while as we continued to dig the damnable roots. Finally I had an idea. "How would you feel about the name: Woman Who Leaps Fire? Personally, I find it rather enigmatic . . . romantic."

Martha brightened perceptibly. "Why yes! I like that very much. Leaps Fire Woman! And I think I know what you are going to suggest."

"Exactly," I said. "From now on, every time you come to one of the fires smoldering outside the lodges, or for that matter, inside Mr. Tangle Hair's own lodge, simply leap over it. You are bound to earn the new name. What else could be construed from such an action?"

Ah, but here is the unfortunate result of our seemingly well-laid plan; Martha is not athletically inclined, a fact which I should have considered. The first fire she came to after she left me, she attempted to leap in the witness of a number of the savages, but, partly because she was still wearing those damnable high shoes of hers, she stumbled and fell directly into the fire pit and was no sooner covered head to toe in black oily soot. The Indians do have an uncanny knack for choosing names and this morning, according to the Reverend, poor Martha is referred to by two names: Falls Down in Fire Woman, and, the even less attractive Ash Faced Woman. I'm afraid that she will never live this down . . . how lucky for me that I made my impulsive dive into the beaver pond . . .

19 May 1875

My dearest sister Hortense,

It occurs to me that I have not written to you for an entire month—certainly the strangest month of my life! How much there is to tell you. But first how is dear Walter? And the children? Father and Mother? Do send news, won't you . . . ah, if only you could . . . if only I could have news of my babies . . .

Of course mail delivery is somewhat spotty out here on the frontier, but you might try addressing your correspondence to: Madame Little Wolf, Queen of the Savages, or, less formally, to Swallow, in care of the Cheyenne Nation, Somewhere in the middle of Nowhere, Nebraska Territory, USA . . . yes that should find me posthaste . . . Hah! . . . if only . . .

Truth be told, I have no idea where we are. Another world certainly . . . Sometimes I try to imagine all of you back in Chicago comfortably ensconced in the bosom of civilization, sitting in Mother's drawing room at teatime, for instance . . . I must concentrate so hard to conjure the image, truly my imagination fails me, just as you cannot possibly imagine the life I am leading . . . not in your wildest dreams, my sister . . . not even in your wildest nightmares can you possibly envisage this Indian village, these people, this landscape.

Let me describe to you a bit of the daily routine of camp life among the savages. The three Mrs. Little Wolves, yes, there are three of us—the old one, the young one, and, most recently the Caucasian one, though as yet we are only betrothed (the Chief is, it occurs to me, what my Harry would have undoubtedly called "one lucky redskin")—all inhabit the same tipi, a lodge it is grandiloquently called in the periodicals but it is certainly not to be mistaken for Father's hunting lodge on the lake—it is actually nothing more than a large round tent, possibly fifteen feet in diameter—you've undoubtedly seen artists' renderings of these primitive habitations—made from buffalo hides and painted with crude aboriginal designs. The floor is earth, there is a fire ring in the center, and our "beds" if such they may be called, are animal skins spread atop tree boughs and leaves, each with a wooden-framed backrest for reclining in a sitting position if one wishes . . . somewhat like a divan. Well, I must admit, finally, that this arrangement is not entirely without its comforts once one grows accustomed to life without furniture and to sleeping on the ground.

There are, I may have neglected to mention not only we three women, and the Chief himself, but a young girl, named Pretty Walker, presumably the Chief's daughter by his first marriage, a young boy who looks after the horses and who I take to be an orphan, and an old crone, who looks exactly like the witch of childhood nightmares, with a large hooked nose and who serves the function of tent organizer and enforcer; she stands guard immediately inside and to the left of the entranceway to the tent, and brandishes a large wooden club at the slightest infraction of a multitude of complicated tipi "rules and regulations" with which I am still not completely familiar.

And finally, completing our big happy family is an infant child, the progeny of the second wife, Feather on Head. The child is so perfectly quiet that I actually lived in the lodge for several days before I was aware of his existence. Indian babies do not cry as do our own; it is quite extraordinary, they are rather like deer fawns, not uttering a sound to give them away. Too, I think his mother may, out of some sort of protective maternal instinct, have intentionally kept the child hidden from me for the first few days of my residency . . . oh, Hortense, when I discovered the baby, or I should say, when Feather on Head finally revealed him to me, how my heart ached, a bittersweet ache of joy at the sight of this tiny infant, and of longing for my own two dears . . . how clearly he brought them back, their pinched smiling faces . . . will I ever see them again?

The child took to me immediately; as you know I have always had an affinity for babies—hah! yes I know, both with bearing them and with caring for them . . . He smiled up at me, truly a little cherub, brown as a chestnut, his eyes as bright as copper pennies, and when Feather on Head witnessed her son's and my obvious mutual affection she became instantly warm toward me. She softened and smiled shyly and we have since become quite friendly, my first friend so far among the Cheyennes! Although perforce our ability to communicate is yet limited by the language barrier. Feather on Head is helping me greatly with my sign language, and although I am trying to make some sense of the Cheyenne tongue itself, I think that I shall never be able to speak it. It is a language that often appears to be without vowels—a language of the crudest sounds rather than words—hisses, grunts, and ululations—strange noises that seem to issue from some older and more primitive earth than the one you and I inhabit. Or I should say than you inhabit . . .

I have recently discovered that a few of the savages do possess an extremely limited command of the English language and even more of them appear to be decently proficient in a kind of bastardized French—which they first learned some years ago from the old-time French fur trappers and traders, and which has been passed down as a kind of patois, barely comprehensible to us but certainly more so than their native tongue. How I wish you could hear their accents, dear sister! The first time this abomination assaulted my ears I didn't even recognize it as the French language—but at least it sounded vaguely familiar. Fortunately, there is one French girl among us, a very pretty dark-haired girl named Marie Blanche de Bretonne, who was touring America with her parents when they were tragically killed by thieves in our fair city of Chicago. Truly, no one is safe any longer in this world. While still in shock and mourning, the poor girl, alone in a strange city, stranded thousands of miles from home, signed up for this program. Like many of our little group, I'm afraid that she is having second thoughts about the matter . . . In any case it was through Marie

Blanche that we first discovered the Cheyennes' ability to speak French, if indeed we may call it that. Why, Hortense, truly it would be enough to make our childhood tutor, Madame Bouvier, turn over in her grave. You remember what a stickler she was for pronunciation? how she would rap our knuckles with her pointer when we got it wrong, and say "Zat eees eencarrect, mademoiselle" . . . But I digress, *n'est-ce pas?* I must stop recalling the past, which comes back to me so vividly when I write to you, as if this new life is but a dream and you, still living in the real world, are trying to pull me back . . . too late, alas, too late . . . would that it could be so . . .

As you might imagine it is hardly an enviable position to find oneself in the home (the word "home" I'm afraid does not properly conjure our bizarre living arrangements) of another woman—in this case, two women—as the soon-to-be third bride of their husband. The older wife, Quiet One, has been far less accepting of me than young Feather on Head. Some nights I lie awake on my bed (such as it is) in mortal fear that she will cut my throat with a knife if I dare to fall asleep . . .

The situation is awkward to say the least. Indeed the word "awkward" hardly describes it. Yes, well we are people from such different . . . backgrounds . . . God, I sound just like Mother when she would lecture us all those years ago about playing with the servant children . . . I begin to understand that this experience requires a new vocabulary altogether—trying to explain it to you would be like trying to describe the world of Shakespeare to the savages . . . the words don't exist, language fails . . . John Bourke was right . . .

Yes, well let me try again. We live in a tent—why mince words, a tent made of animal hides—three wives, a girl, an old crone, an infant child, a young orphan boy, who seems to have been adopted by the Chief's family and who cares for the Chief's considerable string of horses and sometimes helps the women with the chores, and this man Little Wolf, who is a great Chief of his people.

It is quite a spacious tent, as tents go, I'll say that for it. I have my own charming little corner space . . . if it is possible to have corners in a round tent . . . where I sleep upon a bed of pine boughs, animal hides, and trade blankets. The odors in our "home" are quite indescribable—a word that I find myself using often in my attempts at rendering these little scenes on paper. There are the odors of human bodies, of the earth beneath us, of the animal skins used as bedding, of the smoke from the fire . . . Added to these, if the wives have been cooking (which they seem perpetually in the process of doing, for the savages do not seem to observe the custom of breakfast, dinner, and supper at regular hours as we do, but rather eat whenever they are hungry so that there must always be food available) there is generally also an odor inside the tent of food being prepared. Sometimes the cooking scents are actually appetizing, at other times the stench rising from the pot is so perfectly revolting that I can hardly bear it, I feel that I shall be sick and must stumble outside and gasp fresh air and I know that I shall go hungry that day. As you know, Hortense, I have always been interested in the culinary arts as a recreational pastime, but I have not yet offered my services in the "kitchen" such as it is (another excellent example of the inadequacies of language) nor indeed have I been asked to help with meal preparation. However, if I am to live here among these people I fully intend to take a turn at the stove . . . the fire . . . Perhaps I will make my tentmates a lovely little French dish, say a delightful Coq au Vin . . . Harry's favorite repast . . . though, of course, the first question that presents itself is where might I obtain a decent bottle of French burgundy wine? Or for that matter, any bottle of wine . . . Hah! . . . But now I allow myself to drift off again into thoughts of that old life, which can only make this new one so much more precarious and difficult, and . . . insupportable.

Now then, dearest sister, on the brighter side. It has finally been determined that we are to be wed with the others in a group ceremony tomorrow evening. Reverend Hare, an enormous Episcopalian missionary who has accompanied us into the wilderness, will be performing the Christian services. Would that you were here to act as my bridesmaid! Ah, how I love to imagine the family all gathered together . . . staying in our . . . guest tent! Father thin-lipped and appalled, Mother alternately weeping and swooning in abject horror of the heathens. Why, we'd be administering smelling salts to her every quarter hour! God, what fun it would be! I, who have always had such a talent for shocking the family, have this time truly outdone myself, wouldn't you agree?

As I understand it this mass wedding is an unprecedented event and one that does not fit neatly into any of the established ceremonies of the Cheyennes. For the savages, the giving of horses, a feast, and a dance are all that is required to seal the marriage union, it being a simple agreement between the two parties—much as Harry and I took up our life together. Being neither of a particularly religious bent myself, nor, as you know, much interested in the institution of marriage, I find this arrangement to be quite adequate.

However, the addition of Christian nuptials into the upcoming ceremony has got things all complicated both among our women and among the Indians. The savages are unable to reach consensus on even the smallest matters without hours of incredibly laborious deliberation. Now after much "powwowing" and smoking of pipes with Reverend Hare (in this one regard it strikes me that men of all races are similar), the parties seem finally to have come to terms.

In this same way, the savages are absolute sticklers for protocol—some of their customs so peculiar as to simply defy description. Hardly a day goes by that I don't violate some bizarre cultural tabu or other. For instance, it appears that when seated in the lodge the well-brought-up Indian maiden is expected to sit with her feet pointing to the right—except in the case of one particular band to which some of our women have gone and which is encamped slightly separated from the main camp and in which the women are noted for sitting with their feet pointing to the left. Yes, well, I have absolutely no idea how or why these preposterous customs became established in the first place, but the savages take them with the utmost seriousness. My Captain Bourke says that these are due to their innately superstitious nature. On my very first day here, I immediately cast my feet in the wrong direction and there suddenly issued from the women in our tent all manner of disapproving clucking and general distress. The old crone went so far as to wave her stick at me, jabbering like a mad hen. Of course I pay no attention to the position of my feet and shall continue to sit in the lodge with them pointing in whatever direction I damn well choose—regardless of the deep anxiety this appears to cause my tentmates. So you see, Hortense, just as in my "old" life, I am already a fly in the ointment of savage society, already rocking the conventional boat, already considered to be something of a scandal . . . which has always seemed to be my mission in whatever culture I live, does it not?

Ah, but here was a lovely surprise: My fellow wives have sewn for me the most beautiful wedding gown upon which I have ever gazed. It is made of antelope hide—the softest skin imaginable—sewn with sinew thread and intricately embroidered with beads and porcupine quills, and dyed with the essence of roots in exquisite colors and designs. I was completely flabbergasted—and very much touched—when they presented it to me, for it must clearly represent hundreds of hours of the most intensive labor imaginable and would seem to indicate that they have accepted me into their family—and in very gracious fashion, indeed. It is, I understand, common practice for the bride's family to make for her an elaborate wedding dress, but as we are all without our families here, other women of the tribe have taken it upon themselves to dress us properly for the occasion. In fact, all of our other women have also been presented with wedding dresses—in most cases made for them by the sisters and mothers of their intended. I may surely be prejudiced in the matter, but of those dresses I've seen so far, mine is by far the most beautiful, certainly the most elaborately decorated. Perhaps because I am to marry the great Chief, special attention was taken in its creation . . . Even the sullen and unfriendly Quiet One participated in the making of this gown—which is not to suggest that she is warming in any way to my presence.

As you might well imagine, I and most of the other ladies have balked at giving up our own clothing in favor of the savage attire. The clothes and meager personal possessions which we have brought with us into this wilderness represent our last connection to the civilized world, so we are naturally reluctant to part with them—for fear that once we don savage garb, we become perforce savages—not just the brides of savages, but savages ourselves. This is, you understand, an important distinction . . . Some in our group are so intent on keeping up their attire and toilet, no matter how inappropriate these may be, that they can sometimes be seen promenading through the camp—little gaggles of our ladies strolling and chatting and twirling their parasols as if on a garden tour, trying desperately to appear oblivious to our present circumstances. I think that they are quite mad—indeed, some of them really are mad—but while I personally have decided to give up such attempts to forge civilization out of wilderness, I must admit that I have not quite yet resigned myself to dressing exclusively in animal skins.

Fortunately, the Cheyennes are traders, as well as hunters, and some of their attire is not so terribly different from our own. They have available, for instance, cloth and blankets and buttons, and other articles from our world. Indeed, some of the men dress quite ludicrously in bits and pieces of white man's clothing, wearing altered U.S. Army uniforms, and hats—all misshapen and with the tops cut out and eagle feathers protruding from them. This gives the Indians who affect this attire the appearance of children playing dress up; they look more like carnival clowns than soldiers—their outfits bizarre hybrids of the two cultures . . .

I'm pleased to report that my own intended dresses very modestly in traditional Indian garb. The only white man article which he affects is a large silver peace medal around his neck, a gift from President Grant himself.

But I seem to be rambling again . . . where was I? Ah, yes, with the exception of Miss White and some of her more strident followers we are to be married in traditional Cheyenne wedding gowns. We are to be dressed prior to the feast by our Cheyenne "mothers" and "sisters," literally stripped of our civilized clothing and dressed as savages—this is difficult to describe to you Hortense and, I'm certain even more difficult for you to understand, but the prospect is somehow both . . . terrifying and exhilarating.

Without intending to keep you in undue suspense, I shall continue this correspondence after I am officially a bride . . . right now there is much to do.

21 May 1875

Good God, Hortense, so much to tell you, I am only now, two days later awakening from the experience . . . I am still not myself, fear that I shall never again be the same. I have been drugged, my senses assaulted, my very being stripped to its primitive core . . . its savage heart . . . where to begin . . . ?

The music . . . still beats in my mind, throbs through my body . . . dancers whirling in the firelight . . . coyotes on the hilltops and ridges, taking up the song beneath the moon . . .

22 May 1875

Forgive me, dear sister, but I fell back into a deep slumber after my last incoherent ramblings . . . I must have slept the full day and night round and I woke feeling better, stronger, a child grows inside of me . . . is it possible? Or have I only dreamed this, too . . .

Yes, the scene of our wedding night is even more vividly etched now in my mind . . . let me describe it to you:

The moon was full in the sky; it rose early before the sun had set and did not set again until after the sun rose; the moon spent the entire night crossing the sky, illuminating the dancers in an unearthly glow, casting their shadows across the plains as if the earth itself danced . . . all who danced lit by moonlight.

We spent nearly the full day of the wedding in our lodges being dressed by the women, ornaments and totems hung from our clothing and from our hair, our faces painted with bizarre designs so that we would hardly recognize one another later under the pure white moon . . . perhaps this was just as well, perhaps our painted faces were meant as disguises, allowing each of us, savage and civilized alike, to act out these pagan rites in anonymity. It is true that several days later—or so I feel it to be for I have lost all track of time—we "civilized" women are hardly able to look one another in the eye for the madness that overcame us.

The men had recently returned from a successful buffalo hunt—stupidly, it had never occurred to me that the Cheyennes had been waiting for that good fortune to befall them before scheduling the wedding feast, because of course, without the bounty of the hunt, it would be a poor feast, indeed. Clearly, I have as much to learn about the ways of subsistence living as they do about those of civilization.

As it was, individual feasts were held in virtually every lodge in the camp, a kind of large, communal, movable feast. There was a vast amount of food, much of it surprisingly palatable. The first wife, Quiet One, is renowned in the camp for her talents as a cook and outdid herself on this occasion. She roasted the tender ribs and liver of the buffalo over coals, and boiled the tongue, and from another pot served a stew of meat and the wild turnips referred to by their French name, *pommes blanches*. There were other roots and various spring greens with which I am not familiar by name, but all quite interesting to the taste. We "brides" were not allowed to lift a finger—to the point that even our food was cut up for us in small morsels and hand-fed to us by our Indian attendants, as if they were trying to conserve our strength . . . now I understand why.

There was one particular dish that I must tell you about, a dish that most of our women, myself included, were unable to tolerate. Too horrible! Too despicable! Boiled dog! Yes, yes, choked pup! It is considered a great delicacy, saved for just such a special occasion as our wedding. My friend Feather on Head who served the older one as a kind of *sous chef*, performed the gruesome task of wringing the little puppy's neck just prior to cooking—which she did with her bare hands as casually as if she was wringing out a dishcloth. My God! When I tried to intervene, to rescue the poor little thing from her death grip, she merely laughed and pulled away and continued her stranglehold until the flailing puppy was limp and lifeless. It was then scalded in boiling water, scraped of hair, gutted, and roasted over the fire, and all present made such a fuss about its culinary qualities with much satisfied oohing and ahhing and general lip-smacking. I could not bring myself to taste the dog meat—even its odor while cooking sickened me.

Our tipi was crowded with twelve people exactly, the majority of them clearly chosen because they were poor. You would know little about this, Hortense, because you have led such a sheltered and privileged life, but there is a universality to poverty that transcends culture; just as in our own society, there are among the savages both rich and poor—those who are successful hunters and providers who live in well-appointed lodges with many hides and robes and have a good string of horses, and those who have little and depend on the largesse of their neighbors. And never have I seen a more generous, selfless people than these. I believe that those unfortunates who came to our lodge that night—there, you see, already I begin to take a proprietary interest in my living quarters!—were the families of men who had been killed in battle, or possibly the families of some of those poor wretches whom we had encountered at the forts—the drunks and beggars who had deserted their wives and children . . . one can't help but wonder what we are doing to these people that their lives and livelihoods unravel so with our presence—"spoiled" by contact with us, as the Captain put it . . .

It seems to be a primary duty of my husband . . . how strange to say . . . my husband Little Wolf . . . as head Chief to look after the poor of his people. Several women brought children of various ages with them to the feast; they sat quietly in the back of the lodge, silently accepting the food their mothers passed them.

After all had eaten, the younger children, sated, fell asleep on the robes, the men passed a pipe and told stories, which of course, I could not understand, but to which the older children listened raptly. Possibly it was the effect of the food, or the warmth inside the lodge, or simply the soft murmuring of the men's voices—I confess that I am beginning to find the language less objectionable; it possesses a certain rhythm and cadence that though primitive is no longer so displeasing to the ear—I began to fall into a kind of trance, a state that was like sleep, but I was not asleep, just floating as if in a dream, as if drugged.

Then by some unspoken signal, everyone began to leave the lodges to assemble in the communal circle around which the tents are strategically placed . . . this is, I suppose something like our own town square, but of course round rather than square. All is round in this strange new world . . . The musicians (yes, well, again I must use the term loosely for they would hardly be confused for the Chicago Philharmonic Orchestra!), and the singers and dancers also began to assemble. Our own women gathered in small clusters to inspect each other's "wedding gowns," to marvel at each other's painted faces and outlandish costumes. My friend Martha was made up to look like a badger—an uncanny resemblance—with a black mask and white stripe down her forehead and nose. I have no idea for what purpose, but the savages have some meaning for everything. For my part half my face was painted black with white stars forming constellations on my cheeks and the full moon on my forehead, the other side of my face was painted all white with a blue river meandering its length. "You are the day and night," Martha said strangely, marveling, she too appearing to be in some kind of narcotic stupor. "You are the heavens and the earth!"

"*Aye*, and we're a pair of foxes we are, Meggie!" said the Kelly sister Susan appreciatively. Surely the red-haired Irish twins were no less identical got up with real fox heads attached to their hair and fox tails pinned to their rears. An uncanny likeness, and knowing something of the girls' wily natures, a stroke of pure genius on the part of the heathens.

But perhaps most striking of our group was the Negro Phemie, her entire face and body painted white with brilliant red stripes running up her arms, around her neck and eyes, her full Negro lips painted crimson, even her hair painted blood red—my God, she was magnificent to behold . . . a savage dream goddess.

Now appeared the holy man they call Dog Woman and his apprentice, named Bridge Girl—also a *he'emnane'e,* as these half-men/half-women are called. Two stranger creatures I have never before laid eyes upon! The young apprentice, Bridge Girl, speaks in the soft, high voice of a female, but is clearly a young boy. The older man, too, is effeminate in both voice and gesture. Yes, well we've seen similar people on the streets of Chicago—Nancy Boys, Father refers to them.

Now these two set about organizing the dancers, which they did with great solemnity and skill. The men/women are said to possess special abilities at matchmaking and are very popular with the young people, their advice in matters of the heart much sought after. For they know everything of both sexes.

Now at last the music began—an entire savage orchestra! Flute players, drum beaters, gourd shakers . . . a primitive symphony, to be sure, that makes for a crude harmony . . . but one with an undeniably rhythmic power. Then the singers took up the song, the eeriest song I've ever heard, the higher notes of the women floating lightly over the deeper tones of the men, a throbbing steady repetitive beat like a riffle running into a pool . . . it sent chills up my spine and in concert with the otherworldly music actually caused a number of our women to swoon dead away, they had to be revived by the fire—a huge bonfire that had been built in the center of the circle, flames and sparks leaping into the night sky, licking the heavens . . . I assure you, dear sister, not even the lunatic asylum in full riot could prepare one for this bizarre spectacle . . .

Dog Woman announced the different dances, sometimes gently scolding the young people if they did not perform the steps exactly right. Truly, she reminded me of old Miss Williams at our dancing school in Chicago—you remember her don't you, Hortense? . . . you see, still I clutch these memories to draw me back, to keep me from going completely mad in the face of this assault on our sensibilities . . .

The children sat in the back behind the adults on the outside of the circle, watching raptly, beating time with their hands and feet, their faces shining in the moonlight, the flames from the fire sparking in their slate-colored eyes, flickering golden in their oiled black hair.

Now the huge Reverend Hare resplendent in his white clerical gown made his grand entrance. He held his Bible aloft for all to see. Although the savages cannot read, they know it to be a sacred text—being a people to whom totemic objects are of utmost importance—and many crowded around him trying to touch it. The Reverend called out and the grooms began to appear out of the shadows of the fire, seemed to issue from the flames themselves like phantoms. I am to this day not absolutely certain that we had not been unwittingly drugged during the feast, for we all remarked later on the dreamlike state we felt.

If we brides considered ourselves to be elaborately made up for the occasion, the grooms were even more fantastically painted and adorned. It was difficult even to identify some of them and many of our women had simply to take as an article of faith the fact that the man standing beside them was really their intended. I did recognize my Chief Little Wolf, who wore a headdress with buffalo horns on either side, black raven feathers surrounding his head, ringed by eagle feathers, spilling like a tail down his back. He wore spotless new beaded moccasins, a fine deerskin shirt artfully trimmed with what, I now realize, can only have been human hair. Over his shoulders he wore a buffalo robe that had been painted red and was adorned with all manner of intricate designs. In one hand he carried a red rattle, which he shook softly in time to the music, and in the other a lance trimmed with soft fur. He was a picture of savage splendor, and in my altered state of mind, I felt oddly proud to be standing beside him. Well, after all, isn't this how a girl is supposed to feel on her wedding day?

Over the sound of the music and with the dancers still performing in the background, Reverend Hare began reciting the Christian wedding vows. Whatever else may be said of the man he has a commanding and sonorous speaking voice, which managed to rise above the music:

> *"Dearly beloved we are gathered together here in the sight of God, and in the face of this company to join together these men and these women in holy matrimony . . ."*

And each verse, the Reverend repeated in Cheyenne.

> *"Into this holy estate these couples present come now to be joined. If any man can show just cause why they may not lawfully be joined together, let him now speak, or else hereafter forever hold his peace . . ."*

Did Captain John G. Bourke swoop into the camp at this moment atop his big white horse and snatch me away from these proceedings, carry me off to live in a little house set in a grove of cottonwoods on the edge of a meadow, by the banks of a creek, at which safe harbor I would be reunited with my own sweet babies and bear others by my dashing Captain and there live out my life as a good Christian wife and devoted mother? No, alas, he did not . . . Did I pray fervently that at this very moment in the ceremony of matrimony, my Captain would rescue me thusly? . . . Yes . . . I did, I confess that I did . . . God help me.

> *"Wilt thou have this Woman to thy wedded wife, to live together after God's ordinance, in the holy estate of Matrimony? Wilt thou love her, comfort her, honor, and keep her, in sickness and in health; and forsaking all others, keep thee only unto her, so long as you both shall live?"*

When the Reverend uttered his translation of this last verse, a collective *"houing"* arose from the grooms, a strange noise like an unearthly wind blowing through the assemblage.

> *"Wilt thou have this Man to thy wedded Husband, to live together after God's ordinance, in the holy estate of Matrimony? Wilt thou obey him, and serve him, love, honor, and keep him, in sickness and in health; and forsaking all others, keep thee only unto him, so long as ye both shall live?"*

There was a long pause here before there came from among us a scattering of "I will's," some of them barely more than murmurs, remarkable for their general lack of conviction. I know, too, that a number of our women did not answer the question at all, but left it hanging there in limbo as their final escape . . .

> *"And to those whom God hath joined together, let no man put asunder. Foreasmuch as these men and women have consented together in holy wedlock, and have witnessed the same before God and this company, and thereto have given and pledged their troth, each to the other, and have declared the same by joining hands; I pronounce, that they are Husband and Wife; in the name of the Father, and of the Son, and of the Holy Ghost . . . Amen."*

And then it was done . . . A stunned silence fell over our company of women as the full import of this momentous occasion made itself felt. The grooms, seemingly less impressed by their new matrimonial state, faded back into the shadows from whence they came, to rejoin the dancers. Meanwhile we brides came together in small coveys and in some mental disorder, to congratulate one another, or commiserate, whichever the case might be, over our newly wedded state. Some wept, but I do not believe that these were tears of joy. All wondered what was to come now . . .

"Are we truly married, Father, in the eyes of God?" asked the strange woman, "Black Ada" Ware, of the Reverend. She was dressed still in mourning for her wedding, her black veil in place. "Is it so?"

All gathered about, I think hoping that the large Reverend might relieve our minds by telling us that, no, it had been nothing more than a sham ceremony, we were not truly married to these foreign creatures . . .

"Have I married a damn *niggah*?" asked Daisy Lovelace who had also declined to be attired by our hosts and who wore, by contrast, a stunning white lace wedding gown which she had brought with her especially for the occasion. Now the woman pulled her silver flask from under her dress and took a long swallow.

"That's certainly a lovely wedding gown, Miss Lovelace," said Martha, who seemed still to be in a sort of trance.

"It belonged to my dear departed *Motha*," said the woman. "*Ah* was to wear this gown, myself, when *Ah* married Mr. Wesley Chestnut of Albany, Georgia. But after Daddy lost everything in the *wah*, Mr. Chestnut had a sudden change a heart, if you know what *Ah* mean.

"If *Motha* and *Daddy* could only see their little baby girl now," she said, "havin' entered into holy matrimony with a gentleman with the deeply unfortunate name of *Miistah Bluuddy Fuuuut*" (her husband's descriptive name, in fact, was gained by the actions of her brave little dog, Fern Louise). "My *Gawd!*" And then the woman began to laugh, and suddenly I felt a new sympathy toward her, I understood fully and for the first time why she had signed up for this program; she had lost her fortune, had been left standing at the altar by a cad, and was quite possibly no longer as young as she claimed. For all her ugly bigotry, I began to like Miss Lovelace infinitely better for the touching fact that she had brought her mother's wedding gown along with her on this adventure. It proved that for all her apparent cynicism she still held on to hopes, dreams. And I began to laugh with her at the sheer absurdity of our situation, and soon all of us were laughing, looking at each other, some of us made up like demons from hell, married now to barbarians, we laughed until tears ran down our grotesquely painted faces. Yes, surely we had been drugged . . .

After we had spent ourselves laughing and the strange reality of our situation had once again insinuated itself into our befuddled consciousnesses, we wiped our tears and gathered in little coveys, clustered together for protection like confused chickens—indeed, that's what we most resembled, with our painted faces and our colorfully ornamented dresses.

We were naturally shy to take up the dance, but true to her nature, our brave good Phemie was the first to join in. "I must show them how an Ashanti dances," she said to us in her sonorous voice. "The way my mother taught me." For a moment all the Cheyenne dancers paused to watch our bold and unashamed Negress, as she took her place in the dance line. We were very proud of her. She did not dance in the same style as the Indians . . . in fact she was a superior dancer, her step sinuous and graceful, her long legs flashing beneath her dress, she pranced and whirled to the pulsing beat—but careful to follow the steps to the dance, as specified by a stern Dog Woman—who tolerated no unauthorized variations. A general murmuring of approval ran among the Indians who spectated, and then I believe that the dancing became even freer and more frenzied.

"My, that big *niggah* girl can surely dance," said Daisy Lovelace. "Daddy, God rest his soul, always did say they had special rhythm. *Enabuddy* care for a little sip a *medicine,"* she asked, holding out her flask.

"Aye, I'll have a wee nip of it, *shoore,"* said Meggie Kelly. "Loosens my dancin' feet, it does." And she took the flask from Daisy and took a quick pull, making a small grimace and passing it to her sister. *"T'isn't* Irish whiskey, that's *sartain,* Susie, but under the circumstances, it'll 'ave to do."

And then the Kelly sisters themselves melted into the dance—a more fearless pair of twins you could not hope to find; they hiked their skirts up and performed a kind of lively Irish jig to the music. Which made old Dog Woman crazy with anxiety at the impropriety of their steps!

"Oh vat de hell, I *tink* I may as *vell* join *een,* too!" announced dear homely Gretchen, encouraged by the twins' boldness. "I *ben* watching, I *tink* I learn *de* steps now." Gretchen was herself painted up in dark earth tones and wrapped in a rare blond buffalo robe adorned with primitive designs. Indeed, she resembled nothing so much as an enormous buffalo cow. Now she entered the dance line herself, God bless her. *"Yah!"* she called out with her typical gusto, *"Yah!"* and she took up the step with a heavy Slavic polkalike gait, a bovine gracelessness that provided additional humor to the moment. Several of us began to giggle watching her, covering our mouths with our hands, and even some of the native dancers and spectators laughed good-naturedly at her efforts. The savages are not without a sense of humor, and nothing amuses them so much as the sight of someone making a spectacle of herself.

"Lovely! Spiffing good dance!" said Helen Flight, eyebrows raised in perpetual delight. Helen, who has been given the Indian name, Woman

Who Paints Birds, or just Bird Woman, was got up very stylishly to look like a prairie chicken hen with artfully placed feathers about her narrow hips and rump. "Unfortunately I've never had the talent, myself," she said. "That is to say, my dearest companion, Mrs. Ann Hall, would never permit me to dance at balls; she felt that I was always trying to lead the men and that I was 'conspicuously heavy of foot'—her words exactly, I'm afraid."

Miss Flight has already proven to be somewhat scandalous to the natives for her habit of smoking a pipe which, like the morning swim, is a savage activity very much reserved for men—and, at that, is one undertaken with much ritual and ceremony. Whereas Helen is liable to fire up her pipe at any time and in any situation—causing the savages even more consternation than when I sit in the tipi with my feet pointing the wrong way! However, because of her considerable artistic skills, which the heathens hold in the very highest esteem, they have chosen to more or less tolerate Helen's smoking. (A primer on savage etiquette would be most useful to us all.)

Narcissa White came now among us, nearly beside herself with Christian righteousness. Evidently her religious beliefs do not permit dancing. "The recreation of the Devil," she objected. "His evil trick to inflame the passions and overcome the intellect."

"Thank *Gawd* for it," said Daisy Lovelace. "What would we do here with intellect, *Nahcissa?*"

Nor had Miss White allowed herself to be dressed in native attire; she still wore her high-buttoned shoes and high-collared missionary dress. "How can we possibly hope to Christianize these poor creatures," she asked, "if we allow ourselves to sink to their level of degeneracy?"

"Narcissa," I said, gently, "for once why don't you stop sermonizing and try to enjoy our wedding reception. Look, even the Reverend is participating in the festivities." It was true that the Reverend had comfortably ensconced himself fireside on a mound of buffalo robes, surrounded by several of the Cheyenne holy men; he was eating as usual, and chatting animatedly with his savage counterparts.

"Quite, May!" said Helen Flight. "We shall have more than sufficient opportunity to instruct the savages in the ways of civilization. At the present time, I say, 'When in Rome . . . ' Indeed my conspicuous heaviness of foot, notwithstanding, if you don't mind very much, ladies, I believe I'll give it a try. I have studied the grouse on the lek and this is one step I know." With which Helen, too, entered the dance line. "Oh, dear!" I heard her call with delight as she was swallowed by the native dancers, swept away in their midst under the moon until all I could see of her were her hands waving gaily above her head.

"God help you, people," whispered Narcissa White in a small voice.

"Gawd, Nahcissa," drawled Daisy Lovelace, "Don't be such a *damn stick in the mud*. This is our weddin' night, we should all be *celebratin'*. Have a lil' drink, why *don't you."* Daisy held out her flask, and seemed rather drunk herself. "We can repent *tomorah* after we have made passionate *luuuve* to our *niggah Injun* boys tonight," she continued, "because *Ah* have a *daaahk* suspicion that *tomorah* we shall be most in need of *deevine* forgiveness. . . . But what the Hell, *Ah* believe *Ah'll* take a turn on the dance floor *mahself*. I shall pretend that *Ah*'m attendin' the spring debutante ball at the Mariposa Plantation. It is there that I came out to society and where *Ah* danced away the most glorious night of my life. Wesley Chestnut said *Ah* was the most beautiful girl at the ball . . . and afterwards he kissed me for the first time out on the *veranda* . . ." And poor Daisy curtsied and held her arms out, as if joining an invisible partner, and said in a soft dreamy voice, "Thank you, *kind suh, Ah* don't *maahnd* if I do," and she began to do a slow waltz to the music, twirling in among the dancers, soon lost in their midst.

And so, one by one, each of us, trying to hold on to some precious recollection of our past, even if it was only a familiar dance step—any thin lifeline to keep us from falling completely into the abyss of savagery that was opening beneath us—so we joined, one by one, the dance.

What a sight we must have made whirling madly under the full moon . . . waltzes and jigs and polkas, a lively cancan from our pretty little French girl, Marie Blanche—for you see it did not matter what step we did, for all steps were the same finally, faster and faster, a frenzy of color, motion and sound, all the dancers now like breeding birds on the lek, plumage puffed and ruffled, the cocks' chests swelled, the hens' backsides half-turned teasing the air between them—we danced forward and back, round and round—in the music could be heard the steady booming drumming of the grouse, laid over the pulsing rhythmic heartbeat of the earth, and in the singing could be heard the elements of thunder, wind, and rain . . . this dance of earth. How the gods watching must have enjoyed their creation.

And the music and singing filled the sultry night air, washed out over the plains on the breeze so that even the animals gathered on the hills around to watch and listen—the coyotes and wolves took up the song, the bears and antelope and elk appeared—their outlines distinct on the moonlit horizon, and the children watched from behind the embers of the fire, spellbound, a bit frightened by the power of madness they beheld, and the old people watched, nodding to one another approvingly.

We danced. We danced. The People watched. The animals watched. The gods watched.

* * *

Some of the dancers danced all night, for the music played on until the first light of dawn surprised the setting moon. But most of us were claimed earlier by the families of our new husbands; they surrounded us at some point, quietly and without comment, and we followed, meek as lambs, as they led us back to the lodges.

A new tipi had been erected just outside the circle of the Little Wolf family lodges. To this I was taken and at the entrance was made to sit on a soft trade blanket spread on the ground there. Then several of the family members, who included both of the Chief's other wives as well as two young female cousins and the Chief's daughter Pretty Walker, grasped corners of the blanket and wordlessly picked me up and carried me through the entrance into the lodge—much like being carried over the threshold as is our own custom—but by the groom's family women rather than the groom himself. Now I was set down in the new lodge, beside a small fire that burned in the center. The buffalo-hide walls were newly tanned as white as parchment paper and prettily decorated with all manner of primitive drawings, some depicting the hunt, others scenes of warfare, others of men and women in sexual intimacies, of family life, children, and dogs, and still others designs that I could not decipher but were perhaps images of the heathens' gods themselves.

After all had left me alone, I breathed a great sigh of relief—privacy at last! How I hoped that this was to be my own new home. I realized that it was the very first time I had been completely alone since we had arrived here, and what a wonderful luxury it seemed. Exhausted, I stretched out on the soft blanket, before the warm fire, listening to the pulsing music . . .

I fell then into a deep slumber and had the strangest dream . . . at least it happened like a dream . . . It must have been a dream, for my husband was now in the tent with me, he was still dancing softly, noiselessly, his moccasined feet rising and falling gracefully, soundlessly, he spun softly around the fire, shaking his gourd rattle, which made no sound, danced like a spirit being around me where I lay sleeping. I began to become aroused, felt a tingling in my stomach, an erotic tickle between my thighs, the immutable pull of desire as he displayed to me. I dreamed that I saw his manhood grow from beneath his breechclout like a serpent as he danced and I lay on my stomach breathing shallowly and pressing myself against the blanket, feeling that I would explode there. I tried to reach to him but he moved away and behind me and in my dream I could feel him brushing my now naked rump as if with feathers, teasing and brushing so that I became even more aroused. And then, still lying on my stomach I raised my rump toward him, offered myself, and the brushing intensified and I fell again to press against the blanket, a deep pain of longing to be filled.

And still he danced lightly, soundlessly behind me, footsteps rising and falling. Now in my dream a noise rose in my throat, like a sound issuing from another, a sound I had never before heard and I raised my rump again higher and made with it slow circular motion, an act of nature, and the brushing of feathers came again and became finally the faintest touch of flesh, a nipping at my neck, the serpent warm and dry fell across my rump, gently rested between my legs with its own pulse like a heartbeat, moving them apart, opening me, entering me slowly and painlessly and pulling back and entering me again and pulling back so that at last I thrust myself backward toward it as if to capture it once and for all, to take it in. And then it entered me deeply, completely, and the strange sound rose again in my throat and my body trembled, shook, and bucked, and in my dream I was not a human being any longer with a separate consciousness, but became a part of something older and more primitive, truer . . . Like animals, Bourke said . . . this is what he meant . . . like animals . . .

There the dream ended and I remember nothing more until I woke up alone at dawn still lying facedown on the blanket, still dressed in my deerhide wedding dress. I know that it can only have been a dream, an erotic dream the likes of which I had never before experienced. But I also know that, as if by magic, a child now grows inside of me . . .

Well, Hortense, what else is there to say of that night? Would that you could read these words—how shocked you would be by the erotic details of my wedding night! It amuses me to imagine you considering this description over a cup of tea after you've sent Walter off to the bank and the children to school. If only you could know to what depths the family's actions have driven me, finally, surely poor Harry Ames might seem like a less unsuitable mate for your little sister. If only you could know that your accusations against me have led me to a world more lunatic than any you can possibly imagine.

Please give my regards to Mother and Father, and tell them that I shall write to them soon. And kiss my dearest babies for me . . . tell them that not a day passes, not a moment when they are not in my heart and my thoughts . . . and that soon they will have a new brother or sister and one day we shall all be together . . .

I am, your loving sister,
May

NOTEBOOK IV

The Devil Whiskey

"If there is a Hell on earth, being abroad in the camp . . . that night was like walking through its labyrinths. A few dancers still staggered by the dying firelight. Others had fallen down in a jumble of bodies around the fire; some struggled to regain their feet while others lay writhing on the ground. Throngs of drunken savages . . . jostled me as I pushed by. Naked couples copulated on the ground like animals. I stepped over them, pushed aside those who came up against me, and, when necessary, cleared a path by swinging my club. It was as if the whole world had fallen from grace, and we had been abandoned here to witness its final degradation."

(from the journals of May Dodd)

⊁⊀

23 May 1875

So much to report . . . Yesterday, my husband . . . how strange it sounds . . . my husband, Little Wolf, came to our wedding lodge riding his horse, and leading mine, which was saddled. He trailed two packhorses one of which was laden with a "parfleche"—which is the Cheyenne version of our valise—a kind of folding case made of sturdy buffalo rawhide into which household possessions, cooking implements, food supplies etc, are packed. There are several of these parfleches, all of them elaborately painted, in the Chief's lodge. He is obviously a "wealthy" man among his people, for "our" lodge is both larger and better appointed than that of many of the others in camp—as befits a great chief. As Captain Bourke had already explained to us, among the heathens he who owns the most horses is, by definition, the "wealthiest"—at least partly for the simple reason that the more horses one owns, the more goods and the larger lodge one is able to transport from place to place. Even Father, I think, would appreciate the simplicity of these savage economics.

Through the use of sign gestures, Little Wolf, his nut brown face less stern than usual, made it understood that I was to gather some belongings, that we were going off together.

"On our honeymoon, perhaps?" I asked laughing, but of course he did not understand me. I hurriedly put a few items of clothing and toiletries into a beaded buckskin pouch that had been left, along with other items, in my wedding lodge. I can only guess that these were gifts from Little Wolf's family, for there was also a full set of Cheyenne woman's clothing which included a pair of elaborately beaded deerskin moccasins, soft as butter, as well as a pair of leggings that fit over the latter, attaching with a strap just below the knee—somewhat like our own garter. The dress itself was made out of a similarly soft animal skin, sewn with sturdy sinew thread, and rather simply and tastefully decorated with beads and brass buttons. It has a slightly smoky, and not at all unpleasant odor from having been smoked over cottonwood coals in the tanning process. As part of our apprenticeship, we have watched the Cheyenne women fashion these garments in all stages. They are marvelously adept at their various crafts, which we are clearly expected to learn ourselves. In fact, one of our more fortunate ladies, Jeanette Parker, had been a professional seamstress in Chicago before being committed to the State Lunatic Asylum for murdering her husband in his sleep with a leather-stitching needle. I do not know if she is insane or not—and do not care—for it sounds to me as though the lout rather deserved his fate. Jeanette has greatly impressed the Cheyenne women with her sewing skills, having even taught them some stitches with which they were unfamiliar—as a consequence she is held in high esteem among them.

Owing to its smocklike construction, and the fact that the sleeves are open, somewhat like a cape, my new native dress is wonderfully comfortable, as are the leggings and moccasins—all have the effect of a kind of second, loose-fitting skin that lies rather sensuously over one's own. Such practical attire makes our own clothes and shoes seem most constricting. I am very nearly prepared to give up the latter altogether. Even our cavalry-riding breeches seem by comparison overly confining.

But I digress: hurriedly I gathered together a few items, mounted my horse, Soldier, and rode out with my new husband.

The other wives watched us away, Quiet One, dutifully standing in front of her lodge, but still unable to bring herself to look at me. These last several days in my own quarters have provided a much-needed respite—for all of us I am certain. I can hardly fault the woman for her resentment of me and can only imagine what my own reaction would be were I in her position. I have learned that the young second wife, my friend Feather on Head, is the older's sister, which is common among the Cheyennes and designed to help alleviate such stress between wives. At the same time not all of the Cheyennes are polygamous . . . theirs is a complicated culture, and we have much to learn about one another.

As we rode through the camp, my friend Martha came out of her tent, looking every bit the blushing bride. We had not seen each other since our wedding night, but from the glow on her face, I had a suspicion that hers had not been a disappointment. "Oh, May," she said now, running alongside my horse to keep up, "we must speak. I was going to come see you today. Where are you off to?"

"I have no idea, Martha," I said. "As you can see I am simply being a dutiful wife, following my husband. If I'm not mistaken, we're off on our honeymoon!"

"A honeymoon? When will you be back?" Martha asked nervously. "What will I do without you?"

"I don't know, dear," I said, "but you'll manage. You've done quite well without me in the past few days, haven't you? I'm sure we won't be away long."

"May, I must ask you," Martha said, the color rising in her cheeks. "How was your . . . your . . ."

I laughed. "My wedding night?"

"Yes! How was it? Was it strange? Was it wonderful?"

"It was like a dream," I answered. "I'm not sure that it really happened."

"Yes!" Martha said. "That's exactly how mine was—like a dream. Were we drugged, May? I feel certain that I was drugged. Was I only dreaming, or did it really happen?"

"How did you feel the next morning?" I asked.

"Exhausted," Martha said, "I was exhausted, but content . . . and I was . . . I was . . ." Now she blushed even more deeply as she hurried to keep up.

"Sore?" I finished for her. "Was there blood, Martha?"

"Yes," she said. "You know that I was a virgin."

"I would suggest then the possibility that it was more than a dream," I said.

"Do you think it is somehow possible, May, that it was at once a dream but also actually happened?" Martha asked.

"Yes," I said. "Yes, I think that's a fine way of putting it. Like this whole adventure, a dream that's actually happening."

Now we were at the edge of the village, and Martha, not wishing to go on further, stopped and said: "One last thing, May, did you see his face, did you . . . did you . . . were you facing your husband at the moment?"

I laughed. "No, I was like the female swallows we have been watching this spring, Martha, with my tail raised in the air."

"Yes," Martha cried, waving as we rode away from her, "yes, that's it exactly! Good-bye then, May, dear friend. Don't be away long; we need you right here."

"You'll be fine, Martha," I called back to her. "You'll be just fine. I'm sure we won't be gone long. Such an adventure, isn't it!"

Martha waved. "An adventure!" she called back.

And then we were away, swallowed by the immensity of prairie. I was not in the least bit apprehensive at leaving the others behind, and felt secure and perfectly safe in the company of my husband. It was a magnificent summer morning, the prairie in full bloom. Wildflowers of all varieties carpeted the rolling plains, the grass was brilliantly green and waved ever so slightly in a soft breeze, the meadowlarks sang, and in the willows and cottonwoods along the river birds of all kinds took up their morning songs.

As the village faded behind us, I turned on a rise to look back and saw the smoke from the morning fires curling above the tipis, the People going hither and yon about their morning business, the dogs barking, the boys herding the horses out into the meadows, the faint sounds of laughter and life, and suddenly I felt the keenest sense of place—of home—the very first time I have thought of it as such. It was as though I had to leave and look back in order to discover this perspective, in the way that one looks away and then back again at a painting to reaffirm its beauty. And when I did so, and for the first time, I was enveloped by a great sense of peace and contentment. I thought to myself "How extraordinarily fortunate I am."

Yes, for all its savage strangeness and hardships, our new world seemed inexpressibly sweet on this morning; I marveled at how cunningly and perfectly these native people had folded themselves into the earth, into the countryside; they seem as much a part of this prairie landscape as the spring grass. One can't help but feel that they belong here as an integral part of the painting . . .

For the first quarter of an hour, Little Wolf rode well ahead of me, leading the pair of packhorses. He did not speak, nor even turn to check my progress. Finally I nudged my horse forward with my heels and broke into a canter (never have I more fully appreciated the riding lessons that Mother made us take as children! for I am quite comfortable on horseback—a skill that will obviously be of no small usefulness here). I pulled up abreast of the Chief, who looked surprised, and possibly mildly annoyed—as if I were violating yet another point of heathen etiquette.

"I am a New American woman," I said to him, settling my mount into the same gait as his, "and I have no intention of riding twenty paces behind you the whole day long." I know that Little Wolf could not understand my words but I gestured between our horses, to suggest their position side by side and then I gestured between the two of us, and I smiled. And the Chief seemed to consider this, and then he nodded as if he understood and smiled back at me. Yes, we had made a genuine communication! I was very pleased.

I believe now that the Chief has orchestrated this sojourn as a way for us to become acquainted, and, possibly also as a way for him to show me a bit of his countryside. We made camp early yesterday afternoon in a copse of cottonwoods along a creek—the name of which I do not know. The Chief has brought a small hide covering that we strung as shelter between willow branches in case of rain, though the weather has remained clear and mild. Beneath this we made beds of grass, covered by buffalo robes. After we set our camp, I gathered wood in the creek bottom for the fire, happy to be afoot again after a day on horseback.

Little Wolf carried a small rawhide bag containing steel, flint, and a piece of buffalo dung from which he would break a piece and pulverize it to serve as kindling. It seemed terribly ingenious to me how quickly he could spark a fire, to which he would add grass and twigs and soon we had a true blaze over which to cook and take the night chill off.

For our dinner we roasted pintailed grouse that the Chief had killed with his bow earlier in the day, right from the back of his horse, one after the next, when the covey flushed in front of us. Even Father would have been impressed with his marksmanship; I can hardly wait to describe it to Helen Flight; I swear a man (or woman) with a firearm could not have been quicker or truer.

The birds were quite delicious: I stuffed them with tender wild onions and herbs that I had gathered during our day's prairie idyll. Thanks to the education provided by our Indian "mothers" I have become rather adept at identifying some of the edible plants.

This is the first time that we have passed truly alone together, and I think we were both a bit shy at first. However, I have finally devised a means of overcoming the nearly constant frustration of trying to make myself understood, by simply giving up to it. I now babble away in English to Little Wolf, saying whatever nonsense springs to mind—for as he cannot understand me what difference does it make? I must have told him my entire life story last night—I told him about Harry and our children and life in the institution; I told him about Father and Mother, and sister Hortense. I told him about Captain Bourke. I told him everything and I felt the strangest sense of liberation in the unburdening. Little Wolf listened patiently, or at least he appeared to be listening, even if he could not understand, he watched me as if he did, and nodded now and then, and finally even replied, speaking softly to me in his own language, although of course, I have no idea what he said. Thus we sat around our fire half the night, conversing, I, in English, and he in his native tongue, far more sparingly for he is hardly what one would call a loquacious man; I am certain that he, too, told me important things about his life, for sometimes he spoke quite animatedly. I listened carefully, trying to fathom a few words, to make some meaning of what he said, but it seemed that I understood him better when I simply let his words wash over me and did not try to decipher them. In this way, we forged a peculiar closeness: I believe that we both spoke what was in our hearts, and perhaps our hearts, if not our minds, understood one another.

This morning the Chief has gone out early to hunt, while I take this opportunity to record these events in my journal. It is a fine morning and the birds sing merrily in the cottonwoods. I am very comfortable wrapped in my buffalo robe and when the sun is a bit higher in the sky and the air warms, I shall go down to the banks of the creek and have my bath . . .

But dear God, I have had a terrifying encounter, my hand still trembles so to recall it that I can barely hold my pencil. Shortly after I made the preceding entry I went down to the creek. I was delighted to discover there a pool formed by a hot springs. Steam rose from it, and when I felt the water with my toe, it was wonderfully warm. My husband must have chosen this camping site for its proximity to the hot springs.

I removed my clothes as I always do now when bathing—having largely abandoned any pretense of modesty, nakedness being a natural state among the savages. I stepped into the pool, luxuriating in the warmth and silkiness of the water which had a slightly sulfurous odor and was of a perfect temperature. I floated on my back in a state of the purest relaxation.

Suddenly I had the disconcerting sense that I was not alone, that I was being watched. I lay motionless in the water, my heart beginning to pound with an inchoate but no less genuine fear. Finally I sat up, covering my breasts and looked quickly about me. Then I saw him—squatting as still as an animal on the bank was a man, if such he can be called—one of the most fearsome-looking creatures upon whom I have ever laid eyes. He had long matted hair that hung down almost to the ground where he sat, and thick swarthy features that seemed barely human, like those of a wild boar.

The creature was naked but for a breechclout. His skin was blackened with dirt and he was . . . he was in a state of arousal that was not concealed by this garment. When he saw that I had seen him he smiled at me, exposing blackened teeth like the fangs of the Devil's own dog. Then he grasped himself and nodded at me with a disgusting familiarity. I sank back into the water to cover myself as the man stood, still holding himself thus, his intention quite clear. I was shocked to hear him speak to me not in a savage tongue, but in French. *"Salope,"* he said in a low voice, *"je vais t'enculer a sec!"* I will not . . . cannot translate this for the sheer depravity of it.

Now the wretch started into the water toward me, still grasping his manhood like a terrible weapon of violence. My heart rose in my throat, I could not move, my body frozen with fear. "Please, no," I whispered. "Please don't hurt me." Never in my life have I felt more alone, or more terrified. I began to paddle frantically backwards from the man until I came up against the far bank of the pool. I pressed myself against a large boulder there, with no further to go as the creature approached me. Now I could smell him, even above the mineral odor of the water, could smell his filth, his stench of evil . . . He spoke again to me, words so unspeakably vulgar that I felt the bile rise in my throat, and I was certain that I was going to be sick. Just as the wretch reached out toward me I heard the voice of my husband. Yes, thank God! I looked up to see Little Wolf standing on the bank holding his quirt coiled in one hand. He spoke in a calm, even voice, and although I do not know what he said, I sensed from his tone that he knew this man. He addressed the wretch firmly but without a trace of rancor in his voice.

The man replied in Cheyenne, seemed to speak deferentially, almost obsequiously to the Chief, and began to back out of the pool. But then he stopped, as if he had just remembered something, and he turned back to me and smiled his rotten-toothed wolfish grin. This time he whispered in a guttural but surprisingly fluent English, "I am Jules Seminole," he said, and his voice chilled me to the bone. "We will see each other again. And I will do to you those things I promised." Then he waded from the pool without looking back.

Later I attempted to question Little Wolf about the identity of this horrible creature. *"Sas-sis-e-tas,"* he said, or so the word by which the Cheyennes refer to themselves as a people sounded to me. And then he made slashing motions with his right index finger across his left which is the sign they use to identify themselves. "Cheyenne?" I asked in English. "How could he be?" Perhaps Little Wolf understood the question in my voice, for he placed his hand in the center of his breast and made a motion across his left side and said again the word *"Sas-sis-e-tas,"* and then he drew his hand across his breast to his right and said, *"ve'ho'e,"* the Cheyenne word for white man. "He's a half-breed, then," I said.

"O'xeve'ho'e," the Chief answered.

26 May 1875

We have stayed in the same campsite for the past several days. After my terrifying encounter with the half-breed Jules Seminole, I had fervently hoped that we would move to another place, or even return to the camp, but we have not. Although my fear has gradually begun to subside, I have taken the man's threat to heart and I do not let my husband out of my sight. Now when he goes to hunt, I accompany him. If he goes to the creek, I follow him there. I have never been of a particularly timid nature, but for the moment, at least, I feel truly safe only in Little Wolf's company. He does not seem to mind my constant presence and, indeed, the more time we spend together, the more genuinely fond we grow of one another. He is a gentle, solicitous man, and very patient with me.

Little Wolf's hunting expeditions have been most successful. We have killed and dressed, and eaten of, pronghorn, elk, deer, and a variety of small game, including grouse, ducks, and rabbit—the savage's life appears to be one of feast or famine, and when food is bountiful they eat almost constantly. I have been cooking over the fire. We have with us in one of the parfleches a few modern utensils obtained from the white man's trading post and with these I attempt to prepare something more interesting than the standard fare of boiled meat. Besides wild onions and dandelion greens in the meadows, I have found morel mushrooms among the trees in the river bottom. These I recognize from Illinois, where they grew in some profusion in the spring and where I used to gather them with Mother and Hortense.

The rest of the meat has been hung in the cottonwoods well away from our camp, presumably lest bears or other wild creatures should be attracted to it. Besides my cooking duties I have been kept busy learning the finer points of skinning, dressing, and butchering an animal. This, too, is considered to be women's work by the savages, and the Chief has instructed me in the various procedures until I have become, if not precisely expert, at least decently proficient. Fortunately, because Father was himself a hunter, I grew up around wild game and am not in the least bit squeamish about blood and offal. There are those among our group, including my poor friend Martha, who will have some real difficulty adapting to this chore.

The savage life, it strikes me, and particularly a woman's life among them, is one of nearly constant physical effort. There is little time for leisure. Nor has our excursion of the past few days been what most white women might consider an ideal honeymoon! Still it has been an instructive and useful experience.

Never have I been so grateful for my bath at the end of the day's labors—especially in this hot spring. Not only does it give me the opportunity to wash myself of the blood of wild creatures in which I am quite literally "up to the elbows," but it also allows me to scrub the damnable greasepaint from my skin. I and many of our other fair-skinned women have been forced to wear this concoction as protection against the blistering prairie sun. Indeed, many of the savages themselves use the paint for the same reason, and thus I have finally learned the origins of the term "redskin." The paint is made from mixing a brownish red clay, common throughout this country, with fat or tallow. It stinks terribly, and makes one feel perfectly filthy.

Other times the greasepaint is made from a white clay material, which gives the wearer a kind of ghostly appearance. No one looks more ferocious than our Phemie in the white paint which she favors—although her already dark-pigmented skin requires considerably less than ours in the way of protection from the unremitting sun. My own Scottish ancestry and creamy complexion are a distinct disadvantage in this shadeless wilderness of prairie and sky—as it is for Helen Flight and the Kelly girls and nearly all the rest of us of "old world" ancestry. Thank God for the greasepaint, and for our little copse of trees in this campsite.

Per custom Little Wolf takes his bath in the morning when I, too, join him. In the afternoon, he sits on the bank, watching me as I wash again, guarding me I think from any further advances of the wretch Jules Seminole, who still lurks in my nightmares.

The warm water is a perfect temperature, like bathwater heated on the stove at home, and feels wonderful. This afternoon I swam out to the middle of the pool to float there for a few minutes as is my habit. I turned and beckoned to Little Wolf as I often do, making the sign for swim in the hopes of coaxing him into the water, trying to elicit from him some sense of play. I'm afraid that my husband is, if not exactly a dour fellow, a generally serious one, hardly given to displays of merriment. Perhaps this is only a function of his age and position. I had brought with me on our trip Lieutenant Clark's pamphlet on the Indian sign language, which, while hardly complete, has been enormously valuable to us. We practice the gesture language in the evenings by the fire and the Chief has been quite patient with my efforts—trying to teach me a few words of Cheyenne in the bargain. It is slow going, and I still enjoy babbling away in English as a means of release from the frustration of being unable to communicate properly. Yes, well, it occurs to me that anyone who listens so attentively to my incessant ramblings must be a patient man, indeed!

Of course, because he cannot read, it is impossible for Little Wolf to comprehend the nature of a book, but he marvels at the thing, touches it and turns it over in his hands as if it has magical properties—which in a sense I suppose it does. We are able to engage in rudimentary communications (although to be sure we are hardly translating the Bard into sign language as Captain Bourke and I so amused ourselves in attempting!).

Now finally, after much cajoling on my part, Little Wolf slipped into the water himself. He is a physically graceful man. However, the Indians practice a decidedly rudimentary kind of dog paddle, and so I decided, then and there, to teach him a few swim strokes. First I demonstrated the overhand stroke, which, being an athletically inclined fellow, he picked up quickly. Then I showed him the breast stroke. It was great fun and soon we were laughing like . . . well, very much like a pair of honeymooners! I felt that I had "broken the ice."

Impulsively, I put my arms around the Chief's neck, and wrapped my legs around his waist—he looked terribly surprised, even mildly panicked; I do not know if he feared that I was trying to pull him under, or if he only considered it unseemly of a woman to be so forward, for he tried to pull away from me.

"Don't worry," I said in English, grasping him closer, "I am just playing." But truly although I had indeed begun this wrestling entirely in a spirit of play, I found that I liked the touch of him, experienced an unmistakable stirring at the feel of his taut warm skin. Now I felt with my hands the small hard muscles of his shoulders and arms and with my feet explored the firmness of his legs. I found myself pressing more urgently against him. We have, I should mention, had no physical contact whatsoever since our dreamlike wedding night.

"Oh, dear," I whispered now, "Oh my, I had not intended . . ." The Chief seemed to respond to my embrace; I could feel the tension and reluctance drain from his body. For a moment we floated together thus in the warm, buoyant waters of the spring, my legs wrapped lightly around his waist. Then I began to kiss him very softly about his neck and face and on his lips—the savages are not well versed in the art of kissing, and it was rather like kissing a child, but soon he responded in kind. "Isn't that fine?" I whispered. "Yes, isn't that nice, isn't that just lovely?"

This is an indelicate matter . . . I know no other way to address it but directly. As John Bourke suggested the Cheyennes have not encouraged contact with the whites or with the missionaries until now, and although they have traded with them and know something of their ways, this has not included, at least in Little Wolf's case, any knowledge of carnal matters. What the savages have learned on the subject of sexual intercourse between a man and woman they have learned from watching Nature, as John Bourke put it, from watching animals couple . . . and thus they make love . . . like animals . . .

While I am hardly the authority on the subject that Narcissa White would make me out, I am not ashamed to admit that Harry Ames and I enjoyed an active erotic life, or that I am a woman of powerful passions. Men boast of such feelings—women are sent to lunatic asylums for them. Counting my single indiscretion with the Captain and my own "wedding night," I have now had three lovers in my short life. Does this make me a sinner? Perhaps . . . I do not feel like one . . . A harlot? I don't believe so. Am I insane? Hardly.

Now we floated, entwined in the water, my husband and I, my arms wound round his neck, my legs about his waist, floated. Our bodies slid easily against each other, comfortable and familiar, the sulfurous water was warm and oily on our skins. Have we not been sent to instruct the savages in our way of life? Should this not include matters of the flesh? Yes, if the Chief can teach me the finer points of fleshing a hide, so perhaps I can reciprocate by teaching him a few secrets of the human flesh—a fair exchange it seems to me between our worlds.

I slid my hand down Little Wolf's back to his buttocks which was smooth and muscled, hard as river rock, and around to stroke him, sleek as a stallion, slippery as a snake in the oily mineral waters. "Put your hands on me," I whispered, although of course, he could not understand me, and I took his hand and placed it between our bodies and ran it over my belly to my breasts. He has very fine hands, strong but at the same time almost feminine, with a gentle touch unlike that of any I have ever known. I kissed him again and this time he kissed me back and I took him again in my hand, guiding him, settling my hips upon him, legs around his waist, the warmth of the springs entering me, filling me inside with heat and light . . .

28 May 1875

This morning, as I make these hasty scribbles, we prepare to depart—I assume to rejoin the village, for Little Wolf is presently loading our packhorses with all of the meat and hides that we have gathered and prepared in our few days here together. With the exception of my terrifying encounter with the one named Jules Seminole, of whom, thank God, we have seen no further sign, it has been a fine excursion, which I am sorry to see come to an end. We have made, I believe, some valuable progress, Little Wolf and I, in beginning to bridge the gap between our cultures—I do not mean that only as a sly euphemism . . . although there is that, too. I am greatly encouraged and believe now more than ever that there is real hope for the success of our undertaking. Perhaps President Grant's people are right, and the sheer power of American womanhood can knit these worlds together after all. Not only have my husband and I learned to converse on a rudimentary level but we have learned a new respect and a genuine affection for one another. The Chief will be my truest window to the lives of the savages, for within him resides all the qualities so prized by these simple people—courage, dignity, grace, selflessness—

and something else of which I have only seen a glimpse, but that I think would be called fierceness. Little Wolf has the character of a natural leader in any culture, and I'm certain that even John Bourke would have a grudging respect for him—and he for Bourke. For truly it strikes me that they have much in common. Captain and Chief . . . heathen and Catholic. Soldier and warrior . . . tied together now by a woman's love.

And yet, in spite of my best intentions I cannot pretend to have the same feelings for Little Wolf that I had for John Bourke, which was a passion such as I have never before known, a love of both intellect and flesh—body, mind, and soul . . . God I feel that I have lived three lives already, with three loves—my first, Harry Ames, a physical love like a spark, to be extinguished by the darkness of my asylum cell; only to be reignited by the implausible light of a new love like a shooting star. Yes, for if Harry Ames was the bright, erratic spark of my womanhood, then John Bourke was my shooting star, burning brilliantly and intensely. And this man Little Wolf, my lodge fire, offering warmth and security . . . he is my husband, I shall be a good and a faithful wife to him. I shall bear his children.

So Little Wolf and I rode back to the main camp on the Powder River, this morning, our last. I have tried to keep my bearings with the help of a compass and an Army map which Captain Bourke presented to me before our departure—I do not know how accurate the map is and I am far from being skilled as a cartographer, but I know at least the major water courses. The Chief and I rode side by side now—as equals, as it should be—and I chattered as we went, remarking on this and that, pointing to the birds and animals and plants, babbling away as is my wont.

Sometimes the Chief answered me, giving me the names for these things, and sometimes, I suspect, just talking himself, as has become our manner together. I think that I am finally beginning to absorb a bit of the language, though I am yet shy about attempting to speak it.

Now as we came in off the vast silent prairie, the village suddenly seemed by comparison to our last few days of solitude to be a veritable city, bustling with human energy and activity. Indeed, a whole new village had sprung up the opposite bank of the river from ours during our absence—nearly one hundred new lodges had been erected since we left.

The camp dogs came out to bark at us as we approached, and then to sniff and nip harmlessly at our heels as we rode through camp. Packs of small children followed us excitedly; some of the little imps I recognized and was happy to see again. How I love the children! How I look forward to having another of my own!

Several of our ladies greeted me by their lodges as we rode in. I was amused to see that in only the few days of my absence it was becoming more and more difficult to tell some of "our" brides from the natives. Since the wedding ceremony many others have adopted savage garb, and indeed some of the Cheyenne women are now wearing "civilized" attire given them by our women.

Gretchen, attired in a buckskin dress, was carrying a pail of water to her lodge, and she stopped to greet me and to admire our game-laden packhorses. "*Yah,* you got a *goot* man there, May!" she said. "I can hardly get *dat* lazy bum of mine to leave *de* tent," but she spoke with some genuine affection in her voice. "All *de* big *galloop* wants to do is 'wrestle' with me on *de* buffalo robes. *Yah,* you know what I mean, May? *Dat* damn savage of mine can hardly get enough of it! I come see you later, *yah?* I wish to speak to you."

Now we rode past Reverend Hare and Dog Woman's lodge, just in time to witness the latter exit the tipi wearing one of our white women's dresses. He is really rather a sweet old fellow and I couldn't help letting a bark of astonished laughter escape at the sight of him. Hah! Dog Woman glared at me, tugging on his bodice with which he seemed to be having some difficulty. I covered my mouth. "*Je suis désolée,*" I apologized, for the hermaphroditic medicine man speaks a bit of French. "*Alors vous êtes très belle*! You look perfectly beautiful." This seemed to placate Dog Woman somewhat, and indeed, he/she looked rather proud of her new attire. "*Dites-moi, où est le grand lapin blanc?*" I asked.

"Reverend," I called out, "if you are inside there, you must help your roommate arrange her new dress."

"Is that you, Miss Dodd?" the Reverend's oracular voice boomed from inside the tent. "May I remind that you have missed Sunday services again this week. We've got half the camp coming now. We'll make Christians of the heathens yet!"

"Good for you, Reverend!" I answered. "But you'd best hurry before they make heathens of us. I've been thinking myself of converting to the religion of the Great Medicine. It's beginning to make great good sense to me."

Now the Reverend thrust his bald head, pink as a newborn baby, through the opening of his lodge and blinked in the sunlight. "You are a Godless young woman, Miss Dodd," he scolded me. Then he spoke in Cheyenne to Dog Woman, who answered him.

"Reverend, please ask Dog Woman to tell you the new Cheyenne name the Chief and I have given you," I called mischievously as we rode away. "It came about, as these things do, quite naturally on our trip when I was trying to explain to my husband in the sign language the literal meaning of your Christian name."

The Reverend spoke again to Dog Woman, who again replied. In this way, Reverend Hare first learned his new Cheyenne name, which I predict will spread like a prairie fire through the village.

"You're a Godless young woman, May Dodd!" called *Ma'vohkoohe ohvo'omaestse*—the Big White Rabbit—as we rode on through camp. "A Godless young woman! I shall pray for your salvation! And for that of your artist friend Helen Flight, as well. I urge you go to see her immediately, for she has become in your absence Satan's disciple and beguiles the savages with her wicked arts of conjuring, witchcraft, and thaumaturgy!" I began to wonder if perhaps the Reverend hadn't been getting too much sun on his bald pate.

How disappointed I was to discover that my wedding lodge had been dismantled during our absence, and my possessions moved back into the "family" tipi. Thus the honeymoon really is over. Having already grown accustomed to the privacy of my own lodge, I can hardly abide living in such proximity to all the others again.

As I had expected, Martha was the first to come visit me at the lodge, arriving just after I had made this unhappy discovery. She was full of excitement, inquiries, and news.

"Thank God you have returned safely!" she said, breathlessly. Our Horse Boy appeared at that moment, true to his name, to lead my horse away. He's a dear little thing, brown and lithe as an elf. I patted him on the head, and he grinned at me lovingly. "I have so much to tell you, May, but first I must hear about your honeymoon. How was it? Where did you go? Was it terribly romantic?"

"Let's see . . ." I mused, ". . . we traveled by first-class coach into the city where we stayed in the bridal suite of the finest hotel . . . took all of our meals by room service, made love on a feather bed . . ."

"Oh, stop teasing me, May!" Martha said, giggling. "Where did you go, really?"

"We simply roamed the countryside, Martha," I answered. "We camped for several days in a cottonwood copse along a creek, where we bathed in a pool formed by a hot springs . . . in which we made passionate love—"

"Truly?" Martha interrupted. "Is that true? I never know when you are only teasing me, May."

"Tell me news of the camp, dear," I asked. "To whom do the lodges on the other side of the river belong?"

"To the Southern Cheyennes," Martha said, "our 'relatives' who have come visiting from Oklahoma Territory."

"Yes, that would explain the appearance of the wretch Jules Seminole," I said. And I told Martha of my encounter.

"The southerners have got our men all puffed up and strutting about like roosters," Martha said. "Soon they're off to make war against their enemies the Crows. They've enlisted Helen Flight to paint birds on their bodies and on their horses in preparation. She's become very 'big medicine,' quite the *Artiste*-in-residence."

"Ah, so that's what the Reverend was referring to," I said.

We determined to go straightaway to Helen Flight's lodge, where we found the artist sitting outside on a stool in the sun painting the image of a kingfisher on the chest of a young man. The kingfisher was exquisitely rendered just in the act of diving into the water. Seated cross-legged on the ground next to Helen, watching her work, was an elderly fellow with long white braids and a dark, deeply furrowed complexion that resembled ancient, cracked saddle leather.

Helen beamed at our arrival, pausing in her work and removing her pipe from her mouth. "Welcome home, May!" she said, enthusiastically. "We've missed you. My goodness, how pleased I am that you've both come! Do sit down. You must keep me company as I work . . . I've been at it all day. I seem to have been 'discovered' by the savages! I can hardly keep up with the demand for my services.

"Ah, but do please excuse me for failing to make proper introductions," she said. "Have you ladies had the pleasure of meeting the esteemed medicine man, Dr. White Bull?"

"I'm afraid we haven't," I said. "Please don't get up, sir," I joked. The old fellow was much unamused, implacable, rather grumpy, in fact. Both he and the young man wore deathly serious expressions on their faces, and barely glanced at us.

Helen popped her short, beautifully engraved stone pipe back into her mouth and took up her brush again. She has fashioned for herself a very cunning palette made from a rawhide shield, upon which the stretched leather has dried as hard as wood. Here she mixes her colors from an assortment of powders and emulsions made from pounding different-colored stones, earth, grasses, berries, clays, and animal bones, according to ancient savage formulas about which Miss Flight could scarcely be more enthusiastic—for she has available to her nearly the entire color spectrum.

"A fine likeness, Helen," I said with true admiration. Indeed Audubon himself would have been envious, for Helen's kingfisher was a work of art, the colors iridescent, flashing from the boy's taut brown skin as if the bird itself were alive.

"Why thank you," Helen said, pipe clenched firmly between her teeth. "Last night young Walking Whirlwind here had a dream. In his dream he was struck by bullets in battle, but his flesh closed up around the bullet holes and he remained unscathed. The boy has never before been to war, and he is naturally anxious about his prospects. Therefore, this morning he went directly to the medicine man, Dr. White Bull, to tell him of his dream—the interpretation of dreams being a major function of the medicine man." At this point Martha and I both looked again at White Bull, who watched intently and rather critically, as Miss Flight applied her paint to the boy's chest.

"Dr. White Bull," Helen continued, "told the young man that his dream was intended to inform him that the kingfisher was his 'medicine' animal. For when that bird dives under the surface of the water, the water closes up behind it, just as in the boy's dream, the wounds in his flesh closed up after the bullets entered. Bloody ingenious concept, isn't it? Thus this painting, which I am presently executing upon the boy's chest, is intended to protect him from harm. Of course," Helen said, pausing from her work, and removing the pipe from her mouth, her eyebrows raised in ironic surprise, "I offer no guarantees of magic properties with my work!"

"I should certainly hope not!" I said. "Why it's pure superstition, Helen. And quite useless against real bullets."

"I expect so, May," Helen said. "But I am only an artist fulfilling a commission. Guarantees of magic properties are strictly the province of Dr. White Bull here."

At just this point, and as if on cue, the old medicine man started chanting in a low, rhythmic voice.

"There, you see!" Helen said, delighted. "As we speak my collaborator is imbuing my kingfisher with a full complement of special powers."

Hanging from Helen's tent were dozens of bird skins of every species imaginable, many of which she had collected herself in the course of our journey here and others of which have been brought to her by the savages as specimens for the likenesses which she is being "commissioned" to paint on their bodies, and on those of their war ponies. On the ground around her lodge were piles of gifts which the savages have bestowed upon her for her services—articles of finely embroidered clothing, animal hides, an assortment of "medicine" pipes, jewelry, braided horse bridles, and saddles.

"I do encourage you ladies to carry away any of my goods which might be of interest to you," Helen said now. "I hardly have room for them all. I now own a string of a half dozen horses which I have given to my husband, Mr. Hog. Suddenly I find myself a woman of means. I must say it strikes me as frightfully ironic that I've had to come to the middle of the wilderness to achieve economic success as an artist. Ah, and here comes my next commission," Helen said, as another young man rode up on a horse laden with hides.

"Another crane, I'll wager," Helen said, "a perennial favorite among the savages. Which is of particular interest in view of the fact that many other cultures throughout history—both Eastern and Western, primitive and civilized alike—have been known to ascribe special qualities to the noble crane. In the case of our savages, the bird is highly prized for its courage. For even when wounded and unable to fly, it stands its ground and fights heroically. So you see, by wearing these images upon their breasts the warriors believe that they assume these same characteristics."

"But doesn't it concern you, Helen," I asked, "that in spite of the good doctor's assumption of responsibility for magical properties, you may still be held accountable when your art fails them—as it inevitably must?"

"Ah, but Art never fails anyone, May," Helen said cheerfully. "Magic and 'medicine' may certainly fail, but never Art.

"Furthermore," she said, taking a long, thoughtful puff on her pipe, "is it possible that if a warrior believes in his 'medicine,' he can make it come true? A fascinating concept, is it not? And one that lies at the very core of pagan religion."

"And perhaps of our own," I pointed out, "for now you speak of faith, Helen."

"Quite!" said Helen, with customary good cheer. "That is to say, faith in the power of God, in the power of Art, in the power of medicine men and medicine animals—it's all one, finally, don't you agree, May?"

"Your paintings are magnificent, Helen," I said, "but if I had to wager, I'd still put my money on the power of bullets."

"Ah, ye of little faith!" said Helen, in a light tone.

"So the Reverend says of us both, Helen," I answered.

"Quite," she said. "The Episcopalian accuses me of encouraging the worship of false idols. I've explained to him that I'm only a poor artist trying to make my way in the world."

"By encouraging a finer appreciation of art among the heathens," I added.

"Just so, May!" Helen said. "Art being a cornerstone of civilization. And, in any case, what could be false about a kingfisher? There," she said to the boy, sitting back on her stool to inspect her efforts. She made the sign for finished. "All done. Be a good chap, and run along now. He'll do well in battle, that one," she added with satisfaction.

"Ah, the artist begins to believe her own notices!" I teased.

Helen smiled around her pipe and looked down at the old medicine man, White Bull, who appeared to be dozing in the sun. "Wake up, you old charlatan. Here's our next patient."

3 June 1875

With the presence of our visitors from the south the entire camp has been abuzz with activities for the past several days and has much the festive atmosphere of a large family reunion or a county fair.

I have passed my time calling at some of my friends' lodges and watching the various contests of skill that are everywhere being held between the different bands and warrior societies. These include tests of horsemanship, accuracy with bow and arrow, rifle and spear, running events, etc. Nearly everyone in the camp turns out either to spectate or participate.

As Bourke had warned, the savages are relentless gamblers and brisk wagering takes place at every opportunity. Prior to their arrival at our camp the southerners had been to the trading post, and they have brought with them many items of civilization—blankets, utensils, knives, beads, and trinkets—and with these they wager on games of chance and contests of all kinds.

Right in the thick of things I was not surprised to find those scamps the Kelly twins. I can't help but admire their spirit but truly they are a pair of scoundrels! *Hestahkha'e* the savages call them—Twin Woman as if they are one, for it is so difficult to tell them apart. (Martha tells me that a scandalous report is circulating about the camp that the two switched husbands on our wedding night.)

The girls seem to have set themselves up as something like professional bookmakers, and have themselves made a small fortune in trade goods, hides, and horses by organizing and betting upon various games. Yesterday, for instance they put our own Phemie up against several of the Southern Cheyenne men in a running race. Our statuesque Negress offered a great shock to all, Caucasians and savages alike, when she strode to the starting line wearing nothing more than a man's breechclout.

"Good God, Phemie," I said when I first saw her, "you're practically naked!" Truly she was something to behold, her long gleaming black legs muscled like a colt's, her breasts hard and small as a girl's.

Phemie laughed richly. "Hello, May!" she said, greeting me warmly, for I had not seen her since my return. "Yes, when I was a little girl I always ran footraces naked against the other children. I was the fastest child on the plantation. My mother told me this was how our people raced and fought in Africa. Why carry the extra weight of clothing to slow you down?"

"Right *ya* are, too, Phemie," said Meggie Kelly. "They say that the Irish lads of olden days always did battle naked themselves for that very same reason."

"*Aye,* and for the fact that it struck terror into the hearts of their enemies!" added Susie. "And which of you brave laddies'll run against this poor little *goorl* then?"

Several warriors had stepped up to the line by then. Among the Southern Cheyennes were a number who spoke passable English, this branch of the family having had more contact with the whites than ours. With their assistance as translators the Kellys haggled with the other bettors over the odds—a new concept to the savages.

"*Aye,* but she's only a poor *goorl,* you see," Meggie explained through the translator. "It hardly seems fair does it now that she should compete with equal odds against the big strong men? On account of which disadvantage all who bet on Phemie need only put up half as much as those who bet on one of the lads. And those are excellent odds we're givin' *ya,* too, if I may say so."

"I'll take a piece *a* that action *mahself, you rascals,*" said Daisy Lovelace. "*Ah* don't give a damn if she's a *guuurl* or not. *Mah* Daddy always did say that nobody can outrun a *niggah.* Daddy said they got those long legs from runnin' through the jungle *bein' puursued* by lions and other *waahld* creatures. Yessir, *Ah'm* taking all wagers on my dear friend Euphemia *Washin'ton.*"

Then the signal was given, and they were off, Phemie's stride worth two of those of any of the savages. She ran as swiftly and gracefully as a pronghorn, and handily won the race, which led to another challenge and another round of furious wagering. Phemie won a second time, all the other runners now utterly shamed in front of their friends and family, and roundly ridiculed by all.

Of interest to note is the fact that the Cheyenne women were as proud of Phemie's victory as we, and made their funny little trilling noise when she ran across the line ahead of the others. Indeed, where certain obvious tensions and jealousies have existed between us since our arrival here, Phemie's success seemed to bring us all closer together for a moment in a new community of women. This can only be a good thing.

1 June 1875

The festivities to mark the southerners' arrival and the beginning of the summer hunts continue . . . Yesterday afternoon an astonishing thing occurred which makes me—a "nonbeliever" if ever there was one—reassess the discussion we had with Helen Flight on the notion of magic.

The Kellys were taking bets on shooting contests with bow and arrow and rifle when a little girl entered the circle where the competition was being organized. The child led an old man by the hand. The old man had milky eyes that appeared to be entirely blind; he was stooped and wizened with age, his thin hair worn in wispy white braids. The girl whispered shyly to one of the southern Cheyennes who in turn translated to Meggie Kelly.

"Oh, sweet Jesus!" said Meggie to her sister. "The dear little thing says her granddad wants to challenge Black Coyote to a shooting contest." Black Coyote is a brash young warrior married to Phemie's new friend Buffalo Calf Road Woman, who is herself a Cheyenne warrior woman. He was widely considered to be the best shot in the camp and had so far handily beaten all comers.

"*Oih* never *hooord* such a thing, Meggie," said Susie with a laugh. "And who'll bet on the old poor fellow? Why look at him—he's blind as a bat."

"The child says her granddad's got big medicine, Susie," Meggie said. "Isn't that grand? Says the family'll wager two horses on the old fool."

Susan came closer, and took the girl's chin in her hand. "Oh, child, are *ya* quite sure of what you're askin' us?" she said. "Your old granddad cannot even see the target."

"You're not goin' soft on me are *ye*, Susie Kelly?" said her sister. "If the child's family wishes to wager, I'll not stand in their way. And I'll put some of my own winnings on Black Coyote. Haven't we got a regular string of horses now among our winnings?"

"Aye, that *mooch* we do, Meggie," said Susan. "But this is takin' candy from a baby, is it not? I hate to steal from a little girl who believes in her dear old granddad."

"Well, just to make *ye* feel better about it, Susie," Meggie said, "we'll give 'em long odds. How about we put six horses up for their two? Would that salve your precious conscience, then?"

Now a round target was barked off a cottonwood tree, a black circle drawn with charcoal in the center and the distance paced off. Black Coyote, who is a cocksure young fellow, went first. He was shooting a brand-new cartridge rifle that he had won off a southern Cheyenne in an earlier contest. He aimed casually and fired with quick confidence, his bullet lodging just inside the circle. The spectators all *"houed"* approvingly.

Now the old man stepped up to the line. He held his hand closed in a fist and he opened it to reveal one of our seamstress, Jeanette Parker's, sewing needles. Now there was much *houing* of an astonished nature.

"What's the old fool doin', Meggie?" asked Susie. "Where's his damn rifle?"

The old man held his open hand up to his mouth, pointed it toward the target, puckered his lips, and blew a pitiful wheezing breath of air—hardly enough breath to rustle a leaf. But the needle was suddenly gone from his palm and the little girl pointed at the target. All went to examine it closely and there was the needle sticking in the exact center of the circle—a dead bull's-eye!

"T'isn't possible, Meggie," said Susan. "How did the old faker *pool* it off?" Indeed, none of us had ever seen anything like it!

" 'Tis a damn trick they're playin' on us, Susie," said Margaret. "That *moooch* is *shoore*. Got to be rigged somehow."

Now the twins sent a boy to collect their horses to pay off the wager, and while he was gone, they conferred in close confidence. Being no one's fools, they issued a challenge for another contest between Black Coyote and the old man, whose name the translator gave as Stares at Sun. This time they marked a different target on another tree even further away, and all inspected it for any evidence of advance tampering. Many of the savages, who are nothing if not superstitious creatures, had been won over by the old man's magic and this time the wagering was considerably brisker. The twins themselves doubled their bets, with even odds now, and took a number of side bets. They looked to make a killing, and just to further ensure that the old man couldn't play the same trick a second time, right before the contest began they added the stipulation that Stares at Sun must this time use something other than a sewing needle. Clever girls, those Kellys.

Again Black Coyote had the first shot and this time he aimed more carefully before he fired, and his bullet hit the target less than an inch away from the exact center of the circle.

The old man bent down and whispered something to his granddaughter. The child plucked a porcupine quill—which the savages use as ornamentation—off her sweet little dress, and put it very carefully in the old man's open palm. The twins watched closely and suspiciously for any possible sleight of hand.

Again the old man raised his palm to his mouth and, directed by his granddaughter, held it toward the target. He pursed his lips and blew weakly, making a little airless sound like *"pffftt."* Again the little girl pointed at the target, and all went to inspect it, the Kelly girls in the lead so that no further shenanigans could be perpetrated upon them. Incredibly, the porcupine quill was embedded in the precise center of the circle.

"Blooody Hell, Susie!" said Meggie. "The old charlatan has tricked us again! We've been swindled!"

I could only think of Helen Flight's words and wonder if the child's faith in her old grandfather had somehow made his magic work . . .

In any case, we all had a good laugh at the expense of the Kelly twins, and no one minded that they had lost a wager for a change!

4 June 1875

A disturbing encounter today . . . The Kellys have found a veritable gold mine in Gretchen Fathauer, who has been challenging all comers to arm wrestling contests. The girl is strong as a horse and no man had beaten her yet!

This morning Martha and I were standing on the edge of the circle watching as Gretchen handily defeated yet another poor fellow. It was then that I heard a chillingly familiar voice close behind me, *"Je t'ai dit, salope,"* whispered Jules Seminole in my ear with hot stinking breath. *"Je vais t'enculer a sec!"* The wretch so startled me, his filth so filled me with loathing, that I turned on him furiously. "I am not alone here now," I said, "and if you ever touch me, my husband Little Wolf will kill you."

"Good Lord, May," said Martha, frightened as much by my reaction to him as she was by the man himself. "Who is this?"

Seminole laughed, displaying his rotten black teeth. He was dressed in a filthy U.S. Army shirt and a cavalry hat which he removed now to reveal matted hair that spilled in greasy curls down his back and over his chest. "Jules Seminole, *madame,"* he said bowing to Martha. *"Enchantée!"*

"Go find my husband, Martha," I said. "Right now." And to Seminole, I said, "If I tell Little Wolf what filth you speak to me, he will kill you."

"Non, non, ma chère," he said, shaking his head in mock sadness. "You do not understand. A Cheyenne is forbidden to kill a member of his own tribe. It is the greatest sin of which a man is capable. Even if he wished to do so, Little Wolf could never kill me, for my mother was Cheyenne, and I am married to the Chief's own niece. He could not kill me no matter what I choose to do with you. It is the law of the People."

"Then he will certainly take his quirt to you," I said, flushing angrily. "Keep away from me. I will tell him what filth you speak."

"You have much to learn about your new people, my sweet *salope,*" Seminole said. "A more fearless warrior than your husband does not live among the People, but Little Wolf is the Sweet Medicine Chief. He must always put the interests of the People ahead of his own personal affairs. He is forbidden by tribal law from raising a hand against me, because to do so would be an act of selfishness. Why do you think he did not strike me with his quirt at the hot-water hole? Do you think he did not know my intentions toward you? Do you think he did not see my *vetoo-tse*—that one day soon will split you open like an axe splits the crotch of a sapling tree?"

Now Seminole called out to the Kelly girls. "*Oui,* I Jules Seminole will wrestle the German cow! And I'll wager a barrel of whiskey on it."

"Whiskey, you say?" said Meggie Kelly. "And what would you have us put up in return, fine sir?"

"I'll take the cow back to my lodge with me when I beat her," he said. Then Seminole spoke in rapid Cheyenne to Gretchen's husband, who watched on the sidelines and who is himself a rather buffoonish fellow, known by the name *Vonestseahe*—No Brains. The half-breed pulled out a small bottle from his shirt pocket, uncorked it, and handed it to No Brains, who took a long swallow and made a grimace. But he smiled and nodded and spoke again to Seminole.

"*Les jeux sont fait, mesdames,*" Seminole said. "*Vonestseahe* bets Jules Seminole his white wife against a keg of whiskey in an arm wrestling contest."

"You can't do that," I said. "You don't have to do this, Gretchen. He can't bet his wife. Susie, Meggie, don't let this happen. One of you run now and get the Reverend."

"What kind of *hustband* are you, anyhow?" Gretchen demanded, approaching No Brains with her hands on her broad hips. The man already appeared to be a little drunk from the sip of whiskey. "You bet your wife in a *gottdamnt* arm wrestle contest? What kind of man does such a *ting* as *dat?*" Now Gretchen took hold of her husband's nose between the knuckles of her forefinger and middle finger and twisted until tears ran down the man's face and he fell to his knees in agony. Everyone began to laugh.

"*Yah,* OK," Gretchen said, releasing his nose, "*dat* all you *tink* of me, is it, mister? OK, *den* I do it. Come on Frenchy." She pushed up the sleeve of her dress. "Come on, *den,* I take you on."

"Don't do it, Gretchen," I begged. "I know this one. He's evil. He'll hurt you."

"He *haf* to beat me first, May," Gretchen said. "Don't you worry. You seen me lose yet? When I was a girl my *brudders wuld haf* to come get *der* sister to pull *de gottdamnt* oxens out a *de* mud on *de* farm, because I *yam de* strongest one in *de famly*. I beat *dem* all at *de* arm wrestling. I never lose. Don't worry. Come on *den*, Frenchy. We get down here on *de* ground. I show you how *ve Sviss* do it. Susie and Meggie *vill* be judges, *yah?* OK? I beat you, you give me keg of whiskey. You beat me, I go lie on *de* buffalo robes *wid* you." Gretchen raised her stout index finger in the air. "One time, *dat* is. You don't own me, and I don't stay *wid* you, I *yam* not your wife. Understood? One time."

"Oui," said Seminole. And he gave her an evil leer. *"Une fois.* One time is all I could stand with a fat German cow like you."

"Sviss, mister," Gretchen said. "I *yam Sviss*. And you not exactly the kind of fellow a girl dreams about *eider*. You stink like a *gottdamnt* hog."

I begged Gretchen again not to go through with it, but she would not listen to me. Now she and Seminole got situated on the ground, positioning themselves and locking hands. The side-betting was furious. "You know," said Gretchen, "*dis* not really a fair contest, because I liable to pass out from *de* smell *a* Frenchy's breath before we even get started."

Then Susie Kelly gave the signal and the struggle began. Gretchen was all business now, and holding her own, her arm seemingly as stout and immovable as a fence post. We all cheered her on, the Cheyenne women as much as we—making their trilling—for everyone likes Gretchen and clearly all are terrified of the lout Seminole and would not wish such a fate on any woman.

But Jules Seminole is a powerful man, his short swarthy arm thick as a bear's. He began to wear Gretchen down, little by little, gaining slowly, steadily, inexorably. Gretchen's face turned red with blood as she strained against him and the veins in her arm and neck stood out like cording. Now the back of her hand was only inches from the ground. Good God, she was going to lose . . .

"You think my breath *est dégoulas,* eh, my ugly cow?" Seminole said. "*Alors,* wait until you put your fat German tongue up my arse."

And from Gretchen's breast there rose a bellow like the sound of a great dying buffalo, a sound filled with equal measures of anguish and wrath, and, as if infused with an inhuman strength, her arm began to regain the lost ground inch by inch. Now the sweat poured from Seminole's apish brow as his advantage slipped away and soon their arms were locked again at the fulcrum where the contest had begun. Clearly neither had much strength left and it was here at this moment where the match would be decided. And now Gretchen spoke, her face swollen like a blood sausage, her voice barely a whisper as if she had no breath left for words. *"Sviss,"* she hissed, "I told you French pig, I am *Sviss*!" And then with a final roar, this one triumphant, she slammed the wretch's arm to the ground, their locked hands making a thud and a puff of dust like a dropped stone. All cheered heartily as Gretchen stood and wiped the dirt from her dress. She pushed past her well-wishers to her husband. "*Yah,* you go on now," she said to him. "You go on and collect your whiskey, my *hustband.* But don't you come back to my lodge." And then poor brave Gretchen, her great heart broken, looked around at the crowd of people and added, "Someone tell *dis* man what I say to him. You tell him not to come back home to my house."

5 June 1875

Tonight marks the last night of the past days of games, feasts, and dances commemorating the arrival of the southern Cheyenne. It is true that the savages love nothing so much as an excuse to hold festivities. All of our efforts against it notwithstanding, tomorrow the war party goes out against the Crows, and other parties are off on the hunt.

This afternoon Martha and I arranged a conference in Reverend Hare's lodge with our husbands Little Wolf and Tangle Hair, who is himself the Chief of the Crazy Dog soldier society. The intent of our meeting was to enlist the Reverend's aid as translator and moral arbiter in a final effort to dissuade the men from making war against their neighbors.

The *he'emnane'e,* Dog Woman, organized the seating inside the lodge—he's a prissy old thing, and not before everything was just so did he light the pipe which was passed among the men. The women, as usual, were required to sit outside the circle of men, a heathen custom which I find objectionable—particularly given that this "powwow" was our idea in the first place. I suppose that this is not so different from the way women are treated in our own world. Of course, neither were we offered the pipe.

First I expressed through the Reverend our concern about our husbands going off to war. After he had translated, both Little Wolf and Mr. Tangle Hair seemed amused; indeed, they had rather a fine chuckle over it.

"Horse-stealing raids upon enemies, my wife," said Little Wolf, speaking through the Reverend, "are the business of young men, not 'old men' chiefs such as ourselves."

"Well then you must advise the young men not to go," I said.

"I cannot do so," answered the Chief.

"But you are the Chief," I said. "You can advise them as you wish."

"The raid upon the Crows is being organized by the Kit Fox society,"

Little Wolf explained. "I am the leader of the Elks Society and Tangle Hair is the leader of the Crazy Dogs. We are unable to interfere in the affairs of the Kit Fox society. This is tribal law."

"Kit Foxes, Elks, Crazy Dogs!" I said, exasperated. "These are like the clubs of children."

"That I cannot translate," said Reverend Hare.

"And why not?" I demanded.

"Because it's insulting to our hosts," he said.

"As His Reverence has himself pointed out," I said, "our purpose here is to encourage the savages to settle on the reservation. Surely making war against their neighbors does not work toward that end."

"Your government's official position on the matter, madam," explained the Reverend, "is that the heathens are to be distracted from making war upon white people. However any intratribal discord only encourages those who are friendly to us to enlist as scouts against those who oppose us."

"I see," I said, "divide and conquer." I began, then, to understand that not only do we face the obstacle of the heathens' innately warlike nature but also the hypocrisy of our own representatives. "And do you speak for the government or your church, Father?" I asked.

"In this case the two have a common purpose," answered the Reverend.

"Allow me then, please," I said, "to speak to my husband simply as his wife and not as a representative of either your church or our government."

"And what would you like to say to your husband, madam?" asked the Big White Rabbit with a patronizing nod.

"I would like to say: 'Kit Foxes, Elks, Crazy Dogs! These are like the clubs of children.' "

The Reverend smiled benignly, "You are an impetuous young woman, Miss Dodd," he said. "And frequently an irritating one."

"Shouldn't you address me now as Mrs. Little Wolf, Father?" I reminded him. "And isn't your function here to serve as a translator and not a censor?"

"At my discretion, Mrs. Little Wolf," he said. "You must understand that we have interests to protect in this delicate undertaking. That there is a protocol to be observed in all dealings with these people. Believe me, I have a great deal of experience in such matters. One must be diplomatic; one does not order, one must only suggest; one does not insult, one must flatter and cajole."

"Good God, Reverend, you sound more and more like a politician than a man of the cloth," I said.

"I caution you against blasphemy, young lady," he said sharply.

"Then let me rephrase my prior statement in a more politic manner," I said. "Perhaps you will translate the following to my husband: 'We have been sent here by the Great White Father'—No, no let me start over, I loathe that ridiculous term . . . 'We have been sent here by the United States government as a gift. You yourself requested that gift. You asked that we teach you how to live after the buffalo are gone. We are trying to learn from you about your way of life. And, in return, we are trying to teach you the white man's way. Now it is time that you begin to learn these things. That is the reason I have come here to be your wife. As Chief it is your duty to explain to the young men that they must stop waging war against their neighbors.' "

The Reverend translated—or so, at least, I assume. The Chief sat impassively, listening thoughtfully. He took a long puff on the pipe as he seemed to consider my words. Finally he spoke.

Reverend Hare smiled in his irritatingly smug fashion. "The Chief would like to know if white people do not make war upon their enemies?" he asked.

"Why yes, of course they do," I answered, frustrated, for I could see where the conversation was heading.

"He would like to know what difference there is between the Cheyennes making war against their enemies and white people making war against theirs?"

"How do I even know you're translating accurately?" I demanded angrily of the fat Episcopalian.

"Mrs. Little Wolf, please," said the Reverend, raising a pale chubby hand in stern admonishment of my outburst, "do not shoot the messenger."

"Couldn't you just tell my husband that God doesn't want the Cheyennes to go to war against the Crows?" I asked. "Would not that be a fair interpretation of God's position on the matter?"

The Reverend looked at me, the blood beginning to rise in his round pink hairless face, darkening his complexion. He spoke in a low voice. "Madam," he said, "may I remind you that it is hardly within the realm of your responsibilities to determine what God does and does not wish for these people."

"Ah, yes, of course," I said, nodding. "That's up to the church and the United States military, isn't it?"

"I warn you, young lady," said the Reverend pointing at me with a fat trembling finger, "I warn you once and for all not to incur the wrath of God, for the wrath of God is a terrible thing to behold."

"Martha," I said, turning to my friend for support, "please, don't be so timid. Speak up. Tell your husband to discourage the young men from going to war."

"You may repeat Mrs. Little Wolf's sentiments to my husband," Martha said to the Reverend. "Hers is my position exactly."

The Reverend addressed Tangle Hair, who responded curtly. "Your husband says that we should take this matter up with the leaders of the Kit Foxes," said the Reverend. "Which, I'm afraid, is his last word on the subject. And mine."

And this is what we are up against . . . I'm afraid that John Bourke was right about many things . . . that this entire enterprise may have been ill-advised, doomed to failure . . . that we are all of us helpless pawns of higher powers . . . although clearly not high enough.

I scribble these last notes of the day prior to our attending yet another, and, I hope, final feast. I am happy to report that we are not cooking at "home" tonight. Rather we have received an invitation to dine at the lodge of a prominent Chief of the southern Cheyennes, a man named Alights on the Cloud, and then we shall proceed to the dance . . . All this partygoing is beginning to remind me of the Chicago social season, with dinner tonight at the Alights on the Clouds' residence akin to Mother and Father being invited to the McCormicks' estate. I shall give a full report of these festivities tomorrow . . .

7 June 1875

Good God! The flippancy of my entry of two days ago did not presage the coming night's reign of terror . . . a passage through Hell . . . our slender faith in this mission has been shaken to its core . . . our group is in complete disarray, many have vowed to leave here, to return immediately to the safety of civilization—a safety that is, for now at least, to be denied us.

Let me recount, as plainly as I am able, the events that have led us to this dire state. My husband and I attended the aforementioned feast at the lodge of Alights on the Cloud. I was aghast to see upon our arrival that among the half dozen or so other guests was none other than the half-breed wretch Jules Seminole, who was in company with his own wife, a frightened and surely much mistreated girl whom they call by the name Howling Woman . . . yes, well is it any wonder? The poor thing is probably tortured to a state of howling by the miserable lout.

My blood ran cold when first I laid eyes upon Seminole, who leered at me with his disgusting expression of insinuating familiarity, as if we are intimates. Truly, the man makes my skin crawl. My husband hardly seemed to notice, or if he did, said nothing. It is true, I now know, what Seminole told me of the selfless nature of Little Wolf's position among the People.

Because I wished to get out of sight of the wretch as soon as possible, immediately after the feast I told my husband through the sign talk that I could not accompany him to the dance, that I must return to our lodge. However, I was not able to leave immediately, for no one is allowed to enter or depart the lodge while the men are smoking their damnable pipe. It is another of the savages' endless "rules."

While they were smoking, and as usual taking their sweet time over it, Jules Seminole produced a bottle of whiskey. In spite of that which he had lost to Gretchen, he now boasted that he still had several full kegs of the stuff which he had procured at the trading posts en route here. He passed a tin cup around and allowed all the men present one sip of the whiskey. I was disgusted to see that my own husband accepted a drink when the cup was handed to him. And as Little Wolf drank, Seminole looked at me and whispered, "Tonight, my beauty."

All immediately wanted another drink of the stuff, but Seminole only laughed at them, and said that the first taste was free but now they would have to pay for it.

Never have I witnessed a more rapid transformation among the men. Captain Bourke was right on that score, as well—the savages are slaves to whiskey, and have a pitifully low tolerance for it. Many already appeared drunk after the first "free" drink and became immediately belligerent and bellicose. I told my husband again that I was returning to our lodge; I did not care whether the men were finished with their smoke or not, and I began to crawl toward the lodge entrance. There was much *houing* of disapproval from the men at my impropriety, and Little Wolf, acting in uncharacteristically rough fashion, caught me by the ankle and dragged me back. All of the men seemed to find this most amusing and fairly shook with hearty laughter.

But my husband looked at me in a way that I had never before seen, with an expression so debased that it chilled me to the bone. I suddenly no longer knew this man. I wrenched free from his grasp and scrambled as fast as I could out of the lodge and ran back to our own tipi.

Soon the music from the dance began, but it had a different and strangely discordant tone. We began to hear from our lodge all manner of loud shouting and cursing. Our old tipi crone, Crooked Nose, looked at me, shook her head and said, *"ve'ho'emahpe."* Then she made the sign for drinking with her thumb.

Worried for the others I decided to go out again. But when I tried to leave the tent, the crone blocked my way with her club. "Please," I said, and I made the sign for "friends" and for "search." "Please let me pass." The old woman seemed to understand me; she muttered disagreeably, but finally she removed her club from my path.

I skirted the immediate area in which the dance was being held but paused long enough to see that Seminole had set up a kind of makeshift "saloon" there with a keg of whiskey and that a line had formed of men and women holding all manner of drinking vessels and goods with which to trade for the whiskey. These included bows and arrows, carbines, hides, blankets, household goods, beads, clothing, and many other items. It appeared that by the end of the night the wretch would own the entire camp!

Even from a distance I could see that a general state of drunkenness already prevailed and that the *he'emnane'e* had lost all control so that the usually orderly dancing was degenerating into a kind of mad gyration. Those who had been prudent enough not to have imbibed the alcohol were quickly retiring to their lodges, and relatives hurried to cut loose the young girls who are tied together at these affairs with a common rope—a peculiar, but effective, savage custom designed to prevent the girls from being lured away from the fire by young men whose romantic ardor has been inflamed by music and dancing. Or tonight, as was the case, by the devil whiskey.

I hurried on with the idea in mind of finding first Martha, and then as many of the others as possible, so that we might seek refuge at Reverend Hare's lodge—in the same way that one seeks sanctuary in a church. The camp is greatly spread out, and there were several separate dances in progress as I made my way, but it appeared that the whiskey had infected them all.

I reached Martha's lodge and found her there alone in, as I had expected, a state of near panic.

"Good God, what's going on out there, May?" she asked. "It's madness!"

Martha and I made our way to the Reverend's lodge. The situation was deteriorating by the moment—all control appeared to be lost. Bonfires burned everywhere. There was gunfire and brawling, and dancing of the most depraved sort accompanied by a demented music that seemed to issue from the bowels of Hell. We were sickened to witness men dragging their screaming wives and daughters to trade for a drink of whiskey. Fearing for our own lives, we dared not intervene.

When we arrived at the Reverend's lodge, we found that a number of our women were already there, many huddled together, holding each other and weeping in terror. The *he'emnane'e,* Dog Woman, was in the rear of the lodge trying to console and minister to the Reverend, who seemed himself to have suffered a complete breakdown. The latter was in a state of great agitation, and cowered under his buffalo robes like a giant child just awakened from a bad dream. He rocked himself back and forth, wild-eyed and perspiring heavily.

"Qu'est que se passe avec le Reverend?" I asked of the hermaphrodite. *"Il est malade?"*

"Il a perdu sa médecine," said the man/woman sadly.

"Comment?"

"Sa médecine, elle est partie," Dog Woman repeated. He was very sympathetic and now passed a piece of burning sage under the Father's nose. This was presumably designed to help him find his lost medicine again—or as I would have it, his courage.

I knelt beside the giant, trembling, white-robed priest. "Are you ill, Reverend?" I whispered. "Please, what's the matter with you?" I grasped him by his fleshy arm and shook him hard. "Please, these women need you."

"I'm sorry, Miss Dodd," he said, wiping his brow, and trying to collect himself, "the situation is hopeless, it's the worst possible thing that can occur. I have been among the savages before when they were drinking whiskey. It is Satan's tool to possess their soul. It makes them insane. You cannot imagine the atrocities of which they are capable. You cannot imagine. They know no restraint. The only hope, the only defense, is to hide oneself completely from their sight."

"Good God, man," I said. "This is no time to lose your faith. Pull yourself together. Can't you see that the women need you to be strong?"

"Hide yourself," the Reverend said, pulling a buffalo robe over his head. "Hide yourself. It's the only hope."

Even though the Reverend was clearly incapable of defending them, those women already present chose to stay in his lodge, and others soon joined us until it was quite crowded there—all were too fearful to venture forth again into the mad chaos that prevailed throughout the camp.

Jeanette Parker was there, as was the little French girl Marie Blanche, and the strange quiet Ada Ware dressed as always in black, her bleak vision of the world seeming to come true. "A lucky thing for us that the church sent the Reverend to look after us, isn't it?" she said darkly. "I feel so much better for having him here."

Now Narcissa White entered the lodge, disheveled and muttering to herself in a kind of self-absorbed hysteria. "There you see, I told them so, we have failed," she said, "Satan rules the night, I told them, I told them so . . ."

"Told them what for God's sake, Narcissa?" I asked.

"Told them to cast Satan from their hearts," she said. "Told them not to copulate with the heathens until the church had done its proper work and God possessed their miserable souls." She looked at me as if seeing me for the first time. "Did I not?" she asked. "Did I not tell you so? Now look, look what you have done, you Godless whore. You have taken up Satan's ministry, and this . . . this is the result!" She hiked her dress up and I saw the thin rivulet of blood that ran down the inside of her thigh. Evidently, Narcissa's husband had decided, presumably under the influence of the whiskey, to exercise his conjugal privileges after all.

"I'm sorry, Narcissa," I said. "Truly I am. But I don't see how you can blame me or anyone else for this. Have you seen any of the others? Have you seen Phemie or Daisy Lovelace? The Kelly twins? Gretchen? Have you seen little Sara?"

"Sinners, each and every one of them," said Narcissa shaking her head. "You'll all burn in Hell."

"Look around," said Ada Ware. "We're already there."

Worried for the others and for my tentmates, I elected to return to my own lodge. Martha, too fearful to let me out of her sight, accompanied me. We hurried as quickly as we could, keeping to the edge of the dance circles and never looking directly at anyone—trying our best to appear invisible.

There we found my other tentmates cowered together on their robes. As I had expected Little Wolf had not returned. The Chief's daughter, Pretty Walker, who is a lovely girl only a few years younger than myself, had also attended the dance, tied to the others. Thankfully she had been freed and now huddled next to her mother, weeping softly. The young wife, my friend, Feather on Head, anxiously clasped her baby to her breast. I knelt beside the frightened girl, and tried to console her. The old crone, Crooked Nose, sat cross-legged on the ground at her designated place just inside the entrance to the tent, holding her club vigilantly across her lap. For once I was very happy to see her on guard there.

An inhuman howling and wailing rose above the camp—gunfire and savage shrieks, the heartbreaking cries of wives and children. How I worried for our women.

"I must at least find Sara," I said. "Just to know that she is safe. You stay here, Martha," I said. "You'll be fine here."

But when I tried to leave the lodge Crooked Nose again laid her club across the entrance and this time she was implacable. I pleaded with her to let me pass, but finally lost patience and said in English, "Alright you old witch, go ahead and strike me down then. I am going out to look for my friends."

I pushed past her club and opened the flap. As soon as I did so my heart caught in my throat, for there standing in front of the entrance to our lodge was Jules Seminole. I heard Martha scream behind me as Seminole grasped me roughly by the arm and dragged me outside. He pulled my face close to his with an iron grip . . . and then . . . then he licked me like a dog . . . he put the tip of his tongue into my nostril . . . it was like a maggot crawling into my body . . . I was certain I would vomit.

"Yes, now show me your tongue, my little *salope,*" he said. "Give me your tongue."

"Oh, no," I whimpered, trying to pull away. "Oh God, please no."

And then Crooked Nose caught the wretch a terrific blow behind the ear with her club, which made a hollow cracking sound like a gourd splitting. Seminole collapsed on the ground like a dead man, blood running from his ear.

"My God, you've killed him," I said to the crone. But I said so triumphantly.

Martha, useless in her terror, sobbed as Crooked Nose and I each took ahold of one of Seminole's legs and with great effort dragged him some distance away from the lodge, where we left him lying upon the ground. God help me, I wished him dead, but when I bent over him I could see that he was still breathing, his ear beginning to swell like a mushroom.

When we were back inside the tipi I took the old woman by her forearm; it was as hard and sinewy as an old tree root. "Thank you," I said. "You saved my life, thank you." Crooked Nose smiled her toothless crone's smile, her eyes crinkled shut. She nodded and made the sign for "wait," and then she dug about in her parfleche by the head of her bed until she pulled another smaller, stone-headed club from beneath her headrest. Clearly the crone takes her job seriously and is well armed for the task. She waved the club in the air and said something to me in Cheyenne, and then handed it to me. I knew exactly what she was saying: *If anyone bothers you again, knock them over the head with this.* I said, "*Hou,*" to show her that I understood her meaning.

"Please don't go out again, May," Martha begged me. "Stay here with us."

"I'll be back, Martha," I said. "I must check on the child."

If there is a Hell on earth, being abroad in the camp yet a third time that night was like walking through its labyrinths. A few dancers still staggered by the dying firelight. Others had fallen down in a jumble of bodies around the fire; some struggled to regain their feet while others lay writhing on the ground. Throngs of drunken savages, men and women, jostled me as I pushed by. Naked couples copulated on the ground like animals. I stepped over them, pushed aside those who came up against me, and, when it was necessary, cleared a path by swinging my club. It was as if the whole world had fallen from grace, and we had been abandoned here to witness its final degradation. Never had I felt more keenly our precarious situation. Never have I been more fearful. I thought of John Bourke, of all that he had told me, of all his dire warnings. Would that I had heeded him. How I longed now for him to hold me again in his arms, to carry me back to civilization, safe from the horror.

Then I came upon the most shocking sight of all. It was Daisy Lovelace surrounded by a group of men. She was lying on her stomach, covered in blood, her dress pushed up around her waist. The savages appeared to be taking turns upon her. I yelled and pushed through them as another fell atop her. I swung my club with all my strength and hit the man a solid blow on the back of his head. He groaned and went limp upon her, but before I could push him off, another one grasped me from behind and wrenched the club from my hand. Now they had me down, grappling and pinning my arms. I fought for all I was worth, kicking, biting, scratching, and spitting. They tore the dress from my body. I screamed again. Suddenly I heard the crack of a bullwhip, and then another, and one of the savages who squatted upon me grasped his throat and made a gurgling sound as he was lifted backwards like a child's rag doll.

Then I heard a familiar voice, familiar in tone, but because it spoke in Cheyenne I could not place it immediately. But when the voice came a moment later in English I recognized it.

"Git the hell *offa* her, you miserable *stinkin'* heathens!" It was the voice of my old muleskinner friend, Jimmy—my savior Dirty Gertie.

At that same moment two others came to my aid. Another of the savages was lifted off me and I heard Gretchen speak. "I kill you you *gottdamnt* drunken pig!" she said. "You are not my *hustband* no more, I swear to God I kill you!" And she began to kick the man, who was too drunk to walk and crawled along the ground on hands and knees trying to escape her wrath. But Gretchen followed him mercilessly, taking measured aim with a heavy foot that sent him sprawling again and again in the dirt. "You *gottdamn* drunk son of a bitch, what you *tink* you doing? I kill you. You bad man son of a bitch drunken sot. I kill you, you *bastart!"*

By then Phemie had wrenched my club away from the savage who had taken it, and in the same motion backhanded the man in a perfect arc across the face, laying his nose against his cheek in a torrent of blood. And the whip cracked again and now the remaining men were scrambling to escape this fury of women they had unleashed, stumbling and falling over themselves and trying to crawl away in their drunkenness.

"Are you alright, May?" Phemie asked, her voice so calm as to be almost otherworldly. She helped me to my feet.

"I'm fine, Phemie, but what of Daisy?" I had lost track of the poor thing in the confusion.

Now we saw that she still lay facedown in the dirt where I had first discovered her. We knelt beside her. She mumbled something to us, but we were unable to make out her words.

"We have to take her back to her lodge," Phemie said.

Gretchen now had ahold of her drunken husband's hair and was dragging him the way that a child drags a rag doll as he struggled to get his feet under him. "I *yam* so sorry, May, I *yam* so sorry to everyone," she said, and I could see that she was weeping great tears of grief and rage. "I *yam* so sorry to everyone," she said again. "I take this *gottdamn* drunken pig son of a bitch back home now. I see you all tomorrow, *yah?* I *yam* so sorry to you everyone."

"Now that's an old gal I wouldn't want to mess with," Gertie said admiringly. "I bet that ol' boy'll think twice fore he takes hisself another drink a whiskey."

"God bless you, Jimmy," I said to her, gratefully. "You couldn't have arrived at a better time."

"Aw, you can call me Gertie now, honey," she said, "or whatever the hell else you like. The cat's outta the bag. They found me out at Camp Robinson. 'Nother skinner fella caught me just like you did, squattin' to take a pee. It's a dead giveaway, but there ain't no way 'round it, is there now?"

"What are you doing here, Gertie?" I asked.

"Your Cap'n sent me, honey," Gertie said. "Got a message for you. But let's get in out of this damn mess first. I'll give you a hand with her, then we'll talk. Things seem to be winding down some now. Hell, they was so busy partying when I got here I was able to ride right into the goddamn camp without even bein' noticed. Ain't they just plumb lucky I weren't a Crow Injun come to steal me some Cheyenne ponies? Why you folks'd be afoot fer the rest of the damn summer."

Gertie was right, the village had begun to quiet down; most of the dancers and revelers had either passed out or returned to their lodges, or crawled down into the willows along the river to sleep it off. Gertie, Phemie, and I half carried Daisy back to her tent. She had regained consciousness and was able to at least shuffle her feet. "Not a word to *mah* Daddy about this," she mumbled. "Mr. Wesley Chestnut has not conducted himself like a gentleman, *takin'* advantage in this manner of a girl when she is slightly tipsy. Not a word to *mah* Daddy, *Ah* beg of you."

Daisy's tipi crone met us at the entrance to their lodge, and we carried the poor thing inside and laid her gently down on her buffalo robes. The crone dabbed at the blood on her face with a cloth dipped in the water bowl, and made small clucking noises as she did so. The little French poodle, Fern Louise, yapped and ran in agitated circles about Daisy's head.

Daisy's husband, Bloody Foot, returned to the lodge moments after our arrival. The little dog seemed to have made friends with his new master and greeted him enthusiastically. To his credit, the man had not been drinking himself, and now told Gertie in Cheyenne that he had been searching the camp all night for his wife. His unpleasant name notwithstanding, he is a fine-looking fellow and was clearly genuinely concerned for Daisy. We did not tell him what had happened to her; but surely he could see.

It was just dawn by the time Gertie, Phemie, and I finally left Daisy's tipi. Promising to meet later, Phemie went to her own lodge, while Gertie and I walked back toward Little Wolf's.

A strange quiet had descended over the camp. The air was cool and perfectly windless, and the smoke from the dying lodge fires rose in thin straight lines above the tipis. Against the lightening horizon, the faint outlines of the bluffs over the river revealed themselves, and the birds took up their morning songs, tentatively at first and then in full voice. As always, the dawn cast a fresh light on the world; an uncertain hope returned. All seemed calm again, peaceful, as if the earth was a ship at sea and had managed to right itself after the storm.

Gertie and I skirted the half circles of family-grouped tipis where the bodies of some revelers still lay prone upon the ground, insensible as corpses. Fearing the worst, I stopped at Sara's lodge, for which I had started out all those hours ago. I scratched lightly on the covering and called for her. To my great relief, the girl came to the entrance, her face still swollen with sleep. She smiled when she saw me. "I was worried for you," I said. "I've been trying to get to you all night. I just wanted to see that you were safe."

She touched the center of her breast with the tip of her right thumb, the sign for "I," and then she extended her left hand, back down, in front of her body, and placed the tip of her right index finger, held vertically, in the center of her left palm, the sign for "safe." "I am safe," the gesture said.

I peered beyond her into the dimly lit lodge and saw her young husband Yellow Wolf, sleeping soundly on the buffalo robes. The child smiled at me again and swept her right hand, palm down from her breast outwards in a kind of chopping gesture, the sign for "good." Her husband was good, I think she meant to tell me.

"That's wonderful, sweetheart," I said. "I was just worried for you. Go back to sleep. I'll see you later."

And Gertie and I walked on.

"How is it that you speak Cheyenne, Gertie?" I asked her.

"Oh, hell, honey, didn't I tell you that I lived with the Cheyennes for a spell when I was a girl? Not this particular band but I'll betcha I know a few a these folks. I had me a Cheyenne boyfriend, too. Yessir, mighty nice young fella, good-lookin' boy, named *He' heeno*, Blackbird, . . . prob'ly would married Blackbird myself but he got killed by Chivington's army at Sand Creek, Colorado, in sixty-four. We wasn't doin' nothin', we was just camped there."

Now people were starting to stir in their lodges. A few wives and old women came outside to assess the condition, and in some cases, the identity of those who lay on the ground in front of their tipis. Some of the old crones kicked the corpses, squawking at them like angry mother hens to drive them away if they did not belong there. Others dumped bowls of yesterday's tipi water on their faces, which brought them awake sputtering and groaning.

"Goin' to be some sorry sickass *Injuns* around here today," Gertie remarked. "Yessir, whiskey goin' to be the ruination of these folks, that you can bet on, sister. Where'd they get it anyhow?"

"The southern Cheyennes came visiting," I said. "A half-breed among them named Jules Seminole brought whiskey."

Gertie nodded darkly. "Sure, I know Jules Seminole," she said. "A bad character, a very bad character. That's one you want to stay as far away from as you can, honey. Take my word for it."

I laughed, albeit without humor. "Yes, so I have discovered."

"He ain't hurt ya, has he, honey?" Gertie said, stopping to look at me.

"No," I answered, "not really." But then I felt the tears welling up behind my eyes, as if the horror of the past night had finally fully descended upon me. "Oh, Gertie," I said and I began to weep, to sob uncontrollably. It was the first time I had wept since this ordeal had begun, and now I could not stop and had to kneel down on the ground and bury my face in my hands.

"It's OK, honey," said Gertie, kneeling beside me and putting an arm around my shoulder. "You go ahead and have yourself a good cry. There ain't nobody around to see you but old Dirty Gertie, and she ain't goin' to tell nobody on you."

"Tell me your news of the Captain, Gertie," I said through my tears.

"Sure, honey," she said, but I sensed a reluctance in her voice. "When we get back to the lodge, I'll tell ya all about it."

"Has he married the Bradley girl yet?" I asked, composing myself. "Tell me now, Gertie."

"You're a tough gal, honey," she said. "I like that about you. I'll tell ya straight. Weddin's set for next month."

"Fine," I said, nodding and wiping my tears. "That's good. She'll make a fine wife for the Captain."

"Honey, I don't know exactly what went on between you two, but I got a pretty good idea," Gertie said. "Just because the Cap'n was already spoke for, and so was you, don't mean it can't happen. I know how it is out here. You feel like you're out on the edge of the world about to fall off and when somebody like the Cap'n comes along, somebody strong and decent, you grab ahold and you hang on for dear life. And just because he's goin' to marry someone else that don't mean he ain't been moonin' around like a lovesick kid hisself since you left."

"And why did he send you here, Gertie?" I asked, regaining my feet. "Surely not to tell me that." We continued on our way.

"He sent me to warn you, honey," she said. "He couldn't trust anyone from the Army, because what I got to tell you would get him in a heap a trouble. He sent me because I know you and because I speak the language and got ties among these folks."

"Warn me of what?"

"You prob'ly heard the rumors 'fore you come out here about gold in the Black Hills?" Gertie said. "Well, the government give that land to the Sioux and to the Cheyennes in 1868 in the Fort Laramie treaty—it's all on paper. All legal as can be. As long as the Injuns don't bother the whites passin' through, all this country from the Black Hills to the Yellowstone is theirs to roam and hunt—forever. That's what it says right there on the treaty: forever. Well, now word has got out that there's gold in the Black Hills. Just last week, the Army sent out General Custer in charge of an expedition with a bunch of geologist fellas to find out for sure about them reports. Some a my old compadres is skinnin' for 'em—I'd a been with 'em myself if I hadn't got found out fer a gal.

"The scuttlebutt is that if Custer comes back at the end of the summer with his saddlebags full a gold," she continued, "the rush is goin' to be on—in a big way. It's already started strictly on account of the rumors. All them prospectors and settlers and shopkeepers and whores and everyone else who follows the gold rush is goin' to need—is goin' to demand—military protection against the Injuns. Because the Injuns still think that country belongs to them—see? And why shouldn't they? It was give to 'em fair and square. That's the heart of their big medicine country, and they ain't goin' to take real kindly to all them white folks running through it, shootin' it up and scarin' off the game. Now according to what the Cap'n is hearin', Grant's people is fixin' to pull the plug on this whole brides program—for a couple a reasons. For one thing, when the shit storm begins, they don't want a bunch more white women in the way of killin' off the rest of the Injuns. And they sure as hell don't want to get themselves in no situation where the Injuns can use you gals as hostages—then the newspapers would find out about this whole damn mess. How do you suppose that would look for President Ulysses S. Grant? So until further notice you all is the first, an mos' likely the last installment of payment to the Injuns. Now all this is unofficial right now, you understand? The Cap'n is privy on accounta bein' Crook's aide-de-camp, which a course puts him in a tight spot. Now if word gets out among the Injuns that the Great Father in Washington is—number one—backin' out of the brides deal, and—number two—plannin' to take the Black Hills back, well just all kinds a shit's goin' to fall from the skies. The Cap'n don't want you in the middle a that. He wants you to come back to Robinson with me. Right now. After we get a little catnap, we can leave later today."

"All of us?" I asked. "Leave now?"

"Honey, if all you gals was to try to leave at once," Gertie said, "it'd take the damn Injuns about five minutes to track you down and bring you back. And they wouldn't take kindly to it. See, they think you was given to them. And to an Injun a deal's a deal. No, this'd just be you and me, honey. We'd just sneak off and the two of us'd have a pretty good chance a makin' it. Especially after last night. I know this country, and anyhow, Little Wolf might just let you go. It wouldn't hardly look good, see, for the head man to go chasin' off after his wife like a damn jilted lover, if you get my meanin'."

"But Gertie, you know perfectly well that I can't leave my friends here," I said. "Especially after what has just happened."

"That's what I told the Cap'n you was goin' to say," Gertie said. "But he said to tell you that the government's goin' to figure out a way to get the others out, too. It's just a matter of time, and in the meantime at least you'd be safe."

"The government being so reliable," I scoffed. "John Bourke must take me for a fool to believe that. Or a coward to leave my friends here."

"Neither, honey," Gertie said. "You know that, but he figured it was worth a try. You think last night was bad, things is goin' to get a lot worse out here 'fore they get better. They'll get over the whiskey, but once the Injuns get things figured out, which after they start to see all the settlers moving into the Black Hills, will be real quick, this ain't goin' to be no place for a lady. You ain't goin' to be safe here."

I laughed. "We're hardly safe now," I said. "Tell Captain Bourke to come out here with a detachment of troops and provide us all safe escort home," I said. "Like a gentleman."

"Like I say, he can't do that, honey," Gertie said. "He's an Army man.

He'd be facin' a court-martial for sure if his superiors even got wind of the fact that he'd sent me out here to warn you."

"So what is our position, then—officially speaking?" I asked. "Are we nothing more than sacrificial lambs? An interesting, but unsuccessful political experiment? Missionaries stranded in the line of duty? Or perhaps, easiest to explain, white women gone astray, taking up with savages of our own volition?"

"Yup, that's about it, honey," Gertie said. "Take your pick. Like I say, they goin' to try to figure a way to bring you home, but until Custer gets back with a full report on the gold, and until they figure some way to do that, everyone is just settin' tight. Which, you know, honey, has always been the thing the government does best."

"Shame on them!" I said. "Have they no sense of shame?"

"That's the thing they does second best, honey," Gertie said with a wry smile, "is not to have no sense a shame."

We had reached our lodge, Little Wolf's lodge . . . my home. "You must be exhausted, Gertie," I said, "and hungry. Why don't you stay here, have a bite to eat, and sleep for a while."

"Don't mind if I do, honey," she said. "I got to picket my mule, though, first. I left him tied up on the edge of camp."

"I'll have Horse Boy tend to him," I said. "That's his job, and he's very good at it."

"Whooo-eee!" Gertie said, "Ain't you just the lady a the house! Why you got servants to do all the work for ya!"

All were still in their beds inside the lodge, except for old Crooked Nose, who, I believe, never sleeps. She took me by the arm, her fingers like an eagle's claw, and smiled her toothless grin, which was meant, I believe, as an expression of genuine happiness for my safe return. Gertie introduced herself and they whispered briefly in Cheyenne. It did not surprise me that Little Wolf had still not returned to the lodge—the great man was probably passed out somewhere with his drinking cronies of the night.

I went to Horse Boy's bed and knelt beside him. The morning light was still dim inside the tipi but I could see that the child's eyes were open, catching the faint light from the embers of the fire and shining like gunmetal. I stroked his forehead and he smiled slightly. I held my hands open on either side of my ears and wriggled them, the rudimentary sign language for mule. The boy giggled at my antics, and, I think, thought that I was trying to amuse him. Gertie came over and knelt beside me. "Tell the boy where you tied your mule, Gertie," I said. "He'll fetch it and take care of it for you."

She spoke to the lad, who immediately scrambled to his feet, wide-awake and eager as always to perform his duties. I was finally beginning to understand a few words of the language but was still shy about speaking it. "God, I envy you Gertie. I have a terrible time with the Cheyenne language."

"Like I said, I learnt it when I was just a girl. Always easier to pick up at a young age. But you'll get the hang of it. Just remember that everything's done backwards from the way we say things. Let's say you want to say somethin' like, 'I'm heading down to the river to take a swim,' which in Cheyenne is said—'Swim, river, go there, me.' See? It's all backwards."

Without a sound, Quiet One had gotten up herself to stoke the fire with sticks and to put a small pot of meat to heating. Then she left the tipi to fill the paunch water vessel. The savages observe a curious custom of emptying out water that has stood all night—"dead" water they call it—and filling the vessel from the creek each morning with "living" water.

Soon she was back, and she poured some of the water into a small tin trade pan into which she also sprinkled a handful of coffee grounds. She put the pan on the fire to boil. Coffee is a precious commodity among the savages, and she was clearly serving it in honor of the company—without even knowing, or asking, who the company was; generosity is a universal trait of these people. And so in spite of the trials of the night, life went on . . .

The camp was exceptionally well provisioned at the present time. Besides the whiskey that Seminole had brought with him, the southerners had furnished us with the three most prized commodities among the savages—white man tobacco, sugar, and coffee. All these they had brought as gifts from the trading post—although most had probably been squandered last night on the whiskey.

Now I laid a bed of buffalo robes for Gertie next to mine and brought her a bowl of meat and a tin cup of coffee with a generous lump of sugar in it.

"Hell, this ain't so bad now is it, honey?" she said, making herself comfortable against the backrest I had fixed for her. "I always did enjoy sleepin' in a Injun lodge. Cozy, ain't it? Makes ya feel safe."

"I was beginning to feel so until last night," I said. "I have lived in a lunatic asylum, Gertie, but never have I seen lunacy like that."

"It's just the whiskey, honey," she said. "Plain and simple. It's poison to 'em. Turns 'em plumb crazy."

"How long did you live among them, Gertie?"

"Oh, I don't know, let's see . . . 'bout eight years I guess altogether," she said. "I was stole off a wagon train when I was a girl, and I stayed with 'em until after Sand Creek. Someday I'll tell you the whole story . . . when I ain't so plumb tuckered out. But Hell, I liked livin' with these folks just fine. Hated to leave 'em. Yes, ma'am, a person can get mighty accustomed to this life, you understand what I'm sayin'? Besides last night, how are you takin' to it, honey?"

"I've hardly been here long enough to say," I confessed. "And I've hardly had time to reflect upon it, so busy have we been working and learning, adapting to their ways and trying to teach them something of ours. Now that you mention it, it occurs to me that in the past weeks I have hardly stopped to ask myself if I was happy here . . . I had simply resigned myself to it . . . But after the events of the night I shall have to reconsider the question . . ."

"Naw, you don't want to do that, honey," said Gertie, with a dismissive wave of her hand. "Like I say last night was just whiskey talkin'. They'll get over it. You'll get over it. I knew damn well you wasn't comin' back with me. I told the Captain you wasn't no welcher. This is a good band of people you got here. Some of them southerners is a bad influence, that's true. They've spent too much time with the whites, but all in all, if these folks was left alone, things'd be just fine. If the whites'd leave 'em alone, stop lyin' to 'em, stop givin' 'em whiskey, things'd be just fine."

"Stop giving them white brides," I added.

"Yeah, we're always messin' around where it ain't none of our business," admitted Gertie. "An' that's exactly the good thing about the Injun life—you don't have to stop and think about whether or not you're 'happy'—which in my opinion is a highly overrated human condition invented by white folks—like whiskey. You don't have to think about it any more than a bear cub or a pronghorn antelope or a coyote or a damn bird has to think about it. You got a roof over your head? You warm? You got enough food to eat? You got plenty a good water? You got a good man? You got friends? You got somethin' to do to keep you busy?"

I nodded affirmatively to each of these in turn.

"You got a Injun name yet, honey?" Gertie asked. "I forgot to ask ya that. Mine was *Ame'ha'e*—which means Flying Woman because one time I jumped off a runaway horse at a full gallop and landed right in a damned tree and the Injuns all thought I could fly. I always did like that name."

"The name they've given me is *Mesoke*," I said.

"Swallow," Gertie said. "Yup, that's a real purty name. Seems to me that you got everything a body really needs in life. Hell, honey, you tell me, what more does a person need?"

I thought the question over for a moment and then I said: "Safety . . . security . . . love, perhaps."

"Aw, hell, honey," Gertie scoffed, "if them first two things was so important to you, you wouldn't be here. You still be livin' in that asylum you mentioned. And love? Hell, that's the easy part! You see that old girl squattin' by the fire?" she asked pointing to Quiet One. "Now you think she spends her time worrying about whether or not she's happy? You think maybe she ain't got enough love in her life—what with her family, her husband, her children? I'll tell you something. You know when you'll find out if you been happy here? You'll find out after you leave. When you really got some time on your hands to think things over."

"I miss my babies, Gertie," I said. "That's the worst part of it. Do you know that I have two children? It was for them that I signed up for this program, to gain my freedom so that one day I might be with them again. I think of them every day, try to imagine how their lives are, what they look like now. It helps me to go on. I like to imagine how it would be for them if they came to live with me here, grew up among the savages."

"Oh, they'd plumb love it, honey," Gertie said. "Put the damn whiskey aside, and it's a wonderful life for children. I thought I was goin' to die when they first took me, but after a while I practically forgot all about my real folks. It was like livin' a damn fairy tale. Like I say, where the fairy tale comes to end real fast is when you bump against the white man's world again. That's what happened to you last night. An' that's what happened to me at Sand Creek."

"If I give you a letter to my babies, Gertie," I asked, "will you post it for me at the fort when you return? They would not permit us to send any communication to our families before we left, but perhaps you could post one for me?"

"I'll try, honey," she said. "Sure I will." And she laughed. 'You're a long way from mail delivery out here, ain't you?"

"If you liked this life so much, why did you go back to the white world, Gertie?" I asked. "Was it because Blackbird was killed at Sand Creek?"

Gertie was silent for a long time, and I thought perhaps that she had drifted off to sleep. "That was part of the reason," she finally said. "But it was also just because I couldn't get away from the fact that I'm white myself. There's no damn way around that, honey."

And after that we fell silent, as the exhaustion of the night's efforts overcame us. I curled up on my own sleeping place next to Gertie's. I felt like a little girl having a friend spend the night and was especially grateful this morning to have her here with me. She is a rough woman, it is true, and could surely use a bath, but she has a big heart, and what more can be said of a person than that?

The sun had risen, and the camp was going about its business, but it was muffled quiet and safe inside the tipi, the gentle morning sunlight filtering softly through the buffalo skins; the fire was warm and took the early-morning chill off the air, the tent pungent with the mingled scents of human beings and smoke and coffee and meat cooking, the smell of animal hides and earth. All these no longer seemed to me to make for an offensive odor, but rather an oddly comforting one—the smells of home.

Within moments Gertie had started to snore, loud and rhythmic, a snore befitting a muleskinner named Jimmy, but it did not disturb me . . . and soon I drifted off to sleep myself.

15 June 1875

Over a week has passed since our night of terror. I have rested my pen, and with the others thrown myself back into the business of living day to day, trying in the process to repair the dreadful damage done, to refill the empty well of our spirits.

Gertie left this morning, alone, for Camp Robinson. She carried only a letter from me to my children, and a private message to Captain Bourke. In the letter I thanked the Captain for his concern for my welfare but declined his offer to return with Gertie. I wished him well in his new married life. I told him that I was most satisfied in my own . . .

As to the news that she had brought from him, I have not mentioned a word of it to any of the others. Perhaps I err in this decision and should let all decide for themselves what course to follow, but I see no reason to alarm the women about events that are quite beyond their control. To panic them now when all are at their most fragile could only lead to more tragedy and despair. We may have entered into this enterprise as volunteers, but recent events suggest that we are, in reality, captives.

As I had feared, a group of our women, led by Narcissa White—who after the night of drunken debauch and her own violation by her husband, apparently decided to give up her mission here—tried to leave camp the very next day. Just as Gertie predicted, the women's husbands had no difficulty tracking them and returning them to their lodges within a few hours. They wouldn't have gotten far anyway and would only have perished in the prairie or been captured by some other tribe. "If they'd a got caught by the Crows or the Blackfeet," Gertie said, "they'd a found out how cushy life is here with the Cheyennes."

My own husband Little Wolf did not return to our lodge for three days and three nights, nor was he anywhere seen about the camp. He stayed out during that time, alone in the prairie, without shelter, food, or water, sleeping on the ground, doing, I believe, penance for his sins. Perhaps he sought divine guidance from his God.

When he came back in at last he was trailed by a sickly coyote; everyone in camp saw it and everyone remarked upon it—although only we white women seemed to consider this to be a particularly bizarre sight. We are beginning to realize that the savages' world has even a different corporeality than ours, and one quite inaccessible to us.

The coyote was gaunt and losing its hair in patches, and skulked around our lodge for three more days, always keeping a little away. I was frightened of the beast—when I shooed him he skittered sideways like a crab and made a strange hissing sound. Each time that Little Wolf departed the lodge, the coyote followed him, trailed along always the same distance behind. For their own reasons, the camp dogs did not bother the coyote—perhaps they recognized its illness—and they seemed intentionally to keep away from it.

Little Wolf himself never spoke of the coyote, never so much as acknowledged its presence; he remained silent and brooding as if involved in some terrible struggle of his own. He refused even to make the sign talk with me and when I tried to speak to him in English as I had done on our honeymoon outing together, instead of responding in his own language as was our way, he ignored me altogether. There was much speculation in camp about his behavior.

The medicine man, White Bull, told Helen Flight that the coyote was the Chief's medicine animal, that its sickness represented his own sickness and the sickness of the People from drinking the whiskey, and that if the coyote died in the camp, this would be a very bad thing for everyone. But after three days the coyote disappeared—one morning it was simply gone and did not return—and gradually Little Wolf came back to himself.

Other repercussions of that night: a man named Runs From Crow, who was married to our own little French girl Marie Blanche, was killed by a fellow named Whistling Elk—shot dead through the heart. Poor Marie has had a very hard time of it, what with her parents both murdered in Chicago, and now her husband. She is quite beside herself, for she rather liked the fellow. Now Runs From Crow's younger brother, One Bear, has offered to marry her, which is the Cheyenne custom—and rather a civilized one in my opinion. It is my limited experience that French women are, by nature, a practical race, and Marie Blanche, while still grieving for her first husband, is considering the proposal. She will certainly need someone to care for her and her child.

Sadly, the murderer, Whistling Elk, is married to Ada Ware—as if that poor dark thing didn't already have sufficient cause for Melancholia in her life. The affair is a shocking event for the Cheyennes, as killing another member of the tribe is the greatest crime of which a man is capable in their society, and has occurred only rarely in all their history. The murderer, with any members of his family who choose to accompany him, is exiled and must live alone beyond the perimeters of the village. He will be forever an outcast, never fully accepted back into the tribe. People cease to address him, or to so much as acknowledge his presence, and he is not allowed to participate in any tribal activities. He becomes, in effect, an invisible man.

Ada's exiled husband has even been stripped of his name and renamed, Stinking Flesh, for the Cheyennes believe that one who kills a tribal member begins to rot from the inside out. By tribal law, Ada is free to leave the man with no formal divorce decree being required, but for the moment at least has chosen to join him in his banishment. As she is guilty of no crime herself, she is free to come and go among us. However, as the wife of the murderer she is considered to be tainted by her contact with him, and is not allowed to touch anyone or anyone's possessions. Pots or dishes from which she eats at the lodges of others must be broken or discarded for fear that they have been contaminated. I need hardly add that this superstition does not make Ada a popular visitor or dinner guest in anyone's lodge.

"When the doctors at the hospital questioned me about my illness," the poor hapless thing said at our meeting the other day, "I told them that I found it unsupportable being married to an adulterer—especially through the long gray Chicago winter. It was that time of year in particular that I felt the full weight of the black dog crouched on my chest, as if suffocating me. And so that winter the doctors consigned me to a dark room in an insane asylum, where the black dog was my sole company. My husband took the opportunity of my illness and prolonged absence—which was really in payment for his sins—to divorce me and marry his lover. Still the doctors questioned me incessantly: Why was I so sad? Why did I dress always in black? To what did I attribute my Melancholia?

"Now I find myself married to a murderer by the name of Stinking Flesh—who by all accounts is rotting from the inside out . . . and once again I have been exiled for his crime. Now does any among you wonder why I dress in black? Is there no end to a woman's suffering on this earth?" It was the most Ada had ever spoken to us or revealed of herself.

"Aye, but look on the bright side then, Ada," said Meggie Kelly. *"Ya* may be married to a *moordoorer* but now that he's an outcast, at least you don't have to worry about the beggar committin' *adooltory* on *ya,* for no one else'll *tooch* him!"

We all laughed; even Ada smiled, for she is not without a sense of humor, albeit a frequently dark one.

"Meggie's right," said her sister, Susie, "and furthermore, dear, I get a *tooch* of the Melancholia *meself* in Chicago in the wintertime, but *ya 'ave* to admit that *thar's* a great deal more *soonshine* in the prairie in the summertime than ever *thar* was in Chicago in winter. It'll be too damn hot for that old black dog in this country, I'll wager. You won't be seein' *mooch* of him out here."

And in such ways we try to bolster each other's spirits.

This next sad fact I am most loath to report: a number of other girls, both native as well as several of our women, were ravaged that night by drunken savages—in some cases, as in that of Narcissa White, the women's own husbands forced themselves upon them. Daisy Lovelace has grown silent and withdrawn since her terrible ordeal, and we are all filled with concern for her. Her husband, at least, is a kindly and patient man and seems to be caring well for her.

Perhaps most unfortunate, the wretch responsible for the entire night of terror, Jules Seminole, remains still among us, unpunished and by all appearances unrepentant. But for a still swollen ear he seems to have recovered from Crooked Nose's blow, and has already several times come by our lodge to leer at me and make his unspeakably degenerate talk . . . I try to disguise my fear of him, but I am terrified of the man, and make every effort not to go abroad unaccompanied.

Little Wolf, too, is aware of Seminole's skulking and unwholesome interest in me, but has thus far managed to keep vigilant control over his temper when the man comes around. As Sweet Medicine Chief, my husband is powerless to do anything other than speak out against Seminole in council for bringing the whiskey among the People. Truly, but for his own fall from grace as a result, Little Wolf's observance of his duties is monklike . . . nearly Christ-like in its selflessness.

17 June 1875

This morning Helen Flight came to visit, to invite me to a dance tonight in which she is guest of honor. The Kit Fox warriors returned yesterday from their raid against the Crows. Having wisely not imbibed in the drinking on that Hellish night, they had held their own private war dance across the river, and off they went the next morning as planned. All of them were by then painted with Helen's fantastic bird designs—the likes of which the savages, whose own painting skills are limited to the most simple stick figures, had never before seen.

The raid was a great success, and yesterday the Kit Fox warriors came whooping into camp with the usual fanfare, driving an enormous herd of Crow ponies. Not only had the men captured many enemy horses, but also they had not lost a man.

"I'm afraid, *Mesoke,*" Helen told me this morning, "that the Fox chaps are giving me full credit for the success of the venture, after all. 'Medicine Bird Woman'—they call me now *'Ve'kesohma'heonevestsee'*—a frightful mouthful isn't it? so please do continue to call me by my short name, Bird, won't you?"

"Of course, *Ve'ese,*" I answered. (Some of us are making a concerted effort to speak the Cheyenne tongue, and names are an easy place to start.)

"Yes, well one bloke has already been 'round to present me with three Crow horses and to tell me the story of his great success in the raid," said Helen. "I should say—to sing and dance the story. I'm sure you'll see the performance again tonight if you would be so good as to accompany me to the dance. I had the chap painted with the image of a snipe and he showed me how he and his horse had been able to zigzag through the bullets and arrows of the pursuing enemy just as the snipe flies, thus avoiding all injury. All the while as he danced and sang this tale, he held his arms out like bent wings and made the specific winnowing sound of the snipe in territorial display. Quite extraordinary, I should say. Haunting actually . . . never seen anything quite like it. That is to say, he sounded so like the bird, it was as if he had actually become the snipe."

"Perhaps I must revise my opinions of the efficacy of your magic, Helen," I said. "You may make of me a believer yet."

Speaking of which Reverend Hare's staggering loss of faith that terrible night—the dismal failure of his own "medicine"—has greatly diminished his influence among both our women and the savages—who despise more than anything the display of cowardice. They reason that if the Reverend's medicine is so puny in the face of that of his archenemy—the evil God Satan—against whom he is constantly preaching, then what kind of power does the Father's Great White Spirit really have? However childlike in nature it seems, the savages' theological reasoning has a certain simplistic logic. The influence of gods being only as good as their earthly representatives, at the moment Helen Flight's magic seems to hold greater sway among all . . .

The word about the camp is that tomorrow we depart on the summer hunts, I do not know where we go, or for how long . . . I do not know if John Bourke, or Gertie or the Army itself will be able to monitor our movements. This imminent departure to live the life of nomads seems yet another separation, yet another step further into the wilderness—leading us not closer, but seemingly always further away from our eventual return . . .

Having missed my monthly cycle, I am more than ever certain that I am pregnant now. The prospect of being a mother again fills me with both joy and trepidation. Now there are two of us to worry about . . .

→ NOTEBOOK V ←

A Gypsy's Life

"Now we move out again, the horses slipping down off the knoll, following the People, who follow the buffalo, who follow the grass, which springs from the Earth."

(from the journals of May Dodd)

→←

7 July 1875

We have been on the move for weeks—thank God for the calendar I brought to mark off the days or surely I would have lost all sense of time, for, of course, the savages do not observe our calendar, and time itself passes differently among them—impossible to explain this . . . only that there is no time . . .

We have been traveling mostly westward and sometimes north—that much I know for certain—hunting and moving, we follow the buffalo herds.

At present I sit atop my horse Soldier on a slight rise overlooking the green plains below. The sweet child, Horse Boy, light as a feather, his brown skin warmed like a biscuit in the sun, rides up beside me on the saddle as he frequently does. I have grown ever fonder of the boy. He is my little man, my protector, and I his.

Several of us women ride abreast; in this case, I, Martha, Phemie, Helen, and Feather on Head. This traveling time is our best, and in some cases only, opportunity to visit and catch up on each other's news—because, when we are in camp there is too much work for all to do.

For the same reason, I shall try to keep this poor record while on the move, and have taken to strapping my notebook to my back so that when I have a moment to pause thus I can make a few scribbles on the page. Presently I rest my notebook against my little man's back as I write.

Now we watch as the entire band, possibly two hundred lodges strong with the southerners among us, moves out across the prairie, horses and dogs and travois, some people afoot, others riding, with the warrior guards appearing now and then on the distant horizons, before disappearing again into the folds of the land like ships at sea into the swales—it is a sight to behold! How many white people, I wonder, can lay claim to having witnessed such an exodus? Have ever participated in it?

The Cheyennes are a wealthy people and, particularly since the raid against the Crows, we have many horses. Some of the women and older children walk alongside the packhorses or alongside those that drag the travois, occasionally snapping their quirts to move them along. Others ride atop the packs themselves—two or three little girls together on one horse, they play games and chatter away like chicks in the nest. Some of the smaller children ride the huge camp dogs, others ride ponies. From the time that they are able to walk, Cheyenne children are comfortable on horseback, and their little hammerheaded prairie ponies, which are quite distinct in appearance from our own, are superbly even-tempered, well trained, and biddable. Some of the older people, especially if they are ill or in any way infirm, and some of the youngest children who still need to be tended to by adults ride atop the travois—while the infants ride on baby boards strapped to their mothers' backs. Sometimes the baby boards are hung from the pack saddles or the travois poles themselves, where they dangle and bob gently with the movement of the horses much to the comfort and amusement of the infants themselves, who smile and gurgle, and, when they are not sleeping, watch all of the proceedings with wide-eyed interest. In this manner they absorb the nomadic prairie life as naturally as sunlight. The Indian children rarely cry. They are superb, perfect little creatures—but then what children aren't? I think constantly now of our own babies—for many of the others have announced their pregnancies. Our government may have lost faith in our mission, but how can a prospective mother not be filled with hope for the future?

I am in a bright mood today. The constant travel of the past weeks, though hard and frequently exhausting work, rather agrees with me. It occurs to me in response to the conversation I once had with Captain Bourke in which he asked, rhetorically, "Where is the savage's Shakespeare?" that possibly the reason the aboriginals have made scant contributions to world literature and art, is that they are simply too busy living—moving, hunting, working—without the luxury of time to record the process, or even, as Gertie suggested, to ponder it. Sometimes I think that this is not such a bad state . . . and yet here I am, trying to steal a few moments whenever possible that I may faithfully report these events.

I take this opportunity to study the four of us—representatives of our group as it were. Such a ragtag assembly we make! We are nearly natives now, all but indistinguishable from our fellow Cheyenne women, and finally, almost as dark of skin (and Phemie, of course, darker!). Even my fair complexion has gone brown as a chestnut though I am still careful to wear the greasepaint as much as possible.

Weather permitting Phemie dresses still in men's breechclouts and little else, the scandal of her bare breasts long since accepted.

With the increasingly warm weather Helen has given up her heavy knickerbockers and has had our seamstress Jeanette Parker fashion a buckskin suit for her, with fringed blouse and trousers. It is a decidedly eccentric outfit for a lady, but suits Helen perfectly—she looks every bit the frontiersman, especially with her ubiquitous pipe clenched between her teeth.

Like me and my friend and fellow wife, Feather on Head, Martha wears the simple loose-fitting antelope hide dress that the native women favor.

Now we move out again, the horses slipping down off the knoll, following the People, who follow the buffalo, who follow the grass, which springs from the Earth.

14 July 1875

However peripatetic our wandering of the past weeks may seem, there is a genuine method to it. The camp organizes and moves with marvelous efficiency. I am reminded of Mother's stories of the gypsies of Europe. Of course, now I understand why my bridal lodge had to be dismantled—I could hardly have managed it by myself. This is communal life in the purest form. Like a hive of bees, or a colony of ants, all participate for the good of the whole.

The women do all the work of packing the parfleches, dismantling the lodges, rigging and loading the horses and travois, and at the end of the day's travel, remaking the camp in exactly the same formation as the last. In our lodge, the old crone Crooked Nose oversees this process, squawking at us like a cranky magpie while brandishing, at the slightest infraction, a willow switch from her arsenal of weapons. On the morning of our very first move she actually lashed me across the back of the legs with her damnable switch; I was, presumably, packing incorrectly.

"Ouch!" I hollered, leaping at the sting; she'd hit me hard enough to raise a welt. I turned furiously on the old woman, who, instantly recognizing my wrath, began to shrink away from me. I moved toward her, shaking my finger; I put my cupped hand on my throat and pointed at her again and said: "You may be in charge of this operation, you old hag, but if you ever do that to me again, I'll wring your damn buzzard's neck!" I was speaking English, of course, but I was also speaking the universal language of women, and the old crone understood me well. She has not lifted her switch against me again.

The men devote themselves to the hunt, the various military societies to guarding the camp and protecting us as we travel. So far we have had no encounters with enemies nor seen any sign of them but for a few abandoned campsites. It is said that we have recently entered Crow and Shoshone country, and all have noticed an increased vigilance on the part of the warrior societies.

Altogether, having more or less accepted my woman's lot, I would admit that the division of labor among the aboriginals is an equitable one. Far from being a casual pastime as it was for Father and his friends, hunting is quite literally a matter of life and death—extremely difficult and, frequently dangerous, labor. Already this summer we have had one man trampled and killed when he fell off his pony in the middle of the chase. Another was severely gored by a buffalo bull, but survived (the fellow's name has now become Buffalo Not Kill Him), and a third was badly injured when his pony stepped into a badger hole at full gallop and broke its leg (this man now known as Horse Breaks Leg). Still I have not failed to notice that the men embark upon their hunting expeditions with a somewhat keener sense of anticipation than we women are sometimes able to muster for our camp chores and moving activities. Although even these are generally accomplished in a spirit of good cheer and cooperation.

To her own and to the savages' credit, our Negress Phemie, *Mo'ohtaeve'ho'a'e,* which translates interestingly to Black White Woman, is permitted to accompany the men on the hunt. Although women are not allowed membership in council, the Cheyennes are surprisingly egalitarian in recognizing special talents, and Phemie has clearly proven her venatic prowess.

At the same time, women in the tribe wield a great deal of influence in daily affairs and are regularly consulted on all subjects that concern the welfare of the people. My own Little Wolf, for example, values the advice of a prominent medicine woman, Woman Who Moves Against the Wind, above that of all the other medicine men, and, while he hardly agrees with my views on all subjects, he nevertheless listens to them with great respect. Perhaps our own society might learn something from the savages about relations between the sexes.

The scouts have consistently found good-sized herds of buffalo at nearly every place we have been. Thus the men have had excellent hunting, and the larder is full. The buffalo have been further supplemented by elk, deer, pronghorn, a variety of small game, and trout—the streams hereabouts so choked with fish that if one is quick about it one can scoop them up on the bank by hand—another job for the women and children. We have already amassed an abundance of hides, both for the comfort of the tribe and to trade later at the agency trading post for the precious commodities of coffee, sugar, tobacco, cloth, gunpowder, trinkets, cooking utensils, and what other white man luxuries strike the savages' fancies.

Some days I actually find myself hoping that the hunters will not locate game, for its very fecundity makes more labor for everyone. At the expense of my hands which begin to look prematurely like the hands of a crone, I have become competent in all aspects of skinning, butchering, scraping and tanning hides, drying meats, and cooking over the fire—although as to this last, not all members of our family have fully appreciated my culinary efforts.

I have also made a tenuous peace with the old wife, Quiet One—we are hardly friendly, but she tolerates my presence and no longer do I fear for my life at her hands. However, she still becomes sullen every time I insist on taking a turn at the fire—obviously she feels that I am trying to usurp her position as first wife and head cook. Frankly, I should think that she would be grateful for relief from the chore.

If sometimes I find myself complaining about our daily labors, others among our group are shirking their fair share of work altogether. Since her unsuccessful attempt to "escape" Narcissa White has made it plain to our host/captors that she is here against her will and refuses to cooperate in any way whatsoever. The grand scale of her missionary efforts has been similarly reduced. Having largely given up on saving the souls of the savages, whom she has deemed as yet too crude and unformed to be properly Christianized, she has now turned her attentions to teaching them to be obedient servants to their future white masters.

"She wants to teach them to be slaves, first," Phemie has observed. "Then, as my people have done, they will turn to the white God for spiritual salvation. It is the manner in which conquerors have always created a force of laborers."

Toward this end, Narcissa has taken two savage girls under her wing and is trying to teach them certain "civilized" domestic duties—to curtsy and carry her possessions for her, to say "yes, ma'am" and "no, ma'am" and other such things which appear comical, and even mildly insane, in the middle of the wilderness.

Many of the People do own utensils—pots and pans, tin dishes, and even some poor silverware obtained at the trading post, though some still eat with their fingers.

"After they are settled on the reservation," Narcissa explains, "my instruction in such matters will serve them well. For they will always be able to find employment at the forts in the homes of the officers, and in the white towns and settlements that spring up after the frontier is once and for all secured from the heathens that civilization may extend her noble boundaries without constant fear of their vicious depradations." (Speaking of which, Narcissa has never forgiven her husband for the "involuntary" consummation of their marriage—does not allow him in the lodge, and refuses to say whether or not she is pregnant.)

I have no idea why her "servant girls" go along with this treatment, perhaps simply out of curiosity, or mere politeness, for the savages are both curious and polite in abundance. However, I predict that as a rule these people will make poor domestic help.

Now we have reached our afternoon destination, chosen by an advance guard of scouts, and announced by the old camp crier who rides the length and breadth of our procession, spread out by the end of the day over a distance of several miles.

Regardless of whether our new campsite is intended to accommodate us for one day or several, the women set up each as a perfect replica of the last—with every family and each lodge in the same position relative to the whole. The full tribal circle opens always to the east, to face the rising sun, as does each family circle, as does each individual lodge entrance. This is both a religious and practical consideration, for one awakens to the warmth of the morning sun, and by leaving the lodge flap open in the morning the sun lights, warms, and freshens the whole tipi. The symmetry and order is quite lovely—a kind of art form.

Well before sunset, we have the entire village in place and settled—just as if it had been here for weeks or months. Fires burn, food cooks, children play, men smoke and hold their councils—and, as always, women work . . .

1 August 1875

We have been camped for the past six days along the Tongue River, the single longest encampment since we began traveling. It is a lovely spot situated in a natural bowl at the base of the mountains, well protected from the wind and elements. The small valley is green and lush, with ample grass for the horses, surrounded by low hills and bluffs, the river lined by huge cottonwoods whose leaves rustle softly with the slightest breeze.

I walk down to a pool on the river each morning at first light, my favorite time of day, before the camp is fully awake, to fetch the morning water. The wrens have just taken up their lusty morning songs and warblers flicker like bright yellow flames in the green willows' branches. Often ducks, geese, and cranes flare off the water at my approach, and sometimes a doe deer with a fawn bounds away, tails flagging through the undergrowth. At the river's edge, swallows swoop from their nests in the sandy cliffs to skim insects from the surface, and rising trout make concentric rings upon the pool. I drop my paunch vessel into the cool, moving water and as it fills to tug heavily downstream, I feel a part of this world, pulled like the vessel itself to fill up with this life.

This is the best time to make these scribblings in my journal, a few minutes stolen from the beginning of the day, before the bustle and commotion of camp life begins. I sit on my rock overlooking the pool on the river, the air cool and still, the bluffs still shadowed, the sun not yet risen above them, the constant prairie winds not yet come up . . .

Sometimes Helen Flight joins me at dawn on my rock to sketch the bird life. If we sit very quietly, sandhill and whooping cranes might come back into our pool, blue herons and night herons, geese and ducks of many varieties. She holds her sketch pad open on her lap, pipe clenched firmly between her teeth, eyebrows raised as always in delighted anticipation, as if something perfectly extraordinary is taking place. Periodically when I pause in my writing she gently lifts my notebook from my lap and makes a quick study of a bird in the margins of the page—a swallow swooping for insects on the water, or a Kingfisher perched on a tree branch, holding a fish in its beak. "Perhaps *Mesoke*," she says, handing it back to me, "you and I should consider a collaboration of our own, *'A Woman's Life among the Savages of the Western Prairies'* we might entitle it, letterpress by Mrs. May 'Swallow' Dodd Little Wolf, with illustrations by Mrs. Helen Elizabeth 'Medicine Bird Woman' Flight Hog."

"A splendid idea, Helen!" I answer lightly. "Certain to become a classic in frontier literature!"

"Unfortunately human figures have never been my artistic forte," Helen says. "That is to say, I've always been more comfortable drawing animals—specifically birds. Once I undertook a full-length portrait of my companion Mrs. Ann Hall of Sunderland, who, gazing upon it for the first time, exclaimed: 'Why, Helen, you've got me looking exactly like a roseate spoonbill!' "

Besides Helen's company, if I sit long enough on my rock, we may be joined by Gretchen, Sara, Martha, Daisy, or Phemie—often a number of us get together here—a kind of morning girls' club, I, its self-appointed president.

Daisy is happily much recovered from her night of terror at the hands of the drunken savages, and considerably softened around the edges. Oddly (although under the present circumstances of our lives what can any longer be considered odd?) she has become quite close friends with Phemie since her "accident."

"Did *y'all* hear the news about my dear friend, Euphemia Washington?"

Daisy asked us this morning, holding her little poodle Fern Louise in her lap. "She has just been asked to join the Crazy Dogs warrior society—an event without precedent among the savages. And *Ah* do not mean as a ceremonial hostess at social events. *Ah* mean as a *full*-fledged warrior woman. The very *fuust taame* in the history of the tribe that a woman has been so honored—and a *whaate* woman to boot. Aren't *y'all* so proud? Fern Louise and I are, aren't we, darlin'? We believe it is a great honor to us all, *havin'* come about naturally due to Miss Phemie's prowess on the games field and in the *huuunt*."

Now little Sara beams and chatters away in Cheyenne, laughing with Pretty Walker, the daughter of Quiet One and Little Wolf, who often accompanies me to the fetch the water. The Indians call Sara Little White Girl Who Speaks Cheyenne, for she has been the first among us to learn their language fluently; they can hardly appreciate the full irony of the fact that prior to speaking Cheyenne she was mute! Now she has blossomed like a wild rose under the prairie sun—happier and healthier than I've ever seen her. I can hardly believe that she is the same frail and frightened child who clung so desperately to me on the long train ride west. She and her slender young husband, Yellow Wolf, are inseparable, thick as thieves—two people have never been more deeply in love.

Speaking of which, dear Gretchen, *Moma'xehahtahe,* she is now called, or Big Foot, has reconciled with her foolish husband, No Brains, whom she has well cowed and completely under her thumb—or her foot, I should say—since the dark night of whiskey drinking earlier this summer.

He is an indolent, vain fellow with a well-deserved reputation as a poor provider for his family. Often Gretchen must heave him out of the tent with strict instructions to "*Brink* home dinner you *bick* lazy dope!" and on the all too frequent occasions when No Brains has returned from the hunt with an empty packhorse, we have witnessed a bizarre, albeit not unamusing spectacle: a contingent of angry family members, led by Gretchen herself, followed by the man's mother and any children who happen to join in, chasing the fool through the camp with sticks. *"Yah!* You great *bick stupit* idiot," Gretchen, red-faced with Swiss wrath, hollers at him, kicking him in his buttocks and smacking him roundly about the head and shoulders with her stick, as the children lash at his legs. "How you expect to support a family if you can't even *brink* home meat to put on *da* table? *Vee* must depend on your *gottdamnt brudder* and your *udder* friends to feed and clothe us. I *vill* not be a charity case! I always *vork hart* for my own living and I not take handouts now! You *stupit* silly jughead! Look at you, you all *drest* up, you got all *dat* fancy stuff, and you could not bring home meat if the *da gottdamnt* buffalo falls dead at your feet! You great *stupit* nincompoop!"

And poor No Brains stumbles through the camp, trying to escape Gretchen's Big Foot, while warding off the others' battery of blows until inevitably he stumbles and falls to the ground where he is set upon by the smallest children who strike him with their little sticks and shout insulting epithets at him, laughing gaily all the while. Let it not be said that the hunter's life on the prairie is an easy one.

And yet in quieter moments, when we meet, as now, on our rock above the pool of the river in the still of the morning, Gretchen, as placid as a dairy cow, expresses her great fondness for this same buffoon. She is, I think, grateful to have a husband at last, and only wants him to make something of himself.

"I admit *dat* he is not *da* brightest fellow, in *da* whole *vorld, dat* is true," Gretchen says in his defense. "But before *da* children come, I *vill* teach *da* big ninnyhammer how to be a *goot hustband* and provider. I know I *yam* not a pretty girl myself, but I always *vork hart* and I make a nice home for my family *vedder dey* be Indian people or white people—it don't matter to me. I am a *hartvorking,* tidy person, and I *vill* be a *goot mudder* to my children—and a *goot vife* to my *hustband. Dat* is how I was taught by my own *mudder.* And, you know girls, *dat* fellow of mine he may be *da* biggest pumpkinhead in *da* whole tribe, but he is still my man . . . you know, and he likes me . . . *yah*!" she covers her mouth and giggles. "He likes me lots," she adds striking her robust breast with a flat hand. "He loves my *bick* titties! All he wants to do is to roll in *da* buffalo robes with me!" And we all laugh. Bless her heart.

Now the camp begins to stir, and others come down to the water's edge to fill their water paunches, and the men, the members of the Savage Men's Bathing Club arrive at the water for their morning dip, and we can hear them splashing about up- or downriver, and the birds begin to lift off, flushed by the human congress in their domain, the deep sounds of hundreds of heavy wings all along the river, the cacophonous cries of the rising birds like a discordant natural orchestra—yakking and honking and wailing and warbling—fading away to be replaced by the voices of women, children, and men. In the distance, the camp crier begins his rounds . . . calling his messages in a high shrill voice, marking the end of this quiet, best time of day . . .

Sometimes I send Pretty Walker back with the water paunch while I stay on writing or visiting with my friends. She is a lovely thing—the boys can hardly keep their shy eyes off her—slender and long-legged like her father, moves with the grace of a dancer, is not so sullen and suspicious as her mother—an eager, open-natured child, with bright, intelligent eyes. She enjoys the company of us white women, and we have been teaching her a few words of English, while she, in turn, helps us with our Cheyenne. Most of us are less self-conscious about speaking the language now, and can make ourselves understood on a rudimentary level—which, as these people are hardly given to complicated philosophical discourse, is usually quite sufficient. Pretty Walker has been most useful to us in this regard, and we have great fun with her, although I'm afraid that our budding friendship has not entirely met with the approval of her mother.

I have avoided this next topic for the fact that it so exceeds the bounds of propriety, but I must here make mention of one of the most difficult adjustments that we have had to make. That is in the matter of toilet facilities. Fortunately, ours is a very cleanly tribe—unlike some of the others. One might well imagine the stinking mess that would accumulate in a camp of two hundred people if everyone simply went off to do their business at random in the bushes. We have in our recent travels come across the vacated campsites of other tribes—the stench announcing their location from miles away.

The Cheyennes have devised a relatively hygienic solution to this—although one that does not afford a great deal of privacy. In each camp a central area is established, always placed downwind of the village, where all are expected to do their business. Young boys are assigned to guard these communal latrines and to make sure that waste is immediately buried. This is a boy's first job after which he graduates when older to guarding the horses. Latrine duty and the burying of feces is done not only for reasons of basic sanitation, but also because there are many dogs about the camp and, given the opportunity, dogs will . . . forgive me, please, for this is a vile subject . . . roll in, and even eat, human excrement.

For our part, we white women have made certain improvements on the latrine system. Little Marie Blanche, our French girl (who has, after all, "married" her murdered husband's brother), was quite appalled by the whole thing. The French being accustomed to irregular bathing, have devised many clever means of hygienic compensation, and thus Marie Blanche has insisted that water vessels, to serve the function of "bidets," be installed and maintained by the "B.M. boys," as we call them. Thus in this one small—but to a woman, essential—area I think perhaps we have taught the savages something useful. But surely I've said enough on a subject which requires no more graphic description . . .

Despite my present acceptance of our lot, even a certain contentment, I have had an uneasy premonition of late—an indefinable sense of gloom lurks in the background of my general good spirits. I wonder as I strain to see the page in the silvery half-light of dawn, if something were to happen to prevent my return to civilization, who would ever read these words? What would become of my dear children, Hortense and William, should I be unable to make my way back to them? I pray that the letter Gertie took for me will reach them, but how can I know that Father and Mother will ever show it to them when they are old enough to read? Such thoughts fill me with unease. Whatever is to become of me, I should be greatly consoled by the knowledge that my children might one day learn something of their mother's life among the savages, might understand that however eccentric she may have been—however stubborn, foolish, and impetuous—she was not insane . . .

7 August 1875

My recent gloomy premonitions have come more horribly true than ever I could have imagined, for the worst catastrophe possible has befallen us. On this, our darkest day yet, I and several of my compatriots find ourselves in a desperate predicament.

The day began as peacefully and uneventfully as any other. At dawn I sat upon my rock overlooking the pool on the Tongue River near our camp. I was just preparing to unstrap my notebook from my back. Helen Flight sat on one side of me, waiting for the light of day to be favorable for sketching; Martha, Sara, and little Pretty Walker sat on my other side. The Kelly twins, too, had joined us and were squatting on the water's edge about to toss a hook and line into the pool after trout for their breakfast. Gretchen had just lumbered down to fill her own water paunch and squatted now beside the stream.

We all sensed, I think, at exactly the same moment that something was amiss, for the birds which had already taken up their morning song went suddenly silent—a lull broken by the sound of several dozen ducks and geese getting up all at once off the water just downstream from us. We looked up from our respective tasks but no sooner had we done so, than in a heartbeat's time we were each descended upon at once, filthy hands clamped over our mouths, knives held at our throats, arms like iron bounds rendering us immobile. The single sound that could be heard over the wingbeats of the rising waterfowl was a heavy thump from a stone war club and a miserable groan as our friend Gretchen collapsed in a heap at the water's edge.

So well orchestrated was our abduction, that, as I look back on it now,

I believe our attackers must have been watching us, perhaps for several days—assessing our comings and goings, gauging the force necessary to carry us off. And Gretchen, with her great size and obvious strength, must have appeared more to them than they believed one or even two men could comfortably handle, and thus they had rendered her, and her alone, unconscious.

So quickly, stealthily, and powerfully were we overcome, that there was no question of resisting. We knew that if we dared struggle or tried to cry out, our throats would be instantly cut. Now each of us, helpless and paralyzed with terror, was half-dragged, half-carried, downstream from whence our abductors must have come. One particularly large and fearsome-looking fellow hoisted Gretchen over his shoulder and carried her as if she were a sack of potatoes. I did not know yet to what tribe these men belonged, but they were as a rule taller and rather fairer-skinned than our own Cheyennes, were dressed some of them in flannel shirts of white man manufacture, and several wore black Army hats with the tops cut out and the sides wrapped in feathers and variously colored cloth.

At a shallow ford downstream they carried us across the river, where several younger boys waited in a grove of cottonwood trees, holding a string of horses. Among these I recognized a number of our own mounts. Here our hands and feet were bound with rawhide thongs and cloth gags tied over our mouths, and we were very roughly thrown across the pommels of the saddles like so many fresh-killed deer carcasses. One of our savage abductors then climbed up behind each of us.

I do not know exactly how long we traveled thus—it must have been several hours at least, but seemed far longer so great was our pain and discomfort. I was certain that they had killed poor Gretchen for she remained unconscious, and, from the little I could turn my head to look, appeared lifeless where she lay across the pommel. Not until what must have been a full hour had passed was I relieved to hear a moan of life issue from her.

After the hard and agonizing ride, during which we could do nothing but reflect helplessly upon our situation, we arrived at last at a small camp of a half dozen or so makeshift lodges—little more than stick lean-tos covered with canvas—clearly the temporary encampment of a hunting or war party, for there were no women about, only several more young men who met us when we rode in. Now once again we were handled with extreme roughness, thrown off the horses' backs to sprawl in the dirt. This seemed to excite the savages to much laughter and taunting in their unfamiliar tongue.

At last they untied our hands and feet and removed the gags from our mouths. Mine had been so tightly bound that my mouth was split and bleeding at its corners. When free I scrambled on my hands and knees to attend to little Pretty Walker, the youngest and most terrified among us. The Cheyenne children are brought up on tales of being captured thus by other tribes—like the boogeyman stories of our own culture—and this was clearly the girl's worst nightmare come true. *"Ooetaneo'o,"* she wailed in terror. *"Ooetaneo'o."*

So frightened was she that I could not understand what she was trying to say, until Sara spoke up. "Crow," she translated. "She says that these men are Crow." Only later did I realize that it was the first, and the last, time that I would ever hear our Sara speak a word of English.

We all knew the Crow to be the archenemy of the Cheyenne—and a loutish-looking bunch at that with their half-white man clothing and preposterous Army hats, they swaggered and gloated and made merry at our despair. Poor Martha, scared witless herself and in a state of evident shock, began repeating: "They're going to kill us, they're going to kill us all. I know they're going to kill us . . . they're going to kill us all . . ."

Finally, Meggie Kelly spoke sharply to her. *"Showt* up, Martha," she said. "If they were plannin' to kill us, they'd a *doon* so by now. They'd not have gone to all the trouble of carrying us away *loyke* this."

"Aye, Meggie's right," said her sister in a low voice, "They'll not *moorder* us yet. First they're going to *folk* us. Look at that one there. He's *sportin'* a wood, he is."

It was true that one of the men was in a state of erection beneath his breechclout, and the other men, now noticing his condition, laughed and urged him on.

Now the wretch grabbed my little Sara by her hair, and began to drag her toward one of the crude huts. It was less a conscious selection of the girl than that she happened to be in the nearest proximity to him. "No," I screamed, and I grasped the attacker's leg, "not her, please, not her. Take me."

"*Aye,* ya filthy beggar," said Susie Kelly, taking ahold of the man's other leg, "or me! Let that child go, goddamn *ya*!"

Our pathetic entreaties seemed to elicit much further merriment among the man's cohorts. After a short struggle the savage shook loose of Susie's grasp and then caught me square in the jaw with a kick that sent me sprawling. All but Martha, who was too frightened to move, and poor Gretchen, who lay upon the ground half-conscious and groaning, tried to come to our aid, but the savages held them back.

The fiend who dragged her now released his grasp on Sara's hair, fell atop her, and began to force apart her legs. The girl wept and struggled against him. Never as long as I live will I forget the look of silent intensity on her young face, the tears of sorrow that ran down her cheeks. I knew in that instant that this same unspeakable fate must have befallen her as a child growing up in that awful asylum—that her muteness had been her final strength, her final testimony to the cruelty of this world. Held on the ground now by another of them and helpless to stop the crime, I began to weep myself, to plead, to beg, to pray to God . . .

I do not know where the knife came from. Some said later that it belonged to the Crow and that Sara took it from his belt, others that she had it concealed all along beneath her dress. But I saw the flash of steel as it came up in her hand and she plunged the blade into the man's neck as he lay atop her. He made a surprised gurgling sound and clawed wildly at the knife handle, finally pulling the blade free as a great geyser of blood shot like a fountain from his neck. But with his last breath before he bled to death and fell lifeless atop her, he drew the knife across our dear Sara's throat, and in a terrible instant the life drained from her eyes.

Now darkness falls and we sit huddled together upon the ground inside one of the rude stick shelters. Here we try to console one another, weeping softly and whispering together. Several of the younger savages squat in front of the entrance, guarding us, but they have not bothered to bind our hands again for all fight has left us. After they murdered Sara, the filthy brutes violated the rest of us in turn . . . we all simply endured, silently, their vicious assaults . . . I managed only to save the child Pretty Walker from this fate, distracting her would-be assailant by offering myself a second time in her stead . . . I have my notebook, strapped all along to my back, open in my lap and here I make these wretched and perhaps final entries . . .

"Why do you still write in your journal, May?" Martha asked me a moment ago in a small, hopeless voice. "What difference does any of it make now?"

"I don't know, Martha," I said. "Perhaps I write to stay alive, to keep us all alive."

Helen Flight laughed bleakly. "Yes," she said, "I understand perfectly, May. Your pen is your medicine and as long as you're exercising it, you are elsewhere engaged, you are alive. In spite of everything, we are all still alive . . . that is to say, except, of course, for dear little Sara."

We all looked at the child's body, which lay cold and stiffening, where we had dragged her to the rear of the hut.

"I do not wish to live any longer," Martha said. "Perhaps Sara was the lucky one. Surely death would be a blessing after what has befallen us . . . and what we have to look forward to."

"Aw stop *yer* damn whinin', Martha," said Meggie Kelly. "Susie and me are going to *'ave* our babies, and we plan to be alive for that event. Isn't that so, sister?"

"Right, Meggie," said Susie. "We're goin' to be mothers we are. The lads are goin' to come for us, I just know they will."

"Yes, I believe so myself," said Helen. "Chin up, Martha. We've been used abominably ill, it's true, but our husbands aren't going to allow the Crows to just walk off with their wives. Your own husband, Tangle Hair, is, after all, head man of the Crazy Dog soldiers—May's husband, Little Wolf, head man of the Elk warriors, of which society my own Mr. Hog is second-in-command—and a most capable fellow he is, too, if I may say so. I'm quite certain the chaps have already set out to rescue us. That they will swoop down at any moment and exact their vengeance against these criminals."

Brave Gretchen, who was still barely sensible from the terrible blow she took, and whom the savages had at least spared in their ravishment, now raised her head weakly from where she lay beside us. "*Yah* and don't forget my *hustband* No Brains, either," she said. "He come for me. I know he *vill*."

We are allowed no fire and the night air is chilly and so we close in together for warmth and what little comfort we can offer one another . . .

8 August 1875

Yes, thank God! Helen was correct, we have been saved, delivered to safety, returned to our own people! The Crow thieves—kidnappers, murderers, rapists, fiends—are dead. Our warriors killed even some of the young men among them . . . of that I am sorry, for they were little more than boys, though I believe that several escaped in the ensuing melee . . .

The attack came just at dawn after the darkest twenty-four hours of our lives. The Crow guards must have first been silently eliminated, for our other captors were still asleep inside their huts when our brave warriors stormed the camp. The Crows had barely time to exit their shelters before they were struck down, butchered amidst their own cries of surprise and the bloodcurdling shrieks of our men. My husband Little Wolf himself led the charge, seemed not like a man at all but like a God of vengeance, an animal, a bear, fearless, without mercy. He carried a shield and a lance as he rode, striking down the enemy like the wrath of God itself. Truly he was, at that moment, my knight in shining armor.

We women stayed huddled in our shelter but could see the terrible carnage from the open entranceway. Riding right alongside the men, but for her breechclout naked atop her white horse, was our own brave Phemie. The Crows must have been paralyzed with terror at the sight of this howling warrior woman bearing down upon them, drawing her bow like a mythic goddess of war to drive an arrow through the heart of an enemy and then with another bloodcurdling cry, to smote a second with her club. Good God, what a vision . . .

All of our husbands had come for us, just as Helen had predicted, yes, even No Brains, who was finely dressed for battle in an elaborately ornamented war shirt but whom I feel certain held back until the initial charge was over and then came in to count coup upon the already dead and stricken enemy.

The boy Yellow Wolf was the very first to enter our hut and when he saw his beloved bride laid out there cold and dead, a more piteous howling of grief I have never before heard. He went to her, gathered her corpse in his arms, and pressed her to his chest. All of us wept anew for our friend and for her young husband's splendid grief.

Leaving the boy to his private mourning, we exited the shelter to search out our own husbands amidst the chaos of death and dying. The scalps of enemies were being taken . . . other mutilations occurring . . . the scene had an unreal, dreamlike quality to it—as if we were there and yet not there . . . truly we are all of us savages now . . . anointed together in this bloody sacrament of revenge . . . for we took pleasure in our enemies' death and mutilations, and shall never be the same for it . . . we have seen the savagery in our own hearts . . . have exulted in blood and vengeance . . . have danced over the scalps of enemies . . . all that we have done, God help us . . .

The Cheyenne men tend not to be demonstrative in matters of conjugal affection, but when the Kelly girls saw their own twin husbands they ran to them in joy, leapt upon their ponies like sprites, wrapping their legs about the young men's waists, hugging them about the shoulders and kissing them wildly on their faces and necks. "God bless *ya*, lads," they said. "God bless *ya*. We knew *ya'd* come for us. We knew you'd save *yore* dear blessed wives."

Gretchen, much recovered from her injury, but still wobbly and weak-kneed, found her own buffoonish husband, who was afoot leading his horse. No Brains was all puffed up like a cock with his recent coups and himself waved a bloody enemy scalp for all to see.

My husband Little Wolf sat his mount, quiet and still as is his way, watchful and surveying the scene like the dominant wolf of the pack. When he spied me with his daughter Pretty Walker beside me, he rode directly to us and slipped from his horse.

The child began immediately to weep, threw herself into her father's arms.

"Neve'ea'xaeme, nahtona," Little Wolf said, holding her. *"Neve'ea'xaeme, nahtona.* Do not cry, my daughter."

And then he looked over the child's shoulder at me. *"Ena'so'eehovo, Mesoke?* They raped her, Swallow?"

I shook my head, no, and to the next question in my husband's eyes, I cast my own eyes to the ground, and began to weep myself, *"Nasaatone'oetohe, naehame,* I could not stop him, my husband. *Nasaatone'oetohe."*

Little Wolf smiled gently at me, and nodded and when he spoke, I think, it was for the comfort of us both. *"Eesepeheva'e,"* he said. *"Eesepeheva'e.* It is all right now."

Riding back into our camp this afternoon, we were greeted by the joyful trilling of our women as all ran out to meet us. But when the family of Yellow Wolf saw him bringing up the rear, leading a horse with the body of *Ve'ho'a'o'ke* laid across it, a high keening arose from some of the women, and spread throughout the camp.

9 August 1875

This morning we buried Sara and the unborn child she carried. Her body was dressed in her Cheyenne wedding gown and wrapped in a white buffalo hide, covered with rocks in a shallow grave on the prairie.

There had been much discussion among all concerned about whether the girl should have a Christian or a traditional Cheyenne burial. Of course, Reverend Hare and Narcissa White argued for the former. But others of us believed that the only true happiness our Sara had ever known in her short life on this earth had been among these people. And we wished for her soul to go to the place the Cheyennes call *Seano*—the place of the dead—which is reached by following the Hanging Road in the Sky, the Milky Way. Here the Cheyennes believe that all the People who have ever died live with their Creator, *He'amaveho'e*. In *Seano* they live in villages just as they did on earth—hunting, working, eating, playing, loving, and making war. And all go to the place of the dead, regardless of whether they were good or bad on earth, virtuous or evil, brave or cowardly—everyone—and eventually in *Seano* all are reunited with the souls of their loved ones.

"Heaven," I said to the Reverend Hare. *"Seano,* is just like our own Heaven. What difference is there, Father?"

"A substantial difference, Miss Dodd," said the Reverend, "for it is not a Christian heaven and any soul can gain entrance there without regard to baptism, without reward for virtue or punishment for sin. Such a place does not exist, cannot exist, for how can there be a heaven unless there is a hell?"

"This earth, Reverend," I said, "is both a heaven and a hell. No one knew that better than our Sara. She should be allowed a simple heathen burial by her husband."

But the Reverend remained, as I knew he would, implacable on the subject. "The child was baptized in the only true church," he said, "and her body must receive the holy sacraments so that her soul may enter the Kingdom of Our Lord."

And so, finally, both services were conducted, one by Reverend Hare and the other by Yellow Wolf and his family, who carried Sara's body to its final resting place, leading her saddled horse, which to all of our shock the boy killed there beside her grave, drew a knife across its throat—just as his young wife had died herself—so that the horse fell to its knees with a pathetic trumpeting of air escaping its severed windpipe. *"Ve'ho'a'o'ke* must have her horse," Yellow Wolf explained as the horse toppled over on its side and the light faded from its eyes, "to ride the Hanging Road to *Seano.*"

Thus Sara's soul rode her horse wherever she wished to go—a choice of heavens—and all were satisfied.

11 August 1875

Our funeral procession left Yellow Wolf sitting cross-legged beside the grave of his bride. For two days and two nights, we have heard the boy's wails of mourning carried on the wind.

I need hardly say that it has been a difficult time for us all . . . not only dear Sara's tragic end but our own debasement at the hands of the Crows has changed things among us, and within us, things that we can as yet only faintly comprehend.

But for hollow platitudes, the Reverend offers us scant comfort and we have, as always, only each other for solace . . . and thank God for that.

And so we have made a pact together, each of us, never to speak of that night, or the following day, neither among ourselves, nor with any of the others. We cannot change what has happened and so we must go forward away from it.

Our Cheyenne families have taken us back into their generous bosoms, caring for us with great solicitude and kindness, without a hint of reproach—which seems to be the domain of a few of our own women alone. Of course, Narcissa White treats us as if our little group had somehow enticed the Crows to carry us away, that whatever humiliation we may have suffered at their hands was just punishment for our sins and confirmation of her own righteousness.

Since our ordeal I have hardly let my husband out of my sight—truly he is my savior and protector, a good, brave man. I feel a greater attachment to him now than ever, though in a strange way more as a daughter than as a wife. I have taken, the past few nights since our return, to slipping under the buffalo robes with him, after all in our tent sleep—not, of course, for the reason of sexual intimacy, but only to feel him beside me, to curl next to him and take comfort in the smooth warmth of his skin, the fine wild smell of him. The old wife Quiet One has been extremely kind to me; I know that she is aware of these nightly visits but does not begrudge me them. I believe that she knows of my efforts to protect her child, Pretty Walker, who since our return, has herself slept in her mother's bed. The child and I have both now seen the boogeyman in the flesh and are more than ever afraid of him.

20 August 1875

By my estimation I am now approaching the third month of pregnancy. I do not believe that my baby has been injured and for that I am grateful. Martha and the Kelly girls, too, seem healthy in their terms. As does Gretchen. Thank God.

Of my closest circle of friends only Phemie and Helen Flight seem not to be with child. Helen, of course, has already confessed to me about having lied to the medical examiner regarding the matter of her fertility in order to be accepted into this program.

"Mr. Hog is really a most agreeable fellow," she says now, "but he has since our marriage been possessed of the unfortunate male notion that unless he impregnates his wife he is something less than a man. He used to inquire of me almost daily, by rubbing his stomach hopefully, if I was yet with child, and when I answered in the negative . . . well, then he would wish to try again! I must say, it got to be a dreadfully tiresome business.

However since our abduction and safe return he has made no further overtures toward me. I am able henceforth to concentrate my efforts solely on improving my 'medicine.'"

For her part Phemie is still wearing her chastity string, and merely chuckles deeply. "Like you, Helen, I have an occupation," she says. "I am a hunter, and now a warrior, which is hardly a suitable profession for a prospective mother. Moreover from the time that I was a child men have forced themselves upon me whenever they so desired. I am very fond of my husband, *Mo'ohtaeve'ho'e,* and one day perhaps I shall have his child. But I shall decide when I am ready."

As for the rest of us, we have the comfort of all being pregnant together, so that we may share the experience, commiserate, make plans. By our estimation our babies will be born next February, and although we worry about the prospect of being far along in our terms throughout the cold winter months, hopefully we shall be more permanently encamped then. We may even expect to be living at one of the agencies with a doctor and hospital nearby—for there has been talk among some of the men in council recently about going in this year.

23 August 1875

A very ugly thing has occurred today, the repercussions of which will be felt for a long time to come. Hearing shouts of distress from Reverend Hare and angry cries from a mob of savages, a number of us hurried in the direction of the Reverend's lodge. There we came upon a shocking scene.

A man named *Hataveseve'hame,* Bad Horse, was driving the naked Reverend from his and Dog Woman's lodge with a quirt. The Reverend—huge, pink, and hairless—was sobbing and trying to protect himself from the man's lashes, which were raising angry red welts all over the fat man's body. A number of people had gathered, including other members of Bad Horse's family. Bad Horse's wife, a short, squat woman named *Kohenaa'e'e,* Bear Sings Woman, came from the Reverend's lodge carrying their young son—who was also naked, although, especially among the children, such a natural state is not in the least bit unusual. Still it became clear what had occurred, for the Reverend in his confused blubbering combination of Cheyenne and English was trying to explain that he had only been giving the boy instruction in his catechism. Which explanation did not placate the furious father, who continued to drive the Reverend with vicious blows of his quirt.

I stepped up beside Susie Kelly who, with her sister, had joined the small crowd of onlookers. "Should we do something to help him?" I asked, for my dislike of the man notwithstanding, it was a pathetic sight.

" 'Tis a family matter, May," Susie said. "The old hypocrite got caught *booggerin'* the boy. *'Appens* all the time, you know, amongst the Catholics. When Meggie an' me was growin' up in the orphanage, the old priests used to *boogger* the lads *bloody*. Isn't that so, Meggie?"

"Right, Susie, a sad thing, it 'tis, too," said Meggie. "For lads that take it up that chute that way become angry men, that's been my experience. I don't believe they've ever seen such a thing among these people. Even the old Nancy Boys amongst them like the Father's roommate don't fool with the young lads. They say the old *he'emane'e* are celibate."

"He's a lost soul," I said of the pathetic Reverend, "who may not deserve, but still requires, mercy."

"Noothin' to be *doon* for him, May," said Susie. "They won't kill the old *booger*. They're just goin' to teach him a *goood* lesson."

And indeed, the outraged parents' fury soon abated, the family went home with their son, and the crowd dispersed. Then the twins and I went to our fallen spiritual advisor, who lay curled upon the ground, reduced to a quivering mass of torn red flesh. We helped him back into his lodge, where old Dog Woman, clucking his concern, ministered to his wounds.

I'm afraid that the Big White Rabbit's disgrace among the People is final, and irrevocable. I must say, beyond the fact that some of us have fulfilled our end of the bargain by becoming pregnant, we do not seem to be having much success in instructing the savages in the benefits of civilized ways.

28 August 1875

We are on the move again. This time and for the first time since our arrival we are dividing into several groups and heading off in different directions. The game has dispersed and so must the People, for it is easier for smaller bands to feed themselves than one large band all together.

This separation has caused a great deal of anxiety among our women. Martha is nearly hysterical with worry as she and her husband Mr. Tangle Hair belong to a different band than my family, and as a consequence we will be separated—possibly for weeks . . . possibly longer.

"I cannot leave you, May," the poor thing said this morning when we learned of our imminent departure. "Oh, dear God, what shall I do without you?"

"You'll be fine, Martha," I tried to console her. "You'll have others in your group."

"For how long are we to be apart?" Martha asked. "I cannot bear the thought. What's to become of us?"

"You must stop worrying so," I said. "You worry yourself sick and then everything turns out fine after all, does it not?"

Martha laughed. "My friend," she said, "if you call the events of the past months, and especially those of the past weeks, 'fine,' truly you possess a serenity that will never be mine. I cannot survive without you to give me strength."

"Don't be silly," I said. "Of course you can, dear. We will be together again soon enough."

"How can you know that, May?" she asked. "How can we know that we'll ever see each other again?"

"There you go worrying again," I said, trying to be lighthearted. "You are soon to be a mother, and I have always been a believer in the old saw that anxious mothers give birth to anxious babies."

"Of course you're right, May," she said. "But I cannot help myself. I am anxious by nature. I never should have come here to the wilderness . . . I'm too much of a mouse, terrified of everything . . ."

"After what you have been through, Martha," I said, "you have every right to be terrified."

"But you are not, May," she said. "I would give everything to be like you—intrepid and unafraid. I know that we are not to speak of that night, but I must tell you this . . . I must tell you how proud I was of you . . . and I'm sorry, I'm so sorry I didn't help you when they murdered Sara . . ." Now Martha had begun to weep. "I was so frightened, May. I wanted to come to your aid, but I could not, I could not move. Perhaps if I had been able to help you the wretch wouldn't have killed her . . ."

"You must never think that, Martha," I said, sharply. "And you must honor our pact not to speak of that night. There was nothing any of us could have done to save the child."

"Yes, but you protected Pretty Walker," Martha said. "I would never have had the courage to do what you did, May."

"Nonsense," I said. "Enough of that, Martha."

And then she put her arms around me and hugged me with all her might. "Tell me something to give me courage, May."

"I can tell you one thing only, my dearest friend," I said. "And then we will not speak of it again. You must promise me that."

"Yes, of course, I do."

"I was just as terrified as you that night, as everyone else," I said. "I have been from the beginning of this experience. But I've learned to disguise my fear. I made the vow to myself on our very first day, that whenever I was most afraid for my life I would think of my babies, my Hortense and Willie, and I would find peace in knowing that they are safe, I would seek serenity in the image of their little hearts beating calmly. That's what I thought of when the savages set upon me that night. I realized that the worse thing that could happen to me was not that I should be killed—but that this baby I carry would die. And thus I submitted. And I endured. Just as you and the others endured. Because we are women, because we are mothers some of us, and others mothers to be. And some, like Helen Flight, are just plain strong. Do you remember what Helen said once in our discussion on the subject of a warrior's medicine? That if they believed strongly enough in their own power, perhaps they are protected by it?"

"Yes, I remember," Martha said, "and you said it was pure poppycock! Pure superstition!"

"Yes, I did," I admitted, and I laughed. "And truth be known, I still think so! But you must remember, Martha, that you survived that night yourself, you submitted and endured, and by doing so you saved your baby. Your power as a woman, as a mother, is your medicine, and it saved you. Take your courage from that. Do not be afraid of our separation. Have faith that it is only temporary, that you will be well protected by your husband, your family, and the friends who accompany you, and that you and I shall be reunited again in due time."

6 September 1875

Our band heads south. We are told that we are returning to Fort Laramie to trade at the post there for sufficient provisions to see us through the coming winter. Little Wolf also wishes to discuss with the fort commander the matter of the remainder of the white brides that have been promised to his young warriors by the Great White Father. I have neither tried to disabuse him of this notion nor said a word to him of Gertie's report to me on the subject. There have already been disgruntled murmurings of late among some of the Cheyennes that once again the whites are reneging on a treaty provision, for, of course, no more brides have been sent since our arrival—and clearly no more will be.

This will be our first contact with civilization since we were given over to the People in May . . . only five months. But it seems a lifetime. After all that we have endured I am filled with a strange trepidation about the prospect of returning to the fort. Of course, I cannot help but wonder if Captain Bourke will be still stationed there with his new bride. I have had no more word from him since Gertie's visit earlier in the summer. And since that time we have been almost constantly on the move.

Presently we are extremely well supplied with buffalo robes and hides, elk, deer, and antelope skins, so much so that nearly all of our horses are fully packed and more of the People are afoot. There is talk among the young men about launching yet another horse-stealing raid against the Crows. Others talk of stealing horses from some of the white settlements we pass on the way to the fort. The "old men chiefs" such as my husband council against this, for they believe that we are at peace with the whites.

I, myself, am largely afoot, for my own horse Soldier has been pressed into duty carrying parfleches of household goods. And so I walk to lessen his burden. I do not mind to walk, in fact in some ways prefer it. Whatever one may say about the hardships of this nomadic life, we are all of us women in magnificent physical condition. I had hardly realized how sedentary and soft of muscle I had become during my long incarceration in the asylum; one begins to take the inactivity for granted and nearly forgets the joys of healthful outdoor exercise. The first weeks among the savages every muscle and every bone in my body ached with fatigue. But now I am fit as a fiddle. So it is with the other women, some of whom I hardly recognize any longer. Almost all have lost weight, and are darker of skin and sleek as racehorses. I believe from this experience that Caucasian women should also discover the healthful benefits of this open-aired life of physical activity.

I'm happy to report that Helen Flight and her husband are included in our little band as are Phemie and the Kelly girls. Of my closest friends Gretchen, Martha, and Daisy Lovelace are all headed off in separate directions. Poor Ada Ware has loyally remained with her murderer husband and continues to live on the periphery of the Dull Knife band, who themselves are off, God knows where. It is much like keeping track of separate flocks of geese, and while not wishing to alarm poor Martha on the subject, I have no idea how or when we will be reunited.

Both the unfortunate Reverend Hare and Narcissa White have elected to join Little Wolf's band—presumably because ours is headed to the fort. After the former's disgrace, he trails some distance behind us on his white mule, like a penitent or an outcast himself. I never cared for the man, but I feel some pity for him now. I won't be surprised if, after we reach the fort, we will be seeing the last of him. As to Narcissa, after the conspicuous lack of success of her own mission, I have a suspicion that she, too, may be plotting a defection.

Most of the southern Cheyennes have already departed back to their own country, while a few accompany us to Fort Laramie and from there will continue south. I am deeply distressed to report that after a much welcome absence of nearly two months the damnable wretch Jules Seminole is again among us. I hope that we will have seen the last of the lout after we reach Fort Laramie, when he will surely continue on south with the rest of his people. After my experience at the hands of the Crows I am less able than ever to tolerate his presence.

"Exoxohenetamo'ane," I finally said to my husband the last time the man came skulking around our lodge. "He talks dirty to me."

Little Wolf's face darkened in rage. And there the matter rests.

Our smaller group is able to move with even greater dispatch, breaking camp early every morning and traveling hard until nearly dusk. I do not know how many miles we cover each day. The country itself is quite pretty—rolling prairie grassland cut periodically by river courses, the water low now after the dry summer, the whorled grasses already beginning to turn their autumnal shades of yellow. A chill fall wind blows down out of the north reminding us all of the coming winter.

Keeping the Bighorn Mountains to the West, we move roughly south by southeast, across the Tongue, where Hanging Woman Creek flows into it, to the junction of the Clear River and the Powder, following the Powder down to the Crazy Woman Fork and then east and south toward the Belle Fourche. At least this is how I mark the watercourses on my Army map, though some have different names among the whites than the Indians. Beyond the Belle Fourche, the buffalo-grass prairie gives way gradually to a series of desolate, arid buttes, rocky canyons, and dry creek bottoms. We hurry across this inhospitable desert for the only water to be found here is brackish and alkaline, and impossible to drink.

One day we were just able to make out the faint outline of the Black Hills rising up on the eastern horizon, and the next day we were close enough to see the pine-studded slopes but these we kept to our left as we headed south on the prairie's edge.

10 September 1875

A war party of Oglala Sioux has ridden down out of the Black Hills to intercept us. Fortunately these people are close allies of the Cheyennes, and members of the party have relatives in our own camp. Even though they had identified us as friends, the warriors made a spectacular entrance, quite clearly designed to impress us—which it most certainly did—with their faces painted like demons, they were dressed in all manner of elaborately beaded and adorned attire, yipping and wheeling their horses—a more ferocious-looking bunch I have never before seen.

It has been my observation that the savages are showmen of the first order who spend a great deal of time on their personal toilet and appearance and no more so when they prepare for war. The old medicine man, White Bull, has explained to Helen Flight that a warrior must always look his best when going off to wage war in the event that he is killed in battle. For no warrior wishes to embarrass himself by being underdressed when he goes to meet his maker, the Great Medicine. "So you see, May," said Helen Flight with perfect delight, "it's an artist's dream come true, for not only do I adorn the warrior for his protection in battle, but I adorn him so that he might make a good impression on the Great Medicine. That is to say, what more can the artist hope for than to have her work viewed by God in his heaven?" I hardly need mention that Helen, although she professes to be an Anglican, is nearly as irreverent as I.

Although there is much intermarriage between the Sioux people and the Cheyennes, Little Wolf does not speak their language, and does not generally care for them. He believes that their women are unvirtuous. Truly my husband is very much of a tribalist and has kept himself and his family separate from these allies, almost as much as he has from contact with the whites.

Nevertheless, after the warriors—perhaps thirty in number—had finished their display of horsemanship and fierce posturing before us, the Chief emerged briskly from our lodge to speak the sign language with the leader of their party—an enormous fellow named, as I understood it, Hump.

Naturally, before anything important could be discussed between the two Chiefs, the entire Sioux contingent had to be invited to eat and smoke. Not to extend such an invitation would be considered impolite. Several families opened their lodges to the warriors, after which a general council was held in the Medicine Lodge. When all the formalities were completed, and the ceremonial pipe lit, the Sioux at last explained that the intent of their war party was to launch a series of raids against the white gold seekers and settlers who were invading the Black Hills.

Speaking through a Cheyenne interpreter, the Sioux Chief, Hump, then asked Little Wolf if the Cheyennes would join them in a war against the whites. The Black Hills, Hump said, belonged to both the Sioux and the Cheyennes, had been given to them "forever" in the last great treaty talks.

Little Wolf listened politely to this request and then answered that he was quite familiar with the terms of the treaty but that, as the Sioux could plainly see, ours was only a small band with more women and children among it than warriors and that at present we were on our way to do business at the trading post, not to wage war against white settlers.

"Perhaps the Cheyennes will not fight the whites because the soldiers have given you these pale women," Hump said, waving his arm toward us. "Perhaps the white women have made you soft and afraid to fight." At this evident *bon mot* some of the Sioux warriors present made insinuating snickers.

My husband's face darkened and I could see the muscle in his jaw rippling, a sure sign of his well-known temper rising. "The Sioux are certainly aware of the Cheyennes' ability to make war," Little Wolf said. "We claim that we are the best fighters on the plains. It is a foolish thing for the Sioux to say that we are afraid. Ours is not a war party, but a trading party. I have spoken. And that is all I have to say on the subject."

With this Little Wolf stood and left the Medicine Lodge. I followed him home. The next day the Sioux were gone.

14 September 1875

Yesterday we reached Fort Laramie. A more distressing return to the bosom of civilization, I can hardly imagine . . . we are all left now to ponder the question of which world we really inhabit . . . perhaps neither.

We struck our camp as far away as we could from the hangs-around-the-fort Indians, whose appearance and behavior was, if anything, even more shocking to us after living among the Cheyennes these past months. Truly contact with our white civilization has caused nothing but ruination and despair for these unfortunate souls. A number of them, ragged and thin, came straightaway to our camp to beg from us.

After we made camp, Little Wolf himself led our trade contingent to the fort grounds to conduct our business at the trading post there, our packhorses well laden with hides. A few among our group chose to accompany their husbands to the fort, but others had grown suddenly shy faced once again with the prospect of confronting civilization after these many months in the wilderness.

As I look back now with the luxury of twenty-four hours of hindsight, I realize that I, myself, was impulsively bold in my own insistence upon going to the fort with my husband. So anxious was I to catch a glimpse of civilization that I had hardly given a thought to how we would appear to civilized people. I think, too, that in the back of my mind, I must have hoped to catch sight of John Bourke, or at least to hear some word of him.

Phemie and Helen, equally unselfconscious, also elected to go into the trading post, as did the Kelly girls—whose swagger is undiminished by any circumstances. Both the Kellys and Helen Flight, I should mention, have become rather wealthy women by savage standards—the former by the ill-gotten gains of their gambling empire, and Helen for artistic services rendered. Helen hoped to trade her goods for gunpowder and shot for her muzzle loader, as well as for additional painting supplies and sundry "luxuries" of civilization.

"And I intend to post a letter at last to my dear Mrs. Hall!" she said, with great excitement. I, too, had prepared a letter to send to my family, although I felt certain that we would be forbidden still by the military from posting these communications.

Our old crier, *Pehpe'e*, identified us to the fort sentry, and after some delay the gates swung open and a company of Negro soldiers galloped out to meet us. With snappy military precision, they formed lines on either side of our little trade contingent to escort us inside. For all their soldierly discipline, the black men could hardly take their eyes off our Euphemia. *Nexana'hane'e* (Kills Twice Woman) as she is called since our rescue from the Crows, rode her white horse beside her husband Black Man, who rode a spotted pony. It was a mild day and she was bare-chested as is her summer habit, wearing nothing but a breechclout, her long legs, bronzed and muscled, adorned with hammered copper ankle bracelets. She wore copper hoops in her pierced ears, and a necklace of trade beads around her neck and looked as always perfectly regal—more savage than the savages themselves.

Although it must certainly have been in violation of military regulations, one of the soldiers nearest Phemie couldn't resist whispering. "What you *niggers* doin' with these people?" he asked. "Are you prisoners?"

Phemie chuckled deeply. "We live with these people, *nigger,* that's what we're doing," she said. "These are our people. My husband is Cheyenne and does not speak English."

"Cheyenne!" said another soldier behind the first. *"Whooo-eeee,* woman! You is one crazy *nigger!"*

As we entered the fort we could see that a small crowd of curious onlookers, civilians and soldiers, had gathered to observe our procession. Little Wolf rode at the head, followed by a half dozen of his warriors in a tight cluster, followed by the string of packhorses led by the women and some boys, several more warriors bringing up our rear. I, too, was afoot, leading Soldier and two other of our packhorses, walking abreast with Helen Flight, who led her own four horses in a string. I was dressed as usual in my antelope hide dress with leggings and moccasins. I usually wear my hair braided in the Indian fashion now—having found this to be more practical. My fellow wife Feather on Head is very adept at the process. For her part, Helen had her pipe clenched firmly between her teeth, wore her English shooting hat, buckskin trousers and jacket, and carried her muzzle loader in a sling over her shoulder. The Kelly twins sauntered boldly behind us, leading their own string of horses equally well laden with hides.

Only now, incredible to say, does it fully occur to me what a bizarre spectacle we must have presented to those assembled, and even now I flush with embarrassment in recounting the scene.

What other reception we might have expected, I do not know. My own foolish pride blinded me to the fact that far from looking the part of heroic explorers returning in triumph to civilization, we must have appeared in truth not merely comical, but utterly ludicrous.

A number of the soldiers' wives were included in the group of curious onlookers and there arose among them an astonished murmuring which gave way to an excited chattering and pointing as our procession moved past. *"Look, look there, those are a pair of the white girls, the redheads,"* we heard them say. *"Look how filthy they are! Why they look like savages themselves!"*

"Good Lord, that nigger girl is half-naked!"

"And look at the outfit the Englishwoman wears, the painter, doesn't she look like a buffalo hunter!"

"Isn't that fair-haired girl with the braids the one that was so saucy with John Bourke last spring? From the look of her, she's gone completely wild!"

"Wait until the Captain sees her now!"

These last remarks were like an arrow to my heart; and just as suddenly I knew that I did not wish to see Captain Bourke . . . prayed not to see him . . . How could we have been so proud, so foolish? My cheeks colored, I burned with shame, I cast my eyes to the ground.

"Tiny minds, May," said Helen Flight with her usual good cheer, having obviously witnessed my distress. "They have no sense of manners or decorum whatever. And they are to be paid no attention whatever. Tiny, tiny little minds. Let them not concern us, my dear friend. Why you're the smartest little picture of a lady here! And don't you forget it. Keep your head up now, my dear! An *artiste* must never bow her head to the tiny minds. This is a lesson my dearest companion, Mrs. Ann Hall, taught me long ago. Never bow to the tiny minds!" And then Helen, God bless her, her eyebrows raised in delight actually took off her hat and waved cheerfully to the astonished crowd of onlookers.

Her words gave me strength, and I lifted my head again. Still, I continued to pray that the Captain was not here at Fort Laramie after all to witness my humiliation, to see me "gone wild."

But then, for some reason, the mood seemed to change among the onlookers, as if their barbed curiosity spoken in tones loud enough for all of us to hear was not sufficient reproof for our transgression of all things wholesome and Christian. We had almost reached the trading post when someone hissed, *"Whores!"*

And someone else: *"Dirty whores!"*

"Why do you bring your filth here among decent God-fearing Christians?" another said.

Perhaps because she has lived with such intolerance and prejudice for most of her life, the unflappable Phemie knew just how to react to it; she began to sing one of her "freedom songs," as she calls them. Her rich, melodic voice rose above the ugly epithets, covered and finally silenced them:

"I've been buked and I've been scorned,
I've been buked and I've been scorned, children
I've been buked and I've been scorned,
I've been talked about sure's you born."

And though I am certain now that they must have been punished later for it, several of the Negro soldiers who escorted us joined her in the next verse. They shared the community of racial memory and knew the song well. And they sang as if to protect all of us in their charge:

"There'll be trouble all over this world,
There'll be trouble all over this world, children,
There'll be trouble all over this world,
There'll be trouble all over this world."

We were all of us heartened by the singing, given courage by the deep men's voices in harmony with our own Phemie's contralto which rose above the others like that of an angel—a black angel. And we all sang the third verse, which we had heard Phemie sing countless nights in her lodge:

"Ain't gonna lay my religion down
Ain't gonna lay my religion down, children
Ain't gonna lay my religion down
Ain't gonna lay my religion down"

Now we had reached the post store and our procession halted as the trader, with a half-breed interpreter in tow, came out to confer with Little Wolf. As we waited, and for the first time, I took the opportunity to look back at them, to gaze into the crowd at some of the individuals who had witnessed our arrival here in such low mean spirit. They had fallen silent now and regarded us with sullen looks of suspicion and . . . hatred.

Hardly had I begun to peruse their faces than my eyes met those of Captain John G. Bourke . . .

HEF

→ NOTEBOOK VI ←

The Bony Bosom of Civilization

"How strange to recall that six months ago we departed Fort Laramie as anxious white women entering the wilderness for the first time; and now, perhaps equally anxious, we leave as squaws returning home. I realized anew as we rode into the cold north wind on this morning that my own commitment had been forever sealed by the new heart that beats in my belly; that I could not have remained even if I so wished."

(from the journals of May Dodd)

⇻⇺

14 September 1875, Fort Laramie (continued)

This would seem an appropriate place to begin a new notebook, for perhaps it was at the very instant upon first laying eyes again upon John Bourke, that I understood beyond a shadow of a doubt that he was lost to me . . . and I to him. That I had crossed over, finally and irrevocably, to take up residency in "the other world behind this one" as the Cheyennes call the world that exists on the other side of our own.

The Captain could not disguise his horror when our eyes first met, could not hide the flicker of revulsion that crossed his face. We stared at one another thus for a long time before he finally turned his gaze away with something like relief—as though he had decided that he must have been mistaken, after all; that I could not be the person he had at first taken me for.

In the tumult of emotions I felt in seeing him again, I do not know which was more painful to me—the Captain's disgust or his dismissal.

In an attempt to calm the racing of my own heart, I turned my attention to our immediate business here: we began to unstrap our hides from the packhorses and let the bundles slide to the ground, where they fell with a heavy thud—a line of thuds and a cloud of dust billowing up beneath the horses' legs.

The proprietor of the trading post was a short, bandy-legged Frenchman by the name of Louis Baptiste, who now made his way from bundle to bundle, inspecting, counting, jotting figures in the columns of his ledger book. Baptiste had a large hooked nose and small, close-set eyes, and the Indians called him *Pe'ee'ese Makeeta*—Big Nose Little Man.

When Big Nose reached Helen Flight, she said to him: "I shall be negotiating my own trade, sir, independent of the gentlemen. And I authorize Susan and Margaret Kelly to represent me in this matter."

"I only *beezness weeth* the braves," said the trader, *"jamais avec les squaws."*

"On what grounds, may I ask, sir?" Helen inquired pleasantly.

Now Baptiste looked her up and down, his small eyes narrowed meanly. He grinned. *"Mais peut-être vous avez une petite squaw* under your buffalo robes, *madame, non?"*

Helen's smile never wavered. "These are my goods," she said evenly to the man. "And I should be pleased to let those young ladies right there"—she pointed to the Kelly twins—"conduct my business for me, thank you so very much, sir."

By now Susie and Meggie had sauntered forward. "*Aye,* Frenchy, you'll be dealin' with me and sister here," said Susie.

Louis Baptiste raised his palms as if matters were quite out of his hands. "*Comme j'ai dit, mesdames,*" he said, "I do *beezness* with the braves. *Toujours. Jamais avec les squaws.*"

"Yes, well no doubt they are easier to swindle than the women," observed Helen drily.

I spoke up myself then. "We are representatives of the United States government," I said, "officially dispatched by President Grant to instruct these people in the workings of the Caucasian world. This would seem to be an excellent opportunity to begin their economic education."

Baptiste aimed a stream of tobacco juice between his legs; some of it didn't clear the hook on the end of his nose and dripped from it like rusty water from a leaking faucet. He snorted and wiped his nose with the back of his hand, which he then proceeded to study as if it were a matter of the greatest import. "*Oui,* I know who you are, *mesdames,*" Big Nose said with a nod. "You are the white squaw brides of *les sauvages, n'est-ce pas?*" He shook his head with something between astonishment and regret. "*Moi?* I have an Indian squaw woman myself—Arapaho. I find that they are less trouble than white women," he said. And then he shrugged. "Yes, OK, *ça va.* Why not? You may come in the store, but *beeg* Chief he makes deal for everyone." Baptiste moved on down the line of bundles, counting and jotting figures in his notebook.

"Frightfully unattractive little man," said Helen Flight. "Impertinent, too. Never have cared for the French, personally."

"Nor I," said Meggie Kelly. "But he'll not be gettin' the better of the Kelly girls in a trade, I can tell *ya*. Right, Susie?"

Several army officers, including Captain Bourke, had gathered inside the store. Now they stood behind Baptiste, who sat at a long table with his ledger book open before him. Little Wolf was seated across from him, flanked by two of his young Elk warriors standing behind him. Unaccustomed to furniture, the Chief sat stiffly on the edge of his chair. Helen, the Kelly girls, and I stood just inside the door. I was surprised to find that being inside a building after all these months gave me a most peculiar sense of claustrophobia.

John Bourke did not look at me. Indeed, I had the distinct sense that he was trying very hard not to. My heart ached as I watched him . . . I could not help but remember the last time we had seen each other . . .

Big Nose tapped his ledger with a pencil and said, "OK, I *geeve* you four sacks flour, two sacks sugar, one sack baking soda, one sack coffee, six plugs tobacco, one bag wolf poison—"

Before the interpreter, a half-breed hangs-around-the-fort named Little Bat, could finish his translation to Little Wolf, I had pushed forward. "Nonsense," I said. "Those hides and other goods represent an entire summer's worth of labor. What you offer us in trade wouldn't see a dozen of us through half the coming winter."

Captain Bourke looked up from behind the table, seeming at first surprised and then embarrassed by my outburst; he colored and looked down.

"Supply and demand, *madame,*" said Big Nose with a wolfish grin. "*Beeg* Chief he understand that. Too many buffalo *'ides* this year. That *eez* my offer. Take it or leave it."

"Ah, ya beggar!" said Susie Kelly. "*Ya* think we're damn fools, do *ya*? Too many buffalo hides, *me* foot! Never *haird* a *sech* a thing. The buffalo are *scarcer* this year than ever before, and you know it as well as we do."

"I am sorry, *mesdames,*" said Baptiste, raising his hands. "But that *eez* my offer. If *theez* don't seem fair to you, I suggest you may take your *'ides* to the trading post at Camp Robinson. There *mon chèr ami,* Jules Escoffey, make you not nearly such a good deal, I think. *Moi?* Compared to Jules I *yam* Santa Claus."

"What of gunpowder and ammunition?" asked Helen Flight. "We shall require those items for hunting."

"Non, non, madame," said the proprietor, shaking his head. "*Je suis désolé,* I am sorry, no ammunition or gunpowder may be any longer traded to *les sauvages* by order of General George Crook. *C'est vrai, n'est-ce pas, Capitaine?*" he asked, turning to Captain Bourke behind him.

"That is correct, yes," Captain Bourke answered. Now he turned to me and nodded with stiff military formality. "Please explain to your husband, madam," he said, "that the Great Father in Washington has determined that for the Cheyennes' own welfare gunpowder and ammunition will no longer be available to them as articles of trade. In lieu of such items the Great Father is offering a variety of farm implements at wholesale prices."

I could not help letting an astonished bark of laughter escape. "Farm implements?" I said. "Wholesale? Excellent! Yes, well those items will certainly be of great use to us. Why what possible need shall we have for gunpowder and ammunition to procure fresh game when we shall have a 'variety of farm implements' to see us through the coming winter?"

"*Aye,* isn't that grand though!" said Meggie Kelly. "And are we expected to plant potatoes before the *folking* ground freezes?"

"As to the Great Father's paternal concern for the welfare of his Cheyenne children," I continued in a rising voice, "I imagine that although we are no longer allowed to trade our hides for gunpowder and ammunition, if we wished to trade, say, for a keg of rotgut whiskey capable of poisoning the entire tribe, such merchandise might still be available to us?"

Big Nose bared his wolfish teeth beneath his huge hooked nose. "Oh, *mais oui, madame,*" he said, "I throw in a keg of my best *wheesky* if that's what the *Beeg* Chief wishes."

Throughout this conversation, Little Wolf sat impassively, listening to the translation of the interpreter. Now I spoke to him in Cheyenne, surprising myself at the fluency of my anger. "The *vehos* are trying to cheat us," I said. "Our goods are worth ten times what Big Nose offers."

Little Wolf only nodded. "*Pe'ee'ese Makeeta* always tries to cheat us," he answered. "But the People have acquired a taste for sugar and coffee; these goods are important to us, and so we make the best trade that we can manage."

"And you do understand that by order of the Great Father in Washington," I said, "there is to be no more gunpowder or ammunition allowed the People? Instead they offer us farm implements."

Now Little Wolf looked genuinely surprised. As I suspected the interpreter, Little Bat, had not conveyed this last piece of information to him. "Farm implements?" Little Wolf asked. "Of what use are such things to the People?"

"Of no use," I said, "until such time as the People move to the agency and become farmers."

Little Wolf waved his hand in a dismissive backhanded gesture, in the manner that one shoos flies. "We are hunters," he said, "we are not farmers. Tell the soldiers that we have no use for farm implements, that we must have rifles and ammunition." And to Big Nose, he said, "Henceforth my wife, *Mesoke,* and the other women will conduct this trade." With this Little Wolf stood from the table and with his usual great dignity left the room, followed by his soldiers.

Now the Kellys pressed forward to make their case with Big Nose. "There's *noothin'* else to be *doone* now, Frenchy," said Susie, "than to do some *'beezness'* with the squaws, is there, *ya* little cheatin' bastard?"

I took this opportunity to approach John Bourke, who was gathering papers off the table, making quite a show of distracted busy-ness, all transparently designed to avoid having to confront me.

I did not allow him the luxury. "Why does the Army participate in this travesty, Captain?" I asked. "What possible interest does it serve to swindle these people."

The Captain bowed politely. "Mrs. Little Wolf," he said, as if addressing a stranger. "I'm afraid that this is not a matter which I am presently at liberty to discuss with you. Good day," he said, touching the brim of his hat and walking past me.

Before he could do so, I grasped him by the arm. It was, I am aware, a presumptuous act on my part, but I could not help myself. "John," I whispered, near to tears from my racing emotions, "for God's sake, John, it is I, May. Why won't you talk to me, why can't you look at me?"

The Captain stopped and raised his eyes to meet mine, as if seeing me for the first time. "Good God, May," he whispered.

"What did you expect, Captain?" I said. "That I would be dressed in my Sunday finest? Need I remind you that we have been living in the wilderness among savages? I'm sorry if my appearance offends you."

"No, May," John Bourke said. "Forgive me. You offer no offense. You look . . . only . . . very different than I remembered you . . ." And then as if torn by some great internal conflict, his brow furrowed in a storm of anguish, the Captain added, "Please excuse me, madam, I must take my leave. Perhaps we will have an opportunity to speak at a later date." I watched as he strode quickly from the store.

Later that day, my old friend Gertie rode her mule into our camp. I went out to greet her in front of our lodge, alerted to her arrival by the noises of the small pack of children and dogs at her heels. She was roughly attired in woolen trousers and a man's coat several sizes too large for her, wore a red bandanna around her neck, and an old cavalry hat that had been refashioned to a style quite beyond Army regulations, and was jauntily festooned with eagle feathers.

"Damn, honey," Gertie said to me, sliding off her mount, "it's a lucky thing I got a chin strap on this here old hat of mine, or I'd a been relieved of it for sure by now. There ain't nothin' an Injun likes moren' a hat, an' don't ask me why."

Gertie reached into a pocket of her coat and pulled out a handful of hard candies, which she passed out to the children, who chattered gaily and crowded closer around her. "Shoo, now," she said to them, "scoot! I want to talk to the Missus in peace. No, I *awready* told *ya, ya* can't have my *goddamn* hat!" Gertie removed her hat and slapped it against her thigh, raising a cloud of dust. Her hair was sweated and matted greasily on her head, flattened and whorled like the bedding place of a deer in high grass. Her face was streaked with dirt. It was not the first time I have noticed Gertie's lack of attention to matters of personal cleanliness; indeed she possessed a distinct odor that could compete with that of any unwashed savage. I gave her a big hug nevertheless, for I was very glad to see her.

"Damn, but ain't this here a dusty godforsaken country, honey?" she asked. "Coyote ugly, too. I prefer that grass country up north where you been summerin'. You know I trailed you half the goddamn summer with the half-breed scout Big Bat Pourrier. Not a bad sidekick as half-breeds go, old Big Bat. Good tracker, and he never once tried to make no play on me, if you get my meanin' . . ."

I was less astonished by this latter bit of information than the former. "Why did you do that, Gertie?" I asked. "Follow us all summer?"

"The Cap'n asked me to keep an eye on you, honey," she said. "He was awful worried about you, especially after I reported back to him last time—after the little whiskey party. I told him you was makin' out just fine. I figured they would a drunk up all their whiskey that night. One thing about Injuns is that if there's any whiskey around, they'll drink it all up just as fast as they can. Once it's gone and they can't lay their hands on no more that's the end of it. That's about how I figured it would go."

I nodded my head. "But you stopped trailing us after we made our encampment on the Tongue, is that correct?" I asked.

"Yup, figured by then things was goin' real good for you," Gertie said, "so I come back to report in to the Cap'n."

"And since you seem to be in the regular employment of Captain Bourke, Gertie," I said, "may I assume that you've come now with news from him?"

"You can assume exactly that, honey," Gertie said. "He wants to see you. Wants you to meet him underneath the south side of the Platte River bridge this evening after supper. Wants you to wear your white woman duds so as not to attract attention in case anyone spots you two together."

I laughed. "Yes, I suppose it would hardly do for the good Captain to be seen fraternizing with a squaw. Especially the Big Chief's squaw. Unfortunately, I have no white woman clothing, Gertie. I've given them all away. They seemed . . . shall we say . . . unsuitable to our present circumstances."

"Sure, I know just what ya mean, honey," Gertie said. She looked down at her own outfit. "Hell, I suppose I could loan you my duds. I ain't much for dresses, white woman or Injun, but I'd sure be willin' to swap you for a spell."

"That's very kind of you, Gertie," I said quickly, "but it won't be necessary." Although forced to give up many of the standards of civilized hygiene which I once took for granted, I was still not prepared to don Dirty Gertie's aromatic outfit. "The Captain will simply have to receive me in my everyday squaw attire. Please relate to him that I will be at the bridge at the designated hour."

"Will do, honey," she said. Then she scuffed her boot in the dirt. "Well hell, ain't ya goin' to invite me in to set a spell? I figured we'd have some visitin' to do, you and me? Catchin' up."

I smiled tenderly at Gertie, realizing that in my distraction at the idea of seeing John Bourke again in private, I had hurt her feelings, treating her as a messenger rather than a friend. "Of course we do," I said. "I didn't mean to be rude, Gertie. Please, do come in, the ladies will be happy to see you again."

"Honey, 'fore we set down, with the others," Gertie said, "why don't we get one thing over with first, private like. I got a hunch you have a question you're wantin' to ask me."

"A question?" I asked. "You mean regarding John Bourke?"

Gertie nodded. "He broke off his engagement to the Bradley gal, if that's what you're wonderin'," she said. "She went back to her mother in New York."

None of the few pedestrians or drivers of the occasional wagon that passed along the road paid the least bit of attention to one more squaw woman, wrapped modestly in a Hudson Bay trade blanket, as she made her way across the rickety Platte River bridge. On the far side I looked about quickly to be certain that I was not observed and then ducked down the narrow footpath through the willows toward the river's bank.

John Bourke was already waiting for me there. As yet unobserved, I stopped to watch him for a moment, to try to still the pounding of my heart. He stood facing the slow torpid river, his hands clasped behind his back, apparently lost in a reverie. Because I could not bear to see the look of disappointment in his face that I had not metamorphosed back into the comely and properly dressed young white woman with whom he had once recited Shakespeare, I spoke first.

"Do not turn to look at me, Captain," I said.

"Why do you ask this?" he inquired, starting, but he did not turn.

"Because I am as you last saw me," I said. "I am still attired as a savage and I cannot bear the look of revulsion on your face."

And then he did turn. And looking thoroughly distraught, his dark brow riding low over his eyes in a storm of self-reproach, he said: "Forgive me, madam. My behavior toward you was intolerable. It was a shock to see you again after so many months."

I laughed. "Ah, yes, a shock," I said. "Indeed! And to see me then dressed as the enemy. How difficult that must have been for you, Captain!"

"You have every right to be angry with me, madam," he said. "I should not have expected you to be otherwise attired. However, I hope you will believe me when I tell you that it was not revulsion that you saw in my face."

"No?" I asked, approaching him. "And what was it, Captain, that I mistook for revulsion?"

He moved toward me and took my hands in his. His fingers were strong and rough but his touch as gentle as I remembered it. And his eyes softened as he looked into mine with a look that I also remembered. "Heartbreak, perhaps," he said.

"Heartbreak?" I asked, the blood rising to my cheeks. "I'm afraid that I don't understand you, Captain. Heartbreak at my descent into paganism?"

"No, May, heartbreak that you now belong to another man," he answered, "to another people. Once, for the briefest moment, you belonged to me. I let you slip away. What you saw in my face was the look of a man filled with regret for his failures, with self-loathing for his own weakness."

Then I went forward into John Bourke's arms, or he brought me into them, I do not know which . . . I think that neither of us had intended this to happen, particularly not he, whose moral rectitude would hardly allow the embrace of a married woman, but we are like magnets, he and I, and clung to each other, and did not speak . . . for there were no satisfactory words to be said.

I squeezed my eyes shut to keep from spilling tears, but still they fell about his neck and I felt their wetness on my cheek. "John," I whispered. "Dear John. How could we have known . . ."

"I had you, May," he said, "and I let you go. For that I shall never forgive myself."

"And I left you, John," I said. "There could have been no other way. There can be no other way."

The trade blanket had fallen about my feet and as the Captain's arms enveloped me, there was little between the soft, supple skin of the antelope hide from which my garment was so loosely fashioned, and my own skin. We could feel each other . . . the at once familiar contours of our bodies fitting themselves into one form, one being . . .

And then at the same moment we both released our embrace. And into my breast rose the terrible weightless sense of falling from a cliff.

The Captain spoke first, with a kind of husky ferocity in his voice, "This cannot be, May," he said. "You are married to another."

"Of course it can't, John," I said, and I thought my flushed heart would explode in a thousand pieces, "for I am also having his child."

At this he smiled, and stepped toward me again, as if the fact itself released us for that moment from our need for one another. He placed his large hand, his fingers spread, upon my belly as gently as if he were touching the child itself. "I'm very happy for you, May," he said. "Please believe that."

I put my own hand atop his. "Four months so, I make it, John. Isn't it strange where life leads us?"

" 'What fates impose, that men must needs abide;' " he quoted, " 'It boots not to resist both wind and tide.'

"God, I've missed you, May," he said. "I've never stopped thinking of you."

"Nor I you, John," I said. "And what of your fiancée? What of Lydia Bradley? Gertie tells me you've sent her back East."

"Honor dictated that I could not in good faith any longer marry her," he said. "I had fallen in love with you, May. I had lain with you."

"Oh, John, you torture yourself with your damnable sense of honor," I said, "your inflexible Catholic doctrine. She was a pleasant enough young lady, and would have made you a good wife. And you, her, a fine husband."

"Always the practical one, aren't you, May?" John said. And he smiled his old crooked wry smile, his weathered eyes crinkling in the corners. " 'Pleasant enough' is faint praise. In any case she was far too sensitive to be wife to an old Army rat such as myself."

"She'd have been the luckiest woman on earth, John," I said.

"And you, May?" he asked. "How has your luck been running? Tell me, are you in love with your husband? Are you happy in your 'arranged' marriage?"

"I make those three separate questions, Captain," I said. "To the first I would answer that my luck has been mixed. To the second that, yes, I love and honor my husband, Little Wolf. He is a good man and a fine provider for his family. But I am not 'in love' as I think you mean. I do not love him as I once loved you . . . for how could that be so?

"And finally to the question of my happiness, as our mutual friend Gertie once put it, I would answer that 'happiness is a highly overrated human condition invented by white folks.' "

Bourke laughed then, the rich deep laugh that broke my heart to hear again. "A line worthy of the Bard!" he said. "She's a fine piece of work, our Gertie, isn't she though?"

"Yes, she is," I said, "and she's been a dear friend to me."

"But your life among the savages, May?" he asked in a more serious tone. "How does it go for you? You know that I've been worried sick about you."

"And have sent Gertie to watch over me," I said. "I know, John, for which solicitude I am deeply grateful. She arrived the first time at a propitious moment . . . and left the second time only a moment too soon . . ."

The Captain's face filled again with darkness. "What do you mean by that, May?" he asked. "Gertie said that you were in good health, adapting well to your new circumstances. Has something happened?"

"I was, John, and I have," I said, aware that any description of our abduction by the Crow horse thieves could only needlessly torture him. "It is only that, as you yourself warned us, it is a strange and sometimes terrifying life we lead among these people. One of our girls, my little friend Sara, has been killed in an accident."

John touched my face tenderly with the back of his hand. "I'm sorry, May," he said. "I know how you cared for her."

"Other than that we have, most of us, endured," I said.

"I should say that you've at least done so," he said. "Why just look at you, May, fit and brown as a native. If anything you are even more beautiful than I remembered you. I think life in the out-of-doors must agree with you."

"I admit that it has benefits, as well as its discomforts," I said. "Mostly, John, it's been like living a dream, like a suspension of real life. But coming back here and seeing you again . . . I have been abruptly awakened from the dream."

"Your dream is not over yet, May," Bourke said in a serious tone. He turned his back to me and looked out over the river. "You know that I have asked you here for another reason than my desire to see you again."

"I suspected as much, Captain," I said. "Gertie informs me that the government is abandoning us."

"No, not abandoning," Bourke said quickly, turning back to me. "Not as long as General Crook has anything to say in the matter."

"And *does* General Crook have anything to say in the matter?" I asked.

"The Army has been put in a thankless position, May," he answered. "The pendulum has swung even further since Gertie brought you my news this summer. The geologists with Custer's expedition have since returned with glowing reports about the gold discovery in the Black Hills. Parties of miners, their passions inflamed by the prospect of easy riches, are even now making their way toward the region. The Army has been charged with the impossible task of trying to intercept them in order to defend the terms of the Fort Laramie treaty. Of course, this situation is untenable and cannot continue. Public sentiment, fueled by a righteous press, demands that the Black Hills be made safe for white settlers, and the Indians driven from the land."

"Driven from the land?" I asked. "But they believe that they own the Black Hills—indeed, do own them. The Sioux have already been to see us, John. They are forming war parties against the invading miners. It's only a matter of time until some of our people join them."

"Yes, and for this reason and upon the recommendation of Inspector Watkins of the Indian Bureau," the Captain said, "the War Department has been instructed to bring in the remaining free savages, both Sioux and Cheyennes, and to see to their settlement on reservations, which plan is effective immediately."

"I begin to understand why the Army is in collaboration with that wretched little Frenchman," I said. "You sanction the swindling of the savages in trade in order that, like obedient children, they be forced to throw themselves upon the mercy of their benevolent Great White Father."

"Exactly so," said Captain Bourke, nodding. "A peaceful resolution that can be greatly expedited by you and your friends—by encouraging your husbands to give themselves and their families up at the agencies with as much dispatch as possible."

"And, of course, the decision to deny them any further arms and ammunition," I added, "has been made as a precaution in the event that our efforts toward this end fail?"

The Captain did not avoid my eyes when he answered. He nodded glumly. "A campaign under the direction of General Crook is currently being organized—its purpose to round up all those hostiles who have not voluntarily complied by the first day of February 1876. As Chief Little Wolf's wife, May, you are in a unique position to facilitate the process—and possibly save many lives by doing so."

"Ah, so now you've come to believe that the Brides for Indians program is a useful one after all," I said.

"I believe as I have from the beginning," said Bourke, "that it is a contemptible and immoral program that has put you and your friends at tremendous risk. But it is nevertheless in place, you are in the field, and yes, can now be useful."

"My husband is under the impression that as long as the Cheyennes remain on the land that has been given them 'forever' by official treaty, they commit no trespass," I said.

"President Grant has recently dispatched a commission to negotiate the purchase of the Black Hills and the surrounding country from the Cheyennes and the Sioux," said the Captain.

"And if they choose not to sell?" I asked.

"As you may have learned in your travels with them, May," he said, "the savages are hardly united among themselves—even one tribe such as yours has many different factions and many leaders. Rest assured that the President's commission will find someone among the Sioux and the Cheyennes who will be willing to negotiate this sale—after which time all others who remain on the land will be considered trespassers by the United States Army."

"God, it's despicable, isn't it?" I said in a low voice.

"But necessary, I'm afraid," said the Captain. "It is the inevitable course of history."

"And if we are unsuccessful in persuading the Cheyennes to come into the agency before the appointed date," I asked, "will you hunt us down, then John? Shall we be enemies?"

"That must not happen, May," said the Captain firmly. "I'm telling you this in order to avoid any such unthinkable situation. Your husband, Little Wolf, has already requested an audience with General Crook. Perhaps you can exercise some positive influence over the chief."

"My husband wishes to discuss the matter of the remaining brides that have been promised him by the Great White Father," I said. "The Cheyennes may be heathens Captain, but they can count, and the shortage has not escaped my husband's attention."

"You must convince Little Wolf," said Bourke, "that after the savages are peacefully settled on the reservation, they will receive the remainder of their brides."

"Now you ask me to lie for the government, John?" I said, my temper flaring. "To lie to my own husband in order to cover your vile deceptions?"

"Not my deceptions, May," Bourke said quickly, "nor those of General Crook. As you know, we were never consulted by the government and would never have sanctioned this program if we had been. I do not apologize for our role in this affair. We have been charged with protecting those of you who are already afield and at risk. I will arrange for General Crook to meet with your husband. The General is a man of honor who has always dealt fairly with the savages. He will make no promises about delivery of the brides, but he may use the issue as a carrot-on-a-stick. It remains to you to help convince your husband to turn his people in to the agencies before next winter. There they will be given everything they need—food to eat, a roof over their heads, and their children—*your* children—will be educated by Christians; taught to read and write, to farm—to plow and hoe and subdue the Earth as the Bible teaches us we must. Whatever political situations may have changed, May—however you may have changed, do not forget that this was your original mission. To assimilate the savages—to bring them to the bosom of Christian civilization."

"You have heard, perhaps, how our portly Episcopalian brought the children to his ample bosom?" I said.

"I have," said Bourke, coloring, and I could see his temper rising again like water coming to a fast boil. "The Reverend Hare has been recalled by Bishop Whipple, who promises a full investigation of the charges."

"A full investigation is quite unnecessary," I said. "We all know what happened. Are you aware that such acts with children are unknown to the Cheyenne culture? Not just rare—but unknown. As an amateur ethnologist, I should think that you might be interested in this fact. We have much to teach the savages, don't we, John?"

"The Church Missionary Society is looking into finding a Catholic priest to return with you to serve as your spiritual advisor among the heathens. Your husband has, very sensibly I might add," the Captain added with a sly smile, "specifically requested a 'Black Robe' this time."

"Excellent," I said in deadpan tone. "Then our little boys will be safe."

"Good God, May!" Bourke said, shaking his head, and uttering an involuntary laugh. "You're the most irreverent woman I've ever known!" But he laughed again, a deep, delighted belly laugh. And I laughed with him.

We hugged each other quickly before parting, not daring to linger in the other's embrace, lest we allow ourselves once again to become one.

18 September 1875

Little Wolf had his audience with General Crook. None of us white women were allowed to attend or even to leave our camp as several members of the press, including a Mr. Robert E. Strahorn of the *Rocky Mountain News* in Denver had recently arrived at the fort. It was deemed undesirable by the authorities that we be seen by the press, or identified as affiliated in any way whatsoever with the government or the military. In any case, after our initial reception by the fort residents, we have most of us avoided further contact with the whites. It is rarely spoken of, and the newspapers avoid the subject like the plague, but there are other white women, most of them alcoholic, who have taken up residency among the hangs-around-the-fort Indians. These unfortunate souls are referred to as "fallen whores"—and as such, we are passed off.

All I know of the meeting with Crook is what little I have learned from Little Wolf himself and from Gertie, who eavesdropped beneath the window outside. As Captain Bourke had suggested, the General would make no assurances about delivery of the remaining brides. He could only say that if the Cheyennes agreed to come into the agency before winter, the matter would be taken up again with the proper authorities. This was the kind of white man talk that confused and angered Little Wolf, for in his mind the matter had already been agreed upon, the deal struck.

The General further promised that if the Cheyennes came in to the agency, they would be generously cared for by the Great Father.

"Yes," replied Little Wolf, "I have been to the Red Cloud Agency, and I have seen there the generosity of the Great Father. There is no game left in that country and, like the brides that were pledged to the Cheyennes, only a small portion of the provisions that were promised has been delivered to them. So the Sioux have been forced to slaughter their own horses to eat. We have lived free all summer on our own land and we have plenty of meat to see us through the winter. Why should we go to the agency when we have everything we need and live as free people on our own land?"

Little Wolf's logic, simple and childlike, is at once relentless and irrefutable. Even General Crook, an old hand at negotiations with the savages, was somewhat at a loss to explain to what advantage it was to the Cheyennes to come into the agency before winter. The meeting was thus concluded unsatisfactorily.

In the matter of trade negotiations—and in a somewhat brighter vein, Big Nose Little Man had met his match in our Kelly twins. The little wretch's own greed for our hides finally undermined his tenuous alliance with the military who hoped to see us sooner destitute, and we made out rather favorably, after all. At the same time, a flourishing illicit trade and any number of unscrupulous dealers operate outside the fort grounds and from these Little Wolf obtained the rifles, ammunition, and gunpowder we required.

My husband is not stupid and understands that the decision by the Great White Father to withhold arms and ammunition from the Cheyennes is meant to render the People defenseless. As in the matter of the brides due him, it is clear that Little Wolf "smells a rat." Perhaps not incidentally, among the contraband munitions acquired from the illicit traders, our band has purchased a full case of new carbines.

19 September 1875

Yesterday several of our prominent medicine men went into the fort to take up a challenge offered, I was deeply ashamed to learn, by Captain John G. Bourke and several of his Army compadres. The Indians call Bourke "Paper Medicine Man," for as Crook's adjutant he is seen always scratching away in his books.

Had we not been avoiding the fort we white women might have known sooner about the nature of this disgraceful business, and put a quick end to it. As it was I did not learn of it until a boy came running to Little Wolf's lodge to say that the Sweet Medicine Chief must come to challenge the white man's "medicine box," that he must come immediately to save face for the People, for none of our medicine could defeat the box.

I had no idea what the child was talking about but I decided to accompany my husband to the fort to find out. We arrived just in time to witness the latest defeat of yet another of our medicine men at the hands of this so-called "medicine box." This was little more than an old discarded electrical battery that the idle soldiers had rigged up so that when turned by a hand crank it would send a shock through whatever fool was holding the poles. Next to the battery the soldiers had placed a pail of water and in the bottom of the pail a shiny silver dollar.

Now they much amused themselves by challenging any takers to reach into the pail and remove the silver dollar—with the stipulation, of course, that the contestant be holding the pole from the battery in one hand when he did so.

One after another, our medicine men, chanting their medicine songs, attempted to reach into the pail and remove the dollar. As the soldiers merrily sang their own "medicine song"—the Irish ballad "Pat Malloy"—one of them, John Bourke himself, cranked the handle of the damnable machine, which of course shocked the poor savages into submission with a terrible charge of electricity. Thus the medicine men were each, in turn, humiliated in front of the spectators. Some bravely tried a second time, but of course, were helpless against the thing.

At first Bourke did not see me among the crowd, and I pleaded with my husband. "Do not do this," I said. "This is not 'medicine,' it is another white man trick. You will be hurt and disgraced in front of the people if you try."

But others of the tribe urged Little Wolf forward to prove the power of the Sweet Medicine, and the Chief felt obligated to do so.

Still Bourke had not spied me, and when my husband stepped up to the machine, the Captain said: "Ah, and does the great Chief Little Wolf himself wish to challenge our medicine box?" In Bourke's tone of merriment, I detected an undercurrent of malice, which deeply disappointed me.

I could resist no longer and now came forward myself. "Is this how you gentlemen amuse yourself, Captain?" I asked. "By humiliating innocent people? Perhaps you should run along and find some puppies to torture."

Several of the soldiers laughed, but in slightly embarrassed tones, like children caught misbehaving. "Or to eat like the stinkin' heathens," one of them snickered under his breath.

"We're just having a little fun, ma'am," another said. "It's the heathens themselves who keep asking to try their medicine against ours. No harm intended. It's only a game."

Captain Bourke had himself blanched at my words, more in surprise at seeing me there, I think, than at my reprimand. For when he spoke, he did so with no trace of apology in his voice, but with a kind of cocksure defiance.

"We are teaching the savages, in a relatively harmless manner, that their superstitions are helpless against our own superior powers," he said. "It's a lesson better learned here, madam, than elsewhere, I can assure you."

"I see, Captain," I said. "And now you will teach this lesson to my husband, Little Wolf, the Sweet Medicine Chief, the Cheyennes' most esteemed leader and fearless warrior. And the People will learn for certain how powerless they are against the white man."

"Only if the Chief wishes to test his medicine against ours, madam," the Captain said, his dark, shadowed eyes boring into mine.

Little Wolf took one of the poles in hand, and the soldiers began to sing their ditty—"Pat Malloy." My eyes never left those of John Bourke, as he began to turn the crank on the battery and took up the song himself. Little Wolf did not chant but only touched the Sweet Medicine pouch that he wears against his breast, a kind of talisman, and began to put his arm into the pail. Just as he did so, the Captain, still staring at me and singing in a hearty voice, left off turning the crank, and my husband reached into the pail and with impunity removed the silver dollar from the bottom. Now all those assembled began to cheer wildly, as I and the rest of the women made our joyful trilling noise.

John Bourke stood from his seat at the machine, nodded to me with a slight smile, and walked briskly away.

20 September 1875

A change of weather is in the air, and we prepare for departure. The mild early-fall temperatures which we have enjoyed these past few weeks have fallen precipitously overnight. Lying in our lodge last night I could hear the north wind blowing down; it made an ominous rumbling sound like a freight train. And though I was warm under my buffalo robes, I felt the chill of winter in my bones.

This morning my friend Gertie came visiting a last time. "You heard the news of your compadre, Narcissa?" she asked.

"I have not," I answered, "but nothing would surprise me."

"She's in the fort hospital," Gertie said. "They say she lost her baby, miscarried, but I know one a the nurses, and she says the doctor pulled it for her."

"Pulled it?" I asked. "You mean to say she had her baby aborted?"

"That's what I'm hearin'."

"I was wrong, Gertie," I admitted. "I am surprised. None of us even knew she was with child."

"Nurse says that Narcissa begged the doctor to do it on account a her husband forced himself upon her," Gertie said, "an' she couldn't stand the idea of givin' birth to a heathen's baby."

"And she will no doubt be stayin' at the fort to recuperate," I said, "rather than returning north with the rest of us."

"You got it, honey," Gertie said with a nod. "Medical leave. Says her mission can be better served anyhow if she stays here to prepare the way for the heathens' settlement on the reservation. You get my meanin'?"

"Perfectly," I said. "A rat from a sinking ship. That's the part that doesn't surprise me. We all knew the woman was a hypocrite. I just never thought that she would go to such great lengths."

"Somethin' else you might want to know, honey," Gertie said. "She's tellin' folks that you an' some a the others has been on the warpath, that you gone plumb wild yourselves, took some Crow scalps, maybe even . . . maybe even . . . relieved some Crow fellas of some body parts, if you get my meanin' . . ."

"I see," I said. "And to whom is she spreading these rumors?"

"Anyone at the fort who'll listen," Gertie said. "You want to talk about it, honey?"

"No," I answered. "I cannot, Gertie. Only to say that while we were encamped on the Tongue this summer, a group of us were abducted by Crow horse thieves. It must have been shortly after you left. I didn't want to tell you about it because I knew that you'd blame yourself for not being there to look after us. Young Sara was killed in the incident. The rest of us were rescued by our husbands. That's all I can tell you."

Gertie nodded. "Sure, I understand, honey," she said. "I won't ask ya about it again. I just thought you should know what the missionary gal was tellin' folks. It don't make a damn bit a difference to me, see? I been there myself. I know what it's like."

"Thank you, Gertie," I said, grateful that she would not press me on the matter.

"Mostly I come to say good-bye, honey," Gertie said. "We're fixin' to head out ourselves. I don't know where, they never tell us nothin'. But it must be a mighty big expedition, because they give me back my job skinnin' mules, and if they're desperate enough to hire known gals as muleskinners, they must be takin' every damn mule and every damn wagon in the whole country. We're supposed to be ready to march tomorrow morning. My guess is Crook is repositioning some a his troops further north on account a the trouble in the Black Hills. Word is that the Sioux under Crazy Horse and Sitting Bull has been harassing the miners and settlers in that country. I don't know where your folks are headed, honey, but if I had any choice in the matter, I'd sure want to avoid that country. Thing is, when it comes to identifyin' Injun bands, the Army can't tell the difference between buffalo shit and sirloin steak. Even their Injun scouts half the time can't tell the different bands apart. At least not from a distance, and by the time they get up close enough, it's almost always too damn late. So the Army takes the position that any Injuns they come across in hostile territory is a hostile—guilty 'til proven innocent."

"And the Captain hasn't told you anything more specific, Gertie?" I asked.

"I ain't seen him, honey," she said. "When it comes to the movement of troops he'd be skating on awful thin ice to be tellin' military secrets to an old muleskinner, if you get my meanin'.

"But I did hear about that business with the battery," she continued. "You know it took some balls on the Cap'n's part not to juice old Little Wolf when he had the chance. The Cap'n lost face with his own men when he backed down."

"He didn't back down," I said. "He just didn't turn the crank on the machine."

"All the same to the soldiers, honey," she said. "It was their chance to whup the big Chief with their stronger medicine—to teach him a lesson—and the Cap'n let 'em down."

"It was a damn battery, Gertie!" I said. "That's all it was. It was just a damn electrical apparatus!"

"Sure, honey, I know what it was," she said, "but that's just how men are—'I got a bigger battery than you.' He did it for you, honey. You know that, don't you?"

"I know that," I said, "and it was a decent thing for him to do. If you see the Captain, Gertie, will you thank him for me." I laughed. "And if he needs reassurance on the matter, you may tell him that his battery is every bit the equal of the Chief's."

Gertie grinned. "That's what they like to hear, ain't it, honey?" she said.

22 September 1875

On such short notice the authorities failed to locate a priest to take the place of our disgraced Reverend Rabbit, but somehow they managed to find a Benedictine monk to accompany us. We have no idea where the strange fellow came from and know nothing about him except that he rode into our camp yesterday evening on a burro and introduced himself as Anthony—explaining that he had taken his name from Saint Anthony of the Desert, the fourth-century Egyptian hermit monk, and that, like his spiritual namesake, he was seeking a remote spot in the wilderness in which to found his own monastery, and that if we didn't mind, he would be pleased to accompany us.

"Good God," I said under my breath to Helen Flight beside me, "first they send us an overweight Episcopalian pederast on a mule, and now comes a gaunt Benedictine anchorite on a donkey. I think we can see how the authorities value our spiritual needs."

"*Ya've* come to the right place, if you're lookin' for remote, *Broother* Anthony that's for *shooore,*" said Meggie Kelly greeting the fellow. "Me an' Susie are a couple a good Catholic *goorls* ourselves. An' we're *'appy* to *'ave ya* along—right, Susie?"

"Right as rain, with me," said Susie.

"Quite," said Helen. "Anthony of the Prairie we shall dub you! Splendid addition to our little group, I should say."

It is just dawn now as I make this entry. We are to break camp later this morning. I am presently huddled under my buffalo robes and blankets as

Quiet One stokes the morning embers. *"Eho'eeto,"* she whispers when she notices me watching her. *"It is snowing."*

I pull my covers tighter around me. I badly have to make my morning water, but I cannot bring myself to leave the warmth of bed, and shall try to distract myself for a few more moments in these pages.

True to Gertie's report, yesterday we watched as two large companies of cavalry, each with mule-drawn pack trains, departed the fort, one headed northeast toward Camp Robinson and the other northwest toward Fort Fetterman. These had to be General Crook's forces, and Captain John Bourke must have been among them. I suspect that Crook had deployed his troops intentionally while we were still present to witness their strength, so that our band might report back to the others.

I take only some small comfort in knowing that we have at least the fall and part of the winter to come into the agency; that much was made clear by both Captain Bourke and General Crook. I intend to speak with the others when we rejoin them so that we may make a united effort to convince our husbands, and perhaps just as importantly, the women of the tribe, of the wisdom of giving ourselves up. But I fear that after a generally peaceful summer and in a time of tribal prosperity, it may be more difficult to make the People understand why they must relinquish their freedom and vacate land that is theirs "forever"—a word clearly less flexibly defined by their culture than ours.

I begin to worry for us with the coming of winter—especially with our babies on the way. Having been blessed throughout this past summer with a generally mild climate, we "brides" have experienced very little discomfort as a result of inclement weather—other than for the nearly constant prairie winds, which do sometimes provoke anxiety and irritability—and in poor Martha's case have greatly exacerbated her hay fever. Now with this first sudden blast of arctic air blowing down out of the north country I dread the prospect of our confinement. Certainly a more permanent shelter at the agency—perhaps even a real house—seems an attractive proposition compared to a long winter in a tipi. For all that, I must admit that the Indian tipi is marvelously well designed—stays remarkably cool in the heat of summer and quite cozy thus far with this first true cold weather of the season. And with the morning fire burning, it warms quickly.

Now Feather on Head with her dear baby boy—whom I call by the name Willie, after my own sweet William—has joined me under my buffalo robes. It is a game I have taught my tentmates; sometimes in the cool of dawn they steal into my bed and I nuzzle the baby, who smells like a wild prairie plum and we all of us giggle like children and often fall back asleep in each other's arms, curled together like sisters, the baby nestled between us. Sometimes Pretty Walker joins us, her mother, Quiet One, not objecting to these sisterly intimacies. Over these past chilly nights the first wife has resumed her rightful place under the robes with her husband, and I have sufficiently recovered from my own night-terrors to relinquish the position. Truly we are all of us like a pack of dogs, seeking the comfort of another warm body next to ours. Sometimes my little Horse Boy, too, will crawl under the robes with us—although I find of late that he is growing too old to snuggle innocently with the women!—the other day I felt the imp pressing an arousal urgently against my leg! I flicked his little thing, hard as the stub of a pencil, with my finger, causing the child to squeal and quite effectively discouraging his ardor.

Now we girls whisper and giggle under the robes; we trade English words and phrases for those in Cheyenne. The baby coos between us. A happier child I have never before known—he rarely cries and when he does Feather on Head pinches his nose and he stops almost immediately. In this way the Cheyenne mother trains her infant to a perfect animal silence.

It is warm and pungent under our coverings, and we are safe together and none of us wishes to rise to face the frigid air and the crisp fresh snow outside. None of us wishes to pack our belongings today and begin travel in the cold and the snow. But then we hear the old camp crier and all are silent for a moment as we listen for the day's news: *"The People will prepare to depart this morning,"* he cries out. *"We leave for our winter camp to the north. Today we go home. Pack your belongings, take down your lodges, this morning the People will prepare to move."*

Still we do not rise, we snuggle tighter under the buffalo robes until the old crone begins her shrill squawking . . . *"Everybody out of bed, up!, it is time to pack, we leave today."* And if any hesitate she has her willow switch handy and we hear her swacking the covers—any excuse for the old hag to draw on her arsenal of weaponry. Finally Feather on Head slips out from under the robes, suddenly serious again with the often grim business of womanhood in tribal life, which offers scant opportunity for such idle lounging; this morning she leaves her baby in the bed with me—she knows I will care for the sweet Willie, and thus she is free to begin her chores unencumbered. For a few more precious minutes I nuzzle the infant until he coos, coos like a pigeon. But I can wait no longer to make my water, nor can I tolerate any longer the squawking of old *Vohkeesa'e* and so I too, with great reluctance, put away my notebook, and finally slide out from beneath the warmth of my buffalo robes to face the trials of the day. I slip little Willie out behind me and hang him in his baby board, which leans up beside Feather on Head's sleeping place. He does not make a sound in protest, but I think that he looks at me regretfully, as if to say, *"Don't leave me here, don't leave me, auntie."*

When I step out through the lodge opening, the sun is just cresting the eastern horizon, but contains no hint of warmth this morning. The temperature must be well below freezing, the snow crystalline and sparkling and not yet trampled but for one distinct set of footprints heading down toward the river. It is the track of Little Wolf who rose early for his daily morning swim, which he and the others in the Savage Men's Bathing Club continue to take no matter what the weather. Now I follow his prints, stopping in the willows on the way to squat and take my pee, which steams yellow in the snow, melting down quickly to reveal the wet red earth beneath. And then on down to the river where I strip, first removing my leggings and moccasins before giving up the warmth of the heavy buffalo robe I wear and then quickly shedding my dress. Without hesitating, without giving myself time to so much as contemplate the terrible frigidity of the water I wade into the river, quick as I can, the breath catching in my throat, and I make a shallow dive, and come back to the surface gasping, trying to draw a breath out of my frozen breast and emitting a small choked cry of shock! Good Lord, it is cold!

I rush from the water and wrap the buffalo robe, which still holds some trace of the tipi's warmth, round my naked body and grab my dress, moccasins, and leggings and I run, back to the lodge, barefoot through the snow, my feet numb by the time I arrive. I burst through the opening, laughing and making *brrrrrr* sounds much to the delight of my tentmates. The baby dangling from his baby board gurgles delightedly at my grand entrance, his eyes wide. "Yes, *etoneto!*" I say using the Cheyenne word, then the English: *"Coooold! Brrrrrr!"* And the girls, Feather on Head and Pretty Walker, cover their mouths and giggle their soft shy giggles that sound like riffles on a spring creek. And the baby gurgles happily. And the old crone squawks, but even she and the usually undemonstrative Quiet One can't help now but give up small smiles at my antics . . .

In this way our day begins. I think only of my duties. Today we leave. I am a squaw.

23 September 1875

The breaking of camp proceeded somewhat slower yesterday with the cold weather, and it was midmorning before we were finally under way. By then the wind had come up out of the north, and directly into this we rode all day.

Thankfully, all who wanted them had horses for the return trip, for we traveled unencumbered by the several hundred hides with which we arrived here, and the trade goods we bartered for took up somewhat less packing space.

I rode most of the day alongside my friend Helen Flight. Our strange new spiritual advisor, Brother Anthony, trailed behind us on his little burro, the fellow's long legs dangling, his feet very nearly reaching the ground, the poor donkey breaking periodically into a rough-gaited trot to keep from falling too far behind.

With the Kellys' canny representation, Helen had managed, after all, to procure some new painting supplies from the "horrid little frog" as she refers to Big Nose. It seems that some of the garrison wives also enjoy dabbling in the arts as a means of passing the endless days when their husbands are off on expeditions, and so the Frenchman stocks a few such supplies. She has replenished her store of charcoal and sketch paper, and has even obtained a precious roll of painter's canvas. The dear thing also purchased two new notebooks, which she presented to me as a gift. I was terribly grateful to her for I am filling these pages at an alarming rate, and may soon have to stop writing altogether for they are becoming rather cumbersome to transport.

Helen kept a pipe clenched determinedly between her teeth as we rode into the frigid wind; it poked out through her scarf, but she had little success keeping it lit. We both were well covered, I in an extra layer of fur-lined moccasins and leggings and a kind of muff affair, made out of silky beaver fur, to keep my hands warm, and she with a new pair of gloves and men's boots for which she had traded at the store, and also wearing native fur and hide leggings. We both wore heavy coats of buffalo hair which we were particularly grateful to have had made for us during the summer by our camp seamstress Jeanette Parker. On our heads we each wore cossacklike hats of beaver fur pulled low over our ears; these last, an Indian fashion and very snug. Both of us also wore woolen scarves over our faces. In these confining outfits conversation would have been difficult in the best of circumstances—all but impossible with the wind blowing directly into our faces so that the words seemed to be pushed back down our throats before they had time to escape. We would try to holler back and forth and then would look at each other helplessly to see if we had been understood. Finally we gave a kind of mutual shrug and contented ourselves to ride in silence, with nothing but our thoughts for company, hunkered low on our horses, trying vainly to make our profiles as small as possible against the ceaseless wind.

How strange to recall that six months ago we departed Fort Laramie as anxious white women entering the wilderness for the first time; and now, perhaps equally anxious, we leave as squaws returning home. I realized anew as we rode into the cold wind on this morning that my own commitment had been sealed forever by the heart that beats in my belly; that I could not have remained even if I so wished.

Nor can I make room on this page or in my own heart for further thoughts of John Bourke. I push him from my mind. This is no act of easy omission on my part; I do not consign him casually to a forgotten past. It is rather an act of will—a kind of self-performed surgery on my soul . . . the bloodiest of mutilations. Having seen him again, having been held in his arms for that brief moment, having felt again his strong tender hand upon my stomach, the cutting away of him is even more painful this time . . . for in our parting I sense a new finality . . .

I write these few lines from our first night's camp out of Fort Laramie. It did not seem as though we made much progress today, as if the wind itself restrained us. In spite of the fact that I was warmly attired, I felt frozen to the bone by the end of the day—the prairie wind cuts like a razor through any clothing—and the warmth of our lodge this evening seems especially luxurious.

Little Wolf killed an antelope today on the trail and tonight we dine on the fresh backstrap—the most tender and delicious in my opinion of all wild meats. I invited Helen and her husband, Mr. Hog, as well as our new monk Anthony to join us for dinner—which remark as I read it back sounds somewhat more elegant and formal than the occasion warrants.

The guests scratched on the lodge covering at roughly the appointed hour, and were seated in the place of honor by the fire. After Little Wolf had blessed the meat by raising a piece to the four directions, and to the heavens and the earth, and then set it on a little platter off to the side of the fire for *He'amaveho'e*—the Great Medicine himself—to dine upon (although, of course, it is quickly consumed by one of the dogs, which act everyone pretends not to notice), we all fell to eating with hearty appetites. The savages take their meals in a rather serious spirit—perhaps as a matter of life and death—and there is very little conversation around the dining circle.

But Helen and I tend to flout that particular convention (among others, to be sure!), and thus we chattered away, trying to make our new guest feel as much at home as possible in his strange new surroundings.

"Do tell us, Brother Anthony," Helen asked, "are you interested in Nature?"

"It is my life," answered the young Benedictine, with soft reverence in his tone. "I am blessed by all of God's creations."

"Splendid!" said Helen. "That is to say, an appreciation of Nature is nearly a requisite to spiritual survival in the wilderness.

"I don't suppose, if I may be so bold to ask," Helen asked, "that you're a sporting man?"

"A sporting man?" asked the monk.

"No, of course you're not," Helen said, "it's just that this time of year—although at the moment I must say it feels quite like the dead of winter—that is to say, it is the autumn that gets my blood to coursing with thoughts of the hunt—stalking the uplands, the thunderous flush of wings, the crack of guns!

"Indeed, I should like to invite you all very soon over to Mr. Hog and my lodge for a game bird dinner. Do you like to cook, Brother Anthony?"

"I am a baker," Anthony answered softly. I was rather warming to our monk, whose manner is one of great simplicity and quiet attentiveness. I think that he shall do well among these people, that he may be useful in reminding us all that God's work on earth is best accomplished in such a spirit of humility.

"A baker! Splendid!" said Helen, her eyebrows popping up. "That is to say, to my mind there's nothing more useful than a man who can bake. Yes, indeed, fresh-baked bread will be a wonderful addition to our menus," she went on. "You know the natives have gone wild for the stuff—no pun intended. And we are now well supplied with flour and baking powder. Yes, I dare say we'll do a good bit of interesting cooking this fall, wouldn't you agree, May?"

Thus we ate our antelope, chatting and listening to the wind howling outside. It remained snug inside our tent with the fire burning; the wind sliding around the tipi without entering—an advantage to its round design.

When all had finished eating, Little Wolf extracted his pipe and smoking pouch, while Helen, never timid about being unconventional, packed her own short-stemmed pipe with tobacco and lit it from a small stick held to the fire. Then all settled comfortably against their backrests, as Horse Boy and the old crone slipped off to curl up on their sleeping robes.

Even the usually gregarious Helen fell silent and contemplative. The only sounds inside the lodge came from the small cracklings of the fire, and the wind blowing outside. It was a moment of near perfect serenity, and I took the opportunity to study my fellow tentmates, Feather on Head holding her baby, and Quiet One, for once not cleaning or cooking or moving about, just sitting quietly next to her daughter Pretty Walker, both of them staring into the fire. Little Wolf, seated on the other side of them, puffed reverently on his pipe, which he would then hand over gently and with some ceremony to our contemplative guest Anthony, who in turn passed it along to Helen's husband, Hog.

As I looked about, I tried to imagine what the others were thinking of on this night. Surely Helen, like me, had felt the tug of civilization in our short time at the fort, and I think we both wondered now if we would be able to get all the way back when the time came.

Perhaps our Indian families thought about the coming winter, or in Little Wolf's case, about the uncertain future of the people with whose welfare he is forever charged. Perhaps they thought only of the next day's journey, of the friends and family with whom they would soon be reunited.

Surely our new monk prayed to his God to show him the way in this strange new world; I smiled at him when I caught his eye so that he might know that he was among friends.

From his bed, Horse Boy stared into the fire, his bright gunmetal-colored eyes reflecting the flickering flames. Perhaps he thought only of his horses on this cold autumn night, for soon he would bundle himself up in a blanket and leave the tent to sit up with them, guarding against thieves and wolves, before being relieved by another boy just before dawn. Such a hardy race of people these are! God love them . . .

After a time Helen and Hog, who is himself a quiet and dignified fellow, and seems genuinely fond of his eccentric artist wife, rose to return to their own lodge. Although I offered to make a place for Anthony to sleep the night in our lodge, he declined, saying that he had a blanket with him and that he was quite accustomed to sleeping upon the bare ground. It was a part of his devotional labors, he said.

I went outside with the guests when they left, to do my business before bed. Especially with winter coming on I must teach the savages the utility of a chamber pot—a clever white man invention that has some real application to tent living!

Although I had wrapped myself in a blanket, I felt the sting of wind on my cheeks as I exited the tipi. We were camped in the crook of a small creek surrounded only by high, treeless plains—uninteresting and lonely country, with nothing to break the wind, which comes whipping down off the ridges to assault our little grouping of tipis huddled here together, so small and defenseless. How tiny we are, exposed to the huge elements! No wonder these people are superstitious in the face of it. No wonder they try to curry favor with the gods of the four directions, with the gods of Earth and Heaven, with the spirits of wild animals and weather at whose mercy we live. And no wonder, by the same token, that the white man builds his forts and houses, his stores and churches—his flimsy fortifications against the vastness and emptiness of earth which he does not know to worship but tries instead to simply fill up.

Now I pull my dress to my waist and squat alongside a low-growing sagebrush, the only available protection from the wind, and a thin one at that. The most "uninteresting of vegetation," Captain Bourke calls it, and I suppose it is, although at least it has a strong and to my nose not disagreeable scent, and there have been times when I have rubbed it on my body as a kind of hygienic measure—the savage version of French perfume, I should say.

There is no moon tonight and the wind has scoured the clouds from the sky and the heavens shine above me. As I squat to pee I look upward at the billions of stars and planets in the heavens and somehow my own insignificance no longer terrifies me as it once did, but comforts me, makes me feel a part, however tiny, of the whole complete and perfect universe . . . and when I die the wind will still blow and the stars still shine, for the place I occupy on earth is no more permanent than the water I now make, absorbed by the sandy soil, dried instantly by the constant prairie wind . . .

28 September 1875

We take our time making our way back to the Powder River country, describing a circuitous route in the process. The Indians have a peculiar way of traveling that might seem to a white person unplanned and quite random. In this case, the scouts lead the way, the People follow—first north and then veering as if by sudden change of plan to the east and the pine-timbered hills around Camp Robinson, where this journey truly began all those months ago. But this time we skirt the camp itself, and avoid the few white settlements that are springing up around it. These are mostly a hastily contructed and seemingly haphazard grouping of shacks and lean-tos, with sod roofs and mud streets; there is nothing graceful about them and it is difficult to recognize in their shantytown appearance the refined hand of civilization—or for that matter any particular improvement upon the raw countryside itself.

There are cattlemen moving into the country around Camp Robinson, and one day as we were passing through some of our young men went out on a hunting party and killed and slaughtered several beeves. I tried to explain to my husband that the cattle belonged to the settlers and that by killing them we would only bring trouble down upon the People, but Little Wolf answered that the settlers had driven off the buffalo and killed out the game in this country and that the People must eat as they travel. In any case, he said, he could not control the young men who went out to hunt and found cows where once there had been buffalo. As is so often the case, I found it difficult to mount an effective argument against Little Wolf's plain logic.

But at the feasts that followed this hunt, the diners made faces of disdain and much grunting of disapproval at the taste of the beef—and I admit that it is not so flavorful as the wild buffalo to which even I now confess a preference.

From the hills above Robinson we made a short visit to the nearby Red Cloud Agency, where Little Wolf powwowed with some of the Dakota leaders, including Red Cloud himself. They discussed the government commission, which was presently at the Army camp trying to negotiate the purchase of the Black Hills, and which included our former Reverend's superior, Bishop Whipple. Little Wolf chose not to attend these meetings, as did many of the Sioux, for the simple reason that neither he, nor they, had any intention of "selling" the Black Hills, even if authorized to do so, which, of course, none are.

However, as usual, the Indians are very much divided on the question. Perhaps because he is already settled on his own agency, Red Cloud himself seems to be in favor of the sale—even though his people have been so poorly provided for by the Great White Father that they seem nearly destitute compared to ours. At the council, Red Cloud told Little Wolf that so many white miners had already invaded the Black Hills that it was no longer possible to stem the tide, that the tribes might as well receive something for the land, rather than nothing, for one way or another, it was being taken from them, in the same way that the whites took everything. After much, sometimes rather heated, discussion and smoking of pipes, no real consensus on the matter was reached. This division and inability to mount a united front is, as John Bourke suggested, one of the greatest disadvantages that the Indians face in their dealings with the United States government.

While camped briefly at Red Cloud, we were visited by the agent there, a smarmy, unctuous fellow named Carter, who came to our lodge in an effort to enroll Little Wolf's band on the agency rolls. When I spoke to the man in English, he was quite taken aback, having paid me no mind as "just another squaw." Evidently he had no knowledge of the Brides program, for he assumed at first that I must be a captive white woman, and even offered to rescue me! The man became ever more agitated when I explained to him that I was married to the Chief, and that there were others like me also living with the Cheyennes of our own free will. I quite enjoyed Agent

Carter's discomfort and did not feel it necessary to elaborate on the subject of the program which had brought us here.

"Ma'am, you're awful pretty to be in such a terrible mess," he said solicitously, assuming me to be among that unfortunate class of "fallen whores," who in their descent from respectable whoredom had, as a last resort, attached themselves to the savages. And then he told me that he knew a woman who had recently opened a respectable "boardinghouse" in the little town of Crawford, which has sprung up near Robinson. Her establishment is frequented by soldiers at the camp, mail and freight carriers, muleskinners, miners, and the general riffraff that has attached itself to our western outposts—although to hear this fellow tell it, a far more genteel clientele than the savages whom we had been forced to service, and who, he assured me, were not allowed to so much as set foot in Mrs. Mallory's place, let alone fraternize with her girls.

At this I took real umbrage; I explained to the man again that we were wives, not prostitutes—married in the eyes of the church and our own government—that we were here of our own free will, and that, indeed, such a demeaning institution as prostitution did not even exist among the Cheyennes. And I further suggested to him that if he didn't leave our lodge at that very moment, I would inform my husband of his insults and he would very likely be skinned alive as punishment and possibly roasted over a hot fire for our heathen supper to boot! I am happy to report that a faster exit has never before been accomplished!

3 October 1875

From Red Cloud Agency we moved north into the Black Hills; Little Wolf wished to see for himself the influx of whites into the area, and also wishes to make a ceremony at *Novavose*—Medicine Lodge—before winter sets in. This place, called Bear Butte by the whites, is a perfectly symmetrical flat-topped mountain on the northern edge of the Black Hills—sacred ground to the Cheyennes. As I learn more about their beliefs, it strikes me that one reason the savages had not more enthusiastically embraced Reverend Bunny's efforts to convert them to Christianity is that they already have in place an elaborate and to their way of thinking perfectly satisfactory religion of their own—complete with a messiah character, named *Motse'eoeve*—Sweet Medicine himself, a kind of prophet and instructor who rather than coming from such a distant and incomprehensible place as Nazareth, hails right here from *Novavose*—the very heart of the Cheyennes' own country. Is it any wonder they don't wish to give this land up?

According to legend, Sweet Medicine appeared to the People here long, long ago and told them that a person was going to come among them. This person was going to be all sewed up (the Indian manner of saying wearing white man clothing), and that he was going to destroy everything that the People needed to live—he would come among the People and from them take everything, including the game and the earth itself.

While the Indian religion may be rife with superstition, Sweet Medicine's prophecy is lent some credibility by the fact that it is so clearly coming true in our own times.

Regarding matters of spirituality, our anchorite, "Anthony of the Prairie," is already becoming, as I had predicted he would, quite popular among us all. The Cheyennes immediately accepted him as a holy man—for his spirit of simplicity and self-denial is something that they greatly admire—as they do his daily recitation of liturgies, for the Indians are inordinately fond of any form of chanting and religious observance.

I must say that I look forward to our other white women meeting Anthony as well, for I take from him myself a certain strength. He is a quiet, devout man, and yet has a rather mischievous sense of humor. Although I have never been of a highly religious nature myself, I can't help but have the feeling that he has come among us for some reason, and will serve some valuable purpose. Good Lord . . . perhaps I am finding faith after all!

As to the Black Hills, prettier country I have never before seen, timbered with pine, fir, and juniper, and teeming with game of all variety. Thankfully, the weather has turned mild again, perfect autumn temperatures that seem to promise some brief respite from the coming winter. All of our moods have improved immeasurably with the warmer climate and this new, beautiful country. I think we were all rather dispirited by our short visit at the Red Cloud Agency, which seemed so poor, the people there so dejected. Is that, then, to be the inevitable grand end of our mission?—to bring our own people from freedom and prosperity to this state of abject impoverishment and inactivity—hardly assimilated so much as simply confined . . .

Since we left Fort Laramie I have had several conversations with my husband about the necessity for him to give up his People at one of the agencies. I have, toward this end, invoked the name of his child whom I carry and that of all the other expectant mothers, pointing out that if born on the agency, these children will not only be safe from harm but will also have the advantage of attending schools, which will enable them, in turn, to help teach the People the new white man life. "This is what you wanted,"

I say to Little Wolf. "This is what you requested when you went to Washington."

And Little Wolf will only answer that the People are quite prosperous at the moment and have managed to keep away from the whites, and he does not wish to give up this good life just yet. As to your children, he says, they will belong to the white tribe soon enough, but they should have the opportunity to know something about their fathers' world, as well, about how it was to live in the old way—even if this is only for the first year of their lives. They have plenty of time later to learn the new white man way of living.

"We will look back on this life that we have now," Little Wolf said softly, "and we will think that no people on earth were ever happier, were ever richer; we have good lodges and plenty of game; we have many horses and beautiful possessions and I am not yet prepared to give this up to live in the white man way. Not yet. Another fall, another winter, perhaps one more summer . . . then we shall see."

The Cheyennes have a different conception of time than we do; such things as calendar deadlines and ultimatums mean little to them; their world is less static in this way than ours, and does not lend itself well to temporal matters beyond those of the seasons.

"But the Army won't give you that time," I tried to explain to Little Wolf. "This is what I am telling you. You must take the People into the agency this winter."

I wonder now if it was partly for this reason that Little Wolf brought us to Red Cloud, to see the sobering future we can expect for our children in such a place. For truly if that is what we have to look forward to, our present freedom, however temporary, seems more precious than ever.

5 October 1875

All of our efforts to avoid encounters with the invading miners notwithstanding, we have seen much evidence of them in the Black Hills. We have cut the trails of several large wagon trains moving through the country; and have come upon a number of new settlements along the way. Our scouts have also reported the presence of Army troops in the region. Under strict orders from Little Wolf, our warriors have harassed no one, and we passed so stealthily that I doubt the whites were even aware of our presence. However, Phemie told me that some of the young men, including her own husband—Black Man—had slipped off to join a war party of Oglala

Sioux who were making raids upon the immigrants. Nothing good can come of this, I know.

8 October 1875

We have been camped for several days in the vicinity of the mountain called *Novavose*—at which site the savages are holding all manner of religious observances; there is feasting and dancing and vision seeking and the almost constant beating of drums; many of the ceremonies are too elaborate and too complicated to one unversed in the religion to understand or even attempt to record; there has been much fasting and sacrifices made and other self-imposed hardships endured by the men—including sundry bodily mutilations by the younger men, such revolting practices as piercing their breasts and tying themselves to stakes, or to painted shields (Helen's artistic talents again very much in demand!) which they then proceeded to drag about the dance circle in excruciating pain. Whatever accommodations and adaptations we have been able to make to their life and religion—and these have been considerable—no civilized person can find these primitive customs of self-mutilation to be anything less than repugnant. However, our monk Anthony has been extremely interested in these practices and is taking copious notes on all of the heathens' religious observances. He believes that they might have some application to—perhaps even roots in—Christianity itself. Wishful thinking on the part of the holy man, I should say, but then, I suppose that is, after all, his job. On Anthony's behalf I shall also say that he spreads the Gospel of Jesus very gently among the People, with none of the Reverend Hare's fire and brimstone or threats of damnation, and none of Narcissa White's evangelical zeal. Rather he visits from lodge to lodge in such a spirit of honesty, humility, and generosity that the people hardly know that they are being preached to. He is, I think, our best hope yet for the salvation of their souls . . . if salvation they require . . .

Yesterday, Little Wolf's primary advisor, Woman Who Moves Against the Wind, came to our lodge to tell the Chief of a vision she has had. She is a very strange creature, with wild black hair and a peculiar light in her eyes that is like the reflection of flames from a fire. She lives all alone, and because she, too, is a holy person, her needs are met by other members of the tribe. The men bring her game and the women keep her supplied with other necessities. She is considered to be a seer, one who lives with one foot in the other world—the "real world behind this one." My husband the Chief holds her advice in very high esteem.

Now she sat cross-legged and whispered to Little Wolf: I sat as close as possible behind them and strained to hear her. *"In my vision, I saw the People's lodges consumed in flames,"* she began. *"I saw all of our possessions stacked by the soldiers in huge piles and set afire—everything destroyed, everything we own consumed by the flames. I saw the People driven naked into the hills, where we crouched like animals among the rocks."* Here the woman wrapped her arms around herself and rocked back and forth as if freezing. I felt the chill of her words myself. *"It is very cold,"* she continued, *"and the People are freezing, many dying, many babies freezing blue as chunks of river ice in their mother's arms. . . ."*

"No!" I suddenly cried out, as if involuntarily. "Stop that talk! It is nonsense! I do not believe in your visions, they are nothing but pure superstition. I do not listen to such talk! Someone run and find Brother Anthony for me, he will tell us the truth." But I realized as soon as I said it that I was speaking English, and both Little Wolf and Woman Who Moves Against the Wind only looked at me somewhat impatiently, as if waiting for my outburst to be over. Then they huddled closer and I could no longer hear their words.

10 October 1875

Shortly after the seer left our lodge, Little Wolf, without a word to anyone, himself departed. Only later did I learn that he had climbed to the top of the butte to seek his own vision. The Chief is a solitary man and clearly has much on his mind, and presumably he went off to think over what the medicine woman had said.

Little Wolf returned to our lodge after three days and three nights. Of his vision quest he said simply, "I have made offerings to the Great Medicine that he might protect the People from harm. But I had no sign from him."

14 October 1875

From Medicine Lodge we make our way north and again west, moving silently across the undulating plains. After these several days of religious observance the people are reserved and subdued, exhausted by their ceremonies, and—having seen firsthand the continued invasion of the whites into their sacred land—anxious about their future. All have by now learned of the apocalyptic vision of Woman Who Moves Against the Wind. And all know that while Little Wolf made offerings to the Great Medicine, he failed in his own vision quest. This is not considered to be a good thing.

We do not travel hard after our visit to *Novavose* but continue to meander our way back toward the Powder River country. The fine autumn weather continues. The cottonwoods and box elders and ash turn yellow and red in the river bottoms, and the plains roll out before us—a sea of grass, now golden and ocher, the plum thickets in the coulee a deep shade of purple. There is much game along the way—great herds of buffalo already coming into their heavy winter coats, which hang beneath their bellies nearly to touch the ground; there are antelope by the hundreds, deer, and elk in the fall rut so that the bugling of the latter can be heard across the plains like the trumpets of the Gods. The geese and ducks and cranes are on the move, huge flocks that blacken the sky and fill the air with their honkings and cries. Truly it is a spectacle to behold. "We are blessed by God," said Anthony in his pure simplicity as we watched the sky one day. And who can deny it?

Great coveys of pintailed grouse squirt up ahead of our horses, fan off to the horizon like fall seeds spread on the wind. Helen is thoroughly rejuvenated by the shooting and delights our Indian companions with her prowess with the shotgun. She has given some of them instruction in its use, but I am proud to see that none of them can match her shooting skills.

These have been fine days of easy travel and perfect weather, the People quietly harvesting the plenty of the earth—the fall before the winter, the calm before the storm that, since Medicine Lodge, some whisper is coming.

18 October 1875

It was a true homecoming when we reached the winter camp—the other bands had been arriving for several weeks, coming from all directions like spokes on a wheel running to the hub. Some bands had already come in and left again, having decided to make their camps elsewhere. Some have already elected to go into the agencies for the winter, for word has spread from the scouts and between the Sioux and the Cheyennes of the Great Father's recently issued ultimatum that all the free Indians must give themselves up at one of the agencies by the first day of February or pay the consequences. "Three Stars," as the Indians call General Crook, has promised that those who comply early will be favored with the best land for their reservations and a greater share of provisions. Winter at the agency, with all of their food and other needs supplied by the Great White Father, has been promised to be an easy path for all who willingly take it.

We found upon our return that among those who have gone into the agency are a number of our own women and their husbands. Like all of us, they had become increasingly anxious about the prospect of childbirth in the wilds without real doctors and especially in the wintertime. And who can blame them?

With several months yet to go, I remain generally sanguine about my own impending childbirth. I had very little difficulty with either of my former pregnancies, and gave birth to both my children at home with only a midwife in attendance. Still, regardless of what immediate course of action Little Wolf decides for our band, I am pleased that others have already chosen to go into the agency; this can only be a good thing, and our white women will serve as a kind of advance guard to smooth the way for the rest of us when we go—which by all consensus is now only a matter of time. I am certain that before the winter is out the rest of us will succeed in convincing our husbands to "surrender" to "the inexorable march of civilization," as Captain Bourke rather grandly calls it.

So we rode into camp yesterday afternoon, alerting the others to our arrival by singing our song, the song of the Little Wolf band; all the People sang, even the little children, a joyful song of coming together and friendship. I had myself learned the words and sang as we rode in, as did Phemie, Helen, and the Kelly girls. A lively chorus we made of it, too!

The winter camp has been set in a lovely grassy valley formed by the confluence of Willow Creek and the upper Powder River. It is well protected from the wind and elements, defined by rocky pine-studded bluffs on one side of the river, climbing to timbered foothills, and on the other a network of ravines and coulees that rise to the rolling benches and tablelands of the prairie, and on to the faint outline of the Bighorn Mountains against the distant horizon. The valley appears to have everything we need for the moment—sufficient grass for the horses, running water, and an ample supply of cottonwood for our fires. Several large herds of buffalo have also taken up winter residence in the general vicinity and presently feed as placidly as domestic cows on the rich fall grasses.

In this place we will settle for a time—and make our plans for the future. A welcome settling it will be after the constant travel of the past months.

Martha was beside herself with joy at our return. Even from a distance as we rode in and I made her out, I noticed that she was looking quite large with child herself. She waved excitedly to us as we rode down into the valley off the bench above, singing our song, our horses picking their way carefully down the slope. She jumped up and down, clapping her hands like a child. Then I watched as she did something extraordinary; she slipped a rope bridle over the head of one of the horses tethered beside her lodge, grasped it by the mane, and swung onto its back like an Indian! She wheeled the horse and galloped out to meet us! Good God, I thought, can this be my same friend, Martha, who when first we arrived here could hardly take a step without tripping and falling down? Hah! The one they call Falls Down Woman?

She was breathless when she rode up, but hardly more so than I at the sight of her. "May, oh May," she said, "I cannot tell you how pleased I am to see you home! I had begun to worry so for you. Where have you been? You must tell me all about your travels. And I, too, have news for you. Much has happened since you've been away. But first, I must know—did you go all the way to Fort Laramie? Did you dine with the officers? Did you see your Captain?"

I couldn't help but notice how hale and healthy Martha looked. The added weight of pregnancy becomes her; indeed, I'd never seen her look as well. Where, upon our departure all those months ago, she was still mousy and frightened—she has actually grown quite pretty in the interim—her cheeks rosy, her arms brown and strong. I laughed in astonishment and happiness. "All that in good time, dear," I said, "we will have a long visit after we have made camp. And I am so pleased to see you, too. But good Lord, Martha, look at you, you look like a wild Indian! And riding bareback like a trick rider—hardly a proper activity for a pregnant woman!"

"I've never felt better, May, I think that pregnancy and the wilderness life agree with me . . . You were right I was fine without you . . . I suppose I have become a wild Indian!"

And then we both laughed and rode into camp side by side, chattering away like schoolgirls.

NOTEBOOK VII

Winter

"When the end of the village was reached we were to charge at full gallop down through the lines of 'tipis,' firing our revolvers at everything in sight. Just as we approached the village we came upon a ravine some ten feet in depth and of varying width, the average being not less than fifty. We got down this deliberately, and at the bottom and behind a stump saw a young boy about fifteen years old driving his ponies. He was not ten feet off. The youngster wrapped his blanket about him and stood like a statue of bronze, waiting for the fatal bullet. The American Indian knows how to die with as much stoicism as the East Indian. I leveled my pistol . . ."

(John G. Bourke, from his memoir, *On the Border with Crook*)

⊰⊱

1 November 1875

We arrived at winter camp in timely fashion, for two days ago the first snows came. Fortunately, we had nearly a fortnight of mild weather previous to this and the men made a number of successful hunts. Now the larder is full with all manner of game—fresh, dried, and smoked, and we seem to be exceptionally well supplied.

A frigid wind blew down from the north for an entire day before delivering the full brunt of the blizzard. And then the snows marched across the plains like an approaching army, blowing horizontally, at first lightly but soon so thickly that even going outside to do one's business was to risk becoming disoriented and lost in the maelstrom. Fortunately the camp itself is situated so as to be partially protected from the worst of the wind and drifting snow. After another day, the wind began to subside, but the snow continued, falling straighter now, until the air was windless and the flakes, as big as silver dollars, fell steadily. For two days and two nights it snowed thus. And then the wind came again and blew the skies clear and as suddenly stopped. The mercury plunged and the stars in the sky glittered coldly off the fresh snow, which had drifted in huge sculpted mounds across the rolling prairie so that it appeared as if the earth itself had shifted, reformed itself with the storm.

Of course we were very much "housebound" during the storm and there was no visiting among us for those several days. All stayed as much as possible in their lodges; and though ours was warm and snug, the confinement became, finally, quite tedious. After the wind abated I did venture down to the river one morning for a bath, which cold as it is, I do not intend to give up—this activity, at least, allowing me to get out of the "house" however briefly.

5 November 1875

The weather continues clear and cold, but at least we are able to get about now to visit. I should mention that an inventory of our numbers since our band's return from Fort Laramie reveals that well over half of our women chose to move with their husbands and "families" to the agency for the winter—good timing on their parts as a move now with the snow would be virtually impossible. Gretchen and her doltish husband No Brains are still among us, as are Daisy Lovelace and Bloody Foot, of whom Daisy has grown even fonder. "Ah *nevah* would have believed *mahself*," she says, "that I could fall in *luuuve* with a *niggah Injun* boy, but *ah'm* afraid that this is exactly what has happened. I don't care if he is *daaaak* as *naaaght, Ah luuuve* the man, and I am proud to say that *Ah am* carryin' his *chaald*."

As to Phemie, especially since our visit to Red Cloud, she and I have been in some conflict about the matter of enrolling at the agency, and have had several heated discussions on the question. For my part, I argue that such a move is inevitable and in the best interest of the People—while she equates the reservation system with the institution of slavery itself.

"My husband *Mo'ohtaeve'ho'e* and I have discussed the matter," Phemie says. "He does not remember our people's slavery for he has lived most of his life as a free man. Thus we have decided that we will not surrender to the agency. My days of enslavement to white folks are behind me."

"Phemie, there is no slavery on the reservation," I argue. "The People will own the land and will earn their livings as free men and women."

To which Phemie answers in her melodious and imperious manner. "I see," she says. "Then the Cheyennes will enjoy complete equality with the whites, is this what you are telling me, May?"

"That's right, Phemie," I answer, but I hesitate just long enough that she senses my lack of conviction on the matter.

"And if the People are equal to the white tribe, why then are they being restricted to reservations?" Phemie asks.

"They are being asked to live voluntarily and temporarily on reservations as a first step toward assimilating them into our own society," I answer, and already I know that I am walking right into the trap she lays for me.

Phemie laughs her deep, rich chuckle. "I see," she said. "And if they do not 'volunteer' to live on the reservation? Then am I to understand that they may remain on this land which belongs to them and upon which they have been living for many hundreds of years and where some of them, myself and my husband included, are quite content to remain?"

"No, Phemie," I answer, abashed, assuming the role now, involuntarily, of Captain Bourke, "they cannot live here any longer. You cannot. If you try to stay here past the February deadline, you will be breaking the law and you will be punished for it."

"The law made by the whites," Phemie says. "The whites being, of course, the superior race, who make these laws in order to keep the inferior in their place. That, May, is, by definition, slavery."

"Dammit Euphemia!" I answer in frustration. "It's not the same thing at all."

"No?" she asks. "Explain to me then the difference."

And, of course, I cannot.

"My people were once forcibly removed from their homeland," Phemie continues. "My mother was taken from her family when she was just a child. All my life I have dreamed of going back for her. Now, living among these people, I have in a sense done so. This is as close as I will ever get to my mother's homeland, to my family. And I have promised myself, May, that one way or another I will live from now on as a free woman, and I will die, if necessary, to protect that freedom. I could never tell these people that they should surrender and go to live on reservations or at agencies, because to do so is to take from them their freedom, to make of them slaves to a higher order. That, my friend, is my position on the matter and nothing you can say to me will change my mind."

"But Phemie," I plead, "why then did you sign up for this program? You are an educated woman; you must have understood that the process of assimilation that we are facilitating is, inevitably, a process whereby the smaller native population is absorbed into the greater invading one. It is the way of history, has always been."

"Ah, yes, May," Phemie chuckles, seemingly amused at my distress, "*your* version of history, the white man's version. But not mine, certainly, not the history of these, our adopted people. My history, my mother's history, is one of being torn from homeland and family and enslaved in a foreign land. Theirs is one of being pushed from their own land and slaughtered when they refuse to give it up. Absorbed? Assimilated? Hardly. Our common history is one of dispossession, murder, and slavery."

"Perhaps you're right, Phemie," I say. "Which is precisely our purpose here. To see that history does not repeat itself, to prove that there is another way, a peaceful solution in which both races learn from the other, learn to live in harmony together. Our children will be the final proof of this commitment, and the true hope for the future. Let us say, for example, that my son were to grow up to marry your daughter. Think of it, Phemie! Their offspring would be part white, part black, part Indian. In this way we are pioneers, you and I, in a great and noble experiment!"

"Oh May," Phemie says with real sadness in her voice. "The plantations were full of mulattos—people of mixed blood and of all shades of color. I myself am one. I am half-white. My father was the master. Did this make me free? Did this make me accepted by the 'superior' culture? No, I was still a slave. In many cases our lives were more difficult for being of mixed blood, for we were considered neither black nor white, and resented by both. Your Captain was right. You've seen the half-breeds around the forts. Do they appear assimilated to you?"

"They come and go among the two races," I said, without conviction. "But they were all born to women of the exploited culture, fathered by the exploiters. We women hold the key, Phemie, we mothers. We couple with the Cheyennes of our own free will; we bear their children as gifts to both races."

"For the sake of your children I hope you're right," Phemie said. "You asked me a moment ago why I signed up for this program. As I told you months ago on our train ride here, I signed up to live as a free woman, to serve no man, to be inferior to no one. I shall never give up my freedom again, and I shall choose to have children only when I know that they may live as free men and women. If I have to fight first for their freedom, so be it. And to be born on a reservation is not freedom."

And thus Phemie and I go round and round . . . I, advocating peaceful surrender in the interest of future harmony, an idealistic vision of the future perhaps . . . and one, it is true, without precedent in human history. And Phemie advocating resistance, intransigence, militancy—in the process inflaming her husband and her warrior society against the idea of going into the agency, against the invading white man, against the soldiers.

But we have time yet—a long winter to grapple with these questions—to reach some consensus. As always sentiment among those remaining in the camp runs decidedly mixed on the matter of going in. Some of us are making small inroads persuading our own families that this is the only reasonable course of action. Due to the great influence that women hold in the Cheyenne family, I have been concentrating my own efforts on my fellow tentmates. I describe to them the many marvelous inventions of the whites—with some of which they are already familiar—the many comforts they will own in civilization, the conveniences and advantages which are so dear to a woman's heart. . . . For win the women's hearts and those of the People will soon follow.

10 November 1875

Today Gretchen and I have broken yet another barrier between the sexes. If only temporarily . . .

We have all long envied the custom that the men observe of the "sweat lodge." This is a special tipi which serves the same function as a steam house in our own culture, except that this one seems also to hold special religious connotations—and women are strictly *verboten,* as Gretchen puts it. A large fire is built in the center of the sweat lodge, upon which rocks are laid until they are heated nearly red-hot and then water poured over the rocks to create steam—this whole process attended to by a medicine man who also frequently speaks some ceremonial mumbo jumbo and passes a pipe for the men to puff contentedly upon. The participants themselves sit in a circle around the outside of the fire, until they are perspiring freely and when they can bear the heat no longer run outside and roll around in the snow or leap into a hole chopped into the now frozen river. They then return to the sweat lodge to begin the process anew. This strikes me as both a healthful and a hygienic recreation—particularly in the wintertime.

The other day I was visiting with Gretchen in her lodge and she happened to mention—somewhat longingly I thought—that her husband, No Brains, was presently performing a sweat-lodge ceremony. She told me that in the old country her people observed exactly this same practice through the long, dark, northern winters—without the religious overtones, of course, and with no prohibitions upon the sex of the participants. Gretchen's own family had brought the custom with them to America and built a sweat house on their farm in Illinois—which they enjoyed all year.

"Oh, May, *der is nutting bedder dan a goot* steam bath, I tell you *dat,*" Gretchen said, shaking her head mournfully.

"And why should we not be able to take steam baths ourselves?" I asked.

"Oh, no May," she said, "*de* men not allow women in *de* sweat lodge here. My *husband* he tells me *dat.*"

"Why not?"

"Because, it is only for *de* men," Gretchen said. "It is just *de* way *de* People says so."

"Gretchen, what good reason is that?" I said. "Let's you and I march right over there now and have a sweat bath ourselves!"

"Oh, no I don't *tink* so, May," Gretchen said, "I don't *tink dat be sech a goot* idea . . ."

"Of course it is, it's a wonderful idea," I insisted. "And think how invigorating it will be! It is time we taught these people that any activity that is suitable for the men should also be enjoyed by the women. What's good for the goose is good for the gander!"

"Vell, OK, May, *vhat de* hell," said Gretchen. *"Vatch* you going to wear in *de* sweat house, May?"

"I'm going to wear a towel, dear," I answered. "What else would one wear in a sweat lodge?"

"Yah, May, me too," said Gretchen, nodding. *"Dat's* a *goot* idea."

Many of us had brought cotton towels with us when we first came here, a luxury that the Indians have also discovered, and which item is now available at all the trading posts. Thus I fetched my towel from my lodge and went back to meet Gretchen so that we might make our assault on the male bastion of the sweat lodge together.

Truly, living in such close proximity, a sense of modesty regarding our physical bodies is hardly at issue among most of us any longer—and no one pays the slightest attention whether one is clothed from head to toe or half-naked. Going about with one's breasts free seems quite natural. And so Gretchen and I stripped off our dresses, giggling like schoolgirls plotting a prank, wrapped our towels around our enormous pregnant waists, and dashed through the snow to the sweat lodge. We scratched on the covering to the opening. "Hurry up, it's freezing out here!" I cried in my best Cheyenne. I believe now that the medicine man was so shocked to hear a woman's voice demanding entrance, that he opened the flap just a crack out of pure curiosity to see who might have the audacity to challenge this "men only" institution. And when he did so, we did not hesitate for a moment but burst through the opening into the wonderful humid warmth of the sweat lodge, laughing and quite pleased with ourselves. At our sudden appearance, there arose from the men seated around the fire a great grunting of alarm. The medicine man himself, old White Bull, whom I find to be a tiresome and humorless old bag of wind, was not in the least bit amused by our uninvited entrance, and began to speak sternly to us, waving at us a rattle that the Cheyennes use to ward off evil spirits. "You women go away," he said. "Leave here immediately. This is a very bad thing!"

"Not bad at all," I answered. "It's perfectly delightful. And we're staying until we have ourselves a good sweat!" With which Gretchen and I sat ourselves down right in front of the fire.

Several of the men, the most stringent traditionalists, stood and left the sweat lodge, grumbling and grunting indignantly as they did so. Gretchen's husband spoke sternly to her. "What are you doing here, wife? You shame me by coming here in this manner. This is no place for women. Go home!"

"You *gest be quite* you *bick* dope!" she answered (we have all remarked on the fact that Gretchen even speaks Cheyenne with a Swiss accent!), shaking her finger at her husband, her enormous naked breasts flushed pink as scalded suckling pigs in the steamy heat. "A man don't talk to his wife like *dat,* mister! You don't like *dat* I come here *dat gest* too damn bad, *den* you can *gest* go home yourself!" The man was instantly cowed by his wife, and fell silent, much to the evident delight of a number of the other sweat bathers. *"Hemomoonamo!"* someone hissed. ("Henpecked husband!") *"Hou,"* said another, nodding. *"Hemomoonamo!"* And they all nickered softly in amusement.

This bit of humor helped to settle the men, and the sweat-lodge ceremony continued much as if we were not there. Indeed, I think it served the men's purpose simply to pretend that we were not there. After Gretchen and I had both broken into heavy perspiration, and the heat inside the lodge had become nearly unbearable, we crawled to the opening where old White Bull let us out and then we ran buck naked to the river, squealing like crazed children, Gretchen running with her heavy lumbering gait, her massive breasts swinging like well-loaded parfleches.

A thin skin of new ice had already formed on the opening of the water hole and through this we plunged, gasping and trying to catch our breaths, exiting again as quickly as we could and running back lickety-split to the sweat lodge. An ill-advised activity perhaps, for pregnant women, but Indian babies must be hardy to the elements.

But this time, of course, stodgy old White Bull did not answer our entreaties at the entrance, would not untie the lodge flap. "We are freezing out here!" I cried. "You, old man, let us in there right now!" But he did not answer and finally, lest we really did freeze, we ran back to Gretchen's lodge, where we dried ourselves by her fire.

"You know what we shall do, Gretchen?" I suggested. "We shall build our own sweat lodge for the women. Yes, it promises to be a long winter, and we have plenty of hides and nothing but time, so we shall all band together to sew our own sweat lodge, and when we are finished, there will be no men allowed! It will be strictly a girls' club."

"Goot idea, May!" Gretchen concurred. *"Dat's* a damn *goot* idea. No men *allowt!* Girls only!"

And so this is how we shall pass the winter. Making what diversions for ourselves that we can, pranks and make-work projects like our sweat lodge, anything to keep ourselves active. For the days, shorter each in their stingy measure of daylight, can seem interminable if one spends them sitting in the dim lodge. We have our chores, of course, going for the living water in the early morning, and gathering firewood—neither of which activity I object to as at least they get me out of the damn tent. And there is always cooking to be done and food preparation and cleaning and sewing and all the other, sometimes dreary projects of wifedom. But these, too, also serve to prevent idleness.

We remaining white women have become, if anything, even closer in our sisterhood. Without the constant activities of traveling—dismantling and reassembling the lodge, packing and unpacking—we have more time to meet regularly in one or another of our lodges, where we consult each other on the progress or lack thereof that we each make in our efforts to convince our families to go into the agency before February.

In our daily meetings we also compare our respective pregnancies, plan our upcoming births, and offer each other what moral support we can. We gossip and argue, laugh and weep, and sometimes we just sit quietly together around the fire, holding hands, staring into the flames and embers, and wondering at the mystery of our lives, wondering what is to come . . . happy that we have one another, for the winter promises to be long and lonely . . .

We are all much comforted by the presence of Brother Anthony of the Prairie and frequently meet with him in his own spare lodge, which he has erected on the edge of the village. It is a very simple, immaculately clean affair, as befits a monk, and often we sit by his fire and recite the daily liturgy with him.

"In this place I shall build my hermitage in the spring," says Anthony in his soft soothing voice. "In these hills above the river I shall be blessed to have everything I require, for a man needs little to commune with God, but a humble shelter and a pure heart. Later with my hands I shall begin the work of building my abbey. I shall be blessed to have other men of humble minds and simple hearts follow me here, and here we shall pray and study and share the word of God with all who come to us."

It's a lovely image and often we all sit together in contemplative silence and imagine it. I can almost see Brother Anthony's abbey in the hills, can imagine us all worshiping quietly there, can imagine our children and our children's children after us coming to this place . . . it is a fine comforting thought.

Beside reading, reciting the liturgies and instructing us in his Bible, Anthony is teaching us and the native women to bake bread—a fine occupation in the winter and one that fills our tents with wonderful aromas.

The weather continues mostly clear and crisp, with thankfully little wind, and when the sun is up and shining off the pure white prairie, all is very beautiful.

10 December 1875

Nearly a month has passed since my last entry. Time, of course, is not the issue, rather the general torpor of the season and the corresponding lack of interesting occurrences has caused me to rest my pen—to husband and store what little I have to report. Would that we could hibernate like the bears! How wise they are to take their long winter naps and not awake until spring.

The Cheyennes themselves do not appear to suffer from boredom. How lucky they are, for they possess a kind of unlimited patience so that if we are tentbound for days in blizzards, they wait them out without complaint, with a kind of perfect animal-like stillness. Besides simple games that they play, and a bit of gambling among the men, there is little in the way of entertainment—other than storytelling, from which we learn something of the history of these fine people. Of course, they do not read books.

We white women have all read countless times the few volumes that we brought with us or were able to obtain on our last trip to Fort Laramie. I have nearly reduced the Captain's cherished volume of Shakespeare to tatters from my many readings of it, and, of course, much as I may have wished to hoard it for myself, I have made it freely available to the others. Besides our daily visits with Anthony one of our few recreations has been to meet in groups in one or another of our lodges and read the Bard together, passing the book around the circle, each of us reading a different part. But the light is poor in the lodges, especially with the days now so short.

Our women's sweat lodge is now complete and in full operation! It is a perfect delight and we white women have been holding our "councils" there. Hah! We have even encouraged some of the younger and bolder Cheyenne women to join us. Both my tentmates, Pretty Walker and Feather on Head, have attended, with extreme shyness at first, but now more enthusiatically. We have a little girl who tends our fire and keeps a supply of water in the buckets to pour on the hot rocks, and all are welcome—if they are women, that is! We sit, for the most part naked, sweating freely and then dashing for the river. Helen Flight often smokes her pipe and sometimes passes it among the others in a kind of pantomime of the men's dour councils. The Cheyenne women, when they join us, consider this smoking to be quite scandalous, even sacriligious, and will scarcely touch the pipe let alone partake of it.

12 December 1875

I am huge with my baby! Big as a house! I believe that mine is by far the biggest belly in our group! Even Gretchen, herself a hefty woman to begin with, does not seem nearly as large as I. Surely this savage baby of mine is going to be a giant! Fortunately, in spite of the additional bulk I am carrying, I have had a very uneventful pregnancy, almost no illness and, other than the simple act of packing the enormous thing around, very little discomfort. The Cheyennes have all sorts of remedies—teas which they brew from various roots, herbs, flowers, leaves, and grasses—some of which are not disagreeable to the taste; these they give to pregnant women—who are doted over and cared for by the other women, really to the point of distraction.

Much game remains in the vicinity, and the clear weather has been conducive to the hunt, so that we continue to have a steady supply of fresh meat. All of which makes for plenty of work for both men and women so that at least there is less idleness among us—there is always skinning and butchering and tanning to be done.

I have learned to embroider hides with trade beads, and this activity I enjoy—it is a pleasant, time-consuming craft, often peacefully pursued in a group. We sit by the fire, chatting and gossiping and passing the time. Now that most of us white women are so much more proficient in our use of the native tongue, we have achieved a greater intimacy with our fellow Cheyenne wives. Although they have a quite different way of looking at the world than Caucasians, I find that as women we have nearly as much in common as separates us by culture; every day we learn more about one another and have a greater mutual appreciation and respect. Thus we all share the same daily cares and worries, the same labors. And with our pregnancies—for some of the Indian wives are also pregnant—we share the burdens, the responsibilities, and the joys of impending motherhood.

And in our increasing ability to better communicate we also share the fresh glue of humor. At first the Cheyenne women found our white women's irreverence toward the men to be quite scandalous. But now our small jests and banter about the male race in general seems to delight them, seems to unite us all in a new bond of sisterhood. Together we nod and *"hou"* and giggle enthusiastically as, with a little prompting from us, the Indian women discover . . . no, not "discover" . . . I mean to say, "acknowledge" the female's natural superiority to the male.

In spite of her reserve, I am sometimes even able to elicit a tiny sly smile from Quiet One. Like many who speak sparingly she is keenly observant of all that takes place around her. The other day, for example, Little Wolf was holding council in the lodge with several other heads of state in attendance, including the old Chief Dull Knife, and a fellow named *Masehaeke*, or Crazy Mule (he was named this by our Sioux neighbors because one time he rode into their camp on a mule, and one of them said, "Here comes that crazy Cheyenne who rides the mule."). Crazy Mule is a tiresomely long-winded fellow and I always dread when he attends the councils because on he drones—on and on—the only good thing about it, I suppose, being that his voice has the effect of a sleeping potion and instantly puts the children into a deep slumber. I have even sometimes observed Little Wolf and others among the council dozing off while the man is speaking. In any case, the other day, Crazy Mule was going on in his usual fashion and I noticed that Quiet One was looking at me in the shy way she has of observing people from the periphery. I smiled at her and held my hand up to the fire to cast a shadow puppet on the lodge covering above old Crazy Mule's head. Opening and closing my thumb and fingers I made my shadow puppet to be yakking on like the man himself. This woke up the assemblage! There was much stifling of laughter from those who could observe my chattering shadow puppet, and even Quiet One allowed herself a smile large enough to warrant covering her mouth demurely with her hand.

According to Captain Bourke in an opinion expressed to me during our brief meeting at Fort Laramie, the only true hope for the advancement of the savage is to teach him that he must give up this allegiance to the tribe and look toward his own individual welfare. This is necessary, Bourke claims, in order that he may function effectively in the "individualized civilization" of the Caucasian world. To the Cheyenne such a concept remains completely foreign—the needs of the People, the tribe, and above all the family within the tribe are placed always before those of the individual. In this regard they live somewhat like the ancient clans of Scotland. The selflessness of my husband, Little Wolf, for instance, strikes me as most noble and something that hardly requires "correction" by civilized society. In support of his own thesis, the Captain uses the unfortunate example of the Indians who have been pressed into service as scouts for the U.S. Army. These men are rewarded for their efforts as good law-abiding citizens—paid wages, fed, clothed, and generally cared for. The only requirement of their employment, their allegiance to the white father, is that they betray their own people and their own families . . . I fail to see the nobility or the advantage of such individualized private initiative . . .

18 December 1875

A disturbing accident has occurred. Yesterday our Quiet One invited several people to our lodge to partake of a feast of bread that she had just baked. Somehow she confused a bag of arsenic powder for that of baking soda. The Cheyennes obtain the arsenic from the trading post and use it to poison wolves.

The results of this mix-up can be readily imagined. By the grace of God, or perhaps, the grace of the Great Medicine, no one died—but for a pair of hapless dogs who were given bites of the bread in order to confirm the fact that it was indeed poisoned. By then several of the guests had already been stricken. I sent Horse Boy to summon Anthony and some of the others, and together we prevailed upon the afflicted to vomit. Thank God I and none of the other pregnant women had ourselves partaken of the bread, for it would surely have cost us our babies.

All have now recovered, although for everyone, it was a long and painful ordeal. Little Wolf himself became deathly ill. I feared deeply for his life and sat up all night with him. Of course, poor Quiet One was completely distraught at her part in the near catastrophe; and I have tried to comfort her as much as I could.

The event has served as a catalyst to a council being called to discuss this question of poisoning the wolves—a practice the Cheyennes only recently learned from the white agents, who have advised them that by poisoning the wolves, there will be more game for the people. Since its use has become more widespread among the Indians, all have noticed across the prairie the carcasses not only of wolves, but also of coyotes, eagles, hawks, ravens, raccoons, skunks, and even bears, for the poison kills everything that partakes of the arsenic-laced meat or that feeds off the carcasses of its victims.

Our lodge was crowded with a number of prominent chiefs, dignitaries from the various warrior societies, esteemed medicine men, and our own Brother Anthony. Several of our women were also in attendance, the latter, along with a number of Cheyenne women, seated as usual outside the council circle of men.

After the ceremonial pipe had been smoked by the men, the first fellow to speak up was an old medicine man, *Vo'aa'ohmese'aestse,* whose name, unless my Cheyenne is worse than I think, translates to something like, Antelope Bowels Moving.

"It is unfortunate," began the old man, "that Little Wolf's wife confused the wolf poison with the soda for making bread." At this there was much assorted *"houing"* from the assemblage. "Wolf poison is not something that the People should eat in their bread," he continued with a great deal of pomposity. "However, properly used, the poison is a good thing, for it kills the wolves so that there will be more game for the People." Now the old man nodded smugly, and looking extremely self-satisfied with this reasoning, as those assembled *"houed"* enthusiastically.

I could not help myself, and although I knew it was unseemly to do so and would possibly even embarrass my husband, at this point I jumped up from my place and said: "If it is true that there will be more game after we kill the wolves, why is it that our relatives at the agencies who have been using the arsenic for some time now, have no game in their own country?" (Of course, I offer this far more fluent English translation of my remarks.)

Now there arose a small uproar of grunting among the assemblage expressing general disapproval—whether specifically of my remarks or at the fact that a woman had spoken in council at all, is hard to say.

"Vehoae . . ." Little Wolf said with a smile to the assemblage, *"eohkesaahetseveoxohesaneheo'o."* Which roughly translated means, "white women . . . nothing stops them from saying whatever they are thinking."

At this point the "little chief," Black Coyote, spoke up. He is a fine-looking fellow, but with a bit of a reputation as a hothead, and a warmonger, and particularly known for his dislike of white people. "*Mesoke* is right," he said now. "Instead of using the arsenic to poison wolves, we should use it to poison white people. We should make many loaves of poison bread and distribute these among all the whites. We have much more to fear from them than we do from the wolves."

"Well, I didn't say that exactly," I tried to interject over the mixed *houing* of approval from Black Coyote's more militant followers, and the grunting of dissent from his detractors.

"The People have always lived with the wolves and the little wolves (coyotes)," Black Coyote continued. "It is true that sometimes we kill them with arrows or rifles, but there has always been enough game for all of us to share. It was not until the arrival of the white man that the buffalo and the other game began to disappear. The wolf is not our enemy. The white man is our enemy."

This time the young warrior's words were greeted with more *houing* than grunting as he seemed to be winning over the audience.

"I should like to hear what *Maheoneeestseve'ho'e* has to say on the subject," Little Wolf said. This is one of the names the Cheyennes use to refer to Anthony, and means something like "holy-speaking white man."

Anthony spoke softly. He has learned basic Cheyenne in a remarkably short time. "Christ gave the blessing of bread to provide sustenance, not to kill men," he said to Black Coyote. And to the assemblage in general he said, "God put all of the beasts on the Earth for His own divine purpose. He gives abundantly for all to share."

A long silence ensued as all soberly considered Anthony's simple but eloquent remarks.

Finally my husband, Little Wolf, raised his hand and spoke in his usual thoughtful way—without flourish or fanfare, but with plain reason and good sense. "*Mesoke, Mo'ohtaveo'kohome* and *Maheo'neestsevehoe'e* are all correct," said the Chief. "We have always lived with the wolves, and it is true that far more Cheyennes have been killed by the white soldiers than have ever been killed by the wolves." (There was a smattering of *houing* here.) "The wolves and the little wolves have always followed the People wherever we go; eating the offal and cleaning the bones that we leave behind from our hunts. This is not a bad thing, for all thus returns to the earth, and nothing is wasted. Sometimes, it is true that the wolves kill buffalo calves, and deer and elk calves. They kill old and weak animals, this is also true. But the wolves must have meat. If the Great Medicine intended that only the People should be allowed to eat meat, why would he have put wolves upon the earth? With this poison we not only kill the wolves and the little wolves but many other animals who have been our friends and neighbors. I have eaten the poison myself and almost died. I believe that the Great Medicine himself gave me the poison to eat so that I might know that it was a bad thing. It is the white man way to kill all the animals, to drive them away. It is not the way of the People, for we and all the other animals have lived here together, we have always shared, and until the white man came there has always been enough for everyone. Therefore, we will no longer permit the arsenic in this camp. That is my decision."

25 December 1875

Christmas morning! I awoke thinking of my children, feeling the pull of memories . . . the remembrance of Christmas past . . . when I was a child myself and the day still held such promise . . . with St. Nick in his reindeer-drawn sleigh on the roof of our family's house . . . and he would bring me a doll and some sweet candy . . . I had only two Christmases with my dear daughter, Hortense, and only one with sweet Willie before they took me away from them . . .

I woke this Christmas morning, vowing again that one day we would all be reunited, that I will tell my children the stories of their mother's life and adventures.

It has begun snowing again, snowing and blowing, and again we find ourselves tipibound by the weather. But I refused to be so restrained on Christmas Day, and so I rose quietly, dressed warmly, and managed to slip from our lodge before anyone else stirred. All of us sleep more with the snow and cold and short days—in which sense, I suppose, we do hibernate. I took my notebook—strapped to my back—and off I went to visit Martha this Christmas morning.

The wind blew fiercely as I made my way to Martha's lodge, the snow enveloping me in a whirlwind of white that stole my breath away. I could barely see beyond my own nose and at one point I became disoriented, lost all sense of direction, and felt a rising sense of panic. For that moment I was a prisoner of the white wind. But then the driving snow parted just enough that I could make out Martha's lodge coverings—for all of our lodges are painted with different and distinctive paintings.

Martha herself met me at the entrance, surprised to see me so early and out in the storm. "Merry Christmas!" I shouted to her, but she could hardly hear me over the howling of the wind.

"Merry Christmas," I repeated breathlessly after I had entered. It was dark, warm, and snug as a cocoon inside. I shook the snow from my buffalo coat and Martha helped me out of it. The two of us facing each other were like a pair of matching bookends, our protruding bellies touching beneath our antelope skin dresses.

"Christmas?" she said. "Dear God, May, I had completely forgotten. Christmas . . . Come sit by the fire, I'll make coffee for us."

Martha's husband, *Momehexaehe*, still slept in his place before the fire. I have come to know the fellow rather well as Martha and I spend so much time together and his head of frighteningly disarrayed hair notwithstanding, he is a very pleasant, easygoing fellow.

Now Martha and I both sat ensconced on robes, leaning against backrests, which position at least relieved some of the discomfort of our conditions. She stoked the fire with sticks and set a small pot of coffee to boil.

I had made a small gift for Martha—a pair of baby moccasins that I had sewn myself from a butter-soft antelope hide. "I've brought you a little Christmas present, my dear friend," I said, handing her the baby boots which I had enclosed in an embroidered deerskin pouch.

"A present?" Martha said in a small heartbroken voice. "But May, I have nothing for you. I had completely forgotten the day!"

"It makes no difference, Martha," I said. "What's important is that we are together on this day, safe, warm, and healthy."

And then poor Martha began to weep softly—she wept and wept, and I could not make her stop, could not console her.

"What's the matter, Martha," I asked. "Why are you crying?"

But she could only shake her head and weep; could not catch her breath to speak between her pitiful sobs. Finally, when she had calmed herself enough, she said in a tiny choked voice, "I'm sorry, May, I don't know what came over me. Learning that it is Christmas today made me suddenly so desperately homesick and lonely. Not that I have not been happy with my husband, for truly I have, but sometimes I do so miss home. Don't you ever wish that we were home, May? Don't you ever think of it?"

"Every day, Martha," I admitted. "I think of my children, every day of my life. But I do not have a home any longer except for the one that I have right here. Open your gift now, Martha."

She did so, and touched the baby boots lightly with her fingers, tracing the beads, lovingly. "Oh, May, they're absolutely beautiful. These are the most beautiful baby shoes I have ever seen. Thank you. I'm sorry that I have nothing for you on Christmas." And she began to weep anew.

"Hush," I said. "I'm glad that you like them, dear. But please don't cry anymore."

"Do you think that Santa Claus is going to come down the smoke hole in the tipi today?" Martha said, smiling and wiping the tears with the back of her hand.

"I feel certain of it!" I said. "And why shouldn't he? Weren't we always told that Santa visited all children all over the world, wherever they lived. Next year he will visit our new babies, Martha. Think of it! Their first Christmas!"

"I hope that we go to the birthing lodge together, May," Martha said, "that we have our babies at exactly the same time, you and I. But if I go before you, will you promise to come and be with me?"

"Of course I will," I said, "and if I go first, which judging from the size of this enormous belly of mine, I surely will, then you must promise to attend to me."

"I promise," she said. "Oh, May, what a fine friend you have been. Merry Christmas!"

"Merry Christmas to you, Martha," I said. "Let us sing a Christmas hymn together, shall we?"

And so the two of us began to sing . . . while outside the blizzard raged, the wind moaned and howled like a living being, the snow roiled around the lodge, hurtled against it, spinning past to drift out across the prairie. Martha and I sat warm by the fire; we had much to be thankful for on this Christmas morning and we sang with full hearts, with hope and courage for the future:

Oh come all ye faithful,
joyful and triumphant,
Come ye, oh co-ome ye to Be-ethlehem . . .

And now I write these notes by Martha's fire, as she dozes contentedly beside me. Mr. Tangle Hair also sleeps, as does their crone at the entrance. All is quiet and warm inside, and we are safe . . . perhaps I too shall sleep . . .

23 January 1876

I have done something very foolish and in the bargain, risked not only my own life but also the life of my unborn child—and of all those who ventured out to rescue me in the storm. It has been nearly a month since my "accident" and only now am I strong enough to sit up and write. God, how could I have been so careless!

After visiting with Martha on Christmas morning, I dozed off for a time as I reported in my last entry of that day. When I woke, Martha and the others were still asleep. I did not know what time it was and so I crawled to the lodge entrance and peered out to find that while the storm still blew, there was light yet in the sky. I decided that I would make my way back to my own lodge, before darkness fell. I tore a piece of paper from my notebook and wrote a note to Martha and then I bundled myself up in my buffalo coat and slipped out into the storm.

If anything the storm had intensified. But stubbornly I told myself that our lodge was only a short distance away, that if I simply walked slowly in a straight line I would certainly come upon it. After all, I had made it here this morning, had I not? But after only a few steps, a strange and terrifying phenomenon occurred. The maelstrom of wind and snow enveloped me in its own world of chaos. Suddenly I knew no direction—not east or west, north or south, not left or right, not even up and down. I was completely disoriented. I shall turn back, I thought to myself desperately, I can't have come far. But, of course, I did not know where "back" was.

Now I felt the panic overcome me; I fought against it, tried to put one foot in front of the other, but in my state of mental confusion even that proved difficult to do. The snow stung my face and eyes, felt like a million tiny lashes of a whip, cut through my buffalo coat as if I were naked. I had an overpowering urge to lie down, to curl up for warmth until the storm passed, but I knew in what was left of my disarranged mind that if I did so I would surely die there. I staggered on, holding my arms out before me like a blind woman, hoping that I would come across another lodge—any lodge. I tried to cry out but I could barely hear my own words over the screaming of the wind. Tears of terror and pain from the stinging snow streamed down my face to freeze on my cheeks. Finally, I could no longer draw breath from the wind and my own panic; I had no strength to go on. I sank helplessly to my knees in the snow, grasped myself with my arms and rocked back and forth. "Forgive me, child," I whispered to my unborn baby, "forgive me." I fell onto my side, curled up in a tight ball, and felt the sleep of death stealing over me. I knew then that I was going to die . . . but suddenly I was warm and comfortable and I began to have the most extraordinary dream.

I dreamed that I was walking in a beautiful river bottom in the spring, the cottonwoods were in full leaf and the sweet yellow clover was in bloom and the grass across the prairie was as green as the fields of Scotland. I was following a young girl who walked ahead of me, and in a moment I recognized her—it was my dear Sara. I began to weep with joy at seeing her, and I hurried to catch up. Sara turned to wave to me, and I could see that she, too, was pregnant. She smiled and called back to me in Cheyenne. "It is so beautiful in *Seano, Mesoke,*" she said. "I shall have my baby here and later you will join me. I will meet you and show you the way here along the Hanging Road. But it is not quite time yet for you to come. You must go back now." And she turned and began to walk away from me again.

"Wait, Sara," I called out. "Wait for me, dear, please . . ." But I could not catch up to her and she disappeared ahead of me . . .

I do not know how long I slept, but when I woke at last I was in my own bed in my own lodge. My little Horse Boy sat beside me, my little man, his small hand warm as a biscuit upon my cheek. I reached out to see that he was real, cupped his cheek in my own hand. *"Mo'ehnoha hetaneka'eskone,"* I whispered to him.

The boy regarded me solemnly when he saw that my eyes were open, then smiled down at me.

"Mo'ehnoha hetaneka'eskone," I whispered.

"Mesoke," he said.

And then the others gathered excitedly around me and I was startled to see among them my old friend Gertie.

"Name'esevotame?" I asked, speaking unconsciously in Cheyenne.

"Your baby's fine, honey," Gertie said, "but he's mighty lucky and so are you. What the hell were you doin' wanderin' around out there in the blizzard, anyhow? Are you plumb crazy?"

I smiled weakly. "Some people used to say so. How did I get home?" I asked.

"Your little friend here found you," Gertie said, indicating Horse Boy, "found you half-covered in a snowdrift and drug you home all by hisself, although I don't know how the skinny little bastard managed it what with the extra person you're packin' along in there." She placed a hand lightly on my stomach, smiled, and stroked my belly gently.

"Did you ever have children, Gertie?" I whispered weakly. "You've never said."

"Never did, honey," she answered, "never much cared for the little bastards." But I could tell that she didn't mean it. "This little Horse Boy, though, he's OK, and he sure enough saved your fool butt."

"He's my little man," I said.

For days I faded in and out of consciousness. I had contracted pneumonia from my ordeal, with the attendant fever and delirium. I woke and slept, woke and slept, with no sense of time. Through it all I was aware of the steady stream of people who came and went from the tipi, old Crooked Nose overseeing the visitors like a stern head nurse.

My little man Horse Boy hardly left my side, and sometimes curled up on the robe to sleep beside me. Medicine men chanted and passed burning sage under my nose, rattles and other totemic objects around my head. Anthony read passages to me from the Bible, my friends and family were there—their faces blurring one into the next. Martha sat with me, and Gertie, Feather on Head, Helen, Euphemia, the Kelly twins, Quiet One, Gretchen, Daisy, Pretty Walker—all were there. And in my dreams I saw little Sara.

Sometimes the women sang softly to me. Feather on Head and Pretty Walker sang Cheyenne songs, the white women and the Indians taught each other their songs, and my sickbed became a place of joyous singing—until the old crone chased everyone off with her stick.

Always when the others had left, my husband Little Wolf was by my side, sitting silently, motionless as a statue so that when I woke, I was never alone, and when I saw him there I felt always safe, knowing that nothing bad could ever happen to me or to my child as long as my husband was here to protect us. If I was cold and shivering from fever, he would lie down beside me and fold me in his arms to warm me.

I slept and I woke and I slept, I thought that I should never be able to keep my eyes open for more than a few minutes at a time.

But after a time the fever passed and slowly I began to regain my strength. Now I feel the baby move inside me, and I tell myself that all is well.

At the moment I sit propped up against my backrest, scribbling these notes by the dim light of the fire. Feather on Head sits quietly beside me . . . my eyes grow heavy again . . .

26 January 1876

Good God, I can hardly believe the turn of events . . .

After my last entry I drifted off to sleep with my notebook propped against my enormous belly. I woke several hours later, woke with a jolt—the unmistakable tightening of a labor pain. "It cannot be," I whispered to myself. "I am weeks early." And I knew that something must be wrong. Little Wolf sat beside me, and Horse Boy curled against me. I touched the child's shoulder gently, and he woke with perfect animal-like alertness. "Please," I whispered to him, "run and get Martha." And to my husband I said, "The baby comes."

The women came quickly to lift me on my bed and transport me to the birthing lodge—where all Cheyenne babies are born and which gratefully had already been erected in preparation for our group parturition.

The skies were clear as they carried me there, the night air windless and frigid. I lay on my back, borne aloft by the others, looking up toward the heavens at the millions of stars. A shooting star blazed across the sky at that moment. I took this to be a good omen, and I prayed upon the shooting star, prayed that my baby would be born healthy and strong.

A fire already burned in the birthing lodge, tended by Woman Who Moves Against the Wind. The tipi was very clean and beautifully appointed with fine, newly tanned, and exquisitely embroidered hides and blankets, the walls freshly painted with various symbols and a number of Helen Flight's lovely bird designs. "In this way," she had said while painting them, "each of you may choose in turn your own medicine bird for your child." For mine I chose the mighty wren—*ve'kesehesо,* little bird—for its beautiful song, its industriousness and courage.

Now the women laid me gently down on a bed. The Medicine Woman came to my side to examine me, much like one of our own doctors. *"Eane-tano,"* she said to the others.

"Yes, I'm in labor!" I said. "And is the baby healthy?"

"Etonestoheese'hama?" the woman asked, turning to Martha.

"Why don't you ask me that question?" I demanded. "I can tell you perfectly well how far along I am. Just as the others."

"Enehestoheese'hama," Martha answered.

"No, that is not correct, Martha," I said, sharply, "I'm early. I can't possibly be full term yet."

"Close enough, dear," she said, all efficiency now. "You've always been a leader among us, and now you lead us into motherhood. Perhaps your fever has brought on the labor early."

I was still very weak from my recent illness and feared that I had little strength left to spare for the rigors of childbirth. But now the pains came sharply and regularly. The sweat poured from my face. I was certain that something must be wrong with my baby.

The women bathed my brow with damp cloths and spoke their encouragement to me while trying to make me as comfortable as possible. But when at last the time came, I was too exhausted, too weak, I had not the strength left to push; I felt myself fading away, losing consciousness, slipping back into the same wonderful dream I had had before . . . I longed so to go back there, where it was peaceful and green, to be with my little Sara . . .

I found myself in the same beautiful river bottom in the springtime, with the cottonwoods leafing out and the sweet clover blooming yellow in the meadows and up ahead my little Sara, waving to me. "Not yet *Mesoke,"* she called back. "You must stay a little longer, for your baby needs you."

And coming from a great distance away, I heard the voice of Woman Who Moves Against the Wind. *"Ena'tseane,"* she said calmly. *"She is dying in childbirth."* And I wondered who she was talking about.

Ahead of me Sara smiled and waved me back. I wanted so desperately to join her.

"No! No! She cannot be dying," screamed Martha from the distance, "May, your baby is coming, May, you must wake up, you must help!"

And Sara said to me, "It is still not time, *Mesoke*. Another time I will bring you to *Seano*. But now you must go back and bring your daughter into the world."

And then I came awake with a choke and I felt my baby's struggle between my legs as she fought to gain the light.

"Oh, God," I said, gasping for breath, "Oh, my God, *name'esevotame, name'esevotame . . ."*

"Yes, May!" Martha cried. "Yes, your baby is coming! Push, push hard, now, here it comes!"

And then I felt her come free, the wet slickness of her head sliding across the inside of my thigh, the sharp unbearable pain followed by the sweet release as Woman Who Moves Against the Wind took hold of the infant and brought her forward into the world. She lifted my daughter and smacked her on the rump, and my little Wren gave a hearty wail of indignation. Thank God, thank God . . .

I fought to remain conscious, but I felt myself slipping again into a deep exhausted slumber, too weak to raise my head, too weak even to look at my child.

"Ve'ho'me'esevotse," said the woman with a tone of wonder in her voice, *"Ve'ho'me'esevotse."*

"What does she mean, Martha?" I whispered, so spent that I was barely able to speak. "Gertie, tell me what does she mean? Why does she say that? Is my baby healthy?"

"Ve'ho'me'esevotse," repeated Woman Who Moves Against the Wind, as she wiped and swaddled the baby. The other Cheyenne women gathered curiously around and inspected the baby. *"Hou,"* they said in voices filled with astonishment, *"Hou, ve'ho'me'esevotse, ve'ho'ka'kesoas!"*

"Tell me!" I gasped with my last bit of strength. "Why do they keep saying that? What's wrong with my baby?"

"Take it easy, honey, your baby's just fine," Gertie said, "a great big healthy girl baby. But, honey, the medicine woman is right, she ain't no Indian baby, she's a *ve'ho'me'esevotse,* just like she said, a white baby, like them others is saying—*ve'ho'ka'kesoas,* a little white girl if ever I seen one."

" 'Tis God's own truth, May," said Susie Kelly, "the lass is as pale and rosy-cheeked as an Irishman."

"Scots-Irish, I'd say," added her sister Meggie, wryly.

"That is to say, dear," Helen Flight whispered, "your baby appears to be Caucasian."

"Oh, my God," I murmured, giving myself up at last to the death of sleep that dragged me down—and grateful for it I was, too. "Good God, I've had John Bourke's child . . ."

For nearly two more days I slept, waking only long enough to nurse my baby, though sometimes I woke and the child was at my breast already, placed there by Woman Who Moves Against the Wind or one of the others. She was a beautiful child, and from the moment I first laid eyes on her there was never any question in my mind of her parentage. She had

Bourke's nose, Bourke's deep-set intelligent eyes. She was John Bourke's daughter, of that I was certain.

The women fed me broth until I had regained some of my strength, cared for me again as they had before, and finally today I am able to sit up for a time and record this experience in my journal.

Only minutes ago my husband Little Wolf came to see his daughter for the first time. It was a moment that, for obvious reasons, I have been dreading. He sat beside me and looked for the longest time at the baby in my arms. I could only imagine what he must be thinking; I was filled with shame and remorse at my infidelity to this great, kind man—although we had not yet even met at the time of my indiscretion with John Bourke.

Finally Little Wolf reached out and with the greatest tenderness put the back of his fingers against the baby's cheek. *"Nahtona,"* he said, and it was not a question, but a simple statement.

"Hou," I answered in a tiny, tentative voice. "Yes, my husband, your daughter."

"Nahtona, emo'onahe," Little Wolf said, smiling at her, his face filled with fatherly pride.

"Yes, she is, isn't she?" I said. "Your daughter is very beautiful."

"Epeheva'e," he said, nodding with great satisfaction. "It is good that *He'amaveho'e* has given to me, the Sweet Medicine Chief, a white baby to teach us the new way. Woman Who Moves Against the Wind has explained this to me. It is just as the monk said it would be. This baby is the *vo'estanevestomanehe,* our Savior. *Maheo* has sent the white baby Jesus to lead our People to the promised land."

I was deeply touched by Little Wolf's naive acceptance of the child as his own, and I could not help but smile at his muddling of Biblical affairs. After months of listening first to Reverend Hare's sermons, and then to Brother Anthony's quiet explanations, the People have ended up with a strange hybridized religion based partly on their own beliefs and partly on those of Christianity. Perhaps this is as it should be and, surely, makes as much sense as any other.

"My husband," I said gently, "the baby Jesus was a boy child, not a girl. This is not the Savior, this is only our little baby girl. Our daughter. Your daughter and my daughter."

"Hou," he agreed, "I understand. This time the Savior is a girl child. That, too, is a good thing."

I laughed then and spoke in English. "I'm not exactly the Virgin Mary," I said, "but if that's the way you want it, my husband, why the hell not!"

28 January 1876

And so it is that my baby girl, John Bourke's daughter, is considered throughout the camp to be a sacred child—*vo'estanevestomanehe,* the Savior—given by *Maheo,* God Himself, as a gift to the Cheyenne people, a white baby who will lead the next generation of Cheyennes into the new world. A steady stream of visitors have come to see her, to marvel and *hou* approvingly at her milky white skin; many bear gifts for her. Surely Captain Bourke himself would appreciate the irony!

I had not intended to encourage the deceit, but neither have I disabused my husband of his superstitions. I have spoken to Brother Anthony at some length about this, having confessed everything to him. He agrees, as do the others, that to tell Little Wolf the truth of our daughter's parentage would serve no purpose, and that, indeed, this great event can only further encourage the remaining free Cheyennes to go into the agency. "There are no accidents in the Kingdom of God," Anthony said. "Perhaps your child, May, has been chosen to continue His work on Earth, to spread the word of God among the heathens."

"Don't tell me you believe it yourself, Anthony?" I said, with a laugh. "Can't she just be my daughter? That's enough for me."

Of course, some of my white friends, especially the always irreverent Gertie and Daisy Lovelace, tease me mercilessly about the child, upon whom all dote. Any speculation among the general population about the nature of my relationship with the Captain has been finally laid to rest—but none seem to hold it against me, or even be particularly surprised.

Daisy, herself very pregnant, came the first time to see the child, looked at her with her wry hooded eyes, smiled slyly, and said in her purring Southern voice, "*Why* if it *isn't* the *lil'* baby Jesus, herself. *A've huurd* so much about you, *mah deah. Everyone* in camp is talkin' about you." And she shook her head in amusement. "May, you are the only *guuurl* I have *eveh* known, who after havin' committed, if not exactly *adultery,* at least an act of *waaalld* and passionate promiscuity on practically the eve of *hur weddin' naght,* is rewarded for *hur* sins by givin' *buuurth* to a *bastaaad whaate chaald* believed *baah* all to be the baby Jesus. This is an *extraordinary* stroke of good fortune, *mah deah.* How did you *eveh* manage it?"

"Just lucky, Daisy," I admitted with a laugh. "Pure, dumb luck."

"And are you goin' to *infohm* the good Captain that he is a daddy?" she asked.

"If ever he has occasion to see this child, he will certainly know," I replied. "But I am married now to the great Chief Little Wolf, and as far as I'm concerned this child is officially his daughter . . . In any case, imagine how the situation would embarrass the good Catholic Captain among his military friends and cohorts?"

"*Idn't* that just the way of *alll* men?" Daisy said, and she let loose a bark of raw laughter. "It *nevah* occurs to them that they are the very ones who damaged the *guuuuds* in the *fust* place, does it? That was *jest* exactly the attitude of the cad Mr. Wesley Chestnut . . . and all along I thought we were goin' to be married . . ."

"You became with child by him, Daisy?" I asked. "I never knew that."

"Yes I did, and gave her away for adoption," Daisy said, "a decision I've regretted every day of *mah* life since. But this baby *Ah'm* carryin' now? This little *niggah* baby. *Ah'm* keepin' this one come Hell or high water."

29 January 1876

Yesterday offered me the first opportunity since my recovery to speak privately with Gertie, to ask her the question I have been pondering since the first night I saw her here after my accident.

"You rarely come to pay strictly social calls, Gertie," I said, coming right to the point, "and as this is dead of winter, reaching us must have been extremely difficult for you—and a matter of some urgency. Tell me what news you bring."

"Honey, I was just waitin' for things to quiet down some before I was goin' to tell you," Gertie said. "You know, what with your sickness and then the baby comin' the way it did . . . maybe you lost sight of it, but you folks have come right up against the Army's deadline."

"I've had other things on my mind," I said.

"Course ya have, honey," she said, "an' that's why I ain't said nothin' about it. I got news from the Cap'n. I brung you a letter from him. Before you read it, I'd better explain what's up. Crook's army left Fort Fetterman at the beginnin' of the month, headin' for this country. Of course, the Cap'n is with 'em. No telling where they is right now on account of the poor weather, which probably caused them to bivouac up somewhere, but even so they can't be more'n a few weeks away from here. It's a big detachment, honey—this time they ain't foolin' around. They got sixty-one officers with 'em, and over fourteen *hunert* enlisted men. And they're well provisioned, too—they got four *hunert* pack mules, sixty-five packers, a *hunert* and sixty-eight wagons, and seven ambulances. Not only that but they got better n' *three hunert* and *fifty* Injun scouts with 'em—'wolves' the Injuns call 'em when they go over to the other side. You never seen nothin' like it, honey. It's an army itself. They got big bands of Shoshone, Crows, Pawnees—they got Sioux, Arapahos, Cheyennes. Yup, some a your own folks is with 'em. Take a wild guess who's head a the Cheyenne wolves."

"Jules Seminole," I said, without hesitation.

"None other, honey," Gertie confirmed, "an' he's got others with him who are right from this here camp, that got family still here. You know some of 'em on accounta some of 'em just came into the agency this past fall with their white wives. You know that little French gal that was with you, Marie Blanche?—well her husband is one of the wolves, and so is the one they exiled, you know the fella who's married to the gal who always wears black."

"Ada Ware," I said.

"Yup, that's the one—her husband, the one they call Stinkin' Flesh. A course, they won't have no trouble finding you here. They know right where you are. Like I say, honey, the Army don't send out a force like this unless they really mean business. Too many miners and settlers have been getting picked off in the Black Hills, and folks is startin' to really holler for military protection from the Injuns. They been sendin' petitions to General Sheridan in Chicago and to the President hisself in Washington. Crook's orders are to clean out any hostiles they find in this country. And any Injun who ain't enrolled in the agency as of the first of February is a hostile Injun. And that means you, honey."

The irony of having gone from being a volunteer in the service of my government to being considered a "hostile Indian" did not escape my attention. "But with the weather we couldn't have complied if we'd tried, Gertie," I said. "You know that. Especially with all of our pregnant women."

"Sure, honey, I know that," Gertie said. "But what I'm tryin' to tell ya is that this has all been set in motion already. Listen to me on this: A military campaign, once it's set in motion, has a life of its own."

"We can't leave now," I said. "I have a newborn infant. The others are about to have their babies. These are innocent people. We are innocent people. We haven't done anything wrong."

"Honey, I was at Sand Creek in '64," Gertie reminded me. "Those folks weren't doin' nothin' wrong, neither. Last year Captain Henely and the buffalo hunters jumped the Southern Cheyenne on the Sappa, burned the camp, killed everyone in it. Threw the bodies of the smallest babies in the fire. The Army'll do anything it wants. You put a bunch of raw recruits together in hard conditions in winter, fightin' an enemy they don't understand an' that scares the piss out of 'em—anything can happen. Especially when they got orders."

"That's madness, Gertie," I said.

"I know it is, honey," Gertie said softly. "Cap'n knows it is. But it don't make no difference. That's what I'm tryin' to tell you. Them settlers that the Injuns are killin', those are innocent folks, too. What it all comes down to, honey—always comes down to—is that there ain't enough room for the Injuns and the whites in this country. One thing you can be sure of is that the whites ain't goin' to go away. And the other thing is that the Injuns ain't goin' to win this one, either."

Gertie dug into the front of her shirt and brought out Captain Bourke's letter. "Here, honey," she said handing it to me, "I imagine this letter'll tell you pretty much the same thing as I have."

Fort Fetterman, Wyoming Territory
26 December 1875

Madam: I pray that this correspondence finds you in good health. I have news of the most urgent nature to convey to you, and to the other women with you. Thus I have once again dispatched our loyal intermediary "Jimmy" as messenger.

Your people must decamp with as much dispatch as possible and move immediately south toward Fort Fetterman. You must fly a white flag at all times so that your band may be identified as peaceful by Army troops who will intercept you en route. You will be provided safe escort the remaining distance to the fort where arrangements for your future settlement will be made. As I pen this correspondence, General Crook prepares to dispatch the largest winter campaign in the history of the Plains Indian wars. As a member of the General's personal staff, I myself will be traveling with a force that includes eleven companies of cavalry under the command of Colonel Ranald S. Mackenzie. Taking into account vagaries of weather and engagements with hostiles along the way, we expect to reach the Powder River country no later than the middle of February. We have been advised by our scouts of the general location of your camp and the number of people contained within it.

I can not too strongly impress upon you the fact that there is not a moment to spare. Under the direction of General Crook, Colonel Mackenzie and the other commanders have orders to proceed in the clearance of all Indians between the Bighorn and Yellowstone rivers to the Black Hills of the Dakotas. No quarter will be given. All Indians encountered by Colonel Mackenzie's troops are to be considered hostile—with the sole exception of those traveling south toward Fetterman and flying the white flag of surrender. DO YOU UNDERSTAND ME? I urge you to depart immediately. Do not delay.

I am your humble servant,
John G. Bourke
Captain, Third Cavalry, U.S.A.

30 January 1876

Of course we all of us were deeply shaken by Gertie's news and the tone of urgency in Captain Bourke's letter—which the others have also now read. Even with the Army delayed by weather for several weeks it is inconceivable that we will be able to comply with their preposterous demands.

I scribbled a quick note to this effect to Captain Bourke and insisted that Gertie depart immediately to intercept Mackenzie's troops with whom he rides. And I have also prevailed upon Little Wolf to fly a white flag on a lodgepole in the middle of our camp. Surely for all their orders and dire warnings, the Army will not attack a peacefully encamped village in the dead of winter? A village in which, they are fully aware, a dozen pregnant white women reside.

17 February 1876

More than two weeks have passed since Gertie's hasty departure. Still no word back yet, but the weather has remained abysmal, with wind and driving snow. As if in a chain reaction, the others' babies are coming in such rapid succession that the birthing lodge operates at nearly full capacity. Martha and Daisy had theirs on the same day—two strapping boys, beautiful little nut brown infants whose parentage requires less divine explanation than does mine. Indeed, the little fellows make my milky white Irish-Scot daughter look even paler and more exotic by comparison!

"Oh my goodness!" Martha said when first she saw her own son. "Look, May, he's inherited his father's hair!" And it was true, her son was born with a head full of matted tangled black hair! Tangle Hair Jr. we have thus named him.

These were quickly followed by the Kelly girls, who true to form had their labor and births in perfect synchronization—twin daughters both. Twin mothers, twin fathers, twin babies—thus the twins multiply in kind. How extraordinary! "*Roons* in the family," said Susie. The Kelly babies are strange-looking little things, tawny of skin but with deep red hair.

All the children so far seem healthy; we have been extremely fortunate to avoid anything resembling complications during birth. The Cheyennes themselves are quite pleased with these new additions to the tribe and all the women dote on them. Feather on Head loves my little Wren like her own; I can hardly wrest the infant away from her when it is time for her feeding, so attached has the girl become. Indeed, were it not for my milk-swollen breasts I'm not certain that the child would know which of us was her mother. Quiet One, too, seems fascinated by the baby, and Little Wolf still acts the proud father.

22 February 1876

Still no sign of the Army. We have all prayed that Gertie was able to deliver my message to the Captain, and we remain confident that all will end peacefully.

Little Wolf has held a council and most of the chiefs of the remaining warrior bands have agreed that as soon as it is practical to travel we will begin the move toward Fetterman—this decision made, at least partly, as a result of the birth of our daughter. I am very relieved. And proud, for truly we are fulfilling our mission here, after all—facilitating a peaceful resolution. Our anchorite Anthony of the Prairie has also been very helpful toward this end. The People recognize a holy man by his own actions, and the monk's simple faith and self-denial, his fasts and penances are something the Cheyennes well understand and themselves practice as a means of drawing closer to their God.

Anthony has baptized each of our babies thus far and has counseled the People toward the path of peace and harmony. He is a good, pure man, with God in his heart. We had hoped that he might accompany us back to Fetterman, but he remains firm in his pledge to make his hermitage here—to one day found his monastery in the hills above the river. We will greatly miss him. Indeed, a part of me wishes I could remain with him, and I intend to be a regular visitor here, after we are settled on the reservation.

Yesterday, Gretchen had her baby, an oddly small and delicate little thing with none of her mother's bulk. The child's Christian name is Sara.

24 February 1876

These past days have seen a midwinter thaw, with temperatures mild again and the snow rapidly melting. Our scouts have been able to venture farther away from camp and returned today with reports of the movement of Army troops at a distance of several days riding—which means at least a week's travel for the more ponderous military forces. We still fly our white flag over the medicine lodge, and I am now convinced that Gertie safely delivered our message.

However, much to our dismay we have also learned that some of the restless young warriors of the Kit Fox society have taken the opportunity of the springlike weather to slip away with the intention of making a raid upon the Shoshone tribe to the west. This war party was first exposed by the Kelly twins, whose husbands are themselves members of this particular band and who stole off with the others early one morning—telling their wives that the raid was being undertaken in honor of the new babies, and that many horses would be brought back as gifts to them.

"We couldn't stop the lads," said Meggie. "We tried, but they got their damn *bloowd* up. *Ya* think it'd be *enooof* that they got new babies in the house, wouldn't you, but they got to go off an' steal some ponies to prove their damn manhood."

The raid is utter folly, for the Shoshone, like the Crows, while bitter enemies of the Cheyennes, are close allies of the whites. Evidently the recent councils which resulted in the decision to give ourselves up have also caused some of the young men to embark upon this imprudent action as a last opportunity to taste battle, to prove themselves as warriors. Once again the independent nature of Indian society and the lack of central authority acts against their better interests.

On a personal note, I have been recently discussing with Little Wolf our own future at the agency. General Crook has promised that the Cheyennes will be given their own reservation directly upon giving themselves up. Having signed documents, as did all the others, at the outset of this adventure agreeing to stay with the Indians for a minimum of two years, our real work among them will begin in this next year on the reservation—teaching the People the ways of our world.

"One of the first things you will be required to do," I explained to Little

Wolf, "is to give up two of your wives. It is against the white man's law to have more than one wife."

"I do not wish to throw away two of my wives," Little Wolf answered. "I am pleased with all of my wives."

"This is the white man way," I explained. "You must keep only your first wife, Quiet One, and give Feather on Head and me up. She is young enough that she can find a new husband for herself."

"Perhaps she does not wish to have a new husband," Little Wolf said. "Perhaps she is happy to stay with our child in the lodge of her present husband and her sister, Quiet One."

"It does not matter what she wishes; this is the law of the white man," I said. "One man, one wife."

"And you, *Mesoke?*" Little Wolf asked. "You, too, will find another husband?"

"I do not know what I will do," I answered truthfully. "But I could not hope to find a more satisfactory man than you, my husband."

"You will perhaps leave us and take our daughter into the white world where she belongs—as a member of her mother's tribe," Little Wolf said proudly. "If the Great White Father had given us all of the one thousand brides they promised to us, all the children would belong to the white tribe and the People and the whites would thus become one."

"General Crook has promised you that when we go into the agency," I said, "we will take this matter up once again with President Grant."

"Ah, yes," said Little Wolf, nodding, "I am familiar with the promises of white men . . ."

28 February 1876

. . . horror . . . butchery . . . savagery . . . where to begin to tell of it . . . with Meggie Kelly's whisper perhaps, alerting us: "Oh Sweet Jesus," she said as her young husband danced proudly around the fire, displaying to her his unspeakable trophies of war. "Oh Sweet Jesus, God help us all . . . what *'ave ya* done, lads? What *ave ya* done? . . ."

And Martha's bloodcurdling scream of recognition as my own blood ran cold, a chill so profound that my heart shall never warm again. John Bourke was right . . .

The Kit Foxes returned this morning from their raid against the Shoshones, rode into camp howling like banshees, herding before them a herd of horses stolen from the enemy. On the surface a harmless enough act, for the tribes steal horses back and forth, a game of boys and often no one on either side is injured or killed. And so we believed it had been on this raid, for the men returned triumphant, with no keening of mourning and leading no horses bearing the bodies of fallen comrades. They drove the herd of Shoshone horses through camp for all to see, followed by the camp crier who announced the requisite celebratory dance.

Our scouts came in just behind the Kit Foxes to report that Army troops are in the immediate vicinity. I suggested to my husband that he dispatch a courier with a message to Colonel Mackenzie to reiterate our peaceful intentions. Little Wolf answered that before turning his and the council's attentions to other tribal matters, he, and I, were first obligated to honor the Kit Fox raid by attending the feast and dance to be held at the lodge of their leader, a man named Last Bull. This is a bellicose, swaggering fellow of whom I have never been fond.

Thus off we went to a tiresome feast with much loud boastful talk from Last Bull. After the meal was finished all repaired to the bonfire, where the Kit Fox warriors each in turn danced their victory, and told their war tales.

It had snowed last night but now the skies were clear and winter's icy grip was again tightening, with temperatures beginning to plummet. But even the cold weather did not deter the proud warriors from their celebration.

I had left the baby in our lodge with Feather on Head caring for her, and after the feast I went back to check on her and to give her a feeding. "You go to the dance, *naveó a*," I told Feather on Head, as I held my ravenous little Wren to my breast. "I would rather stay here with my baby tonight."

"No, *Mesoke*," she answered. "You must take your baby to the dance with our husband; it was said by the crier that the new babies must all be present to witness their first victory dance—a victory in their honor. Our husband will be displeased if you do not return with his daughter for such an act would be very impolite to the Kit Foxes."

And so, reluctantly, I took my baby and met the others at the dance circle.

All of the other new mothers had also been invited, with the Kelly girls seated in the place of honor. Evidently their own young husbands had performed some great deed to honor the miracle of the birth of twin babies, the miracle of all the babies.

So huge was the fire that it cast sufficient warmth to offset the chill, and, of course, we had our babies well wrapped in furs and blankets. Flames leapt toward the heavens as the warriors began to dance, to recount their tales . . . to raise the first bloody scalps, tied to poles and held aloft and shaken at the Gods for all to admire . . . And some among us cast our heads down, recalling with shame the vengeful satisfaction we had taken in the death and mutilation of the Crows, at whose hands we had suffered so . . . now this memory and its bloody aftermath seemed like a bad dream, not something that had really happened, not something that we had not actually done . . . for we are civilized women . . .

Meggie and Susie's twin husbands danced before them as the girls both held their twins bundled in their laps. Between them the men passed a rawhide pouch, and sang a song of their great deed: *"In this bag is the power of the Shoshone tribe,"* he sang. *"We,* Hestahke, *have stolen this power to give to our children and now it is theirs. The Shoshones will never be strong again for we own their power. Tonight we give this power as a gift to our own babies so that they may be strong. For the children of our white wives are the future of the People. They own the power."*

And *Hestahke* held the pouch aloft and shook it and none could take their eyes from it; surely it held some great treasure, some great Shoshone medicine. The man danced and waved the bag in the air, and handed it to his brother who sang again the same power song, and as he did so, he reached into the pouch and took from it a small object and held it out to his wife Meggie as if offering her a precious jewel. I strained to see what it was that he held in his hand, all of us did, unable to look away.

At first I could not identify the object, but then my curiosity began to turn to stone, my blood to run cold for I knew instinctively that it was some ghastly body part or other, some unspeakable trophy of barbarity.

"Oh Sweet Jesus," whispered Meggie Kelly, "Oh Sweet Jesus, God help us all . . . what *'ave ya* done, lads? What *'ave ya* done . . ."

And now the tears began to run from my eyes, to wash cold across my cheeks. "Please, God, no," I whispered. I looked toward the heavens, the flames from the fire towering into the night sky, its sparks becoming the stars. "No," I whispered, "no, please God, let this not be . . ."

And the man danced and sang, proudly holding his grisly trophy aloft. A soft *houing* of approval and an excited trilling from the Cheyenne women began to rise above the drumbeat. *"In this bag are the right hands of twelve Shoshone babies, this is the power of their tribe and now it is ours. I give this as a gift to our daughters. Our children own this power."* He held the little hand aloft, and I could just make out its tiny curled fingers . . .

Martha screamed, a scream of anguish and condemnation that penetrated the night sky like a siren, cut through the drumbeat and the soft musical trilling of the others. I gathered my baby against my breast and stood, weak-kneed with nausea and horror, from my place beside Little Wolf. My husband himself sat impassively watching the performance . . .

Tears ran from my eyes as I clutched my baby to my breast. *"Me'esevoto!"* I hissed at him like an insane person. *"Babies!* Your people butchered babies! Do you not understand?" I said pointing with a trembling finger. "Do you not understand that one of those innocent babies' hands could just as well belong to your own daughter? Good God, man, what kind of people would do such a thing? Barbarians! You will burn in Hell! Bourke was right . . ."

And I fled, running as fast as I could, cradling my child in my arms as the fresh cold snow squeaked painfully beneath my feet.

I ran back to the lodge, weeping, burst in and fell to my knees. I held my baby to my breast, sobbing and rocking her. "My baby, my baby," were the only words that I was able to speak. *"Naneso, naneso . . ."*

Feather on Head and Quiet One gathered beside me to see what was the matter. Desperate for an answer, sobbing, I asked them please to explain to me how the women of the tribe could permit their husbands to commit such terrible crimes. At first they did not understand my question, for it is not a woman's place to ask such a thing.

"Babies!" I cried. "The men killed and mutilated babies. They cut babies' hands off. These could have been your babies, our babies. Don't you understand? It is a bad thing, a very bad thing that the men did." I wished to say "wrong," but there is no word for such a concept in the Cheyenne language . . . perhaps here lies the difficulty.

Quiet One answered softly, "The Shoshones have always been the enemies of the People, *Mesoke,*" she said. "For this reason the Kit Foxes stole their horses and captured their power to give to our children. The men did so in order that the Shoshones could not use their medicine against us and against our babies. In this way the men protect the People, they protect your baby, *Mesoke.* Our warriors stole the power of the Shoshone babies and gave it to your daughter—*Vo'estanevestomanehe,* the Savior—to make her strong and safe."

"You really don't understand, do you?" I said helplessly, finally too drained of strength to weep any longer. "There is no power in a baby's hand." I reached beneath the covering and pulled my daughter's hand free. She clutched my finger in hers. "Look," I said, "look how tiny and frail it is. You see? There is no power in a baby's hand . . ."

There was no question of sleep on this dark night. Like me, the others had immediately left the dance and, as I suspected, many made their way to Anthony's lodge on the edge of the village, seeking whatever sanctuary and comfort the monk might be able to offer.

The celebration itself had continued after our departure, and now we all sat around Anthony's fire holding our infants and listening to the throbbing drumbeat, the music and singing as the Kit Fox warriors told again and again of their great triumph over babies.

We tried to make some sense of it, to console each other, to give reason to the madness, to make understandable what was simply not. The Kelly girls were the only among us whose husbands were members of the Kit Foxes, who had themselves committed the crimes, and the twins were most inconsolable of all. Gone was all their cheeky Irish bravado.

"I want to go home, Meggie," Susie said. "I can't ever bear to look at the lads again, after what they've *dooone.*"

"Aye, Susie," said Meggie. *"Thar's nooothin'* else to be *doone,* we're finished here, that's for *shoooore.* We'll take the *gaarls* and leave *faarst* thing in the morning. Maybe we can find the Army and give ourselves *ooop.*"

But we all shared their guilt and their failure, and even Anthony's quiet strength, calm counsel, and the prayers we said around his warm fire could not take the chill from our frozen hearts.

"What kind of God allows such things to happen?" I asked the young monk.

"A God who demands faith," he said, "who gave His only son upon the cross that mankind might be saved."

"Aye, and we *aven't* learned a goddamned thing since, *'ave* we now?" said Susie Kelly with a bitter laugh. "We're *gooood* Catholic *gaaarls,* Meggie and me, *Broother,* but such a *tarrable* thing as this stretches our faith mighty thin."

"Now your work among the pagans truly begins," Anthony said. "To these innocent souls we must spread the word of God."

It is nearly dawn now . . . some of the women have returned to their own lodges, others doze fitfully with their babies here in Anthony's lodge. Unable to sleep all night myself, I sit here by the fire, recording these grim events. I look forward now to the arrival of the troops, so that they might escort us safely back to civilization . . .

And even still the drums and the music from the dance continue, the People have danced all through the night . . . a night none of us will ever forget. I prepare now to return to my own lodge . . .

1 March 1876

Yes, truly it is finished now, it is over, the soldiers have come with the breaking light of dawn like the vengeful hand of God to strike us down. I am shot, I fear that I am dying, the village destroyed and burning, the people driven naked into the hills to crouch like animals among the rocks. I have lost track of most of the others, some still alive, some dead, I have taken refuge in a shallow cave with Feather on Head, Quiet One, and Martha. Here we huddle together with our babies as the village burns below, a huge funeral pyre upon which the soldiers pile our belongings, everything that we own and all that we have—hides, furs, and blankets, meat and food supplies, saddles and ammunition—and upon these piles they place the bodies of our dead, and with burning torches set all aflame, they ignite our lodges which burst into flames like trees in a forest fire, the ammunition and kegs of gunpowder inside popping and exploding like fireworks . . . all that we have. Gone. It is the vision of Woman Who Moves Against the Wind come true . . . mankind is mad, all of us savages . . . are we punished for the babies? I cannot find Anthony to ask. I must ask Anthony . . . Anthony will know . . .

I am shot, I fear that I am dying, the breath rattles in my chest, blood bubbles from my mouth and nose. I must not die . . . forgive me my dear William and Hortense for abandoning you, I would have returned to you, truly I would have . . . if I die I pray that you may one day read these pages, know the truth of your mother's life . . . know that she loved you and died thinking of you . . .

I must be quick now, I am so cold I can barely move the pencil across the page, my teeth chatter, the women and children and old people are scattered out among the rocks above the camp, Martha is with me, Quiet One, Feather on Head, our babies . . . I do not know where the others are, some are dead . . . many are dead . . .

As long as I have the strength, I shall continue to record these events . . .

This morning at dawn, just hours ago, I left Anthony's lodge. I took my baby back to our own where I left her under the robes with Feather on Head. Then I went down to the river to where my little man Horse Boy tends the herd. The music from the dance had at last stopped, all had gone to their beds, silence had finally fallen over the camp. From a distance I heard the horses nickering nervously, I sensed that something was terribly wrong. I began to walk faster, dread rising like bile in my throat, faster, I began to run toward the river . . .

I stopped short when I saw him: Horse Boy stood wrapped in his blanket, stood straight as a statue of stone and there before him, mounted and leveling his pistol at the boy like an executioner, was Captain John G. Bourke. Beside him a lieutenant sat his horse, both their mounts as still as stone themselves but for the clouds of vapor they exhaled in the frozen dawn. Behind them, slipping like quicksilver down the draws and coulees, scrambling over the rocks, sliding down the embankments and bluffs, came dozens, hundreds, of mounted soldiers and Indians. I stepped forward. "John, what are you doing?" I cried out. "Put down your gun. He is only a boy. We are all prepared to surrender. Have you not seen our white flag flying."

Bourke looked at me as if he had seen a ghost, with an expression of shock, giving way to horror, and then uncertainty. He hesitated, the gun trembled in his hand. "Good God, May, our scouts have told us that this is the village of the Sioux, Crazy Horse," he said. "What are you doing here?"

"This is the village of the Cheyennes," I said, "Little Wolf's village. My village. Didn't Gertie tell you? Good God, John, put the gun down. He's only a child."

"It's too late, May," the Captain said. "The village is surrounded, the attack begins. Gertie is with another detachment. Our chief scout Seminole assured us that this is the village of the Sioux Chief Crazy Horse. Run the way we have come and hide yourself in the hills. I will find you later."

"Shoot the boy, sir," said the Lieutenant, impatient beside him. "Shoot him now before he cries out to warn the others."

"Fools!" I cried, "Your shot will warn the others! John, for God's sake, don't do this thing. It is madness. This is the village of Little Wolf. We are prepared to surrender peacefully. We fly a white flag of surrender."

Captain Bourke looked at the boy and then back at me. His dark, shadowed eyes went black as coal. "I am sorry, May," he said. "I tried to warn you. We are at war, the attack begins, I have my orders. I am a soldier in the service of my country. Run and hide yourself."

Bourke steadied the gun with a terrible cold certainty and pulled the trigger. Horse Boy crumpled like a rag to the ground, a bullet hole through the center of his forehead.

For a moment there was no other sound but that of the shot, echoing against the rocky bluffs; as if the earth itself stood still in disbelief. As if God in His Heaven had suspended time . . . John Bourke had murdered an unarmed child.

"Charge!" the Lieutenant beside him hollered, and then the gates of hell opened before us.

I ran, stumbling, slipping, falling in the snow, back to our lodge, just as the troops entered the village from both sides; I could think now only of my baby, I must save my child. All were by now alerted to the presence of the invaders whose horses thundered through the camp. Everywhere was gunfire, the screams of terror and death. My husband Little Wolf ran from the front entrance of our lodge carrying his carbine, he stopped to fire, ran, and stopped to fire, as did many of the other men, trying to draw the soldiers to them that the women and children might escape out the back of the lodges.

I ran into our lodge and scooped my baby into my arms. Quiet One slit the back of our tent with a knife, and held it open for Pretty Walker and Feather on Head, who carried her own child on its baby board. Before I went myself through the opening, I turned to old Crooked Nose. "Come, *Vohkeesa'e,* hurry!" I said to her.

But she bared her gums in a smile and shook her club and said in a calm voice, "You run, *Mesoke,* save your baby. I am an old woman and today is a good day to die."

The old woman stepped out through the front entrance of the tipi and as I ran out the hole in the back, I turned to see her swing her club at a soldier riding past. The soldier lost his seat and flailed the air for purchase before hitting the ground with a thud as the old woman set upon him.

I turned and ran for my life. Clutching my baby to my breast, I followed the others toward the rocky bluffs that surrounded the village. All was mayhem and insanity, screams and gunfire, the hollering of soldiers, the cries of our warriors and wails of terror from our women; I cried out for Martha, for Gretchen, for Daisy, but none could hear me over the general din, nor I them.

I caught one glimpse of Phemie, mounted on a white soldier's horse, completely naked, black as death against the whiteness of snow, galloping down upon a soldier who was afoot and trying to extract his bayonet, which was lodged in the breastbone of one of our women. Phemie carried a lance and gave a bloodcurdling shriek that seemed not human and when the soldier looked up at her his eyes widened in terror as she bore down upon him. I turned again and ran following the others into the hills. As I ran I was suddenly knocked down from behind, sent sprawling as if swatted by a lodge pole; I pitched forward, trying to cushion my baby from the fall. But I regained my feet and ran on.

It was very cold, many of the women and children had run naked from their lodges, without time even to put on their moccasins, some of the women carried infants, trying to shield them from the cold with their bodies. Now in the bluffs, old men and women crouched shivering among the rocks. All looked for caves or depressions in which to hide themselves. Stampeded horses from our herd scrambled wild-eyed through the rocks, their hooves clattering in the dry frigid air. Some people had managed to catch a few of the horses and to slit their throats and then open their bellies to plunge their own frozen feet into the steaming entrails.

It was so cold that I feared for my daughter's life. I held her against my skin inside my coat. Thank God that I had been dressed. I caught up at last with Pretty Walker, Feather on Head, and Quiet One, and together we came upon Martha; she, too, was nearly naked, crouched squatting like a trapped animal in the rocks, holding her son to her breast and rocking him back and forth. The baby was blue with cold. I knelt down and took him from Martha and placed him under my coat. He was like an icicle against my skin. Martha was so cold herself and shivering that she was unable to speak. I removed my coat and wrapped it around her and handed Wren to Feather on Head and also placed Martha's child in the girl's arms. "Hold her against your skin," I said. I took the knife from the sheath at Quiet One's waist and together we caught a mare by the mane as she clattered by. I swung onto the horse's back as Quiet One tried to calm her. The mare slipped sideways and tried to keep her feet, and as she did so I leaned forward onto her neck and drew the knife quickly across her throat. There came a deep moan of escaping air and the mare dropped heavily to her knees. I leapt from her back before she toppled, the snow already darkening black with blood beneath her. Then she rolled onto her side, her flanks heaving, the terror in her eyes fading with the light. I slit open her belly with the knife, her steaming entrails spilling forth, and she tried once to rise but fell back dead and I took Martha's son from beneath the robe and thrust him into the hot belly of the mare. "Thank you," I whispered to her, "thank you, mother."

Now Feather on Head and I helped Martha to the horse and we thrust her icy feet, too, into the entrails and at last she stopped her shivering and was able to speak. "My God, May," she said looking at me, "you have been shot. You have been shot in the back."

Now I knew what had knocked me down, and I unstrapped the notebook from my back; it must have absorbed some of the force of the bullet, which had passed completely through it and was now lodged in the flesh between my shoulder blades. "Oh May," Martha said, and she began to weep, "you have been shot. Dear God!"

"Stop it, Martha," I said sharply. "We must find shelter, we must build a fire."

"There is no fuel," Martha cried. "No, we shall all die here in these rocks. Oh my God, May, you have been shot. Our babies, our babies . . ." and she wept.

"Your son is fine, Martha," I said. "Look how little Tangle Hair recovers in the warmth of the mare's innards." It was true. The baby was slick with blood and entrails so that he looked again like a newborn in a strange reverse birth process. But he was regaining his color and now he squalled lustily. "Look at him! How strong he is," I said. "He will stay warm for hours there. But we must find shelter."

My hands are nearly frozen now, my fingers cramp . . . I make these last notes from this shallow cave . . . we have no fire . . . we all freeze to death . . . my breath comes painfully in shallow rattles . . . bloody bubbles run from my lips.

Down below the flames from the burning village crackle in the cold dawn. From these rocks we envy the warmth of flames we see but cannot feel. All that is left when the fires burn down are smoldering piles of ash and rubble, the half-cremated bodies of those who did not escape. Surely some of our friends are down there among them, and their babies . . . God, forgive us all . . . God forgive mankind . . .

From these cold rocks we can see the camp dogs beginning to slink back into the village to pick among the ruins for scraps of meat. The still frigid morning air bears the odors of roasted meats, spent gunpowder, scorched hides, burnt flesh. There are still dozens of soldiers about in the village so that we are unable to go back down to scavenge with the dogs, perhaps find a scrap of meat for sustenance, a flame for warmth . . . a blanket . . .

The soldiers continue to pile our last remaining goods, and atop them place the bodies of our dead, setting each pile afire . . . the funeral pyres blaze cold and fast and burn down quickly to their charred remains.

Now and then from the hills around a puny shot rings out . . . from our warriors, but they are poorly armed and have little ammunition to waste.

"Good brave girl, May," Martha says now, her teeth chattering again with the cold. "Good brave friend, you keep writing in your journal, you keep us alive as before, I love you so, my dear friend."

"And I you, Martha."

"It is over, isn't it?" she says in a small chattering voice. "All over, and for what?"

"For these children," I answer. "Our babies must live. They will be all that remain of us, and they will be enough."

"Let us go down now," Martha says, "and give ourselves up to the soldiers. When they see that we are white women they will take us in."

"They've killed us all, Martha," I say, "whites and Indians. But perhaps their lust is sated now. You go if you like. Go now, my friend, take your son. Tell them who you are and beg the soldiers for mercy."

"I'll find Captain Bourke," Martha says. "I'll bring him back. He'll help us. You wait for me here, May."

"Yes, you go, Martha. I'm finished writing in my notebook now, and I must close my eyes for a moment . . . I am very tired . . . our little friend Sara lives in the most beautiful place you've ever seen, Martha, a beautiful river bottom in the spring where the sun shines warm and the birds sing . . . go now, my dear, dear friend. . . . Pretty Walker, Feather on Head, and Quiet One will sit here with me for a while. . . . I shall wait right here for you to return with Captain Bourke . . .

"Yes, go now. Hurry. Take your son. Tell the soldiers who we are and what they have done. Tell them that this is not the village of Crazy Horse, that this is the village of the great Cheyenne Chief Little Wolf. And tell Captain John Bourke this from me—he will recognize it: tell him 'It is a wise father that knows his own child . . . ' "

→ CODICIL ←

by Abbot Anthony of the Prairie
Saint Anthony of the Desert Abbey
Powder River, Montana
November 15, 1926

⇾⇽

What an extraordinary blessing! God is never in a hurry to divulge His secrets! To bestow His gifts! He has all the time in the world on His hands!

For over a half century I have known of the survival of the preceding journals. But I have told no one. Three days ago they were brought to me at my abbey not far from where the events of these final pages took place. They were delivered here by a young Cheyenne man named Harold Wild Plums, who lives on the nearby Tongue River Indian Reservation. I have known Harold since he was born. I baptized him when he was a child. He is the grandson of the author of these notebooks—May Dodd Little Wolf—*Mesoke,* as she was known by the Cheyennes. Harold is son of the one the Cheyennes call *Ve'keseheso,* Wren, or Little Bird.

Over fifty years! How very different the West is today than it was in 1876. I pray that I am a different man, that I have given up some measure of the pridefulness of youth and in so doing have been blessed to draw closer to God in my old age. I am ill, nearly blind, and I do not have long to live. I wait with a heart full of joy and love to go at last and sit for eternity at the feet of my King. He calls to me. I am blessed to hear His voice, to see His hand in all things.

Truly I have been blessed with a perfect life of prayer and toil, of reading and study. With the sweat of my brow, the labor of my hands, the love of my God, I have been blessed to carve out this humble abbey in the hills above the river. Here I began my hermitage those many years ago in a simple hut upon a hilltop. Here I am blessed to live still, surrounded now by twelve other quiet men of humble mind who have joined me over the years.

For over half a century I have been blessed to walk these hills. I have studied the plants and animals. I have lifted rocks from the Earth and planted my garden. I have been blessed to receive my visitors with a hot meal, a warm bed, and a fresh loaf of bread to take upon their journey. I have prayed.

Fifty years ago I was blessed to come here as a young anchorite with

May Dodd and her friends among a band of Cheyennes led by the great Chief Little Wolf. Fifty years!

"Is your mother well?" I asked Harold Wild Plums on the day he brought these journals to me. "She has not been to visit me in many months. I have been thinking much of her recently."

"She is not well, Father," Harold said. "She is dying of the cancer."

"I shall walk to the reservation to see her," I answered. "For I am old and nearly blind, but I am blessed to be able still to walk, and I can still find my way there."

"No, Father," Harold answered, "my mother asks only that you read these journals and then write down the rest of this story in the last one that still has blank pages. She asks that I come back next week and pick them up and return them to her."

"Tell me, my son," I said. "I have been blessed to know your mother, Wren, since the day that she was born. But we have never spoken of these journals before. Has she always known that they survived the fires of that day?"

"No, Father," Harold said. "They have been kept all these years as a sacred tribal treasure with the Sweet Medicine bundle. Only a few elders knew about them. Old Little Wolf himself kept them in his possession until he died in 1904, but he never told my mother of their existence. He kept them secretly and illegally for twenty-five years after he was exiled by the People for killing Jules Seminole and was stripped of his position as the Sweet Medicine Chief. After his death they were placed in the Sweet Medicine bundle and only recently, because she is dying, were they given to my mother to read."

"And thus after all these years your mother learns the true identity of her father," I said to Harold. "And you, my son, learn the true identity of your grandfather."

"Yes, Father," Harold said. "We know, and now my mother wishes for you to write down in the last notebook that is not yet full the rest of the events of that day so that she may die knowing the whole story."

"You're a fine boy, Harold," I said to him. "Your mother must be very proud of you. I am blessed to do as she requests. Come back next week, and my work will be finished."

And so God in His infinite Grace and Wisdom has set me this final task to complete on Earth at the end of my own life. He has blessed me by placing this great gift of journals in my temporary care. I read them before, many years ago, when old Little Wolf brought them here to me, to read to him, for he never did learn English.

Now as humble scribe I am blessed to take up the last of these notebooks to write this codicil. One side of the notebook is soaked with the dried blood of May Dodd. I press my lips to it in blessing. I write around the brown, burnt edges of the bullet hole that passes through each and every page, to disappear in the flesh of my friend's back.

On the day the soldiers attacked I did not run to the hills with those fleeing. I ran toward the village. There I walked amid the slaughter and burning. In my habit the soldiers did not harm me. God protected me on that day as He has every day of my life, before and since, so that I might spread His Word and offer His Gift of Mercy to all who would accept it.

I tried to protect those who could not flee, the old and the infirm, from the wrath of the attackers. I tried to help those who ran to effect their escape. Where I could I put coverings on the naked children and women. I ministered to the wounded, and offered Last Rites and the Lord's comfort to the dying. I walked amid the death and destruction, the fires of Hell on Earth.

Many died in the village that day, cut down by the soldiers. The Englishwoman, Helen Elizabeth Flight, an extraordinary young woman, died defending her home. The last time I saw her alive, she stood before her tipi, with her feet spread, calmly charging her muzzle loader and shooting at the invading soldiers. She held her pipe in the corner of her mouth. One of the soldiers shot Helen through the forehead and killed her. Later all of her beautiful bird paintings were consigned to the flames. It was a great loss to the world of Art. Helen would have been quite well known had her work survived. All that remains of it are the few sketches included here in May's journals.

The Negro woman, Euphemia Washington, also died that day. She died fighting, but killed many soldiers first. She fought like a demon and terrified the young soldiers. Many of them were just boys. Euphemia had a great calm, but she also had a great anger in her heart. I believe that God would have tamed her anger, for she was a spiritual woman. But He had other plans for her. I remember Phemie less for her anger than for the slave songs of joy, sorrow, and freedom that she used to sing. Sometimes when I am gardening, or baking, or just walking in the hills, I still find myself humming one of these songs. Then I am blessed to recall Euphemia—*Mo'ohtaeve'ho'a'e,* Black White Woman, the Cheyennes called her—and later *Nexana'hane'e.* Yes, the Cheyennes still recall the warrior feats of Kills Twice Woman in their old-time ceremonies. I am blessed by the Lord to recall her songs.

By the time I came upon Gretchen Fathauer she was still alive but mortally wounded. She held her dead daughter to her mighty naked breast and wept great sobs of sorrow. Her husband, No Brains, had run into the hills at the beginning of the attack, leaving his family behind to perish. Gretchen was a dear child of the Lord. I covered her and the infant and tried to make her as comfortable as possible in her last moments. "He left his baby," she sobbed. *"De bick* ninnyhammer forgot to take *de* baby *wit* him when he run away. I tried to save my little Sara, *brudder Antony."*

"Of course you did, my sister," I said to her. I was blessed to administer Last Rites to Gretchen and her child and as I did so I broke down and wept myself.

"It be OK, *brudder Antony,"* Gretchen said trying to console me through her own sobs of grief. *"Yah,* it be OK. Me and baby we go to live with Sara and God in *Seano. Tings* be OK *dare. Yah,* you'll *see."* There amidst the brutality and death, God revealed Himself to me in Gretchen's goodness. He gave me strength for the coming ordeal.

The soldiers were by now largely finished with their grim business of destroying the camp. A mournful keening had arisen from the contingent of Shoshone scouts. They had discovered the Cheyennes' grisly trophy bag of babies' hands and had identified these as their own. Their cries of grief were terrible to hear. I stopped on my way to try to comfort them. I did not speak Shoshone, but I blessed the bag and I prayed for the souls of the children.

Some Cheyennes lived that day and were spared by the soldiers and others escaped into the hills. Later that morning I came across Martha Tangle Hair, wandering dazed through the village, holding her baby son in her arms.

"Help me, Brother Anthony," Martha begged when she saw me. "My baby is so cold."

I had gathered a small pile of blankets saved from the fires. I wrapped one of these around her child, and another around Martha.

"I must find Captain Bourke," she said. "Please help us, Brother. May is wounded. She needs help. I must find Bourke."

"Can you show me where she is, Martha?" I asked. "I will help her."

"May is very cold, Brother, she is shot."

Martha led me into the bluffs above the camp, but she had some difficulty finding the place again. At last we came to it. It was a shallow cave in the rocks. I still go to that place. I have been blessed to make of it a small shrine in May Dodd's memory. There my fellow monastics and I sometimes say our liturgies and there we sit in contemplative silence. The Cheyennes believe that everything that ever happens in a place—every birth, every life, every death—still exists there, so that the past, present and future live on forever in the earth. And so I, too, have come to believe.

I called out to May on that terrible, frigid morning, but no one answered.

When I entered the cave, I found her alone there, dead, sitting up against the rock wall. Quiet One, Feather on Head, and Pretty Walker were all gone, as was May's baby, Wren. In that cave, I administered the Last Rites to May Dodd and from her frozen fingers I removed the pencil. Her notebook, this notebook that I am blessed to hold now in my own hands, was also gone.

I led Martha back down to the smoldering village, and there I personally handed her and her infant over to the care of Captain John G. Bourke. It was the first time that I was to meet this man. But I would come to know him well later. He came often here to my hermitage over the years to pray, and I was blessed to help him do his penance.

The night after the attack the mercury dipped below zero. With everything destroyed by the Army, the Cheyennes had no protection from the elements and hardly any clothing. The survivors fled toward the village of the Lakota chief Crazy Horse, who was encamped on the other side of the mountain. I followed and did what I could to help and comfort the survivors.

It was a two-day journey of unimaginable hardship and suffering. Eleven Cheyenne babies froze to death in their mothers' arms the first night, three more the following night—including all of the remaining white children, with the sole exception of May's daughter, Wren.

Perhaps some scholars of religion might be tempted to find here a lesson in the vengeful hand of God. But God is not vengeful, my children. God is full of Grace, Light, and infinite Mercy. God did not kill the Shoshone babies. Nor did He punish the Cheyennes in retribution by killing their babies. Misguided men on both sides slaughtered the infants. And God took the souls of His children to His Kingdom.

Daisy Lovelace and her son, Wesley, God bless them, succumbed to the cold the first night. To them, too, I administered the sacrament of Extreme Unction under a cold full moon, and Daisy and her child went bravely and in peace to the Kingdom of our Lord. The little dog, Fern Louise, lay curled shivering beside the frozen body of her mistress. I put her beneath my habit and she survived. Fern Louise lived with me for several years before dying peacefully of old age in her sleep.

The Kelly twins, Margaret and Susan, lost both of their sets of twins in the course of the two-night march. The anguish of their grief was a terrible thing to behold. They cursed me, and they cursed the Lord in His Heaven for taking their baby girls.

They were a sprightly pair, Meggie and Susie. Besides Martha, they are the only white women of whom I am aware to have survived the ordeal of Mackenzie's attack and its aftermath. After the death of their infants, they went quite mad. They joined various bands of marauding Cheyennes and

Sioux and fought like demons against the whites in the final days of the Indian wars. They are reported to have ridden with the warriors when Custer and his men were killed later that summer at the Little Bighorn, and to have taken themselves grisly trophies of war there. I made many inquiries on behalf of the Kelly twins over the years and heard many rumors, but I was never able to learn what finally became of those girls. God bless them both.

Little Wolf himself was wounded seven times on the morning of the attack. He fought valiantly to protect his People as they fled from the camp, and somehow survived. With his wives Quiet One and Feather on Head, and his daughter Pretty Walker, he led his ragged band of refugees over the mountain to the camp of Crazy Horse.

The Cheyennes had nothing left, their spirit was broken. Less than a month later many of them began to straggle into Camp Robinson to give themselves up.

The government quietly arranged for the white women who had gone with their Indian families into the agencies earlier that fall to return to their own homes. Some took their children and raised them in the white world, others left their infants with the Cheyennes to be raised on the reservation.

Martha Atwood Tangle Hair, the sole white woman to officially survive the Mackenzie attack, returned to Chicago with her son, whose Christian name was Dodd. I never saw Martha again, but for many years after we kept up a correspondence. She eventually remarried and had several more children. Except to say in her very first letter to me that she had delivered her friend May's last message to John Bourke, Martha never mentioned the affair again. Nor did I ever learn what arrangement she had made with the authorities to purchase her silence. It is not a monk's business to ask such questions. But silent on the subject she remained. Martha joined our Lord in His Kingdom three years ago.

All know the tragic story of Little Wolf's last years. One day several years later he got drunk and shot Jules Seminole dead in the agency store for making a lewd remark to his daughter Pretty Walker. For this crime one of the great men in Cheyenne history was stripped of his position as Sweet Medicine Chief, renamed Stinking Flesh, and banished from the People.

Little Wolf lived in exile for another twenty-five years until he was well into his nineties. He took up a kind of monastic life himself and went everywhere on foot with his faithful first wife, Quiet One. I often used to see the two of them walking across the hills together. Sometimes I was blessed to have them pitch their tipi for a few days next to my hut. It was there that the Chief first gave me these journals to read to him. I always baked a loaf of fresh bread for Quiet One, and Little Wolf would tease her with gentle mischief about the arsenic incident.

Feather on Head had moved out of Little Wolf's lodge when the Cheyennes were required to give up their practice of polygamy. Eventually she married a young man named Wild Plums, and together they raised the child, Wren, as their own daughter. Of course, the People all knew that the sacred white child was the daughter of the white woman May Dodd and Little Wolf—and the Cheyennes still referred to her in their secret old-time ceremonies as *Vo'estanevestomanehe*—the Savior. They still believed, as Little Wolf had always maintained, that the child was *Maheo*'s gift to the People, that she had been sent by God to teach them the new life that must be lived when the buffalo were gone.

Even though I had read all of May Dodd's journals to Little Wolf, and he knew about John Bourke, he never gave up that faith. It was for this reason that he kept the journals secret and never told his daughter of their existence. Before he died he arranged with the keeper of the Sweet Medicine bundle for Wren to be given the journals at the end of her own life. He was a very great man, Little Wolf. I was blessed to know him on Earth.

John Bourke became a great advocate of Indians' rights, and a harsh critic of their treatment at the hands of our government. His outspokenness in such matters largely cost him advancement in his military career. Eventually he married another woman and had a family of his own. His health had been ruined by those terrible years of Indian wars, and he died in 1896.

John Bourke never claimed May Dodd's child, Wren, as his own daughter. But he always secretly watched over her and saw to her welfare as much as he was able. I know this to be true, because I was blessed to be his agent in these efforts. It was I, Brother Anthony of the Prairie, who prayed with John Bourke, and who counseled him to allow these People, and himself, the final miracle of the child's birth. May Dodd was quite right, the children were all that were left of this grand experiment . . . and they are enough.

Blessed be the children of God!

✧ EPILOGUE ✧

by J. Will Dodd
Chicago, Illinois
February 23, 1997

⟩⟨

Abbot Anthony of the Prairie died on the morning of December 7, 1926, just two weeks after he completed the preceding codicil to May Dodd's journals. The Saint Anthony of the Desert Abbey which he founded in the hills above the Powder River is still an operating monastery. It was there, propitiously—perhaps even miraculously Abbot Anthony would surely say—that I began my search when I first came out to the reservation, bearing my own family letter of introduction—the one link that I had between my great grandmother, May Dodd, and the Cheyennes.

The monks at the abbey were very interested in my last name—joyously so—for they know well the legend of May Dodd, and the brothers still say their liturgies and hold their contemplative silences in the rocks where she died. Through them I was put in touch with ninety-six-year-old Harold Wild Plums, said to be the oldest living descendant of the great Cheyenne Chief Little Wolf.

Harold lives with his granddaughter, named, not coincidentally, May Swallow Wild Plums, in a concrete block HUD house in the town of Lame Elk, Montana, on the Tongue River Indian Reservation. Like many such reservation towns in America, it is a bleak place with a distinct third-world feel to it. On an abandoned gutted building across the street from Harold's house, emblazoned in dripping blood red spray paint, is the ghetto legend—*Fuck Tha Police.*

I had already learned from the monks that as a young man Harold had attended college off the reservation and had gone on to become a well-known attorney in the Native American community. For many years he worked on the reservation, representing the Cheyennes, often without pay, on a variety of Native American issues.

The letter I brought to Harold Wild Plums, of course, was the one I had discovered in my own family's archives, the letter that had fueled my initial search, and the rumors of which had haunted mine amd my brother Jimmy's childhood. It was the only surviving correspondence from May Dodd to her children Hortense and William in Chicago.

The letter was written in coarse lead pencil, much faded, on a sheet of yellowed paper that had been torn from a bound notebook. It was dated *10 June 1875* below which date was written, "*Somewhere in Nebraska Territory North of the Niobrara River.*"

According to my own family research, on June 10, 1875, Hortense and William, who was my grandfather, were living with May's parents at their home on Lake Shore Drive in Chicago. May herself, by all family records, was still living in the Lake Forest Lunatic Asylum, a private facility for the insane in the countryside on the banks of Lake Michigan thirty miles north of the city. This institution is still in existence, having undergone several name changes over the years in keeping with the fashions of the times, and presently known as "Serenity Dunes." Of course no patient records from the 1870s survive there, but according to the official family history, May would die in the asylum the following winter of undisclosed causes. She is buried in the Dodd family plot in the Lake Forest Cemetery, or at least she has a stone there. Like all of Chicago's old, monied families ours is a large one, by both birth and marriage, and I have often, over the years, been to the plot for the burials of relatives, including that of my brother, Jimmy, after he was killed in Vietnam. His own grave is not far from that of our great grandmother, May Dodd.

Neither my grandfather William Dodd, nor his sister Hortense, would read their mother's only surviving letter to them until many years after it was written. Not wishing to frighten the children with this mad missive from their mad mother, of whom they knew little—except that she had died when they were infants—May's family kept the letter in a safe deposit box, the existence of which was not revealed to the children until after the death of both May's parents. By then William and Hortense were young adults themselves. Their mother's letter, then, took some twenty years to reach them—slow mail delivery even by the standards of the day. It is a short letter, as if hastily written.

My Dearest Children, Hortense and William,

I have entrusted this letter to my good friend Gertie McCartney, known infamously and variously on the western prairies as "Dirty Gertie" or "Jimmy the Muleskinner." I do not know if this will ever reach you. And if it does, I do not know if you will ever read it. In this way, I feel that sending this letter is much like putting it into a bottle and throwing it into this great sea of grass, all the while hoping desperately that it will wash up one day on your shores.

Even more fervently than that wild hope, I hope and pray daily that you are both well, and that we shall all be soon reunited. I have neither time nor space here to tell you of all that has happened. I am keeping a detailed journal of my journey here so that you may one day know the full story of your mother's life. I can only say now, briefly, that I was unjustly taken from you and committed to an asylum. My love for your father, Harry Ames, was deemed to be my "madness"—of which you are both the cherished result. For that I have no regrets on any score. I do not know what has become of your father. Only perhaps your grandfather can explain this to you—if he has the courage.

Presently I am living on the western prairies with a band of Cheyenne Indians . . . oh, dear, how insane that must seem to you . . . I am married to a man named Little Wolf, a great leader of his people . . . Good God, perhaps this letter is not such a good idea, after all, and will only confirm in your minds that your mother is, indeed, "crazy as a hoot owl," as my friend Gertie would put it. Well, too late for such worries . . . I am with child by Little Wolf, and will give birth to your brother or sister next winter. There are others with me here—by that I mean, other white women. We are members of an important government program, of which you will one day learn. I hope then that you will be very proud of your mother. I cannot here say more.

Please know that you are both kept close to my heart, that not a moment passes when I do not think of you, or long to hold you again in my arms. One day soon I will do so—I will come back to you, I promise you that, my dears. Every fiber of my being lives only toward that end.

Please remember me as your loving mother,
May Dodd

Harold Wild Plums was blind but still keen of mind and his granddaughter, May, read him the letter as I sat on the edge of his ratty, stained sofa. Hearing it read out loud, I understood again how "going West to live with Indians" had become the euphemism it had in our family for insanity. It was a tale for impressionable children, and I think possibly my brother Jimmy and I alone in the family ever actually believed it.

But all I could think of now looking around this bleak concrete block house, a child of privilege myself, was how far away I was from my own world, and how far away my great grandmother must have felt on these prairies. And it was then that I suddenly knew beyond a shadow of a doubt that the story was true.

Harold smiled as the letter was read to him, and nodded. "Yes," he said when she had finished, "those are grandmother's words. Do you recognize her handwriting, May?"

May was an attractive woman in her late thirties. "Yes, Grandfather," she said. "It is the same handwriting as the journals, and the same paper. I'll bet I can find the very page where it was torn out."

"You've got the journals?" I asked in a low voice of wonder.

"May, go and fetch Grandmother's journals from the Sweet Medicine bundle," Harold said to his granddaughter. "Our guest is a relative. He is the grandson of my mother's half brother, Willie. He has finally found us." And then to me Harold looked with his milky blind eyes. "I often thought over the years of searching for my white family," Harold said. And he shrugged. "But I was very busy with other matters. Does your grandfather, William, still live?"

"He died of cancer over thirty years ago," I said.

"Ah, yes," Harold said, nodding thoughtfully. "My mother, Wren, also died of the cancer when she was too young. I do not know why I have lived as long as I have. Perhaps to give you these papers now. That's what Father Anthony would have said." And Harold smiled. "Father Anthony would have said that I am blessed to give you these journals."

At that moment, May came back into the room carrying a stack of old cracked leather-bound notebooks, tied together in a bundle by rawhide thongs.

"Yes, perhaps you would be interested in reading these journals, Will Dodd," Harold said to me.

And very carefully May Swallow Wild Plums placed the bundle in my hands, and with long graceful fingers untied the thongs that bound it.

→ BIBLIOGRAPHICAL NOTE ←

In researching and writing this novel, the author gratefully acknowledges valuable insights and information gained from the following works:

Charles L. Blockson. *The Underground Railroad: Dramatic Firsthand Accounts of Daring Escapes to Freedom* (1987).

John G. Bourke. *On the Border with Crook* (1891).

W. P. Clark. *The Indian Sign Language, with Brief Explanatory Notes of the Gestures Taught Deaf-Mutes in Our Institutions for Their Instruction, and a Description of Some of the Peculiar Laws, Customs, Myths, Superstitions, Ways of Living, Code of Peace and War Signals of Our Aborigines* (1885).

William Cronon. *Nature's Metropolis: Chicago and the Great West* (1991).

Thomas W. Dunlay. *Wolves for the Blue Soldiers: Indian Scouts and Auxiliaries with the United States Army, 1860–90* (1982).

Jeffrey L. Geller and Maxine Harris. *Women of the Asylum: Voices from Behind the Walls 1840–1945* (1994).

Brigitte Georgi-Findlay. *The Frontiers of Women's Writing: Women's Narratives and the Rhetoric of Westward Expansion* (1996).

Josephine Stands In Timber Glenmore and Wayne Leman. *Cheyenne Topical Dictionary* (1984).

Gloria Davis Goode. "Get on Board and Tell Your Story," from *Jump Up and Say: A Collection of Black Storytelling,* Linda Goss and Clay Goss (1995).

George Bird Grinnell. *The Cheyenne Indians,* 2 Vols. (1925).

———. *The Fighting Cheyennes* (1915).

———. *By Cheyenne Campfires* (1926).

E. Adamson Hoebel. *The Cheyennes: Indians of the Great Plains* (1960).

Robert H. Keller, Jr. *American Protestantism and United States Indian Policy, 1869–82* (1983).

John Stands in Timber/Margot Liberty. *Cheyenne Memories* (1967).

Thomas B. Marquis. *Wooden Leg: A Warrior Who Fought Custer* (1931).

Joseph C. Porter. *Paper Medicine Man: John Gregory Bourke and His American West* (1986).

Peter J. Powell. *Sweet Medicine: The Continuing Role of the Sacred Arrows, the Sun Dance, and the Sacred Buffalo Hat in Northern Cheyenne History*, 2 vols. (1969).
Glenda Riley. *Women and Indians on the Frontier, 1825–1915* (1984).
Mari Sandoz. *Cheyenne Autumn* (1953).
Frank N. Schubert. *Outpost of the Sioux Wars: A History of Fort Robinson* (1993).
R. B. Stratton. *Captivity of the Oatman Girls* (1875).
Robert Wooster. *The Military & United States Indian Policy, 1865–1903* (1988).